Industrial Organization

Competition, Strategy, Policy

Second edition

John Lipczynski, John Wilson and John Goddard

 Prentice Hall
FINANCIAL TIMES

An imprint of **Pearson Education**
Harlow, England • London • New York • Boston • San Francisco • Toronto • Sydney • Singapore • Hong Kong
Tokyo • Seoul • Taipei • New Delhi • Cape Town • Madrid • Mexico City • Amsterdam • Munich • Paris • Milan

Pearson Education Limited
Edinburgh Gate
Harlow
Essex CM20 2JE
England

and Associated Companies throughout the world

Visit us on the World Wide Web at:
www.pearsoned.co.uk

First published 2001
Second edition published 2005

ISBN-13: 978-0-273-68802-0

ISBN-10: 0-273-68802-2

British Library Cataloguing-in-Publication Data
A catalogue record for this book is available from the British Library

Library of Congress Cataloging-in-Publication Data
A catalog record for this book is available from the Library of Congress

10 9 8 7 6 5 4 3
09 08 07 06

Typeset in 10/12.5 TimesNewRomanPS by 35
Printed by Ashford Color Press, Gosport

The publisher's policy is to use paper manufactured from sustainable forests.

For my family, Nicole, Sonya, Mark and Anna   JL

For my daughters, Kathryn and Elizabeth   JW

For my parents, Chris and Les   JG

Contents

Part II: Structural Analysis of Industry

Part III: Analysis of Firm Strategy

Part IV: Analysis of Public Policy

17   Competition policy   623

18   Regulation   659

Appendices: Analytical Tools

List of tables

List of figures

List of boxes

List of case studies

Supporting resources

Visit www.pearsoned.co.uk/lipczynski to find valuable online resources

Companion Website for students
- Links to relevant sites on the web
- Online glossary of key terms

Password protected resources for instructors only
- Complete, downloadable Instructor's Manual containing answers to end-of-chapter questions
- PowerPoint slides of the figures in the book that can be downloaded and used as OHTs

For more information please contact your local Pearson Education sales representative or visit www.pearsoned.co.uk/lipczynski

Preface

Industrial Organization: Competition, Strategy, Policy, second edition, is a textbook in industrial organization. It provides coverage of the latest theories of industrial organization, and it examines empirical evidence concerning the strategies, behaviour and performance of firms and industries.

In selecting material for inclusion in *Industrial Organization: Competition, Strategy, Policy*, second edition, we have attempted to provide readers with a flavour of the historical development of industrial organization. The book reflects the development of this subject area from its origins in the classical theories of the firm, followed by its emergence as a recognized subdiscipline within economics around the mid-twentieth century, right through to the present. Today, industrial organization draws on an impressive array of contributions from fields of economic inquiry as diverse as game theory, information theory, organization theory, agency theory and transaction cost analysis. At various stages throughout the book, we examine the work of researchers in the closely related field of strategic management, in order to emphasize the relevance of industrial organization to readers who are approaching the subject primarily from a business or a management standpoint, rather than from a traditional economics perspective.

Industrial Organization: Competition, Strategy, Policy, second edition, contains 47 case studies, which are used to illustrate 'real world' applications of theoretical and empirical research in industrial organization. Many of the case studies have been selected from reports originally published in the *Financial Times*; while others have been compiled from alternative sources. Many of the case studies have been chosen not only for their relevance to industrial organization, but also because they are lively, newsworthy and topical. The case study material certainly bears little or no resemblance to the subject matter of a traditional industrial economics programme of 20 or 30 years ago, when much greater emphasis would have been placed on traditional manufacturing and heavy industry. Instead the case studies focus on key sectors of the modern-day economy, such as IT and telecommunications (Microsoft, eBay, 3G mobile phones technology, open source); banking and financial services (commercial banking, the credit union movement); and sport and leisure (Hollywood movies, English Premier League football).

Industrial Organization: Competition, Strategy, Policy, second edition, is aimed primarily at undergraduate students. The book is intended for use on modules in industrial organization, industrial economics or business economics, by students studying for degrees in economics, business studies, management and other related disciplines. It can also be used as a preparatory, background or reference text by students taking graduate courses in the same subjects. The only prior experience of economics that is assumed is the completion of an introductory *Principles of Economics* module, or a one-semester module in *Microeconomics*.

The style of presentation is non-technical throughout. No knowledge of calculus is required. However, for readers requiring a more rigorous treatment of certain topics, a Mathematical Methods appendix provides formal derivations (using calculus) of a selection of the most important theories and results presented in the main text. Empirical research in industrial organization is also presented throughout the text in a non-technical style. No knowledge of statistics or econometrics is assumed. For readers requiring a primer in the fundamentals of regression analysis, an Econometric Methods appendix provides a brief and non-technical introduction to some of the basic tools, such as regression coefficients, t-statistics and goodness-of-fit.

Structure of the book

Industrial Organization: Competition, Strategy, Policy, second edition, is divided into four parts. In Part I, *Theoretical foundations*, Chapter 1 introduces some of the key elements of industrial organization, starting with the structure-conduct-performance paradigm, which provided the intellectual foundation for the early development of industrial organization as a separate subdiscipline within economics. Chapter 2 reviews the core microeconomic theory from which many of the early and modern theories of industrial organization have developed. Chapter 3 examines a number of alternative theories of firm behaviour, including the neoclassical, managerial and behavioural theories, as well as perspectives drawn from transaction cost analysis and agency theory.

Part II, *Structural analysis of industry*, discusses the approach within the field of industrial organization which emphasizes the role of the structural attributes of an industry in explaining the conduct of the industry's constituent firms. Chapters 4 and 5 examine non-collusive and collusive theories of oligopoly, a market structure whose most important characteristic is the small number of interdependent, competing firms. Chapter 6 examines practical aspects of industry definition, and the measurement of the number and size distribution of an industry's constituent firms, summarized by measures of industry or seller concentration. Chapter 7 examines the determinants of seller concentration. Chapter 8 examines another important structural attribute of industries: barriers to entry. Finally, Chapter 9 provides a link between Parts II and III of the book, by describing the evolution of industrial organization beyond the confines of the structure-conduct-performance paradigm, and the development of new approaches and methods, which are conveniently summarized under the banner of the 'new industrial organization'.

In Part III, *Analysis of firm strategy*, the focus shifts away from industry structure, and towards the newer theories of industrial organization that emphasize conduct or strategic decision making at firm level. Chapter 10 examines a number of pricing practices, including price discrimination and transfer pricing. In recognition of the growing use of auctions as a method for allocating resources and awarding contracts in the commercial and public sectors, Chapter 11 examines the economic theory of auctions. In the rest of Part III, the emphasis shifts towards various non-price strategies that can be adopted by firms, in an attempt to improve their profitability or gain a competitive advantage over their rivals. Chapters 12 and 13 examine product differentiation and advertising. Chapter 14 examines research and development, innovation and technological progress. Chapter 15 examines vertical integration and vertical restraints. Finally, Chapter 16 examines diversification, conglomerate merger and deconglomeration.

Part IV, *Analysis of public policy*, concludes the book, by drawing together the implications for public policy of many of the key findings of Parts I, II and III. Chapter 17 examines competition policy, including government policy towards monopolies, restrictive practices and mergers. Chapter 18 examines the topic of regulation, with particular emphasis given to public scrutiny of the activities and business practices of the recently privatized utilities and other natural monopolies.

Changes for the second edition

We have been gratified and encouraged by the responses to the first edition we have received from instructors and students. However, a new edition provides a welcome opportunity to make improvements, and to update and extend the material that was covered previously. For the second edition, six new chapters have been added to the twelve chapters that comprised the first edition. Chapter 2 *Microeconomic foundations* and Chapter 3 *Theories of the firm* are new to the second edition. These two chapters provide a basis within mainstream microeconomic theory for the material that is covered throughout the rest of the book. Chapter 10 *Pricing* and Chapter 11 *Auctions* are also new to the second edition. Between them, these two chapters cover a range of traditional and more recent economic theories of price formation and resource allocation. The chapter from the first edition covering the topic of concentration has been split into two second edition chapters: this topic is now handled in Chapter 6 *Seller concentration: measurement and trends* and Chapter 7 *Determinants of seller concentration*. Finally, Chapter 12 *Product differentiation* provides full coverage of a topic that was dealt with more concisely, within the chapter on advertising, in the first edition.

In addition to the new chapters, we have revised and updated our coverage of many theoretical and empirical topics in industrial organization throughout the book. We have improved the technical presentation of many of the theories of industrial organization, by grounding our coverage more explicitly within a microeconomic theoretic framework.

The first edition's extensive bibliography has turned out to be a highly popular feature with instructors, and with students wishing to read beyond the confines of a core textbook, perhaps with a view towards choosing a dissertation topic, or towards studying industrial organization at graduate level. Accordingly, in the second edition we have taken the opportunity to extend and fully update our previous bibliography.

We have retained or updated the most interesting and relevant case studies from the first edition, and we have added many more completely new case studies to the second edition. Most of the new case studies describe recent events, which have occurred since the publication of the first edition in 2001. We have significantly increased the number of end-of-chapter discussion questions. Finally, we have extended our website **www.pearsoned.co.uk/lipczynski**, which contains supporting material for instructors in the form of PowerPoint slides and outline answers to discussion questions. The website also contains links to other relevant websites for instructors and students.

Acknowledgements

We would like to thank colleagues and students at the Department of Business and Service Sector Management at the London Metropolitan University, the School of Management at the University of St. Andrews, the School of Business and Economics at University of Wales Swansea, and the School of Business and Regional Development at University of Wales, Bangor for their direct, and at times unknowing help towards the development of this project. We would like to give special thanks to Rick Audas, Chris Carter, Steve Dobson, Derek Eades, David Glenn, Bob Greenhill, Peter Grinyer, Paul Latreille, Donal McKillop, Alan McKinlay, Dave McMillan, George Milios, Phil Molyneux, George Panagiotou, Carlyn Ramlogan, Jeremy Stangroom, Manouche Tavakoli, Riette van Wijnen and Mark Wronski for all of their advice, support and helpful comments. Finally, thanks are due to Marc Jegers and Peter Mottershead for useful feedback on the first edition.

Thanks are due to a number of staff at Pearson Education who have provided excellent support at all stages as this project has progressed. We are especially indebted to Justinia Seaman (Commissioning Editor), Rachael Daily (Editorial Assistant) and Stephanie Poulter (Editorial Assistant) for all of their advice and encouragement during the commissioning stage, and while the preparation of the manuscript was underway. For keeping things on track and reminding us of deadlines during the editing, typesetting and production stages, we are indebted to Georgina Clark-Mazo (Desk Editor). We are also grateful for the assistance provided by Jenny Oates (Copy Editor), Mary Dalton (Proof Reader) and Margaret Binns (Indexer). Any remaining errors are, of course, the authors' joint responsibility.

Finally and most importantly, we would like to thank our families, for their patience, encouragement and support.

We are also grateful to those who have allowed the reproduction of copyrighted material.

Publisher's acknowledgements

We are grateful to the following for permission to reproduce copyright material:

HMSO for an extract from *National Review of Resource Allocation for the NHS in Scotland: Fair Shares For All Technical Report* published on www.scotland.gov.uk © Crown Copyright 1999; Basic Books, a member of Perseus Books LLC, for an extract adapted from *Evolution of Cooperation* by Robert Axelrod, Copyright © 1984 by Robert Axelrod; Sharon Beder for an extract adapted from 'Is planned obsolescence socially responsible?' by Sharon Beder published in *Engineers Australia*, November 1998; Euroabstracts European Commission for material from *Directorate General for Enterprise Euroabstracts European Commission*, vol. 41, August 2003; and Blackwell Publishing and *Journal of Industrial Economics* for an extract adapted from 'Some Simple Economics of Open Space' by J. Lerner and J. Triole published in *Journal of Industrial Economics*, 50, 2002.

Figure 3.6 and Figure 3.7 from 'The science of choice and the science of contract. The theory of the firm as governance structures: from choice to contract', *Journal of Economic Perspectives*, 16, pp. 173 and 181, American Economic Association and Oliver Williamson (Oliver Williamson 2002); Figure 15.4 from OFT, 'BSkyB: The outcome of the OFT's Competition Act investigation', December 2002 (OFT623) Office of Fair Trading; Tables 13.1, 13.2 and 13.3 from The Advertising Association's *Advertising Statistics Yearbook 2003*, World Advertising Research Centre (www.warc.com).

We are grateful to the Financial Times Limited for permission to reprint the following material:

Brand-building: decisions and actions, from FT Mastering Management, © *Financial Times*, 18 December 2000; Case Study 3.1 Bread and circuses from the Emperor Rupert Chairman's pugnacious AGM performance, © *Financial Times*, 15 November 2003; Case Study 3.2 The Walt Disney crisis: Rise of the corporate crusaders, © *Financial Times*, 5 March 2004; Case Study 3.3 Lessons from Railtrack: The collapse has demolished some of the untested assumptions about outsourcing, © *Financial Times*, 9 October 2001; Case Study 3.4 Business schools share the blame for Enron, FT.com, *The Financial Times Limited*, 17 July 2003; Case Study 4.2 BskyB offer set to spark digital TV price war: group to give away set-top boxes in battle for subscribers, © *Financial Times*, 6 May 1999; Case Study 4.3 The prisoner's dilemma in practice: tit-for-tat in the First World War trenches, © *Financial Times*, 18 October 1999; Case Study 5.1 EU bursts into price-fixing cartel's cosy club, © *Financial Times*, 12 June 2002; Case Study 5.2 Watchdog gets shirty with companies over strip price-fixing, © *Financial Times*, 2 August 2003; Case Study 6.2 Industrial clusters and competitive advantage, © *Financial Times*, 6 November 2001; Box 8.1 Does it pay to be a pioneer?, © *Financial Times*, 19 October 1998; Box 8.2 What are the options for later entrants?, © *Financial Times*, 19 October 1998; Box 12.1 The essence of building an effective brand, © *Financial Times*, 18 December 2000; Case Study 13.2 Running a top campaign, © *Financial Times*, 11 November 2003; Case Study 14.1 Strategy for creativity, © *Financial Times*, 11 November 1999; Case Study 15.1 Big media lack creativity, © *Financial Times*, 10 September 2003; Case Study 15.2 Profits in the age of an 'audience of one', © *Financial Times*, 16 April 2004; Case Study 15.3 UK retail group seeks review of PC pricing, © *Financial Times*, 9 April 2000; Case Study 16.2 The myth of the mega-bank: after the failures of diversification, wary lenders scale back their global ambitions (abridged), © *Financial Times*, 6 January 2004; Case Study 17.3 The end of RPM in medicines: medicine prices set to tumble after court ruling, © *Financial Times*, 16 May 2001;

Case Study 17.5 ABB fined heavily over role in cartel: European Commission, ten companies penalized for fixing prices of insulated steel heating pipes, © *Financial Times*, 22 October 1998; Case Study 18.2 Reforms that have failed to work a power of good: liberalisation of the market has brought the UK industry to crisis point, © *Financial Times*, 7 September 2002.

We are grateful to the following for permission to use copyright material:

Case Study 6.1 The media concentration debate, The Financial Times Limited, 31 July 2003, © Eli Noam; Case Study 13.1 For what it's worth: what's in a name? Quite a lot it seems, The Financial Times Limited, 3 February 2004, reproductions by Lauren Henderson and FutureBrand, © Lauren Henderson; Case Study 13.3 Advertising campaigns, The Financial Times Limited, 14 November 2000, © Marc Nohr; Case Study 17.7 Microsoft got what it deserved in Europe, The Financial Times Limited, 29 March 2004, © William Bishop and Robert Stillman; Case Study 18.1 Government and regulation: the past 20 years have seen a marked shift in regulators' role – towards helping businesses and markets to function, 28 August 2002, © Colin Mayer.

In some instances we have been unable to trace the owners of copyright material, and we would appreciate any information that would enable us to do so.

Theoretical Foundations

Industrial organization: an introduction

Learning objectives

This chapter covers the following topics:

- static and dynamic views of competition
- the structure–conduct–performance paradigm
- the Chicago school approach to the study of competition

Key terms

Austrian school
Chicago school
Collusion hypothesis
Distinctive capabilities
Efficiency hypothesis

Five forces model
New industrial organization
Structure–conduct–performance
   paradigm
Value chain

1.1   Introduction

This book deals with the economics of industrial organization. Specific topics that are covered include oligopoly theory, concentration, barriers to entry, pricing and auctions, product differentiation and advertising, research and development, vertical integration, diversification, competition policy and regulation. The aim of this introductory chapter is to provide an overview of some of this subject material, for both the specialist and the non-specialist reader.

The chapter begins in Section 1.2 by examining static and dynamic views of competition in economic theory. The view of competition found in the neoclassical theory of the firm (incorporating the textbook models of perfect competition, monopolistic competition, oligopoly and monopoly) is essentially static. In contrast, a more dynamic approach can be found in the writings of Schumpeter and economists identified with the Austrian school. Section 1.3 describes the structure–conduct–performance (SCP) paradigm, which laid the foundation for the original development of industrial organization as a separate sub-discipline within economics. The key elements of structure, conduct and performance are introduced, and some of the main limitations of the SCP paradigm are discussed. Section 1.4 makes a short diversion into the related sub-discipline of strategic management. Finally, Section 1.5 provides a brief overview of the contents of the rest of this book.

1.2 Static and dynamic views of competition

In microeconomics, the neoclassical theory of the firm considers four main theoretical market structures: perfect competition, monopolistic competition, oligopoly and monopoly. These underpin much of the subject matter of industrial organization. A perfectly competitive industry has six main characteristics: there are large numbers of buyers and sellers; producers and consumers have perfect knowledge; the products sold by firms are identical; firms act independently of each other and aim to maximize profits; firms are free to enter or exit; and firms can sell as much output as they wish at the current market price. If these conditions are satisfied, a competitive equilibrium exists in which all firms earn only a normal profit. If any particular firm is unable to earn a normal profit, perhaps because it is failing to produce at maximum efficiency, this firm is forced to withdraw from the market. In this way perfect competition imposes discipline: all surviving firms are forced to produce as efficiently as the current state of technology will allow.

In reality, however, competition often gives rise to a market or industry structure comprising a relatively small number of large firms. Each firm has sufficient market power to determine its own price, and some or all firms are able to earn an abnormal profit in the long run. One reason competition tends to lead to a decrease in the number of firms in the long run is that as firms grow, they realize economies of scale and average costs tend to fall. In the most extreme case of natural monopoly, a single firm can produce at a lower average cost than any number of competing firms. Among others, Marshall (1890) and Sraffa (1926) formulated the theory of monopoly. The tendency for average costs to fall as the scale of production increases might be a beneficial aspect of monopoly, if the cost savings are passed on to consumers in the form of lower prices. However, if a monopolist exploits its market power by restricting output and raising price in order to earn an abnormal profit, then monopoly may have damaging implications for consumer welfare.

Influenced by Marshall and Sraffa, Chamberlin (1933) and Robinson (1933) brought together the previously separate theories of monopoly and perfect competition, to formulate the theory of imperfect competition, which can be subdivided into the cases of monopolistic competition and oligopoly. The theory of monopolistic competition retains the assumption that the number of firms is large, but emphasizes non-price as well as price forms of competition. In the theory of oligopoly it is assumed the number of firms is small (but greater than one). The firms recognize their interdependence: changes in price or output by one firm will alter the profits of rival firms, causing them to adjust their own prices and output levels. Forms of competition under oligopoly vary from vigorous price competition, which can often lead to substantial losses, through to collusion, whereby the firms take joint decisions concerning their prices and output levels.

Essentially, the neoclassical theory of the firm is based on a static conception of competition. In all of the models outlined above, the main focus is on long-run equilibrium.

> In the end-state conception of equilibrium, the focus of attention is on the nature of the equilibrium state in which the contest between transacting agents is finally resolved; if there is recognition of change at all, it is change in the sense of a new stationary equilbrium of endogenous variables in response to an altered set of exogenous variables; but comparative statics is still an end-state conception of economics.
>
> *(Blaug, 2001, p. 37)*

In the twentieth century, some researchers rejected this static view of competition, and sought to develop a more dynamic approach. According to both Schumpeter (1928, 1942) and the **Austrian school** of economists, the fact that a firm earns an abnormal (monopoly) profit does not constitute evidence that the firm is guilty of abusing its market (monopoly) power at the expense of consumers. Instead, monopoly profits play an important role in the process of competition, motivating and guiding entrepreneurs towards taking decisions that will produce an improved allocation of scarce resources in the long run. Schumpeter and the Austrian school both recognize that knowledge or information is always imperfect.

According to Schumpeter, competition is driven by innovation: the introduction of new products and processes, the conquest of new markets for inputs or outputs, or the reorganization of existing productive arrangements (for example through entry or takeover). By initiating change by means of innovation, the entrepreneur plays a key role in driving forward technological progress. Innovation destroys old products and production processes, and replaces them with new and better ones. The successful innovator is rewarded with monopoly status and monopoly profits for a time. However, following a brief catching-up period, imitators are able to move into the market, eroding the original innovator's monopoly status and profits. Alternatively, another innovator may eventually come along with an even better product or production process, rendering the previous innovation obsolete. According to this dynamic view of competition, monopoly status is only a temporary phenomenon, and is not capable of sustaining a stable long-run equilibrium, as is assumed in the neoclassical theory of the firm.

The Austrian school also views competition as a dynamic process, and sees the market as comprising a configuration of decisions made by consumers, entrepreneurs and resource owners (Kirzner, 1973, 1997a,b). Entrepreneurs play a crucial role by noticing missed opportunities for mutually advantageous trade to take place. Entrepreneurs discover and act upon new pieces of information. By observing the actions of entrepreneurs, other decision makers are able adjust their trading plans and arrive at improved outcomes. Disequilibrium reflects imperfect information or ignorance on the part of buyers and sellers. The entrepreneurial function adds to the flow of information, and helps lubricate the process of adjustment towards a new and superior allocation of scarce resources. Whereas the Schumpeterian entrepreneur actively initiates change, the role of the entrepreneur in Austrian thinking is more passive: the Austrian entrepreneur merely responds more quickly than other agents to new information that is generated exogenously. According to Austrian economists, a monopoly position is attained through the originality and foresight of the entrepreneur; and, as Schumpeter suggests, monopoly profits are unlikely to be sustained indefinitely. As information arrives and new trading opportunities open up, other entrepreneurs appear, who by their actions help propel the economy towards a further reallocation of resources (Young *et al.*, 1996; Roberts and Eisenhardt, 2003).

1.3 The structure–conduct–performance paradigm

The static and dynamic theories discussed above have found an empirical counterpart in the field that has become known as industrial organization. Early work in this area, based predominantly on the **structure–conduct–performance** (SCP) **paradigm**, concentrates on empirical rather than theoretical analysis (Bain, 1951). In the main, the field of industrial organization analyses empirical data and, by a process of induction, develops theories to explain the behaviour and performance of firms and the industries to which they belong (Schmalensee, 1988).

Outline of the structure–conduct–performance paradigm

Seminal early contributions in industrial organization include Mason (1939, 1949) and Bain (1951, 1956, 1959). Mason and Bain are credited with the development of the SCP paradigm. According to this approach, the structure of a market influences the conduct of the firms operating in the market, which in turn influences the performance of those firms. The field of industrial organization is concerned with the investigation of 'the size structure of firms (one or many, "concentrated" or not), the causes (above all the economies of scale) of this size structure, the effects of concentration on competition, the effects of competition on prices, investment, innovation and so on' (Stigler, 1968, p. 1).

The SCP paradigm is useful in a number of ways:

■ It allows the researcher to reduce all industry data into meaningful categories (Bain, 1956).

■ It is consistent with the neoclassical theory of the firm, which also assumes there is a direct link between market structure, and firm conduct and performance, without overtly recognizing this link (Mason, 1949).

■ By defining a workable or acceptable standard of performance, it may be possible to accept an imperfect market structure, if such a structure produces outcomes that are consistent with the acceptable standard (Clark, 1940). By implication, market structure can be altered in order to improve conduct and performance (Sosnick, 1958).

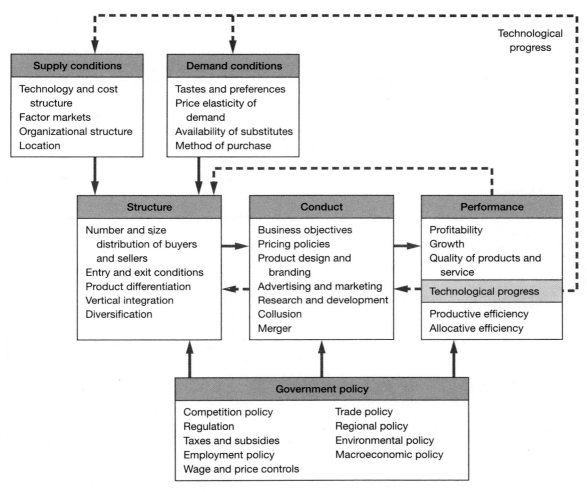

Figure 1.1 The structure–conduct–performance paradigm

A schematic representation of the SCP paradigm is presented in Figure 1.1. In accordance with the fundamental logic of SCP, the main linkages are shown as running from structure through conduct to performance. However, various feedback effects are also possible: from performance back to conduct; from conduct to structure; and from performance to structure (Phillips, 1976; Clarke, 1985). These are represented in Figure 1.1 by dotted arrows. Several specific types of feedback effect are identified in the following discussion of the main components of the structure, conduct and performance categories.

Structure

Structural characteristics tend to change relatively slowly, and can often be regarded as fixed in the short run. Some of the more important structure variables are as follows:

■ *The number and size distribution of buyers and sellers* is an important determinant of the market power exercised by the leading firms in the industry, and the discretion these sellers exercise over their own prices. In consumer goods industries it is normally the case that there are large numbers of small, atomistic buyers. Accordingly, the main focus is on the number and size distribution of sellers. Seller concentration is typically measured using data on the share of total industry sales, assets or employment accounted for by the largest firms in the industry. In capital goods industries, however, it is possible that the number of buyers is also small. If so, there may be market power on the demand side, as well as on the supply side: buyers may exercise discretion over the prices they pay. In such cases, a full assessment of the distribution of market power might require measurement of buyer concentration as well as seller concentration.

■ *Entry and exit conditions* include **barriers to entry**, which can be defined loosely as anything that places a potential entrant at a competitive disadvantage relative to an incumbent firm. The important issue is the relative ease or difficulty that firms may experience when entering an industry: if entry is difficult, then incumbents are sheltered from outside competition (Neven, 1989). Entry barriers may be either natural, deriving from basic characteristics of the product or production technology and cost structure; or strategic, deriving from deliberate actions taken by incumbent firms to discourage or prevent entry. The analysis of entry barriers has shifted from the simple classification developed by Bain (1956) to complex models of strategic behaviour which incorporate threats and irreversible commitments (Dixit, 1982). Irreversible commitments involve an incumbent making sunk cost investments that cannot be recovered in the event of subsequent withdrawal from the market. By raising **barriers to exit** in this way, an incumbent can signal its intention to stick around and fight in order to preserve its market share. The signal may in itself be sufficient to deter a potential entrant from proceeding.

■ *Product differentiation* refers to the characteristics of the product. How similar is each firm's product to those of rival firms? To what extent is each firm's product unique? Any change in the characteristics of the product supplied by one firm, whether real or imagined, may affect the shares of the total market demand that each firm is able to command.

■ *Vertical integration and diversification.* Vertical integration refers to the extent to which a firm is involved in different stages of the same production process. Diversified firms produce a variety of goods or services for several distinct markets. The extent to which a firm is vertically integrated or diversified is likely to have implications for conduct and performance. Vertically integrated firms have greater certainty in obtaining supplies of raw materials, or guaranteed distribution outlets. They have opportunities to engage in certain types of anticompetitive practice (vertical restraints), which may be damaging to non-integrated rivals. Diversified firms may benefit from economies of scope, and are less exposed to risk than their non-diversified counterparts, because losses realized in one market can be offset against profits earned elsewhere. In the long run, of course, firms make their own choices concerning vertical integration and diversification; therefore in the long run these can also be interpreted as conduct variables.

Conduct

Conduct refers to the behaviour of firms, conditioned, according to the SCP paradigm, by the industry's structural characteristics identified above. Conduct variables include the following:

■ *Business objectives.* The objectives that firms pursue often derive from structural characteristics of the industry, in particular the firm size distribution. The neoclassical theory of the firm assumes profit maximization; while managerial theories, developed primarily with large corporations in mind, emphasize the maximization of non-profit objectives such as sales revenue, growth or managerial utility (Baumol, 1959; Marris, 1964; Williamson, 1963).

■ *Pricing policies.* The extent of a firm's discretion to determine its own price depends to a large extent on the industry's structural characteristics. Possible pricing policies include cost plus pricing, marginal cost pricing, entry-deterring pricing, predatory pricing, price leadership and price discrimination (Phlips, 1983). For oligopolists in particular, it may be imperative to avoid direct price competition leading to mutually destructive price wars.

■ *Product design, branding, advertising and marketing.* Natural or inherent characteristics of the firm's basic product are likely to influence the scope for non-price competition centred on product design, branding, advertising and marketing. Although product differentiation is cited above as a structural characteristic, to some extent this is an oversimplification: the extent of product differentiation is at least partly endogenous, influenced or determined by strategies consciously implemented by incumbent firms.

■ *Research and development.* Together with advertising and marketing, investment in research and development provides an obvious outlet for non-price competition between rival firms. The extent and effectiveness of research and development investment, and the pace of diffusion (the speed at which a new idea is adopted by firms other than the original innovator), are critical determinants of the pace of technological progress (Kamien and Schwartz, 1982).

■ *Collusion.* Another option open to firms wishing to avoid direct forms of price or non-price competition is to collude with one another, so as to reach collective decisions concerning prices, output levels, advertising or research and development budgets. Collusion may be either explicit (through an arrangement such as a cartel), or implicit or tacit (through a less formal agreement or understanding).

■ *Merger.* Horizontal mergers (between firms producing the same or similar products) have direct implications for seller concentration in the industry concerned. Vertical mergers (between firms at successive stages of a production process) affect the degree of vertical integration. Conglomerate mergers (between firms producing different products) affect the degree of diversification. Therefore each type of merger decision provides an example of a conduct variable that has a feedback effect on market or industry structure.

Performance

Important indicators of performance, the final component of the SCP trichotomy, include the following:

■ *Profitability.* The neoclassical theory assumes high or abnormal profits are the result of the abuse of market power by incumbent firms. On the other hand, it has also been argued by the **Chicago school** (see below p. 14) that abnormal profit may be the consequence of cost advantages or superior productive efficiency on the part of certain firms, that have consequently been able to achieve monopoly status by cutting price and driving rivals out of business. If this is the case, it is not obvious that market power and abnormal profit should be viewed as detrimental to consumer interests. Similarly, according the the Schumpeterian or Austrian views, abnormal profit is a reward for successful past innovation, or the exercise of superior foresight or awareness by an entrepreneur. To the extent that profitability influences firms' decisions to continue or exit from a market, this performance indicator has direct implications for future structure (the number and size distribution of sellers).

■ *Growth.* Profitability is a suitable performance indicator for a profit-maximizing firm, but may be less relevant for a firm that pursues other objectives, such as sales, growth or managerial utility. Growth of sales, assets or employment might represent a useful alternative performance indicator, by which the performance over any period of firms that were unequal in size at the start of the period can be compared.

■ *Quality of products and service* might be considered an important performance indicator by individual consumers or consumer groups, regulators or governments.

■ *Technological progress* is a consequence of the level of investment in research and development, and the pace of technological progress may be considered a relevant performance indicator. In the long run, technological progress produces perhaps the most fundamental type of feedback effect shown in Figure 1.1, due to its impact on the basic conditions of demand (consumer tastes and preferences change when new products are introduced) and supply (technology and cost structures change when new and more efficient production processes are developed).

■ *Productive and allocative efficiency.* Productive efficiency refers to the extent to which a firm achieves the maximum technologically feasible output from a given combination of inputs, and whether it chooses the most cost effective combination of inputs to produce a given level of output. Allocative efficiency refers to whether social welfare is maximized at the **market equilibrium**. Productive and allocative efficiency are both regarded by economists as important performance indicators.

The role of government policy

As Figure 1.1 suggests, government policy can operate on structure, conduct and performance variables. According to the SCP paradigm, if an industry comprises only a few large firms, the abuse of market power is likely to lead to the level of output

Case study 1.1

Structure, conduct and performance in European banking

The banking sector is of central strategic importance for economic growth, capital allocation, financial stability, and the competitiveness and development of the manufacturing and service sectors. In Europe in 2000, bank assets were valued at the equivalent of 206 per cent of Europe-wide GDP.

The nature of competition in European banking has changed significantly since 1990. Following deregulation (via the Second Banking Directive), the creation of the EU single market in financial services, and the launch of the euro, barriers to trade in financial services have been significantly reduced. Banks are able to trade not only in their own countries, but also elsewhere throughout Europe. Banks have increased the range of products and services they offer to customers, leading to the distinction between banks, building societies, insurance companies and other financial institutions becoming blurred. The arrival of foreign-owned banks in many European banking markets has caused competition to intensify. Furthermore, a wide range of non-bank institutions, including supermarkets and telecommunications firms, now offer financial products and services as well. This has placed additional pressure on established banks to lower costs, limit their risk exposures, improve their management and governance structures, and find new ways of generating revenues from new forms of banking business.

Structure

During the period 1990–2002, there was a decline in the number of banks trading in most European countries. This trend is similar for mutual savings banks, cooperative banks and commercial banks. Table 1 shows data on the total number of banks (domestic and foreign-owned) trading in selected European countries in 1990, 1995, 1998 and 2002. In most (but not in all) countries, there has been a pronounced decline in bank numbers. Over the same period, branch numbers have also declined, as banks have sought to rationalize their branch networks.

This is part of an overall trend towards consolidation in the financial services sector, which has been accompanied by an increase in seller concentration. In 2002, seller concentration measured by the five-firm concentration ratio (the share of the five largest banks in the total assets of the banking sector as a whole) exceeded 60 per cent in Belgium, Denmark, Greece, Netherlands, Portugal, Finland and Sweden. Concentration has also increased, but has remained at lower levels, in Italy, Germany and the UK (where the 2002 five-firm concentration ratios were 31 per cent, 20 per cent and 30 per cent respectively).

However, the number of foreign-owned banks trading in every country included in Table 1 increased over the period 1990–2002. In the UK in 1998, there were 254 foreign banks with a 57 per cent share of total banking sector assets. In Belgium, there were eight foreign banks with a 48 per cent share; in France there were 280 foreign banks with a 15 per cent share; and in Portugal there were 16 banks with a 35 per cent share. In other European countries (except Luxembourg), foreign banks accounted for less than 10 per cent of total banking sector assets.

Table 1 Number of banks by country (selected countries, 1990–2002)

Country	1990	1995	1998	2002
Austria	1,210	1,041	898	823
Belgium	157	145	123	111
Denmark	124	122	212	178
Finland	529	381	348	369
France	2,027	1,469	1,226	989
Germany	4,720	3,785	3,238	2,363
Italy	1,156	970	934	821
Luxembourg	177	220	212	184
Netherlands	111	102	634	539
Portugal	260	233	227	202
Spain	696	506	402	359
Sweden	704	249	148	216
UK	624	564	521	451
EU Total	12,582	9,896	9,260	7,751

Source: Central Bank reports, European Central Bank (various).

Conduct

In response to competitive pressure (brought about by the entry of foreign banks and new financial services providers), many established banks have consolidated by means of merger and acquisition. This strategy has enabled some banks to achieve the large size (or critical mass) required to operate effectively throughout the European single market. Significant recent mergers in the UK include the Royal Bank of Scotland's acquisition of NatWest in 2000, and the merger between the Bank of Scotland and the Halifax in 2001. Cross-border mergers include the Dutch bank ING's acquisition of the Belgium Banque Bruxelles Lambert in 1999, and the acquisition of the UK's Abbey by Spain's Banco Santander in 2004. In 1999, 11 of the 20 largest banks in Europe had achieved top 20 status as a result of large-scale merger deals (Pescetto, 2003).

Many banks have also implemented strategies of diversification and financial innovation. Banks now offer their customers telephone and internet banking services, online share dealing, letters of credit, pensions and insurance, and a wide range of investment services. This has resulted in an increased reliance on revenues from non-traditional banking activities. Non-interest bearing income as a proportion of the total income of European banks increased from 28.3 per cent in 1992 to 42.5 per cent in 2001 (European Commission, 2004).

Performance

Table 2 shows that the average profitability (measured by return on equity) of banks in most European countries improved between 1990 and 2002. Given that competition has become more intense, it seems likely that increased profitability is a consequence of revenues having

Table 2 Return on equity, 1990–2001 (various European countries, %)

Country	1990	1995	1998	2001
Austria	8.63	8.15	9.48	11.29
Belgium	8.29	12.89	14.76	15.31
Denmark	−3.34	18.5	14.60	16.53
Finland	5.61	−7.93	9.86	n.a
France	10.15	3.63	9.93	11.76
Germany	11.93	12.57	17.38	5.12
Italy	16.40	5.91	13.17	14.01
Luxembourg	6.17	19.95	24.67	18.50
Netherlands	12.30	15.81	14.30	15.23
Portugal	12.54	7.65	7.56	6.31
Spain	13.58	9.17	11.07	9.26
Sweden	3.65	22.08	17.33	19.48
UK	14.45	28.59	28.31	20.05
EU Average	–	10.56	15.24	12.33

Source: Various Central Bank reports and OECD (2003) *OECD Bank profitability statistics.* Paris: OECD.

been generated from a wider variety of sources (diversification), and of the more efficient use of technology (such as consumer databases and call centres). This means banks are able to offer a wider variety of products at lower cost than was previously the case. Some of the increase in profitability has been driven by aggressive cost-cutting strategies, including branch closures and manpower reductions.

Overall, the level of competition, both between banks and other banks, and between banks and other financial sector institutions, continues to intensify. Deregulation and technological progress have lowered entry barriers and made banking more competitive. However, continued consolidation has resulted in a larger proportion of the banking sector's assets becoming concentrated in the hands of a relatively small number of institutions.

being restricted, and prices being raised. This stifling of competition is likely have damaging implications for consumer welfare. This suggests there is a role for government or regulatory intervention to promote competition and prevent abuses of market power.

- Competition might be promoted by preventing a horizontal merger involving two large firms from taking place, or by requiring the break-up of a large incumbent producer into two or more smaller firms. Such measures operate directly on market or industry structure.

- Intervention might instead be targeted directly at influencing conduct. A regulator might impose price controls, preventing a firm with market power from setting a profit-maximizing monopoly price. Legal restrictions on permissible forms of collusion might be strengthened, or punishments for unlawful collusion might be increased.

■ Finally, a wide range of government policy measures (fiscal policy, employment policy, environmental policy, macroeconomic policy, and so on) may have implications for firms' performance, measured using indicators such as profitability, growth, productive or allocative efficiency.

In common with the Austrian school, the Chicago school argue vehemently against government intervention in markets in order to promote competition (Reder, 1982). The Chicago school are a group of prominent academic lawyers and economists, whose pro-market, pro-competition and anti-government views were perhaps at their most influential during the 1970s and 1980s. The Chicago school are identified with the argument that large firms are likely to have become large as a result of having operated efficiently, and therefore more profitably, than their smaller counterparts. Therefore punishing the largest firms because they are also the most profitable firms is tantamount to punishing success. Even if certain abuses of market power do take place in the short run, these are likely to be self-correcting in the long run, when competition will tend to reassert itself. For example, there is little point in passing laws against collusive agreements, since such agreements are inherently unstable and are liable to break down in the fullness of time (Posner, 1979). Markets and industries have a natural tendency to revert towards competition under their own steam, without the need for any intervention or assistance from government.

The strident views of the Chicago school have not gone unchallenged. Blaug (2001), for example, accuses the Chicago school of promoting ideology rather than science.

> The Chicago school does not deny that there is a case for antitrust law but they doubt that it is a strong case because most markets, even in the presence of high concentration ratios, are 'contestable'. How do we know? We know because of the good-approximation assumption: the economy is never far away from its perfectly competitive equilibrium growth path! Believe it or not, that is all there is to the 'antitrust revolution' of the Chicago school.
>
> *(Blaug, 2001, p. 47)*

Beyond structure–conduct–performance

Although the SCP paradigm was highly influential in the early development of industrial organization as a sub-discipline within economics, SCP has been subject to fierce criticism from a number of different directions. Below, we provide a checklist of criticisms of the SCP paradigm. Many of these points recur, and will be examined in greater depth, in later chapters of this book.

■ The SCP paradigm draws heavily on microeconomic theory and the neoclassical theory of the firm. However, the theory does not always specify precise relationships between structure, conduct and performance variables. For example, oligopoly theory is largely indeterminate, and sometimes fails to produce clear and unambiguous conclusions.

■ It is often difficult to decide which variables belong to structure, which to conduct and which to performance. For example, product differentiation, vertical integration and diversification are structure variables; but they are also strategies that firms can consciously choose to adopt, and can therefore also be interpreted as conduct variables.

■ What exactly do we mean by performance? Performance is some measure of the degree of success in achieving desired goals. Is it possible to have a set of uniform performance indicators? Differences between the objectives of different firms may render SCP relationships tenuous. For example, if firms are sacrificing potential profits in order to reduce risk by making more secure investments, researchers should be more concerned with variability in profitability than with the profit rate as such (Schwartzman, 1963).

■ As we have seen, the definition of market or industry structure has a number of dimensions. However, many empirical studies based on the SCP paradigm measure structure solely by seller concentration. This is mainly because concentration is easier to measure than other dimensions of structure, such as entry barriers and product differentiation. Consequently there is a danger of overemphasizing the role of concentration. More generally, many of the variables in all three categories of structure, conduct and performance are difficult to measure (Grabowski and Mueller, 1970). How do we quantify the degree of vertical integration in an industry? How do we quantify the extent of collusion, or how do we even know if collusion is taking place? How do we measure the pace of technological progress? How do we determine whether firms are achieving maximum productive efficiency?

> We have concentration measures for most manufacturing markets in many economies for instance, but little comprehensive information is available on more subtle aspects of market structure, and essentially no systematic data aside from accounting profit rates is available on conduct and performance. This leaves a factual vacuum in policy debates that is quickly filled by beliefs and assumptions.
>
> *(Schmalensee, 1990, p. 138)*

■ Empirical research based on the SCP paradigm often finds associations in the anticipated direction between structure, conduct and performance variables. However, such relationships are often quite weak in terms of their statistical significance. Much of the early SCP literature examines the relationship between industry structure and performance, taking conduct as given. For example, in industries with only a few large firms, collusion was simply assumed to take place.

■ The SCP paradigm has been criticized for overemphasizing static models of short-run equilibrium (Sawyer, 1985). No explanation is offered as to the evolution of the structure variables, and the influence of current conduct and performance on future structure. This criticism echoes our previous discussion of feedback links within the SCP framework. At best the SCP paradigm is capable of providing only a snapshot picture of the industry and its constituent firms at one particular point in time.

■ Most early empirical research based on the SCP paradigm focused on the relationship between seller concentration and profitability. According to the **collusion hypothesis**, a positive association between concentration and profitability was interpreted as evidence of collusion or other abuses of market power designed to enhance profits. Later researchers emphasized the possibility that high profitability was achieved through the exploitation of economies of scale, or other cost savings achieved by the managers of large firms. According to the **efficiency hypothesis** (which is closely identified with the Chicago school, discussed above), a positive relationship between concentration and profitability reflects a natural tendency for efficient firms to be successful, and to become dominant in their industries. During the 1970s and 1980s, a large body of literature attempted to resolve the collusion-versus-efficiency debate using tests based on empirical data.

Several of these criticisms, especially the realization that a number of conduct and performance variables have feedback effects on structure, and that causality within SCP is a two-way and not just a one-way process, led eventually to a shift away from the presumption that structure is the most important determinant of the level of competition. Instead, some economists argued that the strategies (conduct) of individual firms were equally, if not more, important (Scherer and Ross, 1990). Theories that focus primarily on strategy and conduct are subsumed under the general heading of the **new industrial organization** (NIO) (Schmalensee, 1982). According to this approach, firms are not seen as passive entities, similar in every respect except size. Instead they are active decision makers, capable of implementing a wide range of diverse strategies. Game theory, which deals with decision making in situations of interdependence and uncertainty, is an important tool in the armoury of the NIO theorists. Theories have been developed to explore situations in which firms choose from a plethora of strategies, with the choices repeated over either finite or infinite time horizons. Some economists believe game theory has strengthened the theoretical underpinnings of industrial organization (Tirole, 1988). Others, however, are highly critical of the game theoretic approach. Schmalensee (1990), for example, complains that just about 'anything can happen!' when game theory is used to analyse competition:

> Game theory has proven better at generating internally consistent scenarios than at providing plausible and testable restrictions on real behaviour . . . Until game-theoretic analysis begins to yield robust, unambiguous predictions or is replaced by a mode of theorizing that does so, any major substantive advances in industrial organization are likely to come from empirical research.

(Schmalensee, 1990, p. 141)

1.4 Strategic management: a short diversion

A number of tools developed in the industrial organization literature have contributed to the growth of the sub-discipline of strategic management. Highly influential in the early development of this literature is Porter (1979a, 1980, 1985, 1996), whose **five forces model** of the firm's competitive environment is heavily SCP-influenced. Porter's five forces are: the extent and intensity of competition; the threat of entrants (new

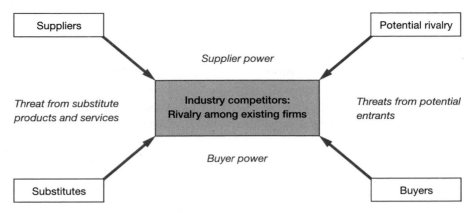

Figure 1.2 Porter's five forces model
Source: Adapted from Porter (1980), p. 4.

competitors); the threat of substitute products and services; the power of buyers; and the power of suppliers. The five forces are illustrated schematically in Figure 1.2.

■ *Extent and intensity of competition.* The intensity of competition depends on the number and size distribution of the industry's incumbent firms. If there are large numbers of similarly sized firms, competition is expected to be more intense than it is if one or a few firms are dominant. Other influences on the extent of competition include the rate of growth of industry sales; incumbent firms' cost structures; and the availability of spare capacity to meet potential increases in demand.

■ *Threat of entrants.* Incumbent firms that are threatened by entry behave differently to those in industries that are sheltered from competition. The perceived threat of entry is likely to be higher in industries where incumbents are highly profitable, and incumbents may search for ways of raising entry barriers. Government regulation also plays a part in determining the ease of entry. The size of the entry threat depends on the importance of economies of scale, the extent of product differentiation and brand loyalty, the level and specificity of capital investments, and the availability of access to distribution outlets.

■ *Threat of substitute products and services.* The availability of substitute products and services naturally tends to increase the intensity of competition. The availability of substitutes increases the price elasticity of demand for existing products, reducing the market power of incumbent firms. Incumbents may respond by seeking to differentiate their products more strongly from those of rivals, through branding or advertising. The attractiveness of substitute products to consumers depends on the prices and quality of the competing products, and the size of any switching costs.

■ *Power of buyers.* The power of buyers of a firm's product depends on their number and size distribution, and their level of dependence on the firm's output. If there are only a few buyers, or if close substitutes are available, buyers are likely to wield significant market power. In order to secure their own supplies, large buyers may seek to integrate backwards (by taking over an input supplier), reducing their reliance on external suppliers.

■ *Power of suppliers*. If suppliers of important inputs into a firm's production process are large in size and small in number, these suppliers can exercise market power by raising price, reducing quality, or even threatening to withhold supplies.

Porter's five forces identify the sources of competition that may confront a firm at any point in time. The firm's strategies and conduct are conditioned by the presence and strength of the five forces. In common with the SCP paradigm, however, Porter's approach is essentially static, and perhaps tends to underemphasize the problem of uncertainty caused by change in the competitive environment.

In contrast to many economists, management strategists tend to emphasize the distinctive internal characteristics of firms, in order to explain how a competitive advantage can be acquired and sustained. In the strategic management literature, the focus is on maximizing firm value through the choice of effective management strategies, rather than minimizing or eliminating abnormal profit in pursuit of wider public policy goals (Ghemawat, 2002; Spulber, 1992, 1994). Competitive advantage is measured by the value a firm is able to create in excess of its costs. Porter (1980) introduces the concept of the **value chain**, which disaggregates the firm into its strategically relevant activities. Primary activities are those associated with the physical creation of the product or service. Support activities are those that support primary activities and each other: for example, activities associated with the purchase of inputs, the management of human resources, or the improvement of technology through research and development. Once the firm's activities are disaggregated in this way, appraisal of their individual contributions can begin. Each support activity is linked to each primary activity to a greater or lesser extent. This approach examines how these links can be improved in order to increase margins on each of the firm's products.

Porter argues that a firm must select and follow a generic strategy in order to add value and gain a competitive advantage over rivals. Generic strategies include cost leadership, differentiation and focus. Under a cost leadership strategy, the firm attempts to keep its costs lower than those of competitors. The firm must be able to identify cost savings at some point in its value chain, or alternatively change the structure of the value chain; for example, by striking an exclusive deal with a supplier of an essential input. Under a differentiation strategy, the firm's product has some unique characteristic which appeals to its customers, leading to higher margins and profits. Finally, focus can apply to both cost leadership and differentiation. The firm focuses its efforts on a particular market segment. In the case of differentiation, for example, this may involve identifying a particular group of customers and gearing the firm's product towards their tastes or needs.

Kay (1993) argues that each individual firm is inherently different, and therefore dismisses the notion of generic strategies. Instead, firms develop **distinctive capabilities** in an attempt to achieve a competitive advantage. This shift of emphasis away from analysing the characteristics of the firm's external environment, and towards examining the each firm's unique attributes and strategies, mirrors the shift of emphasis away from structure and towards conduct that is implicit in much of the NIO (new industrial organization) literature. According to Kay, the main sources of distinctive capability include innovation, architecture and reputation.

■ *Innovation*. Successful innovation provides a firm with advantages over its competitors. However, this advantage only lasts for the time before imitation takes place. Even patents lapse eventually, or are vulnerable to being superseded by further technological change. Advantages from innovation can only be maintained if the firm has other capabilities which make imitation of the technology on its own insufficient to erode the firm's competitive advantage.

- *Architecture*. Architecture refers to the firm's internal organization. For example, Liverpool Football Club's famous boot room, from which several coaches were promoted in succession to the position of team manager, ensured long periods of continuity and success throughout the 1970s and 1980s. If the market changes, however, such advantages can be rapidly eliminated (Kay, 1993, 2003). Arguably, Liverpool failed to adapt as successfully as rivals such as Arsenal and Manchester United to the internationalization of the footballers' labour market that took place during the 1990s.

- *Reputation*. If a firm has a reputation for providing good quality and service, this helps add value and generate sales. Once having been acquired, a positive reputation can be sustainable for long periods, making it difficult for entrants to compete on equal terms with a reputable incumbent.

According to the strategic management literature, the strategic choices and decisions taken by firms are the main determinants of performance. Firms can only maintain a competitive advantage if they can protect their strategies from imitation. The ease of imitation is influenced by institutional and economic factors. For example, restrictive employment contracts, which prevent individuals from using any firm-specific knowledge if they move to a rival firm, may help impede imitation. An organization's corporate culture may be important: for example, a firm that offers secure employment may obtain a greater level of commitment from its workforce than one that relies heavily on temporary workers. Some aspects of corporate culture can be difficult for rivals to imitate. Economic factors affecting the speed of imitation include profitability and risk. Rapid imitation is more likely if the expected profitability from imitation is high, and if the risk is perceived to be low.

The strategic management literature provides many important insights into how firms can obtain and sustain competitive advantages over rivals. Some of these insights have been neglected in much of the industrial organization literature, especially in empirical studies. This is partly due to difficulties in quantifying key variables from the strategic management literature. The strategic management approach has been criticized for placing insufficient emphasis on the interactions between firms at the level of the market or industry. Instead, the focus is mainly on the strategic options available to the individual firm. In this sense, many of the insights derived from strategic management are complementary to those of the more traditional market-oriented microeconomic theory of the firm. We aim to reflect this complementarity at a number of points throughout the course of this book.

1.5 Structure of the book

The book is divided into four parts: Part I, Theoretical foundations; Part II, Structural analysis of industry; Part III, Analysis of firm strategy; and Part IV, Analysis of public policy. The chapter headings with each of the four parts are as follows:

Industrial Organization: Competition, Strategy, Policy

2nd edition

Discussion questions

1. Why is the structure–conduct–performance paradigm so widely used to study the conduct and performance of firms and industries?

2. List the factors that describe market structure. Give examples of ways in which market structure affects conduct.

3. Explain the logic of forward and reverse causation between structure, conduct and performance.

4. What are the limitations of the structure–conduct–performance paradigm?

5. How does the Chicago school view of competition differ from the structure–conduct–performance paradigm?

6. Compare the explanations for differences in firm profitability that are suggested by the collusion and efficiency hypotheses.

7. Compare the neoclassical conception of competition with the views advanced by Schumpeter and the Austrian school.

8. In what ways does the new industrial organization contribute to our understanding of firm behaviour?

9. In what ways does the strategic management literature contribute to our understanding of the decision making and performance of firms?

10. Outline Porter's five forces model of the firm's competitive environment.

11. What are distinctive capabilities, and why are they important?

12. With reference to Case study 1.1, assess the extent to which competition has increased in European banking in recent years. What effect has this had on the performance of banks?

Further reading

Bresnahan, T.F. and Schmalensee, R.C. (1987) The empirical renaissance in industrial economics: an overview, *Journal of Industrial Economics*, 35, 371–8.

Ghemawat, P. (2002) Competition and business strategy in historical perspective, *Business Strategy Review*, 76, 37–74.

Kirzner, I. (1997a) Entrepreneurial discovery and the competitive market process: an Austrian approach, *Journal of Economic Literature*, 35, 60–85.

Neven, D.J. (1989) Strategic entry deterrence: recent developments in the economics of industry, *Journal of Economic Surveys*, 3, 213–33.

Porter, M.E. (1979a) How competitive forces shape strategy, *Havard Business Review*, July–August, 1–10.

Posner, R. (1979) The Chicago school of anti-trust analysis, *University of Pennsylvania Law Review*, 127, 925–48.

Reder, M.W. (1982) Chicago economics: permanence and change, *Journal of Economic Literature*, 20, 1–38.

Roberts, P. and Eisenhardt, K. (2003) Austrian insights on strategic organization: from market insights to implications for firms, *Strategic Organization*, 1, 345–52.

Schmalensee, R.C. (1982) Antitrust and the new industrial economics, *American Economic Review*, Papers and Proceedings, 72, 24–8.

Schmalensee, R.C. (1988) Industrial economics: an overview, *Economic Journal*, 643–81.

Schmalensee, R.C. (1990) Empirical studies of rivalrous behaviour, in Bonanno, G. and Brandolini, D. (eds) *Industrial Structure in the New Industrial Economics*. Oxford: Clarendon Press.

Spulber, D. (1992) Economic analysis and management strategy, a survey, *Journal of Economics and Management Strategy*, 1, 535–74.

Spulber, D. (1994) Economic analysis and management strategy, a survey continued, *Journal of Economics and Management Strategy*, 3, 355–406.

Young, G., Smith, K.G. and Grimm, C.M. (1996) Austrian and industrial organization perspectives on firm-level activity and performance, *Organization Science*, 7, 243–54.

Microeconomic foundations

Learning objectives

This chapter covers the following topics:

- the Law of Diminishing Returns
- short-run and long-run production functions
- the relationship between production and costs
- returns to scale and the minimum efficient scale
- demand, revenue and elasticity
- profit maximization
- the neoclassical theory of the firm: perfect competition, monopoly and monopolistic competition
- allocative and productive efficiency
- welfare properties of perfect competition and monopoly

Key terms

Abnormal profit
Advertising elasticity
  of demand
Allocative efficiency
Average cost
Average fixed cost
Average product of
  labour
Average revenue
Average variable cost
Barrier to entry
Barrier to exit
Complements
Constant returns to
  scale
Consumer surplus
Cross price elasticity
  of demand

Deadweight loss
Decreasing returns to
  scale
Diseconomies of scale
Economic efficiency
Economies of scale
Economies of scope
Elasticity
Fixed cost
Imperfect competition
Increasing returns to
  scale
Interdependence
Isoquant
Law of Diminishing
  Returns
Lerner index
Long run

Marginal cost
Marginal product of
  labour
Marginal revenue
Market demand function
Market equilibrium
Market power
Minimum efficient scale
Monopolistic competition
Monopoly
Natural monopoly
Normal profit
Oligopoly
Opportunity cost
Pecuniary economies of
  scale
Perfect competition
Price elasticity of demand

Price elasticity of supply
Price taking behaviour
Producer surplus
Product differentiation
Production function
Productive efficiency
Real economies of scale
Returns to scale
Short run
Substitutes
Tangency solution
Technical efficiency
Total cost
Total revenue
Variable cost
X-efficient

2.1 Introduction

This chapter reviews the core elements of microeconomic theory that underpin the economic models of firms and industries developed elsewhere in this book. The principal topics covered are production and cost theory, demand theory and the neoclassical theory of the firm, including the models of perfect competition, monopoly and monopolistic competition.

The chapter begins in Section 2.2 with a review of production and cost theory. A key distinction is drawn between the short run (when some inputs are variable and others are fixed) and the long run (when all inputs are variable). The short-run relationship between inputs, output and production costs is governed by the **Law of Diminishing Returns**, and the long-run relationship is governed by economies or diseconomies of scale. Section 2.3 reviews the essentials of demand theory, including the price elasticity of demand, a standard measure of the responsiveness of quantity demanded to a change in price. A profit-maximizing firm should produce the output level at which its marginal revenue *equals* its marginal cost. The relationship between price elasticity of demand and marginal revenue is considered.

Within the neoclassical theory of the firm, different models are used to analyse price and output determination for different market structures. The most important characteristics of market structure are the number of firms, the extent of **barriers to entry**, and the degree of **product differentiation**. The two most extreme cases are perfect competition (the most competitive model) and monopoly (the least competitive). These models are developed in Section 2.4, and their efficiency and welfare properties are compared in Section 2.5. Finally, Section 2.6 develops the model of monopolistic competition. This model describes an industry with large numbers of sellers and no entry barriers (as in perfect competition), but some product differentiation affording the firms some discretion over their own prices (as in the case of monopoly). Accordingly, monopolistic competition represents an intermediate case, falling between the two polar cases of perfect competition and monopoly.

2.2 Production and costs

Microeconomic theory assumes firms combine factor inputs through an efficient method of production in order to produce output. Economists distinguish between factors of production that the firm can vary in the short run, and factors of production that cannot be varied in the short run but can vary in the long run. For example, by offering overtime to its current workforce or by hiring more workers, a firm might easily increase the amount of labour it employs in the short run; similarly, by reducing overtime or by laying workers off, a firm might easily reduce the amount of labour it employs. However, it is not possible for the firm to change the amount of capital it employs at short notice. New factories or offices take time to construct. New capital equipment has to be ordered in advance, and orders take time to be fulfilled. Accordingly, for a firm that employs two factors of production, labour and capital, it is usual to assume labour is variable in the short run, and capital is fixed in the short run but variable in the long run.

A general expression for the long run production function of a firm that uses a labour input and a capital input is as follows:

$$q = f(L, K)$$

where L = units of labour employed, K = units of capital employed, and q = units of output produced.

In the short run, labour is variable and capital fixed. Accordingly, the expression for the firm's short-run production function, obtained by rewriting the long-run production function, is as follows:

$$q = g(L)$$

For example, if the long-run production function is q = f(L, K), but in the short run K is fixed at K = 100, the short-run production function is q = f(L, 100). By incorporating 'K = 100' into the structure of a newly defined function, the short-run production function can be rewritten q = g(L).

Short-run production and costs

Production theory

The short-run relationship between the quantity of labour employed and the quantity of output produced is governed by the Law of Diminishing Returns, sometimes alternatively known as the Law of Diminishing Marginal Productivity. As increasing quantities of labour are used in conjuction with a fixed quantity of capital, eventually the additional contribution that each successive unit of labour makes to total output starts to decline. The Law of Diminishing Returns is illustrated in Columns 1 to 4 of Table 2.1. According to Column 1, the firm can employ between L = 1 and L = 10 workers per week. Column 2 shows the total weekly output in each case. Column 3 shows the **marginal product of labour**, MPL. MPL is the quantity of additional output the firm obtains by employing each additional worker. If one worker is employed, L = 1 and q = 7. But if two workers are employed, L = 2 and q = 26. Effectively, the first worker contributes MPL = 7 units of output, but the second worker contributes MPL = 26 − 7 = 19 units. Similarly, if three workers are employed, L = 3 and q = 54, so effectively the third worker contributes MPL = 54 − 26 = 28 units. One worker can produce relatively little by himself because the factory is severely understaffed. However, two workers combined are more effective than one in isolation, and three are more effective than two. This is reflected in Column 4, which shows the **average product of labour**, APL. APL is the ratio of total output to quantity of labour employed. As L increases from 1 to 2 to 3, APL increases from 7 to 13 to 18.

However, as more and more workers are employed, the point is eventually reached when each additional worker's contribution to total output starts to fall. Once the full contingent of workers that the factory can comfortably accommodate and occupy has been hired, employing even *more* workers will not result in very much more output being produced. If the factory becomes overstaffed, either some

Table 2.1 Short-run production and costs: numerical example

(1) Quantity of labour employed (number of workers per week) L	(2) Total output (units per week) q = g(L)	(3) Marginal product of labour (units per week) MPL	(4) Average product of labour (units per week) APL	(5) Variable cost (£ per week) VC	(6) Fixed cost (£ per week) FC	(7) Total cost (£ per week) TC	(8) Short run marginal cost (£ per unit of output) SRMC	(9) Average variable cost (£ per unit of output) AVC	(10) Average fixed cost (£ per unit of output) AFC	(11) Short-run average cost (£ per unit of output) SRAC
1	7	7	7	200	1,000	1,200	28.6	28.6	142.9	171.4
2	26	19	13	400	1,000	1,400	10.5	15.4	38.5	53.8
3	54	28	18	600	1,000	1,600	7.1	11.1	18.5	29.6
4	88	34	22	800	1,000	1,800	5.9	9.1	11.4	20.5
5	125	37	25	1,000	1,000	2,000	5.4	8.0	8.0	16.0
6	162	37	27	1,200	1,000	2,200	5.4	7.4	6.2	13.6
7	196	34	28	1,400	1,000	2,400	5.9	7.1	5.1	12.2
8	224	28	28	1,600	1,000	2,600	7.1	7.1	4.5	11.6
9	243	19	27	1,800	1,000	2,800	10.5	7.4	4.1	11.5
10	250	7	25	2,000	1,000	3,000	28.6	8.0	4.0	12.0
11	242	−8	22	2,200	1,000	3,200	—	—	—	—

of the workforce will be idle for most of the time, or most of the workforce will be idle for some of the time. In Table 2.1, diminishing returns begin to set in after L = 6 workers are employed. The sixth worker contributes MPL = 37 units of output, but MPL = 34 for L = 7, and MPL = 28 for L = 8. Eventually average productivity, measured by APL, also starts to fall. Average productivity reaches its peak of APL = 28 for L = 7 or L = 8, but APL = 27 for L = 9 and APL = 25 for L = 10. Eventually, the point is reached where the factory becomes so overcrowded that output starts to fall if more workers are taken on. If a tenth worker is employed, total output increases from q = 243 to q = 250, so MPL (=7) is small but still positive. But if an eleventh worker is employed, total output falls from q = 250 to q = 242, so MPL (= −8) becomes negative.

Figure 2.1 illustrates the relationship between MPL and APL. It is important to notice that APL is increasing whenever MPL > APL, and APL is decreasing whenever MPL < APL. This implies APL reaches its maximum value at the point where MPL = APL.

■ If the marginal contribution to total output of the last worker employed is higher than the average output per worker (MPL > APL), the last worker must be pulling the average up (so APL is increasing).

■ If the marginal contribution to total output of the last worker employed is lower than the average output per worker (MPL < APL), the last worker must be pulling the average down (so APL is decreasing).

This relationship between MPL and APL is also visible in the numerical example shown in columns 1 to 4 of Table 2.1.

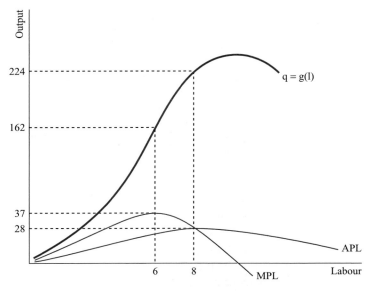

Figure 2.1 Short-run relationship between total, marginal and average product of labour

Cost theory

The short-run relationship between inputs and output that is governed by the Law of Diminishing Returns has direct implications for the firm's cost structure in the short run. However, before discussing the mechanics of cost theory, it is worth commenting that the economist's idea of items that should count towards a firm's 'costs' differs slightly from that of an accountant when preparing a set of company accounts. For an economist, costs encompass 'rewards' as well as monetary payments, since in many cases the supply of an input involves no formal cash or monetary transaction. For example, the owners of a business might not pay themselves for their own time and effort, or for ploughing their own money into the business. Nevertheless, the owners will soon contemplate the closure of the business if the reward or profit from such a personal investment is insufficient to compensate them for their own time and effort *and* match the **opportunity cost** of the financial investment: the return that the owners could have achieved had they invested their money elsewhere. Accordingly, returns that an accountant might consider as part of the firm's 'profit' would be considered by an economist to be part of the 'costs' the firm has to cover if it is to remain in business. An economist would include in the firm's cost functions an allowance for the reward the firm's owners require in order to remain in business. This reward is known as **normal profit**. Finally, any additional return over and above the normal profit is known as **abnormal profit**.

Columns 5 to 11 of Table 2.1 illustrate the implications of the Law of Diminishing Returns for the firm's cost structure in the short run. The previous discussion notwithstanding, for the purpose of constructing this simple numerical example we do not include the firm owner's reward or normal profit explicitly within the cost function (although we could conveniently think of this as forming part of the firm's fixed costs). In addition to the short-run production function data contained in Columns 1 to 4 of Table 2.1, two further pieces of information about costs are used to construct Columns 5 to 11:

■ the firm's weekly cost of employing each worker is £200;

■ the firm also incurs a fixed cost of £1000 per week: the cost associated with the fixed (capital) factor of production. This fixed cost does not vary with the number of workers employed.

Accordingly, columns 5, 6 and 7 of Table 2.1 show the firm's **variable cost**, **fixed cost** and short-run total cost, VC, FC and SRTC, respectively. Column 8 shows the firm's short-run marginal cost, SRMC. **Marginal cost** is the additional cost the firm incurs in order to produce one additional unit of output. For the purposes of Table 2.1, marginal cost is calculated by dividing £200 (the cost of employing each additional worker) by MPL (the additional output contributed by each additional worker). For example, by spending £200 to employ the first worker, the firm obtains MPL = 7 units of output. Therefore at q = 7, the firm's marginal cost (per additional unit of output) is SRMC = 200/7 = 28.6. By spending another £200 to employ the second worker, the firm obtains MPL = 19 additional units of output. Therefore at q = 26, the firm's marginal cost (per additional unit of output) is SRMC = 200/19 = 10.5. It is important to notice that when MPL is rising SRMC is falling, but once diminishing returns set in and MPL starts falling (beyond q = 162), SRMC starts rising. The increase in

SRMC beyond this point is a direct consequence of the Law of Diminishing Returns: as each additional worker employed becomes less productive, the cost to the firm of producing each additional unit of output inevitably increases.

Columns 9 and 10 of Table 2.1 show the firm's **average variable cost** and **average fixed cost**, AVC and AFC, respectively. These are calculated by dividing the total variable and fixed cost (columns 6 and 7) by total output (column 2). Comparing columns 4 and 9, it is important to notice that when APL is rising AVC is falling, but once APL starts falling (beyond L = 8 and q = 244) AVC starts rising. Therefore AVC is 'U-shaped'. If the average productivity of labour is rising, the average labour cost incurred per unit of output produced must be falling. Likewise, if the average productivity of labour is falling, the average labour cost incurred per unit of output produced must be rising. Meanwhile, AFC is decreasing over all values of L and q that are shown in Table 2.1. Reading down column 10, the total fixed cost is spread over larger and larger volumes of output in order to calculate AFC. Therefore AFC falls as q increases. Finally, column 11 of Table 2.1 shows the firm's short-run average cost, SRAC, calculated by summing AVC and AFC. The 'U-shaped' appearance of AVC ensures SRAC is also 'U-shaped'. As q increases, a point is eventually reached at which the downward pull of AFC on SRAC is exceeded by the upward pull of AVC on SRAC. Before this point SRAC is decreasing as q increases, but beyond this point SRAC is increasing as q increases.

Figure 2.2 illustrates the relationship between the firm's marginal and average cost functions, SRMC, AVC, AFC and SRAC. It is important to note that while the MPL and APL functions shown in Figure 2.1 are drawn with labour on the horizontal

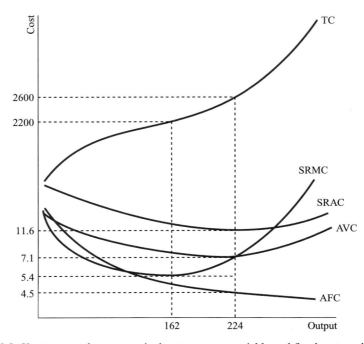

Figure 2.2 Short-run total cost, marginal cost, average variable and fixed cost, and short-run average cost

axis, the SRMC, AVC, AFC and SRAC functions shown in Figure 2.2 are drawn with output on the horizontal axis. It is also important to notice that AVC is decreasing whenever SRMC < AVC, and AVC is increasing whenever SRMC > AVC. This implies AVC reaches its minimum value at the point where SRMC = AVC.

■ If the marginal cost of producing the last unit of output is lower than the average labour cost per unit of output (SRMC < AVC), the cost of producing the last unit must be bringing the average down (so AVC is decreasing).

■ If the marginal cost of producing the last unit of output is higher than the average labour cost per unit of output (SRMC > AVC), the cost of producing the last unit must be pulling the average up (so AVC is increasing).

This relationship between SRMC and AVC is also visible in Columns 8 to 9 of Table 2.1. This relationship is very similar to the relationship between MPL and APL shown in Figure 2.1. In fact, we can think of the SRMC and AVC functions in Figure 2.2 as a 'mirror image' of the corresponding MPL and APL functions in Figure 2.1.

Long-run production and costs

In the long run, the firm has the opportunity to overcome the short-run constraint on production that is imposed by the Law of Diminishing Returns, by increasing its usage of *all* inputs. In addition to employing more workers, it can acquire more plant and machinery and move into a larger building. In other words, it can alter the scale of production.

The long-run relationship between the firm's inputs and output is governed by **returns to scale**. This refers to the proportionate increase in output that is achieved from any given proportionate increase in all inputs. Three types of returns to scale are identified schematically in Figure 2.3. Although the three cases are shown separately, firms can pass through all three phases as they expand the scale of their operations.

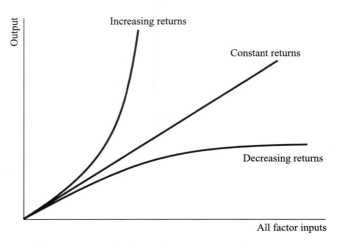

Figure 2.3 Increasing, constant and decreasing returns to scale

- **Increasing returns to scale** occurs when output increases more than proportionately to the increase in inputs. For example, a doubling of all inputs leads to more than a doubling of output. In this case there are **economies of scale**.

- **Constant returns to scale** occurs when output increases proportionately with an increase in inputs. A doubling of all inputs leads to a doubling of output.

- **Decreasing returns to scale** occurs when output increases less than proportionately to the increase in inputs. A doubling of all inputs leads to less than a doubling of output. In this case there are diseconomies of scale.

The sources of economies of scale and diseconomies of scale are considered in some detail below.

In order to derive the firm's long-run cost functions, we initially assume that the firm is faced with a choice between four possible values for the capital input, denoted K_1 to K_4. The firm can therefore choose between four different values for the scale of production. This means that for each of the four values of K, we can use the appropriate short-run production functions (treating K as fixed in each case and allowing L to vary) to derive the firm's short-run cost functions. Figure 2.4 shows the four separate short-run average cost functions, $SRAC_1$ to $SRAC_4$, and the corresponding short-run marginal cost functions, $SRMC_1$ to $SRMC_4$.

Reading Figure 2.4 from left to right, each successive short run average cost curve refers to a larger scale of production.

- Initially, as we move from K_1 to K_2 and $SRAC_1$ to $SRAC_2$, a larger scale of production generates lower average costs. This is due to increasing returns to scale, or economies of scale. Output increases more than proportionately to the increase in inputs, so the average cost (per unit of output produced) decreases.

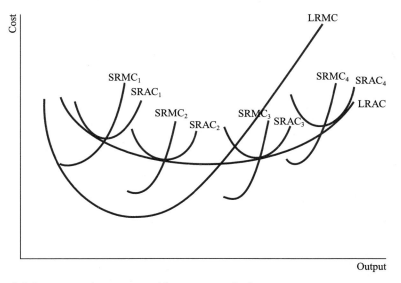

Figure 2.4 Long-run average cost and long-run marginal cost

■ At some point, however, the opportunities for reducing average costs by increasing the scale of production are exhausted. As we move from K_2 to K_3 and $SRAC_2$ to $SRAC_3$, a larger scale of production has no effect on average costs. This is the case of constant returns to scale. Output increases in the same proportion as the increase in inputs, so the average cost (per unit of output produced) remains unchanged.

■ If the scale of production is increased still further, average costs may eventually start to increase. As we move from K_3 to K_4 and $SRAC_3$ to $SRAC_4$, a larger scale of production generates higher average costs. This is due to decreasing returns to scale, or diseconomies of scale. Output increases less than proportionately to the increase in inputs, so the average cost (per unit of output produced) increases.

If we now assume that in the long run, the firm can choose between an infinite number of possible values for the capital input, or between an infinite number of possible scales of production, we can imagine $SRAC_1$ to $SRAC_4$ in Figure 2.4 as representative of an infinite number of possible short-run average cost functions. The smooth 'envelope' that enfolds these curves from below is the firm's long-run average cost function, denoted LRAC. LRAC represents the lowest cost of producing any given output level when the firm can vary both the capital and labour inputs in the long run.

It is important to notice that in order to produce any given level of output at the lowest long-run average cost, the firm does not usually operate at the lowest point on its short-run average cost function. For example, in Figure 2.5 the minimum average cost of producing q_1 units of output is C_1, obtained by operating on $SRAC_1$. If the firm were to increase its output from q_1 to q_2, enabling it to adjust to the minimum point on $SRAC_1$, it could produce at a lower average cost of C_2. However, if the firm really wants to produce q_2 rather than q_1, it can do better still by increasing its scale of production, and shifting onto a new short-run average cost function, $SRAC_2$. By doing so, it produces q_2 at an average cost of C_3, which is lower than C_2 at the

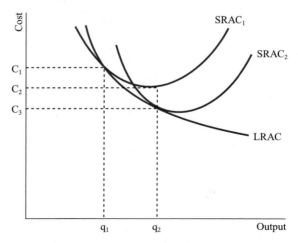

Figure 2.5 Short-run and long-run average cost functions

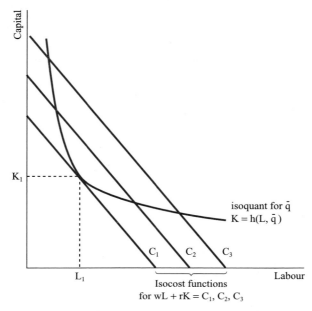

Figure 2.6 Isoquant and isocost functions

minimum point on $SRAC_1$. However, the same argument applies here as well, and the firm does not operate at the minimum point on $SRAC_2$. Only if the firm selects the output level at the lowest point on LRAC does it also operate at the minimum point on the corresponding SRAC function.

The firm's total cost and LRAC functions can also be derived more directly from the production function, using the apparatus of isoquants and isocost functions. This apparatus emphasizes the fact that in order to produce any given quantity of output at the lowest possible cost, the firm needs to select the most cost-effective combination of inputs. This decision will depend not only on the technological conditions embodied in the production function, but also on the prices of the inputs. In other words, there is both a technological dimension and an economic dimension to the firm's decision as to its choice of inputs.

Suppose a firm that employs two inputs, labour and capital, wishes to identify the combination of these inputs that will produce a given quantity of output, say $\bar{q}$, as cheaply as possible. By substituting $\bar{q}$ into the production function $\bar{q} = f(K, L)$ and rearranging, we can identify a relationship between all the combinations of L and K that could be combined in order to produce $\bar{q}$ units of output. This relationship is represented by the function $K = h(L, \bar{q})$, known as the **isoquant** for $\bar{q}$ units of output. h( ) is a new function, obtained by rearranging f( ). In Figure 2.6, which has L and K on the axes, this isoquant is depicted as a downward sloping and curved function. Assuming L and K are substitutable in production to some extent, the downward sloping isoquant implies $\bar{q}$ units of output could be produced either in a capital intensive manner (large K and small L), or in a labour intensive manner (small K and large L), or using some intermediate combination of K and L.

The set of three downward sloping lines shown in Figure 2.6 are the firm's **isocost** functions. Each isocost function shows all combinations of L and K the firm can hire which incur an identical total cost. The further away from the origin, the higher the total cost represented by each successive isocost function. The positions and slope of the isocost functions depend on the prices per unit of L and K, which can be denoted w (the wage rate per unit of labour) and r (the rental per unit of capital), respectively. Finally, Figure 2.6 shows that the most cost-effective method of producing $\bar{q}$ units of output is to hire L_1 units of labour and K_1 units of capital, at a total cost of $C_1 = wL_1 + rK_1$. At any other point on the isoquant for $\bar{q}$, the firm would be located on a higher isocost function than at this point of tangency. This analysis establishes that the lowest possible total cost of producing $\bar{q}$ units of output is C_1. The corresponding LRAC (long-run average cost) is $C_1/\bar{q}$. By repeating a similar analysis for all other possible output levels, we can build up a complete description of the firm's cost structure.

The LRAC function can be used to derive the firm's long-run marginal cost function, denoted LRMC in Figure 2.4. The relationship between LRMC and LRAC is rather similar to the relationship that exists between the firm's short-run marginal cost and average variable cost functions.

■ LRAC is decreasing when LRMC < LRAC. If the marginal cost of producing the last unit of output is lower than the average cost per unit of output, the cost of producing the last unit must be pulling the average down, so LRAC is decreasing. In this case there are economies of scale.

■ LRAC reaches its minimum value at the point where LRMC = LRAC. At this point there are constant returns to scale.

■ LRAC is increasing when LRMC > LRAC. If the marginal cost of producing the last unit of output is higher than the average cost per unit of output, the cost of producing the last unit must be pulling the average up, so LRAC is increasing. In this case there are diseconomies of scale.

Economies of scale

In this subsection, we consider in some detail *why* long-run **average costs** should either decrease or increase as the firm alters its scale of production in the long run. In other words, we examine the sources of **economies of scale** and **diseconomies** of scale.

Economies of scale can be classified as either real or pecuniary. Real economies of scale are associated with savings in average costs due to changes in the quantities of physical inputs. Pecuniary economies of scale are associated with savings in average costs due to changes in the prices paid by the firm for its inputs or factors of production. These categories can be further subdivided according to the specific element of the firm's operations from which the cost savings arise (for example, from labour, technology, marketing, transport or the managerial function). Economies of scale can be realized at the level of the plant, or (in the case of a multi-plant firm) at the level of the firm. Some of the principal sources of economies of scale are described below.

As a firm increases its scale of production, it can benefit from specialization through a greater division of labour. Individual workers can be assigned to specialized tasks.

As workers become more specialized, their knowledge and skills increase and they become more productive. Furthermore, less time is wasted through workers having to switch from one task to another. Accordingly, the firm's average costs are reduced. Similar benefits are also derived from specialization in management. A manager of a small firm may have to perform many tasks (financial planning and control, bookkeeping, marketing, personnel management, and so on). The manager may well lack the necessary expertise to perform some or all of these functons effectively. In contrast, a large firm benefits by employing specialist managers to perform each separate function.

Real economies arise from various technological relationships between inputs and output that underlie the firm's long-run production function. Some examples are as follows:

- *Large-scale production* may simply be more cost-effective than small-scale production. By producing at large volume, the firm can make use of large machines that would not be feasible for a small-scale producer. One large machine may produce more output from any given quantity of inputs than two smaller machines combined.

- *Indivisibilities* of capital and labour inputs are also an important source of economies for the large firm. Some types of capital equipment are 'lumpy' or indivisible. The firm either purchases a whole machine or it does not do so; it cannot acquire 10 per cent or 50 per cent of the machine. A combine harvester is a highly productive input in agriculture, but only a large farm operates at a sufficient scale to justify the purchase of such equipment. The usage of some inputs does not necessarily increase at all as the scale of production increases. A factory perhaps requires one receptionist and one photocopying machine, regardless of whether it produces 5,000 or 10,000 units of output per week. The same might apply to functions such as accounting, finance or health and safety. As the scale of production increases, the total cost of each indivisible input is spread over a larger volume of output, causing average costs to fall. Savings of a similar type might also be realized through a type of balancing process. Assume a firm uses one type of machine to produce and a second type of machine to package its product. If the first machine produces 30,000 units per day and the second packages 40,000 units per day, output has to be at least 120,000 per day (or multiples of 120,000) to fully utilize the capacity of both machines. For an output of 60,000 units, a firm acquires two production machines and two packaging machines, with the packaging machines operating at only three-quarters capacity. For an output of 80,000 units, the firm uses three production machines and two packaging machines, with the production machines operating at eight-ninths of their capacity.

- Learning economies are another important source of cost savings (Spence, 1981). Over time, workers and managers become more skilled as they repeat the same tasks. The length of the production run is therefore an important determinant of the extent to which the firm may benefit from learning economies. For example, Alchian (1963) identifies a learning curve in aircraft production: labour productivity in the manufacture of airframes was a function of the cumulative number of frames already assembled.

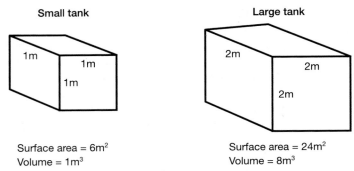

Figure 2.7 Surface area and volume of small and large storage tanks

■ Geometric relationships between inputs and outputs can result in cost savings as the scale of production increases. In some cases, costs may be proportional to surface area while outputs are proportional to volume. In Figure 2.7, a square tank of dimensions 1m × 1m × 1m has a surface area of 6m^2 (square metres) and a storage capacity of 1m^3 (cubic metres). A tank of dimensions 2m × 2m × 2m has a surface area of 24m^2 and a capacity of 8m^3. A fourfold increase in surface area is associated with an eightfold increase in volume. Accordingly, the capacity of an oil tanker increases more than proportionally with an increase in its surface area. Similarly, doubling an oil or gas pipeline's circumference more than doubles its capacity. Some costs (for example, the costs of materials) might be proportional to surface area, while output is proportional to volume. In the oil industry, a '0.6 rule of thumb' is sometimes used by engineers to indicate that a 100 per cent increase in capacity should require only a 60 per cent increase in costs.

Pecuniary economies arise if large firms find it easier than small firms to raise finance. A large firm may be able to offer lenders stronger security guarantees than a small firm. A large firm may have access to sources of finance unavailable to a small firm, such as the stock market or its own bond issues. Lenders may believe a large firm poses a lower risk, perhaps because a large firm can spread its risks through multi-plant operations or diversification, or because a large firm benefits from a reputation effect.

Large firms can buy and sell in bulk, benefiting from *purchasing and marketing economies*. Suppliers of raw materials or other inputs may be willing to offer discounts for large-scale orders. Retailers or distributors may be willing to offer more favourable terms or service to a large-scale producer. A large firm may be able to benefit from using large-scale forms of advertising, such as television advertising, which would be beyond the means of a smaller firm. A large firm that services a national market may be able to realize *transport economies*, by operating separate plants that produce and sell in different regions. A small firm that services a national market from a single plant may incur significant transport costs.

All of the economies of scale described above (both real and pecuniary) are *internal economies of scale*. In every case, cost savings are generated directly by the firm, through its own decision to increase its scale of production. In contrast, *external economies of scale* refer to cost savings that are generated not through expansion on the part of any one firm individually, but through the expansion of all of the industry's member firms collectively. As the size of an industry increases, all firms may realize benefits from factors including: increased specialization of labour; the availability of industry-specific education and training programmes; the availability of specialist facilities, support services or physical infrastructure; the growth of publicly or privately funded research centres; the development of expertise and knowledge of the industry's requirements within banks or other financial institutions; and so on. As the scale of the industry's aggregate production increases, external economies of scale tend to reduce average costs for all of the industry's member firms, large and small.

Case study 2.1

Economies of scale and hospitals in Scotland

The Scottish Office was asked by the Secretary of State for Scotland to recommend how resources in the National Health Service could be best allocated in Scotland. In 1999 the executive reported its findings. One of its chief concerns was to assess the costs of delivering health services to very different geographic areas, so as to ensure an equitable distribution of resources.

One aspect of this analysis was to analyse the implications of remoteness and rurality for the costs of providing hospital services, and other medical services. The costs of running hospitals in rural areas were considered to be higher than those in urban areas because rural hospitals usually operated on a small scale.

The report noted that large scale hospitals had the following advantages.

- They could spread their fixed assets, such as operating theatres and diagnostic equipment over a greater volume of patients, thereby reducing average costs.

- Specialist staff in larger hospitals could be used more efficiently.

- Large hospitals required a smaller margin for reserve capacity to cope with variability of demand. Small hospitals would require proportionately more reserve capacity to deal with unexpected variations in demand such as a sudden increase in births.

- The report also noted that large hospitals provided more staff development, leading to efficiency gains.

The evidence showed that the average cost of providing health services was greater in small hospitals than in large ones. In the case of the large mental illness hospitals, the average cost of patient care was around £700 a week; in the smaller hospitals, the equivalent figure was £900 a week. Similar cost differences were found in acute hospitals, maternity units and institutions caring for the elderly.

Source: Fair Shares for All Technical Report. National review of resource allocation for the NHS in Scotland, Scottish Executive, July 1999. www.scotland.gov.uk/library2/doc02/fsat-00.htm

Diseconomies of scale

Diseconomies of scale arise when long-run average costs tend to increase as output increases for plants or firms operating beyond a certain scale. Managerial diseconomies, arising from difficulties encountered in managing large organizations effectively, are perhaps the most widely cited explanation for diseconomies of scale. Sources of managerial diseconomies include the following:

- Strained communications between different tiers of management, or between different parts of the organization generally.

- Long chains of command and complex organizational structures.

- Low morale among the workforce, who may sense a lack of personal involvement or interest in the performance of the organization.

- Poor industrial relations, due to the complexity of relationships between the workforce and management, or between different groups of workers.

Williamson (1967) elaborates on the causes of managerial diseconomies of scale. The firm can be viewed as a coalition of various teams or groups who are responsible for specialist activities such as production, marketing and finance. Since much of the firm's activity requires teamwork, as in any team there are incentives for opportunistic behaviour such as shirking or free-riding on the part of individuals. This creates a need to monitor the performance of team members. Traditionally, monitoring has been the role of the entrepreneur, but in the modern corporation the entrepreneur has been replaced by salaried managers. Each layer of management is monitored by a higher tier of managers, who in turn are monitored by another tier, and so on. At the apex of the hierarchical structure is the final control exercised by the firm's owners.

An essential function of the hierarchy is to handle, transmit and process or interpret information as it flows between different levels of the organization. This information is subject to two distortions. First, deliberate distortion (information impactedness) occurs when managers, supervisors and team members at lower levels misrepresent their efforts or abilities, so as to appear in the best possible light. Second, accidental distortion (serial reproduction) occurs whenever information has to flow through many channels. Williamson draws an analogy with the children's party game of 'Chinese whispers':

> Bartlett (1932) illustrates this (serial reproduction) graphically with a line drawing of an owl which, when redrawn successively by eighteen individuals, each sketch based on its immediate predecessor, ended up as a recognizable cat; and the further from the initial drawing one moved, the greater the distortion experienced. The reliance of hierarchical organizations on serial reproduction for their functioning thus exposes them to what may become serious distortions in transmission.

> *(Williamson, 1967, p. 127)*

If decision makers do not have access to accurate information, errors tend to occur, and the firm's average cost tends to increase.

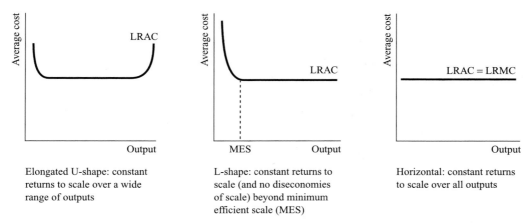

Figure 2.8 Long-run average cost functions with constant returns to scale

The managerial function is not necessarily the only source of **diseconomies of scale**. As the firm or plant expands, transport costs may tend to increase. As the firm's demand for raw materials or other inputs increases, these may have to be shipped in from further afield. Similarly, in order to find sufficient customers, the firm's product may need to be transported over longer geographic distances. External diseconomies of scale might also arise, if the expansion of all of the industry's member firms causes all firms' average costs to increase. This could happen if growth of the industry leads to shortages of raw materials or specialized labour, putting upward pressure on the costs of these essential factors of production.

Some economists have questioned whether one should necessarily assume that diseconomies of scale are inevitably encountered beyond a certain scale of production (Sargent, 1933). At plant level, there may be a natural tendency for average costs to increase as the plant size becomes too large and unwieldy. Therefore it seems reasonable to assume the plant's LRAC function is U-shaped. However, a multi-plant firm might be able to circumvent the tendency for LRAC to increase at plant level, simply by opening more plants and allowing each one to operate at the minimum point on its own LRAC function. In this case, the firm's LRAC function might be L-shaped rather than U-shaped (see Figure 2.8). Eventually, of course, managerial diseconomies at firm level may prevent what might otherwise be potentially limitless expansion of the firm through proliferation of plants. However, even in this case the inevitability of diseconomies of scale has been questioned. The development of decentralized organizational structures, with managers of separate divisions within the firm given considerable individual responsibility and decision-making autonomy, can be interpreted as an attempt to avoid managerial diseconomies that might otherwise arise under a structure of excessive centralized control (see also Section 3.6).

Economies of scope

Economies of scope are cost savings that arise when a firm produces two or more outputs using the same set of resources. Diversification causes average costs to fall if the total cost of producing several goods or services together is less than the sum of the costs of producing them separately. Economies of scope can be realized by bulk-purchasing inputs that are used in the production of several different products. For example the same microchips may be used in the manufacture of several different consumer electronics products. Economies of scope can also be realized by spreading the costs of specialist functions, such as finance, marketing or distribution, over a range of products or services. Computing and telecommunications may provide an important source of economies of scope. Data on the characteristics of customers who have already purchased one product can be stored electronically, and analysed in order to devise targeted marketing strategies for the promotion of other products or services.

Minimum efficient scale

The **minimum efficient scale** (MES) is defined as the output level beyond which the firm can make no further savings in LRAC (long-run average cost) through further expansion. In other words, the MES is achieved when all economies of scale are exhausted. Textbook microeconomic theory suggests a U-shaped long-run average cost function: as soon as economies of scale are exhausted, the firm immediately experiences diseconomies of scale. In practice, however, once MES has been achieved it is possible that a firm may be able to produce at the minimum attainable LRAC over a wide range of output levels. For any range of output levels over which the LRAC function is flat, the firm experiences constant returns to scale. Accordingly, a more realistic LRAC function might have an elongated U-shape, or (as suggested by our earlier discussion of the possible avoidance of diseconomies of scale) an L-shape. These possibilities are shown in the left-hand and middle diagrams in Figure 2.8.

In some of the theoretical models that are widely used in industrial organization, a convenient simplifying assumption is that firms encounter constant returns to scale over all possible output levels they can choose. In other words, it is sometimes convenient to simplify the assumed cost structure by ignoring economies of scale and diseconomies of scale altogether. In this case, the LRAC and LRMC functions are both horizontal and identical to each other, over all possible values of q. For example, suppose the total cost of producing 10 units of output is £100, the cost of producing 20 units is £200, and the cost of producing 30 units is £300. In this case LRAC = £10 (= £100/10 or £200/20 or £300/30) for any value of q. Similarly LRMC = £10 for any value of q, because each additional unit of output always adds exactly £10 to the firm's total cost. This case is shown in the right-hand diagram in Figure 2.8.

For any firm seeking to minimize its costs over the long term, it is important to be able to identify the shape of the LRAC function, or at least identify the output level at which MES is achieved and all possible cost savings arising from economies of scale have been realized. With reference to a textbook LRAC function, locating the MES is of course a trivial task. However, in practice a firm's managers may have little or no idea of the true shape of the LRAC function, and may have to rely on estimates. Some practical methods for the estimation of cost functions are described in Section 7.2 (see Box 7.1).

2.3 Demand, revenue, elasticity and profit maximization

Demand, average revenue and marginal revenue

The **market demand function** for a product or service shows the relationship between market price and the number of units of the product or service consumers wish to buy at that price. In many of the models that are presented in this book, we will assume that the market demand function is linear. Table 2.2 presents a numerical illustration of a linear market demand function. Columns 1 and 2 show that the maximum price any consumer would be prepared to pay is £2. When P = £2, Q = 1 unit is sold. However, if the market price is reduced below P = £2, more buyers are attracted: when P = £1.8, Q = 2 units are sold; when P = £1.6, Q = 3 units are sold; and so on. If the market price is reduced as low as P = £0.2, Q = 10 units are sold; and if (hypothetically) the product or service were being given away for free, Q = 11 would be the quantity demanded when P = 0.

We now suppose that the product or service is being supplied by one firm only, so the industry structure is monopoly. The theory of monopoly is developed in full in Section 2.4. At this stage, however, we have sufficient information to evaluate the

Table 2.2 Demand, revenue, price elasticity and profit maximization: numerical example

(1) Market price (£ per unit of output)	(2) Quantity demanded (Units per week)	(3) Total revenue (£ per week)	(4) Average revenue (= Price, £ per unit of output)	(5) Marginal revenue (£ per unit of output)	(6) Price elasticity of demand	(7) Short-run marginal cost (£ per unit of output)	(8) Total cost (£ per week)	(9) Profit (£ per week)
P	Q	TR	AR	MR	$\lvert$PED$\rvert$	SRMC	TC	π
2.2	0	0				1.0		−1.0
2.0	1	2.0	2.0	2.0	21.00	0.5	1.5	0.5
1.8	2	3.6	1.8	1.6	6.33	0.2	1.7	1.9
1.6	3	4.8	1.6	1.2	3.40	0.5	2.2	2.6
1.4	4	5.6	1.4	0.8	2.14	0.8	3.0	2.6
1.2	5	6.0	1.2	0.4	1.44	1.1	4.1	1.9
1.0	6	6.0	1.0	0.0	1.00	1.4	5.5	0.5
0.8	7	5.6	0.8	−0.4	0.69	1.7	7.2	−1.6
0.6	8	4.8	0.6	−0.8	0.47	2.0	9.2	−4.4
0.4	9	3.6	0.4	−1.2	0.29	2.3	11.5	−7.9
0.2	10	2.0	0.2	−1.6	0.16	2.6	14.1	−12.1
0.0	11	0.0	0.0	−2.0	0.05	2.9	17.0	−17.0

Illustrative calculations at (P = 1.8, Q = 2), columns 3 to 6:

TR = PQ = 1.8 × 2 = 3.6

AR = TR/Q = 3.6/2 = 1.8

MR = ΔTR = TR(Q = 2) − TR(Q = 1) = 3.6 − 2.0 = 1.6

$$\text{PED} = \frac{\Delta Q}{\Delta P} \times \frac{P}{Q} = \frac{2-1}{1.8-2.0} \times \frac{1.9}{1.5} = -6.33 \quad \Rightarrow \quad \lvert\text{PED}\rvert = 6.33$$

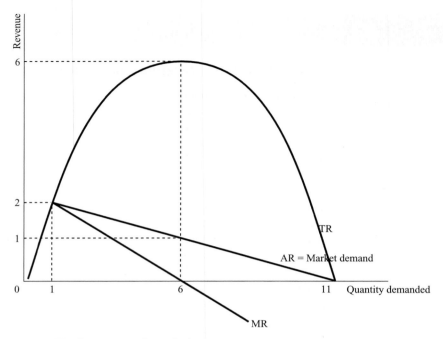

Figure 2.9 Total, average and marginal revenue

monopolist's **total revenue** function, TR. By definition, total revenue *equals* price × quantity, so each entry in Column 3 of Table 2.2 is obtained by multiplying the corresponding entries in Columns 1 and 2. Notice that the monopolist's TR function has an inverted U-shaped appearance: TR = 0 for Q = 0 and Q = 11, and TR attains its maximum value of TR = 6 for Q = 5 and Q = 6.

Columns 4 and 5 of Table 2.2 show the monopolist's **average revenue** and **marginal revenue** functions. The average revenue function, AR, shows the average revenue per unit of output sold, and is calculated by dividing total revenue (Column 3) by quantity demanded (Column 2). Since TR = PQ, AR = TR/Q = PQ/Q = P. In other words, average revenue is identical to price. Therefore Column 4 of Table 2.2 is the same as Column 1. The marginal revenue function, MR, shows the additional revenue generated by the last unit of output sold, and is calculated as the change in total revenue achieved as a result of each one-unit increase in quantity demanded. For Q ≤ 5, TR increases as Q increases, so MR > 0. Between Q = 5 and Q = 6, TR does not change as Q increases, so MR = 0. For Q ≥ 7, TR decreases as Q increases, so MR < 0. Figure 2.9 shows the monopolist's TR, AR and MR functions graphically.

Elasticity

Price elasticity of demand

Table 2.2 and Figure 2.9 demonstrate that a monopolist considering implementing a price reduction could experience either an increase, or no change, or a decrease in its total revenue, depending on the point on the market demand function from which the price reduction is introduced. By definition, TR = PQ. As P falls, Q rises, so the overall effect of a reduction in P on TR could be positive, zero or negative. More specifically:

- If the (positive) quantity effect dominates the (negative) price effect, TR increases as P falls.

- If the quantity effect just balances the price effect, TR remains unchanged as P falls.

- If the quantity effect is dominated by the price effect, TR decreases as P falls.

The effect of a reduction in P on TR therefore depends upon the tresponsiveness of quantity demanded to a change in price. **Price elasticity of demand**, PED, provides a convenient measure of this responsiveness. The formula for calculating PED is as follows:

$$PED = \frac{\text{proportionate change in quantity demanded}}{\text{proportionate change in price}}$$

Let ΔP denote the change in price between any two points on the market demand function, and let ΔQ denote the corresponding change in quantity demanded. Then the proportionate change in quantity demanded is $\Delta Q/Q$, and the proportionate change in price is $\Delta P/P$. The values of P and Q used in the denominators of these expressions are usually taken as the values midway between the two points on the market demand function over which PED is being calculated. Accordingly, we can write:

$$PED = \frac{\left(\dfrac{\Delta Q}{Q}\right)}{\left(\dfrac{\Delta P}{P}\right)} = \left(\frac{\Delta Q}{\Delta P}\right)\left(\frac{P}{Q}\right)$$

Because the changes in P and Q are in opposite directions ($\Delta Q > 0$ if $\Delta P < 0$, and $\Delta Q < 0$ if $\Delta P > 0$), the formula for PED produces a negative value. However, when economists discuss price elasticity of demand, it is quite common to ignore the minus-sign and refer to the corresponding positive value. Therefore a 'price elasticity of demand of 2' refers to the case PED = −2. The mathematical notation used to convert a negative value into its corresponding positive value is the absolute value function, written $|PED| = 2$. Column 6 of Table 2.2 shows the values of $|PED|$ calculated over each successive pair of values for (P, Q) shown in Columns 1 and 2.

We can now amplify the previous discussion of the effect of a reduction in P on TR.

- If $|PED| > 1$, TR increases as P falls. The quantity effect dominates the price effect. The demand function is said to be *price elastic*. Quantity demanded is sensitive to the change in price.

- If $|PED| = 1$, TR remains unchanged as P falls. The quantity effect just balances the price effect. The demand function is said to exhibit *unit price elasticity*.

- If $|PED| < 1$, TR decreases as P falls. The quantity effect is dominated by the price effect. The demand function is said to be *price inelastic*. Quantity demanded is insensitive to the change in price.

Another useful interpretation of price elasticity of demand is obtained by demonstrating the relationship between PED and MR. By definition:

$$MR = \frac{\Delta TR}{\Delta Q}$$

where ΔTR denotes the change in total revenue achieved as a result of a change in quantity demanded, denoted ΔQ. Using the definition $TR = PQ$ and a mathematical rule known as the Product Rule, an expression for MR in terms of P, Q, ΔP and ΔQ is as follows:

$$MR = \frac{\Delta TR}{\Delta Q} = \frac{\Delta(PQ)}{\Delta Q} = P \times \frac{\Delta Q}{\Delta Q} + \frac{\Delta P}{\Delta Q} \times Q$$

Since $\Delta Q/\Delta Q = 1$, we can write:

$$MR = P + \frac{\Delta P}{\Delta Q} \times Q = P + P \times \left(\frac{\Delta P}{\Delta Q} \times \frac{Q}{P} \right) = P + P \times \frac{1}{\left(\frac{\Delta Q}{\Delta P} \times \frac{P}{Q} \right)}$$

$$= P\left(1 + \frac{1}{PED} \right) = P\left(1 - \frac{1}{|PED|} \right)$$

See Appendix 1 for a more formal mathematical derivation of this result. The interpretation of the expression $MR = P\left(1 - \frac{1}{|PED|} \right)$ is as follows:

- If $|PED| > 1$, $1/|PED| < 1$ and $MR > 0$. When the demand function is price elastic, $MR > 0$.

- If $|PED| = 1$, $1/|PED| = 1$ and $MR = 0$. When the demand function exhibits unit elasticity, $MR = 0$.

- If $|PED| < 1$, $1/|PED| > 1$ and $MR < 0$. When the demand function is price inelastic, $MR < 0$.

It is possible to define price elasticity of demand either at market level, or at firm level. In the preceding discussion, we avoided making this distinction by referring to a monopolist. However, in a competitive market in which an identical product is sold by many firms, there might be a big difference between the sensitivity of the total quantity demanded to a change in the market price (assuming all firms make the same price adjustment), and the sensitivity of one individual firm's quantity demanded to a change in its own price (assuming other firms keep their prices unchanged).

Price elasticity of demand is only one of several elasticities used by economists to measure the sensitivity of one variable (in the case of PED, quantity demanded) to changes in another variable (in the case of PED, market price). We will encounter other elasticities, defined in a similar manner to PED, at various points throughout this book. At this stage, however, we will mention three examples in order to illustrate the wide range of applications of the concept of elasticity. In each case, the symbol 'Δ' in front of a variable denotes a change in this variable.

Cross price elasticity of demand

Cross price elasticity of demand, CED, measures the sensitivity of the quantity demanded of Good 1 to a change in the price of Good 2.

$$\text{CED} = \frac{\text{Proportionate change in the quantity demanded of Good 1}}{\text{Proportionate change in the price of Good 2}}$$

$$\text{CED} = \frac{\Delta Q_1}{\Delta P_2} \times \frac{P_2}{Q_1}$$

where Q_1 denotes the demand for Good 1, and P_2 denotes the price of Good 2.

CED provides an indication of whether Goods 1 and 2 are **substitutes** or **complements** in consumption, or whether the demand for Good 1 is unrelated to the price of Good 2:

■ If CED > 0, an increase in P_2 leads to an increase in Q_1. This suggests Goods 1 and 2 are substitutes: as the price of Good 2 increases (and the demand for Good 2 decreases), consumers tend to switch from Good 2 to Good 1, causing the demand for Good 1 to increase.

■ If CED < 0, an increase in P_2 leads to a decrease in Q_1. This suggests Goods 1 and 2 are complements: as the price of Good 2 increases (and the demand for Good 2 decreases), consumers also reduce their consumption of Good 1, causing the demand for Good 1 to decrease.

■ If CED = 0, an increase in P_2 has no effect on Q_1. This suggests Goods 1 and 2 are neither substitutes nor complements: the demand for Good 1 is independent of the price of good 2.

Advertising elasticity of demand

Advertising elasticity of demand, AED, measures the sensitivity of quantity demanded to a change in advertising expenditure.

$$\text{AED} = \frac{\text{Proportionate change in quantity demanded}}{\text{Proportionate change in advertising expenditure}}$$

$$\text{AED} = \frac{\Delta Q}{\Delta A} \times \frac{A}{Q}$$

where Q denotes quantity demanded, and A denotes advertising expenditure.

AED is a measure of the effectiveness of advertising. We would normally expect AED to be positive: an increase in advertising leads to an increase in quantity demanded. Calculated or estimated at the level of the individual firm, AED might be an important indicator of the level of resources the firm should allocate to its advertising budget. If AED is large, the firm might decide to advertise heavily; but if AED is small it might be more cost-effective to look for alternative methods of increasing the demand for its product.

Price elasticity of supply

Price elasticity of supply, PES, measures the sensitivity of quantity supplied to market price.

$$PES = \frac{\text{Proportionate change in quantity supplied}}{\text{Proportionate change in price}}$$

$$PES = \frac{\Delta Q_S}{\Delta P} \times \frac{P}{Q_S}$$

where Q_S denotes quantity supplied, and P denotes price. The s-subscript on Q_S distinguishes the formula for PES from the (otherwise identical) formula for PED. While we would expect an increase in price to be associated with a *decrease* in quantity demanded, we would also expect an increase in price to be associated with an *increase* in quantity supplied. Therefore we would expect PED to be negative and PES to be positive.

In this section, we have focused on the relationship between price and quantity demanded. For most products, however, price is not the only determinant of the level of demand. Case study 2.2 examines a wide range of factors that influence the level of demand for spectator attendance at professional team sports matches.

Case study 2.2

The demand for spectator attendance at professional football

The determinants of the level of demand for spectator attendance at professional team sports matches have been the subject of attention from economists since the 1970s. Some of the earliest contributions to this literature include Demmert (1973), Hart *et al.* (1975) and Noll (1974). The literature is reviewed by Dobson and Goddard (2001) and Sandy *et al.* (2004). This case study examines some of the main factors that influence spectator demand.

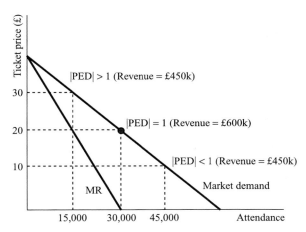

Figure 1 Uniform ticket pricing for profit maximization – zero marginal cost

Price

Economic theory suggests a professional sports club should price its tickets in order to maximize its revenue or profit. In practice, however, there is some empirical evidence to suggest that many clubs fail to achieve this.

Suppose initially the club's marginal cost (the direct cost incurred by attracting one additional spectator into the stadium) is zero. Figure 1 shows the club's demand function for spectator attendance at one match: the number of spectators it would attract at each (uniform) ticket price. In this case, the club maximizes its revenue by charging £20 per ticket and attracting 30,000 spectators: this is, equivalent to maximizing the area of the rectangle beneath the market demand function.

- At prices above £20, price elasticity of demand |PED| is greater than one.
- At prices below £20, |PED| is less than one.
- At a price of £20, at the very centre of the demand function, |PED| *equals* one.

Suppose instead the club's marginal cost (cost of stewarding or policing) is £2 per spectator. Figure 2 shows the club's marginal cost, and the same demand function. In this case profit maximization requires charging £21 per ticket and attracting 28,500 spectators: this is equivalent to maximizing the area of the rectangle between between the market demand and marginal cost functions.

Therefore a profit-maximizing club should always operate on a section of the demand function where |PED| ≥ 1. However, several econometric studies have found that the actual |PED| for football attendance is less than one. There are several possible explanations:

- Football clubs may not be profit maximizers, as the theory assumes.

- The econometric studies could be wrong. It is difficult to estimate price elasticities accurately, because football clubs do not change their prices very often. In recent years,

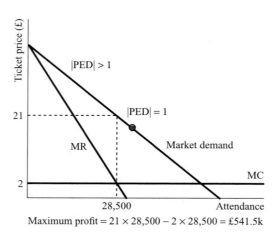

Maximum profit = 21 × 28,500 − 2 × 28,500 = £541.5k

Figure 2 Uniform ticket pricing for profit maximization – positive marginal cost

many stadia are regularly sold out, so it is difficult to obtain good data on the sensitivity of spectator demand to variations in price.

■ Alternatively, the clubs may be operating more sophisticated pricing policies, for which operating with $|PED| < 1$ may be consistent with profit maximization. This is the subject of Case study 10.1.

■ Finally, interrelationships between the demand for match tickets, and the demand for related products or services such as live television broadcasts, merchandise or catering could explain why it is profitable for clubs to price their match tickets so that $|PED| < 1$.

City population and *per capita* income

There is a natural tendency for the strongest teams to be located in the cities with the largest population and/or largest *per capita* incomes. Teams with the largest potential or actual markets tend to generate the most income. In the long term this usually translates into playing success.

In the North American major league sports (baseball, American football, basketball, hockey), membership of the major leagues is closed: there is a fixed number of franchise-holding teams. In the longer term, franchises tend to gravitate towards the largest cities that can afford to pay the highest subsidies. In Europe, membership of the top divisions is regulated through the promotion and relegation system:

■ If a small-market team is promoted to the top division, its lack of spending power often ensures speedy relegation.

■ If a big-market team is relegated to a lower division, its high spending power will usually guarantee promotion back to the top division sooner or later.

Uncertainty of outcome and competitive balance

It is widely assumed by sports economists that spectator interest in sport depends on uncertainty of outcome. There are three (related) types of uncertainty of outcome:

- Degree of uncertainty concerning the result of an individual match.

- Degree of uncertainty concerning the end-of-season outcome of a championship race or a battle to avoid relegation.

- Degree to which championship success is concentrated in the hands of a few teams, or spread among many teams, over a number of years.

In today's English Premiership, there is less of all three types of uncertainty of outcome than in the equivalent competition (the Football League) 20, 30 or 50 years ago. There has been extensive debate concerning the usefulness of policy measures designed to promote competitive balance and increase uncertainty of outcome:

- Capping of teams' total expenditure on players' wages or salaries.

- Sharing or pooling of gate or television revenues.

- The US draft pick system, whereby the weakest teams from the previous season get first choice of new players turning professional for the first time.

Television and newspaper publicity

In most countries, professional sports such as football probably could not survive without the free publicity they receive through newspaper, television and radio coverage. Equally, sports coverage is essential for the ability of the print and broadcasting media to attract readers, viewers, listeners and therefore advertising revenue.

For a long time, it has been assumed by sports administrators and academics that if a sports fixture is the subject of live television coverage, spectator attendance may be adversely affected. However, the statistical evidence for a negative impact of television coverage on attendance is rather mixed: some studies find such an effect, while others find no effect.

Other relevant factors include the following:

- Even if attendance is affected, the loss of gate revenue might be compensated by direct income from the broadcaster, or indirect income from advertising or sponsorship within the stadium.

- The broadcasting rights might be more valuable if the stadium is full, due to the improved atmosphere created by a capacity crowd. Consequently there might be a case for offering cheaper ticket prices to spectators attending televised matches.

Geographic market segmentation

Fifty years ago, the markets served by each English football club were local: most spectators lived within walking distance or a short bus or train journey from the stadium. Today, the most successful clubs attract a national audience. Factors that have contributed to reduced geographic market segmentation have included:

- growth in private car ownership;
- improvements in the road transport system;
- demographic change (population is more mobile geographically);
- increased media coverage of star players and leading teams.

Stadium facilities and hooliganism

In England, anecdotal evidence suggests that hooliganism and the antiquated, delapidated physical condition of many football stadia made a major contribution to the long-term decline in football attendances between the late 1940s and mid-1980s. Aggregate attendances for English league football fell from 41.0m in the 1948–49 season to 16.5m in the 1985–86 season, before recovering to reach 29.2m in the 2003–04 season.

Since the mid-1980s, incidents of hooliganism affecting English football at club level have become much less frequent. Over the same period, the stadia of most leading clubs have been significantly upgraded or completely rebuilt. Since the mid-1990s, Premiership clubs have been required to provide seated viewing accommodation only; many lower-division clubs have done so as well.

Profit maximization

Returning to Table 2.2, columns 7 and 8 summarize the monopolist's short-run cost structure. In accordance with the discussion in Section 2.2, the monopolist's short-run production function is subject to the Law of Diminishing Returns, and short-run marginal costs (SRMC) eventually increase as output (Q) increases. As before, total cost is the sum of the firm's variable cost (which can be inferred from the SRMC function) and fixed cost (assumed to be £1 per week). Column 9 shows the monopolist's profit function. Profit, denoted π, is total revenue *minus* total cost, or $\pi = TR - TC$.

In order to maximize its profit in the short run, the monopolist should select its output level so that marginal revenue *equals* short-run marginal cost, $MR = SRMC$. It is worthwhile to increase output as long as the additional revenue gained by doing so exceeds the additional cost incurred. Once the point is reached at which the additional revenue equals the additional cost, the firm should stop. In Table 2.2, this can be demonstrated by starting from the lowest possible output level of $Q = 0$ and increasing Q in steps of one:

- Increasing from $Q = 0$ to $Q = 1$ increases revenue by $MR = £2$, and increases costs by $SRMC = £0.5$. Therefore profit increases by £1.5, from $\pi = -1.0$ to $\pi = 0.5$.

- Similarly, increasing from $Q = 1$ to $Q = 2$ increases profit by £1.4, from $\pi = 0.5$ to $\pi = 1.9$; and increasing from $Q = 2$ to $Q = 3$ increases profit by £0.7, from $\pi = 1.9$ to $\pi = 2.6$.

■ Increasing from Q = 3 to Q = 4 increases revenue by MR = £0.8, and increases costs by SRMC = £0.8. Therefore profit remains unchanged, at π = 2.6. Between Q = 3 and Q = 4 MR = SRMC, and π = 2.6 is the maximum profit the monopolist can earn.

■ Increasing from Q = 4 to Q = 5 increases revenue by MR = £0.4, and increases costs by SRMC = £1.1. Therefore profit falls by £0.7, from π = 2.6 to π = 1.9. Any further increase beyond Q = 5 also causes profit to fall.

The profit-maximizing rule 'marginal revenue *equals* marginal cost' is quite general, and applies not only to monopolists, but also to firms operating in other market structures such as perfect competition and monopolistic competition. Furthermore, this rule is valid not only for profit maximization in the short run (MR = SRMC, as in Table 2.2), but also for profit maximization in the long run (MR = LRMC).

2.4 Theory of perfect competition and monopoly

It is difficult to decide precisely when the first theory of the firm emerged which was judged to be sufficiently coherent to be acceptable as the 'general' theory. Some people would claim that the credit should go to Edwin Chamberlin and Joan Robinson in the 1930s. Others tend to look back further, to the contributions of Alfred Marshall in the 1890s, or perhaps even Augustin Cournot in the 1830s or Adam Smith in the 1770s. Clearly each development in the theory was built partly on the preceding analyses, and it is impossible to credit any one economist with sole responsibility for the theory. Nevertheless, it is now possible to identify a coherent body of theory that claims to explain the determination of price and output, for both the industry and the individual firm, based on assumptions of **profit maximization** on the part of each individual firm. This body of theory is known as the neoclassical theory of the firm.

Within the neoclassical theory, different models are used to analyse price and output determination for different market structures. The most important characteristics of market structure are the number of firms, the extent of barriers to entry, and the degree of product differentiation. Table 2.3 shows a standard typology of market structures. The two most extreme cases are **perfect competition** (the most competitive model) and **monopoly** (the least competitive). Section 2.4 examines these two cases, and Section 2.5 draws some comparisons between their efficiency and welfare properties. Occupying a large swathe of territory between perfect competition and

Table 2.3 The neoclassical theory of the firm: typology of market structures

	No. of firms	Entry conditions	Product differentiation
Perfect competition	Many	Free entry	Identical products
Imperfect competition			
Monopolistic competition	Many	Free entry	Some differentiation
Oligopoly	Few	Barriers to entry	Some differentiation
Monopoly	One	No entry	Complete differentiation

monopoly is **imperfect competition**, which subdivides into two cases: **monopolistic competition** (the more competitive variant of imperfect competition) and **oligopoly** (the less competitive variant). This chapter concludes in Section 2.6 by examining the first of these two cases: monopolistic competition. Oligopoly theory forms a much larger sub-field within microeconomics and industrial economics, and requires its own separate and more extensive treatment. Accordingly, oligopoly theory provides the subject material for Chapters 4 and 5 of this book.

Perfect competition

In the neoclassical theory of **perfect competition**, the industry is assumed to have the following characteristics.

■ There are large numbers of buyers and sellers. It is sometimes said that buyers and sellers are atomistic. An important implication is that the actions of any individual buyer or seller have a negligible influence on the market price.

■ Firms are free to enter into or exit from the industry, and a decision to enter or exit does not impose any additional costs on the firm concerned. In other words, there are no barriers to entry and exit.

■ The goods or services produced and sold are identical or homogeneous. In other words, there is no product differentiation.

■ All buyers and sellers have perfect information. There are no transaction costs, such as costs incurred in searching for information or in negotiating or monitoring contracts between buyers and sellers.

■ There are no transport costs. Therefore the geographical locations of buyers and sellers do not influence their decisions as to where to buy or sell.

■ Firms act independently of each other, and each firm seeks to maximize its own profit.

These assumptions ensure each individual buyer and seller is a price taker. **Price taking behaviour** means each buyer and seller operates under the assumption that the current market price is beyond his or her personal control. Each firm recognizes its market share is sufficiently small that any decision to raise or lower its output would have a negligible impact on the industry's total output, and therefore a negligible impact on the market price. This also means each firm believes it can sell whatever quantity of output it wishes to sell at the current market price. An important implication of price taking behaviour is that any attempt on the part of an individual firm to increase or decrease its own price directly would be ineffective. If the firm set a higher price than its competitors, all of the firm's customers would immediately switch to its competitors, and the quantity of output sold by the firm would fall to zero. On the other hand, it would be pointless for the firm to set a lower price than its competitors because the firm can already sell as much output as it wishes at the current market price.

With price taking behaviour, each firm faces a horizontal firm-level demand function, located at the current market price. A very small proportionate reduction in price would induce a very large proportionate increase in quantity demanded. This means the perfectly competitive firm's price elasticity of demand (PED) is infinite.

Recall $PED = \frac{\Delta Q}{\Delta P} \times \frac{P}{Q}$. Accordingly, if ΔP is infinitely small (and negative) and ΔQ is infinitely large (and positive), $PED = -\infty$ or $|PED| = \infty$. From Section 2.3, the firm's demand function is also its average revenue (AR) function. Finally, given that the firm's demand or AR function is horizontal, the same function is also the firm's marginal revenue (MR) function. The equivalence between marginal revenue and price when $|PED| = \infty$ can be demonstrated as follows:

$$MR = P\left(1 - \frac{1}{|PED|}\right) = P\left(1 - \frac{1}{\infty}\right) = P(1 - 0) = P$$

The analysis of the perfectly competitive firm's short-run and long-run cost structure is as described in Section 2.2. Accordingly, we can work out the firm's profit-maximizing output decision both in the short run and in the long run. In order to keep the analysis as simple as possible, for the purposes of the short-run analysis we assume each firm is already using the quantity of the fixed factor of production (capital) that will eventually be consistent with the minimization of long-run average costs, or production at the minimum efficient scale, in the long run. For simplicity we also assume fixed costs are zero, so the firm's average variable cost (AVC) and short-run average cost (SRAC) functions are the same. Figure 2.10 shows the determination of the pre- and post-entry market price and the output levels for one representative firm, and for the industry as a whole. In order to understand Figure 2.10, it is important to follow the construction of the firm- and industry-level diagrams in the correct sequence, as follows.

■ The upper left-hand diagram shows the firm's SRAC and short-run marginal cost (SRMC) functions. The firm's MR function is horizontal and equivalent to the market price (P). Profit maximization requires MR = SRMC, so the firm's profit-maximizing output level for any given value of P will be found by reading from the SRMC function. To produce any output at all, the firm must at least cover its SRAC. Therefore the minimum price the firm is willing to accept is determined by the intersection of SRMC and SRAC. The section of SRMC above this intersection is the representative firm's supply function.

■ The upper right-hand diagram shows the market demand function, and the industry supply function. The industry supply function is constructed by summing horizontally the SRMC functions over all N_1 firms in the industry. (Each individual SRMC function is a supply function for one firm; therefore the horizontal sum of the SRMC functions is the supply function for the entire industry.) The pre-entry market price of P_1 is determined by the intersection of the market demand and industry supply functions. Pre-entry industry output is Q_1.

■ Returning to the upper left-hand diagram, we can now locate the representative firm's demand, AR and MR functions, shown by the horizontal line at P_1. The firm maximizes profit by producing q_1 units of output, at which MR = SRMC. By construction $q_1 = Q_1/N_1$, or $Q_1 = N_1 q_1$. At the pre-entry profit-maximizing equilibrium represented by P_1 and q_1, the representative firm earns an abnormal profit shown by the shaded area between P_1 and C_1, the firm's average cost.

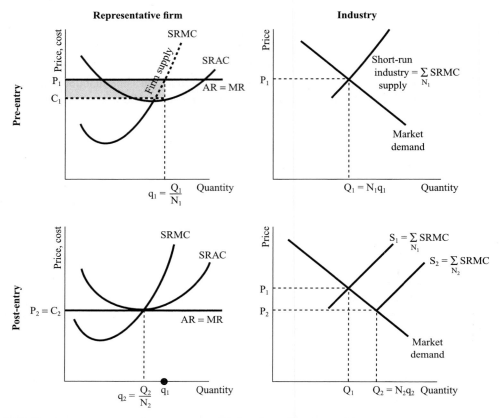

Figure 2.10 Short-run pre-entry and post-entry equilibrium in perfect competition

■ The availability of abnormal profits attracts entrants, so (P_1, Q_1) cannot represent a final or stable equilibrium. Entry increases the number of firms from N_1 to N_2, and in the lower right-hand diagram shifts the industry supply function to the right from S_1 to S_2. Consequently, price falls from P_1 to P_2, and industry output increases from Q_1 to Q_2.

■ In the lower left-hand diagram, we can locate the representative firm's post-entry demand, AR and MR functions, shown by the horizontal line at P_2. The firm maximizes profit by producing q_2 units of output, at which MR = SRMC. By construction $q_2 = Q_2/N_2$, or $Q_2 = N_2 q_2$. At the post-entry profit-maximizing equilibrium represented by P_2 and q_2, the representative firm earns a normal profit only because P_2 coincides with C_2, the firm's average cost. The fall in market price caused by entry and the increase in industry supply has eliminated the pre-entry abnormal profit. Post-entry, each individual firm produces slightly less output than it did pre-entry, but total post-entry industry output has increased due to the increase in the number of firms.

Figure 2.11 shows the equivalent long-run analysis. For simplicity Figure 2.11 shows only the final (post-entry) equilibrium, corresponding to (P_2, Q_2) in Figure 2.10. In Figure 2.11, all short-run functions are identical to the ones in Figure 2.10. In addition,

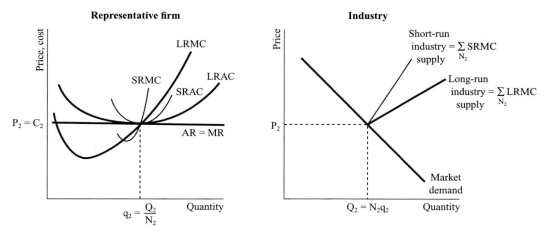

Figure 2.11 Long-run post-entry equilibrium in perfect competition

the left-hand diagram shows the representative firm's long-run marginal cost (LRMC) and long-run average cost (LRAC) functions. Notice that SRAC is nested within LRAC, as in Figure 2.4. In the right-hand diagram, the long-run industry supply function is constructed by summing LRMC horizontally over all N_2 firms, in the same way as before. The equilibrium market price of P_2 is located by the intersection of both the short-run and long-run supply functions with the market demand function.

Monopoly

In the neoclassical theory of **monopoly**, the industry is assumed to have the following characteristics.

■ There are large numbers of atomistic buyers, but there is only one seller. Therefore the selling firm's demand function is the market demand function, and the firm's output decision determines the market price.

■ There are insurmountable barriers to entry. If the monopolist earns an abnormal profit, there is no threat that entrants will be attracted into the industry.

■ The good or service produced and sold is unique, and there are no substitutes. In other words, there is complete product differentiation.

■ The buyers and the seller may have perfect or imperfect information.

■ Geographical location could be the defining characteristic which gives the selling firm its monopoly position. In a spatial monopoly, transport costs are sufficiently high to prevent buyers from switching to alternative sellers located in other regions or countries.

■ The selling firm seeks to maximize its own profit.

As before, the analysis of the monopolist's short-run and long-run cost structure is as described in Section 2.2. Figure 2.12 shows the determination of price and output. In order to understand Figure 2.12, it is important to note the following points.

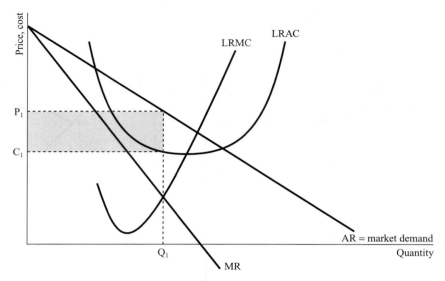

Figure 2.12 Long-run equilibrium in monopoly

■ Since there is only one firm, Figure 2.12 does not distinguish between the firm and the industry. By definition, the monopolist's private price and output decisions immediately establish the market price and the industry output. This means that for a monopoly, there is no industry supply function. Industry output depends on the monopolist's private profit-maximizing output decision, which in turn depends on the shape of the monopolist's cost and revenue functions. In contrast to the case of perfect competition, it is not possible to express this decision in the form of a direct supply relationship between market price and industry output.

■ Since there is no entry, Figure 2.12 does not distinguish between the pre-entry and post-entry equilibria.

■ For simplicity the analysis in Figure 2.12 is limited to the long-run case: the monopolist's short-run average and marginal cost functions are not shown.

The monopolist's profit-maximizing output level of Q_1 is located at the intersection of the marginal revenue (MR) and long-run marginal cost (LRMC) functions. The market price of P_1 is established by reading from the market demand or average revenue (AR) function at Q_1, and the monopolist's average cost of C_1 is established by reading from the long-run average cost (LRAC) function at Q_1. In this case, the monopolist earns an abnormal profit represented by the shaded area between P_1 and C_1. See Appendix 1 for a mathematical derivation of the monopolist's profit-maximizing equilibrium for the case where LRAC and LRMC are horizontal.

2.5 Efficiency and welfare properties of perfect competition and monopoly

In much of the academic, political and media discussion about the role of market forces and competition in allocating resources in a free market economy, there is a strong presumption that competition is somehow a desirable ideal, and conversely monopoly is a state of affairs to be avoided if at all possible. Having examined the determination of market price and output in the theoretical models of perfect competition and monopoly, we are now able to assess the validity of these frequently expressed claims. From a comparison between the right-hand diagram in Figure 2.11 (long-run industry equilibrium under perfect competition) and Figure 2.12 (long-run profit maximization under monopoly), the following points emerge:

- Under monopoly, market price is higher and output is lower than under perfect competition.

- The monopolist typically fails to produce at the minimum efficient scale (MES), and therefore fails to produce at the minimum attainable LRAC. In contrast, the perfectly competitive firm produces at the MES in the long-run equilibrium.

- The monopolist earns an abnormal profit in the long run, while the perfectly competitive firm earns only a normal profit.

Market price is higher under monopoly than it is under perfect competition. In the latter case, price *equals* (short-run or long-run) marginal cost. This suggests that the degree to which price exceeds marginal cost provides a useful indicator or measure of market power. Accordingly, Lerner (1934) proposes the following measure of market power, known as the **Lerner index**:

$$L = \frac{P - MC}{P}$$

The Lerner index is subject to a minimum value of zero, and a maximum value of one. In perfect competition, $P = MC$ so $L = 0$. In monopoly $P > MC$, and if $MC > 0$, $0 < L < 1$. After some simple manipulations, the Lerner index can also be expressed in terms of price elasticity of demand, as follows:

$$MR = P\left(1 - \frac{1}{|PED|}\right) = P - \frac{P}{|PED|} \Rightarrow P - MR = \frac{P}{|PED|} \Rightarrow \frac{P - MR}{P} = \frac{1}{|PED|}$$

For a profit-maximizing firm, $MR = MC$. Therefore we can write:

$$\frac{P - MC}{P} = \frac{1}{|PED|}, \text{ or } L = \frac{1}{|PED|}$$

The Lerner index is the reciprocal of the firm's price elasticity of demand. In perfect competition, $|PED| = \infty$ for each firm, so $L = 0$ (as above). In monopoly, if $MC > 0$ we must also have $MR > 0$. This implies $|PED| > 1$, so $0 < L < 1$ (as above).

The Lerner index provides a convenient measure of a firm's market power based on the relationship between its price and marginal cost. However, does it actually matter that market price and profit are both higher under monopoly than under perfect competition? This might be bad news for consumers, but it is also good news for producers. We should hesitate before claiming, solely on the basis of these comparisons, that competition is more desirable than monopoly. More desirable for whom? In fact, a slightly more sophisticated comparison is required, taking account of the efficiency and **welfare** properties of the two models. On the basis of this kind of comparison, it can be shown that perfect competition is usually preferable to monopoly, because the long-run competitive equilibrium has several desirable properties that are not satisfied by the corresponding long-run monopoly equilibrium. Our first task is to define the relevant notions of efficiency.

Allocative efficiency is achieved when there is no possible reallocation of resources that could make one agent (producer or consumer) better off without making at least one other agent worse off. A necessary condition for allocative efficiency is that the marginal benefit (to society as a whole) of an additional unit of output being produced *equals* the marginal cost of producing the additional unit of output. We can interpret the market price (the price at which the most marginal consumer is prepared to buy) as a measure of the value society as a whole places in the most marginal unit of output produced. Accordingly, allocative efficiency requires that the total quantity of output produced should be such that price *equals* marginal cost.

■ If price exceeds marginal cost, the value that society would place on an additional unit of output (measured by the price the most marginal consumer is prepared to pay) exceeds the cost of producing that unit. Therefore the industry's output is currently too low. Welfare could be increased by producing more output.

■ If price is less than marginal cost, the value that society places on the last unit of output produced (again measured by the price the most marginal consumer is prepared to pay) is less than the cost of producing that unit. Therefore the industry's output is currently too high. Welfare could be increased by producing less output.

Quite distinct from allocative efficiency is the notion of **productive efficiency**, which consists of two components. First, a firm is said to be **technically efficient**, also known as **x-efficient**, if it is producing the maximum quantity of output that is technologically feasible, given the quantities of the factor inputs it is currently employing. In other words, a technically efficient firm operates on (and not within) its own production function (Leibenstein, 1966). Second, a firm is said to be **economically efficient** if it has selected the combination of factor inputs that enable it to produce its current output level at the lowest possible cost, given the prevailing prices of the factor inputs available to the firm (Leibenstein, 1966; Comanor and Leibenstein, 1969). A firm might be technically efficient but economically inefficient, if it uses its selected inputs to produce as much output as is technologically feasible, but if it could have produced the same quantity of output more cheaply by selecting a different combination of inputs. A firm that is both technically efficient and economically efficient operates on (and not above) the lowest attainable long-run average cost (LRAC) function.

Figures 2.13 and 2.14 draw a comparison between the efficiency properties of the perfectly competitive equilibrium and the profit-maximizing equilibrium under monopoly. For simplicity, Figures 2.13 and 2.14 are based on an assumption of constant returns to scale. Therefore the long-run average cost (LRAC) and long-run marginal cost (LRMC) functions are horizontal and identical (see Section 2.2). Figure 2.13 compares perfect competition and monopoly on allocative efficiency criteria, while Figure 2.14 also incorporates productive efficiency criteria.

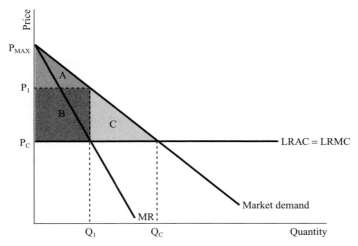

Figure 2.13 Allocative inefficiency in monopoly

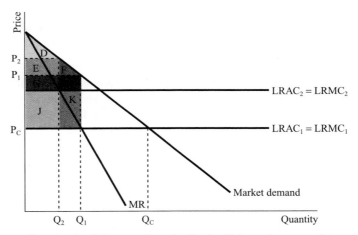

Figure 2.14 Allocative inefficiency and productive inefficiency in monopoly

In Figure 2.13, the horizontal LRMC function is also the industry supply function under perfect competition, and the equilibrium market price and output are P_C and Q_C, located at the intersection of the industry supply and market demand functions. Since P_C = LRMC, the condition for allocative efficiency is satisfied. The profit-maximizing monopolist chooses a price and output level of P_1 and Q_1, located at the intersection of the MR and LRMC functions. Since P_1 > LRMC, the condition for allocative efficiency is not satisfied. Welfare would be increased by producing more output than Q_1. The superior welfare properties of the perfectly competitive equilibrium can also be demonstrated with reference to the welfare economics concepts of consumer surplus and producer surplus.

Consumer surplus is the sum over all consumers of the difference between the maximum amount each consumer would be prepared to pay and the price each consumer actually does pay. Imagine consumers arrayed along the horizontal axis of Figure 2.13 in descending order of their willingness to pay (reading from left to right).

■ At the perfectly competitive equilibrium (P_C, Q_C) consumer surplus is represented by the triangle A + B + C. The first consumer is willing to pay P_{MAX} but actually pays P_C. The second consumer is willing to pay slightly less than P_{MAX} but actually pays P_C. The last consumer (at Q_C) is willing to pay P_C and actually pays P_C.

■ At the monopoly equilibrium (P_1, Q_1) consumer surplus is represented by the triangle A. As before, the first consumer is willing to pay P_{MAX} but actually pays P_1, and so on. The last consumer (at Q_1) is willing to pay P_1 and actually pays P_1.

Producer surplus is the total reward producers receive beyond the reward they require to cover their costs of production, including their normal profit. In the present case, producer surplus is equivalent to abnormal profit.

■ At the perfectly competitive equilibrium (P_C, Q_C) producer surplus is zero because there is no abnormal profit.

■ At the monopoly equilibrium (P_1, Q_1) producer surplus is represented by the rectangle B, equivalent to the monopolist's abnormal profit.

Under perfect competition, consumer surplus is A + B + C and producer surplus is nil. The sum of consumer surplus and producer surplus is A + B + C. Under monopoly, consumer surplus is A and producer surplus is B. The sum of consumer surplus and producer surplus is A + B. The triangle C is known as the **deadweight loss** associated with monopoly. It represents the total welfare loss resulting from the fact that less output is produced under monopoly than under perfect competition. It is important to note that the transfer of surplus of B from consumers to the producer does not form part of the critique of monopoly from a welfare economics perspective, because welfare economics does not make distributional judgements as to *whose* welfare should be maximized. However, the existence of a deadweight loss does form part of this critique, since it implies the welfare of at least one agent could be increased without reducing the welfare of any other agent or agents. For example, if the market structure were changed from monopoly to perfect competition, and the consumers gave the monopolist a compensating side-payment of B, the consumers would be better off (their surplus net of the side-payment having risen from A to A + C) and the producer would be no worse off (the loss of producer surplus of B having been compensated by the side-payment).

Figure 2.13 makes the case that monopoly is less desirable than perfect competition using an allocative efficiency criterion. The possibility that monopoly might also be less desirable based on a productive efficiency criterion rests on the suggestion that a monopolist shielded from competitive pressure (emanating either from rival firms or from actual or potential entrants) may tend to become complacent or lazy, and therefore inefficient in production. A complacent monopolist may cease to strive to make the most efficient use of its factor inputs (technical inefficiency), or it may not bother to identify its most cost-effective combination of factor inputs (economic inefficiency). Consequently the monopolist may operate on a higher LRAC and LRMC function than it would attain if the full rigours of competition forced it to produce as efficiently as possible.

Figure 2.14 identifies the further welfare loss resulting from productive inefficiency on the part of the complacent monopolist. $LRAC_1 = LRMC_1$ is the same as $LRAC = LRMC$ in Figure 2.13, and (P_1, Q_1) is also the same in both diagrams. $LRAC_2 = LRMC_2$ represents the complacent monopolist's cost functions. The complacent monopolist's profit-maximizing price and output are P_2 and Q_2. Examining the welfare implications of shifting from (P_1, Q_1) to (P_2, Q_2), we can draw the following conclusions:

- Consumer surplus falls from D + E + F (= A in Figure 2.13) to D.

- Producer surplus falls from G + H + J + K (= B in Figure 2.13) to E + G.

- Therefore (consumer surplus *plus* producer surplus) falls by F + H + J + K.

- J represents the increase in the cost of producing Q_2 units of output resulting from productive inefficiency.

- F + H + K represents the increase in the deadweight loss resulting from the reduction in output from Q_1 to Q_2.

Is monopoly always inferior to perfect competition on efficiency and welfare criteria? This section concludes by examining one special case for which the comparison is not clear-cut. A **natural monopoly** is a market in which long-run average cost (LRAC) is decreasing as output increases over the entire range of outputs that could conceivably be produced, given the position of the market demand function. In other words, there is insufficient demand for any firm to produce the output level at which all opportunities for further savings in average costs through economies of scale are exhausted, or at which the minimum efficient scale (MES) is attained. In a natural monopoly, monopoly is always a more cost-effective market structure than competition. LRAC is lower if one firm services the entire market than if two (or more) firms share the market between them. Industries where the costs of indivisibilities represent a large proportion of total costs, and where total costs do not increase much as output increases, are most likely to exhibit the characteristics of natural monopoly. Perhaps the most widely cited examples are the utilities, such as gas, electricity and water. A vast and costly physical infrastructure is required in order to distribute these products, but once this infrastructure is in place, fluctuations in the quantities traded cause only relatively minor variations in total costs.

The case of natural monopoly is illustrated in Figure 2.15.

- In order to maximize profit, the monopolist produces Q_1 units of output, and charges a price of P_1. Average cost is C_1, and the monopolist earns an abnormal profit, represented by area A.

- If the monopolist were forced to produce Q_2 units of output, then price would fall to $P_2 = C_2 (< C_1)$ and the monopolist would earn only a normal profit.

- In order to achieve allocative efficiency (price *equals* marginal cost), the monopolist would have to produce Q_3 units of output. Average cost would fall to C_3 $(< C_2 < C_1)$, but price would fall to P_3 and the monopolist would realize a loss, represented by area B.

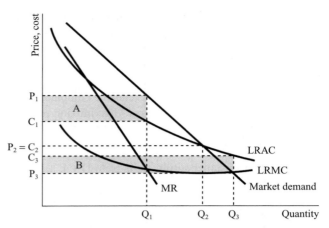

Figure 2.15 Natural monopoly

Therefore in the case of natural monopoly, allocative efficiency might not be attainable because the monopolist would rather go out of business altogether than operate at (P_3, Q_3). However, on efficiency and welfare criteria, it would be preferable for the monopolist to operate at (P_2, Q_2) rather than at the monopolist's preferred (profit-maximizing) position of (P_1, Q_1). This suggests a possible justification for the regulation of natural monopolies by the competition authorities. We return to this issue in Chapters 17 and 18.

2.6 Theory of monopolistic competition

As indicated at the start of Section 2.4, during the 1930s Robinson (1933) and Chamberlin (1933) attempted to draw together the previously distinct theories of perfect competition and monopoly, in order to develop a theory of imperfect competition. Imperfect competition encompasses both oligopoly (the subject of Chapters 4 and 5 of this book) and **monopolistic competition**, described here in this final section of Chapter 2. In the neoclassical theory of monopolistic competition, the industry is assumed to have the following characteristics.

■ There are large numbers of atomistic buyers and sellers.

■ Firms are free to enter into or exit from the industry, and a decision to enter or exit does not impose any additional costs on the firm concerned. In other words, there are no barriers to entry and exit.

■ The goods or services produced and sold by each firm are perceived by consumers to be similar but not identical. In other words, there is some product differentiation. It could be that there are real differences between the goods or services produced by each firm, or it could be that there are imagined differences, with consumers' perceptions of differences reinforced by successful branding or advertising.

- The buyers and the sellers may have perfect or imperfect information. If the product differentiation is perceived rather than real, this suggests that the buyers' information is in some sense imperfect.

- Geographic location could be the characteristic that differentiates the product or service produced by one firm from those of its competitors. In this case, there are transport costs that may to some extent deter buyers from switching to alternative sellers located elsewhere. However, each firm's market is not completely segmented geographically. Any firm that raises its price too far will find that its customers start switching to other sellers.

- Each selling firm seeks to maximize its own profit.

These assumptions ensure each individual firm has some discretion over its own price. Thanks to product differentiation, each firm can exercise some market power. In contrast to the perfectly competitive firm, a firm in monopolistic competition that raises its price does not immediately lose all of its customers, and a firm that lowers its price does not immediately acquire all of its competitors' customers. Therefore we assume non-price taking behaviour on the part of each firm. Each firm faces a demand function that is downward sloping (not horizontal as in the case of perfect competition). However, the firm's discretion over its own price is limited by the fact that its product is quite similar to its competitors' products. This means that if the firm does increase its price, it tends to lose customers to its competitors at a rapid rate; similarly, by cutting its price the firm can attract customers at a rapid rate. Therefore the firm's demand function is relatively price elastic, and certainly more price elastic than the market demand function faced by the monopolist.

The assumption that buyers and sellers are atomistic under monopolistic competition has important implications for the way in which equilibrium is determined. Under atomistic competition, each firm believes its market share is sufficiently small that any decision to raise or lower its own price or output has a negligible impact on its competitors' individual demand functions, and therefore a negligible impact on their price and output decisions. In other words, the firms are sufficiently small and plentiful that the issue of **interdependence** can be ignored: the possibility that any one firm's profit-maximizing price and output decisions carries implications for all of the other firms' decisions. The assumption that interdependence between the firms can safely be ignored distinguishes monopolistic competition from oligopoly, the other market structure that falls under the heading of imperfect competition.

Figure 2.16 shows the determination of the pre- and post-entry market price and output levels for one representative firm in monopolistic competition. Because each firm sells a differentiated product, there is no market demand function and no industry-level analysis. The upper diagram shows the firm's SRAC and short-run marginal cost (SRMC) functions. In accordance with the previous discussion, the firm's AR and MR functions are downward sloping. The firm maximizes profit by producing q_1 units of output, at which MR = SRMC. At the pre-entry profit-maximizing equilibrium represented by P_1 and q_1, the representative firm earns an abnormal profit shown by the shaded area between P_1 and C_1.

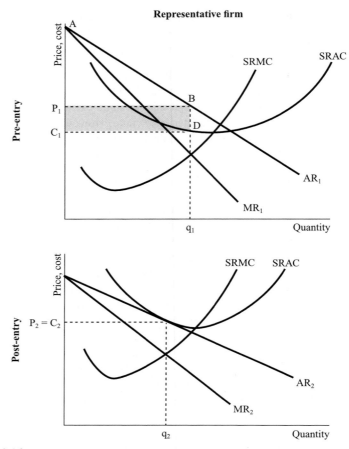

Figure 2.16 Short-run pre-entry and post-entry equilibrium in monopolistic competition

As in perfect competition, the availability of abnormal profits attracts entrants, so (P_1, q_1) cannot be a final or a stable equilibrium. Entry increases the number of firms, and in the lower diagram causes the representative firm's AR and MR functions to shift to the left. The firm maximizes profit by producing q_2 units of output, at which $MR_2 = SRMC$. At the post-entry profit-maximizing equilibrium represented by P_2 and q_2, the representative firm earns a normal profit only. The fall in market price caused by entry has eliminated the pre-entry abnormal profit. Post-entry, each individual firm produces slightly less output than it did pre-entry. (P_2, q_2) represents the well known **tangency solution** to model of monopolistic competition, so called because at this equilibrium the firm's AR function is tangential to its SRAC function. There is a similar tangency solution to the long-run model (not shown in Figure 2.16).

Using the criteria developed in Section 2.5, we can identify the efficiency and welfare properties of the long-run equilibrium under monopolistic competition.

■ The representative firm under monopolistic competition fails to produce at the minimum efficient scale (as is usually the case in monopoly), and therefore fails to produce at the minimum attainable long-run average cost.

- The representative monopolistic competitor earns only a normal profit in the long run (as in the case of perfect competition).

- The representative monopolistic competitor sells at a price that exceeds its marginal cost. Accordingly, there is allocative inefficiency (as in the case of monopoly). Each firm's output, and the total industry output, is lower than is required for the maximization of welfare. There is a deadweight loss.

- The market power enjoyed by the representative monopolistic competitor, thanks to its differentiated product, might enable the firm to operate without achieving full efficiency in production (as in the case of monopoly). Monopolistic competition might be compatible with either technical inefficiency (x-inefficiency) or economic inefficiency, or both. However, in contrast to the monopolist, the monopolistic competitor is not fully shielded from the rigours of competition. A monopolistic competitor that is producing inefficiently is vulnerable to the threat of competition from incumbents or entrants. An efficient incumbent or entrant might imitate the inefficient firm's product characteristics, and be capable of undercutting the inefficient firm on price, because its costs are lower. Therefore the degree to which the monopolistic competitor can operate at less than full efficiency is severely constrained by the lack of entry barriers and the threat of actual or potential competition.

2.7 Summary

This chapter has reviewed the core elements of microeconomic theory that are required for an understanding of the economic models of firms and industries that are developed throughout the rest of this book. We have reviewed the essential elements of production and cost theory, demand theory and the neoclassical theory of the firm, including the models of perfect competition, monopoly and monopolistic competition.

In production and cost theory, an important distinction is drawn between the short run and the long run. For a firm that uses two factors of production, say labour and capital, labour is assumed to be variable and capital fixed in the short run. In the long run, both labour and capital are assumed to be variable. The short-run relationship between inputs, output, and costs of production is governed by the Law of Diminishing Returns. As increasing quantities of labour are used in conjunction with a fixed quantity of capital, eventually the additional contribution made by each successive unit of labour to total output starts to decline. Consequently, as the quantity of output increases, the marginal cost of producing any further output starts to increase.

The long-run relationship between inputs, output, and costs of production is governed by economies and diseconomies of scale. Returns to scale describes the proportionate increase in output achieved from any given proportionate increase in all inputs. Returns to scale are increasing, giving rise to economies of scale, if output increases more than proportionately to the increase in inputs. Returns to scale are decreasing, giving rise to diseconomies of scale, if output increases less than proportionately to the increase in inputs. A firm attains its minimum efficient scale by producing an output level beyond which no further savings in long-run average costs are possible; or in other words, at which all possible opportunities for cost savings through economies of scale have been exhausted.

The market demand function for a product or service shows the relationship between market price and the number of units consumers wish to buy at that price. Price elasticity of demand provides a convenient measure of the responsiveness of quantity demanded to a change in market price. It is possible to define price elasticity of demand either at the market level, or at the firm level. A profit-maximizing firm should produce the output level at which its marginal revenue *equals* its marginal cost. The relationship between price elasticity of demand and marginal revenue has been developed.

In the neoclassical model of perfect competition, there are large numbers of atomistic buyers and sellers, firms are free to enter into or exit from the industry, and there is no product differentiation. All buyers and sellers are assumed to have perfect information, and there are no transaction or transport costs that could otherwise protect individual firms from the full rigours of competition. At the long-run equilibrium, each firm produces at the minimum point on its long-run average cost function, and earns only a normal profit. There is allocative efficiency because the market price *equals* each firm's marginal cost. Competitive discipline ensures that all firms must either achieve full efficiency in production, or fail to realize a normal profit at the long-run equilibrium market price and face being forced out of business.

In the model of monopoly there is only one seller, there are insurmountable barriers to entry, and there is complete product differentiation in the sense that no other firm produces a substitute product that could undermine the monopolist's market power. At the long-run equilibrium, the monopolist charges a higher price and produces less output than would occur if the monopolist were relaced by (or broken down into) a large number of small, perfectly competitive firms. The monopolist typically fails to produce at the minimum point on its long-run average cost function, but it can earn an abnormal profit in the long run. The monopolist charges a price higher than its marginal cost, so there is allocative inefficiency. The lack of competitive discipline suggests that the monopolist may be able to operate without achieving full efficiency in production.

The theory of monopolistic competition falls between the polar cases of perfect competition and monopoly. The industry comprises many firms and entry is possible, but product differentiation affords the firms a degree of market power that is not available to their perfectly competitive counterparts. The absence of barriers to entry ensures the firms are only able to earn a normal profit in the long run. The firms also fail to produce at the minimum efficient scale, and fail to achieve allocative efficiency, because price exceeds marginal cost at the long-run equilibrium. It is possible that the firms' market power may permit them to operate without achieving full productive efficiency. However, the degree of inefficiency that is sustainable is constrained by the threat of competition from incumbents and entrants.

Discussion questions

1. Distinguish between returns to a variable factor of production, and returns to scale.

2. Sketch a typical total product function for a firm with one variable factor of production (labour). At what point on the total product function is the marginal product of labour at a maximum? At what point on the total product function is the average product of labour at a maximum?

3. Relying on your own research from textbooks, newspaper articles or the internet, identify the most important inputs to the production function of a specific industry.

4. Explain why a firm's short-run average cost function may be U-shaped. Explain why a firm's long-run average cost function may be U-shaped.

5. With reference to Case study 2.1, explain why large NHS hospitals may be able to operate with lower average costs than small NHS hospitals in the long run.

6. Explain the concept of consumer surplus. Did you receive any consumer surplus when buying this textbook?

7. With reference to Case study 2.2, assess the relative importance of ticket prices and factors other than price in determining the level of spectator demand for attendance at professional team sports matches.

8. With reference to a large firm or other organization which is familiar to you, give examples of the possible causes of diseconomies of scale.

9. How might the concept of cross-price elasticity of demand be useful when attempting to identify the impact of an increase in the price of petrol on the demand for cars, or the impact of a reduction in the price of butter on the demand for margarine?

10. Explain why a profit-maximizing firm would never operate on the portion of its demand function where the price elasticity of demand is below one.

11. With reference to the theory of production, explain the distinction between allocative efficiency and productive efficiency.

12. Compare the productive and allocative efficiency properties of the long-run profit-maximizing equilibria under perfect competition, monopoly and monopolistic competition.

13. Are all monopolies necessarily bad for social welfare?

14. Is allocative efficiency ever attainable by a natural monopoly?

Theories of the firm

Learning objectives

This chapter covers the following topics:

- the historical development of the neoclassical theory of the firm
- criticisms of the neoclassical theory of the firm
- the separation of ownership from control in the large modern corporation
- managerial and behavioural theories of the firm
- the Coasian view of the firm
- the firm as team-based production; the firm as a nexus of contracts; agency theories of the firm
- transaction costs and the theory of the firm
- property rights and the theory of the firm
- resource-based and knowledge-based theories of the firm

Key terms

Adverse selection	Moral hazard
Agency theory	Organizational slack
Asset specificity	Quasi-rent
Bounded rationality	Residual rights
Cost plus pricing	Satisficing
Governance	Side payments
Incomplete contracts	Specific rights
Minimum profit constraint	Transaction costs

3.1 Introduction

In Chapter 2, we concentrated on the technical analysis of production, costs and demand. This material forms the basis for the neoclassical theory of the firm. In the neoclassical theory, the firm is an idealized abstraction, existing purely to allocate resources and organize production in such a way as to satisfy consumer wants, driven by the desire to maximize profits. Profits are maximized so long as resources are allocated optimally, and the firm has access to full information concerning all relevant market supply and demand conditions. Chapter 3 describes the development of several more modern, alternative theories of the firm, starting from their origins within the neoclassical school of thought. The desire to infuse a greater sense of realism than is perhaps apparent in the neoclassical theory motivates the development of most, if not all, of the alternative theories decscribed in this chapter.

We begin in Section 3.2 with a brief review of the historical development of the neoclassical theory of the firm. This discussion locates the content of the previous chapter within its proper historical context. The historical review is followed in Section 3.3 by a brief discussion of some of the major criticisms of the neoclassical theory. This critique provides the motivation for several of the alternative theories that are described later in this chapter. Some of the earliest challenges to the neoclassical theory developed in the light of growing evidence of the increasing complexity of firms, and the separation of the ownership of large corporations (in the hands of shareholders) from control (in the hands of salaried managers). Where previously it had been assumed that firms were run so as to maximize the interests of their owners, economists began to acknowledge that managers' objectives may differ from those of the shareholders. In Section 3.4 we examine the managerial theories of sales revenue maximization, growth maximization and managerial utility maximization. In Section 3.5 we examine a behavioural theory of the firm that has its roots in both economics and organizational science.

In Sections 3.6 and 3.7, we examine a number of more modern approaches to the theory of the firm. An early paper by Coase (1937) provides a natural point of departure for these theories. Coase asks why institutions known as firms exist at all. Coase's answer is that by implementing certain transactions or taking certain resource allocation decisions consciously (within the domain of the firm) rather than unconsciously (through the medium of the market), a saving in **transaction costs** can be realized. Transaction costs can be defined loosely as costs incurred when using market mechanisms to allocate resources in a world of imperfect information. The firm is viewed as an institution which economizes on transaction costs, or the costs of processing information. Resources are allocated in response to the firm's interpretation of information flows. The firm organizes governance structures that create incentives and provide protection from the threat of opportunistic behaviour made possible by informational asymmetries.

Dissatisfaction within the fields of management science and strategic management with both the neoclassical theory of the firm and its more modern alternatives has led to the development of strategic and knowledge-based theories of the firm, which emphasize strategic choices facing the firm's decision makers. This approach, which defines firms in terms of the resources they own and control, is examined in Section 3.8. Resources include both physical inputs and intangible resources such as technical expertise and organizational structure. A number of insights are borrowed from the transaction costs literature, relating to the boundaries of the firm and decision making under bounded rationality. Knowledge-based theories emphasize knowledge as perhaps the most important of a firm's resources. Firms exist in order to coordinate and protect the unique knowledge that is the firm's key strategic asset.

3.2 The neoclassical theory of the firm: historical development

In *The Wealth of Nations*, Adam Smith (1776) argues that the value of the firm's output is related to its costs of production (a notion which constituted the orthodox view at that time). Costs include an allowance for profit, interpreted as a reward to the firm's owner. Owners maximize profit by attempting to minimize the other costs incurred by the firm. One of the most widely quoted passages is a description of Smith's visit to a Nottingham pin factory, where he observed the potential for the division of labour to increase labour productivity and generate large cost savings.

> To take an example, from . . . the trade of a pin maker; a workman not educated to this business . . . nor acquainted with the use of the machinery employed in it . . . could scarce, perhaps, with his utmost industry, make one pin in a day, and certainly could not make twenty. But in the way in which this business is now carried on, not only the whole work is a peculiar trade, but it is divided into a number of branches, of which the greater part are likewise peculiar trades. One man draws out the wire, another straights it, a third cuts it, a fourth points it, a fifth grinds it at the top for receiving the head . . . ten persons, therefore, could make among them upwards of forty-eight thousand pins in a day.
>
> *(Smith, 1776, pp. 4–5)*

Augustin Cournot (1838) was one of the first economists to attempt a formal mathematical analysis of the behaviour of monopolists and duopolists. Although Cournot was a mathematician by background, he was the first to apply calculus to an analysis of the pricing decisions of firms. Cournot's analysis is considered in detail in Chapter 4, in which we examine the theory of oligopoly.

The idea that the value of a firm's output is dependent on production costs lasted till the late nineteenth century, when this notion was seriously challenged for the first time. According to the new view, the value of the product determines the rewards paid to the factors of production. Firms earning high profits by selling products that are in demand for a high price can pay higher rents, wages and interest. In other words, the price and therefore the value of the product depends ultimately on the level of demand. Stanley Jevons (1871) argued that the value a consumer places on a product depends on utility at the margin, which implies value is judged against all other past units of the product consumed. If marginal utility declines as consumption increases, cuts in price are required to induce an increase in the quantity demanded. This relationship provides an explanation for the downward sloping demand function.

Alfred Marshall (1890, 1892) is considered to have been the first economist to draw the link between costs of production and market demand. Accordingly, value is determined by interactions between the conditions surrounding both supply and demand. Marshall developed the tools of economic analysis that are still familiar to first-year undergraduates: the upward sloping supply function and downward sloping demand function which combine, scissor-like, to determine an equilibrium price and quantity demanded and supplied. If price is set above or below this equilibrium, then firms are faced with excess supply or excess demand. In the case of excess supply or a glut of goods, price tends to fall, encouraging more buyers into the market. Some firms that are no longer able to cover their costs of production are forced to reduce their supply or leave the market. In the case of excess demand or a shortage of goods, price tends to rise, discouraging some buyers who withdraw from the market. Some incumbent firms respond to the price signal by increasing their production, and some entrants are attracted into the market for the first time.

Marshall also introduced the concept of price elasticity of demand, and drew the distinction between the short run and the long run. Like Smith before him, Marshall recognized that in the long run firms benefit from economies of large-scale production. However, this does not necessarily lead to the emergence of monopoly, because there is still the possibility that other producers can compete with a large incumbent, by exploiting distinctive entrepreneurial skills or external economies of scale. To Marshall the dominant market structure seemed to be a variant of competition, although not the textbook perfect competition model of later years. Marshall recognized the importance of rivalry, and that this creates the potential for collusion. However, Marshall viewed oligopoly as a form of quasi-monopoly, and therefore as an exception to the normal competitive market structure.

The theory of perfect competition was developed by John Bates Clark (1899), who believed that competition is fundamentally a force for good in the economy. In competitive markets, everyone receives a reward equivalent to their marginal contribution to production. Accordingly, Clark sought to analyse those forces that have the potential to frustrate competition, especially monopoly and associated restrictive practices. The theory was refined by Frank Knight (1921), who lists a number of conditions required for a market to conform to the model of perfect competition. The most important are that no one buyer or seller is sufficiently powerful to influence prices, that no entry barriers impede the flow of resources into the market, and that all agents have perfect knowledge. Knight explains why perfect competition does not necessarily eliminate abnormal profit in situations where there is a degree of uncertainty. According to Knight, uncertainty describes a situation in which the probabilities that should be assigned to possible future events cannot be determined. Risk, on the other hand, describes a situation in which probabilities can be assigned, and future events can be insured against. Knight argues that even in long-run equilibrium, firms might earn an abnormal profit as a payoff for dealing with uncertainty.

As we have seen in Section 2.6, in the 1930s Joan Robinson and Edwin Chamberlin coined the term imperfect competition to describe the middle ground between perfect competition and monopoly. Robinson (1933) introduces the concept of marginal revenue, and shows that in perfect competition marginal revenue *equals* price. For a firm in imperfect competition, the marginal revenue function is downward sloping. At some levels of production (where marginal revenue is negative), it may be possible to increase total revenue by producing and selling less output. Robinson argues that the tendency for imperfectly competitive firms to restrict production and operate below full capacity helps explain the high unemployment experienced in the UK in the 1930s. In contrast, high unemployment is not consistent with the theory of perfect competition. Robinson's analysis of price discrimination represents another important contribution to the theory of the firm. Chamberlin (1933) developed the theory of monopolistic competition to describe a market in which there are many firms producing goods that are similar but not identical. Accordingly, the firms exercise some discretion in setting their prices. Chamberlin also contributed to the theory of oligopoly. Oligopolists recognize that their actions are interdependent: a change in output by one firm alters the profits of rival firms, perhaps causing them to adjust their outputs as well. Forms of competition under oligopoly vary from vigorous price competition to collusion.

3.3 Critique of the neoclassical theory of the firm

A common criticism levelled at the neoclassical theory of the firm is that it is insufficiently realistic. The theory is largely based on outdated views of competition and entrepreneurial activity. The concept of competition that was developed in the nineteenth century was based on a presumed model of reality. The rise of the textile industry and the growing international trade in staples provided early economists with concepts which dominated early economic thought. Price competition was seen to be both intense and instantaneous, goods were homogeneous, no trade secrets existed, and markets were populated by many buyers and sellers. This model of the firm can be criticized from a number of directions.

- *Organizational goals.* The neoclassical theory assumes that firms seek to maximize profit. In reality, however, firms may pursue other objectives, such as the maximization of sales, growth or market share, or the pursuit of status or job security by the firm's managers, or perhaps the simple enjoyment of a quiet life. Simon (1959) argues that the firm's managers may aim for a satisfactory or sufficient profit to allow the managers to pursue other objectives. By analogy, do firms really search for the sharpest needle in the haystack, or are they content with finding a needle sharp enough to do the job in hand?

- *Uncertainty and imperfect information.* In practice all economic decisions are based on assumptions or predictions about near or future events. Implicit in the neoclassical theory is an assumption that the firm's decision makers can somehow make accurate predictions, or at least be able to assign probabilities to the various possible future events. Therefore decision makers need to be able to anticipate changes in consumer tastes, changes in technology, changes in factor markets and the likely reactions of rivals. In practice, any of these events may be extremely difficult to forsee.

■ *Organizational complexity.* Modern firms are complex hierarchical organizations, bound together by complex communications networks. In practice, breakdowns in communications occur frequently. The greater the number of levels, the greater the likelihood that information is distorted, either deliberately or accidentally. Misinformation reduces the ability of the firm's decision makers to reach correct decisions.

■ *Decision making.* According to the neoclassical theory of the firm, the firm's decision makers solve the problem of which inputs to purchase and how much output to produce by applying the rules of marginal calculus. However, empirical evidence has shown that businessmen and women do not employ such methods; instead, they tend to rely on simpler decision-making conventions or rules-of-thumb. In a seminal article, Hall and Hitch (1939) report the outcomes of interviews with decision makers at 38 firms. Very few had even heard of the concepts of marginal cost and revenue, or price elasticity of demand; instead, most set their prices by calculating their average cost, and adding a mark-up that included a margin for profit. This pricing method is known as **cost plus pricing**. It is examined in more detail in Chapter 10. Neoclassical profit maximization requires that both demand and costs are taken into account in determining price and quantity; cost plus pricing appears to consider only cost while ignoring demand. Hall and Hitch also asked their interviewees why they based their prices on average cost. Some respondents felt that this policy was fair to both producers and consumers. Some claimed not to know the true nature of their demand conditions; they had insufficient information about consumers' preferences or their rivals' reactions. Finally, some felt that frequent changes in price were a nuisance to consumers and their sales teams. For this reason it was preferable to adhere to conventional prices, unless there were significant changes in cost conditions.

In defence of the neoclassical theory, Friedman (1953) argues that some critics miss the point by attacking the validity of the assumptions on which the theory is constructed. The objective of any science is to develop theories or hypotheses which lead to valid and accurate predictions about future outcomes. The only relevant test of the validity of a theory is whether its predictions are close to the eventual outcome. Friedman argues that the proper test of an assumption such as profit maximization is not whether it is realistic, but whether it enables accurate predictions to be generated from the theory on which it is based (Rotwein, 1962; Melitz, 1965).

Machlup (1946, 1967) argues for the essential validity of the profit maximization assumption, even if it does not provide a literal description of reality. Most decision makers have an intuitive feel for what is required to come close to a profit-maximizing outcome, even if they are unable to articulate their practices using the same terminology or with the same precision as economists. The practical implementation of marginal analysis should not require anything more difficult than an ability to formulate subjective estimates, hunches and guesses. By analogy, whenever we drive a car we execute complex manoeuvres such as overtaking intuitively, rather than precisely using complex mathematical formulae. From experience, we can judge the speeds and distances needed in order to overtake successfully; fortunately, it is not necessary that any driver wishing to overtake should solve the problem using differential calculus. Using similar reasoning but adding a Darwinian slant, Alchian (1965) argues that firms that survive in the long run are those that have come close to long-run profit maximization, either deliberately or intuitively, or perhaps even in-advertently. Accordingly, the neoclassical theory accurately describes the behaviour of surviving firms.

An essentially static conception of competition is emphasized in the neoclassical theories of perfect competition, monopolistic competition and monopoly. In the neoclassical theory, the entrepreneur is the personification of the firm, but otherwise plays a rather unimportant role, because at the long-run equilibrium, all buyers and sellers have perfectly anticipated all variations in supply and demand. Price competition is the only form of rivalry. In contrast, Schumpeter (1942) and the **Austrian school** both give the entrepreneur a central role within a more dynamic model of competition. By initiating technological change by means of innovation, the Schumpeterian entrepreneur is the main driving force behind economic progress. Innovation revolutionizes economic conditions by replacing old production methods with new and superior ones. Successful innovation is the fundamental source of monopoly status and abnormal profit. Abnormal or monopoly profit is only a temporary phenomenon, however, because eventually the market for a new product will be flooded by imitators, or the original innovation will be superseded by further technological progress. This Schumpeterian view of the entrepreneur as innovator is examined in more detail in Chapter 14.

The Austrian school also emphasizes the role of the entrepreneur. Here the entrepreneur is seen as crucial in the interaction of decisions made by consumers and resource owners. The entrepreneur spots missed opportunities for trade or investment, by acquiring and processing new pieces of information more quickly than other decision makers. Through his or her actions, the entrepreneur contributes to the spread of new information among other market participants, who are able to adjust their trading plans accordingly.

> The overambitious plans of one period will be replaced by more realistic ones; market opportunities overlooked in one period will be exploited in the next. In other words, even without changes in the basic data of the market (i.e. in consumer tastes, technological possibilities, and resource availabilities), the decisions made in one period of time generate systematic alterations in the corresponding decisions for the succeeding period. Taken over time, this series of systematic changes in the interconnected network of market decisions constitutes the market process.
>
> *(Kirzner, 1973, p. 10)*

In this process the entrepreneur once again plays a central role, by remaining alert to missed opportunities and initiating changes that propel the economy towards a new equilibrium. 'The entrepreneur . . . brings into mutual adjustment those discordant elements which resulted from prior market ignorance' (Kirzner, 1973, p. 73).

Essentially, disequilibrium results from the ignorance of buyers and sellers. Potential buyers are unaware of potential sellers and vice versa. Scarce resources are sometimes used to produce goods for which there is no market; on other occasions, resources that could be used to produce goods for which a market exists are left idle. However, the alert entrepreneur can step in and remedy the situation by noticing these missed trading opportunities, and bringing potential buyers and sellers together.

Casson (1982) develops a synthesis of several of these theories of entrepreneurship. The entrepreneur's main function is the management, coordination and allocation of other scarce resources, using key or privileged information. If this is done efficiently, and the key information remains secret, the entrepreneur is rewarded with profit or income. However, as in the Schumpeterian and Austrian views, in the long run there is a tendency for the entrepreneurial reward to be dissipated. Casson models the entrepreneurial function using a neoclassical-style demand and supply framework. The demand for entreprenuers depends most crucially on the pace of technological change, which determines the level of opportunity for entrepreneurial initiative. The supply of entrepreneurs depends on the educational system and qualifications, social networks, institutions and the general culture of the society, all of which influence the propensity for entrepreneurial behaviour and the availability of capital to finance new ventures. Entrepreneurial rewards tend to be higher when the demand for entrepreneurs is high (due to a high level of technological opportunity) and when the supply of active entrepreneurs is scarce.

3.4 Separation of ownership from control: managerial theories of the firm

As we have seen in Section 3.2, by the end of the first half of the twentieth century the foundations for an economic theory of the firm were well established. The theory had been built largely on a presumed reality of nineteenth-century firms, managed by their owners and specializing in clearly defined activities. In reality, firms were evolving into increasingly complex organizations, buying inputs and selling outputs in many different markets. Some economists were becoming increasingly conscious that these evolving institutions bore little apparent resemblance to the simplifying assumptions of the theory. There were two important implications. First, increasing organizational complexity meant it was impossible for the larger firms to be managed solely by the traditional individual entrepreneur or owner. Instead, there was a tendency for firms to employ large teams of managers, including specialists in individual functions such as marketing, finance and human resource management. Second, it also became impractical for the individual entrepreneur or owner to finance the continued expansion of the larger firms using personal financial resources. Accordingly, large firms needing to raise finance tended to look to the capital markets, with the result that ownership became widely dispersed among large numbers of individual or institutional shareholders. Not only did the number of shareholders grow, but the nature of share ownership also changed. Many large individual shareholdings were effectively broken up by progressive taxation. There was new demand for share ownership from individuals who had become affluent as patterns of income and wealth distribution across society as a whole evolved during the course of the twentieth century.

As share ownership became increasingly dispersed, the control of firms, vested in the ownership of shares, became increasingly diluted. In many cases a type of power vacuum was created, which was filled by an increasingly dominant cadre of managers. This so-called separation or divorce of ownership from control provided ammunition for the critics of the neoclassical theory of the firm, who argued that there was no reason to suppose that the theory's assumed objective of profit maximization would necessarily coincide with the objectives of the managers of large firms, the individuals actually taking the decisions. Managers might well be tempted to pursue objectives other than profit maximization, such as maximizing their own income, status or job security. And given that shareholders are large in number, widely dispersed and perhaps poorly informed and poorly organized, the shareholders' theoretical ability to hire and fire their own managers might not be sufficient to force the latter to act in accordance with the shareholders' interests.

Berle and Means (1932) are widely credited with having first identified and measured the extent of this separation of ownership from control, although the same issue is discussed by Veblen (1923). Classifying a shareholding of between 20 per cent and 50 per cent held by any individual or group as effective control, Berle and Means found that 88 out of 200 large US non-financial corporations (surveyed in 1929) were management controlled. No one individual owned more than 5 per cent of the total stock of any of these 88 firms. Some 30 years later, Larner (1966) replicated the Berle and Means study, but adjusted the ownership threshold from 5 per cent to 10 per cent of shares in the hands of a single owner. Of the 200 top firms, 84 per cent satisfied this criterion and could be regarded as management controlled. The managerial revolution, already in progress in 1929, was close to complete by the mid-1960s. Applying similar methodology (but with a different definition of an owner controlled firm) to a UK data set, Sargent Florence (1961) reports that only 30 of a sample of 98 of the largest UK firms could be classed as owner controlled. In another sample of smaller firms, only 89 of 268 firms were owner controlled.

Prais (1976) and Nyman and Silbertson (1978) question the results, as well as the research methodology, of these studies. First, the presence of interest groups or individuals owning large proportions of shares, does not necessarily imply there are no effective constraints on management. Second, Berle and Means ignore interlocking directorships: an important means of representing the interests of other firms at board level. Third, Berle and Means classify firms according to their ultimate control. If firm A has majority control over firm B and A is management controlled, B is also regarded as management controlled. This method of classification is contentious. Finally, statistical criteria alone are insufficient to determine the extent of ownership or managerial control. It is important to examine the nature of the shareholdings and their inter-relationships including, for example, similar or near-similar interest groups such as kinship. Nyman and Silbertson advocate studying the nature of control on a case by case basis. This approach suggests owner control was much stronger than had previously been realized: 55 per cent of the top 250 UK firms had some degree of owner control, using a 5 per cent threshold for a firm to be classed as owner controlled. Using the same ownership threshold, Leech and Leahy

(1991) find 91 per cent of 470 large UK industrial firms were owner controlled using 1983–85 data. Using a 20 per cent threshold, only 34 per cent were classified as owner controlled.

Although some of the early research concerning the separation of ownership from control has been qualified more recently, the original hypothesis that share ownership in many large corporations is widely dispersed is still essentially valid. Does this imply the managers of these organizations enjoy the freedom to pursue goals and objectives different from those of the owners? In practice, there are several reasons why the managers might not wish to depart too far from the owners' objectives.

■ If the managers are perceived to be running the organization badly, in principle the shareholders can mobilize themselves to dismiss the managers at a share-holders' general meeting. In practice, however, this may be difficult to organize. First, some shareholders might not wish to disrupt continuity by voting for whole-sale dismissals. Second, shareholders might not necessarily be able to assess the degree to which the managers are failing in their duties. Third, even knowledge-able shareholders may be unable to disseminate the relevant information, due to the costs incurred in printing leaflets, arranging meetings, dealing with the press, and so on. Finally, disaffected shareholders can often be outvoted at a general meeting by proxy votes held by the chair. Shareholders not wishing to attend a meeting, normally the majority, can nominate a proxy to vote on their behalf; but proxy votes are often assigned to the firm's managers. It may be that disaffected shareholders can only influence management by selling their shareholdings, depressing the firm's market valuation. Case studies 3.1 and 3.2 discuss two con-trasting examples of the exercise of shareholder power.

■ Although shareholders may suffer from a lack of clear information as to the per-formance of their management, managers of other firms may not be subject to the same constraints. Rival management teams, who perhaps face similar demand and cost conditions, may be in a good position to detect under-performance. If the market valuation of a firm's shares is relatively low but its financial struc-ture is sound, the firm may be vulnerable to a takeover bid. Recognition of this danger reduces the managers' incentives to pursue non-profit-maximizing objectives.

■ If the firm relies on external sources of finance, its managers may face additional constraints in the form of scrutiny by lending institutions such as merchant banks or investment companies. On the whole, firms in the UK tend not to rely heavily on external sources of finance. Nevertheless, merchant banks often arrange new issues, secure external finance and provide advice; a number of large UK companies have merchant bank representation on their boards.

In the 1960s, new developments in the theory of the firm examined the con-tribution of managers to decision making within the firm. The resulting theories are known as the managerial theories of the firm. The best known of these theories are examined below.

Case study 3.1

Bread and circuses from the Emperor Rupert: FT Chairman's pugnacious AGM performance

Annual meetings predicted to be rip-roaring battles rarely live up to their billing, and yesterday's at British Sky Broadcasting was no exception. It was more a stately imperial progress than a war over the Murdoch gene pool.

Many institutional investors have been angered by the appointment of James Murdoch as chief executive of a company where his father Rupert is chairman. Concerned about the corporate governance balance at the top of the company, they at the very least want changes in the composition of the board. Unusually – and rightly – some of the country's largest institutional investors turned up in person to voice their concerns rather than leaving the protesting to the usual band of small investors, few of whom ask pertinent questions. This example should be followed elsewhere.

But from the very start it was clear that Rupert Murdoch was firmly in charge of proceedings. He had the confidence that comes from his News Corporation's ownership of 35 per cent of BSkyB's shares and proxy votes showing the board had won all the resolutions before the meeting had even begun. His manner was brisk, imperial and pugnacious.

However, there were a handful of sops to the protestors. James Murdoch – in his first public outing as chief executive, and looking alarmingly like a pink-cheeked schoolboy – rather woodenly read out a statement in which he reaffirmed 'my pledge to work tirelessly in your interests'.

His father confirmed plans to resume the dividend and announced that two committees would be set up to examine BSkyB's corporate governance and remuneration. The first will be headed by Lord Wilson of Dinton, a newcomer to the board and former cabinet secretary. The second will be conducted by Jacques Nasser, the former chief executive of Ford, and John Thornton, a former Goldman Sachs banker and close confidant of the Murdochs, who has been on the board for nine years. Investors may question the latter's independence.

The board also cleverly finessed a potential row with investors over a pay-off to Tony Ball, the chief executive who has made way for Murdoch Junior. Since he quit of his own volition, he should not be getting a compensation payment for loss of office. Nor, the company announced, will he. Instead, he will have a two-year non-compete contract, of a size yet to be announced. Shareholders simply cannot argue with that.

But while the Murdochs won all the ballots, there was a very heavy institutional vote against Lord St John of Fawsley, the senior non-executive and the man who led the search for a new chief executive. Strip out the Murdochs' block vote and it is clear he has forfeited the support of the big investors. The decent thing would be to resign before the next annual meeting.

Both the Murdochs and the institutions are likely to be pleased by the outcome of the meeting. The former have got what they want.

The latter have put on a display of protest – albeit sometimes in rather hesitant voices – and for the time being they can avoid further uncomfortable questions about BSkyB's governance by noting that they have won a restored dividend and couple of inquiries. Or, the cynical might say, bread and circuses – those sops to the masses from clever emperors since the time of the Romans.

Source: Martin Dickson, Bread and circuses from the Emperor Rupert: Chairman's pugnacious performance, *Financial Times*, 15 November 2003.

The Walt Disney crisis: Rise of the corporate crusaders [FT]

The shareholder revolt against Walt Disney's Michael Eisner poses the question of whether the era of acquiescent shareholders is over. Corporate governance advocates certainly believe the evidence points that way.

Nell Minow, editor of the Corporate Library, a corporate governance watchdog, says: 'It means that shareholders really do care about their ability to send a message to management. They're sending a clear message to Disney and every corporation in America that they're paying attention and not voting with their feet; they're voting with their proxy cards.'

Other corporate governance observers agree that the time when shareholders' only criterion for management success was a rising share price may be passing.

The Disney vote, while unprecedented in terms of disapproval of a high-profile executive, is hardly an anomaly. Last year Hollinger saw a squawk of protest from a major shareholder – Tweedy, Browne, which owned 18 per cent of its shares – grow into a grassroots campaign and an investigation into the unauthorized payments to Conrad Black, chief executive.

There have also been many instances of shareholders approving a proposal by fellow shareholders by hefty margins. But very few have come in the midst of such a high-profile scuffle as the fight over Disney.

In the past, critics complain, large blocks of institutional shareholders often voted with management, 'rubber stamping' decisions. The reason for this pliant behaviour was largely inertia. Fund managers traditionally considered their job to be that of stock pickers, not crusaders for better corporate governance.

The Disney revolt suggests this may be changing.

'What's really interesting is that other types of institutions [that] typically do not show an interest in corporate governance – mutual funds – have gotten involved', says Jay Lorsch, a professor at Harvard Business School. 'The big change would be these guys are suddenly saying we're not just going to buy and sell stock, we're going to exert our influence.'

This August, under changes introduced by the Securities and Exchange Commission, mutual funds will be required to disclose how they vote at annual meetings.

Having to publicly disclose – and perhaps defend – their decisions 'in effect becomes a Big Bang within the mutual fund industry', said Stephen Davis, head of Davis Global Advisors, an international corporate governance advisory firm. 'They're suddenly going to have to prove publicly they do pay attention to ownership issues. Whether the stock price is going up or down in the short term is not the issue at Disney. The issue is that too much power accumulated in the hands of one individual.'

Source: Elizabeth Wine in New York, The Walt Disney crisis: Rise of the corporate crusaders, *Financial Times*, 5 March 2004.

Baumol's theory of sales revenue maximization

Baumol (1959) suggests that the managers of a large firm are primarily interested in maximizing their organization's sales revenue, subject to satisfying a **minimum profit constraint**. There are three reasons why the managers might pursue a sales revenue maximization objective. First, sales are widely regarded as a good general indicator of organizational performance.

> [S]urely it is a common experience that when one asks an executive, 'How's business?', he will answer that his sales have been increasing (or decreasing), and talk about profit only as an afterthought, if at all.

> *(Baumol, 1959, p. 46)*

Second, executive remuneration, as well as the power, influence and status executives can command, tend to be closely linked to their organization's sales performance. Third, assuming lenders tend to rely on sales data as a reasonably simple and visible indicator of organizational performance, a reduction in sales gives cause for concern because it gives rise to difficulties in raising finance from capital markets. The need to satisfy a minimum profit constraint is included in the managers' objective function, because some profit is required in order to provide finance for future expansion; and because executives must ensure sufficient profit is earned to satisfy shareholders and the capital markets. If the shareholders are dissatisfied, they might vote to dismiss the managers at a general meeting; or they might simply sell their shares, causing the company's market valuation to fall and rendering the company vulnerable to take-over. A new group of owners might wish to bring in their own management team. Therefore the minimum profit constraint is included because if profit falls too low, the managers' job security is jeopardized.

> In practice minimum acceptable profit is a rough attempt to provide completely acceptable earnings to stockholders while leaving enough over for investment in future expansion at the maximum rate which management considers to be reasonably marketable.

> *(Baumol, 1959, p. 53)*

Baumol's sales revenue maximization model is illustrated in Figure 3.1. The analysis uses short-run cost functions, and for simplicity it is assumed that the fixed cost is zero. The profit function, denoted π, is the difference between total revenue (TR) and total cost (TC). Therefore $\pi = 0$ at the points where TR = TC. Profit maximization is achieved by producing the output level q_1, at which the vertical distance between TR and TC is maximized. In the absence of any effective shareholder control, the firm's managers might attempt to maximize sales revenue. Sales revenue maximization is achieved by producing the output level q_3, at which the TR function is maximized. However, the need to satisfy the minimum profit constraint shown by the horizontal line π_{MIN}, prevents the managers from increasing output as far as q_3. Sales revenue maximization subject to a profit constraint of π_{MIN} is achieved by producing q_2, the highest output level that is consistent with $\pi \geq \pi_{MIN}$.

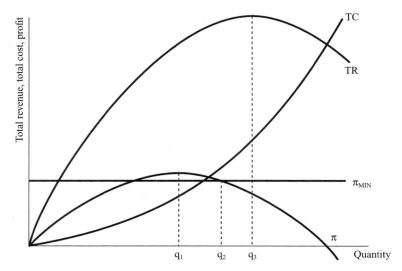

Figure 3.1 Baumol's sales revenue maximization model

Needham (1978) develops a long-run or multi-period version of the same model. The long-run analysis is motivated by the observation that current profit represents an important source of finance for a firm seeking to expand. And by definition, growth is required in order for the firm to increase its sales revenue in the future. Therefore if managers adopt longer time horizons, it is not obvious that they should necessarily wish to produce a level of output greater than that which would maximize current (short-run) profit.

For a firm with a planning horizon of n years, the present value of future sales revenue, denoted PV, depends on current sales revenue, denoted TR_0; the annual rate of growth of sales revenue, denoted g; and the discount rate employed to convert future sales revenue flows into present values, denoted r:

$$PV = \frac{TR_0(1 + g)}{1 + r} + \frac{TR_0(1 + g)^2}{(1 + r)^2} + \ldots + \frac{TR_0(1 + g)^n}{(1 + r)^n}$$

The growth rate g depends on current profit, which is used to finance the firm's future growth. By maximizing profit in the short run, the firm also maximizes g. However, as shown in Figure 3.1, short-run profit maximization implies sales revenue is lower than it could be. By increasing output beyond its short-run profit-maximizing level, the firm achieves an increase in current sales revenue TR_0 at the expense of a reduction in g. Accordingly, in order to maximize PV the firm's managers must decide on an optimal trade-off between current sales revenue and future growth in sales revenue. If we interpret the short-run profit that is required to deliver the chosen long-run growth rate as the firm's short-run profit constraint, the main difference between the short-run model and the long-run model is that in the former this profit constraint is determined exogenously (by the managers' job security requirement), while in the latter it is determined by the trade-off between current sales revenue and future growth. This in turn is determined by the short run trade-off between current sales revenue and current profit.

Not all economists accept Baumol's sales revenue maximization hypothesis. Alchian (1965) argues against the view that firms ignore all other objectives in order to pursue sales maximization. Peston (1959) suggests that the hypothesis might be applied to cases where firms are uncertain about their revenue functions. In an uncertain world, rather than risk producing too little output firms prefer to produce too much, and overproduction may at least enable the firm to realize economies of scale.

> In the nature of things the Baumol hypothesis remains unverified but non-nullified by the evidence. As to that, one would venture the heresy that whether good ideas like Baumol's fit the facts or not . . . is sometimes of small significance compared to the wider possibilities they open up for analysis and investigation. Once one gives up the attempt to formulate a general model in the classical manner, one may expect a model to be useful as for the questions it puts as for any specific answer it might give. The Baumol model certainly asks the right questions.
>
> *(Wildsmith, 1973, p. 65)*

Marris's theory of growth maximization

In view of the separation between ownership and control, Baumol (1962), Marris (1964) and Williamson (1963) all suggest that managers may wish to pursue a strategy of maximizing the growth of the firm. Growth maximization might be achieved at the expense of maximizing the present value of the firm's future profit streams, reflected in the firm's current stock market valuation. Below, we focus on the model developed by Marris.

In Marris's model, the managers' salaries and status depend to a large extent on the size of their departments. Managers are judged by their peers, subordinates and superiors for professional competence. Since each manager's individual contribution to profit is difficult to assess, some other method of evaluation has to be determined. A manager's ability to get on with other people and run his or her department smoothly tends to be used as a performance indicator. However, managers need to do more than this to increase their esteem, especially in the eyes of superiors and peers. Expanding the activities under their own command, and the activities of the firm in general, is the most natural way for a manager to enhance his or her reputation. By so doing, the manager also enhances his or her own job security, and that of subordinates. As a quasi-bureaucratic organization, the firm naturally tends to reward those who contribute most toward its growth and security.

Therefore managers tend to strive for growth, rather than profit maximization. Successful pursuit of a growth maximization objective necessitates achieving balance between the rate of growth of demand for the firm's products, and the rate of growth of the firm's capital.

In the short run, growth of demand for the firm's existing product range might be achieved through measures such as price adjustments, new marketing campaigns, or small changes in product design. However, for any given range of products, there are limits to the effectiveness of such measures in increasing demand; or at the very least, continued reliance on these measures may have damaging and unacceptable consequences for profitability. Eventually, further price reductions become counter-productive as the firm moves onto the price inelastic section of its demand function; or diminishing returns to further advertising or research and development expenditure are encountered. Therefore in order to grow continually over the long run, the firm cannot rely solely on existing products; it must diversify. By adopting a strategy of diversification, the firm can overcome the inevitable constraint on growth of demand imposed by exclusive reliance on any one product or on a fixed product range.

However, even for a firm that is willing to exploit opportunities for diversification into new markets, there are still limits to the rate of growth of demand that can be achieved without causing profitability to decline. This is because there are limits to the number of diversification opportunities the firm's management team can success-fully handle at any one time. If too many new projects are taken on, the firm's managerial resources become too thinly spread. The decision-making and organiza-tional capabilities of the firm's management team become overstretched, mistakes are made, some projects fail, and the firm's capacity to produce begins to exceed the demand for its products. Consequently, profitability starts to decline. Attempts to overcome this problem by recruiting more managers may not succeed; it takes time for new recruits to become familiar with the organization's practices and methods of operation, and in the short run the need to provide training for the newcomers may make matters worse by diverting the attention of the firm's existing managers. In summary, there is a *managerial constraint on growth*, which implies that if a firm attempts to grow too quickly through diversification, profitability will eventually tend to decline.

Firms have available three means of financing growth of capital: borrowing, the issuing of new share capital, and the use of retained profits. However, there are limits to the use of all three sources, which give rise to a *financial constraint on growth*. Reasons for the financial constraint are as follows.

■ If the firm borrows too heavily, its balance sheet debit–equity ratio or gearing ratio (the ratio of long-term debt to share capital) increases. The level of risk faced by lenders and shareholders also increases: earnings may be insufficient to meet the interest payments on the debt; and the higher the fixed charge on earnings required to cover interest, the more volatile (proportionately) is the residual component of earnings that accrues to shareholders.

■ Issuing new share capital is effective as a means of financing expansion only if the financial markets are willing to invest. In order to sell new shares, the firm needs to be able to demonstrate an acceptable rate of current and future profitability.

■ Finally, growth can be financed from retained profit. However, this creates a dilemma for the firm's managers, who must consider the trade-off between using retained profit to finance growth on the one hand, and paying dividends to share-holders on the other. If the shareholders feel the new investments funded from retained profit will be profitable, they may be content to sacrifice dividends; but if the shareholders are not satisfied, they may vote to dismiss the managers or sell their shares. In both cases the managers' job security is jeopardized, for the reasons discussed earlier with reference to Baumol's minimum profit constraint.

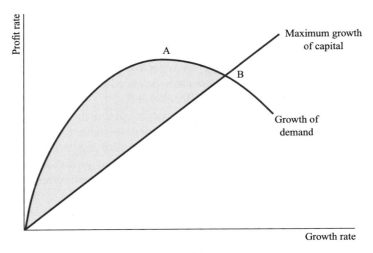

Figure 3.2 Marris's growth maximization model

As a measure of shareholder contentment, Marris suggests using the valuation ratio, defined as the ratio of the firm's stock market value to the book value of its assets. The stock market value represents the market's assessment and expectations of present and future performance, while the book value represents the value of assets employed by the firm. If investors are dissatisfied with the managers' performance, and feel that the firm is not producing an adequate return on the assets it employs, the stock market value will be low relative to the book value of assets, and the valuation ratio will be depressed. The firm is vulnerable to takeover when the valuation ratio is sufficiently low that potential bidders feel they could acquire the firm's assets and then earn a higher return, producing a capital gain through an increase in the share price, market value and valuation ratio.

Marris's model of growth maximization is illustrated in Figure 3.2. The growth of demand function reflects the relationship between the firm's chosen rate of growth of demand (shown along the horizontal axis) and its profitability (shown on the vertical axis). This function is read in an anti-clockwise direction (from the horizontal to the vertical axis). As the rate of growth of demand is increased, at first profitability increases, because it is possible for the firm's managers to identify and successfully exploit profitable diversification opportunities. If the rate of growth increases beyond a certain point, however, profitability starts to fall as the managerial constraint on growth begins to bite.

The maximum growth of capital function shows the relationship between the firm's rate of profit (shown along the vertical axis) and the maximum rate at which the firm is able to increase its capital (shown on the horizontal axis). This function is read in a clockwise direction (from the vertical to the horizontal axis). Marris assumes there is a linear relationship between the rate of profit and the maximum growth rate that can be sustained. Implicitly, the retention ratio (the ratio of retained profit to total profit) is assumed to be constant. In accordance with the preceding discussion of the financial constraint on growth, the higher the profit rate, the higher the maximum rate of growth of capital the firm can sustain. The feasible combinations of profit and growth open to the firm are represented by the shaded area between the growth of demand and maximum growth of capital functions. The shareholders whose objective is profit maximization would prefer the firm to operate at A; but the managers whose objective is growth maximization choose instead to operate at the highest attainable balanced growth rate (at which growth of demand *equals* growth of capital), located at B.

Figure 3.2 and the preceding discussion capture the essential features of the Marris growth maximization model. As with the Baumol sales revenue maximization model, a few refinements have been suggested, which tend to narrow the distinction between the profit-maximizing and growth-maximizing outcomes. For example, shareholders might be willing to forego current profit in favour of growth, if the growth is expected to result in higher profits in the future. Similarly, managers might be willing to forgo some growth in favour of higher current profit, if this produces an increase in the firm's valuation ratio, reducing the likelihood of takeover and enhancing the managers' job security. In both cases there is a trade-off between current profitability and growth, suggesting that an equilibrium might be established somewhere along the section of the growth of demand function inbetween the polar cases of profit maximization at A and growth maximization at B.

The Marris model suggests a few testable hypotheses. First, owner controlled firms achieve lower growth and higher profits than managment controlled firms. Radice (1971) finds that despite differences in average profitability between the two types of firm, owner controlled firms enjoyed faster growth. Second, a low valuation ratio increases the likelihood of the firm being taken over. Using data for some 3,500 UK firms between 1957 and 1969, Kuehn (1975) finds evidence to support this hypothesis. However, Singh (1971) and Levine and Aaronovitch (1981) do not find any such evidence.

Williamson's theory of managerial utility maximization

In Baumol's model, the managers' interests are tied to a single variable, namely sales revenue, which the managers seek to maximize subject to a minimum profit constraint. Williamson (1963) incorporates several variables into the managers' objective or utility function. Managers are assumed to adopt expense preference behaviour, by undertaking large amounts of discretionary spending. This yields satisfaction or utility to the managers, which they seek to maximize. Effectively, expense preference behaviour implies managers divert some of the firm's productive resources for their own uses.

The managerial utility function can be represented as follows:

$$U = f(S, M, \pi_D)$$

S denotes expenditure on staff. It is assumed the manager derives utility from the prestige or power obtained by empire building (increasing the number of staff who report to the manager). M denotes expenditure on managerial emoluments (fringe benefits or perks), such as large offices, expense accounts and company cars. π_D denotes discretionary profit, defined as net profit (after tax and expenditure on managerial emoluments) over and above the minimum level of profit that is required to pay an acceptable level of dividend to shareholders. Again, it is assumed the managers derive utility from discretionary profit: the higher the value of π_D, the greater the managers' job security.

Letting π denote operating profit (before expenditure on managerial emoluments), T denote tax, and π_0 denote the shareholders' minimum acceptable profit level, we can write:

$$\pi_D = \pi - M - T - \pi_0$$

Operating profit, π, is a function of staff expenditure, S. As the level of staff expenditure increases, operating profit initially increases as well. However, eventually diminishing returns set in, and staffing costs start to rise faster than the extra revenue additional staff are capable of generating. As the level of staff expenditure continues to increase, operating profit eventually starts to decrease. We can write:

$$\pi = \pi(S) \quad \Rightarrow \quad \pi_D = \pi(S) - M - T - \pi_0$$

Therefore the problem of managerial utility maximization involves selecting the values of S, M and π_D which maximize the utility function $U = f(S, M, \pi_D)$, subject to the constraint $\pi_D = \pi(S) - M - T - \pi_0$. A diagrammatic representation of this constrained optimization problem can be obtained by assuming, for simplicity, M is constant, and examining the trade-off between S and π_D. This is shown in Figure 3.3. The relationship between S and π_D implied by our discussion of diminishing returns to additional staff expenditure is represented by the inverted U-shaped function $\pi_D = \pi(S) - M - T - \pi_0$. The indifference curves U_1, U_2 and U_3 show the nature of the trade-off between π_D and S that is implied by the managerial utility function.

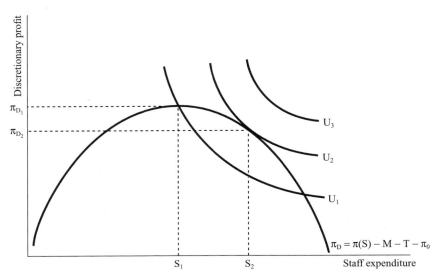

Figure 3.3 Williamson's managerial utility maximization model

In Figure 3.3, a profit-maximizing firm selects a staff expenditure level of S_1, and earns a discretionary profit of π_{D_1}. This produces a managerial utility level of U_1. A managerial firm, whose managers seek to maximize their own utility function, selects a higher staff expenditure level of S_2, and earns a lower discretionary profit of π_{D_2}. This produces a higher managerial utility level of U_2.

Therefore Williamson concludes that a managerial firm tends to overspend on its staff in comparison with a profit-maximizing firm. This result demonstrates the preference of managers for staff expenditure. If M is also made variable rather than fixed (as assumed in Figure 3.3) a similar conclusion emerges in respect of managerial emoluments. At the respective equilibria, $M = 0$ for a profit-maximizing firm, and $M > 0$ for a managerial utility-maximizing firm.

3.5 The behavioural theory of the firm

The behavioural theory of the firm is most closely associated with Cyert and March (1964). This theory defines the firm in terms of its organizational structure and decision-making processes. The boundaries of the firm are defined quite loosely, to include all individuals or groups with influence or interests in the organization's activities. Relevant groups include the firm's managers, shareholders, employees, customers and suppliers of inputs, as well as other parties such as trades unions, consumer organizations, local residents (whose living environment may be affected by the firm's operations), government departments (which may be interested in the implications of the firm's activities for tax revenues, employment or the balance of payments); and so on. (In more recent terminology, these interest groups have been referred to as stakeholders.) Group definitions can be formulated at several different levels; for example, the firm's management team might be subdivided into its constituent parts with responsibilities for functions such as marketing, sales, production, stock-keeping, finance, human resources and so on, with each group tending to emphasize and articulate its own priorities and objectives.

The behavioural theory is based on the observation of actual behaviour within organizations, and it is recognized that all decision making takes place in an environment of uncertainty, or **bounded rationality** (Simon, 1959). No individual or group has complete information about every aspect of the firm's activities and operating environment. But all groups and individuals have some information, and the information they have tends to be most complete in the immediate vicinity of their own activities. Accordingly, decision making is based on bounded rationality rather than global rationality. All decisions are influenced by the beliefs, perceptions and aspirations of the individuals and groups involved. Differences in beliefs, perceptions and aspirations create the potential for conflict within the organization. Conflicts are resolved through a bargaining process, from which corporate goals or objectives emerge. Organizations themselves do not have goals or objectives: corporate goals are the outcome of bargaining within the organization. Agreements between groups or individuals bond the interested parties into coalitions. Corporate goals or objectives are always subject to change, as the aspirations, beliefs and influence of the various parties change over time. Periodically, the parties compare the performance of the firm in the areas in which they are interested with their own aspirations. If performance is consistently above or below their aspirations, aspiration levels may be revised, and new goals or objectives may emerge. Therefore corporate goals and objectives are themselves dependent on past performance.

Corporate goals cannot be reduced to a simple formula, such as profit maximization. In an environment of complexity, imperfect information and uncertainty, the precise set of actions required in order to maximize profit is impossible to determine. Instead, the firm's managers may settle for a satisfactory profit, following rules-of-thumb and decision-making conventions that are determined in the light of past experience. Simon (1959) used the term **satisficing** to refer to the idea that the firm aims for a satisfactory profit, instead of seeking to maximize profit. Rules-of-thumb might include conventions such as 'we must spend 5 per cent of revenue on advertising' or 'we must capture 50 per cent of the market' or 'we must play a lead role in research and development'.

The resolution of conflict through bargaining between groups of stakeholders is often achieved using **side payments**. For example, managers may be keen to adopt a new technology, while individual employees or the trade union that represents them may be reluctant to do so. The adoption of the new technology might be achieved by increasing wages or bonuses. Side payments need not necessarily be in monetary terms. For example, it might be sufficient to allow the workforce some representation at board level. Managers can also bargain over side payments. For example, more resources might be allocated to the department of a key manager who is threatening to leave in order to join a competitor, in an attempt to retain the manager within the firm.

The successful firm holds together, by making side payments that are sufficient to prevent essential individuals or groups from withdrawing. If the side payments are insufficient, workers may go on strike, key personnel may leave, shareholders may sell their shareholdings, suppliers may cease to supply the firm, banks may refuse to grant loans, or local residents may take legal action to force the closure of a plant or factory. Side payments that exceed what is strictly necessary to hold the firm together are possible when there is **organizational slack**. Normally, most parties benefit from organizational slack. For example, shareholders receive dividends above those strictly necessary to prevent them from selling their shares; products are priced at a level some distance below the point at which most customers would switch to a rival firm's product; wages are above the level at which most employees would resign; executives receive remuneration or fringe benefits that are more than sufficient for their services to be retained. When the firm is enjoying increasing sales and profitability, organizational slack expands, and side payments increase accordingly. In times of falling demand and low profitability, organizational slack provides a cushion, enabling cuts or economies to be made without causing key parties to withdraw altogether from the organization.

The behavioural theory of the firm recognizes the complexity of organizational decision making. There is no definitive behavioural theory, since the organizational structure of every firm is different. The theory is based on the observation of actual behaviour within organizations. Accordingly, behavioural theory is strong on explanation, but weak on prediction. In an environment of complexity, imperfect information and uncertainty, it is unlikely that the goals or objectives of the organization can be reduced to a simple formula such as profit maximization. Instead, decisions emerge from bargaining between numerous individuals and groups, pursuing multiple and often conflicting objectives. The emphasis on bargaining over side payments and the resolution of conflict implies the behavioural theory is primarily concerned with decision making in the short run. Accordingly, the theory can be criticized for offering little more than broad generalizations as to how firms tend to develop and grow in the long run.

3.6 The Coasian firm and the transaction costs approach

Over time, increasing awareness of the limitations of both the neoclassical theory of the firm, and the managerial and behavioural alternatives that we have examined in Sections 3.4 and 3.5, has motivated efforts to search for and develop yet more realistic economic theories of the firm. These alternative approaches to the theory of the firm are considered in Sections 3.6 and 3.7.

An important starting point for many of the newer theories that have been developed since the 1970s was an attempt to try to understand *why* firms exist at all, and to identify the fundamental characteristics that distinguish firms from other institutions or organizations. Phelan and Lewis (2000) identify a number of features common to many of the newer theories.

- *Specialization and exchange*. Specialization is a major source of wealth creation. A firm can be regarded as an institution which carries out specialized production for potential buyers, rather than for its own consumption. If the firm were less productive than its buyers, the latter would become self-sufficient and there would be no role for the firm. For gains from specialization to be realized, however, specialization must be accompanied by exchange through the market. Therefore the theory emphasizes the nature of the market transaction, including matters such as the costs of bargaining, delivering, monitoring and enforcing a contracts. It is also relevant to ask exactly what is being exchanged. Some theories emphasize trade in the rights to use or transform an asset. Contracts specify the extent to which rights can be transferred. **Specific rights** are covered explicitly by the terms of a contract, while **residual rights** cover what is left after the terms of the firm's other contracts have been fulfilled. For example, ownership of the firm confers a set of residual rights to the profit earned by the firm, or to the disposal of what remains of the firm's assets, after all other contractual obligations (specific rights) have been met.

- *Coordination and cooperation*. In order to determine the quantities of inputs it requires, the firm has to anticipate the level and the nature of the demand for its product. The level and nature of demand may also determine the way in which the inputs are acquired; for example, should a machine be bought outright, hired or leased? Once the inputs are in place, the firm must decide how best to coordinate the inputs so as to achieve the required output. The suppliers of the firm's inputs (the agents) naturally tend to act in their own interests. The firm (the principal) needs to ensure that contracts are drawn up in a manner that aligns the interests of its suppliers with its own interests. In other words, contracts must provide the right incentives for the agents to act in accordance with the interests of the principal. Cooperation between the suppliers of inputs may also be important. Difficulties associated with coordination and cooperation stem from the fact that the firm operates in a world of imperfect information. If the firm had perfect information, all contracts could be drafted, priced and monitored with complete precision. It is the lack of perfect information that leaves the door open for opportunistic behaviour on the part of agents.

- *Efficiency in production.* It seems reasonable to assume that over the long run, the organizational structures that are observed and that prosper are those that achieve maximum efficiency in production (as defined in Section 2.5). In other words, to survive in the long run a firm needs to be both technically efficient (to produce the maximum quantity of output that is feasible, given the factor inputs it employs) and economically efficient (to operate using the cost-minimizing combination of factor inputs). If there were more efficient ways of organizing production, other firms would have found them and exploited them, forcing the inefficient firm to either adapt or disappear. Therefore the main purpose of the theory of the firm is not to explain how productive activity is most efficiently organized, but rather to explain why different organizational structures tend to emerge and prosper under different conditions.

The Coasian firm

The starting point for Coase (1937) is the observation that in a market economy, many resource allocation decisions are taken unconsciously, through the operation of the price mechanism. Resources tend to flow to wherever they command the highest price. Excluding the possibility of market imperfections, if the price of a factor of production is higher in industry X than in industry Y, the factor moves from Y towards X, until the price differential disappears. However, there is another large class of resource allocation decisions that are not decided in this way. For resource allocation decisions that are taken internally within firms, the price mechanism is suspended. When workers move from one department to another, for example, they do so not because there has been a price signal, but because they have been consciously told to do so. Within the firm we observe something rather similar to economic planning: the conscious coordination of the firm's resources by the entrepreneur or manager. Accordingly, Robertson likens the position of firms within markets to 'islands of conscious power in this ocean of unconscious cooperation' (Robertson, 1930, p. 85).

Why do these 'islands' of conscious power exist? In other words, why should the task of coordination or resource allocation be assigned to the market in some cases, and to the firm in other cases? Coase points out that **transaction costs** are incurred when using markets to allocate resources. Transaction costs include the search costs associated with gathering information about relative prices. Transaction costs also include the costs incurred in negotiating the contract that specifies the terms of the transaction. Finally, transaction costs can be created artificially by governments, through the levying of sales taxes or the imposition of quotas. Coase's explanation as to why some transactions are removed from the domain of the market, and are instead decided consciously within organizations called firms, is that this method of coordination creates a saving in transaction costs.

■ It is not necessary for a factor of production to search for a price signal in order to transfer from one department to another within the firm. The transfer is decided consciously by the entrepreneur or manager.

■ The costs associated with negotiating contracts with suppliers of factors of production can be greatly reduced. For example, instead of hiring labour on a daily basis in a spot market, the firm can hire workers on long-term employment contracts. The precise details of the worker's contractual obligations over the entire duration of the contract are not specified; instead, the employee is expected to comply (within certain limits) with instructions issued by the entrepreneur or manager. The contract needs only specify the limits to the obligations of the contracting parties.

■ Sales tax liabilities or other restrictions on economic activity imposed by government may be circumvented if transactions take place internally within the organization, rather than externally through the market.

According to the Coasian analysis, a firm expands when additional transactions are removed from the sphere of the market and are instead dictated within the boundaries of the firm. A firm declines when it ceases to organize some transactions, which are returned to the sphere of the market. Naturally, a critical question is what determines the boundaries that separate the firm from the market? If the removal of transactions from the market and their incorporation within the firm reduces or eliminates transaction costs, why does the market survive at all as a medium for coordination or resource allocation? Why do we not observe just one very large firm? Fundamentally, the answer is that there are also costs associated with the supply of the entrepreneurial or organizing function. The entrepreneur may be more skilled in organizing some types of transaction than others, so for certain transactions it may be preferable to rely on the market and incur the associated transaction costs. Furthermore, the marginal cost of incorporating additional transactions within the firm increases as the number of transactions already incorporated increases. Due to diminishing returns to the entrepreneurial or organizing function, a point is always reached at which it would be counter-productive to extend the boundaries of the firm any further. Case study 3.3 discusses the policy of outsourcing: using the market to supply essential resources, rather than producing them internally.

Cowling and Sugden (1998) challenge the Coasian view that the analysis of the firm should rest exclusively on identifying the boundaries between market and non-market transactions. Coase (1991) himself draws attention to the fact that within some large organizations, internal markets or quasi-markets are created deliberately in order to settle certain resource allocation decisions, and to introduce an element of competitive pressure or discipline. Coase suggests that in such cases, the firm's competing departments might be viewed as if they were effectively separate firms. However, Cowling and Sugden argue that the market versus non-market (or some intermediate combination) characterization of transactions and resource allocation decisions is largely a superficial construct. The analysis of the firm should concentrate on the nature of the productive activity itself, rather than the method of coordinating this activity. Nevertheless, Coase's interpretation of firms as 'islands of conscious planning' is highly insightful, especially in view of the modern emphasis on strategic decision making within the firm (see Section 3.8).

Case study 3.3

Lessons from Railtrack: The collapse has demolished some of the untested assumptions about outsourcing

The fall of Railtrack, Britain's rail infrastructure operator, has many lessons. But the one that may resonate the longest is the failure of its attempt to rely on a web of subcontractors to carry out maintenance and other routine tasks.

Railtrack had about a dozen prime contractors, which in turn farmed out the work to about 2,000 subcontractors. Getting this web of relationships to work properly was a daunting task. Gaps in communication, and the consequent 'blame culture', are thought to be import-ant causes of the track problems that led to the Hatfield crash which undermined Railtrack's credibility. In adopting this approach, however, Railtrack was merely taking 1990s orthodoxy to its logical conclusion. It was focusing on its core competence – managing and rebuilding the railway network – and outsourcing the routine, low-value tasks. Sir Robert Horton, Railtrack's first chairman, had come from the oil industry. The outsourcing approach he was using is common there, both in running the exploration and production rigs and in main-taining refineries and petrochemical plants. In the 1990s, the outsourcing fashion spread far beyond the oil industry. Its most basic appeal lay in the cost savings potentially achievable by encouraging competitive bidding on contracts. But it also promised to tap into a reservoir of specialist skills within subcontractors, fostered by improved focus and by a career ladder unavailable in big companies. A good track maintenance foreman was never likely to rise to the main board of Railtrack but could realistically hope for a board-level career at a maintenance company.

These practical advantages of wholesale outsourcing rely, however, on unexamined assump-tions. It is these that the Railtrack episode comprehensively demolishes. The first belief holds that properly specified contracts can replicate the operations of an integrated business. Indeed, on this view, they may be better than integration because everyone understands what their responsibilities are, and their incentives are clear and tightly defined. This approach had a par-ticular appeal to governments, as they attempted to step back from the minutiae of delivering public services. British Conservative governments used the approach to break up monolithic nationalized industries into individual entities, such as power generators and distributors.

They put this approach into effect at the top level of the railway system by splitting the task of running the track and the signalling (Railtrack's job) from the role of operating the trains. It is not surprising that Railtrack, born into this environment, carried the approach to its logical conclusion in its internal operations. But former government bodies are not the only candidates for this approach. It is attractive to anyone faced with reforming a big institution. It offers a chance to get away from the producer mentality – 'we know what's good for you' – which is often as pervasive in private sector cost centres, such as corporate information technology departments, as it is in the public sector. The decision to outsource parts of the public sector was political. In private sector companies, there is often a political element to outsourcing, too. It can be seen as the outcome of a victory by departments that consume internal services over their colleagues who supply them. Unfortunately, sometimes those infuriating cabals of specialists do know best.

There is nothing new about this tension. In 1937, the Nobel prize-winning economist Ronald Coase had explained that companies perform internally those tasks for which the transactional costs of outsourcing are too high. What fuelled the outsourcing boom of the 1990s was the second unexamined assumption – that the cost of negotiating, monitoring and maintaining contractual relationships with outsourcing partners had dropped sharply, thanks to the revolution in electronic communications. The management of a much bigger web of contractors – indeed, the creation of a 'virtual company' – became feasible.

In practice, of course, the real costs of establishing and maintaining contracts are not those of information exchange but of establishing trust, alignment of interests and a common purpose. Speedy and cheap electronic communications have only a minor role to play in this process, as Coase himself pointed out in 1997. But the biggest of all the unexamined assumptions that led to the outsourcing boom is also the one that looks most out of date. The move to replace internal corporate activities with a web of external contracts could have come about only in a stable economic and political environment. In such circumstances, contractual relationships are fine. But in a crisis – after a serious rail accident, at a time of a sharp economic downturn or during geopolitical uncertainty – contracts alone are likely to prove an unstable basis on which to build a business.

This is particularly true where the activity is central to a company's credibility. And perhaps that is the most useful lesson from the Railtrack story: it is essential to decide what tasks are vital to your corporate purpose and to devote serious resources to achieving them. Maintaining thousands of miles of steel tracks and stone chippings may be a dull, 19th century kind of task. But as Railtrack found, if you can't keep the railway running safely, you haven't got a business. Given that sort of priority, the outsourcing debate looks very different.

Source: Peter Martin, Lessons from Railtrack: The collapse has demolished some of the untested assumptions about outsourcing, *Financial Times*, 9 October 2001.

Transaction costs and the theory of the firm

Coase's ideas regarding the nature of the firm, outlined above, spawned a number of further contributions to the theory of the firm, which can be grouped under the heading of transaction costs economics. Some of the key ideas are advanced by Cheung (1983), Klein *et al.* (1978) and most notably Williamson (1975; 1985). Coase's original emphasis was on transaction costs incurred before contracts are concluded. These include costs associated with searching for information and negotiating contracts. In contrast, the later transaction costs literature focuses on costs incurred after contracts are concluded. These costs arise from difficulties in monitoring and enforcing compliance, and punishing non-compliance. In this section we focus on Williamson's approach.

Most contracts are **incomplete contracts**, in the sense that the parties cannot identify in advance every possible contingency that might impact on their contractual relationship. In other words, there is bounded rationality (rather than global rationality). Principals and agents may find it impossible to forsee all events that could possibly occur in an uncertain world. Even if the range of possible future events can be forseen, the parties may disagree over the probabilities that should be assigned to different events. And even if events can be forseen and probabilities assigned, this information may be difficult to translate into a meaningful and enforceable contract. Such a contract would have to be exhaustively specified, so as to eliminate all possible ambiguities that could otherwise give rise to expensive litigation.

Contracts that have already been agreed can give rise to unforeseen consequences. The parties may incur renegotiation or switching costs if alternative partners or production technologies are discovered. An important issue which may create a need for the renegotiation of contracts is **asset specificity**. A contract between two parties may involve the creation of an asset that is specific to that relationship, and which has little or no value outside that relationship. This gives rise to the creation of a **quasi-rent** (Klein *et al.*, 1978), related to the difference between the asset's value in its present use and its value in its next best use (or its salvage value). After the contract has been concluded, the parties can act opportunistically by asking to renegotiate the incomplete contract, in an effort to appropriate the quasi-rent.

For example, a principal–agent relationship might involve extensive **sunk cost** investment in the agent's human capital by both parties, with neither party able to recoup the sunk costs if the relationship breaks down. This situation could arise if the principal incurs substantial training costs, and the agent also invests effort in the acquisition of skills that are specific to this particular relationship. Once the specific human capital embodied in the agent has accumulated, on each occasion the contract is renegotiated both parties have an incentive to seek to appropriate a larger share of the return that the principal–agent relationship generates. In a spot market for agents' services, recontracting might take place on a daily or weekly basis. In each renegotiation, the agent can threaten non-renewal causing the principal to incur the training costs all over again with a new agent; but equally, the principal can threaten non-renewal, forcing the agent to sell his services to a new principal with whom the agent's productivity, and therefore his remuneration, might be much lower. As each party issues threats and counter-threats, the costs of renegotiating tend to become prohibitively high. If either party can foresee the possibility that the other party might behave in this manner, the party with foresight might be reluctant to enter into such a relationship in the first place.

The alternative is for the contract between the principal and agent to be integrated or internalized within the sphere of a firm: the relationship becomes one of employer and employee rather than principal and agent. As discussed by Coase, the employee becomes bound by a long-term employment contract, which does not specify every detail of both parties' obligations over the entire contract duration, but which does impose some limits on permissible behaviour. The need for recontracting on a daily or weekly basis is eliminated, and the scope for opportunistic behaviour in an attempt to appropriate quasi-rents is reduced but perhaps not eliminated altogether: threatened strike action or resignation by employees, or threatened dismissal of employees by the employer, are still powerful bargaining instruments once the sunk cost investment in specific human capital has been incurred by both parties. The internalization of market transactions proceeds up to the point where the marginal governance cost associated with running the transaction internally (within the firm) *equals* the marginal transaction cost associated with contracting (via the market).

Although the internalization of transactions is a common remedy according to much of the transaction costs literature, there are some exceptions. Milgrom and Roberts (1988) suggest that under some conditions a series of short-term contracts may be preferable to the internalization of transactions, especially in situations where market conditions and production technologies are subject to change. The empirical transaction costs literature is surveyed by Shelanski and Klein (1995) and Boerner and Macher (2001). Some of this literature explores the relationship between the degree of asset specificity within firms and governance structures, vertical integration and the types and duration of contracts. In a study of subcontracting in the UK engineering industry, for example, Lyons (1996) finds the degree of asset specificity influences not only the duration of contracts, but also the decision whether a firm should subcontract or not. Where firms are more vulnerable to opportunistic behaviour on the part of subcontractors, formal contracts are more likely to be adopted in preference to flexible and informal agreements.

The transaction costs approach has also been used to explore the question of the most effective organizational structure. Figure 3.4 illustrates the unitary or U-form organizational structure, in which the firm's key activities are subdivided into functional areas, such as marketing, finance, production, personnel, and so on. Each department is run by a middle manager, who reports to the firm's chief executive. An advantage of this organizational form is that by specializing, the departmental managers develop functional expertise, allowing the clustering of particular skills or talents within departments. This is particularly useful when a firm produces a single product. Consequently, this organizational structure is common among small and medium-sized firms. The U-form organizational structure is less suited to large organizations that supply a diversified range of goods and services, because in this case each department has to deal with a more diverse range of tasks and functions. Effective coordination of resource allocation decisions and the transmission of information between departments become more difficult as the organization increases in size, and as transaction costs start to increase. Consequently, the departmental managers' workloads become more demanding, and conflict between departments tends to increase.

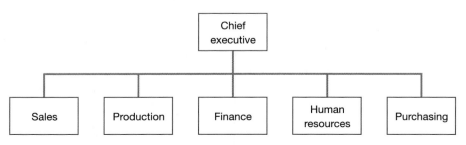

Figure 3.4 Unitary or U-form organizational structure

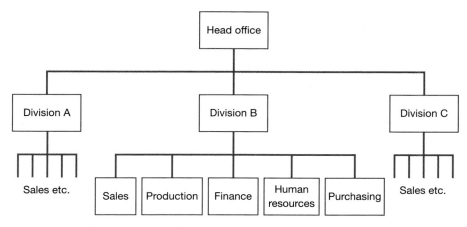

Figure 3.5 Multidivisional or M-form organizational structure

Figure 3.5 illustrates the multidivisional or M-form organizational structure, in which the firm is divided into a number of quasi-independent operating divisions. The M-form was first developed in the US in the 1920s and 1930s, as the scale and scope of large firms such as General Motors grew to such an extent that management structures based on the U-form became overloaded and unable to operate effectively (Chandler, 1977). Within an M-form organizational structure, the operating divisions can be organized geographically (within regional, national or international boundaries), or by product type. Each division is a quasi-firm, comprising all of the key functional areas required to deliver the product or service. Divisional managers exercise a considerable amount of decision-making autonomy over their own operations. The head office is responsible for the longer-term strategic direction of the organization, and plays a supervisory role with respect to the activities of the divisions: the head office monitors performance, allocates finance and sets the parameters within which the divisional managers are permitted to operate. A closely related variant is the holding company or H-form organizational structure, in which a holding or parent company has a significant ownership stake (normally a controlling interest) in other companies or subsidiaries. Again, the managers of the subsidiaries may be granted a considerable amount of decision-making autonomy with respect to operational matters. The H-form structure is especially common among multi-national companies.

Synthesizing a number of insights drawn from his earlier work, Williamson (2002a) proposes a theory of the firm as governance structure. The orthodox approach to economics, popularized by Robbins (1932), can be interpreted as the science of choice on the part of rational utility or profit-maximizing agents. However, this approach is not the only source of insight into economic relationships: there is also the science of contract. Figure 3.6 shows schematically this division between the two sciences. The science of contract branch subdivides into public ordering, covering collective action to secure goods and services which the market fails to deliver; and private ordering, covering issues associated with the alignment of incentives and governance. The alignment of incentives is addressed by **agency theory** and the economics of property rights (see pp. 101–3). **Governance** addresses the ways

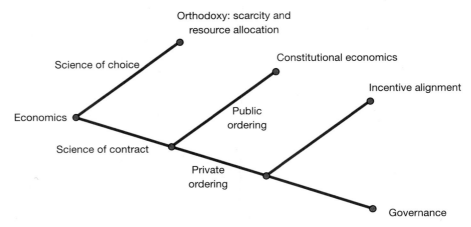

Figure 3.6 The science of choice and the science of contract
Source: Adapted from Williamson (2002), p. 181.

in which organizations can best manage their contractual relationships. Williamson draws the following lessons from organization theory:

■ Bounded rationality is a fact of organizational life, and complex contracts are always incomplete. Parties to a contract have to be ready to adapt to unexpected events, not only because of their lack of information or foresight, but also because of the potential for opportunistic behaviour that may take place due to unanticipated events. The potential for breakdown in contractual relationships encourages the organization to search for the most appropriate governance structures.

■ Governance structures should be designed in the light of all possible outcomes or significant behavioural regularities, both intended and unintended.

■ The most pertinent unit of analysis in the firm is the transaction. The three essential characteristics of transactions which affect the nature of governance are: first, the degree of asset specificity; second, the potential disturbances to which the transaction may be subject; and third, the frequency with which the transaction recurs.

■ Organizational structures are adaptable in the light of changing conditions. With market transactions, agents modify their behaviour in response to price signals. In contrast, organizations rely on skilled or specialized managers to take decisions as to how the organizational structure should adapt and evolve.

Finally, Williamson develops a model of the firm, organization or hierarchy interpreted as a governance structure. Transactions contain elements of conflict and disorder, but also offer the potential for mutual gains by both parties. Governance seeks to reduce conflict, increase order and create the conditions required for mutual gains to be realized. The difference between an organization or hierarchy and the market is that in a hierarchy, incentives tend to be lower, controls are more copious, and conflicts are resolved by diktat. For the reasons we have discussed previously in this section, the degree of asset specificity is perhaps the most important characteristic of

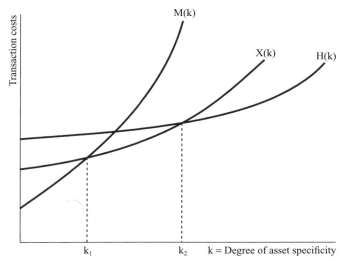

Figure 3.7 Modes of governance and the degree of asset specificity
Source: Adapted from Williamson (2002), p. 173.

a transaction. Figure 3.7 shows the relationship between the degree of asset specificity and transaction costs for three governance modes: the market (M), the hierarchy (H) and a hybrid mode (X). If the degree of asset specificity is zero, transaction costs are highest with H, reflecting the administrative costs associated with the organization's bureaucratic structure. As the degree of asset specificity increases, the cost differential between H and M begins to close, and eventually H emerges as the governance structure with the lowest transaction costs. X occupies the middle ground between M and H, with the lowest transation costs over some intermediate range of values for the degree of asset specificity (between k_1 and k_2). Shelanski and Klein (1995), Dixit (1996) and Lyons (1996) subject this approach to empirical scrutiny.

3.7 Other approaches to the theory of the firm

The firm as team-based production

The development of theories of the firm focusing on contractual relationships between the parties who comprise the organization can be traced back to Alchian and Demsetz (1972). Two important issues are addressed. First, why should the gains from specialization and the coordination of activities be greater if activities are organized within the firm rather than through the market? Second, how can we explain the internal organizational structure of the firm? Alchian and Demsetz challenge the Coasian notion that firms possess the ability to resolve coordination issues by diktat. An employer has no more power over an employee than a customer has over his or her shopkeeper. All the employer can do is assign various tasks to the employee on terms that are acceptable to both parties. As in the case of the shopkeeper and the customer, there is no contractual requirement for the employer and the employee to maintain their relationship permanently. The contract between the parties is renegotiated continually, and can be terminated by either party at any time.

However, the employer–employee relationship within the firm is different from the shopkeeper–customer relationship in one crucial aspect. The firm is characterized by teamwork, which requires coordination and cooperation between large numbers of suppliers of inputs. A central contracting agent, employer or owner carries out this essential coordinating function. To ensure the various inputs are combined effectively, it must be possible for the coordinator to measure and monitor the contribution made by each input, and reward each supplier appropriately. This is known as the metering problem. In many cases, metering works effectively through the medium of decentralized, competitive markets. A consumer who wishes to buy apples can easily establish which supermarket, grocer or fruit seller offers the best deal. For some transactions, however, effective metering may be more difficult to achieve. When hiring a plumber, it is not always straightforward to establish whether the work has been completed properly or whether the price being charged is fair. In cases where the metering of productivity and rewards is weak, effective coordination through the medium of markets may be more difficult to achieve, since one or more of the parties may lack the necessary incentives to comply with their contractual obligations.

With respect to the metering problem, team production poses a number of challenges for the firm. Technically, team production within the domain of the firm may be more efficient than contracting between independent suppliers. With team production, however, it may be difficult to measure accurately each team member's individual contribution to the firm's total output. If individuals are self-employed, any increase in productivity is rewarded directly by an increase in the relevant factor payment. For a team of n members among whom the rewards are divided equally, any increase in effort produces a reward to the individual of only 1/n *times* the extra effort. Consequently, there is a temptation for individual members of a team to shirk or free-ride. Shirking by team members is dealt with by the central contracting agent, employer or owner, who monitors performance and disciplines non-performing team members. The employer's incentive to carry out the monitoring function effectively is provided by his or her claim on the organization's residual return. Essentially, the Alchian and Demsetz argument is as follows. If the total output that can be achieved by organizing team production within a firm exceeds the output that can be produced by contracting between independent suppliers through the market, and if the additional output exceeds the costs of monitoring the team members' individual efforts, team production within the firm supersedes production coordinated through market mechanisms.

The firm as a nexus of contracts

Jensen and Meckling (1976) argue that Alchian and Demsetz's emphasis on team production and monitoring is too narrow, and perhaps even misleading. Instead, the essence of the firm is the entire set of contractual relationships which bind together the firm's owners, employees, material suppliers, creditors, customers and other parties with contractual involvement in the firm's activities. The contractual relationships that bind the parties together raise the issues of agency, incentives and monitoring discussed by Alchian and Demsetz. Therefore the firm encompasses a much wider set of relationships than those defined purely in terms of team production. Jensen and Meckling claim most firms are simply legal fictions, which possess an artificial identity created by law, and serve as a nexus (or link) for the contractual relationships between the individual parties. This wider definition of the firm encompasses non-profit, mutual and public sector organizations.

Jensen and Meckling seek to understand why different sets of contractual relationships develop for different firms, and how these relationships change in response to exogenous changes to the firm's external environment. This approach makes redundant the attempt to distinguish between contractual relationships within the firm on the one hand, and those within the market on the other. Viewing the firm simply as a nexus of contractual relationships renders the personification of the firm analytically misleading. The firm is not like an individual that pursues its own distinct set of objectives. Rather, the firm acts like a clearing house for the multitude of (often conflicting) objectives pursued by the parties linked together by the nexus of contracts.

Agency theory

Agency theory analyses the conflicts that may arise between principals (owners or shareholders) and agents (managers) within a firm. This theory is motivated directly by the analysis of the separation of ownership from control in modern corporations (see Section 3.4). Jensen and Meckling (1976) point out that agents may not always act in the best interests of principals. Under conditions of incomplete contracts and uncertainty, two particular issues arise: adverse selection and moral hazard. The possibility of **adverse selection** arises when a principal is unable to verify an agent's claims concerning the agent's own ability or productivity. There is **moral hazard** when the possibility exists for the agent to act opportunistically in the agent's own private interests, but against the principal's interests as stipulated in the contract that binds the agent to the principal.

Both of these terms originate in the insurance industry. Suppose an insurer wishes to sell health insurance policies to individuals, some of whom are at high risk of sickness while some are at low risk. Suppose the insurer cannot easily distinguish between high-risk and low-risk applicants when the policy is taken out, and therefore decides to charge a premium based on the average sickness rate. This practice is likely to be disastrous for the company, because low-risk applicants will realize it is not worthwhile for them to take out insurance (priced at an average rate that is higher than their own sickness rate). In contrast, high-risk applicants will realize that insurance priced at the average rate (below their own sickness rate) is a bargain, and will buy lots of insurance. The company suffers an adverse selection effect, becaue it finishes up with a loss-making portfolio of high-risk policyholders.

The term moral hazard refers to the tendency for policyholders to become less careful about protecting an interest once it has been insured. If one's house is insured against burglary, when leaving the house one might not bother to lock the doors and windows. If one's car is insured against theft and vandalism, one might not worry about parking in an unsafe part of town. Once insured, the policyholder has little incentive to act in the best interests of the insurer, since it is the insurer who pays the price for the policyholder's carelessness or recklessness.

The implication for the theory of the firm is that a fixed wage contract may not be the best way of organizing the relationship between a principal and an agent. At the point of hiring, a fixed wage offer may result in the principal hiring a group of agents whose actual productivity is lower than the remuneration on offer, because high productivity agents are unwilling to work for less than their actual productivity (an adverse selection problem). And having been hired, an agent may lack sufficient incentive to work to the full limit of his or her capabilities, since the remuneration is the same regardless of the intensity of effort (a moral hazard problem).

A remuneration structure that is to some extent performance-related might offer a solution to both types of problem. Establishing a link between effort and reward reduces or eliminates adverse selection if agents know at the point of hiring they will be rewarded in proportion to their productivity. The same link reduces or eliminates moral hazard if agents know they will pay a price for shirking, in the form of lower remuneration. However, a number of problems still remain. Difficulties involved in monitoring individual contributions to team performance may prevent the design of a remuneration structure that fully reflects individual ability and effort. Furthermore, principals and agents may have different attitudes concerning the trade-off between risk and return. In pursuit of a higher short-run return, managers (agents) may impose higher risks on shareholders (principals) than the latter would prefer. For example, part of the managers' remuneration package might take the form of stock options, allowing the holder the right to buy equity in the company for a set price at a future date. Options provide an incentive for managers to act in a way that increases the firm's market value, helping align the agent's incentives with the principal's interests. But in order to maximize the value of their options, managers might be tempted to pursue exceptionally risky ventures in the short run, to the possible detriment of the firm's long-run profitability and stability.

Property rights and the theory of the firm

Transactions can be viewed as an exchange of rights over various assets such as labour, capital and the use of land. The rights that are exchanged may include the right to use, modify, transfer or extract an income from the asset concerned. Transactions are normally effected through contractual agreements. A distinction is drawn between *specific rights* defined explicitly in the terms of a contract, and *residual rights* that accrue to the owner once all specific rights have been assigned. The property rights approach to the theory of the firm is based on this distinction (Hart and Moore, 1990; Hart 1995). In a world of incomplete contracts, where there is insufficient information or foresight to define a complete contract covering all specific rights, the ownership of the residual rights is of paramount importance. The owner of the asset has the final or *default* control over the asset, and the right to dispose of a good or asset as he or she sees fit.

In contrast to the Alchian and Demsetz (1972) approach, which suggests firms have relatively little control over assets such as their employees, the property rights approach emphasizes the control that is vested in the firm as holder of the residual rights. In cases where an asset such as group of skilled employees are in their most valued use in an organization, they may be willing to follow orders or directions, since the firm, as owner of the residual rights, can appropriate their quasi-rent or even deny them access to the firm's physical assets by dismissing them. It is the ownership of the residual rights that gives the firm control over access to physical assets, or less tangible assets such as brands or reputation.

Suppose two firms, a textbook publisher A and a printing firm B have a long-term contractual agreement. An unforeseen change to the terms of the original contract is now required: A wishes to switch from two-colour to four-colour ink production. If both firms hold the property rights to their own assets, and both have sufficient leverage to damage the other party, it is likely that a mutually acceptable renegotiated contract can be agreed, enabling B to obtain a higher price for its printing services and A to sell more books. However, ownership of the residual rights affects the rewards accruing to the two parties, which may in turn affect the willingness of the parties to commit themselves to specific investments. A may be reluctant to invest in the expensive, specialized software required for the new printing process, as this investment will increase B's bargaining power over A in future contract negotiations. But if A and B are fully integrated, however, the change to four-colour ink production is organized by the owner of the integrated firm, who instructs the manager of the print division to implement the change. The integrated firm neither has to negotiate a new contract, nor increase the manager's remuneration. Furthermore, in the integrated firm the owner has no fear that the benefits of the specific investment will be diluted by opportunistic behaviour. Therefore integrated ownership may encourage specific investment (Grossman and Hart, 1986; Bolton and Scharfstein, 1998).

3.8 Strategic and knowledge-based theories of the firm

So far in Chapter 3, two broad approaches to the theory of the firm have been identified. First, the neoclassical theory of the firm is not really an analysis of the firm as such, but rather a theory of resource allocation in the market. The neoclassical theory gives little attention to internal decision making within the firm: the firm is a simple unit which pursues its goals mechanistically. The firm is like 'a black box operated so as to meet the relevant marginal conditions with respect to inputs and outputs, thereby maximizing profits, or more accurately, present value' (Jensen and Meckling, 1976, p. 307). The second approach views the firm as an institution which minimizes or economizes on transaction costs, or the costs of processing information. Resources are allocated in response to the firm's interpretation of information flows. The firm organizes governance structures that create incentives and protect the organization from the threat of opportunistic behaviour arising from informational asymmetries.

However, dissatisfaction with both of these approaches has led researchers in the field of management science to develop alternative theories of the firm which emphasize strategic choices facing the firm's decision makers. This does not imply a completely new theory is required. 'It appears obvious that the study of business strategy must rest on the bedrock foundations of the economists' model of the firm . . . economic concepts [of Coase and Williamson] can model and describe strategic phenomena' (Rumelt, 1984, p. 557). The strategic and knowledge-based theories of the firm can perhaps best be seen as complements rather than substitutes for the neoclassical and alternative economic theories of the firm. The strategic and knowledge-based theories add further detail and texture to our understanding of the modern organization.

Strategic theory of the firm

Phelan and Lewis (2000) identify three central themes associated with the strategic theory of the firm: the resource-based view of the firm, the determination of the firm's boundaries, and bounded rationality.

Resource-based view of the firm

This theme recognizes that firms can be defined in terms of the resources they own (Penrose, 1959; Wernerfelt, 1984). Resources include inputs used by the firm to produce outputs; but the resource-based approach goes further than the technological relationship between physical inputs and outputs embodied in the neoclassical production function. For example, Grant (1991) distinguishes between tangible and intangible resources, and Barney (1991) distinguishes between physical capital, human capital and organizational capital resources. Miller and Shamsie (1996) argue that each firm's uniqueness derives from the resources it controls, which are unavailable to other firms. More generally, resources are either property-based or knowledge-based. Property-based resources are legally defined property rights held by the firm, such as the right to use of labour, finance, raw material inputs and new knowledge. Other firms are unable to appropriate these rights unless they obtain the owner's permission. Property-based resources are protected by contracts, patents or deeds of ownership. In contrast, knowledge-based resources, such as technical expertise or good relationships with trade unions, are not protected by law, but they may nevertheless be difficult for other firms to access.

'A firm's competitive position is defined by a bundle of unique resources and relationships' (Rumelt, 1984, p. 557). These resources and relationships generate rents; and the more unique a resource, the more valuable it is to the firm. In a competitive market, rents arise because the initial owner and the firm have different expectations as to the value of the resource. To the owner, the value of a resource is its opportunity cost, or its value in its next best use. To the firm, however, value is added by combining and coordinating the resource with other firm-specific resources. The fact that the firm can use the resource in ways the owner cannot envisage creates a differential between the initial owner's valuation and the firm's valuation of the resource.

The term 'capability' defines the specific, unique outcomes when a set of resources are combined and coordinated in complex ways. Foss and Ericksen (1995) suggest resources can be distinguished from capabilities in two ways. Resources are tradeable and uniquely tied to individuals within the organization. Capabilities are not tradeable, and are not necessarily embodied in any particular individual. Capabilities might include a good track record in research and development, a reputation for using only high-quality inputs, a reputation for good customer service, or other aspects of the firm's culture and traditions. Through continued use, these capabilities become stronger, more profitable, and more difficult for competitors to imitate. The firm acts as a repository for the skills, knowledge and experience that have accumulated over time.

> [T]he main interest of the capabilities view is to understand what is distinctive about firms as unitary, historical organizations of co-operating individuals. Moreover, it is becoming an increasingly widespread recognition among contributors to the capabilities view that approaching the firm in this way has fertile implications not only for understanding the sources of firm heterogeneity, competitive advantage, and different rent . . . but also for advancing the economics of organization.
>
> *(Langlois and Foss, 1997, p. 17)*

The boundaries of the firm

As suggested above, the boundaries of the firm can be defined by the ownership of assets. If one firm owns a specific asset, other firms are by definition excluded from using the asset. The boundaries of the firm define which activities or transactions are organized within firms, which are organized by intermediate organizations such as joint ventures, and which remain within the sphere of the market. Strategies of vertical or horizontal integration, franchising, forming strategic alliances, and so on, all involve redefining the boundaries of the firm.

Due to indivisibility of certain inputs, the firm may find itself with spare capacity, which offers the potential for the development of new activities. However, growth is constrained by the limits to the ability of managers to conceive and control movements into new products and markets. In other words, there are cognitive limits to growth. Similar productive activities require similar capabilities, so economies of scale and scope can be realized when firms expand into similar activities. Complementary activities require different capabilities, but as the degree of complementarity increases, the need for greater cooperation and coordination becomes more important. Joint ventures, strategic alliances or full scale integration may assist towards achieving sufficient cooperation and coordination. If managers are rent seekers, growth is constrained by their ability to transfer the firm's resources and capabilities into these new areas.

Bounded rationality

The neoclassical theory assumes firms have complete information. In reality firms are neither fully informed about the best use of resources, nor do they know if they are properly equipped to face future contingencies. It is difficult to predict future changes in market demand, how best to respond to these changes, and what the payoffs are likely to be. Consequently, there is no point in attempting to estimate with any precision a production function of the type associated with neoclassical theory. Instead, strategic theory focuses on how firms can develop and improve their capabilities in order to adapt to a changing market environment. Success depends on the extent to which firms can nurture adaptive capabilities. Firms that tend to rest content with past accomplishments and are slow to innovate tend to decline.

Managers' decisions depend on their technical skills, knowledge, interpersonal and leadership skills. Different managers use similar resources in different ways. Accordingly, over time the capability of different firms tends to diverge, as does their performance. Therefore managers play an active role in a strategic theory of the firm. In contrast, the neoclassical theory identifies a passive role for the manager, who brings together inputs to produce output in accordance with an exogenously determined technology, and sells the output to consumers whose tastes are also exogenous. The Coasian approach recognizes a role for the manager, but this mainly involves dealing with agency problems such as free riding and opportunism.

Case study 3.4

Business schools share the blame for Enron

The corporate scandals in the US have stimulated a frenzy of activity in business schools around the world. Deans are busy pointing out how much their curricula focus on business ethics. New courses on corporate social responsibility are being developed. Old, laudatory case studies on Enron and Tyco are being rewritten to show how bad their senior managers were. In earnest seminars and over lunch, faculty members are asking themselves what more they must do.

Business schools do not need to do a great deal more to help prevent future Enrons; they need to stop doing a lot that they currently do. They do not need to create new courses; they need to stop teaching some old ones. But first, faculty members need to own up to their own role in creating Enrons. It is their ideas that have done much to strengthen the practices they are all now so loudly condemning.

For decades, one of the most popular MBA courses at Harvard was taught by Michael Jensen, the creator of agency theory. This course taught students why, given the fundamental nature of 'man', managers could not be trusted to do their job – which, of course, was to maximize shareholder value – and how to overcome 'agency problems' by aligning managers' and shareholders' interests and incentives. Making large stock options an important part of managers' compensation was clearly one of the most effective ways for achieving such alignment.

At Berkeley and Stanford, business students have been taught the transaction cost economics developed by Oliver Williamson. In essence, this argues that the only reason companies exist is because their managers can exercise authority to ensure that all employees do what they are told. Managers must ensure that staff are tightly monitored and controlled – these courses described this as the exercise of 'fiat' – while creating sharp, individual-level performance incentives.

And wherever in the world one studies management, there is Michael Porter's theory of strategy. This asserts that to make good profits, a company must actively compete not only with its competitors but also with its suppliers, customers, regulators and employees. Profits come from restricting or distorting competition, bad though this may be for society. It is one of the most important tasks that managers are paid to do.

It is not only MBA students who have, for decades, learnt these theories. Many thousands of executives have been taught the same lessons on business courses. Even those who never attended a business school learnt to think this way because these theories were in the air, legitimizing some managerial actions and delegitimizing others and shaping the intellectual background against which day-to-day decisions were made. Is it any surprise, then, that executives in Enron, Global Crossing and scores of other companies granted themselves excessive stock options, treated their employees badly and took their customers for a ride when they could?

Much of the problem has arisen from the excesses of business school academics in pretending that business is a science. Not only economists but also those in areas such as marketing and organizational behaviour increasingly treat business as if it were a kind of physics, in which individual intentions and choices either do not play a role or, if they do, can safely be taken as being determined by economic, social and psychological laws.

The problem is that, unlike theories in the physical sciences, theories in the social sciences tend to be self-fulfilling. A theory of sub-atomic particles does not change the behaviour of those particles. A management theory, if it gains enough currency, changes the behaviour of managers. Whether right or wrong to begin with, the theory becomes 'true' as the world comes to conform with its doctrine.

This is why it is nonsense to pretend that management theories can be completely objective and value-free. Even if the theorists pretend to be objective, the subjects and users of the theory cannot. By incorporating negative and highly pessimistic assumptions about people and institutions, pseudo-scientific theories of management have done much to reinforce, if not create, pathological behaviour on the part of managers and companies. It is time the academics who propose these theories, and the business schools and universities that employ them, acknowledged the consequences.

Source: Sumantra Ghoshal, Business schools share the blame for Enron, FT.com site, 17 July 2003.

Knowledge-based theory of the firm

The knowledge-based theory has developed in recognition of the idea that firms apply knowledge to the production of goods and services, and this knowledge is the most strategically important of a firm's resources (Conner and Prahalad, 1996; Grant, 1996; Kogut and Zander, 1992; Liebeskind, 1996). While neoclassical theory focuses on the problems of coordinating resources and activities within the firm, the knowledge-based theory argues that knowledge, as a strategic asset, must also be coordinated if it is to be used to its full potential. The theory distinguishes between tacit and explicit knowledge. Tacit knowledge cannot be conveyed sufficiently quickly to be appropriated immediately by the learner. For example, learning to ride a bike involves observation and practice, and cannot be done immediately simply by reading a manual. Explicit knowledge, in contrast, is easily absorbed, and can be transferred to various uses immediately. For example, a trade secret might be regarded as explicit knowledge: as soon as the secret is revealed, anyone can make use of the relevant knowledge.

Liebeskind (1996) argues that firms exist in order to protect explicit knowledge. Employment contracts may specify exclusivity and confidentiality clauses, preventing the transfer of economically advantageous knowledge to rival organizations. Firms can protect their explicit knowledge by threats of dismissal of staff who pass on information, making their departure costly through the loss of bonuses, pensions, stock options and promotion opportunities. The firm may try to ensure that its staff have access to no more information than is strictly necessary for them to perform their functions.

Grant (1996) assumes that (tacit) knowledge in the organization is held by individuals, and not by the organization as such. To be useful, this knowledge must be coordinated. The firm exists because its management are better able to perform this coordinating function than the market. How is coordination achieved?

■ Through the use of rules and directives based on corporate etiquette, social norms and procedures.

■ Through the efficient sequencing of tasks by individual specialists.

■ Through the presence of routines that help develop 'mutual adjustments', leading to synchronized outputs. Routines play a key role in the strategic theory of the firm (Coriat and Dosi, 1998; Nelson, 1994; Nelson and Winter, 1982).

■ Where communication between specialists is important, the organization ensures a focus on group decision making and problem solving.

The necessary coordination also depends on the development of common knowledge within the organization. Types of common knowledge include the development of shared meanings in the form of metaphors and analogies understood by members of the organization but not by outsiders, and the sharing of specialized knowledge, which leads to more effective communication within the organization. If there is job rotation, common knowledge becomes more important than specialized knowledge. As the breadth of knowledge held by employees widens, so too does the ability of other firms to acquire the information they require in order to imitate or replicate the organization's most successful characteristics.

3.9 Summary

In Chapter 3, we have traced the historical development of the neoclassical theory of the firm, and we have seen how, over the years, economists have attempted to develop alternative models and theories that are more realistic in describing and explaining the essential or fundamental characteristics of firms. Paradoxically, it has been argued that the neoclassical theory of the firm is not really an analysis of the firm at all, but rather a theory of resource allocation at the level of the market. The neoclassical theory devotes little attention to internal decision making within the firm; instead, the firm is viewed almost as a black box. The firm pursues its goal of profit maximization by converting inputs into outputs in a purely mechanistic fashion.

Some of the earliest challenges to the neoclassical theory of the firm were developed in the 1950s and 1960s, in the light of growing evidence of the increasing complexity of firms, and the separation of the ownership of large corporations (in the hands of shareholders) from control (in the hands of salaried managers). Where previously it had been assumed that firms were run so as to maximize the interests of their owners, economists began to acknowledge that managers' objectives may differ from those of the shareholders. In Baumol's theory of sales revenue maximization, managers are assumed to seek to maximize the size of the firm measured by its sales revenue, since managers' compensation and prestige are assumed to depend more on firm size than on profitability. Profit cannot be ignored altogether, however, because the managers' job security depends upon their ability to earn a satisfactory rate of return for the firm's shareholders.

Marris develops a more dynamic model of growth maximization in the long run, which emphasizes the need for balanced growth in the demand for the firm's products and the firm's capacity to supply. The managers' pursuit of a growth strategy is subject to both a managerial and a financial constraint. Williamson develops a model based on the maximization of managerial utility, which depends on staff expenditure, managerial emoluments and discretionary profit. Finally, the behavioural theory of the firm associated with Cyert and March defines the firm in terms of its organizational structure and decision-making processes, involving all individuals or groups with influence or interests in the organization's activities. Decision making takes place in an environment of uncertainty or bounded rationality, as individuals and groups bargain in an attempt to secure rewards that meet their own aspirations. The resolution of conflict is facilitated by the existence of organizational slack which, in normal conditions, allows parties to receive rewards over and above the level necessary to prevent them from withdrawing their participation and support altogether from the organization.

Coase provides a natural point of departure for many of the more recent, alternative theories of the firm, by raising the question as to why institutions known as firms exist at all. In other words, why should the task of coordination or resource allocation be left within the sphere of the market in the case of some transactions, but handled within the domain of the firm for others? Coase's answer is that the firm's conscious method of coordination creates a saving in transaction costs: the costs incurred when using market mechanisms to allocate resources in a world of imperfect information. Coase's original emphasis was on transaction costs incurred before contracts are concluded, such as the costs of negotiation. The later transaction costs literature, to which Williamson is perhaps the most influential contributor, focuses on costs incurred after contracts are concluded, arising from bounded rationality, asset specificity and difficulties in monitoring and enforcing compliance. The transaction costs approach has been used to explore the question of the most effective organizational structure. With a U-form structure, the firm's activities are subdivided into functional areas (marketing, finance, production, personnel), each of which is run by a specialist manager. However, effective coordination becomes more difficult as the U-form firm increases in size. In the twentieth century, such problems were addressed by the development of the M-form structure, in which the firm is divided into a number of quasi-independent operating divisions. Organizational structures are adaptable in the light of changing conditions. With market transactions, agents modify their behaviour in response to price signals. In contrast, organizations rely on skilled or specialized managers to take decisions as to how the organizational structure should adapt and evolve.

Coase's original insights have also influenced the development of Alchian and Demsetz's theory of the firm as an efficient structure within which to organize team production. A central contracting agent (the employer or owner) carries out essential coordinating and monitoring functions, which cannot be performed effectively through the medium of markets. Jensen and Meckling's nexus of contracts approach focuses attention on the entire set of contractual relationships which bind together the firm's owners, employees, material suppliers, creditors, customers, and so on. The firm encompasses a much wider set of relationships than those defined purely in terms of team production. Echoing the earlier managerial approach, agency theory emphasizes the conflicts that can arise between principals (owners or shareholders) and agents (managers). Under conditions of incomplete contracts and uncertainty, opportunities may arise for agents to act against the best interests of principals, unless the incentive structures confronting principals and agents are properly aligned. Finally, in the property rights approach, a key distinction is drawn between specific rights defined explicitly in the terms of contracts, and residual rights which accrue to the owner once all specific rights have been assigned. In a world of incomplete contracts the ownership of the residual rights is of paramount importance. The ownership of the residual rights gives the firm control over access to physical assets, or less tangible assets such as brands or reputation.

Recently, resource-based or knowledge-based theories of the firm have been developed in the fields of management science and strategic management. These theories emphasize strategic choices facing the firm's decision makers. The resource-based approach defines firms in terms of the resources they own and control. Resources include both physical inputs and intangible resources including technical expertise and organizational structure. The firm's resources combine to produce distinctive capabilities, and the firm acts as a repository for all of the skills, knowledge and experience that have accumulated over time. Knowledge-based theories have developed in recognition of the idea that firms apply knowledge to the production of goods and services. Knowledge is emphasized as perhaps the most distinctive and important of all the firm's resources.

Many of these theories have provided new insights and superior analytical tools with which to understand the modern organization. What seems clear is that no single theory can, by itself, adequately capture the essence of what a firm is, how it acts and how it evolves. Therefore it would be wrong to select one single characteristic, and expect a general theory to emerge from a partial analysis. A more productive approach is draw insights from each of the theories, so as to develop as broad an understanding as possible.

Discussion questions

1. Outline the strengths and limitations of the neoclassical theory of the firm in enhancing our understanding of firm behaviour.

2. With reference to Case studies 3.1 and 3.2, assess the extent to which shareholders can influence corporate objectives.

3. Assess the contribution of the managerial theories of the firm of Baumol, Marris and Williamson to our understanding of the conduct and performance of firms.

4. What is bounded rationality, and why is it important?

5. With reference to Cyert and March's behavioural theory of the firm, give examples of groups and coalitions within a specific organization with which you are familiar. Identify the possible conflicts between these groups, and suggest ways in which such conflicts can be resolved.

6. Explain why Coase believed that the defining characteristic of the firm was the supersession of the price mechanism.

7. In what ways do transaction costs influence the design of the most efficient organizational structure?

8. With reference Case study 3.3, examine the lessons concerning the limits to outsourcing that can be drawn from the experience of the UK's rail industry.

9. The author of Case study 3.4 wrote: 'By incorporating negative and highly pessimistic assumptions about people and institutions, pseudo-scientific theories of management have done much to reinforce, if not create, pathological behaviour on the part of managers and companies.' To what extent do you agree or disagree with this view?

10. Some economists claim the firm is a collection of contracts. If so, in what ways does this differ from the market?

11. Assess the contribution of agency theory to our understanding of firm behaviour.

12. Discuss the extent to which the strategic and knowledge-based theories of the firm can be regarded as substitutes for the neoclassical and alternative economic theories of the firm.

Further reading

Bolton, P. and Scharfstein, D.S. (1998) Corporate finance, the theory of the firm and organizations, *Journal of Economic Perspectives*, 12, 95–114.

Cowling, K. and Sugden, P. (1998) The essence of the modern corporation: markets, strategic decision-making and the theory of the firm, *The Manchester School*, 66, 1, 59–86.

Foss, N.J. (2003) The strategic management and transaction cost nexus: past debates, central questions, and future research possibilities, *Strategic Organization*, 1, 139–69.

Kaplan, S., Schenkel, A., von Krogh, G., and Weber, C. (2001) Knowledge-based theories of the firm in strategic management: a review and extension. *Submitted to Academy of Management Review*, www.mit.edu/people/skaplan/kbv-0301.pdf, retrieved 11 March, 2004.

Kay, J. (1999) Mastering Strategy, *Financial Times*, 27 September 1999 www.johnkay.com/strategy/135, retrieved 2 March 2004.

Koppl, R. (2000) Fritz Machlup and behavioralism, *Journal of Industrial and Corporate Change*, 9, 4.

Moss, S. (1984) The history of the theory of the firm from Marshall to Robinson and Chamberlin: the source of positivism in economics, *Economica*, 51, 307–18.

Shelanski, H. and Klein, P. (1995) Empirical research in transaction cost economics: a review of the evidence, *Journal of Law, Economics and Organization*, 11, 335–61.

Stigler, J. (1957) Perfect competition, historically contemplated, *Journal of Political Economy*, 65, 1–17.

Structural Analysis of Industry

Oligopoly: non-collusive models

Learning objectives

This chapter covers the following topics:

- interdependence and the analysis of price and output determination in oligopoly
- the Cournot, Chamberlin and Stackelberg models of output determination in duopoly
- the Bertrand and Edgeworth models of price determination in duopoly
- the models of the kinked demand curve and price leadership
- game theory and the analysis of decision making in oligopoly

Key terms

Barometric price leadership	First-mover advantage	Price rigidity
Bertrand model	Game theory	Prisoner's dilemma
Collusion	Independent action	Pure strategy
Conjectural variation	Isoprofit curve	Reaction function
Constant-sum game	Joint profit maximization	Repeated game
Cooperative game	Kinked demand curve	Sequential game
Cournot–Nash equilibrium	Mixed strategy	Simultaneous game
Dominant price leadership	Multiple-period game	Stackelberg equilibrium
Dominant strategy	Nash equilibrium	Strategy
Duopoly	Non-constant sum game	Tit-for-tat
Edgeworth model	Payoff	Zero-sum game
Experimental economics	Price leadership	

4.1 Introduction

Oligopoly theory rests on recognition of the importance of the number of firms in the industry, and the nature of the product. These two characteristics are closely related. An industry is defined by the nature of the product it supplies. Firms producing highly differentiated products may not even see themselves as being in direct competition with others. The more homogeneous the products of different firms, however, the greater the awareness of competitors. In all oligopolistic markets, a few sellers account for a substantial proportion of total sales. The fewness of the firms is the chief identifying characteristic of an oligopoly.

As a result of the fewness of firms within a clearly defined industry, producing a fairly homogeneous product or service, the central problem of oligopoly focuses on the recognition of the firms' mutual dependence or **interdependence**. Interdependence means a firm is aware that its own actions affect the actions of its rivals, and vice versa. Profit maximization and survival in an oligopoly depends on how effectively each firm operates in this situation of interdependence.

> For Sartre, hell is dependence on others . . . In every room of Sartre's hell, each person wants something he cannot get except from certain others, who refuse. People sometimes avoid frustration; sometimes, in real life, the others consent. But people are always dependent on others and so they are always vulnerable.
>
> *(Schick, 1997, pp. 82–3)*

This chapter begins in Section 4.2 with a general discussion of the key issues of interdependence, conjectural variation, independent action and collusion in oligopoly. Subsequently, the structure of the chapter reflects the development of theories of independent action in oligopoly, as they have tackled the central issue of interdependence. In Section 4.3, we examine Cournot's original model of output determination in a duopoly, based on a simple assumption that two firms take their output decisions sequentially, each in the expectation that its rival will not subsequently react. Other models that recognize the importance of interdependence include Chamberlin's model of joint profit maximization, in which 'mutual dependence was recognized'. Although this recognition involved some broad theorizing, the process was invaluable in the sense that it asked the right questions concerning short- and long-run reactions, time-lags, imperfect knowledge, irrational conduct, and so on. Stackelberg's leader–follower model builds in an assumption that one firm learns to anticipate its rivals' reactions to its own decisions, and exploits this foresight to increase its own profit at its rivals' expense.

The Cournot, Chamberlin and Stackelberg models focus mainly on the firms' output decisions in duopoly or oligopoly. In Section 4.4, we examine the complementary models developed by Bertrand and Edgeworth, which focus on price-setting. The Bertrand model provides a theoretical justification for the idea that intense price competition might occur in markets with few firms producing a similar or identical product. The Edgeworth model focuses on the possibility that oligopolistic markets might be permanently unstable, with no long-run equilibrium price or output level ever being achieved.

Another attempt to introduce a greater degree of reality into oligopoly theory is Sweezy's **kinked demand curve** model, examined in Section 4.5. Although challenged on empirical grounds, this model rests on the core assumption that firms' behaviour is determined by expectations as to what actions rivals are most likely to take. In this respect, it represents a major contribution to the development of more realistic models of oligopoly. This section also considers models of **price leadership** in oligopoly, in which one firm takes decisions on price and the others simply follow the lead of the price-setting firm.

Finally, Section 4.6 focuses on **game theory**. Game theory is the study of decision making in situations of conflict. It has many applications throughout the social, behavioural and physical sciences; and accordingly, its remit is much wider than just economics. Nevertheless, its focus on uncertainty, interdependence, conflict and strategy makes it ideally suited to the analysis of decision making in oligopoly. Game theory shows how situations can arise in which firms take decisions that may appear rational from each firm's individual perspective, but which lead to outcomes that are sub-optimal when assessed according to criteria reflecting the collective interest of all the firms combined. Theoretically, in many respects game theory is the strongest of all the approaches examined in Chapter 4 as regards its treatment of the key issue of interdependence.

4.2 Interdependence, conjectural variation, independent action and collusion

At the beginning of the twentieth century, classical microeconomic analysis focused on the models of perfect competition and pure monopoly in its attempt to describe the behaviour of firms. While no one pretended what was being presented was an exact copy of real business behaviour, it was felt the two extremes sufficiently defined a spectrum on which reality could be conveniently located. It almost seemed what was being argued was that defining the colours white and black would somehow enable other colours, such as yellow and purple, to be described simply by mixing white and black together in the correct proportions. It soon became apparent, however, that these two models were unable to explain many aspects of business conduct in the real world, such as product differentiation, advertising, price wars, parallel pricing, and tacit and explicit collusion. An additional theory was required to deal with the vast area of industry structure that lies between the two polar cases of perfect competition and monopoly. This middle ground, known as imperfect competition, can be subdivided into two: monopolistic competition, occupying the analytical space closest to perfect competition; and oligopoly, taking up the remaining large portion of the spectrum.

The term 'oligopoly' is derived from the Greek *oligoi* meaning a few and *poleo* to sell. Chamberlin (1957) describes how this term first came into use. He claims to have been the modern-day originator in 1929, when he named one of his articles 'Duopoly and oligopoly'. Unfortunately F.W. Taussig, the editor of the *Quarterly*

Journal of Economics, thought the word was monstrous and crossed it out. The amended title was 'Duopoly and value where sellers are few'. When Chamberlin published his book *Monopolistic Competition* in 1933, he included the original term. However, Chamberlin notes the same term also appears in Thomas More's *Utopia*, first printed in 1516.

Interdependence provides the main challenge for the analysis of oligopoly. Oligopolists are outward turning, and there is an element of circularity in the analysis of their behaviour. Each firm's optimal behaviour depends on its assumptions about its rivals' likely reactions, and even on its assumptions about its rivals' assumptions.

> 'I' (an oligopolist) cannot define my best policies unless I know what 'You' (my rival) are going to do; by the same token, however, you cannot define your best move unless you know what I will do.

> *(Asch, 1969, p. 54)*

Faced with this situation of interdependence, the firms must make some guesses or conjectures as to the likely actions of rivals. Each firm must determine its price or output, while making assumptions about its rivals' likely reactions to its own actions. The term **conjectural variation** refers to the assumptions a firm makes about the reactions it expects from its rivals in response to its own actions.

It is often suggested that the solution to the oligopoly problem is one of two extremes: either pure **independent action**, or pure **collusion**, in which all scope for independent action is extinguished. The possibility of collusion arises when two or more rival firms recognize their interdependence, creating the potential for bargaining to take place between the firms, with a view to formulating some plan of joint action. Bargaining could take the form of explicit negotiations, or it could be clouded in tacit behaviour where the firms reveal their own positions and react to their rivals' positions through various recognized moves and counter-moves. If bargaining does take place in some form, an agreement on the coordination of activity is a likely outcome. Again, any agreement reached could be either explicit, or tacit.

However, in some ways this dichotomy between pure independent action and pure collusion is at odds with reality. Both independent action and collusion are a matter of degree, and while examples may be found that conform to the polar cases, the great majority of cases fall somewhere between these two extremes. The typical oligopoly contains elements of both independence and collusion. For the purpose of identifying various stages along the spectrum of oligopolistic behaviour, it is useful to define the limits as clearly as possible.

Pure independent action implies a firm reaches a unilateral decision on a course of action, without any prior contact with its rivals. However, even this definition could produce outcomes similar to those achieved through collusion, if the firm were subsequently to revise its decisions in the light of its rivals' reactions. Therefore the definition is somewhat incomplete. We must add that we expect the firm to assume its rivals will not react. This implies pure independent action can only exist either in a state of unnatural ignorance, or in an atomistic market where the actions of one firm are too insignificant to have any effect on its rivals.

Pure collusion exists where an agreement or an undertaking is reached regarding the levels of output or price. Bain (1959, p. 272) defined collusion in its purest form as consisting of the following features: all sellers in the industry are covered by the agreement; the agreement is specific and enforceable; the agreement clearly states the price to be charged and outputs to be allocated to each member; there is a formula governing the distribution of benefits to the members of the agreement; and all members rigidly adhere to the terms of the agreement. In fact, Bain's suggestion is really a prescription for a successful cartel. Under pure collusion the firms agree to operate collectively as if they were a single monopolist. All independent action, including the striving for individual benefit, is constrained.

We now describe several types of behaviour that fall between these two extremes of pure independent action and pure collusion. Such behaviour has attracted a diverse array of labels, and no universally agreed terminology exists. For example, the terms 'imperfect collusion', 'unorganized oligopoly' and 'interdependent conduct with no agreement' have all been used by economists to describe similar forms of behaviour.

Machlup (1952a, pp. 504–11) describes four types of conduct under the general heading of 'uncoordinated oligopoly'.

- The first model is 'fighting oligopoly'. Some reasons why firms might slide into economic warfare include the existence of surplus stocks or limited storage facilities, which lead to near-ruinous price wars. Arguably, this type of behaviour was seen in the global petroleum industry in the mid-1980s. On the whole, economists tend to restrict themselves to analyses of rational behaviour, termed vigorous price competition, and ignore other, more extreme forms of conduct. Firms that wish to hurt others, firms that harbour resentments or firms that simply enjoy a fight are difficult to accommodate within the standard methodology.

- The second model is 'hyper-competitive oligopoly'. Typically, a significant number of firms sell a fairly homogeneous product in an imperfect market. Market imperfection is due to lack of precise knowledge as to future prices, sales, changes in quality, and so on. Decisions are often taken on the basis of speculation or rumour. Although conscious of rivals, the typical firm is not inhibited by their presence as it strives for increased market share, believing rival firms to be as aggressive as itself. Individuality and non-conformity tend to preclude cooperation. Buyers are price-conscious, and are quick to play off one seller against another. Although this model approaches perfect competition, interdependence sharpens the potential gains and losses. This form of competition might be regarded as 'demoralized, unhealthy and chaotic' (Machlup 1952a, p. 508).

- The third model is 'chain oligopoly'. In a relatively competitive industry, some firms find themselves effectively competing among smaller subsets of firms, perhaps distinguished by small qualitative differences in product characteristics. Linkages between these subsets create interdependence. For example, L competes directly with K and M; M competes directly with L and N; and so on. Each firm operates within an oligopolistic sub-group, but the sub-groups overlap. Any increase in the total number of firms tends to reduce interdependence. Should any sub-group attempt to exploit its position through collusion, it would soon be swamped by entrants, because the boundaries between sub-groups are fluid. Behaviour therefore tends to be relatively competitive.

■ The fourth model is 'guessing-game oligopoly'. A small group of firms might normally be expected to collude, were it not for the presence of a few stubborn characters who refuse to play ball. Therefore the firms have to operate independently, and try to guess the likely reactions of their rivals to their own decisions. In practice, however, these guesses are not too difficult, as certain behavioural conventions evolve and firms develop the tendency to play safe, by adhering to these conventions. This reduces the degree of uncertainty and the level of guesswork that is required.

The dichotomy between pure independent action and pure collusion identified above encounters one obvious contradiction: that once sellers recognize their interdependence, no truly independent action can occur. Each seller takes into account the likely reactions of its rivals. Therefore the amplitude of price and output changes is dampened by consideration of potential rivalrous reaction. Coordinated or parallel behaviour is more likely the greater the degree of interdependence, and the greater the degree of uncertainty. Indeed, movement towards some form of collusion is often motivated fundamentally by a desire to reduce uncertainty. Accordingly, some economists (Machlup 1952a, p. 439) see all oligopolies as collusive to some extent. Unfortunately for policy makers or regulators, this may imply there is no non-collusive standard of comparison against which to assess the implications of collusion for competition or consumer welfare (Asch and Seneca, 1976).

In contrast, Bain (1959, p. 208) argues that in a number of scenarios, interdependent sellers can still operate independently. With 'implicit bargaining', for example, every announced change in price or output represents an implicit invitation to one's rivals to react in an acceptable manner. If acceptable behaviour results, there is a weak form of tacit collusion. However, this is not tacit collusion in the generally understood sense, since there is no regular action or uniformity of behaviour. Bain also discusses the case where interdependent firms exchange information on matters such as price, sales, or future plans, but then fix their output levels and prices independently. However, no obvious distinction is made between what does and what does not constitute independent action. Can a firm truly be said to act independently if it has to rely on information from its rivals before it can make its own decisions? Nevertheless, despite this ambiguity, the structure of Chapters 4 and 5 of this book adheres to the conventional dichotomy between independent action and collusion under oligopoly. The remaining sections of Chapter 4 discuss theories of oligopoly that focus primarily on independent decision making. Then Chapter 5 examines theories of collusion.

4.3 Models of output determination in duopoly

Cournot's duopoly model

Cournot's (1838) model of output determination in oligopoly was the first successful attempt to describe an oligopoly equilibrium. The type of solution that Cournot proposed almost two centuries ago still plays a central role in many present-day models of oligopoly.

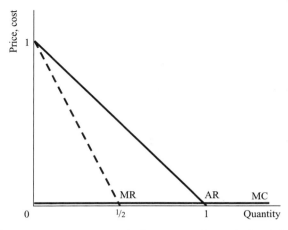

Figure 4.1 Market average revenue, marginal revenue and marginal cost functions, Cournot's duopoly model

Cournot's original formulation assumes a two-firm oligopoly, known as a **duopoly**, operating at zero marginal cost. Cournot suggested a market made up of two proprietors or firms, A and B, both selling mineral spring waters. To ensure both firms operate at zero marginal cost, it is assumed the two firms are located side by side next to the spring, and customers arrive at the spring with their own bottles. The firms are assumed to make their trading plans in turn or sequentially. It is also assumed when making its own trading plans, each firm expects the other firm to maintain *its* output at its current level. In other words, each firm assumes the other firm's reaction (in terms of adjustment to output) is always zero. In the terminology introduced in Section 4.2, this is tantamount to an assumption of zero conjectural variation.

It is assumed the market demand or average revenue (AR) function is linear. For simplicity, the units of measurement for price and quantity are both chosen so that both axes are drawn on a scale of 0 to 1. The market demand or AR function is illustrated in Figure 4.1. In order to understand the derivation of the Cournot model, it is important to note that if the AR function is linear, the marginal revenue (MR) function is also linear, and intersects the horizontal axis at the mid-point between the origin and the intersection of the AR function. In Figure 4.1, this implies if the AR function intersects the horizontal axis at a value of $Q = 1$, the MR function must intersect at a value of $Q = 1/2$. Finally, in accordance with the assumption of zero marginal cost, in Figure 4.1 the MC function is shown running horizontally along the quantity axis.

In the Cournot model, the market equilibrium is reached through a sequence of actions and reactions on the part of the two firms. This is illustrated in Figure 4.2. We assume firm A is the first to open for business. In Round 1, firm A fixes its output and price at the point where MR = MC = 0. Firm A's output in Round 1 is $q_A^1 = 1/2$, and the correponding price is 1/2. Before firm B starts producing, firm A operates as if it were a monopolist.

Now firm B enters the market. B sees A is supplying $q_A^1 = 1/2$. According to the zero conjectural variation assumption, B assumes that whatever B does, A will

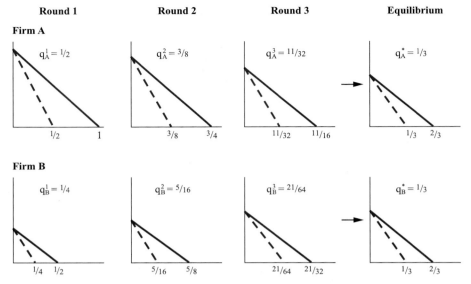

Figure 4.2 The Cournot model: sequence of actions and reactions

continue to produce $q_A^1 = 1/2$. Therefore, B's effective or residual demand function is the segment of the market demand function that is not currently serviced by A. This is the segment of the market demand function that lies to the right of $q_A^1 = 1/2$. If B charges a price of 1/2, B sells zero output. However, if B were prepared to allow the price to fall to 0, B could sell an output of 1/2. In Round 1, therefore, B's AR function runs from $P = 1/2$ to $q = 1/2$, and B's MR function intersects the horizontal axis at $q_B^1 = 1/4$. This is B's profit-maximizing output in Round 1, because at this output MR = MC for B. At the end of Round 1, total industry output is $q_A^1 + q_B^1 = 1/2 + 1/4 = 3/4$. Accordingly, using the market demand function, price is $P = 1/4$.

Before B entered, A was maximizing profit at $q_A^1 = 1/2$ and $P = 1/2$. However, B's intervention causes price to fall to $P = 1/4$, which means A is no longer maximizing profit. According to the zero conjectural variation assumption, A assumes whatever A does, B will continue to produce at $q_B^1 = 1/4$. Therefore A's residual demand function is the segment of the market demand function that lies to the right of $q_B^1 = 1/4$. In Round 2, A's AR function runs from $P = 3/4$ to $q = 3/4$. A's MR function intersects the horizontal axis at $q_A^2 = 3/8$, A's new profit-maximizing output in Round 2.

At the end of Round 1, B was maximizing profit at $q_B^1 = 1/4$ and $P = 1/4$. However, A's adjustment causes price to rise to $P = 3/8$, so B is no longer maximizing profit at $q_B^1 = 1/4$. According to the zero conjectural variation assumption, B assumes whatever B does, A will continue to produce at $q_A^2 = 3/8$. Therefore B's new residual demand function is the segment of the market demand function that lies to the right of $q_A^2 = 3/8$. In Round 2, B's AR function runs from $P = 5/8$ to $q = 5/8$. B's MR function intersects the horizontal axis at $q_B^2 = 5/16$, B's new profit-maximizing output in Round 2. At the end of Round 2, total industry output is $q_A^2 + q_B^2 = 3/8 + 5/16 = 11/16$, and using the market demand function, price is $P = 5/16$.

By this stage, the mechanics of the sequence of actions and reactions should be clear. The Round 3 adjustments are shown in Figure 4.2, but they are not described in full here. At the end of Round 3, total industry output is $q_A^3 + q_B^3 = 11/32 + 21/64 = 43/64$, and price is $P = 21/64$. Of more importance is the equilibrium towards which the industry is converging as each round of actions and reactions takes place. This is shown on the right-hand side of Figure 4.2, where both firms produce identical outputs of $q_A^* = q_B^* = 1/3$. Total industry output is $q_A^* + q_B^* = 1/3 + 1/3 = 2/3$, and price is $P = 1/3$.

With this set of outputs, neither firm has an incentive to make any further change to its trading plans. For example, A assumes B's output is fixed at $q_B^* = 1/3$. Therefore A's residual demand function runs from $P = 2/3$ to $q = 2/3$, so A maximizes profit at $q_A^* = 1/3$. The same is true for firm B. Both firms maximize their own profit subject to the constraint that the other firm's output is fixed at its current level; or equivalently, both firms maximize profit subject to the zero conjectural variation assumption.

Isoprofit curves and reaction functions

The zero marginal cost assumption is an obvious limitation of the version of the Cournot model that is described above. As shown in this subsection, however, it is straightforward to rework the Cournot model so that it can be applied to the case where marginal costs are non-zero. Therefore the zero marginal cost assumption is not a fundamental limitation. In order to rework the Cournot model, we start by developing a new diagrammatic representation of the model, known as an isoprofit diagram. In order to do so, we retain the assumptions of identical firms and a linear industry demand function. In the following discussion we assume non-zero marginal costs, although the derivation is similar if marginal costs are zero.

In Figure 4.3, the output levels of firms A and B are shown on the horizontal and vertical axes, respectively. We begin by selecting a certain combination of outputs represented by the point F, located somewhere towards the bottom-left-hand corner of Figure 4.3. At F, both q_A and q_B are relatively small. Total industry output is also relatively small. We let π_A^1 denote A's profit at F. We consider what happens to A's

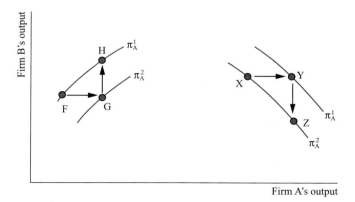

Figure 4.3 Derivation of firm A's isoprofit curves

profit if A increases its output by a small amount, while B holds its output constant. This adjustment is represented by a horizontal shift from F to G. We can infer A's profit at G *increases* to π_A^2, for two reasons:

■ Total industry output at F is small. The industry is operating on a relatively price-elastic section of the market demand function. Therefore an increase in q_A (and the corresponding fall in market price) produces a large increase in A's revenue.

■ q_A at F is small, and A's marginal cost is relatively low. Therefore an increase in q_A produces only a small increase in A's costs.

We now consider what happens to A's profit if B increases its output by a small amount, while A holds its output constant. This adjustment is represented by the upward vertical shift from G to H. We can infer A's profit *decreases*, back to π_A^1. The fall in market price caused by B's increase in output produces a decrease in A's revenue, while A's output and costs are unchanged.

Firm A's **isoprofit curves** show all combinations of q_A and q_B which produce identical profit for firm A. Comparing the values of A's profit at points F, G and H, we can conclude firm A's isoprofit curves are upward-sloping in this region of Figure 4.3.

We now repeat the exercise by selecting a new combination of outputs represented by the point X, located somewhere towards the bottom-right-hand corner of Figure 4.3. At X, q_A is relatively large, but q_B is relatively small. Because q_A is large, total industry output is also relatively large. We assume A's profit at X is π_A^2, and we consider what happens to A's profit if A increases its output by a small amount, while B holds its output constant. This adjustment is represented by a horizontal shift from X to Y. We can infer A's profit at Y *decreases* to π_A^1, for two reasons:

■ Total industry output at X is large. The industry is operating on a relatively price-inelastic section of the market demand function. Therefore an increase in q_A (and the corresponding fall in market price) produces only a small increase, or perhaps even a decrease, in A's revenue.

■ q_A at X is large, and A's marginal cost is relatively high. Therefore an increase in q_A produces a large increase in A's costs.

We now consider what happens to A's profit if B decreases its output by a small amount, while A holds its output constant. This adjustment is represented by the downward vertical shift from Y to Z. We can infer A's profit *increases*, back to π_A^2. The increase in market price caused by B's decrease in output produces an increase in A's revenue, while A's output and costs remain unchanged. Comparing the values of A's profit at points X, Y and Z, we can conclude firm A's isoprofit curves are downward-sloping in this region of Figure 4.3.

The concave curves shown in Figure 4.4 represent firm A's complete set of isoprofit curves. In accordance with the preceding discussion, successive isoprofit curves represent higher levels of profit for A as they approach the horizontal axis. Furthermore, for any given value of q_B, the profit-maximizing value of q_A can be found by identifying the isoprofit curve that attains a peak at that value of q_B. For example, if $q_B = \bar{q}_B$ in Figure 4.4, A's profit-maximizing output level is q_A^*, where

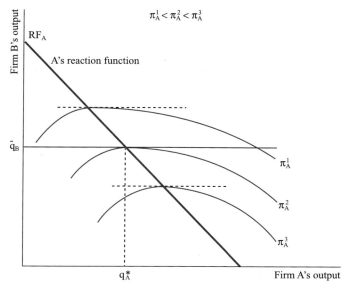

Figure 4.4 Firm A's isoprofit curves and reaction function

the horizontal line at $\bar{q}_B$ is tangential to the isoprofit curve for π_A^2, the highest isoprofit curve that is attainable by A anywhere along this horizontal line. At any other point on the line, A's profit is less than π_A^2.

Reading Figure 4.4 from top to bottom, as firm A's profit increases, the peaks of successive isoprofit curves lie further to the right. The lower the value of q_B, the more of the market there is available for A to exploit, and so the higher the profit-maximizing value of q_A. Firm A's **reaction function** denoted RF_A shows, for each value of q_B (assumed fixed), the profit-maximizing value of q_A. In Figure 4.4, RF_A is the line connecting the peaks of successive isoprofit curves

The next stage in the analysis involves the construction of isoprofit curves and a reaction function for B. Firm B's isoprofit curves show all combinations of q_A and q_B which produce identical profit for firm B. Firm B's reaction function shows, for each value of q_A (assumed fixed) the profit-maximizing value of q_B. Thanks to our earlier assumption that the firms are identical, this task is straightforward. B's isoprofit curves and reaction function have exactly the same appearance relative to the vertical axis as A's isoprofit curves and reaction function relative to the horizontal axis. Figure 4.5 shows one (representative) isoprofit curve for each firm, together with the two firms' reaction functions, on the same diagram.

Cournot–Nash equilibrium

Using the apparatus of isoprofit curves and reaction functions, we can now locate the outputs q_A and q_B that represent an equilibrium solution to the duopoly model. Using the same reasoning as in our earlier derivation of Cournot's model, we assume both firms seek to maximize their own profit, subject to the constraint that the other firm's output is fixed at its current level. In other words, both firms maximize profit subject

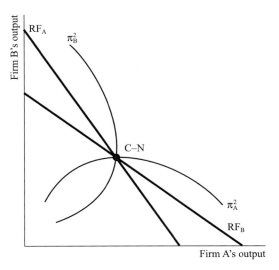

Figure 4.5 Cournot–Nash equilibrium

to the zero conjectural variation assumption. In the terminology of this subsection, this is equivalent to assuming that both firms seek to operate on their own reaction functions (recall, each firm's reaction function shows its profit-maximizing output treating the other firm's output as given). The point in Figure 4.5 at which both firms are simultaneously located on their own reaction functions is the point where RF_A and RF_B intersect, denoted C–N. C–N denotes a **Cournot–Nash equilibrium**, named after Cournot and the American mathematician Nash. The centrepiece of Nash's PhD thesis, prepared in 1950, was a solution to the problem of determining an equilibrium in a non-cooperative game (see Section 4.6), based on similar principles to the solution to the two-firm duopoly model proposed by Cournot more than a century before. Nash was eventually awarded the Nobel Prize in economics in 1994 for his contributions to game theory.

It is interesting to note that our original description of the Cournot model can also be represented (more concisely) using reaction functions. Figure 4.6 shows a pair of reaction functions derived under the zero marginal cost assumption; as noted above, assuming MC = 0 does not change the general shape of the isoprofit curves and reaction functions, although it does affect their precise locations. Figure 4.6 represents the process of convergence towards the market equilibrium at C–N as a process of 'zigzagging' between points located on RF_A and RF_B.

■ In Round 1 before B has entered, A's profit-maximizing output is $q_A^1 = 1/2$, at the very bottom of RF_A (where $q_B = 0$). When B does enter, B's profit-maximizing output subject to $q_A^1 = 1/2$ is $q_B^1 = 1/4$, at the point on RF_B corresponding to $q_A = 1/2$. Therefore at the end of Round 1, ($q_A^1 = 1/2$, $q_B^1 = 1/4$) is attained, as before.

■ In Round 2, A's profit-maximizing output subject to $q_B^1 = 1/4$ is $q_A^2 = 3/8$ (the point on RF_A corresponding to $q_B^1 = 1/4$). Similarly, B's profit-maximizing output subject to $q_A^2 = 3/8$ is $q_B^2 = 5/16$ (the point on RF_B corresponding to $q_A^2 = 3/8$). At the end of Round 2, (3/8, 5/16) is attained.

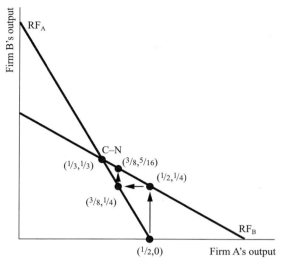

Figure 4.6 Cournot model: sequence of actions and reactions shown using reaction functions

- At the end of Round 3, (11/32, 21/64) is attained (not shown in Figure 4.6).

- Equilibrium is attained at ($q_A^* = 1/3$, $q_B^* = 1/3$), represented by the point C–N in Figure 4.6 located at the intersection of RF_A and RF_B.

The Cournot–Nash solution can also be derived for cases in which an oligopoly consists of more than two firms. Under the zero conjectural variation assumption in an N-firm model, each firm sets its output so as to maximize its own profit, treating the outputs of the other N − 1 firms as fixed at their current levels. A general formula for the market equilibrium is:

$$Q_n = Q_C \frac{N}{N+1}$$

where Q_n represents total industry output at the Cournot–Nash equilibrium and Q_C represents total industry output if the industry structure was perfectly competitive. In our original case, the maximum value of market demand (when price *equals* zero) is one, and marginal cost is zero. The perfectly competitive industry output level is $Q_C = 1$, because P = MC implies price is driven down to zero. The formula for Q_n implies the following:

- N = 1 corresponds to the case of monopoly. In Round 1 before B enters, A maximizes profit by producing the monopolist's output, $Q_n = q_A^1 = 1/2$.

- N = 2 corresponds to the case of duopoly. $Q_n = q_A^* + q_B^* = 2/3$ is consistent with ($q_A^* = 1/3$, $q_B^* = 1/3$) at the Cournot–Nash equilibrium.

- As N increases and approaches infinity, Q_n increases and approaches $Q_C = 1$.

What can we conclude from the Cournot model? The model can be criticized in several ways. First, it is based on a naive and unrealistic assumption that each firm believes its rival will not change its output (the zero conjectural variation assumption), in spite of each firm continually observing behaviour that contradicts this assumption. Each time either firm adjusts its own output, it does so on the basis of the zero conjectural variation assumption. But on each occasion this assumption turns out to be false, because the other firm does react and does also change its output. It is natural to wonder why the firms fail to learn from experience to anticipate each other's reactions.

In defence of the Cournot model, it can be argued that the solution to the problem of oligopoly is more important than the story about how this equilibrium is attained. This story does not need to be taken too literally: in practice there are many ways for the two firms to arrive at C–N, where both are maximizing their own profits subject to the constraint that the other firm's output is treated as fixed.

> (T)he assumption that each firm believes that its rival will hold output constant is implausible. But the general prospect that in oligopoly firms will misunderstand the way rivals behave is quite plausible.
>
> *(Martin, 1988, pp. 109–10)*

Further support is provided by Scherer (1980, p. 155) who claims 'some decision-makers do exhibit myopic tendencies in certain rivalry situations'.

Cournot can be criticized for ignoring the possibility that firms may seek co-operative or collusive solutions, in order to maximize their joint profits. This is, and almost certainly was in Cournot's time, a fact of economic life in oligopolistic markets. Cournot has also been criticized for focusing on output-setting, and ignoring price-setting decisions. Price adjustments in the Cournot model are the consequence of output decisions, rather than being primary courses of action.

Nevertheless we can point to some positive contributions of the theory. It provides economists with important tools of analysis, such as conjectural variation, isoprofit curves and reaction functions. It identifies an oligopoly equilibrium that is located reassuringly between the extremes of perfect competition and monopoly. It can also be used as a benchmark for all further discussion of oligopoly.

> A realistic approach to oligopoly problems cannot be based on Cournot's theory. Yet now, after more than a century, it is still difficult to see what is involved in an oligopoly theory without showing how the theory is related to Cournot's basic construction.
>
> *(Fellner, 1949, p. 57)*

Chamberlin's solution: Joint profit maximization

The apparatus of isoprofit curves and reaction functions developed in the previous subsection can be used to identify several solutions to the duopoly model other than the one proposed by Cournot. Chamberlin (1933) suggests an alternative solution, in which the firms recognize their interdependence when making their output decisions.

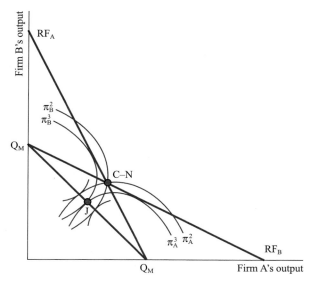

Figure 4.7 Cournot–Nash equilibrium and joint profit maximization

Accordingly, Chamberlin departs from the zero conjectural variation assumption. No longer does each firm set its output so as to maximize its own profit, while treating the other firm's output as fixed. Instead, the firms recognize it is in their mutual interest to produce and share equally among themselves the output that would be delivered if the market was serviced by a single monopolist. In this way, the firms also share equally among themselves the monopoly profit.

Starting from the Cournot–Nash equilibrium C–N in Figure 4.7, it is apparent that if both firms were to simultaneously reduce their output, both firms could simultaneously achieve an increase in profit. In other words, moving 'south-west' from C–N, it is possible for both firms to simultaneously move onto isoprofit curves representing higher levels of profit than at C–N. In fact, starting from any point above and to the right of the line $Q_M Q_M$, it is always possible for both firms to simultaneously increase their profits by moving 'south-west' in Figure 4.7. $Q_M Q_M$ is the line identifying all points of tangency between the isoprofit curves of firms A and B.

The points at which $Q_M Q_M$ cuts the horizontal and vertical axes of Figure 4.7 are labelled Q_M because these points represent the profit-maximizing outputs if either firm were operating as a monopolist. For example, along the horizontal axis $q_B = 0$, so firm A operates as a monopolist with a profit-maximizing output of Q_M. Similarly, along the vertical axis $q_A = 0$ and firm B's profit-maximizing output is also Q_M. $Q_M Q_M$ is simply a 45-degree line linking these two points. At any intermediate point on $Q_M Q_M$, total output is Q_M, and this output is shared between firms A and B. At point J, at the middle of this line, the monopoly output of Q_M is shared *equally* between firms A and B. Point J represents Chamberlin's **joint profit maximization** solution to the duopoly model.

In Chamberlin's formulation, both firms recognize their interdependence and realize that sharing the monopoly profit is the best they can do. It is important to note that Chamberlin does not suggest firms achieve this solution through collusion. The outcome rests on the assumption that each firm recognizes that the monopoly ideal can be achieved through independent action; and this view is shared by its rival. In this way, both firms achieve a higher payoff than in Cournot's formulation.

Chamberlin's solution allows for no unilateral aggression, cheating or back-sliding on the part of the two firms. Starting from point J, A may be aware that if it were to unilaterally increase its output (moving 'east' in Figure 4.7 towards RF_A) it could achieve an increase in profit, provided B does not react by also increasing its output. However, moving 'east' from J causes B's profit to fall, so it seems unlikely B would fail to react. Similarly at J, B is aware that if it were to increase its output (moving 'north' towards RF_B) it could increase its profit provided A does not do the same. But again, moving 'north' from J causes A's profit to fall, and it seems unlikely A would fail to react. Therefore Chamberlin's solution is always liable to break down, if either or both firms succumb to the temptation to act unilaterally and ignore their interdependence.

Stackelberg's solution: the leader–follower model

Stackelberg (1934) suggested yet another solution to the Cournot duopoly model. The Cournot model assigns equal status to both firms as they progress towards the final equilibrium. Both firms operate according to the zero conjectural variation assumption, and each firm fails to anticipate the other's reaction on each occasion it adjusts its own output. Suppose, however, we drop the zero conjectural variation assumption for firm A, but retain this assumption for firm B. B continues to select its profit-maximizing output by treating A's output as fixed at its current level. But A learns to recognize that B behaves in this manner. A therefore learns to take B's behaviour into account whenever A makes its own output decisions.

How should firm A select its own output, given that it has this insight into firm B's behaviour? A's awareness of B's behaviour is tantamount to A's recognition that whatever output A selects, B always reacts by selecting an output that returns the two firms to an output combination that lies on B's reaction function, RF_B. A should therefore select the output that maximizes A's profit subject to B's expected reaction. Accordingly, A should select q_A^L and aim for S_A in Figure 4.8: the point on RF_B where A's profit is maximized. A anticipates, correctly, that B will react by producing q_B^F. S_A is the point of tangency between RF_B and the highest isoprofit curve A can attain, given that the final equilibrium must lie on RF_B. At any other point on RF_B, A's profit is lower than it is at S_A.

By learning to anticipate and take account of firm B's behaviour, firm A earns a higher profit than at C–N, while B earns a lower profit. A is rewarded, and B is punished, for the fact that A has insight into B's behaviour, while B does not have corresponding insight into A's behaviour. An alternative (but only slightly different) interpretation of Stackelberg's solution is as a model of **first-mover advantage**. Returning to Cournot's original story of sequential decision making, if A recognizes that B always follows the zero conjectural variation assumption, in Round 1 A should produce q_A^L, in the knowledge that B will react by producing q_B^F. Accordingly, the two firms arrive directly at the **Stackelberg equilibrium** at the end of Round 1, with A producing the higher output and earning the higher profit. In this interpretation, A is the leader and B is the follower, and A is rewarded for its first-mover advantage.

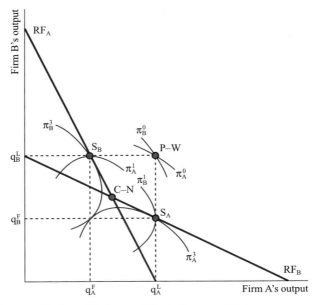

Figure 4.8 Cournot–Nash equilibrium and Stackelberg equilibria

Generalizing the preceding discussion, we can identify four possible outcomes, as shown in Figure 4.8:

- At S_A, firm A is the leader and firm B is the follower, as discussed above.

- S_B represents the opposite case, where B is the leader and A is the follower. A follows the zero conjectural variation assumption. B recognizes A behaves in this way, and aims for S_B, the point on A's reaction function RF_A that maximizes B's profit.

- If both firms are followers, C–N, the Cournot–Nash equilibrium, is achieved as before.

- Finally, and quite realistically in many oligopolistic markets, both firms might similtaneously attempt to be leaders. If both simultaneously produce the higher level of output $q_A^L = q_B^L$, the result is a Stackelberg disequilibrium or price war at P–W. At this conflict point there is overproduction, and the firms are forced to cut their prices in order to sell the additional output. Accordingly, both firms earn less profit than at C–N. A costly price war might eventually determine a winner and a loser, but it is also possible the firms may realize the futility of conflict and search for a more cooperative solution.

In Section 4.3, we have identified a number of possible solutions to the problem of output determination in duopoly. A mathematical derivation of these results can be found in Appendix 1. To conclude this section, it is useful to return to the numerical example that was used to introduce the Cournot model at the start of this section, and compare the numerical values of price and quantity for each of the solutions to the model. Accordingly, we now consider a duopoly in which the market demand

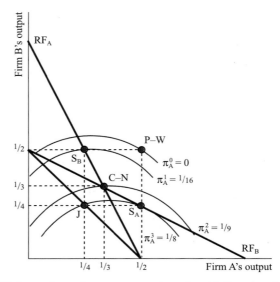

Figure 4.9 Equilibrium values of q_A, q_B, π_A, π_B: duopoly with linear market demand and zero marginal cost

function is linear and the units of measurement for price and quantity are scaled from 0 to 1; and both firms produce at zero marginal cost. Figure 4.9 shows the numerical values of q_A and q_B at the Cournot, Chamberlin and Stackelberg equilibria. The following table contains the same numerical data, and also compares the equilibrium prices and profits of the two firms.

	P	**Q**	**q_A**	**q_B**	**π_A**	**π_B**
Cournot–Nash	1/3	2/3	1/3	1/3	1/9	1/9
Chamberlin	1/2	1/2	1/4	1/4	1/8	1/8
Stackelberg – A as leader	1/4	3/4	1/2	1/4	1/8	1/16
Stackelberg – B as leader	1/4	3/4	1/4	1/2	1/16	1/8
Stackelberg disequilibrium (price war)	0	1	1/2	1/2	0	0

The Chamberlin joint profit maximization equilibrium corresponds to the monopoly price and output, with the firms sharing the monopoly profit equally between them, with $\pi_A = \pi_B = 1/8$. Both are better off than at the Cournot–Nash equilibrium, where price is lower, total output is higher, and $\pi_A = \pi_B = 1/9$. At the Stackelberg equilibrium with A as leader, price is lower still, and total output is higher. A does better ($\pi_A = 1/8$) and B does worse ($\pi_B = 1/16$) than at the Cournot–Nash equilibrium. At the Stackelberg equilibrium with B as leader, these positions are reversed. Finally, the Stackelberg disequilibrium (price war) corresponds to the perfectly competitive price and output, with price driven down to zero (equal to marginal cost), output raised to one, and both firms earning zero profit.

4.4 Models of price determination in duopoly

The Bertrand model: price competition

In another famous and influential contribution to duopoly theory, Bertrand (1883) criticizes Cournot's emphasis on output-setting. Bertrand argues that price, rather than output, is the key decision variable for most firms. In Cournot's model, the firms decide their output levels, and then allow the market price to adjust accordingly. In the **Bertrand model** each firm sets its own price, and then sells as much output as it can at the chosen price. Bertrand uses a zero conjectural variation assumption as regards prices: each firm assumes its rival will stick to the rival's current price. The model rests on implicit assumptions that the output of the two firms is identical, and there are no transaction or search costs. Therefore customers flow effortlessly to the firm that is currently offering the lowest price.

To locate the equilibrium in the Bertrand model, we assume, as in the case of the Cournot model, that the firms take their price decisions sequentially. We also assume both firms face a horizontal marginal cost function $MC_A = MC_B$. In Round 1, firm A sets its price initally at the monopoly level, P_M, and earns the monopoly profit. Then firm B arrives. How should B react to A's initial price decision? By setting its price fractionally below P_M, say at $P_M - \varepsilon$ where ε is a very small amount, B undercuts A and gains all of A's customers. By doing so, B earns a profit fractionally below the monopoly profit.

In Round 2, how should A react to B's intervention in Round 1? Using the same reasoning, by setting its price fractionally below $P_M - \varepsilon$, say at $P_M - 2\varepsilon$, A undercuts B and gains all of B's customers. A earns a profit a little further below the monopoly profit. Then, by setting its price at $P_M - 3\varepsilon$, B undercuts A again and regains all of A's customers. B's profit is now a little further still below the monopoly profit.

Similar reasoning also applies in Round 3 and in subsequent rounds, when further price-cutting takes place. Is there ever an end to the price-cutting sequence? The answer to this question is yes. When price has fallen to the perfectly competitive level $P_C = MC$, there is no incentive for either firm to cut price any further. Although by so doing, either firm could still gain all of the other's customers, this would not be worthwhile if it required setting a price below marginal cost, at which normal profit would not be earned. If firm A is the first to reach P_C, at the next decision point firm B simply follows firm A, and also charges P_C. Because consumers are indifferent between the two firms at this price, it is assumed each firm captures a 50 per cent share of the market at P_C. The solution is illustrated in Figure 4.10. At the equilibrium price $P_C = MC$, both firms produce output levels of $q_A = q_B = 1/2Q_C$.

Our earlier criticism of the zero conjectural variation assumption applies to the Bertrand model, as it does to the Cournot model. We might well expect each firm to learn from experience to anticipate its rival's reactions to its own price-cutting decisions. Furthermore, Bertrand's conclusion that in equilibrium, the two duopolists finish up charging the perfectly competitive price may seem surprising. In contrast to the Cournot model, the Bertrand model appears to suggest there is no intermediate case lying between the polar cases of monopoly and perfect competition. In fact, this conclusion is due to Bertrand's assumption that the two firms produce

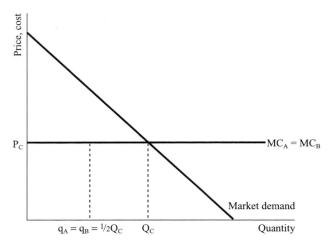

Figure 4.10 Equilibrium in the Bertrand duopoly model

an identical product. In Chapter 12, we develop a model of Bertrand competition with product differentiation, in which a price cut by one firm allows it to gain some, but not all, of its rival's customers.

However, in the case described above where the firms produce identical products, there is no option other than to compete on price. Equilibrium is only achieved when price is driven down to the perfectly competitive level. It has been suggested that price competition in the airline industry, especially since the arrival of low-cost airlines, may approximate to Bertrand competition. Although the number of airlines is small, from the customer's perspective they offer essentially an identical product. Intense price competition on many routes has driven down fares to levels close to marginal cost, which (in an industry with high fixed costs and low variable costs) is quite close to zero.

The Edgeworth model: price competition with a production capacity constraint

Edgeworth (1897) modifies Bertrand's model of price competition in duopoly to allow for the possibility that the firms are subject to a production capacity constraint. At relatively low prices, this constraint precludes each firm from gaining all of the other firm's customers by implementing a further small price cut. Edgeworth retains Bertrand's zero conjectural variation assumption as regards prices: each firm assumes its rival will stick to the rival's current price. In this capacity-constrained case, the conclusions are very different from those of Bertrand. In fact, Edgeworth shows that there is *no* stable equilibrium solution to the capacity-constrained duopoly model.

Figure 4.11 illustrates **Edgeworth's model**. The horizontal marginal cost function of Figure 4.10 is replaced with a vertical section located at $1/2Q_C$, which is assumed to represent each firm's full-capacity output level. Suppose through a process of Bertrand competition, the two firms have arrived at the Bertrand equilibrium, with

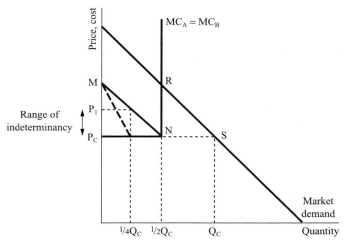

Figure 4.11 Price-setting in the Edgeworth duopoly model

each firm producing an output of $1/2Q_C$ and selling at a price of P_C. Why is this no longer a stable equilibrium if the firms are capacity-constrained? The answer is that either firm can now consider raising its price without the fear it will lose all its customers to the other firm. For example, if A is incapable of producing more than $1/2Q_C$, B can set a price anywhere between P_C and M, and still sell some output to those customers whom A is incapable of servicing. These customers are forced to pay the higher price charged by B. In Figure 4.11, MN represents B's residual demand function. The triangle P_CMN is the segment of the market demand function that cannot be serviced by A (equivalent to the triangle NRS). To maximize profit using B's residual demand function, B should charge a price of P_1, at which B produces and sells an output of $1/4Q_C$.

However, a situation where A produces $1/2Q_C$ and charges P_C, and B produces $1/4Q_C$ and charges P_1, is also not a stable equilibrium. A now has an incentive also to raise its price to P_1. By doing so A can still produce and sell its full-capacity output of $1/2Q_C$. However, A now sells twice as much output and earns twice as much profit as B. But B then realizes that by reducing its price slightly, say to $P_1 - \varepsilon$, B can undercut A, increasing its own output to B's full-capacity level of $1/2Q_C$, and reducing A's output to (slightly more than) $1/4Q_C$. A then realizes that if A reduces its price further, it can once again increase its own output and profit, at B's expense. The sequence of price-cutting continues until price returns to P_C and both firms produce their full-capacity output levels of $1/2Q_C$. But at this point, one of the firms realizes it can do better by raising its price, and the entire cycle begins all over again! And so it goes on, prices fluctuating continually between P_1 and P_C. The model is inherently unstable, and the solution is indeterminate.

As before, we can criticize Edgeworth's model for its reliance on the zero conjectural variation assumption. The model seems to be built on the idea that firms' conjectures are *always* wrong. We can also criticize the model for the assumption that firms can continually and effortlessly adjust their prices and outputs. A charitable assessment of the model is to see it as an improvement on some of the previous models discussed, in that it identifies the possibility of *instability* in oligopoly. Some economists believe that oligopolies are inherently unstable. Although prices may at times appear stable, often the stability is imposed, either by tacit or explicit collusion. Perhaps the temptation to collude is irresistible, if the alternative is perpetual instability as Edgeworth suggests. Solberg (1992, pp. 603–4) suggests that Coca-Cola and Pepsi Cola, both subject to capacity limits in local markets, have frequently resorted to aggressive price-cutting strategies, as suggested by the Edgeworth model.

Case study 4.1

Oligopoly price wars

Price wars in oligopolistic markets are frequent events. In this Case study we note three examples reported in the British press in May and June 2002.

German airlines price war

The established German airline, Lufthansa, was faced with competition from a low-cost carrier, Germania. This operator offered cheap flights between Berlin, Frankfurt and Cologne. In response, Lufthansa reduced fares on 50 of its domestic routes, by up to 60 per cent. These cheaper fares were available for off-peak flights, and had to be booked at least two days in advance.

Supermarket petrol price war

In May 2002, the British supermarket chain Asda announced petrol price cuts of around 2 per cent at its 140 filling stations. This was sufficient to force its rival Morrisons to react with similar price reductions at its 90 stations. Tesco, Britain's largest supermarket chain, which boasts a local pricing policy that guarantees cheaper prices than local rivals, was immediately forced to follow suit.

Tabloid newspaper price war

In May 2002, *The Mirror* newspaper announced price reductions from its normal cover price of 32p to 20p (10p in Scotland). After three weeks, having claimed circulation had risen by 9 per cent, the newspaper announced an end to the price cut, though it decided to retain the 20p cover price in certain important regions, such as London and the Midlands. The *Mirror*'s main rival, News International's *Sun*, interpreted this move as a 'surrender' on the part of the *Mirror* in this price war. However, the *Sun* did not react immediately; instead it decided to await developments before determining its next move.

Case study 4.2

BSkyB offer set to spark digital television price war: group to give away set-top boxes in battle for subscribers

British Sky Broadcasting, the satellite broadcaster, armed itself for a fierce battle for digital television subscribers yesterday when it said it would give away the £200 set-top boxes needed to receive the new services. BSkyB, which launched 140 digital channels last year, said it would give away the equipment from next month to 'remove all possible barriers to digital take-up'. It also intends to stop broadcasting using analogue technology by 2002. The move looks set to spark a price war in the industry. On Digital, BSkyB's rival, which launched 30 digital terrestrial channels via roof-top aerials last year, confirmed it planned to give away its own set-top boxes for a month. Analysts said yesterday On Digital would have to extend that offer to match BSkyB's. A feeling that BSkyB would win the battle for digital subscribers sent its shares soaring 65.5p to 607p. Meanwhile, shares in Carlton Communications and Granada Group, the two ITV companies that own On Digital, closed down 48.5p at 544.5p and down 24p at £13.43 respectively. BSkyB also announced it would offer free internet access via personal computers from 1 June and a 40 per cent discount on British Telecommunications telephone calls. In addition, it revealed it had signed up 551,000 digital customers by 3 May. Mark Booth, BSkyB's chief executive, said the announcements were aimed at competing more effectively with the cable industry, which has yet to launch a digital service. Cable customers have discounted phone calls and will not have to pay an upfront charge for digital boxes. Mr Booth brushed off suggestions that BSkyB was feeling threatened by competition from On Digital. 'On Digital will be a successful niche player but it will always be in a niche', he said.

Stephen Grabiner, chief executive of On Digital, welcomed BSkyB's plans. He said BSkyB's decision to cease analogue transmissions would enable the government to feel more comfortable about switching off the terrestrial analogue signal. He hinted that On Digital would match BSkyB's offer.

BSkyB said the cost of acquiring each new subscriber would be £155. It is suspending dividend payments in favour of investing in digital. BSkyB is setting aside £315m to pay for the free transfer of its analogue subscribers to digital. However, Martin Stewart, chief financial officer, said switching off analogue transmissions would give BSkyB annual savings of £50m. BSkyB is increasing the monthly charge for many of its channels.

Cable & Wireless Communications, the UK's biggest cable operator, said its 200-channel digital television service would be launched in Manchester and the north west on 1 July. It hoped to sign up about 200,000 customers during the first year and said it would always be able to charge less than BSkyB. But it warned that launching the channels would hit pre-tax profits.

Source: BSkyB offer set to spark digital television price war: group to give away set-top boxes in battle for subscribers, *Financial Times*, 6 May 1999. Reprinted with permission.

The Bertrand and Edgeworth models are among the earliest attempts to theorize about the behaviour of oligopolists. The one major drawback these models have in common with the Cournot model, but not with the Chamberlin and Stackelberg models, is the zero conjectural variation assumption: the belief that rivals will not respond to any price or output change by altering their own prices or outputs, *despite* continually observing behaviour that contradicts this assumption. We now examine some other models in which this assumption is relaxed, and the firms are aware their actions will prompt rivals to reconsider their own decisions.

4.5 The kinked demand curve and models of price leadership

The kinked demand curve

This famous model was developed almost simultaneously by Sweezy (1939) and Hall and Hitch (1939). The model seeks to explain an observed tendency for price to be rather inflexible or 'rigid' in many oligopolistic markets. The idea behind the kinked demand curve model is that each firm in an oligopoly may be reluctant to initiate either a price increase or price cut, for the following reasons:

■ The firm believes if it increases its price, its rivals will not follow suit, but will instead seek to take advantage by encouraging the firm's customers to switch to them. Consequently the firm stands to lose a sizable portion of its market share if it increases its price.

■ The firm also believes if it cuts its price, its rivals will follow suit, in order to protect their own market shares. Consequently the firm does not stand to gain market share if it cuts its price.

In other words, the firm tends to take a rather cautious or pessimistic view of its rivals' likely reaction to any decision to either increase or reduce its own price. If all firms think in this way, prices throughout the industry tend to be inflexible or rigid, because no firm wishes to be the first to implement a price change in either direction.

Sweezy's model is shown in Figure 4.12. P_1 is the firm's current price. dd is the firm's demand function, drawn on the assumption that if it raises or lowers its price from P_1, its rivals do not follow suit. dd is relatively price elastic, because if the firm is the only one raising its price, it loses most of its customers; and if it is the only one cutting its price, it gains customers rapidly from its rivals. DD is the firm's demand function, drawn on the assumption that if it raises or lowers its price from P_1, its rivals do follow suit. DD is less price elastic, because if all firms simultaneously raise or lower their prices, they only gain or lose sales to the extent that total industry sales rise or fall; the firms do not tend to gain or lose customers from one another.

In Figure 4.12, the firm faces two possible demand functions, drawn on differing assumptions about rivals' reactions to any price change. What is the firm's perceived demand function? On the pessimistic assumptions described above, we should consider dd to be the demand function applicable for a price rise above P_1 (or for quantities less than q_1). DD is the demand function applicable for a price cut below

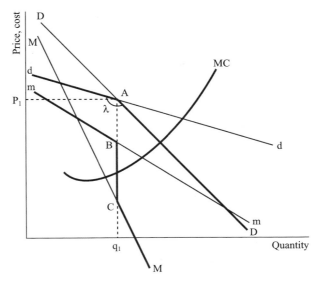

Figure 4.12 Sweezy's kinked demand curve model

P_1 (or for quantities greater than q_1). Therefore dAD is the firm's perceived demand function. There is a kink at point A, which identifies the current price and quantity, P_1 and q_1.

What is the shape of the firm's perceived marginal revenue (MR) function? Applying similar logic, mm is the MR function associated with the demand function dd, applicable for quantities less than q_1. MM is the MR function associated with the demand function DD, applicable for quantities greater than q_1. Therefore mBCM is the firm's perceived MR function. There is a discontinuity between points B and C located at the current quantity q_1, at which point a switch between the two MR functions takes place.

Profit is maximized where MR = MC. MR > MC to the left of q_1, and MR < MC to the right of q_1. Therefore profit is maximized at P_1 and q_1, because MC intersects the discontinuous section of the perceived MR function at q_1. Even if MC rises or falls slightly, as long as the point of intersection remains within the discontinuity BC, the profit-maximizing price and quantity are unchanged. This provides a more formal demonstration of the property of price rigidity or 'sticky prices'.

The degree of price rigidity depends on the length of the discontinuity in the MR function, BC. This in turn depends on the angle of the kink (λ), which has been called the barometer of **price rigidity**. Stigler (1947) identifies several factors that might affect the angle of the kink.

- If there are very few rivals, both price increases and price cuts are *more* likely to be followed, since the firms are highly conscious of their interdependence. The perceived demand function may approach DD. If there are many rivals, price increases and price cuts are *less* likely to be followed, as competition approaches the atomistic case in which each firm's actions have a negligible effect on its rivals. Stigler thought an intermediate number of firms would generate the most acute λ, and the longest discontinuity in the MR function.

■ The size of the rivals may also affect the size of the kink. If there is one large firm, or a clique of firms, it may act as a price leader, with others following its price decisions. In this extreme case there may be no kink. The same applies if there is collusion.

■ Product homogeneity (or a large and positive cross-elasticity of demand) produces an acute λ and a long discontinuity, as customers are more likely to shift when facing a price differential.

This list is extended by Cohen and Cyert (1965, p. 251):

■ If entrants are unsure about the market structure, or incumbent firms are unsure about the intentions of entrants, firms may adopt a wait-and-see attitude and be reluctant to initiate price rises.

■ The same may also be true in a new industry, where firms are attempting to size each other up.

■ If there is substantial shareholder control, risk-averse managers may decide to play safe, by avoiding actions that could provoke damaging reactions from rivals.

The kinked demand curve model can be criticized for not explaining how price is formed at the kink. The model begins with the price as given; it does not explain how price is determined. It explains the existence of the kink but not its location. Furthermore, price rigidity might be explained in other ways. Firms may be reluctant to raise price for fear of alienating their customers. Firms may wait for a convenient time to introduce one large price rise, rather than revise prices continuously, the latter being a strategy that might annoy customers. Levy *et al.* (1997) suggest that changing price is itself a costly and complex operation. Accordingly, in businesses where menu costs are high, price changes are less frequent.

Stigler (1947) found little empirical evidence of price rigidity. Having examined the evidence in seven oligopolistic markets (cigarettes, automobiles, anthracite, steel, dynamite, refining and potash) he claimed price changes were quite frequent, although there was some evidence to suggest the smaller the number of firms, the less frequent were price changes.

> But is this adverse conclusion really surprising? The kink is a barrier to changes in prices that will increase profits, and business is the collection of devices for circumventing barriers to profits. That this barrier should thwart businessmen – especially when it is wholly of their own fabrication – is unbelievable.
>
> *(Stigler, 1947, p. 435)*

In a later article, Stigler said he was amazed at the continuing popularity of the model. 'The theory has received no systematic empirical support and virtually no theoretical elaboration in these decades, but these lacks have been no handicap in maintaining its currency' (Stigler, 1978, p. 183). However, there is some evidence to support Sweezy's reasoning. For example, Kashyap (1995) examined price changes for 12 retail goods over 35 years, and found prices were typically fixed for more than a year. In a study based on 80 industries, Domberger and Fiebig (1993) found price cuts were more readily followed than price increases in tight oligopolies.

Sweezy's basic assumption that price increases will not be followed and that price cuts will, has been challenged. A price cut need not send signals to rivals that a firm is aggressively seeking to capture a larger market share. Rivals may reason that the firm's product is of lower quality, or the firm has financial problems. Rivals react according to how they interpret the price cut. Likewise, price increases may be followed if firms believe market conditions warrant such an increase, or if they face temporary capacity shortages and are unable to meet increases in demand. In times of increasing demand and possible price inflation, producing any additional output increases costs substantially for a firm approaching capacity (Brofenbrenner, 1940; Efroymson, 1955). Accordingly, a capacity-constrained firm may be eager to follow a rival's price rise and reluctant to follow a price cut, which would only increase demand further.

This case is illustrated in Figure 4.13, where the perceived demand function is DAd, the marginal revenue function is MCBm, and the kink has become reflexive. In this case, profit is not maximized at (P_1/q_1) the current price and quantity P_1q_1. By reducing output to q_2, the firm could increase profit by X (the area between MC and MR over the range q_2 to q_1). Alternatively, by increasing output to q_3, the firm could increase profit by Y (the area between MR and MC over the range q_1 to q_3). In Figure 4.13, since Y is larger than X, the firm should select output q_3. However, this outcome is not inevitable. During times of inflation in particular, both MC and the demand functions dd and DD tend to rise. If the increase in MC is greater than the increase in demand, perhaps (as suggested above) because the firm is approaching a production capacity constraint, Y tends to become smaller than X. Therefore a profit-maximizing firm would eventually switch to the lower output level q_2.

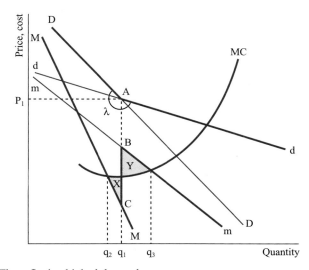

Figure 4.13 The reflexive kinked demand curve

Models of price leadership

Models of price leadership or parallel pricing are yet another type of oligopoly model, in which the firms recognize their interdependence. It is a frequently observed phenomenon that firms in oligopolistic markets change prices in parallel. One firm announces a price change, and the other firms rapidly follow suit.

Dominant price leadership

In one class of price leadership model, **dominant price leadership**, it is assumed that the industry is dominated by one firm, owing to its superior efficiency (lower costs), or perhaps its aggressive behaviour. The firm sets the price, and other firms follow passively, whether through convenience, ignorance or fear. In fact there is no oligopoly problem as such, since interdependence is absent.

In Figure 4.14, it is assumed that there is one large dominant firm, and a competitive 'fringe' comprising a large number of small firms. The dominant firm is the price leader, and sets the market price. The competitive fringe are the followers. These firms are price takers, and each firm faces a perfectly elastic demand function at the price set by the dominant firm. It is assumed that the dominant firm has complete information regarding its own demand and cost functions, as well as those of its smaller competitors.

In Figure 4.14, D_{TOTAL} is the market demand function. S_{FRINGE} is the total supply function of the competitive fringe, obtained by summing the marginal cost functions of each firm in the competitive fringe horizontally. Each firm in the competitive fringe maximizes profit by producing the quantity at which price *equals* marginal cost. Therefore the horizontal sum of all of the marginal cost functions represents the total quantity supplied by the competitive fringe at any price. In order to obtain

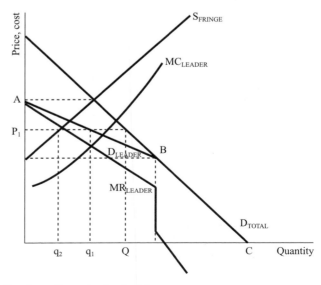

Figure 4.14 Dominant firm price leadership

D_{LEADER}, the residual demand function of the dominant firm, we subtract the quantity supplied by the competitive fringe at any price from the total market demand function at that price. Therefore $D_{LEADER} = D_{TOTAL} - S_{FRINGE}$. Notice at A, $S_{FRINGE} = D_{TOTAL}$, so $D_{LEADER} = 0$. At B, $S_{FRINGE} = 0$, so $D_{LEADER} = D_{TOTAL}$. Beyond B, the leader operates along D_{TOTAL}, so over the entire range of output levels the leader's demand function is ABC. The kink in this demand function at B implies the leader's marginal revenue function (MR_{LEADER} above B) has a discontinuity at B.

The dominant firm maximizes profit by choosing the output at which MR_{LEADER} *equals* MC_{LEADER}, the dominant firm's marginal cost function. The dominant firm's price and output are (P_1, q_1). At a price of P_1, the output of the competitive fringe is q_2. Total industry output *equals* $Q = q_1 + q_2$. By construction, $q_2 = Q - q_1$, because the horizontal distance between D_{TOTAL} and D_{LEADER} *equals* S_{FRINGE}.

Barometric price leadership

Barometric price leadership exists where a firm announces a price change that would, in time, be set by the forces of competition. It is simply the first to announce the price change. The leader is not necessarily the dominant firm, and the leader does not necessarily have any market power with which it could impose its will on others, as in the dominant firm price leadership model. Indeed, one would expect the identity of the leader to change from time to time. The leader acts as a barometer for the market, and if it fails to interpret market signals correctly leadership will soon pass to some other firm.

Markham (1951) suggests barometric price leadership is of two types: the competitive type and the (more dangerous) monopolistic type, known as effective or collusive price leadership. The more benign, competitive type is characterized by:

- Frequent changes in the identity of the leader.

- No immediate, uniform response to price changes: followers take their time to consider the suitability of a price change implemented by the leader.

- Variations in market share.

Effective or collusive price leadership is characterized by:

- A small number of firms, all relatively large.

- Substantial entry barriers.

- Limited product differentiation, reinforcing the firms' awareness of their interdependence.

- Low price elasticity of demand, deterring price-cutting.

- Similar cost functions.

As will be shown in Chapter 5, these characteristics are not too dissimilar to the characteristics of successful cartels. When the agreed price leader changes its price, the other firms immediately follow suit. There is no overt or explicit collusion: all firms act independently. However, they realize it is better to cooperate tacitly in an orderly market than to slide into the anarchy of a price war. Nevertheless, the effect is similar to explicit price fixing. 'The monopolistically barometric form of price leadership is dire, and it may serve all the ends of a strong trade association or a closely knit domestic cartel' (Bain, 1960, p. 198).

4.6 Game theory

Game theory is an approach to decision making under conditions of uncertainty developed by the mathematicians von Neumann and Morgenstern (1944). A game is a situation in which two or more decision makers, or players, face choices between a number of possible actions at any stage of the game. A game that is played only once is a single-period game. A game that is played more than once is a **multiple-period** or **repeated game**. A multiple-period game can be repeated either infinitely, or a finite number of times. A player's **strategy** is a set of rules telling him which action to choose under each possible set of circumstances that might exist at any stage in the game. Each player aims to select the strategy (or mix of strategies) that will maximize his own **payoff**. The players face a situation of interdependence. Each player is aware that the actions of other players can affect his payoff, but at the time the player chooses his own action he may not know which actions are being chosen by the other players. A game in which all players choose their actions simultaneously, before knowing the actions chosen by other players, is a **simultaneous game**. A game in which the players choose their actions in turn, so that a player who moves later knows the actions that were chosen by players who moved earlier, is a **sequential game**. The outcome of a game is the set of strategies and actions that are actually chosen, and the resulting payoffs. An equilibrium is a combination of strategies, actions and payoffs that is optimal (in some sense) for all players.

Broadly speaking, games fall into two categories: **cooperative games** and non-cooperative games. In a cooperative game, it is assumed the players can negotiate a binding agreement. When a seller and a buyer haggle over a price, this 'game' can be solved by an agreement (either verbal or written) over a mutually acceptable price. When two producers collude over price or outputs, there is also a *de facto* binding agreement. If an agreement is not possible, however, the game is non-cooperative. Games can also be classified according to their outcomes. In a **constant-sum game**, the sum of the payoffs to all players is always the same, whatever strategies are chosen. In a **non-constant sum game**, the sum of the payoffs depends on the strategies chosen. A **zero-sum game** is a constant-sum game in which the sum of the gains and losses of all players is always zero. A game of poker is a zero-sum game: one player's winnings are exactly matched by the losses of rival players.

In many ways, the property of **interdependence** is the key defining characteristic of a game, and it is this property that makes game theory relevant to an understanding of decision making for firms in oligopoly. In most of the game theory examples that are discussed in Section 4.6 and elsewhere in this book, the players are two or more oligopolistic firms. Strategies and actions concern the decisions the firms have to take about price or output, or other commercial decisions on matters such as advertising, product differentiation, research and development, entry, location, and so on. Payoffs are usually defined in terms of the implications for the firms' profitability of the strategies and actions that are chosen. However, it is worth noting that game theory has many applications other than decision making under oligopoly. Examples include strategy and tactics in professional team sports, military strategy and nuclear deterrence.

Dominant strategies and Nash equilibrium

For our first game theory example, Figure 4.15 shows the payoff matrix for two firms, A and B. Firm A's strategies are α and β, and firm B's strategies are γ and δ. The elements in the matrix represent the payoffs (for example profit) to the two firms. Within each cell, the first figure is A's payoff and the second figure is B's payoff. For example, if A selects strategy β and B selects strategy γ, A's payoff (profit) is +3 and B's payoff is +2.

First, we consider the choice between strategies α and β from A's perspective. One method A could use in order to make this choice would be to examine which of α and β is best for A if B selects γ, and which of α and β is best for A if B selects δ:

- If B selects γ, α yields a payoff of +4 for A, while β yields a payoff of +3. Therefore if B selects γ, it is best for A to select α.

- If B selects δ, α yields a payoff of +2 for A, while β yields a payoff of +1. Therefore if B selects δ, it is best for A to select α.

In this game, no matter what strategy B selects, it is best for A to choose α rather than β. α is said to be a **dominant strategy**, because it is the best strategy for A no matter what strategy B selects.

Second, we consider the choice between strategies γ and δ from B's perspective, using a similar approach:

- If A selects α, γ yields a payoff of +4 for B, while δ yields a payoff of +3. Therefore if A selects α, it is best for B to select γ.

- If A selects β, γ yields a payoff of +2 for B, while δ yields a payoff of +1. Therefore if A selects β, it is best for B to select γ.

Accordingly, no matter what strategy A selects, it is better for B to select γ rather than δ. Therefore γ is B's dominant strategy. Following this approach, it appears A should select α and B should select γ, so that both firms earn a payoff of +4. In fact, the game shown in Figure 4.15 is rather trivial, in the sense that +4 is the best payoff achievable by either player under any circumstances, so it seems natural that

Firm B's strategies

		γ	δ
	α	(+4, +4)	(+2, +3)
Firm A's strategies	β	(+3, +2)	(+1, +1)

Figure 4.15 Payoff matrix for firms A and B

the players should choose the combination of strategies that produces this payoff for both of them. Below, we will see that not all games are structured in a way that always produces such a pleasing outcome for the players! There is, however, one further desirable and important property of the current example: at the equilibrium, neither firm can improve its payoff given the current strategy of the other firm. Given that B selects γ, if A switches from α to β, A's payoff falls from +4 to +3. And given that A selects α, if B switches from γ to δ, B's payoff also falls from +4 to +3.

Suppose now the strategies are the firms' output decisions, and the payoffs are their profits. If A selects α and B selects γ, both firms maximize their own profit, subject to the constraint that the other firm's output is fixed at its current level. Therefore both firms maximize profit subject to a zero conjectural variation assumption. We have previously identified an equilibrium of this kind, in our discussion of the Cournot duopoly model. In the terminology of Section 4.3, this kind of solution is known as a Cournot–Nash equilibrium. In the terminology of game theory, it is known simply as a **Nash equilibrium**. In a Nash equilibrium, neither player can improve his payoff given the strategy chosen by the other player.

Prisoner's dilemma

Figure 4.16 presents a second example, with a similar structure but a different set of payoffs. Applying the same reasoning as before, from A's perspective:

- If B selects γ, α yields a payoff of +3 for A, while β yields a payoff of +4. Therefore if B selects γ, it is best for A to select β.

- If B selects δ, α yields a payoff of +1 for A, while β yields a payoff of +2. Therefore if B selects δ, it is best for A to select β.

And from B's perspective:

- If A selects α, γ yields a payoff of +3 for B, while δ yields a payoff of +4. Therefore if A selects α, it is best for B to select δ.

- If A selects β, γ yields a payoff of +1 for B, while δ yields a payoff of +2. Therefore if A selects β, it is best for B to select δ.

Therefore β is a dominant strategy for A and δ is a dominant strategy for B. Accordingly, it seems that A should select β and B should select δ, in which case both firms earn a payoff of +2. As before, this solution is a Nash equilibrium:

Firm B's strategies

		γ	δ
	α	(+3, +3)	(+1, +4)
Firm A's strategies	β	(+4, +1)	(+2, +2)

Figure 4.16 Payoff matrix for firms A and B: prisoner's dilemma example

given that B selects δ, if A switches from β to α, A's payoff falls from +2 to +1; and given that A selects β, if B switches from δ to γ, B's payoff also falls from +2 to +1. However, this time something appears to be wrong. If both firms had selected the *other* strategy (α for A, γ for B), either by cooperating or perhaps by acting independently, both firms would have earned a superior payoff of +3 each, rather than their actual payoff of +2 each.

Figure 4.16 is an example of a special class of single period non-constant sum game, known as the **prisoner's dilemma**. In a prisoner's dilemma game, there are dominant strategies for both players that produce a combined payoff that is worse than the combined payoff the players could achieve if they cooperate, with each player agreeing to choose a strategy other than his dominant strategy. In other words, in a prisoner's dilemma, there are gains to be made if the players collude.

To see why this type of game is known as a prisoner's dilemma, consider a situation where the police hold two prisoners, Jeffrey and Jonathan, who are suspected of having committed a crime together. However, the police have insufficient evidence to secure a conviction unless one or both prisoners confess. The prisoners are separated physically and there is no communication between them. Each is told the following:

- If you both confess, you both receive a reduced punishment of five years in prison.

- If neither of you confesses, you both go free.

- If you confess and your fellow prisoner does not, you go free and receive a reward of £50,000.

- If you do not confess and your fellow prisoner confesses, you receive the normal punishment of ten years in prison.

The payoff matrix is shown in Figure 4.17. Jeffrey's reasoning might be as follows: if Jonathan confesses, I should confess because minus 5 years is better than minus 10 years; and if Jonathan does not confess, I should confess because +£50k is better than 0. Therefore I will confess. Jonathan's reasoning is the same, because the payoffs are symmetric between the two prisoners. Therefore both confess, and both receive the five-year sentence. But if they had been able to cooperate, they could have agreed not to confess, and both would have gone free. Even acting independently, they might be able to reach the cooperative solution. Jeffrey knows that if he does not confess, he goes free as long as Jonathan does the same. However, Jeffrey is worried because he knows there is a big incentive for Jonathan to 'cheat'

		Jonathan's strategies	
		Not confess	Confess
Jeffrey's strategies	Not confess	(0, 0)	(–10 years, +£50,000)
	Confess	(+£50,000, –10 years)	(–5 years, –5 years)

Figure 4.17 Payoff matrix for Jeffrey and Jonathan: classic prisoner's dilemma

on Jeffrey by confessing. By doing so Jonathan can earn the £50k reward and land Jeffrey with a ten-year sentence!

Jonathan is in a similar position: if he does not confess, he goes free as long as Jeffrey also does not confess. However, Jonathan also knows there is a big incentive for Jeffrey to cheat. The cooperative solution might be achievable, especially if Jeffrey and Jonathan can trust one another not to cheat, but it is also unstable and liable to break down.

In Section 4.3, we analysed the choices of output levels by two duopolists. Comparing the Cournot–Nash and the Chamberlin solutions to the duopoly model shown in Figure 4.9, it is apparent that if the two firms operate independently according to the zero conjectural variation assumption, and each firm produces a relatively high output level of 1/3, the Cournot–Nash equilibrium is attained. In the terminology of the present section, this is a non-cooperative outcome. If on the other hand the two firms recognize their interdependence and aim for joint profit maximization, and each firm produces the lower output level of 1/4, the Chamberlin equilibrium is attained. In present terminology, this is the cooperative outcome.

In Figures 4.18 and 4.19, we show that if the two duopolists have to make their output decisions simultaneously, without knowing the other firm's decision, effectively they play a prisoner's dilemma game. The assumptions underlying Figures 4.18 and 4.19 are the same as in the original Cournot model developed in Section 4.3, with one exception. The two duopolists are assumed to produce an identical product,

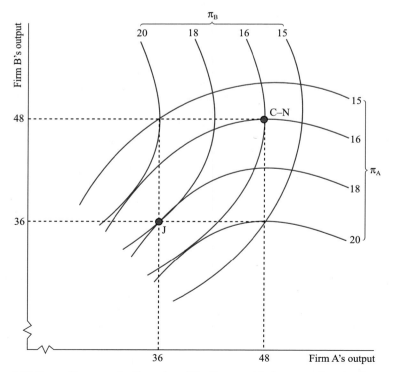

Figure 4.18 Isoprofit curves for firms A and B: Cournot–Nash versus Chamberlin's prisoner's dilemma

Firm B's strategies

		'Low' output	'High' output
Firm A's strategies	'Low' output	(+18, +18)	(+15, +20)
	'High' output	(+20, +15)	(+16, +16)

Figure 4.19 Payoff matrix for firms A and B: Cournot–Nash versus Chamberlin's prisoner's dilemma

and incur zero marginal costs. The one change involves a rescaling of the quantity axis for the market demand function, so that the maximum quantity that could be sold if the price falls to zero is 144 units (rather than one unit). As before, the price axis for market demand function is on a scale of $P = 0$ to $P = 1$, so when $P = 0$, $Q = 144$ and when $P = 1$, $Q = 0$. The only effect of the rescaling of the quantity axis is to avoid the occurrence of fractional prices, quantities and profits. You can verify that the prices, quantities and profits or payoffs shown in Figures 4.18 and 4.19 are equivalent to their counterparts in Figure 4.9 multiplied by a factor of 144.

In Figure 4.18, we assume each firm has to choose between producing a 'high' output level of 48 units, or a 'low' output level of 36 units. If both firms produce 'high', the Cournot–Nash equilibrium is attained, and both firms' profits are +16. If both firms produce 'low', the Chamberlin joint profit maximization equilibrium is attained, and both firms' profits are +18. If one firm produces 'low' while the other produces 'high', the 'low' producing firm suffers and earns +15, while the 'high' producing firm prospers and earns +20. Figure 4.19 represents these outcomes in the form of a payoff matrix. Applying the same reasoning as before, from A's perspective:

■ If B selects 'low', 'low' yields a payoff of +18 for A, while 'high' yields a payoff of +20. Therefore if B selects 'low', it is best for A to select 'high'.

■ If B selects 'high', 'low' yields a payoff of +15 for A, while 'high' yields a payoff of +16. Therefore if B selects 'high', it is best for A to select 'high'.

Accordingly, it is best for A to select 'high', no matter what strategy B selects. The same is also true for B, because the two firms are identical. 'High' is the dominant strategy for both firms, and if both firms select their dominant strategies, both produce 'high' and the suboptimal non-cooperative Cournot–Nash outcome is attained. As before, the cooperative or collusive outcome might be achievable if the firms can trust each another to stick to the 'low' output strategy and not defect and produce 'high' output. However, as before, this outcome is unstable and liable to break down. For the cooperative solution to hold in an oligopoly, any agreement between the firms might have to be accompanied by an enforceable contract (legal or otherwise).

Not all prisoner's dilemma games generate suboptimal outcomes, especially when the assumptions are relaxed. First, the optimal (cooperative) outcome might be achieved if there is good communication between the players. If firms meet frequently, they can exchange information and monitor each other's actions. If the two prisoners, Jeffrey and Jonathan, were not segregated, they could determine their best strategies by a continual examination of their options. The nuclear deterrence 'game' played by the United States and the Soviet Union in the 1960s and 1970s was likened to a prisoner's dilemma game. The choices were whether to attack the rival with a preemptive strike, or abide by the the 'non-first use' agreement. Perhaps one reason why the optimal outcome (sticking to the agreement) was achieved was that the installation of a telephone hotline between Washington and Moscow permitted rapid communication and exchange of information at the highest levels of government.

Second, in practice an important characteristic of any game is the length of the reaction lag: the time it takes for a player who has been deceived to retaliate. The longer the reaction lags, the greater the temptation for either player to act as an aggressor. If Jonathan cheats on Jeffrey, Jeffrey may have to wait ten years to take revenge, unless he has friends on the outside prepared to act more quickly. In cartels, the main deterrent to cheating is immediate discovery and punishment. In the nuclear deterrence game, short reaction lags were crucial to ensuring both sides kept to the agreement. Each side boasted that it could retaliate within minutes if attacked by the other, ensuring there was no first-mover advantage. This policy became known as mutually assured destruction (MAD).

Third, the dynamics of rivalry may also be relevant. Is the rivalry continuous, or 'one-off'? If rivalry is continuous in a repeated game, players learn over time that cooperation is preferable to aggression. Professional criminals have no problem with the prisoner's dilemma: experience has taught them that silence is the best option. In an oligopoly, firms change prices, alter product lines, determine advertising strategies, continuously. The firms may learn over time that aggressive behaviour leads to hostile reactions from rivals, that tend to cancel out any short-term gains (see Case study 4.3). Repeated or multiple-period games are examined in more detail below.

Mixed strategies

In many games, there is no strictly determined solution. Consider the payoff matrix shown in Figure 4.20. This is a constant-sum game: whatever combination of strategies is chosen, the sum of the payoffs to both players is +5. However, there is no dominant strategy for either player. From A's perspective:

■ If B selects γ, α yields a payoff of +1 for A, while β yields a payoff of +4. Therefore if B selects γ, it is best for A to select β.

■ If B selects δ, α yields a payoff of +3 for A, while β yields a payoff of 0. Therefore if B selects δ, it is best for A to select α.

And from B's perspective:

■ If A selects α, γ yields a payoff of +4 for B, while δ yields a payoff of +2. Therefore if A selects α, it is best for B to select γ.

■ If A selects β, γ yields a payoff of +1 for B, while δ yields a payoff of +5. Therefore if A selects β, it is best for B to select δ.

Firm B's strategies

		γ	δ
Firm A's strategies	α	(+1, +4)	(+3, +2)
	β	(+4, +1)	(0, +5)

Figure 4.20 Payoff matrix for firms A and B: mixed strategies example

There is no simple solution to this game because there are no dominant strategies. A is in a difficult position. If A selects strategy α, B might select strategy γ and A only earns a profit of +1. But on the other hand, if A selects strategy β and B selects strategy δ, A earns a profit of zero. Of course, B also faces a similar dilemma.

The solution lies in the concept of a **mixed strategy**, developed by von Neumann and Morgenstern (1944). A player follows a mixed strategy by choosing his action randomly, using fixed probabilities. Each player's optimal mixed strategy involves the selection of probabilities that maximize his expected payoff, regardless of the strategy that is being employed by the other player. In contrast, our earlier examples resulted in the choice of a **pure strategy** by both players. According to the non-cooperative solution to the prisoner's dilemma game shown in Figure 4.16, for example, A should only select β and B should only select δ, because β and δ are dominant strategies.

Returning to Figure 4.20, suppose A assigns a probability of x to the choice of α, and a probability of $(1 - x)$ to the choice of β. We can evaluate A's expected payoffs (in terms of x) as follows:

■ If B chooses γ, A's possible payoffs are +1 (if A chooses α, with a probability of x) and +4 (if A chooses β, with a probability of $1 - x$). A's expected payoff is $1x + 4(1 - x) = 4 - 3x$.

■ If B chooses δ, A's possible payoffs are +3 (if A chooses α, with a probability of x) and 0 (if A chooses β, with a probability of $1 - x$). A's expected payoff is $3x + 0(1 - x) = 3x$.

The left-hand diagram in Figure 4.21 plots A's expected payoffs against all possible values of x, for each of the two possible choices available to B. Setting x = 1 is equivalent to 'A always chooses α'. In this case, the worst A can do is earn a profit of +1 (if B chooses γ). Similarly, setting x = 0 is equivalent to 'A always chooses β'. In this case, the worst A can do is earn a profit of 0 (if B chooses δ). However, according to Figure 4.21, A can improve on the worst possible outcomes under both of these pure strategies by selecting a mixed strategy of x = 2/3. In this case, A earns an expected profit of +2, whichever of γ and δ is chosen by B. In fact, it can be shown that A still earns an expected profit of +2 if B selects any mixed strategy which involves choosing randomly between γ and δ, no matter what probabilities B assigns to these two choices.

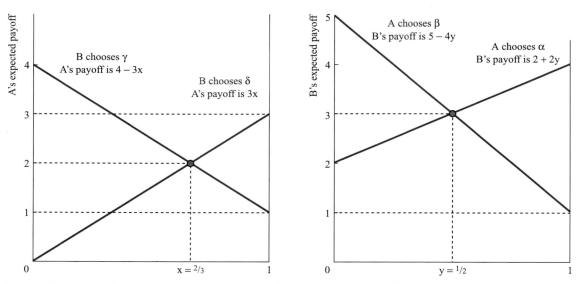

Figure 4.21 Expected payoffs for firms A and B and mixed strategy Nash equilibrium

We can also evaluate B's optimal mixed strategy, again with reference to Figure 4.20. Let B assign a probability of y to the choice of γ, and a probability of $(1 - y)$ to the choice of δ. B's expected payoffs (in terms of y) are as follows:

- If A chooses α, B's possible payoffs are +4 (if B chooses γ, with a probability of y) and +2 (if B chooses δ, with a probability of $1 - y$). B's expected payoff is $4y + 2(1 - y) = 2 + 2y$.

- If A chooses β, B's possible payoffs are +1 (if B chooses γ, with a probability of y) and +5 (if B chooses δ, with a probability of $1 - y$). B's expected payoff is $1y + 5(1 - y) = 5 - 4y$.

The right-hand diagram in Figure 4.21 plots B's expected payoffs against all possible values of y, for each of the two possible choices available to A. Setting $y = 1$ is equivalent to 'B always chooses γ'. In this case, the worst B can do is earn a profit of +1 (if A chooses β). Similarly, setting $y = 0$ is equivalent to 'B always chooses δ'. In this case, the worst B can do is earn a profit of +2 (if A chooses α). However, B improves on the worst possible outcomes under both of these pure strategies by selecting a mixed strategy of $y = 1/2$. In this case, B earns an expected profit of +3, whichever of α and β is chosen by A. In fact, B earns an expected profit of +3 for any mixed strategy selected by A.

If A sets $x = 2/3$ and B sets $y = 1/2$, the game shown in Figure 4.20 achieves a **mixed strategy** Nash equilibrium. Each player selects the probabilities that maximize his own expected payoff, given the mixed strategy that is being employed by the other player. In fact, by selecting the probabilities in this way, each player guarantees his own expected payoff, whatever the probabilities selected by the other player. Selecting $x = 2/3$ guarantees A an expected payoff of +2 for any value of y selected by B; selecting $x = 2/3$ makes A indifferent to B's selection of probabilties. Likewise, selecting $y = 1/2$ guarantees B an expected payoff of +3 for any value of x selected by A; selecting y = 1/2 makes B indifferent to A's selection of probabilities. Although the mathematics is beyond the scope of this text, it has been shown that for any game with a fixed number of players, each of whom chooses between a fixed number of possible actions, a Nash equilibrium involving either pure strategies or mixed strategies always exists.

Sequential games

In the games we have examined so far in Section 4.6, the players act simultaneously and decide their strategies and actions before they know which strategies and actions have been chosen by their rivals. However, there are other games in which the players' decisions follow a sequence. One player makes his decision, and the other player observes this decision before making his response. For example, firm A decides to launch a new brand, and firm B then decides how best to respond. Should B imitate A and launch a brand with identical characteristics, or should B aim for a segment in the market that is not serviced by A, and launch a brand with different characteristics? For a **sequential game**, it is convenient to map the choices facing the players in the form of a game tree.

Assume two breakfast cereal producers are both considering a new product launch. They each have a choice of launching one of two products: one product's appeal is 'crunchiness', and the other's appeal is 'fruitiness'. We also assume the crunchy cereal is more popular with consumers than the fruity cereal. Figure 4.22 shows the payoff matrix in the same form as before, assuming both firms move simultaneously, ignorant of what their rival is planning. According to Figure 4.22, it is better for both firms if they each produce a different product than if they both produce the same product. The structure of the payoffs is such that there is no dominant strategy for either firm. If B produces 'crunchy' it is better for A to produce 'fruity', but if B produces 'fruity' it is better for A to produce 'crunchy'. Using the methods of the previous subsection, you can verify that the mixed strategy Nash equilibrium requires both firms to choose their actions randomly, with probabilities of 3/4 assigned to 'crunchy' and 1/4 assigned to 'fruity'.

In a sequential game, however, where A is the first to launch its new product and B then responds after having observed A's action, the outcome is different. Using the same figures for the breakfast cereals example, Figure 4.23 shows the game tree representation of the payoffs, also known as the *extensive form representation*.

		Firm B's strategies	
		Crunchy	Fruity
Firm A's strategies	Crunchy	(+3, +3)	(+5, +4)
	Fruity	(+4, +5)	(+2, +2)

Figure 4.22 Sequential game: strategic form representation

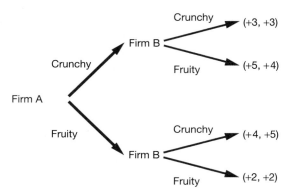

Figure 4.23 Sequential game: extensive form representation

(The equivalent terminology for the payoff matrix we have used previously is the *strategic form representation*.) Consider A's decision:

- If A produces 'crunchy', B's 'fruity' payoff of +4 exceeds B's 'crunchy' payoff of +3, so B will produce 'fruity' and A will earn a profit of +5.

- If A produces 'fruity', B's 'crunchy' payoff of +5 exceeds B's 'fruity' payoff of +2, so B will produce 'crunchy' and A will earn a profit of +4.

In fact, A realizes that whatever product A launches, the rational response of B is to launch the alternative product. A's best action is to produce 'crunchy', and A earns the higher payoff of +5. B produces 'fruity' and earns the lower payoff of +4. A finishes up with the higher payoff because A benefits from a first-mover advantage, as in the case of the Stackelberg duopolist examined in Section 4.3.

Repeated games

In our discussion of single-period prisoner's dilemma and other games, we assumed the game is played only once. However, some games may be played repeatedly by the same players. Suppose firms A and B are hotdog sellers located outside a sports stadium. If the occasion is a one-off event such as the Olympics, and the two hotdog sellers are unlikely to ever see each other again subsequently, the game between them is a single-period game. In this case, the two hotdog sellers are less likely to cooperate. Suppose, however, the event is one that is repeated at regular intervals. Suppose the stadium is Old Trafford, the event is Manchester United home matches, and the hotdog sellers see one another at regular, fortnightly intervals. In this case, it is more likely that cooperative behaviour will evolve as the two sellers observe and learn from each others' behaviour. In a **repeated** or **multiple-period game**, each firm may attempt to influence its rival's behaviour by sending signals that promise to reward cooperative behaviour, and threaten to punish non-cooperative behaviour.

With reference to the prisoner's dilemma game shown in Figure 4.16, we refer to β and δ as the (sub-optimal) non-cooperative choices, which produce payoffs of +2 for firms A and B; and α and γ as the (optimal) cooperative choices, which produce payoffs of +3 for both firms. As we have seen, in a single-period game in which the firms act independently, β and δ are the dominant strategies, and the non-cooperative outcome is likely to occur. However, suppose the game is to be repeated over an indefinite number of periods. Firm A could adopt the following strategy, known as **tit-for-tat**, in an attempt to encourage firm B to always select the cooperative choice:

- In period 1 A chooses α.

- If B chose γ in period t − 1, in period t (for t > 1) A chooses α.

- If B chose δ in period t − 1, in period t (for t > 1) A chooses β.

In each period after the first, provided B chose the cooperative strategy last time, A rewards B by choosing the cooperative strategy this time. But if B chose the non-cooperative strategy last time, A punishes B by choosing the non-cooperative strategy this time. For as long as B cooperates, A also cooperates and the (optimal) cooperative solution is achieved. But if B attempts to exploit A's cooperation for short-term gain by defecting from γ to δ, A punishes B in the following period by also switching, from α to β. However, B's punishment does not necessarily have to be long-lasting. Provided B learns from his error and switches back from δ to γ, A also switches back from β to α, and cooperation is restored.

Since it is difficult to observe situations which replicate the structure of many theoretical games in practice, a sub-field of economics known as **experimental economics** has been developed in order to test the predictions of game theory. Laboratory experimentation allows economists to determine the structure of games and test relevant hypotheses. Some economists are particularly optimistic about the future of this development:

> a hundred years from now, game theory will have become the backbone
> of a kind of micro-economics engineering that will have roughly the relation
> to the economic theory and laboratory experimentation of the time that
> chemical engineering has to chemical theory and bench chemistry.

> *(Roth, 1991, p. 107)*

In the present context, experiments have shown the adoption of a tit-for-tat strategy by one or both players is a highly effective method for ensuring adherence to co-operative behaviour in repeated games with a prisoner's dilemma structure. Usually, both players rapidly learn it is best for them to adhere to the cooperative strategy on each occasion the game is repeated.

However, there is one important caveat. Tit-for-tat is effective in infinitely repeated games, in which there is no period when the game is played for the last time. Tit-for-tat may also be effective in games that are repeated only a finite number of times, but on each occasion neither player knows whether or not this *is* the last time the game will be played. However, tit-for-tat is likely to be ineffective in games that are repeated only a finite number of times, and on the final occasion the players know they will not play the game again.

Suppose the game is played for the last time in period T. In period T, B knows 'defecting' from γ to δ will go unpunished, because the game will not be played again in T + 1. Therefore there is no deterrence, and B defects. Realizing that B will behave in this way, A may as well abandon tit-for-tat in T, and also defect from α to β. Therefore the non-cooperative outcome occurs in T.

From this reasoning, we might suppose that the usefulness of the tit-for-tat strategy now finishes in period T − 1. In fact, however, the situation is actually worse than this, because in period T − 1 the same difficulty occurs. In T − 1, B knows 'defecting' from γ to δ will go unpunished, because non-cooperation is going to happen anyway in T. Therefore there is no deterrence in T − 1 either, and B defects. Realizing that B will behave in this way, A may as well abandon tit-for-tat in T − 1, and also defect. Therefore the non-cooperative outcome also occurs in T − 1.

Similar reasoning will also apply in periods T − 2, T − 3, and so on, all the way back to the start of the game. In other words, the usefulness of tit-for-tat as a means for ensuring adherence to cooperative behaviour unravels completely due to the finite lifetime of the repeated game. A has no means of punishing B for non-cooperative behaviour in period T, so the tit-for-tat strategy fails in period T. But if tit-for-tat fails in period T, it also fails in T − 1; and if it fails in T − 1, it also fails in T − 2; and so on.

Case study 4.3

The prisoner's dilemma in practice: tit-for-tat in the First World War trenches

The original prisoner's dilemma story involves two criminals who are arrested after committing a serious crime. The police have no proof of their involvement except for a minor infraction. The prosecutor offers them a deal whereby the one who implicates the other escapes all punishment and the other gets a heavy prison sentence. If both implicate the other, both end up in prison for a long time. The dominant strategy is for each criminal to implicate the other. Consequently they both end up getting relatively heavy prison sentences. When the game is repeated, however, co-operation can be sustained implicitly through dynamic strategies. In his classic book, *The Evolution of Co-operation,* University of Michigan political scientist Robert Axelrod studied empirically and experimentally the strategies that lead players involved in prisoner's dilemma situations to co-operative outcomes. His starting point was an unexpected experimental result. When experts were asked to submit strategies for repeated prisoner's dilemma games and these strategies were matched with each other in a computer tournament, tit-for-tat, the simplest strategy, won. This was a strategy under which each player started by co-operating, and then did to the other player what that player had done to him previously. Axelrod's analysis of the data found tit-for-tat had four properties making a strategy successful. A successful strategy should be nice: confronted with a co-operative player, it should reciprocate. It should also be provocable: faced with an uncalled defection, it should respond. It should be forgiving: after responding to a defection, it should go back to co-operation. And it should be easy to understand: other players should be able to anticipate the consequences of their actions. Axelrod presents a surprising example of the usefulness of a variant of this strategy: First World War trench warfare. Here is a summary of his account.

The historical situation in the quiet sectors along the Western Front was a (repeated) prisoner's dilemma. At any time, the choices of two small units facing each other are to shoot to kill or deliberately to shoot to avoid causing damage. For both sides, weakening the enemy is important because it promotes survival. Therefore, in the short run it is better to do damage now, whether the enemy is shooting back or not. What made trench warfare so different from most other combat was that the same small units faced each other in immobile sectors for extended periods of time. This changed the game from a one-move prisoner's dilemma in which defection is the dominant choice, to an iterated prisoner's dilemma in which conditional strategies are possible. The result accorded with the theory's predictions: with sustained interaction, the stable outcome could be *mutual co-operation* based upon *reciprocity* [emphasis added]. In particular, both sides followed strategies that would not be the first to defect, but that would be provoked if the other defected. As the lines stabilized, non-aggression between the troops emerged spontaneously in many places along the front. The earliest instances may have been associated with meals served at the same times on both sides of no-man's land. An eyewitness noted that: 'In one section the hour of 8 to 9 a.m. was regarded as consecrated to private business, and certain places indicated by a flag were regarded as out of bounds by the snipers on both sides.' In the summer of 1915 [a soldier noted that] 'It would be child's play to shell the road behind the enemy's trenches, crowded as it must be with ration wagons and water carts, into a bloodstained wilderness but on the whole there is silence. After all, if you prevent your enemy from drawing his rations, his remedy is simple: he will prevent you from drawing yours.' The strategies were provocable. During the periods of mutual restraint, the enemy soldiers took pains to show each other they could indeed retaliate if necessary. For example, German snipers showed their prowess to the British by aiming at spots on the walls of cottages and firing until they had cut a hole.

Source: Extracted from Robert Axelrod (1984) *The Evolution of Co-operation*. © The Financial Times Limited, 18 October 1999. Reprinted with permission.

4.7 Summary

The fewness of the firms is the chief defining characteristic of oligopoly. The central problem of oligopoly focuses on the recognition of the firms' interdependence when they are few in number. Interdependence implies each firm is aware its actions affect the actions of its rivals. There are as many different models of oligopoly as there are assumptions about how firms behave when faced with this situation of inter-dependence. It is often suggested that the solution to the oligopoly problem is one of two extremes: either pure independent action, or pure collusion where all scope for independent action is extinguished. In reality both independent action and collusion are matters of degree, and the great majority of cases fall somewhere between these two extremes. However, Chapters 4 and 5 are structured in accordance with this traditional dichotomy. Chapter 4 has dealt mainly with models of independent action; in Chapter 5, the emphasis shifts towards collusion.

The Cournot duopoly model is the earliest theory of output determination in oligopoly. Cournot assumes the firms maximize their own profit subject to the constraint that the other firm's output is fixed at its current level; or equivalently, both firms select their outputs so as to maximize profit subject to a zero conjectural variation assumption. Zero conjectural variation is equivalent to the behavioural assumption that leads to what is known in game theory terminology as a Nash equilibrium. Under this assumption, the Cournot duopolists achieve a market equilibrium that lies somewhere between the polar cases of monopoly and perfect competition. Other possible solutions to the model of output determination under duopoly include Chamberlin's model of joint profit maximization; Stackelberg's leader–follower model; and Stackelberg disequilibrium, in which both firms simultaneously behave aggressively, leading to overproduction and a price war.

In the Bertrand and Edgeworth models of price determination under duopoly, there is a zero conjectural variation assumption with respect to price. Both firms maximize their own profit subject to the constraint that the other firm's price is fixed at its current level. In Bertrand's model, the firms' output levels are unconstrained. Edgeworth considers the implications of a production capacity constraint. These models recognize the possibility that oligopolistic markets may deliver outcomes such as intense price competition (Bertrand) or perpetual instability with no determinate market equilibrium (Edgeworth). In contrast, the kinked demand curve model suggests price under oligopoly may become 'sticky'; while models of price leadership suggest that one way for oligopolists to deal with their situation of interdependence is to delegate responsibility for price-setting to a single dominant firm or price leader.

Game theory is an approach to decision making in which two or more decision makers or players face choices between a number of possible courses of action or actions at any stage of the game. The property of interdependence is the key defining characteristic of a game. Although game theory has many applications throughout the social and physical sciences, it is the treatment of interdependence that makes game theory relevant to an understanding of decision making in oligopoly. Game theory shows how situations can arise in which players take decisions that appear rational from an individual perspective, but lead to outcomes that appear suboptimal when assessed according to criteria reflecting the players' collective interest. However, games do not always generate unique solutions, since strategic decisions and outcomes are dependent on sociological and psychological as well as economic behavioural patterns and conventions. For this reason, game theory is often better at explaining observed patterns of behaviour after the event than it is at predicting behaviour in advance.

It should be apparent from Chapter 4 that oligopoly can generate many possible outcomes. It seems that almost anything can happen in oligopoly, from outright collusion to bitter price wars. As a result some economists (for example, Rothschild, 1947) have suggested that oligopoly theory is indeterminate. The consensus, however, is still largely in favour of developing better theory and better models.

But it would be misleading to conclude that we cannot develop theories which predict oligopolistic conduct and performance with tolerable precision. A more constructive interpretation is this: to make workable predictions we need a theory much richer than the received theories of pure competition and pure monopoly, including variables irrelevant to those polar cases. In our quest for a realistic oligopoly theory we must acquire Professor Mason's 'ticket of admission to institutional economics', at the same time retaining the more sharply honed tools with which economic theorists have traditionally worked.

(Scherer, 1980, p. 152)

Nevertheless, it is still the case that we have no clear and unambiguous solution to the central issue of interdependence. Firms and individuals may react in many different ways, and this is reflected in the large number of models examined in this chapter. It is the presence of the rival firms in oligopoly that creates uncertainty, which in turn makes oligopoly theory so difficult and challenging.

Discussion questions

1. Explain the relevance of the concepts of interdependence, conjectural variation, independent action and collusion to our understanding of oligopoly.

2. What types of conduct are associated with Machlup's notion of uncoordinated oligopoly?

3. Does Cournot's original duopoly model have any relevance to our understanding of price and output determination under oligopoly?

4. Explain the role played by the assumption of zero conjectural variation in the derivation of the Cournot–Nash equilibrium.

5. Compare and contrast the Cournot, Chamberlin, Stackelberg and Edgeworth models of price and output determination for a duopoly.

6. Suggest examples from the real world that approximate to each of the classical theories of oligopoly.

7. With reference to each of the examples quoted in Case study 4.1, identify product or cost characteristics that may have contributed to the tendency for competition to be manifested in the form of a price war.

8. Quote real world examples of oligopolistic firms that have benefited from a first-mover advantage.

9. With reference to Sweezy's model of the kinked demand curve, explain the reasons why we might expect price to be unresponsive to small variations in cost in the case of oligopoly. What are the main limitations of the kinked demand curve model?

10. Explain the distinction between dominant and barometric price leadership. How are price leaders chosen?

11. Explain the relationship between Cournot's solution to the problem of output determination in duopoly, and the game theory concept of the Nash equilibrium.

12. Explain what is meant by the term mixed strategy. Under what circumstances is it advisable for the players in a non-cooperative game to adopt mixed strategies?

13. In repeated games, it is often assumed that rivals are more likely to cooperate with one another than to compete. Under what conditions might competition be likely to break out in a repeated game?

14. With reference to Case study 4.2, which theoretical model of oligopoly best explains the behaviour of the leading firms in the UK's market for digital television services?

15. With reference to Case study 4.3, outline the contribution of the model of the prisoner's dilemma to our understanding of strategic behaviour.

Further reading

Asch, P. and Seneca, J. (1976) Is collusion profitable? *Review of Economics and Statisitics*, 58, 1–10.

Hall, R.L. and Hitch, C.J. (1939) Price theory and business behaviour, *Oxford Economic Papers*, 2, 12–45.

Haskel, J. and Scaramozzino, P. (1997) Do other firms matter in oligopolies? *Journal of Industrial Economics*, 45, 27–45.

Kashyap, A. (1995) Sticky prices: new evidence from retail catalogues, *Quarterly Journal of Economics*, 110, 245–74.

Machlup, F. (1952a) *The Economics of Sellers' Competition*. Baltimore, MD: Johns Hopkins University Press.

Robinson, J. (1969) *The Economics of Imperfect Competition*, 2nd edn. London: Macmillan.

Roth, A.E. (1991) Game theory as a part of empirical economics, *Economic Journal*, 101, 107–14.

Stigler, G.J. (1978) The literature of economics: the case of the kinked oligopoly demand curve, *Economic Inquiry*, 16, 185–204. Reprinted as Reading 10 in Wagner, L. (ed.) *Readings in Applied Microeconomics*. Oxford: Oxford University Press (1981).

Oligopoly: collusive models

Learning objectives

This chapter covers the following topics:

- the tendency for firms to collude in oligopoly
- degrees and forms of collusion
- collusive institutions
- economic models of collusion and cartel behaviour
- factors conducive to cartel formation
- influences on cartel stability

Key terms

Buyer concentration
Cartel
Degrees of collusion
Explicit collusion
Forms of collusion
Joint venture

Seller concentration
Semi-collusion
State-sponsored collusion
Tacit collusion
Trade association

5.1   Introduction

Collusion between firms attracts much attention from the public, the press and government. One manifestation of collusion is price-fixing, which is easily recognized as having adverse consequences for consumer welfare.

> [P]eople of the same trade seldom meet together, even for merriment and diversion, but the conversation ends in a conspiracy against the public, or in some contrivance to raise prices.
>
> *(Smith, 1776, p. 128)*

However, price-fixing in order to boost profitability is not the only reason for firms to collude. For a group of oligopolists, collusion may represent an obvious way of dealing with the uncertainties that would otherwise arise due to their situation of interdependence. Collusion may be simply a means of easing competitive pressure and creating a manageable operating environment through unified action, rather than necessarily a strategy for maximizing joint profits. A central theme of this chapter is that many collusive agreements are highly unstable. History is littered with examples of cartels that have eventually broken down, often because individual members have succumbed to the temptation to act selfishly in pursuit of private interests, rather than adhere to arrangements aimed at furthering the collective interest of group members.

The chapter begins in Section 5.2 with a discussion of the principal forms that collusion may take. In Section 5.3 we focus on the institutions that help to shape and determine collusion. To assume that all collusion is organized through the medium of cartels is an oversimplification. Alternative vehicles, including trade associations, joint ventures and state-sponsored collusion, are also considered. Section 5.4 examines economic models of cartel behaviour. Some of these models are based on assumptions of joint profit maximization. Others focus on issues arising when cartel members bargain over the allocation of production quotas or the distribution of joint cartel profits. In Section 5.5 we consider factors other than joint profit maximization that may motivate firms to explore avenues for cooperation. Section 5.6 discusses aspects of market structure that tend to be conducive to collusion and the formation of cartels. Finally, Section 5.7 examines factors that affect cartel stability or instability. As well as standard market structure variables like seller concentration, the degree of product differentiation and entry conditions, these include the effectiveness of mechanisms for monitoring compliance and punishing non-compliance on the part of cartel members. We also consider sociological and psychological factors that are often ignored in the economics literature, including the quality of leadership and the degree of social cohesion among cartel members.

5.2 Collusive action and collusive forms

In the idealized free market, all firms are assumed to act independently in their desire to seek the highest economic return. However, as we saw in Chapter 4, in oligopolies characterized by interdependence and uncertainty, firms may seek to avoid taking independent action. The uncertainties and risks associated with independent action provide a spur for the firms to participate in some form of collusive arrangement.

Unlimited competition may be a fine thing from the point of view of the political philosopher speculating about the welfare of people, but surely it is a nuisance from the point of view of most businessmen. There may be a few hardy individualists among them who enjoy vigorous competition as long as they are stronger than their opponents, can take pride in their success, and make enough money for comfort. But those that are losing ground and those that are losing money, or fear that they may lose, and all those who prefer an easy life to one of strain and strife – the majority, I dare say – regard unrestrained competition as an uncivilized way of doing business, unnecessarily costly of nervous energy and money, and disruptive of friendly relations with their fellow men.

(Machlup, 1952a, p. 434)

Collusion is best seen as a way of easing competitive pressure through unified action, rather than purely as a strategy to maximize joint profits. It has been claimed that the collusive solution to the oligopoly problem is the often most obvious solution.

What, then, do oligopolists really do . . . Undoubtedly they do many things, but the specific suggestion offered here is that they frequently 'collude', 'conspire', or, otherwise 'agree' on coordinated policies.

(Asch, 1969, p. 5)

Asch suggests three reasons for believing that collusion in oligopoly is widespread. First, it is plausible. Collusion obviates the uncertainties of independent action, and in some weak forms it need not be illegal, or it need not be easily detected. Second, it is realistic. Evidence shows that throughout the world, competition authorities are never short of work in investigating the sharper end of collusive practices. It therefore seems probable that the weaker forms of collusion are widespread. Third, collusion is simple. Cooperation reduces the complexities of interdependence: firms no longer need to speculate about the likely reactions of rivals.

Collusion is not a uniform mode of behaviour. Machlup (1952a) draws an important distinction between **degrees of collusion** and **forms of collusion**. The first degree of collusion, the weakest, is the expectation that rivals will not act independently unless the level of business activity warrants such action. We can move up several degrees to identify states where firms, even those suffering from slack business, will refrain from independent action. In the strongest degree of collusion, each firm has complete trust that its rivals will stick to all agreements and rules of conduct, so long as the firm itself abides by such codes.

There is not necessarily any close correlation between the form of collusion and the degree of collusion. Collusion of a high degree may be based on a highly informal understanding. Conversely, highly structured forms of collusion may be developed to determine a relatively low degree of collusion. Machlup separates the forms of collusion into two: those that rely on no formal agreement or communication, and those based on explicit agreements.

Six forms of informal collusion are identified, as follows:

1. Industry tradition: the belief, based on past observation of consistent behaviour, that rivals will act or react in a predictable way.

2. Informal expressions of opinion within the industry regarding trade practices.

3. Sales representatives from different firms exchange information about strategic decisions taken by their firms.

4. Trade association announcements regarding proposed courses of action to be taken by firms.

5. Similar announcements made by individual firms.

6. The active participation of firms in trade association activities.

In all of these cases, there is an expectation that firms will adhere to the courses of action identified by the information that is in circulation. One could argue that the six forms are differentiated by the degree of expectation as to likely conduct, the first form reflecting greater uncertainty than the second, the second reflecting greater uncertainty than the third, and so on; although to some extent this type of interpretation blurs Machlup's original distinction between forms and degrees of collusion.

Tacit collusion is a term often used to describe a collusive outcome that requires no formal agreement, and where there is no direct communication between firms. NERA (2003, p. 42) note that the European Court outlined three conditions which can sustain tacit coordination. First, for tacit collusion to operate there must be transparency, so that all firms are aware of each other's behaviour. Second, there must be an incentive for firms to stick to a common policy. In other words, any firm that breaks the agreement is made worse off and not better off. Third, potential entry and buyer reactions should not be seen by firms as potentially destabilizing threats.

Tacit collusion may develop through personal contacts, a group ethos, or live-and-let-live attitudes. Personal and social contacts among competitors lessen rivalrous attitudes: perhaps one does not undercut or poach customers from people with whom one socializes. Social groupings, whether by social class, ethnic origin or even religion, may help stabilize an otherwise potentially unstable collusive arrangement. This feeling of belonging can be strengthened by the existence of trade associations, trade journals, conferences and social activities.

> [C]lose communication and contact among the members of [the US steel] industry had created such mutual 'respect and affectionate regard' that they regarded themselves as honor-bound to protect one another, and that each felt that this moral obligation was 'more binding on him than any written or verbal contract'.
>
> *(Machlup, 1952b, p. 87)*

Forms of collusion based on explicit agreements include verbal and written agreements. A widely quoted example of the former is the so-called Gary Dinners, hosted by Judge Gary, president of US Steel, between 1907 and 1911. Leaders of the steel industry met socially, but also used the opportunity to negotiate verbal agreements concerning pricing and production strategies. The colluders believed that they were operating within the law, as long as no formal agreement existed. Written agreements can be regarded as higher forms of collusion. These may be characterized as formal contracts, stipulating rights and obligations, sanctions, fines, deposition of collateral, and so on. Case study 5.1 provides a recent example of a price fixing cartel.

Case study 5.1

EU bursts into price-fixing cartel's cosy club

Mario Monti, European Competition Commissioner, yesterday fined eight Austrian banks a total €124.3m ($117.5m) for 'one of the most shocking' price-fixing conspiracies ever uncovered by the Brussels authorities. The penalty punishes some members of the 'Lombard Club' – a long-standing group of leading Austrian financial institutions that met in the Bristol Hotel, Vienna – for fixing interest rates for loans and savings and other fees between 1995 and 1998. Erste Bank, the country's second-largest bank, received the biggest fine – €37.7m. Bank Austria, a unit of Germany's HVB group, will have to pay €30.4m, like its rival RZB. Five other banks – BAWAG, PSK, ÖVAG, NÖ Hypo and RLB – received smaller fines.

The Lombard Club cartel may be one of the most shocking offences ever punished by the Brussels trust-busters, but it was also one of the least secret – and possibly one of the least successful. The Commission's five-year investigation unearthed evidence of a complex set of price-fixing committees, which covered the whole of Austria and most banking products in breach of EU antitrust laws.

Between 1994 and 1998, more than 300 meetings of such committees took place in Vienna alone, the Commission said. But the existence of a bankers' gentlemen's club that met regularly to discuss business matters was never a mystery. Unlike most other cartels – which are agreed in cloak-and-dagger meetings in secret hideaways – this one took place before cigars and Sachertorte in the smart Viennese hotel. The Lombard Club was initiated in the aftermath of the second world war by the Nationalbank, the Austrian central bank, to prevent cut-throat competition between the commercial banks and steer credit into those sectors favoured by the state planners.

Every first Wednesday of each month – apart from August – bank CEOs met for lunch in the plush Marie Therese Room of the central Vienna hotel to talk about monetary and financial topics and agree on common interest rates and fees. The meetings went on even after Austria joined the EU in 1995, but neither the banking nor the political establishment seemed to notice that these arrangements violated EU law.

Mr Monti made a veiled reference to this yesterday when he warned: 'Banks should be in no doubt that they are the subject to EU competition rules just like any other sector.' The meetings stopped only in 1998 when, alerted by press reports and a series of complaints including one by the leader of the rightwing Freedom party Jörg Haider, the Brussels investigators raided the offices of some of the Lombard Club members.

Mr Haider's complaint was written by his lawyer Dieter Böhmdorfer, now justice minister. Mr Haider has demanded compensation for bank customers who had been hurt by the cartel. He estimated the damage at €7bn, which is much higher than most other estimates. According to the banks, which are set to appeal against the Commission's decision, Mr Monti has been unduly harsh on a deal that was well-known and had only a limited affect on consumers and businesses. Erste Bank said the decision was 'unacceptable' and the fines 'disproportionate' as the Commission had failed to take into account the fierce competition among Austrian banks in the late 1990s.

The banks say that, as competition heated up during the period, the Lombard Club agreements became increasingly irrelevant. Bankers broke their promises the second they walked out of the room. In their view, this is proven by the fact that, by the late 1990s, Austria had one of the smallest interest rate spreads and lowest fee structures among any European country, a third lower than the EU average. This also made Austrian retail banks far less profitable than institutions in Italy, Spain or other countries, they say. The Commission disagrees. It says the banks should be punished because they acted in such an open, anti-competitive way for so long. The Brussels investigators said that the cartel was comprehensive, well-structured and covered the entire country – 'down to the smallest village' in the words of one participant. The Commission dropped a parallel investigation into the efforts by some Austrian banks to fix foreign exchange fees. However, Mr Monti said yesterday's decision and the size of the fine – the sixth-largest ever levied – were proof of Brussels' renewed determination to crack down on cartels.

Source: EU bursts into price-fixing cartel's cosy club, *Financial Times*, 12 June 2002.
© The Financial Times Limited. Reprinted with permission.

Machlup's highest form of collusion operates within the sphere of governmental influence and guidance. Recognized (or tolerated) national and international cartels fall within this category. Although this form of collusion may appear highly formalized, this is no guarantee of a successful outcome. Inherent conflicts of interest between industry members may more than outweigh the benefits of a sophisticated and officially sanctioned organizational structure.

5.3 Collusive institutions

In Section 5.3, we examine the various institutions that have been set up to promote and organize cooperation between producers. Our main emphasis will be on **trade associations** and **cartels**, since these types of institution occur most frequently in oligopolistic markets. However, several other institutional forms are also considered, including **joint ventures**, **semi-collusion** and **state-sponsored collusion**.

What are the differences, if any, between trade associations and cartels? Both can be regarded as a group of independent firms pursuing a joint course of action. In a practical sense, the difference often seems to rest on legal interpretation. Trade associations, when seen as cooperative ventures that foster competition (for example by circulating information), or at least as organizations that do not impede competition, are usually tolerated by legal authorities. 'Unless trade associations promote competition and except as they do, there is little justification for their existence' (Dolan, 1977, p. 273). The implication is that if trade associations abstain from anticompetitive practices, they somehow undergo a metamorphosis to become champions of competition. In reality, the formation of a trade association is often motivated by anticompetitive objectives, and such organizations may subsequently find it difficult to change their ethos.

> Many entrepreneurs, having grown up in this tradition of cooperation, will find it difficult to adjust themselves to different conditions. It may take more than the formal determination of agreements by the Restrictive Practices Court to ensure that they act competitively.
>
> *(Cuthbert and Black, 1959, p. 52)*

A cartel is a form of organization adopted by firms in an oligopoly in an attempt to achieve a collusive outcome. Almost by definition, cartels foster collusion, while trade associations may or may not pursue similar objectives. The dividing line is fine and easily blurred. Liefmann (1932) sees cartels as organizations that seek to enhance the monopoly power of a group of producers through combined action. To achieve this aim, most firms in the industry must be included. This is another distinguishing feature of cartels. Trade or professional associations that attempt to improve the economic situation of their members do not necessarily require monopoly power in order to achieve their aims.

Trade associations

Although it is difficult to specify the precise functions of **trade associations**, it is possible to provide a general description of their role.

> Trade associations can be enormously helpful to their memberships. They can expand and upgrade education and consumer information programs, launch new research and development programs, encourage ethical business practices and communicate the viewpoint of business in the political forum.
>
> *(Clanton, 1977, p. 307)*

One of the chief functions of trade associations is to provide members with industry data on sales, productive capacity, employment, creditworthiness of customers, quality of products and innovation. They also promote activities intended to reduce inefficiency and promote better relations with customers, trade unions and government. To achieve this goal they publish trade journals, stimulate cooperative research programmes, instigate market research surveys, define trade terms and recruit lobbyists.

The dividing line between legitimate and collusive action is open to interpretation. For example, moves to standardize output could be interpreted either as a legitimate policy to improve product quality, or an illegitimate vehicle for price-fixing by reducing the ability of firms to price differentially. The popularity of price reporting systems or open price associations, through which members inform each other, as well as outsiders, of current and future product prices, reached a peak in the US in the early years of the twentieth century. Many schemes were developed by the lawyer Arthur Jerome Eddy, and became known as Eddy Plans. Associations which undertook such plans became known as open price associations, defined as follows:

> an organization which provides a medium for the exchange of business information among members of a given industry whereby they may arrive at an intimate acquaintance with competitive conditions as they exist among themselves and in the whole industry.

(Nelson, 1922, p. 9)

Nelson (1922) sees these organizations as distinct from other trade associations, characterized by fairly loose structures and more general aims. Nelson quotes the case of the American Hardwood Manufacturers' Association, which was quite open in its price deliberations, inviting customers, the press and any other interested parties to its meetings. Price reporting schemes or open price associations might be justified on the grounds that they promote fair competition: information is an essential lubricant for competitive markets. But on the other hand, a price-reporting agreement could simply provide a form of cover for price-fixing.

If a price reporting scheme is intended to promote competition, it should be neither doctored, nor prevented from being disclosed to all parties including buyers (Wilcox, 1960). Comments or suggestions as to likely future pricing policy should not accompany such reports, which should be neutral and informative. In practice, it is doubtful whether trade associations can always divorce themselves from self-interest in this manner. Mund and Wolf (1971) suggest agreements can be tolerated if they are limited to closed transactions. Reported prices should be actual prices. To report quoted prices could increase pressure from the more dominant or militant members to standardize all prices. If waiting periods are stipulated (so each member undertakes to maintain the price for a given period) open price agreements are tantamount to price-fixing (Machlup, 1952b). A waiting period allows firms to set a price, confident in the knowledge that rivals will not immediately reduce their prices.

To conclude the discussion of price reporting schemes, we refer to the Danish ready-mix concrete industry in the early 1990s. The Danish Competition Council decided to gather and publish market prices for three Danish regional markets. It believed the provision of price information would provide greater transparency and enhance competition. However, Albaek *et al.* (1997) find as a consequence of the scheme, average prices rose by some 15–20 per cent in one year. The scheme appears to have improved the scope for tacit collusion. The relevant trade association would have been unable to provide a price reporting scheme, as there was insufficient trust amongst the members. Without costly monitoring of members' price reports, the system would not have been credible.

To determine whether a trade association is acting competitively or not, Herold (1977) and Dolan (1977) identify seven areas that might be examined:

1. Any agreement amongst trade association members to fix prices or allow courses of action resulting in stable prices is an obvious restraint of trade.

2. The exclusivity of membership can serve as an indicator of specific economic advantage to existing members. An association which bars or impedes membership to some firms is likely to be acting anticompetitively.

3. The provision of statistical data should not be used as a vehicle for uniformity of action.

4. A trade association's wish to standardize output by various certification procedures might be aimed at maintaining minimum standards of quality, but could also be used to ensure symmetry of decision making or a boycott of uncertified producers.

5. Lobbying activity is not in itself anticompetitive; however, lobbying can be directed towards the pursuit of anticompetitive goals.

6. The involvement of a trade association in negotiations with trades unions could involve price-fixing in the labour market.

7. Any agreement over joint research could be instrumental in weakening the competitive pressures for innovation, rather than being a spur to the development of new products and ideas.

The impact of trade associations on competition is uncertain. If a trade association does not itself help foster collusion, it might provide a convenient stepping-stone towards full-blown collusion, perhaps by gathering, processing and disseminating the information that subsequently forms the basis of an agreement.

> [T]he process of formation is easier if there have been already opportunities for communication between the parties which combine. Such opportunities are furnished by Chambers of Commerce, by associations of masters with reference to the demands of labour, by Institutes and Congresses, or by temporary associations such as are formed to make representations to the Legislature regarding the claims of an industry.
>
> *(MacGregor, 1906, p. 123)*

> In both the electrical equipment and bleacher industries, and in the earlier cases as well, conspiratorial meetings were held at, or immediately after, the regular trade association meetings.
>
> *(Erickson, 1969, p. 87)*

The vast majority of price and other cartel agreements in the UK, prior to their abandonment or modification in the late 1950s, operated through trade associations.

> Participating in industry associations could also be regarded as a facilitating practice especially where associations are used to promote or disguise the exchange of sensitive information, adoption of anticompetitive standards, or changes in government regulations which would facilitate coordinated interaction.
>
> *(OECD, 1999, p. 8)*

However, any advantages stemming from the circulation of information on prices may be undermined by the use of price data to reinforce and police collusive agreements. It is difficult to generalize, and a case-by-case approach is required to establish the direction taken by any particular trade association.

Cartels

The term **cartel** derives from the German word *Kartelle* meaning a producers' association. Liefmann (1932) claims that the term was coined to describe phenomena first observed in Germany in the late nineteenth century. The word *Kartelle* is derived from the Latin *charta*, which means a paper or letter. The word was often used in a military context, to refer to a written agreement for an exchange of prisoners. It is interesting to note that the reference is to a temporary truce, and not a permanent peace. Perhaps the simplest and most concise definition is suggested by Liefmann (1932), who sees cartels as associations with monopolistic aims. The notion of monopolistic intent has caused much controversy. The term monopoly has emotional connotations which may blur a reasonable description of collective action. Some see the monopolistic intent of cartels as simply a corollary of any restrictions imposed upon unfettered competition (Piotrowski, 1932).

Cartels are associations of independent firms in the same industry that exist in order to impose some form of restraint upon competition. To many observers, cartels are associated with actions taken by small groups of firms determined to exploit their market power to the full. Benton (1943, p. 1) sees the term surrounded 'with a strange aroma suggesting some new social disease'. For the *New York Times*, 'The word cartel has become the label for something "bad". As an emotional symbol, it calls for the response of a "secret" or "un-American" contact with foreigners.' (*New York Times*, September 14 1943).

However, there is evidence suggesting that firms join cartels mainly for reasons of self-protection, rather than to exploit their customers (Hunter, 1954). Agreements tend, on the whole, to impede entry or the development of new products that might threaten the profitability or survival of incumbent firms. Price-fixing seems only to be of secondary importance, usually as a means to support the less efficient members. Profits are not spectacularly higher than one would suppose. Asch and Seneca (1976) argue that firms may aim at reasonable profits, rather than maximum joint profits. Fog (1956) draws a similar conclusion:

> [I]t seems that the main purpose of many cartels is to obtain security rather than maximum profit *per se*. Of course, 'security' requires a good profit; but not necessarily maximum profit. From my own interviews I got the definite impression that the participants did not meet at the negotiations with any ideas about which cartel price would give the best profit. But each of them had an idea about a certain minimum price that nobody should be allowed to cut.
>
> *(Fog, 1956, p. 22)*

Hexner (1946) and Brems (1951) both provide more detailed definitions of a cartel:

a voluntary, potentially impermanent, business relationship among a number of independent, private entrepreneurs, which through coordinated marketing significantly affects the market commodity or service.

(Hexner, 1946, p. 24)

a voluntary, written or oral agreement among financially and personally independent, private, entrepreneurial sellers or buyers fixing or influencing the values of their parameters of action, or allocating territories, products or quotas, for a future period of time.

(Brems, 1951, p. 52)

Hexner identifies four elements that define a cartel. First, the *plurality of independent entrepreneurs* ensures that cartels are a collective marketing control, rather than one exercised by a single entrepreneur. The firms must be effectively independent, rather than merely legally independent. If firms are already close, cartelization may not generate anything new. Similarly, different divisions and subsidiaries within one parent company cannot be regarded as independent. Second, the cartel must be voluntary. There is a distinction between free and compulsory cartels. Hexner cites Nazi Germany in the 1930s, when free cartels were transformed into compulsory agreements, designed to ensure that signatories acted in accordance with specific social and macroeconomic objectives, directed and controlled by government. Third, a cartel must be of at least potential impermanence. Much of the discussion in this chapter reflects the temporary nature of cartels. Finally, the cartel should serve the interests (whether real or imagined) of its members.

In Brems' formulation, *personal independence* is included to ensure that interlocking directorships are excluded from cartel definitions. *Private* ensures that cartels are limited to non-governmental organizations. *Entrepreneurial sellers* excludes trade unions. Finally, 'sellers *or* buyers' eliminates vertical integration from the definition.

It is interesting to note that Piotrowski's (1932) key concept of restriction of competition does not appear in many definitions, especially the ones quoted above. The reason is that competition may survive within cartels, albeit in a modified form. Competition in the market may be replaced by competition around the negotiating table, as part of the bargaining process.

But even in a well established cartel the members may retain a competitive and even hostile attitude towards one another and all the time be on their guard – first of all the cartel may be dissolved again and be replaced by competition. This fact definitely limits the potentialities of a cartel. In the extreme case there may still be a high degree of competition even within a well organized cartel . . . [It] is possible under the guise of a well-established cartel to have competition so strong that it may be termed price warfare.

(Fog, 1956, p. 23)

Some observers have tried to classify types of cartel. OECD (1965) identify seven types: price cartel, quota cartel, allocation cartel, standardization agreement, specialization agreement, costing agreement and rebate agreement. Wilcox (1960, p. 73) identifies four main categories according to the methods employed: cartels that control the conditions surrounding a sale; cartels that control costs, prices and profit margins; cartels that allocate territories or customers; and cartels that award members fixed shares in the industry's total productive capacity. Many cartels fall under more than one of these headings.

Joint ventures, semi-collusion and state-sponsored collusion

A **joint venture** is an association between two or more otherwise competing firms. Joint ventures might take the form of a consortium or a syndicate, although the latter is generally limited to the fields of banking and insurance. Consortia are usually estab-lished when firms undertake speculative activities, for which the risk is sufficiently high to discourage individual involvement. In so far as joint ventures prevent or distort competition by coalescing the interests of several firms, they are similar to cartels. It could be argued, however, that joint ventures stimulate innovation, by enabling projects to proceed that would not otherwise be feasible. Alternatively, joint ventures may enable a group of new firms to band together and overcome entry barriers.

Joint ventures have often been sponsored by governments and international bodies. '[European] Community action must . . . create an environment or conditions likely to favour the development of cooperation between undertakings' (European Com-mission, 1985, p. 34). In a more recent report, however, the European Commission (1997a) is concerned that this type of cooperation could inhibit competition. It identifies three main reasons why firms are keen to form joint ventures: to com-bine their resources in such a way as to increase efficiency; to enter a new market; and to develop joint research and development programmes. The report finds that only the latter motive provides 'convincing efficiency justifications for cooperation' (European Commission 1997a, p. 175).

Not all joint ventures result in cooperation. Partnerships such as joint ventures and strategic alliances may encounter difficulties when managers behave non-cooperatively so as to advance the private interests of their own firms (Minehart and Neeman, 1999). The issue is how best to design contracts that encourage managers to maximize joint (partnership) profits.

Semi-collusion occurs in cases where it is difficult to formulate specific agreements covering all aspects of the firms' behaviour. For example, agreements covering research and development, advertising and capital investment strategies may not be possible, because it is too difficult to monitor compliance. Accordingly, it has been suggested that firms may opt to collude in some activities and compete in others. Matsui (1989) argues that if collusion takes place in the product market, but there is competition in other areas of activity, firms may be worse off and consumers better off. In a study of Japanese cartels in the 1960s, Matsui argues that firms accumulated excess capacity in the belief that cartel quotas would be based on capacity. The combination of cartelization and excess capacity led to increased output and reduced profits. Similar conclusions are reached by Steen and Sørgard (1999) regarding semi-collusion in the Norwegian cement industry. However, Brod and Shivakumar

(1999) show that where the non-production (competitive) activity is research and development, the welfare effects are indeterminate: spillovers can make producers and consumers either better off or worse off.

The discussion of cartels has concentrated on private, voluntary organizations that are free of government control or intervention. **State-sponsored collusion** is a further variation. Governments may either meet the demands of a group of producers, or they may impose cartelization on reluctant firms. The justification might be to promote rationalization, as in Britain and Germany in the 1930s, or to encourage 'orderly marketing': the objective behind the UK's Agricultural Marketing Acts of 1931 and 1933.

5.4 Economic models of price and output determination for a cartel

Several models of price and output determination for a cartel are considered in Section 5.4. We begin by considering some models of joint profit maximization. We then examine some alternative approaches that focus mainly on issues that arise during bargaining between cartel member firms.

Joint profit-maximizing models

First, we consider a model in which all of the firms in an industry are members of a centralized cartel, which has complete control over price and output decisions. It is assumed that each firm produces an identical product. However, the firms' cost functions need not necessarily be identical. Finally, it is assumed that entry is successfully deterred. The maximization of the cartel members' combined profit is essentially a problem of joint profit maximization, with the cartel firms seeking to act collectively as if they were a single monopolist.

Figure 5.1 shows a three-firm model. The cost functions of firms A, B and D are shown in the first three diagrams, reading from left to right. The industry marginal cost function shown in the right-hand-side diagram is obtained by summing the three firms' marginal cost functions horizontally. Joint profit maximization is achieved by

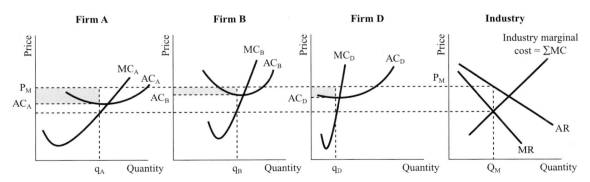

Figure 5.1 Joint profit maximization in a three-firm cartel

choosing the industry output at which marginal revenue derived from the industry average revenue function *equals* the industry's marginal cost. This output level is Q_M, and the corresponding price is P_M. The individual production quotas of firms A, B and D are q_A, q_B and q_D, and by construction $Q_M = q_A + q_B + q_D$. The total cost of producing Q_M is minimized by allocating quotas in such a way that the marginal costs of each firm, when producing its own quota, are the same (Patinkin, 1947). Suppose the quotas were such that the cost to firm D of producing its last unit of output was higher than the cost to firm A of producing its last unit of output. Then it would be profitable to reallocate some of firm D's quota to firm A. This would be so until the marginal costs are brought into equality. It can be seen from Figure 5.1 that the least efficient producer with the steepest marginal cost function, firm D, is assigned a smaller quota than the more efficient producers, firms A and B.

Our second joint profit-maximizing model examines the case where an industry consists of two groups of firms: a group that forms a cartel, and a group of non-cartel firms. The total number of firms is N, and the number of firms that form the cartel is K; therefore there are N – K non-cartel firms. There are assumed to be large numbers of small firms in both groups. In this model, it is assumed that all firms produce an identical product, all firms have identical cost functions, and entry is successfully deterred. Finally, price-taking behaviour on the part of the non-cartel firms is assumed. The model is similar to the dominant firm price leadership model that was introduced in Section 4.5.

The diagram on the right-hand-side of Figure 5.2 shows the non-cartel firms' collective marginal cost function, obtained by summing the non-cartel firms' individual marginal cost functions horizontally. Because the non-cartel firms are price-takers, their collective marginal cost function can be interpreted as their supply function. The middle diagram shows the cartel firms' collective marginal cost function, also obtained by summing their individual marginal cost functions horizontally. The middle diagram also shows the residual demand function for the cartel firms, obtained by subtracting the non-cartel firms' total supply at each price from the industry demand function. The cartel firms maximize their joint profit by choosing the output

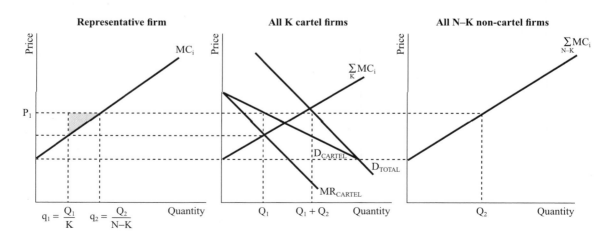

Figure 5.2 Equilibrium with K cartel firms and N – K non-cartel firms

level Q_1, at which the residual marginal revenue *equals* the cartel firms' collective marginal cost. The cartel firms' output decision also determines the industry price, P_1, obtained from the cartel firms' residual demand function at Q_1. Returning to the right-hand-side diagram, the non-cartel firms' total output when the price is P_1 is Q_2. Total industry output is $Q_1 + Q_2$, which by construction *equals* the industry demand when the price is P_1.

Finally, the diagram on the left-hand-side of Figure 5.2 compares the outputs and profits of an individual cartel firm and a non-cartel firm. These can be drawn on the same diagram because it is assumed that both firms have identical cost functions. As shown in the middle diagram, for the cartel firm the joint profit-maximizing price of P_1 exceeds marginal cost. Each individual cartel firm produces $q_1 = Q_1/K$ units of output. Each non-cartel firm is a price-taker, and produces $q_2 = Q_2/(N - K)$ units of output, at which price *equals* marginal cost. This means the non-cartel firm produces more output than the cartel firm. The non-cartel firm also earns a higher profit than the cartel firm. In the diagram on the left-hand-side of Figure 5.2, the difference in profit is represented by the shaded area between P_1 and MC_i over the output range q_1 to q_2.

This comparison between the profits of the cartel and non-cartel firms has important implications for the theory of cartels. In Figure 5.2, the cartel firm deliberately reduces its output in order to raise price and earn a higher profit. However, the non-cartel firm also benefits from the increased price, but without bearing any burden in the form of profit foregone as a result of producing a reduced output. Essentially, there is a free-rider problem. The free-riding non-cartel firms earn higher profits than the cartel firms, thanks entirely to the sacrifices made by the latter.

This situation may have serious implications for the viability or the stability of the cartel. Why should any firm agree to join the cartel if, by doing so, it earns a lower profit than it would earn by remaining outside? Clearly, it is better to let others bear the burden of reducing their outputs, and meanwhile sit back and enjoy the benefit of the increased price. Of course, the difficulty is that if all potential cartel members think in this way, the cartel may never be formed. Moreover, even if the cartel has already been formed, its stability is threatened by the possibility of defection or cheating. In Figure 5.2, each cartel member knows that by increasing its output from q_1 to q_2, it can increase its profit by an amount represented by the shaded area. If the number of cartel members is large and only one firm defects, the effect of this additional ouput on the profits of the remaining loyal cartel members might be quite small. The remaining cartel members may be prepared to tolerate the situation, since the costs of disciplining the recalcitrant firm might exceed the profits that would be recouped. However, the danger is that more than one firm defects, in which case the cartel could quickly disintegrate. If all cartel members simultaneously increase their outputs, the market ends up at the competitive price and output, with all firms earning only a normal profit.

> And this is the first difficulty of forming a cartel. Every firm would prefer to be the outsider, and yet if enough stay outside, the cartel becomes futile: a large group of free riders will find that the streetcar won't run.
>
> *(Stigler, 1966, p. 233)*

D'Aspremont *et al.* (1983) discuss an important qualification to these conclusions concerning the free-rider problem and cartel instability. With reference to the model shown in Figure 5.2, we consider the case in which N, the number of firms, is small rather than large (see also Donsimoni *et al.*, 1986). In this case, any decision by a cartel firm to break the cartel agreement has a non-negligible effect on the profits of both the cartel firms that remain loyal, and the non-cartel firms. In the model shown in Figure 5.2, a decision by one cartel firm to produce q_2 rather than q_1, effectively leaving the cartel, would shift the non-cartel supply function to the right and the cartel residual demand and marginal revenue functions to the left. This would reduce the equilibrium price, and reduce the profits of both the cartel and the non-cartel firms. Before any defection takes place, the profit of a non-cartel firm always exceeds the profit of a cartel firm. However, this does not rule out the possibility that the post-defection profit of the cartel firm that defects is less than its pre-defection profit when it was still part of the cartel.

Accordingly, for a firm considering leaving the cartel or defecting, the relevant comparison is not between the current profits of a cartel firm and a non-cartel firm. Instead, the relevant comparison is between the current profit of a cartel firm and the adjusted (post-defection) profit of a non-cartel firm. There are two conditions for the stability of the cartel. First, there is internal stability if no cartel member can increase its profit by leaving the cartel; and second, there is external stability if no non-cartel firm can increase its profit by joining the cartel. D'Aspremont *et al.* (1983) show that a cartel that is both internally and externally stable can always be achieved if the number of firms is finite. A corollary is that the greater the number of firms in the industry, the smaller the effect of any one firm's actions on price and profits, and the greater the likelihood that any cartel agreement will turn out to be unstable.

Apart from the free-rider problem and cartel instability, Stigler (1966) discusses two other difficulties likely to be encountered in forming a cartel. The first, which also derives from the free-rider problem, is that of potential or actual entry. If entry is not successfully deterred, and outside firms are attracted by the relatively high cartel price, industry output increases and price falls, destroying the cartel. The cartel may have to modify its pricing policy in order to exclude potential entrants; or alternatively, seek some form of accommodation with actual entrants (Patinkin, 1947).

Stigler's remaining difficulty is administrative. How should the output quotas be determined and profits divided? In theory, and as shown in Figure 5.1, the quotas should be determined so as to ensure the marginal costs of all cartel firms are equal. However, this implies that each firm earns a different profit. Low-profit firms might not be willing to accept such an outcome. One solution might be to introduce a system of side-payments to compensate low-profit earners. However, this solution implies complex negotiations, monitoring and sanctions for non-compliance. The administrative costs might outweigh the benefits. Alternatively, quotas could be set at sub-optimal levels (different from those necessary to maximize joint profits) in order to make mutual compliance more likely. For example, quotas might be fixed as a percentage of each firm's capacity, or quotas might be fixed as a percentage of pre-cartel output levels. However, this type of arrangement might also lead to instability. Firms might invest unnecessarily in spare capacity in order to gain a larger quota (Stigler, 1966). Or firms might increase their outputs unnecessarily shortly before the agreement takes effect, with the same objective in mind.

The conclusions of economic theory as to the output policy of cartels have been criticized widely. For example, Bain (1948) criticizes Patinkin's (1947) original recommendation that output quotas should be determined on the basis of minimization of total industry costs, and that the firms in the cartel should accept different quota levels, or even a complete shutdown of plants, in return for an equitable slice of the profits. Patinkin's strategy is based on questionable assumptions that cartels possess workable mechanisms to redistribute revenues among member firms if the agreed distribution of profits differs from the distribution that is implied by the cost-minimizing output quotas. It is also assumed there is sufficient mutual trust to overcome the temptation for firms to act independently. According to Bain, in US industry there was little evidence of profit-sharing, the inevitable outcome of Patinkin's strategy.

Bargaining models

This subsection discusses two alternative theoretical approaches to modelling cartel behaviour, both of which which focus directly on the bargaining process and the divergent interests of cartel members. Fog (1956) develops a model in which the members recognize the need to negotiate a mutually acceptable price. It is assumed that three firms A, B and D, produce a similar or identical product and wish to agree a price. Figure 5.3 shows the relationship between the cartel price and the profits of the three firms. The horizontal axis shows the amount by which the cartel price exceeds the competitive price. The point at which each firm's profit curve intersects the vertical axis represents the firm's profit under competition, if the cartel fails to agree a higher price. As before, the competitive price and output level are determined at the intersection of industry marginal cost function (the horizontal summation of the three firms' individual marginal cost functions) with the industry demand function. And as before, if the firms agree a cartel price above the competitive price,

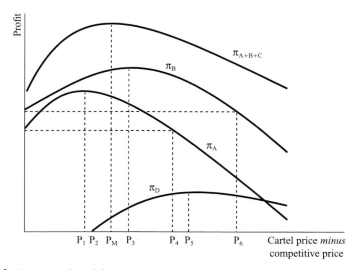

Figure 5.3 Fog's cartel model

their market shares are determined by the cost-minimizing condition that their individual marginal costs should all be the same. The differences between the three profit curves shown in Figure 5.3 are due to differences between the three firms' fixed and variable cost functions.

At the competitive price, firms A and B earn positive profits, but firm D suffers a loss. Firms A, B and D would favour cartel prices P_1, P_3 and P_5, respectively. However, their scope for negotiation is restricted by the following constraints. A will not accept a cartel price above P_4, since this would cause A's profits to fall below those realized under competition. If the cartel price rises above P_4, A would prefer the cartel to break up. For similar reasons, B will not accept a price above P_6. D does not wish to accept a price below P_2, and does not wish to see the cartel break up, because D suffers a loss under competition. The scene is set for negotiations to determine a mutually agreed cartel price. D is in a relatively weak position because of D's need for the cartel to hold together. Perhaps the most likely outcome is that A and B agree a price somewhere between P_1 and P_3, and D simply accepts this solution.

Negotiations become even more complex if the firms formulate objectives with different time horizons, perhaps due to concern that a high agreed price might attract entry or regulatory intervention. Firms that have made large sunk cost investments may be more concerned about such threats. Sunk cost investments are expenditures that cannot be recouped if the firm subsequently leaves the industry. Sunk cost investments, which often involve expenditure on items such as advertising or research and development, are discussed in Chapter 7. Effectively, sunk cost investment lengthens a firm's time horizons.

The bargaining skills of the individual participants are also likely to influence the outcome of the negotiations. Bluff, give-and-take and compromise may all have a part to play. Certainly, the agreed price need not necessarily be the joint profit-maximizing price P_M, at which the sum of the three profit curves π_{A+B+D} attains its maximum value. The firm that dominates or has greatest influence in the negotiations may impose a different outcome. However, a merger between the three firms would presumably result in P_M being attained. Indeed, the merged firm might decide to close down the relatively unprofitable plant D, resulting in shifts in the positions of the profit curves of the other two plants (not shown in Figure 5.3).

Another bargaining approach, developed by Williamson (1975), views collusion primarily as a problem of contracting. Collusive agreements may or may not be lawful, but in either case participants cannot necessarily rely on the courts to enforce agreements. Therefore firms must develop their own armoury to ensure compliance and punish non-compliant behaviour. The ease with which collusion can be established and sustained through contractual arrangements depends on a number of factors.

■ *The ability to specify contractual relations correctly.* It is difficult to formulate a comprehensive statement of obligations and responsibilities. Any such statement requires information on the production costs of each firm, the nature of the product, the permitted levels of expenditure on research and development or innovation, as well as the 'interaction effects between the decision variables within and between firms' (Williamson, 1975, p. 244). Not only is this information expensive to gather, interpret and transform into specific policies for each firm, but it is also necessary to formulate these policies for an unknown future context. If the contract is to be comprehensive, all future contingencies must be anticipated. Joint profit maximization is not easily translated from theoretical abstraction to practical application. '[When] the optimization problem is cast in a multiperiod framework under conditions of uncertainty, abstract analysis breaks down' (Williamson, 1975, p. 240).

■ *The extent to which agreement can be reached over joint gains.* Even if joint profit maximization can be specified contractually, a number of problems immediately arise. Joint profit maximization might require the reduction of some firms' output and the expansion of others. Those firms faced with demands to reduce their output may be reluctant to agree to, or tolerate, any reduction in their market share. These firms may fear that if the agreement were to break down, they would be left in a less powerful position than the position they occupied before the agreement.

■ *Uncertainty.* The agreement is also subject to uncertainty. Firms must agree on how to adapt to changes in the economic environment. This may require costly renegotiation if the firms subsequently discover new opportunities to profit from such changes.

■ *Monitoring.* Individual firms may not be able to detect fellow conspirators' price cuts. In Williamson's terminology, information is impacted, giving rise to opportunistic behaviour. Monitoring is necessary to detect and deter non-compliance with the cartel argreement. Monitoring and policing an agreement is more complex in cases where there are non-price forms of competition.

■ *Penalties.* Successful collusion must eventually rest on the availability of effective sanctions against firms that fail to comply with the terms of the agreement. In the absence of legal protection, the cartel must impose its own penalties through the market. For example, cartel members might retaliate by reducing their own prices to the level set by the non-compliant firm; or by ceasing inter-firm cooperation; or by head-hunting the non-compliant firm's key employees. The success of such penalties depends on the effectiveness of the deterrent as well as the willingness of the loyal firms to impose penalties. The enforcers (the loyal cartel members) also incur costs by introducing sanctions. Indeed, some of these firms might also defect and secretly assist the non-compliant firm, if they feel the benefits of so doing outweigh the costs they incur through enforcement.

Some theorists tend to view oligopolistic collusion as an attempt to achieve a monopolistic outcome, and to treat successful cartels as effective monopolies. In contrast, Williamson's contracting approach clearly underlines the difference between the problems of a monopolist, and those that confront a group of interdependent oligopolists.

> The monopolist . . . enjoys an advantage over oligopolists in adaptational respects since he does not have to write a contract in which future contingencies are identified and appropriate adaptation thereto devised. Rather, he can face the contingencies when they arise; each bridge can be crossed when it is reached, rather than having to decide *ex ante* how to cross

all bridges that one may conceivably face. Put differently, the monopolist can employ an adaptive, sequential decision-making procedure, which greatly economises on bounded rationality demands, without exposing himself to risks of contractual incompleteness which face a group of oligopolists.

(Williamson, 1975, p. 245)

5.5 Other motives for collusion

As we have seen in Section 5.4, the higher profits resulting from the exercise of near-monopoly power can be described by traditional microeconomic models. In Section 5.5, we focus on other motives for collusion in general, and for the formation of cartels specifically. The factors considered in this section are risk management and the enhancement of security, exchange of information, and unsatisfactory financial performance on the part of potential cartel members.

Risk management and the enhancement of security

To some, the reduction of risk is the principal motive for collusion. Some of the earliest writers emphasize this point. '[I]t is the pressure of risk which first arouses producers to the possibilities of another method of organization' (MacGregor, 1906, p. 46). The nature of risk is twofold. First, risk arises from changes in consumer tastes.

> No method of industrial organization will standardize the consumer.
> His demand for even such routine goods as food and clothing changes
> both quantitatively and qualitatively by accidents of time, place and value
> of money. Even a whole industry must face these changes, and provide
> whatever defences may lessen their influence.
>
> *(MacGregor, 1906, p. 51)*

Second, risk results directly from competition between producers. In the absence of any central control, firms may tend to overproduce, driving price below average cost.

> The market may be able to bear the increment of supply caused by himself
> [the firm]; but not an equivalent increment from all his rivals, if they
> retaliate by his own means, or if even they communicate panic to each other.
> This is the road which leads to crises.
>
> *(MacGregor, 1906, p. 52)*

Under this dual pressure, MacGregor feels the natural outcome is an environment of insecurity brought about by firms speculating about rivals' behaviour, prices and outputs. This could generate restrictive practices on the part of firms seeking to retain their market shares. 'There is some ground for saying that the lack of a well coordinated system of control makes industry resemble a mob rather than an army' (MacGregor, 1906, p. 53).

The firm might attempt to escape from these risks by developing market power independently through product differentiation, product innovation or vertical integration (strategies that are explored in subsequent chapters of the book). However, all such strategies are costly and uncertain. Collusion represents an alternative method for reducing risk.

Liefmann (1932) sees the development of collusion as resulting from the increased divergence between what he calls the 'risk of capital' and the 'profit of capital'. Modern mass-production technology raises the risk to entrepreneurs' fixed capital, if they are unable to keep their plants in continuous operation. Entrepreneurs also risk their working capital if they are unable to find sufficient customers for their finished goods. Due to these pressures, entrepreneurs had experienced a steady erosion of profit. This divergence reached a critical point when the capital risks could no longer be offset by profit. As soon as this occurred, common agreements became an accepted solution, and 'competition had killed competition'(Liefmann, 1932, p. 21).

However, neither the pre-war nor the more recent evidence necessarily supports this view. Industries prone to rigorous competition are not always made up of sickly firms, limping their way towards collusive agreements. '[C]laims that competition has cutthroat and destructive propensities, and hence that cartelization [collusion] is warranted, deserve to be taken with several grains of salt' (Scherer and Ross, 1990, p. 305).

Another possible source of risk and uncertainty is a firm's reliance on large orders that are placed infrequently (Scherer and Ross, 1990). Such orders may make tacit collusion more difficult, and force firms to consider explicit collusion. Any price reduction from some tacitly agreed norm involves a cost in the form of lower future profits, owing to retaliation from rival firms. This cost is independent of the size of the order, but the short-term gain depends on the order size. Undercutting is therefore more likely if orders are large and irregular than if they are small and regular. Furthermore, firms that operate with short time horizons are likely to accept the immediate gain from a price reduction, and be unconcerned about future retaliation that may or may not occur. Firms with large overheads or excess capacity may also be tempted to break rank and breach a tacit price agreement. In the US cast-iron pipe, electrical equipment and antibiotics industries, large and infrequent orders led to the formation of 'bidding cartels to restrain industry members' competitive zeal' (Scherer and Ross, 1990, p. 307).

In a study of pricing in the UK electrical equipment industry, Richardson (1966) finds evidence of excess capacity, due to the variability of the government's electricity investment programmes, technical advances, and lack of any coordination on the part of independent manufacturers. The fact that price competition could not resolve this problem, suggests a role for price agreements among producers and with government. Agreed prices would guarantee a return to firms that had installed capacity to meet variable levels of government demand.

The degree of collusion attributable to risk in an industry is difficult to measure. High risk may bring about collusion, but the intended result of such collusion is to reduce risk. Ambiguity as to the direction of causation is inevitable. Measuring risk as the standard deviation of the residuals from a time trend fitted to each firm's time-series profit data, Asch and Seneca (1975) find little evidence of causation in either direction.

A more common thesis is that the firm attaches importance to its relative position when all producers in the industry are ranked in descending order of their market shares. Any move towards the guarantee of position through collusion is attractive. Perfect competition and monopoly, as theoretical ideals, are not concerned with position. A perfectly competitive firm regards itself as too insignificant to be concerned with position; and a monopolist, as sole supplier, does not need to consider its position as a goal or objective. On the other hand, an oligopolist may be acutely aware of its own market share, which in many ways defines its status within the industry. The oligopolist may wish to increase its market share, or at least ensure that its market share is not eroded. Maintaining or improving position is therefore a central objective in the oligopolist's strategic decision making.

The above arguments are closely related to security. So long as the firm in perfect competition maximizes profits, it enjoys as much security as it can attain. The monopolist in the pure form fears no one, and is rewarded with absolute safety. The oligopolist does not have the same luxury. It faces continual challenges to its position, both internally from rivals and externally from potential entrants.

Exchange of information

Many of the factors that motivate collusion are associated with uncertainty. Accordingly, such concerns might be reduced by the provision of useful market information, which may itself be a powerful motive for collusion. O'Brien and Swann (1969) develop a theory of information exchange. All firms require information on which to base their decisions. The importance of information depends on the degree of interdependence, or the extent to which firms are vulnerable to damage by the actions of rivals. Firms are most vulnerable when undertaking investment, which involves long-term and possibly irreversible financial commitments. It may be in the interests of all firms that each firm invests wisely, since miscalculations which create excess capacity may lead to price-cutting or other panic measures, threatening industry stability.

The type of information required, its timing (pre- or post-notification), and the means of communication (oral or written; trade gossip or more formal, detailed memoranda) depend on the required degree of stability. Regular, strict pre-notification agreements, identifying individual parties and their terms of sale, produce greater uniformity and stability than information that is supplied informally or intermittently. Information exchange reduces firms' vulnerability and increases industry cohesion, enabling firms to react more consistently and efficiently when some potentially destabilizing event occurs. Firms become more sensitive to one another and more aware of their positioning in terms of market share. By itself, sharing information may drive firms towards more cooperative forms of behaviour. Firms may no longer wish to threaten industry stability with overtly competitive behaviour. It might be argued that the circulation of information acts as the gel for collusion.

Unsatisfactory performance

Firms are naturally concerned with profitability. Years of poor profitability, perhaps caused by intense competition and frequent price-cutting, may eventually prompt firms to explore the possibility of establishing an accommodation with rivals. This type of pressure forced the American Plumbing Fixtures Manufacturers to develop price-fixing agreements in the 1960s. The price conspiracy was rationalized by the executives of the 15 companies involved as not ' "gouging" the public, just seeking an adequate profit' (*Fortune*, 1969, p. 96). Profits may also be low as a result of depressed demand conditions for a particular product or industry. The frequently quoted price agreements in the American bleachers, electrical equipment and pipe industries all followed periods of decline and poor performance at industry level. 'Certain economic conditions – depressions, recessions, or downward movements in industry demand – provide both a favourable climate and a powerful incentive for conspiracy' (Erickson, 1969, p. 83).

Asch and Seneca (1976) estimate the effect of collusion on the profitability of US manufacturing corporations between 1958 and 1967. They also reverse the causation, to examine the effect of profitability on the level of collusion. They find an inverse relationship between the level of collusion and profitability. This is consistent with the hypothesis that unsatisfactory profits encourage collusion. However, an alternative explanation is that their sample was largely made up of collusion-prone firms. Since the data were based on unsuccessful examples of collusion, poor collusive perform-ance was likely to be discovered. The bleacher manufacturers earned low profits during the Second World War, owing to their inability to obtain steel and other materials. Collusive price and tendering agreements could not resolve the underlying problem of supply shortages. Consequently, these agreements were unstable.

Schmitt and Weder (1998) examine the factors that propelled firms in the Swiss dyestuff industry into cartel agreements after the First World War. Two major factors are identified: first, a reduction in foreign demand owing to increased protection and an increase in foreign productive capacity; and second, the entry of German firms into the world market.

A firm's growth record can also reflect its profitability. Asch and Seneca (1975) suggest that growth and profits can be correlated, and growth might be included among the factors encouraging firms to collude. Firms in a declining industry are perhaps more likely to collude in an attempt to restore profitability to some historical level. Declining industries may also see the breakdown of orderly marketing, or other forms of tacit collusion, as firms attempt to undercut rivals in a desperate bid to maintain their own profitability. This sudden indiscipline may encourage firms to search for more explicit or specific forms of collusion. Palmer (1972) tests the hypothesis that firms in declining industries are more likely to collude than firms in expanding industries, using US data to examine the growth in industries that were subject to antitrust suits between 1966 and 1970. The evidence is consistent with the declining industry hypothesis.

5.6 Factors conducive to cartel formation

In Section 5.6, we identify a number of factors that influence whether the firms in an industry are likely to be able to succeed in forming a cartel. These include the degree of **seller concentration** and the number of firms in the industry, the degree of similarity in the firms' cost structures, product characteristics and market shares, and the extent to which firms are vertically integrated.

Seller concentration and the number of firms

A common hypothesis is that firms find it easier to collude in industries with small numbers of firms, or high levels of concentration. This hypothesis is based on theories of group and coalition behaviour which suggest that as numbers increase, the unanimity of goals diminishes. With a dilution of unanimity, the group incurs heavier bargaining, monitoring and enforcement (or transaction) costs.

> [T]he single most important factor in the development of collusive pricing is the structure of the industry, particularly the number of firms. Studies of specific industries have revealed again and again the significance of structure here. In bleachers, an industry where there was a particularly successful conspiracy, the market was dominated by four, then six, and finally eight firms. In electrical equipment, another industry that had a particularly successful set of conspiracies, the various markets were again dominated by a very few firms.
>
> *(Erickson, 1969, p. 84)*

> The formation of a Trust or Cartel requires in the first place that the parties shall be few enough to come to terms readily.
>
> *(MacGregor, 1906, p. 120)*

Phillips (1962) and Scherer and Ross (1990) provide a theory of the effect of numbers on the extent of collusion. First, as the number of firms increases, the contribution of each firm to total output decreases, and the firms become more likely to ignore their interdependence. Second, as the number of firms increases, there is more temptation for a rogue firm to undercut the agreed price, as it perceives a low risk of detection. Finally, since firms often have different views as to the optimal cartel policy, communication and negotiation between firms is required to reconcile differences. Coordination becomes more difficult as numbers increase. In the absence of a central agency or trade association, the number of channels of communication increases exponentially with the number of firms: based on the expression $N(N - 1)/2$, one channel will suffice for two firms, but six are required for four firms, fifteen for six firms, and so on. A breakdown in any one channel may precipitate retaliation; and the resulting disruption may extend far beyond the two parties originally responsible.

The importance of concentration and the number of firms seems to be confirmed by the empirical evidence. Hay and Kelley (1974) find that of 50 cases of reported conspiracy for which CR_4, the four-firm concentration ratio (the percentage share of industry sales accruing to the four largest firms; see Chapter 6) could be calculated, 38 had CR_4 greater than 50 per cent. The average number of firms involved in a conspiracy was 7.25, and in 79 per cent of all cases examined, 10 or fewer firms were involved.

High concentration also ensures that the fringe of non-colluding firms is relatively small. If the non-colluding fringe makes negligible inroads into the markets of cartel members, it may be tolerated. Indeed, any other action might run the risk of alerting the regulatory authorities. If the non-colluding fringe makes serious inroads into the cartel members' market shares, defensive strategies such as price-cutting may be instigated. In the case of Laker Airways, an early low-cost airline which eventually failed in 1982, the liquidator alleged (and he was in the main vindicated by the US courts) that the major airlines (British Airways, Lufthansa, Swissair, Pan Am and TWA) had conspired to drive Laker out of business by reducing their fares. Laker was regarded by one chairman (Thompson of British Caledonian) as 'the most disruptive airline on the North Atlantic' (*Sunday Times*, 3 April 1983). If there is a sizeable fringe of firms which cannot be induced to join the cartel, there is little chance of success in maximizing joint profits. The tacitly set collusive price in the American tobacco industry was:

> significantly influenced and limited by the threat of aggressive independent competition. Cigarette prices, though collusively determined, appear to have been held below the industry profit-maximizing level in part because of the rivalry and independence of action of a limited group of independents.
>
> *(Bain, 1959, p. 307)*

Armentano (1975) finds that price-fixing conspiracies in the electrical equipment industry were always threatened by small firms, which, when geographically close to potential customers, would quote a price just sufficient to cover costs in times of falling demand. The industry was also threatened by a fringe of low-quality producers, which regularly undercut the nationally agreed price.

The level of industry concentration in the past may also be a relevant factor. It might be expected that the more stable the level of concentration historically, the greater the likelihood that collusive behaviour has become established. However, little systematic research has been done to investigate this hypothesis, and most of the arguments are based on anecdotal evidence. One historical example refers to collusion in the heavy woollens industry.

> The number of firms regularly engaged in heavy woollen cloth contracting does not seem to have varied greatly in the period 1820–50 except during the years of deep general depression in the early 1840s, which brought many desperate bidders into this market, and structurally the trade had the appearance of a concentrated core of enterprises of efficient size with a more or less competitive fringe of smaller firms continuously fluctuating in size and composition.
>
> *(Glover, 1977, p. 231)*

However, there are many cases where high seller concentration did not lead to collusion. Asch and Seneca (1975) find no significant association between the number of firms and the degree of collusion. To resolve this contradiction, one might argue that very high concentration should lead to tacit cooperation, but at slightly lower levels of concentration a more explicit form of collusion is required as numbers increase. An industry comprising three or four firms may well be able to organize itself informally, but if new firms enter, tacit collusion may no longer suffice. Fraas and Greer (1977) suggest that at one extreme, perhaps two firms with an identical product, explicit collusion is possible but hardly necessary. At the opposite extreme, with many firms selling differentiated products at irregular intervals, explicit collusion, although desirable for firms seeking joint profit maximization, is much more difficult to achieve. It is in the intermediate cases that explicit collusion is most likely to take place.

> [T]he evidence indicates that as the number of parties increases and/or as the structural conditions become increasingly complex, conspirators must increasingly resort to arrangements of more elaborate design or greater efficiency if they are to achieve their joint maximizing objectives.
>
> *(Fraas and Greer, 1977, p. 43)*

Similar cost functions

Firms with similar cost structures find it easier to collude than those with pronounced differences in costs. A firm faced with an average cost function that decreases as output increases may be reluctant to restrict its output as a condition of cartel membership. In the absence of side-payments to offset the opportunity cost incurred by membership, the firm may be reluctant to join the cartel in the first place. Furthermore, a requirement to restrict output might run counter to a smaller firm's ambition to eventually overtake the larger producers. Obviously, this can only be achieved by growth in sales, and not by moves to restrict sales (Rothschild, 1999).

If quotas are determined by the cartel on the basis of equal percentage reductions from prior competitive output levels, unequal shares of cartel profits will accrue to firms with different marginal cost functions. The formation of the uranium cartel in 1980 rested on recognition that there were a wide variety of deposits, of different depths and thicknesses, and consequently widely differing marginal costs (Rothwell, 1980). Quotas, devised to ensure an equitable distribution of cartel profits, were an important precondition for the formation of a cartel.

Similar market shares

MacGregor (1906) suggests that if most of the firms in an industry are similar in size, the likelihood of successful collusion is enhanced. Other symmetries conducive to collusion might include similar patterns of firm evolution, similar technologies, similar product ranges and similar productive capacities. If market shares are symmetric, it is possible that the large firms have already eliminated the smaller firms through competition. Asymmetric market shares, on the other hand, are likely to be associated with a divergence of views between the large and the small firms (Harrington, 1989, 1991; Schmalensee, 1987). The small firms may, for example, be reluctant to adopt quotas based on existing market shares, while the large firms may collude with each other to enhance their (collective) dominance. Compte *et al.* (2002) consider a situation in which colluding firms have similar costs and produce similar goods, but have different capacities. Firms with spare capacity are tempted to defect from a price-fixing agreement, while firms with limited capacity are unable to issue credible threats to punish the firms that defect.

However, it can be argued that asymmetric market shares enhance the ability of a few large firms to initiate and enforce a profitable agreement. Phillips (1962) suggests that unequal market shares can create a degree of stability and order. Some firms act as leaders, while others accept the role of followers. The leaders have the authority to enforce cooperative behaviour, while the followers are aware that as higher-cost producers, they can easily be punished by the leaders through price-cuts. Vertically integrated leaders can also punish the followers by impeding their access to inputs or markets. The fear of economic loss need not be the only reason for coordination:

> [a] number of other factors might be mentioned, [including] such vague influences as historical prominence and a reputation for wisdom and fairness. But whatever the source of power, it tends to diminish the degree of rivalry.
>
> *(Phillips, 1962, pp. 31–2)*

Similar products

Similar products (or a lack of product differentiation) may be another factor conducive to successful collusion. Firms selling similar goods need only focus on a narrow range of pricing decisions. If many characteristics contribute to (either real or perceived) product differences, it becomes difficult to achieve agreement over price.

> [C]ombination is much easier if there is some degree of uniformity in the products of the firms . . . There is also abundant evidence that the process of formation is impeded by differences in quality . . . and for this reason finishing industries are not easily combined. Thus the German Steel Cartel has not yet been able to take complete control of finished products, which are still sold by the individual works. Syndication is as a rule possible only for raw material and half-finished goods.
>
> *(MacGregor, 1906, pp. 122–3)*

> Consumer goods industries, with their usual emphasis on diversity and differentiation, would appear to be poor candidates for successful price collusion.
>
> *(Armentano, 1975, p. 307)*

Switching costs are defined as costs incurred when a buyer switches between suppliers, but not incurred when remaining with the original supplier. Effectively, switching costs make similar products more heterogeneous, as a buyer is no longer indifferent between the two suppliers. Types of switching cost include transaction costs incurred when changing a bank or internet service provider; compatibility costs incurred when changing products that are linked to one another, such as Microsoft Windows and Office; and the learning costs incurred in using a new product or service (Klemperer, 1995). Switching costs reduces the incentive for producers to join or adhere to cartel agreements (NERA, 2003).

Even products that are very similar may be supplied under varied conditions and specifications. For example, while a product such as steel springs for upholstery seems to be fairly homogeneous, the price list used by the Spring and Interior Springing Association (Office of Fair Trading Register, Agreement 1132) records over 400 separate prices, according to height, thickness of spring, alloys used, status of buyer and so on (Lipczynski, 1994). Negotiating, monitoring and renewing such an array of prices is inevitably a complex task. Furthermore, if product characteristics are subject to change over time, perhaps due to technological progress or evolving consumer tastes, a price agreement is more difficult to negotiate and sustain.

Measuring the relationship between the degree of product differentiation and the level of collusion is a difficult task. Most empirical research relies on measures indirectly related to the degree of product differentiation. Asch and Seneca (1975) distinguish between producer and consumer goods industries, on the grounds that the former are more homogeneous than the latter. The expectation is that collusion is more likely in producer goods industries. Symeonides (1999) suggests product differentiation achieved through investment in advertising or research and development tends to frustrate collusion, since low-quality producers are less likely to collude with high-quality producers. In the 1950s, UK firms with high levels of research and development and advertising expenditures relative to sales were less likely to collude.

Kantzenbach *et al.* (1995) modify the general conclusion that product differentiation inhibits successful collusion. High product differentiation may have implications primarily for the form of collusion, rather than the ability to conclude an agreement at all. Firms might abandon price-fixing, but still segment the market by product type or geography. In this case successful collusion is possible, because in segmented markets price elasticity of demand tends to be low, and punishment is not costly if price cuts are required in only a few market segments (Davidson, 1983; Ross, 1992).

There is another reason why price-fixing is more likely to succeed if price elasticity of demand is low: if high prices are to generate significantly increased revenues, it is implicit that demand is price inelastic. There is circumstantial and subjective evidence that many cases of collusion are associated with price-inelastic demand (Erickson, 1969). However, if demand is currently price-elastic, this could be because collusion has already succeeded in increasing price, enabling firms to operate at the joint profit-maximizing position on the market demand function (Posner, 1976). If demand is price-inelastic at current prices, producers are failing to maximize joint profits, which in turn suggests they are not colluding.

Vertical integration

A successful cartel requires member firms to be reassured that fellow members are abiding by the terms of the agreement. Effective monitoring is important. If one member is vertically integrated downstream, perhaps with ownership of retail outlets, it may be able to undercut the cartel price by reducing its transfer price to its own retailers. Unless other cartel members are fully aware of the true cost structure of the retail business, they may be unaware that the cartel agreement is being undermined.

5.7   Influences on cartel stability

Impermanence appears to be a pervasive characteristic of most, if not all, cartels. Ironically, those agreements that have lasted for longer durations, may have been among the least effective in promoting joint profit maximization. Brozen (1975) devotes an entire section of his book to readings on the instability of price conspiracies, with each reading dwelling on the ineffectiveness and fragility of the agreements.

The fundamental reason so many cartels fail to live up to expectations is that what appears optimal for the group as a whole may not be optimal for each member individually. Therefore bargaining is required to find a form of agreement that reconciles this divergence of interests. Fellner (1965) believes the basic reason for the instability of coordinated action is that the bargaining strengths of members tend to change in unpredictable ways. For an agreement to remain effective, the group must create outlets for these changes. For example, individual firms might be permitted some freedom to introduce new product lines or experiment with new cost-saving technologies. If outlets of this kind are insufficient to channel and control the competitive zeal of members, skirmishes and wars may break out from time to time. Since firms are aware of this possibility they may seek to remain prepared, perhaps by maintaining some spare capacity. However, this might directly contravene one of the requirements for joint profit maximization, namely the elimination of spare capacity. Joint profit maximization may therefore be a difficult target to achieve.

In Section 5.7 we examine specific factors that tend to frustrate long-term cooperation. Levenstein and Suslow (2004) survey the literature on cartel stability; notable contributions include Asch and Seneca (1975), Dick (1996), Fraas and Greer (1977), Hay and Kelley (1974), Marquez (1994) and Posner (1970).

Seller concentration and the number of firms

In Section 5.6, we argued that high seller concentration and small numbers of firms are factors conducive to cartel formation. Similarly, the level of concentration and the number of firms may also affect the stability of a cartel after it has been formed, particularly if effective communication and monitoring are easier when numbers are small. With small numbers, in the event that non-compliance is detected retaliation is likely to be quicker and more effective. If the time taken to retaliate is long, the short-term gains from non-compliance may outweigh the long-term costs; if the time-lag is short, the opposite applies. Research in the field of experimental oligopoly, reviewed by Huck *et al.* (2001), supports the idea put forward by Dolbeur *et al.* (1968) that stability is affected by the number of firms:

> The number of firms in the market had a significant effect upon average profit and price under both information states [incomplete and complete information] . . . Finally, stability increased as [the number of firms] decreased.

(Dolbear et al., 1968, p. 259)

It is widely assumed that cartels are always threatened by competition from firms outside the cartel. Non-cartel firms earning profits higher than those of cartel members may tempt members to desert the cartel, undermining its existence (Kleit and Palsson, 1999; Posner, 1976). In an analysis of agreements at the OFT, however, Lipczynski (1994) finds that some cartels are able to tolerate sizeable portions of the industry outside the cartel.

Different goals of members

If a cartel comprises a heterogeneous collection of firms, it is probable that individual members have differing goals. Conflicting objectives might remain lightly buried in the interests of group solidarity, but might resurface at any time. Members may disagree over issues such as the balance between short-run and long-run profit maximization, the regard that should be paid to potential competition, or how best to respond to changes in government policy. The literature on cartels contains numerous examples of conflict among members.

Fog (1956) suggests that larger firms often tend to seek stable, long-run policies, while smaller firms are more interested in exploiting short-run opportunities. For example, Pindyck (1977) finds that some members of the International Bauxite Association in Australia, faced with high transport costs and excess capacity, were tempted to sell bauxite outside the cartel. In US Major League Baseball, some team owners appear to be less concerned with profit maximization than others:

> Agreement within the cartel is also hampered by the fact that not all members are profit maximizers. Some owners view baseball as largely a sporting activity, with profitability at most a secondary concern. Even today, teams like the Red Sox and the Cubs behave quite differently from teams like the Dodgers. Given the relatively small size of the cartel and the protected positions of its members, this divergence of goals tends to produce instability.
>
> *(Davis, 1974, p. 356)*

Davis (1974) notes a further divergence of goals between the rich and the poor teams over the distribution of gate receipts. In 1901, a plan had been agreed to ensure visiting teams received 30 cents for each grandstand ticket sold and 20 cents for each 'bleacher' ticket, amounting to around 40 per cent of total gate receipts. By 1953, the increase in ticket prices had reduced this percentage to 21 per cent.

> Bill Veeck argued for a return to the old percentage but was voted down. In his words, 'Five clubs voted for the change I suggested and three voted against it. Since it takes six to make a change, I was licked. And who do you think lined up against me? You're right – the rich ones. The Yankees, Tigers and Red Sox'.
>
> *(Davis, 1974, p. 356)*

The process of cartel formation and the assignment of quotas

It is possible that the process of cartel formation might have implications for stability. Prokop (1999) develops several game theory models of cartel formation, in which firms decide whether to join the cartel or remain on the non-cartel fringe either sequentially or simultaneously. Cartel stability is shown to be more likely if decision making is sequential rather than simultaneous. A similar conclusion was reached in our discussion of the likelihood of players behaving cooperatively in a sequential game in Section 4.6.

Osborne (1976) argues that the assignment of production quotas when the cartel is established can have important implications subsequently for its stability. This argument is illustrated in Figure 5.4, based on the isoprofit curves and reaction functions diagrams that were originally developed in Section 4.3. At any point on the line Q_MQ_M, the combined output of firms A and B *equals* the profit-maximizing output for a monopolist, Q_M. At all points on Q_MQ_M, the firms maximize their joint profits, but the quotas assigned to each firm vary between different points on Q_MQ_M. At F, firm A takes the larger share of output; at H, B takes the larger share; while G is an intermediate case. If the two firms are identical so the model is symmetric, at G both firms are assigned an equal quota of $1/2Q_M$.

Starting from any of points F, G and H, there is an incentive for either firm to cheat by raising its output, if it believes the other firm will not retaliate. If firm A increases its output while firm B's output is unchanged (moving 'east' from F, G or H), A increases its profit; or if B increases its output while A's output stays

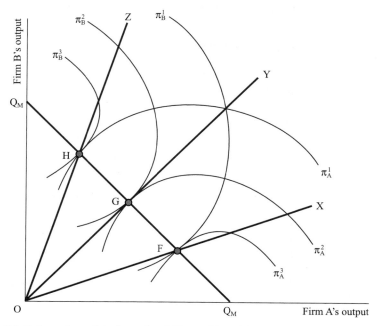

Figure 5.4 Osborne's model of cartel stability and instability

unchanged (moving 'north' from F, G or H), B increases its profit. Exactly the same kinds of incentive underlie the prisoner's dilemma model discussed in Section 4.6: both players have an incentive to adopt non-cooperative behaviour, provided the other player does not do the same.

Suppose however the rules or established practices of the cartel are such that if one firm cheats by increasing its output, the other firm punishes it by also increasing its output, until the market shares implied by the quota agreement are restored. In this case, a decision by either firm to cheat would invite retaliation, resulting in a diagonal shift up the rays OX, OY or OZ, along which the market shares of both firms are the same as at points F, G and H respectively.

An examination of the implications of diagonal shifts up the rays OX, OY and OZ demonstrates the importance for cartel stability of the initial quota assignment. Beginning from G and moving up OY, both firms experience a decrease in profits. Therefore if retaliation of the kind described above is anticipated, neither firm has an incentive to cheat. If the quotas are assigned such that the firms locate at G, the cartel is stable. However, beginning from either F or H, the cartel is unstable. Beginning from F and moving up OX, A's profit increases while B's decreases, so A has an incentive to cheat. Similarly, beginning from H and moving up OZ, B's profit increases while A's profit decreases, so B has an incentive to cheat.

Notice that at F and H, it is the firm with the larger initial quota (firm A at F, and firm B at H) that has the incentive to cheat. This is because the retaliation always restores the original quotas. For example, beginning from F, at which A has the larger market share, a large increase in output by A only provokes a small increase by B, so overall A gains and B loses. Diagrammatically, the condition for cartel stability is that the ray from the origin should be tangential to the two isoprofit curves at their point of tangency on the line $Q_M Q_M$. This condition is satisfied at G, but it is not satisfied at either F or H.

Non-price competition

A cartel is likely to be unstable if there are significant opportunities for non-price competition. Little purpose is served by agreeing to fix prices if, soon afterwards, intense non-price competition between cartel members breaks out in the form of expensive rival advertising campaigns, or the simultaneous launch of new and competing brands. Symeonides (2003) reports evidence for the UK of a negative relationship between the level of advertising and the degree of collusion.

Monitoring and detection of cheating

Stigler (1964) argues that collusion is successful when it is accompanied by efficient mechanisms for monitoring compliance with the agreement. The most effective method for detecting secret price-cutting might be to check transaction prices in the market. However, such audits can present practical difficulties. For example, Stocking and Mueller (1957) find evidence of sophisticated methods of breaking price agreements by recourse to reciprocal trade.

Stigler argues that evidence of cheating can be inferred by observing unexpected changes in the market shares of individual firms. If a firm discovers that it is systematically losing business which it would normally expect to secure, it might infer that another cartel member is guilty of price-cutting. The greater the degree of regular variation in the cartel firms' market shares, the greater the potential for secret price-cuts, since it is more difficult for loyal firms to detect suspicious changes in their market shares. Stigler draws the following conclusions:

- collusion is more effective where actual transaction prices are correctly reported, as in government contracts;

- collusion is less effective where the identity of the buyers changes frequently;

- the effectiveness of collusion varies inversely with the numbers of sellers and buyers and the entry of new buyers.

Stigler's approach can be criticized in several respects. Implicitly, Stigler assumes the threat of detection is a sufficient deterrent. The non-compliant firm incurs no penalty other than that of having to discontinue its non-compliance (Yamey, 1970). By concentrating on the detection of non-compliance, many other aspects of collusion are ignored. Stigler's approach can at best be regarded as a partial theory of collusion.

> [Stigler] takes as given that the collusive agreement has already been reached. Attention is focused instead on cheating and on statistical inference techniques for detecting cheaters. While this last is very useful and calls attention in an interesting way to aspects of the oligopoly problem that others have neglected, it is also incomplete . . . monitoring is only one of a series of contracting steps, and not plainly the one that warrants priority attention.
>
> *(Williamson, 1975, p. 244)*

Sanctions

The ability of a cartel to impose effective sanctions if cheating does occur is another important determinant of cartel stability. If additional profits can be realized through non-compliance, then non-compliance probably will occur unless some policy of deterrence is adopted. 'It is surely one of the axioms of human behaviour that all agreements whose violation would be profitable to the violator must be enforced' (Stigler, 1968, p. 42). The ability of a cartel to discipline its own members for breaches of agreement is essential, as the courts cannot be used to enforce an illegal contract. Ayres (1987) argues that punishment can be effected either by taking action that reduces the demand for the non-compliant firm's product, or by increasing its costs. Increasing costs may be difficult, but reducing demand is often straightforward. Accordingly, a common sanction is the matching of price cuts.

> Enforcement consists basically of detecting significant deviations from the agreed-upon prices. Once detected, the deviations will tend to disappear because they are no longer secret and will be matched by fellow conspirators if they are not withdrawn.
>
> *(Stigler, 1968, p. 42)*

Rees (1993a) finds that in the British salt duopoly, any gain from cheating was outweighed by losses from credible short-term price cuts. Levenstein (1996, 1997) also observes such use of effective short-term price-cutting in the bromine cartel prior to the First World War; although it is also suggested that severe price wars may have provided signals that a new round of bargaining to fix prices was required.

Sealed bidding provides a useful mechanism for ensuring detection if a firm breaks a cartel agreement. Sealed bid competition occurs when a buyer (frequently the government) requests bids for a contract, and subsequently announces the result publicly. The firms submit their bids secretly. The bidding firms might decide to meet in order to consider their bids, and perhaps decide which firm will win the contract. If a firm should cheat by submitting a lower bid than has been agreed, it will be detected when the winning bid is announced.

> The system of sealed bids, publicly opened with full identification of each bidder's price and specifications, is the ideal instrument for the detection of price cutting. There exists no alternative method of secretly cutting prices.
>
> *(Stigler, 1968, pp. 44–5)*

It has been suggested that sealed bidding may be so effective in ensuring discipline, that collusion might be limited to the sealed bid part of the relevant market. An interesting account of sealed bidding in practice can be found in Herling's (1962) description of the electrical equipment conspiracy. However, a note of caution is sounded by Hay and Kelley (1974), who find in some cases that bids for government contracts were actually excluded from cartel agreements, in the belief that collusion would easily be detected by the government.

In a study of restrictive practices in the food trade, Cuthbert and Black (1959) find evidence of the use of two other types of direct sanction: fines and expulsion. Members breaking the terms of the agreement were fined, sometimes heavily. Expulsion implies that any advantage of cartel membership is lost. This may be serious if, for example, raw material suppliers cooperate with the cartel and agree not to supply non-members. A cartel may also use the services of third parties in an attempt to deter cheating. A joint sales agency through which all output is channelled should prevent price-cutting, though problems of allocating the proceeds between the cartel members might surface. Finally, the threat or use of physical force might be an effective means of encouraging compliance. Kuhlman (1969) discusses the role of organized crime in policing cartel agreements.

Buyer concentration

It seems plausible that cartel stability should be enhanced if buyers lack market power or if **buyer concentration** is low. Buyers with market power may threaten agreed prices by switching to alternative suppliers, or by suggesting reciprocal transactions with individual producers. '[T]he better organized and more efficient are the other groups with which an interfirm organization has conflict relations, the greater the tendency for rivalry within the interfirm organization' (Phillips, 1962, p. 35).

Erickson (1969) fails to find strong evidence that powerful buyers had a significant effect on stability, although this was based on an examination of only two cases. In contrast, Snyder (1996) and Dick (1996) find evidence that large buyers encourage suppliers to deviate from cartel agreements. When an industry supplies a small number of large buyers, orders are often large and infrequent. Under these conditions, it is tempting for parties to a collusive agreement to defect by offering secret price reductions, in an effort to secure these valuable contracts. In such cases it may be difficult for other cartel members to detect and punish defection.

> The relevance of big buyers to coordinated interaction does not stem from their sophistication or self-proclaimed ability to protect themselves. Instead, the issue is whether sellers will have the incentive to deviate from terms of coordination because the gains from securing a large long-term contract outweigh any losses from being caught after the fact.
>
> *(Dennis, 1992, p. 9)*

On the other hand, if buyers are atomistic, defection becomes more difficult: the more buyers there are, the greater the chance of being found out. 'No one has yet invented a way to advertise price reductions which brings them to the attention of numerous customers but not to that of any rival' (Stigler, 1968, p. 44). To illustrate the point, let p denote the probability that a firm's rivals detect a price cut that the firm offers to only one customer. Therefore the probability that a price cut offered to only one customer remains undetected is $1 - p$. Suppose, however, the price cut is offered to n customers. Under certain assumptions, the probability that the price cut remains undetected is $(1 - p)^n$. Suppose p is small, say $p = 0.01$. If $n = 100$, the probability that the price cut is undetected is $0.99^{100} = 0.366$. In this case, the firm contemplating the price cut might think it has a reasonable (more than one-in-three) chance of not being detected. But if $n = 1000$, the probability that the price cut is undetected is $0.99^{1000} = 0.00004$. In this case, there is almost no chance that the price cut remains undetected.

Fluctuations in demand

A reduction in total demand may place strains on a cartel agreement (Briggs, 1996; Haltwanger and Harrington, 1991). As demand falls, firms are tempted to undercut the cartel price in a bid to protect their sales volumes. This temptation need not affect all firms equally. Some may regard the recession in sales as temporary and may urge others to keep their nerve; others may view the decline as a real threat to their futures and will consider any strategy for survival. A climate of mutual suspicion and uncertainty may eventually cause the cartel to break apart.

In the sense that they must adapt to fluctuating demand, cartels are no different from individual firms. If they fix prices, they have to make accommodating changes in production and employment. If they fix output quotas, they have to accept the burden of fluctuating prices. No cartel has complete control over demand, and history is full of instances of cartels and agreements that collapsed in the face of fluctuating demand. In the early 1920s, the demand for timber in Scotland fell, owing to the adoption of new house-building styles. Soon after, an agreement amongst timber firms in northern Scotland, which had endured for 13 years, collapsed (Perren, 1979).

If cartel members have spare capacity or if fixed costs are a large proportion of total costs, the cartel is likely to be unstable. If demand is falling, the temptation to cut price in an attempt to increase output and cover the fixed costs is even stronger. It has been claimed the existence of spare capacity allows for greater stability, so long as the capacity is under the control of loyal cartel members. By adjusting production and price as demand conditions fluctuate, a dominant cartel member can use spare capacity to maintain order and discipline in the market. The behaviour of Saudi Arabian crude oil producers is often quoted as evidence for this hypothesis (Youssef, 1986). For such a strategy to be effective, however, the costs of maintaining spare capacity must not be excessive. It is questionable whether such a strategy is often applied in practice.

Posner (1976) argues collusion may be more difficult to enforce in times of increasing demand. In an expanding market, a firm being undercut by rivals may not immediately detect that cheating is occuring, since its own sales are rising (Bagwell and Staiger, 1997; Ellison, 1994; Rotemberg and Saloner, 1986). Rey (2002) suggests collusion is easier in times of expanding demand, as current profits are lower than future profits. In this case, the long-term costs imposed by rivals' retaliation should exceed the short-term benefits gained from non-compliance with the agreement.

Porter (1983) and Green and Porter (1984) argue cartel breakdowns occur when there is an unanticipated change in demand, evidenced by unusually low market shares for at least one firm, rather than a general long-term decline in demand. Demand can vary for a number of predictable reasons. However, at some critical level, when no rational explanation can be deduced for the falling sales, firms will take action. If the price drops below a certain level (a trigger price), firms that have previously been maximizing joint profits may revert, for a time, to Cournot-type competition (see Section 4.3).

Entry

In the long run, the stability and profitability of collusion depends on the ease or difficulty of entry. If a cartel shelters behind effective entry barriers, it may enjoy the necessary time and space to prosper and resolve the conflicting demands of its members. If entry barriers are low, the cartel faces competitive pressure from potential entrants. If a cartel has agreed to fix the price above the competitive level, there is an incentive for an entrant to move in and set a price just below the cartel price, encroaching on the profits of group members. In the most extreme case, unrestricted entry will lead to the destruction of the cartel. The survival of the cartel may therefore require implementation of measures to raise entry barriers, or policies that increase the time required to achieve successful entry. In this subsection, the term entry barrier is used in both of these senses. Entry barriers are discussed in full in Chapter 8.

Entry-type threats to cartel stability need not emanate only from rival firms. The development of new products can have similar destabilizing implications. In the American incandescent lamp industry in the 1930s, General Electric operated a system of licence agreements and quota allocations. A minor firm, Sylvania, which had been allocated a 5.5 per cent quota, decided to market the new fluorescent lamp without a General Electric licence. It rapidly increased its market share to 20 per cent (Brems, 1951). Sultan (1974) notes similar destabilizing effects in the electrical equipment industry when, in 1959, General Electric announced the development of a new transformer without notifying its competitors.

Case study 5.2

Watchdog gets shirty with companies over strip price-fixing

After lacklustre performances by England at last year's World Cup, some soccer fans might have thought the replica strip they were wearing was not worth the price they paid. Yesterday they were proved right as the Office of Fair Trading slapped a £18.6m fine – the second-highest it has awarded – on 10 companies, including Manchester United Football Club and the Football Association, for keeping the prices of team shirts artificially high. The OFT had been keeping an eye on the replica shirt market for some time. In 1999 the watchdog had already investigated complaints about price-fixing in the sector and had received assurances from the FA and clubs that such practices would be rooted out. In August 2000, however, it received a further complaint and began a new inquiry into the sector, which culminated in yesterday's ruling.

The OFT said it had covered three main instances of collusion. First there were agreements between Manchester United, Umbro, the licensed manufacturer of replica shirts, and a number of sports retailers to fix prices at key times, such as Euro 2000 or the launch of new team strips. The agreement had kept shirts for the England team, Manchester United, Chelsea, Glasgow Celtic and Nottingham Forest at £39.99.

There was also an agreement to keep the price of England kits high on the internet, the OFT said, with JJB Sports, the UK's largest sportswear retailer, the FA, Umbro and Sportsetail colluding to keep prices at the same level as those on the high street. Separately the OFT found that Umbro and Florence Clothiers, a retailer now in receivership, had agreed to fix prices for replica Glasgow Celtic shirts for a short time in 2001. The OFT said the price-fixing had been serious and, in some cases, long-term, stretching over 21 months, and that a large fine had been set to reflect that.

JJB Sports, which was given the highest fine – £8.37m – said the ruling was 'politically motivated'. David Greenwood, finance director, said: 'They were on a mission to nail someone for the high price of replica kits and refused to accept any evidence to the contrary.' JJB Sports claims that far from inflating prices, it has been a key force in keeping the price of football shirts under the £40 mark. While JJB plans to appeal against the decision, observers agree the OFT is trying to send a tough message to the business community as it takes on increased powers. In addition to being able to fine companies up to 10 per cent of their turnover for competition infringements, in June it gained the power to impose jail sentences on executives in cartel cases.

Paula Riedel, competition partner at Linklaters, the law firm, said: 'It is quite convenient that the first case for the OFT after it gained these new powers has been one with lots of household names. The fact that it is very high profile is a good way of spreading the message that they are getting tough a bit further.' Earlier this year, in another high-profile ruling, the OFT imposed a record fine of £22.5m on Argos and Littlewoods for fixing the prices of toys and games. So far this year, Ms Riedel calculates, the OFT has imposed fines totalling just under £50m, compared with £10m last year.

The OFT argues, however, that such tough tactics are having the desired effect. John Vickers, chairman said: 'Since we launched our investigation the prices of replica football shirts have fallen and consumers can now shop around and get a better price.' An England 2003 shirt can be bought for as little as £24, and that is what matters, says the OFT.

Source: Watchdog gets shirty with companies over strip price-fixing, *Financial Times*, 2 August 2003.

Non-economic influences on cartel stability

In a classification of influences on cartel stability, non-economic factors such as leadership, trust and social background may also be relevant.

> In my view the propensity of an oligopoly to behave monopolistically or competitively is unlikely to depend upon industry characteristics alone. The 'personalities' of the oligopolists, the presence or absence of an *esprit de corps* or sense of group loyalty or mutual confidence and trust among them . . . may in some cases be as important as industry characteristics.
>
> *(Yamey, 1973, p. 315)*

Cowen and Sutter (1999) define cooperative efficacy as a belief in the benefits of cooperation. In general, cooperative efficacy appears to have declined in American society, with many Americans preferring to bowl alone rather than join leagues. In the specific case of cartels, a lack of cooperative efficacy is a major threat to stability.

Leadership

Many economists are reluctant to recognize the importance of leadership, which perhaps sits more comfortably in the domain of disciplines like organizational behaviour or sociology. However, the formation of a cartel requires that someone takes the lead and organizes discussions and negotiations. People need to be persuaded, coaxed or even threatened to join the cartel, and leadership qualities are necessary to create and sustain a successful agreement. Likewise, a strong personality hostile to the notion of cooperation might prevent the formation of a cartel.

Phillips (1962) describes the Trenton Potteries Case, in which the president of the Association of Sanitary Earthenware was reduced to pleading with his members to be honourable in maintaining Association prices.

> This attitude, coupled with the persistence of price cutting, the lack of any evidence of threats, coercion or pressure on any member, demonstrates that no one in the market had enough power to lead the group effectively.
>
> *(Phillips, 1962, p. 174)*

With reference to the Chrome Cartel, Phimister (1996) emphasizes the role played by Edmund Davis in developing a successful international cartel in the early twentieth century. Davis's talents were also put to good use in the exploitation of other extractive industries in Africa.

> Davis increasingly devoted his time to constructing cartels. Monopoly or near-monopoly control over large sections of the base mineral industry was a key to much of his subsequent success. It was a strategy which he employed to marked effect in coal, asbestos, chrome, copper, tungsten and tin mining.
>
> *(Phimister, 1996, p. 79)*

Trust

Trust between cartel members is another important requirement for successful collusion (Yamey, 1973). If trust is lacking, even sophisticated pricing and output agreements may be insufficient to hold a cartel together. Through the medium of his famous dinners, Judge Gary, president of US Steel in the early 1890s, attempted to develop a spirit of cooperation. A firm considering a significant change of strategy would feel duty-bound to inform the other firms.

> They were not obligated to do it except as two men who profess to be friends, or professing to give information to one another as to what they were doing, naturally ought to tell the truth about it.
>
> *(Nelson, 1922, p. 37)*

Again, the historical literature is full of examples of trust, or, more commonly, the lack of trust, among cartel members. One British cutlery manufacturer, who did not wish to attend his trade association meetings, claimed:

> I don't go because the fellows there are too insincere. A manufacturer gets up and makes a speech condemning the prices we are getting. We all ought to agree to charge, say, 19s. a dozen. There are cries of Hear! Hear! all round. The speaker finishes, walks into the next room and takes up the telephone – Get out a new price list! We are charging 18s. 6d.
>
> *(Sonkondi, 1969, p. 100)*

James (1946) reports a lack of trust amongst the late nineteenth-century lumber manufacturers in the US. Effective collusion was often held back by the strong individualism which, he claimed, was typical of the so-called American frontier spirit.

Social homogeneity

If the participants to an agreement share the same social background, group stability is likely to be enhanced. Consider the following account of the American electrical equipment conspiracy:

> The industry is tightly-knit with many friendships among the executives of competing firms; indeed, officials of smaller firms sometimes are former General Electric or Westinghouse Electric executives. The men involved oftentimes had similar educational backgrounds – college graduates in engineering with a rise through technical ranks into the world of sales. And the friendships were not only professional but often quite personal. Trade association meetings fostered these. It was perhaps easy in the camaraderie of these meetings at upper bracket hotels, amid speeches typical of any association lauding the industry's members and 'mission', to draw even closer than business and background indicated.

> *(Wall Street Journal, 10 January 1962)*

If most owners and managers come from a similar and preferably closely knit social background, stability is likely to be enhanced. To cheat on one's peers is to run the risk of suffering not only economic retaliation, but also social stigmatization. The cheat is branded as an outsider, and denied the support and comfort of the social group. In an extreme case, Gupta (1995) finds collusion in the Indian tea industry in the 1930s was organized by managing agents belonging to a small and socially cohesive group of British nationals. Any agent who violated the norms of business and social behaviour risked the sanction of social exclusion. Podolny and Scott Morton (1999) find the social status of an entrant to the British merchant shipping industry influenced the reactions of incumbent members. Entrants from a higher social background were less likely to trigger a price war than those from a lower social class.

> The writers of the historical sources we use . . . are actually attuned to this feature [social status] of owners. Many of the sources were written around the Second World War when social status still mattered. Consequently owners are described as from 'a prominent family in Yorkshire that founded the University of X' or a knight, or a member of Parliament. These owners were coded as high status . . . the lack of a description of family background or accomplishments probably indicates there were none . . . we therefore assume that entrants whose economic actions are described, but social background omitted, are not high status.

> *(Podolny and Scott Morton, 1999, pp. 54–5)*

Even where collusion would seem to be unenforceable, a common social background can help establish effective joint action. Common value systems are also built on efficient communications, so that potential or actual conflict can be quickly resolved through the auspices of trade association meetings, clubs, lodges, and so on. Low (1970, p. 260) quotes an example of failed collusion in the US steel industry due to the exclusion, on religious grounds, of two Jewish executives from association meetings that were held in a 'waspish' (white anglo-saxon protestant) country club in Pittsburgh.

However, Phillips (1972) suggests the importance of class and social background may tend to diminish over time. Eventually competing firms' value systems tend to converge because they are producing similar products, attracting similar customers or encountering similar technical problems. Consequently, rivalry decreases and cooperation increases. Phillips uses the number of trade associations in an industry as an indicator of homogeneity: the more trade associations, the less homogeneity. Price-fixing is found to be more effective in industries with few trade associations, although there was a greater propensity to attempt price-fixing in industries with a larger number of trade associations.

Group homogeneity

Other notable attempts to locate the study of oligopoly within disciplines such as sociology and psychology, are made by Cyert and March (1964), Phillips (1962) and Stern (1971). This tradition stresses the notion that oligopolists are members of a group, and many decisions are essentially group decisions. Group behaviour exhibits quite different traits from individual behaviour, but economic theory seems almost totally concerned with the latter. If sociologists and psychologists find no evidence to support economists' assumptions concerning rational individualistic behaviour, it might be argued that alternative theories based on sociology and psychology are required.

According to Sherif and Sherif (1956) and Benz and Wolkomir (1964), individuals frequently come into contact with each other as a result of some focal issue: for example, stallholders in a market, or students attending a lecture course. If this focal issue helps develop common goals, this may lead to the development of an informal group, defined as follows:

> [a] social unit which consists of a number of individuals who stand in (more or less) definite status and role relationships to one another and which possesses a set of values or norms of its own regulating the behaviour of individual members, at least in matters of consequence to the group.

> *(Sherif and Sherif, 1956, p. 144)*

Naturally, conflict arises when groups with mutually exclusive goals collide. If subordinate goals are introduced which require collective interaction, conflict is reduced and cooperative action may develop. When firms compete for a market share, inter-firm conflict breaks out. Firms initially view rivals as members of an *out-group*. Raw material suppliers, trades unions, regulators or the government, as well as rival firms, may all be seen as out-group members. In time, however, certain norms of behaviour and attitudes arise, owing to the similarity of the environment within which all parties operate: all are exposed to the same technologies, customers, labour demands, regulatory framework, and so on. Rival firms or other parties move closer together and begin to view the industry as a reference group; they develop a sense of mutual belonging. Agents formerly regarded as part of the out-group might eventually form part of the *in-group*.

The focal issue or common goal which unites firms is the desire to organize their environment. The initial impetus comes from the conflict inherent in any oligopolistic industry. Paradoxically, this conflict may eventually create the cohesion necessary for group solidarity. For example, independent firms, in effect members of different out-groups, may unite to form an in-group in order to put an end to price-cutting. This objective becomes their common (uniting) goal. Competition may be channelled into less disruptive areas, such as product differentiation or research and development. The cohesiveness of the group is even stronger when the conflict is perceived to originate outside the industry. The common goal, in the face of external threat, is perhaps simple survival. The greater the external threat, the greater the cohesiveness of the group, and the less likely the chance of defection.

While this kind of approach stands in stark contrast to mainstream economic theory, there are obvious difficulties in attempting to develop an explicit model to test the relationship between group structures and associated behaviour. Indeed, one would have to redefine whole industries, not according to output, but perhaps according to group affinities. To define meaningful structures within which groups function, an exhaustive and difficult firm-by-firm and industry-by-industry classification would be required.

5.8 Summary

This chapter has discussed the various methods used by groups of firms to facilitate cooperative or collusive actions in pursuit of their collective interests. Collusion is best seen as a means of easing competitive pressure and reducing the uncertainty that stems from oligopolistic interdependence by taking unified action, rather than solely as a strategy for maximizing joint profits. Collusion might be effected though the medium of a cartel, but might alternatively take place through mechanisms such as trade associations, joint ventures or state-sponsored agreements.

The prescription in terms of output quotas and pricing policy for cartel members to maximize their joint profits is easy to define in theory, but often harder to implement in practice. For example, the less efficient firms might be required to accept relatively low production quotas, and may demand a share of the profits emanating from elsewhere in the cartel as the price that must be paid for their compliance. This raises numerous questions about the bargaining process between the prospective cartel members, the outcome of which may be theoretically indeterminate. Furthermore, if the cartel does succeed in reducing total industry output, this creates a free-rider problem in the sense that non-cartel firms reap the benefits of a higher price, without bearing any of the costs of having to produce a lower output. If it is obviously more profitable for an individual firm to remain outside the cartel, this misalignment of private and collective interests might prevent agreement from ever being reached, or might cause the cartel to break down almost as soon as it has been formed.

The success or failure of collusive arrangements depends on many factors, some of which are beyond the direct control of the group of colluding firms. In the absence of legal sanctions, what are the factors most likely to determine the success or failure of collusion?

■ Fewness of numbers helps in the handling and evaluation of information.

■ Similarity of cost conditions reduces a significant potential source of conflict.

■ Demand that is relatively inelastic at the pre-cartel price ensures that revenues can be increased significantly by reducing output levels and raising price.

■ An equitable and fair mechanism for determining the allocation of production quotas and distribution of profits helps make an agreement possible.

■ The fewer decisions the members of a cartel are required to take in order to conclude an effective agreement, the greater the likelihood of success.

■ Members must perceive that the gains from cooperative action outweigh the benefits of private action.

■ Mechanisms for detecting and punishing non-compliance with the terms of the agreement should be effective.

■ Higher prices and improved profitability should not attract non-cartel entrants into the industry.

■ The cartel must guard against other external threats to its stability, including significant changes in demand or technology.

■ The quality of leadership and the degree of mutual trust and social cohesion among cartel members may be important influences on stability.

Discussion questions

1. Explain what is meant by Machlup's distinction between the degrees of collusion and the forms of collusion.
2. With reference to Case study 5.1, outline how the Lombard Club of leading financial institutions organized price fixing.
3. Explain why trade associations can be useful as vehicles for facilitating collusion.
4. Using a suitable theoretical model, show how the divergent interests of the members of a cartel can be resolved through a process of bargaining.
5. Are there ever any motives for collusion other than the desire to maintain prices at a level higher than would be achieved in a competitive market?
6. Why is it often necessary to police cartel agreements? Who polices OPEC?

7. Typical characteristics of industries that are prone to collusion include high concentration, high entry barriers, price inelastic demand, large numbers of buyers, homogeneous products and static demand. Explain why each of these characteristics may help foster collusion. Give real world examples of industries that exhibit some or all of these characteristics.

8. Auctions in which participants are required to submit sealed bids often seem to be prone to collusion among bidders. Why?

9. Explain why producers in certain industries set recommended retail prices.

10. Given the difficulty in detecting overt acts of collusion, suggest evidence that might provide investigators with proof of collusive behaviour.

11. In what ways might the assignment of production quotas when a cartel is first established have important implications for its subsequent stability?

12. Quoting examples drawn from Case studies 5.1 and 5.2, suggest factors that may tend to help or hinder collusion.

Further reading

Asch, P. and Seneca, J. (1975) Characteristics of collusive firms, *Journal of Industrial Economics*, 23, 223–37.

Christie, W.G. and Schultz, P.H. (1995) Policy watch: Did Nasdaq market makers implicitly collude? *Journal of Economic Perspectives*, 9, 199–208.

European Commission (1997a) *Competition Issues. Impact on Competition and Scale Effects*. Single Market Review, subseries 5:3.

Jacquemin, A. and Slade, M.E. (1989) Cartels, collusion and horizontal merger, in Schmalensee, R. and Willig, R.D. (eds) *Handbook of Industrial Organization*. Cambridge, MA: MIT Press.

Osborne, D.K. (1976) Cartel problems, *American Economic Review*, 66, 835–44.

Phlips, L. (ed.) (1998) *Applied Industrial Economics*. Cambridge: Cambridge University Press, sections II and III.

Podolny, J.M. and Scott Morton, F.M. (1999) Social status, entry and predation: the case of British shipping cartels 1879–1929, *Journal of Industrial Economics*, 47, 41–67.

Shepherd, W.G. (1997) *The Economics of Industrial Organization*. Englewood Cliffs, NJ: Prentice-Hall, ch. 11.

Concentration: measurement and trends

Key terms

Aggregate concentration	Industrial district
Cluster	Industry concentration
Concentration ratio	Lorenz curve
Concentration measures	Market concentration
Entropy coefficient	Numbers equivalent
Geographic market definition	Porter's Diamond Model
Gini coefficient	Product market definition
Hannah and Kay index	Regional concentration
Herfindahl–Hirschman index	Specialization

6.1 Introduction

Any analysis of a firm's competitive environment involves identifying the key elements of industry structure. Usually, the most important characteristics of industry structure include the number and size distribution of firms, the existence and height of barriers to entry and exit, and the degree of product differentiation. **Seller concentration** refers to the first of these elements: the number and size distribution of firms. In empirical research in industrial organization, seller concentration is probably the most widely used indicator of industry structure. Any specific seller concentration measure aims to reflect the implications of the number and size distribution of firms in the industry for the nature of competition, using a relatively simple numerical indicator. Both the number of firms and their size distribution (in other words, the degree of inequality in the firm sizes) are important. For example, the nature of competition in an industry comprising 10 equal-sized firms might be very different from the nature of competition in an industry comprising one dominant firm and nine smaller firms. A useful concentration measure should be capable of capturing the implications of both the number of firms, and their relative sizes, for the nature of competition.

In view of the importance of concentration in empirical studies of competition, we devote two entire chapters to this topic. This chapter focuses on the measurement of concentration, and on patterns and trends in concentration data. Chapter 7 focuses on the factors that determine the levels and trends in concentration in particular industries.

Before producing concentration measures for specific markets or industries, it is necessary to take decisions concerning the boundaries of the markets or industries that are being measured. Section 6.2 discusses the issues involved in market and industry definition, from both a theoretical and a practical perspective. Section 6.3 describes the schemes that are used to classify industries for the purposes of compiling the official UK and EU production and employment statistics. Section 6.4 describes the calculation of a number of alternative concentration or inequality measures, assuming we have individual size data for the firms that are members of the industry. The concentration or inequality measures include the n-firm concentration ratio, the Herfindahl–Hirschman index, the entropy coefficient and the Gini coefficient. Worked examples are used to illustrate the method of calculation for each measure, and to compare the properties and limitations of the various measures. Section 6.5 discusses some of the issues that should be considered when interpreting concentration measures. Finally, Section 6.6 presents some facts and figures concerning patterns and trends in seller concentration in the UK and EU. Patterns of specialization and geographic concentration, reflected in spatial patterns of firm and industry location within the EU, are also considered.

6.2 Market and industry definition

Markets and industries

In the calculation of any specific concentration measure, the definition of the relevant market is likely to be a crucial decision. The definition of a market is straightforward in theory, but often more problematic in practice. Serviceable theoretical definitions can be found in the works of the earliest, nineteenth-century economists. For example, Cournot defined a market as:

the entire territory of which parts are so united by the relations of unrestricted commerce that prices there take the same level throughout, with ease and rapidity.

(Cournot, 1838 pp. 51–2Fn)

Similarly, Marshall defined a market as an area in which:

prices of the same goods tend to equality with due allowance for transportation costs.

(Marshall, 1920, p. 270)

For practical purposes, the definition of any market contains both a product dimension and a geographic dimension. The **product market definition** should include all products that are close substitutes for one another, both in consumption and in production. Goods 1 and 2 are substitutes in consumption if an increase in the price of Good 2 causes consumers to switch from Good 2 to Good 1. The degree of consumer substitution between Goods 1 and 2 can be measured using the **cross-price elasticity of demand**. Good 1's elasticity of demand with respect to a change in the price of Good 2 is:

$$CED = \frac{\text{Proportionate change in quantity demanded for Good 1}}{\text{Proportionate change in price of Good 2}}$$

$$CED = \left(\frac{\Delta Q_1}{\Delta P_2}\right) \times \left(\frac{P_2}{Q_1}\right)$$

A large and positive cross-price elasticity of demand indicates that the two goods in question are close **substitutes** in consumption (for example, butter and margarine). If the price of Good 2 rises, the demand for Good 1 also rises. Goods 1 and 2 should therefore be considered part of the same industry. But how large does the cross-elasticity have to be; or in other words, how close is 'close'? Presumably Coke and Pepsi are very close substitutes, and Coke and Tango are quite close substitutes. But what about Coke and mineral water, or Coke and coffee?

In contrast, a large and negative cross-price elasticity of demand indicates that the two goods are close **complements** (for example, camera and film). However, this could also imply that they should be considered part of the same industry. CD players and amplifiers might be grouped together as part of the hi-fi equipment industry. But what about cars and petrol? These goods are also complementary, but would it be sensible to include motor manufacturers and oil companies in the same industry group?

Good 1 produced by firm A, and Good 2 produced with similar technology by firm B are substitutes in production if an increase in the price of Good 1 causes firm B to switch production from Good 2 to Good 1. In this case, firms A and B are close competitors, even if from a consumer's perspective Goods 1 and 2 are not close substitutes. For example, Good 1 might be cars and Good 2 might be military tanks. No consumer would decide to buy a tank simply because there has been an increase in the price of cars. But on receiving the same price signal, a tank producer might decide to switch to car production. The degree of producer substitution between Goods 1 and 2 can be measured using the cross-price elasticity of supply. Good 1's elasticity of supply with respect to a change in the price of Good 2 is:

$$\text{CES} = \frac{\text{Proportionate change in quantity supplied of Good 1}}{\text{Proportionate change in price of Good 2}}$$

$$\text{CES} = \left(\frac{\Delta Q_1^S}{\Delta P_2}\right) \times \left(\frac{P_2}{Q_1^S}\right)$$

A negative value for CES would suggest that Goods 1 and 2 are substitutes in production: if the price of Good 2 rises, the supply of Good 1 falls, as producers switch from Good 1 to Good 2. In this case as well, there can be difficulties in implementation. For example, if 'engineering' is defined as 'a process using lathes', we might classify aerospace and bicycle manufacturers as direct competitors.

The **geographic market definition** involves determining whether an increase in the price of a product in one geographic location significantly affects either the demand or supply, and therefore the price, in another geographic location. If so, then both locations should be considered part of the same geographic market. In principle, a similar analysis involving spatial cross-price elasticities could be used to determine the geographic limits of market boundaries.

In practice, however, the problems are similar to those that arise in defining product markets. Should any specific market be defined at the local, regional, national, continental or global level? Substitution in consumption or production is always a matter of degree, but any operational market definition requires specific boundaries to be drawn, not only in 'product space', but also in geographic space. Elzinga and Hogarty (1973, 1978) suggest a practical procedure for defining geographic boundaries. This requires data on the extent to which consumers in a regionally defined market purchase from regional producers (internal transactions) and from producers outside the region (external transactions). A regional market exists if the ratio of internal to total transactions is high; Elzinga and Hogarty suggest a critical value of 75 per cent.

National Economic Research Associates (1992) and Bishop and Walker (2002) describe the methodology used to determine market definitions in the application of UK and EU competition policy (see also Chapter 17). The SSNIP (small but significant non-transitory increase in price) test is widely used. For product markets, this test assesses whether a (hypothetical) monopolist producing Good 1 would find it profitable to increase price by between 5 per cent and 10 per cent. If so, the relevant market for Good 1 is market 1. If not, this suggests the producers of other goods constrain the monopolist's pricing policy. Therefore the market definintion should include Good 1 and related Goods 2 and 3. A similar procedure is used to define a geographic market: would a (hypothetical) monopolist located in geographic area X find it profitable to increase price by between 5 per cent and 10 per cent? If so, X is a geographic market; if not, a wider geographic market definition is required. In order to implement the SSNIP test, various price and cross-price demand elasticity measures are used (OFT, 1999a; Stigler and Sherwin, 1985; Werden and Froeb, 1993).

Throughout much of microeconomics and industrial organization, the terms *market* and *industry* tend to be used rather loosely, and sometimes interchangeably. Although the distinction is not rigid, it seems natural to use the term *industry* to refer specifically to a market's supply side or productive activities, while the term *market* encompasses both supply/production, and demand/consumption. Throughout this book, we will usually adhere to this terminological convention. However, such a convention is not universal. Kay (1990) sees markets as representing demand conditions, while industries represent supply conditions. In Kay's terminology, the *strategic market*, defined as the smallest geographic or product area in which firm can successfully compete, brings the industry and market together.

> The characteristics of the strategic market are influenced both by those demand factors which determine the economic market which the firm serves, and by those supply factors which determine the boundaries of the industry within which the firm operates.

> *(Kay, 1990, p. 3)*

Nevertheless, we will normally use the term 'industry' to refer to a group of firms producing and selling a similar product, using similar technology, and perhaps obtaining factors of production from the same factor markets.

> [A]n individual business must be conceived as operating within an 'industry' which consists of all businesses which operate processes of a sufficiently similar kind . . . and possessing sufficiently similar backgrounds of experience and knowledge so that each of them could produce the particular commodity under consideration and would do so if sufficiently attractive.

> *(Andrews, 1951, p. 168)*

A focus on factor markets might provide a yardstick for grouping firms into industries that differs from the criteria for market definition discussed above. However, once again there are practical difficulties. This type of classification might suggest that soap and margarine belong to the same industry, while woollen gloves and leather gloves belong to different industries. Finally, in order to emphasize the degree of overlap between markets and industries, it is interesting to note that Stigler's (1955) industry definition provides a succinct summary of the criteria for identifying the boundaries of markets:

> An industry should embrace the maximum geographical area and the maximum variety of productive activities in which there is strong long-run substitution. If buyers can shift on a large scale from product or area B to area A, then the two should be combined. If producers can shift on a large scale from B to A, again they should be combined. Economists usually state this in an alternative form: All products or enterprises with large long run cross elasticities of either supply or demand should be combined into a single industry.

> *(Stigler, 1955, p. 4)*

6.3   Official schemes for industry classification

Although in principle the definition of markets and industries may raise a number of difficult issues, for the practical purpose of compiling official production and employment statistics, some specific scheme for defining and classifying industries is required. In the UK, the official classification of industries is known as the *Standard Industrial Classification*, or SIC. This system was first introduced in 1948, and was subsequently updated in 1980 and 1992. The 1980 SIC (SIC 1980) is divided into 10 divisions, each assigned a digit from 0 to 9. These are reproduced in Table 6.1. The 10 divisions of SIC 1980 are subdivided by the addition of further digits, to provide more refined definitions at the class (two-digit), group (three-digit) and activity (four-digit) levels. For example, a typical subdivision within Division 3 'Metal goods, engineering and vehicle industries' is as follows:

Division 3   Metal goods, engineering and vehicle industries
Class 34   Electrical and electronic engineering
Group 345   Other electronic equipment
Activity 3454   Electronic consumer goods

In 1992, the European Commission introduced a new classification system for use throughout the European Union (EU), known as *Nomenclature générale des activités économiques dans les communautés Européennes* (NACE). At the same time, the UK's Standard Industrial Classification was revised to achieve consistency with NACE. The objective was to standardize industry definitions across member states, making inter-country comparisons easier and providing a statistical basis for the harmonization of competition and industrial policy within the EU. The UK's 1992 SIC (SIC 1992) is based on a four-digit numbering system, while NACE adds a fifth digit in some cases. The 10 SIC 1980 divisions are replaced by 17 SIC 1992 sections, labelled alphabetically from A to Q. These are reproduced in Table 6.2, which also provides a comparison with SIC 1980. One important difference between the 1980 and 1992 classifications is the more detailed breakdown of the services industries provided by the 1992 system, reflecting the increase in the importance of the service sector (European Commission, 1997a).

Table 6.1 The UK's SIC 1980, by division

Division	Description
0	Agriculture, forestry and fishing
1	Energy and water supply industries
2	Extraction of minerals and ores and other fuels; manufacture of metals, mineral products and chemicals
3	Metal goods, engineering and vehicle industries
4	Other manufacturing industries
5	Construction
6	Distribution; hotels and catering; repairs
7	Transport and communication
8	Banking, finance, insurance, business services and leasing
9	Other services

Table 6.2 The UK's SIC 1992 and the EU's NACE, by section

Section (SIC 1992/NACE)	Description	Division (SIC 1980)
A	Agriculture, hunting and forestry	0
B	Fishing	0
C	Mining and quarrying	1, 2
D	Manufacturing	1, 2, 3, 4
E	Electricity, gas and water supply	1
F	Construction	5
G	Wholesale and retail trade; repair of motor vehicles and household goods	6
H	Hotels and restaurants	6
I	Transport, storage and communication	7, 9
J	Financial intermediation	8
K	Real estate, renting and business activity	8, 9
L	Public administration and defence, compulsory social security	9
M	Education	9
N	Health and social work	9
O	Other community, social and personal service activities	9
P	Private households with employed persons	9
Q	Extra-territorial organizations and bodies	9

Although there is consistency between the industry definitions used in the UK's SIC 1992 system and the EU's NACE system, there are minor differences in the numerical presentation of the various levels of both systems. For example, NACE contains more levels in total than SIC 1992. Most of the NACE sections are subdivided into subsections by the addition of a second letter. Not all sections are subdivided: for example, section B, Fishing, has no subsections. In contrast, section D, Manufacturing, has 14 subsections. Susections are then subdivided into divisions, which correspond to a two-digit classification. The full list of NACE divisions is reproduced in Table 6.3. Divisions are further subdivided into three-digit groups, four-digit classes, and in some cases, five-digit subclasses. For example, Table 6.4 shows all layers of classification between the most general 'Manufacturing' section D, and the most specific 'Bacon and ham' subclass 15.13/1.

6.4 Measures of concentration

Seller concentration, an indicator of the number and size distribution of firms, can be measured at two levels:

1. for all firms that form part of an economy, located within some specific geographical boundary;

2. for all firms classified as members of some industry or market, again located within some specific geographical boundary.

Table 6.3 The EU's NACE, by division

NACE Division (two-digit) code	Description
A.1	Agriculture, hunting and related service activities
A.2	Forestry, logging and related service activities
B.5	Fishing; operation of fish hatcheries and farms; service activities incidental to fishing
CA.10	Mining of coal and lignite; extraction of peat
CA.11	Extraction of crude petroleum and natural gas; service activities incidental to oil and gas extraction
CA.12	Mining of uranium and thorium ores
CB.13	Mining of metal ores
CB.14	Other mining and quarrying
DA.15	Manufacture of food products and beverages
DA.16	Manufacture of tobacco products
DB.17	Manufacture of textiles
DB.18	Manufacture of wearing apparel; dressing and dyeing of fur
DC.19	Tanning and dressing of leather; manufacture of luggage, handbags, saddlery, harness, footwear
DD.20	Manufacture of wood, wood and cork products except furniture
DE.21	Manufacture of pulp, paper and paper products
DE.22	Manufacture of publishing, printing and reproduction of recorded media
DF.23	Manufacture of coke, refined petroleum products
DG.24	Manufacture of chemicals and chemical products
DH.25	Manufacture of rubber and plastic products
DI.26	Manufacture of non-metallic mineral products
DJ.27	Manufacture of basic metals
DJ.28	Manufacture of fabricated metal products, except machinery and equipment
DK.29	Manufacture of machinery and equipment not elsewhere classified
DL.30	Manufacture of office machinery and computers
DL.31	Electrical machinery and apparatus not elsewhere classified
DL.32	Manufacture of radio, television and communication equipment and apparatus
DL.33	Manufacture of medical, precision and optical instruments, watches and clocks
DM.34	Manufacture of motor vehicles, trailers and semi-trailers
DM.35	Manufacture of other transport equipment
DN.36	Manufacture of furniture, manufacture not elsewhere classified
DN.37	Recycling
E.40	Electricity, gas, steam and hot water supply
E.41	Collection, purification and distribution of water
F.45	Construction
G.50	Sale, maintenance and repair of motor vehicles; retail sale of automotive fuel
G.51	Wholesale trade and commission trade, except motor vehicles and motorcycles
G.52	Retail trade, except motor vehicles and motor cycles and repairs of household goods
H.55	Hotels and restaurants
I.60	Land transport; transport via pipelines
I.61	Water transport
I.62	Air transport
I.63	Supporting and auxiliary transport activities; activities of travel agencies
I.64	Post and telecommunications
J.65	Financial intermediation
J.66	Insurance and pension funding
J.67	Activities auxiliary to financial intermediation

Table 6.3 (*continued*)

NACE Division (two-digit) code	Description
K.70	Real estate activities
K.71	Renting of machinery and equipment without operator and of personal and household goods
K.72	Computer and related activities
K.73	Research and development
K.74	Other business activities
L.75	Public administration and defence; compulsory social security
M.80	Education
N.85	Health and social work
O.90	Sewage and refuse disposal, sanitation and similar activities
O.91	Activities of membership organization n.e.c.
O.92	Recreational, cultural and sporting activities
O.93	Other service activities
P.95	Activities of households as employers of domestic staff
P.96	Undifferentiated goods producing activities of private households for own use
P.97	Undifferentiated services producing activities of private households for own use
Q.99	Extra-territorial organizations and bodies

Table 6.4 Comparison between the UK's SIC 1992 and the EU's NACE

SIC 1992	NACE	Description
Section D	Section D	Manufacturing
n/a	Subsection DA	Manufacture of food products; beverages and tobacco
Division 15	Division DA.15	Manufacture of food products and beverages
Group 151	Group DA.151	Production, processing and preserving of meat and meat products
n/a	Class DA.1513	Production of meat and poultry products
n/a	Subclass 15.13/1	Bacon and ham

The first type of seller concentration, known as **aggregate concentration**, reflects the importance of the largest firms in the economy as a whole. Although in practice data are relatively hard to come by, in principle aggregate concentration is relatively straightforward to measure. Typically, aggregate concentration is measured as the share of the n largest firms in the total sales, assets or employment (or other appropriate size measure) for the economy as a whole. The number of firms included might be n = 50, 100, 200 or 500. Aggregate concentration might be important for several reasons:

■ if aggregate concentration is high, this might have implications for levels of seller concentration in particular industries;

■ aggregate concentration data might reveal information about the economic importance of large diversified firms, which is not adequately reflected in indicators of seller concentration for particular industries;

■ if aggregate concentration is high, this might indicate that the economy's largest firms have opportunities to exert a disproportionate degree of influence over politicians or regulators, which might render the political system vulnerable to abuse.

The second type of seller concentration, known as **industry concentration** or (alternatively) **market concentration**, reflects the importance of the largest firms in some particular industry or market. In some cases, it may also be relevant to measure buyer concentration, in order to assess the importance of the largest buyers. This might arise in the case of an industry which supplies a specialized producer good, for which the market includes only a very small number of buyers.

In the rest of Section 6.4, we focus on the measurement of seller concentration at industry level. Clearly, the number and size distribution of the firms is a key element of industry structure. Any specific measure of seller concentration at industry level aims to provide a convenient numerical measure reflecting the implications of the number and size distribution of firms for the nature of competition in the industry concerned. In empirical research in industrial organization, concentration is probably the most widely used indicator of industry structure.

As we will see below, economists have employed a number of alternative **concentration measures** at industry level. To assist users in making an informed choice between the alternatives that are available, Hannah and Kay (1977) suggest a number of general criteria that any specific concentration measure should satisfy if it is to adequately reflect the most important characteristics of the firm size distribution:

■ Suppose industries A and B have equal numbers of firms. Industry A should be rated as more highly concentrated than industry B if the firms' cumulative market share (when the firms are ranked in descending order of size) is greater for industry A than for industry B at all points in the size distribution.

■ A transfer of market share from a smaller to a larger firm should always increase concentration.

■ There should be a market share threshold such that if a new firm enters the industry with a market share below the threshold, concentration is reduced. Similarly, if an incumbent firm with a market share below the threshold exits from the industry, concentration is increased.

■ Any merger between two incumbent firms should always increase concentration.

As will be shown below, not all of the seller concentration measures that are in use satisfy all of the Hannah and Kay criteria. This section examines the construction and interpretation of the most common measures of seller concentration. These are the n-firm concentration ratio, the Herfindahl–Hirschman index, the Hannah-Kay index, the entropy coefficient, the variance of the logarithms of firm sizes, and the Gini coefficient.

In order to demonstrate the calculation of the various concentration measures that are described below, Table 6.5 shows sales data for six hypothetical industries, I1 to I6, all of which have the same total sales.

Table 6.5 Firm size distribution (sales data): six hypothetical industries

	I1	I2	I3	I4	I5	I6
Firm 1	5,066	1,644	2,466	7,412	3,564	5,066
Firm 2	3,376	1,644	2,466	3,706	3,564	3,376
Firm 3	2,250	1,644	2,466	1,854	3,564	2,250
Firm 4	1,500	1,644	2,466	926	1,500	1,500
Firm 5	1,000	1,644	2,466	464	1,000	1,000
Firm 6	666	1,644	2,466	232	666	666
Firm 7	444	1,644		116	444	938
Firm 8	296	1,644		58	296	
Firm 9	198	1,644		28	198	
Total	14,796	14,796	14,796	14,796	14,796	14,796

- The nine firms in I1 have a typically skewed distribution of sales figures.

- The nine equal-sized firms in I2 all have the same sales figures.

- In I3, the number of equal-sized firms is six (rather than nine).

- I4 is similar to I1, except the size distribution is more heavily skewed (with the largest firm in I4 taking a larger market share than its counterpart in I1, and the smallest firm in I4 taking a smaller market share than its counterpart in I1).

- I5 is the same as I1 except for the three largest firms, which are equal-sized in I5.

- Finally, the six largest firms in I1 are the same as their counterparts in I6, but the three smallest firms in I1 have been merged to form a single firm in I6.

For each of I1 to I6, Table 6.6 shows the numerical values of the concentration measures that are presented below. For I1, Tables 6.7 to 6.11 show the calculations for each concentration measure in full. We refer to the numerical examples shown in Tables 6.5 to 6.11 at various points throughout this section.

n-firm concentration ratio

The n-firm **concentration ratio**, usually denoted CR_n, measures the share of the industry's n largest firms in some measure of total industry size. The most widely used size measures are based on industry sales, assets or employment data. The formula for the n-firm concentration ratio is as follows:

$$CR_n = \sum_{i=1}^{n} s_i$$

where s_i is the share of i'th largest firm in total industry sales, assets or employment. In other words, $s_i = x_i / \sum_{i=1}^{N} x_i$, where x_i is the size of firm i, and N is the number of firms in the industry. There are no set rules for the choice of n, the number of large

Table 6.6 Seller concentration measures: six hypothetical industries

	I1	I2	I3	I4	I5	I6
n-firm concentration ratio						
CR_3	.7226	.3333	.5000	.8767	.7226	.7226
CR_4	.8240	.4444	.6667	.9393	.8240	.8240
CR_5	.8916	.5556	.8333	.9707	.8916	.8916
Herfindahl–Hirschman and Hannah–Kay Indexes						
$HK(1.5)$	.4376	.3333	.4082	.5485	.4236	.4440
$HH = HK(2)$	.2108	.1111	.1667	.3346	.1924	.2133
$HK(2.5)$	.1076	.0370	.0680	.2158	.0906	.1084
Entropy and Relative entropy						
E	1.7855	2.1972	1.7918	1.3721	1.8236	1.7191
RE	.8126	1.0000	1.0000	.6245	.8299	.8835
Numbers equivalent						
$n(1)$	5.96	9.00	6.00	3.94	6.19	5.58
$n(1.5)$	5.22	9.00	6.00	3.32	5.57	5.07
$(I/HH) = n(2)$	4.74	9.00	6.00	2.99	5.20	4.69
$n(2.5)$	4.42	9.00	6.00	2.78	4.96	4.40
Variance of logarithms of firm sizes						
VL	1.0960	0	0	3.2223	1.1040	.4669
Gini coefficient						
G	.4482	0	0	.6035	.4101	.3219

Table 6.7 Calculation of three-, four- and five-firm concentration ratios

	I1
Firm 1	5,066
Firm 2	3,376
Firm 3	2,250
Firm 4	1,500
Firm 5	1,000
Firm 6	666
Firm 7	444
Firm 8	296
Firm 9	198
Total	14,796

$$CR_3 = \frac{5,066 + 3,376 + 2,250}{14,796} = 0.7226$$

$$CR_4 = \frac{5,066 + 3,376 + 2,250 + 1,500}{14,796} = 0.8240$$

$$CR_5 = \frac{5,066 + 3,376 + 2,250 + 1,500 + 1,000}{14,796} = 0.8916$$

firms to be included in the calculation of CR_n. However, CR_n for n = 3, 4, 5 or 8 are among the most widely quoted n-firm concentration ratios.

For most practical purposes, both the choice of n and the choice of size measure may not be too crucial. For example, Bailey and Boyle (1971) find that n-firm concentration ratios for several values of n are highly correlated. Similarly, Smyth *et al.* (1975) find that a number of alternative size measures are all highly correlated with each other (Shalit and Sankar, 1977). White (1981) discusses the criteria for appropriate measurement of firm size:

> In the case of concentration in individual markets, we are searching for some inferences as to the likelihood of oligopolistic co-ordination concerning prices and sales. The [sales] shares of the oligopolists themselves will be a prime determinant of the likelihood of that co-ordination. Hence, industry sales are the proper measure of concentration calculations in individual industries.
>
> *(White, 1981, pp. 223–4)*

In practice, an attractive property of the n-firm concentration ratio is that it requires size data on the top n firms only, together with the corresponding aggregate size measure for the entire industry. In other words, the data requirements are less demanding than for the other concentration measures that are described below, each of which requires individual size data for all of the industry's member firms. However, the use of data for the top n firms only is also a limitation, in the sense that no account is taken of the number and size distribution of firms that are outside the top n. Furthermore, no account is taken of the size distribution within the top n firms.

These points are illustrated in Tables 6.5 and 6.6 by I5 and I6, both of which have the same CR_3 as I1. However, we might well regard I5 as *less* highly concentrated than I1, and I6 as *more* highly concentrated:

- The top three firms in I5 are equal-sized, while the size distribution of the top three in I1 is skewed, making I5 look more competitive than I1.

- The three smallest firms in I1 have been merged in order to form one larger firm in I6, making I6 look less competitive than I1.

These comparisons show that the n-firm concentration ratio fails to meet several of the Hannah and Kay criteria for a satisfactory concentration measure. For example, a transfer of sales from a smaller to a larger firm does not necessarily cause CR_n to increase; and a merger between two or more industry member firms does not necessarily cause CR_n to increase.

Herfindahl–Hirschman (HH) index

Working independently, Hirschman (1945) and Herfindahl (1950) both suggested a concentration measure based on the sum of the squared market shares of all firms in the industry. The **Herfindahl–Hirschman (HH) index** is calculated as follows:

$$HH = \sum_{i=1}^{N} s_i^2$$

where s_i is the market share of firm i, and N is the total number of firms in the industry. For an industry that consists of a single monopoly producer, HH = 1. A monopolist has a market share of $s_1 = 1$. Therefore $s_1^2 = 1$, ensuring HH = 1. For an industry with N firms, the maximum possible value of the Herfindahl–Hirschman index is HH = 1, and the minimum possible value is HH = 1/N.

■ The maximum value of HH = 1 occurs when the size distribution of the N firms is highly skewed. In the most extreme case, one dominant firm has a market share only fractionally smaller than 1, and N − 1 very small firms each has a market share only fractionally larger than zero. Essentially, this is the same as the case of monopoly, for which HH = 1 as shown above.

■ The minimum value of HH = 1/N occurs when the industry consists of N equal-sized firms. In this case, each firm has a market share of $s_i = 1/N$. Therefore $s_i^2 = (1/N)^2$ for i = 1 . . . N, and $HH = \sum_{i=1}^{N}(1/N)^2 = N(1/N)^2 = 1/N$.

In Tables 6.5 and 6.6, I2, I1 and I4 each have N = 9 firms, and the respective size distributions are equal-sized, skewed and highly skewed. We obtain HH = 0.1111 (or 1/9) for I2, HH = 0.2108 for I1, and HH = 0.3346 for I4. This confirms that HH increases as the size distribution becomes more unequal. It is important to notice also that HH succeeds where CR_3 fails in identifying I5 as less concentrated than I1, and I6 as more concentrated than I1. For I5, I1 and I6, the values of HH shown in Table 6.6 are 0.1924, 0.2108 and 0.2133, respectively. Of all the concentration measures considered in this section, the HH index and the closely related **Hannah and Kay index** (see below) are generally the most satisfactory in respect of their ability to satisfy the Hannah and Kay criteria.

A practical difficulty with the HH index is its requirement for individual size data on all of the industry's member firms. In contrast, CR_n only requires individual data on the top n firms, and an industry total. However, it can be shown that even if individual data are not available for the smaller firms, a reasonable approximation to HH is obtained using data on the larger firms only. In I1, suppose we had individual sales data for firms 1 to 6 only, and the industry's total sales, but suppose we did not know how many other firms there were apart from these six. Then the maximum value HH could take (if one other firm accounted for all of the remaining sales) is HH = 0.2133. The minimum value HH could take (if a large number of very small firms accounted for the remaining sales, each with a very small share) is HH = 0.2093. The actual value of HH for I1 is 0.2108. Therefore the range of values HH can take is not very large. Whatever assumptions we make about the missing individual firm size data, we get a reasonably close approximation to the true value of HH.

A reciprocal measure, known as the **numbers equivalent** of the HH index, is defined as (1/HH). The numbers equivalent is an inverse measure of concentration. For an industry with N firms, the minimum possible value of the numbers equivalent is (1/HH) = 1, and the maximum possible value is (1/HH) = N.

Table 6.8 Calculation of Herfindahl–Hirschman and Hannah–Kay indexes

Firm	Sales	s_i	$s_i^{1.5}$	s_i^2	$s_i^{2.5}$
1	5,066	.3424	.2003	.1172	.0686
2	3,376	.2282	.1090	.0521	.0249
3	2,250	.1521	.0593	.0231	.0090
4	1,500	.1014	.0323	.0103	.0033
5	1,000	.0676	.0176	.0046	.0012
6	666	.0450	.0095	.0020	.0004
7	444	.0300	.0052	.0009	.0002
8	296	.0200	.0028	.0004	.0001
9	198	.0134	.0015	.0002	.0000
Sum	14,796	1.0000	HK(1.5) = 0.4376	HH = HK(2) = 0.2108	HK(2.5) = 0.1076

Numbers equivalent: $n(1.5) = 0.4376^{1/(1-1.5)} = 0.4376^{-2} = 5.22$
$(1/HH) = n(2) = 0.2108^{1/(1-2)} = 0.2108^{-1} = 4.74$
$n(2.5) = 0.1076^{1/(1-2.5)} = 0.1076^{-0.6667} = 4.42$

- The minimum value of $(1/HH) = 1$ occurs when $HH = 1$, and corresponds to the case of one dominant firm and $N - 1$ very small firms.

- The maximum value of $(1/HH) = N$ occurs when $HH = 1/N$, and corresponds to the case of N equal-sized firms.

Accordingly, the numbers equivalent is useful as a measure of inequality in the firm size distribution. For an industry with N firms, the minimum possible value, $(1/HH) = 1$, corresponds to the most unequal size distribution; and the maximum possible value, $(1/HH) = N$, corresponds to the most equal size distribution. In Tables 6.5 and 6.6, I2 with N = 9 equal-sized firms has $(1/HH) = 9$, and I3 with N = 6 equal-sized firms has $(1/HH) = 6$. I1 with N = 9 firms and a skewed size distribution has $(1/HH) = 4.74$, and I4 with N = 9 and a highly skewed distribution has $(1/HH) = 2.99$. However, even I4 falls some way short of the maximum inequality case of $(1/HH) = 1$.

Hannah and Kay index

It is possible to interpret the Herfindahl–Hirschman index as a weighted sum of the market shares of all firms in the industry, with the market shares themselves used as weights. A general expression for a weighted sum of market shares is

$\sum_{i=1}^{N} w_i s_i$, where w_i denotes the weight attached to firm i. By setting $w_i = s_i$, we obtain

$$HH = \sum_{i=1}^{N} w_i s_i = \sum_{i=1}^{N} s_i^2.$$

Therefore HH is a weighted sum of market shares, with larger weights attached to the larger firms and vice versa.

Hannah and Kay (1977) suggest the following generalization of the HH index:

$$HK(\alpha) = \sum_{i=1}^{N} s_i^{\alpha}$$

where α is a parameter to be selected. α should be greater than zero, but not equal to one, because $HK(1) = 1$ for any firm size distribution. In terms of the 'weighted sum' interpretation of the HH index, the choice of α in the $HK(\alpha)$ index enables the relative weights attached to the larger and small firms to vary from the proportions used in the HH index. For the $HK(\alpha)$ index, the weights can be defined $w_i = s_i^{\alpha-1}$.

Accordingly, we obtain $HK(\alpha) = \sum_{i=1}^{N} w_i s_i = \sum_{i=1}^{N} s_i^{\alpha-1} s_i = \sum_{i=1}^{N} s_i^{\alpha}$.

■ If $\alpha = 2$, the Hannah–Kay index is the same as the Herfindahl–Hirschman index, or $HK(2) = HH$.

■ If $\alpha < 2$, $HK(\alpha)$ attaches relatively more weight to the smaller firms and relatively less weight to the larger firms than HH.

■ Conversely, if $\alpha > 2$, $HK(\alpha)$ attaches relatively more weight to the larger firms and relatively less weight to the smaller firms than HH.

The last two points are illustrated in Table 6.8. For I1 the contribution to the HK(1.5) index of firm 1 (the largest firm) is 45.8 per cent (0.2003 out of 0.4376). But firm 1's contribution to the HK(2.5) index is 63.8 per cent (0.0686 out of 0.1076). Our earlier comments about the favourable properties of the HH index apply in equal measure to the $HK(\alpha)$ index. Furthermore, the larger the value of α, the smaller the degree of inaccuracy if the $HK(\alpha)$ index is calculated using accurate individual data for the largest firms, but estimated data for the smaller firms.

The expression for the corresponding inverse concentration measure, the numbers equivalent of the Hannah–Kay index, is as follows:

$$n(\alpha) = \left(\sum_{i=1}^{N} s_i^{\alpha} \right)^{1/(1-\alpha)}.$$

Notice that when $\alpha = 2$, $n(2) = \left(\sum_{i=1}^{N} s_i^2 \right)^{1/(1-2)} = \left(\sum_{i=1}^{N} s_i^2 \right)^{-1} = 1/\sum_{i=1}^{N} s_i^2 = 1/HH$, as before.

The numbers equivalent can be defined for any value of α that is greater than zero apart from $\alpha = 1$. The properties and interpretation of the numbers equivalent are the same as before: for an industry with N firms, the minimum value is 1 (one dominant firm and $N - 1$ very small firms); and the maximum value is N (all N firms are equal-sized). In Tables 6.5 and 6.6, $n(\alpha) = 9$ for I2 (with $N = 9$ equal-sized firms) and $n(\alpha) = 6$ for I3 (with $N = 6$ equal-sized firms), regardless of which value is chosen for α.

Entropy coefficient

The **entropy coefficient**, E, is another 'weighted sum' concentration measure. In this case, however, the weights are inversely related to the firms' market shares. The weights are the natural logarithms of the reciprocals of the firms' market shares. E is defined as follows:

$$E = \sum_{i=1}^{N} s_i \log_e(1/s_i)$$

E is an inverse concentration measure: E is small for a highly concentrated industry, and E is large for an industry with low concentration. In Tables 6.5 and 6.6, E is 1.3721 (for I4), 1.7855 (I1) and 1.8236 (I5). Therefore E correctly identifies I4 as more concentrated than I1, and I1 as more concentrated than I5. The minimum possible value is E = 0, for an industry comprising a single monopoly producer. The maximum possible value is E = $\log_e$(N), for an industry comprising N equal-sized firms. Because the maximum value of E depends on the number of firms, it may be inconvenient to use entropy coefficients to compare concentration for two different-sized industries. However, it is straightforward to define a standardized entropy coefficient, whose maximum value does not depend on the number of firms. This is known as the relative entropy coefficient, RE, and is defined as follows:

$$RE = E/\log_e(N) = [1/\log_e(N)] \sum_{i=1}^{N} s_i \log_e(1/s_i)$$

The minimum possible value is RE = 0 for a monopoly, and the maximum possible value is RE = 1 for an industry comprising N equal-sized firms.

Finally, as noted above, both E and the numbers equivalent of the HK index are inverse concentration measures. Hannah and Kay (1977, pp. 56–7) demonstrate the

Table 6.9 Calculation of entropy coefficient

Firm	Sales	s_i	$1/s_i$	$\log_e(1/s_i)$	$s_i \log_e(1/s_i)$
1	5,066	.3424	2.9206	1.0718	0.3670
2	3,376	.2282	4.3827	1.4777	0.3372
3	2,250	.1521	6.5760	1.8834	0.2864
4	1,500	.1014	9.8640	2.2889	0.2320
5	1,000	.0676	14.7960	2.6944	0.1821
6	666	.0450	22.2162	3.1008	0.1396
7	444	.0300	33.3243	3.5063	0.1052
8	296	.0200	49.9865	3.9118	0.0783
9	198	.0134	74.7273	4.3138	0.0577
Sum	14,796	1.0000			E = 1.7855

Relative entropy: RE = E/$\log_e$(N) = 1.7855/$\log_e$(9) = 1.7855/2.1972 = 0.8126
Numbers equivalent: n(1) = exp(E) = exp(1.7855) = 5.96

mathematical relationship between them. The numbers equivalent of the HK index,

$$n(\alpha) = \left(\sum_{i=1}^{N} s_i^{\alpha} \right)^{1/(1-\alpha)}$$

is not defined for $\alpha = 1$. However, it can be shown that as α approaches one, the limiting value of $n(\alpha)$ is $\exp(E)$ or $e^E = \prod_{i=1}^{N} (1/s_i)^{s_i}$. Therefore we can think of $\exp(E)$ as a numbers equivalent-type measure that corresponds to the case $\alpha = 1$.

Variance of the logarithms of firm sizes

In statistics, a variance provides a standard measure of dispersion or inequality within any data set. In the case of data on the sizes of firms in an industry, the statistical property of dispersion or inequality is closely related to (but not identical to) the economic property of seller concentration. In Table 6.5, dispersion in I2 is zero (because all firm sizes are the same), but dispersion in I4 is much higher (due to the inequality in the firm size distribution). Clearly, seller concentration is higher in I4 than in I2. Accordingly, the variance of the logarithms of firm sizes, VL, can be included among the list of concentration measures (Aitchison and Brown, 1966). VL is defined as follows:

$$VL = (1/N) \sum_{i=1}^{N} [\log_e(x_i) - \bar{x}]^2 \text{ where } \bar{x} = (1/N) \sum_{i=1}^{N} \log_e(x_i)$$

and x_i is the size of firm i (as before, measured using sales, assets, employment or some other appropriate size indicator).

Table 6.10 Calculation of variance of logarithmic firm sizes

Firm	Sales, x_i	$\log_e(x_i)$	$\log_e(x_i) - \bar{x}$ ($\bar{x} = 6.9078$)	$[\log_e(x_i) - \bar{x}]^2$
1	5,066	8.5303	1.6225	2.6325
2	3,376	8.1244	1.2167	1.4802
3	2,250	7.7187	0.8109	0.6575
4	1,500	7.3132	0.4054	0.1644
5	1,000	6.9078	0.0000	0.0000
6	666	6.5013	−0.4065	0.1652
7	444	6.0958	−0.8120	0.6593
8	296	5.6904	−1.2174	1.4821
9	198	5.2883	−1.6195	2.6229
Sum	14,796	62.1072		9.8643

$\bar{x} = $ mean value of $\log_e(x_i) = (1/N) \sum_{i=1}^{N} \log_e(x_i) = 62.1072/9 = 6.9078$

$VL = (1/N) \sum_{i=1}^{N} [\log_e(x_i) - \bar{x}]^2 = 9.8643/9 = 1.0960$

For the purposes of calculating VL, the firm size data are expressed in logarithmic form for the following reasons:

■ Most industries have a highly skewed firm size distribution, with large numbers of small firms, fewer medium-sized firms and very few large firms. The variance of the (untransformed) firm size data would therefore tend to be unduly influenced by the data for the largest firms. The log-transformation reduces or eliminates the skewness in the original distribution, enabling VL to provide a more reasonable measure of inequality across the entire firm size distribution.

■ The variance of the (untransformed) firm size data would be influenced by the scaling or units of measurement of the data. VL, in contrast, is unaffected by scaling. For example, if inflation caused the reported sales data of all firms to increase by 10 per cent, the variance of the (untransformed) sales data would increase, but VL would be unaffected. In this case, there is no change in concentration or dispersion because the sales of all firms are increased in the same proportions. VL reflects this situation accurately.

Although VL has occasionally been used as a measure of seller concentration, it is more accurate to interpret VL as a measure of dispersion or inequality in the firm size distribution. The distinction can be illustrated using the following examples taken from Tables 6.5 and 6.6:

■ Both I2 and I3 have VL = 0 because in both cases all firms are equal-sized, so there is no inequality. From an industrial organization perspective, however, it seems clear that I3 is more highly concentrated than I2. I3 has fewer firms than I2, making it more likely that a cooperative or collusive outcome will be achieved.

■ An economist would regard I6 as more concentrated than I1. However, the merger between the three smallest firms in I1 to form I6 implies I6 has a lower degree of inequality in its firm size distribution than I1. Accordingly VL is smaller for I6 than for I1. When we switch from I1 to I6, VL moves in the opposite direction to HH and HK(α), and in the wrong direction from the economist's perspective.

Lorenz curve and the Gini coefficient

A **Lorenz curve** (named after Lorenz, 1905) shows the variation in the cumulative size of the n largest firms in an industry, as n varies from 1 to N (where N is the total number of firms). Figure 6.1 shows a typical Lorenz curve. The firms are represented in a horizontal array, from the largest to the smallest (reading from left to right) along the horizontal axis. The vertical axis shows the cumulative size (the sum of the sizes of all firms from firm 1 to firm n, as a function of n).

■ If all of the firms are equal-sized, the Lorenz curve is the 45-degree line OCA. At point C, for example, exactly half of the industry's member firms account for exactly half of the total industry size, represented by the distance OD.

■ If the firm size distribution is skewed, the Lorenz curve is the concave curve OBA. At point B, exactly half of the industry's member firms account for three-quarters of the total industry size, represented by OD.

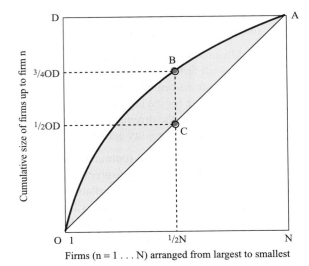

Figure 6.1 The Lorenz curve

The Lorenz curve can be used to define a concentration measure due to Gini (1912), known as the **Gini coefficient**. With reference to Figure 6.1, the Gini coefficient is defined as follows:

$$G = \frac{\text{area of the crescent between OBA and OCA}}{\text{area of the triangle ODA}}$$

- The maximum possible value of G = 1 corresponds to the case of one dominant firm with a market share approaching one, and N − 1 very small firms each with a negligible market share. In this case the Lorenz curve approaches the line ODA, so the numerator and denominator in the formula for G are the same.

- The minimum value of G = 0 corresponds to the case of N equal-sized firms. In this case the Lorenz curve is the 45-degree line OCA, so the numerator in the formula for G is zero.

The formula definition for the Gini coefficient is as follows:

$$G = \left\{ \frac{\displaystyle\sum_{n=1}^{N}\sum_{i=1}^{n} x_i}{0.5(N+1)\displaystyle\sum_{i=1}^{N} x_i} \right\} - 1$$

where x_i is the size of firm i (as before, measured using sales, assets, employment or some other appropriate size indicator) when the firms ranked in descending order of size.

Like the variance of logarithmic firm sizes measure, the Gini coefficient is most accurately interpreted as a measure of inequality in the firm size distribution. In fact,

Table 6.11 Calculation of Gini coefficient

Firm, n	Sales, x_i	Cumulative sales, up to firm n, $\sum_{i=1}^{n} x_i$
1	5,066	5,066
2	3,376	8,442
3	2,250	10,692
4	1,500	12,192
5	1,000	13,192
6	666	13,858
7	444	14,302
8	296	14,598
9	198	14,796
Sum	$\sum_{i=1}^{N} x_i = 14{,}796$	$\sum_{n=1}^{N}\sum_{i=1}^{n} x_i = 107{,}138$

$$\text{Gini coefficient, } G = \left\{ \frac{\displaystyle\sum_{n=1}^{N}\sum_{i=1}^{n} x_i}{0.5(N+1)\displaystyle\sum_{i=1}^{N} x_i} \right\} - 1 = \left\{ \frac{107{,}138}{0.5 \times 10 \times 14{,}796} \right\} - 1 = 0.4482$$

elsewhere in economics one of the best known applications of the Gini coefficient is for the measurement of inequality in household incomes. In our case, Tables 6.5 and 6.6 show that both I2 and I3 have G = 0, because in both cases all of the firms are equal-sized. As before, however, an industrial economist might regard I3 as more highly concentrated than I2. Furthermore, I6 has G = 0.3129, smaller than G = 0.4482 for I1. But an industrial economist would regard I6 as more concentrated than I1.

Case study 6.1

The media concentration debate

One of the most rancorous political battles in Washington today is over the rules limiting media concentration. Michael Powell, chairman of the Federal Communications Commission, has narrowly pushed through a set of rules that relax ownership restrictions. The share of population that can be reached by the television stations owned by any one company was raised from 35 to 45 per cent. The cross-ownership limits of newspapers and television stations in the same market were rescinded or reduced, depending on the size of the market. And local ownership ceilings for television stations were raised. The result has been a political firestorm, in which the political right and left have joined forces against free-market advocates, resulting in a lopsided congressional vote of 400:21. The Senate is in no better a mood. The White House has threatened a veto if such a law is passed. It would be President George W. Bush's first veto; and judging from the congressional vote tally and the desertion of the FCC's Republican allies, an uphill struggle. Powell, meanwhile, seems disgusted enough to contemplate departing.

Opponents of the FCC's new rules view themselves as a last line of defence against homogenized news controlled by five giant media conglomerates: AOL Time Warner, Disney, General Electric, News Corporation and Viacom. They fear a situation like that of Italy, where Silvio Berlusconi has used his media empire to achieve power and office. Defenders of the FCC argue that new technologies have made the media market wide open and reduced the importance of broadcasting stations. Both sides project themselves as defenders of the first amendment, protecting media from government, or, alternatively, shielding the public from communications empires.

The American media concentration debate and the principles that are at stake were cogently analysed in June by my fellow New Economy Forum columnists Tom Hazlitt and Richard Epstein. This column, in contrast, will be empirical. It is useful to step back and look at the facts. Are American media more concentrated today, nationally and locally, than they were in the past? This is largely an empirical question. It is true that large media companies have become larger; but so has the entire sector. The answer is therefore not as obvious as it seems.

Fortunately for its readers, the FT Online New Economy Forum is in possession of the world's best data set on media ownership and market shares, covering about 100 information sector industries and going back about 20 years. We are therefore able to provide some real but still preliminary empirical findings. What follows might be dry but it is directly relevant to the debate in Washington.

It is important to understand the difference between national and local media concentration. A newspaper company may own 25 papers that give it in the aggregate a moderate national market share among newspaper companies; but each of these papers may be the only local paper in its town, giving it substantial powers there over local news coverage and advertising prices. Other media are national rather than local, for example most magazines, books, music, and content network of television and cable. It is therefore necessary to look at both national and local concentrations.

What is market concentration? We use an index known as 'CR$_4$', which is the share of the top four companies in a market. Just to be sure, we also look at another index, the 'HH' used by the US Government to define concentration for antitrust purposes. We compare concentration trends over the past 20 years.

The concentration of broadcast television is the most contentious issue in the debate. Let us therefore look at the facts. For local television station ownership, the national share of the top four companies just about doubled, from 12 per cent in 1984 to 21 per cent in 2001/2. But by the standards of the US antitrust authorities, this leaves the industry still firmly in the range of 'unconcentrated'. During that period, market concentration also declined for television networking, which provides the bulk of broadcast station evening and weekend programmes, from a three-network oligopoly of nearly 100 per cent to a four-company share of 92 per cent, still very high but dropping. If we combine networks for broadcast television and for cable television, as most viewers would, national network concentration declined from 82 per cent to 68 per cent.

At the same time, the local concentration of broadcast television stations, based on an analysis of 30 representative markets, did not increase as many have feared, but actually declined, owing to the shift of viewership away from the affiliates of three networks to a wider range of broadcast stations. Whereas the largest four stations in a local market accounted for 90 per cent of audiences in 1984, that number had declined to 73 per cent 20 years later. Furthermore, most of that decline took place in the past five years. If we put all these elements together into a composite index, the results show a decline in the overall concentration of broadcast television over the past 20 years.

In contrast, market concentration grew considerably for radio stations, where the owner-ship rules until the 1990s kept any company from owning more than a few stations, in an industry of 12,000 stations. Today, with no national ownership ceilings, the top four station groups, led by Clear Channel and Viacom, account for 34 per cent of stations by revenues. This is more than four times the 8 per cent of two decades ago, and marks a growth un-paralleled by any other medium; but even this, in terms of the US government's guidelines on market concentration, is well within the 'unconcentrated' range. Furthermore, most of that growth has taken place between 1992 and 1996 and has slowed down more recently. Local radio concentration is perhaps the most important issue to worry about. It has grown from an average of 44 per cent of an audience held by the top four station owners in each local market 20 years ago to 84 per cent, and falls definitely within the range of 'highly concentrated industries'.

For multi-channel television (cable and satellite), the four-company concentration tripled nationally from 21 per cent to 60 per cent, an increase that is more troubling than that of broadcast television. Most important is the extent of local concentration. Here, cable used to be for a long time the only option, wielding considerable gatekeeper power. Today, with satellite television a viable option for national programmes, cable's share has declined to 78 per cent and keeps sliding.

It is interesting to look at which local medium is most concentrated: newspapers. While their national concentration is moderate but rising (27 per cent, up from 22 per cent), local concentration levels are astonishingly high. Whichever index one uses, local newspapers are at the top for local media concentration.

Finally, to get an overall picture, we aggregated the trends for all mass media: television, cable and radio but also print, music, and film. On average their concentration is low by the definition of the US antitrust authorities but steadily increasing, especially after 1996. Average four-company concentration in each of the industries rose from 31 per cent to 46 per cent, to a level that is still unconcentrated (but barely) by the government's guidelines.

Contrast this with the higher concentrations in the telecom services sector (76 per cent) or even the internet sector, whose wide-open fragmentation increasingly exists more as a founding myth than as a reality (up from 63 per cent in 1996 to 73 per cent in 2001/2.)

We can also look at the presence of the top four mass media companies in the entire mass media sector. Their revenues tripled from $26bn in 1984, in today's money, to $78bn last year. The share of these companies in the overall mass media sector has doubled from about 11 per cent in 1984 to 21 per cent in 2001/2. This is a considerable relative increase – but the absolute level would be considered low in most sectors of goods and services. The low percentages, defying conventional wisdom, are explainable by the sheer size and diversity of the mass media market and its segments: about $400bn, if one adds up the revenues of print, music, broadcasting, cable, and film.

These dry numbers are relevant to the hot debate in Washington, assuming that evidence has a role besides the rhetoric. Outside of radio, the data do not show a rapid trend to media concentration and dominance. This should not suggest that media concentration is low or that there is no need for vigilance. But it is quite another matter to call it a crisis, as many have done in the heat of the battle. Congress has clearly signalled its unwillingness to see the radio scenario replay itself for television. Society is entitled to determine the proper balance between the economic and speech rights of media companies and the public's right to diverse sources of information. And economics is not the only factor to consider. The ownership of news and entertainment media is important to the health of democracy. But the debate over it must be healthy, too, and relate to facts rather than be driven by some dark fear that a handful of media giants (liberal or conservative, take your pick) are taking over nationally and locally, a fear which is not supported by the data.

Source: Eli Noam, The media concentration debate, FT.com site, 31 July 2003. © The Financial Times.

6.5 Interpretation of concentration measures

Subject to the availability of data, the calculation of any of the concentration indicators detailed above is straightforward. Some of the technical limitations of individual measures have already been identified and discussed. However, even if we disregard the technical issues, the broader interpretation of concentration indicators can still be problematic, due to inherent difficulties in defining the boundaries of the relevant industry or market (Curry and George, 1983). Some of the key issues are as follows.

■ *Choice of appropriate industry definition.* A concentration measure is specific to some industry, but any industry definition is arbitrary to some extent. Industry definitions should allow the calculation of concentration measures that sensibly reflect economic power. Therefore a properly defined industry should include producers of all substitute products. But how close does an alternative product have to be in order to count as a substitute? Substitution is a matter of degree, and the difficulty lies in knowing where to draw the line. By defining the limits very tightly, almost any firm could be considered as a monopolist. In one case in the US, the relevant market was described as 'the industry supplying paint to General Motors'. Since DuPont was at the time the only supplier of paint to General Motors, DuPont immediately achieved monopoly status. In general, the more refined the industry definition (the greater the number of digits), the higher measured concentration is likely to be. The choice of suitable industry or market definitions for decision making in competition policy is discussed in Chapter 17.

■ *Defining the boundaries of the market*. The selection of the cohort of firms whose size data are to be used to measure concentration also includes a geographical dimension. The relevant market for one firm might be local; another firm might service an international market. Naturally, concentration measures calculated from international or national data tend to suggest lower levels of concentration than regional or local measures. For example, the bus services industry consists of small numbers of carriers in each city. Therefore locally, seller concentration tends to be high. Measured at national level, however, concentration tends to be much lower.

■ *Treatment of imports and exports*. If (as is likely) producers of imported goods are excluded from the calculation of a concentration measure for some industry in the national economy, measured concentration might either overstate or under-state the true importance of the largest firms. For example, if a single foreign firm imported goods that accounted for 40 per cent of the market, making it the largest single producer, CR_n calculated using data on domestic firms only would seriously understate the true degree of concentration. If on the other hand the imported goods' 40 per cent market share was accounted for by a large number of small foreign producers, CR_n would overstate true concentration. Similar issues arise if (as is also likely) the reported sales of domestic firms include sales in export markets. One firm might have extremely high sales relative to all the rest, but if these sales are dispersed across several highly competitive export markets, the firm does not have much real market power. But a high concentration ratio might easily be misinterpreted to suggest the exact opposite. These and other similar issues are discussed by Utton (1982).

■ *Multi-product operations*. Concentration measures based on a firm's reported company accounts data might not take account of diversification: many larger firms sell goods or services across a wide range of separate markets. Typically, a plant or firm is classified as part of the census industry to which its main product belongs. If 60 per cent of a firm's sales revenues are derived from an industry A product, and 40 per cent from an industry B product, then all of that firm's sales (or other firm size data) may simply be attributed to industry A. Concentration measures calculated from data of this kind might tend to overstate or understate true concentration in both industries. Only by pure chance (if all of these 'diversified firm' effects cancel each other out) will concentration be measured accurately.

Although at first sight the choice between the various concentration measures might seem almost bewildering, this decision often turns out not to be too crucial in practice. Most of the measures described above tend to be highly correlated with one another (Davies, 1979; Kwoka, 1981). For example, using Belgian data Vanlommel *et al.* (1977) compare 11 concentration measures for 119 industries, and find that most of the measures are highly correlated.

However, in the final analysis it may be impossible to quantify all relevant aspects of an industry's competitive nature in a single numerical measure. For example, the number of firms in an industry might be small, but if their objectives and modes of operation differ fundamentally, they may disregard their interdependence and behave like atomistic competitors. Even the narrower and purely 'economic' characteristics may be hard to pin down. '[N]o single concentration measure effectively considers the three underlying determinants of competition: sector size, inequality of market shares and coalition potential' (Vanlommel *et al.*, 1977, p. 15). But if proper attention is also paid to broader industry characteristics such as historical tradition, the objectives and social background of owners and managers, and so on, it quickly becomes impossible to summarize all of the information that might be relevant using a single, one-dimensional numerical measure.

6.6 Trends in concentration and the location of industry

In this section we describe patterns and trends in seller concentration at the aggregate level, and for particular industries. We also describe influences on the geographical location of industry.

Trends in aggregate concentration

Hart and Prais (1956) examine trends in aggregate concentration for the UK (by examining the distribution of firm sizes of all quoted companies, measured by stock exchange valuation) for the period 1895–1950. Aggregate concentration increased throughout most of the pre-Second World War period up to 1939. Subsequently, aggregate concentration appears to have declined between 1940 and 1950. Evely and Little (1960) report similar findings. Hannah and Kay (1977) examine trends in aggregate concentration (measured by the proportion of assets accounted for by the top 100 firms) between 1919 and 1969. Aggregate concentration appears to have increased over the period 1919–30, declined during 1930–48, but then increased again during the 1950s and 1960s. Merger activity appears to have contributed significantly to the rise in concentration both during the 1920s, and during the 1950s and 1960s. The fall in concentration during the period 1930–48 is attributed to the faster growth of medium-sized firms, relative to their larger counterparts.

Large-scale mergers and an improvement in the competitiveness of large manufacturing firms appear to have contributed to a further increase in aggregate concentration in the UK during the 1970s (Clarke, 1985; Hart and Clarke, 1980). During the 1980s, however, the long-term trend was reversed, and aggregate concentration began to decrease (Clarke, 1993). At the start of the 1980s, the UK's manufacturing sector was subjected to an unprecedented squeeze from a combination of high interest rates and a high exchange rate. Faced with a sharp fall in demand in both the domestic market (as the UK economy became mired in recession) and in export markets (as the high exchange rate damaged competitiveness), a large number of manufacturing firms were forced out of business altogether. Many of those that survived did so only by shedding labour and downsizing. This led to a reduction in average firm size, and a fall in aggregate concentration.

Davies *et al.* (2001) examine changes in aggregate concentration at the European level (measured by the aggregate market shares of the 100 largest European manufacturing firms) over the period 1987–93. Aggregate concentration appears to have fallen slightly from 29.6 per cent to 28.6 per cent. While concentration remained relatively stable, there was a substantial turnover (entry and exit) among the top

100 firms. Between 1987 and 1993 there were 22 exits from the top 100. In nine cases, this was caused by slow internal growth, bankruptcy or takeover by firms from outside the top 100. In four cases, it was caused by takeover by other top 100 firms. In the remaining nine cases, it was caused by a relative decline in sales, resulting in these firms slipping from the top 100. Of the 22 entrants, two were created by divestment of assets by existing top 100 firms, and 13 achieved top 100 status through relative sales growth. The remaining seven firms were classified as completely 'new' entrants.

Pryor (2001a, 2001b, 2002) examines the trend in aggregate concentration in the US, over the period 1960–97. Aggregate concentration appears to have declined over the period 1962–85. However, this trend was reversed and aggregate concentration began to increase from the late 1980s onwards. Deconcentration during the 1980s is attributed to factors such as an increase in import penetration, deregulation, stronger competition policy and technological change which tended to lower the minimum efficient scale (MES). During the 1990s, phenomena such as globalization, improvements in information technology and e-commerce appear to have pushed in the direction of further deconcentration. However, this tendency has been more than offset by an increase in merger activity, which caused aggregate concentration to increase during the 1990s.

Trends in industry concentration

Naturally, seller concentration varies considerably from industry to industry. Economists have often been most concerned with concentration in manufacturing, in which large-scale production techniques became prevalent during the 1920s and 1930s (Chandler, 1990). For example, Shepherd (1972) reports that average four-digit, five-firm industry concentration ratios were lower for UK (52.1 per cent) than for US manufacturing (60.3 per cent) for the period 1958–63. This pattern is attributed to differences in technologies, more intense competition and a more rigorous competition policy regime in the UK. Table 6.12 shows CR_5 (five-firm concentration ratios) for selected UK manufacturing industries in 1992. At a European

Table 6.12 Five-firm concentration ratios for selected industries, UK, 1992

Industry	Five-firm concentration ratio
Tobacco	0.99
Iron and steel	0.95
Motor vehicles and engines	0.83
Pharmaceuticals	0.51
Grain milling	0.63
Footwear	0.48
Brewing	0.38
Clothing	0.21
Printing and publishing	0.16

Source: Census of Production PA 1002 (1995), National Statistics © Crown Copyright 2000.

level, Davies *et al.* (2001) report an increase in CR$_5$ for all manufacturing industries over the period 1987–93, from 24.8 per cent to 25.7 per cent.

All EU member countries experienced a pronounced shift in the distribution of economic activity away from manufacturing and towards services towards the end of the twentieth century. Over the period 1991–2001, GDP in services (distribution, hotels and restaurants, transport, financial intermediation, real estate and public administration) grew at an average rate of around 3 per cent per annum, while GDP in industry (mining and quarrying; manufacturing; and electricity, gas and water supply) grew at around 1.5 per cent per annum (European Commission, 2003a). By the start of the twenty-first century, industry accounted for 22 per cent of GDP in the EU, services accounted for 71 per cent, agriculture accounted for 2 per cent and construction accounted for 7 per cent. In all EU member countries with the exception of Portugal, more than 60 per cent of the labour force was employed in services (European Commission, 2003a).

The trend towards increasing seller concentration was repeated in many service sector industries towards the end of the twentieth century. Table 6.13 summarizes the size distribution of firms by industry classification across all EU member countries in 1997. Table 6.13 suggests there is considerable variation in patterns of concentration between industries, with the largest employers (firms of 250 employees or more) accounting for the largest shares of sales in motor manufacturing and financial services, and the smallest shares of sales in hotels and restaurants, construction and real estate.

The location of European industry

Specialization reflects whether a country's production is composed mainly of a small number of products or services, or whether the country's production is widely dispersed across a broad range of goods and services. Table 6.14 shows some examples of high-specialization manufacturing industries for selected EU member countries. **Geographic concentration** (or **regional concentration**) reflects whether a large share of an industry's total output is produced in a small number of countries or regions, or whether the industry is widely dispersed geographically (Aiginger, 1999).

A recent study by European Commission (2000) compares patterns of specialization in Europe, the US and Japan. While Europe tends to specialize in traditional industries such as building materials, tiles, footwear and textiles, Japan and the US specialize in technology-oriented industries such as electronic components and motor vehicles. Cockerill and Johnson (2003) suggest this is due to the higher absolute and relative expenditures on research and development in the US and Japan. For example, in 2001 private sector research and development expenditure as a percentage of GDP was 1.28 per cent for the 15 states that were EU members at the time (the EU-15), 2.11 per cent for Japan, and 2.04 per cent for the US. Within Europe, Sweden and Finland had the highest percentages (2.84 per cent and 2.68 per cent, respectively), and Portugal and Greece had the lowest (0.17 per cent and 0.19 per cent, respectively). The UK figure was 1.21 per cent (European Commission, 2003a).

Observed patterns of specialization and geographic concentration in European industry are rather complex, and often dependent on definitions and methods of

Table 6.13 Firm size distributions for selected industries, EU, 1997 (distribution of sales by employment size class)

NACE two-digit code	Description	Micro	Small	Medium	Large
13 and 14	Mining of metal ores; other mining and quarrying	21.1	29.6	22.4	26.9
15 and 16	Manufacture of food products and beverages; manufacture of tobacco products	7.8	14.0	23.5	54.6
17, 18 and 19	Manufacture of textiles; manufacture of wearing apparel; dressing and dyeing of fur; manufacture of tanning, leather; luggage, handbags, saddlery, harness, footwear	11.8	27.8	30.3	30.1
20, 21 and 22	Manufacture of wood, wood and cork products except furniture, manufacture of pulp, paper and paper products, manufacture of publishing, printing and reproduction of recorded media	12.5	20.4	23.5	43.5
24 and 25	Manufacture of chemicals and chemical products; manufacture of rubber and plastic products	3.7	9.9	20.1	66.3
26	Manufacture of non-metallic mineral products	8.8	20.7	26.2	44.2
27	Manufacture of basic metals	1.7	7.6	15.4	75.3
28	Manufacture of fabricated metal products, except machinery and equipment	14.8	29.5	25.9	29.9
29	Manufacture of machinery and equipment not elsewhere classified	5.7	15.5	22.5	56.3
30, 31 and 32	Manufacture of office machinery and computers; electrical machinery and apparatus not elsewhere classified; manufacture of radio, television and communication equipment and apparatus	4.2	7.9	13.4	74.6
33	Manufacture of medical, precision and optical instruments, watches and clocks	11.3	18.6	23.3	46.8
34 and 35	Manufacture of motor vehicles, trailers and semi-trailers; manufacture of other transport equipment	1.3	3.5	6.1	89.1
36	Manufacture of furniture, manufacture not elsewhere classified	16.2	26.2	26.4	31.2
40	Electricity, gas steam and hot water supply	5.9	4.2	28.3	61.7
45	Construction	33.9	28.9	18.4	18.8
50, 51 and 52	Sale, maintenance and repair of motor vehicles; retail sale of automotive fuel; wholesale trade and commission trade, except motor vehicles and motorcycles; retail trade, except motor vehicles and motor cycles and repairs of household goods	29.1	24.7	19.7	26.5
55	Hotels and restaurants	49.7	20.2	10.7	19.4
60, 61, 62 and 63	Land transport; transport via pipelines; water transport; air transport; supporting activities; travel agencies	23.5	18.9	14.9	42.8
64 and 72	Post and telecommunications; computer and related activities	11.4	9.1	11.5	68.1
65	Financial intermediation	4.1	7.3	23.6	65.0
66	Insurance and pension funding	6.6	6.1	15.2	72.2
67	Activities auxiliary to financial intermediation	8.1	13.2	9.2	69.4
70	Real estate activities	53.6	20.3	20.2	6.0
71, 73 and 74	Renting of machinery and equipment without operator and of personal and household goods; research and development; other business activities	33.3	20.5	16.8	29.4

Source: Adapted from European Commission (2000) *Panorama of EU Business*. Luxembourg: Office for Official Publications of the European Communities. Selected table entries, chapters 2–21.

Size bands: Micro: 0–9 employees; Small: 10–49 employees; Medium: 50–249; and Large: 250+ employees.

Table 6.14 Specialization in European manufacturing

Country	Industry	Industry	Industry
Belgium	Cells and batteries	Iron and steel processing	Other textiles
Denmark	Fish	Games and toys	Optical equipment
Finland	Pulp and paper	Sawmilling and planing of wood	Telecommunications equipment
France	Aircraft and spacecraft	Processing of nuclear fuel	Steam generators
Germany	Electricity distribution	Machine tools	Motor vehicles
Italy	Ceramic tiles	Motorcycles and bicycles	Tanning of leather
Netherlands	Audio-visual household goods	Oils and fats	Other transport equipment
Sweden	Pulp and paper	Sawmilling and planing of wood	Tubes
UK	Aircraft and spacecraft	Pesticides and other agro-chemical products	Publishing

Source: Adapted from European Commission (2000) *Panorama of EU Business*. Luxembourg: Office for Official Publications of the European Communities; and European Commission (2003a) *EU Business: Facts and Figures*. Luxembourg: Office for Official Publications of the European Communities.

measurement. Consequently, different studies have drawn different conclusions as to the existence or direction of any long-term trends in these patterns. Amiti (1997, 1998) examines changes in specialization and geographic concentration for 27 European manufacturing industries over the period 1968–90. Specialization increased for Belgium, Denmark, Germany, Greece, Italy and the Netherlands, but decreased for France, Spain and the UK. A similar exercise for selected countries using a more disaggregated industry classification finds that Belgium, France, Germany, Italy and the UK all became more specialized. Geographic concentration increased in 17 out of 27 industries, predominantly those in which producers were heavily reliant on intermediate inputs from suppliers, and where there were significant economies of scale. Brulhart (1998) reports geographic concentration increased throughout Europe during the 1980s. However, Aiginger and Davies (2000) report that while specialization in European manufacturing increased during the period 1985–98, geographic concentration decreased. A number of smaller countries overcame historical disadvantages and increased their shares of production in specific industries.

Hallet (2000) measures specialization and geographic concentration in order to examine changes in the spatial distribution of 17 economic activities within Europe for the period 1980–95. Southern (peripheral) regions were more highly specialized than their northern counterparts. Specialization tended to increase in poorer regions, and in regions that underwent major change in industrial structure. Geographic concentration is captured using four measures:

■ The extent to which production is spatially dispersed.

■ The extent to which production is concentrated at the EU's core or periphery.

■ The degree of 'clustering', reflected by the geographic distance between branches of similar activity.

■ The extent to which production is concentrated in high- or low-income regions.

Manufacturing industries with significant economies of scale tend to be geographically concentrated. Production in sectors such as agriculture, textiles and clothing takes place predominantly at the EU's periphery, while sectors such as banking and financial services are concentrated at the centre. Production of a number of products, including ores and metals, chemicals, and transport equipment, is clustered around specific locations, perhaps due to historical links to raw material suppliers. Finally, labour-intensive sectors tend to be located in low-income regions, while capital-intensive or technology-oriented sectors are concentrated in the higher-income regions.

Clusters are groups of interdependent firms that are linked through close vertical or horizontal relationships, located within a well defined geographic area (European Commission, 2002). Porter (1998a) provides a more detailed definition:

> a geographically proximate group of inter-connected companies and associated institutions in a particular field, linked by commonalities and complementarities. The geographic scope of a cluster can range from a single entity or state to a country or even a group of neighbouring countries. Clusters take varying forms depending on their depth and sophistication, but most include end-product or service companies; suppliers of specialized inputs, components, machinery and services; financial institutions; and firms in related industries. Clusters also often involve a number of institutions, governmental and otherwise, that provide specialized training, education, information and technical support (such as universities, think tanks, vocational training providers); and standard setting agencies. Government departments and regulatory agencies that significantly influence a cluster can be considered part of it. Finally, many clusters include trade associations and other collective private sector bodies that support cluster members.
>
> *(Porter, 1998a, p. 254)*

Some researchers use the term **industrial district** to refer to a production system 'characterized by a myriad of firms specialized in various stages of production of a homogeneous product, often using flexible production technology and connected by local inter-firm linkages' (Jacobson and Andrésso-O'Callaghan, 1996, p. 116). For example, several well-known clusters or industrial districts are located in northern Italy and southern Germany. A tendency for many company owners to originate from similar social backgrounds facilitates communication, and tends to blur the boundaries between individual firms and the communities in which they are based. This phenomenon has been documented in Italy, where there are several clusters or industrial districts comprising networks of small, specialized firms that are internationally competitive in the production of goods such as furniture, ceramic tiles and textiles (Becattini *et al.*, 2003; Markusen, 1996). Case study 6.2 provides a discussion of the importance of industrial clusters for competitive advantage.

Clusters typically include distributors and retailers, suppliers, banks, and firms producing related products and services. They can also include public or semi-public bodies such as universities, voluntary organizations and trade associations. Relationships are most effective if the firms are in close geographical proximity to one another,

Industrial clusters and competitive advantage FT

There is consensus among academics and policymakers about the importance of industrial districts, or clusters, as a source of national competitiveness. To take three examples, Silicon Valley in electronics, Baden-Wurttemberg in machine tools and the City of London in financial services are all places where companies operating in the same or related businesses cluster together, competing and collaborating in a network of mutually supportive activities. These and other cases have prompted national and regional governments to look for ways of promoting new clusters, especially in high-technology sectors such as computers and biotechnology.

What remains uncertain, however, is how much weight should be placed on clustering, as distinct from other factors, in explaining why particular industries do well in some countries but not in others. In this context Italy is of special interest since it is there, especially in northern and central parts of the country, that clustering is most pervasive. Many observers believe that Italy's industrial districts, most of which specialize in traditional sectors such as engineering, textiles and building materials, give manufacturers a unique competitive advantage.

Comparing British and Italian performance in two of these industries, wool textiles and machine tools, there is no doubt that Italian companies have surpassed their British counterparts. In the 1950s the UK was the largest exporter of wool textiles, though Italian competition was starting to bite; now Italy is far ahead. In machine tools, the UK exported twice as much as Italy in 1960; last year Italy had 10 per cent of the world market (in third place behind Japan and Germany), while the UK had only 4 per cent.

Are clusters, or the lack of them, responsible? In wool textiles, one of Italy's greatest successes has been in high-quality worsted cloth for men's wear, most of which comes from Biella, a small town in Piedmont. The Biella cluster consists mainly of small, specialist, family-owned companies, although a few, such as Zegna and Loro Piana, have integrated forward into garment manufacture and retailing.

As in other industrial districts, the Biella companies benefit from access to a pool of skilled labour, easy availability of experienced suppliers and sub-contractors, and industry-wide associations providing common services; one of the biggest co-operative efforts is the lavish Ideabiella exhibition, held every autumn near Como.

But the West Riding of Yorkshire, where the bulk of the British industry is concentrated, was also a well functioning industrial district in the early postwar decades – and not obviously worse equipped than Biella with co-operative institutions. A more significant difference between the two regions lay in the domestic market.

Italy had a fragmented retailing structure, creating opportunities for garment makers – and to some extent fabric producers – to promote their brands either through independent retail shops or through their own outlets. To this should be added the rise of Italian fashion houses such as Gucci, Prada and Armani, which catered to a strong domestic demand for stylish clothing and used that base to create an international business.

In the UK, retailing was far more concentrated. In the 1950s the larger Yorkshire weavers were heavily dependent on Montague Burton and the other 'multiple tailors', supplying a huge demand for the made-to-measure working man's suit. With the demise of bespoke tailoring, buying power shifted to Marks and Spencer and its competitors, which sold ready-made suits at affordable prices. Their requirements were for long runs of standard fabrics, made to their own specifications and used in garments that were sold under the retailer's name. In wool textiles, as in other parts of the textile industry, the UK has not been helpful for manufacturer-owned brands, except at the top end of the trade.

There were, and still are, weavers in Yorkshire and in Scotland that produce top-quality worsted fabric largely for export. Their reputation stands high but their number is much smaller than in Italy. The Italian industry benefited from a virtuous circle – strong local demand for fashionable clothing, supplied through a variety of retail outlets and feeding into textile companies, which were under constant pressure to upgrade their design and manufacturing skills so that they could respond quickly to changing styles.

In machine tools, industrial districts cannot account for Italian success, since the industry is spread widely around the country; there are no concentrations of machine tool makers comparable to Biella in wool textiles.

Part of the explanation for Italy's superior record in this field lies in the way Italian metal-using companies – the buyers of machine tools – developed after the war. The Italian 'economic miracle' depended not so much on large companies (of which there were only a handful, such as Fiat, Eni and Pirelli) as on small, entrepreneurial firms that operated in medium- or low-technology industries. They had neither the financial nor the technical resources to take on the world leaders and they concentrated on sectors that called for flexibility, short production runs and relatively little capital. This, in turn, generated a demand for general purpose machine tools, which were cheaper and simpler to maintain than, say, those typically made in Germany.

Lacking the institutional support that existed in Germany – for example, a well developed apprenticeship system – the Italians made a virtue of the limited resources at their disposal and the result was a distinctive approach to machine tool design that suited domestic users. This approach later proved adaptable to overseas customers that were looking for equipment less technically sophisticated than the Germans offered and more tailored to their needs than the standard machines in which the Japanese specialized.

The size and character of domestic demand is not the only factor that determines an industry's ability to compete internationally but, as Michael Porter, the Harvard business academic, has argued, it has an important influence on product strategy. If that strategy also meets the needs of overseas buyers, exporting becomes feasible and attractive; if it does not, breaking out of the home market is harder.

Where does this leave public policy? One lesson is that artificially created clusters, not closely linked to user industries, are unlikely to prosper. It is also worth noting that in neither wool textiles nor machine tools can Italy's outstanding performance be attributed to government intervention. Success came about almost by accident, just as it did in Silicon Valley in the 1950s and 1960s. What mattered there was the rapid growth in US demand for semiconductors, first from the federal government for defence and space exploration and later from the computer industry. Several countries tried to create Silicon Valleys of their own – but mostly without success, because the demand factor was lacking.

Source: Industrial clusters and competitive advantage, *Financial Times*, 6 November 2001, p. 18.
© The Financial Times.

Table 6.15 Location of EU science-based (S) and traditional (T) clusters

Country	Cluster name
Austria	Cluster biotechnology and molecular medicine science in Vienna (S); wooden furniture cluster, upper Austria (T)
Belgium	Flanders multimedia valley (S); Flemish plastic processing (T)
Denmark	Communication cluster in northern Jutland (S); Herning-Ikast textiles and clothing industry (T)
Finland	Technology cluster in Oulu (S); shipbuilding in Turku (T)
France	Evry Genopole (biotechnologies), Evry (S); Technic Valle (screw-cutting and mechanics), Haute-Savoie (T)
Germany	Chemical industry, northern Ruhr area (S); Enterprise – information – system, Lower Saxony (S); media cluster, north Rhine-Westphalia (T)
Greece	Industrial district of Volos (sundry metal products and foodstuffs) (T); industrial district of Herakleion (foodstuffs, non-metallic minerals) (T)
Ireland	Dublin software cluster (S); dairy processing industry (T)
Italy	Biomedical cluster in Emilia-Romagna (S); Eye-glass cluster in Belluno country (T)
Liechtenstein	Financial services (T)
Luxembourg	CASSIS (IT and e-business consultancy for SMEs) (S); Synergie (Technical facilities industries) (T)
Netherlands	Dommel valley (information and communication technology), Eindhoven/Helmond (S); Conoship (shipbuilding), Freisland and Groningen (T)
Norway	Electronics industry in Horten (S); shipbuilding at Sunnmore (T)
Portugal	Footwear cluster with several geographical concentrations in northern and central parts of the country (T); manufacture of metallic moulds in Leiria (T)
Spain	Machine-tools in the Basque country (S); shoe manufacturing in the Vinapolo valley (T)
Sweden	Biotech valley in Strangnas (S); recorded music industry in Stockholm (T)
United Kingdom	Cambridgeshire (High-Tech) (S); British motor sport industry, Oxfordshire/Northamptonshire (T)

Source: European Commission (2002) *Regional Clusters in Europe, Observatory of European SMEs* 2002/No. 3, p. 28.

and if there is effective communication. Firms within a cluster do not always always compete, but sometimes cooperate by serving different niches of the same industry. However, they face the same competitive threats and opportunities. Because clusters are made up of what often seem to be a collection of disparate firms, standard industry classifications may not be useful in identifying them (Porter, 1998b).

The European Commission (2002) survey 34 clusters located in the EU-15 plus Norway. The clusters are characterized as traditional (transactions are based on long-term market relationships; collaboration is between service suppliers and government bodies; innovation takes place through product development and distribution), and science-based (transactions are based on temporary and long-term relationships; collaboration is between research and development institutions and government bodies; innovation takes place through new product and process development and new organizational forms). Table 6.15 shows the locations of some of these clusters.

Enright (1998) discusses the importance of clusters for firm-level strategic decision making and performance. Many regions contain vital resources and capabilities that can be exploited by individual firms in order to gain a competitive advantage.

However, firm-level strategy and performance are affected by interdependence, cooperation and competition between firms within the same cluster. Efficiency or productivity gains are realized if firms can access resources and inputs (skilled personnel, raw materials, access to customers, training facilities for staff) from elsewhere within the cluster, or take advantage of complementarities such as joint marketing and promotion, or accumulate specialized information and knowledge (Porter and Sovall, 1998). The formation of new firms may be encouraged and entry barriers kept low. If firms diversify within a cluster they not only take advantage of firm-specific economies of scope, but can also draw on the human capital or other resources that already exist elsewhere within the cluster. Clusters foster a sense of trust (or 'social glue') that helps bind participants together (Morosini, 2004).

Porter (1990) identifies clusters as key to the interactions between location, competition and national competitiveness. The competitive environment influences the way in which firms use their endowments of resources in order to formulate their strategies, which in turn determine performance. Innovation and technological spillovers are crucial to the development of firms. **Porter's Diamond Model** (1990) illustrates the determinants and dynamics of national competitive advantage. Competitive rivalry, factor and demand conditions, and the existence of related and supporting industries are the key determinants of the extent to which firms can develop and maintain a competitive advantage over rivals.

Porter's Diamond is illustrated in Figure 6.2. Domestic competitive interaction and rivalry stimulates firms to innovate and improve efficiency. For example, the Japanese car manufacturing and consumer electronics industries were intensely competitive within Japan, before the most successful firms also became dominant players at the international level. Changes in demand conditions provide an important stimulus for innovation and quality improvement. German firms are the dominant producers of high-speed cars, partly because there are no speed limits on the autobahns. Belgian and Swiss chocolate makers service discerning, up-market customers. The varied preferences of consumers allow firms and industries to transfer locally accrued advantages to a global arena. Factor conditions comprise natural, human and capital resources, and the quality of the physical, administrative and technological infrastructures. Some of these resources are natural, but others, such as concentrations

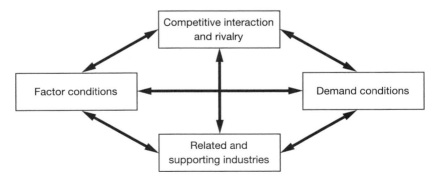

Figure 6.2 Diamond framework of competitive advantage
Source: Adapted from Porter (1990), figure 3.1, p. 72.

of specialized labour or capital, have developed in tandem with the historical growth of specific industries in particular locations. The quality and quantity of specialized high-quality inputs influences national competitiveness. Clusters of related and supporting industries, which engage in complementary or support activities, often strengthen successful industries. Examples of mutually supporting clusters include semi-conductors, computers and software in the US, and chemicals, dyes, textiles and textile machinery in Germany.

Porter's Diamond has stimulated academic and policy-maker interest in regional clusters of small and medium-sized firms. A number of schools attempt to explain the emergence of clusters. Many of the ideas date back to the work of Marshall (1890), who identifies a number of positive externalities that arise when firms are located in close proximity. These include benefits from the exchange of knowledge, sharing of labour and access to suppliers. Locational advantages or agglomeration economies accumulate through the growth of related industries and the development of specialized labour markets. The availability of agglomeration economies means that over time, specialization is likely to increase.

According to organization theory, during the last two decades of the twentieth century technological change and the changing nature of production tended to push in the direction of smaller-scale production. Another common theme has been the fostering of long-term relationships between buyers and suppliers, and the development of cooperative networks of firms. Specialized knowledge is a crucial determinant of firm performance. Consequently, firms tend to cluster in specific geographic areas, in order to take advantage of learning opportunities and the sharing of knowledge (Lundvall and Johnson, 1994).

Industrial organization and strategic management literature views clusters as a consequence of specialized firms coming together in order to reduce transaction costs (see Chapters 7 and 16). According to this approach, an industry is most accurately defined by identifying commonalities across firms situated at different stages of the production process or value chain. This might involve the grouping together of raw material, intermediate input suppliers, end-user manufacturers and retailers into a single cluster (Enright, 1998, 2000; Porter, 1998a,b, 2001; Porter and Sovall, 1998).

The economic geography literature emphasizes the effect of agglomeration economies on the dynamics of growth and trade (Harrison *et al.*, 1996; Martin and Sunley, 1997). In seeking to explain geographic concentration, Krugman (1991, 2000) observes that much trade that takes place is intra-industry (between firms within the same industry). Trade theory based on notions of comparative advantage has little to say about this phenomenon. The geographic location of industry is driven primarily by regions seeking to exploit agglomeration economies. The initial location of trade is partly a product of historical accident, but as the gains from trade are realized, spatial patterns of location, specialization and trade become entrenched. Transport costs are an important influence on the location of industry, but even if transport costs are low, early patterns in the location of production (which may initially have been partly accidental) tend to persist. The role of forward and backward linkages is also important, and can lead to the appearance of vertically integrated clusters of firms. However, increased specialization can leave non-diversified regions highly exposed to business cycle fluctuations.

Kay (2004) notes that the location of industry and clusters is the result of historical accident and the coevolution of capabilties and specialization.

> Since mutually reinforcing capabilities and specialisms depend on past choices, forgotton or now irrelevant historical events still influence the location of production today. Film producers in the 1920s sought the light of southern California. Films are rarely made in California any more, but Hollywood remains the centre of the world film industry. London is still a marketplace for shipbroking and marine insurance because of Britain's historical past. Similar accidents of history – the site of Leland Stanford's University and Xerox Corporation's research facility – made Silicon Valley the centre of the international software industry.
>
> *(Kay, 2004, p. 73)*

Porter (1998a) argues that the advantages of locating within a cluster might represent a countervailing factor that helps check the widespread tendency for the international relocation of production, a pervasive feature of the globalization phenomenon. Globalization has resulted in improvements in communication, transport and distribution networks, enabling firms to switch productive activities between countries in order to reduce labour costs or tax liabilities. However, many low-cost locations are unable to offer adequate supplies of essential factor inputs or business support facilities; such locations may also fail to provide a suitable environment for innovation. Therefore savings in labour costs or tax liabilities can be more than offset by losses in productivity. By locating within a cluster, firms can attract and retain key factor inputs and exploit opportunities for innovation. However, Steiner (2002) argues that current and future improvements in information technology and telecommunications may eventually permit the development of clusters that are not confined to specific geographic locations.

> Clusters are a system of production which is more than just a territorial concentration of specific firms working in the same sector, but one which involves complex organizations with tight trans-sectorial relationships implying a change from 'industrial district' to 'network' forms of organization at the interregional and international level. Instead of interpreting the globalization process as an external constraint and a risk to their survival, the increasing regional production systems is viewed as the gradual extension to the international level of tight inter-firm relationships, which have traditionally existed at the local and interregional level.
>
> *(Steiner, 2002, p. 208)*

6.7 Summary

Seller concentration, the number and size distribution of firms in a industry, is one of the key characteristics of industry structure. Chapter 6 has dealt with the measurement of seller concentration. Any specific measure of seller concentration aims to reflect the implications of the number of firms and their size distribution for competition in the industry concerned. Before attempting to measure concentration for any specific industry or market, it is necessary to take decisions as to the boundaries of the markets or industries that are being measured. For practical purposes, the definition of any market contains both a product dimension and a geographic dimension. The product market definition should include all products that are close substitutes for one another, both in consumption and in production. Similarly, the geographic market definition involves determining whether an increase in the price of a product in one location significantly affects demand or supply elsewhere. In principle, various price and cross-price elasticities can be used to determine the limits of product and geographic market boundaries. In practice, however, substitution is always a matter of degree, and decisions concerning boundaries are always arbitrary to some extent. The UK's Standard Industrial Classification and NACE, its EU counterpart, are currently the official standard used in the compilation of government statistics.

The most widely used seller concentration measures include the n-firm concentration ratio, the Herfindahl–Hirschman index, the Hannah–Kay index, the entropy coefficient, the variance of the logarithms of firm sizes, and the Gini coefficient. The method of calculation for all of these measures has been described in detail, and their strengths and limitations have been assessed.

When these measures are applied to real world data it is apparent that seller concentration varies considerably between sectors. However, some general patterns do emerge. For example, the trend towards increased seller concentration in manufacturing, which was evident throughout much of the twentieth century, was repeated in many service industries towards the end of the century, as the distribution of economic activity shifted away from manufacturing and towards services. Patterns of specialization and geographic concentration, which influence the spatial distribution of production within the EU, have also been considered. In particular, the phenomenon of clustering, whereby groups of interdependent firms located within a specific geographic area realize economies by establishing close vertical or horizontal relationships, is a locational pattern that has received much attention in the industrial organization, strategic management and economic geography literatures.

Discussion questions

1. Explain the terms substitutes in consumption, and substitutes in production. What is the relevance of these terms to the issue of market definition?

2. Examine the issues involved in defining the geographic boundaries of a market. With reference to Case study 6.1, illustrate your answer with reference to issues that have arisen in the political debate concerning media concentration in the US.

3. What is the distinction between a market and an industry?

4. What is a strategic market?

5. Explain the distinction between aggregate concentration and industry concentration.

6. Outline Hannah and Kay's (1977) general criteria for a concentration measure to adequately reflect the most important characteristics of the firm size distribution.

7. Examine the main advantages and disadvantages of the n-firm concentration ratio as a measure of seller concentration.

8. Does the Herfindahl–Hirschman index provide a more satisfactory method for measuring seller concentration than the n-firm concentration ratio?

9. Explain the distinction between concentration and inequality. How much does an inequality measure such as the variance of the logarithms of firm sizes tell us about market structure?

10. Explain the construction of the Gini coefficient as a measure of inequality in an industry's firm size distribution.

11. Explain the distinction between specialization and geographic concentration.

12. What factors may give rise to the appearance of clusters of related and supporting industries in particular geographic areas? Illustrate your answer with examples drawn from Case study 6.2.

13. Outline the main elements of Porter's Diamond Model. To what extent does this model shed light on the sources of national competitive advantage?

Further reading

Bell, G.G. (2005) Clusters, networks and firm innovativeness, *Strategic Management Journal*, 26, 287–95.

Curry, B. and George, K. (1983) Industrial concentration: a survey, *Journal of Industrial Economics*, 31, 203–55.

Davies, S.W. (1989) Concentration, in Davies, S. and Lyons, B. (eds) *The Economics of Industrial Organization*. London: Longman.

Davies, S.W. and Lyons, B.R. (1996) *Industrial Organisation in the European Union*. Oxford: Clarendon Press.

Davies, S., Rondi, L. and Sembenelli, A. (2001) European integration and the changing structure of EU manufacturing, 1987–1993, *Industrial and Corporate Change*, 10, 37–75.

Porter, M.E. (2001) Regions and the new economics of competition, in Scott, A.J., *Global-City Regions*. Oxford: Oxford University Press.

Utton, M.A. (1970) *Industrial Concentration*. Harmondsworth: Penguin.

Determinants of seller concentration

Learning objectives

This chapter covers the following topics:

- systematic determinants of seller concentration
- theoretical motives for horizontal merger
- empirical evidence on the impact of horizontal merger on profitability
- the random growth hypothesis

Key terms

Accounting profitability approach	Sample selection bias
Core competencies	Statistical cost approach
Engineering cost approach	Sunk cost
Gibrat's Law	Survivor approach
Horizontal merger	Survivorship bias
Industry life cycle	Type 1 industry
Law of Proportionate Effect	Type 2 industry

7.1 Introduction

In Chapter 6, we have discussed the measurement of seller concentration, and identified a number of patterns and trends in the data on seller concentration across regions and countries, and over time. In Chapter 7, we turn our attention towards an examination of some of the main determinants of seller concentration. Why do some industries tend to become more highly concentrated than others? What are the factors that cause seller concentration to vary over time? Section 7.2 identifies the principal theoretical determinants of seller concentration, and the role that these factors play in influencing the historical evolution of industry structure. Relevant factors include economies of scale, entry and exit barriers, regulation, the scope for discretionary sunk cost investment on items such as advertising and research and development, the stage reached in the industry's life cycle, and the firm's distinctive capabilities and core competencies.

Evaluation of horizontal mergers often focuses on the possibility of anticompetitive effects. A merger between two firms producing goods or services that are direct substitutes in consumption naturally has direct implications for seller concentration and industry structure, perhaps conferring significantly enhanced market power upon the merged organization. However, enhancement of market power is not necessarily the only reason why horizontal integration may be an attractive strategy. It may be motivated by a desire to realize cost savings through economies of scale in production, purchasing, marketing or research and development. The target firm may have its own reasons for wishing to be acquired. Section 7.3 discusses the principal motives for horizontal merger; and Section 7.4 describes some of the empirical evidence as to whether horizontal mergers lead to increased profitability through cost savings or the enhancement of market power.

In the earlier sections of this chapter, we search for specific economic explanations for observed patterns of seller concentration. Section 7.5 describes an alternative approach towards explaining the evolution of industry structure, which is based on the notion that the growth of individual firms is inherently unpredictable. According to the random growth hypothesis, there is a natural tendency for concentration to increase gradually over the long term, even if the growth patterns of individual firms are completely random. We explain why this is so, and review the empirical evidence on the accuracy of the random growth hypothesis as a descriptor of actual growth patterns.

7.2 Seller concentration: systematic determinants

This section examines the main systematic determinants of seller concentration. These factors include economies of scale, entry and exit barriers, regulation, the scope for discretionary **sunk cost** expenditure on items such as advertising and research and development, the stage reached in the industry's life cycle, and the firm's distinctive capabilities and core competencies.

Economies of scale

The structure of costs may have important implications for industry structure and the behaviour of firms. Economies of scale result from savings in long-run average cost (LRAC) achieved as a firm operates at a larger scale. The output level at which the firm's LRAC attains its minimum value is the firm's minimum efficient scale (MES) of production. The comparison between the total output that would be produced if each incumbent firm operates at its MES, and the total demand for the industry's product at the price required in order for at least normal profit to be earned, has important implications for the number of firms that the industry can accommodate. This in turn has implications for seller concentration and industry structure.

If the total demand for the product *equals* the MES, the most cost
ment is for the industry to be serviced by a single firm, and industr
likely to be monopolistic. If the total demand for the product is 1,
as the MES, then the industry can accommodate 1,000 firms a¹
MES, and the industry structure might approximate perfect competition. However,
if average costs are approximately constant over a range of output levels beyond
the MES, the actual number of firms might be less than the number that could be
accommodated if all were operating at (but not beyond) the MES. In Box 7.1, we
describe four possible methods for estimating the LRAC function or the MES for
a plant or a firm. These are the **engineering cost approach**, the **statistical cost
approach**, the **survivor approach**, and the **accounting profitability approach**.

Box 7.1

Estimation of cost functions and minimum efficient scale

For firms seeking to minimize their costs over the long term, or for policy makers or
researchers seeking to understand the implications of an industry's cost structure for its performance, it may be useful to be able to identify the shape of the LRAC function, or at least
identify the output level at which minimum efficient sale (MES) is achieved and all possible
cost savings arising from economies of scale have been realized. Box 7.1 describes four
methods for estimating cost functions and MES.

Engineering cost approach

This method, which relies on technical experts (engineers) to estimate costs, is the closest to
cost theory as outlined in Chapter 2. The production function details the physical relationships between inputs and outputs. By costing these physical relationships, an average cost
function (based on hypothetical rather than actual data) can be determined. Possible practical
difficulties include the following:

- All such estimates must specify a time dimension. The quality and durability of inputs may
  differ considerably if planning is for five years or 20 years. Any learning economies which
  will reduce future costs should be anticipated and incorporated.

- Engineers may disagree over the precise nature of technological relationships, and all
  estimates are in any event subject to human error. Engineering estimates might be incorrect
  about either the absolute level of costs, or the location of the MES, or both.

- While engineers may find it relatively easy to estimate the productivity of capital equipment,
  they may find it more difficult to anticipate labour productivity, in view of uncertainties
  about worker behaviour.

- An engineer may also find it difficult to assess the costs of the non-productive activities of the firm, such as the administrative and marketing functions. Accordingly, engineering cost estimates are more suitable for plants rather than firms.

- If an engineer lacks evidence based on past experience, it may be very difficult to make an estimate. If the largest plant to date produces 30,000 units, any estimate of the cost of producing 300,000 units is likely to be highly speculative.

Pratten (1971) uses the engineering method to find the MES for 25 UK manufacturing industries. For practical purposes, MES is defined as the point at which a 100 per cent increase in output results in a reduction in average costs of less than 5 per cent. In several industries, including commercial aircraft and diesel engines, the MES was large relative to industry output, implying a tendency for high levels of seller concentration. In other industries, including machine tools and iron foundries, the MES was small relative to industry output. Scherer *et al.* (1975) report a similar analysis for 12 US manufacturing industries. The larger firms appeared to have market shares greater than those required for production at the MES. Emerson *et al.* (1988) use a similar methodology and obtain similar results.

Statistical cost approach

Using the statistical cost approach, the average cost for each firm is plotted against a suitable firm size measure, and an average cost function is estimated by fitting a curve through the resulting set of points. Therefore the statistical cost approach relies on actual (rather than hypothetical) costs and output data. Cross-sectional data is generally preferred to time series data, since the latter may reflect changes in technology. This approach often works better with plant-level than with firm-level data, since larger cross-sectional data sets are likely to be available. Possible practical difficulties include the following:

- Analysis of multi-product firms or plants requires the identification of specific costs associated with specific products. This may be impossible to achieve without making arbitrary adjustments to accounts-based cost data. Accounting practices may themselves differ between different firms or plants. Furthermore, estimation using cross-sectional data is based on an implicit assumption that firms are using similar production technologies; if this is not the case, the interpretation of the estimated average cost function is unclear.

- Knowledge and experience that an incumbent firm has built up may be an important determinant of its current and future costs. However, accounts-based cost data may fail to reflect the implications of learning economies on future costs.

- Faced with a set of cross-sectional costs and output data, the researcher does not know whether all firms are already operating at the average cost-minimizing points on their short-run or long-run average cost functions, or whether some firms are undergoing a process of adjustment towards long-run equilibrium. For example, some firms may be waiting for their existing capital equipment to wear out before installing new equipment or introducing new production methods. Therefore the statistical cost method cannot distinguish between short-run and long-run average costs.

Application to the banking industry

The statistical cost approach has recently been used to assess the extent to which banks take advantage of economies of scale. Various measures of inputs and outputs and various functional forms for the cost function have been used, to test for economies of scale. Two broad approaches have been followed. With the production approach, the bank collects funds and uses these to offer goods and services. Banking output can be measured by the number of accounts offered or number of loans granted, and costs by the capital and labour costs incurred in this production process. With the intermediation approach, banks are treated as financial intermediaries, which put borrowers in touch with lenders. The value of loans granted or investments are the output measures, while operating costs and interest payments to depositors are measures of costs. Early research adopted the production approach, and found either economies of scale or constant costs at fairly low levels of output, suggesting that economies of scale exist for small and medium-sized banks only (Gilbert, 1984). Later research adopted the intermediation approach, and found evidence that banks face U-shaped average costs curves, so there may be substantial cost penalties for operating at a sub-optimal scale. Altunbas and Molyneux (1993) test for scale and scope economies for French, German, Italian and Spanish banks for 1988. Using a highly flexible functional form to specify the banking cost function, they estimate the sensitivity of total costs to variations in output levels and the prices of factor inputs. The estimations are carried out separately for banks operating in each country, and for banks in different size bands (measured by the value of assets). This procedure allows for the possibility that the cost function coefficients vary either by country, or by size of bank. Evidence of economies of scale (an inverse relationship between outputs and the value of LRAC) is found in all banking markets. For Italy, economies of scale are found for the sample as a whole and for each size band. For Spain economies of scale are found for banks with assets less than $100million. For France economies of scale are found for the sample as a whole and for banks with assets below $3,000 million. No significant evidence of economies of scale is found for German banks, although there is some evidence of diseconomies of scale at low levels of output. Overall, early research suggests economies are exhausted at low levels of production. More recent research for US and European banks has found stronger evidence of scale economies for large banks (Berger and Humphrey, 1997; Molyneux *et al.*, 2001).

Survivor approach

Modern usage of the survivor approach was pioneered by Stigler (1958).

> The survivor technique proceeds to solve the problem of determining the optimum size of firm as follows: Classify the firms in an industry by size, and calculate the share of the industry output coming from each class over time. If the share of a given class falls, it is relatively inefficient, and in general is more inefficient the more rapidly the share falls. An efficient size of firm, on this argument, is one that meets any and all problems the entrepreneur actually faces: strained labour

relations, rapid innovation, government regulation, unstable foreign markets, etc. This is of course, the decisive meaning of efficiency from the point of view of the enterprise.

(Stigler, 1958, p. 56)

However, the relationship between survival and efficiency was noted much earlier, by nineteenth-century economists including John Stuart Mill and Alfred Marshall. The latter was undoubtedly influenced by the ideas of Charles Darwin. To illustrate the survivor approach, we assume there are four sizes of plant in an industry, with size measured by employment. Suppose the shares in total employment by plant size in two periods are as shown in the Table.

Size	Employment	Employment share % Period 1	Employment share % Period 2
1	1–100	20	15
2	101–300	35	55
3	301–600	30	20
4	601–1,000	15	10

In this case, size band 2 appears to be the optimum plant size, on the grounds that the employment share of plants in this size band has increased significantly, while the employment share of plants in the other size bands has declined. An obvious attraction of the survivor approach is that its data requirements are less onerous than the engineering or statistical cost approaches. However, because the survivor approach does not require detailed costs data, no average cost function can be directly inferred. The survivor approach reflects the ability of a plant or firm to be flexible, to adapt and to grow. This is not necessarily the same as the ability to minimize long-run average costs. The survivor approach implicitly assumes that competition will tend to eliminate sub-optimal firms or plants. Consequently this approach is not applicable at firm level in the case of monopoly or collusive oligopoly. However, in such cases it may still be applicable at plant level, if a multi-plant monopolist views its plants as being in competition with one another.

Sometimes the survivor approach can produce results that are difficult to interpret. In the previous example, suppose the employment share of plants in size bands 1 and 3 increased, while employment in bands 2 and 4 decreased. This could imply that the industry is able to accommodate two different plant sizes: perhaps one is labour intensive and the other capital intensive. Alternatively, it could imply that the industry has been incorrectly defined. For example, convergence towards two different optimum plant sizes could suggest that two different market segments, such as performance cars and family saloon cars, are produced with completely different technologies, and should therefore be analysed as two separate industries.

Accounting profitability approach

Finally, it has been suggested that the optimal firm size should be correlated directly with accounting profitability. Identification of a smooth relationship between firm size and profitability might give managers all the guidance they really need, circumventing the need for precise estimation of the firm's cost structure. However, accounting rates of return are difficult to measure with any degree of consistency between firms. Furthermore, accounting profits reflect not only economies of scale, but also many other factors, such as demand conditions and market power, and the firm's relationships with its suppliers and distribution networks. To isolate the relationship between firm size and accounting profitability, it would be necessary to control for the impact on profitability of all such factors.

Barriers to entry

Microeconomic theory views entry (and exit) as an important driver in the process by which markets adjust towards equilibrium. The more dynamic Schumpeterian and Austrian schools emphasize the innovative role of entry in driving industry evolution. There is plentiful empirical evidence to show that entry is higher in profitable or fast-growing industries (Baldwin and Gorecki, 1987; Geroski, 1991a,b), and exit is higher from low-profit industries (Dunne *et al.*, 1988). Other things being equal, entry is likely to reduce concentration, assuming the average size of entrants is smaller than that of incumbent firms. However, the effect could be the opposite if entry takes place at a large scale, perhaps as a result of a diversification strategy on the part of a large established firm from some other industry or geographic area. Meanwhile, by reducing the numbers of incumbent firms, exit is likely to increase concentration. In practice entry and exit rates themselves tend to be correlated (Caves, 1998). For example, Dunne *et al.* (1988) report evidence of a negative relationship between annual entry and exit rates for US manufacturing industries over the period 1963–82. In this case, it is the net effect on concentration that is most important. Barriers to entry are discussed in detail in Chapter 8.

Scope for discretionary, sunk cost expenditures

Sutton (1991, 1998) examines the implications of a long-run increase in market size for the market shares of individual firms and for seller concentration. Sutton identifies two basic industry types, classified according to the nature of their sunk costs. In a **Type 1 industry**, also known as an *exogenous sunk cost industry*, each firm incurs some fixed sunk cost in order to enter the industry. This expenditure might include the cost of establishing a plant, or the cost of achieving some threshold level of advertising expenditure. Sunk costs are exogenous, in the sense that the firm has limited discretion in choosing the levels of such expenditures. There are no other entry barriers. In a **Type 2 industry**, also known as an *endogenous sunk cost industry*, the amount of sunk cost expenditure allocated to items such as advertising and research and development is discretionary. Some sunk cost expenditure may be required in order to enter; but further substantial sunk cost expenditures are incurred subsequently, as incumbents compete to maintain or increase their own market shares. Advertising and research and development are important vehicles for discretionary sunk cost investment in Type 2 industries.

The following summary of Sutton's argument draws on Bagwell's (2005) recent survey. We consider first a Type 1 industry with a homogeneous product. For any given level of total industry sales, the profit earned by each individual firm is assumed to be inversely related to N, the number of firms, and influenced by θ, an industry-level parameter reflecting the intensity of price competition. The polar cases of θ are joint profit maximization, in which the firms operate a cartel, setting their prices as if they were a single monopolist; and Bertrand competition, in which price is driven down to the perfectly competitive level. Costs comprise a variable component that is linear in output; and a fixed component σ, the exogenous sunk cost.

In this model, N adjusts so that each firm earns only a normal profit in the long run. The equilibrium condition can be written $S\pi(N, \theta) = \sigma$, where S denotes total consumer expenditure in the market, and $S\pi(N, \theta)$ is each firm's operating profit (revenue *minus* variable costs). Each firm must earn sufficient operating profit to cover its fixed cost. This analysis has two implications. First, for any given N, an increase in S increases $S\pi(N, \theta)$, enabling each incumbent firm to earn an abnormal profit. This tends to encourage entry. Therefore an increase in S leads an increase in N. As S increases, seller concentration, measured by 1/N, tends towards zero. Therefore there is a tendency towards the fragmentation of industry structure as the size of the market increases.

The second implication follows from the assumption that $\pi(N, \theta)$ is dependent on θ. This implies a relationship between θ and the equilibrium value of N. With joint profit maximization, the operating profit per unit of output is at its maximum. Many firms can earn a normal profit, so N is large and industry concentration is relatively low. With Bertrand competition, the operating profit per unit of output is at its minimum. Fewer firms can earn a normal profit, so N is small and concentration is high. Within any Type 1 industry, the performance of all firms is similar; but when comparisons are drawn between firms in different Type 1 industries, variations in the industry-level parameter θ are the main drivers of differences in firm performance.

We now consider a Type 2 industry with vertical product differentiation. This means the products of different producers are differentiated by product quality: some producers concentrate on the high-quality end of the product range, while others produce lower-quality lines for a mass market. Each firm's product is defined by a vertical attribute u, which reflects product quality. Suppose by advertising, each firm can increase consumers' perceptions of u. In a Type 2 industry, the tendency towards fragmentation as the market expands is offset by a competitive escalation in advertising expenditures. By advertising sufficiently heavily relative to its competitors, a firm can always induce a certain proportion of consumers to buy its product at a price that exceeds its variable cost. Therefore as the market expands, at some point a firm that deviates from the established equilibrium by incurring an increased advertising outlay can earn sufficient operating profit to cover its (increased) sunk cost. At that point, it becomes profitable for a firm to deviate, resulting in the creation of a new equilibrium. Each time there is an escalation in sunk cost expenditure, the deviating firm's market share attains at least some minimum value (which does not change over time). Therefore concentration does not tend towards zero, and industry structure does not fragment, as the size of the market increases. Over time, the industry's member firms become increasingly dispersed in size, with each firm's relative position dependent on its historical record of achievement in ratcheting up its sunk cost expenditures.

Several attempts have been made to classify Type 1 and Type 2 industries. Type 1 industries include household textiles, leather products, footwear, clothing, printing and publishing. Type 2 industries include motor vehicles, tobacco, soaps and detergents, pharmaceuticals and man-made fibres (Bresnahan, 1992; Davies and Lyons, 1996; Lyons et al., 1997; Schmalensee, 1992). Lyons et al. (1997) and Robinson and Chiang (1996) test Sutton's hypothesis empirically, and report some supporting evidence. The European Commission (1997b) examines the evolution of concentration in 71 industries between 1987 and 1993. Average concentration was found to be significantly higher in Type 2 than in Type 1 industries, in accordance with Sutton's hypotheses.

Regulation

Government policy can also influence levels of concentration. Competition policy and regulation are primarily aimed at correcting various types of market failure, increasing competition and giving consumers a wider choice of products and services. Policies aimed at increasing competition by discouraging restrictive practices or disallowing mergers on grounds of public interest tend to reduce concentration, or at least prevent concentration from increasing. Conversely, policies that restrict the number of firms permitted to operate in certain industries, or grant exclusive property rights to selected firms, tend to increase concentration. Industrial policy and the regulation of industry are examined in Chapters 17 and 18.

The industry life cycle

The stage that has been reached in the industry life cycle may have implications for seller concentration (Dosi et al., 1997; Klepper, 1997; McGahan, 2000). Figure 7.1 illustrates the four stages of a typical **industry life cycle**: the introduction, growth, maturity and decline stages. Case study 7.1 provides an application to the US credit union sector.

During the introduction phase, firms invest heavily in research and development in order to develop a completely new product. The firms that are initially successful in bringing the product to market benefit from a first-mover advantage. Although they are able to charge high prices, sales volumes may be relatively small, and there is no guarantee that revenues will be sufficient to recoup the initial research and development expenditures. Competing producers may offer similar products with incompatible technological specifications. At this stage, there may be lack of awareness or confusion on the part of consumers as to the usefulness of the product. Seller concentration is likely to be relatively low.

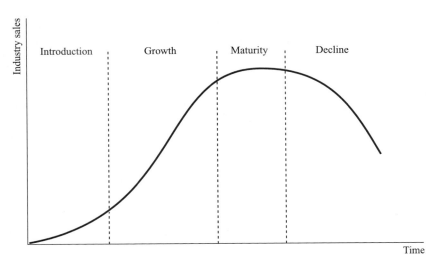

Figure 7.1 The industry life cycle

During the growth phase, a particular technological specification becomes established as the industry standard. The market starts to expand, and by producing at higher volumes, successful producers whose brands become established start to realize cost savings through economies of scale. Prices fall rapidly, stimulating further growth in consumer demand. Success may also attract entry, with new firms seeking to imitate the successful specification, perhaps by introducing brands embodying only minor or superficial variations in product characteristics. The consequent increase in industry supply and competition places further downward pressure on prices. However, because consumer demand is expanding rapidly, incumbent firms can tolerate the presence of entrants, and seller concentration remains relatively low.

During the maturity phase, growth of sales and profitability level off as consumer demand for the industry's product approaches the saturation level. Opportunities for additional growth in demand, through further price-cutting or further introduction of minor variations in product characteristics, are eventually exhausted. Incumbent firms may respond more defensively to threatened or actual competition from entrants by seeking to raise entry barriers, perhaps by undertaking large-scale advertising campaigns or through brand proliferation. Merger and takeover is likely to be the principal means by which incumbents can achieve further economies of scale or further growth. At this stage, seller concentration increases to levels higher than those seen during the introduction and growth stages, as production at high volume becomes essential if firms are to maintain acceptable levels of profitability.

Finally, during the decline stage, the sales and profits of incumbent firms begin to fall. Collusion or mergers between incumbent firms may well take place, primarily for defensive purposes: to eliminate competition and strengthen the parties' market power, thereby providing some compensation for the decline in consumer demand. Some firms may decide to withdraw from the industry altogether, perhaps having identified new opportunities in alternative markets. Incumbents that are unable to implement effective defensive strategies may be faced with a loss of investor confidence, a falling share price and eventual bankruptcy. With the market only capable of sustaining a declining number of producers, seller concentration remains relatively high.

Stigler (1951) examines the interaction between the industry life cycle and the extent of vertical integration, and considers the implications for concentration in vertically linked industries. Before the market has achieved sufficient volume to sustain specialist suppliers of raw materials and specialist distribution channels, producers may seek to ensure their own input supplies and provide their own sales service, through backward and forward integration. Accordingly, concentration in the supply of raw materials and in distribution may be relatively high during the introduction stage. As the market starts to expand, however, specialist suppliers of raw materials and specialist distribution services begin to appear, and concentration in these adjacent sectors tends to decline. In the later maturity and decline stages of the industry life cycle, vertical integration may constitute part of the incumbents' defensive strategies. Accordingly, concentration in the raw materials and distribution sectors may tend to revert back towards higher levels. Klimenko (2004) elaborates on the nature of vertical integration towards the end of the industry life cycle:

> [A]t mature stages of industry evolution, firms rarely introduce new products and most of the time routinely produce standardized goods and services. The existence of stable interface standards between segments of the industry's value chain implies that upstream firms can mass-produce intermediate products to satisfy standardized downstream demands instead of customizing them to individual specification of downstream firms. At the same time, the downstream firms are able to pick standardized inputs 'off the shelf' without worrying how well they fit in the assembly of the final product.
>
> *(Klimenko, 2004, p. 178)*

The mobile phone industry provides a recent example. At the birth of the industry, mobile phone manufacturers were required to have expertise in designing radio chips, batteries, software, the assembly of electronic components, and the design of cases. Incumbent firms such as Nokia, Motorola and Ericsson integrated vertically to produce base stations in order to provide mobile-phone coverage. However, as the industry has evolved and matured, specialist producers have entered the market, producing radio chips, software and handsets. Consequently, a process of vertical dis-integration is taking place as incumbent firms outsource the manufacturing of component parts (*The Economist*, 2004a).

Distinctive capabilities, strategic assets and core competences

According to Kay (1993), the performance of firms depends on **distinctive capabilities**. Distinctive capabilities include architecture, innovation and reputation. Architecture refers to the firm's internal organization, its relationships with suppliers, distributors and retailers, and its specialized industry knowledge. Architecture

Case study 7.1

Industry life cycle for the credit union sector

Credit unions are cooperative, member owned, not-for-profit financial institutions, which are based on the underlying principle of self-help. Credit unions offer loans to their members out of a pool of savings that is built up by the members themselves. In the US, credit unions are constituted according to provisions set out in their common bond statutes, which define (and restrict) their target membership. Consequently, credit unions in different categories exhibit differences in the membership characteristics, operational structure and the subsidies that are available. Common bond categories include the following: community; associational; educational; military; federal, state and local government; manufacturing; service; and low income.

The interwoven relationship that exists between a credit union's members, who are the customers for its financial products, the suppliers of its funds, and in some cases its managers and shareholders, has led to credit unions being described by Croteau (1963) as the purest form of cooperative institution. In many countries, credit unions are viewed as playing a crucial role in tackling financial exclusion, by providing low-cost financial services to groups often excluded from obtaining credit from banks, or access to other banking services. It is estimated that more than 100m people in 84 countries belong to a credit union. The total assets of credit unions worldwide are estimated at US $430.5bn. However, the pace of development of the credit union movement differs widely between different countries. Ferguson and McKillop (1997) detail four discrete stages in the development of a credit union sector.

■ *Nascent stage.* In this stage, credit unions are run by volunteer workers, and receive financial aid and other forms of assistance from local government agencies and charitable organizations. This model still characterizes the UK's relatively under-developed credit union sector.

■ *Transition stage.* Once a particular critical mass has been achieved, the industry moves into the second, transition stage of development. At this stage, objectives of saving costs by achieving economies of scale are largely forgone in favour of maintaining smallness as a defining credit union attribute. However, in the transition stage credit unions tend to hire paid employees (full-time or part-time) rather than rely solely on volunteers. They have professional management, but retain volunteer directors. They may offer a range of financial services, rather than just one or two basic products. Membership becomes more socially diverse, including some middle-class income earners. This model characterizes the credit union sector in the Republic of Ireland.

■ *Mature stage.* At the mature stage, a more business-like philosophy tends to prevail. Mature credit union sectors are characterized by much larger asset and membership sizes. Concentration within the sector tends to increase, as dominant institutions begin to emerge. This trend is strengthened by means of consolidation, in the form of horizontal mergers between some individual institutions. Professional staffs operate multiproduct services, and state-of-the-art information technology is empoyed in marketing and administration. Mature credit union sectors include those in the US, Canada and Australia.

■ *Post-mature stage*. During the post-mature stage, the distinctiveness of the credit union movement tends to be eroded or lost, as the largest and most successful institutions become increasingly similar to market-oriented financial services competitors. In the US, a small number of credit unions have recently been converted into banks.

While the industry life cycle approach is a useful tool to analyse the development of the credit union sector, there are some limitations.

■ Not all credit union sectors pass through the four stages identified above. Changes in general economic conditions or technology might significantly influence the development of a particular credit union sector.

■ The importance of strategic decisions taken by the managers of individual credit unions may influence the path taken by a credit union sector. As a sector reaches maturity, credit unions are unlikely to remain passive spectators while the demand for their products and services stagnates or declines. Instead, they may decide to invest in financial innovation, or diversify into new product or geographic areas.

■ A credit union sector might comprise several distinct strategic groups (see Section 9.3). These may reach each stage in the life cycle at different times. In the case of credit unions, the common bond may be an important determinant of strategic group formation.

that allows the firm to maintain a competitive edge over rivals or entrants. Innovation, combined with mechanisms to protect intellectual property, provides some firms with assets that can be used to maintain high levels of performance. A firm that has established a name, reputation of brand associated with high quality and service may also enjoy a decisive advantage over competitors. Accordingly, firms that can draw on distinctive capabilities may be able to grow and sustain a large or dominant market share over long periods.

In the terminology of Prahalad and Hamel (1990), a firm's **core competences** are the key to its performance. Core competences derive from the firm's specialized knowledge, and the ways in which this knowledge is used in order to establish and maintain an edge over competitors. The key to staying ahead of the competition is being able to protect the firm's specialized resources and competences from imitation. Especially in industries where technological change occurs at a rapid pace, incumbent firms must be capable of adapting quickly, and initiating change themselves. Only firms with sufficient ambition ('strategic intent') and sufficient flexibility or adaptability ('strategic stretch') are likely to succeed (Hamel and Prahalad, 1994).

This approach emphasizes the firm itself, rather than industry characteristics, as the ultimate source of a competitive advantage that may eventually have major ramifications for industry structure indicators such as seller concentration or barriers to entry. Singh *et al.* (1998) attempt to identify the types of strategy that were most frequently used by UK firms in the food, electrical engineering, chemicals and pharmaceuticals industries. Questionnaire data obtained from marketing executives suggests that research and development and advertising are among the most common instruments employed with long-term strategic objectives in view. There was little indication of reliance on price-based strategies or the patenting of new products.

7.3 Horizontal mergers: theoretical motives

There are three types of merger: horizontal, vertical and conglomerate. **Horizontal mergers** involve firms producing the same products. Vertical mergers involve firms operating at different stages of the same production process. Conglomerate mergers involve firms producing different goods or services. Section 7.3 examines the direct consequences of horizontal mergers for seller concentration. Other things being equal, horizontal mergers naturally tend to increase concentration directly. Assuming the partners occupy different industrial classifications, vertical or conglomerate mergers do not affect concentration directly, but they may do so indirectly if they enable the merged entity to benefit from increased market power. For example, a vertical merger might allow a producer to secure control over access to raw materials or distribution channels, enabling it to force competitors out of business. Economies of scope achieved as a result of a conglomerate merger might give a producer a crucial cost advantage, enabling it to cut prices and force competitors out of business. However, in this book vertical and conglomerate mergers are treated as separate topics in their own right, and are examined elsewhere in Chapters 15 and 16.

The UK's economic history is peppered with 'waves' of merger activity. The twentieth-century decades of peak merger activity were the 1920s, when mergers were motivated primarily by a desire to achieve economies of scale associated with the new mass-production techniques; the 1960s, when mergers were actively encouraged by the UK government; and the 1980s and 1990s, when renewed high levels of merger activity were prompted by increased international market integration and globalization.

In theory, there are two principal reasons why firms may choose to merge horizontally. First, a merger can enable the realization of savings in the costs of production. Second, a merger can leave the newly integrated firm with enhanced market power.

Cost savings

One of the most common arguments in favour of horizontal mergers is that the combined size of two (or more) firms allows various cost savings to be realized, perhaps to a greater extent than would be possible through internal expansion. The following classification is based on Roller *et al.* (2001).

- *Rationalization.* Suppose two firms own a number of plants, each operating at a different marginal cost. Differences in marginal cost might be due to differences in the quantities of the capital input, differences in the technologies employed, or differences in the scale of production. Following a merger, the firm can shift production from the high marginal cost plants to the low marginal cost plants. This should continue until marginal costs in all plants are the same. It is possible that rationalization requires some plants to close altogether.

- *Economies of scale* are realized when long-run average cost decreases as the scale of operation increases (see Chapter 2). According to Parsons (2003), horizontal mergers in the US cable television industry during the 1990s allowed many firms to benefit from economies of scale in areas including personnel, marketing, advertising and, importantly, the ability to exploit new fibre-optic and digital-server technologies. The trend toward merger and clustering led to many large cities being dominated by single cable companies.

- *Research and development.* The integration of research and development activity may allow cost savings, by avoiding unnecessary duplication of effort. Diffusion of new technology may be achieved more efficiently within an integrated organization. Since a horizontal merger reduces the number of competing firms, the integrated organization may feel more confident in undertaking speculative investments, since there is less risk of ideas being stolen by a rival. Accordingly, the benefits of research and development are internalized.

- *Purchasing economies.* A horizontal merger increases the bargaining power of the integrated firm, which may be able to extract lower prices from upstream suppliers. Similarly, an integrated firm may be able to raise finance from the capital markets at a lower cost than its constituent parts.

- *Productive inefficiency and organizational slack.* In the absence of competitive pressure, a monopolist may fail to achieve efficiency in production (see Chapters 2 and 3). There is technical inefficiency (x-inefficiency) if the firm fails to achieve the maximum output that is technically feasible given the set of inputs it employs. There is economic inefficiency if the firm fails to employ the most cost-effective combination of inputs, given the current levels of factor prices. Closely related to the notion of productive inefficiency in the microeconomics literature is the idea of organizational slack in the organizational behaviour literature. To the extent that a horizontal merger increases the size or market power of the merged entity and reduces competitive pressure, it may increase the likelihood that the firm fails to achieve efficiency in production, or it may increase the scope for the firm to operate with organizational slack. On the other hand, however, a highly active market for corporate ownership can itself help impose discipline, reducing the scope for firms to operate inefficiently. A firm that fails to achieve efficiency in production (or operates with too much slack) may find its share price reduced, making it an acquisition target for new owners who believe they can operate more efficiently, increase profits and increase the firm's share price.

Farrell and Shapiro (2000) suggest that horizontal mergers which produce cost savings through economies of scale are relatively few in number. Where the potential exists for economies of scale, these can often be realized through internal expansion, and do not require a merger to take place. In assessing the benefits and costs of any specific merger, only merger-specific gains, which cannot be achieved in any other way, should be considered. Merger-specific gains, also known as *synergies*, include gains arising from the integration of specific, hard-to-trade assets owned by the merging firms. Some examples are as follows.

■ *Coordination of joint operations*. When two firms are linked by the joint management of a resource, such as an oil field, frequent contractual disputes might tend to increase costs. By reducing or eliminating disputes of this kind, a merger might result in cost savings.

■ *Sharing of complementary skills*. Consider a situation where one firm is more skilled in manufacturing than a rival, while the rival is more skilled in distribution. In time it might be possible for both firms to become skilled in their areas of current weakness; but a merger might enable this to happen sooner or more effectively. Similarly, one firm might own a patent that could be more fully or quickly exploited using another firm's resources.

■ *Improved interoperability*. Two firms might develop what they consider to be separate products; for example, two pieces of software that can be used interchangeably by end-users. However, because the two pieces of software were developed separately, they may be incompatible when used jointly. Moves to develop compatible software may be thwarted if there is a culture of competition between the two firms. By eliminating rivalry of this type, a horizontal merger may enable the benefits of compatibility or interoperability to be achieved more easily.

■ *Network configuration*. Suppose two firms operate a rail service between two cities, with each firm owning a single track. If each firm offers a return service, 'down' trains meet 'up' trains, so passing points have to be built, making route planning more complex and creating the potential for delays. However, if the two firms merge, the two tracks can each be used to serve traffic in one direction, resulting in a cost saving through a synergy effect.

Market power

As we saw in Chapter 4, oligopoly as a market structure is characterized by the problem of interdependence. A firm's success (or lack of success) depends on how its rivals act and react to its strategies. Interdependence creates uncertainty in strategic planning. One way of reducing uncertainty is for firms to collude, either explicitly or tacitly, over prices, output levels, the extent of product differentiation, and so on. In cases where collusion is difficult to organize or control, however, horizontal integration might be seen as a viable alternative strategy that would yield similar benefits, perhaps more effectively.

A horizontal merger may leave the newly integrated firm with a larger market share, or it may imply the direct removal from the market of a close rival. One or both of these outcomes increases the ability of the merged firm to increase its price, without having to worry about its rivals' reactions. Furthermore, the merger may make collusion easier to achieve. With fewer firms operating in the industry, there is a better chance of being able to achieve agreement and monitor compliance. These kinds of outcome may cause concerns for the competition authorities. A merger is more likely to be regarded as anticompetitive if it not only increases the degree of seller concentration, but also makes the entry of new firms more difficult. The treatment of mergers as part of competition policy is discussed in Chapter 17.

As well as increasing market power, a horizontal merger might be motivated by a desire to protect the dominance of an incumbent firm. Should a dominant incumbent be threatened by an entrant with a new product, it might attempt to acquire the entrant as a way of preserving the status quo. The alternative strategy might be to invest in the development of a rival product. To do so might take time, and might carry a high financial risk. Therefore acquisition of the rival firm might be a cheaper and less risky strategy, even if relatively generous terms are required for the takeover bid to be accepted.

Motives of the acquired firm

When examining horizontal mergers, it is important to consider the motives of the firms that is being acquired. These might include the following:

- The acquired firm may have suffered a loss of market share, or may be faced with decreasing revenue and financial difficulties. Being taken over might guarantee the continued operation of some or all of the firm's current resources: for example, its plants or its workforce.

- The owners or managers of the acquired firm may feel they have insufficient technical or organizational expertise, or insufficient finance, to be able to continue to manage the growth of the firm.

- The owners of the acquired firm might be forced to sell in order to meet tax or other financial liabilities.

Owners of a weak firm, who are desperate to find a buyer, might be prepared to accept a price below the firm's true value. In a competitive market for corporate ownership, in which there are many potential buyers with perfect information, competition among buyers should see the acquisition price bid up to the acquired firm's true value. In practice, however, there may be relatively few potential buyers with sufficient knowledge or skill to successfully rescue ailing firms through an acquisition strategy. Horizontal mergers may therefore take place on terms that significantly undervalue the acquired firm.

Horizontal merger as a mechanism for disseminating management theory and practice

Drawing on ideas developed by Dawkins (1998), Vos and Kelleher (2001) provide an interesting and radical analysis of the motivation of managers in their pursuit of mergers and acquisitions, arguing by means of analogy with the natural sciences.

'Memes' are ideas that spread much like genes and viruses. Human beings, through their abilities to imitate or 'replicate' become 'hosts' to new ideas. Through natural selection, evolution generates successful memes which spread throughout the host population. Memes exist purely to be replicated. Dawkins argues that the successful replication of ideas (the ability to create many copies) is based on fidelity, fecundity and longevity.

In the field of management, Vos and Kelleher suggest mergers increase managerial power and provide a vehicle for the transfer or replication of the corporate identity, which they refer to as the 'corporate story'. With an increase in the power of managers, the ideas transferred by these managers gain in credibility. Their 'corporate story' is more likely to be believed and imitated, so more exact copies are likely to be made. In other words, successful managers are the 'carriers' for new corporate ideas. The memes responsible for such thought-contagion are 'fitter': they are able to replicate more accurately (fidelity) and more extensively (fecundity) than other memes, and survive for longer (longevity).

> Merger and acquisition increases management power so that memes can spread more widely. Access to more resources provides memes with more chance to selfishly attempt to replicate themselves. When observed from this perspective, merger and acquisition activity appears to be an arena where power is not the end goal, but rather the means to the end. Memetic transference is the end goal.

(Vos and Kelleher, 2001, p. 10)

7.4 Horizontal mergers: some empirical evidence

The empirical evidence as to whether horizontal mergers lead to increased profitability through increased market power or cost savings is rather contradictory, and on the whole inconclusive. For example, Cosh *et al.* (1980) examine 211 mergers in the UK between 1967 and 1969, comparing profitability during a five-year period before the merger with profitability during the five years following the merger. The merged firms are found to have experienced an increase in average profitability. On the other hand, in a study of mergers in the UK between 1964 and 1972, Meeks (1977) finds that profitability fell on average during the seven-year period following the merger. Rydén and Edberg (1980) examine 25 mergers in Sweden between 1962 and 1976. The merged firms experienced lower profitability in comparison to a control group. Ravenscraft and Scherer (1987) examine the pre-merger profitability of 634 US target firms in the late 1960s and early 1970s. The target firms' profitability (ratio of operating income to assets) was 20 per cent, much higher than the average profitability of all firms of 11 per cent. Using a different sample, Ravenscraft and Scherer report a negative effect of merger on (post-merger) profitability. In contrast, Healy *et al.* (1992) report that while performance declined on average following the largest 50 US mergers between 1979 and 1984, it fell by less than the industry averages for the firms involved. Pesendorfer (2003) examines the effect of mergers in the US paper industry during the mid-1980s. Post-1984 (when merger guidelines were revised to allow a more liberal interpretation by the competition authorities) 31 mergers occurred. The analysis suggests that cost savings were typically realized post-merger.

Gugler *et al.* (2003) report a large-scale study of around 15,000 mergers world-wide, over the period 1981–99. The aim is to examine whether mergers are motivated by an objective of increasing market power, reducing costs or furthering managerial aims such as growth maximization. The test for market power is based on sales and profit data. A merged firm with increased market power should increase price, moving onto a more inelastic portion of its demand function. While profits increase, sales tend to fall. The test for cost savings is based on the notion that a reduced marginal cost leads to a reduction in price and an increase in both profit and sales. If managerial objectives are dominant, neither costs nor profit need be affected in the long run, although in the short run costs are incurred in integrating the two organizations. Therefore both profit and sales may tend to fall. A broad conclusion is that just over half of the mergers resulted in profits greater than would have been expected had the merger not occurred. A similar proportion resulted in a fall in sales. The combination of rising profit and falling sales is consistent with the market power hypothesis.

An alternative approach to analysing the performance of merged firms is to study the effect of merger announcements on the stock market prices of the firms involved, using what is known as an *event study*. An event study compares a company's share price immediately before and after the occurrence of an event that is expected to influence the company's market valuation. Share prices reflect the present value of investors' estimates of potential future profits. If investors expect a merger to result in greater market power or future cost savings, the share prices of the merger partners should increase. Empirical studies focus on the share prices of the 'target' firms, 'bidding' firms, or a combination of both. For example, Bradley *et al.* (1988) examine 236 US merger bids between 1963 and 1984, and find that the mean increase in share prices was 32 per cent. Schwert (1996) examines 1,814 US target firms in both successful and unsuccessful merger bids between 1975 and 1991, and calculates an average share price increase of 17 per cent. However, Jarrell *et al.* (1988) find evidence of share price reductions for bidding firms during the 1980s. Roller *et al.* (2001) report that across a large number of studies, the average gains of target firms are around 30 per cent, while bidding firms tended to break even on average.

Weiss (1965) examines the effects of horizontal mergers on seller concentration for the period 1926–59 for six US manufacturing industries (steel, cars, petrol, cement, flour and brewing). Changes in concentration ratios over approximate 10-year intervals are decomposed into effects arising from the internal growth of firms, the exit of incumbent firms, mergers, and turnover or changes in the identity of the largest firms in each industry. Internal growth and exit appear to have played a more important role than mergers in influencing changes in concentration.

Hannah and Kay (1981) find that mergers played an important role in increasing seller concentration in the UK over the period 1919–69. Furthermore, if growth attributable to merger was excluded, small firms would have grown by more than large firms. Accordingly, '[m]erger has been the dominant force in increasing concentration in the UK since 1919 . . . Its role has been growing and it now accounts for essentially all of currently observed net concentration increase' (Hannah and Kay,

1981, p. 312). Utton (1971), Aaronovitch and Sawyer (1975) and Hannah (1983) report similar findings. However, Hart (1981) suggests Hannah and Kay may have overstated the impact of mergers on concentration: 'even if all the 122 large mergers [involving over £5 million] had been prohibited, aggregate concentration would have continued to increase' (Hart, 1981, p. 318). As a cause of increasing concentration, mergers are less important than internal growth. A more recent study by the European Commission (1994) finds that mergers increased concentration over the period 1983–89 in a number of industries, including rubber, plastics, chemicals and pharmaceuticals. Other UK studies of the impact of mergers on concentration include Hart and Clarke (1980), Hart *et al.* (1973), Kumar (1985) and Utton (1972).

Overall, studies of merger activity tend to suggest that a large proportion of mergers have not been successful in increasing the profitability of the merged organization. Perhaps there is a systematic tendency to underestimate the practical difficulties involved in linking different product and distribution systems. Merged information systems may also prove to be inefficient, and senior managers may face distorted information flows for a significant period after the merger. Finally, if the two parties to a merger have separate and incompatible corporate 'cultures', staff from the two firms may find it difficult to integrate. The empirical evidence as to the importance of horizontal merger as a factor driving trends in seller concentration also appears to be rather mixed and inconclusive.

7.5 The random growth hypothesis

In Section 7.2, we have emphasized the importance of a large number of systematic factors in determining the structure of an industry. All of these explanations assume that observable characteristics of an industry or its incumbent firms are the ultimate source of the competitive advantages that will determine the performance of the industry's most successful firms. In turn, the most successful firms' performance has major implications for the number and the size distribution of firms the industry is ultimately capable of sustaining. In Section 7.2, the emphasis on *observable* characteristics of the industry and its constituent firms is crucial.

An alternative school of thought within industrial organization emphasizes the role of chance, or random factors, in determining the growth of individual firms and their eventual size distribution. According to the random growth hypothesis, individual firms' growth over any period is essentially random, as if determined by means of a draw in a lottery. Some firms do well and some do badly, but the distribution of strong and weak growth performance between firms is essentially a matter of chance. Furthermore, past growth is no reliable indicator of the rate at which a firm will grow or decline in the future. The growth of individual firms cannot be foreseen, any more than the winners of next Saturday's lottery can be predicted from the characteristics of last week's winners and losers, the strategies they employed when selecting their numbers, or their past records of success or failure.

It is important to note that the random growth hypothesis does not rule out the possibility that *ex post* (with the benefit of hindsight), strong growth performance can be attributed to 'systematic' factors such as managerial talent, successful innovation, efficient organizational structure or favourable shifts in consumer demand.

Rather, it implies that growth originating from these factors cannot be predicted *ex ante* (before the event). 'Systematic' factors of this kind may determine growth, but these factors are themselves distributed randomly across firms. As before, their effects cannot be foreseen or predicted in advance using data on the firms' observable characteristics.

If successful growth performance is essentially a matter of luck or chance, is the tendency to hero-worship successful entrepreneurs (Bill Gates, Richard Branson) in certain quarters of society (some sections of the business press, for example) fundamentally misconceived? In support of this view, Schwed's (1955) analogy of the 'great coin flipping contest' is worth quoting at some length.

> The referee gives a signal for the first time and 400,000 coins flash in the sun as they are tossed. The scorers make their tabulations, and discover that 200,000 people are winners and 200,000 are losers. Then the second game is played. Of the original 200,000 winners, about half of them win again. The third game is played, and of the 100,000 who have won both games half of them are again successful. These 50,000, in the fourth game are reduced to 25,000, and in the fifth to 12,500. These 12,500 have now won five straight without loss and are no doubt beginning to fancy themselves as coin flippers. They feel they have an 'instinct' for it. However in the sixth game, 6,250 are disappointed and amazed they have finally lost, and perhaps some of them start a Congressional investigation. But the victorious 6,250 play on and are successively reduced in number until less than a thousand are left. This little band have won nine straight without a loss, and by this time most of them have at least a local reputation for their ability. People come from some distance to consult them about their method of calling heads and tails, and they modestly give explanations of how they have achieved their success. Eventually there are about a dozen men who have won every single time for about fifteen games. These are regarded as the experts, the greatest coin flippers in history, the men who never lose, and they have their biographies written.
>
> *(Schwed, 1955, pp. 160–61, quoted in Sherman, 1977, p. 9)*

Kay (2004) makes a similar observation.

> When you buy a lottery ticket, you make a mistake – you almost certainly should not bet at such poor odds. But if the winning ticket is yours, chance redeems your mistake. When people succeed in risky situations, the outcome is a mixture of good judgement and good luck, and it is impossible to disentangle the elements of the two. This is of central importance to considering successful businesses and successful business people. To what extent were Henry Ford, William Morris and Bill Gates people who had the judgement to choose the right number, or lucky people whose number came up?
>
> *(Kay, 2004, p. 402)*

What are the implications of random growth for the long-run trend in seller concentration? The fact that the growth or decline of individual firms cannot be predicted using data on the firms' observable characteristics does not imply the trend in seller concentration is also purely a matter of chance. Proponents of the random growth hypothesis have developed simulation models to show that there is a natural tendency for industry structure to become increasingly concentrated over time, even if the growth of the industry's individual member firms is completely random. These models involve tracing the effects on seller concentration of the imposition of a sequence of random 'growth shocks' upon simulated (hypothetical) firm size data. This random growth hypothesis is embodied in the **Law of Proportionate Effect** (LPE). The LPE is also known as **Gibrat's Law** after the French statistician Gibrat (1931), who is credited with the first discussion of the implications of the random growth hypothesis for seller concentration.

A simple and highly stylized illustration of the implications of a random growth process for the trend in seller concentration is shown in Table 7.1. Suppose in year 1 an industry comprises eight equal-sized firms, each with sales of 100. The assumed random growth process is as follows: in any subsequent year, each firm has an equal chance of either doubling or halving its sales. For simplicity, it is assumed that no other outcome is possible. It is important to emphasize that this is only one of many possible ways in which a random growth process could be specified. A more realistic formulation might select the individual firms' growth rates randomly from some continuous range of values, rather than allowing only two (extreme) outcomes. However, the binary formulation keeps the arithmetic as simple as possible.

In Table 7.1, it is assumed that every year, half of the firms in each size category grow and the other half decline. Therefore four of the eight equal-sized firms in year 1 double in size in year 2, and four halve in size. From each group of four equal-sized firms in year 2, two double in size and two halve in size in year 3; and so on. The CR_3 and HH seller concentration measures (see Section 5.3) are reported at the bottom of Table 7.1. These reflect a progressive increase in concentration, with the firm size distribution becoming increasingly skewed in successive years. By year 4, only one firm has experienced the good fortune of three consecutive years of positive growth. Accordingly, this firm (firm 1) achieves a market share of more than 50 per cent in year 4.

Table 7.1 Trend in seller concentration with random firm growth

	Year 1	Year 2	Year 3	Year 4
Firm 1	100	200	400	800
2	100	200	400	200
3	100	200	100	200
4	100	200	100	200
5	100	50	100	50
6	100	50	100	50
7	100	50	25	50
8	100	50	25	12.5
CR_3	.375	.6	.72	.768
HH	.125	.17	.231	.314

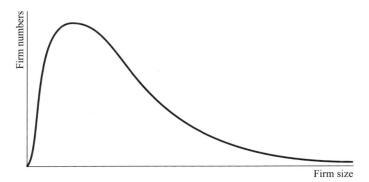

Figure 7.2 Distribution of firm sizes

Hannah and Kay (1977) use a gambling analogy to illustrate the same point.

> [I]f a group of rich men and a group of poor men visit Monte Carlo, it is likely that some of the rich will become poor and some of the poor become rich: but it is also probable that some of the rich will get richer and some of the poor will get poorer, so that the extent of inequality within each group and over the two groups taken together is likely to increase. The process works to increase industrial concentration in much the same way.
>
> *(Hannah and Kay, 1977, p. 103)*

Therefore if firms' growth rates are determined randomly, the firm size distribution tends to become skewed, with the industry comprising a few very large firms and a much larger number of smaller firms. This pattern is illustrated in Figure 7.2. Furthermore, the degree of skewness tends to increase progressively over time.

The long-run implications of the random growth hypothesis for seller concentration have been analysed using more realistic and less highly stylized simulation models. For example Scherer (1980) traces the evolution of a firm size distribution for a hypothetical industry initially comprising 50 equal-sized firms. Each firm's growth rate in each year was drawn from a normal probability distribution, whose parameters (mean and variance) were calibrated using data on a sample of 369 of the 500 largest US firms over the period 1954–60. The evolution of industry structure over a 140-year time period was simulated 16 times, and the average four-firm concentration ratio calculated. The results showed that the concentration ratio increased from 8 per cent in period 1 to approximately 58 per cent in period 140. McCloughan (1995) develops a more elaborate stochastic growth model that also incorporates entry and exit.

Table 7.2 reports the average results across 20 replications of a simulation over 50 time periods of an industry comprising 20 firms. The firms are equal-sized (each with a size value of 1 unit) at period 0. In each subsequent period, their logarithmic growth rate is drawn randomly from a normal distribution with zero mean and a standard deviation of 0.1. Over 50 periods, the average market share of the largest firm increases from 5 per cent to 15.1 per cent, and the average market share of the top five firms increases from 25 per cent to 49 per cent. Table 7.2 also shows the corresponding adjustments in the HH index and the numbers equivalent of the HH index.

Table 7.2 Simulated evolution of industry structure and concentration under the random growth hypothesis

Period	Mean size	St.Dev. of size	CR_1	CR_2	CR_5	HH	Numbers equivalent, n(2)
0	1.00	–	.050	.100	.250	.050	20.0
1	1.00	.10	.060	.117	.282	.050	20.0
2	1.00	.14	.064	.124	.291	.051	19.6
5	1.02	.23	.075	.142	.324	.052	19.2
10	1.03	.33	.087	.161	.354	.055	18.2
15	1.05	.41	.096	.177	.383	.058	17.2
20	1.10	.49	.105	.191	.400	.060	16.7
25	1.14	.59	.117	.208	.419	.063	15.9
30	1.18	.67	.127	.218	.435	.066	15.2
35	1.21	.74	.133	.226	.454	.068	14.7
40	1.22	.78	.138	.236	.462	.070	14.3
45	1.22	.83	.143	.245	.471	.072	13.9
50	1.26	.91	.151	.257	.490	.076	13.2

Some of the earliest empirical research on the random growth hypothesis examines whether the actual size distribution of firms is consistent with the size distribution that would be expected if firm growth is truly random. Clarke (1979), Quandt (1966), Silberman (1967) and Stanley *et al.* (1995) all report tests which assess how accurately certain theoretically skewed statistical probability distributions (including the log-normal, Yule and Pareto distributions) describe observed firm size distributions. Although these studies are unable to identify any specific theoretical distribution that always provides the best description of reality, the tendency for observed firm size distributions to be highly skewed, and therefore amenable to representation using these types of distribution, is almost universal.

An alternative approach to testing the LPE is based on the idea that if growth is random, there should be no relationship between the size of a firm at the start of any period and its growth over that period. In other words, firm size should have no predictive capability for future growth. Furthermore, past growth should also have no predictive capability for future growth. Regression analysis can be used to test for these non-relationships. A typical specification is as follows:

$$(x_{i,t+T} - x_{i,t}) = \alpha + \beta_1 x_{i,t} + \beta_2(x_{i,t} - x_{i,t-T}) + u_i$$

where $x_{i,t}$ represents the natural logarithm of the size of firm i in year t. Growth is observed over the T-year period between years t and t + T, and $(x_{i,t+T} - x_{i,t})$ represents firm i's logarithmic growth rate over this period. Similarly $(x_{i,t} - x_{i,t-T})$ represents firm i's logarithmic growth over the previous T-year period between years t – T and t. The disturbance term u_i represents the random component of firm i's growth for the period t to t + T. According to the random growth hypothesis, the regression coefficients β_1 and β_2 should both be zero. $\beta_1 = 0$ implies there is no relationship between firm size in year t and growth over the period t to t + T; and $\beta_2 = 0$ implies there is no relationship between growth over the period t − T to t, and growth over the period t to t + T. Using firm size data for a sample of firms observed at points t − T, t and t + T, we can estimate the model as a cross-sectional regression, and test the hypotheses $\beta_1 = 0$ and $\beta_2 = 0$ in order to determine whether the data supports the random growth hypothesis.

In the event that the random growth hypothesis is not supported by the data, two of the most likely alternatives are as follows.

- If $\beta_1 < 0$, there is a negative relationship between initial size and subsequent growth. In other words, $\beta_1 < 0$ implies the smaller firms tend to grow faster than the larger firms. Over the long run, there is a tendency for *convergence* in firm sizes. In this case, there would be some eventual limit to the tendency for concentration to increase over time. Accordingly, the long-run implications for the trend in seller concentration of $\beta_1 < 0$ are very different from the implications of $\beta_1 = 0$.

- If $\beta_2 > 0$, there is a positive relationship between growth in consecutive T-year periods. In other words, a firm that grew relatively fast over the period t − T to t is likely to do so again over the period t to t + T. Such a pattern could reflect distinctive capabilities on the part of the firm, enabling it to deliver above-average growth consistently. In this case, the tendency for concentration to increase over time would be strengthened relative to the case in which growth is completely random.

Empirical research that tests the LPE has produced mixed results. Several early studies, based on data up to and including the 1970s, report either no relationship or a positive relationship between firm size and growth. A number of more recent studies find a consistent tendency for small firms to grow faster than large firms. As we have seen, a growth pattern that is in accordance with the LPE ($\beta_1 = 0$) implies seller concentration tends to increase over time. A tendency for small firms to grow faster than large firms ($\beta_1 < 0$) implies no long-term increase in seller concentration. Broadly speaking, the results of the empirical literature are consistent with what is known about trends in seller concentration (see Section 6.4): until the 1970s concentration tended to increase consistently, but since the 1970s there has been no consistent trend.

Table 7.3 summarizes a number of empirical studies of the LPE. We conclude this section by commenting on some general features of this literature. As noted above, much of the recent LPE literature consistently reports a tendency for small firms or plants to grow faster than their larger counterparts (Blonigen and Tomlin, 2001; Dunne and Hughes, 1994; Evans, 1987a,b; Hart and Oulton, 1996, 1999). While this might reflect genuine growth patterns, it has also been suggested that a negative size–growth relationship might, at least in part, be an artifact of the way in which many empirical tests are constructed. Specifically, their reliance on data for firms that survived over the sample period raises the possibility that a type of **sample selection bias** or **survivorship bias** might be responsible for a negative reported size–growth relationship. Some of the earliest literature recognized that the validity

Table 7.3 Tests of the Law of Proportionate Effect (LPE): a selective review

Study (chronological order)	Sample characteristics	Results
Hart and Prais (1956)	UK firms, 1885–1950. London Stock Exchange valuation size measure.	No size–growth relationship before 1939. Negative size–growth relationship for 1939–50.
Hart (1962)	UK brewing, spinning and drinks firms, 1931–54. Gross profit depreciation size measure.	No size–growth relationship. Large brewing firms have more variable growth than small firms.
Hymer and Pashigian (1962)	1,000 large US manufacturing firms, 1946–55. Assets size measure.	No size–growth relationship. Variability in growth greater for small firms.
Mansfield (1962)	Varying numbers of US steel, petroleum and tyre firms, 1916–57. Firm output size measure.	Reports tests for all firms, for survivors, and for firms operating above industry MES (minimum efficient scale). No size–growth relationship above MES.
Samuals (1965)	322 UK manufacturing firms, 1951–60. Net assets size measure.	Larger firms grew faster than smaller firms, due to economies of scale.
Samuals and Chesher (1972)	2,000 UK firms from 21 industry groups, 1960–69. Net assets size measure.	Large firms grew faster than small firms. Variability in growth greater for small firms. Departures from LPE greatest in oligopoly. Some evidence of persistence of growth.
Utton (1972)	1,527 UK firms from 13 manufacturing industries, 1954–65. Net assets size measure.	Large firms grew faster than small firms in five industries; small firms grew faster in one industry.
Aaronovitch and Sawyer (1975)	233 quoted UK manufacturing firms, 1959–67. Net assets size measure.	No size–growth relationship.
Singh and Whittington (1975)	Approx. 2,000 UK firms in 21 industry groups, 1948–60. Net assets size measure.	Large firms grew faster than small firms. Variation in growth rates declines with firm size. Some evidence of persistence of growth.
Chesher (1979)	183 UK manufacturing firms, 1960–69. Net assets size measure.	No size–growth relationship. Some evidence of persistence of growth.
Kumar (1985)	UK firms, 1960–76. Three sub-periods are: 1960–65 (1,747 firms), 1966–71 (1,021 firms), 1972–76 (824 firms). Net assets, fixed assets, total equity, employees and sales size measures.	Negative size–growth relationship for 1960–65 and 1972–76. No size–growth relationship for 1966–71. Some evidence of persistence of growth.
Evans (1987a)	42,339 small US firms, 1976–80. Employees size measure.	Failure rates, growth and variability of growth decrease with age. Overall, rejects LPE in favour of an inverse relationship between size and growth.
Evans (1987b)	17,339 small US manufacturing firms, 1976–82. Employees size measure.	Finds an inverse relationship between firm size and firm growth. Strong evidence of an inverse relationship between age and growth.
Hall (1987)	Varying numbers of US firms, 1972–83. Three sub-periods are: 1972–83 (962 firms); 1972–79 (1,349 firms); 1976–83 (1,098 firms). Employees size measure.	Negative size–growth relationship. Variability of growth greater for small firms.

Table 7.3 (*continued*)

Study (chronological order)	Sample characteristics	Results
Dunne *et al.* (1988)	200,000 US manufacturing plants, 1967–77. Employees size measure.	Negative size–growth relationship, and negative age–growth relationship for multi-plant firms. Variability of growth declines with plant size.
Contini and Revelli (1989)	467 small Italian manufacturers, 1973–86. Employees size measure.	Negative size–growth relationship. LPE holds for largest firms in the sample.
Acs and Audretsch (1990)	408 four-digit US industries, 1976–80. Employees size measure.	No size–growth relationship in the majority of industries (245 out of 408).
Reid (1992)	73 small UK firms, 1985–88. Sales and employees size measures.	Negative size–growth relationship. Younger firms have faster growth.
Wagner (1992)	7,000 small German firms, 1978–89. Employees size measure.	No size–growth relationship. Some evidence of persistence of growth.
Dunne and Hughes (1994)	2,149 UK firms, 1975–85. Assets size measure.	Accepts LPE for majority of size classes in 1980–85, but rejects in all classes 1975–80, finding that small firms had faster and more variable growth than larger counterparts.
Hart and Oulton (1996)	87,109 small independent UK firms, 1989–93. Net assets, employees and sales size measures.	Negative size–growth relationship This pattern is robust with respect to size category and size measure.
Hart and Oulton (1999)	29,000 small independent UK firms, 1989–93. Employees size measure.	Negative size–growth relationship, except for the very largest firms.
Wilson and Morris (2000)	264 manufacturing and 163 service firms, UK, 1991–95. Net assets size measure.	Negative size–growth relationship. Small firms had more variable growth. Persistence of growth for manufacturing.
Wilson and Williams (2000)	400 European banks, 1990–96. Total assets and equity size measure.	Small Italian banks grew faster than large ones. No size–growth relationship for France, Germany and the UK.
Blonigen and Tomlin (2001)	Japanese-owned US manufacturing plants, 1987–90. Employees size measure.	Small plants grew faster than large plants.
Dobson *et al.* (2001)	All English professional football clubs, 1926–97. Gate revenue size measure.	Some evidence of convergence for certain periods (1930–59 and 1970–89). No convergence in other periods.
Goddard *et al.* (2002a)	443 Japanese manufacturing firms, 1980–96. Total assets size measure.	Some evidence of convergence in firm sizes towards firm-specific average values.
Goddard *et al.* Wilson (2002b)	7,603 US credit unions, 1990–99. Assets and membership size measures.	Large credit unions grew faster than small credit unions.
Audretsch *et al.* (2002)	1,170 Dutch service firms, 1987–9. Sales size measure.	In contrast to recent manufacturing evidence, no size–growth relationship.
Geroski *et al.* (2003)	147 quoted UK firms, 1948–77. Net assets size measure.	Growth among surviving firms is mainly random. Little evidence of long run convergence in firm sizes.

of the LPE might be limited to firms operating above a certain size threshold, or minimum efficient scale (MES) (Simon and Bonini, 1958). The long-term survival of small firms depends upon their ability to achieve at least the MES, so that they can realize the full benefits of economies of scale. Small firms that fail to achieve the MES reasonably quickly tend to exit. Therefore we might expect to observe faster-than-average growth among a cohort of surviving small firms, during the phase when such firms are still striving in order to attain the MES.

In most instances empirical tests of the LPE are based on a cross-sectional regression of logarithmic growth rates over a given period on initial log sizes. However, Gibrat's original formulation and many subsequent interpretations of the LPE emphasize the implications for trends in the size distribution of firms and seller concentration over the long run. In view of recent improvements in the time coverage of firm-level databases, and advances in econometric methods for analysing time-series data sets and panel data sets (containing both a cross-sectional dimension and a time dimension), it is unsurprising that empirical tests of the LPE based on time-series or panel models, rather than on cross-sectional regression, have recently started to appear. For example, Goddard *et al.* (2002a) test the validity of the LPE for a Japanese manufacturing sample with 15 years of annual size and growth data for more than 300 firms. Some evidence of a negative size–growth relationship is reported. For the majority of the 147 large, quoted UK firms in Geroski *et al.*'s (2003) 30-year study, there is little or no evidence of any relationship between size and growth. Accordingly, the study comes down strongly in favour of the random growth hypothesis.

> Our results suggest that the growth rates of firms who survive long enough to record 30 years of history are random . . . Among other things, this means that there is no obvious upper bound on levels of concentration in individual industries or across the economy as a whole. A metaphor for convergence might tell a story of ships all reaching the same harbour despite coming from different directions. In fact, the metaphor that describes our data is ships passing in the night.
>
> *(Geroski et al., 2003, p. 55)*

Several researchers develop models in which growth is part-random, but partly influenced by systematic factors. For example, Davies and Lyons (1982) include firm numbers, economies of scale and barriers to entry among the systematic determinants of growth. Small firms need to grow rapidly in order to achieve the MES. The systematic influences are most important in determining growth, and (implicitly) concentration, up to the point at which economies of scale are exhausted. Once the MES has been attained, however, growth is mainly random. Geroski and Mazzucato (2002) examine the extent to which corporate learning (which can be either systematic, arising from technological innovation and spillovers, internal resources and learning economies of scale; or random) is evident in the growth patterns of large US car manufacturers over an 85-year period. There is only limited evidence of any systematic learning effect on observed growth. Learning effects appear to be mainly random.

Davies and Geroski (1997) apply a variant of the random growth model to firm-level market share data on 200 large UK firms within 54 manufacturing industries. The empirical model is as follows:

$$\Delta MS_{i,j} = \alpha_j + \beta_j MS_{i,j} + \gamma_1 x_{1,i} + \gamma_2 x_{2,i} + \ldots + \gamma_k x_{k,i} + u_{i,j}$$

$MS_{i,j}$ represents the market share of firm i in industry j at the start of the observation period, and $\Delta MS_{i,j}$ the change in firm i's market share in industry j over the course of the observation period. $u_{i,j}$ is a disturbance term that incorporates the random element in variations in the firms' market shares. The regression coefficients α_j and β_j play a similar role in this model to their counterparts in the random growth model (as specified previously in this section). However, the j-subscripts indicate that the values of these coefficients are permitted to vary between industries. Davies and Geroski use a number of industry characteristics to model the variation in α_j and β_j. These include estimates of the MES, growth in industry sales, the advertising-to-sales ratio, the research and development expenditure-to-sales ratio, and the initial level of concentration. The additional covariates $x_{1,i}, x_{2,i}, \ldots, x_{k,i}$ represent a number of firm-specific determinants of growth. $\gamma_1, \gamma_2, \ldots, \gamma_k$ are the regression coefficients on these covariates. Indicators of expenditure on advertising and research and development that are specific to the firm itself and its nearest rivals are found to be significant determinants of changes in market share. The model suggests that relative stability in an industry's concentration ratios can conceal significant 'turbulence', or turnover, in the identities and rankings of the firms with the largest market shares.

7.6 Summary

In Chapter 7, we have examined some of the main theoretical determinants of seller concentration. Why do some industries tend to become more highly concentrated than others, and what are the factors driving trends in seller concentration over time? The main theoretical determinants of seller concentration that have been examined in this chapter include the following:

- *Economies of scale*. The comparison between the total output that would be produced if each incumbent firm operates at minimum efficient scale, and the total demand for the industry's product, has major implications for the number of firms that the industry can profitably sustain.

- *Entry and exit*. Entry tends to reduce concentration if the average size of entrants is smaller than that of incumbents. However, the effect could be the opposite if entry takes place at a large scale, perhaps as a result of a diversification strategy on the part of a large established firm from some other industry. By reducing the numbers of incumbents, exit usually tends to increase concentration.

- *Scope for discretionary, sunk cost expenditure*. Advertising, product differentiation and research and development are more important vehicles for discretionary investment in some industries than others. In industries which provide scope for these forms of sunk cost expenditure, incumbent firms tend to respond to an increase in demand by increasing their discretionary expenditures, leading to raised entry barriers, a larger minimum efficient scale and increased seller concentration. In industries without scope for significant sunk cost expenditures, any increase in demand may create opportunities for entrants, and seller concentration may tend to decrease.

■ *Regulation.* Government competition policy directed towards monopolies, mergers or restrictive practices may have direct implications for seller concentration. Policies that restrict the number of firms permitted to operate may tend to increase concentration.

■ *The industry life cycle.* New and rapidly expanding industries may be capable of sustaining large numbers of firms, with small firms able to prosper by innovating or finding niches. Mature and declining industries are likely to accommodate smaller numbers of firms, as incumbents attempt to offset the effects on profitability of slow growth in demand by realizing economies of scale, and eventually by eliminating competition through collusion or merger.

■ *Distinctive capabilities and core competences.* According to the resource-based theory of the firm, the successful firm itself, rather than the industry structure, is the ultimate source of the strategies and capabilities that will eventually determine structural indicators such as seller concentration.

Evaluation of horizontal mergers often focuses on the possibility of anticompetitive effects which enhance the market power of the merged organization, and economies of scale in production, purchasing, marketing or research and development. A merger between two firms producing goods or services that are direct substitutes in consumption naturally has direct implications for seller concentration, although the empirical evidence as to the importance of horizontal merger as a driver of long-run trends in seller concentration is rather varied and inconclusive. The empirical evidence based on company accounts or stock market data of merged firms before and after mergers have been announced and concluded appears to suggest that a large proportion of mergers have not been particularly successful in increasing the profitability of the merged organization.

According to the random growth hypothesis that is expressed by the Law of Proportionate Effect (also known as Gibrat's Law), strong or weak growth performance is distributed randomly across firms. In any given period some firms may perform well and others perform badly, but the distribution of strong and weak growth performance between firms is essentially a matter of chance. Furthermore, past growth is no reliable indicator of the rate at which a firm will grow or decline in the future. According to this view, the growth performance of individual firms can neither be explained by specific identifiable characteristics of the firms themselves, nor foreseen or predicted in advance. If individual firms' growth is random, stochastic theory and simulation models show there is a natural tendency for industry structure to become increasingly concentrated over time. Broadly speaking, the empirical evidence on the random growth hypothesis is consistent with what is known about long-run trends in seller concentration: until the 1970s growth was pretty random and concentration tended to increase quite consistently; but since the 1970s there is some evidence that small firms have grown faster than large ones, and the long-run trend in seller concentration has become less consistent.

Discussion questions

1. What are the implications of the relationship between MES (the minimum efficient scale of production) and the level of market demand for the degree of seller concentration in an industry?

2. Compare and contrast four approaches that have been used to estimate the extent of economies of scale.

3. Explain Sutton's (1991) distinction between Type 1 and Type 2 industries. If there is a sustained increase in market size in the long run, how is the trend in seller concentration expected to differ between these two industry types?

4. Outline the model of the industry life cycle. For what reasons might the degree of seller concentration be expected to change as an industry progresses through the four stages of its life cycle?

5. With reference to Case study 7.1, consider the extent to which the historical development of the US credit union sector conforms to the industry life cycle model.

6. What are distinctive capabilities, and what are core competences? Why are they important?

7. In what ways might a horizontal merger be expected to lead to increased profitability as a result of cost savings?

8. To what extent does the empirical evidence support the view that most horizontal mergers are primarily profit-motivated?

9. Explain the implications of the random growth hypothesis (Gibrat's Law, also known as the Law of Proportionate Effect) for the long-run trend in seller concentration.

10. Explain how the random growth hypothesis might be subjected to empirical scrutiny.

Further reading

Campbell, J.R. and Hopenhayn, H.A. (2005) Market size matters, *Journal of Industrial Economics*, 53, 1–25.

Caves, R.E. (1998) Industrial organization and new findings on the turnover and mobility of firms, *Journal of Economic Literature*, 36, 1947–82.

Curry, B. and George, K. (1983) Industrial concentration: a survey, *Journal of Industrial Economics*, 31, 203–55.

Davies, S.W. (1989) Concentration, in Davies, S. and Lyons, B. (eds) *The Economics of Industrial Organisation*. London: Longman.

Davies, S.W. and Lyons, B.R. (1996) *Industrial Organisation in the European Union*. Oxford: Clarendon Press.

Dosi, G., Malerba, F., Marsila, O. and Orsenigo, L. (1997) Industrial structures and dynamics: evidence interpretations and puzzles, *Industrial and Corporate Change*, 6, 3–24.

Geroski, P.A. (1999) *The Growth of Firms in Theory and Practice*, Centre of Economic Policy Research Discussion Paper Series, No. 2092. London: Centre of Economic Policy Research.

Geroski, P.A. (2003) *The Evolution of New Markets*. Oxford: Oxford University Press.

Sutton, J. (1991) *Sunk Costs and Market Structure*. London: MIT Press.

Sutton, J. (1997) Gibrat's legacy, *Journal of Economic Literature*, 35, 40–59.

Winter, S.G. (2003) Understanding dynamic capabilities, *Strategic Management Journal*, 24, 991–95.

Barriers to entry

8.1 Introduction

Barriers to entry can be defined in several ways. Bain (1956) defines entry barriers as conditions that allow established firms or incumbents to earn abnormal profits without attracting entry. Stigler (1968, p. 67) defines entry barriers as 'a cost of producing (at some or every rate of output) which must be borne by a firm which seeks to enter an industry but is not borne by firms already in the industry'. Demsetz (1982) suggests entry barriers persist in the long run only if they are erected and supported by the state. Spulber (2003, p. 55) defines an entry barrier as 'any competitive advantage that established firms have over potential entrants'. Caves and Porter (1977) suggest entry barriers apply not only to entrants, but also between different groups of established firms within industries. Groups may be defined by product characteristics or ownership structure.

Paradoxically, the extent of **barriers to exit** may be an important factor determining the incentive for new firms to enter. It is costly to exit if production requires sunk cost investment expenditures. **Sunk costs** are costs that cannot be recovered if the firm subsequently decides to exit from the industry. For example, expenditure on capital equipment which can only be used to manufacture the product in question, and which will be scrapped if the firm exits, is an example of a sunk cost expenditure. Entry is therefore riskier in cases where the entrant is unable to recover its costs if its decision to enter subsequently turns out to be unsuccessful.

Even if the entrant is confident it can succeed, perhaps because it knows it can produce at a lower average cost than an incumbent, barriers to exit facing the incumbent may still be an important consideration for the entrant. If the incumbent has already incurred significant levels of sunk cost expenditure, so its exit barriers are high, the incumbent is likely to resist attempts by the entrant to capture part or all of its market share, perhaps by initiating a price war. If there has been no sunk cost expenditure and exit barriers are low, the incumbent threatened by competition from a low-cost entrant might simply prefer to withdraw quietly. If entrants take account of the probable reaction of incumbents before deciding whether or not to enter, the extent of exit barriers facing incumbents may be an important factor influencing this decision.

This chapter begins in Section 8.2 by discussing the classification of types of barrier to entry that may arise from an industry's demand, product or technological characteristics. Structural barriers are examined in Section 8.3. These are entry barriers over which neither incumbents nor entrants have direct control. This category includes entry barriers arising from economies of scale, an absolute cost advantage held by an incumbent over an entrant, and natural product differentiation. Other types of structural entry barrier include legal barriers, erected by government and enforced by law; and geographic barriers, which create difficulties for foreign firms attempting to trade in the domestic market. Strategic barriers to entry are those created or raised by incumbents through their own entry-deterring strategies. Such strategies are examined in Section 8.4. These include limit pricing, predatory pricing, strategic product differentiation, and signalling commitment by deliberately increasing sunk cost investment expenditure.

Contestable markets theory is examined in Section 8.5. In industries where barriers to entry are surmountable, the threat of entry may keep prices close to the competitive level, even if there are few firms and the industry appears to be highly concentrated. Contestable markets theory breaks the direct link between the number and size distribution of sellers and the extent of market power or the discretion incumbents have in setting their own prices. Section 8.6 examines a more dynamic view of entry and market evolution over the long run. Entry is seen as a disequilibrating force that plays a central role in shaping the evolution of market or industry structure in the long run. The chapter concludes in Section 8.7 with a brief review of some of the empirical evidence on the determinants of entry and the main sources of barriers to entry.

8.2 Classification of barriers to entry

Although most industrial economists would agree that the study of entry barriers began formally with Bain's pioneering work in the mid-1950s, one should note that there were some notable earlier contributions on this topic. For example, Harrod (1952) analyses entry by identifying firms as either *snatchers*: firms that are interested only in high prices and short-run profits, and not worried about attracting entry; or *stickers*: firms that have committed long-term investments to the industry and do not wish to attract entrants by setting too high a price. Bain (1956) identifies three main sources of barrier to entry, arising from economies of scale, absolute cost advantage and product differentiation. Bain's original classification has since been extended and refined. Shepherd (1997, p. 210), for example, lists no fewer than 21 types of entry barrier.

There is no unique, agreed system for classifying the many factors that may impede entry. Broadly speaking, however, entry barriers may be subdivided into those that stem from the structure of the industry itself, providing shelter for the incumbent firms, and those that are created by the incumbent firms deliberately, in order to keep out potential entrants or at least retard the rate of entry. Howe (1978, p. 64) refers to the former type as natural and the latter as artificial. Shepherd (1997, pp. 210–11) also divides entry barriers into two types: exogenous, reflecting structural conditions such as the prevailing state of technology, and normally considered beyond the control of incumbents (at least in the short run); and endogenous, deriving from strategies actively implemented by incumbents in order to deter entry.

Below, we follow the traditional dichotomy. We examine first structural barriers, and then turn to entry-deterring strategies. Before commencing, however, we should bear the following points in mind:

- Groupings and definitions are not always straightforward. Undoubtedly there is some overlap between different categories of entry barrier. For example, product differentiation might be both a structural barrier and an entry-deterring strategy.

- The status of the entrant will often define the ease of entry. What might appear to be a formidable barrier to a small, independent start-up firm might appear a lesser problem to a large multi-product firm that is already dominant in other markets.

- The effect of entry on incumbents might well depend on the speed at which entry is executed. Entry at a slow rate alerts incumbents to the danger of additional competition, and allows them time to develop effective strategies to counter the threat. Faster entry may not allow incumbents to react so effectively.

8.3 Structural barriers to entry

Structural barriers are entry barriers over which neither incumbent firms nor entrants have direct control. Under this heading, we consider the three types of entry barrier originally discussed by Bain: **economies of scale**, **absolute cost advantage** and **product differentiation**. We also discuss **legal** and **geographic entry barriers**.

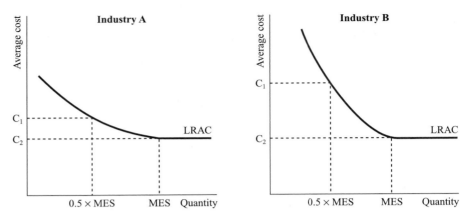

Figure 8.1 Economies of scale as a barrier to entry

Economies of scale

Economies of scale can act as a barrier to entry in two ways. First, there is an entry barrier if the MES (minimum efficient scale) is large relative to the total size of the market. As we have seen in Section 2.2, MES is the output level at which all potential economies of scale have been exploited, and the firm is operating at the lowest point on the LRAC (long-run average cost) function. The nature of the technology may be such that firms must claim a large market share in order to produce at the MES. A natural monopoly, in which long-run average costs decrease as output increases over all possible output levels the market can absorb, is the most extreme case. As we have seen in Section 2.5, in a natural monopoly average costs are minimized if one firm occupies the entire market. This situation tends to arise in industries where fixed costs are high relative to variable costs.

The second way in which economies of scale can act as an entry barrier is when average costs associated with a production level below the MES are substantially greater than average costs at the MES. This is illustrated in Figure 8.1. In both industry A and industry B, the penalty for producing at 50 per cent of the MES is $C_1 - C_2$. This penalty is much greater in industry B than in industry A, due to the difference in slope between the two LRAC functions.

Economies of scale present the potential entrant with a dilemma. Either the entrant accepts the risk associated with large-scale entry in order to avoid the average cost penalty; or the entrant enters at a smaller scale and absorbs the average cost penalty. Large-scale entry is risky because the expansion in industry capacity might disrupt the status quo, depressing prices and inviting retaliatory action from incumbents. On the other hand, small-scale entry may not be viable, because the average cost penalty may make it impossible for the entrant to operate profitably alongside incumbents already producing at (or beyond) the MES.

Pratten (1988) provides some empirical estimates of the extent to which economies of scale acted as a barrier to entry for a number of European industries in 1986. Table 8.1 shows estimates of the additional average cost that would be incurred by operating at 50 per cent of the MES, beyond the average cost incurred when operating at the MES, expressed as a percentage of the latter.

Table 8.1 Economies of scale as a barrier to entry

Industry	Increase in average cost if operating at 50% of MES
Motor vehicles	6–9%
Chemicals	2.5–15%
Metals	> 6%
Office machinery	3–6%
Mechanical engineering	3–10%
Electrical engineering	5–15%
Instrument engineering	5–15%
Paper, printing and publishing	8–36%
Rubber and plastics	3–6%
Drink and tobacco	1–6%
Food	3.5–21%
Footwear and clothing	1%

Source: Adapted from Pratten (1988), table 5.5, pp. 88–92.

Absolute cost advantage

An incumbent has an absolute cost advantage over an entrant if the LRAC function of the entrant lies above that of the incumbent, and the entrant therefore faces a higher average cost at every level of output. This situation is illustrated in Figure 8.2.

There are several reasons why an entrant may operate on a higher LRAC function. First, an incumbent may have access to a superior production process, hold patents, or be party to trade secrets. For example, the Monopolies and Mergers Commission (1968) estimated that it would take an entrant to the cellulose fibre industry between five and seven years to catch up with state-of-the-art production technology. Patenting involves the deliberate creation of a property right for new knowledge, intended to protect an innovator from imitation by rivals. From a public

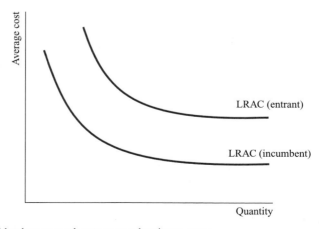

Figure 8.2 Absolute cost advantage as a barrier to entry

policy perspective, the motive for allowing patents may be to increase consumer welfare. Patents encourage firms to invest in research and development, with the promise of monopoly profits for successful innovators, as well as increased choice and utility for consumers.

However, patenting can also be used by an incumbent strategically, in an attempt to deter entry. For example, a firm in possession of a new technology may apply for multiple patents to cover all possible spin-offs, so as to deny rivals the opportunity to invent around the new technology. In chemicals, for example, minor variations in molecular structure can easily lead to the creation of new product spin-offs (Needham, 1976). In the defence industry, new firms incur substantial entry costs related to technology and research and development expenditure in order to produce sophisticated defence equipment (Hartley, 2003). Langinier (2004) presents a theoretical model that assesses the extent to which patents and patent renewals act as a barrier to entry. In cases of low demand and asymmetric information regarding market demand, patent renewal is shown to deter entry. However, if market demand is high, patent renewals do not discourage entry. The economics of patenting is examined in more detail in Section 14.5.

Second, incumbent firms may have exclusive ownership of factor inputs. They may control the best raw materials, or have recruited the most qualified or experienced labour or management personnel. Consequently entrants are forced to rely on more expensive, less efficient or lower-quality alternatives. For example, British Airways exercises influence over landing slots at London's Heathrow Airport, forcing competitors to use less attractive airports. However, through a variety of innovative strategies low-cost entrants have been able to overcome this entry barrier, and operate profitably. For example, low-cost airlines have unbundled their core product by charging separate prices for the flight itself and extras such as meals; reduced costs by using cheaper airports; simplified ticket purchase and check-in arrangements; reduced airport turnaround times; and made more intensive use of their aircraft (Johnson, 2003).

Third, incumbents may have access to cheaper sources of finance, if they are viewed by capital markets as less risky than new firms. For example, in pharmaceuticals large incumbents with well established research and development programmes are deemed less likely than their smaller counterparts to develop products that subsequently go on to fail drug trials. Lower risk means that preferential financial backing is easier to attain (Nightingale, 2003). If the new firm's management is previously unknown, any funds loaned are likely to carry a risk premium. Some authors have identified this as a separate barrier, referred to under an all-embracing term such as capital requirements barriers. This covers all difficulties that an entrant may encounter in raising sufficient finance to be able to operate at a realistic scale of production.

Finally, the presence of vertically integrated incumbents in industries such as biotechnology, brewing, iron, mobile telephones, steel or chemicals may force an entrant to operate at more than one stage of production if it wishes to overcome the incumbents' absolute cost advantage. In European brewing, for example, any new firm would not only manufacture beer, but also be able to source supplies, promote the finished product and establish an efficient network of distribution outlets (Lawler and Lee, 2003). Denying rivals access to inputs or markets through various forms of vertical exclusion may be subject to legal challenge under competition law (see below, Chapter 17), but this is not to say that such practices never take place.

It is worth noting that an absolute cost differential need not always work in favour of the incumbent. It is possible that an incumbent has overpaid for its assets, in which case the entrant may be favoured. This might be true in industries reliant on rapidly changing technologies, such as computer hardware or software, whose costs fall rapidly over time. In some cases the entrant may be spared the costs of persuading consumers to accept a new idea or a new product, such costs having already been incurred by incumbents.

Demsetz (1982) argues that Bain's absolute cost advantage does not reflect the abuse of market power by incumbents, but simply reflects the scarcity of resources and the associated rents. However, this comment does not invalidate the preceding discussion, in so far as it concerns structural barriers to entry. These additional costs are real enough to potential entrants, and they do not necessarily derive from the exploitation of market power.

Natural product differentiation

A structural entry barrier exists if customers are loyal to the established brands and reputations of incumbents. A successful entrant will need to prise customers away from their existing suppliers, or at least stir customers out of their inertia. This might be achieved either by selling the same product at a lower price, or launching advertising, marketing or other promotional campaigns. Due to price-cutting or increased costs (or both) the entrant is faced with a squeeze on profit, at least during the initial start-up phase. Comanor and Wilson (1967a,b) identify the following natural product differentiation barriers:

- High advertising imposes additional costs upon entrants. In order to overcome existing brand loyalties or customer inertia, the entrant must spend proportionately more on advertising for each prospective customer. In other words, market penetration costs are high. This is an absolute cost advantage barrier. For example, in European brewing it is estimated that the establishment of a leading brand through advertising takes around 20 years (Competition Commission, 2001; Lawler and Lee, 2003).

- If entry takes place on a small scale, the entrant will not benefit from economies of scale in advertising. Large-scale advertisers may benefit from an increasingly effective message, and decreasing average advertising costs.

- The funds needed to finance an advertising campaign may incur a risk premium, as this type of investment is high risk. Furthermore, it creates no tangible assets that can be sold in the event of failure.

- Entry barriers arising from product differentiation are complex to analyse, because successful differentiation can not only raise entry barriers, but may also stimulate entry with the promise of higher profits if a successful new brand can be established. Stigler (1968) argues product differentiation is only a barrier to entry if the entrant faces higher costs of product differentiation than the incumbent.

Legal barriers

Legal barriers to entry are some of the most effective of all entry barriers, as they are erected by government and enforced by law. Both the Chicago and Austrian schools view legal barriers as the most difficult to surmount, and the most damaging to competition. Examples of legal barriers include:

- *Registration, certification and licensing of businesses and products.* Some industries are characterized by the need to seek official permission to trade, for example pubs, taxis, airlines, and defence equipment (Hartley, 2003). For pharmaceuticals, legal entry barriers facing new firms or products are high, arising from the framework of safety rules and regulations requiring products to satisfy a myriad of standards and tests (Nightingale, 2003). In some cases, incumbents may press for more stringent regulation, in an attempt to keep out firms that do not meet industry standards. Under this guise of maintaining standards, low-cost entrants may be denied access to the market.

- *Monopoly rights.* Monopoly rights may be granted by legislation. Government may allow certain firms exclusive rights to produce certain goods and services for a limited or unlimited period. An example is franchised monopolies in industries such as the railways, mobile telephones and television broadcasting. Franchised monopolies are often awarded in situations of natural monopoly, where average costs are minimized when one firm occupies the entire market, or in cases where firms require the guarantee of a relatively large market share in order to invest in technology and product development.

- *Patents.* As noted above, patenting involves the deliberate creation of a property right, enforced by law. Ownership of a patent confers monopoly rights and the potential to earn an abnormal profit, usually for a fixed period. The intention is to encourage research and development and innovation, by enabling successful innovators to appropriate the returns from their original investment. The disadvantage, from a public policy perspective, is that by granting an incumbent exclusive rights to use a piece of technology or produce a particular product, competition is impeded and the pace of diffusion of a technology is inhibited.

- *Government policies.* Government policies can also raise legal barriers to entry. Friedman (1962) suggests tariffs, tax policies and employment laws may all impede entry, either directly or indirectly. For example, in several European countries car tax is related to engine capacity. This has the effect of increasing the price of cars imported from the US, which have greater engine capacity on average.

Geographic barriers

Geographic barriers are the restrictions faced by foreign firms attempting to trade in the domestic market. Such barriers affect the extent and type of entry (either through greenfield investments, acquisitions and joint ventures) pursued by foreign firms (Elango and Sambharya, 2004). Examples of geographic entry barriers include:

- *Tariffs, quotas, subsidies to domestic producers.* All such measures place foreign producers at a disadvantage.

Case study 8.1

Legal barriers to entry in UK industries

Casinos

In 1997, the Monopolies and Mergers Commission (1997) investigated a proposed acquisition of one London casino company by another. Both firms controlled casinos in the relevant market, defined as the up-market segment of London casinos. Seventy-eight per cent of turnover was controlled by these two firms. Entry barriers were considered to be high. Casinos were regulated by both the Gaming Board and local licensing authorities. To obtain a certificate from the Gaming Board, casinos had to show that there was an unsatisfied demand for their services. This was extremely difficult for a new entrant to show. There were further entry barriers due to location constraints. Potential sites for the location of up-market casinos would only be considered in the most expensive parts of London. Finally the commission noted that regulation of the industry was strict. Gaming odds were fixed by law and no advertising was allowed. Again, these constraints deterred potential entrants. The merger was prevented. One of the reasons cited was that the merger would result in the ability of the two firms to absorb any increase in demand, preventing the appearance of any gaps in the market. It was concluded that the proposed merger was designed to send just such a signal to all potential rivals with casino interests elsewhere.

Pharmacies

In 2003, the Office of Fair Trading examined whether the existing system of entry regulations for retail pharmacies in the UK operated in the best interests of consumers. More than 12,000 retail (community) pharmacies offer prescription and over-the-counter medicines, professional advice and other health-related products. The most important source of revenue is NHS prescriptions, accounting for around 80 per cent of pharmacy income. In 1987, the government introduced regulations that placed a limit on the number and location of pharmacies. Any new outlet would have to pass a local needs test. The OFT concluded that the existing system limited consumer choice and restricted price competition between pharmacies in over-the-counter medicines. If the existing regulatory system were abolished, consumers might pay £25–£30 million less for over-the-counter medicines per year. Compliance costs incurred by pharmacies might fall by £16 million per year; and NHS administration costs might fall by £10 million per year. Consumers would benefit from service quality improvements; while pharmacies would become more efficient, leading to a reduction in the costs of NHS prescriptions.

Sources: Based on Monopolies and Mergers Commission (1997) *London Clubs International and Capital Corporation PLC: A Report on the Merger Situation*. London: HMSO. OFT (2003) *The Control of Entry Regulations and Retail Pharmacy Services in the UK*. London: Office of Fair Trading.

- *Physical barriers.* Frontier controls and customs formalities create administrative and storage costs, and lead to delays in transactions being completed.

- *Technical barriers.* Technical barriers include requirements to meet specific technical standards, employment regulations, health and safety regulations and transport regulations.

- *Fiscal barriers.* Aspects of a country's fiscal regime may disadvantage foreign firms. Exchange controls may impose costs on foreign firms that need to convert currencies in order to trade.

- *Preferential public procurement policies.* Purchasing policies practised by national governments may give preferential treatment to domestic firms, placing foreign competitors at a disadvantage.

- *Language and cultural barriers.* Language or other cultural differences between countries may also be considered as a geographic barrier to entry (Ghemawat, 2003).

Bain (1956) argues structural entry barriers arising from economies of scale, absolute cost advantage and product differentiation are generally stable in the long run. However, this does not imply these barriers should be regarded as permanent. The same comment also applies to legal and geographic entry barriers. Market structures can and do change eventually, and the importance of any specific entry barrier can increase or decrease over time. For example, new technology may re-shape the LRAC functions of both incumbents and entrants, transforming the nature of an economies of scale entry barrier. New deposits of a raw material may be discovered, reducing the absolute cost advantage enjoyed by an incumbent. One highly original or innovative marketing campaign might be sufficient to completely wipe out long-established brand loyalties, or other product differentiation advantages of incumbents. However, Bain believes that in general such changes occur gradually. Therefore his main point, that entry barriers are a key and stable defining characteristic of industry structure, remains valid.

However, this view has been contested by the Chicago school. It is argued that Bain's definition of entry barriers, which includes any obstacle a new firm must overcome to enter a market, is meaningless. All firms at some time face such requirements, including incumbents that were once themselves entrants. More meaningful is Stigler's definition: entry barriers are factors that impose a higher long-run production cost on the entrant than on the incumbent, enabling the incumbent to charge a higher price without attracting entry. This, the Chicago school argue, is rare. More important is not the existence of entry barriers, but rather the speed with which such barriers can be surmounted (Demsetz, 1982; Stigler, 1968).

8.4 Entry-deterring strategies

Structural barriers stem from underlying product or technological characteristics, and cannot be changed easily by incumbent firms. There is however a second class of entry barrier over which incumbents do exercise some control. Incumbents can create or raise barriers of this second kind through their own actions. Relevant actions might include changes in price or production levels, or in some cases merely the threat that such changes will be implemented if entry takes place. A credible threat of this kind may be sufficient in itself to deter potential entrants from proceeding. The extent to which it is possible for an incumbent to adopt entry-deterring strategies depends on the degree of market power exercised by the incumbent.

In this section we discuss four major entry-deterring strategies. The first two are pricing strategies: **limit pricing** and **predatory pricing**. The third is strategic product differentiation. The fourth, creating and signalling commitment, involves an incumbent demonstrating its willingness to fight a price war in the event that entry takes place, by deliberately incurring sunk cost investment expenditure.

Limit pricing

Suppose a market is currently serviced by a single producer, but entry barriers are not insurmountable. The incumbent therefore faces a threat of potential entry. According to the theory of **limit pricing**, the incumbent might attempt to prevent entry by charging a price, known as the limit price, which is the highest the incumbent believes it can charge without inviting entry. The limit price is below the monopoly price, but above the incumbent's average cost. Therefore the incumbent earns an abnormal profit, but this abnormal profit is less than the monopoly profit.

In order to pursue a limit pricing strategy, the incumbent must enjoy some form of cost advantage over the potential entrants. In the limit pricing models developed below, this is assumed to take the form of *either* an absolute cost advantage *or* an economies of scale entry barrier. It is therefore assumed that a structural barrier to entry exists, but this barrier may be surmountable unless the incumbent adopts a pricing strategy that makes it unattractive for the entrants to proceed.

A critical assumption underlying models of limit pricing concerns the nature of the reaction the entrants expect from the incumbent, if the entrants proceed with their entry decision. A key assumption of these models, which has been termed the Sylos Postulate, is that entrants assume the incumbent would maintain its output at the pre-entry level in the event that entry takes place. Therefore the incumbent is prepared to allow price to fall to a level determined by the location of the combined post-entry output (of the incumbent and entrants) on the market demand function (Sylos-Labini, 1962). Notice that the Sylos Postulate is analogous to the zero **conjectural variation** assumption that we have encountered previously in the development of the Cournot duopoly model (see Section 4.3).

Figure 8.3 shows the limit pricing model in the case of an absolute cost advantage entry barrier. In this case it is assumed there is a single incumbent and a fringe comprising a large number of small competitive potential entrants. $LRAC_1$ is the incumbent's average cost function, and $LRAC_2$ is the entrants' average cost function. In order to concentrate solely on the effects of absolute cost advantage (and exclude economies of scale), it is assumed both LRAC functions are horizontal, and therefore equivalent to the long run marginal cost (LRMC) functions. The incumbent's monopoly price and output are (P_M, Q_M). At all output levels, the entrants' average cost is below P_M. Therefore if the incumbent operates at (P_M, Q_M)

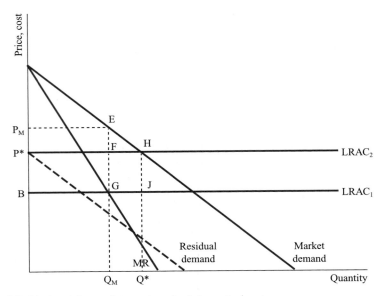

Figure 8.3 Limit pricing to deter entry: absolute cost advantage

initially, entry takes place subsequently. The entrants produce $Q^* - Q_M$, reducing the price to P^*, and reducing the incumbent's abnormal profit from $BP_M EG$ (pre-entry) to $BP^* FG$ (post-entry).

Suppose instead the incumbent pursues a limit pricing strategy in the short run. This involves operating at (P^*, Q^*) initially. If entry takes place, industry output is increased above Q^*, causing price to fall below $P^*(= LRAC_2)$. The entrants' residual demand function shows the relationship between industry price and the entrants' output, assuming (in accordance with the Sylos Postulate) the incumbent maintains its output at Q^*. The residual demand function is equivalent to the segment of the market demand function that lies to the right of Q^*. Since the residual demand function lies below $LRAC_2$ at all output levels, the entrants conclude they cannot earn a normal profit, and abstain from entry. The incumbent's position at (P^*, Q^*), and its abnormal profit of $BP^* HJ$, are sustainable in both the pre-entry and post-entry periods. $BP^* HJ$ exceeds $BP^* FG$, the long-run abnormal profit in the previous case where the incumbent starts at (P_M, Q_M) and allows entry to take place.

Figure 8.4 shows the limit pricing model in the case of an economies of scale entry barrier. In this case, it is more natural to consider the case of a single incumbent and a single entrant (rather than a fringe of small competitive entrants), because both firms would need to operate at a reasonably large scale in order to benefit from economies of scale. For simplicity, only the limit pricing solution (and not the comparison with the monopoly pricing solution) is shown. LRAC is the average cost function of both the incumbent and the entrant. The incumbent can prevent entry by operating at (P^*, Q^*). As before, the residual demand function is the entrant's effective demand function when the incumbent is producing Q^*, equivalent to the section of the market demand function to the right of Q^*. The residual demand function lies below LRAC at all output levels. If the entrant produces a low output,

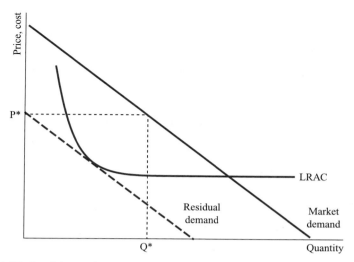

Figure 8.4 Limit pricing to deter entry: economies of scale

it fails to benefit from economies of scale. If the entrant produces a high output, it benefits from economies of scale, but the extra output causes price to drop to a level that is unprofitable. Therefore the entrant concludes it cannot earn a normal profit at any output level, and abstains from entry.

There is relatively little empirical evidence concerning the use or effectiveness of limit pricing strategies. Much of the evidence that is available is anecdotal. For example, Scherer and Ross (1990) observe that the pricing policy of the Reynolds Pen Corporation, manufacturers of the first ballpoint pens, invited entry on a large scale. In 1945 the price was between US$12 and US$20, but by 1948 the price had fallen to 50 cents and Reynolds' market share was close to zero. In the 1960s Xerox implemented a strategy of charging low prices to low-volume users (less than 5,000 copies per month). An alternative technology (wet copying) was available, and Xerox's pricing strategy was designed to deter low-volume users from switching to this alternative product.

Stigler (1968) and Yamey (1972b) have criticized the theory of limit pricing on the following grounds:

■ Why is it more profitable to attempt to restrict all entry rather than retard the rate of entry?

■ Why should the entrant believe the incumbent would not alter its pricing and output policies if entry takes place?

■ If an industry is growing, it may be difficult to persuade a potential entrant that there is no market available if entry takes place.

■ Market structure is ignored. Applied to the case of oligopoly, the theory assumes all incumbent firms would implement a limit pricing strategy. For this strategy to succeed, a high level of coordination or collusion would be required.

- Limit pricing implies perfect information regarding the market demand function, the incumbent's own costs, the entrants' costs, and so on. These would be impossible to estimate with any degree of precision. Predatory pricing (see below) might offer an easier alternative: the incumbent would simply set a price below that of the entrant until the entrant withdraws.

- The status of the entrant is all-important. An incumbent may wish to seek an accommodation with a large potential entrant.

Predatory pricing

A strategy of **predatory pricing** on the part of an incumbent firm involves cutting price in an attempt to force a rival firm out of business. When the rival has withdrawn, the incumbent raises its price. The incumbent adopts the role of predator, sacrificing profit and perhaps sustaining losses in the short run, in order to protect its market power and maintain its ability to earn abnormal profit in the long run (Myers, 1994). Strictly speaking, predatory pricing is a post-entry strategy. However, an incumbent faced with threatened entry might attempt to ward off the threat by convincing the potential entrant it would implement a predatory pricing policy in the event that entry takes place.

Faced with the threat or the actuality of price-cutting on the part of a predator, how might an entrant or other rival firm respond? The rival might be able to convince the predator it is in their mutual interest to merge, or find some other way of sharing the market between them. Alternatively, the rival might be able to convince customers it is not in their interest to accept price cuts from the predator in the short run, if the consequence is that the predator achieves monopoly status in the long run.

Another possible response would be for the rival firm to reduce its output, forcing the predator to produce at an even higher volume than it might have planned, in order to maintain the reduced price. If the reduced price is below the predator's average variable cost, the predator's losses are increased, and the length of time over which it can sustain the price-cutting strategy might be reduced. If the rival firm does not have large sunk costs, it might be able to redeploy its assets to some other industry and (temporarily) withdraw altogether, in the expectation that it will return when the predator raises its price.

The (anti-interventionist) Chicago school is rather sceptical about the reality of predatory pricing. First, the predator's gain in profit in the long run must exceed the loss resulting from price-cutting in the short run. It may be difficult for a predator to be certain this condition will be met. Second, for a predatory pricing strategy to succeed in deterring entry, the predator has to convince the entrant it is prepared to maintain the reduced price and sustain losses for as long as the entrant remains in business. It may be difficult or impossible for the predator to signal this degree of commitment to the entrant. Third, as suggested above, for a predatory pricing strategy to be worthwhile, the predator has to be sure that having forced its rival out of business and raised its price, the entry threat will not return, either in the form of the same rival, or some other firm. In order to prevent this from happening, the predator might attempt to acquire the rival's assets. Finally, if an incumbent and an entrant have identical cost functions, a predatory pricing strategy could just as easily be used by the entrant against the incumbent as the other way round. Therefore predatory pricing is not necessarily or solely an entry-deterring strategy.

For regulators, it is often difficult to determine whether a specific price-cutting campaign constitutes predatory pricing, which is likely to be unlawful under competition legislation, or whether it constitutes a legitimate strategy to acquire market share that will also benefit consumers. From 26 proven cases of predatory competition in the US, in only six was there clear economic evidence of predatory pricing (Koller, 1975).

Case study 8.2

Predatory competition

Buses

Predatory competition can come in many forms, and is by no means merely confined to pricing. For example, firms can adopt predatory strategies in relation to the quantity or quality of products and services supplied. In 1994, the Office of Fair Trading investigated two bus companies in Scotland suspected of non-price forms of predatory competition.

In 1990, Moffat & Williamson (M&W) won a contract to operate bus services that were subsidized by Fife Regional Council. On some of the routes M&W faced a competitor, Fife Scottish, which operated a commercial service. In 1992 Fife Scottish duplicated the subsidized service provided by M&W, by running additional bus journeys. This had the effect of reducing the demand for M&W services. The OFT found that as a dominant local operator, Fife Scottish was guilty of cross-subsidizing loss-making services that were introduced purely in order to compete directly with M&W.

Newspapers

In 1996, after launching a free weekly newspaper, the *Aberdeen and District Independent* newspaper complained to the Office of Fair Trading about the actions of its rival, *Aberdeen Herald and Post* (part of the Aberdeen Journals newpaper group). The *Herald and Post* was accused of predatory competition, by reducing advertising rates for its own newspaper in order to discourage customers from buying advertising space in the *Aberdeen and District Independent*. In July 2001, the *Aberdeen Herald and Post* was found guilty of predatory competition: deliberately incurring losses in order to eliminate its rival from the market.

Strategic product differentiation

For many product types, a certain amount of product differentiation is quite natural, in view of basic product characteristics and consumer tastes. Accordingly, in Section 8.3 natural product differentiation was interpreted as a structural barrier to entry. In some imperfectly competitive markets, however, incumbents may employ advertising or other types of marketing campaign in order to create or strengthen brand loyalties beyond what is natural, in order to raise the start-up costs faced by entrants. In this case, product differentiation crosses the line that separates structural entry barriers from entry-deterring strategies that are consciously initiated by an incumbent.

For example, in an investigation of a proposed merger in 1996 between Kimberley-Clark and Scott Paper in the toilet tissues industry, the European Commission found that advertising expenditures relative to sales are relatively high in the UK. The main objective of heavy advertising is to strengthen brand loyalties and raise entry barriers. Many firms wishing to establish a new brand incur significant sunk costs in the form of advertising and other promotional expenditure.

Spurious product differentiation or brand proliferation (common, for example, in detergents and processed foods) refers to efforts by an incumbent firm to crowd the market with similar brands, denying an entrant the opportunity to establish a distinctive identity for its own brand. From the incumbent firm's perspective, however, a strategy of brand proliferation could simply cannibalize existing brands. The incumbent firm might also raise its own average costs relative to those of an entrant. The entrant might be able to benefit from economies of scale by producing a standardized product, or specialize in providing a segment-specific service to its customers (Spulber, 2003).

Existing brand loyalties, and therefore entry barriers, are strengthened in cases where consumers incur significant **switching costs**: costs associated with switching to another supplier. Customers with high switching costs are committed to remaining with their existing suppliers, and cannot easily be lured elsewhere. Examples of products which may have high switching costs include bank accounts, computer software, and supermarkets and other stores that offer loyalty cards.

Loyalty discounts, exclusive dealing and refusal to supply are all strategies intended to deny entrants access to supplies of inputs or access to customers. For example, Capital Radio's practice of offering 'solus' deals to advertisers was investigated by the Office of Fair Trading in 1994. In return for agreeing to advertise exclusively on Capital Radio, the advertiser received a discount. The effect of these agreements was to exclude Capital's competitors from a significant segment of the radio advertising market (OFT, 1994). One of the most famous contracts was in petrol retailing in the UK in the 1960s, when many independent retailers signed long-term contracts to receive petrol supplies from a sole supplier. Vertical relationships of this kind are examined in more detail in Chapter 15.

Signalling commitment

Dixit (1982) uses a game-theoretic model to describe a situation in which an incumbent firm attempts to deter entry by deliberately increasing its sunk cost expenditure before

Case study 8.3

Switching costs as a barrier to entry

In 2003, National Economic Research Associates (NERA) produced a report for the Office of Fair Trading on the role of switching costs. Switching costs arise when consumers have invested time and money in learning how to use specific products and services. As such, this knowledge is not always tranferable to substitute products (Klemperer, 1987). For example, a consumer wishing to switch from using Microsoft Excel to an alternative spreadsheet program incurs additional costs in learning how to use the new software. Firms often entice new customers with low introductory prices and supplement these with loyalty reward schemes. Once consumers are locked in, switching costs make consumer demand less price elastic, providing opportunities for incumbents to increase prices in the long run.

The extent to which substitute products are successful in capturing market share from incumbents depends partly on the extent to which they are superior in quality, and partly on the level of switching costs. Effectively, switching costs create a barrier to entry. Common examples of switching costs are bank accounts, computer software, hotels, shops (loyalty cards), airlines (airmiles reward programmes), mobile phone contracts and gas and electricity services. The tendency for switching costs to restrain competition is increased in cases where actual or virtual network effects exist, leading consumers to rely on complementry products and services.

NERA (2003) argue the assessment of switching costs must examine the short-run and long-run effects on competition. For example, in the short run a firm may price its products below marginal cost (predatory competition) in order to attract customers. But in the long run, the same product might be priced above marginal cost (abuse of market power) in order to earn an abnormal profit.

Source: NERA (2003) Switching costs. Part One: Economic models and policy implications, *OFT Economic Discussion Paper, Number 5*. London: Office of Fair Trading.

entry takes place. The incumbent creates and signals a commitment to fight entry by engaging the entrant in a price war, in the event that entry subsequently occurs.

A **passive incumbent** does not pre-commit to fighting the entrant, in the event that entry subsequently takes place. In other words, a passive incumbent waits to see if entry occurs, before investing in the additional productive capacity or the aggressive marketing campaign that will be required in order to fight a price war. In contrast, a **committed incumbent** does pre-commit, by incurring the sunk cost expenditure that will be required in order to fight in advance, before it knows whether or not entry will actually take place. Figure 8.5 shows the array of possible outcomes in a sequential game (see also Section 4.6) played by an incumbent and an entrant, in the form of realized final profits or losses for each firm. These depend upon whether the incumbent is passive or committed, and upon whether entry actually does occur.

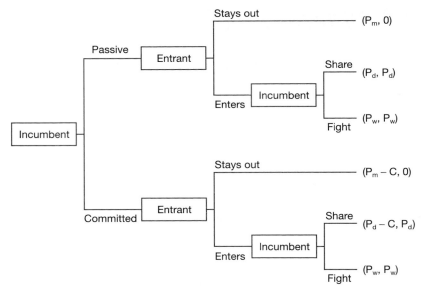

Figure 8.5 Sequential entry game

Passive incumbent

First, we consider the case in which the incumbent is passive. If the entrant stays out, the incumbent earns monopoly profit and the entrant earns zero. In Figure 8.5, this outcome is denoted $(P_m, 0)$. If entry does occur, the incumbent can either fight a price war, or accommodate the entrant by sharing the market. In the event of a price war, both firms earn a loss of P_w. This outcome is denoted (P_w, P_w). In the event that the firms share the market, both earn duopoly profit and the outcome is (P_d, P_d). It is assumed $P_d > 0$, $P_d \leq \frac{1}{2}P_m$ and $P_w < 0$.

In this case, the incumbent might attempt to threaten the entrant with the prospect of a price war in the event that entry occurs. However, if the entrant has perfect knowledge of the array of outcomes shown in Figure 8.5, the entrant will realize this threat is not credible. Suppose entry actually does occur. At that point, the incumbent is faced with the choice of fighting, in which case it suffers a loss of P_w, or accommodating, in which it earns a profit of P_d. In other words, if entry actually does take place, it makes no sense for the the incumbent to carry out the threat to fight. Realizing this and attracted by the prospect of a profit of P_d, the entrant proceeds, and (P_d, P_d) is the final outcome.

Committed incumbent

Second, we consider the case in which the incumbent is committed, and incurs sunk cost investment expenditure of C. This time, if the entrant stays out, the incumbent's monopoly profit is reduced as a result of having incurred the sunk cost expenditure. As before the entrant earns zero. In Figure 8.5, this outcome is denoted $(P_m - C, 0)$. If entry does occur, as before the incumbent can either fight a price war, or accommodate and share the market. In the event of a price war, the outcome is (P_w, P_w). Crucially, the fact that the sunk cost expenditure needed to fight was incurred in advance does not affect the incumbent's realized losses if the price war occurs. In the event that the firms share the market, the outcome is $(P_d - C, P_d)$. It is assumed $C > 0$, $P_m > C > P_d$ and $P_d - C < P_w$.

In this case, the incumbent's threat to launch a price war is credible. Suppose entry actually does occur. At that point, the incumbent is faced with the choice of fighting, in which case it earns a loss of P_w, or accommodating, in which it earns an even greater loss of $P_d - C$. This time, if entry actually takes place, it makes sense for the incumbent to carry out the threat to fight. Faced with the prospect of suffering a loss of P_w if it proceeds, the entrant is deterred, and $(P_m - C, 0)$ is the final outcome.

For a numerical illustration of this model, let $P_m = 100$, $P_d = 20$, $P_w = -20$, and $C = 60$. Summarizing the logic of the previous paragraphs, if the incumbent is passive and entry takes place, the incumbent realizes -20 by fighting and 20 by accommodating. Therefore post-entry, it is in the incumbent's interests to accommodate. Faced with the prospect of realizing a profit, the entrant proceeds and the final outcome is $(20, 20)$. If the incumbent is committed and entry takes place, the incumbent realizes -20 by fighting and -40 by accommodating. Therefore post-entry, it is in the incumbent's interests to fight. Faced with the prospect of realizing a loss, the entrant does not proceed and the final outcome is $(40, 0)$.

Are there any circumstances in which the incumbent could remain passive (avoiding incurring the sunk cost expenditure), but still be successful in deterring entry? Dixit (1982) discusses the case in which the game described in Figure 8.5 is repeated an infinite number of times. In this case, it may be in the interests of an incumbent who is passive in each period (as defined above) to fight whenever entry actually occurs, in order to establish a reputation for fighting. Observing that the incumbent always reacts by fighting, the entrant learns from experience that there is nothing to be gained by entering, and abstains from doing so. As we have seen in Section 4.6, however, this type of model unravels if there is a limit to the number of times the game is repeated. Reputation then becomes unimportant in the final period, when there is no incentive for the incumbent to fight. Knowing this, the entrant proceeds in the final period. But this implies reputation also becomes unimportant in the second-last period, so the entrant proceeds then as well, and so on.

In the setting of a repeated entry game, another case in which a passive incumbent might succeed in deterring entry (without incurring sunk cost expenditure) occurs if there is imperfect knowledge, and the entrant does not know whether the incumbent is passive or committed. An incumbent who is actually passive might attempt to deceive the entrant into believing the incumbent is committed, by launching a price war in the event that entry takes place. After observing a fighting response in one period, and knowing that a committed incumbent always fights, the entrant's subjective probability that the incumbent is committed increases, making it less likely that the entrant will decide to proceed in subsequent periods.

Alternatively, incumbent firms can attempt to deter potential entrants by announcing new versions of existing products well in advance of their actual launch. This deters potential entrants from developing similar products, as they may anticipate it will be unprofitable to do so. Haan (2003) cites a number of instances of so-called vaporware (excessively early announcement of a new version of a product) in the information technology industry. These include Microsoft's Windows 2000 (promised in 1997, but not launched until 2000), and Intel's 64-bit Itanium chip (promised in early 2000, but not launched until 2001).

Box 8.1

Does it pay to be a pioneer?

The timing of market entry is critical to the success of a new product. A company has two alternatives: it can compete to enter a new product market first or it can wait for a competitor to take the lead and then follow once the market has been proven viable.

Companies such as Sony, Intel, Merck and 3M are examples of companies that try to enter new markets first. They aggressively search for new products and markets and invest heavily in research and development to support their strategic objectives.

By contrast, Matsushita typically follows Sony in introducing consumer electronic products. AMD and Cyrix let Intel introduce new processor generations and then follow quickly with lower-priced alternatives. Many pharmaceutical companies, such as Novopharm or Ratiopharm, do not invest in developing new drugs but focus instead on generic versions of existing drugs.

All this raises an intriguing strategic question: is it generally better to take the lead and pioneer a new product market or to wait and follow a pioneer?

'Be first to market' is one of the more enduring strategic principles in marketing. It is based on the belief that pioneers have persistent advantages in the form of higher market share and superior distribution, product lines and quality. However, during the past few years the wisdom of this principle has been increasingly criticized despite generally strong empirical support. The criticism typically centres on three issues.

Survivor and reporting bias

The various databases used to study the effects of pioneering only contain data for surviving companies. Further, the classification of companies as pioneers or followers relies on responses from current employees. These problems are suspected to lead researchers to overestimate the pioneering effect.

Causation versus correlation

The conclusion that pioneers have an advantage has been based on observed differences between pioneers and followers. In the Pims (Profit Impact of Market Strategies) database, market shares for a large cross-section of business units are approximately 29 per cent for pioneers, 20 per cent for early followers and 15 per cent for late entrants.

However, this observation alone is insufficient to conclude that pioneering causes a market share advantage. Let us assume that well managed companies are more likely to be pioneers. At the same time, we would expect well managed companies to achieve higher market shares. This situation would lead to the same observed market share pattern but the differences would not be caused by pioneering.

Market share versus profit

Research has focused on market share and paid little attention to the effect of pioneering on profitability. Higher market share does not automatically lead to higher profits.

The purpose of this article is to reconsider the validity of the 'be first to market' principle. It uses recent research results to draw a more differentiated picture of the impact of pioneering on company performance.

Customer-based sources of pioneering advantage

Despite the limitations of existing research, nobody denies that there are potentially advantages to being a pioneer. Over the years, a long list of sources that could yield an enduring performance advantage for pioneers has been developed. These can be divided into two main types: customer-based sources and operation- or cost-based sources. We shall consider customer-based sources first.

Customer learning and preference formation

For many new products, customers are initially uncertain about the contribution of product attributes and features to the product's value. Preferences for different attributes and their desired levels are learned over time.

This enables the pioneer to shape customer preferences in its favour. It sets the standard to which customers refer in evaluating followers' products. The pioneering product can become the prototypical or 'original' product for the whole category, as exemplified by Walkman, Kleenex, Polaroid or Hoover.

Access to customers

The pioneering product is a bigger novelty when it appears on the market and is therefore more likely than followers to capture customer and distributor attention. In addition, a pioneer's advertising is not cluttered by messages from competitors. Even in the long term, followers must continue to spend more on advertising to achieve the same effect as pioneers.

The pioneer can set standards for distribution, occupy the best locations or select the best distributors, which can give it easier access to customers. For example, in many US cities Starbucks, as the first entrant, was able to open coffee bars in more prominent locations than its competitors.

In many industrial markets, distributors are reluctant to take on second and third products, particularly when the product is technically complex or requires large inventories of products and spare parts.

Switching costs

Switching costs arise when investments are required that would be lost when switching to another product. For example, many people have developed skill in using the traditional qwerty keyboard. Switching to the presumably more efficient dvorak keyboard would require relearning how to type, an investment that in many cases would exceed the expected efficiency gains.

Switching costs also arise when the quality of a product is difficult to assess. People who move abroad often experience this 'cost' when simple purchase decisions such as buying detergent, toothpaste or coffee become harder because the trusted brand from home is no longer available.

Pioneering products have the first chance to become this trusted brand. Consequently, followers must convince customers to bear the costs and risks of switching to an untried brand of unknown quality.

Network externalities

The value to customers of many high-technology products depends not only on their attributes but also on the total number of users. For example, the value of a videophone depends on the number of people using the same or a compatible system. A pioneer obviously has the opportunity to build a large installed base before competitive entry. This reduces followers' ability to introduce differentiated products.

There are other advantages from a large user base, such as the ability to share documents with other computer users. Thus, software companies are often willing to give away products to build the market quickly and set a standard.

Operation- or cost-based sources of pioneering advantage fall into three main categories:

Experience effects and economies of scale

Being first means that pioneers can build production volume and accumulate research and development and market experience before any other competitor. This potential cost advantage can be used to achieve higher margins or to protect customer-based advantages through lowering prices to discourage competitors from entering the market.

A pioneer can maintain this advantage only when it is able to keep the accumulated experience proprietary. However, different studies have shown that inter-company diffusion of technology and knowledge occurs rapidly in most industries. Mechanisms for diffusion include reverse engineering, research publications, plant tours, workforce mobility, use of external consultants, and so on.

Patents

Patents offer a means of keeping experience proprietary and limit imitation. However, they offer a significant barrier in only a few industries, such as pharmaceuticals. On average, patents are imitated within about four years at about 65 per cent of the innovator's cost. Moreover, filing for and enforcing patents is time-consuming and costly and requires the release of detailed information that could be useful to potential followers.

Pre-emption of scarce resources

Pioneers have the opportunity to acquire scarce resources when demand for them is still low and they are therefore cheaper. In some cases, they might be able to monopolize an important input factor. For example, Minnetonka, a small US manufacturer of consumer goods, was able to protect Softsoap, the first liquid soap, against competitors such as Procter & Gamble by buying up a full year's supply of the small plastic pump required for the dispenser. Subsequently however, P&G's size told and its Ivory brand ousted Softsoap.

However, if a resource remains scarce, its value increases and so do incentives to search for alternative sources or substitutes. And it is often unclear at the time of entry which resources will be critical. A scarce resource also provides its owner with the opportunity to extract the benefits from the pioneer. For example, Drexel, Burnham & Lambert was a pioneer in junk bonds but one of its employees – Michael Milken, who was the driving force behind the company's success – earned more than his employer at one point.

Potential sources of follower advantage fall into two categories: free-riding and incumbent inertia.

Free-riding

By definition, pioneers are the first to invest significant resources into such areas as research and development, market infrastructure, buyer education and employee training. These investments cannot always be kept proprietary. In other words, followers can free-ride on them. For example:

- IBM, although not the pioneer, was the first to push its personal computer (PC) as a standard for the whole product category. This offered clone makers such as Compaq, which followed IBM, a larger market without bearing the cost of market development.

- Convincing retailers to carry a second brand in a successful new product category may require less effort than to induce them to use limited shelf space for an unproven new category.

- Before Starbucks, few Americans were willing to pay a premium for good-tasting coffee. Today, any coffee bar can benefit from the consumer education effort by Starbucks.

- The widespread use of electric cars will require a network of battery recharging stations. Early market entrants will be likely to carry these investments disproportionately.

Incumbent inertia

When followers enter the market, they have significantly more information than pioneers had at their time of entry. They can worry less about customer or technology uncertainty. They can imitate best practices and avoid the pioneers' mistakes. Before a market exists, market research is often unreliable. Once customers have gained experience with a product, they can better describe what they like.

For example, before entering the US market, Toyota interviewed owners of Volkswagens, the leading small car at the time, to learn what they liked and disliked about small cars. Though pioneers have access to the same new information, they are often less able or willing to take advantage of it.

Inertia is not necessarily irrational. Companies have investments in specific assets. Thus, switching costs faced by pioneers may make new practices less attractive to them than to followers. With fixed assets, incremental changes often look more attractive than radical changes.

For example, IBM was afraid that PCs would cannibalize its mainframe business, a concern that clone makers did not share. Dell can take better advantage of the internet to sell directly to customers than PC manufacturers such as IBM or Compaq, which must consider how their existing retailers will be affected.

But even when economic arguments favour radical changes, many companies and their employees are highly resistant to change.

The long-term impact

The existence and persistence of customer-based sources of pioneering advantage is strongly supported by theoretical, empirical and experimental research. Customer-based sources enable the average pioneer to achieve and maintain higher market shares. Recent re-examinations of research have shown that this finding holds even when the first two criticisms mentioned above – survivor and reporting bias and the causation versus correlation problem – are taken into account.

In contrast to customer-based sources, the operation- or cost-based sources of pioneering advantage do not yield a long-term cost advantage. While the average pioneer cannot build a persisting advantage from these sources, followers are generally able to leverage their own sources to achieve and maintain a cost advantage. This pattern holds especially for consumer product markets.

In summary, the average pioneer obtains higher market share, while the average follower counters this advantage with lower cost. This raises the question: which of the two advantages is stronger? Or are they equally strong?

One way to answer this is to examine the long-term effect of pioneering on profitability (net income or return on investment, say). If the market share advantage is stronger, pioneers should be more profitable; and if the cost advantage is stronger, followers should be more profitable.

In 1997, the present author and a colleague carried out a study of the Pims database to determine which was the case. We found that the average follower is more profitable than the average pioneer. A pioneer's profit handicap is generally smaller in business markets than in consumer markets. However, in the first few years after entry the average pioneer has higher profits, especially in consumer markets. This advantage evaporates over time and then turns into a disadvantage.

Conclusion

In general, companies considering pioneering a new market should base their decision on a careful evaluation of the potential sources of advantage and disadvantage. Expectations of a sustainable long-term advantage due to pioneering should remain moderate. Market share advantages are often more easily established but generally at the expense of operational efficiency. Thus after entry, pioneers should remain operationally flexible and not hesitate to learn from followers.

The research cited above calls into question the 'be first to market' principle, which is based on the expected long-term effects of pioneering. So if it yields lower long-term profits than following, why should companies continue to pioneer?

There are four main reasons. First, according to the study just mentioned, pioneers may not have a long-term profit advantage but they enjoy higher profits in the early years after entry. With high enough discount rates, long-term profits could play only a limited role in the entry timing decision. In other words, pioneering may be justified by its short-term rather than its long-term benefits.

Some companies plough the short-term profits of pioneering into research and development that will form the basis for another bout of pioneering. The idea is to generate a continuous cycle of pioneering – to never wait for followers to catch up and profits to sag. Gillette pursues a strategy of this sort.

The second reason for pioneering is that, while it may not be best for an individual product or business unit, it can be the optimal strategy for a company to implement across all its markets. For example, 3M builds its long-term success less on a single pioneering product such as Post-it notes than on a continuous stream of new, innovative products. Its corporate goals are set accordingly. 3M wants 30 per cent of sales to come from products that are less than five years old and 10 per cent from products that are less than 12 months old.

Third, deciding on market entry timing requires an assessment of the advantages and disadvantages associated with pioneering and following. Among the companies considering entering a market first, the one that expects the biggest gain from doing so is likely to invest more resources and to take more risks to beat the competition to market. Unfortunately, this company is also more likely to overestimate the magnitude of the obtainable advantages. This phenomenon is known as 'the winner's curse' and has been observed, for example, in auctions of oil drilling licences.

Finally, while pioneering may not pay off on average, under specific conditions the advantages may exceed the disadvantages. For example, when customers are unmotivated or unable to learn about alternatives once a first product has been adopted, pioneers can build lasting profit advantages.

Customers may be unmotivated to learn because the product is not considered important enough to justify the effort of a renewed product evaluation. Certain habit purchases fall into this category. Customers are unable to learn when a product's quality is not observable, it is relatively expensive and it is purchased infrequently. This description applies to many consumer durables.

In contrast, industrial buyers are often better able and more motivated to evaluate different alternatives before purchase. This is one explanation of why the effects of pioneering are generally weaker for industrial products.

Source: Mastering marketing survey, © *Financial Times* 19 October 1998.

Box 8.2

What are the options for later entrants?

It is not easy for a company to decide whether to pioneer a market or to enter later. Both strategies have the potential to offer substantial benefits.

Research shows that pioneers obtain better returns for advertising and promotion and can charge higher prices than later entrants. If consumer preferences are ambiguous in a new category, a pioneer can shape them to suit. In cases where uncertainty about the performance of a new product is high or switching costs are large, the pioneer is also at an advantage.

Later entrants, on the other hand, can free-ride on the pioneer's efforts to build a new category. They can also learn from the pioneer's mistakes and enjoy a greater response to perceived product quality. For those companies with innovative products, the benefits of later entry are even greater. They can grow faster than pioneers, making pioneers' marketing efforts less effective, and can enjoy higher repeat purchase rates.

How then should companies plan their entry strategies? When should they pioneer? When should they follow?

To pioneer or enter later?

What is the likely life of the product category?

One benefit of pioneering is the potential for profits during the monopoly period. The shorter the life of the category, the longer is the monopoly period relative to it.

In product categories with a short life cycle, it pays to be the first mover. Certain software products fall under this classification. Year 2000 software, for example, has a very short business horizon.

What are the expected costs of imitation?

In many product categories, the cost of imitation may be quite low compared to the pioneer's cost of development. For example, a study of chemical, drugs, electronics and machinery industries shows that, on average, imitation costs are only 65 per cent of the pioneer's development costs. If this is likely to be the case, it may be better to enter later than to pioneer.

In some cases, however, pioneers may gain valuable patents that substantially increase the cost of imitation. For example, Polaroid benefited from large margins on its pioneering instant cameras thanks to its long-running patent.

What are my resources?

A company with large resources need not be a first mover. It may be a better idea to let some other company undertake the risk of pioneering a new market. By waiting and entering later, it can cash in on the pioneer's effort and muscle the pioneer out.

Corporate history contains many examples of large companies pushing aside small pioneers. Minnetonka produced the first dispenser soap in the US market but was ousted by Procter & Gamble's Ivory brand. Microsoft is another company that has succeeded in many markets by entering later with greater resources.

What are the expected switching costs in this market?

In some markets, it is highly expensive for customers to switch from one brand to another. A pioneer can lock customers in before later entrants. This creates an uphill task for later entrants, which are often reduced to competing only for new customers to the market. This is particularly true in many industrial and business-to-business markets.

How important is brand equity in customer choice?

Brand equity can be critical in some markets but is far less important in others. Consider the Personal Digital Assistant (PDA) market. Palm Pilot, built by US Robotics (now 3Com), was a late entrant, following products such as Apple's Newton and Motorola's Envoy.

Both Apple and Motorola are better known and have greater brand equity. However, these earlier entrants lacked high-quality handwriting-recognition software, which is critical for the functioning of a PDA. Palm Pilot was the first to use this software and improved on other features as well. By producing a better product, it overcame the brand equity handicap. The other brands subsequently tried to match Palm Pilot on quality but many customers still preferred Palm Pilot.

Brand equity matched with reasonable product quality does favour pioneers. Hewlett-Packard pioneered laser printing in the desktop market. The power of the HP name along with high product quality has made the HP Laserjet the technical and psychological standard in the market.

What are the likely costs of market education?

If it costs a lot to educate customers in a new market, the chances are that later entrants will free-ride on the pioneer. Hence later entry may be preferable.

The Cat scanner market is a good example. EMI went to a lot of trouble to teach medical institutions about the usefulness of the Cat scanner that it pioneered in 1972. To encourage trials, it agreed to service newly purchased Cat scanners at no extra cost for a year so that customers could learn more about them.

General Electric entered the market in 1976. It did not have to sell the idea of Cat scanners. It simply had to persuade customers that its model was better than EMI's, which is just what it did. GE's task was made easier by the fact that it already supplied traditional X-ray equipment and thus had access to the market. It also helped that GE's third-generation scanner succeeded whereas EMI's failed.

EMI had a solid 50 per cent market share at the time of GE's entry. In 1978, however, GE surpassed EMI to become the market leader.

The answers to these questions may not always point in the same direction. Companies will have to weigh them carefully. Successful companies will be those that are able to think clearly about all these issues before making a final decision.

Late entrant strategy

For many companies, pioneering is not an option. In many markets, some company always beats others to the market to become the pioneer. So what can later entrants do to compete with the pioneer or, more generally, the dominant incumbent?

A later entrant's strategy will depend upon the answers to three questions:

■ How substantial are my resources?
■ How able am I to come up with an innovative product?
■ What is the perceived quality of the dominant incumbent's product?

A company's resources are typically reflected by its financial position, capital, cash and other assets. Its ability to innovate depends on its research and development expertise. A dominant incumbent's perceived quality can be heavily influenced by its marketing efforts.

Depending on the combination of these factors, a late entrant has *numerous* strategic options. An innovative, well resourced late entrant that faces a dominant brand with low perceived quality has the easiest challenge.

The best strategy is to come up with a product that is innovative compared to the incumbents' offerings. A good example of a company that has adopted this strategy is Gillette, which has built a powerful position in the razor market through continuous innovation. This has enabled it to overtake the pioneer in the US, Star, and many others.

Similarly, Boeing surpassed the UK's De Havilland Comet 1, the pioneer in commercial jet aircraft, through product innovation – by building a safer, larger, more powerful jet.

The role of innovation is particularly strong in evolving or so-called 'high-technology' markets, such as the video cassette recorder market, in which the pioneer Ampex was overtaken by Matsushita. Another example is the microwave market, in which the pioneer Amana was eclipsed by Samsung.

Innovation also plays a role in so-called 'low-technology' markets. In the US, Tide dominates the liquid laundry detergent market pioneered by Whisk, and Eveready is the leader in the flashlight battery market launched by Bright Star.

At the other end of the spectrum, the most daunting task falls to a late mover with scarce resources and little research and development expertise that faces a dominant incumbent with a high perceived quality. Such a late mover may have to settle for a lower market share but could remain very profitable – sometimes more profitable than the dominant player – by focusing on niches.

Hon Industries is a good example of a successful niche marketer in the office furniture market, which is dominated in the US by Steelcase. Although it is only the fourth largest office furniture manufacturer in the US, Hon is the leader in the US $4bn 'medium-priced' niche, where it has a share of over 20 per cent. Although Steelcase is three times larger than Hon, Hon generates about twice its rate of return.

How did Hon achieve this position? It has developed an excellent reputation for offering good products at attractive price points and backs this with a broad product line in its market niche. Unlike Steelcase, it focuses on distribution through office products wholesalers. It can offer quick delivery from a nationwide network of 135 wholesalers.

Many later entrants are small companies with a limited ability to innovate but which face markets where the dominant brand's perceived quality is low. Their best strategy is to enter soon after the pioneer, when the market is in the growth stage. One such company is Lycos, which entered the market for web search engines after Yahoo!, the pioneer. Although the search offered by both these brands is rated as less powerful than that offered by Hotbot (for example), today Lycos enjoys a market share that is close to Yahoo!'s.

Some later entrants may have the ability to produce a superior product but lack resources. If they face a dominant incumbent with a low perceived product quality, their best strategy is to innovate. An example is computerized ticketing services, which were pioneered by Ticketron, a subsidiary of Control Data. Ticketmaster, a start-up company, competed by making innovations around the basic product: it helped customers promote shows, carried out demand analysis for them and offered superior customer service.

Ticketmaster also stressed continuous product improvements. It kept improving its ticketing software by increasing the speed of processing and adding features such as translations into other languages to serve foreign markets. With all these, it took only five years for Ticketmaster to dethrone Ticketron, a pioneer that had been a market leader for over 10 years.

By understanding consumer preferences better than incumbents do, even a later entrant with limited resources can identify a superior but overlooked product position and differentiate itself. Consider the bookselling sector. In 1995 Amazon.com was a start-up company with few resources. It succeeded by differentiating its product (selection of books) from the highly rated US incumbent, Barnes & Noble.

It accomplished this by offering its products on the internet, allowing customers to browse its selection electronically and customizing book suggestions for individual customers. Today, with a market capitalization of over $6bn, it is one of the biggest start-up success stories of recent years.

When a later entrant has plenty of resources but little capacity for innovation, it should try to beat the incumbent at its own game by out-advertising or out-distributing it.

When the dominant brand's perceived quality is low, the later mover simply has to outspend or undercut it; but when its perceived quality is high, the later mover should enter as soon as possible. Microsoft has successfully pursued this strategy. In the market for software suites, it has eclipsed Corel Suite, which is widely seen as of lower quality, by out-advertising and out-distributing it.

In the market for spreadsheets, it has beaten Lotus 1-2-3, which is generally perceived as a high-quality incumbent, by entering early and outspending it. Interestingly, Lotus 1-2-3 is itself another example of a successful later entrant that surpassed the pioneer, Visicalc.

Microsoft is pursuing a similar strategy in the web browser market. It is steadily gaining market share for its internet Explorer at the expense of the market pioneer, Netscape.

While Microsoft has mainly outspent its rivals, Sunbeam is an example of a later entrant that overtook the dominant brand by undercutting its price. In the food processor market

Cuisinart, the pioneer, is known for its high quality. Sunbeam capitalized on an increasingly price-sensitive market by offering a no-frills compact processor at a low price. In contrast, Cuisinart continued selling a high-end processor at a substantially higher price.

When a later entrant is resource-rich, is renowned for its technological expertise and faces an incumbent whose product is perceived to be of high quality, it should innovate and out-spend or undercut the incumbent.

Glaxo's Zantac in the anti-ulcer drug market is a classic example. The pioneer, SmithKline Beecham's Tagamet, was a highly rated product that took the market by storm. Glaxo followed with Zantac, which was effective in smaller dosages and had fewer side-effects. Further, Glaxo teamed up with Roche's sales force and outspent Tagamet in marketing. The result was that Zantac became not only the highest-selling anti-ulcer drug but also the best-selling prescription drug in the world by 1986.

Although pioneering advantage is real and seemingly insurmountable, all is not necessarily lost for later entrants. By adopting the right strategies, they may be able to turn the conventional wisdom of pioneering advantage on its head.

Source: 'Mastering marketing survey', © *Financial Times*, 19 October 1998.

8.5 Potential entry and contestability

The theory of **contestable markets**, originally developed by Baumol *et al.* (1982), considers an industry comprising a small number of incumbent firms or a single incumbent, whose market power is constrained by the threat of potential entry. Despite the fact that the incumbents are few in number, the entry threat forces them to keep their prices at a relatively low level, and constrains their ability to earn abnormal profits. Accordingly, even in highly concentrated industries, it is possible that incumbent firms can earn only a normal profit, because of threatened competition from potential entrants. Having a large number of competing firms in existence is not a necessary condition for industry price and output to be set at a level consistent with perfect competition; threatened competition from potential entrants may be sufficient to produce the same effect.

For a market to be perfectly contestable, there must be no significant entry or exit barriers. The theory of contestable markets therefore excludes structural entry barriers, entry-deterring strategies on the part of incumbent firms, and sunk costs. Baumol *et al.* introduce the idea of **hit-and-run entry**, based on the following assumptions:

■ A potential entrant can identify consumers who will purchase its output at or below the current market price.

■ The entrant has sufficient time to sell to these consumers before the incumbent has time to react.

■ At the prices quoted, the entrant earns sufficient revenue to cover its fixed and variable costs.

For unrecoverable investments, the length of time for which the asset is employed is important. If the asset can be used solely in the current period, the sunk costs are essentially a current fixed cost. The ability to recover all costs quickly is a crucial characteristic of a contestable market, because if sunk costs cannot be recovered quickly, the incumbent has the opportunity to respond to the entrant's presence strategically. By cutting price aggressively, the incumbent might be able to make the entrant's continuing operation unprofitable. If hit-and-run entry is profitable, however, the entrant can move in and realize its profit before the incumbent has time to react.

Call and Keeler (1985), Graham *et al.* (1983), Moore (1986), and Morrison and Winston (1987) discuss some of the limitations of the theory of contestable markets.

- The exclusion of sunk costs is generally unrealistic, as entry into most markets requires a significant amount of sunk cost investment. There are some possible exceptions (see below), but in most industries 'sunk costs are found to weaken the support for "strong" interpretations of the contestable market hypothesis and thus yield a wide diversity of dynamic patterns of market performance' (Coursey *et al.*, 1984, p. 69).

- By restricting the analysis to the short-run period within which the incumbent does not have sufficient time to respond, the reaction of the incumbent to attempted hit-and-run entry is excluded by assumption. Schwartz and Reynolds (1983) argue that an analysis of entry should focus not on the existing price charged by incumbents before entry, but on the post-entry price. 'The theory is naïve and static, with only one price. It ignores possible strategic price discrimination by the incumbent, which would decisively defeat entry while permitting excess profits' (Shepherd, 1997, p. 220).

- The assumption that the potential entrant faces no cost disadvantage relative to the incumbent is unrealistic. The latter may have acquired technical expertise and built up goodwill in the past.

Commercial airline services and bus services on specific routes have been regarded as promising testing grounds for contestable markets theory. While the construction of an airport or a bus station represents a form of sunk cost investment (since these assets cannot be moved geographically), the purchase of a fleet of aircraft or buses by a service provider does not entail sunk costs. Such assets can easily be transferred from one route to another, making hit-and-run entry (on the part of service providers) a realistic possibility.

Several researchers have subjected contestable markets theory to empirical scrutiny using data on commercial airlines. Hurdle *et al.* (1989) tested for contestability in 867 airline routes in 1985. Regression analysis is used to examine the effects of potential entry and industry concentration on the level of fares charged on any specific route. Industry concentration, and not potential entry, is found to be the most important determinant of fares. Similarly, Strassmann (1990) tested for contestability using data on 92 US airline routes in 1980. If contestable markets theory is relevant, there should be no relationship between industry concentration and fares, or between entry barriers and fares. In a regression analysis, structural variables such as concentration and entry barriers are found to be the most significant determinants of fares. Therefore both of these studies find that factors other than potential entry have the greatest influence on price. Neither study provides much support for the contestable markets theory. More recent evidence suggests established airlines benefit from learning economies of scale and brand loyalty advantages, which result in barriers to entry (Button and Stough, 2000; Johnson, 2003).

Accordingly, the practical relevance of contestable markets theory is questionable. Although the theory provides some insights concerning the possible behaviour of incumbents threatened by potential entry, early predictions that the notion of contestability might revolutionize the theory of the firm were wide of the mark.

> As often happens, a bright idea has been exaggeratedly oversold by its enthusiastic authors. The ensuing debate trims the concept and claims to their proper niche, taking their place among all the other ideas. In this instance, contestability offers insights, but it does not affect the central role of market structure.
>
> *(Shepherd, 1997, p. 220)*

8.6 Entry and industry evolution

Most of the models of entry and exit that have been examined in this chapter are static, in the sense that they are based on direct comparisons between a pre-entry and a post-entry market equilibrium. Essentially, entry is modelled either as a once-and-for-all game, or an equilibrating mechanism whose principal economic function is the elimination of abnormal profit. In contrast, and echoing many of the earlier insights of Schumpeter (1928, 1942), Geroski (1991a) views entry as part of a dynamic model of competition. In this context, entry and exit play a central role in shaping the evolution of industry structure in the long run.

Geroski discusses two fundamental types of entry:

■ Imitative entry, which occurs when the entrant can earn a profit by copying an incumbent's product or method of production. Imitative entry is primarily an equilibrating force, in the sense that it helps propel the industry towards an equilibrium whose location and characteristics remain fundamentally unaltered. The incumbent's abnormal profit is reduced or eliminated as part of the adjustment process.

■ *Innovative entry, which occurs when an entrant introduces a product with new* characteristics, or finds a new method of producing an existing product more cheaply than before. Innovative entry is primarily a disruptive or disequilibrating force, in the sense that it changes fundamentally the location and characteristics of an existing market equilibrium, and propels the industry in a new direction.

Innovative entry in particular makes a crucial contribution to the formation and growth of new industries and the decline of old ones. Entry by more innovative or more efficient outsiders encourages incumbent firms to improve or replace their existing product lines, or reduce their costs. Competition will eventually force the withdrawal of incumbents that fail to innovate.

Entry can also play a more creative role in markets, serving as a vehicle for the introduction and diffusion of innovations which embody new products or processes that fundamentally alter conditions of supply and demand. Further, the mere threat of entry of this type may induce incumbents to generate new innovations or to adopt existing ones more rapidly.

(Geroski, 1991a, p. 210)

The turnover of firms due to entry and exit is likely to be higher in technology-oriented industries such as electronics and pharmaceuticals, in which non-price competition tends to prevail. In these industries, variation in firm-level profit rates may be extreme, due to the uncertainties associated with the outcomes of innovation. Successful entrants may benefit significantly from first-mover advantages, which arise in several ways:

The first springs from its headstart in travelling down learning functions and exploiting economies of scale . . . The second comes from the fact that first movers have an opportunity to monopolize scarce inputs . . . Third, the purchase decisions of early consumers are effectively investments in learning about the product – what it does and how to use it – and when consumers have made such investments and are content with how the product works for them, they will be reluctant to try alternatives . . . Fourth and finally, first movers who bring a winning product to the market often enjoy an enhanced brand identity and status.

(Geroski, 2003, pp. 194–5)

Summarizing this dynamic view of entry and market evolution, the most important economic role of entry is not to facilitate a once-and-for-all adjustment from an old market equilibrium to a new one. Instead, markets are in a permanent state of disequilibrium, transition and flux. In a capitalist economy, the urge to invent and the incentive to innovate are ever-present. The Schumpeterian model of competition between firms (also discussed in Chapter 14) bears some similarities to the Darwinian model of natural selection or survival of the fittest, which accounts for the evolution of species in the natural sciences. The forces of competition enable the stronger and more efficient members of a population of firms to survive and prosper. Meanwhile the weaker and less efficient firms decline and face the prospect of elimination.

8.7 Empirical evidence on entry

There is a substantial empirical literature on the determinants of entry in manufacturing (Siegfried and Evans, 1994). Typical findings are that rates of entry are relatively high in profitable industries and fast-growing industries (Baldwin and Gorecki, 1987; Geroski, 1991a,b). Rates of entry are relatively low in industries where incumbents have absolute cost advantages over potential entrants, or where entrants' capital requirements are substantial (Orr, 1974). Evidence concerning the relationship between rates of entry and factors such as scale economies, excess capacity and incumbents' pricing practices (such as limit and predatory pricing) is both limited and inconclusive.

As discussed above, the size of barriers to exit depends on the level of sunk costs. A complete absence of sunk costs is unusual, given that many assets are specific, and cannot easily be transferred to other uses (Harbord and Hoehn, 1994). There is some manufacturing evidence to suggest that exit is higher when profits are low and sunk costs are insignificant (Dunne et al., 1988); although Schary (1991) finds no relationship between profitability and exit. Other characteristics of the firm's financial and operational structure may be more important influences on the exit decision. Duetsch (1984) suggests conflicts of objectives between owners and managers sometimes makes it difficult to achieve a decision to exit. It is also possible that there is a direct association between entry and exit rates, if there is a tendency for entrants to displace some incumbents. However, using US manufacturing data for the period 1963–82, Dunne et al. (1988) find a negative correlation between annual entry and exit rates.

In a well known study, Orr (1974) examines the determinants of entry into 71 Canadian manufacturing industries for the period 1963–67. The regression model is as follows:

$$E = \beta_1 + \beta_2\pi_p + \beta_3Q + \beta_4X + \beta_5K + \beta_6A + \beta_7R + \beta_8r + \beta_9C + \beta_{10}S$$

E is the average number of entrants in the sample period; π_p is the average industry profit rate; Q is past industry growth; X is the ratio of MES to industry sales (representing an economies of scale barrier to entry); K is an estimated fixed capital entry requirement; A is advertising intensity (ratio of advertising expenditure to industry sales); R is research and development intensity (ratio of research and development expenditure to industry sales); r is the standard deviation of industry profit rates (representing business risk); C is the level of industry concentration (measured on an ordinal scale: low = 1, high = 5); and S is total industry sales.

Orr finds a positive relationship between E and each of π_p, Q and S. Therefore high values of profitability, growth and industry size are all associated with high rates of entry. Orr finds a negative relationship between E and each of X, K, A, R, r and C. Therefore there is evidence of entry barriers resulting from economies of scale, capital requirements, high advertising or research and development intensities, business risk and high industry concentration.

Smiley (1988) and Bunch and Smiley (1992) examine entry-deterring strategies adopted by incumbents in new and established product markets. A total of 293 completed questionnaires were obtained from product managers, brand managers, directors of product management, division managers and marketing managers. Respondents were asked to identify the types of entry-deterring strategy they employed, and how frequently. In new product markets, entry-deterring strategies include:

■ Charging low prices and spending heavily on advertising and promotion.

■ Building excess capacity as a signal that incumbents are able to meet future demand.

- Pre-emptive patenting in order to prevent entrants from producing identical or similar products.

- Using the media to signal that entry would provoke retaliation.

- Engaging in limit pricing to make entry unprofitable.

Additional strategies used in established product markets include:

- Brand proliferation, intended to occupy product space, so that entrants cannot establish their own differentiated products or brands.

- Masking the profitability of any single product line through the use of appropriate reporting practices in company accounts.

For new products, advertising (78 per cent of firms) and pre-emptive patenting (71 per cent) were the most widely used entry-deterring strategies. Limit pricing was rarely used. There was little systematic difference between manufacturing and services, except that manufacturers were significantly more likely to use pre-emptive patenting.

For existing products, brand proliferation (79 per cent of firms), advertising (79 per cent) and masking the profitability of individual product lines (78 per cent) were the most widely used entry-deterring strategies. Building excess capacity was rarely used. Manufacturers were more likely than service firms to mask the profitability of product lines, and to use pre-emptive patenting. Service firms typically concentrated on advertising and promotions and product differentiation to create brand loyalties.

Khemani and Shapiro (1990) argue that entry is expected if an incumbent's current profit, denoted π_0, exceeds the expected long-run profit, denoted $\hat{\pi}_p$. Exit is expected if current profit is below the expected long-run profit. Expressions for entry and exit can therefore be specified as follows:

$$\text{ENT} = \alpha_1 + \gamma_1(\pi_0 - \hat{\pi}_p)^R + \beta_1\log_e(N) + \varepsilon_1$$
$$\text{EXT} = \alpha_2 + \gamma_2(\pi_0 - \hat{\pi}_p)^R + \beta_2\log_e(N) + \varepsilon_2$$

ENT and EXT are the logarithms of the numbers of firms entering or exiting an industry; N is the number of firms in the industry; and R is an indicator variable for positive or negative values of $(\pi_0 - \hat{\pi}_p)$. Observed patterns of entry and exit are found to correspond to this model specification.

Geroski (1991b) examines the extent of entry by domestic and foreign firms in 95 UK manufacturing industries for the period 1983–84. The number of entrants per industry was similar in both years, but the market share of entrants was relatively small (the average across industries was between 7 per cent and 8 per cent of total industry sales). On average, domestic entrants succeeded in capturing a higher market share than foreign entrants. Exit rates were relatively stable over time, but entry and exit rates were positively correlated, suggesting a displacement effect. High profitability and large industry size are reported to have encouraged entry, but (surprisingly) there was a negative relationship between industry growth and entry. The significance of these effects is greater for domestic entrants than for foreign entrants.

Sleuwaegen and Dehandschutter (1991) examine the determinants of entry for 109 Belgian manufacturing industries for the period 1980–84. Schwalbach (1991) does the same for 183 German manufacturing industries for the period 1983–85. In these studies, entry rates are positively related to expected profits and industry growth, but negatively related to barriers in the form of initial capital requirements, and product differentiation advantages accruing to incumbents. For the early 1980s, Cable and Schwalbach (1991) report entry and exit rates for Belgium, Canada, Germany, Korea, Norway, Portugal, UK and US averaging at around 6.5 per cent of the relevant population of firms. Entry and exit rates also tend to be positively correlated with each other.

Rudholm (2001) assesses the determinants of entry to 22 Swedish pharmaceutical markets between 1972 and 1996. Entry is higher in markets where incumbent firms earn high profits. Entry is lower in markets where incumbent firms enjoy long periods of patent protection. Overall, entrants tend to enjoy a high probability of survival.

Roberts and Thompson (2003) examine the population of Polish manufacturing firms drawn from 152 three-digit industries over the period 1991–93 to assess the determinants of entry and exit. Concentration, profitability, capital requirements and state ownership all tend to reduce entry. There is a positive association between the rate of entry and industry size, and the rate of previous exit of incumbent firms. Exit is less likely when concentration, industry growth and profitability are high, but more likely in large industries or in those with a past history of high entry and exit.

Disney *et al.* (2003) examine the Annual Business Inquiry Respondents Database (ARD) for evidence on entry, exit and survival for UK manufacturing establishments over the period 1986–91. The results suggest small entrants are more likely to fail than their larger counterparts, but this danger recedes if fast growth is achieved. The rate of exit is higher for single establishments than for those that form part of a larger group.

Finally, Geroski (1995) presents a series of stylized facts on entry, based on accumulated past theoretical and empirical research:

- Rates of entry by new firms are often high (relative to the numbers of incumbents), but new entrants rarely capture large market shares.

- Entry often leads to the displacement and exit of some incumbent firms.

- Small entrants are less likely to survive than large entrants.

- Entry by new firms is more common than entry by existing firms by means of diversification. However, diversified entrants are more likely to succeed.

- Entry rates tend to be high during the early stages of an industry's development, when consumer preferences are unsettled, and core brands, products and processes are not yet established.

- Entry by new firms leads to increased competition, stimulates innovation and encourages incumbents to make efficiency savings.

- Incumbents tend to prefer non-price strategies to price strategies in order to deter entry.

- Large or mature entrants are more likely to succeed than small or young entrants.

8.8 Summary

Structural barriers to entry are barriers over which neither incumbents nor the entrants have direct control. This category includes the three types of entry barrier originally discussed by Bain: economies of scale, absolute cost advantage and product differentiation. Economies of scale can act as an entry barrier in two ways. First, there is an entry barrier if the minimum efficient scale (MES) of production is large relative to the total size of the market. Second, economies of scale can act as an entry barrier when average costs associated with a production level below the MES are substantially greater than average costs at the MES. Economies of scale present the potential entrant with a dilemma. Either the entrant accepts the risks associated with large-scale entry in order to avoid the average cost penalty; or the entrant enters at a smaller scale and absorbs the average cost penalty.

An incumbent has an absolute cost advantage over an entrant if the long-run average cost function of the entrant lies above that of the incumbent, and the entrant therefore faces a higher average cost at every level of output. An absolute cost advantage might arise in several ways. The incumbent might have access to a superior production process, hold patents or be party to trade secrets. The incumbent might have exclusive ownership or control over factor inputs. The incumbent might have access to cheaper sources of finance. Finally, the entrant might incur costs in the form of expensive advertising or marketing campaigns, in an effort to create a reputation or establish its own brand identities and brand loyalties.

A structural entry barrier also exists if customers are loyal to the established brands and reputations of incumbents. A successful entrant will need to prise customers away from their existing suppliers, or at least stir customers out of their inertia. Therefore, natural product differentiation can represent a structural barrier to entry. Other types of structural entry barrier include legal barriers, erected by government and enforced by law; and geographic barriers, which create difficulties for foreign firms attempting to trade in the domestic market.

Entry-deterring strategies create strategic barriers to entry, defined as those created or raised by incumbents through their own actions. The extent to which it is possible for incumbents to adopt entry-deterring strategies is likely to depend on the degree of market power in the hands of the incumbent. Under a limit pricing strategy, the incumbent seeks to prevent entry by charging the highest price possible without inviting entry. To do so, it exploits either an absolute cost advantage or an economies of scale advantage, in order to set a price such that if entry takes place, the entrant is unable to earn a normal profit.

A strategy of predatory pricing on the part of an incumbent involves cutting price in an attempt to force an entrant to withdraw from the market. When the entrant has withdrawn, the incumbent raises its price. The incumbent sacrifices profit and perhaps sustains losses in the short run, in order to protect its market power in the long run. An incumbent faced with threatened entry might attempt to ward off the threat by convincing the potential entrant that it would implement a predatory pricing policy in the event that entry takes place.

For many product types, a certain amount of product differentiation is quite natural, in view of basic product characteristics and consumer tastes. In some imperfectly competitive markets, however, incumbent firms may employ advertising or other types of marketing campaign in order to create or strengthen brand loyalties beyond what is natural to the market, raising the initial costs entrants will incur in order to establish a presence. In this case, product differentiation becomes a strategic entry barrier. Finally, it has been suggested that incumbents can attempt to deter entry by deliberately increasing their sunk cost investment expenditure before entry takes place. The incumbent signals a commitment to fight entry by engaging the entrant in a price war.

Contestable markets theory considers an industry comprising a small number of incumbent firms or a single incumbent, whose market power is constrained by the threat of potential entry. Even though the incumbents are few in number, and the industry appears to be highly concentrated, the threat of hit-and-run entry keeps prices close to the competitive level. Therefore, having a large number of competing firms in existence is not a necessary condition for industry price and output to be set at the perfectly competitive level; threatened competition from potential entrants may be sufficient to produce the same effect. Contestable markets theory breaks the direct linkage between the number and size distribution of sellers and the amount of discretion exercised by incumbents in determining their own prices.

A more dynamic view of entry and market evolution over the long run regards entry not as an equilibrating mechanism, as assumed in the neoclassical theories of perfect and monopolistic competition, but rather as a disequilibrating force which, by changing and disrupting established market equilibria, plays a central role in shaping the evolution of industry structure in the long run.

Most of the empirical evidence on the determinants of entry in manufacturing confirms that high industry profitability and growth are effective stimulants to entry. There is also some empirical evidence that, in accordance with the theory, entry barriers resulting from economies of scale, heavy capital requirements, high advertising or research and development intensities, high levels of business risk and high levels of industry concentration are effective in slowing the rate at which entry takes place.

Discussion questions

1. Distinguish between structural, legal, geographic and strategic barriers to entry. Provide examples of each type of entry barrier.
2. With reference to Case study 8.1, quote examples of UK and European industries that are subject to legal barriers to entry.
3. How might the height of entry barriers to a particular industry be measured in practice?
4. To what extent does the theory of limit pricing provide a useful contribution to the theory of entry deterrence?
5. Is limit pricing preferable to monopoly pricing on social welfare criteria?
6. With reference to Case study 8.2, explain how a strategy of predatory pricing might be used to eliminate competition.

7. What factors are likely to influence the credibility of a threat by an incumbent to engage an entrant in predatory competition, in the event that entry takes place?

8. With reference to Case study 8.3, explain how switching costs can act as a barrier to entry. Quote examples of ways in which incumbent firms can increase the costs to consumers of switching away from their products.

9. Explain how an incumbent might attempt to deter entry by increasing its own sunk cost investment.

10. What factors are relevant for a firm in deciding whether to be a pioneer in a new market, or to enter an established market at a later stage?

11. Examine the options for a late entrant that is seeking to compete with a dominant incumbent.

12. Explain the theory of contestable markets. To what extent does the empirical evidence justify the idea that potential competition is an important influence on pricing behaviour?

13. Examine the role of entry and exit in determining the evolution of industry structure.

14. According to the empirical evidence, what are the most commonly used entry-deterring strategies adopted by incumbent firms in new and established product markets?

Further reading

Bain, J.S. (1956) *Barriers to New Competition.* Cambridge, MA: Harvard University Press.

Baumol, W.J., Panzer, J. and Willig, R.D. (1982) *Contestable Markets and the Theory of Industry Structure.* New York: Harcourt Brace Jovanovich.

Bresnahan, T.F. and Reiss, P.C. (1994) Measuring the importance of sunk costs, *Annals of Economics and Statistics*, 34, 181–217.

Geroski, P.A. (1991a) *Market Dynamics and Entry.* Oxford: Blackwell.

Geroski, P.A. (1995) What do we know about entry? *International Journal of Industrial Organization*, 13, 421–40.

Geroski, P.A. (2003) *The Evolution of New Markets.* Oxford: Oxford University Press.

Kor, Y.Y. and Mahoney, J.T. (2005) How dynamics, management and governance of resource deployments influence firm-level performance, *Strategic Management Journal*, 26, 489–96.

Neven, D.J. (1989) Strategic entry deterrence: recent developments in the economics of industry, *Journal of Economic Surveys*, 3, 213–33.

Siegfried, J.A. and Evans, L. (1994) Empirical studies of entry and exit: a survey of the evidence, *Review of Industrial Organisation*, 9, 121–55.

Spulber, D.F. (2003) Entry barriers and entry strategies, *Journal of Strategic Management Education*, 1, 55–80.

Market structure, firm strategy and performance

Learning objectives

This chapter covers the following topics:

- empirical controversies surrounding the use of the structure–conduct–performance paradigm
- the strategic groups approach
- variance decomposition of firm-level profitability
- the new empirical industrial organization
- persistence of profit

Key terms

Accounting rate of profit
Business unit effects
Corporate effects
Industry effects
Internal rate of return
Mark-up test
New empirical industrial
  organization

Persistence of profit
Price–cost margin
Revenue test
Strategic group
Tobin's q
Variance decomposition analysis

9.1 Introduction

This chapter discusses empirical research in industrial organization that has examined the links between market structure and the conduct and performance of firms and industries. The SCP (structure–conduct–performance) paradigm which was introduced in Chapter 1 represents a natural starting point for empirical research in this area. However, the SCP approach has been subject to intense criticism, and later empirical research in both industrial organization and strategic management has sought to shift the focus of attention away from industry structure and towards conduct or strategic decision making at firm level.

This chapter begins in Section 9.2 by reviewing some early empirical research based on the SCP paradigm, which sought to identify the impact of structural industry-level variables such as concentration, economies of scale, and entry and exit conditions on firm performance, usually measured by profitability indicators. We also consider a powerful critique of the SCP paradigm which was developed in the 1970s by the Chicago school, who suggested a positive association between concentration and profitability might reflect not an abuse of market power, but an association between firm size and efficiency: the most efficient firms are the most profitable, and also tend to grow and achieve large market shares. This suggests the analysis of performance should be based less on industry structure, and more on the conduct and strategic decision making of the individual firm.

The strategic management literature on strategic groups is reviewed briefly in Section 9.3. A strategic group is a group of firms whose conduct is similar, and which tend to view other members of the same group as their main competitors. The members of a strategic group recognize their interdependence, and this recognition conditions their behaviour. Mobility barriers impede the rate at which non-members can join a strategic group. In some respects, strategic groups theory represents a middle way between the competing industry- and firm-oriented approaches of the industrial organization literature.

Section 9.4 reviews variance decomposition studies of firm-level profitability data, which involve the decomposition of the variation in profit rates into components specific to the industry, the parent corporation and the line of business. This approach is capable of providing further insights into the debate as to whether the industry or the firm is the most appropriate unit of observation in industrial organization. Section 9.5 reviews a body of research known as the new empirical industrial organization, which attempts to draws inferences about market structure and competitive conditions from direct observation of conduct at firm level. Finally, Section 9.6 examines the persistence of profit literature, which analyses the process of adjustment towards equilibrium by observing patterns of persistence and convergence in firm-level profit rate data. In this literature, the degree of persistence of profit is interpreted as another indicator of the nature of competitive conditions.

9.2 Empirical tests of the SCP paradigm

The performance of firms is one of the central research themes in industrial organization. There is a substantial body of empirical research that seeks to explain variations in performance between firms, most commonly measured by profitability. Early research within the SCP tradition developed and extended frameworks to analyse competitive conditions in industries. According to much of the earliest empirical literature, based on the SCP paradigm, industry-level variables such as concentration, economies of scale, and entry and exit conditions are the main determinants of firm performance. However, this literature has subsequently been criticized for providing (at best) limited explanations as to why profitability varies between firms.

For example, the Chicago school argue that market power deriving from monopolization is only temporary, except perhaps in the case of monopolies that are created and maintained by government. A positive association between concentration and profitability may reflect a positive association between productive efficiency and firm size: the most efficient firms earn the highest rates of profit, and their success enables them to grow and achieve a relatively large market share. Consequently, the relationship between market structure and profitability has nothing to do with the exploitation of market power by large firms; instead, it is due to the association between efficiency, profitability and firm size. If differences in efficiency between firms are important in determining the performance of individual firms, the firm rather than the industry is the most appropriate unit of analysis. This view, which is in contrast to the SCP paradigm, has been termed *revisionist* by Schmalensee (1985) and Amato and Wilder (1990).

> The debate between the revisionist and traditional schools can be summarized in terms of their differences regarding the appropriate unit of observation in industrial economics. The revisionist view is a story of industries consisting of both successful and unsuccessful firms, implying that there are important inter-firm differences in profitability. The traditional view focuses on industry effects which are assumed to be measured by concentration. The revisionist view thus focuses on the firm and firm-level efficiencies, while the traditional view focuses on the market and industry specific sources of market power.
>
> *(Amato and Wilder, 1990, p. 93)*

These opposing views have motivated an extensive empirical debate. Many of the earlier studies suggest concentration and other industry-level variables are important in determining performance, the **collusion hypothesis**. Many later studies emphasize the importance of efficiency differences between firms, the **efficiency hypothesis**. Naturally, for all of these studies the measurement of profitability is an important methodological issue. This topic is examined in Box 9.1.

Box 9.1

Measurement of company profitability

Profitability is the perhaps most relevant and certainly the most widely used performance measure in empirical studies based both on the SCP paradigm and on most of the other empirical methodologies that are reviewed in Chapter 9. However, the measurement of profitability is not always a straightforward task. For example, measures of profitability based either on company accounts data or on stock market data do not always correspond precisely or even closely to the theoretical concepts used by economists in the neoclassical theory of the firm, such as normal profit or abnormal profit. Section 9.1 examines some of the measures of profitability that are most commonly used in practice.

Measure 1: Tobin's q

Tobin's q is the ratio of the firm's stock market value to the replacement cost of its capital:

$$q = \frac{M_c + M_p + M_d}{A_r}$$

M_c and M_p are the market values of the firm's ordinary and preference share capital, respectively; M_d is the firm's outstanding loan capital; and A_r is the firm's total assets valued at replacement cost.

$q = 1$ implies the market value of the firm is equal to the book value of the assets owned by the firm, while $q \neq 1$ indicates the market value diverges from the book value of the firm's assets.

If $q > 1$, the firm's market value exceeds its book value. This situation exists when a firm has resources or advantages that contribute positively to its market value (in other words, from which it can expect to earn a positive return in the future), but which do not feature among the assets valued in the firm's balance sheet. Such advantages might stem from intangible assets that rival firms are unable to replicate, or from the exercise of market power that enables the firm to earn a return in excess of the normal profit the assets deployed by the firm would ordinarily be expected to yield.

If $q < 1$, the firm's market value is below its book value. This situation exists when the firm fails to earn a return equivalent to the normal profit the firm's assets would ordinarily be expected to yield. This might be due to lazy or incompetent management. A firm whose stock market value is significantly lower than its book value is usually considered to be vulnerable to being taken over. Outside investors (other than the firm's current shareholders) might believe they can make more profitable use of the firm's assets, and might therefore bid for the firm in the hope of acquiring it at a price from which they can subsequently realize a capital gain by increasing the firm's profitability.

A stock market-based profitability measure may be attractive for several reasons. Under assumptions of capital market efficiency, a firm's current market value should reflect all currently known information about its future profitability. An allowance for the level of risk is automatically incorporated, eliminating distortions arising from the fact that company accounts-based measures of returns or profits are not risk-adjusted. Stock market valuations should be unaffected by distortions to company accounts arising from the treatment of items such as tax and depreciation. One obvious limitation, however, is that stock market valuation data is, by definition, only available for listed firms. Furthermore, the firm's stock market valuation depends on expected future profitability. This tends to be subjective, and likely to fluctuate with investor sentiment, making stock market performance measures rather volatile. Finally, the denominator of Tobin's q is based on company accounts data, and is therefore subject to all of the limitations associated with the use of such data. In particular, the replacement cost of assets can be difficult to assess or measure.

Measure 2: Price–cost margin

The **price–cost margin** is the ratio of profit to sales revenue:

$$PCM = \frac{TR - TC}{TR} = \frac{P \times Q - AC \times Q}{P \times Q} = \frac{P - AC}{P}$$

where TR = total revenue, TC = total cost, P = price, Q = quantity and AC average cost. If AC is constant so AC = MC, PCM is equivalent to the Lerner index, $L = (P - MC)/P$ (see Section 2.5). In perfectly competitive equilibrium, PCM = 0. If the firm exercises some market power, and can elevate price above average cost, PCM > 0.

The price–cost margin is not an accurate proxy for the Lerner Index in the absence of constant returns to scale. Consequently, the greater the positive or negative difference between average cost and marginal cost, the greater the tendency for the price–cost margin to overstate or understate the Lerner index.

Measure 3: Accounting rate of profit

An **accounting rate of profit** (ARP) is usually defined as the ratio of profit (before or after tax) to capital, equity or sales. Discretionary expenditure, depreciation, debt, tax, inflation and mergers can all cause difficulties for the calculation and interpretation of company accounts-based profitability measures.

Discretionary expenditure

Discretionary expenditure on items such as advertising and research and development is usually treated as a current cost item in company accounts. However, such expenditures are essentially investments, that are expected to yield returns over a number of future years. Consequently, ARP for a firm that has invested heavily in advertising or research and development in the current year may be understated. Conversely, ARP for a firm currently benefiting from past advertising or research and development expenditure (that has already been written off at the time as a current cost) may be overstated.

Depreciation

Variation in practice regarding the treatment of depreciation can create difficulties in arriving at a fair valuation of a firm's capital. Different firms may use different accounting methods when allowing for depreciation (such as straight line depreciation or reducing balance depreciation). Some firms may deliberately choose to adopt a policy of accelerated depreciation.

Debt

The capital structure of most firms contains a mix of debt and equity. On an ARP measure with equity in the denominator, a firm with a high debt-to-equity ratio will naturally tend to appear more profitable. For an ARP measure with assets in the denominator, interest payments should be added back into the profit figure in the numerator, in order to make the numerator consistent with the sources of funds in the denominator that generated the profit. If interest payments are not added back into the profit figure, a firm with a relatively low debt-to-equity ratio (and therefore smaller interest payments) will tend to appear more profitable.

Risk

ARP may not be properly adjusted for risk. Finance theory suggests risk-averse investors require a higher return on a high-risk investment, and a lower return on a low-risk investment. Accordingly, performance should be measured using a risk-adjusted profit rate. However, ARP is unadjusted for risk. The firm's debt-to-equity ratio also has implications for the level of risk borne by its shareholders. The higher the debt-to-equity ratio, or the higher the firm's *gearing*, the greater the risk that the firm's earnings (before interest) will be insufficient to provide a return to the shareholders after the debtholders (who have a prior claim on the firm's earnings and assets) have been paid. Therefore the higher the firm's debt-to-equity ratio, the higher the risk borne by the shareholders, and the higher the return the shareholders are likely to demand. Again, a risk-adjusted profit rate is required to measure performance appropriately.

Tax

ARP may be defined either on a pre-tax (gross) or a post-tax (net) basis. In theory, post-tax (net) profit is perhaps superior, since it likely that firms' investment or entry and exit decisions are based on an assessment of post-tax rather than pre-tax profitability.

Inflation

Inflation tends to create accounting bias, because most firms value their assets using a historical cost convention, rather than in accordance with the actual replacement cost. In periods of inflation, historical values tend to understate the true value of older capital, causing older assets to be undervalued relative to newer ones. Slow-growing firms (with a high proportion of older assets) tend to report an overstated ARP; conversely, rapidly growing firms (with a high proportion of newer assets) tend to report an understated ARP.

Mergers

After a merger has taken place, it can be difficult to value the assets of the new, combined firm, due to accounting bias. Suppose one firm has taken over another firm with some degree of market power. The acquiring firm may have paid more for the assets than would have been the case had there been no market power. If the acquiring firm incorporates the acquired firm's assets into its accounts at market value rather than book value, these assets are over-valued, and the merged firm's stated return on capital is biased downwards. If a wave of merger activity takes place, expectations of abnormal profits tend to become capitalized in this way throughout the entire industry. This results in ARP being generally understated.

Do accounting rates of profit tell us anything?

The use of accounts-based profit rate measures to assess the degree of market power or the intensity of competition has caused some controversy (Fisher and McGowan, 1983; Martin, 1984). It has been argued that serious errors can arise if an accounting rate of return is inter-preted directly as an economic return.

> [I]t is clear that it is the economic rate of return that is equalized in an industry competitive equilibrium. It is an economic rate of return (after risk adjustment) above the cost of capital that promotes expansion under competition and is produced by output restriction under monopoly. Thus the economic rate of return is the only correct measure of the profit rate for economic analysis. Accounting rates of return are useful only insofar as they yield information as to economic rates of return.
>
> *(Fisher and McGowan, 1983, p. 82)*

By economic rate of return, Fisher and McGowan mean the **internal rate of return** (IRR) on a single project. IRR is the discount rate at which the net present value of a project is zero. In theory, an economist should be concerned with the average value of IRR over all of the firm's investment projects. If a firm persistently earns returns higher than its cost of capital, this could be an indication of market power. However, the data that would be required in order to calculate the IRR over the lifetime of each project are not likely to be available from company accounts.

In contrast, ARP is income net of depreciation earned in a single accounting period, deflated by total assets (valued after depreciation has been subtracted). While IRR is calcu-lated over the lifetime of a single project, ARP reflects the returns on a collection of projects in a single year. Therefore these measures describe different types of return over differing periods. Only if the ARP is constant over the entire life of the project are the two measures the same. To calculate IRR, data are required over the entire lifetime of the project or firm; but most empirical studies examine profitability at a single point in time or for a fixed period (Edwards *et al.*, 1987; Kay and Mayer, 1986).

In an empirical study of these issues, Bosch (1989) examines the relationship between the accounting rate and internal rate of return for 1,030 large US industrial firms over a 20-year period. He finds a correlation coefficient of 0.63 between the two rates. This suggests that an accounting return may represent a useful indicator, but by no means a perfect indicator, of the corresponding economic return.

Bain (1951) tests the relationship between concentration and profitability using data for 42 US manufacturing industries between 1936 and 1940. Profitability is measured using return on equity, and concentration is measured using the eight-firm concentration ratio CR_8. Average profitability is significantly higher in industries with CR_8 above 70 per cent (at 9.2 per cent) than in those with CR_8 below 70 per cent (at 7.7 per cent). These results are interpreted as indicating that exploitation of market power leads to enhanced profitability. Numerous other studies from the 1950s and 1960s report results similar to those of Bain. This literature, which is reviewed by Weiss (1974, 1989), was influential in shaping the direction of competition policy in a number of countries during the same period.

In a representative study based on the SCP paradigm from the 1960s, Collins and Preston (1966) examine the relationship between concentration (measured using CR_4) and a **price–cost margin** profitability measure, for a sample comprising 32 US four-digit (SIC) food manufacturing industries observed in 1958. The regression model includes terms in CR_4 and CR_4^2, to allow for a possible non-linear (quadratic) relationship between concentration and profitability. Collins and Preston obtain an R^2 (goodness-of-fit) of 0.80, and statistically significant coefficients on both CR_4 and CR_4^2. This is interpreted as supportive of a quadratic relationship between concentration and profit. There are no systematic increases in the price–cost margins accompanying increases in concentration when concentration is low ($CR_4 < 0.3$). For $0.3 < CR_4 < 0.5$, concentration and the profitability appear to increase in similar proportions. However, as CR_4 increased beyond about 0.5, profitability appeared to increase at an accelerating rate. For $CR_4 = 0.6$ the average price–cost margin was around 0.25; but for $CR_4 = 0.85$ the average price–cost margin was around 0.45.

Demsetz (1973, 1974) points out that if the positive relationship between market concentration and profitability reflects the exercise of market power, then it should affect all firms equally. However, if the profitability of large firms in concentrated industries is higher than the profitability of small firms in concentrated industries, then the correlation between profitability and concentration is due to a relationship between efficiency and profitability. Demsetz's empirical results are based on 1963 US Internal Revenue Service data for 95 manufacturing industries. The profitability measure is profit *plus* interest divided by total assets. The results are summarized in Table 9.1. The profitability of firms in size classes R1, R2 and R3 does not appear to be related to concentration. However, in the largest size class, R4, profitability and concentration are positively related, lending support to the efficiency hypothesis. Demsetz argues against Bain's view that highly concentrated industries are uncompetitive. An implication is that specific government policies intended to promote competition directed at highly concentrated industries are not required. Overall, the empirical evidence does not allow us to adjudicate definitively between the collusion and efficiency hypotheses (Weiss, 1989). Below, we review a representative selection of studies.

Ravenscraft (1983) analyses 1975 US data for 3,186 lines of business (LOB) in 258 Federal Trade Commission categories (FTC). Price–cost margins are positively associated with LOB market shares, but negatively associated with seller concentration. However, Ravenscraft's regression only explains about 20 per cent of the variation in profits, even though 21 additional explanatory variables are included to account for industry and LOB effects. Scott and Pascoe (1986) use the FTC LOB

Table 9.1 Rates of return by size and concentration (weighted by assets)

CR_4 (%)	Number of industries	R1 %	R2 %	R3 %	R4 %	All firms %
10–20	14	7.3	9.5	10.6	8.0	8.8
20–30	22	4.4	8.6	9.9	10.6	8.4
30–40	24	5.1	9.0	9.4	11.7	8.8
40–50	21	4.8	9.5	11.2	9.4	8.7
50–60	11	0.9	9.6	10.8	12.2	8.4
Over 60	3	5.0	8.6	10.3	21.6	11.3

CR_4 is the four-firm concentration ratio measured on industry sales in 1963.
R1 is average rate of return for firms with assets < US$500,000.
R2 is average rate of return for firms with US$500,000 < assets < US$5 million.
R3 is average rate of return for firms with US$5 million < assets < US$50 million.
R4 is average rate of return for firms with assets > US$50 million.

Source: H. Demsetz (1973) Industry structure, market rivalry and public policy, *Journal of Law and Economics*, 16, p. 6, table 2.

data for 261 industries for the period 1974–76. The importance of firm and industry effects is tested by allowing for firm- and industry-specific coefficients on variables such as concentration, market growth and market share. Both firm and industry effects are important determinants of profitability, although much of the variation in profitability remains unexplained.

Smirlock *et al.* (1984) test the validity of the collusion and efficiency hypotheses using *Fortune* data on 132 US manufacturing firms for the period 1961–69. The performance measure is Tobin's q, defined as the ratio of the firm's market valuation to the replacement cost of the firm's assets. The independent variables are market share, CR_4, indicators of the height of entry barriers (classed as high, medium or low), and the growth of the firm's market share over the period 1961–69. If the efficiency hypothesis is valid, there should be a positive relationship between profitability and market share, and no relationship between profitability and concentration. Conversely, if the collusion hypothesis is valid, there should be a positive relationship between profitability and concentration, and no relationship between profitability and market share. On this basis, the results tend to support the efficiency hypothesis. There is also a positive relationship between profitability and growth, perhaps because growth influences investors' expectations of future profitability reflected in the firm's valuation ratio. Finally, no relationship is found between profitability and the height of entry barriers.

Clarke *et al.* (1984) also test the validity of the collusion and efficiency hypotheses, using UK data on 155 three-digit manufacturing industries for the period 1971–77. Little difference is found between the average profitability of large and small firms within highly concentrated industries. This finding lends support to the collusion hypothesis.

Eckard (1995) uses US data for five cohorts of firms (based on size) to examine the relationship between changes in profitability (measured by the price–cost margin) and changes in market share over the periods 1967–72 and 1972–77. Under the efficiency hypothesis, there should be a positive relationship between changes in profitability and changes in market share, assuming the more efficient firms are more profitable and grow faster. The empirical results are consistent with this hypothesis.

The collusion and efficiency hypotheses have also been investigated extensively in the banking literature. For example, Berger (1995) compares the validity of two variants of the collusion hypothesis and two variants of the efficiency hypothesis, using US banking data. According to the collusion hypothesis, banks exploit their market power either by charging higher prices for differentiated banking products, or by colluding in order to raise prices. Large banks produce at lower average cost either by becoming more efficient through superior management or by being innovative; or by realizing economies of scale. In both cases, according to the efficiency hypothesis, the most efficient banks are likely to have the largest market shares. In the empirical model, the dependent variable, profitability, is measured using both return on assets and return on equity. Independent variables include concentration, measured using the HH index (see Section 6.4); measures of the effect on average cost of economies of scale; and measures of the efficiency implications of managerial talent. The efficiency measures were significant determinants of profitability, but there was little association between economies of scale and profitability. Profitability was positively related to market share, but not to concentration. These results suggest product differentiation contributes positively to profitability, but collusion does not do so.

Berger and Hannan (1998) examine the relationship between operational efficiency and concentration. According to the *quiet life hypothesis*, market power may enable banks to operate without achieving full efficiency in production; in other words, there may be x-inefficiency. The relationship between concentration and efficiency is examined using data on a sample of 5,263 US banks, with controls included for differences in ownership structure and geographic location. Banks in more highly concentrated markets are found to be less efficient. This finding lends some support to the quiet life hypothesis.

Slade (2004) examines the relationship between concentration, market share and profitability from both a theoretical and an empirical perspective. In a data set comprising 14 metal, mining and refining industries, concentration is found to be positively related to profitability, but there is no relationship between market share and profitability. These results tend to support the collusion hypothesis. Using data on 45 Korean manufacturing industries for 2002, Yoon (2004) finds a negative relationship between market growth and profitability and between concentration and profitability; and positive relationships between expenditures on advertising and research and development, and profitability.

9.3 Strategic groups

The **strategic groups** approach steers a middle way between the original industry-level and the later firm-level approaches discussed in Section 9.2 (Oster, 1999). A strategic group can be defined as a group of firms whose conduct is similar, and which tend to view other firms from the same group as their main competitors (Oster, 1999). The members of a strategic group recognize their interdependence, and this recognition conditions their behaviour. For strategic groups, mobility barriers play a role similar to entry barriers, by preventing non-members from joining the group. For example, entry barriers to the UK pharmaceutical industry depend on whether an entrant wishes to compete with branded or generic products; and an existing generic producer would face mobility barriers if it were to attempt to move into branded products. Mobility barriers can account for a tendency for some groups of firms consistently to earn higher rates of profit than others within same industry (Caves and Porter, 1977; Newman, 1978). More specifically, the amount of variation in average profitability between firms in different strategic groups depends on the following factors:

■ *The number and size of groups*. If the strategic groups are numerous and similar in size, competition is likely to be more intense than if there is a small number of strategic groups that are heterogeneous in size.

■ *The extent to which groups follow different strategies*. If strategic groups differ in respect of their propensities to invest in discretionary expenditures such as advertising and research and development, differences in average profitability are likely to be magnified.

■ *The extent to which groups are interdependent*. If the markets served by different strategic groups tend to be segmented, differences in profitability are likely to be larger than in the case where the groups tend to compete to attract the same customers.

According to McGee and Thomas (1986), strategic groups can be delineated on the basis of similarities in market-related strategies (similarities in product quality or design, pricing, extent of product differentiation, branding and advertising); firm-specific characteristics (firm size, ownership structure, the extent of vertical integration or diversification); or industry characteristics (reliance on economies of scale or scope, production technologies used, types of distribution methods and networks).

If the strategic group is a meaningful or useful concept, there should be greater variation in profitability between groups than within groups. Porter (1979b) aims to identify strategic groups using US data for 38 consumer good industries. The firms within each industry are categorized as leaders or followers, with leaders defined as firms accounting for at least 30 per cent of industry sales revenue. In cross-sectional regressions for profitability, for the leader group concentration, economies of scale, advertising-to-sales ratio, capital requirements and industry growth all contribute positively to profitability. For the follower group, profitability is inversely related to concentration, but there is a positive association between industry growth and capital requirements and profitability. The fact that there are differences between the two groups is interpreted as evidence favouring the strategic groups approach.

Tremblay (1985) tests for the existence of strategic groups in the US brewing industry. Data for the period 1950–77 are used to estimate demand equations for firms classified as national and regional producers. There are significant differences in marketing costs between the two groups, giving rise to a type of mobility barrier making it difficult for regional producers to break into the national market.

Using data on 16 UK retail grocery firms, Lewis and Thomas (1990) use multiple discriminant analysis and cluster analysis to identify the principal sources of variation in profitability between their strategic groups. The most important factors include firm size, discretionary expenditures on advertising and research and development, and geographic location. The strategic groups consist of major and medium-sized supermarkets, small independent stores and cooperatives. The empirical results suggest there are significant differences in capital intensity between groups. However, there is greater variation in profitability within groups than between groups. This finding casts some doubt on the usefulness of the strategic groups concept in the case of the UK retailing sector.

An obvious difficulty with the strategic groups approach is the subjective element involved in the definition of a strategic group. Barney and Hoskisson (1990) argue there is no theoretical basis for choosing a set of variables that could be used to identify strategic groups, or for determining the weightings to be attached to any given set of variables. In practice, cluster analysis is often used to identify groups of firms with similar characteristics. However, the detection of a cluster does not necessarily imply the existence of a strategic group; the clusters that are detected could just as easily be an artifact of this particular statistical technique. Nevertheless, it seems likely that the strategic group is a meaningful concept in many industries, even though it is impossible to define a list of objective criteria that can be used to identify strategic groups. Because of these difficulties, the strategic groups approach has received relatively little attention from economists; however, this approach is more popular in the field of management science.

9.4 Sources of variation in profitability: industry, corporate and business unit effects

In the literature reviewed in Sections 9.2 and 9.3, it is assumed various industry-level and firm-level variables can be used to explain the variation in firms' performance measured using profitability data. However, in many studies only a relatively low proportion of the total variation in profitability is explained by the independent variables. In a seminal paper, Schmalensee (1985) suggests an alternative approach, known as **variance decomposition analysis**, which involves the decomposition of the variation in profitability data into a component that is specific to the industry, a component specific to the corporation, and a component specific to each line of business of a diversified corporation. A statistical technique known as analysis of variance (ANOVA) is used to determine the proportions of the total variation in profitability that can be explained by **industry effects**, **corporate effects** and **business unit effects**, and the proportion that is left unexplained by each type of effect.

The details of the Schmalensee study are as follows. The sample contains 1975 data on 456 diversified US corporations, with lines of business that are classified into 261 different industry groups. A diversified corporation reports separate accounts data for each of its lines of business. Therefore, a separate accounting rate of profit is available for each line of business within each corporation. The following equation is estimated:

$$\pi_{i,k} = \mu + \alpha_i + \beta_k + \eta S_{i,k} + \varepsilon_{i,k}$$

The dependent variable, $\pi_{i,k}$, is the accounting rate of profit reported for corporation k's line of business in industry i. μ is the overall mean profit rate, across all firms and all industries (or lines of business). α_i is the component of $\pi_{i,k}$ that is specific to industry i. α_i is the same for all lines of business (across all corporations) that are classified under industry i. In other words, α_i is the average deviation of the profit belonging to industry i from the overall mean profit rate, μ. α_i can therefore be interpreted as the effect that is specific to industry i. β_k is the component of $\pi_{i,k}$ that is specific to corporation k. β_k is the same for all of corporation k's lines of business. In other words, β_k is the average deviation of the profit rates belonging to corporation k from the overall mean profit rate, μ. $S_{i,k}$ is corporation k's share of total sales in industry i. This market share variable is included in order to obtain an approximation to the effect that is specific to corporation k's line of business in industry i; or in other words, to obtain an effect that corresponds to the interaction between the industry effect α_i and the corporate effect β_k, μ is the coefficient on $S_{i,k}$. Finally, $\varepsilon_{i,k}$ is a disturbance term that captures any variation in $\pi_{i,k}$ that is not attributed to any of the other effects.

Although the variance decomposition approach is mainly descriptive, it is capable of providing powerful insight into the fundamental debate as to whether the industry or the firm is the most appropriate unit of observation in industrial organization. If the industry effects account for a larger proportion of the variation in profitability than the firm (corporate or line of business) effects, this suggests the industry is more important; conversely, if the firm effects dominate the industry effects, this suggests the firm is more important. Schmalensee's empirical results suggest industry effects are more important than firm effects; however, a number of later studies based on a similar empirical methodology came to the opposite conclusion.

Schmalensee's analysis, based on data for a single year, is exclusively cross-sectional. However, a number of subsequent contributions to the variance decomposition literature draw on panel data sets comprising several annual profitability observations on each line of business within each firm. If the data set includes both a cross-sectional and a time-series dimension, an analysis of the sources of variation in profitability richer than the one developed by Schmalensee becomes possible. Specifically, it is possible to identify the following effects:

- Industry effects that are common to all corporations operating a line of business in any particular industry. There is a unique effect pertaining to each industry. These effects derive from industry characteristics such as seller concentration, the extent of entry and exit barriers, and product differentiation.

- Corporate effects (or firm effects in Schmalensee's original terminology) common to all lines of business operated by any particular corporation. There is a unique effect pertaining to each corporation. These effects reflect the impact of strategic decisions taken at head office level, concerning matters such as the firm's scale and scope, horizontal and vertical integration and other forms of long-run investment or divestment.

- Line of business or business unit effects that are specific to each line of business operated by each corporation. These effects capture the impact of operational decisions on performance within each of the corporation's lines of business, concerning matters such as production levels, resource allocation across departments, research and development and marketing.

■ Year effects capture the effects of macroeconomic fluctuations and changes in government policy or taxation that impact equally on the profitability of all lines of business for all corporations. In addition, it is possible to include interactions between year effects and industry effects, and between year effects and corporate effects. These allow for the presence of a transitory component within each of these effects. For example, macroeconomic fluctuations or government policy changes might have a different impact on different industries; therefore the industry effects should be time-varying. Alternatively, it might be that strategic decisions confer only a temporary rather than a permanent competitive advantage; therefore the corporate effects should also be time-varying.

One of the first panel studies was published by Rumelt (1991), who takes Schmalensee's sample of 1975 data on 1,775 business units, and appends 1974, 1976 and 1977 data for the same business units, thereby obtaining a panel data set. The following equation is estimated:

$$\pi_{i,k,t} = \mu + \alpha_i + \beta_k + \gamma_t + \delta_{i,t} + \phi_{i,k} + \varepsilon_{i,k,t}$$

Time-subscripts are added to the dependent variable and the disturbance term, $\pi_{i,k,t}$ and $\varepsilon_{i,k,t}$ respectively, to identify the year to which each observation belongs. μ, α_i and β_k are interpreted in the same way as before. The year effect γ_t allows for year-to-year variation in the overall mean rate of profitability. The industry–year interaction term $\delta_{i,t}$ allows for these year-to-year variations to differ by industry. Finally, the industry–corporate interaction term $\phi_{i,k}$ incorporates a business unit effect: an effect that is specific to corporation k's line of business in industry i. This term replaces the market share variable $S_{i,k}$ in Schmalensee's formulation. The panel structure of Rumelt's data set enables a separate effect to be estimated for every business unit, without the need for any assumption that the business unit effects are proportional to market share. By fitting this model, Rumelt obtains an industry effect that explains 17.9 per cent of the variation in profitability; the industry–year interactions explain a further 9.8 per cent; the corporate effects explain 14.8 per cent; and the business unit effects explain a further 33.9 per cent. Accordingly, Rumelt infers the business unit effect is actually very much larger than the one reported by Schmalensee.

A number of later contributions have reported similar models estimated using more recent or more extensive data sets; similar models for alternative performance indicators; or models with extended specifications that incorporate various refinements. As alternative performance indicators, Wernerfelt and Montgomery (1988) use Tobin's q; Chang and Singh (2000) use business unit market share data; and Hawawini *et al.* (2003) use residual income. McGahan (1999a) reports analyses of accounting profitability and Tobin's q, observed at corporate rather than at business unit level. This study includes an analysis of the effect of corporate focus (the extent to which a corporation is diversified) on performance. Corporate focus is found to be unimportant in explaining variations in profitability at corporate level.

Several contributors, starting with Roquebert *et al.* (1996), have suggested that Schmalensee and Rumelt may have understated the importance of the corporate effect. In a simulation study, Brush and Bromiley (1997) show that even if the corporate effect is of a similar magnitude to the one reported in the earliest studies, it still has a non-negligible influence on the averages of their simulated business unit profit rates. The simulations suggest the statistical techniques used in most variance decomposition studies lack sufficient power to identify the smaller effects on performance accurately. It may be possible to improve the power of the tests by estimating non-linear transformations of the effects. Bowman and Helfat (2001) argue that the inclusion of single business units in many samples deflates the estimated corporate effect for corporations comprising multiple business units. If corporate strategy exerts a varying effect on different businesses within the corporation, the effect may be incorrectly attributed to business rather than corporate level. According to Ruefli and Wiggins (2003), a small estimated corporate effect may be due to the importance of corporate strategy, rather than the opposite: if the performance of management improves in all corporations, competitive forces may tend to erode the magnitude of the corporate effect. Adner and Helfat (2003) estimate a time-varying corporate effect, using press reports to identify the timings of major strategic decisions by US petroleum corporations.

Using accounting profitability data, McGahan and Porter's (2002) reported industry, corporate and business unit effects turn out to be smaller when estimated over a 14-year period than when estimated over a seven-year period. This suggests these effects may contain a temporary component, which may be present for several successive years, but which may disappear in the long run. Therefore the industry, corporate and business unit effects appear bigger when estimated using short-duration data sets (where any temporary effect is more prominent) than when they are estimated using longer-duration data sets (where temporary effects are likely to have disappeared). Accordingly, McGahan and Porter (1997) and Chang and Singh (2000) incorporate an adjustment for persistence, or first-order autocorrelation, in the disturbance term of their profitability models. Persistence or first-order autcorrelation is present when there is non-zero correlation between successive values of the disturbance term for the same firm: a likely feature if the industry, corporate or business unit effects contain a temporary component, as described above.

McGahan and Porter (1999) develop a more general analysis of the persistence or sustainability over time of the industry, corporate and business unit effects. Estimates of these effects are split into a fixed component, and a time-varying, incremental component. The empirical analysis allows for different degrees of persistence in each of the incremental components. This approach appears more informative than modelling persistence solely through the disturbance term, because persistence can be directly related to questions concerning the sustainability of competitive advantage at different levels (industry, corporation or business).

According to the view that the industry is the most appropriate unit of observation in industrial organization, an industry's structural characteristics are more stable than the fortunes of individual firms: therefore we should expect to find greater persistence in incremental industry effects than in incremental corporate or business unit effects. According to the view that the firm is the most relevant unit of observation, entry and exit to and from industries should eliminate inter-industry differences rapidly; but the incremental corporate or business unit effects should be more persistent. For example, high-performing corporations and businesses should be able to keep at least some of their advantages proprietary; while past sunk cost investment may delay the transfer of resources away from from low-performing corporations and businesses into more productive uses. McGahan and Porter's (1999) empirical results generally tend to favour the industry view: the incremental industry effects turn out to be more persistent than the incremental corporate and business unit effects. In a more recent study, McGahan and Porter (2003) test for the presence of asymmetries in these results. For example, they find both the magnitude and the persistence of industry effects is greater for above-average performers than for below-average performers; conversely, business unit effects are more important for low-performers.

Most variance decomposition studies of the sources of variation in profitability used pooled data from a large number of industries. One example of a sector-specific study is Amel and Froeb's (1991) analysis of the Texan banking sector, based on 1982–87 data. Banks are classified by the geographic market they serve, rather than by line of business. In this case, it is argued that a geographic classification provides a more appropriate market definition than the Standard Industrial Code. Using a similar methodology to Schmalensee, Amel and Froeb find the variation in profitability between banks within geographic markets is greater than the variation between markets. This is interpreted as evidence that firm effects are more important than industry (or in this case geographic market) effects in determining performance.

The empirical studies reviewed above draw exclusively on US data, and at present the profitability variance decomposition literature includes relatively limited evidence from outside the US. However, Furman (2000) reports comparisons between four countries using 1992–98 data: Australia, Canada, the UK and the US. Khanna and Rivkin (2001) examine the effects of business group membership on profitability for a sample of firms drawn from 14 developing countries. Business group and industry membership are important determinants of the variation in profitability. In a study using 1994–98 data on non-diversified Spanish manufacturing firms, Claver *et al.* (2002) report a business unit effect of around 40 per cent, together with very small industry and year effects. Spanos *et al.* (2004) analyse a sample of 1,921 Greek firms using 1995–96 data, and find business unit and industry effects account for 15 per cent and 6.5 per cent of the variance in profitability, respectively.

Table 9.2 provides a summary of the profitability variance decomposition literature.

9.5 The new empirical industrial organization (NEIO)

Empirical research based on the SCP paradigm has been widely criticized for placing too much emphasis on industry structure, while the analysis of firm conduct is often underemphasized. However, the observed relationship between commonly used SCP structure and performance indicators, such as concentration and profitability, is often quite weak. These considerations have motivated a number of attempts to collect direct empirical evidence on the nature of competition, by observing conduct directly (Bresnahan, 1982, 1989; Lau, 1982; Panzar and Rosse, 1982, 1987). This approach has become known as the **new empirical industrial organization** (NEIO). One of the major strengths of NEIO is that it is grounded firmly in microeconomic

Table 9.2 Firm and industry effects in determining profitability

Study (chronological order)	Sample	Performance measure	Industry effects (%)	Business unit effects (%)	Corporate effects (%)
Schmalensee (1985)	456 US firms with 1,775 lines of business in 242 manufacturing industries, 1975	ROA	19.5	0.6	
Wernerfelt and Montgomery (1988)	247 US firms drawn from the FTC line of business database, 1976	Tobin's q	20.1	3.7	2.3
Kessides (1990)	456 US firms across 242 industries and 1,775 lines of business, 1975	Return on sales	20.1	27.5	9.8
Rumelt (1991)	457 US firms across 242 industries and 1,774 lines of business, 1974–77	ROA	17.9	33.9	14.8
Powell (1996)	Survey of top executives of a sample of 54 US manufacturing firms	ROA	20		
Roquebert et al. (1996)	10 samples comprising 94–114 US firms, drawn from 223–266 industries, covering 387–451 lines of business, 1985–91	ROA	10.2	37.1	17.9
McGahan and Porter (1997)	7,003 US firms with 12,296 lines of business in 628 industries, 1981–94	ROA	9.4	35.1	11.9
Mauri and Michaels (1998)	264 US firms from 69 manufacturing industries, 1978–92	ROA	6.2	36.9	
McGahan (1999a,b)	4,947 US firms with 9,904 lines of business in 668 industries, 1981–94	ROA	29.4	66	1
Chang and Singh (2000)	305 US firms with 1,519 lines of business in 142 industries, 1983, 1985, 1987, 1989	Market share	4.8	11.6	0.9
Furman (2000)	2,518 firms from Australia, Canada, UK and US, 1993–96	Operating income	Australia: 12.2 Canada: 24.8 UK: 5 US: 10.9	Australia: 51 Canada: 9.4 UK: 18.1 US: 52.5	Australia: 5.5 Canada: 5.9 UK: 18.7 US: 9.3
Claver et al. (2002)	679 Spanish firms over the period 1994–98 from 100 3-digit industries, 1994–98	ROA	2.1		42.7

Table 9.2 (*continued*)

Study (chronological order)	Sample	Performance measure	Industry effects (%)	Business unit effects (%)	Corporate effects (%)
McGahan and Porter (2002)	7,793 firms drawn from the US Compustat Business Segment Reports, 1981–94	ROA	9.6	12	37.7
Hawawini et al. (2003)	562 firms drawn from top 1,000 US and European listed firms for 55 3-digit industries, 1987–96	(i) Economic Value Added (EVA); (ii) Total market value (TMV); (iii) ROA	EVA: 6.5 TMV: 11.4 ROA: 8.1		EVA: 27.1 TMV: 32.5 ROA: 35.8
McGahan and Porter (2003)	7,005 firms drawn from US Compustat Business Segment Reports for 638 industries and 58,340 business segments, 1985–92	ROA	(a) above average performers: 29.6 (b) below average performers: 22.5	(a) 38.7 (b) 54.3	(a) 29.9 (b) 22.8
Ruefli and Wiggins (2003)	4,792 US firms, 1980–96	ROA	0.14	12.3	7.1
Adner and Helfat (2003)	30 US energy firms, 1977–97	ROA	2.1	19	7.3
Spanos et al. (2004)	1,921 Greek firms, 1995–96	ROA	6.5	15	
Caloghirou et al. (2004)	280 Greek manufacturing firms, 1994–96. Split into small (<250 employees) and large (>250 employees) firms	Profit measured on an ordinal scale: CEOs asked to rate their firm's performance relative to rivals	(a) small firms 14.6 (b) large firms 48.2	(a) 6 (b) 16.3	
Hawawini et al. (2004)	Sample of 1,314 non-financial firms from US, UK, Germany, Belgium, the Netherlands and Luxembourg, 1987–96	(i) Economic value added (EVA); (ii) Total market value (TMV); (iii) ROA	US: 1.6 UK: 6.7 Germany: 3.2 Benelux: 3.2		US: 46 UK: 45 Germany: 9.6 Benelux: 0

(oligopoly) theory. SCP measures structure–performance relationships across a number of industries, and draws inferences about what these relationships might mean for conduct. In contrast, NEIO makes direct observations of conduct in specific industries, and draws inferences about what these observed patterns of conduct might mean for structure.

Empirical research in the NEIO stream attempts to estimate the behavioural equations that specify how firms set their prices and quantities. However, a behavioural relationship such as marginal revenue *equals* marginal cost cannot be estimated directly, because we do not observe data on marginal revenue and marginal cost. We might be able to estimate such a relationship indirectly, by specifying a model in which the application of a pricing rule such as marginal revenue *equals* marginal cost has implications for the patterns of variation in other variables that we can observe. For example, one of the approaches described below compares variations in the prices of the firms' factor inputs with variations in their total revenues. If the firms are profit maximizers, this comparison produces different results under market conditions of perfect competition, monopolistic competition and monopoly. One of the main methodological challenges for NEIO research is to find ways of transforming behavioural relationships that are unobservable in their original theoretical form into relationships involving variables that can be observed, so that tests are available that can be implemented in practice. Two such approaches, the revenue test and the mark-up test, are reviewed in the next two subsections.

The Rosse–Panzar revenue test

Rosse and Panzar (1977) develop a test that examines whether firm conduct is in accordance with the models of perfect competition, imperfect or monopolistic competition, or monopoly. The Rosse–Panzar test is also known as the **revenue test**. This test is based on empirical observation of the impact on firm-level revenues of variations in the prices of the factors of production that are used as inputs in the production processes of a group of competing firms. Built into the test is an explicit assumption of profit-maximizing behaviour on the part of the firms.

Rosse and Panzar show that the H-statistic, defined as sum of the elasticities of a firm's total revenue with respect to each of its factor input prices, differs under perfectly competitive, imperfectly competitive and monopolistic market conditions. The intuition is straightforward in the polar cases of perfect competition and monopoly; but more complex in the intermediate case of imperfect or monopolistic competition. The following discussion focuses on the two polar cases. In each of these, we consider the impact of a simultaneous equiproportionate increase in all of the firm's factor input prices. This implies an equiproportionate increase in the total cost of producing any given level of output, and an upward shift in the positions of the LRAC (long-run average cost) and LRMC (long-run marginal cost) functions.

Figure 9.1 illustrates the adjustment under perfect competition. As each firm's LRAC and LRMC functions shift upwards ($LRAC_1$ to $LRAC_2$; $LRMC_1$ to $LRMC_2$), the market price must increase in exactly the same proportion, so that each firm continues to earn only a normal profit when long-run equilibrium is restored. The increase in market price implies a reduction in the level of demand. The required adjustment in the total quantity of output (from Q_1 to Q_2) is achieved by a reduction

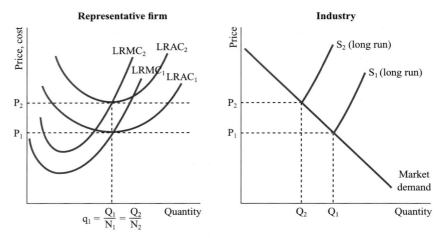

Figure 9.1 Effect of an increase in factor input prices on long-run post-entry equilibrium in perfect competition

in the number of firms (from N_1 to N_2). However, for those firms that survive, total revenue increases in the same proportion as total cost; and in the same proportion as the original increase in factor prices. Therefore in perfect competition, the H-statistic (the sum of the elasticities of revenue with respect to each factor price) is one.

Figure 9.2 illustrates the adjustment under monopoly. For simplicity, in this case we assume horizontal LRAC and LRMC functions. As these functions shift upwards, the monopolist's profit-maximizing price and output adjust from (P_1, Q_1) to (P_2, Q_2). Note that a monopolist with non-zero costs always operates on the price-elastic

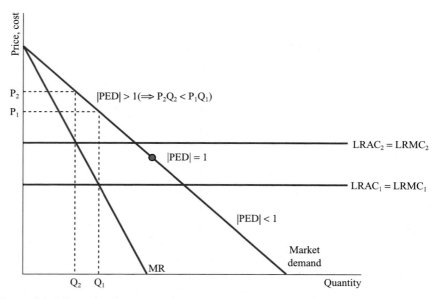

Figure 9.2 Effect of an increase in factor input prices on equilibrium in monopoly

portion of the market demand function. This must be so, because for profit maxi-mization, marginal revenue *equals* marginal cost, so if LRMC > 0, we must have MR > 0. And if MR > 0, price elasticity of demand, |PED| > 1. This implies the shift from (P_1, Q_1) to (P_2, Q_2) causes a reduction in the monopolist's total revenue (if |PED| > 1, an increase in price causes total revenue to fall). Therefore in monopoly, the H-statistic (the sum of the elasticities of revenue with respect to each factor price) is negative.

The Rosse–Panzar revenue test is implemented by estimating the following linear regression using firm-level data:

$$\log_e(TR_{i,t}) = \beta_0 + \beta_1\log_e(w_{1,i,t}) + \beta_2\log_e(w_{2,i,t}) + \beta_3\log_e(w_{3,i,t})$$

where $TR_{i,t}$ = total revenue of firm i in year t; $w_{j,i,t}$ = price of factor input j paid by firm i in year t. In this formulation, it is assumed there are three factors of produc-tion (for example, labour, capital and land). If the prices of the factor inputs cannot be observed directly, they are usually imputed, using the ratio of the quantity of each factor employed (number of employees, for example) to the level of expenditure on the same factor (expenditure on wages and salaries).

An advantage of specifying this revenue equation in log-linear form is that the coefficients can be interpreted as elasticities. Therefore, with three factor inputs, the Rosse–Panzar H-statistic is defined as:

$$H = \beta_1 + \beta_2 + \beta_3$$

The estimated version of the revenue equation can be used to obtain an estimated value of H, and the numerical value of H permits us to draw inferences about the firms' conduct. The interpretation is as follows:

- If H = 1, conduct is in accordance with the model of perfect competition.

- If H < 0, conduct is in accordance with the model of monopoly.

- 0 < H < 1 represents the intermediate case of conduct in accordance with imper-fectly competitive market conditions.

Bresnahan and Lau's mark-up test

Another method for examining the nature of firm conduct, known as the **mark-up test**, is suggested by Bresnahan (1982, 1989) and Lau (1982). This test involves estimating a structural model incorporating demand and cost equations, together with the profit-maximizing condition marginal revenue *equals* marginal cost. The parameters of the model can be estimated using data either at industry level or at firm level.

In this subsection, we provide a detailed description of the construction of one such model, which is employed by Shaffer and DiSalvo (1994) to test for then nature of competitive conduct in a banking market in south central Pennsylvania. Although this model is implemented using banking data, the model specification is quite gen-eral, and the same model can be used for other industries. To describe the mark-up test, our style of presentation is more technical than in the previous subsection.

Shaffer and DiSalvo begin by specifying a market demand function in log-linear form, to be estimated using industry time series data.

$$\log_e(P) = a_0 + a_1\log_e(Q) + a_2\log_e(Y) + a_3\log_e(Z) + a_4t$$

where P = market price; Q = total industry output; Y = aggregate income; Z = price of a substitute product; t = linear time trend. This market demand function is specified in inverse form (with price on the left-hand-side and quantity demanded on the right-hand-side). However, the expression can easily be rearranged to provide an expression for quantity demanded in terms of price:

$$\log_e(Q) = -a_0/a_1 + (1/a_1)\log_e(P) - (a_2/a_1)\log_e(Y) - (a_3/a_1)\log_e(Z) - (a_4/a_1)t$$

As before, by specifying the market demand function in log-linear form, we can interpret the coefficients as elasticities. Therefore PED (price elasticity of demand) *equals* $(1/a_1)$. The income elasticity of demand *equals* $-(a_2/a_1)$, and the cross-price elasticity of demand *equals* $-(a_3/a_1)$. If $a_1 < 0$, $a_2 > 0$ and $a_3 > 0$, PED is negative, and the income and cross-price elasticities are both positive, as the relevant theory suggests. Furthermore, since $PED = \dfrac{1}{a_1}$ we can also write $\dfrac{1}{PED} = a_1$.

Having specified the market demand function, Shaffer and DiSalvo also specify a marginal revenue and a marginal cost function for each firm. An expression for the total revenue of firm i is:

$$TR_i = Pq_i$$

where q_i = output of firm i, such that $\sum_i q_i = Q$.

Therefore firm i's marginal revenue can be written as follows:

$$MR_i = P + q_i\frac{\Delta P}{\Delta q_i}$$

This expression says that if firm i increases its output by one unit, the effect on firm i's total revenue consists of two components. First, firm i obtains the current market price, P, for the additional unit of output produced and sold. Second, if the extra output causes the market price to fall, firm i loses some revenue over each unit of output it is already producing. Firm i's current output level is q_i, and the rate at which price falls as firm i's output increases is $\Delta P/\Delta q_i$. In perfect competition, firm i does not expect price to change when it increases its output, so $\Delta P/\Delta q_i = 0$. In imperfect competition or monopoly, however, firm i expects price to fall as it increases its output, so $\Delta P/\Delta q_i < 0$. Some simple algebraic manipulation of the previous expression enables us to write:

$$MR_i = P + q_i\frac{\Delta P}{\Delta q_i} = P\left(1 + \frac{q_i}{P} \times \frac{\Delta P}{\Delta q_i}\right) = P\left(1 + \frac{1}{PED_i}\right)$$

where PED_i is firm i's price elasticity of demand.

What is the relationship between PED and PED_i? The answer depends on firm i's conjectural variation: how does firm i expect its competitors to react if firm i implements a small increase in output? Shaffer and DiSalvo introduce a parameter λ_i to represent firm i's conjectural variation. λ_i is defined in such a way that we can write:

$$\text{PED}_i = \frac{\text{PED}}{1 + \lambda_i} \Rightarrow \frac{1}{\text{PED}_i} = \frac{1 + \lambda_i}{\text{PED}} = a_1(1 + \lambda_i) \Rightarrow \text{MR}_i = P[1 + a_1(1 + \lambda_i)]$$

The numerical value of the parameter λ_i provides important information about the nature of competition that is perceived by firm i:

- Under perfect competition, when firm i increases its output level, it assumes there will be no impact on the market price. In order to represent this in the model, we require $\lambda_i = -1$. This ensures $\text{PED}_i = \infty$, and $\text{MR}_i = P$.

- Under joint profit maximization, the firms set their prices as if they were a single monopolist. When firm i increases its output level, it assumes the market price will adjust in accordance with the market demand function. In order to represent this case in the model, we require $\lambda_i = 0$. This ensures $\text{PED}_i = \text{PED}$, and $\text{MR}_i = P\left(1 + \dfrac{1}{\text{PED}}\right)$.

- Finally, intermediate values of the parameter λ_i such that $-1 < \lambda_i < 0$ correspond to various forms of imperfect competition, including Cournot competition (each firm chooses its profit-maximizing output level, treating other firms' output levels as fixed at their current levels).

Next, Shaffer and DiSalvo specify firm i's marginal cost function:

$$\text{MC}_i = \text{AC}_i \left[b_0 + b_1\log_e(q_i) + b_2\log_e(w_{1,i}) + b_3\log_e(w_{2,i}) + b_4\log_e(w_{3,i})\right]$$

where AC_i = firm i's average cost; $w_{j,i}$ = price of the j'th factor input used by firm i (as before, we assume firm i uses three factors of production). This type of specification is commonly used to estimate cost functions. The numerical values of the parameters of the total cost function from which this marginal cost function is derived can be chosen to allow for diminishing returns to each factor input; and either increasing, constant or decreasing returns to scale. For present purposes, the following features of the marginal cost function are important:

- Marginal cost, which we cannot measure or observe directly, is expressed as a function of average cost, which we can measure and observe.

- If $b_1 > 0$, $b_2 > 0$, $b_3 > 0$ and $b_4 > 0$, marginal cost increases as output increases, and marginal cost increases as each factor input price increases.

Firm i's condition for profit maximization is $\text{MR}_i = \text{MC}_i$. Therefore we can write:

$$P[1 + a_1(1 + \lambda_i)] = \text{MC}_i \Rightarrow P = \text{MC}_i - Pa_1(1 + \lambda_i)$$

Unfortunately, this expression contains MC_i, which we cannot observe. Some further algebraic manipulation is therefore required, in order to express firm i's profit-maximizing condition in terms of variables we can observe and measure. We divide all three terms in the second expression (above) by AC_i; multiply top and bottom of the first term by Q; and multiply top and bottom of the third term by q_i, to obtain:

$$\frac{PQ}{Q \times AC_i} = \frac{MC_i}{AC_i} - \frac{Pq_ia_1(1 + \lambda_i)}{q_iAC_i} \Rightarrow$$

$$\frac{TR}{Q \times AC_i} = [b_0 + b_1\log_e(q_i) + b_2\log_e(w_{1,i}) + b_3\log_e(w_{2,i}) + b_4\log_e(w_{3,i})] - \frac{TR_ia_1(1 + \lambda_i)}{q_iAC_i}$$

where TR = industry total revenue = $PQ = \sum_i TR_i$. This final expression is a rearranged statement of firm i's profit-maximizing condition $MR_i = MC_i$, expressed entirely in terms of variables that we can observe and measure. In order to implement the mark-up test, the following linear regressions are estimated using time-series data at industry and firm level. For clarity, all firm and time-subscripts are included.

Market demand function (one equation, based on industry-level time-series data):

$$\log_e(P_t) = a_0 + a_1\log_e(Q_t) + a_2\log_e(Y_t) + a_3\log_e(Z_t) + a_4t$$

Profit-maximizing condition (one equation for each firm, based on firm-level time series data):

$$y_{i,t} = b_{0,i} + b_{1,i}\log_e(q_{i,t}) + b_{2,i}\log_e(w_{1,i,t}) + b_{3,i}\log_e(w_{2,i,t}) + b_{4,i}\log_e(w_{3,i,t}) + \beta_ix_{i,t}$$

$$\text{where} \quad y_{i,t} = \frac{TR_t}{Q_tAC_{i,t}}; \; x_{i,t} = \frac{TR_{i,t}}{q_{i,t}AC_{i,t}}; \; \beta_i = -a_1(1 + \lambda_i)$$

The estimated versions of these equations can be used to obtain an estimated value of λ_i for each firm. The value of λ_i (within the range $-1 \leq \lambda_i \leq 0$) provides an indication of the nature of firm i's conjectural variation. This in turn indicates whether price-setting conduct by each firm is based on perfectly competitive, imperfectly competitive or monopolistic (joint profit maximization) assumptions.

Empirical evidence

The revenue and mark-up tests have been applied quite extensively using banking data. Using the revenue test for a sample of New York banks, Shaffer (1982) finds $0 < H < 1$, and infers competition is in accordance with the model of monopolistic competition. Although the New York banking sector is highly concentrated, entry and exit conditions are relatively free. Nathan and Neave (1989) run similar tests for Canadian banks, trust companies and mortgage companies with data for the period 1982–84. In each case the results indicate $0 < H < 1$. 'The significantly positive values of the elasticity measure indicate that Canada's financial system does not exhibit monopoly power' (Nathan and Neave, 1989, p. 576). Using European banking data for the period 1986–89, Molyneux *et al.* (1994) obtain $0 < H < 1$ for France, Germany,

Spain and the UK, and H < 0 for Italy. In a later study using 1992–96 data, De Bandt and Davis (1999) obtain 0 < H < 1 for France, Germany, Italy and the US. Competition appears to be most intense in the US, while French and German small banks have a certain degree of market power. For other recent banking applications, see Bikker and Groeneveld (2000), Hondroyiannis *et al.* (1999) and Shaffer (1989, 2001, 2004); and for applications to other industries, see Fischer and Kamerschen (2003), Genesove and Mullin (1998) and Nebesky *et al.* (1995).

The results of many of these empirical studies tend to be consistent: commonly, price-setting behaviour in accordance with the intermediate competitive models (imperfect or monopolistic competition) is detected. Accordingly, some critics have argued that while NEIO models are 'potentially useful if there is concern over the specification of the structural model, or if data required to estimate the structural model are not available', they are also limited in the sense that they offer 'a determination of only what the market structure of degree of monopoly is not, and do not suggest what it is' (Church and Ware, 2000, p. 450).

Furthermore, the revenue test in particular is based on assumptions that markets are observed in a state of long-run equilibrium.

> Where available data are sufficient to implement it, the Bresnahan–Lau technique is superior to the Rosse–Panzar approach in terms of econometric identification and ability of the estimated conduct parameter to map into specific oligopoly solution concepts. Moreover, the Rosse–Panzar statistic is not reliable for samples that are not in long run equilibrium, but may exhibit a downward bias in that case.
>
> *(Shaffer, 2001, p. 82)*

9.6 The persistence of profit

As we have seen, the SCP and NEIO approaches are based on microeconomic theory, in which optimizing behaviour is assumed. The main focus is on equilibrium, and little is said about the process by which equilibrium is reached. Problems such as imperfect information and uncertainty are ignored. Another strand in the empirical literature, known as the **persistence of profit** (POP) approach, examines the time-series behaviour of firm-level profit data.

POP constitutes a departure from the static, cross-sectional methodology that is prevalent in most of the literature based on the SCP paradigm. It can be argued that the SCP view of competition is typically based on a snapshot, taken at one particular moment in time, and does little to explain the dynamics of competition (Geroski, 1990). There is no certainty that a profit rate, or any alternative performance measure observed at some specific moment in time, represents a long-run equilibrium value of the variable in question. Therefore an empirical association between concentration and high profitability may simply appear by chance, from observation during a period when the relevant market is in a state of disequilibrium. If so, cross-sectional data does not capture (unless by luck) the long-run equilibrium relationship. Furthermore, cross-sectional data usually does not contain enough information on which to base reliable policy decisions. For example, an abnormal or monopoly profit realized in one period could disappear in the next, rendering intervention by government or other regulatory organizations unnecessary.

Brozen (1971) criticizes Bain's (1951) study, suggesting that a disequilibrium phenomenon was being observed (in the data used). If high profitability is the result of the exercise of market power by a monopolist in long-run equilibrium, then similarly high returns should be realized over a number of years. Brozen replicates Bain's empirical analysis over a later period (1953–57), and finds that in highly concentrated industries, average profitability was only 0.6 per cent above the average; and in unconcentrated industries, average profitability was 0.5 per cent below the average. This suggests that over time, profitability in the more profitable industries tends to fall, and profitability in the less profitable industries tends to rise. In other words, there is a tendency for profit rates to converge towards a common long-run average value. This finding lends support to the disequilibrium hypothesis.

Brozen's findings motivated a body of empirical research that has examined patterns of industry and firm performance over an extended period. Research at industry level suggests industry profits tend to converge quite slowly, over periods of several years' duration. Significant correlations between past and present profit rates are therefore observed. Firm-level studies suggest there are significant differences between firms in long-run equilibrium profit rates, and differences in the speed of convergence. The remainder of this section provides a selective review of this literature.

Industry-level studies

Qualls (1974) uses US data on 30 industries observed over the period 1950–65. There is no significant weakening in the relationship between concentration and profitability. Therefore Qualls rejects Brozen's position. Qualls also reports an analysis of firm-level profitability data, using a sample of 220 firms observed over the period 1951–68. Again, there is no evidence of convergence in firm-level profit rates.

Using data for a sample of 197 US industries observed in 1963, 1967 and 1972, Levy (1987) develops a model in which expectations of future profitability are formed with reference to market structure variables such as entry barriers, concentration, advertising intensity and industry growth; and anticipated changes in these variables. If current profitability is higher than expected, entry should take place, causing profitability to fall. The same process should happen in reverse if current profitability is lower than expected. The empirical results suggest the process of adjustment towards long-run equilibrium takes about four years. Industry-level variables such as entry barriers, concentration and growth in demand are important in determining the speed of adjustment. These results provide support for Brozen's critique.

Using data for a sample of 48 US industries observed over the period 1958–82, Coate (1989) estimates the following model:

$$\pi_{i,t} = \beta_0 + \beta_1 \pi_{i,t-1} + \beta_2 \text{GROWTH}_{i,t} + \beta_3 \text{CR}_{4\,i,t} + \varepsilon_{i,t}$$

where $\pi_{i,t}$ is the average price–cost margin in individual i industry for year t; $\pi_{i,t-1}$ is the average price–cost margin for the previous year t − 1; $\text{GROWTH}_{i,t}$ is a measure of the growth of industry i in year t; $CR_{4\,i,t}$ is industry i's four-firm concentration ratio in year t; and $\varepsilon_{i,t}$ is a disturbance term. The empirical results suggest a tendency for profits above or below the long-run equilibrium to converge towards a long-run equilibrium within 10 years. These results provide partial support for Brozen's critique.

Using a sample of US data on 2,438 large firms in 230 industries covering the period 1969–81, Keating (1991) finds profitability in highly concentrated industries was less persistent than profitability in unconcentrated industries. The average profitability of the 50 industries with the highest average profitability at the start of the period declined over the course of the period. There is no evidence of long-run persistence in industry-level average profitability.

Droucopoulos and Lianos (1993) examine data on 20 Greek manufacturing industries over the period 1963–88, to investigate convergence in industry-level average profit rates. In most cases, the speed of adjustment towards long-run equilibrium is slow: 90 per cent of any abnormal return earned in year t persists into year t + 1. High concentration or high advertising intensity tend to slow the speed of adjustment. Bourlakis (1997) examines data on 85 Greek manufacturing industries observed over the period 1958–84. Again there is evidence of a tendency for profitability to persist, especially in highly concentrated industries.

Firm-level studies

At the firm level, the POP literature focuses on the persistence of a firm's standardized profit rate, defined as the difference between the firm's actual profit rate and the average profit rate across all firms in each year. If firm i's standardized profit rate in year t is denoted $\pi_{i,t}^s$, we can write $\pi_{i,t}^s = \pi_{i,t} - \bar{\pi}_t$, where $\pi_{i,t}$ is firm i's actual profit rate in year t and $\bar{\pi}_t$ is the average profit rate in year t. The standardization eliminates from the analysis the effects of any macroeconomic fluctuations, which tend to impact equally on all firms' profit rates, causing $\bar{\pi}_t$ to vary from year to year.

Firm-level POP studies investigate two forms of persistence in $\pi_{i,t}^s$. First, short-run persistence refers to the degree of correlation between consecutive values of $\pi_{i,t}^s$ for the same firm: in other words, the correlation between $\pi_{i,t-1}^s$ and $\pi_{i,t}^s$.

- In perfectly competitive markets with no barriers to entry, abnormal profit is only a very temporary (short-run) phenomenon, which is rapidly eliminated by the forces of competition. Therefore any abnormal profit (positive or negative) should disappear quickly. This implies there should be little or no correlation between consecutive values of any firm's standardized profit rate, or between $\pi_{i,t-1}^s$ and $\pi_{i,t}^s$.

- If competition is anything less than perfect, and there are barriers to entry (which may or may not be surmountable in the long run), it may take some time for any abnormal profit to be eroded by the forces of competition. This means if an abnormal profit (positive or negative) is realized by a firm in one year, it is more than likely the same firm will earn a similar abnormal profit the following year. This implies there should be a positive correlation between consecutive values of the standardized profit rate, or between $\pi_{i,t-1}^s$ and $\pi_{i,t}^s$.

The second type of persistence of profit, long-run persistence, refers to the degree of variation in the long-run average standardized profit rates between firms.

■ In competitive markets with no barriers to entry, or with entry barriers that are surmountable in the long run, short-run abnormal profits are eventually competed away. Each firm's profit rate should eventually converge towards a common value that is the same for all firms. In other words, all firms should earn only a normal profit in the long run.

■ In markets where barriers to entry are permanent and insurmountable, there is no convergence of firm-level profit rates towards a common long-run average value. Differences in firm-level average profit rates may persist permanently or indefinitely.

The POP model can be formulated using a first-order autoregressive model for each firm's standardized profit rate:

$$\pi_{i,t}^s = \alpha_i + \lambda_i \, \pi_{i,t-1}^s + \varepsilon_{i,t}$$

The parameters α_i and λ_i have i-subscripts to denote that it is usual to estimate a separate version of this model for each firm. λ_i represents the strength of short-run persistence in firm i's standardized profit rate. $\lambda_i = 0$ implies there is no association between $\pi_{i,t-1}^s$ and $\pi_{i,t}^s$, and therefore corresponds to the case of perfect competition. $0 < \lambda_i < 1$ implies there is a positive association between $\pi_{i,t-1}^s$ and $\pi_{i,t}^s$, or positive short-run persistence of profit.

In the first-order autoregressive model with $0 \leq \lambda_i < 1$, there is a tendency for firm i's standardized profit rate to converge towards an average or equilibrium value of $\mu_i = \alpha_i/(1 - \lambda_i)$ in the long run. The sign of the parameter α_i determines whether firm i's long-run average standardized profit rate is positive or negative; in other words, whether firm i's actual long-run average profit rate is above or below the average for all firms. If $\mu_i = 0$ for all firms, then all firms' profit rates converge to the same long-run average value. In this case there is no long-run persistence of profit. If $\mu_i > 0$ for some firms and $\mu_i < 0$ for others, there is long-run persistence: there is variation between the long-run average profit rates of different firms.

The implications of different patterns of short-run and long-run persistence for some typical time series plots of firm-level profit rates are illustrated in Figure 9.3. The graphs show stylized plots of standardized profit rates for two firms (1 and 2) when short-run persistence is either zero or positive; and when long-run persistence is either zero or non-zero. Figure 9.3 illustrates the following features:

■ When short-run persistence is zero ($\lambda_i = 0$), the time-series plots of the standardized profit rates are jagged. The value of $\pi_{i,t-1}^s$ (above or below zero) conveys no information about whether $\pi_{i,t}^s$ will be above or below zero, because the year-to-year variation in $\pi_{i,t}^s$ is essentially random. In contrast, when short-run persistence is positive ($\lambda_i > 0$), the time-series plots of the standardized profit rates are smoother. If $\pi_{i,t-1}^s$ is above zero, it is likely $\pi_{i,t}^s$ will also be above zero (and vice versa), because sequences of positive or negative standardized profit rates tend to persist over several consecutive time periods.

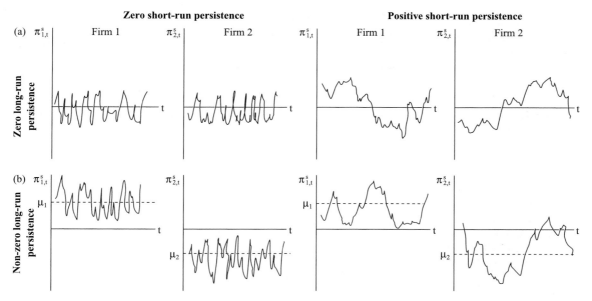

Figure 9.3 Short-run and long-run persistence of profit

- When long-run persistence is zero ($\mu_i = 0$ for all i), the standardized profit rates of all firms tend to fluctuate around the same long-run average value of zero. When long-run persistence is non-zero ($\mu_i \neq 0$ for all i) the standardized profit rates tend to fluctuate around different long-run average values ($\mu_1 > 0$ and $\mu_2 < 0$ in Figure 9.3(b)).

The idea that by observing patterns in the time-series variation of firm-level profit rate data, we can draw inferences about the nature of competition (whether barriers to entry exist, and if so, whether they are temporary or permanent) has motivated a body of research that was first pioneered by Mueller (1977, 1986). The hypothesis tested in these studies is that (potential and actual) entry into and exit from any market are sufficiently free to bring any abnormal profits quickly into line with the competitive rate of return. In other words, competitive forces are sufficiently powerful to ensure no firm persistently earns profits above or below the norm. Firms never achieve a stable equilibrium in the conventional sense, however, because each period brings new random shocks. If the market is responsive to excess profits and losses, returns tend to gravitate towards the competitive level. But if some firms possess and are able to retain specialized knowledge or other advantages, these firms may be able to earn profits that remain above the norm persistently, in the long run.

In the empirical POP literature, the average value (over a number of sample firms) of the estimated short-run persistence parameter λ_i provides a useful indicator of the strength of persistence, which has been reported on a consistent basis in most studies. Most researchers have obtained a value of this statistic in the range 0.4–0.5. Most studies have also reported evidence of significant differences between firms in long-run average profit rates. In other words, it appears all firms' profit rates do not tend to converge towards the same equilibrium or average value in the long run. A summary of some of the main empirical POP studies is shown in Table 9.3.

Table 9.3 Summary of firm level persistence of profit studies

Study	Country	Sample period	No. of firms	Mean λ_i
Geroski and Jacquemin (1988)	UK	1949–77	51	0.488
	France	1965–82	55	0.412
	West Germany	1961–81	28	0.410
Schwalbach *et al.* (1989)	West Germany	1961–82	299	0.485
Mueller (1990)	US	1950–72	551	0.183
Cubbin and Geroski (1990)	UK	1950–72	243	0.482
Jenny and Weber (1990)	France	1965–82	450	0.363
Odagiri and Yamawaki (1990)	Japan	1964–82	376	0.465
Schohl (1990)	West Germany	1961–81	283	0.509
Khemani and Shapiro (1990)	Canada	1964–82	129	0.425
Goddard and Wilson (1996)	UK	1972–91	335	0.458
Waring (1996)	US	1970–89	12,986	0.540
Goddard and Wilson (1999)	UK	1972–91	335	0.450
Marayuma and Odagiri (2002)	Japan	1964–82	376	0.464
		1983–97	357	0.543
Glen *et al.* (2001, 2003)	Brazil	1985–95	56	0.013
	India	1982–92	40	0.229
	Jordan	1980–94	17	0.348
	Korea	1980–94	82	0.323
	Malaysia	1983–94	62	0.349
	Mexico	1984–94	39	0.222
	Zimbabwe	1980–94	40	0.421
Villalonga (2004)	US	1981–97	1,641	0.284

9.7 Summary

The performance of firms is one of the central research themes in industrial organization. There is a now a substantial body of empirical research that seeks to explain variations in performance between firms, most commonly measured by profitability. Early research, based mainly on the SCP (structure–conduct–performance) paradigm, identified structural industry-level variables such as concentration, economies of scale, and entry and exit conditions as the most important determinants of firm performance. However, this approach has been subject to intense criticism. Many of the structure–performance relationships identified in SCP-based empirical research are relatively weak. Some economists, including those associated with the Chicago school, argue market power deriving from monopolization is only a temporary phenomenon. A positive association between concentration and profitability may reflect an association between productive efficiency and firm size: the most efficient firms earn the largest profits, enabling them to grow at the expense of their competitors. If efficiency differences between firms are more important than industry structure in determining performance, attention should presumably be directed less towards the industry and more towards the individual firm. Accordingly, later empirical research in both industrial organization and strategic management has sought to shift the focus of attention towards conduct or strategic decision making at firm level.

The strategic management literature on strategic groups perhaps offers a middle way between the industry-level and firm-level approaches discussed above. A strategic group is a group of firms whose conduct is similar, and which tend to view other members of the same group as their main competitors. The members of a strategic group recognize their interdependence, and this recognition conditions their behaviour. For strategic groups, mobility barriers play a role similar to entry barriers, by preventing non-members from joining the group. The variation in average profitability between firms in different groups depends on the number and size of groups; the extent to which groups follow different strategies; and the degree of interdependence between groups. Cluster analysis is often used to identify groups of firms with similar characteristics; but the strategic groups approach can be criticized for failing to provide a clear theoretical basis for deciding group membership. The strategic groups approach has been more influential in the strategic management literature than in the industrial economics literature.

A variance decomposition analysis of firm-level profitability data involves the decomposition of the variation in profit rates into components specific to the industry, the parent corporation and each line of business within a diversified corporation. It is possible to identify the proportions of the total variance in profitability that are explained by each type of effect. The variance decomposition approach is mainly descriptive. However, it is capable of providing powerful insights into the debate as to whether the industry or the firm is the most appropriate unit of observation in industrial organization, by comparing the relative contributions made by the industry effects or the corporate and business unit effects in explaining the variation in profitability. Some of the earliest studies of this kind found industry effects to be more important than firm-level effects; however, this finding has been challenged by several later researchers. Recently, several researchers have explored the persistence or sustainability over time of the industry, corporate and business unit effects. Estimates of these effects are split into a fixed component, and a time-varying, incremental component. The notion of persistence can be directly related to questions concerning the sustainability of competitive advantage at different levels (industry, corporation or business).

In industrial organization, empirical research based on the SCP paradigm has been widely criticized for placing too much emphasis on industry structure, while the analysis of conduct is underemphasized. This critique has motivated several attempts to assess the nature of competition by observing conduct directly. This approach is known as the new empirical industrial organization (NEIO). NEIO makes direct observations of conduct and draws inferences about market structure. The revenue test of Rosse and Panzar involves estimating the sum of the elasticities of revenue with respect to each of the firm's factor input prices. The sign and magnitude of this statistic indicate whether firms' price-setting behaviour is consistent with the theoretical models of perfect competition, monopolistic competition or monopoly. The mark-up test of Bresnahan and Lau involves estimating a structural model incorporating demand and cost equations, linked by the profit-maximizing condition marginal revenue *equals* marginal cost. An estimate of the firm's price elasticity of demand again provides evidence about the nature of competition the firm perceives.

Both the SCP and NEIO methodologies are based on assumptions of profit maximization and long-run equilibrium. In contrast, the persistence of the profit strand in the empirical industrial organization literature focuses on the process of adjustment towards equilibrium, by analysing time-series data on firm-level profit rates. Short-run persistence refers to the degree of correlation between consecutive values of a firm's standardized profit rate (in successive years). In perfectly competitive markets with no barriers to entry, abnormal profit is rapidly eliminated by competition, so there is little correlation between consecutive profit rates. In imperfectly competitive markets with high barriers to entry, abnormal profits may tend to persist for several years. Therefore consecutive profit rates tend to be more highly correlated. Long-run persistence refers to the degree of variation between firms in the long-run average (standardized) profit rates. Empirical studies at industry and firm level consistently report evidence of significant short-run and long-run persistence of profit.

Discussion questions

1. Distinguish between the traditional and revisionist views of the ultimate source of profitability.

2. To what extent is it reasonable to infer that high profits earned by firms in highly concentrated industries are the result of these firms abusing their market power?

3. Examine the strengths and limitations of company accounts-based measures of firm profitability.

4. In order to calculate a reliable measure of a firm's performance, why is it important to adjust a profit rate calculated from company accounts data for risk?

5. Explain carefully the construction and interpretation of Tobin's q as a measure of performance.

6. Explain the construction of an empirical test for the relative merits of the collusion and efficiency hypotheses as explanations for variations in firm profitability.

7. What are strategic groups? What criteria might be used to identify strategic groups in practice? With reference to an industry of your choice, attempt to identify two or three strategic groups.

8. Compare and contrast the SCP (structure–conduct–performance) and the NEIO (new empirical industrial organization) approaches to empirical research in industrial organization.

9. Explain how the application to firm-level profitability data of variance decomposition techniques such as analysis of variance can shed new light on the long-standing debate as to whether performance depends primarily on industry-level or on firm-level factors.

10. Summarize the intuition underlying the following tests that are used to draw inferences about market structure and competitive conditions, based on observation of firms' conduct under assumptions of profit maximization: the Rosse–Panzar revenue test, and Bresnahan and Lau's mark-up test.

11. What can we infer about the intensity of competition by observing patterns of variation in firm-level time-series profit rate data?

12. Explain the distinction between short-run and long-run persistence of profit.

Further reading

Bresnahan, T.F. (1989) Empirical studies of industries with market power, in Schmalensee, R. and Willig, R.D. (eds) *Handbook of Industrial Organization*, vol. 2. Elsevier Science Publishers, 1011–58.

Caves, R.E. (1986) *American Industry: Structure, Conduct and Performance*, 6th edn. Englewood Cliffs, NJ: Prentice-Hall.

The *Economist* (1998) The economics of antitrust, May 1998.

Glen, J., Lee, K. and Singh, A. (2003). Corporate profitability and the dynamics of competition in emerging markets: a time series analysis. *Economic Journal*, 113, F465–84.

Martin, S. (2002) *Advanced Industrial Economics*, 2nd edn. Cambridge, MA: Blackwell, chs 5, 6 and 7.

McGee, J. and Thomas, H. (1986) Strategic groups: theory, research and taxonomy, *Strategic Management Journal*, 7, 141–60.

Mueller, D.C. (ed.) (1990) *The Dynamics of Company Profits: An International Comparison.* Cambridge: Cambridge University Press.

Neuberger, D. (1998) Industrial organization of banking: a review, *International Journal of the Economics of Business*, 5, 97–118.

Scherer, F.M. and Ross, D. (1990) *Industrial Market Structure and Economic Performance*, 3rd edn. Boston: Houghton Mifflin, ch. 11.

Schmalensee, R.C. (1989) Inter-industry studies of structure and performance, in Schmalensee, R.C. and Willig, R.D. (eds) *Handbook of Industrial Organization*, vol. 2. Amsterdam: North-Holland, ch. 16.

Weiss, L.W. (1974) The concentration–profits relationship and antitrust, in Goldschmid, H., Mann, H.M. and Weston, J.F. (eds) *Industrial Concentration: The New Learning*. Boston, MA: Little Brown, 183–233.

Weiss, L.W. (1989) *Concentration and Price*. Boston, MA: MIT Press.

Young, G., Smith, K.G. and Grimm, C.M. (1996) Austrian and industrial organization perspectives on firm-level activity and performance, *Organization Science*, 7, 243–54.

PART 3

Analysis of Firm Strategy

Learning objectives

This chapter covers the following topics:

- cost plus pricing
- first-degree, second-degree and third-degree price discrimination
- price discrimination in practice
- peak-load pricing
- transfer pricing under various market conditions

Key terms

Cost plus pricing
Dumping
First-degree price discrimination
Intertemporal price discrimination
Peak-load pricing

Perfect price discrimination
Second-degree price discrimination
Third-degree price discrimination
Transfer pricing
Two-part tariff

10.1 Introduction

Price determination is an essential component of each of the theories of decision making and resource allocation at firm level and industry level that has been developed in the previous chapters of this book. In particular, price formation in perfectly competitive, imperfectly competitive and monopolistic market conditions was one of the central themes of Chapters 2, 4 and 5. In Chapter 10, we examine a number of further aspects of pricing behaviour, from both a theoretical and a practical perspective.

One possible critique of the neoclassical theory of the firm can be developed by questioning whether in practice firms have sufficient information to determine their prices by applying the profit-maximizing rule marginal revenue *equals* marginal cost.

In Section 10.2, we examine an alternative pricing rule known as cost plus pricing, whereby price is determined by adding a percentage mark-up to average variable cost. The mark-up includes a contribution towards the firm's fixed costs, and a profit margin. The relationship between profit-maximizing pricing and cost plus pricing is considered, and the conditions are identified under which both methods produce similar outcomes.

The pricing models developed earlier in this book assume firms set uniform prices that are identical for all consumers, and are identical no matter what quantity each consumer buys. In Section 10.3, we examine an alternative pricing policy known as price discrimination, whereby a firm either sells at different prices to different consumers, or makes the price per unit each consumer pays dependent on the number of units purchased. For such a policy to be possible, the firm must enjoy some degree of market power, and the market must be divisible into sub-markets between which secondary trade or resale is not possible. Three types of price discrimination, known as first-, second- and third-degree price discrimination, are considered. Several examples of price discrimination commonly encountered in practice are identified. Section 10.4 examines the related (but conceptually distinct) practice of peak-load pricing, in which a supplier facing a level of demand that varies at different times of the day or on different days of the year can vary its prices accordingly, but must also decide on a fixed capacity level that is the same for all periods.

In multidivisional organizations, the choice of transfer prices at which intermediate products are traded internally between divisions affects the imputed divisional profitability. Decisions taken at divisional level with a view to the maximization of divisional profits do not necessarily ensure the maximization of the firm's aggregate profits. In Section 10.5, several profit-maximizing models of transfer pricing are developed. The analysis suggests that incentives for divisional managers, and decisions concerning the viability of loss-making divisions, should not be based solely on imputed divisional profitability, but should reflect the implications for the profitability of the firm as a whole.

10.2 Cost plus pricing

According to the neoclassical theory of the firm under the assumption of profit maximization, price is determined through the application of the behavioural rule marginal revenue *equals* marginal cost (MR = MC). As we have seen in Section 3.3, one of the earliest attacks on the neoclassical theory of the firm was developed by economists who questioned whether firms have sufficient information to apply this rule in practice. In a highly influential study, Hall and Hitch (1939) report the results of interviews with 38 businesses, 30 of whom reported the use of some form of **cost plus pricing** formula. Under cost plus pricing, the firm calculates or estimates its AVC (average variable cost), and then sets its price by adding on a percentage mark-up that includes a contribution towards the firm's fixed costs, and a profit margin:

Price = AVC + % mark up
or P = (1 + m)AVC

where P denotes price, and the mark-up (expressed as a percentage) is $100 \times m$ per cent. A number of advantages are claimed for cost plus pricing over pricing using the profit-maximizing rule MR = MC.

- The cost plus pricing formula is simple to understand, and can be implemented using less information than is required for profit-maximizing pricing. For the latter, the firm requires detailed information about its MC, MR and AR (demand) functions. For cost plus pricing, the firm only requires an estimate of its AVC, and a decision concerning the size of the mark-up.

- Cost plus pricing may produce greater price stability than profit-maximizing pricing. The latter implies price should change every time there is a minor variation in demand. In contrast, with cost plus pricing, provided AVC is relatively flat over the relevant range of output levels, minor variations in the level of demand need not lead to changes in price. Price stability may be valued by consumers, as it reduces their search costs, and by producers, as it reduces the likelihood that destructive price competition may break out.

- Cost plus pricing appeals to a sense of fairness: in determining its mark-up, the firm can claim to allow for a reasonable profit margin, rather than the maximum profit. Price changes can be attributed solely to changes in costs, rather than fluctuations in market demand.

However, in some cases these claimed advantages might be open to question. Fluctuations in demand can only be ignored safely when setting price if AVC is constant over the relevant range of output levels. If AVC varies with output, the firm needs to know its output level before it can determine its price. This means it needs to estimate its demand function. Cost plus pricing does not imply price stability if costs themselves are changing, or if there are fluctuations in demand and AVC varies with output. Cost plus pricing may not be simple to implement for a multi-product firm, since it may be difficult to apportion fixed and variable costs accurately between a number of product lines (Hanson, 1992).

Finally, the question arises as to what profit margin to include in the mark-up. If the size of the profit margin varies with market conditions, the difference between cost plus pricing and pricing for profit maximization using the rule MR = MC might not be as large as it first appears. Suppose for instance the cost plus pricing firm always selects approximately the same profit margin as a profit-maximizing firm would achieve by applying the rule MR = MC. Naturally, this profit margin tends to be higher when demand conditions are strong, and lower when demand is weak. In this case, cost plus pricing and profit-maximizing pricing would both yield approximately the same outcome. The widespread reported use of cost plus pricing might suggest cost plus is a convenient rule-of-thumb for firms that are really profit maximizers, even if they do not themselves explicitly recognize this form of behaviour.

Under what conditions do cost plus pricing and profit-maximizing pricing using the rule MR = MC produce identical results? In Section 2.3, it was shown that MR can be written as follows:

$$MR = P\left(1 - \frac{1}{|PED|}\right)$$

where $|PED|$ is the absolute value of the firm's price elasticity of demand. A necessary condition for MR > 0 is $|PED| > 1$, or PED < −1. Rearranging the previous expression, we can write:

$$MR = P\left(\frac{|PED| - 1}{|PED|}\right)$$

Under the profit-maximizing rule MR = MC, we can write:

$$MC = P\left(\frac{|PED| - 1}{|PED|}\right) \quad \Rightarrow \quad P = \left(\frac{|PED|}{|PED| - 1}\right)MC$$

If we assume AVC is approximately constant over the range of output levels within which production takes place, then MC ≅ AVC. Under this assumption, we can write:

$$P = \left(\frac{|PED|}{|PED| - 1}\right)AVC$$

Using our earlier expression for the cost plus pricing formula P = (1 + m)AVC, we can write:

$$1 + m = \frac{|PED|}{|PED| - 1} \quad \Rightarrow \quad m = \frac{1}{|PED| - 1}$$

Therefore cost plus pricing is equivalent to profit-maximizing pricing if AVC is approximately constant, and the mark-up is set to a value of $1/(|PED| - 1)$. Note that this formula for the mark-up only produces a positive (and therefore meaningful) value for the mark-up in the case $|PED| > 1$, the same condition that is required for MR > 0. The more price inelastic the firm's demand, the larger the mark-up required for profit maximization. When economic conditions are depressed, $|PED|$ is likely to be high, in which case the mark-up consistent with profit maximization is small. When economic conditions are more buoyant, the mark-up consistent with profit maximization is larger. Similarly, when competition is intense, $|PED|$ is likely to be high, in which case the mark-up consistent with profit maximization is small. When competition is weaker, the mark-up consistent with profit maximization is larger.

Since Hall and Hitch's (1939) original paper on cost plus pricing, several other researchers have investigated firms' pricing practices, mostly using survey methods. For example, Fog (1960) presents evidence for a sample of 139 Danish firms, suggesting that the use of cost plus pricing is widespread. Barback (1964) carried out a similar survey for a sample of seven UK firms, four of which reported using a cost plus pricing formula. The firms acknowledged they would abandon cost plus pricing if market conditions deteriorated. Using case study evidence for 13 UK firms, Hague (1971) suggests cost plus pricing is widely used, albeit in a modified form taking account of market conditions and the actions of competitors. Using a sample of 193 UK distributors, Shipley and Bourdon (1990) find over 50 per cent of the firms used cost plus pricing.

Table 10.1 How UK firms set their prices

Pricing method	All	Manufacturing	Construction	Retail	Other services
Reference to market conditions	39	41	51	18	48
Competitor prices	25	26	11	30	23
Direct cost + variable mark-up	20	20	22	21	17
Direct cost + fixed mark-up	17	16	19	24	14
Customer set	5	6	3	0	6
Regulatory agency	2	1	0	0	3

Note: Data are percentages of sample firms reporting use of the method shown in the left-hand column. Percentages may exceed 100 per cent because firms are permitted to indicate more than one choice.

Source: Adapted from Hall, S., Walsh, M. and Yates, A. (1996) How do UK companies set prices? *Bank of England Quarterly Bulletin*, May, 36, 180–92, Table A, 13.

Using a sample of 728 UK manufacturing firms, Shipley (1981) asked respondents to assess the importance of various objectives that might be considered when formulating prices: these included target profitability; target sales revenue; target market share; price stability; stability of sales volume; comparability of own prices with those of competitors; and prices perceived as fair by customers. Many firms reported considering multiple objectives when pricing their products. While profitability was important, it was not the only consideration. Firms were more likely to be profit-oriented in industries where competition (measured by the number of competing firms) was more intense. Large firms (measured by the number of employees) were more likely than small firms to admit to profit-maximizing behaviour. However, only 16 per cent of all firms considered profit maximization to be an overriding objective.

Hall *et al.* (1996) report a survey of 654 UK firms, which were asked to assess the most important factors they consider when setting prices. The results are summarized in Table 10.1. Market conditions were the most important factor, especially in the case of firms in the construction industry. Competitors' pricing policies were also important, especially in retailing. Around 40 per cent of the firms surveyed reported the use of a cost plus pricing method. Smaller firms in particular were unlikely to have collected sufficient data on demand conditions to be able to use a profit-maximizing (MR = MC) pricing rule.

10.3 Price discrimination

In most of the theoretical models of firms' production and pricing decisions that have been considered previously in this book, we have assumed the firm sets a uniform price which is the same for all consumers, and which is the same no matter how many units of the product each consumer buys. In practice, however, a firm that enjoys some degree of market power might consider adopting a more complex pricing policy. Consider a product that is produced under uniform cost conditions. It might be in the firm's interest to sell at different prices to different consumers, or to make the price per unit that any consumer pays dependent on the number of units purchased. The policy of selling different units of output at different prices is known as price discrimination (Phlips, 1983; Pigou, 1920).

It is important to note that there is price discrimination only in cases where there are variations in the prices charged for a product that is supplied under an identical cost structure no matter who the buyer is, or how many units are produced and sold. For example, a petrol retailer who charges different prices at an inner-city petrol station and at a remote rural petrol station does not adopt a policy of price discrimination if the price differential is proportional to the difference in costs (transport costs perhaps being higher in the rural location). Conversely (and perhaps paradoxically) a petrol retailer who charges the same price in two locations where there is a cost difference *does* practice price discrimination, favouring consumers in the high-cost location who under a uniform pricing policy would pay a higher price to reflect the cost difference.

There are three types of price discrimination, as follows:

■ **First-degree price discrimination**, also sometimes known as **perfect price discrimination**, involves making the price per unit of output depend on the identity of the purchaser *and* on the number of units purchased. First-degree price discrimination is a theoretical construct that is encountered only rarely in practice. A possible example would be a private doctor in a small village who does not operate a fixed price structure, but instead simply charges his patients on the basis of his or her assessment of their ability to pay.

■ **Second-degree price discrimination** involves making the price per unit of output depend on the number of units purchased. However, the price does not depend on the identity of the purchaser: all consumers who buy a particular number of units pay the same price per unit. Discounts for bulk purchases are a common example of second-degree price discrimination. Other examples of industries that adopt this type of pricing structure include the utilities (water, gas and electricity) and some high technology industries such as mobile phones and internet services.

■ **Third-degree price discrimination** involves making the price per unit depend on the identity of the purchaser. However, the price does not depend on the number of units purchased: any consumer can buy as few or as many units as he or she wishes at the same price per unit (Schmalensee, 1981). Common examples of third-degree price discrimination include the practice of offering discounts to children, students or senior citizens for products such as transport or entertainment. Firms that trade internationally sometimes adopt this type of price structure. The term **dumping** describes the practice of charging a lower price to consumers in poorer countries than to those in richer ones.

For a policy of price discrimination to be possible, two conditions must be satisfied. First, the price discriminating firm must enjoy some degree of market power, so that it has the discretion to choose its own price structure. For a perfectly competitive firm, a policy of price discrimination is not possible. If the firm attempts to charge a price in excess of its marginal cost to any segment of the market, entry takes place and the increase in supply forces price down until price *equals* marginal cost at the perfectly competitive equilibrium. The existence of successful price discrimination is sometimes interpreted as proof that a firm exercises some degree of market power.

The second necessary condition for successful price discrimination is that the market for the product must be divisible into sub-markets, within which there are different demand conditions (or different price elasticities of demand). These sub-markets must be physically separate either through space or time, so that secondary trade or resale between consumers in different sub-markets is not possible. A firm cannot force Jack to pay more than Jill if it is possible for Jill to purchase at the lower price on Jack's behalf. For example, in the markets for accounting, legal and medical services, there is often simultaneity between production and consumption, making it difficult or impossible for consumers to resell the service between themselves. Similarly, simultaneity between production and consumption enables a cinema to offer discounted admission to children, because it is not possible for a child to purchase the right to watch the movie at the cheaper price, and then pass on or resell this right to an adult. But on the other hand, the cinema does not allow children to buy ice cream at a discounted price, because it would be easy for children to buy ice cream on their parents' behalf.

Simultaneity between production and consumption is not the only way in which effective separation of sub-markets can be achieved. Some newspapers are made available to students at a discounted price, despite the fact that resale would be possible in theory. However, in practice it would not be worthwhile incurring the transaction costs involved in organizing the resale of a newspaper for which a cover price discount of (say) 50 per cent represents a saving of only a few pence. Significant transport costs can also help achieve an effective physical separation of sub-markets. For example, the practice of dumping surplus agricultural produce in poorer countries relies on the fact that transport costs would be prohibitive if the consumers in poorer countries attempted to resell to their counterparts in the richer countries.

First-degree price discrimination

Figure 10.1 illustrates a policy of **first-degree price discrimination**, exercised by the monopoly supplier of some good. First, we consider the polar case where the market demand function represents a large number of consumers. Depending on the price, each consumer either buys one unit of the good, or abstains from buying altogether. Each consumer's reservation price is the maximum price the consumer is willing to pay. We can imagine the consumers arrayed along the horizontal axis of Figure 10.1, in descending order of their reservation prices or willingness to pay. Therefore the first consumer has a reservation price of P_1; the second consumer has a reservation price of P_2; and so on. In the standard case where the monopolist charges the same price to each consumer, the profit-maximizing price and quantity is (P_M, Q_M). Notice that if the monopolist did not have to offer the same price to all consumers, it would be worthwhile to supply the consumer located just to the right of Q_M, whose reservation price or willingness to pay is slightly lower than P_M but still higher than the monopolist's marginal cost. But in the standard case, the monopolist would have to offer the same price cut to all of its existing Q_M consumers who are located to the left of this point. The loss of revenue that this would entail exceeds the benefit the monopolist would gain by attracting the additional customer. By

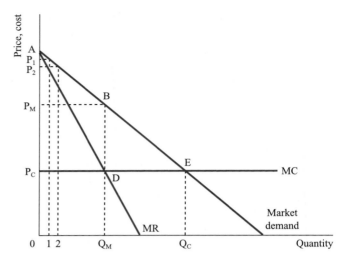

Figure 10.1 First-degree price discrimination

implementing a policy of first-degree price discrimination, however, the monopolist can exploit the differences in willingness to pay, by charging each consumer his or her own reservation price. Therefore the first consumer pays a price of P_1, the second consumer pays a price of P_2, and so on. It is worthwhile for the monopolist to supply all consumers whose reservation prices exceed the monopolist's marginal cost. Therefore total output is Q_C, and the most marginal consumer pays a price of P_C.

It is also possible to implement a policy of first-degree price discrimination in a second polar case, where the market demand function represents one consumer, who is prepared to buy any number of units of the good, but whose willingness to pay decreases as the number of units purchased increases. If the monopolist offers a price of P_1, the consumer buys only one unit. But if the monopolist offers to sell a second unit at a reduced price of P_2, the consumer buys two units. If reductions in the prices of further units are offered, the consumer is induced to buy three, four or five units, and so on. The monopolist could continue in this way until the price of the last unit sold equals the monopolist's marginal cost. As before, the monopolist's total output is Q_C, and the selling price is P_C. At (P_C, Q_C) the monopolist obtains a surplus of P_CAE.

An alternative way in which the monopolist could obtain the same surplus is by charging a two-part tariff. The monopolist offers the consumer a price structure requiring the payment of a fixed fee (which is mandatory if the consumer wishes to make any purchases at all), and an additional uniform price for each unit that is purchased. In Figure 10.1, the monopolist's optimal two-part tariff is to charge a fixed fee of P_CAE, and a uniform price per unit of $P_C = MC$. As before, the total quantity of output produced and sold is Q_C, and the most marginal unit is sold at a price of P_C. A two-part tariff price structure is often used by golf, tennis or bowling clubs, which charge a fixed annual membership fee, and make an additional charge for use of the facilities on each occasion. Two-part tariffs are also used by amusement parks and theme parks such as Disneyland, where there is a fixed entry fee and an additional price charged for each ride (Oi, 1971).

It is worthwhile to use Figure 10.1 to compare the efficiency and welfare properties of the monopolist's standard profit-maximizing equilibrium at (P_M, Q_M), and the equilibrium that is achieved with first-degree price discrimination. With first-degree price discrimination, the total output of Q_C is higher than Q_M in the standard case of monopoly. In fact, Q_C is the total output that would be produced if the monopolist were replaced by a large number of perfectly competitive producers. Furthermore, the equilibrium achieved with first-degree price discrimination satisfies the necessary condition for allocative efficiency (see Section 2.5), that the price of the most marginal unit of output produced *equals* the marginal cost of producing the last unit.

As we have seen in Section 2.5, for a non-discriminating monopolist operating at (P_M, Q_M) consumer surplus is represented by the triangle $P_M AB$; producer surplus is the monopolist's abnormal profit of $P_C P_M BD$; and the deadweight loss is DBE. With first-degree price discrimination there is no consumer surplus, because each consumer pays a price equivalent to his or her maximum willingness to pay for each unit. There is a producer surplus of $P_C AE$, which represents the total abnormal profit earned by the monopolist by selling each unit at a varying price. Finally, the deadweight loss that exists in the non-discriminating case is eliminated.

We therefore reach what might at first sight seem a rather paradoxical conclusion. The monopolist who adopts a policy of first-degree price discrimination earns an even higher abnormal profit than the monopolist who charges a uniform price; but on allocative efficiency criteria, the outcome under first-degree price discrimination is preferable to the outcome in the case of monopoly with uniform pricing. The policy of first-degree price discrimination allows the monopolist to convert all of the consumer surplus that exists in the non-discriminating case into producer surplus, and to eliminate the deadweight loss. In other words the monopolist extracts all of the available surplus, and earns an even higher abnormal profit. However, this outcome is superior on allocative efficiency criteria, for the following reasons:

■ In the non-discriminating case, it is possible to make someone better off without making anyone else worse off, because there is a consumer who is willing to pay a price for an extra unit that would exceed the cost of producing this extra unit.

■ With first-degree price discrimination it is not possible to make someone better off without making anyone else worse off, because price *equals* marginal cost for the most marginal unit produced and sold.

The paradox is resolved by noting that for allocative efficiency, it does not matter whether the surplus accrues to consumers or to producers: welfare economists do not make judgements as to whether monopoly profits are good or bad. All that matters is that there should be no unexploited opportunities for welfare gains that could be achieved without causing losses elsewhere. And as we have seen above, such opportunities do exist at the non-discriminating monopoly equilibrium (which is therefore allocatively inefficient); but no such opportunities exist at the equilibrium under first-degree price discrimination. First-degree price discrimination is sometimes known as perfect price discrimination, because all of the available surplus is extracted by the monopolist. As we will see below, this is not the case with either second-degree or third-degree price discrimination.

Second-degree price discrimination

In the case where the market contains a number of consumers with different demand functions (or differences in willingness to pay), first-degree price discrimination requires the monopolist to be able to sell to different consumers on different terms. However, while the monopolist may be aware that different consumers have different demand functions, the monopolist may have no practical method for distinguishing between individual consumers. How is the monopolist to tell which consumer has which demand function? The consumers themselves are not likely to be willing to reveal this information, since doing so enables the monopolist to extract all of their consumer surplus. In the case where the monopolist cannot distinguish between consumers, the best policy is to offer the same menu of prices and quantities to all consumers, and allow the consumers to self-select. In other words, the monopolist designs a menu of prices and quantities such that each consumer chooses a price–quantity combination that is optimal for the consumer, but which also allows the monopolist to discriminate profitably between consumers.

The two-part tariff that was discussed above can be used to implement a policy of **second-degree price discrimination**. Suppose there are two groups of consumers with different demand functions, and different price elasticities of demand. In Figure 10.2, Consumers 1 and 2 are representative consumers from each group (and for simplicity we assume there are equal numbers of consumers in each group). Consumer 2 buys more units than Consumer 1 at any price, and at any given price Consumer 2 has a higher price elasticity of demand than Consumer 1. For simplicity, we assume the maximum price any consumer is prepared to pay is the same for both groups: in other words, the demand functions of Consumers 1 and 2 touch the vertical axis at the same point. With a policy of first-degree price discrimination, the monopolist would set a fixed fee of P_CAF for Consumer 1; a fixed fee of P_CAG for Consumer 2; and a uniform price of P_C per unit purchased for both consumers. For second-degree price discrimination, however, the monopolist must offer both consumers the same menu of prices. Suppose the monopolist continues with the uniform price of P_C per unit. Which fixed fee should the monopolist set?

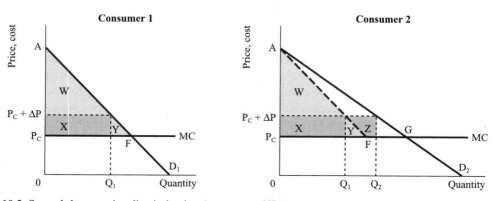

Figure 10.2 Second-degree price discrimination (two-part tariff)

- If the fixed fee is set at the larger value of P_CAG, the monopolist extracts all of Consumer 2's surplus, but Consumer 1 drops out of the market altogether, and the monopolist fails to extract any surplus from Consumer 1.

- On the other hand, if the fixed fee is set at the smaller value of P_CAF, the monopolist extracts all of Consumer 1's surplus and extracts the same amount of surplus from Consumer 2, but fails to extract FAG of Consumer 2's surplus.

In fact, it can be shown that in some cases neither of these two options is optimal for the monopolist. Suppose the second of the two options is preferred to the first and the monopolist chooses to supply to both consumers (in which case $2P_CAF > P_CAG$). Using Figure 10.2, we can show that the monopolist can earn a producer surplus higher than $2P_CAF$ by setting a fixed fee slightly lower than P_CAF, and charging a uniform price per unit slightly higher than P_C. Suppose the monopolist increases the price per unit from P_C to $P_C + \Delta P$. In order for Consumer 1 to remain in the market, the fixed fee must be reduced from area $W + X + Y$ ($= P_CAF$) to area W. Consumer 1 purchases Q_1 units, and the producer surplus earned from Consumer 1 is $W + X$. Previously the producer surplus earned from Consumer 1 was $W + X + Y$. Therefore the producer loses Y from Consumer 1. However, Consumer 2 purchases Q_2 units, and the producer surplus earned from Consumer 2 is $W + X + Y + Z$. Previously the producer surplus earned from Consumer 2 was $W + X + Y$. Therefore the producer gains Z from Consumer 2. By construction, area Z exceeds area Y. This ensures the monopolist gains overall by increasing the price per unit from P_C to $P_C + \Delta P$, and by reducing the fixed fee from $W + X + Y$ to W.

The analysis illustrated in Figure 10.2 establishes that in the case where it is profitable for the monopolist to supply both consumers, the optimal two-part tariff includes a uniform price that is set at a level higher than the monopolist's marginal cost. The precise determination of the optimal two-part tariff is a rather complex mathematical problem, and is beyond the scope of this book. The complexity is even greater in the more realistic case in which there is a large number of consumer types, each with their own demand functions. However, one important result is that with second-degree price discrimination, the monopolist cannot extract as much surplus as is possible with a policy of first-degree price discrimination. In Figure 10.2, if the monopolist sets a uniform menu of prices which does not vary between the two consumers, no uniform two-part tariff will enable the monopolist to extract a surplus as large as $P_CAF + P_CAG$. It is natural to expect that a policy of first-degree price discrimination, which is based on perfect information about consumers' preferences, is more profitable than second-degree price discrimination, which is based on imperfect information.

Third-degree price discrimination

In the case of second-degree price discrimination, the monopolist cannot segment the market by distinguishing between consumers, and must offer the same menu of prices to each consumer. However, the menu of prices is constructed in such a way that the price per unit that each consumer pays depends on the number of units purchased. This is true even in the case of the two-part tariff: if a larger quantity is purchased, the average price per unit is lower because the fixed fee is spread over a larger number of units. In contrast, with a policy of **third-degree price discrimination**, the price per unit that each consumer pays is constant, but the monopolist can segment the market by offering different prices to different consumers.

As we have argued above, in practice the monopolist is unlikely to have sufficient information to achieve complete market segmentation, since this would require perfect information about each consumer's individual demand function. However, partial market segmentation may be achieved quite easily in cases where consumers can be divided into groups based on easily identifiable characteristics, such as age or membership of particular groups such as students or pensioners. For market segmentation based on characteristics such as these to be effective, the nature of the individual's demand function must be correlated with the identifying characteristic. This condition is often satisfied. A child's demand for admission to a cinema is likely to be more price elastic than that of an adult. A pensioner's demand for bus travel, or a student's demand for a newspaper, is probably more price elastic than that of other adults.

Therefore with third-degree price discrimination, the monopolist segments the market into groups; charges the same price per unit sold within each group; but charges different prices to members of different groups. Figure 10.3 illustrates the case where there are two groups of consumers. As before, consumers 1 and 2, shown in the two left-hand diagrams, are representative consumers from each group. We assume consumer 2's demand is more price elastic than that of consumer 1. Since the price must be uniform within each sub-market but the sub-markets are perfectly segmented, it turns out that the monopolist's optimal pricing policy is to operate as a monopoly supplier to each sub-market. The monopolist should select the price–quantity combination for each sub-market at which the sub-market's marginal revenue *equals* the monopolist's marginal cost. Therefore in Figure 10.3, the monopolist charges a relatively high price of P_1 to consumer 1 whose demand is price inelastic, and a relatively low price of P_2 to consumer 2 whose demand is price elastic. For reference, in Figure 10.3 the right-hand diagram shows the market demand function (obtained by summing the consumers' individual demand functions horizontally), and the profit-maximizing price–quantity combination (P_M, Q_M) in the standard case where the monopolist charges a uniform price to all consumers.

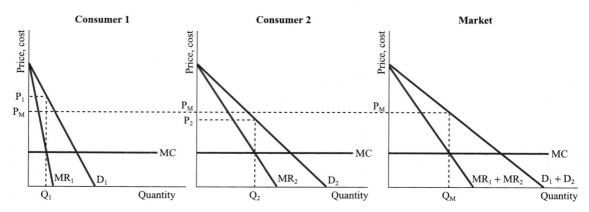

Figure 10.3 Third-degree price discrimination

Price discrimination in ticket price structures for English Premier League football

In Case study 2.2, it was shown that understanding the determinants of spectator demand is important to clubs when making decisions about stadium capacity and ticket pricing. In a survey of English Premier League football clubs carried out during the 1998–99 season, Clowes and Clements (2003) find clubs use a wide range of sophisticated ticket-pricing structures.

In accordance with the economic theory of price discrimination, several of these price structures are designed to extract more value from spectators with differing degrees of willingness-to-pay than would be possible with a uniform ticket price structure. Several examples can be found of both second-degree price discrimination (charging different prices depending on the number of matches attended) and third-degree price discrimination (charging different prices to different spectators or groups of spectators).

Season tickets

Buying an annual season ticket normally offers three benefits:

- A guaranteed seat for every home match.
- Priority allocation of tickets for away matches, cup finals, and so on.
- An effective discount on the price of buying tickets for each match individually (second-degree price discrimination).

In the 1998–99 survey, the size of the discount varied from zero to about 35 per cent. Two clubs charged season ticket premiums: a policy that might be justified in economic terms if the stadium is regularly filled to capacity.

Membership schemes

Membership schemes that require payment of a fixed membership fee, but then allow members to purchase match tickets at a discounted price, are a form of two-part tariff (second-degree price discrimination).

Some clubs run separate membership schemes for juniors, with separate prices. Some junior membership schemes give members the right to receive a package of 'free' merchandise.

Personal seat licence (PSL)

In the US, some major league teams charge a fee that guarantees the right to purchase a season ticket for a particular seat over the long term (20 or 30 years). PSLs typically lapse if the holder dies or fails to renew the season ticket (Sandy *et al.*, 2004). A PSL is also a form of two-part tariff (second-degree price discrimination).

In the US, PSLs are common among new (expansion) teams or teams that have relocated to a new city. Unsurprisingly the idea has been more difficult to sell to the existing season ticket holders of established teams. Several attempts to introduce similar schemes by English football clubs in the early 1990s were unpopular with spectators, and the idea failed to take off.

Price concessions

Price concessions to specific groups are a form of third-degree price discrimination. The 1998–99 survey found that all Premier League clubs that responded offered discounts on season tickets or match-day tickets (or both) to juniors, pensioners and people with disabilities. Some (but not all) clubs offered discounts to students and the unemployed. However, perhaps surprisingly only a small number of clubs offered discounts to family groups.

Price banding

In the 1998–99 survey, seven English Premier League clubs indicated that ticket prices were dependent on the attractiveness of the opposition, with home fixtures classified into two or three price bands.

This practice is consistent with profit maximization. If the PED (price elasticity of demand) is lower for a fixture against Manchester United than for a fixture against average Premier League opposition, the profit-maximizing club should charge a higher price for the more attractive fixture. This policy is not price discrimination, since different prices are charged for different matches with different characteristics.

Good and bad seats

Most English football clubs charge different prices for seats in different locations within the stadium. This policy is not price discrimination, since different prices are charged for what are essentially different products.

The demand functions for seats in different locations are likely to be interdependent:

■ If the club sets too large a price differential, there is likely to be excess demand for the cheaper seats.
■ If the price differential is too small, demand will tend to switch towards the dearer seats.

Most clubs tend to rely on experience or trial-and-error in order to determine the most appropriate price differential.

Price bundling

In the 1998–99 survey, eight English Premier League clubs operated a policy of bundling. Either tickets for two or more matches must be bought simultaneously; or proof of purchase of a ticket for one match is required to purchase a ticket for another match.

A common practice is to bundle a sell-out match together with a match that is unlikely to sell out. Bundling is also justified as an attempt to reduce the possibility of away supporters of popular teams purchasing tickets in the home sections of the stadium.

Source: Clowes, J. and Clements, N. (2003) An examination of discriminatory ticket pricing practice in the English football Premier League, *Managing Leisure*, 8, 105–20.

It is not possible to draw many general conclusions about the welfare effects of third-degree price discrimination (Layson, 1994). In comparison with the non-discriminating case (where the monopolist charges a uniform price to all consumers regardless of sub-group membership) the sum of producer surplus and consumer surplus may be higher, lower or the same, depending on the exact positions of the sub-market demand functions. However, two unequivocal conclusions can be drawn. First, the monopolist's abnormal profit (producer surplus) is always higher in the case of third-degree price discrimination than in the non-discriminating case (Yamey, 1974). The monopolist does not segment the market and charge different prices to different sub-markets unless it is profitable to do so. Second, in the case where there are two sub-markets, one price will always be higher and the other price lower than the uniform monopoly price in the non-discriminating case. Consumers in the sub-market with the higher price have less consumer surplus and are always worse off than in the non-discriminating case; conversely, consumers in the sub-market with the lower price have more consumer surplus and are always better off than in the non-discriminating case. Appendix 1 contains a mathematical derivation of profit maximization under third-degree price discrimination.

Examples of price discrimination

Section 10.2 concludes by identifying a number of examples of price discrimination other than those that have been discussed previously in this section.

Intertemporal price discrimination

With **intertemporal price discrimination**, the supplier segments the market by the point in time at which the product is purchased by different groups of consumers. Video games, mobile phone handsets, books, CDs and DVDs are examples of goods that are often more expensive if they are purchased sooner, but cheaper for consumers who are prepared to delay purchase. In the case of books, there is a physical difference between the expensive hardback edition that is available when the book is first published, and the cheaper paperback edition that appears several months later. However, the retail price differential is usually much larger than the difference in production costs between hardbacks and paperbacks. Therefore despite the physical difference, this case conforms to the model of intertemporal price discrimination. Case study 10.2 describes an empirical study of intertemporal price discrimination in the book publishing industry.

Figure 10.4 shows the market demand function in the case where there is a large number of consumers, each of whom either buys one unit of the good, or abstains from buying altogether (as in Figure 10.1). Each consumer's reservation price is the maximum price the consumer is willing to pay, and as before we can imagine the consumers arrayed along the horizontal axis of Figure 10.4 in descending order of their reservation prices or willingness to pay. For the model of intertemporal price discrimination, we assume each consumer is willing to make his or her purchase in one of two time periods. Consumers who make a purchase in period 1 do not make a repeat purchase in period 2; but consumers who abstain from purchasing in period 1 (because the period 1 price exceeds their reservation price) still have the same reservation price in period 2. It is also assumed that consumers who purchased in period 1 do not subsequently resell to consumers who abstained from purchasing in period 1.

Intertemporal price discrimination by book publishers

Book publishing is often cited in the economics literature as an example of an industry that practices intertemporal price discrimination. Publishers divide consumers into submarkets based on their time preferences for the purchase of a given title. Consumers with a high willingness to pay (low price elasticity of demand) are prepared to buy the expensive hardback edition, available when the title is first published. Consumers with a low willingness to pay (high price elasticity of demand) are prepared to wait for the publication of the cheaper paperback edition, usually available between nine and 18 months after initial publication.

Clerides (2002) assesses these claims based on an analysis of price, cost and sales data for 1,108 titles published by Yale University Press over the period 1980–95. Around 50 per cent of the titles in the sample were not published in a paperback edition. A total of 136 titles were published in hardback and paperback editions simultaneously (SIM), while 434 were published sequentially as hardback and then paperback (SEQ). The hardback editions accounted for 12 per cent and 38 per cent of the total sales for SIM and SEQ, respectively. Evidence of price discrimination is collected in several stages, by investigating:

■ Price spreads between hardback and paperback editions for both SIM and SEQ titles.

■ Cost differentials between hardback and paperback editions.

■ Differences in price–cost margins between hardback and paperback editions.

Price spreads

Theory suggests the price differential between the hardback and paperback editions of SIM titles should be smaller than the equivalent differential for SEQ titles. However, this turns out not to be the case. For SIM titles, average prices were US$46.11 (hardback) and US$20.11 (paperback). For SEQ titles, the average prices were US$44.16 and US$19.52.

Cost differentials

Publishers sometimes justify the higher prices charged for hardback editions on the basis of costs. Clerides estimates fixed costs at US$5,182 per title. Fixed costs account for around one-third of total production costs on average. Marginal costs (per unit) are estimated as $2.95 for a hardback and $1.74 for a paperback. The marginal cost differential is mainly due to the higher cost of binding a hardback.

Differences in price–cost margins

To test for price discrimination, price and cost data are combined to construct price–cost margins for a subsample of 73 titles published in both hardback and paperback editions. A simple indicator of price discrimination is $P_{hardback} - MC_{hardback} > P_{paperback} - MC_{paperback}$. For all but five of the 73 titles, the hardback price–cost margin was larger than the paperback price–cost margin, and in tests the difference between the price–cost margins was found to be statistically significant. This is interpreted as evidence that price discrimination is practised by book publishers.

Source: Clerides, S.K. (2002) Book value: intertemporal pricing and quality discrimination in the US market for books, *International Journal of Industrial Organization*, 20, 1385–1408.

For simplicity, in Figure 10.4 we assume a monopoly supplier with a constant marginal cost function. In period 1, the monopolist's profit-maximizing price and output combination is (P_1, Q_1). However, under the conditions outlined above, in period 2 the monopolist effectively faces a residual demand function comprising all consumers whose reservation price is below P_1, equivalent to the triangle Q_1AB. MR_2 is the marginal revenue function associated with the residual demand function, and in period 2 the profit-maximizing price and output combination is $(P_2, Q_2 - Q_1)$. The $Q_2 - Q_1$ consumers who purchase in period 2 pay a lower price than the Q_1 consumers who purchase in period 1. If the model were extended over further periods with similar assumptions, more consumers (to the right of Q_2) could be induced to make purchases by means of further price cuts.

Coase (1972) points out that the ability of a monopolist to practise intertemporal price discrimination may be limited by strategic behaviour on the part of consumers.

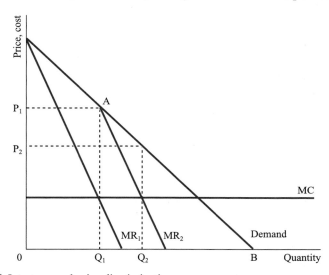

Figure 10.4 Intertemporal price discrimination

If the monopolist acquires a reputation for price-cutting, even those consumers with a high willingness to pay may decide to delay their consumption, so as to obtain an increased surplus by purchasing at the reduced price at a later date. The extent to which consumers are prepared to do so depends on the durability of the good (is it worth the same tomorrow as it is worth today?) and the discount rate consumers use to evaluate the present value of future consumption. In an extreme case in which the good is perfectly durable and the discount rate is zero (consumers are indifferent between present and future consumption), the monopolist is forced to charge the competitive price in all periods. Anticipating the monopolist will eventually reduce the price to the perfectly competitive level, all consumers decide to delay purchase rather than pay more than the perfectly competitive price. This forces the monopolist to charge the perfectly competitive price from the outset.

Brand labels

The practice of charging different prices for similar or identical goods differentiated solely by a brand label can be interpreted as a form of price discrimination. In supermarkets, value brands sell at a substantial discount relative to the brands of recognized manufacturers, even though in some cases the difference in quality is small or non-existent. In the clothing market, some consumers are willing to pay £20 or £30 more for a small badge or emblem sewn onto an otherwise identical T-shirt or pair of jeans. But it can be argued that branding does not conform to the model of price discrimination, because the status or prestige conferred by the purchase or ownership of the branded product should be recognized as a genuine product characteristic, for which suppliers of branded products are entitled to charge if consumers are willing to pay.

Loyalty discounts

Major airlines offering airmiles schemes that can be used by frequent travellers to earn free tickets, practise a form of second-degree price discrimination. Consumers who travel frequently pay a lower average price per journey than consumers who make only single or occasional journeys. Many airlines allow airmiles to be earned from purchases of other products, making it possible to travel without ever paying directly for a ticket. Supermarkets such as Tesco, which operate loyalty or bonus points schemes providing coupons or rebates to regular customers, operate a similar form of second-degree price discrimination.

Coupons

Some retailers supply coupons that provide price discounts, perhaps through advertisements printed in the newspapers or through leaflets delivered directly to people's homes. In principle the price discount is available to any consumer, but in practice only those consumers willing to spend the time and make the effort required to cut out, retain and present the coupon will obtain the discount. This practice can be interpreted as a form of price discrimination, favouring those consumers with more time or lower opportunity costs, who are prepared to make the effort to collect and present the coupon.

Stock clearance

A department store that conducts a sale in which the price of merchandise is successively reduced until all sale items have been purchased exercises a form of price discrimination, if this practice results in different consumers paying different prices on different days for identical goods. This pricing practice can be interpreted as a form of intertemporal price discrimination (see pp. 367–70). For a single item that is successively reduced in price until it is eventually sold, this procedure for finding a buyer is known as a Dutch auction. The theory and practice of auctions is discussed in Chapter 11.

Free-on-board pricing

In some markets, producers or distributors absorb transport costs, so that all buyers within a specific geographic area (country or region) pay a uniform price, despite the variation in transport costs within this area. This pricing system is known as free-on-board pricing. Ironically, even though all prices are the same, free-on-board pricing is a form of price discrimination, which favours buyers in the more remote locations where transport costs are higher. The difference in costs means these buyers should pay more. Therefore the policy of charging the same price is a form of price discrimination. From the point of view of suppliers, a uniform pricing policy may be attractive because by eliminating price discrepancies it reduces the risk that price competition may break out among suppliers. Free-on-board pricing removes any temptation for an individual supplier to implement a price cut, which might be justified to competitors on grounds of reduced transport costs, but might actually be motivated by an attempt to capture an increased market share.

10.4　Peak-load pricing

In some markets, demand varies at different times of the day or on different days of the year. Examples of products or services for which demand is variable include gas and electricity; public transport services; roads, tunnels and bridges; gyms and fitness clubs; package holidays and amusement parks. In each of these cases, it is unlikely the supplier can adjust capacity to meet the higher level of demand in peak periods, or reduce capacity in response to the lower level of demand in off-peak periods. Furthermore, none of these products or services is storable. It is not possible for consumers to build up stocks during off-peak periods, and then run these stocks down during peak periods. Under such conditions, the supplier faces a **peak-load pricing** problem. Specifically, two issues need to be addressed: first, what level of capacity should be installed; and second, for any given capacity what are the optimal peak period and off-peak period prices.

In order to develop a model to address these questions, it is assumed there are separate peak period and off-peak period market demand functions, denoted D_1 and D_2 respectively. In Figure 10.5, it is assumed these two demand functions are completely independent of one another: purchases made in one period do not in any way affect demand in the other period. Capacity can be installed and maintained at

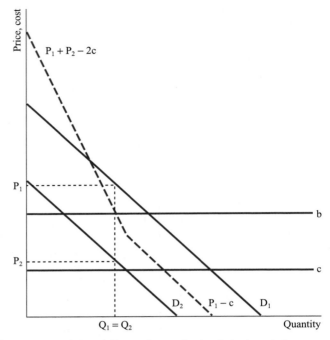

Figure 10.5 Peak-load pricing: full capacity production in both periods

a constant marginal cost per unit of capacity of b, which allows the industry to operate in both the peak period and the off-peak period. Production costs in each period are directly proportional to output, so there is also a constant marginal production cost of c per unit of output.

In many countries, some (although not all) of the industries that are subject to the peak-load problem are either in state ownership, or in private ownership but heavily regulated. Accordingly, much of the theoretical literature on peak-load pricing is based on an assumption of social welfare maximization, rather than profit maximization. As we have seen in Section 2.5, the standard condition for social welfare maximization is price *equals* marginal cost. In the present case, this condition needs to be amended, because for each additional unit of capacity that is installed, one additional unit of output can be produced and sold in each of the two periods, at different prices. If the industry operates at full capacity in both periods, the equivalent condition for social welfare maximization is:

$$P_1 + P_2 = b + 2c$$
$$\text{or} \quad P_1 + P_2 - 2c = b$$
$$\text{or} \quad P_1 = b + 2c - P_2 \text{ and } P_2 = b + 2c - P_1$$

In these expressions, P_1 and P_2 are the prices charged per unit of output in the peak period and off-peak period, respectively. The first of the three expressions says the total proceeds obtained by creating an additional unit of capacity enabling the industry to produce and sell one additional unit of output in both periods, $P_1 + P_2$, *equals* the marginal cost of installing the additional capacity, b, *plus* the marginal production cost for the two additional units of output, 2c. The second expression is a rearrangement of the first, used to identify the optimal prices and capacity in Figure 10.5. The third expression says the optimal price for each period is the total marginal cost incurred through the installation of additional capacity and the additional production in both periods, b + 2c, *minus* the price charged in the other period.

In Figure 10.5, the dotted line shows, for each per-period output level shown on the horizontal axis, the value of $P_1 + P_2 - 2c$ implied by the two market demand functions. Over the range of output levels where $P_1 > c$ and $P_2 > c$, the dotted line is constructed by summing the two demand functions vertically, and subtracting 2c. Over the range of outputs where $P_1 > c > P_2$, the dotted line is $P_1 - c$. According to the expressions for social welfare maximization, in Figure 10.5 the optimal capacity is $Q_1 = Q_2$, and the optimal values of P_1 and P_2 are obtained from the peak and off-peak demand functions (D_1 and D_2 respectively) at this point. The peak-period consumers, whose demand or willingness to pay is stronger, are charged a higher price than the off-peak consumers. However, the willingness to pay of consumers in both periods is taken into account in determining the optimal capacity, because the system operates at full capacity in both periods.

It need not always be the case that the industry operates at full capacity in both periods. If the marginal cost of installing additional capacity were lower than is shown in Figure 10.5, it might be optimal (again in terms of social welfare maximization) to operate at full capacity during the peak period, but to maintain some spare capacity in the off-peak period. This case is shown in Figure 10.6, in which the marginal cost of installing additional capacity is lowered from b to b'. For the peak

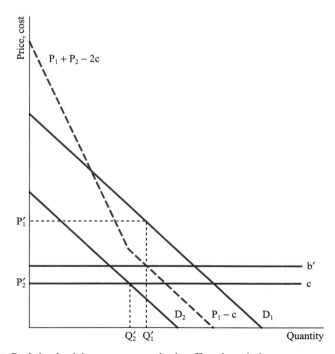

Figure 10.6 Peak-load pricing: spare capacity in off-peak period

period, it is now worthwhile to install capacity of Q_1', and sell Q_1' units of output for a price of $P_1' = b' + c$. For the off-peak period, however, if Q_1' units of output were produced, the price would fall below the marginal production cost of c. In the off-peak period, the industry should operate below full capacity, and sell Q_2' units of output for a price of $P_2' = c$. In this case, the willingness to pay of the off-peak consumers becomes irrelevant in determining the optimal capacity, because the system only operates at capacity during the peak period.

10.5 Transfer pricing

The multi-divisional or M-form organizational structure, and the holding company or H-form structure (see Section 3.6) can raise particularly difficult issues for managers when taking pricing and production decisions. It is often the case that one division will use the output of another division as one of its inputs. In the simplest case, an M-form or H-form organization might include quasi-independent production and distribution divisions. The distribution division buys the output of the production division, and sells the product to the final consumer. The question immediately arises, at what price should the trade take place between the production division and the distribution division? In general, the M-form or H-form organization requires a system of **transfer pricing** to determine the prices of intermediate products that are produced by one divison and sold to another division, when both divisions form part of the same organization (Hirschleifer, 1956).

In M-form or H-form organizations where the individual divisions are quasi-independent, the choice of transfer price can be a crucial decision, because it affects the imputed revenues of the selling division, the imputed costs of the buying division, and therefore the imputed profitability of both divisions. For example, if the transfer price is set too low, the imputed profits of the distribution division are articificially inflated, and the profits of the production division are artificially depressed. This may have implications for head office's perceptions of managerial performance or labour productivity in both divisions, which in turn may affect future investment or other internal resource allocation decisions (Eccles, 1985). Moreover, suppose the divisional managers are encouraged to operate in such a way as to minimize costs or maximize profits at divisional level. Through its effect on the divisional revenue and cost functions, the transfer price affects the divisional managers' production decisions, the volume of internal trade, the quantity of inputs purchased from outside the firm or the quantity of intermediate outputs sold outside the firm, and therefore the profitability of the firm as a whole. As we shall see below, when there is internal trade within the organization, decisions taken at divisional level with a view to the maximization of divisional profits do not necessarily ensure the maximization of the total profit of the firm as a whole. Case study 10.2 provides an application.

Below, we develop profit-maximizing models of transfer pricing between the production and distribution divisions of an M-form organization, for the following three cases:

- In the first case, it is assumed all of the production division's output is passed on to the distribution division to be sold to final consumers. There is no alternative, external market in which the production division can sell its intermediate output. Similarly, the distribution division obtains its supplies only from the production division, and has no alternative external sources.

- In the second case, it is assumed there is a perfectly competitive external market, in which the production division can sell any surplus intermediate output that is not taken up by the distribution division. Similarly, the distribution division has the option of obtaining additional supplies (over and above those it obtains from the production division) through the external market.

- In the third case, it is assumed the external market for the intermediate product is imperfectly competitive rather than perfectly competitive.

Transfer pricing with no external market for the intermediate product

Figure 10.7 presents a model of transfer pricing for trade between a production division (producer) and a distribution division (distributor) in the simplest case where there is no external market for the internally transferred product. In the left-hand diagram, MC_1 represents the producer's marginal cost function, and in the right-hand diagram D_2 and MR_2 represent the distributor's demand and marginal revenue functions. MC_2 is the marginal cost function associated with the distributor's own activities (excluding the cost of the units of output the distributor must purchase from the producer).

Suppose initially the distributor sets the transfer price, and the producer follows price-taking behaviour in respect of this price. The distributor knows the chosen transfer price will be treated by the producer as the latter's marginal revenue function, and the producer will choose the output level at which the transfer price *equals* the producer's marginal cost, MC_1. In order to maximize the profit of the firm as a whole,

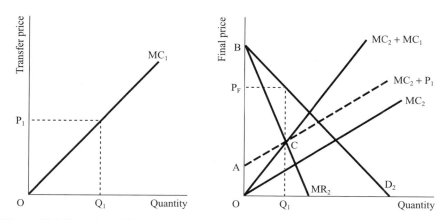

Figure 10.7 Transfer pricing: no external market for intermediate product

the distributor should operate as if its total marginal cost function is $MC_2 + MC_1$, obtained by adding the value of MC_1 at each output level vertically onto MC_2. The distributor chooses the output level Q_1 at which $MC_2 + MC_1 = MR_2$. This determines the transfer price P_1, which induces the producer to produce Q_1 units of output. The distributor sells the product to the final consumers at a price of P_F.

Suppose instead the producer sets the transfer price, and the distributor follows price-taking behaviour. In this case, the same result is obtained. The distributor's total marginal cost function is $MC_2 + P$, where P is the transfer price chosen by the producer. The producer knows that for any value of P the producer chooses, the distributor is willing to purchase the output level at which $MC_2 + P = MR_2$. In order to maximize the profit of the firm as a whole, the producer should set a transfer price of P_1, as before.

In both cases, P_1 is the transfer price that maximizes the firm's total profit. In Figure 10.7, the area OBC represents the firm's total profit; OAC represents the profit imputed to the producer; and ABC represents the profit imputed to the distributor. However, it is interesting to note that a transfer price of P_1 does not maximize the profits of either the producer or the distributor individually. In the case where the distributor sets the transfer price, the distributor maximizes its own profit by choosing the output level at which the distributor's marginal outlay function *equals* MR_2 (see Figure 10.8). The distributor's marginal outlay function is steeper than $MC_2 + MC_1$, because it takes into account the fact that for each extra unit the distributor buys from the producer, the distributor pays not only the producer's marginal cost of producing that unit, but also an increased transfer price over all the other units the distributor was already buying. It would be in the distributor's private interest to buy a smaller quantity Q_1' at a lower transfer price of P_2, increasing the distributor's imputed profit from ABC to A'BDE in Figure 10.8. The producer's imputed profit falls from OAC to OA'E, and the firm's total profit falls from OBC to OBDE.

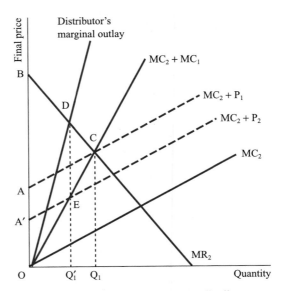

Figure 10.8 Transfer pricing: profit maximization for the distributor

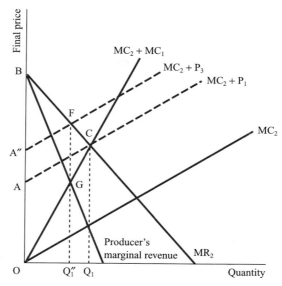

Figure 10.9 Transfer pricing: profit maximization for the producer

Similarly, in the case where the producer sets the transfer price, the producer maximizes its own profit by choosing the ouput level at which the producer's marginal revenue function *equals* $MC_2 + MC_1$. The producer's marginal revenue function takes account of the fact that at very low output levels, the distributor would be willing to pay a high transfer price, but as the output level increases, the transfer price is reduced not only on the most marginal unit bought, but also over all the other units the distributor was already buying (see Figure 10.9). It would be in the producer's private interest to supply a smaller quantity Q_1'' at a higher transfer price of P_3, increasing the producer's imputed profit from OAC to OA''FG in Figure 10.9. The distributor's imputed profit falls from ABC to A''BF, and the firm's total profit falls from OBC to OBFG.

Transfer pricing with a perfectly competitive external market for the intermediate product

Some intermediate products may be traded between the divisions of an M-form or H-form firm, but may also be traded between the production divisions and external buyers from outside the firm. For example, a car manufacturer might be one division of an M-form organization, which includes a separate tyre manufacturing division. The latter sells tyres not only to the car manufacturing division, but also externally to garages and car repair shops, or direct to consumers. There are many other tyre manufacturers, so the external market for tyres is highly competitive. Returning to our previous case of the production division and distribution division, if the external market is perfectly competitive the production division has the option to sell as much of the intermediate commodity as it likes on the external market at the perfectly competitive price. Similarly, the distribution division has the option to buy as much of the intermediate commodity as it likes, again at the perfectly competitive price.

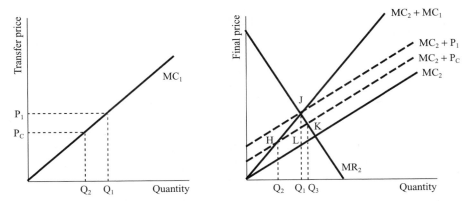

Figure 10.10 Transfer pricing: perfectly competitive external market (price below P_1)

Under these circumstances, the transfer price is effectively constrained to be equal to the perfectly competitive price. If the transfer price were higher than the competitive price, the distributor would prefer to make all of its purchases of the intermediate commodity on the external market; and if the transfer price were lower than the competitive price, the producer would prefer to sell all of its output on the external market. However, it is also likely that the quantity of internal trade and the quantity of production will diverge, with external trade accounting for the difference between the two. Figures 10.10 and 10.11 illustrate two possible cases.

First, in Figure 10.10 the perfectly competitive price P_C is lower than P_1 in Figure 10.7. The distributor's total marginal cost function is $MC_2 + P_C$, and the distributor selects the quantity Q_3 at which $MC_2 + P_C = MR_2$. At a price of P_C, the producer is willing to supply only Q_2 units. The distributor purchases the additional $Q_3 - Q_2$ units on the external market. In comparison with the case where the transfer price is P_1 and Q_1 units are traded, the triangle HJL represents the cost saving to the firm resulting from buying $Q_1 - Q_2$ units of the intermediate commodity on the external

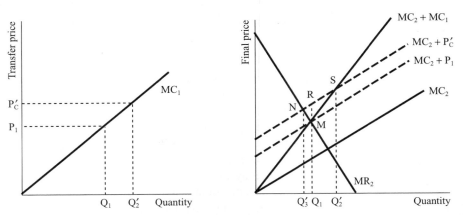

Figure 10.11 Transfer pricing: perfectly competitive external market (price above P_1)

market rather than producing these units internally, and LJK represents the additional profit earned because the distributor's total output increases from Q_1 to Q_3 (with the extra $Q_3 - Q_1$ units also purchased on the external market).

Second, in Figure 10.11 the perfectly competitive price P'_C is higher than P_1 in Figure 10.7. The distributor's total marginal cost function is $MC_2 + P'_C$, and the distributor selects the quantity Q'_3 at which $MC_2 + P'_C = MR_2$. At a price of P'_C, the producer wishes to supply Q'_2 units. The producer sells the additional $Q'_2 - Q'_3$ units on the external market. In comparison with the case where the transfer price is P_1 and Q_1 units are traded, the triangle NRM represents the extra profit to the firm resulting from selling $Q_1 - Q'_3$ units of the intermediate commodity on the external market rather than internally, and MRS represents the additional profit earned because the producer's output increases from Q_1 to Q'_2.

The analysis shown in Figures 10.10 and 10.11 suggests that if a competitive external market exists, the firm should participate in this market. It is damaging to the firm's interests to insist that all units of the intermediate commodity used by the distributor are produced internally, if the commodity can be purchased more cheaply on the external market. And it is equally damaging to insist that the producer can only sell the intermediate commodity to the distributor, if the commodity can be produced and sold more profitably on the external market. By participating in the external market, in both cases the firm achieves an increase in its total profit. Of course, these conclusions could change if the firm had some other strategic motive for non-participation in the external market. For example, the firm might not wish to purchase externally because it seeks to prevent a competitor from selling its output, hoping to force the competitor to exit from the production industry; or similarly, the firm might not wish to sell externally because it seeks to prevent a competitor from gaining access to supplies of the intermediate commodity, hoping to force the competitor to exit from the distribution industry.

Transfer pricing with an imperfectly competitive external market for the intermediate product

A further possibility is that the intermediate product may be traded not only between the divisions of an M-form or H-form firm, but also between the production division and one or more external buyers in an imperfectly competitive market. A car manufacturer might be one division of an M-form organization, which buys inputs from a separate division which manufactures specialized electrical components. There are very few other manufacturers of similar components, so the external market for components is imperfectly competitive.

Returning to our theoretical model, with an imperfectly competitive external market, the transfer price for internal trade between the production and distribution divisions differs from the price paid by buyers in the external market. In Figure 10.12, the analysis is restricted to the case where the transfer price, denoted P_4, turns out to be higher than P_1 in Figure 10.7. This means the producer's output of Q_5 is larger than the distributor's output of Q_4, and the producer sells the surplus output of $Q_5 - Q_4$ in the imperfectly competitive external market for the intermediate product. The two left-hand diagrams in Figure 10.12 are constructed in the same way as before. The right-hand diagram shows the producer's demand function and marginal revenue

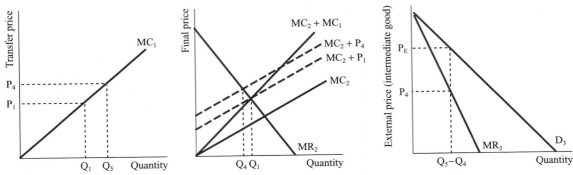

Figure 10.12 Transfer pricing: imperfectly competitive external market (price above P_1)

function in the external market, denoted D_3 and MR_3 respectively. The optimal transfer price of P_4 is the only value that satisfies the following conditions:

■ At the producer's total output level of Q_5, the producer's marginal cost *equals* the transfer price, or $MC_1 = P_4$.

■ At the transfer price of P_4, the distributor's total marginal cost *equals* the distributor's marginal revenue, or $MC_2 + P_4 = MR_2$, yielding an output level for the distributor of Q_4.

■ When the surplus intermediate output of $Q_5 - Q_4$ is sold in the external market, the producer's marginal revenue in the external market *equals* the transfer price, or $MR_3 = P_4$. The producer's selling price in the external market is P_E, which is higher than the transfer price of P_4. Effectively, the producer practices third-degree price discrimination (see Section 10.2), by charging different prices in the segmented internal and external markets for the intermediate output.

Transfer pricing: some implications

The analysis in Section 10.5 has shown that the imputed profitability of each division is not the same as the contribution of each division to the profitability of the firm as a whole. There are several implications.

■ The rewards and incentives for divisional managers should not be based solely on the imputed profitability of their own divisions, but should reflect the implications of their decisions for the profitability of the firm as a whole. If divisional managers seek to maximize the imputed profitability of their own divisions, in the case where there is no external market for the intermediate product a situation of bilateral monopoly exists. The distributor would prefer to use its monopsony power (as sole buyer) to reduce output and reduce the transfer price (see Figure 10.8), while the producer would prefer to use its monopoly power (as sole producer) to reduce output and increase the transfer price (see Figure 10.9). However, both of these outcomes reduce the profitability of the firm as a whole.

■ Strategic decisions concerning the closure of (imputed) loss-making divisions or the expansion of profitable divisions should take account of the implications for the profitability of the firm as a whole. For example, the firm as a whole does not benefit from the closure of a loss-making production division if this decision reduces the profitability of the distribution division by more than the direct saving achieved by not producing the intermediate product in-house. If there are significant transaction costs associated with buying or selling on the external market, these should also be taken into account when assessing the viability of (imputed) loss-making divisions.

Tax avoidance through transfer pricing

Professor Prem Sikka of the University of Essex, writing in *The Guardian* (30 June 2003), identified ways in which some large multinational companies avoid taxes by deliberately overpricing inputs (imports) from their foreign upstream activities, or underpricing outputs (exports) destined for their downstream activities abroad. Through such transfer pricing practices, vertically integrated multinationals can shift profits to subsidiaries in countries with low corporate tax rates.

Professor Sikka found the following transfer prices charged by some US multinationals. Overpriced imports included:

Czech plastic buckets at US$972.98 each;
Canadian fence posts at US$1.853.50 each;
Chinese toilet paper at US$4,121.81 per kilo;
Israeli apple juice at US$2,052 per litre;
Trinidadian ballpoint pens at US$8,500 each; and
Japanese tweezers at US$4,896 each.

Underpriced exports included:

A toilet bowl and tank to Hong Kong for US$1.75;
Prefabricated buildings to Trinidad for US$1.20 each;
Bulldozers to Venezuela for US$387.83 each; and
Missile and rocket launchers to Israel for US$52.03 each!

These practices have a dramatic impact in reducing company tax liabilities. Professor Sikka cited the following example. A UK subsidiary produces a bulldozer at a cost of £27,000, but sells it to a downstream subsidiary in Venezuela (for example) for £300. The Venezuelan plant sells the bulldozer at the market price of £60,000. The UK subsidiary records a loss and pays no corporation tax, although the firm has made a global pre-tax profit of £33,000. The US Treasury has been estimated to have lost US$175 billion in tax revenues in this way over three years (2000, 2001 and 2002).

Source: The Guardian, 30 June 2003.

■ Transfer pricing is a particularly controversial topic in the case of multinational firms. The fact that decisions concerning transfer prices have implications for the profits imputed to each division within the firm provides strong incentives for firms to set their transfer prices in such a way as to shift profits towards divisions located in countries with low rates of corporation tax (tax on company profits). A multinational firm may therefore declare artificially high or low transfer prices, so that its profits are declared in a way that minimizes its overall corporation tax liability. The tax authorities may attempt to impose rules or controls on transfer pricing; for example, by insisting that transfer prices are comparable with prices at which the intermediate product can be traded on the external market. However, often such controls are easily circumvented, especially in developing countries where the influence of the tax authorities over the accounting practices of large foreign-owned multi-nationals may be weak.

10.6 Summary

One of the earliest attacks on the neoclassical theory of the firm questioned whether in practice firms have sufficient information to apply the profit-maximizing rule marginal revenue *equals* marginal cost when setting their prices. Cost plus pricing is an alternative pricing rule, whereby price is determined by adding a percentage mark-up to average variable cost. The mark-up includes a contribution towards fixed costs, and a profit margin. Under some conditions, the cost plus pricing method may be simpler and less demanding in terms of its informational requirements than profit-maximizing pricing. However, the advantages of cost plus pricing are only likely to materialize if the firm's costs are stable, and if average variable cost is constant over the relevant range of output levels. If the cost plus pricing firm always selects approximately the same profit margin as a profit-maximizing firm would achieve, cost plus pricing and profit maximization are equivalent. For this to be the case, the margin must be an inverse function of the firm's price elasticity of demand. Although the use of cost plus pricing is quite widely reported in the empirical literature on pricing, it could be that cost plus is just a convenient rule-of-thumb for firms that are really profit maximizers, even if they do not explicitly acknowledge this form of pricing behaviour.

Firms with a degree of market power need not always set uniform prices that are identical for all consumers, and identical no matter how many units of the product each consumer buys. With a policy of price discrimination, the firm might sell at different prices to different consumers, or make the price per unit each consumer pays dependent on the number of units purchased. For price discrimination to be possible, the firm must have market power, and the market must be divisible into sub-markets with different demand conditions, so that secondary trade or resale between consumers in different sub-markets is not possible.

There are three types of price discrimination.

■ First-degree price discrimination involves making the price per unit of output depend on the identity of the purchaser and on the number of units purchased. The monopolist exploits differences in consumers' willingness to pay, by charging each consumer his or her own reservation price for each individual unit purchased. First-degree price discrimination yields a higher abnormal profit than the standard case of profit maximization with a uniform price in monopoly, because all consumer surplus that exists in the standard case is converted into producer surplus, and deadweight loss is eliminated. The outcome under first-degree price discrimination is allocatively efficient, because price *equals* marginal cost for the most marginal unit produced and sold.

■ Second-degree price discrimination involves making the price per unit of output depend on the number of units purchased. The price does not depend on the identity of the purchaser. The monopolist designs a menu of prices and quantities such that each consumer chooses a price–quantity combination that allows the monopolist to discriminate profitably between consumers. A two-part tariff, requiring the payment of a fixed fee if the consumer wishes to make any purchases at all, plus an additional uniform price per unit purchased, is a form of second-degree price discrimination.

■ Third-degree price discrimination involves making the price per unit depend on the identity of the purchaser. The price does not depend on the number of units purchased. However, the monopolist is able to segment the market by offering different prices to different consumers. The monopolist charges a relatively high price to consumers whose demand is price inelastic, and a relatively low price to consumers whose demand is price elastic.

Forms of price discrimination used in practice include the following:

■ Intertemporal price discrimination, whereby the supplier segments the market by the point in time at which the product is purchased.

■ Branding, whereby different prices are charged for similar or identical goods differentiated solely by a brand label.

■ Loyalty discounts for regular customers, operated by airlines, supermarkets and other retailers.

■ Coupons that provide price discounts discriminate beween consumers on the basis of willingness to make the effort to claim the discount.

■ Stock clearance sales involving successive price reductions are a form of intertemporal price discrimination.

■ Free-on-board pricing involving the producer or distributor absorbing transport costs, and representing a form of price discrimination favouring buyers in locations where transport costs are higher.

In markets where demand varies at different times of the day or on different days of the year, but the supplier is unable to adjust capacity to meet the higher level of demand in peak periods (or reduce capacity in off-peak periods) the supplier faces a peak-load problem. If the levels of demand and costs are such that it is efficient to operate at full capacity in both periods, the social welfare maximizing price for each period is the marginal cost of installing an extra unit of capacity *plus* the marginal production cost in both periods *minus* the price charged in the other period. If it is efficient to operate at full capacity during the peak period, the willingness-to-pay of the off-peak consumers becomes irrelevant in determining the optimal capacity, because the system only operates at capacity during the peak period.

In multi-divisional organizations, the choice of transfer prices at which intermediate products are traded internally between divisions affects the imputed profitability of the divisions involved. Decisions taken at divisional level with a view to the maximization of divisional profits do not necessarily ensure the maximization of the total profit of the firm as a whole. In this chapter, profit-maximizing models of transfer pricing have been developed for the cases where there is no external market for the intermediate product; and where the intermediate product can be traded on an external market that is either perfectly competitive or imperfectly competitive. The analysis suggests incentives for divisional managers should not be based solely on imputed divisional profitability, but should reflect the profitability of the entire organization. Strategic decisions concerning the closure of (imputed) loss-making divisions should also take account of the implications for the profitability of the firm as a whole, including any additional transaction costs associated with trade on the external market that are not considered when calculating imputed divisional profits. The transfer pricing practices of multinational firms can raise particularly difficult policy issues in cases where firms use transfer pricing to minimize their corporation tax liabilities.

Discussion questions

1. For what reasons might a firm depart from a policy of pricing for profit maximization, and adopt a cost plus pricing formula instead? Under what conditions do these two pricing methods produce identical outcomes?

2. What conditions must be satisfied for a producer to be able to implement a policy of price discrimination?

3. Explain carefully the distinction between the three degrees of price discrimination.

4. In the case of a monopolist, why might a policy of first-degree price discrimination produce an outcome that is preferred on social welfare criteria to a policy of setting a uniform price in order to maximize profit?

5. With reference to Case study 10.1, examine the conditions under which intertemporal price discrimination might be a profitable pricing strategy.

6. Consider two medium-sized English Premier League football clubs, one of which has a small stadium, which is regularly filled to capacity, while the other has a larger stadium in which often there are many empty seats. In what ways might you expect the ticket price structures of these two clubs to differ? Your answer should refer to Case study 10.2.

7. Explain why economists have interpreted supermarket (or other retailer) loyalty cards as a form of second-degree price discrimination.

8. The demand for gas and electricity varies between different times of the day, and between different months of the year. What factors should be considered by a utility company when deciding how much capacity to install, and what prices to charge during peak and off-peak periods?

9. To maximize the aggregate profits of a multi-divisional firm, it is not sufficient to ask each division to attempt to maximize its own profit. Explain why not, and discuss the implications for corporate governance.

10. Explain how a multi-divisional firm should set its transfer price when there is an imperfectly competitive external market for the intermediate product.

11. With reference to Case study 10.3, explain how a multinational firm can use transfer pricing to minimize its tax exposure.

Further reading

Armstrong, M. (1999) Price discrimination by a many product firm, *Review of Economic Studies*, 66, 151–68.

Eccles, R. (1985) *The Transfer Pricing Problem*. Lexington, KY: D.C. Heath.

Marx, L.M. and Shaffer, G. (2004) Opportunism and menus of two-part tariffs, *International Journal of Industrial Organization*, 22, 1399–1414.

Nayle, T. (1984) Economic foundations of pricing, *Journal of Business*, 57, 23–39.

Phlips, L. (1983) *The Economics of Price Discrimination*. Cambridge: Cambridge University Press.

Stole, L. (2005) 'Price discrimination in competitive environments', in Armstrong, M. and Porter, R. (eds) *Handbook of Industrial Organization*, vol. 3. Elsevier Publishing. Forthcoming.

CHAPTER 11

Auctions

Learning objectives

This chapter covers the following topics:

- English and Dutch auctions, first and second price sealed bid auctions
- the pure common value model and the independent private values model
- the winner's curse
- optimal bidding strategies
- the seller's optimal reserve price, risk aversion, asymmetric bidders and affiliated valuations
- experimental and field evidence on buyer and seller behaviour in auctions

Key terms

Affiliated valuations model
Ascending bid auction
Descending bid auction
Dutch auction
English auction
First price sealed bid auction
Independent private values model

Pure common value model
Reserve price
Revenue equivalence theorem
Second price sealed bid auction
Vickrey auction
Winner's curse

11.1   Introduction

Goods have been bought and sold through auctions throughout history. The Romans, for example, auctioned slaves and property looted from their foreign conquests. Auctions are still used today for a wide variety of transactions in the modern-day economy. Houses, cars, paintings and antiques are commonly sold by auction, while farmers often use auctions to trade livestock and other agricultural produce. Governments commonly sell the rights to drill for oil or gas within a particular tract of land or sea by auction. In many countries, large sums have been raised in recent years from the auction of licences to operate mobile phone services. Governments also use auctions to sell treasury bills and other government securities. Government procurement contracts require contractors to submit tenders, with the lowest tender winning the right to become the supplier. The expansion of the internet has created new opportunities for trading by auction. For example, a huge variety and volume of goods are now traded on a daily basis through the eBay website. Even your local department store conducts a certain type of auction each time it announces a sale, in which the prices of sale items are successively reduced until all such items have been sold.

An auction is a market mechanism for converting bids from market participants into decisions concerning the allocation of resources and prices, through a specific set of rules. In general terms, auction theory raises a number of issues that we have already encountered in previous chapters. Specifically, auction theory is concerned with price formation under conditions of uncertainty, asymmetric information and interdependence. Auctions can be characterized by the rules for the submission of bids, for determining the identity of the winning bidder, and for determining the price the winning bidder pays. Section 11.2 describes the four basic auction formats, which provide the cornerstone for the economic theory of auctions, and which (subject to certain possible variations or embellishments) describe most auctions in practice. In auction theory, the assumptions concerning the way in which bidders assess the value of the item under auction turns out to be a crucial ingredient. Two polar cases, known as the **pure common value model** and the **independent private values model**, are introduced in this section.

Section 11.3 develops the pure common value model, in which bidders form individual estimates of the value of an item that has the same intrinsic value to all of them. This section introduces the phenomenon of the **winner's curse**: an apparent tendency for winning bidders in auctions requiring the submission of sealed bids to systematically overvalue the item in question, and consequently to overbid.

Section 11.4 considers optimal bidding strategies for all four basic auction formats, in the case where bidders form independent private valuations of the item under auction. A central result in auction theory, known as **revenue equivalence**, suggests that with the independent private values model, all four basic auction formats yield the same expected price to the seller.

Section 11.5 discusses a number of extensions to the basic theory covered in the two previous sections. These include the theory governing the seller's optimal choice of reserve price; risk aversion, which raises the possibility that in certain auctions bidders may bid more aggressively in order to improve their chances of winning; asymmetric bidders, who can be divided into different sub-groups with different average valuations of the item under auction; and the **affiliated valuations model**, in which bidders' valuations of the item under auction contain elements of both the pure common value and the independent private values models. Finally, Section 11.6 reviews some of the empirical evidence on buyer and seller behaviour in auctions. This review is subdivided into studies based on experimental evidence, and those based on field evidence.

11.2   Auction formats, and models of bidders' valuations

Section 11.2 introduces the four basic auction formats which provide the cornerstone for the economic theory of auctions. Also considered in this section are the assumptions that can be used to model the way in which bidders value the item under auction. Two polar cases, known as the pure common value model and the independent private values model, are considered. We begin, however, with a brief description of the four basic auction formats.

- The **English auction**, also known as the **ascending bid auction**, involves the price being set initially at a very low level which many bidders would be prepared to pay, and then raised successively until a level is reached which only one bidder is willing to pay. The last remaining bidder secures the item at the final price and the auction stops. This type of auction can be conducted by having the seller call out the prices continuously, with individual bidders withdrawing when the price reaches a level they are unwilling to pay, until only one bidder remains. Alternatively, the bidders themselves might be required to call out their bids; or the bids might be submitted electronically with the highest current bid posted. The English auction is widely used to sell items such as paintings, antiques and (sometimes) houses and cars. Over the years, its dramatic potential has also made it the favourite auction format of numerous movie directors.

- The **Dutch auction**, also known as the **descending bid auction**, works in the opposite way. The price is set initially at a very high level which no bidder would be prepared to pay, and is then lowered successively until a level is reached which one bidder is prepared to pay. The first bidder who is prepared to match the current price secures the item at that price, and the auction stops. The Dutch auction is used in a number of countries to sell agricultural produce, including tulips in the Netherlands (the source of the name Dutch auction).

- In the **first price sealed bid auction**, each bidder independently submits a single bid, without seeing the bids submitted by other bidders. The highest bidder secures the item, and pays a price equal to his or her winning bid. The first price sealed bid auction has been used by governments to sell drilling rights for oil and gas, and the rights to extract minerals from state owned land. Another example of this type of auction is the English Premier League's regular auctions of the live television broadcasting rights for Premier League football.

- The **second price sealed bid auction** is also sometimes known as a **Vickrey auction**, after the author of a seminal paper on auction theory (Vickrey, 1961). The bidding process works in the same manner as a first price sealed bid auction: each bidder independently and privately submits a single bid. Again, the highest bidder secures the item, but pays a price equal to the second-highest submitted bid. This format has a number of interesting theoretical properties, but it has only occasionally been used in practice.

Asymmetric information is a key element of most theoretical models of auctions. First, the seller typically does not have perfect information concerning the distribution of bidders' valuations of the item being auctioned. Second, the bidders themselves do not have perfect information about each others' valuations. The simplest theoretical models of auctions are based on two alternative assumptions concerning the distribution of bidders' valuations.

■ In the **pure common value model**, the item has a single, intrinsic value that is the same for all bidders. However, no single bidder knows what this true value is. On the basis of private information or signals that differ between bidders, each bidder makes an independent assessment or estimate of the item's true value. For example, in an auction for the drilling rights to an oilfield, there is a certain amount of oil under the ground which determines the intrinsic value of the rights, and this value might be considered identical by all oil firms. At the time the drilling rights are auctioned, no firm knows exactly how much oil is present, although each firm has made its own private assessment based on its own survey work. In this case, one bidder's private estimate of the value would be influenced by knowledge of the estimates of other bidders. For example, if firm A initially valued the rights at £100m, but subsequently discovered that nine other firms had each carried out a similar survey that valued the rights at less than £100m, firm A would probably conclude that its own survey was overoptimistic or inaccurate, and would revise its estimate downwards.

■ In the **independent private values model**, each bidder knows the true value of the item to himself or herself personally. However, personal valuations of the item differ between bidders, and there is no single, intrinsic value that all bidders can agree on. For example, my valuation of a painting might depend solely upon my personal appreciation of the item, and anyone else's opinion might be completely irrelevant to me in forming my personal valuation.

The pure common values model and the independent private values model can usefully be interpreted as theoretical, polar extremes. In practice, elements of both models may be required in order to represent the actual distribution of bidders' preferences. In the first example cited above, the value of the drilling rights might not be the same for all oil firms. Firm A might possess some specific assets (physical assets, or specialized or experienced labour) that are productive only in certain geological conditions, and which make these particular drilling rights of greater value to firm A than to any other oil firm. In the second example, your personal valuation of a painting might depend partly on your own personal tastes, but it might also depend partly on other people's tastes, which determine how much prestige you gain by becoming the painting's owner, or how much cash you expect to realize if you subsequently decide to sell. In such cases, it may be necessary to use a third model known as the **affiliated valuations model**, which includes elements of both the pure common value model and the independent private values model (Milgrom and Weber, 1982). Although the full details of the affiliated valuations model are beyond the scope of this text, this model is considered briefly in Section 11.5.

11.3 The pure common value model and the winner's curse

In this section, we examine some of the properties of auctions when there is a single, intrinsic value of the item being auctioned that is the same for all bidders, but which is unknown precisely to any individual bidder. As we have seen in Section 11.2, the auction of the drilling rights to a particular tract of land or sea provides a classic example of an auction that may conform to the pure common values model. A second example, which has been widely used in classroom or laboratory experiments, is as follows. Your lecturer brings a jar filled with penny coins into the classroom, and allows each student to take a quick look at the jar, which is sufficient for the student to form an estimate of the number of coins, but insufficient to count the number of coins precisely. The lecturer then auctions the jar. In this case, the jar has an intrinsic value (determined by the actual number of coins) which is unknown to any of the students but is the same for every student; and each student forms an imperfect estimate of this intrinsic value, which may turn out to be either too high or too low.

In a classic paper on auctions of oilfield drilling rights, Capen *et al.* (1971) identify a phenomenon known as the **winner's curse**, which appears to be a rather common feature of many auctions in which bidders' valuations conform to the pure common value model. In order to describe the winner's curse, we make the following assumptions:

■ The auction format is first price sealed bid. Only this auction format is considered in the current section. Detailed consideration is given to all four basic auction formats in the discussion of the independent private values model in Section 11.4; and in Section 11.5 some consideration is given to the other three auction formats in the case where bidders' valuations conform to the pure common value model.

■ Each bidder forms an unbiased private estimate of the true value of the item being auctioned. In other words, in any particular auction each bidder is equally likely to undervalue or overvalue the item, but if there were a large number of auctions no bidder would systematically overvalue or undervalue the items on average.

■ Each bidder submits a sealed bid that is strictly increasing relative to his or her own private estimate of the intrinsic value. This implies the bidder with the highest private estimate always submits the highest bid, and this bidder always wins the auction.

Suppose initially all bidders submit bids equivalent to their own private estimates. Since these private estimates are equally likely to be above or below the true value, it is very likely that the winning bidder, with the highest private estimate, has overestimated the true value of the item. Therefore the bidder with the highest private estimate wins the auction, having submitted a bid that is very likely to turn out to be higher than the true value of the item! Paradoxically, the winning bidder is very likely to turn out to be a loser, in the sense of having overpaid for the item. The winning bidder falls victim to the winner's curse. In their analysis of auctions for oil and gas drilling rights in the Gulf of Mexico during the 1950s and 1960s, Capen *et al.* note a consistent tendency for the winning oil firms to have overestimated the true values of the rights they were successful in securing.

> In recent years, several major companies have taken a rather careful look at their record and those of the industry in areas where sealed competitive bidding is the method of acquiring leases. The most notable of these areas,

and perhaps the most interesting, is the Gulf of Mexico. Most analysts turn up with the rather shocking result that, while there seems to be a lot of oil and gas in the region, the industry is not making as much return on its investment as it intended.

(Capen et al., 1971, p. 641)

In experiments replicating the second example cited above, in which a jar containing an (unknown) number of penny coins is auctioned and sold to the highest bidder, a similar tendency is observed very frequently: the winning bid often exceeds the true value of the jar, and the winning bidder consequently experiences the winner's curse. Experimental and field evidence on the winner's curse is reviewed in greater detail in Section 11.6.

The paradox of the winner's curse can also be described in the following terms. In the oil firms' example, if firm A's own private valuation of the drilling rights is the only information available to A, this private valuation represents A's best estimate of the true value of the rights. However, if A also has information concerning the private valuations of other firms, this information might well cause A to revise its estimate of the true value. For example, if A's private survey produces a valuation of £100m, but A subsequently discovers that nine other firms have all (independently) valued the rights at less than £100m, A might well infer that its own valuation of £100m is very likely to be an overestimate. A's best estimate of the true value, conditional on the news that its own private valuation of £100m is the highest of 10 similar private valuations, is now considerably less than £100m. If A also discovers that the other nine valuations are all within the range £50m to £95m, A might perhaps revise its estimate downwards towards the middle of this range: this would produce a revised estimate of around £75m.

Therefore firm A has two possible estimates of the true value of the rights on which it could base its sealed bid:

■ A's original private estimate of the true value of the rights, unconditional on any information about the private estimates of the other bidders.

■ A's revised estimate of the true value of the rights, conditional on A's private estimate being the highest private estimate of any bidder, and A's bid therefore being the winning bid.

At the time it submits its bid, firm A has only its own original estimate to go on, but if A bases its bid on this estimate, A is very likely to experience the winner's curse if A wins. In order to avoid the winner's curse, A's sealed bid should be based on a revised estimate, conditional on A's original estimate being the highest estimate. Since A only wins if A's bid does turn out to be the highest, and A's bid is irrelevant to A if some other bidder submits a higher bid, A's revised estimate of the true value should be made conditional on the assumption that A's original estimate will turn out to be the highest, and that A's bid will therefore turn out to be the winning bid.

Using mathematical notation, the situation can be described as follows. Let V represent the true value of the item that is being auctioned. V is unknown to any of the bidders, but each bidder obtains a signal, denoted S_i for bidder i. For simplicity we assume S_i is drawn randomly from a uniform distribution with a minimum value of zero and a maximum value of 2V. In other words, if we select a bidder at random, this bidder's private signal is equally likely to take any value between zero and 2V, and is therefore equally likely to provide an underestimate or an overestimate of V. Therefore each bidder's signal is an unbiased estimate of V. We can write $E(V | S_i) = S_i$, where $E(V | S_i)$ denotes the expected value of V, conditional on i's signal but unconditional on any information about the signals obtained by other bidders.

Suppose, however, we wish to write down bidder i's estimate of the true value of the item conditional on S_i being the highest signal obtained by any bidder, and i's bid therefore being the winning bid. In order to do so, the following result is useful:

$$E[S_{(1)}] = \underline{v} + [N/(N + 1)]\bar{v}$$

where $S_{(1)}$ denotes the highest signal obtained by any bidder, $E[S_{(1)}]$ is the expected value of $S_{(1)}$, $\underline{v}$ and $\bar{v}$ are the minimum and maximum values (respectively) that any bidder's signal can take, and N is the number of bidders. The result is derived in Appendix 1. In our case, $\underline{v} = 0$ and $\bar{v} = 2V$, so $E[S_{(1)}] = 2VN/(N + 1)$.

We let $E[V | S_i = S_{(1)}]$ denote the expected value of V, conditional on S_i being the highest signal obtained by any bidder. If the true value of the item is V, on average we would expect S_i (if it is known to be the highest signal) to equal $2VN/(N + 1)$. Rearranging, we obtain:

$$E[V | S_i = S_{(1)}] = (N + 1)S_i/(2N)$$

Alternatively, we can write $E[V | S_i = S_{(1)}] = d(N)S_i$, where $d(N) = (N + 1)/(2N)$ is the discount factor that should be applied to S_i in order to obtain an expected value for V conditional on i's signal being the highest signal, or $S_i = S_{(1)}$. As Table 11.1 shows, as N (the number of bidders) increases, d(N) decreases. Therefore as N increases the size of the discount increases.

Note that if bidder i is the only bidder (N = 1), by definition bidder i has the highest signal, so d(N) = 1 (there is no discount). The larger the value of N, the greater is the likelihood that by being the highest signal, S_i represents an overestimate of V. Therefore as N increases, d(N) decreases and the size of the discount increases. When the number of bidders is very large, bidder i should apply a 50 per cent discount; in other words, i's valuation conditional on S_i being the highest signal obtained by any bidder is only 50 per cent of S_i.

The preceding analysis suggests that in the pure common value model, to avoid the winner's curse bidder i's submitted bid should be based on $E[V | S_i = S_{(1)}]$. This is not quite the same as saying that bidder i's submitted bid should actually *be*

Table 11.1 Relationship between N, the number of bidders, and d(N)

N	1	2	5	10	100	1000
d(N)	1	0.75	0.6	0.55	0.505	0.5005

$E[V \mid S_i = S_{(1)}]$. In fact, in a first price sealed bid auction it pays to submit a bid some distance below the bidder's opinion as to the true value of the item. Therefore when formulating his submitted bid, bidder i should apply a further discount to $E[V \mid S_i = S_{(1)}]$. The reasons for doing so are examined in Section 11.4, in which the formulation of optimal bidding strategies for all four basic auction formats is examined, in the context of the independent private values model.

11.4 Optimal bidding strategies and revenue equivalence in the independent private values model

In this section, we examine some of the properties of auctions when bidders form independent private valuations of the item being auctioned. Each bidder privately and independently forms an opinion of the value of the item, and even if one bidder's opinion as to the value of the item were to be revealed, this information would be completely irrelevant to other bidders when formulating their own private valuations. In this section, we analyse the optimal bidding strategies for an individual bidder in each of the four basic auction formats that were introduced in Section 11.2, in an independent private values setting. The discussion of optimal bidding strategies also enables us to demonstrate an important result in auction theory, known as the revenue equivalence theorem.

Optimal bidding strategies

In order to determine a bidder's optimal bidding strategy in each of the four basic auction formats, it is assumed for simplicity that all bidders' private values of the item under auction are drawn randomly from a uniform distribution, with a minimum value of zero and a maximum value of one. In other words, if a bidder is selected at random, this bidder's private value is equally likely to take any value between the lowest possible value of any bidder (equal to zero) and the highest possible value (equal to one). This choice of minimum and maximum values of zero and one is purely a scaling decision, and does not affect the generality of the results derived below. The assumption that the values are distributed uniformly is a simplifying assumption, introduced in order to keep the mathematics as simple as possible. In fact, this assumption is not required for our treatment of the first two auction formats (English and second price sealed bid) examined below; but it is required for our treatment of the other two formats (first price sealed bid and Dutch). For these two formats a more general treatment would require the use of an arbitrary probability distribution for the bidders' private values; however, the mathematics involved is beyond the scope of this text.

One other assumption introduced at this stage is that the bidders are risk neutral. The meaning of risk neutrality, and the implications of relaxing this assumption, are discussed in Section 11.5. Under these assumptions, it is a simple task to determine the optimal bidding strategies for an individual bidder in two of the four auction formats: the English (ascending bid) auction and the second price sealed bid auction. The discussion begins by considering these two cases.

The English (ascending bid) auction

In an English auction, a bidder's optimal bidding strategy is to continue bidding for as long as the price is below his or her private value, and to withdraw as soon as the price *equals* or exceeds this private value. If another bidder is currently offering a price that is below your own private value, it is certainly worthwhile for you to enter a revised and higher bid (as long as this bid is also below your private value) for the following reasons:

■ If your revised bid is successful, you gain a rent equal to the difference between your private value and your winning bid;

■ If your revised bid is unsuccessful, you gain and lose nothing through having entering the revised bid.

Therefore if another bidder is currently offering a price that is below your private value, you might possibly gain something, and you certainly cannot lose anything, by entering a revised bid. It is a trivial matter to show that if another bidder is currently offering a price that is above your private value, you can only lose and you cannot possibly gain by entering a revised bid.

The second price sealed bid auction

As we have seen in Section 11.2, according to the rules of a second price sealed bid auction, the bidder who submits the highest bid pays a price equivalent to the second-highest entered bid. In this case, a bidder's optimal bidding strategy is to enter a bid equivalent to his or her own private value. To show why this is necessarily the optimal strategy, we consider the implications of raising or lowering the submitted bid slightly, in the region of this optimal bid.

■ Suppose you raise your submitted bid so it is now slightly above your private value. This only affects the outcome of the auction if your original bid (equal to your private value) was not the highest bid, but your raised bid is the highest bid. In this case, by raising your bid you must have overtaken some other bid, which now becomes the second-highest. This bid determines the price you will now pay. But this price must be higher than your private value! Therefore you would not wish to be the winner under these circumstances. By raising your bid, you can only lose, you cannot possibly gain.

■ Suppose you lower your submitted bid so that it is now slightly below your private value. This only affects the outcome of the auction if your original bid (equal to your private value) was the highest bid, but your lowest bid is not the highest bid. In this case, by lowering your bid you must have dropped below some other bid, which now becomes the highest. This rival bid determines the price you would have paid if you had bid your private value (because the rival bid would then have been the second highest). But this price must be lower than your private value! Therefore by lowering your bid you have forfeited an opportunity to buy the item for less than your private value. As before, by lowering your bid you can only lose, you cannot possibly gain.

In both an English auction and a second price sealed bid auction, it pays to tell the truth. In an English auction each bidder's optimal bidding strategy is to continue bidding up to his or her private value; and in a second price sealed bid auction the optimal strategy is to submit a bid equivalent to this private value. This strategy is optimal no matter what other bidders decide to do. In other words, in the terminology of game theory it is a dominant strategy (see Section 4.6). When all bidders implement this dominant strategy, a dominant equilibrium is achieved.

Furthermore, at the dominant equilibrium the outcomes of the English auction and the second price sealed bid auction are always the same. The bidder with the highest private value of the item always wins, and always pays a price equal to the second-highest bidder's private value. At first sight this result may seem surprising: the rules of these two auction formats appear very different, so one might expect the outcomes to differ as well. However, if bidders behave rationally there is in fact no difference between the outcomes of these two auction formats, which can be described as strategically equivalent.

The first price sealed bid auction

Does our conclusion for the two auction formats we have analysed so far, that truth-telling (bidding in accordance with your private value) pays, extend to the first price sealed bid auction? The answer is no. In a first price sealed bid auction, it pays to submit a bid that is below your own private value. Figure 11.1 illustrates why this is so. For the purposes of constructing this diagram, we consider bidder i with a private value of V_i, and in accordance with the assumptions made at the start of this section, we assume $0 \leq V_i \leq 1$. We assume bidder i is considering submitting a bid of B, where $0 \leq B \leq V_i$. It is never worthwhile to submit a bid of $B > V_i$, because if this turns out to be the winning bid, the price exceeds bidder i's private value. We assume for each bid in the range $0 \leq B \leq V_i$, a probability that B will turn out

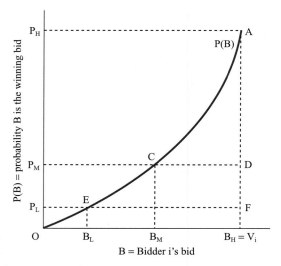

Figure 11.1 Bidding strategies: first price sealed bid auction (independent private values model)

to be the winning bid, denoted P(B), can be calculated. The factors that determine P(B) are considered below. At this stage, however, we simply take P(B) as given. The following assumptions about P(B) are uncontroversial:

- P(0) = 0: a submitted bid of zero will always be beaten by at least one other bidder, so the probability that a bid of zero wins the auction is zero.

- P(B) is an increasing function of B: the higher the submitted bid, the higher the probability that the bid wins the auction.

- P(B) is a decreasing function of N, the number of bidders. On the assumptions we have made so far, all bids lie somewhere in the range zero to one. Assume for example you intend to submit a bid of 0.8. If there is only one other bidder, the probability that this rival bid is below 0.8 and you win the auction is perhaps quite high. If there are two other bidders, the probability that *both* rival bids are below 0.8 is somewhat lower, but still reasonably high. But if there are 100 or 1,000 other bidders, the probability that these rival bids are *all* below 0.8 is extremely small.

In Figure 11.1, the curve OA represents the relationship between B and P(B), drawn on the assumption that N, the number of bidders, is fixed. Three possible bids are shown on the horizontal axis: $B_H = V_i$ (high), B_M (medium) and B_L (low).

- Suppose bidder i submits the high bid of B_H, equal to his or her private value. The probability that B_H turns out to be the winning bid is $P(B_H)$. The expected value of the payment is $B_H \times P(B_H) = OP_HAB_H$ in Figure 11.1, and the expected value of the acquisition is $V_i \times P(B_H) = OP_HAB_H$. Therefore if bidder i submits the high bid of B_H, the expected rent is zero, because the expected values of the payment and the acquisition are the same.

- Suppose bidder i submits the medium bid of B_M. The probability that B_M turns out to be the winning bid is $P(B_M) < P(B_H)$. The expected value of the payment is $B_M \times P(B_M) = OP_MCB_M$, and the expected value of the acquisition is $V_i \times P(B_M) = OP_MDB_H$. Therefore if bidder i submits the medium bid of B_M, the expected rent is positive and equal to the area B_MCDB_H.

- Finally, suppose bidder i submits the low bid of B_L. The probability that B_L turns out to be the winning bid is $P(B_L) < P(B_M) < P(B_H)$. The expected value of the payment is $B_L \times P(B_L) = OP_LEB_L$, and the expected value of the acquisition is $V_i \times P(B_L) = OP_LFB_H$. Therefore if bidder i submits the low bid of B_L, the expected rent is positive and equal to the area B_LEFB_H.

By visual inspection of Figure 11.1, it is apparent that $B_MCDB_H > B_LEFB_H$. Therefore in this case, it is better to submit the medium bid of B_M than the low bid of B_L. However, both B_M and B_L are better options than submitting the high bid $B_H = V_i$ (although as B_L approaches zero, the expected rent also approaches zero). By reducing the submitted bid below $B_H = V_i$, bidder i gains by committing to pay a lower price, but also loses by accepting a lower probability of winning the auction. Choosing the optimal bid involves selecting the optimal trade-off between these two effects.

The analysis in Figure 11.1 is only partial, because as yet the determination of the curve OA has not been explained. In fact, the position of this curve depends on the bidding strategies of the other bidders. Clearly, the probability that any given bid submitted by bidder i turns out to be the winning bid depends not only on the number of other bidders, but also on whether the others are bidding high (close to their own private values) or low (well below their own private values). In other words, each bidder faces a situation of interdependence. In such a situation, we can search for the Nash equilibrium solution to the auction. Each bidder should submit the bid that maximizes his or her expected rent, based on the conjectural variation assumption (which turns out to be correct at the equilibrium) that all other bidders also submit the bids that maximize their expected rents.

Under the assumptions we have used to develop the model to this point (uniformly distributed independent private values, and risk neutrality), it can be shown that at the Nash equilibrium the optimal bidding strategy for each bidder is to submit a bid equal to $(N - 1)/N$ *times* the bidder's own private value, where N is the number of bidders. In other words, the optimal bid of bidder i is:

$$B_i^* = b^*V_i$$

where $b^* = (N - 1)/N$ and $V_i =$ bidder i's private value. Accordingly, when there are $N = 2$ bidders, $b^* = (N - 1)/N = 1/2$, so each bidder submits a bid equivalent to one-half of his or her private value. When there are $N = 3$ bidders, $b^* = (N - 1)/N = 2/3$, so each bidder submits a bid equivalent to two-thirds of his or her private value. When there are $N = 100$ bidders, $b^* = (N - 1)/N = 99/100$, so each bidder submits a bid equivalent to 99 per cent of his or her private value. As the number of bidders increases, the optimal bid approaches the bidder's private value. The mathematical derivation of this result is examined in Appendix 1.

The Dutch (descending bid) auction

In a Dutch auction, a bidder's optimal bidding strategy is to wait until the price has fallen a certain amount below his or her private value, and then (assuming no other bidder has already done so) to call out what will instantly become the winning bid.

Why is this the optimum bidding strategy? In a Dutch auction, there is clearly no point in bidding while the price is higher than your private value, because if you do so you pay more than the item is worth to you. There is also no point in bidding when the price *equals* your private value, because if you do so you pay exactly what the item is worth to you, so you gain nothing. But if you allow the price to drop a little further: *either* another bidder will enter a bid before you, in which case you have not lost anything; *or* you will still be the first to bid, in which case you obtain the item for a price that is lower than your private value, and you gain a positive rent. So by allowing the price to drop, you can only gain and you cannot possibly lose.

How far below your private value should you allow the price to drop before entering your bid? The answer turns out to be the same as in the case of the first price sealed bid auction. Your bidding strategy should maximize your expected rent, based on the conjectural variation assumption that all other bidders' strategies also maximize their expected rents. And it turns out that the bidding strategy, which satisfies this condition, and which produces a Nash equilibrium, is exactly the same as in the case of the first price sealed bid auction. Under our assumptions (uniformly distributed independent private values, and risk neutrality), bidder i should bid when the price reaches $B_i^* = b^*V_i$, where $b^* = (N - 1)/N$ and $V_i =$ bidder i's private value, as before.

At the Nash equilibrium, the outcomes of the first price sealed bid auction and the Dutch auction are always the same. The bidder with the highest private value of the item always wins, and always pays a price equal to $(N - 1)/N$ *times* his or her own private value. Again, this result may seem quite surprising, because the rules of these two auction formats appear to be very different. However, in both cases the information available to bidders when they submit their bids is identical: no bidder learns anything about other bidders' willingness to pay before submitting his or her own bid. If bidders behave rationally, there is no difference between the outcomes of these two auction formats. Therefore the first price sealed bid auction and the Dutch auction are said to be strategically equivalent.

The revenue equivalence theorem

The final stage in our analysis of the four basic auction formats (based on assumptions of uniformly distributed independent private values and risk neutrality) involves a comparison of the seller's expected proceeds in each case. This enables us to answer a very important question for the seller: which auction format is expected to yield the highest price; or in other words, which auction format should the seller select? And the answer based on the preceding analysis, which again may seem surprising, is that it does not matter! All four auction formats are expected to yield exactly the same price to the seller on average. This powerful result in auction theory is known as the **revenue equivalence theorem**. The intuition is as follows:

- In an English auction, bidders continue to participate until the price reaches their own private values. The auction stops when the bidder with the second-highest value drops out, and at this point the price payable by the winning bidder is determined. Therefore the seller's expected price is the expected value or expectation of the second-highest private value.

- In a second price sealed bid auction, each bidder submits a bid equivalent to his own private value. Under the second price principle, the winning bidder therefore pays a price equivalent to the second-highest private value.

- In a first price sealed bid auction, each bidder submits a bid some distance below his private value. The seller's expected price is the expected value of the highest private value *minus* the amount by which this bidder shades his bid. If all bidders *behave rationally when deciding how far to shade their bids, the seller's expected* price turns out to be the expectation of the second-highest private value.

- In a Dutch auction, each bidder plans to call out when the price has fallen some distance below his private value. The seller's expected price is the expected value of the highest private value *minus* the further amount by which this bidder allows the price to drop before calling out. Again, the seller's expected price turns out to be the expectation of the second-highest private value.

When the bidders' private values are distributed randomly in the range zero to one, a general formula for the average price each of the four auction formats is expected to yield to the seller is $(N - 1)/(N + 1)$, where N is the number of bidders, as before. The mathematical derivation of this result is examined in Appendix 1. When there are $N = 2$ bidders, on average the seller expects to receive a price of $1/3 = 0.33$. When there are $N = 3$ bidders, the expected price is $2/4 = 0.5$. With $N = 4$ bidders the expected price is 0.6; with $N = 10$ the expected price is 0.82; and with $N = 100$ the expected price is 0.98. As the number of bidders increases, two factors tend to work in the seller's favour. First, in a second price sealed bid and in a Dutch auction, increased competition between bidders results in higher bids being entered. Second, in all four auction formats, the probability increases that some bidders will have private values very close to the maximum value of one. The higher the bidder's private value, the higher the submitted bid in all four auction cases.

Table 11.2 summarizes the results of the analysis of optimal bidding strategies and revenue equivalence for the independent private values model. It is important to remember that the revenue equivalence theorem relies heavily on the independent private values assumption. As we will see in Section 11.5, for example, if the pure common value model applies, an English auction produces a higher expected price than a first price sealed bid auction (Milgrom and Weber, 1982).

Evidence concerning the empirical validity of the revenue equivalence theorem is rather limited. However, Lucking-Reiley (1999) describes an analysis of the secondary market for collectable cards. Cards were traded over the internet using all four basic auction formats (English, first price sealed bid, second price sealed bid and Dutch). The revenues obtained using the Dutch auction format were significantly higher than those obtained using the first price sealed bid format, even though these two formats are strategically equivalent. However, revenues obtained using the English auction format were not significantly higher than those obtained in second price sealed bid auctions.

Table 11.2 Optimal bidding strategies and revenue equivalence for the independent private values model

Auction format	Optimal bidding strategy	Price paid by winning bidder	Seller's expected proceeds
English (ascending bid)	Be prepared to remain in the bidding until price *equals* your private value	Second-highest private value, denoted $V_{(2)}$	$E[V_{(2)}] = \dfrac{N-1}{N+1}$
Second price sealed bid	Submitted bid *equals* your private value	Second-highest private value, $V_{(2)}$	$E[V_{(2)}] = \dfrac{N-1}{N+1}$
First price sealed bid	Submitted bid *equals* $[(N-1)/N]$ *times* your private value	$[(N-1)/N]$ *times* winning bidder's private value = $[(N-1)/N]V_{(1)}$ where $V_{(1)}$ denotes the highest private value	$\left(\dfrac{N-1}{N}\right)E[V_{(1)}]$ $= \left(\dfrac{N-1}{N}\right) \times \left(\dfrac{N}{N+1}\right)$ $= \dfrac{N-1}{N+1}$
Dutch (descending bid)	Be prepared to wait and bid when price *equals* $[(N-1)/N]$ *times* your private value	$[(N-1)/N]$ *times* winning bidder's private value = $[(N-1)/N]V_{(1)}$	$\dfrac{N-1}{N+1}$ (as above)

11.5   Extensions and additional topics in auction theory

The seller's optimal auction design, and the reserve price

The revenue equivalence theorem demonstrates that under the assumptions adopted in Section 11.4, all four of the basic auction formats yield the same expected price to the seller in the independent private values model. Therefore the choice between the four formats should be a matter of indifference to the seller. However, this does not mean that any (or all) of these four formats are optimal from the seller's perspective, in the sense of producing the highest expected proceeds under any possible set of rules the seller could devise.

In fact, there is one very obvious reason why these auction rules might be sub-optimal from the seller's perspective. If the item being sold has a positive private value to the seller, all four basic auction formats (as described so far) leave open the possibility that the seller ends up selling the item at a price below the seller's own private value. If the seller's private value is V_0 (assuming $0 \le V_0 \le 1$, as before) and $V_0 > V_{(1)}$ (where $V_{(1)}$ is the private value of the bidder with the highest private value, as before), the seller's proceeds are certainly below V_0 in all four auction formats, because no bidder ever bids more than his own private value. Even if $V_{(1)} > V_0$ but $V_0 > V_{(2)}$, in an English auction the seller's proceeds are below V_0, because the bidder with the second-highest private value drops out when the bidding reaches $V_{(2)}$. In a second price sealed bid auction the seller's proceeds are below V_0, because the bidder with $V_{(1)}$ pays a price of $V_{(2)}$. In a first price sealed bid auction or a Dutch auction, if $V_{(1)} > V_0 > V_{(2)}$ the seller's proceeds are below V_0 if the submitted bid of the bidder with $V_{(1)}$ is below V_0.

This discussion suggests the seller can always increase his expected proceeds by specifying a **reserve price**, and introducing a rule that the item is not sold if the price payable by the winning bidder does not at least match (or exceed) the reserve price. Suppose initially the seller sets a reserve price, denoted r, equivalent to his own private value, so $r = V_0$. (In fact, as we will see below, the seller can do better than this by setting $r > V_0$.) In comparison with the case where there is no reserve price at all, setting $r = V_0$ can sometimes increase and can never reduce the seller's proceeds. Suppose the price paid by the winning bidder in the absence of the reserve price would have been below $r = V_0$. With the reserve price imposed, *either* the winning bidder pays a higher price of r, *or* the seller retains the item which is worth V_0 to the seller. Either way the seller is better off. Suppose instead the price paid by the winning bidder in the absence of the reserve price would have been above $r = V_0$. In this case the existence of the reserve price becomes irrelevant and the outcome is unchanged. Therefore in this case the seller is no worse off.

It can be shown mathematically that it is optimal for the seller to set a reserve price that is higher than his own private value, so $r > V_0$. It is interesting to note that this leaves open the possibility of an inefficient allocation of resources: if $r > V_{(1)} > V_0$ the seller retains the item even though there is a bidder who values the item more highly than the seller. However, as in the standard case of monopoly, an inefficient allocation of resources can be consistent with the maximization of the seller's (or monopolist's) private proceeds (or profit).

What reserve price is optimal from the seller's perspective? As the seller increases the reserve price slightly within the region $r > V_0$, there is a trade-off, which can be illustrated simply in the case of an English auction. Suppose r is already above V_0, and the seller is considering a small increase in the reserve price from r to $r + \Delta r$.

- If $V_{(1)} > r + \Delta r > r > V_0$, the price paid by the winning bidder increases by Δr. The item is still sold, and seller's rent increases from $r - V_0$ to $r + \Delta r - V_0$.

- If $r + \Delta r > V_{(1)} > r > V_0$, the bidder with the highest value, who would have paid the old reserve price of r, drops out of the bidding before the new reserve price of $r + \Delta r$ is reached. The item is no longer sold, and the seller loses out on a rent of $r - V_0$.

The optimal reserve price is the one that maximizes this trade-off from the seller's perspective. In the case where all private values are distributed uniformly within the range zero to one, the formula for the optimal reserve price is simple: the seller should set $r = (1 + V_0)/2$. The mathematical derivation of this result for the case of $N = 2$ bidders is shown in Appendix 1. Accordingly, even if the item has no value to the seller, the reserve price should be set at $r = 1/2$; if the seller's private value is $V_0 = 1/2$, the reserve price should be set at $r = 3/4$; if $V_0 = 0.8$, $r = 0.9$; if $V_0 = 0.9$, $r = 0.95$; and so on. It is interesting to note, and perhaps counterintuitive, that under these conditions the optimal reserve price does not depend at all on the number of bidders.

Risk averse bidders

The analysis in Section 11.4 is based on an assumption that the bidders in the auction are indifferent to risk, or risk neutral. From the bidder's perspective, the outcomes of all of the auctions examined in this chapter are binary: either the bidder wins the auction, and gains some rent; or the bidder fails to win the auction, and gains and loses nothing. Consider the following three auctions:

- Auction A1, in which the bidder is certain to win the auction, and by doing so gains a rent of +5.

- Auction A2, in which the bidder has a probability of 0.5 of winning the auction, and gains a rent of +10 if he does win.

- Auction A3, in which the bidder has a probability of 0.25 of winning the auction, and gains a rent of +20 if he does win.

In A2 and A3, if the bidder fails to win the auction, he gains zero rent. The expected rent (calculated by multiplying the rent by the probability of winning) is the same in all three cases: $5 \times 1 = 10 \times 0.5 = 20 \times 0.25 = +5$. A risk neutral bidder is indifferent between these three auctions, but a risk averse bidder prefers A1 to A2, and A2 to A3. With A1 there is zero risk, because the bidder is certain to gain a rent of +5. A2 is more risky than A1, because the certain rent of +5 is replaced by possible rents of either +10 or 0. And A3 is riskier still, because the variance or spread in the distribution of possible outcomes is even larger: in A2 the possible outcomes are +10 or 0, but in A3 the possible outcomes are +20 or 0. This implies a risk averse bidder would be prepared to trade a reduction in the rent gained from winning the auction for an increase in the probability of winning. If a risk averse bidder prefers A2 to A3, for example, the same bidder might perhaps be indifferent between A2′ and A3, where A2′ also offers a probability of 0.5 of winning, but a rent of only +8 rather than +10 if the bidder does win. The expected rent is lower in A2′ than in A3, but the probability of winning is higher, which implies there is less risk.

How does risk aversion affect the optimal bidding strategies considered in Section 11.4? The answer to this question is straightforward in the cases of the English and Dutch auctions.

■ In an English auction, risk aversion makes no difference to the optimal bidding strategy. The only decision the bidder has to make at each stage of the bidding is whether to remain in the bidding or drop out. By remaining, the bidder retains a chance of gaining a rent for as long as the price is below his private value, but by dropping out the bidder is immediately certain that the rent will be zero. Therefore as before, the bidder remains in the bidding until the price reaches his private value, and then withdraws.

■ In a Dutch auction, in contrast, risk aversion does affect the optimal bidding strategy. As soon as the price has fallen below the bidder's private value, and as it continues to fall further, the bidder has to trade the risk that someone else will call out first (so the opportunity of obtaining the item at a price below the bidder's private value is lost) against the possible benefit of allowing the price to fall a little further (the possibility of obtaining the item even more cheaply). From our previous discussion, we can infer that a risk averse bidder will adopt a more cautious attitude to this trade-off than a risk neutral bidder. In other words, in a Dutch auction a risk averse bidder will call out earlier. The risk averse bidder is prepared to trade a reduction in the rent he gains by winning the auction for a higher probability of winning.

Summarizing, risk aversion makes no difference to bidders' behaviour in an English auction, but it causes bidders to bid more aggressively (in other words, higher) in a Dutch auction. Therefore the revenue equivalence theorem breaks down if bidders are risk averse: a Dutch auction yields a higher expected price to the seller than an English auction.

For sealed bid auctions the logic is similar:

■ In a second price sealed bid auction (strategically equivalent to an English auction), risk averse bidders submit bids equivalent to their private values. Therefore a second price sealed bid auction yields the same expected price to the seller, regardless of whether bidders are risk neutral or risk averse.

■ In a first price sealed bid auction (strategically equivalent to a Dutch auction) risk averse bidders tend to bid closer to their private values than risk neutral bidders. In other words, risk averse bidders bid more aggressively (higher) than risk neutral bidders.

Therefore with risk averse bidders, a first price sealed bid auction yields a higher expected price to the seller than a second price sealed bid auction; and again, revenue equivalence breaks down. This means the seller is no longer indifferent between the four basic auction formats. With risk averse bidders, the seller should select a Dutch auction or a first price sealed bid auction in preference to an English auction or a second price sealed bid auction.

Asymmetric bidders

In some auctions where bidders have independent private values, it may be necessary to relax the assumption that all bidders' private values are drawn from an identical probability distribution. It might be the case that bidders can be split into two (or even more) groups, with members of one group systematically tending to value the item more highly than members of the other group. For example, bidders for a work of art might divide into dealers and private collectors. All dealers' valuations might be drawn from one specific probability distribution, and all collectors' valuations might be drawn from another distribution.

With asymmetric bidders, the English auction (and the second price sealed bid auction) operates in the same way as in Section 11.4. In the English auction, the second-last bidder withdraws when the bidding reaches the second-highest private value across both groups. However, the existence of asymmetric bidders complicates the analysis of the first price sealed bid auction (and the Dutch auction). As we have seen, in a first price sealed bid auction the bidder submits a bid below his or her private value. How far below depends on the optimal trade-off between the increased rent if the submitted bid still wins, and the reduced probability of winning. With asymmetric bidders, however, bidders from the two groups will tend to form different assessments of this trade-off. Suppose, for example, there are four bidders in total: two dealers and two collectors. Suppose also that dealers tend to value the item more highly on average than collectors, and all bidders are aware of this fact.

- Each collector knows he is competing against two dealers and one other collector. The collector perceives the competition he faces to be quite fierce: to win the auction, he needs to outbid two dealers (who are both likely to value the item more highly than he does) and one other collector. To have any realistic chance of winning, the collector feels he must bid aggressively; in other words, he submits a bid close to his own private value.

- Each dealer knows he is competing against one other dealer and two collectors. The dealer does not perceive the competition to be very fierce: to win the auction, he only needs to outbid one other dealer and the two collectors (who are both quite likely to value the item less highly than he does). The dealer feels he can afford to bid conservatively; in other words, he submits a bid that is some considerable amount below his own private value.

In this situation, it is possible that the winning bidder turns out not to be the bidder with the highest private value. Suppose dealer 1 has a higher private value than collector A, but collector A ends up submitting a higher bid than dealer 1 for the reasons outlined above. Then collector A wins the auction, despite not having the highest private value. The fact that this outcome has a non-zero probability invalidates the revenue equivalence theorem in the case of asymmetric bidders: the first price sealed bid auction (or the Dutch auction) generally yields an expected price different from that of the English auction (or the second price sealed bid auction). Which auction format yields the higher expected price depends on the precise nature of the two distributions of private values. Furthermore, the fact that the bidder with the highest private value may not always win the auction implies the first price sealed bid auction with asymmetric bidders is allocatively inefficient.

McAfee and McMillan (1987) show that the theory of optimal auction design in the case of asymmetric bidders can, in some cases, explain or justify (on strictly economic criteria) the practice whereby local government departments give preferential treatment to local suppliers for the award of procurement contracts. Suppose non-local suppliers have a cost advantage over local suppliers. Then the department might find it optimal to allow a local price preference of (say) 5 per cent; in other words, the lowest local tender wins the contract provided it is not more than 5 per cent higher than the lowest non-local tender. At any given price the contract is worth more to a non-local supplier than it is to a local supplier, due to the former's cost advantage. The price preference policy increases the degree of competition perceived by the non-local supplier, encouraging the latter to bid more aggressively (tender more cheaply) in the hope that it might still win the contract. This tends to operate in the local government department's interest, by lowering the price it expects to pay.

Affiliated valuations, and the winner's curse revisited

In the independent private values model, the individual bidders' private values of the item are completely unrelated: one bidder's opinion of the value of the item is completely irrelevant to other bidders in forming their valuations. In contrast, in the pure common value model, in which bidders independently estimate a single true value of the item that is the same for all of them, each bidder's opinion is highly relevant to other bidders. If a bidder could collect information about other bidders' valuations, he could assess the true value of the item more accurately.

As we have seen in Section 11.2, the independent private values model and the pure common value model are theoretical extremes, and in many cases bidders' actual valuations of an item may contain elements of both models. In Section 11.2 we cited the example of a painting, for which a bidder's personal valuation depends partly on his personal tastes, and partly on other people's tastes, which influence the resale value or the prestige the bidder obtains by becoming the owner. Broadly speaking, bidders are said to have affiliated valuations if the revelation that one bidder perceives the value of the item to be high would cause other bidders to increase their assessments of the value of the same item.

When bidders' valuations are affiliated, bidders tend to bid more aggressively in an English auction than they do in the other three basic auction formats. This statement is true both in the special case of the pure common value model, and in the more general case of affiliated valuations. Therefore the English auction yields a higher expected price to the seller than the other three basic auction formats. This is because the bidders who remain in the bidding as an English auction progresses can observe the fact that other bidders have also remained in the bidding, and can therefore infer that these other bidders' valuations of the item are at least as high as the current price. The acquisition of this information lessens the effect of the winner's curse. The bidder who can observe that other bidders are still interested at the current price does not have to form such a cautious estimate of the item's true value (conditional on being the winning bidder) as the bidder in the first price sealed bid auction, whose bid effectively is submitted in a 'blind' condition.

When bidders' valuations are affiliated (including the special case of the pure common value model) revenue equivalence breaks down. The seller should use an

English auction in preference to any of the other three auction formats, because an English auction yields the highest expected price. It can also be shown that with affiliated valuations, a second price sealed bid auction yields the seller a higher expected price than either a first price sealed bid auction or a Dutch auction, both of which yield the same expected price (McAfee and McMillan, 1987; Milgrom and Weber, 1982).

Finally, when bidders' valuations are affiliated (including the pure common value model), the seller's optimal reserve price depends on the auction format and on the number of bidders. This also follows from the fact that in the affiliated valuations case, any bidder's valuation of the item conditional on being the winning bidder depends on the auction format and on the number of bidders. This result is in contrast to the equivalent result for the independent private values model (see p. 390), in which the optimal reserve price is the same for all four auction formats, and is independent of the number of bidders (Klemperer, 2002a,b).

11.6 Empirical evidence

Much of the empirical research into auctions examines cases that approximate to the pure common value model, where the true value of the item is the same for all bidders, but this value is not known to any bidder with certainty. A number of studies have considered how auctions should best be designed to maximize the price received by the seller. From the seller's perspective, it is important to design the auction in such as way as to maximize competition among bidders; minimize the possibility of collusion among bidders; and minimize the tendency for bidders to reduce their submitted bids in an effort to avoid falling victim to the winner's curse. Case study 11.1 describes the auction of licences to operate third generation (3G) mobile telephone services in the UK in 2000. This section provides a selective review of empirical studies of auctions. Extended reviews can be found in Kagel and Levin (2002), Klemperer (1999, 2004), McAfee and McMillan (1987), Milgrom (2004) and Smith (1989).

Experimental evidence

Auction theory lends itself quite favourably to empirical scrutiny using experimental methods, which allow the researcher the opportunity to observe buyer and seller behaviour under controlled conditions (Plott, 1989). This subsection describes some representative examples. Bazerman and Samuelson (1983) report tests for the existence of a winner's curse that were conducted using 12 classes of postgraduate students at Boston University. Students were asked to submit sealed bids for four jars of objects containing either coins or paperclips. The true value of each jar (based on retail prices in the case of jars containing paperclips) was $8. Across 48 auctions, the average sub-mitted bid was $5.13, but the average winning bid was $10.01. Therefore the winning bidders fell victim to the winner's curse, realizing an average loss of $2.01.

Kagel and Levin (1986) conducted experiments in which students participate in a sequence of first price sealed bid auctions. The students are each given $10 accounts, with winning bidders' balances adjusted for their expenditure and the values of any items acquired. Losing bidders' balances remain unchanged, with no monies added or subtracted. Before submitting bids, the students were informed of a minimum and

Case study 11.1

The auction of the UK 3G mobile telephone spectrum licences

The sale by auction of spectrum licences to operate third generation (3G) mobile telephone services in the UK, completed in April 2000, raised more than £22.4bn, equivalent to around 2.5 per cent of GNP. 3G technology provides mobile phone users with high-speed internet access. When the earlier second generation (2G) licences were sold, telecom firms were required to submit business plans detailing costs and timescales for the roll-out of services. Each licence was sold for as little as £40,000, plus an annual licence fee. By 2000–01 the total annual 2G licence fee had risen to about 1 per cent of the rental value implied by the 3G auction prices. Objectives which informed the design of the 3G auctions, both in the UK and elsewhere in Europe, included achieving an efficient allocation of the spectrum, promoting competition, realizing the full economic value of the licences, and enabling UK or European operators to play a leading role in the development of new technology in telecommunications (Binmore and Klemperer, 2002).

Auction design features

There is extensive evidence that incumbents are more likely to win auctions for licences in cases where incumbents have incurred sunk cost investment expenditure in the past. This was likely in the case of incumbent 2G licence holders, who had more to lose in the 3G auction than entrants (Klemperer, 2004). Furthermore, the incumbents were likely to enjoy absolute cost advantages over entrants, derived from their existing 2G infrastructure (Binmore and Klemperer, 2002). Therefore the UK government anticipated (correctly, as it turned out) that the four existing 2G licence holders would submit winning bids for 3G licences. To encourage competition from new bidders, it was decided to grant a fifth licence, guaranteeing there would be at least one successful bid from an entrant.

The five 3G licences that were auctioned (labelled A to E) were variable in size: licences A and B were both significantly larger than licences C, D and E. To give maximum opportunity to entrants, none of the four incumbents was permitted to bid for the largest licence A. The auction design involved multiple ascending bids, with full disclosure of the present state of the bidding between each bidding round. In the first round, each bidder submits a bid for one of the five licences. In subsequent rounds, any bidder who is not currently the top bidder for one of the five licences must raise one of the current top bids by at least the minimum bid increment, or withdraw. The process continues until only five bidders remain. These bidders obtain the licence for which they are the current top bidder, at their current bid price.

The design of the 3G bidding process offered several advantages from the UK government's perspective. Its simultaneous nature ensured that bidding competition would spill over from one licence to another. As in an English auction, each bidder's optimal bidding strategy was relatively simple to determine: bidders should stay in the bidding until the current prices of all licences exceed the bidder's own private valuations. And as in an English auction, publication of current bids while bidding was underway would tend to mitigate the effect of the winner's curse, enabling each bidder to see that other bidders are still involved in the bidding at the current price. The outcome of the auction should be efficient, in the sense that at the final prices no reallocation of licences among bidders could increase the rent of any bidder. Finally, because this was the first auction of its kind, the designers were confident that bidders lacked the experience to collude effectively.

Participants in the auction were TIW, Vodafone, BT, Deutsche Telecom, Orange, NTL, France Telecom, Telefonica, Worldcom, Nomura, Sonera, Global Crossing and Eircom. The bidding process took place over a six-week period from March to April 2000, and lasted for 150 rounds. The entrant TIW took licence A at a price of £4.4bn. The incumbent Vodaphone secured licence B for £6bn. The other successful incumbent bidders were BT, Deutsche Telecom and Orange, who each paid just over £4bn for the other three licences.

Other European 3G auctions

Perhaps surprisingly, the successful design of the UK auction appears to have been ignored to some extent when similar auctions were held in several other European countries (Klemperer, 2002a,b). For example, in the Netherlands five licences were auctioned to an industry comprising five dominant incumbent firms. This design feature appears to have discouraged firms other than the five incumbents from bidding, and consequently the revenue raised from the auction was disappointing. The Italian government threatened to postpone the auction and withdraw licences if no new bidders were forthcoming. In the event only one nominal bid was received from a non-incumbent, and this firm withdrew from the bidding at an early stage, raising suspicions of collusion. Eventually five licences were awarded to five incumbents, and the revenues raised were lower than expected. In Switzerland, joint bids were invited for four licences. Four relatively modest joint bids were duly submitted, with the revenues only slightly higher than the government's reserve prices. Denmark had a more successful experience. A sealed bid design was adopted, so as to minimize opportunities for collusion between bidders, and encourage bids from entrants. A new entrant displaced an incumbent to secure one of the five licences, and the total revenue was higher than expected (Klemperer, 2002b).

Was there a winner's curse?

Cable *et al.* (2002) use share price data for the successful and unsuccessful bidders in the UK 3G licence auction to assess the effect of the announcement of the outcome of the auction on the share prices or market values of the companies involved. Event-study methodology examines movements in company share prices immediately before and after some event that is expected to influence the stock market valuation of the companies involved, controlling for the company's typical response to any general stock market movement that may have occurred on the day of the event. This methodology is applied to the share price data of the winning and losing bidders, around the time of the announcement of the outcome of the auction in April 2000. One winning bidder, Orange, was excluded from the analysis due to several changes of ownership during the estimation and event periods. By the time of the auction Orange was owned by Vodaphone, which submitted a separate winning bid, thereby contravening a rule preventing ownership of more than one licence. Vodaphone was subsequently required to divest itself of Orange.

On the first trading day following the announcement, the shares of three of the successful bidders (BT, TIW, Vodaphone) increased in value, while Deutsche Telekom (One2One) declined in value. Several of the losing bidders (NTL, Worldcom, Nomura, and Sonera) increased in value but a number of others (France Telecom, Telefonica, Global Crossing and Eircom) declined in value. Overall, the pattern was rather inconsistent. Over a 30-day period following the announcement, of the winning bidders only Vodafone increased in value. Among the losing firms, there was again little consistent pattern in the change in the share price over the same 30-day period.

To assess whether the successful bidders were subject to the winner's curse, cumulative returns on the combined values of portfolios of winning and losing bidders are calculated over the rest of the calendar year following the announcement of the auction result. Over a 30-day period following the announcement, the portfolio of losing firms recorded a 1 per cent loss, while the portfolio of winning firms recorded a 7 per cent loss. Subsequently, however, the performance of the two portfolios converged, and there was no lasting difference in performance. Overall, there is little systematic evidence of any winner's curse.

> There is no evidence that the outcome of the auction was anything but efficient and, further, no case for easing the regulatory stance in the industry on the grounds that the successful licence bidders paid too much.
>
> *(Cable et al., 2002, p. 459)*

Between 2000 and 2003 most telecom firms experienced large share-price reductions. This was a global phenomenon, which affected the winners and losers in the UK's 3G auction in equal measure. With the benefit of hindsight, it seems clear that winning bidders paid far more for the licences in 2000 than they would have paid two or three years later. The auction appears to have distributed wealth from the shareholders of the winning bidders to the UK government (Klemperer, 2002c). However, it has been suggested that the winning bidders have subsequently used their ownership of the licences to impede entry and retard the rate of take-up of 3G technology, while at the same time seeking to renegotiate terms and conditions. Delaying the take-up of 3G technology has enabled these firms to extend the profitable lifetime of the older 2G technology (Ozanich *et al.*, 2004).

maximum possible value of each item for sale. Participants were allowed to bid until the balance in their account reached zero. Outcomes are compared with the predictions of a theoretical model that assumes risk neutrality and rational bidding. In auctions with small numbers of bidders, there was a tendency for profits to be realized on average: in auctions with three or four bidders, for example, the average profit was just over $4 per auction. Losses were realized on average in auctions with more than about six bidders. In contrast, the theoretical model predicts average profits of $7.48 and $4.82 at the Nash equilibrium, for small and large groups of bidders, respectively.

Laboratory experiments of this kind have been subject to criticism from several directions. Kagel *et al.* (1989) and Kagel and Richard (2001) demonstrate that learning and experience gained by bidders over a series of auctions tends to reduce the impact of the winner's curse. However, even with experienced bidders, outcomes are not always fully consistent with the theoretical model's prescriptions for rational bidding behaviour. Hansen and Lott (1991) attribute the average losses realized by bidders in the Kagel and Levin study to a tendency for aggressive bidding, in a rather artificial case in which participants can lose no more than their initial balances.

Reliance upon inexperienced student volunteers might represent a significant shortcoming in many experimental studies, if there are systematic differences between the behaviour of volunteers and that of experienced professional decision makers. Dyer *et al.* (1989) report an experiment in which the behaviour of construction industry executives was compared with that of student volunteers, in a common value auction in which participants submitted tenders to become the lowest-cost supplier. Perhaps surprisingly, there was little difference in the behaviour or performance of students and executives, with both falling victim to the winner's curse.

Cox and Hayne (1998) investigate possible differences in behaviour between experiments in which bidders are organized into teams, and experiments with individual bidders. The hypothesis is that team decision making may help reduce the impact on bidding behaviour of individual judgemental errors. In experiments where individuals and teams receive one signal each, there is little difference in performance, and susceptibility to the winner's curse is mainly a function of the experience of the participants. However, in experiments with multiple signals (for example, each member of a team of five receives a separate signal, while an individual bidder receives all five signals) teams appear to handle the multiple signal data significantly less effectively than individuals.

Field evidence

Capen *et al.* (1971) are widely credited for providing the first field evidence relating to the phenomenon of the winner's curse. As noted in Section 11.3, this study examined the bidding for oil and gas drilling rights in the Gulf of Mexico during the 1950s and 1960s. In a number of auctions the winning bids were many times higher than the next-highest bids, suggesting that some form of winner's curse was operative. For example, in Alaska in 1969 the winning bids were at least twice as large as the next-highest bids in 77 per cent of all cases. In follow-up studies, Mead *et al.* (1983) found after-tax rates of return to have been below the average return on equity for US manufacturing corporations, and expressed qualified support for the existence of a winner's curse. Hendricks *et al.* (1987) report that firms granted leases between 1954 and 1969 in auctions involving more than six bidders earned low or negative returns. The bids submitted by around two-thirds of the firms investigated were significantly higher than those that would produce a Nash equilibrium in the theoretical model.

> The results of the experiments indicate that a few firms did not behave optimally, and that, in at least one case, a firm [Texaco] consistently overestimated the value of the tracts. Most firms seemed aware that their valuations of tracts they win are biased upward, although a subset of the firms may have underestimated the extent of this bias.
>
> *(Hendricks et al., 1987, p. 518)*

Drawing on the results of an earlier study by Cassing and Douglas (1980), Blecherman and Camerer (1998) test for the winner's curse in wage offers made to players in US major league baseball in 1990. Two groups of players were examined: players who were free agents at the time of signing (and who were eligible to sell their services to the highest bidder); and players who were already on unexpired contracts and therefore ineligible for free agent status. In the absence of a winner's curse, players' salaries should be equivalent to their marginal revenue products (MRP). MRPs are estiamted for both groups of players, and compared with actual salaries. The average salary of free agents was $934,000, and the average estimated MRP of $605,000. For players without free agent status, the equivalent figures were $712,000 and $704,000. This suggests a tendency for teams that signed free agents to have overpaid and experienced the winner's curse. The contract system can be interpreted as a form of collusion between team owners who seek to avoid becoming involved in competitive bidding wars and overpaying for the services of star players.

The market for corporate takeover is another in which the possibility of a winner's curse arises. In cases where a number of bidders are competing to take over a firm, and the highest offer wins, it seems likely there may be a systematic tendency for winning bidders to overbid. Assessing the evidence presented in a number of empirical studies, Roll (1986) finds acquiring firms do tend to pay a substantial premium over and above the market value of the firms they acquire. This premium cannot be explained by subsequent increases in post-acquisition performance (see Section 7.4). Many merger decisions may be driven by either peer pressure or hubris, and may not be explicable in terms of rational economic calculus.

Case study 11.2

What determines the prices of goods traded in online auctions?

The growth of the internet has created new opportunities for trading by auction. A huge volume of goods is now traded daily through the eBay websites around the world. Online auctions provide a convenient low-cost environment for buyers and sellers to trade. The search engine technology underlying online auctions allows buyers and sellers to trade specialized products in liquid markets.

Founded in 1995 by Pierre Omidyar, eBay created an electronic platform for the sale of goods and services. eBay is not a traditional firm, even by the standards of the internet, because it does not hold any stock. Instead it acts as a broker to facilitate trade between buyers and sellers, by bringing them into contact with one another. In any transaction, the seller can set the opening price, a (secret) reserve price (if they wish), and the duration of the auction (between three and ten days). Bidders submit bids, which can be raised at any time within the auction period. Because the duration is fixed, many bidders post their bids during the last few hours or minutes of the auction period. When the auction closes and a winning bid is selected, the buyer and seller make contact. At this point the buyer pays for the goods via a PayPal account (an online payments system purchased by eBay in 2002); and the seller ships the goods to the buyer.

Information concerning the reliability of buyers and sellers can be obtained from published data concerning their previous trading history. Under this system, buyers and sellers rate the experience of trading with each other (following a transaction) as positive (+1), negative (–1), or neutral (0). Cumulative ratings are displayed for each trader. A rating exceeding +10 receives a star, while a rating below –4 leads to a trader being banned from further use of eBay. For the use of its services, eBay charges sellers a listing fee and a commission based on the value of the transaction. In 2004, eBay operated in 29 countries, and the total value of items traded was US$34 billion.

Several academic economists have investigated the behaviour of buyers and sellers in auctions. Particular interest has focused on the impact of asymmetric information, reputation effects and the degree of trust between buyers and sellers on traders' behaviour. This literature is surveyed by Bajari and Hortacsu (2004). For example, Lucking-Reiley *et al.* (2000) analyse the determinants of the prices of 461 collectable coins (Indian Head pennies) that were traded on eBay during July and August 1999. Data were collected on the age and grade of the coin; the minimum submitted bid; the final submitted bid; the number of bids; the reserve price (if any); the seller's rating; the duration of the auction; and whether or not the auction period included a weekend. Results from the analysis included the following:

■ Positive (negative) seller ratings lead to higher (lower) prices. Negative ratings have more impact on price than positive ratings.

■ Longer auctions fetch higher prices.

■ Reserve prices fetch higher prices (especially when only one bidder participates).

11.7 Summary

An auction is a market mechanism for converting bids from market participants into decisions concerning the allocation of resources and prices. Auctions can be characterized by the rules for the submission of bids, for determining the identity of the winning bidder, and for determining the price the winning bidder pays. There are four basic auction formats:

■ The English auction or ascending bid auction requires bids to be raised successively until a price is reached which only one bidder is willing to pay.

■ The Dutch auction or descending bid auction requires the offer price to be lowered successively until a price is reached which a bidder is prepared to pay.

- The first price sealed bid auction requires bidders to submit sealed bids independently. The highest bidder pays a price equivalent to the winning bid.

- The second price sealed bid auction also requires bidders to submit independent sealed bids. The highest bidder pays a price equivalent to the second-highest submitted bid.

The simplest theoretical models of auctions are based on two alternative assumptions concerning the distribution of bidders' valuations of the item under auction.

- In the pure common value model, there is a single, intrinsic value of the item that is the same for all bidders. No single bidder knows what this true value is. Each bidder estimates the item's true value independently.

- In the independent private values model, each bidder knows the true value of the item to himself or herself personally. Personal valuations of the item differ between bidders.

The winner's curse is a common feature of auctions where the pure common value model applies, especially those conducted using the first price sealed bid format. If all bidders submit bids equivalent to their private estimates of the item's intrinsic value, it is likely the winning bidder will have overestimated the intrinsic value. To avoid the winner's curse, each bidder's sealed bid should be based on a revised estimate of this value, conditional on the original estimate being the highest estimate made by any bidder.

In the independent private values model, if risk-neutral bidders pursue optimal bidding strategies which maximize their own private rents, all four basic auction formats are expected to yield the same expected price to the seller. This result is known as the revenue equivalence theorem.

In all four basic auction formats, the seller increases his expected proceeds by specifying a reserve price, such that the item is not sold if the selling price does not at least match (or exceed) the reserve price. The optimal reserve price is usually some distance above the seller's private valuation of the item. If bidders are risk averse, the optimal bidding strategy in an English auction or a second price sealed bid auction is unaffected. Risk-averse bidders tend to bid more aggressively in a Dutch auction or a first price sealed bid auction, in an effort to reduce the risk of not winning the auction. If bidders are asymmetric (split into two groups with private values drawn from different distributions), revenue equivalence breaks down. In this situation, it is possible that the winning bidder is not the bidder with the highest private value.

The pure common values model and the independent private values model are theoretical extremes. An affiliated valuations model allows bidders' valuations to be partly dependent on the intrinsic value of the item, but also partly subjective. When bidders' valuations are affiliated, revenue equivalence breaks down. An English auction yields the highest expected price to the seller, because the bidders' ability to observe each other's behaviour while bidding is underway mitigates the effects of the winner's curse. In the UK, this result helped inform the design of the government's successful auction of licences to operate mobile phone services using 3G technology, which took place in April 2000.

Discussion questions

1. Describe the four basic auction formats.
2. Explain the distinction between the pure common value model and the independent private values model of bidder valuations.
3. In a sealed bid auction in which bidders form independent private values, why might a bidder be well advised to abstain from submitting a bid equivalent to her private estimate of the item being sold?
4. 'In a sealed bid auction, it would pay to bid more aggressively if you knew you were competing against 10 other bidders than you would if you knew you were only competing against two other bidders.' Do you agree or disagree with this statement? Explain your reasoning.
5. Explain why the English auction and the second price sealed bid auction are strategically equivalent.
6. Explain why the Dutch auction and the first price sealed bid auction are strategically equivalent.
7. Why does it 'pay to tell the truth' in a second price sealed bid auction, but not in a first price sealed bid auction?
8. What are the implications of the revenue equivalence theorem for the seller's choice of auction format?
9. Under what conditions does revenue equivalence break down?
10. Assess the extent to which field evidence supports the phenomenon of the winner's curse.
11. Assess the extent to which experimental evidence supports the phenomenon of the winner's curse.
12. Referring to Case study 11.1, assess the effectiveness of the auction designs used to sell licences to operate mobile phone services using 3G technology in the UK and elsewhere in Europe.
13. Are bidders who use the eBay website (see Case study 11.2) at risk of experiencing the winner's curse? Justify your answer by referring to relevant aspects of auction theory.

Further reading

Bajari, P. and Hortacsu, A. (2004) Economic insights from internet auctions, *Journal of Economic Literature*, 42, 457–86.

Bergstrom, T.C. and Miller, J.H. (2000) *Experiments with Economic Principles*, 2nd edn. New York: McGraw Hill.

Binmore, K. and Klemperer, P. (2002) The biggest auction ever: the sale of the British 3G Telecom licences, *Economic Journal*, 112, C74–96.

Cohen, A. (2002) *The Perfect Store: Inside eBay*. London: Piatkus Publishers.

Klemperer, P. (1999) Auction theory: a guide to the literature, *Journal of Economic Surveys*, 13, 227–86.

Klemperer, P. (2002b) How not to run auctions: the European 3G telecom auctions, *European Economic Review*, 46, 829–45.

Klemperer, P. (2004) *Auctions: Theory and Practice*. Princeton, NJ: Princeton University Press.

McAfee, R. and McMillan, J. (1987) Auctions and bidding, *Journal of Economic Literature*, 25, 699–738.

Milgrom, P. (1989) Auctions and bidding: a primer, *Journal of Economic Perspectives*, 3, 3–22.

Thaler, R. (1991) *The Winner's Curse: Paradoxes and Anomalies of Economic Life*. New York, ch. 5.

Learning objectives

This chapter covers the following topics:

- vertical and horizontal product differentiation
- natural and strategic product differentiation
- the socially optimal amount of product differentiation
- Lancaster's product characteristics model
- Hotelling's location model
- Salop's location model

Key terms

Horizontal product differentiation
Location model
Natural product differentiation
Near-neighbour brands

Representative consumer model
Spatial model
Strategic product differentiation
Vertical product differentiation

12.1 Introduction

Most markets are typified by some degree of product differentiation. There is no single homogeneous brand of car, soap powder, hotel, T-shirt or breakfast cereal. Product differentiation can be viewed as the ability of producers to create distinctions (in a physical or in a psychological sense) between goods that are close substitutes, so that consumers no longer regard them as identical or near-identical.

In Chapter 12 we deal with product differentiation as a topic in industrial organization in its own right for the first time. However, product differentiation has already had an important role to play in several earlier chapters; and it will do so again later in this book. For example, in Chapter 2 the degree of product differentiation was cited as one of the defining characteristics of market structure. The theoretical model of monopolistic competition refers to an industry in which a large number of firms compete to produce and sell similar but slightly differentiated products or services. In Chapters 4 and 5, product differentiation is one of the principal forms of non-price competition open to oligopolists seeking to avoid becoming embroiled in damaging price competition. In Chapter 6, the issue of market definition was seen to depend on decisions as to where to draw the dividing line between groups of products that, on the basis of degree of similarity, might be considered either as part of the same market, or as comprising separate markets. In Chapter 8, product differentiation (or brand proliferation) was cited as one of the strategies an incumbent firm can adopt in order to raise barriers to entry.

Section 12.2 begins by drawing a distinction between **vertical** and **horizontal product differentiation**, and identifying a number of natural and strategic sources of product differentiation. This section also draws a distinction between two types of economic model of product differentiation. In representative consumer models, consumers have tastes or preferences for goods or services, and firms compete to attract consumers by differentiating the products they offer. In **spatial** or **location models**, consumers' tastes or preferences are defined in terms of the individual characteristics that are embodied in the goods or services. Section 12.3 develops an analysis of the implications of product differentiation for social welfare in the representative consumer model of monopolistic competition. This analysis suggests that in this model, only by accident does the degree of product differentiation at the post-entry equilibrium maximize social welfare.

The next three sections present a series of spatial or location models of product differentiation. Section 12.4 develops Lancaster's product characteristics model, in which goods are viewed as bundles of characteristics, and differentiated goods or brands contain the same characteristics in varying proportions. Section 12.5 develops Hotelling's model of spatial competition. In the original version of this model, geographic location is the characteristic that differentiates one supplier's product from another. However, the same model has been widely used to model competition in product characteristic space. In one variant of the model, two firms choose locations on a straight line, with prices assumed fixed. An alternative variant allows for price determination with fixed locations. Finally, Section 12.6 examines Salop's adaptation of the Hotelling model, in which both firms and consumers are located around the circumference of a circle. In this case, both locations and prices are endogenous, and there is free entry. The model's solution is analogous to the post-entry equilibrium in the neoclassical (representative consumer) model of monopolistic competition.

12.2 Types of product differentiation

In the economics literature, it is customary to distinguish between vertical and horizontal product differentiation (Beath and Katsoulacos, 1991). First, **vertical product differentiation** means one product or service differs in overall quality from another. For example, one brand of fruit juice may have higher fruit content and lower sugar content than another brand, and as such may be recognized as a higher-quality brand by all consumers. If the prices of the high-fruit brand and the high-sugar brand were the same, most or all consumers would purchase the high-fruit brand. Second, **horizontal product differentiation** means products or services are of the same or similar overall quality, but offer different combinations of characteristics. For example, a Ford Focus, Vauxhall Astra, Honda Civic, Volkswagen Golf and Toyota Corolla are all similar brands or models of car, but each one offers a slightly different package of attributes. Most drivers of cars in the relevant class would be able to express a preference in favour of one of these brands or models, but different drivers might well express different preferences.

The distinguishing characteristics of differentiated products and services may be classified as either natural or strategic. With **natural product differentiation**, the distinguishing characteristics arise from natural attributes or characteristics, rather than having been created through the actions of suppliers. With **strategic product differentiation**, the distinguishing characteristics are consciously created by suppliers: for example, through a decision to create a new brand and promote it by means of advertising or other types of marketing activity.

Sources of natural product differentiation include the following:

■ *Geographic variation.* In this case, the location of a seller automatically differentiates a product or service in the minds of consumers. Clearly the corner shop and the out-of-town superstore offer competing services that are differentiated in the minds of consumers on the basis of location (as well as other characteristics such as choice and price). In the residential property market, houses that are identical in every other respect might be highly differentiated in terms of the town, city or region in which they are located.

■ *New technology.* New technology can be used to differentiate a product: for example, through the addition of internet and e-mail features to a mobile telephone. Procter & Gamble has been successful in differentiating many of its products through the introduction of new technological features. Examples include the *Swiffer* mop that captures dust, and the *Nutri-Delight* orange drink, which has a special formula allowing iodine to coexist with certain vitamins and minerals, and which it is claimed permits children to gain weight.

■ *Brands and trademarks.* Brands and trademarks are used widely to differentiate similar products. Trademarks are words or symbols used to identify particular brands. In many cases, a firm that has developed a trademark will also hold exclusive property rights to use the trademark. Examples include a crocodile or a polo player on horseback (Lacoste or Ralph Lauren clothing). In some cases, the brand or trademark eventually becomes synonymous with the product. For example, the brand name Hoover has become widely used as a generic term for any vacuum cleaner. In such cases the brand owner may eventually lose its exclusive property rights (Bryson, 1994).

■ *Community or national differences.* Here the country or community of origin is the defining attribute that differentiates goods and services. In other words, products and services from certain parts of the world are deemed to be different and of higher quality. Examples include Devon custard, Russian vodka, Scottish whisky, Swiss watches, curry from the Indian subcontinent, Italian designer clothes, Hollywood movies.

■ *Consumer tastes and preferences*. Consumers themselves have different attributes, tastes and preferences. Consequently, the product characteristics that are most desired vary from one consumer to another. Product differentiation targeted at meeting these varied wants is often horizontal. Examples include the colour of cars and the style of clothes.

Sources of strategic product differentiation include the following:

■ *Factor variations*. Factor inputs such as labour and capital are rarely homogeneous. This creates opportunities for final outputs produced using differentiated factors of production to be marketed as distinct from those of other firms. For example, a supplier might claim its employees are more highly skilled, better trained or less prone to make errors; or that its components or raw material inputs are superior to those used by rival suppliers. Case study 12.2 (see pp. 433–4) suggests the use of star performers in Hollywood movies is an example of this type of differentiation.

■ *Additional services*. Additional services can often be used to differentiate products. Even if the same product is available from two suppliers, the conditions surrounding the sale might be different. Suppliers might differentiate their products by offering cheaper credit, faster delivery times or a more comprehensive after-sales service. By offering after-sales guarantees or warranties, the supplier sends signals to consumers that it has confidence in the quality of its product.

■ *Rate of change of product differentiation*. Products with a short natural lifespan can be subjected to planned obsolescence, especially in cases where the product accounts for a relatively small proportion of most consumers' budgets. Case study 12.1 discusses some of the issues involved. Consumers might be urged to purchase new styles, or models with superficial changes in characteristics. Products such as clothing and video games are often subject to this form of strategic product differentiation. Monopolies and Mergers Commission (1966) and Schmalensee (1978) present evidence of such behaviour in the UK detergents and US ready-to-eat cereals markets, respectively.

■ *Consumer ignorance*. Ignorance on the part of consumers can allow firms to exaggerate the extent of differentiation of their products and services. Suppliers sometimes exploit consumer ignorance through misleading advertising. Sometimes suppliers attempt to convince consumers that higher prices reflect higher quality (Scitovsky, 1950, 1971). If such attempts are successful, the level of consumer demand might even increase as price increases. Chawla (2002) discusses the role of consumer ignorance in determining prices for health treatment in private practice. In the Egyptian private health sector in the late 1990s, patients were poorly informed, and prices were relatively high as a consequence.

Case study 12.1

Planned obsolescence

It has been claimed (Beder, 1998) that an engineer working for General Electric in the 1930s argued that sales of flashlight bulbs could be increased if their efficiency was increased, but their lifespan was shortened. Instead of a bulb lasting over three batteries it could be made to last over just one battery. Similar suggestions and strategies were discussed and developed in many other industries. More recently, firms have become more sophisticated in their obsolescence strategies. Rather than manufacture products that break down or wear out physically, a new generation of products suggests to the consumer that the product has come to the end of its working life. The Gillette disposable blade has blue stripes which fade with use, suggesting the blade is wearing out. Goods can also become obsolete when individual parts and accessories are deliberately no longer produced. The fear is that high-quality products with long lifespans would lead to saturated markets and a depressed economy. But the outcome is that the consumer is sold an inferior product, which could be more durable at little additional cost. Apart from the ethical consideration, such strategies may provide opportunities for rival firms or entrants to supply longer-lasting or higher-quality products.

Marketing specialists discuss obsolescence under four main headings.

- *Intentional physical obsolescence*. The design of the product determines its lifespan. Examples include car batteries and lightbulbs.

- *Style obsolescence*. Suppliers deliberately alter the style of clothes, trainers, cars and other consumer goods, so as to make consumers of older styles feel out of date.

- *Technical obsolescence*. Sometimes a new technology replaces an older one, such as recordable DVD replacing VHS videotape. The new product has different attributes to the old one. If it is known that a product will be out of date after a certain period for stylistic or technical reasons, the producer might not bother to ensure the product has a longer physical lifespan. This might result in savings in production costs, which might be passed on to consumers in the form of lower prices, or which might simply be used to boost profits.

- *Postponed obsolescence*. In some cases, producers might be capable of introducing a more technically advanced product, but prefer instead to ration the technology. Consumers are offered improved products at planned intervals, and not necessarily as soon as they are technologically feasible. For example, improvements in computer operating systems are not necessarily incorporated into consumer products at the same pace as advances in computer science and technology.

In the economics literature, there are two basic approaches to the specification of consumer preferences and the modelling of firm behaviour in the case of horizontal product differentiation (Waterson, 1994). First, in **representative consumer models** consumers have tastes or preferences for goods or services, and firms compete to attract consumers by differentiating the goods or services they offer. Each firm's demand is a continuous function of its own price and the prices set by competing firms. This is true even in models where competition is atomistic. In the neoclassical model of monopolistic competition, developed in Section 2.6, each firm assumes its own individual pricing decision provokes a negligible response from its rivals.

Second, in **spatial** or **location models** consumers have tastes or preferences for the characteristics embodied in goods or services. In this case, consumer demand for a particular firm's product might be highly dependent on small changes in the price set by another firm whose product embodies a very similar bundle of characteristics; but independent of small changes in the price set by a third firm, whose product characteristics are further removed. Consider the high street food chains McDonald's, Burger King and Pizza Hut. If Burger King implements a small price cut, this might have a significant effect on demand at McDonald's; but if Pizza Hut does the same, this might have no effect on demand at McDonald's (or at Burger King). Only if Pizza Hut implements a large price cut would consumers who normally buy burgers consider switching to pizzas. This suggests McDonald's' demand might be a smooth function of Burger King's price, because the product characteristics are so similar, but a discontinuous function of Pizza Hut's price, because the product characteristics are further removed.

12.3 Monopolistic competition revisited: the socially optimal amount of product differentiation

In this section, we develop an analysis of the implications of product differentiation for social welfare in the representative consumer model of monopolistic competition that was originally developed in Section 2.6. Dixit and Stiglitz (1977) provide an extended treatment of some of the issues that are raised below.

We begin by recalling Figure 2.16, which shows the pre-entry and post-entry equilibria for a representative firm in monopolistic competition (see p. 64). At the pre-entry equilibrium, the firm earns an abnormal profit equivalent to the area C_1P_1BD. This abnormal profit attracts entrants; whose presence reduces the quantity the representative firm can sell at any price, and shifts the firm's demand or average revenue function to the left. At the post-entry equilibrium, the tangency solution is attained, and the representative firm's abnormal profit has disappeared.

For the purposes of examining the welfare implications of product differentiation, we interpret the pre-entry equilibrium shown in Figure 2.16 as depicting the situation when the representative firm is the only firm in the industry. This interpretation was not used in our previous discussion in Section 2.6, where it was simply assumed that there are fewer firms present at the pre-entry stage than at the post-entry stage. Logically, however, there is no difficulty in carrying out the pre-entry analysis for the extreme case where only one firm is present. This implies we can interpret the shift from the pre-entry to the post-entry equilibrium in Figure 2.16 as depicting a change in the number of firms from $N_1 = 1$ to N_2, the number of firms at the post-entry equilibrium at which each firm earns only a normal profit.

In order to establish the welfare implications of increasing product differentiation, it is necessary to determine the implications for total producer surplus or abnormal

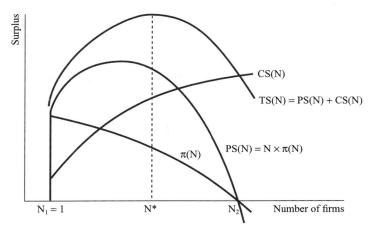

Figure 12.1 Monopolistic competition: too much product differentiation

profit, and for total consumer surplus, as the number of firms increases from $N_1 = 1$ to N_2. This relationship is derived in Figure 12.1. The construction is as follows.

- The function $\pi(N)$ shows the relationship between N, the number of firms, and the abnormal profit earned by the representative firm (represented by the area C_1P_1BD in Figure 2.16 for the case $N = 1$). It is assumed as N increases and the average revenue functions of incumbent firms start shifting to the left, their abnormal profits decrease smoothly. $\pi(N_2) = 0$ because at the post-entry equilibrium, the representative firm earns zero abnormal profit.

- The function $PS(N) = N \times \pi(N)$ shows the relationship between the number of firms and the total producer surplus or abnormal profit earned by all firms collectively. Starting from $N = 1$, a second firm can enter and earn an abnormal profit that exceeds the reduction in the first firm's abnormal profit resulting from this entry decision. Therefore total abnormal profit increases as the number of firms increases from $N = 1$ to $N = 2$. Similarly, for other small values of N, further entry causes the total abnormal profit to increase, since each entrant's abnormal profit exceeds the total loss of abnormal profit to the incumbents. Eventually, however, as N continues to increase, total abnormal profit must start to decrease. $PS(N) = N \times \pi(N)$ must attain a value of zero when the number of firms reaches N_2, since $\pi(N_2) = 0$.

- The function $CS(N)$ shows the relationship between the number of firms and the total consumer surplus. In the case $N_1 = 1$, consumer surplus is represented by the area P_1AB in Figure 2.16. As the number of firms increases and each incumbent firm's average revenue function starts shifting to the left, total consumer surplus increases for two reasons: first, entry causes total industry output to increase and prices to fall; and second, as more variety is introduced, each consumer is more likely to find a brand that matches his or her tastes more closely.

- Finally, the function $TS(N) = PS(N) + CS(N)$ shows the relationship between the number of firms and the total surplus, calculated as the vertical summation of $PS(N)$ and $CS(N)$. In Figure 12.1, $TS(N)$ attains its maximum value at $N = N^*$,

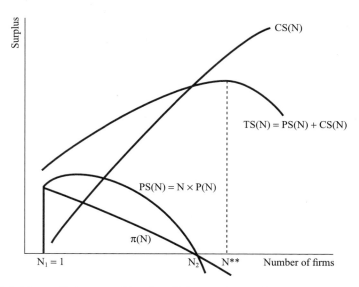

Figure 12.2 Monopolistic competition: insufficient product differentiation

which is smaller than N_2. Therefore in this case there is too much product differentiation at the post-entry equilibrium. However, the opposite case is also possible. In Figure 12.2, TS(N) attains its maximum value at $N = N^{**}$, which is larger than N_2. In this case there is too little product differentiation at the post-entry equilibrium.

The main conclusion that emerges from this analysis is that only by coincidence is social welfare maximized at the post-entry equilibrium in monopolistic competition. The number of firms at the post-entry equilibrium is determined by entrants examining whether or not they obtain a positive private benefit (abnormal profit) if they enter. However, each entry decision also imposes costs and benefits on other parties, which are not considered by the entrant. By increasing industry output and reducing prices, entry tends to reduce the producer surplus (abnormal profits) of incumbent firms, but it also tends to increase consumer surplus. Whether the number of firms, and therefore the amount of product differentiation, at the post-entry equilibrium is too high or too low (from a social welfare maximization perspective) depends on which of these two effects dominates. If the negative producer surplus effect dominates, there is too much product differentiation; but if the positive consumer surplus effect dominates, there is too little product differentiation. Only by coincidence, if these two effects are evenly balanced, is the degree of product differentiation optimal.

12.4 Lancaster's product characteristics model

In Sections 12.4 to 12.6, we turn our attention away from the representative consumer model of monopolistic competition, towards a number of spatial or location models of product differentiation. The first model we consider is Lancaster's (1966) product characteristics model. In this model, consumers derive utility not from the goods they consume, but from the characteristics that are embodied in the goods consumed. Goods are viewed as bundles of characteristics, and differentiated goods or brands are goods that contain the same characteristics in different proportions. For example, when you decide which car to buy, you consider an array of characteristics. Car manufacturers produce glossy brochures which list characteristics such as safety features, performance, comfort, seating, security, styling, in-car entertainment, and so on. Similarly, mobile phones are marketed by product characteristics: does the phone have a camera, personal organizer, polyphonic ring tones, predictive text, vibrating alert, video capture, voice-activated dialling, FM radio, and so on? The average car or mobile phone purchaser is not interested in every available model. He or she narrows the choice down to those models that come close to delivering the desired bundle or mix of characteristics. Many product markets are saturated with huge numbers of models and product types. During a visit to his local store, Schwartz (2004) counts 85 varieties of crackers, 285 varieties of cookies, 85 brands of juices, 75 iced teas, 15 flavours of bottled water, 61 varieties of sun protection products, 80 pain relievers, 40 toothpastes, 150 lipsticks, 75 eyeliners, 90 nail polishes, 116 skin creams, and 360 brands of shampoo and other hair care products.

In Figure 12.3, a consumer obtains utility from the consumption of two characteristics. The quantities of each characteristic are shown along the axes of the diagram, and IC is the consumer's indifference curve. Indifference curves for characteristics have the usual properties: more of each characteristic is always preferred to less of the same characteristic, and the indifference curves are convex to the origin. The four rays represent the proportions of characteristics 1 and 2 that are available from brands A, B, C and D. For example, brand A offers lots of characteristic 1 but very little of characteristic 2. Brand D offers the opposite combination. Brands B and C offer more balanced combinations of characteristics 1 and 2. Here are some examples of products and the characteristics they might embody.

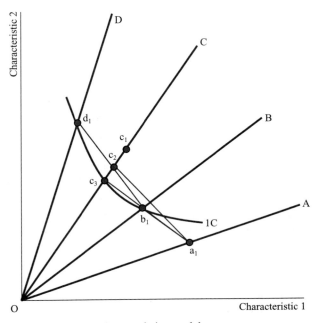

Figure 12.3 Lancaster's product characteristics model

Product	Characteristic 1	Characteristic 2
Breakfast cereals	Crunchiness	Fruitiness
Curry sauces	Flavour	Hot, medium or mild
Musical acts	Beat	Melody
Cars	Spaciousness	Manoeuvrability

The consumer with indifference curve IC normally prefers the characteristics to be combined in proportions similar to those provided by Brand C. Initially, the prices of the four brands are such that for a given level of expenditure, the consumer can afford to locate at b_1 if he or she allocates all of the budget to brand B, c_1 if he or she purchases brand C, or likewise, a_1 or d_1. Faced with this set of choices, the consumer chooses brand C and locates at c_1. Utility at c_1 is higher than at b_1 or d_1, both of which are located on the same indifference curve, IC. Utility at c_1 is also higher than at a_1, which is located on a lower indifference curve than IC.

Consider the implications of an increase in the price of Brand C. Let P_1 denote the price of C that enables the consumer to locate at c_1. Suppose the price of C increases to P_2, so that if the same budget is allocated to good C, the consumer can only attain c_2. If it is possible to achieve a desired mix of characteristics by consuming combinations of brands in varying proportions, there is another way of attaining c_2. If the quantities of brands B and D can be mixed in this way, any combination of characteristics along the arc $b_1 d_1$ is attainable. The consumer could also achieve c_2 by splitting the budget between purchases of brands B and D. If the price of C increases beyond P_2, the consumer prefers combined consumption of brands B and D to sole consumption of brand C. At prices beyond P_2, this consumer is eliminated from the market for brand C.

In practice, can a desired mix of characteristics actually be achieved by consuming different brands in varying combinations? For products like breakfast cereals or curry sauces, it is easy to imagine purchasing two different brands and mixing them together. For musical acts or cars, it is harder to imagine consuming different brands in combination, unless perhaps alternative combinations of characteristics are required at different times of the day or week. If manoeuvrability is required for town driving during the week, but spaciousness is more important for long trips at weekends, a family might decide to run two cars.

If it is not possible to consume combinations of alternative brands in varying proportions in order to achieve a desired mix of characteristics, in Figure 12.3 the consumer would stick with brand C unless the price increases beyond P_3 (at which the point c_3 is attainable). Beyond P_3, the consumer would derive higher utility by switching altogether to either brand B or brand D.

In the case where brands can be consumed in combination, in Figure 12.3 the purchase of brand C is not ruled out altogether at prices above P_2. Consider a second consumer with a different set of indifference curves, who normally prefers the characteristics to be combined in proportions similar to those provided by brand B. If the points attainable by allocating the entire budget to one brand are a_1, b_1, c_2 and d_1, it is better to purchase a combination of brands A and C than to allocate the entire budget to brand B. In this way, a point on OB beyond b_1 is attainable.

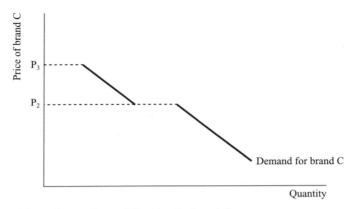

Figure 12.4 Discontinuous demand function for brand C

However, if the price of brand C increases beyond P_3, combined consumption of A and C is no longer preferable. In this case, the second consumer is also eliminated from the market for brand C.

This analysis suggests there are sharp discontinuities in the demand curve for brand C, illustrated in Figure 12.4. Above P_3, neither consumer purchases brand C. At P_3, however, C captures the second consumer (who normally prefers B), and there is a sudden jump in the demand for C. Similarly at P_2, C captures the first consumer (who normally prefers C), and there is a further jump in the demand for C. Variation in the price of C also produces sharp discontinuities in the demand for C's **near-neighbour brands**, in this case brands B and D.

These discontinuous demand functions, and the interdependencies between them, are likely to have major implications for competition and pricing strategy. Archibald and Rosenbluth (1975) consider the implications of variations in the number of characteristics and the number of competing brands.

- When there are many competing brands and there are many rays in Figure 12.3, small price changes cause smoother and more continuous switching between brands. The effect of a change in the price of brand C on the total demand for brand D is negligible from the viewpoint of the producers of brand D, because brand C is only one of a very large number of competitors in brand D's near-neighbourhood. In this case the Lancaster model approximates to the neoclassical model of mono-polistic competition described in Section 2.6.

- In Figure 12.3, strong product differentiation produces rays that are further apart, while weak product differentiation produces rays that are closer together. If the rays are far apart, large price variations are needed to trigger switching between brands. If the rays are close together, only small price variations are needed for the same effect.

- In Figure 12.3, non-substitutable characteristics make the indifference curves more L-shaped, while easily substitutable characteristics make the indifference curves flatter. If the indifference curves are L-shaped, large price variations are needed to trigger switching between brands. If the indifference curves are flat, only small price variations are needed for the same effect.

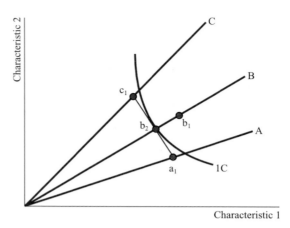

Figure 12.5 Positioning of new brand B

The Lancaster product characteristics model also provides insights into the decision to introduce a new brand. The market depicted in Figure 12.5 is currently occupied by Brands A and C. As before, A and C can be combined in varying proportions to produce a preferred combination of characteristics. A consumer with the indifference curve IC maximizes utility by consuming a combination of A and C at point b_2. However, the gap that exists in the product characteristic space between brands A and C represents an opportunity for the creation of a new brand B. If brand B can be priced so that the consumer can attain a position such as b_1, the consumer will switch from the combined purchase of brands A and C at b_2 to the sole purchase of brand B at b_1. The essence of building an effective brand is discussed in Box 12.1.

Box 12.1

The essence of building an effective brand

The role of brands and their contribution to business performance have been a source of controversy over the years. In the mid-1990s, following the rise of private labels in fast-moving consumer goods industries, many were quick to announce the decline and fall of brands such as Coca-Cola, Marlboro and Gillette.

However, those predictions were premature. By the end of the decade not only had most of the fallen brands recovered, but a number of non-consumer goods and service companies had joined the club of sophisticated brand builders.

Who would have thought, for instance, that Intel – an industrial label for a semiconductor chip that computer users do not see, touch, smell or taste – was on its way to becoming one of the world's most recognized and valuable brand names? Intel's management, with a keen eye on the growing number of first-time PC buyers, saw the potential for creating and then protecting a highly differentiated branded position in an increasingly commodity-like market for semiconductor chips.

Intel's success, confirmed by the premium prices PC customers are willing to pay for a product with an Intel sticker, has been an inspiration for many raw material and component manufacturers. Like Intel, they seek ways of enhancing their competitive position through the effective use of their brands.

The controversy surrounding brands was re-ignited most recently with the rise of electronic commerce. Once again, many predicted the decline of brands. They argued that brands had little to contribute in internet markets, where price transparency is the rule. As experience accumulated, however, sceptics were again proved wrong.

While products and prices can be compared endlessly, internet consumers are nonetheless sticking to a few established sites with recognized names – such as Amazon.com and Charles Schwab, and even old-economy labels such as Barnes & Noble and IBM.

The realization that brands are just as important online as offline has encouraged many e-commerce companies to invest heavily in advertising. At the height of the dotcom frenzy, many e-commerce start-ups spent sums several times their sales revenues in an attempt to establish a dominant presence in the internet's crowded market space.

The logic of brands

What explains the persistence and growth of brands in both the old and new economy, and the endemic scepticism about their role? What is the enduring logic of brands? A closer analysis of Intel's campaign may provide some answers.

In the early 1990s, a court gave Intel's rival AMD the right to copy the company's microchips – an unforeseen byproduct of a licensing agreement between them. Managers were faced with the challenge of finding new ways of differentiating Intel's chips from those produced by its competition. Competing on price was not an appealing option. Branding computer chips itself was a new idea, but reaching the consumer with a brand statement was totally unconventional, especially in an industry where differentiation had always been fought on technical superiority.

After all, the sceptics argued, Intel's customers were PC makers, not PC users. Why should the consumers care about the brand of a component inside their PC?

However, Intel's managers understood the psychology of a growing number of first-time PC buyers who wanted reassurance that their investment in a computer was a safe one. The 'intel inside' sticker on each PC communicated quality and power – exactly what the consumers needed. All the company's press and broadcast advertisements emphasized the brand values of assured quality and high-tech power. Intel's brand was to stand for a safe choice.

The message fell on receptive consumer ears, but consumers were not the only beneficiaries of Intel's logic. Intel had also recognized that many lesser-known manufacturers would be interested in buying the company's premium-priced microchip and displaying the Intel logo on their products and advertising. While the brand on the computer, often an IBM clone, might not be well known, consumers had no difficulty recognizing the Intel sticker that had come to represent assured quality and computing power.

Sales benefits

Market research indicated that consumers were willing to pay a premium for PCs containing Intel's chip. Intel decided to offer the PC makers a rebate on chip purchases to be spent on advertising, which displayed the Intel logo. It was an offer clone makers could not refuse.

By the late 1990s even big names such as IBM and Hewlett-Packard had joined the bandwagon. Intel's logo appeared on the computers of more than 1,600 manufacturers and its chips held a 75 per cent market share.

Intel's campaign also led to benefits for PC retailers. Consumer preference for the brand increased stock turnover for computers carrying the company's logo. It also raised margins. The computer retail trade thus shared in the payoffs from a well-recognized brand.

As Intel's example shows, the logic of brands can be compelling across the value chain. Effective brands facilitate consumer choice, provide retailers with added incentives and help differentiate a company's products or services.

In the final analysis, though, a brand-differentiated business must produce higher returns or else the branding exercise is futile. The good news for such businesses is that strong brands do confer such superior returns. For example, Interbrand, a company that specializes in valuing brands, places Intel among the world's four most valuable brand names (after Coca-Cola, Microsoft and IBM) and estimates the brand to be worth nearly US$40bn. This is the highest value ever seen for an ingredient brand; it is proof that when fully understood and exploited, brands have tangible payoffs.

Brand-building

The process

What turns a name into a great brand? There are no simple answers to this, but an important principle underlies all attempts at creating brands. Strong brands do not just happen; they are built over time through a deliberate management process involving strategic decisions and corresponding actions. The quality of this process can make all the difference between a desirable brand and the also-rans.

There are six key decision and action elements of brand-building: anchor values, customer value proposition, media communications, promotion and point-of-sale. These elements define the strategic and operational imperatives of a given brand; they provide a structured blueprint for building a brand.

Anchor values

Every brand needs to be based on values and attributes that are permanent, purposeful and fundamental to its strategy. Anchor values give depth of meaning to an otherwise inert name and, in so doing, provide a strategic ambition and direction to the brand.

For example, when Ericsson launched its cellular phones, managers decided on 10 anchor values: simplicity, dependability, independence, co-operation, ambition, fulfilment, innovation, social interaction, up-to-date, accomplishment.

These values were to inspire everything the company did, from choice of technology and design to how the brand communicated to its target consumers. They were also meant to reflect the unique corporate attributes of Ericsson, a 120-year-old telecommunications company that believes in human interaction above cold technology.

Anchor values can be thought of as genetic codes for everything that might relate to a brand, not just its communication. Deciding on these values is the first step towards defining a long-term brand strategy.

Customer value proposition

Second, managers should define what anchor values would mean for the customer. This element, referred to as customer value proposition (CVP), is about translating general anchor values into specific statements on the benefits that drive the buying decision. Simplicity of design and use, a tangible functional benefit, is part of Ericsson's CVP for its mobile phones.

Non-differentiated products and services cannot credibly rely on tangible and functional benefits as drivers of consumer choice. Their CVPs should be based on less tangible, more emotional or aspirational propositions. 'The Pepsi generation', for example, was a CVP for younger drinkers who saw themselves as belonging to an up-and-coming generation with new habits and lifestyles.

CVP is inspired by anchor values but is more targeted towards benefits that are highly regarded by customers. Like the security associated with Intel's chips, CVP gives customers reasons to seek the brand. An effective CVP is based on deep insights into customer needs and behaviour; it adds a customer-led trajectory to brand strategy.

Positioning

The third element in brand-building consists of two decisions: one concerning target segments, the other a differentiation platform. Together, they define a brand's positioning.

Segment definition identifies customers for whom the anchor values are most relevant and whose wishes are best addressed by the brand's CVP. They also constitute the target for future brand-building. For example, Nescafé's redefined strategy targets consumers who welcome new ways of drinking coffee and are willing to 'open up' to the idea of a good cup of instant coffee. Not all coffee drinkers fall into this definition. For Intel, the target segment was the first-time PC buyer who wanted a safe choice. Knowledgeable computer buffs were not part of Intel's target group.

The second decision concerning a differentiation platform attempts to answer the question: 'Why this brand?' Unlike CVP, which is focused on customer benefits, differentiation is about how a brand is different. For Sony, what differentiates its brand is the excitement embedded in its products, a streamlined but intelligent simplicity that often hides a complex technology. Accordingly, when the company uses a label saying 'It's a Sony', it tries to communicate the essence of its differentiation: that the product is simpler on the outside, more sophisticated on the inside and, as a consequence, more fun to use.

Anchor values, customer value propositions and positioning constitute the three strategic elements of brand-building. They set in place clear guidelines for management implementation; actions that consistently convey the brand values through the use of media, promotional schemes and point-of-sale customer interaction.

Media communication

The most visible part of brand strategy implementation is advertising. Huge sums are spent each year on print, outdoor, television, radio and website advertising. But, to the dismay of brand builders, most spending is wasted because advertisements either do not reach the target audiences or, when they do, they fail to leave lasting impressions. Two factors contribute to this problem: clutter and decay.

Clutter results from the average consumer being exposed to an estimated 200 to 300 commercial messages a day. The challenge for an advertiser is to cut through this clutter. The brand-builder faces a second factor, decay, which means that most of the message is forgotten minutes later.

Clutter and decay put special demands on media communication, where often the largest resources are spent. It remains an advertiser's challenge to relate in a more intimate way with target customers, not only for the brand message to be better noticed, but also to leave a longer-lasting impression. These aims were behind Nescafé's recent 'open up' international television campaign. This uses unusual people and situations to stand out from other coffee advertisements and to convey the essence of its brand message for drinkers of roast and ground coffee – open yourself up to a new experience, that of instant coffee.

Promotions

Not all great brands are built on the back of high-budget mass advertising. Promotion can be even more effective. Consider, for example, the Body Shop, the pre-eminent retailer for cosmetics and personal care products. The founder's philosophy of doing business precludes the use of advertising along with, among others, excessive packaging and animal testing. Yet, Body Shop's unorthodox promotional schemes, including sponsorship of social activism and environmental causes, have greatly contributed to the brand's success among progressive and affluent youth. Other examples of promotional activities include Swatch's sponsorship of sports events and Harley-Davidson's owners' clubs.

The ever-rising cost of advertising, media clutter and the emergence of highly targeted promotional vehicles have contributed to the increasing reliance on non-media promotions. Effective promotions create synergies with other marketing vehicles and support the brand strategy. Accordingly, any promotional activity that fails this test must be avoided as it risks diluting, or even conflicting with, the brand's anchor values.

Point of sale

The final element in the brand-building process involves activities affecting the customer experience at the point of sale. These are 'moments of truth' when decisions are made for or against buying a given brand. In supermarkets, where brands reach out from the crowded shelves for attention, the point-of-sale experience may be as short as three seconds. Availability and location on the shelf, packaging, the words and images on the product are all factors that shape a customer's experience and choices at the point of sale, in seconds.

The importance of the point of sale is not limited to bricks-and-mortar businesses. The customer interface on a website can also be a determining factor, affecting the outcome of a given online transaction. Evidence suggests that the rate of 'online drop-outs' (shoppers who considered buying online but decided against it) is directly related to the customer's experience on the website. Research shows that the simplicity and convenience of a site are crucial to repeat shopping and customer loyalty.

Where personal selling is part of the buying experience, as is the case for many industrial products and services, the point-of-sale interaction can have an overwhelming impact on brand values as they are experienced by the customer.

Consider Hilti, a manufacturer of construction power tools and fastener systems with a 7,500-strong direct sales force. These salespeople communicate Hilti's CVP of superior product quality and end-user service to customers around the world. For Hilti, every day represents nearly 70,000 customer contacts, each offering an opportunity to create a branded customer experience.

From the rigorous training of field salespeople to their unified appearance (including a bright red hardhat and toolkit) and well-programmed sales pitch, managers make a conscious effort to use every interaction to reinforce Hilti's brand values. The company knows that no other communication vehicle can be as powerful as the customer experience.

As important as customer interface tends to be at the point of sale, it is often left out of the brand-building process, given to chance and possibly to divergent localized actions. McDonald's has well understood the importance of customer experience in its fast-food outlets. Its speedy service, friendly atmosphere and cleanliness are as much a part of McDonald's brand values as are its consistent food quality and family orientation.

At the sharp end of the brand-building process, where strategy is finally translated into a specific customer interface, it is the experience that speaks louder than commercial words. Accordingly it is important to ensure that every moment of truth leads to a reinforcement of what the brand stands for and, as such, to a uniquely branded customer experience.

Beyond the talk

While the above brand-building model highlights important process decisions and actions, a brand-builder's ultimate aim should be one of establishing and managing a relationship with the customer – a task far more complex than following a decision guide. Effective brands evoke a trusting relationship, which is reinforced with every customer transaction.

Trust in brands, as in any relationship, comes from consistency and continuity. On consistency, every customer experience with the product or service must reaffirm and reinforce the values it communicates. Anything short of this is cause for distrust and termination of the relationship. Consistency puts a special demand on managers to question the fit between every brand-related action and the core values of strategy.

Continuity is critical because strong brand relationships are only built over a long time. (Awareness may be built quickly, but this does not constitute a relationship. It takes accumulated positive experience for people to bond closely with brands.) Shifting brand values and irregular investments in communication, both signs of erratic management priorities, are two culprits for a discontinuous relationship. Customers reward those brands that stand for continuity and invest for the long term.

Source: Kamran Kashani, Survey – mastering management © Financial Times, 18 December 2000.

12.5   Hotelling's location model

In an early and highly influential contribution to the literature on spatial competition and product differentiation, Hotelling (1929) develops a model of competition in which geographical location is the characteristic that differentiates one supplier's product from another. The products themselves are identical, but if all firms were charging the same price, all consumers would prefer to purchase from their nearest supplier. This means each firm has a certain amount of market power. A firm that raises its price does not automatically lose all its customers to its competitors. Some customers (those located nearest to the firm concerned) are willing to pay a slightly higher price in order to continue buying locally, rather than incur the costs of travelling further afield in order to buy more cheaply.

Although the original version of the Hotelling model describes competition in geographic space, the same model can easily be adapted to describe competition in product characteristic space. Case studies 12.2 and 12.3 provide applications for Hollywood movies and air travel, respectively. In the case of breakfast cereals, we can imagine different brands as being situated at different locations on a two-dimensional plane such as Figure 12.6, in which the horizontal dimension measures one characteristic such as degree of crunchiness, and the vertical dimension measures another characteristic, degree of fruitiness. Each consumer has a preferred location on the two-dimensional plane, reflecting the consumer's ideal brand which, if it existed, would embody the consumer's preferred combination of these two characteristics. The consumer can either buy a brand that is situated close to her own location (which provides the highest utility), or a brand that is situated further away (which provides less utility). As before, if all firms were charging the same price, all consumers would prefer to purchase from their nearest supplier (in characteristics space). If there are significant price differences, however, it might be worthwhile to purchase from a more distant supplier,

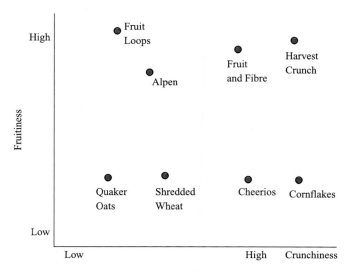

Figure 12.6 Product characteristic space for breakfast cereals

Product differentiation at the movies

Hollywood movies have dominated the market for movies for a century. While audiences now consume movies through a wide range of media including television, video, DVD and the internet, until the mid-1960s cinema was the main medium. In the US, during the post-war period aggregate cinema attendances declined from a high of 4.5 billion in 1946 to just 0.8 billion in 1972. The revenues of the major movie studios declined, but not uniformly across all types of movies. By the mid-1960s the most successful hit movies were still earning revenues comparable to the highest-earning movies of the late-1940s. However, lower ranked movies tended to perform much worse in the 1960s than in the 1940s.

Traditionally, the strategies of the large studios (such as MGM, RKO, Paramount, 20th Century Fox and Warner Brothers) were based on selling and distributing movies through their own cinemas, and using the more certain revenue associated with low-budget movies to offset the more uncertain revenues associated with high-budget movies. However, the revenues obtained from low-budget movies in particular declined with the fall in audience numbers during the 1950s and 1960s. Demand side explanations for the fall in cinema attendances include the trend towards suburbanization, which increased the distances cinema-goers had to travel in order to attend. Increased home ownership and a booming birthrate imposed new demands on people's leisure time, while the growth of television provided a cheaper and more convenient source of entertainment. Also, adverse antitrust decisions against the big studios required the divestment of large numbers of cinemas. In response to these adverse demand side and supply side developments, movie companies implemented a range of product differentiation strategies.

In the movie industry, horizontal product differentiation involves the development and extension of movie genres. Sedgewick (2002) develops a genre continuum (based on clusters of dominant genres) to examine the characterstics of the 1,820 most successful movies during the period 1946–65. The extremes of the continuum are comedies and musicals (for gaiety and light-heartedness) at one end; and westerns, war and crime movies (for violence, bloodshed and death) at the opposite extreme. Intermediate genres include animation, drama, fantasy, historical, horror, mystery, romance, sci-fi, spy movies and thrillers. The development of such a continuum is 'based on the likelihood of near- and distant-neighbour characteristics attracting distinct taste publics' (Sedgwick, 2002, p. 692). The number of movies in the leading genres is spread quite evenly: the top four genres were drama (408 movies), comedy (343), musicals (243) and westerns (217). During the period, new genres emerged targeted at the youth market, with greater emphasis on sex and rock-and-roll music. In general it appears the market became more fragmented by genre, with only the biggest-budget blockbuster movies being capable of transcending genre and attracting mass audiences.

Vertical product differentiation in the movie industry implies the existence of quality differences within genres. Quality differences and vertical differentiation might suggest that consumers should be willing to pay more to watch box office blockbusters; however, the movie companies and cinemas generally did not tend to charge higher prices for hit movies. Consequently, vertical differentation can be measured directly from audience or revenue data.

Films such as *Gone with the Wind* (1939), *The Sound of Music* (1965), and the more recent *Titanic* (1998) can be thought of as supreme examples of vertically differentiated film commodities: films that were considered to be attractions superior in almost all respects to other films on offer at the time by filmgoers at large, many of whom only rarely went to the movies.

(Sedgwick, 2002, p. 694)

Another way of measuring vertical differentiation is based on data on the incidence of appearances in movies by the leading stars of the period. Between 1946 and 1965, Elizabeth Taylor appeared in 10 movies that were among the top 10 earners for the year in which they were released. The next highest numbers of appearances in top 10 movies were by Bing Crosby and Gregory Peck (9 each); John Wayne (7); and Marlon Brando and Carey Grant (6 each). However, by itself casting a star in a movie is not enough to guarantee success.

Rather, it was their conjunction with other idiosyncratic and intangible inputs, such as director, screenplay, and genre, which led to the success or otherwise of the films in which they starred. In other words, charisma needs good guidance, good story material and co-stars to work with, and an appropriate setting if it is to be fully effective.

(Sedgewick, 2002, p. 701)

Source: Based on J. Sedgewick (2002) Product differentiation at the movies: Hollywood, 1946 to 1965, *Journal of Economic History*, 62, pp. 676–705.

provided the saving in price is at least sufficient to compensate for the loss of utility. In order to develop the Hotelling location model, the examples cited below refer to competition in geographic space and competition in product characteristic space interchangeably. We begin building the model, however, using the geographic interpretation. We consider a town, which consists of one street running from west to east. The street is perfectly straight, and consumers live at addresses distributed evenly (or uniformly) along the street. For simplicity, distances are standardized so that the total length of the street is 1. Each consumer's address is represented by a number between 0 and 1, with 0 denoting the address at the far west end of the street, and 1 denoting the address at the far east end.

Therefore for simplicity, our model of competition in geographic space is one-dimensional: all consumers are located on a single east–west dimension. For the model of competition in product characteristic space, the equivalent condition is that there is only one relevant product characteristic: degree of crunchiness, for example, in the breakfast cereals case. Each consumer's location, or ideal brand (in terms of degree of crunchiness), can be represented by an address number between 0 (soft) and 1 (crunchy), in the same way as before.

Case study 12.3

Hotelling in the air

The Norwegian economists Salvanes *et al.* (2004) have analysed the dispersion of scheduled flight departure times by Norwegian airlines using the Hotelling model. An important objective is to examine the effect of deregulation on the clustering of flight times on routes that were served by two (duopoly) carriers. The timetabling decision might be governed by two broad considerations. An airline might wish to locate close (offer similar flight times) to a rival in an attempt to poach some of the rival's customers. Alternatively, an airline might wish to locate far away (offer different flight times) from its rival, in order to differentiate its service and appeal to a different segment of the market.

Before 1994, the market was heavily regulated. Each route was allocated to one airline, with regulated prices and flight times. After 1994, routes were deregulated and airlines were free to operate on any route and to set their own prices and flight times. Post-1994, two airlines, SAS and Braathens, became the dominant carriers in the Norwegian market. There was virtually no price-cutting in the business sector, and only very modest price reductions in the leisure sector. This might be explained by the market being dominated by two similar-sized firms, with a similar capability to increase sales by reducing price. Therefore each airline had the capacity to inflict damage on its rival, should the rival behave aggressively. Under these conditions, both airlines may have consciously sought to avoid triggering a price war.

If deregulation did little to reduce prices, did it result in more aggressive flight scheduling? Before 1994, the authorities determined the time schedules for particular routes with the intention of ensuring greater consumer choice as regards flight times. Flights covering the same route and taking off at the same time (pairwise flights) were not allowed. On the basis of casual observation of the Oslo–Bodo and Oslo–Stavanger routes, deregulation appears to have had no effect on timetabling by the dominant airline on each route. The dispersion of departure times before and after deregulation showed little change.

However, following deregulation there was a tendency for more pairwise flights, especially in the morning and afternoon segments: those most popular with business travellers. A clustering index, calculated for 12 routes, confirms this pattern. This outcome appears to be consistent with the notion that if suppliers tend to avoid price competition, there is likely to be clustering in product characteristics space at the competitive or Nash equilibrium.

Sources: K.G. Salvanes, F. Steen and L. Sorgard (2005) Hotelling in the air? Flight departures in Norway. *Regional Science and Urban Economics*, 35, 193–213. Borenstein, S. and Netz, J. (2000) Why do all flights leave at 8am? Competition and departure differentiation in the airline markets, *International Journal of Industrial Organization*, 17, 611–40.

In the case where suppliers are differentiated by geographic location, it is assumed that every day, each consumer wishes to make a single purchase from one of two firms, both of which supply an identical product. The utility obtained by consuming a unit of the product can be standardized to a value of one. When making his or her daily purchase, each consumer incurs a transport cost dependent on the distance travelled. Transport cost is quadratic in distance, so as distance increases, transport cost increases at an increasing rate. Suppose initially the two firms are located at opposite ends of town: firm A at address 0 and firm B at address 1. For a consumer located at address d between 0 and 1, the utility gained and total cost incurred (purchase price *plus* transport cost) are as follows:

	Utility	Purchase price *plus* transport cost
Purchase from firm A	1	$P_A + kd^2$
Purchase from firm B	1	$P_B + k(1 - d)^2$

In the case where suppliers are differentiated by the characteristics of their brands, again it is assumed that every day, each consumer wishes to make a single purchase from one of two firms. The utility that would be obtained by consuming a brand corresponding precisely to the consumer's ideal brand (if such a brand existed) is standardized to a value of one. When making his or her daily purchase of one of the two available brands, each consumer incurs a utility loss dependent on the distance between the location of the brand purchased, and the location of the consumer's ideal brand. The utility loss is quadratic in distance, so as distance increases, the utility loss increases at an increasing rate. Again, suppose initially firms A and B are located at addresses 0 and 1, respectively. For a consumer located at address d between 0 and 1, the (net) utility gained and cost incurred (just the purchase price in this case) are as follows:

	Utility (net)	Purchase price
Purchase from firm A	$1 - kd^2$	P_A
Purchase from firm B	$1 - k(1 - d)^2$	P_B

The parameter k plays a vital role in the model. In the model of competition in geographic space, a higher value of k implies a higher transport cost. In the model of competition in product characteristic space, a higher value of k implies a higher degree of consumer brand loyalty: as k increases, it costs consumers more (in terms of utility foregone) to switch from a brand situated close to their ideal brand to a brand situated further away. In both models, as k increases consumers become less likely to switch between firms A and B in response to small changes in P_A and P_B. Therefore k is a measure of the consumers' rate of substitution between firms A and B. The higher the value of k, the lower the rate of substitution, and the lower the intensity of competition between firms A and B.

In both models, the consumer buys from the firm from which she receives the highest surplus, defined as the difference between the utility gained and the cost incurred, provided this surplus is positive:

- If $P_A + kd^2 < P_B + k(1-d)^2$ and $P_A + kd^2 \leq 1$, the consumer buys from firm A.

- If $P_A + kd^2 > P_B + k(1-d)^2$ and $P_B + k(1-d)^2 \leq 1$, the consumer buys from firm B.

Hotelling considers the case where the price is determined exogenously and is the same for both firms ($P_A = P_B = \bar{P}$), but the firms are free to choose where (in geographic space or product characteristic space) to locate. However, the model can be extended to cover a second case where the two firms' locations are fixed, but prices are endogenous and each firm is free to set its own price. A third case, in which both locations and prices are endogenous and chosen by the firms, is more complex. In fact, this third case turns out not to have a stable equilibrium solution at all. Accordingly, in Section 12.5, we restrict our attention to the first two cases. In both cases, for simplicity we assume production costs are zero. A modified version of the Hotelling model, in which there is an equilibrium in the third case (endogenous locations and prices) is examined in Section 12.6.

Case 1: Locations endogenous, price exogenous (fixed)

In this case, each firm chooses its location so as to maximize its own profit. Under the fixed price and zero cost assumptions, each firm's profit is a linear function of the number of consumers it serves. At which addresses (on the scale 0 to 1) should the two firms locate? Intuitively, we might guess that firm A should locate at the address 0.25, and firm B should locate at the address 0.75. In this case, firm A would serve all consumers living at addresses between 0 and 0.5, and firm B would serve all consumers living at addresses between 0.5 and 1. This situation is shown in the upper section of Figure 12.7.

But is this choice of locations a Nash equilibrium? The answer is no. If firm A assumes B's location is fixed at its current address of 0.75, A can increase its market share by relocating to a point just fractionally to the west of B, say 0.749. By doing so, A now serves all consumers at addresses between 0 and 0.7495, and B's

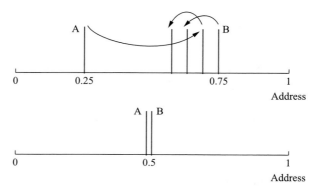

Figure 12.7 Hotelling's location model with fixed prices and endogenous locations

market share is reduced to consumers at addresses between 0.7495 and 1. However, this position is also unstable, and is also not a Nash equilibrium. If B now assumes A's location is fixed at its current address of 0.749, B can increase its market share by relocating to a point just fractionally to the west of A, say 0.748. By doing so, B now serves all consumers at addresses between 0 and 0.7485, and A's market share is reduced to consumers at addresses between 0.7485 and 1.

According to this reasoning, the two firms are engaged in a leap-frogging process, as each seeks to acquire more market share at the expense of its competitor. Is there ever an end to this process? The answer is yes. Notice that as leap-frogging takes place, both firms are moving in the direction of the centre of town. And when both firms are located at the very centre, at addresses just fractionally on either side of 0.5, neither is able to increase its market share (or profit) by changing its location any further. Therefore a stable Nash equilibrium is achieved when both firms locate in the same position, in the very centre of town, as shown in the lower section of Figure 12.7. All firms locating in the central position is not a property of the Nash equilibrium in the general case with more than two firms. However, even in this case there is a tendency for bunching, whereby several firms locate together in the same position.

Is this solution simply a feature of a highly stylized and unrealistic theoretical model, or does it have any relevance in the real world? Perhaps it does. In the case of competition in geographic space, a tendency for several petrol stations to cluster together at important traffic intersections or other busy locations is often notice-able when driving around towns and cities. In the case of competition in product characteristic space, the perception that all brands of soap powder are the same has long been something of a cliché in public discussion of the role of branding and advertising in modern society. Hotelling's location model provides a plausible explanation as to why it might make sense for more than one brand of soap powder to have similar or identical characteristics.

Case 2: Locations fixed (exogenous), prices endogenous

In this case, the locations of the two firms are assumed to be fixed, and each firm sets its price so as to maximize its own profit. We assume the two firms are located at the opposite ends of the spectrum of addresses, with firm A at address 0 and firm B at address 1. We consider two versions of a model of price determination:

- A collusive model, in which the two firms behave as if they were a single mono-polist, and charge the price that maximizes their joint profit.

- A non-collusive model, in which the two firms set their prices independently. At the Bertrand (or Nash) equilibrium, each firm sets its price so as to maximize its own profit, treating the other firm's price as fixed at its current level.

The mathematical details of both models can be found in Appendix 1.

Collusive model: joint profit maximization

In the collusive model, the monopoly (joint profit-maximizing) price is always the same for both firms. Whenever $P_A = P_B$, the consumer located at address 0.5

is indifferent between buying from either firm. The price at which this consumer is indifferent between buying (from either firm) and withdrawing from the market is denoted $\tilde{P}$, and defined as follows:

$$\tilde{P} + kd^2 = \tilde{P} + k(1 - d)^2 = 1$$

Substituting $d = 1/2$ into this expression, it is easily shown:

$$\tilde{P} = 1 - k/4$$

When k is small, transport costs or brand loyalties are low, and the rate of sub-stitution or the propensity for consumers to switch between suppliers is high. When k is small, $\tilde{P}$ turns out to be the joint profit-maximizing or monopoly price. The two firms' common price should be set so that the most marginal consumer is just willing to stay in the market.

However, when k is large, transport costs or brand loyalties are high, and the rate of substitution or propensity for consumers to switch between suppliers is low. When k is large, it is profitable for the two firms to set their common price higher than $\tilde{P}$. Although some consumers withdraw from the market, the firms increase their joint profit by raising the common price, and exploiting the market power that arises from the reluctance to switch of those consumers who remain in the market.

Figure 12.8 shows the determination of the monopoly (joint profit-maximizing) price for k = 1.00, 1.33 and 1.67. In each case the left-hand diagram shows the total cost of buying from either firm as a function of location, represented on the horizontal axis. The right-hand diagram shows marginal revenue as a function of price: the effect on revenue (or profit in a model with zero costs) of a small increase in price. At prices below $\tilde{P}$, marginal revenue (in terms of price) is always positive and constant. The monopoly (joint profit-maximizing) price is never less than $\tilde{P}$, because in this range price can always be increased without causing any consumer to withdraw. Above $\tilde{P}$, however, marginal revenue (in terms of price) tends to be negative when k is low, but positive when k is high.

Let P_M denote the monopoly (joint profit-maximizing) price.

- When k = 1.00, $P_M = \tilde{P} = 0.75$. The marginal effect on revenue or profit of a further increase in price is negative, so a further increase in price would not be profitable.

- When k = 1.33, $P_M = \tilde{P} = 0.67$. The marginal effect on revenue or profit of a further increase in price is just equal to zero. Again, a further increase in price would not be profitable.

- When k = 1.67, $\tilde{P} = 0.6$. In this case, the marginal effect on revenue or profit of a further increase in price is positive, so price should be increased beyond $\tilde{P}$. Joint profit maximization occurs at $P_M = 0.67$, where this marginal effect is equal to zero.

In fact, it can be shown that for any value of k > 1.33, $P_M = 0.67$ is the joint profit-maximizing price. When transport costs or brand loyalties are sufficiently high, each

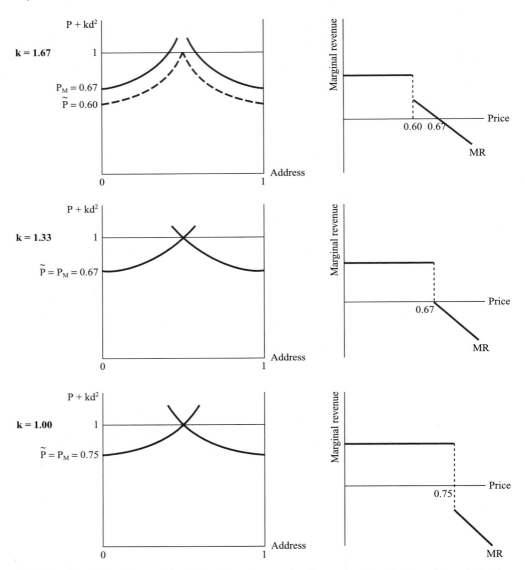

Figure 12.8 Hotelling's location model with fixed locations and endogenous prices: joint profit maximization

firm operates like a monopolist within its own market segment (addresses 0 to 0.5 for firm A and 0.5 to 1 for firm B). For $k > 1.33$ it is worthwhile to raise price beyond the level at which all consumers remain in the market, exploiting fully the reluctance to switch (brand loyalties) of those consumers who do remain.

Non-collusive model: Bertrand (or Nash) equilibrium

In order to locate the Bertrand (or Nash) equilibrium in the non-collusive model, we need to use the apparatus of isoprofit curves and reaction functions for firms A and B. In Section 4.3, isoprofit curves and reaction functions were derived for a quantity-adjustment duopoly model (in which two firms take profit-maximizing decisions about their output levels), with quantities shown on the horizontal and vertical axes. In the present case, we require isoprofit curves and reaction functions for a price-adjustment model, with prices rather than quantities shown on the horizontal and vertical axes.

In order to derive isoprofit curves and reaction functions in terms of prices, we assume initially that both firms are operating at prices sufficiently low that no consumer is priced out of the market. All consumers are willing to buy from at least one of the two firms. In Figure 12.9, we consider the following shifts:

(i)   Both firms initially charge the same price and are located at point F in Figure 12.9. A decides to increase its price, represented by a shift from F to G.

(ii)   A initially charges a higher price than B, and the firms are located at point X in Figure 12.9. A decides to increase its price, represented by a shift from X to Y.

In both (i) and (ii), there are two effects on firm A's profit, which operate in opposite directions:

■ By charging a higher price to each consumer it retains, A tends to earn more profit than before.

■ However, A also loses some business, because A's price increase causes A's most marginal consumers to switch to B. A loses the profit it was earning previously from those consumers who switch.

In (i), A's most marginal consumers who switch to B are those located at addresses close to 0.5, at the centre of town. These consumers incur relatively high transport costs in order to buy from A. For any given price increase by A, the rate at which these marginal consumers switch from A to B is low (if transport costs are a large

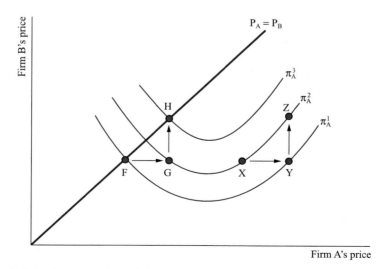

Figure 12.9 Derivation of firm A's isoprofit curves

proportion of the total cost of buying from A, a small increase in P_A makes only a small difference). The first of the two effects identified above tends to dominate, and A's profit increases due to the move from F to G.

In (ii), A's most marginal consumers who switch to B are located at addresses closer to firm A than before. These consumers incur lower transport costs than before in order to buy from A. For any further price increase by A, the rate at which these marginal consumers switch from A to B is high (if transport costs are only a small proportion of the total cost of buying from A, a small increase in P_A makes a big difference). The second of the two effects identified above tends to dominate, and A's profit decreases due to the move from X to Y.

To complete the derivation of A's isoprofit curves, suppose B now implements a small price increase, while A holds its price constant. This is represented by the shift from G to H, or from Y to Z in Figure 12.9. In both cases, some consumers switch from B to A, causing A's profit to increase. Similarly, if B cuts its price while A holds its price constant, consumers switch from A to B, causing A's profit to decrease. This establishes that A's isoprofit curves are convex to the horizontal axis, or U-shaped. Reading Figure 12.9 from the bottom to the top, each successive isoprofit curve represents a higher level of profit to firm A. Similarly, B's isoprofit curves are convex to the vertical axis.

For each value of P_B, firm A's reaction function, denoted RF_A, shows the profit-maximizing value of P_A. Accordingly, RF_A runs through the minimum points of each of A's isoprofit curves. But what is the shape of RF_A? In fact, the precise shape and location depend on the value of the parameter k. As we have seen, this parameter determines the rate of substitution, or the rate at which consumers switch between A and B in response to a small price change by either firm.

Figure 12.10 shows a sketch of the typical shape of RF_A. RF_A is upward-sloping between points M and N; backward-bending between points N and R; and vertical between points R and S. The logic is based on an analysis of the effect of a small increase in P_B on the profit-maximizing values of P_A in different regions of Figure 12.10.

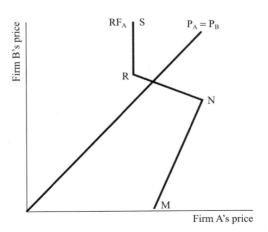

Figure 12.10 Firm A's reaction function

■ Between M and N, P_B is relatively low and B captures most of the market. As P_B increases from point M, the most marginal consumers whom B loses are located close to A. These consumers prefer to switch to A rather than drop out of the market altogether, so A's demand increases. To maximize profit, A should respond by increasing P_A, until the marginal profit gained from those consumers A retains (despite the increase in P_A) *equals* the marginal profit lost from those consumers who switch back to B (due to the increase in P_A). RF_A is upward sloping between M and N because A reacts to an increase in P_B by *increasing* P_A.

■ Between N and R, P_B is higher than before. As P_B increases from point N, the marginal consumers whom B loses are located further away from A than before. Also, P_A is higher than before. Accordingly, the consumers whom B loses prefer to drop out of the market altogether, rather than switch to A. However, this decision is sufficiently borderline that they could be enticed back if A were to reduce P_A. A does so until the marginal profit A gains from the extra consumers enticed back matches the marginal profit lost from A's existing consumers (due to the cut in P_A). RF_A is backward bending between N and R because A reacts to an increase in P_B by *reducing* P_A.

■ Finally between R and S, P_B is higher still. As P_B increases from point R, the marginal consumers whom B loses are located close to B and far away from A. They prefer to drop out of the market altogether rather than switch to A. This decision is not borderline, and these consumers would not be enticed back by a small reduction in P_A. They might be enticed back by a large reduction in P_A, but it is not profitable for A to implement a sufficiently large price cut: the loss of revenue from A's existing customers would be too great. A's demand is unaffected by the increase in P_B, and the profit-maximizing value of P_A is also unaffected. RF_A is vertical between R and S because A reacts to an increase in P_B by leaving P_A *unchanged*.

Figure 12.11 shows the determination of the Bertrand (or Nash) equilibrium price for k = 0.33, 0.67, 1.00, 1.33 and 1.67. In each case, the left-hand diagram shows the intersection of the two firms' reaction functions, and compares the Bertrand (or Nash) equilibrium price, denoted P_N, with the monopoly (joint profit-maximizing) price, P_M. The right-hand diagram shows the total cost of buying from either firm as a function of location on the horizontal axis, when the selling price is either P_N or P_M. As before, the precise solutions depend heavily on k, or the consumers' rate of substitution between firms A and B.

Small k; high rate of substitution; intense competition

Small values of k (k = 0.33, 0.67) represent high rates of substitution between firms A and B. Price competition between A and B tends to be intense. The Bertrand (or Nash) equilibrium prices are located on the upward sloping sections of RF_A and RF_B. These turn out to be $P_N = 0.33$ and $P_N = 0.67$, respectively. In fact, when the model is parameterized as assumed here, it can be shown $P_N = k$ for all $k \leq 0.67$ (see Appendix 1). In the most extreme case of price competition, when k = 0 and the rate of substitution between firms A and B in response to small changes in P_A and P_B is

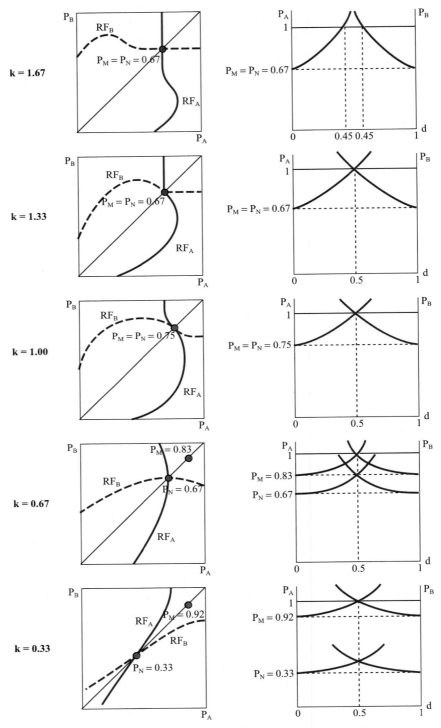

Figure 12.11 Hotelling's location model with fixed locations and endogenous prices: Bertrand (or Nash) equilibrium

infinite, the present model becomes equivalent to one of Bertrand price competition between two duopolists selling an identical product. As we saw in Section 4.4, equilibrium in the Bertrand model is reached when the prices set by the two duopolists have been driven down to the perfectly competitive level (price *equals* marginal cost). In the present case, marginal cost is zero, so when $k = 0$ the Bertrand (or Nash) equilibrium price is $P_N = 0$.

Medium k; medium rate of substitution; medium competition

Higher values of k ($k = 1.00$, 1.33) represent medium rates of substitution and less intense price competition between firms A and B. The Bertrand (or Nash) equilibrium prices are located on the backward-bending sections of RF_A and RF_B. Each firm acts as a monopolist within its own market segment, and P_N and P_M coincide, at $P_N = P_M = 0.75$ for $k = 1.00$, and at $P_N = P_M = 0.67$ for $k = 1.33$. In both cases, however, the rate of substitution is still sufficiently high that it is profitable to set prices in such a way that all consumers are served.

Large k; low rate of substitution; weak competition

Finally, the highest value of k considered in Figure 12.11 ($k = 1.67$) represents the lowest rate of substitution and the least intense price competition between firms A and B. The Bertrand (or Nash) equilibrium prices are located on the vertical sections of RF_A and RF_B. Each firm acts as a monopolist within its own market segment. For all values of $k \geq 1.33$, P_N and P_M always coincide at $P_N = P_M = 0.67$. But for $k > 1.33$, the rate of substitution is so low that it is profitable to set prices in such a way that some consumers are excluded from the market.

The results of the analysis of the collusive and non-collusive versions of the Hotelling model with fixed locations and endogenous prices are summarized in Figure 12.12, which shows the relationship between the parameter k and P_M, the joint profit-maximizing (monopoly) price and P_N, the Bertrand (or Nash) equilibrium (competitive) price. The findings can be summarized as follows.

- Over small and medium values of k, P_M is decreasing in k. As k increases, it is worthwhile for the firms to reduce P_M in order to retain those consumers who would otherwise withdraw from the market. However, if k becomes sufficiently large, it ceases to be profitable to continue cutting P_M in order to retain the consumers from the more distant locations. Instead, it becomes more profitable to hold P_M constant and allow the most marginal consumers to withdraw.

- In perfect competition ($k = 0$), $P_N = 0$. Any increase in k beyond $k = 0$ confers some market power on the two firms, so initially P_N is increasing in k. Over medium values of k, the firms acquire sufficient market power to begin to act like monopolists within their own sub-markets. Consequently P_N approaches P_M, and eventually P_N and P_M become equivalent. Over high values of k, P_N (like P_M) is unaffected by further increases in k. It is interesting to note that over some values of k ($1.00 \leq k \leq 1.33$), P_N is decreasing in k: as the market becomes less competitive, the Nash equilibrium price decreases. This is because within this range, the two duopolists are already operating effectively as if they were local monopolists.

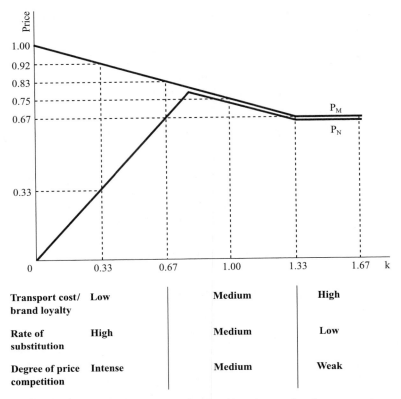

Figure 12.12 Hotelling's location model with fixed locations and endogenous prices: summary of results

12.6 Salop's location model

Salop (1979) develops a modified version of the Hotelling model, in which the firms and consumers are located around the circumference of a circle. In contrast to the Hotelling model (where the firms and consumers are located on a straight line with two end points), an equilibrium exists in the Salop model in the case where both locations and prices are endogenous. The presence of the two end points accounts for the non-existence of an equilibrium solution in Hotelling's model; and conversely, the fact that a circle does not have any end points explains the existence of an equilibrium in Salop's model. In order to develop the Salop model, we make one further modification to the specification of the Hotelling model: we assume non-zero production costs, including both a fixed cost and a variable cost component.

The theoretical properties of Salop's model are quite interesting, but with reference to competition in product characteristics space, it is difficult to think of many real world examples where the characteristics of a group of differentiated products might realistically be represented in the form of a circular array. One case that might correspond to this formulation, however, is a group of rival airlines offering flights on a particular route at different hours of the day and night, around a 24-hour clock. Each airline offers a flight at a particular time, and each passenger has a preferred

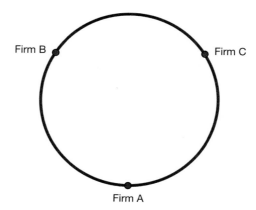

Figure 12.13 Salop's location model with three firms

departure time, which varies between passengers (and which might be anytime, day or night). A passenger whose preferred departure time is 1100 might be indifferent between a 0900 and a 1300 departure (but with lower utility than at 1100), and indifferent between a 0700 and a 1500 departure (but with still lower utility). This passenger's least favoured departure time might be 2300.

Assuming consumers are located uniformly around the circumference of the circle, in the Salop model each firm wishes to locate as far as possible from its nearest competitors. This means it is always optimal for the firms to spread out as much as possible, locating at equidistant points around the circumference. If the length of the circumference is standardized to one, and the number of firms is N, the optimal distance between each firm is $1/N$. Figure 12.13 illustrates a three-firm version of the Salop model, in which the optimal distances between the firms are $1/3$.

The formulation of each consumer's transport cost in the model of competition in geographic space, or the consumer's utility cost of consuming a product with characteristics different from the consumer's ideal characteristics, is the same as in the Hotelling model. The transport or utility cost is kd^2, where d represents distance, and the parameter k determines the consumer's rate of substitution between suppliers. The utility gained from consuming one unit of the product (the product with the ideal characteristics in the product differentiation model) is one, as before. If the firms are equidistant, the maximum distance of any consumer from his or her nearest supplier is $1/(2N)$. We let $\bar{P} = 1 - k/(2N)^2$ denote the price at which the most distant consumer is indifferent between buying and withdrawing from the market. If all three firms charge a price of $\bar{P}$, all three firms achieve a quantity demanded of $1/3$.

Figures 12.14 and 12.15 examine the relationship between firm A's pricing decision and demand, on the assumption that firms B and C both charge a price of $\bar{P}$. In Figure 12.14, the circle has been redrawn as a straight line (but without end points). Suppose initially firm A also charges $P_1 = \bar{P}$, but A is considering either reducing its price to P_2, or increasing its price to P_3.

- With a price reduction below $P_1 = \bar{P}$, A acquires some consumers from B and C, so A's quantity demanded increases, from $1/3$ to $2d_2$. Because consumers switch between suppliers at prices such as P_2 (below $\bar{P}$), P_2 lies within what Salop terms the *competitive region*.

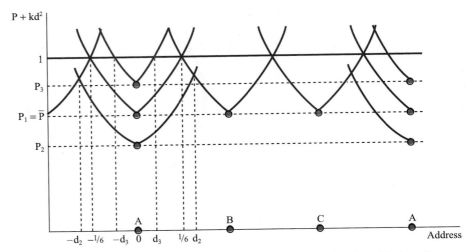

Figure 12.14 Salop's location model: effect of changes in firm A's price with three firms

■ With a price increase above $P_1 = \bar{P}$, A loses some consumers, who prefer to withdraw from the market altogether rather than switch to either B or C. A's quantity demanded decreases, from 1/3 to $2d_3$. Because A's former consumers either continue to buy from A or withdraw from the market altogether at prices such as P_3 (above $\bar{P}$), P_3 lies within the *monopoly region*.

Figures 12.14 and 12.15 show that the rate at which firm A loses consumers by increasing its price in the monopoly region exceeds the rate at which A gains consumers by reducing its price in the competitive region. Consequently, A's demand function has a kink located at price $P_1 = \bar{P}$.

What happens if a new firm is allowed to enter the market, increasing the number of firms from three to four? Assuming the three incumbent firms can relocate costlessly, the four firms will choose to arrange themselves at equal distances of 1/4

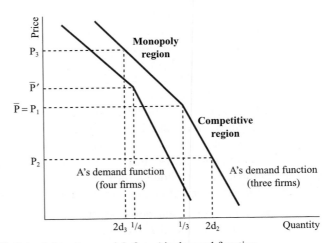

Figure 12.15 Salop's location model: firm A's demand function

from one another. The maximum distance of any consumer from his or her nearest supplier is now less than before. Therefore $\bar{P}'$, the new price at which the consumer who is most distant from any firm is indifferent between buying and withdrawing, is higher than $\bar{P}$. If all four firms charge a price of $\bar{P}'$, all four firms achieve a quantity demanded of 1/4. Therefore the position of the kink in firm A's demand function shifts up and to the left, as shown in Figure 12.15.

Suppose all firms face a constant marginal cost, denoted c, per unit of output *plus* a non-zero fixed cost, denoted f. Salop shows that entry will take place until a Nash equilibrium is reached, at which no incumbent firm wishes to change its price and no outside firm wishes to enter. This equilibrium is analogous to the post-entry equilibrium in the (representative consumer) monopolistic competition model (see Section 2.6 and Figure 2.16). At the equilibrium in the Salop model, each incumbent firm earns a normal profit, and if another firm were to enter, this would cause all firms (including the entrant) to earn negative profits. The equilibrium number of firms is established using the following relationships:

Each firm's quantity demanded $= 1/N$
Each firm's price $= \bar{P} = 1 - k/(4N^2)$
Each firm's total revenue $= (1/N)[1 - k/(4N^2)]$
Each firm's total cost $= (1/N)c + f$

Each firm earns zero abnormal profit when total revenue equals total cost. Therefore the equilibrium value of N is determined by the following condition:

$$(1/N)[1 - k/(4N^2)] = (1/N)c + f$$

This condition can be rearranged to obtain a cubic equation in N, which can be solved to determine the equilibrium value of N, which in turn determines the equilibrium value of $\bar{P}$.

According to Figure 12.15, the Nash equilibrium price in the Salop model rises as the number of firms increases from three to four. This result may seem surprising: we usually expect to find prices falling as competition increases. But in fact, the tendency for price to rise as the number of firms increases (due to entry) is a feature of this model throughout the entire process of adjustment towards the Nash equilibrium. As the number of firms increases, each individual firm services a smaller segment of the market, but obtains some compensation by raising its price. It is possible for the firms to do so, because as each firm's market segment becomes narrower, the preferences of the consumers the firm retains become more closely aligned with the characteristics of its own product. Therefore although consumers pay a higher price, they obtain a product with characteristics that are closer on average to their own ideal product specification.

12.7 Summary

There are two forms of product differentiation. Vertical differentiation means one product or service differs in overall quality from another. If the prices of both products were the same, most or all consumers would purchase the higher-quality product.

Horizontal differentiation means products or services are of the same or similar overall quality, but have different attributes. Different consumers would express different preferences favouring one or other of the products. There is natural product differentiation when the distinguishing characteristics of products or services are natural attributes, rather than having been created through the actions of suppliers. There is strategic product differentiation when the distinguishing characteristics are consciously created by suppliers.

Sources of natural product differentiation include location, which might automatically differentiate a product or service in the minds of consumers; technology, which can be used to add new features to an existing product; brands and trademarks, which help differentiate products that are physically similar; associations in consumers' minds between particular products and particular countries; and consumers' own preferences for attributes such as colour or style. Sources of strategic product differentiation include the quality of factor inputs used by a supplier; variations in the conditions of sale, guarantees or after-sales service; planned obsolescence and frequent changes in design or style; and misleading advertising which attempts to exploit consumer ignorance.

In the economics literature, the two basic approaches to modelling horizontal product differentiation are: representative consumer models, in which consumers have tastes or preferences for goods or services, and firms compete to attract consumers by differentiating the goods or services they offer; and spatial or location models, in which consumers have tastes or preferences for the characteristics that are embodied in goods or services. The neoclassical model of monopolistic competition and several of the standard models of duopoly or oligopoly with product differentiation are representative consumer models. Several of the models that are introduced in Chapter 12 fall into the category of spatial or location models.

An analysis of the implications of product differentiation for social welfare in the representative consumer model of monopolistic competition suggests that only by coincidence is social welfare maximized at the post-entry equilibrium in monopolistic competition. The number of firms at the post-entry equilibrium is determined by entrants examining whether or not they obtain a positive private benefit if they enter. By increasing industry output and reducing prices, entry tends to reduce the producer surplus (abnormal profits) of incumbent firms, but it also tends to increase consumer surplus. Whether the number of firms, and therefore the amount of product differentiation, at the post-entry equilibrium is too high or too low depends upon which of these two effects dominates.

In Lancaster's product characteristics model, goods are viewed as bundles of characteristics, and differentiated goods or brands are goods that contain the same characteristics in varying proportions. The quantities of each characteristic are shown along the axes of an indifference curve diagram, and rays reflect the proportions in which the characteristics are available from competing brands. The demand functions for each brand are discontinuous functions of the brand's own price and the prices of adjacent brands. Consumers sometimes respond to small price changes by making small adjustments to the quantities of the brands they are currently consuming. However, sometimes small changes in price trigger switches between brands, in which case there are large, discrete changes in the quantities purchased.

Hotelling's model of spatial competition, in which geographic location is the characteristic that differentiates one supplier's product from another, has been widely used to model competition in product characteristic space. In the duopoly model in which price is exogenous and the firms choose where to locate along a straight line drawn in geographic or product characteristic space, an equilibrium is achieved when the firms locate in the same position, at the very centre of the straight line. In the case where locations are exogenous and the firms are free to select their own prices, it is possible to develop collusive and non-collusive versions of the model of price determination. The main conclusions are as follows:

■ When transport costs or brand loyalties are low, the collusive or joint profit-maximizing price is higher than in the case where transport costs or brand loyalties are high. In the latter case, it pays the duopolists to lower the price to some extent in order to prevent some consumers from withdrawing from the market altogether. If transport costs increase beyond a certain point, however, it is better to allow some withdrawals, rather than cut the price any further. In this case, both duopolists effectively operate as local monopolists within their own sub-markets.

■ The equilibrium price in the non-collusive model tends to be low when transport costs or brand loyalties are low. In this case the non-collusive model tends towards one of perfect competition. When transport costs or brand loyalties are high, it becomes profitable for the duopolists to operate as local monopolists within their own sub-markets. In this case the non-collusive and collusive models yield identical outcomes.

Finally, in Salop's adaptation of the Hotelling model, the firms and consumers are located around the circumference of a circle. In this case, it is possible to derive an equilibrium for the case where both locations and prices are endogenous, and there is free entry. The solution to the Salop model is analogous to the post-entry equilibrium in the neoclassical model of monopolistic competition. A feature of this model is that the equilibrium price rises as the number of firms increases. Each firm's market segment becomes narrower, and the preferences of the consumers each firm retains become more closely aligned with the characteristics of that firm's product. Although consumers pay a higher price, they obtain a product with characteristics closer on average to their ideal product specification.

Discussion questions

1. What is the distinction between vertical and horizontal product differentiation?

2. What is the distinction between natural and strategic product differentiation?

3. Explain the methodological difference between representative consumer models and spatial or location models of product differentiation.

4. With reference to Case study 12.1, examine the factors that a producer should consider when introducing a product that has planned or built-in obsolescence.

5. Can a free market be expected to deliver a socially optimal level of product differentiation?

6. According to Lancaster's product characteristics model, why might the demand functions for competing brands exhibit discontinuities with respect to small changes in the prices of each brand?

7. What factors should be taken into account by a firm that is seeking to strengthen the loyalties of consumers to its brand?

8. With reference to Case study 12.2, quote examples of vertical and horizontal product differentiation in the Hollywood film industry.

9. Under what circumstances might it make sense for two rival bus companies to charge the same fares, and schedule identical departure times, for a daily long-distance bus service?

10. In the Hotelling model with fixed locations and endogenous prices, a decrease in the consumers' rate of substitution between competing brands might result in a decrease in the equilibrium collusive price, but an increase in the equilibrium non-collusive price. Explain why.

11. With reference to Case study 12.3, explain why commercial flights operated by rival airlines are sometimes clustered around similar or identical departure times.

12. In the Salop model with endogenous locations and prices, explain why an increase in the number of competing suppliers (due to entry) might be associated with an increase in the equilibrium price for each competing brand.

Further reading

Bagwell, K. (2005) Advertising, in Porter, R. and Armstrong, M. (eds), *Handbook of Industrial Organization*, vol. 3. Amsterdam: Elsevier Publishing.

Beath, J. and Katsoularos, Y. (1991) *The Economic Theory of Product Differentiation*. Cambridge: Cambridge University Press.

Caves, R.E. and Williamson, P.J. (1985) What is product differentiation really? *Journal of Industrial Economics*, 113–32.

Degryse, H. (1996) On the interaction between vertical and horizontal product differentiation: an application to banking, *Journal of Industrial Economics*, 44, 169–86.

Phlips, L. and Thisse, J-F. (1982) Spatial competition and the theory of differentiated markets, *Journal of Industrial Economics*, 31, 1–9.

Waterson, M. (1994) Models of product differentiation, in Cable, J. (ed.) *Current Issues in Industrial Economics*. London: Macmillan.

Learning objectives

This chapter covers the following topics:

- the determinants of advertising expenditures
- advertising intensity measures
- informative and persuasive advertising
- advertising and welfare
- advertising and barriers to entry
- the relationship between advertising and industry concentration and profitability
- advertising and prices

Key terms

Advertising intensity	Experience good
Advertising response function	Informative advertising
Advertising-to-sales ratio	Persuasive advertising
Convenience good	Search good
Credence good	Shopping good
Dorfman-Steiner condition	

13.1 Introduction

Advertising is a method used by producers to communicate information to consumers about the goods or services they have to sell. Advertising is perhaps the most widely used method for informing or persuading consumers of the benefits of choosing a particular product or service, or a particular brand. Advertising can involve a number of practices including direct mail, in-store promotion, telemarketing, product placements, sponsorship and exhibitions.

> [E]xpenditure on advertisement is expenditure (over and above the costs of producing and transferring the commodity to the consumer) which is increased by the seller with a view to increasing sales of his commodity. Thus in addition to the costs of the printed advertisement, it includes expenditure on travelling salesmen, 'free offers', competitions, coupons, and on displays and other services for attracting buyers.
>
> *(Braithwaite, 1928, p. 18)*

Producers often use advertising to persuade consumers that there are genuine differences between competing brands of a product or service. Over longer periods of time, advertising can be used to construct an attractive image for a brand, and strengthen the loyalties of the brand's consumers. In the days before there was meaningful regulation of advertising, firms often made outrageous claims in promoting their products. In the US in the 1930s, for example, many products were portrayed as having miraculous properties (Bryson, 1994). One company boasted that its brand of cigarettes could cure a smoker's cough.

> Coca-cola advertising a century ago told you that the beverage was healthful, refreshing, the preferred drink of ladies, available at any drug store. Today, the same company tells you only that 'Coke is it'.
>
> *(Kay, 2004, pp. 215–16)*

According to Tedlow (1993), large-scale marketing in the US really began as long ago as the 1880s, when large industrial firms started to appear for the first time selling mass-produced and highly standardized products to the newly emerging mass market. Typical examples include Coca-Cola, Johnson & Johnson, Procter & Gamble, and Heinz, all of which are still prominent in their respective industries today. The reliance upon mass-production technologies to achieve economies of scale meant marketing, like production, had to be carried out on a large scale, and tended to treat consumers as homogeneous agents.

From the 1950s onwards, the introduction and wide-scale penetration of commercial television and radio created new advertising and marketing opportunities. Advertising messages could now be transmitted directly into the homes of consumers. By choosing the time of day and the type of program within which advertisements were embedded, advertisers could segment audiences according to key demographic or socio-economic categories, such as age, sex, income, education, and so on. Tedlow (1993) notes that from the 1990s onward, there has been a trend toward micro-marketing, where each consumer represents a potential segment. These changes are driven by changes in production and information technologies that have given firms more flexible systems to deliver goods, services and advertising messages to consumers. For example, Dell allows consumers to order tailor-made versions of personal computer products online. However, Tedlow (1993, p. 31) acknowledges that such trends may not necessarily continue if 'confused consumers are confronted in the marketplace with scores of distinctions without differences', or if constraints in distribution networks are met. Producers can now more easily measure the effectiveness of any given advertising strategy. The increasing sophistication of advertising links on the internet means firms only have to pay each time a consumer accesses the advertisement. 'This is the equivalent of paying for junk mail only to households that read it' (*The Economist*, 2004b, p. 84). American Airlines are reported as using 'behavioural targeting', by monitoring the interest shown by readers of the online version of the *Wall Street Journal* in travel stories. It then targets the selected readers with flight offers (*The Economist*, 2004b).

Advertising is one of the main weapons of competition between firms. From a theoretical perspective, we might expect the importance of advertising to vary according to market structure.

- In the theoretical model of perfect competition, there appears to be no role for advertising, because each firm faces a perfectly elastic demand function and can sell as much output as it wants at the current price, which is determined through the interaction between supply and demand across the entire market. In any case, all market participants are assumed to have perfect information, which appears to eliminate the need for firms to advertise.

- At the other extreme in the case of monopoly, there appears to be some scope for advertising, although this scope is still perhaps limited. The monopolist faces an inelastic demand function and is insulated from competition by entry barriers. The monopolist can therefore choose the price it charges. There may be some incentive to advertise if advertising is effective in increasing total industry demand. But there is no incentive to advertise in order to tempt consumers away from competitors, since by definition a monopolist has no competitors.

- Finally, in the intermediate case of oligopoly, oligopolists who recognize their interdependence may prefer to avoid price competition, and instead engage in non-price forms of competition such as advertising or research and development. There may be strong incentives to advertise, both in order to increase total industry demand, and to attract customers at the expense of competitors.

Chapter 13 discusses theoretical ideas and empirical evidence concerning the role of advertising. Section 13.2 presents some facts and figures about the economic importance of advertising in modern societies, and about patterns of advertising expenditure across different types of product and service. Section 13.3 examines the relationship between certain key attributes of products, services and brands, and the likely effectiveness of advertising. The distinction between **search goods** and **experience goods** is introduced. Section 13.4 develops an optimizing model of advertising behaviour. The relationship between market structure and the optimal level of advertising that is discussed informally above is developed more formally, under profit-maximizing assumptions.

Section 13.5 examines ways in which advertising acts as a barrier to entry. Thanks to past advertising expenditure, an incumbent firm may achieve more sales for any given level of current advertising than an entrant, leading to an absolute cost advantage. Alternatively economies of scale in advertising may make it difficult for small-scale entrants to compete with incumbents. Section 13.6 examines the role of advertising in situations where consumers have limited information, and an informational asymmetry exists between producers and consumers. The role of informative advertising in reducing consumers' search costs is considered. A signalling model is developed in which the actual content of advertising messages is unimportant, but consumers receive useful signals about product quality from the simple fact that some brands are advertised more heavily than others.

Section 13.7 considers the question whether there is too much advertising in modern societies. Some economists have argued that advertising leads to a misallocation of resources, because advertising distorts consumer preferences. Others believe advertising improves the flow of information concerning product and service attributes, and therefore improves the allocation of resources. Finally, Section 13.8 provides a selective review of empirical evidence concerning many of the issues raised in Chapter 13.

13.2 Determinants of advertising expenditure

Advertising is a huge global business. In the UK, total expenditure on advertising increased from £121 million in 1948 to £16.7 billion in 2002. As Table 13.1 shows, the contribution of advertising to Gross Domestic Product (GDP) varies widely across countries. In 2002, while advertising accounted for 1.21 per cent of GDP in the US and 1.12 per cent in the UK, in France, Germany, Italy and Japan the corresponding percentage figures were only 0.63 per cent, 0.84 per cent, 0.6 per cent and 0.73 per cent, respectively (Advertising Association, 2003).

Some of the factors that affect a country's aggregate expenditure on advertising are as follows.

- *Disposable income.* A positive relationship between disposable income and advertising expenditure is expected. When national income is high or increasing, consumers tend to have more disposable income to spend on goods and services. This encourages firms to spend heavily on advertising.

- *Unemployment.* A negative relationship between unemployment and advertising expenditure is expected. When unemployment is low advertising tends to increase, for two reasons. First, when unemployment is low, disposable incomes are high (see above). Second, when employment is high, firms tend to experience difficulties in hiring workers to fill vacant positions. This leads to increased advertising by recruitment agencies (Howard, 1998).

- *Government regulation.* In recent years, many governments have tended to reduce or eliminate restrictions on advertising. For example, total advertising expenditure in Sweden increased by 250 per cent in the year following the introduction of commercial television in 1988 (Howard, 1998).

Many economists draw a distinction between informative and persuasive advertising. **Informative advertising** provides consumers with factual information about the existence of a product, service or brand, or about attributes such as its price, features or uses. Informative advertising aims to give consumers information with

Table 13.1 Advertising as a percentage of gross domestic product (at market prices)

Country	1996	1998	2000	2002
Austria	0.72	0.83	0.97	0.90
Belgium	0.65	0.74	0.81	0.83
Denmark*	0.82	0.87	0.77	0.68
Finland	0.87	0.91	0.93	0.81
France*	0.65	0.64	0.71	0.63
Germany*	0.89	0.93	1.00	0.84
Greece	0.79	0.85	1.02	0.95
Ireland	0.96	0.95	1.13	0.96
Italy*	0.49	0.55	0.69	0.60
Japan	0.76	0.75	0.79	0.73
Netherlands*	0.90	0.95	0.97	0.84
Norway	0.81	0.85	0.73	0.73
Portugal*	0.76	0.87	1.14	1.08
Spain	0.83	0.83	0.89	0.75
Sweden*	0.75	0.85	0.83	0.67
Switzerland*	0.93	0.94	1.07	0.97
UK	1.16	1.24	1.30	1.12
United States*	1.28	1.30	1.39	1.21

Data are net of discounts. They include agency commission and press classified advertising expenditure, but exclude production costs. * data for 2002 are estimates.

Sources: The European Advertising and Media Forecast, National Data Sources, NTC Publications Ltd. Reproduced from Advertising Association (2003) *Advertising Statistics Yearbook 2003*, table 19.4, p. 183. Oxon: NTC Publications. Reprinted with permission.

which to make informed choices that will help them maximize their (exogenously determined) utility functions, subject to their budget constraints. **Persuasive advertising**, on the other hand, makes claims which may not be objectively verifiable, and which aim to change consumers' perceptions of a product, service or brand with a view to stimulating sales. Drinking a sophisticated brand of coffee will make you sexually attractive; driving a sporty car will help you become rich, glamorous or powerful; wearing a certain brand of trainers will turn you into a world champion. One interpretation of persuasive advertising is that it seeks to shift consumers' tastes and thereby change the shape of their utility functions (no longer exogenous) in a direction favouring the advertising firm.

Economists often take a positive view of informative advertising, and a more critical view of persuasive advertising. Informative advertising is 'good' because reliable information is a powerful lubricant, needed to ensure the smooth functioning of competitive markets. But persuasive advertising is 'bad' because it (perhaps deliberately) sets out to mislead or confuse, and may even tend to distort competition. In practice, however, it is often difficult to make a clear distinction between informative and persuasive advertising. Many advertisements seek to inform and persuade at the same time.

> [T]o interpret advertising effort as primarily designed to persuade consumers to buy what they really do not want, raises an obvious difficulty. It assumes that producers find it more profitable to produce what consumers do not want, and then to persuade them to buy it, with expensive selling campaigns, rather than to produce what consumers do already in fact want (without need for selling effort).
>
> *(Kirzner, 1997b, p. 57)*

In general, therefore, advertising seeks to either inform or persuade or do both. However, we can be more specific as to the reasons why firms invest in advertising campaigns:

■ *To launch a product or service.* Advertising can be used to provide potential consumers with information concerning a new product or service. Such advertising may be primarily informative rather than persuasive. For example, the UK government and firms in the financial services sector advertised heavily in order to provide the public with detailed information before and after the launch of Individual Savings Accounts (ISAs) in 1999.

■ *To provide information on price and quality.* Advertising can be used to provide consumers with information concerning price and quality attributes of products and services. This is particularly important if these attributes tend to change rapidly over time, as a result of competition or technological change. For example, mobile phone providers in the UK advertise heavily in order to inform consumers of the attributes of the products and services they offer. Advertising can also be used to provide consumers with information on the location of the firm's sales outlets. Recent estimates suggest consumers in the US are exposed to average of 3,000 advertising messages each day (*The Economist*, 2004b).

■ *To increase or protect market share.* Advertising campaigns may be designed to persuade consumers that a firm's products and services are superior to those of its competitors. In a rapidly expanding market, there may be less need for advertising of this kind, as there is a large pool of potential customers available for all firms. Where consumer demand is stagnant or decreasing, firms may tend to advertise more heavily, in an effort to protect their individual shares of a dwindling market.

■ *To establish a brand's image or strengthen consumers' brand loyalties.* Advertising can be considered as a type of investment expenditure, whereby a firm seeks to create positive associations in consumers' minds with its own brand, which may yield benefits to the firm in the form of lasting consumer brand loyalty. Goodwill and positive reputation effects can act as significant entry barriers, making it difficult for outside firms to establish a presence in a market dominated by an established brand that has been heavily advertised in the past. In 2001 McDonald's spent over £41 million in the UK promoting its brand image (Advertising Association, 2003).

Brands are insubstantial things, mere signals, names, associations. Sometimes they signal real differences between products. Sometimes they are pure illusion. Either way, brands are akin to a product's or company's reputation, and they influence consumers' perceptions. The wearer of a Rolex watch is concerned with more than keeping time; the BMW driver with more than getting from place to place.

(The Economist, 1991)

Klein (2000) criticizes the use of brands by large multinationals. She argues the power of brands has reduced consumer choice and increased the dominance of large multinational firms at the expense of their local counterparts. Case study 13.1 assesses the importance of brands.

Case study 13.1

For what it's worth, what's in a name? Quite a lot, it seems. Brands are like any other asset: they require investment, but they can also boost the value of a company
Creative business – Marketing

Given the extreme market volatility of recent years, investors are seeking new ways to assess the viability of their investments. While there are multiple reasons behind a company's success or failure on the stock market, one key indicator which should be considered is the strength of the brand.

Reviewing historical trends in markets shows that, on average companies with strong brands consistently outperform their key stock market indices, while companies with weak brands will usually underperform. By analysing markets around the world, our research has found this holds true for most leading stock markets and their indices including the S&P 500, Fortune 100 and the FTSE 100.

Our study categorised listed companies as strongly or weakly branded, based on metrics such as awareness, customer preference and loyalty; ad and marketing spend and its effectiveness versus industry peers; the brand's role in influencing purchase decisions; and other quantitative metrics such as longevity in the market and the brand's economic value. The study also took into consideration interviews with analysts and executives to determine which listed companies were strongly-branded and which were considered weakly-branded. For example, on the FTSE HSBC qualified as a strong brand, while Friends Provident was weakly branded.

How can the brand play a role in affecting company performance to such an extent? It does so by influencing every step of a business's value chain. A strong brand generates revenue and sustains earnings by giving customers reasons, emotional and rational, to purchase from that company again and again. This strong brand ensures a level of security, premium pricing and greater market share: look at Starbucks selling a few pence worth of coffee for £3.

In an economic downturn, the gap in share price between those companies with strong brands and those with weak is even more remarkable. In a recession people go with brands they trust. This is why Heinz stays a market favourite. Strong brands help companies weather the bad times.

Strong brand strategies among consumer goods companies is one thing, but branding presents a tremendous opportunity for companies operating in vertical markets, often B2B, where brand building might have taken a strategic back seat to capital investments and resources procurement.

A significant gap in share performance exists for those industries not traditionally focused on brand building. Strong brands operating in the utilities, financial services, oil and gas and commodities markets support much higher share prices for their companies than players with weaker brands. They are competing in a space not yet saturated with strong brands. For them, brand building done with strategic focus should produce a better return on marketing investment than for companies in industries such as consumer goods, retail and media. Companies which have identified the supreme value of a strong brand are positioning themselves well to become dominant forces in their market.

In financial services, it is evident which companies strive to build their brands and which might be ignoring them. The historical share performance of strong brands such as Barclays, Lloyds, HSBC and Prudential solidly surpasses the likes of Royal and Sun Alliance and Old Mutual. Among operational and cyclical reasons for share price fluctuations, the brand is one factor behind these differences.

A striking gap also appears in the oil and gas and commodities industries, where strongly branded such as BP outperform weakly branded companies including Premier Oil and Dana Petroleum. In telecoms, BT and Vodafone's performance towers over Cable & Wireless.

It is not only the influence on share performance that highlights the brand's role as an important asset. Over the past 25 years the balance between a company's tangible and intangible assets has shifted. On average, 70 per cent of company value is linked to intangible assets – the largest of which is usually the brand. Given this, the brand should be treated as any other asset, measured and held accountable for a certain level of return.

Leading companies rely on brand valuation tools to measure the return on branding investments. Nissan, for example, uses brand valuation to measure the return on its marketing investments – it determined that its last rebranding efforts in 2000 provided a return of more than 3,500 per cent. Marketing peers will agree on the importance of brand but understanding brand as a financial asset and key driver of shareholder value is rapidly elevating brand management to CEO and board level.

Source: Lauren Henderson, For what it's worth, what's in a name? Quite a lot it seems. Brands are like any other asset: they require investment, but they can also boost the value of a company. © *Financial Times*, 3 February 2004, p. 6.

Theoretical models of oligopoly suggest firms may prefer to engage in non-price rather than price competition. Industry advertising expenditure as a proportion of industry sales, known as **advertising intensity** or the industry's **advertising-to-sales ratio** provides an indication of the importance of advertising as a form of non-price competition. As shown in Table 13.2, the advertising-to-sales ratio varies considerably between product groups (Advertising Association, 2003). In the UK in 2001, bleaches and lavatory cleaners, shampoos, soaps and vitamins all had relatively high advertising-to-sales ratios, 26 per cent, 20 per cent, 12 per cent and 8.5 per cent, respectively. In contrast, carbonated drinks, DVD players, floor coverings, and domestic fuel and lighting all had much lower advertising-to-sales ratios, 0.49 per cent, 0.43 per cent, 0.22 per cent and 0.06 per cent, respectively. However, these percentages can sometimes be misleading. In some cases, absolute expenditure on advertising is huge, but sales are so large that advertising intensity turns out to be quite low. The motor industry, with an advertising-to-sales ratio of only 1.19 per cent in Table 13.2, is an obvious example.

Table 13.2 Advertising-to-sales ratios of selected UK product groups, 2001

Product group	Advertising-to-sales ratio
Bleaches and lavatory cleaners	25.51
Shampoos	20.17
Soaps	11.88
Vitamins	8.46
Air fresheners	6.79
Deodorants	6.35
Cereals	5.25
Electric razors	5.20
Home computers	4.64
Sportswear	4.16
Coffee	4.05
Video games	2.76
Confectionery	2.40
Tea	1.47
Cars	1.19
Gambling	0.91
Televisions	0.83
Rail travel	0.77
Beer	0.65
Cheese	0.60
Cinema	0.54
Carbonated soft drinks	0.49
DVD players	0.43
Carpets, floor coverings and tiles	0.22
Domestic fuel and lighting	0.06

Source: Adapted from Advertising Association (2003) *Advertising Statistics Yearbook 2003*, table 18.1, 170–4. Oxon: NTC Publications. Reprinted with permission.

Table 13.3 Top 10 advertisers and brands in the UK, 2002

Top advertisers in 2002		Top brands in 2002	
Procter & Gamble	£161.89 m	McDonald's	£41.9 m
COI Communications	£119.5 m	PC World	£32.2 m
British Telecom	£96.6 m	Sainsbury's	£31.5 m
Ford	£94.9 m	Tmobile network	£30.6 m
L'Oréal Golden	£70.8 m	DFS	£26.3 m
Masterfoods	£66.9 m	B & Q	£25.9 m
Renault	£66.1 m	Toyota Corolla	£23.9 m
Toyota	£65.5 m	DFS sofas/suites	£22.3 m
Vauxhall Motors	£63.4 m	Orange Network	£20.3 m
Nestlé	£62.9 m	Ford Fiesta	£19.3 m

Source: Adapted from Advertising Association (2003) *Advertising Statistics Yearbook* 2003, pp. 210–11. Oxon: NTC Publications.

Albion and Farris (1981) identify a number of influences on advertising intensity for any particular industry or product.

■ *Firm objectives*. The level of advertising intensity may depend on the business objectives of incumbent firms. If incumbent firms are profit maximizers, advertising is only considered if it makes a positive contribution to profit. If firms seek to maximize sales or market share, advertising may be considered even if the additional cost outweighs the extra sales the advertising generates, provided the effect on sales is positive. Different firms within the same industry may pursue different objectives, making it difficult to interpret industry-level advertising intensity data of the type presented in Table 13.2.

■ *Market structure*. As argued above, the incentive to advertise may differ systematically between different market structures. This relationship is examined in greater detail in Section 13.3.

■ *The age of the product*. With new products, firms often advertise heavily in order to increase consumer awareness and establish a presence in the market. Firms producing established products may be able to trade by exploiting brand loyalties that have been built up in past advertising campaigns. Therefore there may be a relationship between the age of the product and advertising intensity.

■ *The number of brands and the extent of product differentiation*. If there is a high degree of product differentiation or if consumers have strong brand loyalties, and consumers perceive that no close substitutes exist, advertising campaigns designed to capture market share from rivals are likely to be expensive. Cable (1972) finds a positive relationship between the number of brands and advertising intensity at industry level. Schmalensee (1978) argues brand proliferation tends to raise entry barriers, insulating incumbent firms from competition. *The Economist* (1999, 2001) highlights the importance of brands, as does Case study 13.1.

■ *Type of product or service produced*. It seems apparent from Table 13.2 that advertising intensity varies quite significantly by product type. Are there any systematic patterns in this data? This issue is examined in detail in Section 13.3.

In a recent study, Paton and Conant (2001) report a survey of senior managers to assess the determinants of internet advertising for a sample of 864 UK firms. Internet advertising is more likely in industries where competition is intense, and for firms with low debt levels that are consumer-oriented. There is evidence that internet advertising is complementary to traditional forms of advertising. Case studies 13.2 and 13.3 assess the scope and effectiveness of some specific advertising campaigns.

Running a top campaign. Television advertisements featuring hairy marathon men have left The Number's directory inquiry competitors gasping for breath

Whether they tickle your fancy or irk your sensibilities, the hairy 118 runners featured in one of this year's most ubiquitous advertising campaigns have run off with the lion's share of the UK directory inquiry market. According to a recent Mori survey conducted on behalf of telecommunications regulator Oftel, during the period in which 192 ceased to exist and the new entrants launched their products to market, The Number had streaked ahead of all its competitors – including BT – in terms of both familiarity and usage.

Aside from the pervasiveness of its ad campaign, what stands out about the success of the company called 'The Number' is that it discarded the usual tactics of competitive pricing or leveraging an established brand to sell its service. Instead it traded off the memorability of the 118 118 number and the cult status of its 'mystery runners'.

The hirsute human faces of the company's directory inquiries offering have bored their way into the public consciousness with an arsenal of guerrilla marketing tactics that pushed well beyond the normal realms of promotion. These ranged from staged appearances of the runners at high-profile events, to supplying Cancer Research charity shops with thousands of the 118 running shirt – elevating it to the stag-night costume-of-choice over the summer.

According to Julian Hough, business development director at WCRS, the agency behind the campaign, its success is based on the left-field approach to boring subject matter.

'We went into the pitch with very heavy hearts. When you look at all the other deregulated markets, most had created ads with crappy jingles featuring gimps dressed up in big foam numbers. Our idea came from the idea of having more energy and going farther – like long-distance runners.'

But choice of medium also proved crucial in the run-up to the launch. One of the more telling statistics from the Oftel survey was the extent to which television advertising had an impact on awareness, benefiting The Number – which chose to use television as its main advertising vehicle. BT, on the other hand, maintained a low-key, below-the-line marketing approach in the lead-up to the changeover.

Of the respondents that were aware of the introduction of new numbers, 82 per cent found out via television. A further 12 per cent heard about the directory inquiry changeover via press advertising; 6 per cent were informed by radio advertising; and posters, word of mouth and direct mail was cited by a further 4 per cent.

BT, which would normally trade on its brand status and extensive customer base, had to start from scratch with other entrants when 192 was abolished. Simon Lubin, head of marketing at BT directories, says: 'Our strategy was to spend our money at a time it would have maximum effect and to wait until 192 switch-off occurred.'

But this meant that its 118 500 number lost ground in the lead-up to the changeover, and 59 per cent of the fixed-line customers surveyed recognized 118 118 above all other new entrants.

Conduit's offering, 118 888, which was also supported by an extensive television campaign, had market recognition of 16 per cent, while BT came in fourth behind 118 811 from One.

Of the 17 per cent of fixed-line customers that had actually used one of the inquiry numbers in August, The Number again led the field with 10 per cent, followed by Conduit with 4 per cent and BT with 1 per cent.

BT has since launched a multi-million-pound television and outdoor advertising campaign based on the concept of Post-it notes, which Lubin says has raised its call volumes by 35 per cent. According to research gathered by The Number, BT now claims the number two position with between 20 and 30 per cent of the market in terms of volume, trailed by Conduit, which has slipped to about 7 per cent. The Number says its market share has held steady at about 50 per cent.

William Ostrom, director of communications at The Number, says: 'We were taken aback by the volume of calls. We had 50 per cent of the market from day one and that did put pressure on operations such as recruitment.' But despite some problems with staff service levels that were widely reported in the media, notoriety actually lifted market awareness.

This tallies with findings from the Oftel survey, where 36 per cent of respondents based their number choice purely on advertising recall, 21 per cent said they had called the only number they knew, and only 17 per cent selected what they believed was the cheapest service.

But is the recall of a number enough to retain customers in the long term? Not according to BT.

Lubin says that the market has already lost 50 per cent of its volume since the changeover.

SOURCE OF AWARENESS OF NEW DIRECTORY INQUIRY NUMBERS

% (August 2003)
Television ads: 82
Press ads: 12
Radio ads: 6
Posters: 4
Word of mouth: 4
Leaflet with BT bill: 4

Source: Oftel.

Source: Louisa Hearn, Running a top campaign. Television advertisements featuring hairy marathon men have left The Number's directory inquiry competitors gasping for breath. *Financial Times*, 11 November 2003, p. 6. louisa.hearn@ft.com

Case study 13.3

Advertising campaigns
(Survey – creative business)

'You see these guys waiting for a big wave to surf, and you hear this really distorted bass line. Meanwhile, these white horses come striding over the ocean.'

Try describing the Guinness campaign, recently named as Britain's best television ad of all time, in a way that sounds vaguely evocative. Hard isn't it?

Or try, for that matter, any other advertising campaign. Renault's Nicole and Papa? 'There's this nubile French teenager and her lascivious elderly father, both of whom keep nipping off in the car for surreptitious sexual encounters.'

And the PG Tips chimpanzees? 'There are these monkeys dressed in wigs drinking tea.'

It doesn't get any easier, does it?

And yet, that's what goes on in the advertising, marketing and design industries, day after day. People selling creative ideas. And other people buying them.

For those of us whose job it is to purvey the applied art of creativity, there are, of course, recognised academies of learning, from art schools to advertising colleges. And as an industry, we have developed all sorts of techniques for presenting creative work, and a vast array of tools to lend credibility to our hypotheses.

But few people are ever taught how to 'buy' creative work. It's a lot like parenting; you're just expected to know how to do it.

There are as many different ways to do it as there are clients. From the assiduously constructed brief which resembles the specification for a large engineering project, to the client who was once irresponsible enough to say to me forget the brief just excite me.

There are just as many ways for a client to evaluate creative work once the agency has produced it. From the reductionist method of checking every element against an identifiable item on a checklist, to the altogether more subjective assessment of whether the client and his/her wife/husband/boss/tea lady like it.

Agencies abound with stories of clients and their idiosyncratic methods of assessing creative work. And some clients have come up with as many methods of evaluating consumer reaction as the agencies who originate the ideas.

All of which hints at what a responsibility buying creative work is. And it is. Partly because there's so much at stake be it market share, stock price or even people's careers. And partly because it can require as much vision, ambition, courage and creativity to buy a piece of creative work as it does to produce it. It is an oft-repeated truism, but agencies can only be as creative as their clients will let them be.

But lest agencies get off the hook too easily, I feel honour-bound to report that they are themselves sometimes ill-qualified to judge creative work.

Be it a new corporate identity, a promotional brochure or a piece of advertising, often the most vexed projects of all are those which we refer to as 'house jobs'. Why? Because on such projects, we have the most irksome, inconsistent and unforgiving clients of all. Ourselves.

Source: Mare Nohr, Advertising campaigns, *Financial Times*, 14 November 2000, p. 58.

13.3 Advertising and product characteristics

Several economists have suggested product characteristics may be an important determinant of advertising intensities. For example, it has been suggested that goods whose attributes consumers can assess accurately before they are purchased and consumed are unlikely to be the subject of large-scale advertising campaigns. In contrast, goods whose attributes are difficult to assess may be more heavily advertised. For products that are purchased regularly, consumers are unlikely to search for detailed information prior to purchase, and are unlikely to be persuaded by advertising that the brands they consume have qualities other than those consumers can discern for themselves. For products that are purchased less frequently, consumers may be more open to persuasion through advertising prior to purchase. Consumers are more likely to search for detailed information prior to purchase of products whose price accounts for a significant proportion of a typical consumer's budget. For such products, persuasive advertising may be ineffective in swaying the consumer's eventual purchase decision. For inexpensive products or services, on the other hand, mistakes tend to matter less, and consumers may be content to be swayed by advertising messages.

Nelson (1974a,b) defines **search goods** as those whose attributes can easily be determined by inspection, either by touch or by sight, prior to purchase. Common examples include clothes, carpets, household and office furniture. **Experience goods** are those whose attributes can only be determined when they are consumed, after they have been purchased. Common examples include foods, toothpaste, washing-up liquid, cars and hi-fi systems. Nelson argues the probable effectiveness of persuasive advertising differs systematically between search goods and experience goods. There may be a role for informative advertising of search goods, to ensure consumers are aware of the product's price, capabilities or existence. But persuasive advertising of search goods is unlikely to be effective, because it is easy for consumers to assess the quality of the product for themselves before deciding whether or not to purchase. The truth (or otherwise) of advertising claims about the qualities of search goods is in any case transparent.

For experience goods, in contrast, there is likely to be a role for both informative and persuasive advertising. If consumers cannot assess the quality of the product for themselves prior to purchase, the purchase decision may be swayed by persuasive advertising. The truth (or otherwise) of advertising claims about the qualities of experience goods only becomes apparent after the consumer is already committed, and purchase has already taken place. Accordingly, Nelson concludes that advertising intensity is likely to be higher for experience goods than for search goods.

Darby and Karni (1973) extend this classification to include **credence goods**; see also Mixon (1994). A credence good is one whose quality cannot easily be assessed before or after consumption, because a judgement about quality requires the consumer to have specialized knowledge of the product or service. Common examples are dental services, medical care, car repair services and (perhaps) university courses. Applying similar reasoning, both informative and persuasive advertising may be effective in the case of credence goods.

Frequency of purchase may also have implications for the effectiveness of persuasive advertising, especially in the case of experience goods. Arterburn and Woodbury (1981) use the term **convenience goods** to describe goods that are relatively cheap and that are purchased frequently. In contrast, **shopping goods** are expensive and purchased infrequently. For example, washing-up liquid and hi-fi equipment are both experience goods, because their qualities cannot easily be identified prior to purchase and consumption; but washing-up liquid is a convenience good, while hi-fi equipment is a shopping good. Bin-liners and furniture are both search goods, because their qualities can easily be assessed prior to purchase and consumption, but bin-liners are a convenience good, while furniture is a shopping good.

Suppose there are two new brands of washing-up liquid, one of which is of high quality and the other low quality. In both cases, persuasive advertising might be effective in persuading consumers to try either brand for the first time. However, once consumers have had the opportunity to assess the qualities of the brands for themselves, only the high-quality brand is likely to attract repeat purchases. The advertising expenditure devoted to the low-quality brand is mostly wasted if this brand turns out to be incapable of attracting repeat purchases. This discussion suggests advertising might sometimes have a role to play in signalling quality to consumers. The content of the advertising message itself may be irrelevant, but the very fact that a brand is advertised heavily suggests the producer is confident that consumers who try the brand will be satisfied, and will make repeat purchases. A model of quality signalling through advertising is described in Section 13.6.

Many consumer durables, such as cars, washing machines, video and hi-fi equipment, can be classified as experience goods and as shopping goods. Other things being equal, the infrequency of purchase might suggest advertising intensities for shopping goods should be higher than for convenience goods. But there is a countervailing factor. Shopping goods are expensive, and their purchase accounts for a large proportion of a typical consumer's budget. When purchasing shopping goods that are also experience goods, consumers are likely to make efforts to gather reliable information about the attributes of competing brands. Mistakes made in purchasing a hi-fi system are costly, so it makes sense to consult specialist publications such as *What Hi-Fi?* or *Hi-Fi Choice*, rather than rely solely on advertising messages.

> Repeat purchases of the brands they like is the major source of control that consumers have over the market for experience goods. However, experimenting with unknown brands is a fairly expensive way for consumers to learn about the qualities of goods. Whenever possible, consumers seek to make their experiments less costly. One of the ways they do this is to choose their experiments guided by the recommendations of relatives and friends or of consumer magazines.
>
> *(Nelson, 1974a, p. 48)*

In contrast, mistakes made when purchasing convenience goods such as washing-up liquid do not matter very much. Consumers may be more open to persuasion by advertising messages, even if these are perceived or known to be unreliable.

13.4 Advertising and profit maximization

Whether informative or persuasive advertising is employed, firms spend money on advertising campaigns in order to increase the demand for their products or services, in the hope that increased consumer demand will yield a higher profit. In this section, we analyse the firm's advertising decision within a traditional framework of profit maximization. In order to select the level of advertising expenditure that maximizes its profit, the firm advertises until the marginal benefit (in terms of increased revenue) gained from the last unit of advertising *equals* the marginal cost. Below, the problem of selecting the profit-maximizing level of advertising is considered separately for the market structures of monopoly, oligopoly and perfect competition.

Monopoly

In the case of a monopoly, only a simple extension of the neoclassical model of profit maximization is needed in order to identify the optimal level of advertising. In Figure 13.1, it is assumed that the position of a monopolist's average revenue function, which is the same as the market demand function, depends on the level of advertising expenditure. Advertising expenditures of a_1, a_2, a_3 and a_4 are shown in Figure 13.1, and it is assumed the difference between each successive level of advertising expenditure ($a_2 - a_1$, $a_3 - a_2$ and so on) is the same, and equal to Δa. It is assumed there are diminishing returns to advertising, so on each successive occasion advertising expenditure is increased by Δa, the outward shift in the average revenue function becomes smaller. For simplicity, production cost is assumed to be linear in output. The firm's total cost is the sum of its production cost and its advertising expenditure.

■ When advertising expenditure is a_1, the firm's optimal output is Q_1, where $MR_1 = MC$.

■ By increasing advertising expenditure from a_1 to a_2, the firm increases its optimal output to Q_2, where $MR_2 = MC$. The increase in operating profit (revenue *minus* production cost) of $\Delta\pi_2$ exceeds the advertising expenditure of Δa. The decision to advertise is beneficial, and the shift from Q_1 to Q_2 is profitable. In fact, the firm should continue to increase its advertising expenditure until the marginal increase in operating profit is just equal to the marginal increase in advertising expenditure.

■ By increasing advertising expenditure from a_2 to a_3, the firm increases its optimal output to Q_3, where $MR_3 = MC$. The increase in operating profit of $\Delta\pi_3$ is just equal to the additional advertising expenditure of Δa. The effect of the extra advertising is neutral, and the firm is indifferent between operating at Q_3 and Q_2. If advertising is continuous ($\Delta a \rightarrow 0$) rather than discrete, there is a unique profit-maximizing level of advertising expenditure.

■ Finally, by increasing advertising expenditure from a_3 to a_4, the optimal output increases to Q_4, where $MR_4 = MC$. The increase in operating profit of $\Delta\pi_4$ is less than the additional advertising expenditure of Δa. The extra advertising is not worthwhile, and the firm should not seek to operate at Q_4.

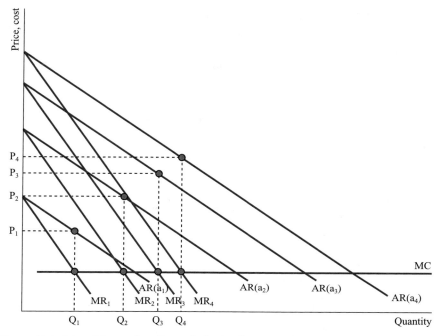

Figure 13.1 Advertising and profit maximization in monopoly

In a seminal article, Dorfman and Steiner (1954) develop an analysis of the monopolist's optimal advertising decision using an algebraic model. Their results are insightful, and working through the formal algebraic derivation is worthwhile. The Dorfman–Steiner framework is essentially the same as in Figure 13.1, except we now assume advertising expenditure is continuous rather than discrete, and we no longer assume the firm's demand (or average revenue) function and production costs are necessarily linear in output. The monopolist's demand (or average revenue) function is:

$$Q = Q(P, a)$$

where Q denotes quantity demanded, P denotes price and a denotes advertising expenditure. The monopolist's cost function is:

$$c = c(Q) + a$$

where Q denotes quantity produced, and c denotes cost. The monopolist's profit is:

$$\pi = TR - c(Q) - a = P \times Q(P,a) - c(Q) - a$$

For profit maximization, the additional profit gained from a marginal increase in advertising expenditure should be zero. For simplicity, Dorfman and Steiner assume that when the firm changes its advertising expenditure it adjusts its quantity produced but does not alter its price. Let ΔQ, Δc and Δa denote the changes in output, cost and advertising expenditure, respectively. For profit maximization, the following relationship must hold between these quantities:

$$P\left(\frac{\Delta Q}{\Delta a}\right) - \left(\frac{\Delta c}{\Delta Q}\right)\left(\frac{\Delta Q}{\Delta a}\right) - 1 = 0 \quad \text{or} \quad \left\{P - \left(\frac{\Delta c}{\Delta Q}\right)\right\}\left\{\frac{\Delta Q}{\Delta a}\right\} = 1$$

We now multiply both the left-hand side and the right-hand side through by $\frac{a}{PQ}$, and note that $(\Delta c/\Delta Q) = MC$:

$$\left(\frac{P - MC}{P}\right)\left(\frac{\Delta Q}{\Delta a}\right)\frac{a}{Q} = \frac{a}{PQ}$$

From Chapter 2, we know $(P - MC)/P = 1/|PED|$ where $|PED|$ is the price elasticity of demand. We also know $(P - MC)/P$ is the Lerner index, which is widely used as an indicator of market power, as discussed in Section 2.5.

Applying the general definition for any elasticity, we can write $\left(\frac{\Delta Q}{\Delta a}\right)\frac{a}{Q} = AED$, where AED is the advertising elasticity of demand (defined as the ratio of the proportionate change in quantity demanded to the proportionate change in advertising expenditure). By substitution and re-ordering the previous expression, we can write:

$$\frac{a}{PQ} = \left(\frac{P - MC}{P}\right)AED \quad \text{or} \quad \frac{a}{PQ} = \frac{AED}{|PED|}$$

This expression is known as the **Dorfman–Steiner condition**. It implies for profit maximization, the ratio of advertising expenditure to total revenue, or the advertising-to-sales ratio, should be proportional to the ratio of advertising elasticity of demand to price elasticity of demand. The intuition underlying this result is as follows. When the advertising elasticity is high relative to the price elasticity, it is efficient for the monopolist to advertise (rather than cut price) in order to achieve any given increase in quantity demanded. Accordingly, the monopolist spends a relatively high proportion of its sales revenue on advertising. On the other hand, when the price elasticity is high relative to the advertising elasticity, it is efficient to cut price (rather than advertise) in order to achieve any given increase in quantity demanded. Accordingly, the monopolist spends a relatively low proportion of its sales revenue on advertising.

Oligopoly

The preceding analysis refers to a monopolist, and the reactions of competing firms are therefore irrelevant. In order to apply the same kind of analysis to the case of oligopoly, the analysis needs to be extended to take account of the interdependence between the oligopolistic firms. We now consider a market in which there are two duopolists, firms A and B. Initially, for simplicity we assume firm B's advertising expenditure is fixed, and we consider the profit-maximizing advertising decision of firm A. Adapting our previous notation, we let q_A denote firm A's quantity demanded and a_A denote firm A's advertising expenditure. Q denotes total industry demand, equal to the combined demand for firms A and B, $q_A + q_B$; m_A denotes firm A's share of industry demand, or q_A/Q; and AED_A denotes firm A's advertising elasticity of demand.

The revised expression for AED_A is as follows:

$$AED_A = \frac{a_A}{Q}\left(\frac{\Delta Q}{\Delta a_A}\right) + \frac{a_A}{m_A}\left(\frac{\Delta m_A}{\Delta a_A}\right)$$

The two terms on the right-hand-side of this expression represent the following effects of a small change in a_A on q_A. First, there is an increase in total industry demand, ΔQ, part of which goes to firm A. Second, there is an increase in firm A's share of total industry demand, m_A. The expression for AED_A justifies the idea that the advertising elasticity of demand under oligopoly should be higher than it is under monopoly. When firm A increases its advertising expenditure, it benefits not only from an increase in total industry demand (as does the monopolist) but also from an increase in its own market share. This 'market share' effect does not apply in the case of the monopolist. In other words, for a monopolist, $m_A = 1$ and $\Delta m_A = 0$, so the second term on the right-hand-side of the expression for AED_A is zero. For an oligopolist, $m_A < 1$ and $\Delta m_A > 0$, so the second term on the right-hand side of the expression for AED_A is positive.

Using the Dorfman–Steiner condition as before, we can write:

$$\frac{a_A}{P_A q_A} = \left(\frac{P_A - MC}{P_A}\right)AED_A = \left(\frac{P_A - MC}{P_A}\right)\left\{\frac{a_A}{Q}\left(\frac{\Delta Q}{\Delta a_A}\right) + \frac{a_A}{m_A}\left(\frac{\Delta m_A}{\Delta a_A}\right)\right\}$$

P_A denotes firm A's price. We can infer the advertising-to-sales ratio for an oligopolist should be higher than for a monopolist. The oligopolist has an additional incentive to advertise: not only does advertising increase total industry demand, but it also increases the advertising firm's share of industry demand.

The final extension to the analysis of firm A's profit-maximizing advertising decision under duopoly builds into the formula for AED_A an allowance for the effects of firm B's reaction to firm A's decision to increase its advertising expenditure. Firm B's advertising expenditure is denoted a_B, and the change in advertising expenditure implemented by firm B is Δa_B. The revised expression for AED_A is as follows:

$$AED_A = \frac{a_A}{Q}\left\{\left(\frac{\Delta Q}{\Delta a_A}\right) + \left(\frac{\Delta Q}{\Delta a_B}\right)\left(\frac{\Delta a_B}{\Delta a_A}\right)\right\} + \frac{a_A}{m_A}\left\{\left(\frac{\Delta m_A}{\Delta a_A}\right) + \left(\frac{\Delta m_A}{\Delta a_B}\right)\left(\frac{\Delta a_B}{\Delta a_A}\right)\right\}$$

The two terms of the right-hand side of this expression represent the same two effects of a small change in a_A on q_A as before. But as well as the direct effect of Δa_A on Q and on m_A, there are also indirect effects resulting from Δa_B, the change in firm B's advertising expenditure implemented in response to the change in firm A's advertising expenditure. Assuming $(\Delta a_B/\Delta a_A)$ is positive, firm B responds to an increase in firm A's advertising by increasing its own advertising. Firm A gains to the extent that firm B's action increases total industry demand, but firm A also loses to the extent that firm B's action reduces firm A's market share.

Using the Dorfman–Steiner condition, we can write:

$$\frac{a_A}{P_A q_A} = \left(\frac{P_A - MC}{P_A}\right)\left[\frac{a_A}{Q}\left\{\left(\frac{\Delta Q}{\Delta a_A}\right) + \left(\frac{\Delta Q}{\Delta a_B}\right)\left(\frac{\Delta a_B}{\Delta a_A}\right)\right\} + \frac{a_A}{m_A}\left\{\left(\frac{\Delta m_A}{\Delta a_A}\right) + \left(\frac{\Delta m_A}{\Delta a_B}\right)\left(\frac{\Delta a_B}{\Delta a_A}\right)\right\}\right]$$

Because $(\Delta Q/\Delta a_B) > 0$ and $(\Delta m_A/\Delta a_B) < 0$, we cannot say unambiguously whether firm A's advertising-to-sales ratio in the case where firm B reacts to firm A's actions is higher or lower than in the case where firm B's behaviour is fixed.

However, suppose the effect of advertising on each firm's market share generally tends to dominate the effect on total industry demand. In the most extreme case, we could assume $(\Delta Q/\Delta a_A) = (\Delta Q/\Delta a_B) = 0$. Suppose also each firm tends to ignore or underestimate its rival's reaction to its own advertising decisions. In the most extreme case, suppose firm A assumes $(\Delta a_B/\Delta a_A) = 0$, when in fact $(\Delta a_B/\Delta a_A) > 0$. Then according to the previous expression, firm A will tend to set its advertising-to-sales ratio at a level too high for profit maximization. Firm A's advertising-to-sales ratio under the (false) assumption $(\Delta a_B/\Delta a_A) = 0$ is:

$$\frac{a_A}{P_A q_A} = \left(\frac{P_A - MC}{P_A}\right)\left\{\frac{a_A}{m_A}\left(\frac{\Delta m_A}{\Delta a_A}\right)\right\}$$

But firm A's (true) profit-maximizing advertising-to-sales ratio is:

$$\frac{a_A}{P_A q_A} = \left(\frac{P_A - MC}{P_A}\right)\left[\frac{a_A}{m_A}\left\{\left(\frac{\Delta m_A}{\Delta a_A}\right) + \left(\frac{\Delta m_A}{\Delta a_B}\right)\left(\frac{\Delta a_B}{\Delta a_A}\right)\right\}\right]$$

The second of these expressions is smaller than the first, because $(\Delta m_A/\Delta a_B) < 0$ and $(\Delta a_B/\Delta a_A) > 0$. Accordingly, in this case firm A tends to overspend on advertising. If firm B has a similar tendency to underestimate the size of firm A's reactions, there will be a general tendency for the firms collectively to advertise more heavily than they would if they took proper account of their interdependence.

Perfect competition

The Dorfman–Steiner condition, which states that the profit-maximizing advertising-to-sales ratio *equals* the ratio of the firm's advertising elasticity of demand to its price elasticity of demand, provides a straightforward justification for the assertion made in Section 13.1, that there is no role for advertising in perfect competition. The demand function of the perfectly competitive firm is horizontal, and the firm's price elasticity of demand is infinite. Accordingly, the ratio of the firm's advertising elasticity of demand to its price elasticity of demand is zero. The profit-maximizing advertising-to-sales ratio is also zero. If the firm can sell as much output as it likes at the current market price, there is no point in advertising.

The alternative formulation of the Dorfman–Steiner condition, which states that the profit-maximizing advertising-to-sales ratio equals the product of the Lerner index and the advertising elasticity of demand, produces the same conclusion. For the perfectly competitive firm, the Lerner index is zero because price *equals* marginal cost. Therefore the profit-maximizing advertising-to-sales ratio is also zero.

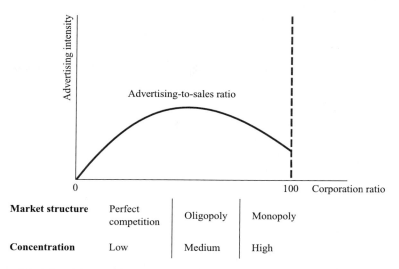

Figure 13.2 Advertising, market structure and concentration

Figure 13.2 summarizes the conclusions of Section 13.4 concerning the relationship between market structure and the profit-maximizing advertising-to-sales ratio. The latter should be zero under perfect competition, positive under oligopoly and positive under monopoly, but larger under oligopoly than under monopoly. Section 13.8 includes a review of a number of empirical studies of this relationship between advertising intensity and market structure or concentration, as summarized in Figure 13.2.

13.5 Advertising as a barrier to entry

Advertising can act as a barrier to entry in several ways.

- *The need to advertise increases start-up costs.* Entrants may have to spend heavily on advertising in order to establish name recognition and a presence in the market. This raises entrants' initial costs. It may be difficult for an entrant to raise the required finance because the returns to advertising outlays are usually uncertain (Weiss, 1963).

- *High levels of advertising build up reputation effects.* Past advertising by incumbents creates goodwill and strengthens consumer brand loyalties. These advantages may be difficult for entrants to overcome. Reputation effects may be particularly strong for first-movers: firms that have in the past pioneered a particular product or brand. Pioneering firms are often able to shape consumer tastes in favour of their own products or brands (Glazer, 1985). Robinson *et al.* (1994) survey the sources of first-mover advantages.

- *Economies of scale in advertising.* According to Scherer and Ross (1990), there are two sources of economies of scale in advertising. First, firms must advertise a large number of times before advertising messages permeate the minds of consumers, and produce increased sales. Second, large-scale advertisers may pay less per unit of advertising than small-scale advertisers. Furthermore, an indirect 'distribution effect' arises when retailers increase stocks of products in response to a manufacturer's advertising campaign, in the expectation that demand will increase (*The Economist*, 2004b).

Figure 13.3 shows the possible **advertising response functions** of an incumbent firm and an entrant. These functions reflect the responsiveness of sales to the volume of advertising expenditure. For the entrant, assumed to be advertising its product or brand for the first time, a threshold level of advertising expenditure of a_1 must be achieved before its advertising begins to have any positive effect on sales. The entrant must spend at least a_1, in order for its brand to achieve name recognition among potential purchasers. Further advertising beyond a_1 increases the entrant's sales, although diminishing returns eventually set in. Saturation point is reached at an advertising expenditure level of a_2. Any further advertising beyond a_2 has a harmful effect on sales: consumers become fed up with receiving the firm's advertising messages, and stop buying the product or brand.

The incumbent is assumed to have advertised its product or brand in the past. Past advertising is assumed to have been effective in building up name recognition and consumer brand loyalty. Therefore in contrast to the entrant, the incumbent does not have to overcome an advertising threshold before it reaps any benefits from advertising: any advertising expenditure in the current period produces some increase in sales. Like the entrant, however, the incumbent is subject to diminishing returns to advertising, and may reach a saturation point beyond which further advertising has a harmful effect on sales.

Advertising response functions such as those shown in Figure 13.3 may contribute to entry barriers due to both an absolute cost advantage favouring the incumbent, and economies of scale (see Section 8.3). Thanks to its past advertising investment, the incumbent achieves more sales for any given amount of current advertising expenditure. This implies the incumbent has an absolute cost advantage over the entrant.

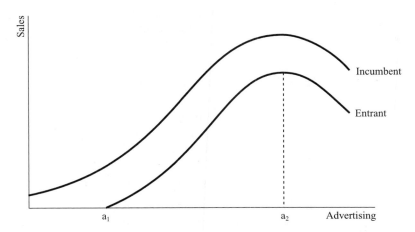

Figure 13.3 Advertising response functions

Furthermore, because the gradient of the advertising response function is increasing over the lower end of the range of values for a, and because the threshold level of advertising expenditure is effectively a fixed cost from the entrant's perspective, there are economies of scale in advertising. Within the relevant range of values for a, the effectiveness of each unit of advertising expenditure increases as the volume of advertising expenditure increases. If advertising costs are incorporated into the firms' total cost functions, economies of scale in advertising may change the location of the minimum efficient scale of production. This in turn may alter the extent to which the cost structure, and in particular the need to be producing on a scale sufficiently large to be cost-efficient, acts as a barrier to entry.

The importance of advertising as a barrier to entry is disputed by King (1983), who refers to the UK's processed cheese industry. Cheese slices produced by Kraft Foods held a dominant position in this market between 1971 and 1975, when Kraft's advertising expenditure was relatively low. In 1976, Kraft doubled its advertising expenditure, but this did not prevent several new brands from successfully entering the market. King suggests the costs of plant and machinery contributed much more than advertising costs to the entrants' total cost functions. Scott Morton (2000) examines the extent to which the advertising of patented branded pharmaceutical products in the US immediately prior to the loss of patent protection deterred the entry of generic drugs. The sample comprises drugs that lost patent protection over the period 1986–91, while the advertising data is monthly from three years before to one year after patent expiration. There is little evidence that advertising deterred entry.

Advertising response may vary not only between incumbent firms and entrants, but also among incumbent firms. Fare *et al.* (2004) examine the cost-efficiency of advertising by media (television, radio, print) for a sample of six large US brewers over the period 1983–93. A linear programming technique called data envelopment analysis is used to assess the extent to which brewers choose the appropriate mix of media consistent with profit maximization. Only one of the six firms (Anheuser Buesch) is found to use advertising efficiently. In a second-stage analysis, advertising efficiency estimates are found to be positively linked to profitability.

13.6 Advertising, information search and quality signalling

Information plays a crucial role in competition. In the perfectly competitive model, all buyers and sellers have perfect knowledge. Consequently one price prevails, and all firms earn normal profit. However, if information is imperfect or if there is an informational asymmetry between producers and consumers, consumers may not be capable of making an informed choice about the products and services they purchase. This may have serious implications for the effectiveness of competition and the nature of market equilibrium.

Some economists have suggested that advertising improves the speed and efficiency with which consumers search for information. Consumers gather information through a search process, which imposes costs in the form of wages or leisure time forgone. From the consumer's perspective, advertising reduces the cost of obtaining this information. Equivalently, if products are heavily advertised the consumer can

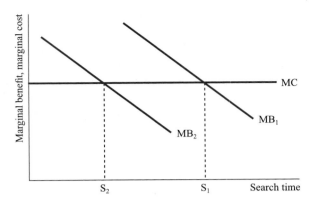

Figure 13.4 Optimal search time

obtain a given amount information more cheaply, since the information obtained from advertisements reduces the need for independent search.

In Figure 13.4, the marginal cost function MC represents the cost of each additional hour of search, and is assumed to be constant. The benefit to the consumer from each additional hour of search is represented by the downward-sloping marginal benefit function MB_1. The benefit gained from spending additional time searching declines as the time already spent increases. The search process continues until the marginal benefit *equals* the marginal cost, with S_1 hours devoted to search.

The provision of information through advertising reduces the marginal benefit gained from each additional hour of information search, shifting the marginal benefit function to the left from MB_1 to MB_2. The optimal search time decreases from S_1 to S_2. If, as seems likely, information is disseminated more efficiently through advertising than it is through having large numbers of consumers searching for information independently, the sum of the product price and the search cost is likely to be lower due to advertising.

> Advertising is among other things, a method of providing potential buyers with knowledge of the identity of sellers. It is clearly an immensely powerful instrument for the elimination of ignorance – comparable in force to the use of the book instead of the oral discourse to communicate knowledge.
>
> *(Stigler, 1961, p. 182)*

Advertising also plays an important role in some signalling models, which deal with situations of asymmetric information between producers and consumers. In a classic analysis of the market for secondhand cars, Akerlof (1970) argues that sellers tend to have more information than potential buyers about the true quality of each car on the market, and a potential buyer may not be able to tell which cars that are for sale are of good quality and which ones should be avoided. In the terminology of the advertising literature, secondhand cars are an experience good. Faced with this uncertainty, the maximum price a rational buyer is willing to pay falls somewhere between the true value of a high-quality car and the true value of a low-quality car. However, if sellers of high-quality cars are unwilling to sell at a price below the true value of a high-quality car, they withdraw from the market. The market for high-quality cars collapses, and only low-quality cars are traded. The title of Akerlof's article, 'The market for lemons', refers to American slang terminology for a low-quality secondhand car.

A similar situation might exist in the market for a product with competing high-quality and low-quality brands. If the product is an experience good and potential buyers cannot distinguish between the low- and high-quality brands before purchase, there may be a tendency for high-quality brands to be driven out of the market by low-quality brands, for the reasons discussed by Akerlof. However, Kihlstrom and Riordan (1984) and Milgrom and Roberts (1986) show that if there are repeat purchases of the product, the producer of a high-quality brand may be able to use advertising as a signal of quality. The idea is that for advertising to be worthwhile, it has to persuade consumers to buy the product more than once. It is not worthwhile for a low-quality producer to advertise its brand as high-quality, because consumers who are initially misled into purchasing the inferior brand discover from experience that the brand is low-quality, and will not make the same mistake again. However, it is worthwhile for a high-quality producer to advertise, because consumers who purchase this brand and confirm from experience that it *is* high-quality, will make repeat purchases.

To demonstrate the signalling model, we assume each brand of a certain product has a two-period lifetime. A low-quality brand that is known by consumers to be low-quality earns a profit of 10 per period. However, a low-quality brand can earn a profit of 30 per period, if it is mistakenly perceived by consumers to be high-quality. A high-quality brand can earn a profit of 25 per period, provided consumers can distinguish between the high-quality brand and its low-quality imitators. If consumers cannot make this distinction, in each period the high-quality brand is driven out of the market by a flood of low-quality imitators, and the high-quality brand earns zero profit.

Suppose initially there is no advertising, and the low-quality producer can pretend its brand is high-quality at zero cost.

- A low-quality brand that is known to be low-quality earns a combined profit in periods 1 and 2 of $10 + 10 = 20$.

- A low-quality brand that pretends to be high-quality earns a profit of 30 in period 1. However, in period 2 consumers know from experience the brand is actually low-quality, so the period 2 profit is 10. The combined profit in periods 1 and 2 is $30 + 10 = 40$.

Accordingly, it is profitable for low-quality producers to pretend their brands are high-quality in period 1. The high-quality brand is driven out of the market and earns zero profit. In period 2, the same thing happens again. Although the low-quality brands that existed in period 1 are now perceived by consumers to be low-quality, new brands appear that are actually low-quality but pretend to be high-quality. Again, the high-quality brand is driven out of the market and earns zero profit.

We now suppose producers of either brand can only convince consumers their brand is high-quality in period 1 by advertising, at a cost of 25. No advertising is necessary in period 2, because by then consumers have established for themselves the true quality of the brand they purchased in period 1.

■ The producer of a low-quality brand that is not advertised and is known to be low-quality earns a combined profit in periods 1 and 2 of $10 + 10 = 20$, as before.

■ The producer of a low-quality brand that is advertised and pretends to be high-quality earns a profit of $30 - 25 = 5$ in period 1. Despite the advertising, in period 2 consumers know the brand is actually low-quality, so the period 2 profit is 10. The combined profit in periods 1 and 2 is $5 + 10 = 15$.

Accordingly, it is not profitable for producers of low-quality brands to advertise and pretend to be high-quality in period 1. The producer of the high-quality brand, on the other hand, does advertise, and is not driven out of the market. The period 1 profit is $25 - 25 = 0$. In period 2, however, this producer earns a profit of 25. The combined profit in periods 1 and 2 is $0 + 25 = 25$.

In the signalling model, it is not the advertising message itself that is effective in convincing consumers that the advertised brand is high-quality. Rather, the simple fact that this brand is being advertised provides the necessary signal of high quality. Consumers realize the producer only advertises if it is confident of attracting repeat purchases. Similarly, the fact that the low-quality brand is not advertised provides a signal of low quality. Consumers realize that if the brand was high-quality the producer would advertise; therefore the fact that the brand is not advertised signals that it is low-quality.

> [If] the consumer believes that the more a brand advertises, the more likely it is to be a better buy . . . in consequence, the more advertisements of a brand the consumer encounters, the more likely he is to try the brand.
>
> *(Nelson, 1974b, p. 732)*

> It is clear that if high-quality brands advertise more and if advertising expenditures are observable (even if not perfectly so), then rational, informed consumers will respond positively to advertising even if the ads cannot and do not have much direct informational content.
>
> *(Milgrom and Roberts, 1986, p. 797)*

> Costly and wasteful advertisement demonstrates that the advertiser is also investing in the quality of the product and a continued relationship with customers, because otherwise the costly and wasteful advertising would serve no purpose.
>
> *(Kay, 2004, p. 217)*

Advertising is not necessarily the only method by which producers can send signals of quality. Hertzendorf (1993) argues if price signalling is effective, advertising is unnecessary. Advertising is only useful if price does not provide consumers with enough information to assess quality. More recently, Fluent and Garella (2002) developed a theoretical model that examines whether firms use advertising or price to signal quality to consumers. They find advertising is an appropriate signalling device in differentiating products when quality differences are small, but price is preferred when quality differences are large. Horstmann and MacDonald (2003) suggest advertising is an important tool in informing consumers about product quality and characteristics; but as consumer awareness increases, the need for advertising should decline. However, data from the US market for compact disc players over the period 1983–92 suggests a tendency for prices to fall and advertising intensity to increase over time.

13.7   Is there too much advertising?

As we have seen, advertising is often categorized as either informative or persuasive. Informative advertising is widely regarded as useful because it helps provide consumers with information, with which they can make more informed choices. Persuasive advertising, in contrast, distorts the information consumers receive, making it more difficult for them to make informed choices on the basis of objective information. Reliable information is a prerequisite for effective competition, which ensures resources are used efficiently to produce the goods and services that consumers actually want. Persuasive advertising changes the preference functions of consumers and can even damage competition, if firms that have invested in building up brand loyalties exploit their market power by charging higher prices and earning abnormal profit.

The traditional view of advertising, expressed by Bain (1956), Comanor and Wilson (1974), Galbraith (1958, 1967) and Kaldor (1950), takes a critical view. Advertising tends to distort consumer preferences, by persuading consumers to buy products and services that are heavily promoted.

> Most advertising is not informative. The typical Marlboro ad, with a cowboy smoking a cigarette, or a Virginia slims ad, or a Budweiser beer ad, conveys no credible information concerning the nature of the product being sold, the price at which the product is sold, or where the product may be obtained. Firms spend money on ads such as these because they believe it increases their profit, because such ads have an effect on demand curves.
>
> *(Stiglitz, 1991, p. 842)*

> The goal of persuasive advertising is to change customers' perceptions of a product. If persuasive advertising works, it means that a branded product is considered in some non-tangible way to be 'different' to its rivals. If successful, therefore, persuasive advertising may generate brand loyalty – customers may be unwilling to switch to competitors' products if they are convinced that their preferred brand offers something that no other product would be able to provide.
>
> *(Nawaz, 1997, p. 3)*

> Persuasive advertising interferes with the exercise of innate preferences, it alters choices away from the efficient lines that 'consumer sovereignty'

would yield. Thus persuasive image instilling advertising is largely a form of economic waste.

(Shepherd, 1997, p. 111)

In one of the most famous critiques of advertising, Kaldor (1950) argues that because advertising is supplied jointly with goods and services, consumers are forced to pay for advertising they do not want, and are therefore unwilling accomplices in a waste of resources. The amount of advertising supplied exceeds that demanded because it is provided as a 'free' service not only to purchasers, but also to consumers who will never buy the good or service under consideration. Advertisers do not charge a positive price for advertising, since to do so would result in less advertising being demanded than is required for advertisers to maximize profit. Consequently, there is an oversupply of advertising, and a waste of resources that is financed by consumers who have no choice other than to pay a higher price for the advertised goods.

The main criticisms of Kaldor's argument are as follows:

■ Consumers have a choice between advertised and non-advertised goods. If consumers did not buy advertised products, there would be no market for advertising (Telser, 1966b).

■ By supplying advertising jointly with goods and services, savings may be realized. Collecting separate fees for the provision of information might be more expensive than incorporating advertising costs into the price of the product or service.

■ Kaldor's view is consistent with the underlying assumptions of microeconomic theory, in which a consumer with fixed tastes possesses perfect information (Koutsoyannis, 1982). In reality, however, consumers inhabit societies that are dynamic by nature. Tastes are socially and culturally conditioned, and are not exogenous. Consumers continuously acquire new information from their own experiences and through the media. The static equilibrium methodology used in consumer theory, based on assumptions of fixed tastes and perfect information, is therefore misleading (Hoschman and Luski, 1988; Nichols, 1985).

An alternative view, articulated by Littlechild (1982), Nelson (1974a,b, 1975, 1978), Stigler (1961) and Telser (1964, 1966a) is that advertising provides consumers with valuable information which allows them to make rational choices. Under this view, advertising plays a positive role in ensuring the efficient allocation of resources. The extent to which consumers are able to make informed choices depends on the knowledge and certainty they have about the attributes of products and services. Informed consumers are unlikely to pay higher prices for any particular product or service unless 'real' differences exist. 'Consumers are not completely helpless pawns in the hands of greedy businessmen. Though they have far less than perfect information, consumers have far more than zero information' (Nelson, 1974a, p. 47).

Ozga (1960) and Stigler (1961) argue that if consumers have perfect information about price and quality, firms must charge similar if not identical prices for comparable products or services.

Evaluation of the welfare effects of advertising is made difficult by the fact that persuasive advertising changes consumer tastes and preferences. This means there is no consistent standard for making welfare comparisons before and after advertising takes place. We cannot easily say whether a consumer is better off or worse off as a result of advertising, if the consumer has a different utility function in each case.

However, Dixit and Norman (1978) suggest a method for avoiding this difficulty. If it can be shown that welfare is increased by advertising if the assessment is made using pre-advertising consumer preferences, *and* if it can also be shown that welfare is increased if the assessment is made using post-advertising consumer preferences, then we can conclude unambiguously that welfare is increased no matter how the comparison is made.

Dixit and Norman's analysis for the case of a monopolist is shown in Figure 13.5, which is drawn on the same assumptions as Figure 13.1. As before, following an advertising campaign costing $\Delta a = a_2 - a_1$, the monopolist's average revenue function shifts from $AR(a_1)$ to $AR(a_2)$, and the profit-maximizing price and quantity shift from P_1Q_1 to P_2Q_2. What are the welfare implications of this shift? As argued above, there are two possible answers, depending whether we use pre-advertising or post-advertising preferences to make the comparison.

■ Using the pre-advertising demand function $AR(a_1)$, the welfare gain from the extra production is the area between $AR(a_1)$ and MC over the range Q_1 to Q_2, *minus* the advertising expenditure. The welfare gain is $B - \Delta a$. This expression could be positive or negative.

■ Using the post-advertising demand function $AR(a_2)$, the welfare gain from the extra production is the area between $AR(a_2)$ and MC over the range Q_1 to Q_2, *minus* the advertising expenditure. The welfare gain is $B + C + D - \Delta a$. This expression could also be positive or negative.

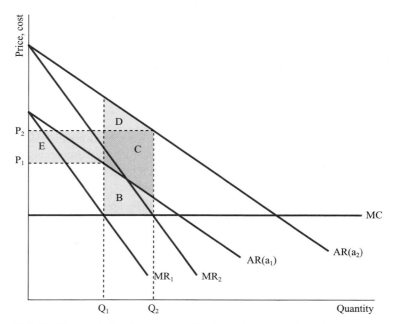

Figure 13.5 Welfare analysis of an increase in advertising expenditure in monopoly

In order to ascertain whether advertising is always welfare-enhancing if it is also profitable, one further assumption concerning Figure 13.5 is introduced at this point: it is assumed area D < area E. From the construction of Figure 13.5 it is clear that for sufficiently small changes in a, the condition D < E is very likely to be satisfied, and below we assume this is in fact the case.

The gain in monopoly profit resulting from the shift from P_1Q_1 to P_2Q_2 is B + C + E − Δa. The monopolist only advertises if B + C + E − Δa ≥ 0, which is a necessary (but not a sufficient) condition for B − Δa > 0 and (assuming D < E) for B + C + D − Δa > 0. This means advertising can only be welfare-enhancing if it is also profitable. There can never be a case in which welfare could be improved by advertising more, but the monopolist fails to increase advertising because it is not profitable to do so.

The profit-maximizing monopolist increases its advertising until B + C + E − Δa = 0. We can now examine the welfare effects of the last unit of advertising expenditure at the profit-maximizing equilibrium.

■ Using pre-advertising preferences, the welfare effect of the last unit of advertising expenditure is B − Δa. If B + C + E − Δa = 0, B − Δa must be negative, because C and E are both positive.

■ Using post-advertising preferences, the welfare effect of the last unit of advertising expenditure is B + C + D − Δa. If B + C + E − Δa = 0, B + C + D − Δa must be negative, because it is assumed D < E.

Therefore at the profit-maximizing equilibrium, the welfare effect of the last unit of advertising expenditure is negative. From a welfare perspective the profit-maximizing monopolist tends to overspend on advertising, and a small reduction in advertising would be welfare-improving. Dixit and Norman show similar results also hold in oligopoly and monopolistic competition.

13.8 Empirical evidence

Information content and effectiveness of advertising

Resnick and Stern (1977) assess the information content of advertising, by searching for the presence or absence in advertisements of 'cues', which contain various types of information. Relevant cues include information on price, quality, performance, component parts or contents, availability, special offers, taste, packaging or shape, guarantees or warranties, safety, nutrition, independent research, company sponsored research and new ideas. Advertisements are classed as informative if they include one or more cues. Of 378 advertisements assessed, 49.2 per cent are classed as informative. However, the results are sensitive to definitional changes. 'If the criterion would have been the communication of three different information cues, only four commercials, or 1 per cent of the total sample, would have been classed as informative' (Resnick and Stern, 1977, p. 52).

Drawing on the work of Clarke (1976), who summarizes the findings of 69 studies of sales responsiveness to advertising, Leone (1995) examines the responsiveness of sales to advertising for a range of products, including household cleaning products, food, beverages, petrol, electrical appliances, cigarettes, cars and alcohol. In the case of established brands, advertising tends to have some affect on sales for between six and nine months, but in most cases the effect of advertising on sales is short-lived.

Using data from 60 previous studies, and analysing a sample of 91,438 advertisements, Abernethy and Franke (1996) find an average number of information cues of 2.04 per advertisement. The percentages of advertisements providing at least one, two or three information cues are 84 per cent, 58 per cent and 33 per cent respectively. Advertisements for durable goods provided 35 per cent more cues on average than those for non-durable goods. Outdoor advertising and television advertising contain less information than magazine and radio advertising.

Becker and Murphy (1993) argue advertisements should be treated as valuable complements to the goods they promote, and not as products that distort consumer tastes and preferences. In cases where advertisements appear on television and radio, these tend to lower consumer utility. However, consumers are compensated for exposure to advertising by the provision of free television and radio programmes. Similarly, companies such as Qualcomm, producers of the Eudora email package, provide free access to email and other software in exchange for exposure to advertising. Advertising does not necessarily reduce utility in all forms of media. In media where consumers can easily ignore advertising, such as the print media, advertising is more likely to be informative and utility-increasing.

Paton (1998) uses survey data on UK manufacturing, service and distribution firms to assess the extent to which advertisements incorporate price information. Over 1,000 firms are surveyed, in order to obtain a usable sample of 325 firms; 70 per cent of the sample included no price information in their advertisements. Price information tends to be included in advertising more commonly in distribution than in manufacturing and services, and more commonly when consumers are the end-users of a product or service.

Advertising and concentration

Most empirical studies of the link between advertising and concentration seek to test for the existence of a relationship similar to the one summarized in Figure 13.2. The methodology used to test this hypothesis is SCP-based, and accordingly most of these studies were published during the 1960s, 1970s and 1980s. Taken as a whole, the empirical evidence favouring the hypothesis that advertising intensity should be higher under oligopoly than under either perfect competition or monopoly appears to be reasonably strong and convincing (Leahy, 1997).

Some of the earliest studies test for a linear relationship between concentration and advertising intensity. For example, according to Telser (1964), if there is an association between advertising and market power, then industry concentration and advertising intensity should be positively related. In Telser's empirical analysis, industry advertising-to-sales ratios for a sample of 42 three-digit consumer goods industries for 1947, 1954 and 1958 are correlated with concentration ratios. Evidence of a positive but statistically insignificant relationship between concentration and advertising intensity is obtained.

Mann *et al.* (1967) argue that a four-digit industry definition comes closer than Telser's three-digit classification to the theoretical concept of the market. Data are used for 42 firms, divided into 14 four-digit industries. Average advertising-to-sales ratios for various groups of firms (such as the dominant firms in each industry) are calculated for the periods, 1952–56, 1957–61 and 1962–65. There was a significant positive association between industry concentration and industry advertising-to-sales ratios for all three periods.

Most later studies test for a non-linear relationship between concentration and advertising intensity (Leahy, 1997). If a quadratic functional form is assumed, the specification of the regression equation is as follows:

$$\left(\frac{A_i}{S_i}\right) = \alpha + \beta_1 + \beta_2 CR_i + \beta_3 CR_i^2 + u_i$$

where the dependent variable is (A_i/S_i), the advertising-to-sales ratio of industry i; and the independent variables are linear and quadratic terms in CR_i, the industry i concentration ratio, or some other suitable industry concentration measure. A necessary (but not always sufficient condition) for an inverted U-shaped relationship between concentration and advertising intensity is $\beta_2 > 0$ and $\beta_3 < 0$.

Using data on 25 UK consumer goods industries, Sutton (1974) finds evidence of an inverted U-shaped relationship between concentration and advertising intensity. Cable (1972) and Buxton *et al.* (1984) also report similar results. Taken together, these findings lend some support to the view that advertising is higher under oligopoly than other market structures. However, using similar UK data, Reekie (1975) and Rees (1975) find no significant relationship between concentration and advertising intensity. Overall, therefore, the UK evidence from the 1970s and 1980s is somewhat ambiguous.

Using US data, Ornstein (1978) finds a evidence of positive linear relationship between concentration and advertising intensity. However, a quadratic term in CR_i^2 is statistically insignificant. More recently, Weiss *et al.* (1983) and Uri (1987) report evidence in favour of an inverted U-shaped relationship between concentration and advertising intensity.

In an international study, Lambin (1976) examines the relationship between several variables, including price elasticity of demand and concentration, and advertising intensity, for a sample of 16 product groups covering over 100 brands across eight countries, for the period 1960–70. '[N]o systematic association is observed between market concentration and advertising intensity'. However, '[a]dvertizing increases the capacity of the firm to charge higher prices to the consumer' (Lambin, 1976, p. 147).

More recently, Lee (2002) uses a sample of 426 (five-digit) manufacturing industries to examine the relationship between advertising and concentration. An inverted U-shaped relationship is found for consumer goods industries, but a J-shaped relationship is observed in the case of producer goods.

Advertising and profitability

Using data on 42 consumer goods industries for the period 1954–57, Comanor and Wilson (1967) find a positive relationship between the industry advertising-to-sales ratio and profitability. Miller (1969) and Weiss (1969) obtain similar results from different data sets. Vernon and Nourse (1973) find a significant relationship between profit and advertising-to-sales ratio at industry level, which they interpret as evidence that advertising represents a barrier to entry. However, Bloch (1974) argues that these studies are flawed, because they treat advertising expenditures as a current expense. Instead, advertising should be treated as capital expenditure and depreciated accordingly. When Bloch's profit data are adjusted, no empirical relationship between advertising and profit is found.

Paton and Vaughan Williams (1999) find a positive relationship between advertising expenditures and current and future profitability for a large sample of UK firms. Greuner *et al.* (2000) examine the long-run relationship between advertising and profitability for three dominant US car manufacturers (GM, Ford and Chrysler) for the period 1970–94. There is little evidence that advertising influenced profitability. Notta and Oustapassidis (2001) examine the relationship between four advertising media (television, radio, newspapers and magazines) and profitability for a sample of 350 Greek food manufacturing firms for the period 1993–96. Only television advertising appears to increase profitability.

Advertising-to-sales ratios, widely used in many empirical studies, are prone to measurement error. If a firm actively pursued a strategy based on promotions other than advertising, the correlation between concentration, profitability and advertising may be biased (Lambin, 1976). Furthermore, for diversified firms it is often difficult to assess from company accounts which product lines are being heavily advertised. This problem can be tackled using data at the line-of-business level. Using US data for 3,186 lines-of-business drawn from 258 industry categories, Ravenscraft (1983) finds no relationship between advertising expenditure and profitability.

A few methodological problems arise in empirical studies of the relationship between advertising and profitability. First, it is often difficult to determine the direction of causation between advertising and profit. Does advertising lead to increased profit, or do profitable firms advertise more? (Vernon and Nourse, 1973). Second, size measures such as sales, assets and employment are often highly correlated. These measures are used in the denominators of both the advertising and profitability measures, leading to the possibility that spurious relationships may be identified (Miller, 1969). Third, advertising may be a useful instrument for firms wishing to adjust their reported profit for tax reasons. A high profit in any particular year, and the tax liability this would create, might be massaged and reduced by spending heavily on advertising. This type of behaviour might distort the results of empirical studies which attempt to identify a statistical relationship between advertising and profitability.

From the empirical evidence reviewed above, it is unclear whether advertising reduces competition by increasing entry barriers, or whether advertising helps producers realize economies of scale in production, in which case cost savings may be passed on to consumers in the form of lower prices. This has led some researchers to examine the direct relationship between advertising and price (see pp. 486–90).

Advertising and market share

In studies of the link between advertising and market share, the main hypothesis is that if advertising promotes competition, the market shares of the top firms should be unstable; but if advertising restricts competition the opposite applies (Willis and Rogers, 1998). Eckard (1987) examines the relationship between advertising intensity and the combined market shares of the four largest firms in 228 manufacturing industries for the period 1963–82. As advertising expenditure increased, the ranking of firms by market share tended to change more frequently, and market shares became less stable. This implies support for the view that advertising promotes competition. Das *et al.* (1993) obtain similar results for a sample of 163 US industries for the period 1978–88.

> While our results cannot be interpreted to mean that advertising is not ever used anticompetitively, the empirical findings suggest that advertising and promotional activities on balance work to increase the competitiveness of markets across a large set of industries over an extended period of time.
>
> *(Das et al., 1993, p. 1412)*

Advertising and product quality

Tellis and Forell (1988) test for an empirical relationship between advertising intensity and product quality, using data on 749 firms for the period 1970–83. Products are grouped into those at early stages (introductory and growth) and those at advanced stages (maturity, decline) of the product life cycle. There are strong positive relationships between product quality and each of advertising expenditure, market share and profitability for products at advanced stages of the product life cycle.

In an analysis of the advertising strategies of leading car manufacturers, Thomas *et al.* (1998) find evidence that car producers use advertising expenditures to signal quality.

> [This observation] is consistent with game theory models that show that since high-quality products enjoy greater repeat sales and profits, their producers find it more profitable to spend large unrecoverable sums on advertising to signal product quality.
>
> *(Thomas et al., 1998, p. 429)*

Similarly, using information produced by leading specialist magazines on the quality of running shoes, Archibald *et al.* (1983) find advertising expenditures are closely related to product quality after information on quality is published. Caves and Greene (1996) find a positive association between product quality and advertising intensity for experience goods and new products.

Advertising and price

The traditional view of the effect of advertising on price is that the prices of advertised goods tend to be higher than those of non-advertised goods, due to the higher selling costs; and because advertising reduces the price elasticity of demand, resulting in higher prices. Furthermore, producers or retailers who market generic or own-brand products at a lower price are simply exploiting the information spread by the advertised goods. They are essentially free-riders (Porter, 1976).

An alternative view, implicit in the notion of informative advertising (Stigler, 1961), suggests an informed consumer is better able to select products at a lower price for given level of quality. Therefore advertising reduces consumer ignorance and increases the price elasticity of demand, resulting in lower prices.

This subsection reviews a number of studies of the relationship between advertising and price in manufacturing, services and distribution. Much of this research compares the level and dispersion of prices between markets in which there are restrictions on advertising and those where advertising is unrestricted. Kaul and Wittink (1995) review 18 studies covering a 20-year period. On the balance of evidence, the following generalizations emerge:

■ Advertising containing price information increases consumer sensitivity to price changes (price elasticity of demand).

■ Advertising containing price information leads to intensified competition and results in lower prices.

■ Non-price advertising reduces consumer sensitivity to price changes.

Below, we review a number of sectoral studies of the relationship between advertising and price.

Spectacles and optometry services

Benham (1972) examines the differences between the prices paid by consumers for spectacles (eyeglasses) in US states where advertising restrictions exist, and in states where they do not. Data from a national survey of 634 consumers is used to compare the prices of spectacles between states. In the empirical model, the dependent variable is the price paid for spectacles by each consumer, and the independent variables include a dummy variable indicating whether the spectacles were purchased in a state where advertising restrictions exist, and controls for income, age, sex and family size. Benham finds spectacles were more expensive in states where advertising was restricted, and estimates a price differential of US$6.70. Between the most and least restrictive states, the estimated price differential was US$19.50.

> The results . . . are consistent with the hypothesis that in the market examined, advertising improves consumer knowledge and that the benefits derived from this knowledge outweigh the price-increasing effects of advertising.
>
> *(Benham, 1972, p. 349)*

Mackintosh and Frey (1978) examine the dispersion of prices for spectacles in New Orleans and Louisiana, where advertising restrictions were in force. Using a sample of 15 dispensers, data on price differentials for three types of lens (based on three types of sight deficiency) and two types of frame were obtained by volunteers who visited the dispensers. Evidence was found of significant price differences due to a lack of price transparency. Consumers could not always judge whether they were receiving a good deal. It is suggested that if the advertising restrictions were removed, these price differences would diminish.

Maurizi *et al.* (1981) examine the effects of the removal of advertising restrictions on spectacles in California. They find no difference between the prices of glasses from opticians who advertised and those who did not. However, the prices of opticians who advertised contact lenses were on average 17 per cent lower than those of their counterparts who did not advertise.

Legal services

Cox (1982) examines the relationship between advertising and the price of legal services in six US states in 1978. Advertising regulations are classed as restrictive in Alabama and Mississippi, moderate in Arizona and Indiana, and permissive in California and Wisconsin. The sample comprises 250 lawyers drawn from six states. Lawyers operating in states with permissive regulation were 11 times more likely to advertise than their counterparts operating under restrictive regulation.

In Cox's regression analysis, the dependent variable is the price charged by each lawyer for a particular service. Independent variables include a measure of the extent to which the lawyer advertises, income per head in the lawyer's geographical area (capturing demand effects), the number of lawyers in the practice (firm-size effects), the length of time the lawyer has practised in the same area (reputation or goodwill effects), and a measure of the time the lawyer takes to perform the service (efficiency effects).

Cox finds a negative relationship between advertising and price, lending some support to the notion that heavier advertising leads to lower prices. For example, uncontested bankruptcies were on average US$47 more expensive where advertising restrictions were in force, although divorces were US$16 cheaper. Prices charged by larger legal firms were higher, as were prices charged by inefficient firms. Reputation also had a positive effect on price. In another study, Cox *et al.* (1982) find evidence of large variation in the prices charged for some legal services, suggesting a high level of consumer ignorance. However, both the level and dispersion of prices was lower in cases where lawyers advertised, which suggests advertising helps consumers make more informed choices.

Using fees and advertising data on lawyers from 17 US states, Schroeter *et al.* (1987) examine the effects of advertising on individual legal firm price elasticities of demand. If advertising provides information, demand should become more elastic; but if advertising alters consumer preferences, demand should become more inelastic.

In Schroeter *et al.*'s regression model, the dependent variable is an estimate of an individual lawyer's price elasticity of demand for a specific service. The independent variables include the lawyer's individual advertising intensity for the service and the industry-level advertising intensity for the same service, and a set of controls for location and average disposable income levels. A positive association is found between advertising and price elasticity of demand.

Using data on 275 Scottish legal firms Stephen (1994) estimates a regression model in which the dependent variable is the individual firm's price elasticity of demand for a specific service. Independent variables include a firm size measure, the number of offices operated by the firm, the unemployment rate in the firm's geographic area, a concentration measure for the same area, and a dummy variable capturing whether or not the firm advertises. A negative relationship between advertising and price suggests firms that advertise have more price elastic demand functions than those that do not. Price elasticity is positively associated with firm size and concentration, but negatively associated with the number of branches and the local rate of unemployment.

Medicines

Cady (1976) examines the impact of restrictions on advertising on prices in the retail drugs market. Cady suggests prices are likely not only to be higher in markets where advertising is restricted, but also to be more dispersed. The sample comprises data on 10 common products, compiled from a national survey of 1,900 US retail pharmacies. Cady finds greater variation in prices where advertising was restricted. In a regression model which examines the relationship between the extent of advertising and price, the dependent variable is the price of an individual drug from a particular pharmacy, and the independent variables capture environmental characteristics (location, population, average income) of the area where the pharmacy is located, structural and organizational characteristics of the pharmacy, and a dummy variable indicating whether restrictions on advertising were in force.

Pharmacies located in states where advertising restrictions were in force are found to have charged up to 9 per cent more than their counterparts in unrestricted states. Consumers could save an estimated US$150 million if advertising restrictions were removed.

> [A]dvertising can act as a significant stimulus to market competition through the provision of salient, useful information. To ignore this effect and to view all advertising as abusive, deceptive, and contributing to imperfect market conditions is potentially detrimental to consumer welfare.
>
> *(Cady, 1976, p. 29)*

Alcohol

Milyo and Waldfogel (1999) examine the impact of the lifting of advertising restrictions on alcoholic beverages in Rhode Island in 1996. The prices of advertised goods are found to have declined after the restrictions were lifted, but the prices of beverages that were not advertised were roughly unchanged.

Physician services

Rizzo and Zeckhauser (1992) examine the impact of advertising on the price of physician services using data from the American Medical Association between 1987 and 1988. The dependent variable is a measure of the average price charged by each individual physician, and the independent variables are the numbers of physicians in the same geographical area, and a variable reflecting the extent to which the physician advertises. Although preliminary estimations suggest advertising lowered the price of physician services, after controls are added for sample selection bias and measurement error in the advertising variable, advertising is found to cause prices to increase.

On balance the evidence suggests advertising appears to reduce the variability and level of prices. The empirical evidence for several service industries suggests advertising aids consumer search, and enables consumers to make more informed choices (see also Love and Stephen, 1996). However, some evidence suggests the price information contained in advertisements produced by service sector firms is often low (Paton, 1998; Paton and Vaughan Williams, 1999).

13.9 Summary

This chapter has examined the role of advertising in the modern economy. Some advertising messages provide useful information about the attributes of the products, services or brands they promote, enabling consumers to make more informed choices. However, advertising which seeks to persuade consumers of the superiority of particular goods by transmitting messages whose truth (or otherwise) may be unreliable, or at least not objectively verifiable, may represent a waste of resources or may damage competition or reduce welfare. It has been shown that the effectiveness of advertising may depend on whether the product's attributes are easily identifiable prior to purchase and consumption (search and experience goods), and upon cost and frequency of purchase (convenience and shopping goods).

There are good theoretical reasons to expect that the relationship between market structure and advertising intensity should have an inverted U-shaped appearance. Advertising intensity should be zero under perfect competition, positive under both oligopoly and monopoly, but larger under oligopoly than under monopoly. A monopolist's only incentive to advertise is to try to increase total industry demand, whereas oligopolists have the additional incentive of trying to capture market share from one another. During the 1960s, 1970s and 1980s a number of empirical studies based on the structure–conduct–performance paradigm identified evidence of a relationship of this kind between industry concentration and advertising-to-sales ratios.

Advertising can help raise barriers to entry. An incumbent firm may benefit from an absolute cost advantage in advertising if its past advertising investment has helped establish name recognition or brand loyalty among consumers. Consumer familiarity makes current advertising more effective than it is for an entrant attempting to establish a presence in the market for the first time. Economies of scale in advertising may also make it difficult for small-scale entrants to compete effectively with incumbents who are already producing and advertising on a large scale.

The competitive model relies on an assumption of perfect information, but in situations where consumers have limited information advertising may play an important role in signalling information about product quality. The content of advertising messages may be unimportant, but the fact that a producer is prepared to invest in advertising suggests the producer is that confident consumers, having made an initial purchase, will return and make repeat purchases.

Some economists believe advertising tends to mislead or distort the truth, and is usually wasteful or even damaging. Others argue advertising contributes positively to the circulation of information through society, and in any event consumers have choices and are not forced to purchase advertised goods if they do not wish to do so. Perhaps this debate will never be resolved conclusively. However, some of the empirical evidence, at least, seems to suggest that advertising has beneficial effects for competition and for consumers. For example, increased advertising appears to be associated with rapid turnover in firm-level market shares, which suggests competition is effective; advertising seems to increase price elasticity of demand as consumers become better informed; and prices appear to be lower in markets where advertising is deregulated than in those where restrictions exist. All of this is supportive of the view that some, if perhaps not all, advertising does play a positive role in transmitting useful information and stimulating competition.

Discussion questions

1. At the national level, identify factors that might be expected to influence a country's aggregate level of expenditure on advertising.

2. With reference to Case study 13.1, assess the importance of brand image for a firm's value.

3. Explain the distinction between search goods and experience goods. Quote examples of goods that belong in each category.

4. Explain the distinction between convenience goods and shopping goods. What are the implications of this distinction for the likely effectiveness of persuasive advertising?

5. With reference to Case studies 13.2 and 13.3, consider whether tea, beer, cars and directory enquiries services should be categorized as search goods or experience goods, and as convenience goods or shopping goods. In what ways are these categorizations reflected in the types of advertising campaign that have been run in each case?

6. On theoretical grounds, explain why we might expect to observe a higher level of advertising in an oligopoly than in either of the polar cases of perfect competition or monopoly.

7. Assess the validity of Kaldor's view that most advertising is simply a waste of resources.

8. According to the Dorfman–Steiner condition, a monopolist's optimum ratio of advertising expenditure to sales revenue is given by the ratio of the advertising elasticity of demand to price elasticity of (market) demand. Explain the intuition underlying this theoretical result. Would you give an oligopolist the same advice?

9. In what ways might a heavy advertising campaign by an incumbent firm raise barriers to entry? Illustrate your answer by drawing possible advertising response functions for an incumbent and an entrant.

10. With reference to a quality-signalling model of advertising, explain carefully why the content of the advertising message might be less important than the simple fact that the product is being advertised for consumers who are considering buying the product.

11. 'Evaluation of the welfare effects of advertising is made difficult by the fact that persuasive advertising changes consumer tastes and preferences.' Explain how Dixit and Norman (1978) avoid this difficulty. What are the main conclusions of their analysis of the social welfare implications of advertising?

12. Explain carefully how we might test empirically for the existence of an inverted U-shaped relationship between concentration and advertising intensity. Does the available empirical evidence support such a relationship?

Further reading

Albion, M.S. and Farris, P. (1981) *The Advertising Controversy*. Boston, MA: Auburn House.

Bagwell, K. (2005) The economics of advertising, in Armstrong, M. and Porter, R. (eds) *Handbook of Industrial Organization*, vol. 3. Amsterdam: Elsevier.

Bearne, A. (1996) The economics of advertising: a re-appraisal, *Economic Issues*, 1, 23–38.

Gabszewicz, J.J., Laussel, D. and Sonnac, N. (2005) Does advertising lower the price of newspapers to consumers? A theoretical appraisal, *Economics Letters*, 87, 127–34.

Comanor, W.S. and Wilson, T. (1979) Advertising and competition: a survey, *Journal of Economic Literature*, 17, 453–76.

Kaul, A. and Wittink, D.R. (1995) Empirical generalisations about the impact of advertising on price sensitivity and price, *Marketing Science*, 14, 151–60.

Leahy, A.S. (1997) Advertising and concentration: a survey of the empirical evidence, *Quarterly Journal of Business and Economics*, 36, 35–50.

Lee, C.Y. (2002) Advertising, its determinants and market structure, *Review of Industrial Organization*, 21, 89–101.

Love, J.H. and Stephen, F.H. (1996) Advertising, price and quality in self regulating professions: a survey, *International Journal of the Economics of Business*, 3, 227–47.

Luik, J. and Waterson, M.J. (1996) *Advertising and Markets: A Collection of Seminal Papers*. Oxford: NTC Publications.

Schmalensee, R.C. (1972) *The Economics of Advertising*. Amsterdam: North Holland.

The Economist (2005) Target practice: Advertising used to be straightforward. 2 April 2005.

Learning objectives

This chapter covers the following topics:

- the stages of research and development
- market structure, firm size and the pace of technological change
- research and development strategies
- investment appraisal of research and development programmes
- measuring and identifying the determinants of the pace of diffusion
- patents
- empirical evidence on the determinants of the pace of technological change

Key terms

Creative destruction
Diffusion
Innovation
Invention

Patent
Process innovation
Product innovation
Schumpeterian hypothesis

14.1 Introduction

Technological change can be defined as the introduction of superior qualities to products or methods of production, which eventually render existing products or production processes obsolete. In most studies of industrial organization, research and development undertaken by firms is assigned a high level of importance. Technological change affects output, product quality, employment, wages and profits. Not only does successful research and development activity confer significant advantages on the firm concerned, but it is also a major driving force behind economic growth and the improvement in social welfare.

This chapter begins in Section 14.2 with an examination of the relationship between market structure, firm size and the pace of technological change. A five-stage classification of the components of a successful research and development programme is introduced, and some of the key ideas of Schumpeter, perhaps still the most influential thinker in this area, are examined. The **Schumpeterian hypothesis**, that there is an association between successful **innovation** and monopoly, has provided the motivation for an extensive body of theoretical and empirical research. In a well known contribution, Arrow shows that the incentive to innovate may be greater under perfectly competitive conditions than it is under a monopoly. Several economists have suggested that oligopoly might be the market structure most conducive to a fast pace of technological change. Finally, the case for a positive association between firm size and the pace of technological change is assessed.

Section 14.3 discusses the decision to invest in research and development activity. A distinction is drawn between offensive, defensive, imitative and dependent research and development strategies. Like any other investment decision, the decision to commit resources to a research and development programme can be subjected to investment appraisal analysis. Relevant considerations include the anticipated levels of demand and costs, the marketing strategy (in the case of a new product), and the means of financing the research programme.

The rate of **diffusion** measures the pace at which a piece of new technology spreads from the original innovating firm to other firms for which the technology is applicable. Section 14.4 describes the Mansfield model of diffusion, which provides a benchmark for measuring and modelling the factors that influence the pace of diffusion. One such factor is the patenting system, discussed in Section 14.5. The granting of a **patent** to the inventor of a new product, process, substance or design confers a property right over the knowledge that is embodied in the invention. In designing a patenting system, a balance needs to be struck between providing sufficient incentives to encourage research and development activity on the one hand, and avoiding excessive monopolization and possible abuses of market power on the other.

Finally, Section 14.6 reviews some of the empirical literature on the economics of research and development, including studies which present evidence on a number of the issues covered in the previous sections of this chapter. Overall, the empirical research on the relationships between market structure, firm size and innovation is shown to be rather inconclusive.

14.2 Market structure, firm size and the pace of technological change

As a process, research and development can subdivided into several different stages. Different economists and management scientists have developed their own taxonomies. Probably the best known of these, described in Stoneman (1995), pp. 2–8, is the trichotomy which identifies three stages: **invention**, **innovation** and **diffusion**. This three-stage classification was first developed by Joseph Schumpeter (1928, 1942). A slightly more elaborate five-stage classification is as follows:

- *Basic research*. An invention is the creation of an idea and its initial implementation. Basic research corresponds to the invention stage in the Schumpeterian trichotomy. At its extreme, basic research may be carried out without any practical application in view. For example, early research in molecular physics was carried out without any foreknowledge of the use of the valve in broadcasting and communications. Industrial firms may be reluctant to undertake basic research, due to the uncertainty of outcome. Consequently, basic research is often the province of government agencies and universities. In a study of the petroleum and chemical industries, Mansfield (1969) finds only about 9 per cent of the firms' total research and development expenditure was on basic research, while 45 per cent was on applied research and 46 per cent on development.

- *Applied research*. Unlike basic research, applied research has a stated objective. Following an investigation of the potential economic returns, research is undertaken to determine the technological feasibility of the proposed application.

- *Development*. Generally this can be considered as the bringing of an idea or invention to the stage of commercial production. At this stage, resources are heavily committed, and pilot plants or prototypes may have to be built. Although it is clear that at every stage of research and development the firm must review its progress, it is at the development stage that the selection process for the next (commercial production) stage is most important. The failure of a new product that has already entered into commercial production would be very costly to the organization.

- *Commercial production*. This stage refers to the full-scale production of a new product or application of a new process. Regardless of the amount of research and development already undertaken, there is still a large element of risk and uncertainty. A major difference between invention and innovation arises from the level of risk involved: the main interest of the inventor is in the generation of ideas and not the production of goods and services on a commercial basis. Together, the applied research, development and commercial production stages correspond to the innovation stage in the Schumpeterian trichotomy.

- *Diffusion*. The final stage refers to the spread of the new idea through the firm, as well as the imitation and adoption of the innovation by other firms in the same industry, or in other industries where the innovation may be applicable. There is also a spatial element to the diffusion process, as ideas spread geographically through foreign direct investment, licensing agreements or joint ventures.

An important distinction is often drawn between product and process innovation. A **product innovation** involves the introduction of a new product. A **process innovation** involves the introduction of a new piece of cost-saving technology. However, the distinction between product and process innovation is not always clear cut. New products often require new methods of production; and new production processes often alter the characteristics of the final product. Furthermore, one firm's product innovation may be another firm's process innovation. For example, a new piece of capital equipment might be classed as product innovation by the producing firm; but from the point of view of the user, the machine would represent a process innovation.

Schumpeter and the gale of creative destruction

At several points in this book, we have encountered the argument that monopoly may be associated with inefficiency in production. Shielded from the full rigours of competition, the monopoly producer may tend to become complacent, and fail to produce at the lowest attainable average cost. A similar case can be made to suggest that among all possible market structures, monopoly may not be the most conducive to a rapid pace of technological progress. A complacent monopoly producer that is already earning an abnormal profit may feel reasonably content with its existing production technology, even if it might be possible for the firm to realize cost savings and increase its abnormal profit by investing in research and development.

However, it has also been argued that high levels of seller concentration and market power may be associated with a fast pace of technological change. Much of the theoretical and empirical analysis of the economics of research and development and innovation is based on ideas developed by Schumpeter (1928, 1942), who saw technological change as the fundamental driving force behind the growth and development of the capitalist economy. Schumpeter coined the term **creative destruction** to describe the economic impact of technological change. The creative aspect of technological change results in new and improved goods and services being brought to market, and more cost effective technologies being used in production.

> The fundamental impulse that sets and keeps the capitalist engine in motion comes from the new consumers' goods, the new methods of production or transportation, the new markets, the new forms of industrial organization that capitalist enterprise creates.
>
> *(Schumpeter, 1942, p. 83)*

But there is also a destructive aspect to technological change, because the introduction of new technologies inevitably challenges the market power of incumbent firms that remain wedded to the older, less effective technologies. In other words, the process of creative destruction simultaneously rewards successful innovators, and punishes those firms whose technologies are superseded and become obsolete. The process of creative destruction 'incessantly revolutionizes the economic structure from within, incessantly destroying the old one, incessantly creating a new one. This process of creative destruction is the essential fact about capitalism' (Schumpeter, 1942, p. 83). Successful innovators are rewarded with market power: for a time the firm becomes a monopoly supplier of the new product; or its mastery of a new process enables it to produce at a lower cost than its rivals, and perhaps capture some or all of their market share by setting a reduced price they are unable to match. However, the market power conferred by successful innovation is always temporary, and never permanent. The firm must continually guard against the possibility that others will encroach into its market by introducing further improvements in technology, new sources of supply, or new forms of organization.

Schumpeter claims the textbook neoclassical models of oligopoly and monopoly cannot convincingly account for the huge increases in production and consumption that took place during the late nineteenth and early twentieth centuries. The popular view of large quasi-monopolistic concerns, reducing output in order to maximize profit and thereby denying society a higher standard of living, was not a credible representation of the reality of modern capitalist economies.

> As soon as we go into details and inquire into the individual items in which progress was most conspicuous, the trail leads not to the doors of those firms that work under conditions of comparatively free competition but precisely to the doors of the large concerns which, as in the case of agricultural machinery, also account for much of the progress in the competitive sector and a shocking suspicion dawns upon us that big business may have had more to do with creating that standard of life than with keeping it down.
>
> *(Schumpeter, 1942, p. 82)*

The Schumpeterian analysis has several important implications. Perfect competition is not the ideal market structure: large corporations that have acquired market power as a result of having been successful innovators in the past are the main drivers of technological change and economic growth. Economists should focus less on price competition, and more on other forms of competition, especially competition by means of product and process innovation. In one remarkable passage, Schumpeter even comes close to anticipating the theory of contestable markets (see Section 8.5) by about 40 years:

> It is hardly necessary to point out that competition of the kind we now have in mind acts not only when in being but also when it is merely an ever present threat. It disciplines before it attacks. The businessman feels himself to be in a competitive situation even if he is alone in his field or if, though not alone, he holds a position such that investigating government experts fail to see any effective competition between him and any other firms in the same or a neighboring field and in consequence conclude that his talk, under examination, about his competitive sorrows is all make believe.
>
> *(Schumpeter, 1942, p. 85)*

The Schumpeterian hypothesis, that there is an association between successful innovation and monopoly, has provided the motivation for a substantial body of theoretical and empirical research. Clearly, Schumpeter's approach lies beyond the confines of the neoclassical theory of the firm and the SCP paradigm, which concentrate mainly on decisions concerning price, output or other conduct variables within a pre-determined market structure. For Schumpeter, causation lies in the opposite direction: the conduct of a successful innovator is rewarded with the creation of a (temporary) monopoly based on exclusive ownership of the intellectual property rights embodied in the new technology. Nevertheless, some economists have attempted to reposition the Schumpeterian hypothesis within a neoclassical economics framework, by examining the theoretical relationship between market structure and the incentive to invent or innovate. Other contributions examine the closely related (but nevertheless conceptually distinct) question of the relationship between firm size and the pace of technological change.

The pace of technological change: monopoly versus perfect competition

Is monopoly more conducive than perfect competition to a high level of effort being committed to research and development, or a high level of innovative activity? As suggested above, arguments pointing in either direction can be developed. In favour of monopoly, one can point out that firms in highly concentrated industries may earn abnormal profits, which can be invested in risky research and development programmes. Firms in more highly competitive industries may earn only a normal profit, leaving no uncommitted resources available to finance speculative investment in research and development. Furthermore, the lack of competitive pressure in a monopoly creates an environment of security, within which it is possible for the firm to undertake high-risk investment in projects whose returns may be uncertain at the outset. In the event that the investment succeeds, there is less risk of imitation; and in the event that the project fails, there are no rivals waiting to step in and take advantage of the firm's temporary financial difficulties (for example, by initiating a price war at a time when the firm's ability to sustain losses might be diminished). In other words, the lack of competitive pressure gives the firm the time and space it needs to develop and grow.

On the other hand, and as noted above, in the absence of competitive pressure, the managers of a monopoly firm might tend to become become complacent or lazy; or excessive internal bureaucracy within the firm's organizational structures might lead to a loss of managerial control, or other forms of technical inefficiency (x-inefficiency). Another line of reasoning suggests the probability of a successful product or process invention emerging is positively related to the number of research teams that are simultaneously working on similar a idea or challenge. Under a competitive market structure, there may be more research teams competing to be the first to come up with a solution, and therefore a higher probability that at least one of these teams will succeed. Finally, a monopolist that owes its market power to a successful innovation in the past may be so tied to its existing technology that to switch resources to a new product or process would be considered too costly.

A slightly more subtle variant of this final argument in favour of competition points out that if a new piece of technology displaces a monopoly firm's current technology, the monopolist's incentive to innovate is governed by the *net* effect on its profit. Under a competitive market structure, the incentive to innovate is governed by the *gross* return from the innovation. Accordingly, the incentive to innovate may be greater under competitive conditions than it is under a monopoly.

This argument is developed more formally by Arrow (1962), in a widely cited theoretical contribution to the debate surrounding the relationship between market structure and the pace of technological change. Arrow compares the impact of a cost-saving process innovation under market structures of perfect competition and monopoly. In both cases, constant returns to scale and horizontal LRAC and LRMC (long-run average and marginal cost) functions are assumed. The innovation causes a downward shift in the position of the LRAC (=LRMC) function. Under perfect competition, it is assumed the inventor charges each perfectly competitive firm a royalty per unit of output for use of the cost-saving technology. The inventor's return is the total value of the competitive firms' royalty payments. Under monopoly, it is

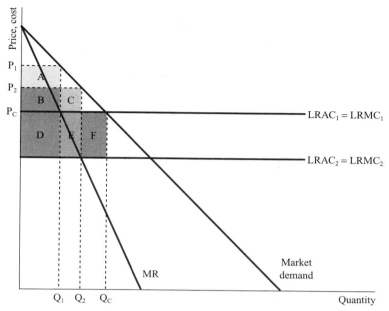

Figure 14.1 Arrow's incentive to innovate: small cost-saving innovation

assumed the monopoly firm itself is the inventor. The inventor's return is the increase in abnormal (or monopoly) profit realized due to the adoption of the cost-saving technology. There are two alternative versions of Arrow's analysis, covering the cases where the innovation produces a small reduction and a large reduction in the LRAC function. However, both analyses produce the same conclusion: that the incentive to invent or innovate is greater under perfect competition than it is under monopoly.

Figure 14.1 shows Arrow's analysis for the case of a small reduction in the LRAC function, from $LRAC_1$ to $LRAC_2$.

■ Before the innovation, the monopolist maximizes profit by operating at (P_1, Q_1). The monopolist's abnormal profit is A + B.

■ After the innovation, the monopolist maximizes profit by operating at (P_2, Q_2). The monopolist's abnormal profit is B + C + D + E. Therefore the monopolist's reward for the innovation is (B + C + D + E) − (A + B) = C + D + E − A.

■ Before the innovation, the perfectly competitive industry reaches equilibrium by operating at (P_C, Q_C). At P_C, price *equals* average cost and normal profits are earned. Q_C represents the combined output of all of the perfectly competitive firms.

■ The maximum royalty per unit of output the inventor can charge for use of the technology is given by the amount of the cost saving, $LRAC_1 − LRAC_2$. Therefore from the viewpoint of the perfectly competitive firms, nothing really changes. Before the innovation they incur a production cost of $LRAC_1$ per unit

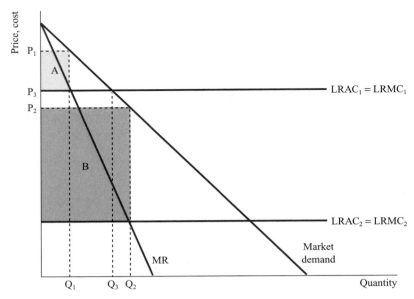

Figure 14.2 Arrow's incentive to innovate: large cost-saving innovation

of output. After the innovation they incur a production cost (per unit) of $LRAC_2$, and a royalty payment of $LRAC_1 - LRAC_2$, so effectively their average cost is $LRAC_1$. The industry equilibrium remains at (P_C, Q_C) and the inventor's total royalty payment is $D + E + F$.

■ To show the reward for the innovation is greater under perfect competition than it is under monopoly, we must show $D + E + F > C + D + E - A$, or $F + A - C > 0$. A sufficient condition is $A - C > 0$. This condition is satisfied because $A + B$ is the largest rectangle that can be constructed within the triangle formed by the market demand function and $LRAC_1$ ($A + B$ being constructed by setting $MR = LRAC_1$). Therefore $A + B > B + C \Rightarrow A > C \Rightarrow F + A - C > 0 \Rightarrow D + E + F > C + D + E - A$.

Figure 14.2 shows Arrow's analysis for the case where the shift from $LRAC_1$ to $LRAC_2$ represents a large saving in average costs.

■ Before the innovation, the monopolist maximizes profit by operating at (P_1, Q_1). The monopolist's abnormal profit is A.

■ After the innovation, the monopolist maximizes profit by operating at (P_2, Q_2). The monopolist's abnormal profit is B. Therefore the monopolist's reward for the innovation is $B - A$.

■ Before the innovation, the perfectly competitive industry reaches equilibrium by operating at (P_3, Q_3). At P_3, price *equals* average cost and normal profits are earned. Q_3 is the combined industry output.

■ The inventor maximizes the royalty payment by setting the charge for use of the technology in such a way as to force the perfectly competitive industry to operate as if it were a monopolist. This implies the royalty per unit of output should be set at $P_2 - LRAC_2$ (so that $MR = LRMC_2$). After the innovation the perfectly competitive firms incur a production cost (per unit) of $LRAC_2$, and a royalty payment of $P_2 - LRAC_2$, so effectively their average cost is P_2. The industry equilibrium shifts to (P_2, Q_2), the firms continue to earn normal profits, and the inventor's total royalty payment is B.

- In this case, it is obvious the reward for the innovation under perfect competition is greater than the reward under monopoly, because $B > B - A$.

Arrow's analysis is criticized by Demsetz (1969). Because the pre-innovation output levels of the perfectly competitive industry and the monopoly are different, Arrow fails to compare like with like. Arrow's comparison tends to favour the perfectly competitive industry because the benefits of the cost-saving technology are spread over a larger volume of output than in the monopoly case. In order to make a fair comparison, we should set aside the usual tendency for a monopolist to produce less output than a perfectly competitive industry. Instead, the comparison should be based on an assumption that the pre-innovation output levels are the same under both market structures. In order to achieve this effect, it is necessary to assume the market demand function differs between the two cases. A simple way in which this can be achieved is to assume the market demand function in the perfectly competitive case coincides with the marginal revenue function in the monopoly case.

Figure 14.3 shows Demsetz's analysis for the case of a large reduction in the LRAC function, again from $LRAC_1$ to $LRAC_2$. D_M and MR_M are the monopolist's

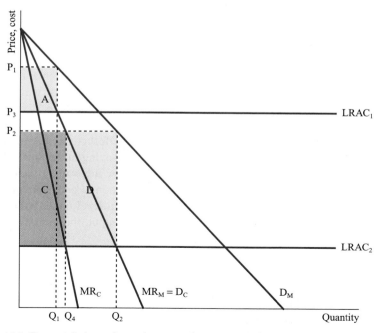

Figure 14.3 Demsetz's incentive to innovate: large cost-saving innovation

demand and marginal revenue functions. D_C (= MR_M) and MR_C are the market demand and marginal revenue functions of the perfectly competitive industry.

■ Before the innovation, the monopolist maximizes profit by operating at (P_1, Q_1). The monopolist's abnormal profit is A.

■ After the innovation, the monopolist maximizes profit by operating at (P_2, Q_2). The monopolist's abnormal profit is C + D (= B in Figure 14.2). Therefore the monopolist's reward for the innovation is C + D − A, as before.

■ Before the innovation, the perfectly competitive industry reaches equilibrium by operating at (P_3, Q_1). At P_3 (= $LRAC_1$) price *equals* average cost and normal profits are earned. Q_1 is the competitive industry output, identical to the monopolist's pre-innovation output.

■ As before, the inventor maximizes the royalty payment by setting the charge for use of the technology in such a way as to force the perfectly competitive industry to operate as if it were a monopolist. This implies the royalty per unit of output should be set at P_2 − $LRAC_2$ (so that MR_C = $LRMC_2$). The competitive industry equilibrium shifts to (P_2, Q_4), the firms continue to earn normal profits, and the inventor's total royalty payment is C.

■ To show the reward for the innovation is greater under monopoly than it is under perfect competition, we must show C + D − A > C, or D − A > 0. This condition is satisfied because by construction, the height of rectangle D exceeds the height of rectangle A, and the width of D also exceeds the width of A.

In other contributions to the Arrow–Demsetz debate, Kamien and Schwartz (1970) argue that a fair comparison between the incentives to invent and innovate under perfect competition and monopoly should be based on a starting position at which not only the industry output levels, but also the price elasticities of demand, are the same. This is not the case in Figure 14.3: the monopolist's demand function (D_M) at (P_1, Q_1) is more price elastic than the perfectly competitive industry's market demand function (D_C) at (P_3, Q_1). In an analysis that assumes identical pre-innovation output levels and price elasticities (which involves constructing a more price elastic market demand function for the perfectly competitive industry passing through (P_3, Q_1)), Kamien and Schwartz show the incentive to innovate is stronger under monopoly than it is under perfect competition. Yamey (1970) observes Arrow's analysis focuses solely on a cost-saving innovation. Therefore Arrow does not consider the case of a completely new innovation, which allows production of a good that was previously either uneconomic or technologically infeasible. In this case, the assumed pre-innovation output level under both market structures is the same: zero. With zero pre-innovation output, the incentive to innovate is identical under perfect competition and monopoly.

The pace of technological change: oligopoly

It is clear from the preceding theoretical analysis that there is no unequivocal answer to the question as to whether monopoly or perfect competition is the market structure that most favours high levels of research and development activity, high levels of innovation, and a fast pace of technological change. Some economists have suggested that the correct answer to this question is 'neither', and that oligopoly might be the market structure most conducive to a fast pace of technological change. This suggests we might expect to observe an inverted U-shaped relationship between seller concentration and the level of inventive or innovative activity.

■ In perfect competition, abnormal profits are zero. Consequently competitive firms may not have the means to invest in risky or speculative research programmes. They also may not have much incentive to do so, unless competitive pressure dictates that such investment is a necessary condition for minimizing costs and remaining in business.

■ In monopoly, abnormal profit is positive, so a monopoly firm has the means to invest in research if it chooses to do so. But as argued above, a lack of competitive pressure may imply there is little incentive to do so.

■ In oligopoly, abnormal profits may be positive (depending on the precise form of competition that develops given the firms' situation of rivalry and interdependence). There is also competitive pressure; indeed, the firms' very recognition of their interdependence suggests they may perceive this pressure to be especially keen or acute. Therefore oligopolistic firms have both the means and the incentive to invest in research and development. Research and development is one form of discretionary expenditure (advertising being another) that might provide a channel for the firms' competitive rivalry that does not entail potentially destructive price competition.

The arguments for an inverted U-shaped relationship between concentration and the levels of inventive or innovative activity are of course very similar to those suggesting a similar relationship between concentration and advertising intensity (see Section 13.4). Scherer (1967b) reports empirical evidence in support of an inverted U-shaped relationship. Using 1960 data on 56 US manufacturing industries, Scherer finds employment in research and development as a share of total employment increased with seller concentration (measured using a five-firm concentration ratio) up to about $CR_5 = 0.5$, but declined for higher values of CR_5.

It is important to note that the pace of technological progress may depend not only on firms' decisions as to whether to embark on particular research and development programmes, but also on the speed at which these programmes are implemented. In an oligopoly in which interdependence is recognized, speed may have a critical influence on the eventual success or failure of a research project. If the research proceeds too slowly, a rival firm might develop a similar idea sooner, and take out a patent. On the other hand, if the firm moves too quickly and takes insufficient care to protect its ideas from imitation, it might fail to appropriate the benefits from its own investment.

Scherer (1967a) develops a model which makes explicit the speed or time dimension involved in the firm's research and development decision. The model is illustrated in Figure 14.4. The curved function C represents the trade-off between development time (shown on the horizontal axis) and cost (vertical axis). A research programme can be implemented at a slow and leisurely pace, or at a very fast

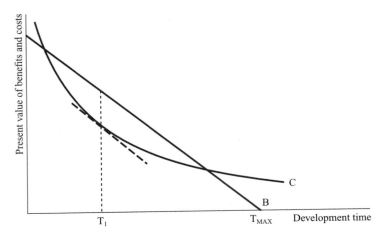

Figure 14.4 The optimal development time

pace, or at various speeds in between. However, by increasing the pace and aiming for a shorter development period, the firm incurs additional costs for the following reasons:

- Over a short development period, research activity may be subject to the Law of Diminishing Returns. For example, hiring more scientists may tend to produce diminishing marginal returns if the quantity of equipment or the size of the laboratory is fixed in the short run. Similarly, diminishing returns may set in if a firm is obliged to recruit from a finite pool of properly qualified or fully trained research staff.

- Errors are likely to occur if researchers tend to move from one stage of the research to the next without waiting for detailed results from experiments or tests that took place at earlier stages.

- In order to generate results quickly, researchers may need to pursue several alternative research paths simultaneously, in the hope that one or more will deliver results. Costly effort is devoted to ideas that eventually fail to materialize. This might have been avoided had there been less pressure to produce positive results quickly.

- A slower pace of development implies a smaller up-front cost, as the total cost of the research is spread over a longer development period. Accordingly, due to the usual effects of discounting future values in order to calculate a present value, the longer the development period, the smaller the present value of the total cost.

In Figure 14.4, the function B represents the relationship between the development time and the benefit the firm receives from the innovation. B is negatively sloped for two reasons. First, early completion of the project maximizes the firm's first-mover advantage, and maximizes the period over which the firm will reap the maximum reward, before rivals are able to catch up by developing their own alternative technologies. The benefit function B attains a value of zero at development time T_{MAX}, because if the firm delays for too long, allowing all its rivals to precede it in

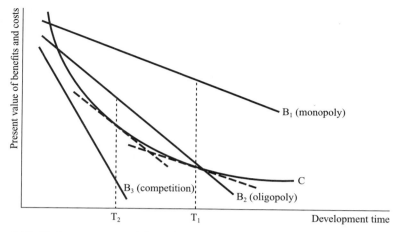

Figure 14.5 Market structure and the optimal development time

introducing comparable innovations, it may receive no benefit whatsoever from the research. (In contrast, the cost function C is tapered, because the present value of the future costs is non-zero and positive, however far ahead in the future the costs are incurred.) Second, earlier completion implies the benefits are less heavily discounted; as with costs, the present value of the benefits naturally tends to vary inversely with the duration of the development period, due to the discounting effect. The profit-maximizing firm selects the optimum development time, at which the slope of the benefits function *equals* the slope of the cost function, and the vertical distance between B and C is maximized. Therefore, in Figure 14.4, a development time of T_1 is chosen.

The shape of the cost function C is determined primarily by the nature of technology, but the slope of the benefit function B is determined by market structure. In Figure 14.5, the benefit functions B_1, B_2 and B_3 represent possible benefit functions under monopoly, oligopoly and perfect competition, respectively. The relative slopes of B_1, B_2 and B_3 are determined by the level of competition the innovating firm faces under each market structure.

■ Under monopoly there are no competitors, so the innovating firm reaps the full benefit regardless of the development time. The discounting of future benefits to obtain a present value creates a negative relationship between the development time and the present value of the benefit, but this value is not affected by the risk that rivals will introduce comparable innovations if the development is delayed.

■ In contrast, under oligopoly the innovating firm does have to worry about the actions of its rivals. The number of competitors is small and entry barriers are significant, although not insurmountable. Delay will not necessarily reduce the benefit to the innovating firm to zero: with only a small number of competitors, it is unlikely that any of the firm's rivals will produce an identical or very similar innovation immediately. But the longer the delay, the more likely that one or more of them will do so.

■ Finally, under perfect competition there are many competitors and no entry barriers. In this case, rapid speed is essential. With large numbers of competitors, it is very likely that one or more other firms are already working on an identical or very similar idea. The first firm to bring the idea to fruition captures most of the benefit, so there is a steep negative relationship between development time and the present value of the benefit.

Figure 14.5 has been constructed so as to produce an inverted U-shaped relationship between seller concentration and the pace of technological change. Under monopoly, the benefit curve B_1 produces a relatively long profit-maximizing development time of T_1. Under oligopoly, the steeper benefit curve B_2 produces a shorter development time of T_2. Finally, under perfect competition, the benefit curve B_3 is so steep that it fails to exceed the cost function C at any value of T. In this case, there is no investment in research and development at all. Accordingly, technological change proceeds at the fastest pace under oligopoly, at an intermediate pace under monopoly, and at the slowest pace under perfect competition.

This analysis can be criticized on the grounds that the theorizing underlying Figure 14.5 is rather intuitive, and not based on any explicit model of firm conduct under alternative market structures. '[T]he results of this theoretical research are sensitive to the assumptions made, and with the appropriate constellation of assumptions, virtually anything can be shown to happen' (Scherer, 1992, p. 149). For example, another case that has been examined using a similar approach involves a market containing one dominant firm and one small firm. The dominant firm faces a benefit curve similar to B_1, provided the small firm does not attempt to innovate. If the small firm does innovate, however, the dominant firm risks losing its dominant position unless it quickly follows suit. Therefore the dominant firm's benefit curve shifts to something similar to B_2, and the dominant firm responds quickly by imitating the small firm's innovation. For example, Netscape's initial success in developing the first internet browser proved to be short-lived once the dominant firm Microsoft decided to launch its own rival product.

Price competition tends to reduce the profits of all of the firms in an oligopolistic market, and oligopolists often attempt in one way or another to avoid direct competition on price. To the extent that discretionary expenditure on advertising and research and development represents a form of non-price competition, it is natural to ask whether there is also a tendency for oligopolists to collude, either tacitly or explicitly, in order to avoid wasteful and mutually damaging competition in these areas as well.

In an oligopoly comprising a small number of firms, it may be quite simple to agree a common price, but more difficult to determine an optimal level of research and development activity. The implications of a price agreement for the sales and profitability of the parties may be simple to predict; in contrast, the consequences of research and development cannot be forseen in advance. Prices are visible and transparent, so monitoring compliance and punishing non-compliance is relatively straightforward. Research and development is complex and opaque, so effective monitoring and enforcement may be more difficult.

If a price agreement breaks down, the long-run consequences may be relatively minor. If a research and development agreement breaks down, those firms that have already invested heavily may suffer more severely than those that have made a smaller commitment. If one firm is selected to carry out the research on the others' behalf, the others run the risk of subsequently being excluded from ownership of the property rights. For example, if the research turns out to have more far-reaching applications than were originally envisaged, the firm that undertook the original research might attempt to appropriate all of the unanticipated benefits for itself. If the research effort is shared, it may be difficult to achieve coordination; and given the numbers of firms involved, there may be a temptation for some firms to free-ride, allowing others to do most of the work.

Nevertheless, despite the potential difficulties, cooperative research and development ventures do sometimes happen. Some agreements cover the pre-competitive stage, when firms share basic scientific or technical knowledge, but continue to compete as suppliers of products based on this knowledge. In other agreements, cooperation is extended to cover the firms' activities as suppliers to the product's ultimate buyers (Hagedoorn, 2002). D'Aspremont and Jacquemin (1988) find little evidence to suggest cooperation over research and development that aims to eliminate wasteful duplication has any adverse consequences in the form of lost output through the creation of quasi-monopolies. Therefore the liberal attitudes of most governments to joint research and development ventures appear to be justified. Baumol (2001) takes a similar view, suggesting that with a few exceptions, the wider social benefits of joint research usually outweigh the costs.

The pace of technological change: firm size

The Schumpeterian hypothesis is often interpreted in terms of an association between market structure and the pace of technological change. However, this hypothesis is also consistent with the idea that only large firms have the resources to implement the large-scale research and development programmes that are required to generate ideas for new products and new production processes, and to develop these ideas to the point that they are capable of being implemented commercially. In a series of books and articles published during the 1950s and 1960s, John Kenneth Galbraith (1956, 1967) argued more explicitly that large firms were mainly responsible for driving the process of technological change in modern capitalist economies.

> Thus mention has been made of machines and sophisticated technology. These require in turn, heavy investment of capital. They are designed and guided by technically sophisticated men. They involve, also, a greatly increased elapse of time between any decision to produce and the emergence of a saleable product. From these changes come the need and the opportunity for the large business organization. It alone can deploy the requisite capital; it alone can mobilize the requisite skills. It can also do more. The large commitment of capital and organization well in advance of result requires that there be foresight and also that all feasible steps be taken to insure that what is foreseen will transpire. It can hardly be doubted that General Motors will be better able to influence the world around it – the prices and wages at which it buys and the prices at which it sells – than a man in suits and cloaks.

(Galbraith, 1967, p. 4)

The argument that technological change is most likely to be driven by large firms rather than small firms or independent inventors is based mainly on economies of scale or scope (in one form or another) in research and development, or in adjacent functions such as finance.

■ Modern research laboratories are expensive to build, equip and staff. It may be that only a large firm has the capability to operate at the scale required to justify the purchase of sufficiently specialized equipment, or the hiring of specialist staff in sufficient numbers. In other words, if there is a minimum efficient scale (MES) for cost-effective research and development, the small firm might be unable to attain the required threshold.

■ A large firm can spread risk over several projects, reducing the damage to the firm that the failure of any one project might cause. In contrast, a small firm might be forced to place all its eggs in one basket, and bear the risk that the failure of the project could force the firm's closure.

■ For a large diversified firm, knowledge acquired from research in one area might have applications in other areas. For a small specialized firm, such economies of scope might not be available.

■ Because investment in research and development is highly risky, it might be necessary to rely heavily on internally generated finance rather than finance raised from capital markets. A large firm might have larger internal cash flows than a small firm. If capital markets are efficient, external finance might provide a solution for a small firm lacking the financial resources to develop a promising idea. However, in practice the small firm might be at a disadvantage here as well: the large firm might be able to borrow more cheaply because it is perceived to be less risky, or because it has a positive reputation. Alternatively, a group of small firms might attempt to collaborate in a joint research venture. But in this case transaction costs may be incurred, initially in negotiating an agreement and subsequently in monitoring compliance.

The counter-argument that technological progress is more likely to originate from outside the confines of large corporations is based on the idea that large organizations provide insufficient incentive for creative or original thinking. An employee with a bright idea might find it difficult to appropriate the eventual commercial rewards. Alternatively, the bureaucratic nature of many large organizations tends to reward behaviour that conforms with established institutional norms, and discourages creativity, originality or non-conformity.

The empirical evidence for a positive association between firm size and the level of inventive or innovative activity is not particularly strong, and in some cases it may even point in the opposite direction. For example, Hamberg (1966) finds only seven out of 27 major inventions during the period 1947–55 emanated from company research and development departments. In a more extensive study covering 61 major inventions during the period 1900–56, Jewkes *et al.* (1969) find that the majority emanated from small private inventors, rather than from the research departments of large firms. However, this finding is not necessarily entirely contrary to the Schumpeterian view. While private inventors may be successful as originators of completely new and original ideas, the resources of large firms may still be required to carry out most of the development work required to bring these ideas to commercial fruition.

With reference to the construction industry, Oster and Quigley (1977) find several innovations in organization, systems design and the integration of housing components would have required a scale of production uncommon among the majority of construction firms. Using data on Spanish manufacturing firms, Martinez-Ros and Labeaga (2002) find a significant relationship between firm size and the level of innovation. On the other hand, Fritsch and Meschede (2001) find process and product innovation do not increase in proportion to firm size.

14.3 Investment in research and development

Research and development strategies

In many cases, the decision to invest in research and development is strategic, and is not determined exclusively by considerations of short-run profit maximization. A number of strategic issues that may inform or influence this investment decision can be identified. The following discussion is based on Freeman and Soete (1997).

Offensive strategy

An offensive strategy seeks to enable a firm to dominate its market through the introduction of a new technology. The main focus of activity within the firm is to generate new ideas, and to protect these ideas and associated spin-offs by acquiring patents. The firm typically invests heavily in capital equipment and in developing the human capital of its research workers. Major twentieth-century innovations that were originally developed in this manner include DuPont's development of nylon (in 1928) and lycra (in 1959), IG Farben's development of PVC (in 1929), and RCA's development of colour television (in 1954). The firm may be willing to invest in basic research, although not of the purest type. In order to stay ahead of actual or potential competitors, the firm must undertake some experimental development work, and it requires a capability to design, build and test prototypes and pilot plants. The firm may need to educate its customers and its own employees about the benefits of the new technology, through seminars, videos, training manuals and other support services. An important element of Microsoft's innovation strategy has always been to ensure new products are accompanied by sufficient investment in customer education.

Defensive strategy

For some firms, investment in research and development may be necessary for survival, in order to keep pace with product improvements or technical change in production processes initiated by competitors. If it does nothing, the firm's market share could collapse if rivals are offering more advanced products, or if rivals are able to sell at a lower price because their production costs are lower. A firm that adopts a defensive strategy tends to follow the lead set by a rival whose strategy is offensive. The defensive firm may lack the large technical resources needed to pursue an offensive strategy, or it may be risk averse, preferring to invest only in proven products or processes. A defensive strategy may include efforts to introduce small improvements to existing technologies, permissible within the constraints of the patent breadth. Defensive firms must also invest in sufficient technical resources to be able to respond quickly to new ideas generated by offensive firms.

Imitative strategy

Unlike the defensive firm, the imitator does not attempt to improve on the innovations of the offensive firm. Instead it is content to copy, either by acquiring a licence in the short run or by exploiting free knowledge in the long run. Investment in technical resources is relatively low, as the firm does not need to acquire new knowledge. Nevertheless, for an imitative strategy to be profitable, the imitator must have some advantage that it can exploit, such as cheap labour or a captive market. As well as increased competition from alternative products such as orlon, dacron and nylon, a major reason for DuPont's withdrawal from the US rayon market in 1960 was its inability to compete with low-cost producers. Imitators might have access to captive markets, such as their own subsidiaries or other markets that are protected by political patronage or tariff barriers, from which the offensive firm is excluded. In some countries governments actively seek to encourage imitative strategies, in order to exploit technologies that have been developed elsewhere.

Dependent strategy

A firm that adopts a dependent strategy adopts a subservient role in relation to stronger offensive or defensive firms, perhaps as a supplier or subcontractor. Dependent firms do not themselves initiate research and development. They adopt technologies that are passed down to them, often as a condition for preserving the relationship. A new technology may be accompanied by technical assistance, the loaning of skilled labour, or other forms of assistance or support. This type of relationship is common in the Japanese electronics and car industries. A dependent relationship may in some cases be a precursor towards full vertical integration, especially if the dominant firm sees this as necessary in order to protect its investment in the relevant technology.

Investment appraisal of research and development projects

Often, it is clear how a firm should apportion its research and development budget. In small firms, the direction of research often reflects the aspirations and hunches of the owner or technical director. In industries where the direction of technological change is clear, it may be straightforward for individual firms to decide the direction their research expenditures should take. However, for firms with large research and development budgets and no overwhelming technological priorities, there may be an element of discretion concerning the allocation of the budget. Perhaps the main difference between a decision to invest in the replacement of capital goods and a decision to invest in research and development lies in the level of uncertainty attached to the latter investment. The risk attached to research effort differs from other risks in that it is not repetitive and measurable. It is therefore unlikely to be insurable. The risk naturally tends to be less for research into the application and modification of an established technology than for basic research and radical product or process development.

In principle, the relevant issues are captured by standard models of investment appraisal.

> Conceptually, the decisions made by an administrator of research funds are among the most difficult economic decisions to make and to evaluate, but basically they are not very different from any other type of entrepreneurial decision.

> *(Griliches, 1958, p. 431)*

In this section, we list the main factors that need to be considered in the investment appraisal decision.

Demand

Perhaps the most fundamental issue is whether the new idea meets an unsatisfied market demand. This is not always as difficult as it may sound, since in some cases it may be customers who alert their suppliers to a gap in the market. For example, Minkes and Foxall (1982) find that a large proportion of research and development is stimulated by requests for product or process improvement from users. Recent advances in mobile phone technology have in part been driven by consumer demand for a wide variety of handset types and styles (*The Economist Technology Quarterly*, 12 June 2004). However, the firm still has to assess the growth potential of the relevant market. This might involve long-run forecasting, which can be highly speculative. Alternatively, the Delphi technique, developed by the RAND Corporation in the late 1960s, is based on the assessments of a number of experts or specialists. Individuals drawn from various fields of expertise are asked to present opinions as to the future of a market. Each opinion is circulated to all members of the group, who are then asked to revise their original opinions in the light of what they have read. Through a process of iteration, an expert consensus is eventually reached. According to Madu *et al.* (1991), Taiwan used this method to reorganize its entire information technology industry:

> these decisions reflect the experts' world views, life experiences, cognitive feelings and perceptions. Thus, these results are based on the participants' subjective assessments which may also be influenced by data. Decision-making in itself is subjective. However, the use of experts in a systematic manner will yield a satisfactory solution to sociotechnical problems.

> *(Madu et al., 1991, p. 109)*

The Delphi technique assumes a collective consensus is better than the views of one individual. This may not always be the case. An alternative approach to techno-logical forecasting is trend extrapolation, whereby historical sales data is used to forecast future developments. An obvious difficulty is that one has to assume the parameters remain the same in the future as they were in the past. Over a 10-year or 20-year forecast period this may be a dangerous assumption. Of course, many of the most dramatic innovations have also been among the least expected.

> Almost every major innovation [in electronics and synthetic materials] was hopelessly underestimated in its early stages, including polyethylene, PVC and synthetic rubber in the material field, and the computer, the transistor, the robot and numerical control in electronics.
>
> *(Freeman and Soete, 1997, p. 249)*

The strength of competition from other incumbents or entrants is another important issue. In the 1970s, for example, the success of Lestoil, a small US producer of liquid household cleaners, attracted the attention of major manufacturers such as Lever Brothers, Procter & Gamble and Colgate Palmolive, whose entry Lestoil was unable to prevent.

Costs

Given that the full costs of development projects are often uncertain and spread over relatively long durations, it is difficult to produce reliable cost estimates. The uncertainty can be reduced by concentrating on less speculative projects, but even then the likelihood of error is high.

> Those firms who speak of keeping development cost estimating errors within a band of plus or minus 20 per cent are usually referring to a type of project in which technical uncertainty is minimal, for example, adapting electronic circuit designs to novel applications, but well within the boundaries of existing technology.
>
> *(Freeman and Soete, 1997, p. 246)*

There is a very high variance attached to cost estimates for innovations involving anything more than a straightforward application of an existing technology. Furthermore, there is a common tendency to underestimate costs, perhaps to a greater extent than with other types of investment. Particular interest groups within an organization might deliberately underestimate or overestimate costs in an attempt to influence the likelihood of a particular project being adopted, or at least allow their assessment to be clouded by their own views or interests.

Under the general heading of costs, a firm needs to evaluate the demands placed on its production capabilities when considering investment in the development of a new product or process. Does the firm have the capacity, capital, trained staff and technical expertise required to see the project through? Does a new technology require new inputs, involving the firm in new and unfamiliar supply relationships? Will the production of a new product be hindered by a capacity constraint, or is the idea of developing the product motivated by a need to exploit spare capacity that already exists?

Marketing

Several issues may need to be considered when devising a marketing strategy for a new product. Can the firm exploit its own reputation to help the development of a new market? Conservatism or suspicion on the part of consumers may place a new firm's attempt to market a new product at a disadvantage. Does the new product have distinctive marketable features? If the idea is too complex for the average consumer to understand, a market may never fully develop. Does the firm have well developed distribution channels or dealer networks, through which the new product can be promoted? The alternative is to rely on independent distributors, who may need to be persuaded or prised away from their existing suppliers. Finally, what sort of pricing strategy might be required to overcome consumer inertia or resistance? If a new product is subject to what Leibenstein (1950) calls a *taboo effect*, and consumers are reluctant to buy the product until a large number of other consumers have already done so, it might be necessary to charge a loss-making price, or perhaps even give the product away for a time, in order to break the taboo. In the UK, BSkyB's policy of giving away satellite dishes in order to encourage take-up of its subscription television services may be a case in point.

Case study 14.1

Strategy for creativity

Corporate leaders and government ministers are forever exhorting UK business to do more to develop new ideas. But what are the qualities that mark out the most innovative companies? Some of the answers can be found by going to the pub. At Bass, the brewing group, new brands such as All Bar One and O'Neill's represent a novel partnership between corporate might and individual spark. Bass's traditional market on the housing estates in the Midlands and the north of England was flagging in the early 1990s. 'We needed a radical "break-out" strategy of new product development and concept innovation', says Tim Clarke, chief executive of Bass Leisure Retail. Senior executives went talent-spotting in the pub business and persuaded two young entrepreneurs, Amanda Wilmott and David Lee, to come and work with the group for a fixed period in exchange for a share of profits if the venture succeeded.

Ms Wilmott developed All Bar One, the upmarket, female-friendly chain that has opened 50 outlets in city centres in the past five years. Mr Lee was responsible for It's a Scream, a 75-strong chain of student venues. 'They've had the personal satisfaction of expressing their creativity, which is very important to them', says Mr Clarke. 'We take ownership of the brand and the intellectual property, but they have corporate cashflow behind them and an extremely attractive earn-out.' Other brands, including Vintage Inns and Hollywood Bowl, were conceived in house by aspiring entrepreneurs who were taken off regular duties and encouraged to put their ideas into practice in a kind of 'fit-out studio'. The retail brands Bass has developed over the past five to six years are now contributing a third of turnover, he says. Top-level backing in the company is crucial. 'Senior management spends two or three nights a week out and about in the business, understanding where the creative ideas are and tying them back in with the formal process of consumer market research.'

Bass's experience accords with new research from PA Consulting, the management consultancy group, that emphasises the importance of creativity and leadership for stimulating innovation. PA questioned chief executives, marketing directors and technical directors at 150 companies, identifying nine elements of innovative companies. 'There's no silver bullet to making innovation happen,' says John Buckley, PA's head of technology. 'You have to have all the jigsaw in place, the infrastructure, the technology and so on. But the surprise for me was that without this vision and committed leadership from the top, it's not going to happen.' PA finds that high R&D expenditure does not necessarily lead to greater innovation or bigger turnover from new products. Indeed, companies spending most on R&D are getting the least return, says Mr Buckley. Larger, more mature companies are often under considerable pressure to improve existing products rather than develop new ones, he says. They often have a greater aversion to risk than smaller or younger companies. 'Although they have much larger R&D budgets in absolute terms, they spend much less of them on really innovative products', he says. 'The leaders of smaller companies are showing more vision and leadership and fostering a creative culture.' Both he and Mr Clarke at Bass argue that companies need to pursue both risky new projects and straightforward product improvements if they are to increase total shareholder return. 'For every All Bar One that emerges, there has to be a willingness to take the failures', says Mr Clarke. 'The investment in pilots would be anything from £1m to £3m per outlet, and you never know whether they're going to be successful or not.' From nothing, Bass put £25m to £30m of revenue investment a year over three years into new brand development. 'The payback can be quite dramatic. If you do a concept trial on five outlets and write that off, it's completely dwarfed by the results from 75 It's a Scream pubs.'

How do companies make the necessary shift to a more creative environment? They may only be forced into it by finding themselves in a strategic cul-de-sac, as Bass was. This was the case with Kenwood, the appliance maker that is undergoing a painful restructuring and switching the bulk of its production from Hampshire to China. 'We took the decision to encourage innovation as part of our turnround strategy', says Colin Gordon, chief executive. Last year, Kenwood launched 28 products ranging from dishwasher-safe deep fat fryers to a bathroom steam-cleaner for the Italian market. This was more than double the number of new products two years ago, he says. The changes have included recruiting more 'creative' people, improving the timing of launches, learning from mistakes, ensuring successes are widely broadcast in the company, and introducing multi-disciplinary development teams. Designers can get the chance to see their product through to the manufacturing stage and ensure it is made to the right specifications. Innovation is now part of a broader strategy, not something locked away in the R&D department, he says. 'People can push their ideas forward and have them listened to. This was missing before.'

The most profitable companies put far more emphasis than less profitable ones on innovation in the marketplace, the research finds. Yet there are serious disagreements between technical directors on one side and chief executives and marketeers on the other about whether innovation is primarily a technological issue or a customer issue. 'Far too many companies are trying to focus on the product', says Mr Buckley. 'If I'm a shareholder in a food company, do I want them spending my investment on basic research or getting a better product on to the market faster? I think it should be the latter. Innovation is a chief executive issue, not an R&D issue.'

Finance

The returns from investment in research and development and innovation are uncertain and difficult to estimate. The managers initiating the research probably have more information as to the likely success of the project than the financier. Therefore it may be difficult to raise finance externally, and the firm may need to rely mainly on internally generated funds. Consequently research is often underfunded (Bougheas *et al.*, 2003). The venture capital market exists to fill this gap, providing external finance for risky projects. According to Kortum and Lerner (2000), increased activity in the venture capital market in the US was associated with an increase in the pace of innovation, when measured by data on patents taken out.

14.4   Diffusion

The pace at which new technologies filter through into common use varies enormously from one case to another. The rate at which technological change spreads throughout the economy is known as the rate of **diffusion**. Some new technologies are adopted rapidly, and spread like wildfire among firms or among consumers. Others seem to languish in oblivion for several years, and then suddenly take off. Others, despite seeming to be brilliantly conceived from a scientific or technological point of view, may never succeed in challenging or superseding the established product or process that is dominant in the relevant market or industry.

A mathematical model of the diffusion process

In a seminal study, Mansfield (1961) develops a mathematical framework that provides the basis for many subsequent attempts to measure the pace of diffusion and to investigate the determinants of the pace of diffusion empirically. This framework has furthered knowledge and understanding on both the microeconomics of technology adoption and the macroeconomic impact of technology on economic competitiveness and growth (Diamond, 2003). Suppose we observe the diffusion process for a successful innovation that is eventually adopted by all of the firms in the relevant industry, and we count the number of firms that have adopted the innovation at regular time intervals. Let N_i denote the total number of firms that will eventually adopt innovation i, and let $n_{i,t}$ denote the number of firms that have adopted by time t. Therefore the proportion of firms that have adopted by time t is $n_{i,t}/N_i$. Figure 14.6 shows the pattern we would typically expect if we plot this proportion against time. The positively sloped and elongated S-shaped curve is interpreted as follows:

- When the innovation first appears, there are very few adopters, and the pace of diffusion is rather slow. At this stage the costs may be quite high, and the benefits uncertain. Only the most innovative or far-sighted firms are willing to take the decision to adopt.

- As time passes, the benefits of the innovation become clearer, and the costs of adoption start to fall. The pace of diffusion increases, as larger numbers of firms take the decision to adopt.

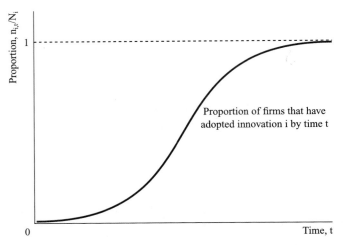

Figure 14.6 Growth over time in the proportion of firms that have adopted an innovation

■ Eventually, however, a point is reached when most firms have already adopted. Consequently the pace of diffusion tends to slow down again. Only the most cautious firms, or those that are the most resistant to change, have still not yet taken the decision to adopt.

How can we represent this logic in mathematical form? A suitable mathematical expression for the pace of diffusion, measured by the number of firms adopting between time t and time t + 1, is as follows:

$$n_{i,t+1} - n_{i,t} = k_i \left(\frac{n_{i,t}}{N_i} \right) \left(1 - \frac{n_{i,t}}{N_i} \right)$$

k_i is a positive constant. This expression captures the logic of the previous discussion in the following manner:

■ At the start of the diffusion process when $n_{i,t}/N_i \cong 0$, the pace of diffusion is also close to zero.

■ Mid-way through the diffusion process when $n_{i,t}/N_i \cong 0.5$ and $1 - n_{i,t}/N_i \cong 0.5$, the pace of diffusion is non-zero and positive.

■ At the end of the diffusion process when $n_{i,t}/N_i \cong 1$ and $1 - n_{i,t}/N_i \cong 0$, the pace of diffusion again approaches zero.

It is worth commenting that very similar models are widely used in the natural or biological sciences, for tasks such as modelling the spread of contagious diseases among a human or animal population. By analogy, a successful innovation can be likened to a contagious disease; or even a *meme*, defined as 'good ideas, good tunes, good poems, . . . Anything that spreads by imitation' (Dawkins, 1998, p. 304).

Returning to the previous mathematics, some manipulations can be applied to the expression for $n_{i,t+1} - n_{i,t}$, in order to obtain expressions for the proportions of firms that have adopted and have not adopted by time t. The derivations of the following expressions are shown in Appendix 1.

$$\frac{n_{i,t}}{N_i} = \frac{1}{1 + e^{-(\alpha_i + \beta_i t)}} \quad \text{and} \quad 1 - \frac{n_{i,t}}{N_i} = \frac{N_i - n_{i,t}}{N_i} = \frac{e^{-(\alpha_i + \beta_i t)}}{1 + e^{-(\alpha_i + \beta_i t)}}$$

α_i and β_i are constants, and e is the exponential function. It is also useful to consider the ratio of these two expressions, $n_{i,t}/(N_i - n_{i,t})$, equivalent to the ratio of adopters at time t to non-adopters at time t. Taking the natural logarithm of this ratio, we obtain:

$$\log_e[n_{i,t}/(N_i - n_{i,t})] = \alpha_i + \beta_i t$$

According to this expression, the natural logarithm of the ratio of adopters to non-adopters follows a linear time trend. Using data on $n_{i,t}$ for each successive time period, it is possible to obtain numerical estimates of the parameters α_i and β_i. This is done quite simply, by running a regression with $\log_e[n_{i,t}/(N_i - n_{i,t})]$ as the dependent variable and a linear time trend as the independent variable. The estimate of the parameter β_i is of particular interest, because this parameter represents a direct measure of the pace of diffusion.

Using adoptions data on 12 innovations which took place in the US coal mining, brewing, iron and steel, and railroads industries, in the first stage of his analysis Mansfield obtains an estimate of the parameter β_i for each of the 12 cases. He then estimates a second-stage cross-sectional regression, using on data on all 12 innovations, in an attempt to identify factors that influence the pace of diffusion. As independent variables in the cross-sectional regression, Mansfield uses an average profitability measure for each innovation, and a variable measuring the size of the investment required for each innovation. In accordance with prior expectations, the pace of diffusion is found to be positively related to average profitability, and negatively related to the size of the initial investment.

In a follow-up study, Mansfield (1969) examines the adoption of numerical control (a process of operating machine tools via numerical instructions on cards or tape) in the US tool and die industry in the 1960s. The industry was made up of many small firms, and decision-making processes were relatively simple. An analysis of the characteristics of the earliest adopters suggests larger firms were likely to adopt earlier than smaller firms. Mansfield also examines whether more highly educated managers are better informed about the potential of a new technology, and younger managers are less resistant to change. The survey results support these conjectures. The chief executives of the majority of adopting firms were college graduates, with a median age of 48. Many chief executives of non-adopting firms were educated to high school level only. The median age in this group was 55. Around 10 per cent of chief executives who were close to retirement had decided to stay with the existing technology. 'Judging by the interviews and other evidence, the diffusion process seems to have been slowed perceptibly by misunderstanding of the innovation and resistance to change' (Mansfield, 1969, p. 71).

Although Mansfield's methodology for measuring and modelling the pace of diffusion has been employed widely, it has occasionally been subject to criticism. For example, Karshenas and Stoneman (1995) raise the following objections.

- The first criticism is aimed at the implicit assumption that all imitators are homogeneous, and that their number, the technology and profitability of the investment are all constant over time. In addition it is assumed the adopters are passive recipients, rather than active seekers, of technological change. More sophisticated models include controls for adopters' search costs, and the effects of networking on the dissemination of information (Midgley *et al.*, 1992).

- The second objection is that the Mansfield model is fundamentally demand-oriented, and ignores the role of supply side factors. Taking the supply side into account, the pace of diffusion is influenced by suppliers' cost functions, the market structures in which suppliers operate, and technological change in supply industries (Stoneman, 1989).

- The third criticism is that the adopting firms' costs are not properly analysed. Actual costs of adoption include more than just the cost of acquiring new capital equipment. The technology may require adaptation of the firm's training practices or organizational structures. 'In the limit, technology may be purpose built for a firm in which case the study of diffusion becomes a study of customer supplier relationships' (Karshenas and Stoneman, 1995, p. 279).

Determinants of the pace of diffusion

Mansfield's pioneering research in the 1960s identifies several factors that may either help or hinder the diffusion of new technologies. However, it is possible to extend the list of determinants of the pace of diffusion beyond those influences originally considered by Mansfield. This subsection considers a number of industry- and firm-level factors.

Communication

An important potential barrier to rapid diffusion is poor communication between inventors, innovators and the business community (National Economic Development Council, 1983). In the UK, the development of science parks and other initiatives was motivated by the wish to bring universities (the producers of new knowledge) and the immediate users, closer together. According to the definition provided by the UK Science Parks Association (1999), a science park is a business support and technology transfer initiative with the following objectives:

- To encourage and support the start-up and incubation of innovation-led, high growth, knowledge-based businesses.

- To provide an environment in which larger and international businesses can develop specific close interactions with a particular centre of knowledge creation, for the mutual benefit of all parties concerned.

In other words, science parks are a channel for the dissemination of academic ideas and discovery to industry and commerce. Science parks are more likely to grow and thrive where there is an abundance of new knowledge and specific types of infrastructure. The closer science parks are to universities, the greater the cross-fertilization of ideas. Most commentators agree that universities are influential in fostering new ideas that will eventually contribute towards technological progress (Jacobsson, 2002; Salter and Martin, 2001). However, it is difficult to measure universities' direct contribution to technological progress with any precision. Pavitt (2001) suggests only a small proportion of the scientific research carried out within universities transfers seamlessly into commercial application. According to Klevorick *et al.* (1995), in some sectors, such as biotechnology and chemicals, the relationship between universities and business is very close; while in others, such as textiles and foodstuffs, the relationship is more distant.

Case study 14.2

University–industry links in the EU

ERSTI (European Report on Science and Technology Indicators) 2003 examines European performance at the interface between research institutions and enterprises from a number of different angles. The relatively low share of total expenditure on research and development financed by industry in Europe has been well publicised. At 56.5 per cent in 1999, it falls far short of the US (68.2 per cent) and Japan (72.4 per cent). Indeed, the Barcelona Council not only called for the EU's overall investment in research and development to rise to 3 per cent of GDP by 2010, but also for industry to put up two-thirds of the 3 per cent.

Less attention has been paid to the contribution made by business to the research undertaken by universities and public research institutions. In this area, the EU outperforms both the US and Japan. In Europe in 1999, industry financed 8.8 per cent of governmental research

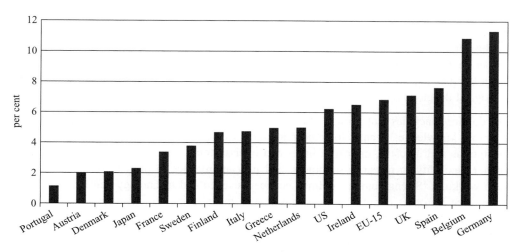

Share of higher education R&D expenditure financed by industry, 1999
Source: DG Research, www.madrimasd.org/MadridIRC/documentos/doc/Euroabstracts_200304.pdf, p. 15.

in 1999: more than in Japan (1.8 per cent) and the US (zero). In Europe in 1999, industry financed 6.9 per cent of university research (up from 5.9 per cent in 1991): also more than in Japan (2.3 per cent) and the US (6.3 per cent).

These figures indicate strong university–industry links in Europe. Is European business at least beginning to draw on the knowledge-creation capacity of Europe's research base? To test this hypothesis, ERSTI 2003 presents the results of a study by Incentim at the University of Leuven, which brings an innovative methodological approach to the examination of science–technology linkages. The dossier uses scientific citations in patent documents, termed non-patent references, as an indicator of flows from academic science to commercial application. This novel approach produces some startling new insights, as well as confirming a number of long-held assumptions:

■ Technology is becoming more science intensive. The average number of scientific articles cited in all European patents rose from 2.78 in 1987–91 to 3.39 in 1992–96. In US patents, the number rose from 1.05 to 1.83.

■ Between 1992 and 1996, biotechnology was the technological field in which science was most extensively cited. The most cited scientific fields over the same period were biochemistry and molecular biology.

■ The study examined the relationship between the geographical sources and destinations of the scientific knowledge cited in European and US patents. European inventors made significantly greater use of local science than their US or Japanese counterparts. 'For the period 1992–96, 59 per cent of the science cited by European inventors in the patent applications to the European Patent Office related to scientific research carried out in the EU. This compares with 35 per cent of US citations that related to research of US origin, and only 25 per cent of Japanese citations that related to research of Japanese origin.'

■ As a corollary of the relatively weak dependence of US inventors on US science, the dossier confirms the leakage of European science. 'In patent applications at the EPO, 45 per cent of all US inventor cited scientific literature is of European origin (36 per cent in US patents), indicating an important spillover from European research to US technological development.'

The dossier concludes that Europe should do even more to facilitate local exploitation of its scientific knowledge. It calls for closer interactions between universities, public research institutions and industry, improved intra- and inter-sectoral mobility of research personnel, greater flexibility in research structures, and new approaches to project management and team working. 'Strengthening the links between science and technology can help not only to enhance Europe's competitiveness, but also to increase its attractiveness as a place for researchers to work and as a place for firms to invest.'

Source: Euroabstracts European Commission, Directorate General for Enterprise, 41, August 2003, p. 15.

Cohen *et al.* (2002), Spencer (2001) and Laurensen and Salter (2003) identify factors that influence the relationship between universities and business. For example, Laurensen and Salter find research and development intensity, firm size, and factors relating to the industrial environment are most important in explaining the propensity of firms to draw on links with university research. Based on a survey carried out in 1993, Battisti and Stoneman (2003) assess the importance of within (intra) and between (inter) firm effects in determining the diffusion of a process technology (known as Computerised Numerically Controlled Machine Tools) across 343 UK engineering and metalworking establishments. Inter-firm diffusion is measured by the number of firms using the innovation; and intra-firm diffusion is assessed from the extent of usage within any firm. Overall, the pace of diffusion was slower within firms than between firms. Given the differences in inter- and intra-firm diffusion, 'we know much less about industry diffusion than it might have been thought from a reading of the inter-firm literature' (Battisti and Stoneman, 2003, p. 1654).

The quality of communication between firms within the same industry is also likely to influence the pace of diffusion. If the firms that comprise an industry are clustered geographically, the pace of diffusion tends to be faster (Baptista, 2000). In Aharonson *et al.*'s (2004) study of the Canadian biotechnology industry, firms that are clustered geographically are eight times more likely to innovate than firms in remote locations. In a study of the car industry in eastern Europe, Lorentzen *et al.* (2003) find the existence of networks and the presence of multi-national companies are important determinants of the pace of diffusion. However, in a study of the role of clusters in the UK and Italy, Beaudry and Breschi (2003) find clustering alone does not ensure a rapid pace of diffusion, because firms within clusters can be negatively influenced by the presence of non-innovating firms.

Management inertia

An important reason some firms may be slower to adopt new products or processes than others relates to the education, experience and attitudes of managers. Managers who are scientifically educated to a high level, and conversant with the characteristics of current scientific and technological developments, are likely to be more imaginative, more flexible and more open to persuasion as to the commercial potential of a promising new product or process. Managers with a poor technical background may be reluctant to recognize the superiority of a new technology, and may adopt it only when their existing equipment needs replacement. Firms that are run by a lethargic and over-bureaucratic cadre of managers are likely to be slow, excessively cautious or unimaginative in seizing technical opportunities.

Patel and Pavitt (1987) find the rate of diffusion of four specific engineering innovations was much lower in the UK than in Germany. This may reflect a lack of commitment to develop and commercialize new technologies, as well as a lack of engineering expertise on the part of management. Blair (1972) cites a case in which managers were apparently content to stick with an existing technology for several decades, despite the availability of a superior alternative. In 1959, Pilkington Brothers, a UK glass manufacturer, developed a new float glass process which revolutionized the production of flat glass. When attempting to patent the process in the US, Pilkington's management was astonished to discover that an identical patent had been in existence in the US since 1907; but no US or foreign firm had previously attempted to exploit the idea.

> The most charitable explanations are ignorance of the US patents, which would hardly be a tribute to their technical awareness, or satisfaction with the existing technology and a consequent disinclination to embark on the development work ultimately and successfully pursued by a smaller British firm.
>
> *(Blair, 1972, p. 236)*

Protecting an older technology

Reluctance to innovate need not be solely due to stubbornness, inertia or resistance to change on the part of managers. In some cases a dominant firm may wish protect its existing market share or preserve the current market structure either by either keeping new ideas secret, or denying entry to firms with a new ideas or newer technologies. Maclaurin (1950) details the resistance of several major US communications firms (Western Union, Postal Telegraph and American Telephone and Telegraph) to the development of radio. These firms sought to buy up competitors, to enter into restrictive agreements, and (in the case of the attempt by the Marconi Company to start operating in Newfoundland) to block the award of franchises. Similarly, the UK Post Office attempted to block Marconi's attempt to enter the UK market by refusing to connect its overseas service to Post Office telegraph lines.

The speed at which new technology replaces older technology is partly dependent on the age profile of the industry's existing capital stock. Firms with a high proportion of older machines that are already due for replacement are likely to adopt the new technology at a faster rate than those that have only recently installed machines dependent on the older technology.

Employee or trade union resistance

Organized labour might attempt to resist the adoption of a new technology, if they view it as a threat to their employment. For example, in the 1970s print unions in the UK were reluctant to accept technology which allowed journalists to electronically transfer their copy direct to the photosetting department, bypassing the composing rooms (Storey, 1979). Three trades unions representing workers in the composing rooms successfully resisted this and a number of other innovations for several years. Consequently, Fleet Street was slow in adopting new technologies that were being widely introduced elsewhere in newspaper publishing. On the other hand, Linter *et al.* (1987) find trade unions were not a significant barrier to the adoption of new technologies in a number of industries.

Regulation

If an industry is subject to a cumbersome regulatory framework, which perhaps requires standards for materials, design and safety, the adoption of a new technology may be sluggish, because amending the regulations may be a slow and bureaucratic process. For example, Oster and Quigley (1977) find local building codes significantly reduced the diffusion of new technology in the construction industry. On the other hand, Hannan and McDowell (1984) suggest that in the case of the adoption of automated telling machines (ATMs) by US banks, regulation may have stimulated the rapid diffusion of new technology. The adoption of ATMs was seen as a way of circumventing state-level restrictions on the number of branches a bank was permitted to operate.

Risk and liquidity

A new technology may be adopted slowly or reluctantly if its introduction involves significant risk. For example, the technology might require certain inputs that are difficult to obtain, or which may be unfamiliar to the firm. Risk may also stem from uncertainty over the level of demand. Oster and Quigley (1977) find wide fluctuations in the demand for housing were driven partly by changes in the market for credit. These fluctuations inhibited the adoption of new technology in the construction industry. The use of more capital intensive production methods can increase a firm's vulnerability to fluctuations in demand. It might be argued that the more profitable the firm, the more able it is to generate internal finance for the development and application of a new technology. It is implicit in this view that investment in new technology is risky, and it is difficult for firms to raise external finance. However, Hannan and McDowell (1984) find little evidence to support this conjecture.

Patents

In a free market, new knowledge is a free resource, available to all firms. A possible consequence is that there may be too little, or no research and development, as the firms undertaking the investment would be reluctant to see free-riders reap the benefits of the knowledge acquired from costly and risky research and development investment (Gallini, 2002). Accordingly, governments offer patents to protect innovators from over-rapid diffusion. In the UK, a successful patent application grants the holder a 20-year monopoly. A patent system that is over-protective may result in an excessively slow pace of diffusion. However, there seems to be little evidence that the UK's patenting system does significantly impede the pace of diffusion. It is common for patent holders to enter into patent sharing or licensing agreements. Taylor and Silberston (1973) find large UK firms were relatively liberal about granting licences, especially to foreign firms operating in non-competing markets. Patents are discussed in detail in Section 14.5. Some international comparisons concerning the pace of technological change are drawn in Box 14.1.

Box 14.1

The pace of technological change: some international comparisons

Most observers would agree that productivity and competitiveness are important ingredients for economic growth and development, and that productivity and competitiveness in turn depend on the pace of technological change. For example, the UK's Department of Trade and Industry (2003) identifies several reasons why innovation is important for individual businesses and for the economy as a whole. This DTI report refers specifically to the UK, but similar points would be equally applicable to many developed economies.

■ Liberalization of international markets has exposed UK firms to competition from firms with relatively low labour costs, yet high levels of technical education. For example, similar proportions of the population in the relevant age group attend university in South Korea and the UK, but average wages in South Korea are around half those in the UK.

■ Reductions in transportation and communication costs have reduced barriers to international trade, making product characteristics (including the level of technology) a more significant determinant of a firm's ability to attract customers in the global market.

■ The adaptation of science and technology to the development of new products and industries (such as biotechnology) is an important source of international competitive advantage.

■ Service industries (including banking and financial services), which in total account for more than 70 per cent of GDP in most developed economies, have become more technology-intensive.

■ Increased awareness and concern over environmental issues have increased demands for businesses to find technological solutions in order reduce harmful externalities.

Table 14.1 compares the levels of expenditure on research and development in the corporate sector as a proportion of GDP, for several European countries and the US, for selected years between 1992 and 2001. On this criterion, the UK's performance is close to the EU average, but lags some distance behind the US. Figure 14.7 shows the number of patents taken out per million population for selected countries in 1998. On this criterion, the UK lags behind Japan, the US and Germany, and is below the EU average.

Similar concerns are expressed by the European Commission (1995a), who refer to a European paradox. Relative to the US and Japan, Europe's scientific performance has deteriorated in several key areas, such as electronics and information technology. A major weakness is Europe's inferiority in translating research output into innovative output. More recently, the European Commission (2003c) reports that the US leads the EU in no fewer than 10 out of 11 innovation indicators. The European Commission (1995a) identifies a number of factors that hinder the realization of a more productive innovation culture.

Table 14.1 Expenditure on corporate research and development as percentage of GDP, 1992–2001

	1992	1997	1998	1999	2000	2001
Finland	1.21	1.79	1.94	2.20	2.41	2.42
Germany	1.66	1.54	1.57	1.70	1.75	1.76
France	1.49	1.39	1.35	1.38	1.37	1.37
UK	1.39	1.16	1.17	1.23	1.19	1.23
EU	1.18	1.13	1.14	1.19	1.22	1.24
US	1.90	1.91	1.94	1.98	2.04	2.10
OECD	1.49	1.48	1.49	1.53	1.56	1.62

Sources: OECD/ONS; Department of Trade and Industry (2003) *Innovation Report: Competing in the Global Economy : The Innovation Challenge*. London: HMSO.

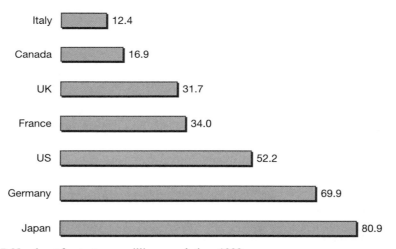

Figure 14.7 Number of patents per million population, 1998
Source: Department of Trade and Industry (2003) *Innovation Report: Competing in the Global Economy: the Innovation Challenge*. London: HMSO.

Weak research base

- *Inadequate inputs*. Corporate expenditure on research and development as a proportion of GDP is less in Europe than in the US and Japan. This gap has widened since the 1980s.

- *Fragmentation*. While US and Japanese firms tend to concentrate on a limited number of areas, there may be a tendency for European firms collectively to pursue research in too many fields.

- *Lack of anticipation*. European firms may have been relatively unsuccessful in anticipating technological developments, as well as identifying and overcoming constraints on innovation.

Human resources

■ *Education and training*. It is suggested that European education systems may be too rigid to meet the challenges posed by technological change. The standard of technical education in Europe is a particular concern. Technical subjects are often viewed as non-academic, while scientific teaching tends to avoids technological application and personal experimentation.

■ *Barriers to intra-EU mobility*. Within Europe, goods, capital and services tend to transfer more freely than people. The US and Japan are culturally and linguistically homogeneous, while the countries of Europe are diverse. Other factors include housing market rigidities which make migration within the EU difficult (in contrast to the US); the reluctance of individual countries to recognize qualifications from other EU member states; and characteristics of national taxation and welfare systems that also tend to deter mobility.

Finance

■ *The financial system*. Although a high proportion of basic research tends to be self-financed, many European firms rely on financial institutions for assistance with the development costs for new products and processes. Financial markets may not work effectively from the firms' perspective, however, if lenders take an unduly cautious view of the risks associated with investment in new technology. Globalization and the deregulation of financial markets have given lenders more opportunities for short-run, low-risk investments. Between 1987 and 1994, the quantity of venture capital raised in Europe is reported to have quadrupled, but the share devoted to high-technology investment fell from 37 per cent in 1985 to 10 per cent in 1994. The formation of exchanges such as Easdaq in Brussels in November 1996 and TechMARK in London in November 1999, specializing in high-technology investment, represents an attempt to provide a European equivalent to the NASDAQ exchange in the US.

■ *Public finance*. Public financing of research can be either direct (grants to research agencies and firms) or indirect (investment in education, vocational training, infrastructure, and so on). It is estimated that US firms receive about twice as much state funding as EU firms. Much of the difference is accounted for by strategic sectors such as defence, aerospace and electronics.

■ *The fiscal environment*. The personal taxation systems in most EU countries may not encourage individuals to invest in unlisted high-technology firms. Most EU company taxation systems tend to favour financing by borrowing, rather than internally generated finance. Since a large portion of investment in research is self-financed, this tends to place innovative firms at a disadvantage. The taxation of intangible investments (such as training) tends to be harsher than the taxation of tangible investments. National taxation systems for risk capital are diverse, and the level of complexity may frustrate investment that crosses EU national borders.

Legal and regulatory environment

- *Patenting.* The number of patent applications in the EU is relatively low in comparison with the US and Japan. This may be due to the high costs of applying for and maintaining patents, the costs of litigation in the case of disputes, and a lack of awareness of the revenues that can be earned from licensing patents.

- *Standards, certification and quality systems.* Systems governing standards, certification and quality can either encourage or hamper innovation. For example, the development and subsequent success of Wireless Fidelity (Wi-Fi) technology was a direct consequence of close cooperation between a number of rival firms (Intersil, 3Com, Nokia, Aironet, Symbol and Lucent), which set up a central body known as the Wireless Ethernet Compatibility Alliance (WECA) to determine a common industry product specification (*The Economist Technology Quarterly*, 12 June 2004). The design of new products or processes may be constrained by the need to meet what firms consider to be unrealistic performance, safety or environmental standards.

- *Administration and bureaucracy.* It is a common complaint that excessive bureaucracy and red tape within the EU tends to deter innovation, and that US firms benefit from less onerous administrative arrangements.

14.5 Patents

The granting of a **patent** to the inventor of a new product, process, substance or design confers a property right over the knowledge that is embodied in the invention. The relevant knowledge is legally recognized as an economic asset, which can either be exploited by the patent holder, or licensed or sold by the patent holder for exploitation by others. In exchange for this legal recognition, the inventor discloses information about the existence of the invention to the public. In most countries patents are awarded for a finite period. In the UK the lifetime of patents was increased from 16 to 20 years (the current figure at the time of writing) by the 1977 Patents Act. In most countries, to be patented an invention must meet the following criteria:

- *The invention must be new*, in the sense that it has not been previously used, published or demonstrated in the public domain. There are certain ideas that cannot be patented, including pure scientific discoveries, mathematical formulae, mental processes and artistic creations.

- *The invention must be non-obvious*, in the sense that it does not represent a trivial modification of something that is already known to specialists in the relevant scientific field. It must embody a genuine advance in knowledge that would not have seemed obvious to any reasonably well informed specialist.

- *The invention must be capable of commercial application.* It is not possible to patent pure scientific knowledge that has no practical application.

In the UK in 2004, the application fee for a patent was £200 (£130 for search and £70 for examination), and the annual renewal fee (payable from the fourth year onwards) was £50. However, other expenses may be incurred in making an application. For example, it may be necessary to hire the services of consultants (patent agents) to ensure the application is correctly drafted, so as to avoid possible imitation around the patent and minimize the risk of future litigation. It may also be necessary to take out patents in foreign countries, to prevent imitation by foreign competitors. The costs and effort involved can act as a deterrent, perhaps especially in the case of inventions emanating from small and medium-sized firms or from independent inventors.

Patents exist in order to provide incentives for investment in research and development and for innovation. Granting a property right over the knowledge creates a monopoly, conferring market power upon the patent holder. The opportunity to earn an abnormal profit through the exploitation of this market power may represent the main incentive for the original research and development investment. Expressing this argument in other terminology, it can be argued that the knowledge that is created through successful research and development activity possesses the characteristics of public goods known as non-excludability and non-rivalness. In the absence of a patenting system, these characteristics might reduce or eliminate the incentive for investment in the acquisition of new knowledge.

■ *Non-excludability* implies once new knowledge has been created, it is difficult to exclude others from gaining access to the knowledge. In other words, it is difficult to establish property rights in the knowledge. This means that in the absence of a patenting system, the inventor may encounter difficulties in appropriating the rewards from the effort invested in originally acquiring the knowledge.

■ *Non-rivalness* implies making knowledge available to one person does not diminish the quantity of the same knowledge that could be made available to other people. In other words, the marginal cost of disseminating knowledge to more and more people is either very small or zero. This creates a conflict between the inventor's private interest in preventing or restricting access to the knowledge, and the social objective of welfare maximization, which requires the knowledge to be disseminated as widely as possible.

In designing a patent system, policy makers need to strike a balance between providing sufficient incentives to encourage research and development activity on the one hand, and avoiding excessive monopolization and the abuse of market power on the other. The dilemma is illustrated by the example shown in Figure 14.8. As in Figure 14.2, we consider the incentive to invest in the development of a new process that has the potential to produce a large saving in average costs for the firms in a perfectly competitive industry. The inventor's initial development cost is X. The benefits from using the process accrue over two periods.

■ In period 1 (the short run), the inventor has exclusive knowledge of the process, and can license it to the perfectly competitive firms. We assume imitation is not possible in the short run, so paying for the right to use the process is the only way for the firms to gain access.

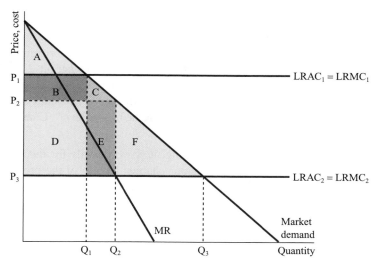

Figure 14.8 Welfare implications of patenting

- In period 2 (the long run), if the invention is not patented imitation is possible, and any firm can use the process (without incurring the development cost). If the invention is patented, the inventor can continue to charge the licence fee or royalty.

In Figure 14.8, $LRAC_1$ represents the average cost under the old technology, and $LRAC_2$ represents the average cost using the new process. Q_1 is the industry output before the innovation, and P_1 is the market price. While it is possible to control access to the process, the profit-maximizing royalty is $P_2 - LRAC_2$ per unit of output. Q_2 is the industry output, P_2 is the market price, and $D + E$ is the total royalty payment. If it is not possible to control access (because the inventor's property rights are not protected by patent), Q_3 is the industry output and P_3 is the market price.

Does the option for the inventor to take out a patent increase welfare by improving the inventor's incentive to proceed; or does this option reduce welfare by conferring market power upon the inventor, which can be used to restrict output and raise the market price? In fact, either outcome is possible. Suppose initially $X < D + E$.

- Even if there is no patenting, it is still worthwhile for the inventor to proceed with the innovation. The inventor's period 1 (short-run) reward of $D + E$ exceeds the development cost of X. In period 1 industry output adjusts to Q_2. In period 2, however, imitation takes place. The inventor receives no further return in period 2, and industry output adjusts to Q_3. In period 2 there is allocative efficiency, because price *equals* marginal cost. Consumer surplus is $A + B + C + D + E + F$.

- If there is patenting, the same analysis applies in period 1. In period 2, however, the inventor continues to charge for the use of the process, and in period 2 once again earns a return of $D + E$. The inventor's total return over the two periods is $2(D + E)$. Industry output remains at Q_2. In period 2 there is allocative inefficiency, because price exceeds marginal cost. Consumer surplus is $A + B + C$, and producer surplus (in the form of the royalty payment) is $D + E$.

Now suppose $D + E < X < 2(D + E)$.

■ If there is no patenting, it is not worthwhile for the inventor to proceed with the innovation. The inventor's period 1 (short-run) return of $D + E$ does not repay the development cost of X, and in period 2 the inventor receives no further reward. The innovation does not take place, and industry output remains at Q_1 in periods 1 and 2. There is allocative efficiency only in the narrow sense that price *equals* marginal cost (at the higher level). Consumer surplus is A and there is no producer surplus.

■ If there is patenting, it is worthwhile for the inventor to proceed. In periods 1 and 2, the inventor charges for use of the process, and earns a total royalty of $2(D + E)$, which exceeds the development cost of X. Industry output is Q_2 in periods 1 and 2. There is allocative inefficiency, because price exceeds marginal cost (at the lower level). However, consumer surplus is $A + B + C$ and producer surplus is $D + E$.

Therefore in the case $X < D + E$, combined consumer and producer surplus in period 2 is higher if there is no patent system. But in the case $D + E < X < 2(D + E)$, the opposite is true. In this latter case, the equilibrium of (P_2, Q_2) with patenting is a second-best solution. The best outcome would be (P_3, Q_3), but this outcome is not feasible because of the problem of inappropriability: without a patent the inventor cannot recoup the development cost due to imitation. However, the second-best outcome of (P_2, Q_2) is preferable to (P_1, Q_1), the actual outcome in the absence of a patenting system.

This kind of analysis raises practical questions as to how long patents should be issued for, and how wide their coverage should be. Clearly the duration of a patent should be sufficient to enable the inventor to earn a reasonable return on the original research and development investment. If the duration is too short, the return may not justify the cost, and the invention may never happen. But if the duration is too long, the inventor earns an excessive profit and welfare is damaged by the usual deadweight loss caused by monopolization. Since every invention has a different time profile of costs and proceeds, it is difficult for policy makers to determine a patent duration suitable for all cases. Yang and Tsou (2002) examine the propensity to patent following a change in the Taiwanese patenting system in 1994, which increased the duration of patents. Although the number of patents increased after the change, this may have been mainly due to factors other than the change in duration.

Determining the optimal scope or breadth of a patent is even more difficult, since the concept of breadth is inherently difficult to measure or generalize, unlike duration which is straightforward. As a generalization, a new idea should differ sufficiently from an existing idea to prevent other firms inventing around the existing idea, and reducing the patent holder's profit. However, too broad a protection encourages firms to invest in fundamental technologies, but discourages further investment in second- and third-generation applications or smaller improvements (Scotchmer, 1991). Taken together, the issues of duration and breadth are complex, and it is difficult to make general recommendations (Denicolò, 1996; Takalo, 2001). O'Donoghue *et al.* (1998) define the effective patent life as the duration at which the idea either reaches the end of its useful lifetime, or is superseded by a newer innovation. The effective patent life is shown to depend on the breadth of the patent.

To this point, our discussion has focused on the possibility that insufficient research may be undertaken if the patent system provides either insufficient incentive to the inventor to initiate the research, or perhaps too much incentive in the form of excessive market power once the innovation has taken place, which inhibits diffusion. However, it is also possible to envisage situations in which too much research, or the wrong kind of research, is produced, either with or without a patenting system (Cockburn and Henderson, 1994; Hall and Ziedonis, 2001; Hirschliefer, 1971). This could arise if firms launch competitive research and development programmes or patent races, in an effort to be the first to acquire a patent and the monopoly position this confers. Not only is much of the research effort duplicated unnecessarily, but the paramount importance of speed in a patent race may lead to errors being committed and a further waste of resources. The existence of a patent system may produce distortions in the allocation of resources to research activity, favouring activities for which patenting is likely to be feasible. There seems no reason to assume that patented work is necessarily that which produces the greatest economic benefit.

Case study 14.3

Economics of open source

With open source software, programmers at many different locations and institutions cooperate and share code in order to improve and extend software programs. It is intended that such cooperation should lead to the continual improvement and refinement of the basic product. Access to open source code is freely available to anyone who wishes to use it. The open source movement is based on principles that are in marked contrast to the usual business practice of guarding one's intellectual property by means of copyright and patents. However, open source does appear to be capable of generating innovative, reliable and low-cost technological progress.

Two of the most successful open source software products are the Linux operating system and the Apache web server.

- Linux was created by Linus Torvalds, a 21-year-old graduate student, in 1991. It was based on Minix, a version of the Unix operating system that was used on personal computers. After posting Linux on a university server, Torvalds invited contributions from other programmers. By 1994 the number of users had increased to half-a-million, and by the start of the twenty-first century estimates of the number of Linux users worldwide ranged from 7 to 16 million. Linux had become established as a significant competitor to Microsoft Windows. Throughout, Torvalds has retained overall leadership and decision-making authority for the Linux project.

- The development of Apache began in 1994. Brian Behlendorf, a 21-year-old programmer who was working on one of the world's first commercial internet servers, which ran on Unix-based software written at the National Center for Supercomputer Applications (NCSA) at the University of Illinois, started posting patches for the NCSA server to mailing lists of individuals. The decision to collect and integrate these patches led to the creation of

Apache. Many individuals were permitted to report problems and suggest changes, but only a limited number were permitted to write new code. Despite the subsequent launch of rival web server products by Microsoft and Netscape, Apache retained its dominant market position: out of 24 million internet domains surveyed in 2000, around 60 per cent were powered using Apache software.

According to Lerner and Tirole (2002), the interest of economists and policy makers in the open source movement has been stimulated by several factors: the rapid pace of diffusion of open source software; the launch of projects by large corporations based on open source software (Hewlett Packard, IBM and Sun); the creation of commercial firms specializing in applications of open source products (Red Hat and VA Linux); and innovation in the organizational structures that have been developed in order to deliver cooperative effort.

The open source movement raises a number of interesting questions for economists. In particular, why should researchers or programmers devote effort to the production of public goods, for which they receive no direct monetary remuneration? One possibility is that programmers obtain direct benefits (bug fixing or customization) for their own organizations from solving a problem that has arisen with an open source program. Another possibility is that programmers derive enjoyment or satisfaction from tackling and solving open source problems, which may be more interesting or challenging than their routine work. In the long run, a contribution to the development of open source projects may benefit a programmer professionally, by signalling talent to prospective employers or venture capital financiers. Alternatively, some programmers may be motivated by the desire for peer recognition from other programmers, rather than by prospective monetary reward. The Apache project recognizes all contributors on its website, and highlights its most prolific contributors.

Other advantages of open source include the following. Open source projects benefit by obtaining free programmer training from schools and universities. In contrast, owners of proprietary code have to train their own programmers in-house. Suppliers of proprietary software cannot easily allow users to modify and customize their code for the user's own purposes. Because of the tendency for commercial firms to hide the visibility of their key employees, it may be difficult for these staff to signal their talents to the outside labour market. This may create disincentive effects.

There have been attempts to develop open source projects in other fields such as medical research, on-line encyclopaedias (Wikipedia) and on-line academic journals. There are, however, some factors that may impose limits on the extension of the open source movement to other fields. For example, manufactured products require less intellectual or knowledge-based inputs and more physical capital and labour inputs than software programming. Therefore the open might source model may not be applicable. The altruistic tendencies of contributors to open source software might derive partly from a personal or sociopolitical stance against the dominant software firms, which might not exist in other fields. Finally, the open source model works best in the field of incremental research, and is less capable of generating revolutionary or first generation innovations.

Source: Lerner, J. and Tirole, J. (2002) Some simple economics of open source, *Journal of Industrial Economics*, 50, pp. 197–234.

By granting monopoly status, patents may in practice offer more protection to innovators than to genuine inventors. Some firms may even implement a strategy of pre-emptive patenting in an attempt to limit competition. In other words, patents might tend to provide protection at the wrong stage in the process: inventors require protection, but at the innovation stage competition is preferable, in order to maximize the pace of diffusion. Some implications of an open-source technology are examined in Case study 14.3.

Several of the points discussed above are reflected in the empirical research into the effects of patents on the incentives for inventive or innovative activity. Examining a sample of research-intensive firms, Taylor and Silberston (1973) find the majority would still have carried out research even in the absence of patent protection. Schankerman (1998) investigates patent renewals in France for four technology fields: pharmaceuticals, chemicals, mechanical engineering and electronics. There are differences in the importance of patent protection across different fields. Patent protection appeared to be least important in the pharmaceutical field, perhaps due to a strong tradition of price regulation:

> The finding that patent rights are surprisingly less valuable in pharmaceuticals, where there is stringent price regulation in France, highlights the important point that R&D incentives are shaped not only by patent law but also other institutional constraints that effect the appropriability environment.
>
> *(Schankerman, 1998, p. 104)*

14.6 Empirical evidence

The Schumpeterian hypothesis

As we have seen in Section 14.2, the Schumpeterian analysis suggests two distinct hypotheses: first, that market structure affects the quantity of inventive or innovative activity or the pace of technological change; and second, that large firms are more likely to invest in research and development than small firms owing to economies of scale. In this section, we examine some of the empirical evidence concerning these two hypotheses. However, at the outset it is important to draw attention to some general problems that often confront researchers in this field.

Typically, three types of measure of the level of research and development activity are used:

■ Input-based measures, usually based on levels of research and development expenditure (the hiring of scientific personnel and spending on research equipment) reported in company accounts.

■ Output-based measures, usually based on the numbers of patents issued.

■ Lists of inventions or innovations.

Input-based measures are of limited value, for several reasons. First, all of a firm's research and development expenditure may be attributed to that firm's principal activity, whereas in reality the effort may be directed towards subsidiary activities.

Second, some research activity may be located outside the firm's research and development department, for example in a design office. Third, official statistics may not reflect research undertaken by small and medium-sized firms, if these firms do not identify their research expenditures specifically in their accounts. Finally, an input-based measure is by definition a measure of effort, but not necessarily a measure of achievement.

The use of data on patent applications or patents granted offers the implicit advantage that, in most cases, patent applications are made with a view to the commercial application of new ideas. Nevertheless, patents are not homogeneous, and outcomes can range from commercially successful to completely useless. A patent count of two should reflect twice as much technical output as a count of one, but clearly this is not always the case. Cross-sectional comparisons (between firms in different industries) are subject to the difficulty that the propensity to patent varies widely from one industry to another. For example, defence contractors seldom patent their inventions, since government is the exclusive purchaser of their products. In organic chemicals and petrochemicals, on the other hand, small changes to the molecular structure of compounds can have major implications for product characteristics. Consequently, there is a natural tendency for the proliferation of manipulated molecule patenting. International studies face the further difficulty that the institutional barriers that need to be surmounted in order to secure a patent vary quite widely between countries.

Patel and Pavitt (1995) recommend using lists of inventions and innovations as an alternative to data based on patents. With the benefit of hindsight, the economic contribution of each technological advance can be assessed. However, a lot of specialized knowledge may be required in order to draw up a list, and decisions as to which innovations to include and exclude are subjective to some extent. One possibility is to identify relevant technological innovations as those that are 'important enough to warrant annotation in the vast array of trade journals covering particular industries' (Scherer, 1992, p. 1423).

Fortunately, input- and output-based measures of research and development activity seem to be quite highly correlated. Therefore the decision as to which measure to use might not be critical. Based on a sample of 57 US pharmaceutical firms for the period 1955–60, Comanor and Scherer (1969) report that the correlation between the average number of research employees and the number of patents issued was more than 0.8.

A simple test of the relationship between market structure and the level of inventive or innovative activity is based on a cross-sectional regression of a suitable input- or output-based measure against an industry seller concentration measure. However, the causation between concentration and the quantity of research and development is not necessarily all one-way (Phillips, 1966). As a result of technological change, opportunities for new innovations arise, and some firms take advantage while others are slow to adapt. Over time, the more innovative firms increase their market shares, and seller concentration increases.

According to Geroski (1994), factors such as increased product differentiation, economies of scale and the natural tendency for seller concentration to increase over time even if growth is essentially random (see Sections 7.2 and 7.5) made a larger contribution than innovation to the rise in seller concentration in most developed countries during the twentieth century. Geroski tests Blair's (1972) hypothesis that over the long run technological change (specifically, the advent of new materials and electronics) reduced the MES (minimum efficient scale) at plant level, and was a force for deconcentration. '[O]ur results suggest that innovative activity does affect the evolution of market structure in particular industries, and that innovation plays a deconcentrating role wholly consistent with Blair's hypothesis' (Geroski, 1994, p. 40).

Tests of the Schumpeterian hypothesis based on cross-sectional regressions of industry research activity indicators against industry concentration can be criticized as unsound, because different industries offer widely differing technological opportunities for research and development and innovation. For example, the cotton textile industry is less technology-oriented than the pharmaceutical industry. To a large extent technological opportunity may be an inherent product characteristic, although it may also depend partly on whether a vigorous scientific culture forms part of industry tradition.

Cohen and Levin (1989) discuss the issue of differing technological opportunity at greater length. Methods used to address this issue are often impressionistic. For example, a sample might be subdivided into high- and low-technology industries. Scherer (1965) excludes firms from industries classified as low in technological opportunity, and elsewhere uses dummy variables to distinguish between different levels of technological opportunity. Comanor (1967a) makes similar impressionistic choices. Jaffe (1986) classifies firms according to 20 technological opportunity clusters. Levin *et al.* (1987) define technological opportunity on the basis of interviews conducted with research and development executives, which seek to measure receptiveness to scientific advance based on information flows from government, universities, suppliers and clients.

Much of the empirical research on innovation focuses on the twin hypotheses that firms in highly concentrated industries and large firms are most likely to invest heavily in research and development. Since a thorough coverage of the literature can be found in survey articles by Cohen (1995), Cohen and Levin (1989), Kamien and Schwartz (1982) and Scherer (1992), we focus only on a small number of representative studies.

Scherer (1965) obtains data on input-based (scientists employed) and output-based (patents) research and development activity measures for 448 of the *Fortune 500* list of US companies in 1955. There is a positive relationship between sales and research and development output, but at a less-than-proportionate rate. Differences in technological opportunity are mainly responsible for inter-industry differences in research output. Research output does not appear to be systematically related to variations in market power, profitability, liquidity or product-line diversification. There is a dip in innovative output at high levels of concentration.

> These findings among other things raise doubts whether the big, monopolistic, conglomerate corporation is as efficient an engine of technological change as disciples of Schumpeter (including myself) have supposed it to be. Perhaps a bevy of fact-mechanics can still rescue the Schumpeterian engine from disgrace, but at present the outlook seems pessimistic.

> *(Scherer, 1965, p. 1122)*

Comanor (1967a) subdivides industries into two groups: those where product and design differences are an important feature of market structure (examples include consumer durables); and those where these features are unimportant (examples include cement and aluminium). Although this classification is subjective to some extent, the implication is that the first group requires a higher research input than the second group. This hypothesis is supported by the data. In order to investigate the relationship between concentration and the amount of research and development, each group is further subdivided into high- and low-concentration industries. In industries where product differentiation is an important factor, concentration is not a significant determinant of research and development; but where product differentiation is less important, concentration plays a bigger role. In the latter group, research tends to focus on process innovation, which is less likely to provoke reactions from rivals. The Schumpeterian hypothesis appears to apply in this case. In industries where research is an important instrument of strategy, there is no apparent relationship between concentration and the amount of research and development; this finding is consistent with the conclusions of Scherer. However, Comanor suggests inter-industry differences in technological opportunity could account for some of the patterns in the data.

Comanor also investigates the role of research and development as an entry barrier. The chosen indicator of the height of entry barriers is an estimate of MES (average size of the top 50 per cent of plants by industry output) divided by total industry shipments. Where barriers to entry are high, there is no association between concentration and research and development, but where barriers to entry are low, there is such a relationship. A possible interpretation is that high entry barriers make it less important for firms to undertake research and development as a form of non-price competition.

Using a data set covering 4,378 innovations produced and used between 1945 and 1983 in the UK, Geroski (1994) examines whether monopoly or competition is the market structure most conducive to innovation. The dependent variable is the level of innovative output (measured by the number of innovations produced). The explanatory variables include the following: the expected price–cost margin following the innovation; the five-firm concentration ratio (CR_5); the change in CR_5 during the study period; the extent of market penetration by entrants; the market share of imports; the relative number of small firms; the market share of exiting firms; measures of industry size and growth; capital intensity; export intensity; and a measure of industry unionization.

Geroski is reluctant to rely solely on CR_5 as a market structure measure. The entry, imports, small firm and exit variables are intended to capture further aspects of competition and rivalry. For example, an industry with a high rate of entry, many small firms, a low and falling CR_5 and a low exit rate would be regarded as competitive; conversely, low entry, few small firms, a high and rising CR_5 and high exit would indicate limited rivalry and elements of monopoly.

The results suggest only a limited relationship between market power and the pace of technological change. The reported coefficients on CR_5 and the change in CR_5 are negative and significant. These results suggest industries that are highly concentrated, and becoming more so, tend to produce a slower pace of technological change than more competitive industries. There is a positive relationship between expectations of abnormal profit and the pace of technological change, although the measurement of expected profitability may be problematic. Industry size, export intensity and unionization appear to be unrelated to innovative activity, and the relationships between innovative activity and growth and capital intensity are relatively weak. Overall, the results do not appear to support the Schumpeterian hypothesis. 'There is, in short, almost no support in the data for popular Schumpeterian assertions about the role of actual monopoly in stimulating progressiveness' (Geroski, 1994, p. 59).

Using cross-sectional data on 26 international pharmaceutical firms for the period 1987–89, Alexander et al. (1995) re-examine the question of the relationship between firm size and the pace of technological change. Research output is measured as the number of new compounds the firm has in its research and development pipeline. A more traditional measure of output per research and development employee is also used. Explanatory variables include an employment measure of firm size; the levels of research and development investment per employee; past research and development expenditure; and a domestic or foreign ownership dummy variable. The results suggest there is a positive relationship between firm size and the pace of technological change. Research and development activity was lower in firms owned outside the US. Although there is a positive relationship between research and development expenditure and output, this relationship is subject to diminishing returns.

Geroski et al. (1993) examine the empirical relationship between innovation and profitability. Using pooled cross-sectional and time-series data on a sample of 721 UK manufacturing firms observed between 1972 and 1983, including a subset of 117 firms that are identified as innovative, Geroski et al. estimate a regression model in which the dependent variable is the firm's average profit margin. The key explanatory variable is the number of innovations produced by the firm in each year. Controls are also included for the number of innovations produced and used within the firm's two-digit industry group, in an attempt to capture innovation spillover effects. There are also controls for the firm's market share, industry concentration, import intensity and the degree of unionization. A lagged dependent variable allows for effects related to technological opportunity and appropriability, as well as the usual mechanism for partial adjustment towards equilibrium.

The results suggest there is a positive relationship between the number of innovations produced by a firm and its profitability, although the relationship is relatively weak. Spillover effects are less important than in similar research based on US data. An attempt is made to distinguish between the contributions of research and development inputs and outputs to profitability, and to determine whether 'the correlation between innovative output and profitability [reflects] transitory or permanent performance differences between innovating and non-innovating firms' (Geroski et al., 1993, p. 199). The results suggest permanent effects are more apparent during periods of recession. Therefore innovating firms are better able to withstand cyclical downturns than non-innovating firms.

In a survey of the empirical literature on the relationship between firm size and innovation, Scherer (1992) draws the following conclusions:

- Large firms are more likely to invest in formal research and development and to obtain patents. However, most manufacturing firms, even those of a modest size, appear to be involved in some form of innovative activity.

- Traditional measures of innovation based on research and development expenditure ignore a large amount of informal activity, especially within smaller firms.

- There is some evidence that research and development activity and patenting tend to increase linearly with firm size.

- The ratio of research and development expenditure to sales at firm level varies more between industries than within industries.

- In general, large size achieved through a strategy of diversification does not tend to result in a higher research and development expenditure to sales ratio, unless the diversification strategy is pursued specifically in order to develop research and development synergies.

Based on the observation that research output tends to increase less than proportionately with firm size, and may even decline at large sizes, Cohen (1995) infers small firms achieve more innovations per unit of research and development expenditure than larger firms. However, this could be because large firms tend to pursue fewer ideas more intensively. Therefore the average innovation of the large firm might be of a higher quality than that of a smaller firm.

Although there is some empirical evidence suggesting a positive relationship between seller concentration and the level of research and development activity, this relationship appears to be rather weak, and becomes even more fragile if factors such as technological opportunity and appropriability are considered. Even if a positive relationship between concentration and innovation does exist, its interpretation can be problematic. As we have seen previously, causation between market structure and innovation can run in either direction. Furthermore, and contrary to the Schumpeterian hypothesis, it is possible that the smaller or medium-sized firms in highly concentrated industries are primarily responsible for the positive association between concentration and research and development activity.

Rosenberg (1976) and Williamson (1975) report evidence to suggest small or medium-sized firms tend to search more intensively for innovative ideas, perhaps because as relatively marginal players in their own industries, they need to be innovative in order to enhance their survival prospects. Conversely, the larger the firm, the less it has to gain from being innovative. Overall, the empirical research on the relationships between firm size, market structure and innovation has failed to produce clear and unambiguous conclusions. Many studies are based on limited data sets, and many are faced with serious problems of defining and quantifying key variables. One general conclusion that does emerge, however, is that a simplistic or mechanistic interpretation of the Schumpeterian hypothesis is not supported by the empirical evidence.

The pace of diffusion

Romeo (1975) applies Mansfield's methodology to the US machine-tools industry, to examine the relationship between seller concentration, the scale of production and research and development expenditure and the pace of diffusion, reflected in the shape of the S-curve (Figure 14.6). The results suggest the pace of diffusion tends to be faster in less highly concentrated industries. Industries operating on a larger scale experience a slower pace of diffusion, partly because they have to spend more in absolute terms in order to match the rate of diffusion in industries operating on a smaller scale.

Several recent studies examine the pace of diffusion of new technologies in banking and financial services. As with tangible goods, technological progress in financial services can be achieved through both product and process innovation. Product innovations include new types of bonds and securities. These often fall under the heading of *off-balance sheet business*, which covers a range of non-traditional banking activity that generates fees and other types of non-interest income. Process innovations include new ways of distributing financial services such as Automated Teller Machines (ATM), Electronic Funds Transfer at the Point of Sale (EFTPOS), telephone banking, call centres, internet banking, and Customer Relationship Management Systems (CRMS) (Tufano, 2003). Jagtiani *et al.* (1995) examine the diffusion of several off-balance-sheet product innovations (stand-by letters of credit, loan sales, swaps, options, futures and forwards) in 86 large US banks over the period 1984–91. Regulatory changes in capital requirements for banks had little effect on the speed of adoption in most cases, although the rate of adoption increased for stand-by letters of credit, as banks substituted these for more traditional forms of lending. The adoption decision was not explained by bank size or other measurable characteristics of banks (such as capital ratios and creditworthiness indicators). For many banks, the timing of adoption may be influenced by a bandwagon effect.

Molyneux and Shamroukh (1996) examine the diffusion of off-balance-sheet business product innovations (junk bonds and note-issuance facilities) among 505 European, Japanese and US banks over the period 1977–86. Adoption of junk bonds appears to have been driven by assessments of future profitability, based on market conditions. Adoption of note-issuance facilities appears to have been a more defensive strategy, in response to a perceived threat to traditional lending business. Fung and Cheng (2004) examine the diffusion of three financial innovations (contingent liabilities, exchange-rate contracts, and interest-rate contracts) over the period 1990–2000 for a sample of Hong Kong banks. Information complementarity (using customer information to market a number of different financial products) and individual bank creditworthiness appear to be the main drivers of diffusion.

Canepa and Stoneman (2004) examine the factors that might explain differences in the pace of diffusion between countries, using survey data on the take-up of new technologies in manufacturing from six countries: the UK, Italy, Portugal, Switzerland, Canada and the US. The pace of diffusion is heavily dependent on the nature of the technology, and no one country achieved a faster pace of diffusion consistently across all technologies. Adoption costs, information and learning effects, and firm or industry characteristics including size, location and the level of competition are the major influences on the pace of diffusion.

Massini (2004) examines the pace of diffusion in the UK and Italian mobile phone industries. Rapid diffusion in Italy was encouraged by handsets being made available to consumers at relatively low prices; while in the UK, other factors, including rising real incomes, were at least as important. Sundqvist *et al.* (2004) examine the diffusion of wireless communications over the period 1981–2000 across 64 countries. Wealthy countries adopt earlier than poorer ones; the rate of adoption is similar across countries deemed to have similar cultures; and the pace of diffusion tends to be faster in countries that adopted later (lag markets), perhaps due to an ability to learn from the experiences of the early adopters (lead markets). According to Beise (2004), lead markets that have a competitive advantage related to low-cost production, buoyant demand, intense rivalry between existing producers and a strong export orientation are best able to produce innovations that later become globally adopted. The mobile phone industry conforms to the lead market hypothesis. In this case Scandinavia took the lead in production and adoption. Eventually cellular telephony and the associated cellular mobile phone standard achieved global acceptance, displacing rival technologies such as pagers.

14.7 Summary

Much of the theoretical and empirical analysis of the economics of research and development and innovation is based on ideas developed by Schumpeter, who saw technological change as the main driving force for economic growth. The process of creative destruction simultaneously rewards successful innovators and punishes those firms whose technologies are superseded and become obsolete. Large firms that have become monopolies through successful past innovation are the main drivers of technological progress.

The Schumpeterian hypothesis, that there is an association between successful innovation and monopoly, has provided the motivation for an extensive body of research, including several attempts to reposition Schumpeter's approach within a neoclassical economics framework. In a well known contribution, Arrow shows the incentive to innovate may be greater under competitive conditions than it is under a monopoly. However, Arrow's analysis has been subject to criticism for failing to present a fair comparison, based on equivalent output levels or price elasticities before the innovation takes place, in both the perfectly competitive case and the monopoly case. Several economists have argued for an inverted U-shaped relationship between seller concentration and the amount of research and development activity, with oligopoly being the market structure most conducive to a fast pace of technological change. An oligopolist has both the means to devote resources to research and development (being capable of earning an abnormal profit, unlike the perfect competitor); and the incentive (being subject to intense competitive pressure from rivals, unlike the monopolist).

Although the Schumpeterian hypothesis is often interpreted in terms of an association between market structure and the pace of technological change, this hypothesis is also consistent with the notion of a relationship between firm size and the amount of research and development. It may be that only large firms have the resources to implement large-scale research programmes, or to bear the risks associated with a form of investment whose returns are inherently uncertain. On the other hand, large organizations may fail to provide sufficient incentives for creative or original thinking on the part of their managers or other employees. The bureaucratic nature of many large organizations may tend to discourage originality or non-conformity.

In many cases, the decision to invest in research and development is strategic. Relevant strategic issues that may influence this investment decision include the choice between an offensive strategy, whereby a firm seeks to pioneer new ideas; a defensive strategy, whereby a firm seeks to undertake sufficient research to keep pace with competitors; an imitative strategy, whereby a firm merely seeks to copy ideas that have been developed elsewhere; or a dependent strategy, whereby a firm borrows or acquires a licence to use a piece of technology that has been developed elsewhere. Like any other investment decision, the decision to commit resources to research and development can be subjected to investment appraisal analysis. Relevant considerations include the anticipated levels of demand and costs, the marketing strategy (in the case of a product innovation) and the means of financing the research programme.

The rate of diffusion measures the pace at which a piece of new technology spreads from the original innovating firm to other firms for which the technology is applicable. The Mansfield model provides a benchmark for measuring and for investigating the factors that determine the pace of diffusion. Industry- and firm-level determinants include the following:

- Quality of communications: effective channels of communication between firms that are members of the same industry, and between firms and university researchers, are likely to produce a faster pace of diffusion.

- The education, experience and attitudes of a firm's managers may influence or determine their receptiveness to new ideas.

- A dominant firm that hopes to maintain an entrenched position as market leader might be reluctant to experiment with new technologies; so too might a firm that has recently upgraded its capital stock based on an older technology.

- Organized labour might also have an interest in resisting the adoption of new technology, it is viewed as a threat to current employment levels.

- A cumbersome regulatory framework may slow down the pace of adoption of new technology.

- A new technology may be only adopted slowly or reluctantly if its introduction involves significant risk.

- The design of a country's patenting system can affect the pace of diffusion in either direction.

The award of a patent to the inventor of a new product, process, substance or design confers a property right over the knowledge embodied in the invention. In most countries patents are awarded for a finite period; the current UK duration is 20 years. In order to be patented, an invention must be new, non-obvious and capable of commercial application. Patents exist in order to provide incentives for investment in research and development and for innovation. Granting a property right over the knowledge creates a monopoly, conferring market power upon the patent holder. The opportunity to earn an abnormal profit through the exploitation of this market power may represent the main incentive for the original investment. In designing a patent system, policy makers need to strike a balance between providing sufficient incentives to encourage research and development on the one hand, and avoiding excessive monopolization and abuses of market power on the other. Determining how long patents should be issued for, and how narrow or wide their coverage should be, are difficult issues, which may have major implications for the pace of technological change.

Although there is some empirical evidence suggesting a positive association between seller concentration and the amount of research and development, the relationship appears to be relatively weak. If factors such as technological opportunity and appropriability are taken into account, the evidence for such a relationship becomes even more fragile. Furthermore, causation between market structure and innovation can run in either direction. Overall, empirical research on the relationships between market structure, firm size and innovation has failed to deliver clear and unambiguous conclusions.

Discussion questions

1. Explain the distinction between the basic research, applied research, development, commercial production and diffusion stages in the commercial application of a new technology.

2. Explain the distinction between product innovation and process innovation. Quote examples of new technologies that required elements of both forms of innovation.

3. What is the distinction between the creative and destructive aspects of Schumpeter's process of creative destruction?

4. Is the level of effort devoted to research and development likely to be higher if an industry is monopolized than if it is perfectly competitive? Consider this issue with reference to the theoretical analyses of Arrow and Demsetz.

5. The author of Case study 14.1 wrote: 'The most profitable companies put far more emphasis than less profitable ones on innovation in the marketplace . . . Yet there are serious disagreements between technical directors on one side and chief executives and marketeers on the other about whether innovation is primarily a technological issue or a customer issue.' Assess the contribution of marketing to the processes of innovation and technological change.

6. With reference to Case study 14.2, quote evidence to support the claim that university–industry links are becoming increasingly important in stimulating the commercial application of new technologies.

7. What factors are relevant to a firm in determining the speed at which it intends to execute a planned research and development programme? Why might the market structure in which the firm operates be a relevant factor in this decision?

8. For what reasons did Galbraith believe that most private sector research and development in a developed economy would be carried out by large firms, rather than by small firms or independent inventors? Do you think Galbraith's arguments are correct?

9. What are the strengths and limitations of Mansfield's mathematical model of the process of diffusion?

10. What factors are influential in determining the pace of diffusion?

11. Distinguish between offensive, defensive, imitative and dependent research and development strategies.

12. What factors might be relevant in explaining why Europe's performance in innovation may have been relatively weak compared with that of the US and Japan?

13. What factors should be considered by policy makers when deciding the duration of patents? Is it possible that patents might slow the pace of technological change?

14. Are effective arrangements for the protection of intellectual property rights always a necessary prerequisite for innovation to take place? Consider this question with reference to Case study 14.3.

Further reading

Battisti, G. and Stoneman, P. (2005) The intra-firm diffusion of new process techniques, *International Journal of Industrial Organization*, 23, forthcoming.

Cohen, W.M. and Levin, R.C. (1989) Empirical studies of innovation and market structure, in Schmalensee, R. and Willig, R. (eds) *Handbook of Industrial Organization*, vol. 2. Amsterdam: North Holland, 1059–107.

Dodgson, M. and Rothwell, R. (eds) (1994) *The Handbook of Industrial Innovation*. Cheltenham: Edward Elgar.

European Commission (1995a) *Green Paper on Innovation*, COM(95)688.

Freeman, C. and Soete, L. (1997) *The Economics of Industrial Innovation*, 3rd edn. London: Pinter.

Gallini, N.T. (2002) The economics of patents: lessons from recent US patent reform, *Journal of Economic Perspectives*, 16, 131–54.

Geroski, P. (1994) *Market Structure, Corporate Performance and Innovative Activity*. Oxford: Clarendon Press.

Hamberg, D. (1966) *Essays in the Economics of Research and Development*. New York: Random House.

Jewkes, J., Sawers, D. and Stillerman, R. (1969) *The Sources of Invention*, 2nd edn, London: Macmillan.

Karshenas, M. and Stoneman, P. (1995) Technological diffusion, in Stoneman, P. (ed.) *Handbook of the Economics of Innovation and Technical Change*. Oxford: Blackwell, ch. 7.

Kato, A. (2005) Market structure and the allocation of R&D expenditures, *Economics Letters*, 87, 127–34.

Klepper, S. and Simons, K. (2005) Industry shakeouts and technological change, *International Journal of Industrial Organization*, 23, forthcoming.

Mansfield, E. (1969) Industrial research and development: characteristics, costs and diffusion results, *American Economic Review, Papers and Proceedings*, 59, 65–79.

Patel, P. and Pavitt, K. (1995) Patterns of technological activity: their measurement and interpretation, in Stoneman, P. (ed.) *Handbook of the Economics of Innovation and Technical Change*. Oxford: Blackwell, ch. 2.

Scherer, F.M. (1992) Schumpeter and plausible capitalism, *Journal of Economic Literature*, 30, 1416–33.

Schumpeter, J. (1942) *Capitalism, Socialism, and Democracy*. New York: Harper.

Stoneman, P. (1995) *Handbook of the Economics of Innovation and Technical Change*. Oxford: Blackwell.

Suetens, S. (2005) Cooperative and non-cooperative R&D in experimental oligopoly markets, *International Journal of Industrial Organization*, 23, forthcoming.

Vertical integration and restraints

Learning objectives

This chapter covers the following topics:

- motives for vertical integration: enhancement of market power
- motives for vertical integration: cost savings
- measurement of vertical integration, and empirical evidence
- franchising and networks
- forms of vertical restraint
- resale price maintenance, foreclosure, territorial exclusivity, quantity-dependent pricing

Key terms

Backward vertical integration
Bundling
Double marginalization
Downstream vertical integration
Foreclosure
Forward vertical integration
Franchise agreements
Network

Non-linear pricing
Quantity-dependent pricing
Quantity forcing
Resale price maintenance
Tying
Upstream vertical integration
Vertical integration
Vertical restraint

15.1 Introduction

The topic of vertical relationships covers a wide range of issues involving firms operating at different stages of the same production process. **Vertical integration** refers to a situation where a single firm has ownership and control over production at successive stages of a production process. Activities located at the initial stages of a production process are known as *upstream* activities, and those located closer to the market for the final product are known as *downstream* activities. Therefore **upstream** (or **backward**) **vertical integration** refers to a situation where a firm gains control over the production of inputs necessary for its own operation; and **downstream** (or **forward**) **vertical integration** refers to a situation where a firm gains control over an activity that utilizes its outputs. Since capacity may differ at different stages of production, even a vertically integrated firm may have to rely on external market transactions to achieve its required capacity. Balanced vertical integration occurs if capacities at successive stages are equal.

The explanations for vertical integration are varied and do not lend themselves to simple classification. The earliest theories tended to focus on issues such as the the desire to secure enhanced market power; the technological benefits of linking successive stages of production; the reduction in risk and uncertainty associated with the supply of inputs or the distribution of a firm's finished product; and the avoidance of taxes or price controls. Section 15.2 describes motives for vertical integration associated with the enhancement of market power, and Section 15.3 describes motives associated with cost savings. The discussion of cost savings motives starts by interpreting vertical integration as a strategy for reducing transaction costs (see also Chapter 3), and interprets the various opportunities for cost savings using a transaction costs framework. Section 15.4 reviews some of the empirical evidence on the motivations and consequences of vertical integration.

As an alternative to vertical integration, some firms may decide to develop vertical relationships of a looser nature than full-scale vertical integration. Advantages include the preservation of some (or all) of both parties' independence, and the avoidance of costs that might be associated with vertical integration. Examples of agency or vertical relationships that stop short of full-scale integration include franchising, involving a specific contractual agreement between a franchisor and franchisee; and networks of independent firms that are linked vertically, and establish non-exclusive contracts or other relationships with one another. Franchising and networks are examined in Section 15.5.

Finally, some firms may find vertical integration or other types of vertical relationship too costly to organize and monitor. Instead, they may develop various forms of vertical restraint in order to achieve similar outcomes. Vertical restraints are conditions and restrictions on trade imposed by firms that are linked vertically. For example, if a producer makes it a condition of supply that a retailer should charge a minimum price, this constitutes a vertical restraint or restriction. In Section 15.6 we examine the motives for the creation of vertical restraints. Finally, in Section 15.7 we examine some of the main forms vertical restraints may take, including resale price maintenance, foreclosure, territorial exclusivity and quantity-dependent pricing.

15.2 Motives for vertical integration: enhancement of market power

A major debate in industrial organization concerns the implications of vertical integration for market power. In this section, we discuss a number of incentives for vertical integration that raise issues concerning possible uses and abuses of market power.

Double marginalization

One of the strongest arguments in favour of vertical integration derives from an analysis of the problem of **double marginalization** or double mark-up (Machlup and Taber, 1960; Spengler, 1950; Tirole, 1988). Consider an industry in which there are two vertical stages: an upstream production stage and a downstream retail stage. The problem of double marginalization arises when the production stage is under the monopoly control of a single producer, the retail stage is under the monopoly control of a single retailer, and both the producer and the retailer add their own mark-ups to the price. The outcome is that price is higher and output is lower than in the case where the two stages are vertically integrated with a single monopoly producer–retailer.

Although the problem of double marginalization arises only in the case where both the production and retail stages are monopolized, in theory it is possible for both of these stages to be either competitive or monopolized. In order to develop the analysis of double marginalization, it is useful to analyse the four possible combinations of competition and monopoly that could arise. These are illustrated in Figures 15.1 to 15.4.

In Figure 15.1, D_2 is the market demand function faced by the competitive retailers, and MC_1 is the marginal cost function of the competitive producers. The producers sell to the retailers at a price of P_1, equal to the producers' marginal cost, MC_1. Therefore $P_1 = MC_1 = MC_2$ becomes the retailers' marginal cost function. The retailers sell an output of Q_1 to consumers at a price of P_1, equal to the retailers' marginal cost; therefore the market price is P_1. Producer surplus (abnormal profit) is zero, and consumer surplus is P_1AB.

In Figure 15.2, D_2 and MC_1 represent the monopoly retailer's market demand function and the competitive producers' marginal cost function, as before. MR_2 represents the retailer's marginal revenue function. The producers are competitive, so they sell to the retailer at a price of P_1, equal to the producers' marginal cost, MC_1.

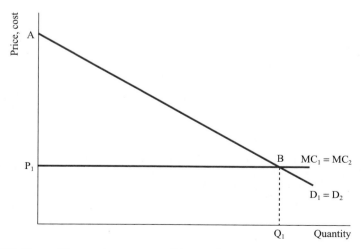

Figure 15.1 Competitive producers, competitive retailers

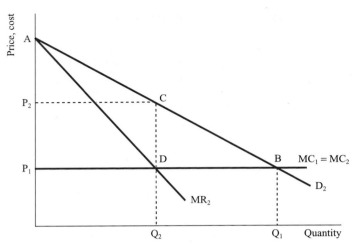

Figure 15.2 Competitive producers, monopoly retailer

As before $P_1 = MC_1 = MC_2$ is the retailer's marginal cost function. In this case, however, the monopoly retailer sets $MR_2 = MC_2$, and sells an output of Q_2 to consumers at a market price of P_2. The competitive producers earn zero abnormal profits, but the monopoly retailer earns an abnormal profit of P_1P_2CD. The combined producer surplus is P_1P_2CD, and consumer surplus is P_2AC. The usual deadweight loss associated with monopoly is DCB.

In Figure 15.3, the monopoly producer knows the price it sets will become the competitive retailers' marginal cost function. The retailers will trade at a price equal to their marginal cost, and will sell whatever quantity the market will bear at this price. Therefore D_2, the market demand function facing the retailers, is also the

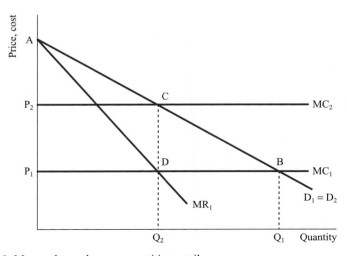

Figure 15.3 Monopoly producer, competitive retailers

producer's demand function, D_1. Accordingly, MR_1 is the producer's marginal revenue function. MC_1 is the producer's marginal cost function, as before. The producer sets $MR_1 = MC_1$, and sells an output of Q_2 at a price of P_2. P_2 becomes the competitive retailers' marginal cost function, MC_2, so they sell the output of Q_2 to consumers at a market price of P_2. The monopoly producer earns an abnormal profit of P_1P_2CD, but the competitive retailers earn zero abnormal profit. As before, the combined producer surplus is P_1P_2CD, and consumer surplus is P_2AC. The only difference between this case and the previous one is that in Figure 15.2 the abnormal profit of P_1P_2CD accrues to the monopoly retailer, while in Figure 15.3 the same abnormal profit accrues to the monopoly producer.

Finally, Figure 15.4 shows the case of double marginalization. The monopoly producer knows the price it sets will become the monopoly retailer's marginal cost function, and it also knows the retailer will sell a quantity such that the retailer's marginal revenue and marginal cost are equal. In other words, the quantity that is sold to consumers (also the quantity the producer can sell to the retailer) is located using the retailer's marginal revenue function MR_2. Effectively, MR_2 represents the producer's demand function, D_1. The producer maximizes profit by setting the marginal revenue associated with this demand function, MR_1, equal to the producer's marginal cost, MC_1 (as before). The producer sells an output of Q_3 at a price of P_2, which becomes the retailer's marginal cost function, MC_2. The retailer maximizes profit by setting the marginal revenue associated with the market demand function, MR_2, equal to MC_2. The retailer sells the output of Q_3 to consumers at a market price of P_3. The monopoly producer earns an abnormal profit of P_1P_2FG and the monopoly retailer earns an abnormal profit of P_2P_3EF. The combined producer surplus is P_1P_3EG, and consumer surplus is P_3AE. However, $P_1P_3EG < P_1P_2CD$, because P_1P_2CD is the maximum profit that can be earned from a market demand function of D_2 when the marginal cost function is MC_1. Moreover $P_3AE < P_2AC$, and the deadweight loss of GEB is larger in Figure 15.4 than the equivalent deadweight loss of DCB in Figures 15.2 and 15.3.

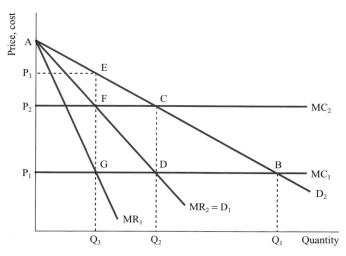

Figure 15.4 Monopoly producer, monopoly retailer

Figure 15.2 can be used again to illustrate the profit-maximizing price and output in the case where the producer and retailer are vertically integrated. In this case, MC_1 is the integrated producer–retailer's marginal cost function, and D_2 is its market demand function. The integrated firm sells an output of Q_2 to consumers at a market price of P_2. The integrated firm earns an abnormal profit (producer surplus) of P_1P_2CD, and consumer surplus is P_2AC. Both consumers and the integrated producer–retailer are better off than in the double marginalization case (Figure 15.4), and the deadweight loss is reduced from GEB (Figure 15.4) to DCB. In the double marginalization case, the problem facing the non-integrated producer is that the retailer's additional mark-up operates against the producer's interests, by reducing the output that is sold to a level below the producer's profit-maximizing output. However, there are some other possible solutions to this problem for the producer, short of full-scale vertical integration. One solution might be to impose a maximum resale price. Another might be to require the retailer to stock an output of Q_2; the alternative being that the retailer received no supplies at all. These practices are examined in further detail in Section 15.7.

Forward vertical integration

If a monopolist supplies input A to a competitive downstream industry which produces output X, by entering the downstream industry the monopolist could use its control over the supply of inputs to become the dominant firm. But is this worthwhile? The traditional answer is that the monopolist has no incentive to integrate forward if industry X is already competitive. The monopolist cannot produce X any more cheaply. However, if industry X is not competitive and efficient in production, cost savings could be achieved through vertical integration. For example, expenditure on marketing could be reduced, or lower stock levels could be maintained.

This argument, known as the Adelman–Spengler hypothesis (Adelman, 1949; Spengler, 1950), is based on an assumption of fixed factor proportions. Suppose, however, firms in industry X can vary the proportions used of the input A and a substitute input B that is produced under competitive conditions; in other words, suppose input substitution is possible. The supplier of A might have an incentive to integrate vertically with firms in industry X (Scherer and Ross, 1990; Vernon and Graham, 1971) for the following reasons. In Figure 15.5, the isoquant x_1 shows combinations of A and B that can be used to produce x_1 units of the output X. Prior to vertical integration, the isocost line is C_1C_1. The relatively steep slope of C_1C_1 reflects the ratio of the monopoly price charged for A and the competitive price (equal to the marginal cost) of B. The economically efficient (lowest-cost) method of producing x_1 is represented by point D. If input A were supplied at marginal cost, the isocost line passing through D would be C_2C_2. The shallower slope of C_2C_2 reflects the ratio of the marginal cost of A to the competitive price (marginal cost) of B. The abnormal profit of the monopoly supplier of A (measured in units of B) is represented by the vertical distance C_1C_2.

If the monopoly supplier of A integrates into industry X, however, the relevant cost per unit of A is not the monopoly price, but the marginal cost of producing A. With the new relative factor prices, it is no longer economically efficient to produce x_1 units of X at point D. Instead, in order to produce x_1, the vertically integrated firm

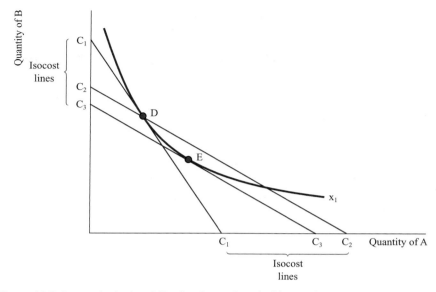

Figure 15.5 Input substitution following forward vertical integration

should switch to point E on the lower isocost line C_3C_3. By doing so, a further cost saving (again measured in units of B) of C_2C_3 is achieved. Furthermore, since the cost of producing X has fallen, it might be profitable to increase production of X to a higher level than x_1 (not shown in Figure 15.5). C_2C_3 is therefore a lower bound for the increase in the profit of the vertically integrated firm: if it is optimal to produce more than x_1, profit must increase by more than C_2C_3.

Backward vertical integration

Suppose an industry is monopolized by firm A. Effectively, firm A imposes a tax on the users of A's output in industry B, in the form of a monopoly price. As shown in Figure 15.6, industry B firms have an incentive to vertically integrate backward. Firm B5 is able to produce an alternative input (B_A), and does so if it considers firm A's

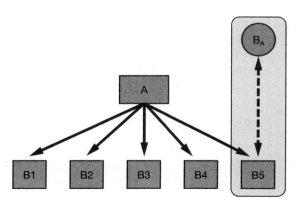

Figure 15.6 Backward vertical integration: case 1

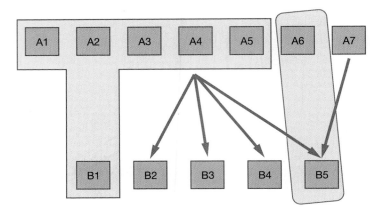

Figure 15.7 Backward vertical integration: case 2

price to be excessive. The incentive only exists if firm B5 can replace A's activity at a cost lower than the price charged by A. If a monopolist feels some of its customers are actively pursuing a policy of backward vertical integration in order to avoid the tax, it may be willing to accommodate them with special price concessions, in order to avoid losing their custom.

A mid-1980s example involving forward vertical integration was News International's reluctance to use the UK's railway network to distribute its newspapers to wholesalers. News International instead used its own subsidiary TNT, a road haulage company (Monopolies and Mergers Commission, 1993). Oi and Hunter (1965) analyse the conditions under which firms might develop their own private distribution channels, rather than rely on contracting carriers through the market.

Another case in which a firm might consider backward vertical integration is illustrated in Figure 15.7. Firm B1, one of a number of firms in downstream industry B, has been seeking to secure control over an essential input produced by upstream industry A, by vertically integrating backward and acquiring firms A1 to A5. In order to prevent B1 from gaining monopoly control over the A-industry, firm B5 vertically integrates backward by acquiring firm A6. In the long run, rival suppliers such as A7 might enter in order to challenge the emerging monopoly, but in the short run it would be extremely damaging for B5 to allow A6 to go the same way as A1 to A5 and fall into B1's ownership. B5's non-integrated competitors B2, B3 and B4 are already weakened, because they have no alternative other than to buy from the A-firms that have been acquired by B1. Colangelo (1995, 1997) discusses a variation on a similar theme, in which vertical integration, either forward or backward, is used as a strategy for avoiding being taken over in a horizontal merger.

Price discrimination

Vertical integration could provide a means for implementing a policy of price discrimination, which might otherwise be ineffective or ruled unlawful by the competition authorities. As we have seen in Section 10.3, three conditions are required for successful price discrimination. First, the supplier must exercise monopoly control over the market. Second, the price elasticities of demand must be different for different classes of buyer. Third, the supplier must ensure that no resale or seepage occurs: customers who can buy at the lower price cannot resell to customers who are charged the higher price.

The Alcoa case in the US (Perry, 1980; Stuckey, 1983) involved a monopoly supplier of aluminium, which sold to both the aircraft industry and the kitchen utensils industry (pots and pans). Many substitute materials can be used to produce pots and pans, so the price elasticity of demand is high and the price discriminating supplier sets a low price. In the aircraft industry there are few substitutes for aluminium, so the elasticity is low and the price is high. This suggests kitchen utensils producers have an incentive to resell surplus aluminium ingots to the aircraft industry. By forward vertical integration into the kitchen-utensils industry the aluminium supplier can prevent seepage, and can perhaps more easily conceal the policy of price discrimination.

15.3 Motives for vertical integration: cost savings

Williamson (1971, 1975, 1989, 2002a) argues that vertical integration may enable the integrated firm to reduce transaction costs. '[T]he firm is not a simple efficiency instrument . . . but possesses coordinating potential that sometimes transcends that of the market' (Williamson, 1971, p. 112). As we have seen in Section 3.6, Williamson's transaction costs paradigm is based on Coase's (1937) seminal article on the nature of the firm. Coase raises the fundamental question as to why firms exist within a market economy. Coase argues that there are costs associated with the use of the price mechanism to allocate resources and coordinate economic activity. Within a firm, coordination is achieved through management direction and not through the price mechanism. The supersession of the price mechanism is the defining characteristic of the firm.

In cases where the market fails to work well, and a particular transaction proves costly to execute through the market, there may be a cost saving if the firm internalizes that transaction. In other words, the market fails in the case of any transaction involving costs that could be reduced by substituting internal organization for external market exchange. Accordingly, whenever there is a large differential between the costs of external (market) coordination and internal organization for transactions involving producers at successive stages of a production process, there is an incentive for vertical integration. Many of the cost-savings explanations for vertical integration can be located within the transaction costs framework.

Technological conditions

A familiar argument for vertical integration is that technical conditions may dictate that production should be integrated under one coordinating unit. In the steel industry, for example, blast furnaces that produce steel and the strip mills that shape and cut steel are not only controlled by the same firm, but are also located within the same plant so as to conserve heat. In general, where there are closely related or technologically complementary production processes, a vertically integrated firm may be able to achieve better planning and coordination, longer production runs and better use of capacity. In many cases, however, this justification for vertical integration does not lead to vertical merger, because if such obvious technological advantages exist, it is likely that integrated plants have been built from the outset. One might even argue that the two successive stages of production have really evolved into one stage. However, technological change may create new opportunities for integration. Pickering (1974, p. 57) quotes the case of ICI in the synthetic fibres industry. In the early 1970s, when the bulking process had become more closely associated with a new texturizing process, ICI integrated vertically so as to achieve better coordination between these previously separate processes.

However, Williamson (1989) argues the technical economies realized through common ownership of technologically adjacent production processes are often exaggerated. The fundamental reason why closely related technical processes are integrated is that the alternative of achieving coordination using market mechanisms is too expensive. For example, the costs of drawing up and monitoring a contract between an owner of a blast furnace and an owner of steel mill would be prohibitively high. Any attempted contract would probably be incomplete, because the codification of the obligations and responsibilities of both parties under all circumstances that could conceivably arise, is impossible.

Uncertainty

Uncertainty creates a number of problems affecting firms' efforts to organize production. Coordination requires foresight concerning many possible events, some of which can be predicted while others cannot. As we have seen in Section 3.5, Simon (1959) coins the term 'bounded rationality' to describe the limited ability of economic agents to absorb and process the information needed to make optimal decisions. The firm's performance depends on how well its managers react and adapt to unanticipated events. Helfat and Teece (1987) discuss two types of uncertainty. Primary uncertainty arises from factors external to the firm, such as technological change, change in consumer demand, and change in government policy. Secondary uncertainty arises from a lack of information available to the firm's decision makers. Vertically adjacent firms may fail to disclose information to each other; or even worse, may distort information in an attempt to gain an unfair advantage.

A vertically integrated firm may also be able to take advantage of opportunities to conceal information. When a vertically integrated firm produces goods for its own consumption, it avoids making publicly observable market transactions. In certain cases this can create uncertainty in the minds of rivals. According to Choi (1998), many Japanese software companies develop most of their products for specific customers; these products are rarely or never sold on the open market. This strategy, which is in marked contrast to common practice in the US, makes it difficult to assess whether or not customers are receiving a good deal in terms of price or quality.

Transactions between firms at different stages of production are subject to many forms of uncertainty. For example, raw material supplies might be affected by political instability or climatic variation, which may interfere with the smooth flow of inputs. Carlton (1979) notes that most market prices do not adjust automatically to ensure a balance between supply and demand. The firm never knows the exact demand for its product in the short term. The adjustment of production in response to fluctuations in demand is never instantaneous; decisions often have to be taken in the absence of any clear price signal; and the firm is continually at risk of over- or underproducing. However, some of these uncertainties can be reduced through vertical integration. An integrated firm might obtain information about changing supply and demand conditions earlier than a non-integrated firm (Arrow, 1975).

Another possible cause of uncertainty is the quality of the inputs. Without directly observing a supplier's production process, a firm is faced with the risk that it may be in receipt of substandard inputs. The desire to monitor the production of inputs may provide an incentive for vertical integration. For example, Hennessy (1997) finds that in the food industry, the cost of determining quality is a significant transaction cost involved in the marketing of intermediate goods.

Uncertainty need not always lead to vertical integration. In an industry charac- terized by rapid technological change, a firm might be able to manage risk and uncertainty most effectively by buying in its inputs, rather than producing them itself. Jacobson and Andréosso-O'Callaghan (1996) cite the case of major software firms such as Microsoft and Lotus, which did not publish their own users' manuals, preferring instead to use specialist firms which bore the uncertainty over the demand for manuals. In the event, the market did eventually decline, as online help functions largely superseded the printed manual.

Carlton (1979) suggests an optimal partial integration strategy might involve integrating to meet high-probability demand, while leaving low-probability demand to specialist producers. Emons (1996) considers the case of a downstream firm whose demand for inputs varies randomly. The downstream firm can either integrate vertic- ally so as to produce its own inputs, or buy them through the market. If the vertically integrated firm invests in the capacity required to meet demand in good times, it incurs additional costs because it has spare capacity in bad times. However, when the downstream firm produces its own inputs, the market demand for inputs falls, leading to a reduction in input prices. This price effect may outweigh the costs of maintaining spare capacity.

Assured supply

Monteverde and Teece (1982) find the higher the level of investment undertaken by engineering firms in the production of components, the greater the tendency towards vertical integration. Buyers of technologically complex and strategically important inputs can find themselves at the mercy of suppliers, and backward integration is an obvious strategy for downstream producers to ensure supplies. Similarly, Acemoglu *et al.* (2003) find when producers are more technology- intensive than their suppliers, it is more likely the producer will integrate backward than when the opposite is the case. The implication is that interruptions to the supply of inputs could threaten the producer's investment. If this is a frequent or serious problem, the producer may consider backward integration in order to secure its own supply of inputs. However, it is important to identify the ultimate cause of the supply shortage. In industries where this may be due to factors beyond the supplier's control, such as political instability or variations in climate, backward integration does not protect the downstream producer.

Adelman (1955) and Langlois and Robertson (1989) suggest vertical integration may be linked to the industry life cycle (see also Section 7.2). In the introduction and growth stages, producers may integrate backward in order to develop their own specific components, and integrate forward in order to ensure efficient promotion, marketing and after-sales service. As growth continues and the industry approaches the maturity stage, specialist supply industries and independent distribution channels evolve, allowing producers to divest themselves of upstream and downstream activities. Eventually, during the maturity and decline stages, the extent of vertical integration may increase, as incumbent firms attempt to compensate for stagnant or declining consumer demand by increasing their market power.

Case study 15.1

Big media lack creativity

Thomas Edison, founder of General Electric, invented a process by which you could record sounds and play them back, over and over again. The modern media business was born. And now, after dabbling successfully in aero engines, medical equipment and financial services, GE is returning to these roots. Through Universal Studios, Jeff Immelt and his colleagues are now promoters of Eminem and producers of *Seabiscuit*.

The prospect of media industries inevitably being dominated by large international conglomerates has long excited investment bankers and depressed creative people. But, more recently, it has seemed to be yesterday's idea rather than today's. Time Warner, whose appetite for acquisitions was always greater than its capacity to finance or absorb them, made a deal too far and gave away half the company in exchange for AOL. AOL has now cheekily announced that its brand is tarnished by association with the struggling AOL Time Warner. And two European adventures in America have come to grief. Thomas Middelhoff was fired from Bertelsmann, Jean-Marie Messier from Vivendi Universal, and the empires they built are being dismantled. Although other media giants are in better shape, their experience does not offer strong support for the inevitable consolidation of the industry. News Corporation and Viacom are the creations of business geniuses with an exceptional eye for undervalued assets and the evolution of their industries. But with Rupert Murdoch aged 72 and Sumner Redstone 80, the direction of these businesses is bound to change. Michael Eisner's vision for Disney is that you make money for Disney's shareholders – and chief executive – by exploiting the existing repertoire far more exhaustively than anyone had imagined possible.

The argument for vertical integration is that delivery needs content and vice versa. This is why the AOL Time Warner deal was, briefly, thought to be a marriage made in heaven. Content does need delivery – but it does not need to own it; the FT needs the newspaper delivery boy's bicycle but does not need to buy it. The notion that Disney required the ABC network for distribution was ludicrous. And there are good arguments for keeping these businesses apart. The newspaper round will be more efficient if one bicycle carries several titles – and there will never be much rapport between a rap artist and a telephone company.

Perhaps horizontal integration is required by technological convergence, as new media blur boundaries between print, film and music. But assembling disparate groups of people with past success in established production and distribution systems is not necessarily the best way to exploit these opportunities. Music publishers have been more concerned to defend their existing businesses against the internet than to exploit it. New thinking comes most often from new companies.

Some people emphasize the opportunities for cross-selling in a multi-media business. Warner Bros can use AOL to promote Harry Potter films on the internet. But you do not need common ownership for this. The originator of the Potter phenomenon is Bloomsbury, the independent book publisher, and subsidiary rights are licensed to many different companies. Books with television tie-ins are today's fashion but it is only fortuitous if the network and the publisher are part of the same corporation.

Media conglomerates are the product of the ambitions of those who run them rather than the imperatives of the market. Media businesses depend on talented, often difficult, individuals and their well founded suspicion of multinationals is an obstacle to the success of such businesses. The low-risk, bureaucratic way to run a media company is to focus on products similar to those that have already succeeded. And you need only look at television, music and films today to see that this is exactly what happens. Current bestsellers, for instance, tend to be diet guides, courtroom thrillers and sporting biographies. I counted three genuinely original works among them: *The Life of Pi*; *The No. 1 Ladies' Detective Agency*; and *Schott's Miscellany*. Each was brought to market by a small, independent, specialist publisher.

Source: John Kay, Big media lack creativity, *Financial Times*, 10 September 2003. © The Financial Times Limited. Reprinted with permission.

Externalities

Externalities can be created when property rights are poorly defined. Suppose firm A discovers a new process that only firm B can develop and produce. A asks B to keep the idea a secret from A's rivals, and to sell the finished product only to A. However, once A has passed the necessary information to B, there may be no incentive for B to comply with A's original request, in which case A fails to benefit from its own discovery. In this case, A has a clear incentive to integrate with B, in order to protect its property rights in the discovery. In the US in the 1920s, the development and profitability of the automobile and petrol industries were retarded by the slow pace of innovation of petrol retailing: petrol was still sold in canisters by small cornershops. To speed up the development of retailing, petroleum producers integrated forward. The producers did not wish to invest in petrol stations *and* allow them to stay independent, because the new stations could have sold other firms' petrol. Similar examples can be found in the UK brewing, tailoring and airlines industries. Some producers argue forward integration into distribution is necessary in order to protect their investments. The final, retail stage may be too important to be left in the hands of inexperienced or inefficient independent retailers.

Complexity

When two successive stages of a production process are linked by potentially complex legal relations, it may be efficient to integrate vertically. To guarantee a more certain supply of inputs or distribution outlets, a producer may attempt to negotiate long-term contracts with its suppliers or distributors. However, if the product is nonstandard, perhaps due to frequent changes in design or technology, it may be difficult to specify an exhaustive contract capable of forseeing all possible circumstances or pre-empting all possible ambiguities that could subsequently result in expensive litigation. An alternative approach might be to negotiate only a short-term contract. However, where a long-term investment is involved, the producer might feel it requires long-term guarantees. In such cases, neither long-term nor short-term contracts are effective, and vertical integration may provide a better solution.

The production and retailing stages of the movie industry provide an example of the issue of complexity. Each movie is unique, and distribution patterns for one movie never quite coincide with those of another: issues such as pairing, regional exposure, repeat showings, television sales and degree of promotional effort determine a unique distribution strategy for every movie. This implies complex contractual relations between producers, distributors and exhibitors. Contractual agreements would also have to be monitored by a sophisticated and costly inspectorate. It may be simpler for producers to integrate forward with distributors and cinema chains, or for the latter to integrate backward.

Gil (2004) examines vertical relationships between distributors and exhibitors in the movie industry. Since contracts are inherently uncertain and subject to externalities, they are incomplete, especially as regards the length of time for which movies will be screened. It is particularly difficult to write contracts specifying the degree and effectiveness of the promotional activities supplied by the distributor and exhibitor. The distributor is generally responsible for national, regional and local promotion, while the exhibitor concentrates on point-of-sale promotion and pricing policy. The exhibitor also decides which movie to show on which screen in the cinema. Decisions taken by the exhibitor affect ancillary markets supplied by the distributor, such as the DVD and video purchase and rental markets. In addition, the exhibitor may have other sources of revenue dependent on the screening of specific movies, such as concessionary sales and on-screen advertisements. Consequently the incentives of both parties may be misaligned. In the case of the Spanish movie industry, Gil finds movies shown by vertically integrated distributor–exhibitors are screened for up to two weeks longer than movies screened by independent exhibitors. Movies of uncertain quality are more likely to be distributed by integrated firms.

Moral hazard

In general, a moral hazard problem arises when an agent lacks the incentive to work in the best interests of the principal, and the principal cannot monitor the actions of the agent. Moral hazard issues can affect contracts between firms at a different stages of a production process. Suppose a buyer of inputs arranges a contract under conditions of uncertainty. It is possible for the input supplier to bear the risk, but this requires a risk premium to be added to the supply price. The buyer might regard this premium as excessive, and might decide to bear the risk itself by offering terms under which the buyer reimburses the supplier for all costs incurred, and adds a mark-up for profit. Many government contracts are structured in this manner. However, contracts of this kind provide no incentive for the supplier to control its own costs. The buyer might insist on monitoring the supplier's work, but if monitoring proves too difficult or costly, vertical integration may be a better alternative.

Asset specificity

Asset specificity occurs when two firms are dependent on each other, as a result of investments in specific physical capital, human capital, sites or brands. The specialized nature of the asset creates a situation of bilateral monopoly, in which only one firm buys and one firm sells the specialized asset or resource. Figures 15.8 and 15.9 show a microeconomic analysis of bilateral monopoly. In Figure 15.8, it is assumed there is one (monopoly) upstream seller and many downstream buyers of the specialized asset. This case corresponds to a standard model of monopoly. The upstream seller maximizes profit by producing at the point where marginal revenue *equals* marginal cost. Using the buyers' demand function to identify the corresponding price, the seller's profit-maximizing price and output combination is (P_1, Q_1).

In Figure 15.9 it is assumed there are many upstream sellers and one (monopsony) downstream buyer of the specialized asset. The construction is as follows.

- The downstream buyer's demand function (the same as the buyers' collective demand function in Figure 15.8) is interpreted as the downstream buyer's marginal revenue product function: the maximum amount the buyer is prepared to pay for each additional unit of the asset is the extra revenue it obtains by using the marginal unit of the asset to produce and sell more of its own product.

- The upstream sellers' collective supply function corresponds to the monopolist's marginal cost function in Figure 15.8.

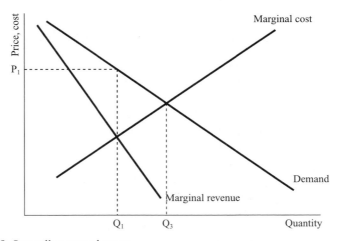

Figure 15.8 One seller, many buyers

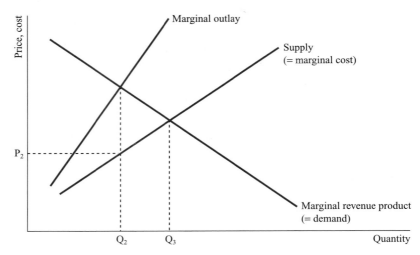

Figure 15.9 Many sellers, one buyer

■ The downstream buyer's marginal outlay function is the marginal function corresponding to the upstream sellers' supply function. The marginal outlay function lies above the supply function. For each additional unit of the specialized asset the buyer wishes to purchase, in order to induce more supply the buyer has to offer a slightly higher price, not only for the marginal unit but also for all the other units (up to the marginal unit) to which the buyer is already committed.

In Figure 15.9 the downstream buyer should buy the quantity of the specialized asset at which marginal revenue product *equals* marginal outlay. Using the sellers' supply function to identify the corresponding price, the buyer's profit-maximizing price and output combination is (P_2, Q_2). P_2 in Figure 15.9 is certainly lower than P_1 in Figure 15.8: a monopsony buyer is able to impose a low price on a group of atomistic sellers, and a monopoly seller is able to extract a high price from a group of atomistic buyers. Depending on the relative slopes of the revenue and cost functions, Q_2 might be higher or lower than Q_1.

Combining the analyses in Figures 15.8 and 15.9, there is no determinate solution to the bilateral monopoly case, in which a single seller confronts a single buyer. The equilibrium price could fall anywhere between P_1 and P_2, depending on relative negotiating or bargaining strengths of the monopoly seller and monopsony buyer of the specialized asset. It would be in the joint interest of both parties to agree to exchange the quantity Q_3, at which the downstream buyer's marginal revenue product *equals* the upstream seller's marginal cost. Collusion between the two parties might permit this outcome to be achieved (Machlup and Taber, 1960). However, the usual difficulties of negotiating, monitoring and enforcing an agreement can be avoided if the two firms integrate vertically.

Using transaction costs terminology, the difficulties of the situation can be illustrated with reference to the following example. Suppose a shipper of antique furniture is the only firm that requires specialized padded wagons for long-distance rail transport; and in view of the low level of demand, only one firm produces such wagons.

The producer and the shipper are locked in by the specific nature of the asset. Both can behave opportunistically, in an attempt to extract more favourable terms. The seller may demand a higher price, threatening a refusal to supply, knowing the buyer has no alternative source of supply. Equally, the buyer may demand a lower price, threatening to refuse to buy, knowing the supplier has no alternative market. 'Because non-redeployable specific assets make it costly to switch to a new relationship, the market safeguard against opportunism is no longer effective' (John and Weitz, 1988, p. 340). Consequently, the market transaction is characterized by expensive haggling and high contractual costs, which may propel the firms to integrate vertically.

Williamson (1983) identifies four types of asset specificity.

- *Site specificity*. By having plants located close to one another, there is a saving on transportation, processing and inventory costs. The assets cannot be moved to other locations without increasing costs.

- *Physical asset specificity*. Plant and machinery that is designed with a limited end use, either for use by one buyer or with one input, is specific to one market transaction. Such investments offer little or no return in alternative uses.

- *Human asset specificity*. Human capital, in the form of specialized knowledge and experience that has been developed by a firm's managers or workers, may be essential for one supplier but irrelevant and therefore worthless elsewhere.

- *Dedicated assets*. A firm may be forced to make large-scale investments in dedicated assets in order to meet the needs of one large buyer. If the buyer decides to go elsewhere, the firm is left with excess capacity.

The Fisher Body case provides an early example of asset specificity (Klein *et al.*, 1978; Klein, 2000). In 1919, Fisher Body and General Motors (GM) signed a 10-year contract stipulating that Fisher Body would be the sole supplier of car body parts to GM, on condition that Fisher would invest in specialized machinery and processes. However, the length of the contract, together with the cost plus pricing formula agreed by GM, appears to have given Fisher the chance to behave opportunistically. In the mid-1920s, GM's demand for Fisher's bodies grew unexpectedly. Fisher refused to invest in more machinery and labour training, and refused to locate closer to the GM plant at Flint, Michigan. GM eventually solved the problem through backward vertical integration.

Using data from ten large computer manufacturers between 1950 and 1970, Krickx (1995) tests the hypothesis that vertical integration is more likely when asset specificity is high, by analysing three major components: receiving tubes, transistors and integrated circuits. As the specificity of the components increased, so did the tendency towards vertical integration. By the late 1960s, the top six computer producers had all vertically integrated backward into the integrated circuit industry. John and Weitz (1988) base a measure of specificity on the amount of staff training and experience required to sell a product. There is a positive relationship between the degree of specificity and the degree of vertical integration. For other asset specificity examples, referring to the automobile components, aerospace parts, electronic components, aluminium industry and coal-burning plants industries, see Joskow (1985, 1987), Masten (1984), Monteverde and Teece (1982) and Stuckey (1983).

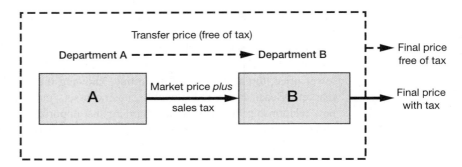

Figure 15.10 Vertical integration to avoid a sales tax

Avoidance of tax or price controls

Vertical integration between downstream and upstream firms, either within or across national boundaries, can be a means of avoiding tax or price controls. A market transaction that is subject to a sales tax or price control can be replaced by an internal transaction, escaping the liability or restriction. For example, if A is liable to pay a sales tax, from which B (the next stage of production) is exempt, there is a clear incentive for A to integrate vertically with B in order to escape the tax (see Figure 15.10). Alternatively, vertical integration might enable firms to avoid minimum or maximum price controls inposed by governments or regulators.

Of course, the authorities are aware of these possibilities, and may attempt to tax or regulate upstream firms as well. Scherer (1980, p. 305) shows that in the US and Europe, integrated petroleum firms reported low pre-tax profits at the refining and marketing stages of production, but much higher profits at the crude oil extraction stage, which was subject to a lower rate of tax on profits. Within the EU, there is wide variation in national rates of corporate taxation, providing an incentive for firms to locate their subsidiaries in low-tax countries (Jacobson and Andréosso-O'Callaghan, 1996).

15.4 | Vertical integration: some empirical evidence

In this section, we outline a number of ways in which vertical integration can be measured, and we review some empirical studies of vertical integration.

Measurement of vertical integration

Number of stages of production

The first method used to measure the extent of vertical integration is a simple count of the number of stages of production a firm is involved in. The more stages, the greater the degree of vertical integration. However, a major difficulty is to decide what constitutes a stage of production. How should the boundaries between different stages be defined? This measure does not lend itself to comparisons between different industries. In one industry, complete vertical integration might involve only a few stages, while in another industry it might involve many more.

Value added-to-sales ratio

Adelman (1955) recommends a measure of vertical integration based on the ratio of value added-to-sales. This ratio reflects the degree of self-sufficiency: the less self-sufficient a firm is, the smaller the ratio. As an illustration, suppose upstream firm A supplies an input to downstream firm B.

Firm A		Firm B	
Purchases	50	Purchases from A	100
Value added	50	Value added	50
Sales to B	100	Sales	150
Value added-to-sales ratio	0.5	Value added-to-sales ratio	0.33

Now suppose firms A and B vertically integrate.

Firm A/B	
Purchases	50
Value added	100
Sales	150
Value added-to-sales ratio	0.66

The vertically integrated firm A/B has a higher value added-to-sales ratio than either firm A or firm B individually. In general, a perfectly integrated firm would have a value added-to-sales ratio of one. In other words, value added corresponds exactly to final sales. There are several difficulties associated with this measure.

■ Value added represents factor payments such as wages, interest and rents. If the price of any of these factors changes, the value of purchases also changes, affecting the calculation of the value added-to-sales ratio. Therefore this ratio can change for reasons unrelated to the degree of vertical integration.

■ Technological change affects the firm's usage of factors of production. Again, this affects the value of purchases, and the value added-to-sales ratio.

■ Similarly, if the market structure evolves from competition to oligopoly or monopoly, price may increase as the firm starts to exercise its enhanced market power, affecting the value of sales. Again, the value added-to-sales ratio is affected by factors unrelated to the degree of vertical integration.

■ Figure 15.11 illustrates the problem of directional bias. Each of three vertically related firms has a value added of 40. The upstream firm A makes no purchases and is totally self-sufficient. Firm B is considering a vertical integration strategy. B's original value added-to-sales ratio is 40/80 = 0.5. If B vertically integrates backward with A, firm A/B's value added-to-sales ratio is 80/80 = 1. But if B vertically integrates forward with C, firm B/C's value added-to-sales ratio is 80/120 = 0.67. An upstream merger increases the ratio by more than a downstream merger. The value added-to-sales ratio is subject to directional bias: its value is (positively) influenced by the nearness of integration to primary production.

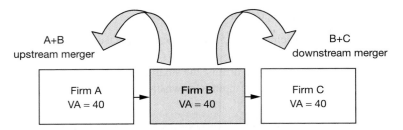

Figure 15.11 Directional bias of value added-to-sales ratio

Employment in auxiliary activities

Gort (1962) suggests that vertical integration can be measured by a ratio of employment in a firm's auxiliary activities to its total employment. The greater the ratio, the greater the degree of vertical integration. Across a sample of industries, Gort reports that this ratio varied between 9.7 per cent for transportation to 67.3 per cent for the petroleum industry. However, the definition of primary and auxiliary activities is to some extent arbitrary.

Internal (within-firm) and external (market) coordination

According to Davies and Morris (1995), a good measure of vertical integration should be based on the theory of the firm; it should avoid subjective assessments and be based on objective census data; and it should be sufficiently general to be applied at firm level and at industry level, so that firm-level measures can be aggregated to obtain the corresponding industry-level measure. They suggest a measure based on the transaction costs paradigm, recognizing that vertical integration involves substituting internal (within-firm) coordination for external (market) coordination. Since data on within-firm transactions are difficult to obtain, Davies and Morris impute such flows indirectly from input–output tables and inter-industry comparisons of firms' market share data.

Empirical evidence on vertical integration

The topic of vertical integration has been extensively dealt with in the theoretical industrial organization literature. In contrast, the empirical literature on the motives for vertical integration, and the impact of vertical integration on performance, is surprisingly sparse. This may be due partly to the difficulties involved in measuring vertical integration accurately, as discussed above. Below, we review a selection of empirical studies that tackle issues associated with vertical integration.

Spiller (1985) evaluates two competing hypotheses as to the motives for vertical integration. The first is a neoclassical hypothesis that vertical integration increases profit by permitting savings in average costs, risk reduction, tax evasion or the imposition of price controls. The second is a transaction costs hypothesis, which emphasizes the benefits of integration arising from asset specificity. The study is based on 29 vertical mergers that took place in the US during the 1970s and early 1980s. Asset specificity is inferred from the locations of vertically related plants, and the extent of correlation between firm-specific shocks. The gains from the mergers are inferred from share price data. The findings generally seem to favour the asset specificity hypothesis.

John and Weitz (1988) develop a transaction costs analysis of forward vertical integration. The study identifies direct and indirect distribution channels used by producers. The use of direct channels implies vertical integration, while indirect channels comprise a variety of institutional structures. It is suggested four particular factors may increase the use of direct channels: asset specificity, environmental uncertainty, behavioural uncertainty and the availability of savings in average costs. Asset specificity is discussed in Section 15.3; environmental uncertainty refers to unforeseen fluctuations in supply and demand in the markets for the firm's inputs and outputs; behavioural uncertainty refers to opportunistic behaviour on the part of one of the contracting parties in a vertical relationship; and the cost savings argument is based on the notion that integration is more likely if there is potential for savings through economies of scale or scope.

Much of the data for the empirical analysis is obtained from interviews with managers. The dependent variable is the firm's use of direct channels, measured as a percentage of sales that are direct to end-users. Among the independent variables, the degree of asset specificity is inferred from the time spent training newly hired but experienced sales staff. Environmental uncertainty is measured from responses to questions concerning the ability to predict sales. Behavioural uncertainty is represented by the time-lag between the initial contact with a buyer and the eventual order; the assumption being that where time-lags are short, there is less scope for opportunistic behaviour. Two scale variables are included: the value of sales and the spatial density of customers. If spatial density is low, sales staff spend much of their time travelling, and are unlikely to be cost effective.

The estimated model explains 28 per cent of the variation in sales through direct channels. The coefficients on the independent variables measuring asset specificity, environmental uncertainty and behavioural uncertainty are all significant. The coefficient on the scale effect measured by sales is insignificant, but when the spatial density measure is used, a significant coefficient is obtained. Overall the results tend to support the transaction costs hypothesis.

D'Aveni and Ravenscraft (1994) examine the effects of vertical integration on costs. First, vertical integration can reduce costs by reducing the number of market transactions, integrating administrative functions and allowing better access to information on upstream or downstream operations. Second, vertical integration can increase costs, through managerial diseconomies of scale (the difficulties in managing a larger organization), or an absence of competitive pressure allowing the managers to get away with technical or x-inefficiencies. The results suggest vertical integration does produce some cost savings, through lower overhead, marketing and innovation costs. However, these cost savings are often offset by technical inefficiencies resulting from reduced competitive pressure.

Using a historical rather than an empirical approach, Krickx (1995) applies transaction costs methodology to the computer mainframe industry by observing changes in vertical governance patterns over a 20-year period. The institutional analysis focuses on 10 firms, and three separate governance patterns are identified: vertically integrated, intermediate exchange and market exchange. Vertical integration appears to be consistent with both transaction costs and production cost arguments. Factors such as technology, appropriability (determined by the ease with which a new technology can be copied) and industry maturity also played an important role in determining the degree of vertical integration.

Gertner and Stillman (2001) examine vertical relationships, and the ability of firms to respond to sudden changes in their competitive environment. The response of integrated and non-integrated clothing firms to the internet is examined. In general, vertically integrated firms offered online services earlier than their non-integrated counterparts, and offered a wider product range. Kwoka (2002) examines the economies of vertical integration in the electricity generating industry in the US; Nemoto and Goto (2002) explore similar issues for Japan. Vertical integration between the power generation, transmission and distribution stages is a common feature of the electricity industry. The US industry is characterized by large vertically integrated utililies, operating alongside non-integrated generators, transmission and distribution firms. Kwoka finds the large vertically integrated utilities benefit from economies of scale in distribution, through the packaging and selling of power and the billing and servicing of accounts. Enforced deintegration would result in the loss of these vertical economies.

15.5 Agency and vertical relationships

In Sections 15.2 and 15.3, we examined reasons why a strategy of vertical integration might be attractive to some firms. However, vertical integration is only one of a number of possible vertical structures. In this section, we examine some alternative vertical relationships, which fall within the general category of principal–agent relationships. For example, a producer (acting as the principal) contracts a supplying firm (the agent) to produce its inputs. The fundamental reason for developing contractually specific vertical ties is harmonization of production, processing and distribution activities. But why should firms choose this approach, rather than rely on the advantages of vertical integration? In general there are two reasons: first, to maintain some degree of independence; and second, to avoid costs that may be associated with full-scale backward or forward vertical integration. Firms that value their independence or wish to operate only in familiar stages of production may develop vertical relationships short of full-scale integration (Aust, 1997; Gal-Or, 1991, 1999; Harrigan, 1983). Vertical separation, as opposed to vertical integration, might allow the development of sufficiently friendly relations among the principals to facilitate effective collusion (Bonanno and Vickers, 1988). Below we examine two common forms of vertical relationship: **franchise agreements** and **networks**.

Franchise agreements

Franchising refers to a vertical relationship between two independent firms: a franchisor and a franchisee (OECD, 1993b). The franchisor sells a proven product, process or brand to a franchisee on a contractual basis, in return for set-up fees, licence fees, royalties or other payments. The contract typically covers issues such as the prices to be charged, services offered, location and marketing effort. One of the commonest models of **franchise agreement** involves retail franchising, in which a producer develops a vertical relationship with a retailer.

Several types of franchise agreement can be identified.

■ The *business format franchise* covers not only the sale of a product or brand, but also the entire business format, comprising a marketing strategy, staff training, manuals, quality control processes, store layout and close communications between the franchisor and franchisee. Kentucky Fried Chicken, Dynorod and Prontoprint operate franchises of this type.

■ The *product* or *trademark franchise* allows greater independence to the franchisee and gives the franchisor less control. For example, a relationship between a car manufacturer and a car dealer may allow the dealer a large degree of independence. Car dealers supplying identical brands can differentiate their service; in contrast, Kentucky Fried Chicken outlets are characterized by their homogeneity.

■ The *producer-to-wholesaler franchise*, such as Coca-Cola, and the *wholesaler-to-retailer franchise*, such as the grocery chains Spar and Mace, complete the list. In the case of the former, the wholesalers of Coca-Cola are independent bottlers who hold perpetual Coca-Cola franchises with exclusive territories. In the latter case, a wholesaler, such as BWG group in Ireland, owns the franchise to supply independent chain stores trading under brand names such as Spar and Mace.

It is natural to ask why the relationship between the franchisor and franchisee is subject to contractual control. The fundamental reason is that decisions taken by one party concerning price, quality, service offered, quality of factor inputs employed and so on, affect the profit and performance of the other party. Furthermore, the decisions of one franchisee may well impact on rival franchisees. While individual decisions may maximize the profit of one of the parties, externalities may reduce aggregate profits for the entire vertical operation. Accordingly, contractual control is necessary in order to reduce or eliminate the effects of negative externalities. 'The crucial economic fact that underlies franchising contracts is that the incentives of the transacting parties do not always coincide' (Klein, 1995, p. 12).

Klein (1995) identifies four potential sources of conflict.

■ When franchisees jointly use a common brand, a free-rider problem arises. Each franchisee has an incentive to reduce the quality of the product in order to save costs, but the consequences of any such action are borne by all franchisees. The probable future reduction in customer demand is spread across the entire market, and does not fall directly on the free-rider.

■ If an initial pre-sales service is required in order to persuade customers to buy the product, free-riding franchisees might be able to avoid providing such a service by relying on other firms to do so. For example, online car dealers might be able to charge a lower price by selling cars over the internet, avoiding the costs of providing showrooms, test drives and sales staff to answer queries. Customers might first obtain these services from franchised outlets, and then purchase more cheaply from the free-riding online supplier.

- A franchisee may have some degree of market power in the setting of a price for the final product, perhaps because the franchisor has granted exclusive distribution rights. In this case, a situation of double marginalization may arise (see Section 15.2). The higher price charged by the franchisee might not necessarily be in the franchisor's best interests.

- If the price at which the franchisor sells the product to the franchisee exceeds the franchisor's marginal cost, there is an incentive for the franchisor to increase its output, requiring the franchisee to increase the supply of its complementary input (for example, marketing or other promotional effort). However, the amount of the complementary input a franchisee may wish to supply is not dependent on the franchisor's profit-maximizing output level. For example, suppose a franchisor sells its product at a wholesale price of £4.50, and the franchisee sells to consumers at a retail price of £5. The £0.50 mark-up covers the average distribution cost and the franchisee's normal profit. Suppose a particular buyer has a reservation price of £4, but if the buyer is exposed to marketing services costing £3, the reservation price would increase to £5. Clearly, the franchisee cannot afford to spend £3 in order to secure this sale. However, if the franchisor's marginal cost is below £1.50, it would benefit the franchisor to spend £3 in order to attract a sale worth £5. If the producer were vertically integrated with the distributor, the additional marketing service would be funded. Under a franchise agreement, the franchisor would need to subsidize the franchisee's marketing effort in order to achieve the same outcome.

Three basic forms of contractual control or vertical restraint can be identified, that reduce or eliminate conflict due to negative externalities.

- Relationships can be coordinated by giving the franchisor direct control over the franchisee's decisions, such as price-setting, quality of product or service and marketing effort.

- A structure of rewards and penalties can be designed to ensure the incentives facing both parties are properly aligned. For example, the contract could specify that the franchisee pays the franchisor a fixed fee, and buys all variable inputs at marginal cost. Under this structure, the franchisee's profit-maximizing output decision coincides with that of the franchisor.

- To reduce competition between franchisees (intra-brand competition), a franchisor might offer exclusive territorial contracts, or fix a minimum retail price.

In practice, contracts between franchisors and franchisees may include aspects of all three forms of contractual control. Macho-Stadler and Pérez-Castrillo (1998) view franchise contracts as a mix of centralized and decentralized decision making. In the fast-food industry, for example, decisions such as menu selection and building design are taken centrally by the franchisor, while employee recruitment and local advertising are taken locally by the franchisees.

Under some circumstances, it might be in a franchisor's interest to give certain franchisees ownership of several units (Kalnins and Lafontaine, 2004). Multi-unit ownership may increase the franchisee's bargaining power and lead to opportunistic behaviour. However, there are several reasons why a franchisor might be willing to accept this risk. First, a franchisee might possess specialized knowledge that can be deployed productively in more than one unit. Second, franchisees may be tempted to free-ride, by using lower quality inputs or offering poor service, while enjoying the benefits of brand recognition and loyalty. This externality tends to diminish as the size of the franchisee's operation expands. Third, by concentrating franchise ownership the franchisor can prevent excessive local competition between franchisees in the same chain. Kalnins (2001) finds prices in fast-food restaurants are influenced more by the pricing strategies of competitors in the same chain than by the prices set by rival chains. Finally, multi-unit owners may benefit from economies of scale in marketing.

In some cases, a franchisor might decide to maintain centralized control by running some outlets itself. According to Macho-Stadler and Pérez-Castrillo (1998), the geographic location of outlets is a key determinant of the degree of centralization or decentralization. Outlets far from the franchisor's headquarters, outlets in rural areas and outlets close to motorways are more likely to operate with less centralized control. Focusing on the nature of contracts in oligopolistic markets, Gal-Or (1999) suggests the extent to which interdependence is recognized may have a major bearing on the terms of contracts.

Networks

Networks are groups of firms linked vertically by regular contact and relationships that may eventually develop into formal relations. For example, upstream firms might train staff in downstream firms, provide technical expertise, and customize their products in order to meet specific requirements of buyers. The relationship is non-exclusive, and both parties sell to and buy from other firms. In contrast, independent firms rely solely on market transactions for standardized products, and do not develop special relationships with upstream suppliers or downstream customers. Kranton and Minehart (2000) cite the clothing industry in New York and the Japanese electronics industry as examples of networks. In the face of uncertain demand, it is suggested networks can sometimes offer better solutions than full-scale vertical integration. First, buyers reliant on multiple sourcing arrangements may be able to reduce the bargaining power of sellers. Second, firms in networks can make specific investments, in order to meet the needs of buyers or sellers. Accordingly, vertical integration is not the only possible solution to specificity problems. Third, the aggregate level of investment in specific assets by the network may be less than in a vertically integrated firm (Bolton and Whinston, 1993).

According to Robertson and Langlois (1995), networks can be located within the transaction costs paradigm, encompassing independent, market-oriented firms at one extreme, and firms that have internalized transactions through common ownership or contractual agreements at the other extreme. However, networks can also be analysed within a second dimension. This approach focuses on two alternative definitions of the firm, introduced in Section 3.7. First, the firm as nexus of contracts approach (Cheung, 1983; Jensen and Meckling, 1976) characterizes the firm by the nature of its internal and external contracts: contracts within the firm are informal, subject to revision, and need to be coordinated administratively. The essence of a firm is its ability to manage these internal contracts efficiently. Second, the property rights approach characterizes the firm by its ownership of assets. Accordingly, vertical integration involves the ownership of successive stages of production. In order to understand vertical relationships, both definitions are useful. For example, it may be possible for two independent firms to be linked via administrative coordination, or for an integrated firm to deal with its subsidiary through the market. In Figure 15.12 these two defining characteristics, integration of coordination and integration of ownership, are represented by the horizontal and vertical axes, in order to locate the following organizational forms:

■ *Marshallian district*. This refers to the loosest of all networks, based on Alfred Marshall's analysis of nineteenth-century British manufacturing firms. Groups of small firms, producing the same or similar products, tend to cluster in specific geographic areas. Being vertically separated, the firms rely purely on local market transactions. However, the network (or district) allows for the realization of external economies, through the development of pools of specialized labour, and the rapid diffusion of new technologies.

■ *'Third Italy' district*. This refers to the system developed in north-east Italy, where clusters of relatively small firms have developed into industrial districts (see also Section 6.6), often located in the vicinity of smaller towns or cities. The firms often specialize in the production of standardized products, such as ceramics or textiles. The major difference from the Marshallian district is the level of cooperation between the firms. Cooperation is often sponsored by government, and may involve shared accounting services, domestic and international marketing initiatives and investment in infrastructure.

■ *Venture capital network*. Venture capitalists are often involved in financing small, high technology start-up businesses. Well known high-technology clusters include Silicon Valley in the US and the Cambridge Science Park in the UK. The degree of integration of coordination is low; although perhaps higher than in the Marshallian district, since some coordination is provided by venture capitalists who supply the initial finance. Venture capitalists help protect their investments by ensuring producers have at their disposal entrepreneurial and managerial expertise, as well as contacts with upstream suppliers and downstream customers. The involvement of venture capitalists implies producers cede some control to their investors, so there is an element of centralization and outside control.

■ *Japanese kaisha network*. Where production is characterized by the availability of significant economies of scale, industrial districts comprising clusters of small firms are less likely to develop. An alternative core network model involves many small satellite firms located in the vicinity of one large firm, often an assembler. For example, US (and British) car manufacturers often rely on suppliers with relations governed through short-term contracts. The large manufacturer ensures discipline by exercising market power as a single (monopsony) buyer: if suppliers do not meet the manufacturer's requirements regarding price, quality and timing, the manufacturer buys its inputs elsewhere. The manufacturer's detached attitude towards its upstream suppliers does not inspire loyalty, and fails to provide incentives for innovation, or for any action other than sticking rigidly to the terms of the contract. However, under the *kaisha* network system, large Japanese

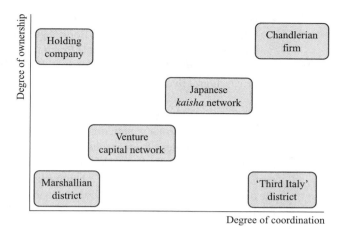

Figure 15.12 Robertson and Langlois' two dimensions of integration

manufacturers typically offer long-term contracts to their suppliers, and share technical and design knowledge. Japanese manufacturers often have significant ownership stakes in their suppliers. Owing to their interconnectedness, upstream and downstream firms tend to share similar business and financial goals.

■ *Chandlerian firm.* Chandler (1977) describes the traditional vertically integrated firm. Successive stages of production are centrally owned, and market relationships between upstream suppliers and downstream buyers have been internalized.

■ *Holding company.* This structure combines integration of ownership, with non-integration of coordination. Consequently, divisions or subsidiaries owned by the parent are allowed to operate in an independent, market-oriented manner. The development of multi-divisional structures can be interpreted as a form of decentralization. Although vertically integrated, the core firm retains only very narrowly defined strategic functions, and the divisions or subsidiaries operate almost autonomously.

15.6 Motives for vertical restraints

In some cases, firms may find that vertical integration or other types of vertical relationship are too costly to organize and monitor. Instead, they may develop various forms of **vertical restraint**, in an attempt to achieve similar outcomes. Vertical restraints are conditions and restrictions on trade imposed by firms that are linked vertically.

It is perhaps unfortunate that the words 'restraint' and 'restriction' have negative connotations, because some conditions surrounding the sale of goods may have beneficial rather than harmful effects on economic welfare. For example, referring to the UK bookselling industy at the start of the 1990s, Kay (1990b) identifies the following types of vertical restraint:

■ No part of a published book could be copied and distributed without the permission of the copyright owner.

- Books could not be sold below a minimum price set by the publisher. In the UK this was known as the Net Book Agreement (NBA), a legal agreement that had satisfied the Restrictive Trade Practices Court. In recent years, however, this agreement has all but disappeared as the large retail booksellers have discounted prices aggressively. The NBA was officially abandoned in 1995.

- No paperback could be rebound by a buyer as a hardback.

Each of these restraints is anticompetitive: the first acts an entry barrier preventing non-copyright holders from producing books; and the second inhibits price competition between booksellers. The third sustains a form of price discrimination: the cost differential between binding a hardback and a paperback is much smaller than the hardback–paperback price differential, and publishers' pricing policies exploit the relatively low price elasticity of demand for hardbacks (see Chapter 10). However, defenders of these arrangements argued that there were considerable benefits to consumers. If books could be copied and sold by rivals freely, publishers would be unable to recoup the costs of publishing a book. Rivals would be able to free-ride, having avoided the costs of contracting an author, typesetting and marketing; consequently, fewer books would be published. The NBA protected small booksellers that provided useful services to customers, such as information and local shopping. Small booksellers may have been unable to cover their costs if book prices were lower. Finally, price discrimination allows a wide variety of books to be published and sold at a reasonable price, cross-subsidized by a small number of bestsellers.

In general terms, vertical restraints may serve two purposes: to enhance market power, and to generate cost savings. The principal motives for vertical restraints are discussed under these headings.

Enhancement of market power

Market power due to monopoly control over one stage of production or distribution can be extended to an adjacent stage through vertical restraints. For example, banks can notify their financial service subsidiaries of potentially suitable customers, while denying their rivals access to the same information. One of the motives for regulation of the privatized utilities is to ensure their market power is not extended downstream.

One way of extending market power is through a price or profit squeeze. An integrated monopolist can narrow the margin between the price of a raw material input and the price of the finished product. Table 15.1 summarizes an example based on the Alcoa case (Shepherd, 1997, p. 276). Under pricing policy A, the dominant firm sells aluminium ingots to its own manufacturing division and to other firms at a price of 1,000 per ton, and earns a profit of 200 from ingot production. After processing at an additional cost of 500, aluminium products are sold to final consumers for 2,000 per ton. The dominant firm and the non-integrated rival both earn a profit of 500 at the manufacturing stage. The dominant firm's total profit is 700. The 1,000 price the dominant firm charges its division is known as a transfer price (see Section 10.5). Under pricing policy B, the dominant firm increases ingot prices to 1,490, and earns a profit of 690 from ingot production. The accounting costs of its manufacturing division rise to 1,990 and profit falls to 10, but the dominant firm's

Table 15.1 Enhancement of market power through a price/profit squeeze

Pricing policy	Integrated dominant firm		Non-integrated rival firm	
	A	B	A	B
Aluminium ingot production				
Cost	800	800		
Price	1,000	1,490		
Profit	200	690		
Manufacturing aluminium products				
Cost – ingots	1,000	1,490	1,000	1,490
– other	500	500	500	500
Price	2,000	2,000	2,000	2,000
Profit	500	10	500	10
Total profit	700	700	500	10

total profit remains 700. However, the non-integrated rival experiences a profit squeeze, from 500 to 10. This might be sufficient to force the rival to withdraw from the manufacturing industry.

Other general methods for enhancing market power through vertical restraints include the following:

■ *Increase in final prices and deterioration of service.* Any restraint which results in customers being forced to concentrate their orders on a narrow range of suppliers results in the denial of access to alternative (more efficient) sources of supply, and of access to alternative products. This can lead to a reduction in intra-brand competition and inter-brand competition. Unable to exploit alternative sources, consumers may face higher prices and poorer conditions of supply.

■ *Increased opportunities for collusion.* The practice of forcing distributors to resell the product at a minimum price reduces intra-brand price competition and presents opportunities for effective horizontal price-fixing.

■ *Raising entrants' costs.* Vertical restraints discourage entry by raising sunk costs. Exclusive distribution agreements deny outlets to entrants, who are obliged to develop their own distribution networks. If potential rivals are denied access to cheap or high-quality inputs by an integrated firm, they face an absolute cost advantage entry barrier. Potential entrants could also be fearful about certainty of supply. An upstream firm could deny sufficient inputs to a downstream firm, frustrating its attempts to produce at the minimum efficient scale (MES). Finally Banerjee and Lin (2003) suggest rivals' costs as well as potential entrants' costs can be raised through increased innovative effort on the part of downstream firms. An innovative downstream firm benefits from reduced costs, which can be passed on to consumers in the form of lower prices, leading to increased demand. The downstream firm buys more inputs from upstream suppliers, leading to increased input prices which increase production costs, not only offsetting some of the benefits to the innovative downstream firm (a negative effect from this firm's perspective), but also increasing the costs facing the firm's rivals (a positive effect).

Case study 15.2

Profits in the age of an 'audience of one'

As the media move into the digital age, one thing is certain: there is more to come. 'An endless multiplication of bandwidth and channels', is the prediction of David Hiller, senior vice-president at Tribune Company, the Chicago-based television and publishing group.

For media companies this represents a huge challenge. Those with business models based on advertising – television networks and newspapers, for example – are finding it increasingly hard to reach a mass audience. 'The mass media don't exist any more', says Bob Liodice, chief executive of the US Association of National Advertisers. Meanwhile, companies with business models based on taking money directly from consumers – such as record labels, film studios and pay-television operators – are struggling to maintain control over when and how their content is consumed. Fragmentation is 'the single most important trend across all media platforms', says John Lavine, head of the media management centre at Northwestern University in Chicago. Fragmentation is not new. In the early 1950s, most US households received fewer than four television channels. Today, the average is 50. But digitization is supercharging the process. Digital cable and satellite television services offer up to 200 channels where only a few dozen analogue channels would fit before. The internet is the digital conduit for countless sources of news, information and entertainment. Some have seen this as indicating the end-point of fragmentation: the 'audience of one'.

Digital technology has already produced one entertainment market – video games – that is bigger than Hollywood. Sales of DVDs now exceed box-office takings. Ring tones, the irritating cell-phone jingles, generate more revenues than traditional singles in some markets. Personal video recorders equipped with large hard discs, which allow viewers to control not only what they watch but also when and how, are the next wave. The PVR market got off to a slow start, reaching only 3m homes between its launch in 1999 and the end of last year. By 2007, however, 20m–40m US households are expected to have one. To consumers, this looks like personalization: tailor-made media. To industry executives, it is fragmentation gone wild.

So far, the industry's responses have fallen into three main groups: horizontal integration, vertical integration, and the search for new sources of revenue.

The logic behind horizontal integration is this: in a fragmenting market, media companies can no longer reach a mass audience with a single flagship programme or publication. Instead, reach comes from a portfolio of media properties, each targeted at a different group, across a range of platforms. 'The rules of programming have changed', says Bill Halloran at Bain & Co., the management consulting firm, 'it used to be about appealing to the broadest possible audience. Now it is about striking a chord with a particular group.' In television, examples of this more targeted approach include HBO, with its reputation for edgy and controversial drama, and the overtly right-leaning coverage of Fox News. Companies are also being more selective about their customers. In Europe, British Sky Broadcasting is leaning towards premium customers, where its Sky Plus service offers the benefits of a PVR linked to a line-up of 400 channels. Benefits include much lower churn – the rate at which subscribers cancel – and higher revenues per user. In newspapers, Tribune Group has supplemented the reach of the *Chicago Tribune*, one of the biggest US 'metro' newspapers, with sister titles including *Red Eye*, a tabloid aimed at the 18–34 age group, and *Hoy*, a Spanish-language newspaper. It also owns television and radio stations in its home market and has a stake in Careerbuilder.com, a classified employment advertising internet site.

The *New York Times* and other publishers have followed suit, adding television assets and websites to their core product. By stretching across titles and channels, they hope to reach an audience broad enough to satisfy advertisers. It is an approach that favours large companies with deep resources. 'Industry leaders are recognising that scale is critical and they need to be in a lot of places to meet consumers' needs,' says Michael Wolf, head of McKinsey's media and entertainment practice.

'If they are a television broadcaster, they can no longer just be on television. They need a web presence, possibly a print magazine, or a DVD strategy. If they are a newspaper, they can't just be available on news-stands or thrown on doorsteps. They need to be available to customers when and where they want, whether it's in tabloid rather than broadsheet or on a laptop screen or a wireless device.' In other words, media companies need to re-aggregate audiences by diversifying across types of media and taking a portfolio approach to content. 'Wherever you get fragmentation, eventually you get re-aggregation', says Prof Lavine.

Vertical integration, the marriage of content with distribution, is an alternative approach. Comcast's unsolicited bid for Disney was, among other things, an attempt at vertical integration: marrying Comcast's national cable television network to Disney's content-producing movie studios and ABC television network. It was not the first of its kind. AOL merged with Time Warner; Rupert Murdoch's News Corp last year added DirecTV, the US satellite broadcaster, to its Fox studios and television assets. The argument for vertical integration is based on market power. Distributors might hope to strike better deals with content providers if they have content of their own to offer in return. The snag is that content creation demands different management skills from the asset-intensive business of distribution. Certainly, content companies such as Disney and Viacom (owner of the CBS broadcast network and cable television channels including MTV) argue distribution is not vital to remain competitive. Moreover, the experience of the music industry suggests that owning distribution may become a precarious income model.

Peter Gabriel, the former Genesis rock star and founder of OD2 – Europe's largest online music service – says: 'I think the way people are thinking about the business is a barrier to change. We see two revenue streams: pay-as-you-go subscription and artists selling directly from their own websites.' Citing direct sales by artists such as Prince or David Bowie, Mr Gabriel claims the content creators will become retailers, setting their own pricing and cutting out traditional distributors. 'You can certainly make the case that digital distribution at some point is free', says Mr Hiller.

Media companies are already exploring alternative sources of revenue – either the subscription model advocated by music retailers such as OD2 and Napster, or the pay-per-download system pioneered by Apple. In subscription, digital radio stations such as Sirius and XM in the US have created a business with customers paying a flat monthly fee for more than 100 channels of advertising-free radio. Similarly in television, TiVo – the pioneer of PVR technology – has won 1m subscribers. Analysts also expect BSkyB to double its Sky Plus (PVR) customer base to more than 800,000 by the end of 2005. In principle, these subscription services could enable precision marketing. Service providers could use their detailed knowledge of viewing habits to deliver targeted advertising. TiVo and BSkyB are already working towards this goal, presenting themselves to advertisers as a platform on which to build interactive ads. Content producers are also starting to explore programming opportunities offered by PVRs: for example, DirecTV's NFL Sunday Ticket, which offers American football highlights delivered overnight to TiVo for viewing the next day. Other attempts at new media business models include services such as Movielink (a joint venture between MGM, Paramount, Sony Pictures, Universal and Warner Brothers) and MovieBeam (owned by Disney), a bold attempt to place a fully managed store of digital content in the consumer's home. Even SES Astra, the world's largest satellite operator, is moving into such businesses – offering point-to-point satellite internet connections and high-definition television capacity to media companies.

Romain Bausch, SES chief executive, says: 'High-definition television could be the way forward. Our Asian partners tell us that by 2005 China would like all television stations to be HDTV. That's good for us because they require additional capacity and that means more satellites.' But success is uncertain. All these companies are experimenting with delivery systems without knowing which will be profitable.

One thing is true. Companies must adapt to consumer demand. Mr Wolf says: 'If music lovers can burn a mixed CD with all their favourite songs on it, why can't they order one custom-made? Why is there not easy access to out-of-print books straight from publishers, rather than forcing readers to buy used books? Why not give people the best television shows of the previous week via video-on-demand?'

The media and entertainment industry is struggling to answer those questions. Only the companies that pass the test will survive in the digital age.

Source: Profits in the age of an 'audience of one', *Financial Times*, 16 April 2004. © The Financial Times Limited. Reprinted with permission.

Cost savings

Vertical restraints have the potential to produce cost savings in cases where arm's length dealing between producers and distributors via the market leads to suboptimal outcomes. A free-rider or externality problem occurs when a retailer is willing to invest in marketing, but is deterred from doing so because it is unable to appropriate the full benefits of this effort. For example, the retailer may wish to invest in a large retail space, where customers can browse at their leisure and be advised by fully trained staff. However, a rival discount retailer could prosper by attracting customers who have already accessed the pre-sales service, and undercutting the price. Consequently the service-oriented retailer may be unwilling to invest in providing the service, which damages the producer because sales are reduced if the service is not available. To prevent such an externality, the producer may refuse to supply the discount retailer, or adopt a policy of resale price maintenance (see Section 15.7).

The European Commission (1998a) suggests three tests to ascertain whether the free-rider problem is a valid reason for imposing vertical restraints: first, the free-riding issue should relate to pre-sales rather than after-sales service; second, the product should be new or technically complex, so that consumers actually need information; and third, the product should be relatively expensive, so that it would pay a consumer to obtain information from one source but purchase elsewhere.

Other issues relating to the free-rider problem include the question of certification. This arises where retailers with a high reputation effectively certify the quality of a good by stocking it. This may be particularly important for new products, which might require such recognition in order to become established. If the product were stocked by downmarket stores, it might fail to acquire the necessary credibility. A further issue arises when a producer is committed to making a specific investment with a particular retailer for the distribution of its product. Once the investment is made, the producer is committed to its chosen retailer. The fear of becoming dependent on other parties could prevent or delay the investment.

15.7   Types of vertical restraint

In this section we examine some of the principal types of vertical restraint.

Resale price maintenance

Resale price maintenance (RPM) is defined as an arrangement whereby an upstream firm retains the right to control the price at which a product or service is sold by a downstream firm, usually in the retail market (Mathewson and Winter, 1998). RPM most commonly involves the fixing of a minimum price (price floor), although a maximum price (price ceiling) is also possible. RPM has been subject to criticism from two directions, one legal and the other economic. From a legal viewpoint RPM can be interpreted as contrary to the principle of alienation, which implies that as an individual relinquishes ownership of goods, he or she should have no further say in their use and disposal. From an economic viewpoint, the principal concern is that RPM is anticompetitive:

■ *Retailer collusion*. Retailers or dealers often share information or communicate for perfectly benign reasons, although it is possible that informal contact develops subsequently into full-blown collusion. As seen in Chapter 5, any collusive agreement is potentially unstable, due to the possibility that one or more of the parties decides to take independent action. RPM may be a means by which price discipline, and therefore stability, can be achieved (Julien and Rey, 2000). Furthermore, RPM can protect the retailer cartel from entry by other retailers offering price discounts. This view is attacked by the Chicago school (Bork, 1978; Ornstein, 1985; Posner, 1981), who claim that retailer cartels are rare, owing to relatively low entry barriers. Furthermore, there is no reason why a producer should wish to support a retailer cartel that might work against the producer's own interests.

- *Producer collusion.* Normally one would expect producers wishing to collude on price to fix the wholesale price. This policy may be effective if retailers' cost and demand conditions are stable. If these conditions vary, however, the producers may not know whether differences in the prices charged by different retailers are due to genuine differences in cost or demand conditions, or cheating by one or more of the colluding producers. RPM eliminates price variations, since retailers are prevented from adjusting the retail price.

Arguments in favour of RPM can be developed from both a legal and an economic perspective. From a legal perspective, it can be argued the owner of a good has the right to offer any contract associated with the sale of the good that he or she wishes. From an economic perspective, it can be argued RPM permits cost savings in distribution. Success in the production and marketing of a product depends on the actions of both producers and retailers. It is possible for individually rational behaviour to lead to suboptimal outcomes for both the producer and the retailer.

One case in point arises when the demand for a product depends not only on price, but also on associated pre-sales services, such as convenient location, availability of parking space, short waiting times, displays and demonstrations, and information provided by staff. Producers have an incentive to ensure retailers provide such services. However, the free-rider problem (see Section 15.6) may explain why certain retailers are unable to provide the necessary service. For example, the UK bicycle manufacturer Raleigh argued at the Monopolies and Mergers Commission (1981) that the demand for bicycles depends on pre-delivery services such as pre-sales inspection, final assembly and adjustments, as well as post-delivery services such as advice, repairs and stock of spare parts. Raleigh argued discount stores such as Halfords could not offer these services and sell at a discounted price (Hardt, 1995).

Historically, however, RPM has covered products such as confectionery, tobacco and clothing which perhaps do not require much pre-sales service. Marvel and McCafferty (1984) suggest RPM enables retailers to provide an informal quality certification service (see Section 15.6). Butz and Kleit (2001) suggest producers often set low price floors, in order to limit the level of discounting without excluding it altogether. By narrowing the price differential between discount store prices and stores offering full service, producers may hope the presence of the discount stores encourages full-service stores to maximize the quality of their service.

The pre-sales service and certification arguments assume producers are unable to contract for the provision of these services directly. A contractual solution may be difficult to achieve, because of problems associated with the monitoring of contractual obligations. Klein and Murphy (1988) and Blair and Lewis (1994) suggest RPM can help provide the necessary discipline for a contractual solution to be feasible. If the producer is happy with the level of service provided, retailers earn an abnormal profit, assuming the cost of providing the service is within their margin. However, if the producer is unhappy with the service, the dealer's quasi-rents would be lost when the producer terminates the contract.

Gilligan (1986) attempts to distinguish between allocative efficiency and market power as motives for RPM, by examining the effect on the profits of firms that were subject to complaints under competition law for the use of RPM. Using share price changes as a proxy for changes in future profits, Gilligan finds share prices were significantly affected by these challenges. This suggests RPM makes an important contribution to profit. Share price changes appear to be related to structural characteristics of the firms and their industries; this relationship is consistent with the retailer and producer collusion hypotheses.

> [T]he findings of this study do not support the recent recommendations that RPM should enjoy benign treatment under contemporary antitrust policy . . . The results from our study of a sample of firms that were the object of antitrust adjudication clearly suggest that RPM sometimes causes allocative distortions in manufacturing and distribution. When RPM appears to promote efficiencies in the distribution process, its use is outlived and persists only because of marketing inertia. Calls for *per se* legality of RPM must, given the findings of this study, be based on grounds other than economic efficiency.
>
> *(Gilligan, 1986, pp. 554–5)*

Using a different methodology, Hersch (1994) examines the share prices of high-volume retailers and producers associated with high RPM usage, following the 1951 US Supreme Court Schwegmann verdict, which severely limited the enforcement of RPM. Hersch finds little effect on share prices, but there are significant differences in the impact of RPM based on firm and market characteristics. This conclusion lends support to the retailer collusion hypothesis. In other recent contributions, Deneckre *et al.* (1996) argue that producers facing uncertain demand have an incentive to resort to RPM in order to maintain adequate levels of stock, by preventing the emergence of discount stores. Wang (2004) examines the incentives for an upstream oligopoly to impose RPM.

Foreclosure

Foreclosure refers to the practice of refusing to supply a downstream firm, or to purchase from an upstream firm. Complete or absolute foreclosure occurs either when a supplier obtains control over all of the downstream outlets; or a purchaser obtains control over all of the the supplying outlets. In each case, non-integrated rivals are denied a share in the relevant market. For example, vertically integrated cable operators, which make programmes and distribute them, tend to exclude rival programmes from access to their distribution network (Chipty, 2001; Rubinfeld and Singer, 2001).

Foreclosure need not always be total (Comanor, 1967b). With reference to exclusive distribution and exclusive purchasing agreements, Dobson (1997) identifies three conditions for the effectiveness of foreclosure:

- A sufficient proportion of upstream or downstream firms are covered by the exclusive agreement.

- There are substantial barriers to entry or an inability to expand output internally at the upstream or downstream stage.

- The agreements are of relatively long duration.

In addition to the possible anticompetitive effects, Heide *et al.* (1998) identify a number of other factors that might influence the extent to which a firm pursues an exclusive dealing strategy. Firm size may influence the degree of exclusive dealing. Large firms may benefit from economies of scale and scope in distribution by developing exclusive dealerships, or from promotional economies which enhance the reputation of their brands. This can bring benefits to producers, retailers and customers through the coordination of sales efforts, enabling customers to make informed choices. However, exclusive dealing makes it difficult or impossible to compare different brands at one location. Customers save on search costs by shopping at outlets that carry a large selection of brands. The implication is that exclusive

---

Case study 15.3

UK retail group seeks review of PC pricing

John Lewis Partnership, the retail group, has threatened legal action unless the Office of Fair Trading reopens an investigation into alleged price fixing in the home computer market. The OFT cleared Dixons, the electrical retailer, in October 1999 of allegations that it abused its market position to overcharge for PCs. But John Lewis and rival group Comet – part of the Kingfisher chain – claim the 10-month investigation improperly measured Dixon's market share and that exclusive supply agreements with Compaq Computers and Packard Bell had further increased its market power. Dixons dismissed the claims that it was fixing the market as 'utter nonsense'.

An executive close to the affair said on Sunday: 'The OFT has made a mistake in law and unless it takes another look at this, John Lewis will seek a judicial review.' The group claims Compaq and Packard Bell computers accounted for 60 per cent of its PC sales last year. It has warned Kim Howells, minister for consumer affairs, that other big name brands may enter into similar exclusive supply deals, threatening the government's aim of putting a PC into every home. 'Even the loss of these two (brands) would severely limit our ability, and that of other high street retailers, to present a competitive range of products', it said.

The OFT investigation concluded that no retailer or manufacturer was in a position of market power because equivalent computers were available through mail order and internet suppliers. However, Nick Palmer, Labour MP for Broxtowe and secretary of the Commons cross-party internet working group, rejected this and will call on Stephen Byers, trade and industry secretary, on Tuesday to re-examine the home computer market. 'The average first time buyer still prefers to deal with traditional high street shops, which are dominated by Dixons and its subsidiaries Currys and PC World', he said. The OFT said it had not received an official complaint from John Lewis or Comet, but that the exclusivity agreements could be prohibited under the Competition Act if there was evidence of them leading to higher prices. Dixons said: 'Our objective is to secure the lowest prices and the widest range of products for our customers, and that is all we are doing.'

Source: *Financial Times*, 9 April 2000. © The Financial Times Limited.

dealing may cause distributors to lose custom, reducing the incentive for distributors to enter into such agreements.

Does foreclosure or exclusivity damage competition? Bork (1978) argues the anticompetitive effects are exaggerated. Essentially, foreclosure is an irrelevancy: what matters is the degree of concentration in upstream and downstream markets. Vertical mergers and foreclosure are of little consequence in competitive horizontal markets. On the other hand, Comanor and Frech (1985), Ordover *et al.* (1990) and Bolton and Whinston (1993) argue vertical mergers may reduce competition in input markets. As a firm vertically integrates downstream, it has less incentive to compete on price with other upstream suppliers. Accordingly, the upstream rivals can also increase their prices. In the markets for hardware and software systems, there is evidence that foreclosure can lead to monopolization of the hardware market (Chen and Riordan, 2003; Church and Gandal, 2000). Bernheim and Whinston (1998) are more agnostic: under different conditions, exclusive dealing can be anticompetitive, efficiency enhancing, or simply irrelevant.

Krattenmaker and Salop (1986) suggest a number of conditions that could be used to determine whether competition is harmed by foreclosure.

- *Is the ability of excluded rivals to compete reduced?* Exclusion might lead to an increase in rivals' costs in the following cases. First, if a firm gains control over the entire supply of a low-cost or high-quality input, rivals might have to acquire inputs that are more costly or of lower quality. Second, if exclusion reduces the supply of inputs available on the open market, rivals are forced to bid up the prices of the remaining inputs. However, foreclosure need not necessarily increase rivals' costs if abundant supplies are available from alternative sources.

- *Is market power increased by exclusion?* The ability to foreclose need not necessarily increase the firm's market power, if it has powerful rivals or if entry is possible. Exclusion may harm certain competitors, without necessarily damaging competition.

- *Is exclusion profitable?* Foreclosure implies some sales forgone. The increase in profit from enhanced market power might not be enough to compensate for the loss of revenue.

Territorial exclusivity

Producers can impose territorial restrictions, which allow dealers to operate only in specified locations. In some cases, the dealer is restricted to operating in a particular territory, but can serve any customer who approaches them. Alternatively, the dealer may be obliged to serve only customers from a specified location. Katz (1989) suggests territorial agreements affect final consumers' search costs. In order to draw comparisons, consumers may have to visit a range of outlets in different locations. As a result of increased search costs, consumers may be unwilling to shop around, in which case inter-brand competition is reduced and industry profits are increased. However, territorial agreements may help foster dealer collusion, by limiting the number of dealers in a given area. This could work against the producer's interests.

Quantity-dependent pricing

Quantity-dependent pricing implies the price per unit paid by a buyer depends on the quantity purchased (Katz, 1989). Several specific types of vertical restraint fall under this heading.

Quantity forcing

Quantity forcing occurs when a buyer is obliged to buy more than he or she would wish under normal circumstances. This might be achieved by forcing the buyer to make a minimum payment for purchases up to a certain level. Forcing buyers to stock and sell more than they wish may have the effect of improving service and reducing prices to final consumers. This latter effect could help overcome the problem of double marginalization (see Section 15.2).

Non-linear pricing

A **two-part tariff** (see Section 10.3) is an example of a non-linear pricing structure. With a two-part tariff, a buyer pays a fixed franchise fee, *plus* a price per unit. As the quantity bought increases, the average cost per unit falls. The policy of charging a fixed franchise fee for the opportunity of stocking and selling the product on top of a constant per-unit charge can also be used to eliminate double marginalization, without resorting to full-scale vertical integration. In Figure 15.4, (P_3, Q_3) is the price and quantity combination chosen by the monopoly retailer, with double marginalization. The monopoly producer earns an abnormal profit of P_1P_2FG, and the retailer earns an abnormal profit of P_2P_3EF. From the producer's perspective, a better solution would be to charge the retailer a franchise fee of P_1P_2CD, and to make the product available at a price per unit equivalent to the producer's marginal cost, MC_1. In this case, (P_2, Q_2) is the price and quantity combination chosen by the retailer. The producer's abnormal profit is provided by the franchise fee of P_1P_2CD.

Kay (1990b) suggests two reasons why a non-linear pricing structure might be attractive to a producer. First, if a retailer's profit increases more than proportionately with the total amount of business done with the producer, this should increase the incentive to promote the product. For example, an insurance company might wish independent brokers to recommend its policies above others, or a breakfast cereal producer might wish a supermarket to display its brand prominently on the shelves. A non-linear price structure should provide incentives. Second, if retailers stock only one product or a narrow range of products, the switching and search costs to consumers are increased. This policy increases the producer's market power.

Tying

The European Commission (1999a) defines **tying** as the selling of two or more distinct products, where the sale of one good is conditioned on the purchase of another. Products are distinct if, in the absence of tying arrangements, the products are purchased in separate markets. For example, the supply of shoes with laces is not generally considered as the supply of two distinct products. In contrast, if the purchase of a machine entails a contractual obligation to have the machine serviced by the producer's engineers, two distinct supply markets are tied: one for the machine, and the other for servicing. Singer (1968) suggests a number of reasons why tying might be an attractive option for a supplier (producer or retailer):

■ *Evasion of price controls.* If the price a supplier can charge for one product is regulated, the supplier might force its buyers also to stock an unregulated product at a high price, effectively evading the price control.

■ *Protection of goodwill.* A supplier may wish to protect the quality of its product by insisting repairs and spare parts are supplied only by itself. The supplier might argue that to have the product serviced by non-approved engineers may cause damage, and may harm the firm's reputation. Whether this argument is justified depends on whether efficient alternatives to the tying arrangement exist.

■ *Economies of distribution.* Producers may tie two or more complementary products in order to benefit from economies in distribution. In principle, assembled products such as cars involve tying many separate products such as engines, crankshaft, axles, wheels, tyres and other parts.

■ *Price discrimination.* Suppose a monopoly supplier sells colour printers (the tying product) and ink cartridges (the tied product). The supplier charges a competitive price for its printers but prices the cartridges above their marginal cost. Large customers (with a low price elasticity of demand) are forced to pay a higher price overall, since they use proportionately more of the expensive cartridges than the smaller customers. Resale is ruled out since the price of cartridges is the same for all customers. A form of price discrimination is achieved indirectly. The common practice of selling machines and expensive service contracts can be interpreted as a similar case of covert price discrimination.

■ *Leverage.* A tying arrangement can extend the power of a monopolist into related markets, enhancing market power in the market for the tied product. The leverage a monopolist can exert depends on the proportion of the tied market covered by the tying arrangement, and on the effectiveness of the tying arrangement as a barrier or deterrent to entry (Carlton and Waldman, 2002; Chen and Ross, 1999; Choi and Stefanadis, 2001; Whinston, 1990).

Bundling

Under the practice of **bundling**, a supplier offers several goods as a single package. For example, hotels offer rooms bundled with the use of facilities such as in-house gyms and swimming pools. The prices of all these additional services are included in the price of the room, whether they are used or not. Adams and Yellen (1976) show that bundling is profitable since customers can be sorted into different groups with different willingness-to-pay, and their consumer surplus appropriated accordingly. In other words, bundling can be used as a form of price discrimination. Case study 15.4 discusses a recent example, involving an OFT investigation of the UK's dominant pay-television provider, BSkyB.

Case study 15.4

BSkyB and vertical restraints

In late 2002 the Office of Fair Trading reported on an investigation of the satellite broadcaster BSkyB, the UK's leading pay-television supplier. The investigation examined whether BSkyB was guilty of abusing its market power in the market for pay-television services, in the following ways:

- Forcing a margin squeeze on rival pay-television service providers.
- Bundling its channels.
- Giving selective price discounts to distributors.

The structure of the industry is illustrated schematically in the diagram below. Programmes are created upstream, either through BSkyB's ownership of exclusive rights (primarily for the live broadcast of sports events, and for the screening of certain movies), or by programme production companies. BSkyB's acquisition of the exclusive rights for certain sports and movies was at the core of the investigation. Programmes are sold to the channel providers, which put together packages of programmes in order to produce distinctive channels. The channels are then sold to the distributors, who bundle the channels together for sale to the final consumer (the pay-television subscribers). At the time of the investigation, pay-television was offered through the media of satellite (BSkyB), cable (NTL and Telewest) and terrestrial television (On Digital, later ITV Digital, and subsequently Freeview). BSkyB was involved in both channel provision and the distribution of pay-television. This form of vertical integration could have implications for competition at the distribution stage.

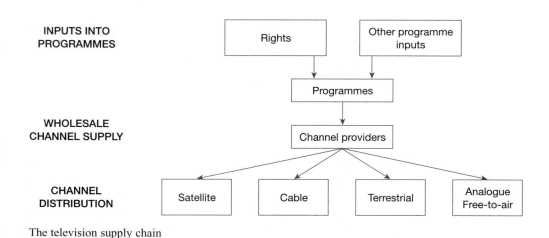

The television supply chain
Source: OFT 623, 17 December 2003.

The OFT first needed to establish whether BSkyB occupied a dominant position in the relevant market. This raised a number of issues of market definition. The relevant market was seen as the supply of English Premier League football, as well as top movies (defined as those that had grossed over $50m at the US box office). The OFT concluded that BSkyB did occupy a dominant position in this market.

The next step was to determine whether there was any evidence that BSkyB was abusing its market power.

Margin squeeze

The OFT had received complaints from all other pay-television distributors (NTL, Telewest and ITV Digital) that BSkyB was squeezing their profit margins for the supply of sports and movie channels. A margin squeeze takes place if a vertically integrated firm sells its output to its downstream competitors at prices that generate very little profit, even though the competitors are as efficient as the vertically integrated supplier in the downstream market. The alleged squeeze may also have distorted competition in the retail market, leaving consumers facing higher prices, lower quality and less choice. To address this question, the OFT used cost estimates for BSkyB and its competitors. The results were borderline, and in the absence of strong evidence, the OFT concluded the allegation of anticompetitive practice through a margin squeeze was unproven.

Mixed bundling

Mixed bundling involves two or more products being sold at a price below the sum of their individual prices. The OFT argue that bundling can result in the foreclosure of rival suppliers, if they cannot offer similar price discounts by similar means. The OFT noted that offering price discounts is natural in cases where the provider has a high ratio of fixed costs to marginal costs. The appropriate test of anticompetitive practice was to examine whether the incremental price charged for the additional service was equivalent to its marginal cost. No evidence was found to suggest the incremental price was either above or below the marginal cost.

Selective discounting

It was also alleged that BSkyB offered price discounts to distributors based on factors such as: sales of premium BSkyB programmes; number of subscribers to BSkyB channels; and level of market penetration. The latter was calculated on the basis of sales of BSkyB packages to homes with access to cable in their street. Such discounting could be anticompetitive, if it discouraged distributors from broadcasting non-BSkyB channels. However, there was no evidence to substantiate the allegation of anticompetitive practice through selective discounting.

Source: Office of Fair Trading (2002) *BSkyB: The Outcome of the OFT's Competition Act Investigation, December 2002, OFT62*. London: Office of Fair Trading.

With reference to the movie industry, Stigler (1963) discusses the practice of block booking, which can be interpreted as a form of bundling. Block booking refers to the practice of offering an exhibitor a collection of movies in a package, rather than making them available individually. Assume a London distributor knows the reserve prices of two exhibitors. One exhibitor owns an arthouse cinema in Hampstead, and the other owns a West End cinema which shows popular movies. The reserve prices each exhibitor is willing to pay for two movies, *Citizen Kane* and the latest *Harry Potter*, are:

Exhibitor	*Harry Potter*	*Citizen Kane*
Hampstead	7,000	4,000
West End	8,500	3,000

If each movie is sold separately and the distributor is able to prevent resale, perfect price discrimination can be achieved. The total rental is £22,500 (= 7,000 + 4,000 + 8,500 + 3,000). However, if it is not possible to prevent resale, the best the distributor can do is to charge £7,000 for *Harry Potter* and £3,000 for *Citizen Kane*. This generates a total rental of £20,000 (= 7,000 + 7,000 + 3,000 + 3,000). If the distributor practises block booking non-discriminatingly, the two-film package can be sold for £11,000 to both exhibitors. The total rental rises to £22,000.

Vertical restraints: anticompetitive or benign?

Are vertical restraints always anticompetitive? Or are they sometimes desirable on efficiency or welfare criteria? Or is their effect simply neutral? Much of the debate in Europe and the US has centred on the views of the Chicago school (Bork, 1978; Posner, 1981; Telser, 1960), a group of academic lawyers and economists who stress a strongly pro-market and pro-competition approach. Before the views of the Chicago school came to prominence, it was widely believed that vertical restraints, by their very nature, reduce the independence of distributors and are therefore anticompetitive. Resale price maintenance (RPM), for example, was seen as little different from horizontal price-fixing, and was banned in most countries. In contrast, the Chicago school distinguish between vertical and horizontal restraints. Competition takes place within a market, and is therefore impeded by horizontal restraints, but not by vertical restraints. Producers do not normally impose restrictions downstream that would reduce the level of demand for their own products. If restrictions are imposed, it is because a potential cost saving or efficiency gain can be realized, perhaps through the elimination of externalities or opportunism (Baake *et al.*, 2004).

Since the 1970s the tide has turned somewhat against the Chicago view (Comanor, 1985; Rey and Tirole, 1986). It is now more fashionable to analyse vertical restraints on a case-by-case basis. Restraints may sometimes raise entry barriers or facilitate collusion, leading to a distortion of competition. For example, RPM might be used as an alternative to horizontal price-fixing, the latter being more obvious as well as illegal. However, why upstream firms should wish to cooperate in enhancing market power downstream is not always clear. Grimes (2002) analyses the approach of the US legal system to vertical restraints. The US Supreme Court recognizes that vertical restraints can be justified as a cost-effective method for promoting an upstream supplier's brands. In some cases vertical restraints may foster competition, and blanket condemnation of such practices is unwarranted.

15.8 Summary

The topic of vertical relationships covers a wide range of issues involving firms operating at different stages of the same production process. Vertical integration refers to a situation where a single firm has ownership and exercises control over production at successive stages of the production process. Vertical integration may be used as a strategy for restricting competition, and either using or abusing market power. However, one of the strongest arguments in favour of vertical integration derives from an analysis of the problem of double marginalization, which arises when successive stages of a production process are under the control of independent (non-integrated) monopoly firms. For example, if a producer and retailer are both monopolists, and both add their own mark-ups to the price, the outcome is a higher price and lower output than in the case where the two firms are vertically integrated. Both producer and consumer surplus are higher if the production and retail stages are vertically integrated.

Williamson's transaction costs paradigm provides another very general and wide-ranging explanation for vertical integration. Specific sources of cost saving include the following:

- *Technological conditions*. Vertical integration may lead to the reduction of production costs. This may occur where complementary processes are best completed together.

- *Uncertainty*. The relationship between firms in successive stages of production is subject to uncertainty arising from incomplete information. Vertical integration can help reduce such incompleteness.

- *Assured supply*. Firms may be concerned about the risks of being let down by a supplier. Backward vertical integration may help ensure a steady supply of inputs.

- *Externalities* arise when a firm incurs additional costs brought about by the actions of its suppliers or distributors. Vertical integration may help eliminate these costs.

- *Complexity*. Vertical relationships may be characterized by complex technical and legal relations. The resulting difficulties may be reduced through vertical integration.

- *Moral hazard*. A firm's independent suppliers or retailers may have insufficient incentive to act in the firm's own best interests; within an integrated organization these disincentives may be eliminated.

- *Asset specificity* arises when a firm invests in the production or distribution of custom-made products for specific clients. High bargaining costs in a case of bilateral monopoly may be reduced or eliminated through integration.

- *Avoidance of tax or price controls* may also be possible through a strategy of vertical integration.

In empirical studies, the degree of vertical integration can be measured using a simple count of the number of stages of production a firm is involved in; the ratio of value added-to-sales (which reflects a firm's degree of self-sufficiency); the ratio of employment in a firm's auxiliary activities to its total employment; and an estimate of the ratio of a firm's internal (within-firm) transactions to external (market) transactions. However, empirical evidence on the impact of vertical integration on performance is surprisingly sparse, perhaps partly because of the difficulties involved in measuring vertical integration accurately.

As an alternative to vertical integration, vertical relationships of a looser nature, stopping short of full-scale merger, are also possible. Examples include franchise agreements, involving a specific contractual agreement between a franchisor and franchisee; and networks of independent firms that are linked vertically through non-exclusive contracts or other relationships. Potential advantages of franchising or networks include the preservation of some (or all) of both parties' independence, and the avoidance of some of the costs that might otherwise be associated with full-scale vertical integration.

Vertical restraints are conditions and restrictions on trade that are imposed by firms that are linked vertically. Such restrictions may be motivated by factors similar to those that motivate other types of vertical relationship: specifically, the enhancement of market power and the potential for the realization of cost savings. Principal types of vertical restraint are as follows:

■ *Resale price maintenance* (RPM) involves a producer controlling the price at which a product or service is sold by a retailer. RPM usually involves the fixing of a minimum price, although a maximum price is also possible. RPM may eliminate disincentives for retailers to supply pre-sales service, or provide an informal quality certification service.

■ *Foreclosure* refers to the practice of refusing to supply a downstream firm, or to purchase from an upstream firm. The extent to which foreclosure damages competition is controversial; some economists argue that only horizontal competition matters, and vertical restraints of this kind are irrelevant.

■ *Territorial exclusivity* is a form of geographic foreclosure, whereby a producer requires its retailers to trade only in specified geographic locations.

■ *Quantity-dependent pricing* implies the price paid by a buyer depends on the quantity purchased. A retailer might be obliged to stock more than he or she would wish; the price the retailer pays might include a fixed component and a variable component that depends on quantity (two-part tariff); the supply of one product to a retailer might be made conditional on the retailer's willingness to stock a second product (tying); or several products might be sold together to consumers as a single package (bundling).

The many types of vertical relationship that have been examined in this chapter may help promote efficiency or economic welfare; may be anticompetitive; or may simply have a neutral effect. In the 1970s and 1980s, the views of the Chicago school, who took an essentially benign view of the implications of vertical integration and vertical restraints for competition influenced the formulation of competition policy in many countries. More recent thinking suggests a slightly more sceptical and cautious approach is appropriate. Although blanket condemnation of vertical integration and vertical restraints is unwarranted, it is advisable to examine the implications for competition, efficiency and welfare of each case on its own individual merits.

Discussion questions

1. In a certain industry, both the production stage and the distribution stage are controlled by separate monopoly firms. Why might acquisition of the distributor be an attractive proposition for the producer? Would such a takeover be likely to make consumers better off or worse off?

2. Outline the cost-saving motives for vertical integration.

3. In the market for a certain intermediate product, there exists a single seller and a single buyer. Why are the equilibrium price and quantity traded theoretically indeterminate? For what reasons might it be profitable for the buyer and the seller to integrate vertically?

4. Quote examples of firms that have vertically integrated backward in order to guarantee their sources of supply, and firms that have vertically integrated forward in order to safeguard their distribution outlets.

5. With reference to Case studies 15.1 and 15.2, assess the arguments for and against vertical integration in the media industry.

6. How might a strategy of vertical integration help a firm to reduce its tax exposure?

7. Describe the methods that can be used to measure the extent of vertical integration.

8. Examine the potential sources of conflict in franchise relationships. Give examples of types of contractual relationship between franchisor and franchisee that might help reduce or eliminate conflict.

9. Explain the categorization of networks of vertically related firms according to the degree of integration of coordination, and the degree of integration of ownership.

10. What are vertical restraints? Examine the market power and cost saving motives for vertical restraints. Are vertical restraints necessarily damaging to consumer interests?

11. With reference to Case study 15.3, explain the criteria that were used by the UK's Office of Fair Trading to determine whether the electrical retailer Dixons was guilty of abusing its market power in the personal computers retail market, by operating exclusive supply agreements with the manufacturers Compaq and Packard Bell.

12. Explain the distinction between the practices of tying and bundling. For what reasons might a supplier consider adopting such practices?

13. With reference to Case study 15.4, examine the basis on which the Office of Fair Trading acquitted the satellite broadcaster BSkyB of allegations concerning the abuse of market power in the UK's market for pay-television services.

Further reading

Bork, R. (1978) *The Antitrust Paradox: A Policy at War with Itself*. New York: Basic Books.

Combs, J., Michael, S.C. and Castrogiovanni, G.J. (2004) Franchising: a review and avenues to greater theoretical diversity, *Journal of Management*, 30, 907–31.

Dobson, P.W. and Waterson, M. (1996) *Vertical Restraints and Competition Policy*. Office of Fair Trading Research Paper No. 12. London: OFT.

Jensen, M.C. (2000) *Foundations of Organizational Strategy*. Cambridge, MA: Harvard University Press.

Joskow, P.J. (2003) Vertical Integration, in *Handbook of New Institutional Economics*, Forthcoming, Kluwer econ-www.mit.edu/faculty/download_pdf.php?id = 833 accessed 27 April 2004.

Katz, M.L. (1989) Vertical contractual relations, in Schmalensee, R. and Willig, R.D. (eds) *Handbook of Industrial Organization*, vol. 1. Amsterdam: North Holland, ch. 11.

Motta, M. (2003) *Competition Policy, Theory and Practice*, Cambridge: Cambridge University Press, ch. 6.

OECD (1993b) *Competition Policy and Vertical Restraints: Franchising Agreements*. Paris: OECD.

Phlips, L. (ed.) (1998) *Applied Industrial Economics*. Cambridge University Press, chs 9, 15 and 21.

Scherer, F.M. and Ross, D. (1990) *Industrial Market Structure and Economic Performance*. Boston, MA: Houghton Mifflin, chs 14 and 15.

Williamson, O.E. (1971) The vertical integration of production; market failure considerations, *American Economic Review*, 61, 112–27

Williamson, O.E. (1989) Transaction cost economics, in Schmalensee, R. and Willig, R.D. (eds) *Handbook of Industrial Organization*, vol. 1. Amsterdam: North Holland, ch. 3.

16 Diversification

Learning objectives

This chapter covers the following topics:

- product, market extension and pure diversification
- the rationale for diversification
- diversification and corporate coherence
- why firms may decide to reduce their commitment to diversification
- evidence related to the direction and determinants of diversification in the UK and Europe

Key terms

Conglomerate
Conglomerate merger
Corporate coherence
Cross-subsidization
Deconglomeration

Direction of diversification
Internal capital market
Predatory competition
Reciprocity
Tie-in sales (tying)

16.1 Introduction

A diversified firm or **conglomerate** is a firm involved in the production of a number of different goods and services. In other words, a diversified firm is a multi-product firm. Large diversified firms operate in many sectors of the economy. Examples are Unilever, which produces a large array of packaged food and personal care products; BAA, which is involved in airport management services, building projects, railways, property management and consultancy services; and ABB, which is involved in various power and automotive technologies as well as oil, gas and petroleum. Large diversified firms account for a significant proportion of the total economic activity in most developed economies. Naturally, this raises a number of questions concerning the implications of diversification for competition and performance. Chapter 16 addresses these issues.

In Section 16.2 we begin by identifying three principal types of diversification: first, diversification by product extension, where a firm supplies a new product that is closely related to its existing products; second, diversification by market extension, where a firm moves into a new geographic market; and third, pure diversification, where a firm moves into a completely unrelated field of activity. There are two ways in which a diversification strategy may be implemented: either through internally generated expansion, or through merger and acquisition. Section 16.3 examines the theories that have been developed to explain why a firm might decide to pursue a diversification strategy. These are considered under four broad headings: enhancement of market power; realization of cost savings; reduction of transaction costs; and managerial motives for diversification.

Section 16.4 discusses the **corporate coherence** approach to explaining the growth of the diversified conglomerate, that has been developed in the management science literature. A starting point for this approach is the observation that most conglomerates tend to pursue a coherent diversification strategy over the long run. Typically the direction of diversification is not determined randomly; instead, the products of most conglomerates tend to be related. Nevertheless, during the 1980s and 1990s there appears to have been a shift of emphasis away from diversification, and in some cases towards the divestment of unrelated activities in pursuit of increased corporate focus. Section 16.5 considers reasons why some conglomerates have been subject to a strategy of divestment or **deconglomeration**.

Finally, Section 16.6 discusses practical methods for the measurement of the extent of diversification based on the degree of relatedness of a firm's primary and secondary activities. Some of the empirical evidence on the determinants of the extent and direction of diversification among UK and European conglomerates is reviewed. In general the empirical evidence seems to suggest most conglomerates are rather cautious in their diversification strategies, preferring in most cases to diversify in a manner that leaves them operating relatively close to their current technological and market bases.

16.2 Types of diversification

In Section 6.2, we have seen that the definition of a market contains both a product dimension and a geographic dimension. The product market definition includes all products that are close substitutes for one another, either in consumption or in production. The geographic market definition involves determining whether an increase in the price of a product in one geographic location significantly affects either the demand or supply, and therefore the price, in another location. If so, both locations form part of the same geographic market. Based on this definition of markets, the US Federal Trade Commission's annual *Statistical Report on Mergers and Acquisitions* suggests a convenient three-part classification of types of diversification:

- *Product extension.* A firm can diversify by supplying a new product that is closely related to its existing products. A sweet manufacturer that sells a milk chocolate bar may decide to produce and sell a dark chocolate bar as a product extension. Diversification by product extension could also include a move slightly further afield; for example, a chocolate bar producer might decide to supply closely related products such as ice cream or snack foods. Diversification by product extension should not be viewed as a discrete series of easily identifiable steps, but rather as part of a continuous process. Since almost all firms produce more than one product line or offer more than one service, all firms are to some extent diversified.

- *Market extension.* Diversification by market extension involves moving into a new geographic market. For example, the sweet manufacturer who produces chocolate bars for the UK market might decide to venture further afield, by marketing the same chocolate bars elsewhere in the EU.

- *Pure diversification.* A pure diversification strategy involves movement into unrelated fields of business activity. Firms that supply unrelated products to unrelated markets are known as **conglomerates**. The UK conglomerate Virgin plc represents a well known example of a firm that has grown mainly through a strategy of pure diversification. Virgin began in the early 1970s as a music store, before diversifying into numerous other fields including airlines, train services, financial products, soft drinks, mobile phones, holidays, cars, wines, publishing and bridal wear. Diversification by product extension or market extension refers to a strategy based on core product specialization. Conglomerates or purely diversified firms do not specialize in this way. As we shall see, pure diversification is a relatively unusual strategy. Most firms tend to diversify by entering adjacent markets, rather than totally unrelated ones. Sometimes it might appear that a firm is involved in pure diversification, but on closer examination there is a logical explanation as to why a particular direction has been chosen. For example, in 1982, Mars UK, the confectionery firm, developed marine radar, aimed at the small boat market. At first glance, this appears to be a case of pure diversification. However, Mars Electronics had developed a successful electronics business on the basis of technical expertise accumulated through its vending machine operations. Having spotted a gap in the market for a cheap and reliable radar system, the company diversified into this niche market.

There are two ways in which a diversification strategy can be implemented: first, through internally generated expansion; and second, through merger and acquisition. **Conglomerate merger** involves the integration of firms that operate in different product markets, or in the same product market but in different geographic markets. Internally generated expansion is likely to require the simultaneous extension of the firm's plant and equipment, workforce and skills base, supplies of raw materials, and the technical and managerial expertise of its staff. A strategy of diversification through conglomerate merger may be a lot less demanding in this respect. Another important distinction is that diversification through internal expansion is likely to result in an increase in the total productive capacity in the industry concerned, while diversification through conglomerate merger involves only a transfer of ownership and control over existing productive capacity. The main requirements for the latter strategy are an ability to select an appropriate target firm; access to the financial resources required to secure a controlling interest in the target firm; and an ability to manage the integrated organization effectively after the merger has taken place.

De Jong (1993) suggests the choice of diversification strategy might depend on the stage reached in the industry life cycle (see also Section 7.2). Firms operating in newer industries where rivalry is low are likely to face plentiful opportunities to extend their product lines as their markets expand. Firms operating in mature industries are likely to find their opportunities for new product developments constrained by slow growth in market demand, and more intense rivalry. Diversification through conglomerate merger rather than through internally generated expansion may be a more attractive strategy, especially since, as noted above, it avoids increasing the industry's total productive capacity. During the late 1940s, 1950s and 1960s when most European economies were still undergoing reconstruction following the Second World War, diversification in Europe was typically implemented through internally generated expansion, while diversification by conglomerate merger was more common in the US (Chandler, 1990; Jacobson and Andréosso-O'Callaghan, 1996). During the post-war reconstruction phase, most European industries were at an earlier stage of their lifecycles than the equivalent US industries. Furthermore, Chandler (1990) suggests the ability of European firms to finance conglomerate mergers was constrained by the small size and lack of flexibility of European capital markets relative to their US counterparts.

16.3 Motives for diversification

In Section 16.3, we examine a number of theories that have been developed to explain why a firm might decide to pursue a strategy of diversification. We begin by examining motives related to the enhancement of the firm's market power, and motives related to the potential for cost savings. We then consider theories of diversification based on some of the alternative theories of the firm that were examined in Chapter 3.

Enhancement of market power

The diversified firm which operates in a number of separate geographic and product markets may enjoy a competitive advantage over a specialized firm, because it can draw on resources from its full range of operations in order to fight rivals in specific markets. Furthermore, a firm that already has significant market power in one market may be reluctant to expand further within the same market, for fear of alerting the competition authorities. A superior and less confrontational strategy might be to move into other related or unrelated markets. There are several specific anti-competitive consequences of diversification.

Cross-subsidization and predatory competition

Through a policy of **cross-subsidization** the diversified firm may be in a strong position to compete against a specialized rival in the rival's market, drawing on cash flows or profits earned elsewhere within the organization to cover the costs of engaging the rival in either price or non-price forms of predatory competition (Aron, 1993; Myers, 1994). Under a predatory pricing strategy, for example, the diversified firm might undercut the specialized firm's price in an attempt to force it out of the market (see also Section 8.4). Once the rival has withdrawn, the price is reset to the original level or a higher level. In order for this strategy to succeed, the predator must have a deeper pocket than its rival (OECD, 1989; Scherer and Ross, 1990). A predatory pricing strategy is only likely to be profitable if there are barriers to entry. Otherwise the sacrifice of profit in the short run may be in vain. 'Predatory competition is an expensive pastime, undertaken only if monopoly and its fruits can be obtained and held' (Adelman, 1959, p. 369). However, by signalling commitment the predator may develop a reputation as a willing fighter, which itself serves as an entry barrier (Chen, 1997; Milgrom and Roberts, 1982).

There may be limits to the usefulness of a predatory competition strategy for a diversified firm. The specialized rival might turn out to be a more effective fighter, as it would be fighting for its very survival. For any firm wishing to eliminate rivalry, there may be alternative, less costly strategies than predatory competition, such as collusion or acquisition (McGee, 1958; Telser, 1966a). **Predatory competition** involves diverting resources from one operation in order to fight elsewhere. Although the diversified firm might have the capability to carry out such a strategy, it might refrain from doing so if this places its other operations at risk. For example, one of Rockefeller's associates remarked that Standard Oil 'gained or lost on a titan's scale while our opponents did so on a pygmy's' (Nevins, 1953, p. 65).

Reciprocity and tying

Reciprocity involves an agreement that firm A purchases inputs from firm B, on condition that firm B also purchases inputs from firm A. In other words, reciprocity is 'the practice of basing purchases upon the recognition of sales to the other party, rather than on the basis of prices and product quality' (Weston, 1970, p. 314). It can be argued that in effect, all economic transactions involve an element of reciprocity; and in the extreme case of barter, transactions are based solely on reciprocal arrangements. Reciprocity only becomes anticompetitive if one of the parties is forced to take part in a reciprocal transaction in which it would not participate voluntarily.

The US Federal Trade Commission argues that reciprocal trade increases existing entry barriers or creates new ones if entrants are effectively excluded as a result of reciprocal trade arrangements (Utton, 1979). A specialized firm has only a limited range of input demands, whereas a diversified firm has a much wider spread of purchasing requirements. Therefore the diversified firm is in a stronger position. Much of the evidence on reciprocity draws on anecdotal evidence based on cases that were brought before the courts. Needham (1978) argues that reciprocity is just one method by which a firm can exploit its existing market power, rather than a strategy for extending market power. Consequently the practice itself should not be viewed as particularly damaging to competition.

Tying involves the linked selling of two distinct products: in order to purchase good X, the buyer must also purchase good Y. This practice may be an attractive

Diversification as a growth strategy

The brewer Guinness believed, by the 1960s, that it had achieved saturation point in the stout market. Brewed and sold all over the world, the company's proud boast had been that 6 million pints were drunk every day. To achieve greater growth, new products had to be developed and marketed. Guinness decided to diversify into the lager market by launching a new brand, Harp. It was then forced to integrate vertically into pubs to guarantee outlets for the new drink. It also diversified into microbiology, biochemistry and confectionery.

In the 1960s, Cadbury also faced limited growth prospects for its confectionery products. It believed chocolate consumption in the UK (already the highest *per capita* in the world) could not grow any further. The firm also faced a powerful rival, Rowntree-Macintosh. Cadbury diversified into a range of foods such as instant milk, instant mashed potato, tea, jams, and most importantly of all, soft drinks, acquiring Schweppes in 1969. By the 1980s, Cadbury-Schweppes concentrated further expansion on its core confectionery and soft drinks businesses.

At the start of the twentieth century, Hoover's business was the manufacture of harnesses. Concerned about the decline in the horse-drawn carriage industry due to the advance of the motor car, W.H. Hoover was keen to diversify out of harness-making. In 1907, he acquired the rights to J.M. Spangler's vacuum cleaner and, by applying the company's technical skills, was able to market a superior product with great success.

There are also many examples of unsuccessful diversification strategies. In the mid-1960s British Match, a monopoly producer of matchsticks in the UK, was facing a decline in the demand for matches. It diversified into wood, chipboard and fireworks. During an investigation by the Monopolies and Mergers Commission of its acquisition of the razor producer Wilkinson Sword, British Match claimed its past diversification had not been successful (Monopolies and Mergers Commission, 1973, para. 74). In 1973, its non-match businesses accounted for 47 per cent of total group sales, but only 26 per cent of profits. The group blamed this on the poor growth of the acquired companies, and difficulties experienced in managing these businesses post-acquisition.

Source: The Monopolies Commission (1973) *British Match Corporation Ltd and Wilkinson Sword Ltd: A Report on the Proposed Merger*, Cmnd. 5442. London: HMSO.

strategy for a diversified firm that is seeking to generate sales across a number of distinct product lines. The practice of tying is discussed in more detail in Section 15.7.

Cost savings

In theory, a diversification strategy can result in cost savings in three ways: first, through the realization of economies of scope; second, by reducing risk and uncertainty; and third, by reducing the firm's tax exposure.

Economies of scope

As we have seen in Section 2.2, economies of scale are realized when the firm reduces its long-run average cost by increasing its scale of production, while economies of scope are realized when long-run average cost savings are achieved by spreading costs over the production of several goods or services. Douma and Schreuder (1998) quote a farming example. A fruit-grower must leave enough space between the trees to allow access for labour and farm equipment. This land can be used to graze sheep. The farmer uses one input, land, to produce two products, fruit and wool. However, the availability of cost savings through economies of scope does not necessarily imply the fruit-grower must diversify into sheep farming. Instead the land could be rented to a sheep farmer. This market transaction delivers the same outcome as the diversification strategy. However, if the market transaction costs are too high, diversification might be the more cost-effective approach.

Needham (1978) expresses scepticism as to the importance of economies of scope as a motivating factor for a diversification strategy. First, if the economies of scope are achieved by spreading the costs of indivisible inputs over a wider range of outputs, the specialized firm could realize similar cost savings through economies of scale, by increasing its scale of production. Second, the inputs must be non-specific, and capable of being spread over different activities. This requirement might only be satisfied by certain inputs, such as the marketing or finance functions.

Reduction of risk and uncertainty

All firms are vulnerable to adverse fluctuations in demand, and increased competition in their product markets. The three examples discussed in Case study 16.1 illustrate the impact of threats of this kind. The more products a firm develops, the lower is this vulnerability. According to Penrose (1995), the unpredictability of demand creates uncertainty, which in turn might motivate a diversification strategy:

> Except for seasonal variations, it is rarely possible accurately to predict fluctuations in demand. The less accurate the firm feels its predictions are, the more uncertain are profit expectations; consequently the firm will give more weight to the possibilities of obtaining a more complete utilization of its resources and a more stable income stream and less weight to the possible restriction on its ability to meet fully the peak demand for its existing product.

> *(Penrose, 1995, p. 140)*

A diversification strategy can help smooth out seasonal fluctuations in cash flows, if the firm is able to establish a presence in markets with different seasonal peaks. Examples of offsetting activities include Walls' ice cream and meat products; Valor Gas's heating and gardening equipment product ranges; and the newsagent W.H. Smith's involvement in travel agency services.

The ability to manage risk through diversification may help the firm to raise finance at a lower cost. From the point of view of the lender, however, it is not immediately obvious why a diversified firm should receive more advantageous terms than a specialized firm. A lender can manage his or her own risk by spreading a diversified portfolio of investments across a number of specialized firms. It could be argued that for a small investor in particular, holding shares in one diversified firm might be more attractive than holding a diversified portfolio of investments in many firms. For the small investor, the transaction costs incurred in making multiple investments and the cost of monitoring their performance might be onerous. However, vehicles such as unit trusts exist in order to channel funds from small-scale investors into managed diversified portfolios, reducing their investors' exposure to risk.

Obi (2003) examines whether the diversification of US bank holding companies into non-bank activities reduced the amount of unsystematic risk. Unsystematic risk is specific to the individual firm. This is in contrast to systematic or market risk, which affects all firms equally and cannot be managed through a strategy of diversification. Fifty financial institutions that moved from traditional banking business into areas such as life insurance, share dealing and real estate between 1984 and 1995 are examined. The results suggest unsystematic risk was reduced through diversification, although market risk appears to have increased over the same period.

Reduction of tax exposure

Under some taxation regimes, diversification can enable a firm to reduce its tax liability. Profits in one activity can be offset against losses in another. A specialized firm which makes a loss pays no tax on profit, but the tax payable by other profitable specialized firms is not reduced. A diversified firm may make greater use of debt rather than equity finance. If interest payments on loans are tax deductible, the overall effect might be a reduction in the firm's taxable profit (Needham, 1978). These arguments were tested by Berger and Ofek (1995), who express scepticism as to whether such factors are significant in most diversification or divestment decisions:

> Two potential benefits of diversification are increased interest tax shields resulting from higher debt capacity and the ability of multi-segment firms to immediately realize tax savings by offsetting losses in some segments against profits in others. Our estimate of tax saving, however, is only 0.1 per cent of sales, far too small to offset the documented value loss.
>
> *(Berger and Ofek, 1995, p. 60)*

Diversification as a means of reducing transaction costs

Motives for diversification or conglomerate merger can also be identified using the transaction costs approach. Below, these are considered under two headings: the conglomerate as an **internal capital market**; and the conglomerate as a vehicle for the exploitation of specific assets.

The conglomerate as an internal capital market

In theory, the financial or capital markets should always reward efficient management by increasing the market value of the firm. In practice, however, investors may be unable to access accurate information in order to judge the performance of management, especially since managers are likely to exercise influence or control over the flow of information. It would require a great deal of altruism for managers to pass on information which might reflect badly on their own performance. Information impactedness (Williamson, 1971) creates a transaction cost that frustrates the efficient allocation of investment funds.

With an M-form corporate structure (Williamson, 1975) the headquarters of the conglomerate performs the task of allocating funds for investment between a number of divisions (see Section 3.6). The managers of the divisions have autonomy in their day-to-day decision making. In this coordinating role, the M-form headquarters has two advantages over the capital market. First, the divisional managers are subordinates to the senior managers, and can be ordered to provide reliable information. An implicit disciplinary threat can be used to encourage compliance (Harris and Raviv, 1996). It might be easier for divisional managers to share confidential information with senior managers than with external investors. Second, the headquarters can conduct internal audits to guard against mismanagement at divisional level. Effectively, the conglomerate acts as a miniature capital market, but enjoys better access to information and is able to monitor performance at divisional level more effectively. Of course, as the conglomerate grows larger, limits may be reached to the ability of the senior managers to monitor and coordinate effectively.

There is also an opposing view, that the managers of a large diversified conglomerate might perform the task of allocating funds less efficiently than the capital markets. The managers might be excessively willing to prop up ailing divisions at the expense of the profitable ones. Divisions within a conglomerate bargain for funds, and the bargaining power of a division might be enhanced by investments that do not benefit the organization as a whole. The head office might buy the cooperation of divisions by diverting investment funds in their direction (Berger and Ofek, 1995; Berlin, 1999; Scharfstein, 1998).

Van Oijen and Douma (2000) elaborate on the factors that determine whether or not central management can exercise effective control over the divisions of a large, diversified conglomerate. Diversification eventually presents a challenge to the control exercised by central management in the following areas:

- *Planning.* A corporate strategy identifies the portfolio of industries and geographic markets in which the firm will be involved. This is distinct from a business strategy, which concerns individual divisions in different industries and countries. The centre is responsible for corporate strategy, but the extent of its involvement in business strategy depends on the level of diversification. The greater the participation of the centre in business strategy, the greater the likelihood that decisions benefit the corporation, rather than the individual division. If the divisions are to benefit from synergies in marketing and distribution, some central coordination is required. Central coordination is easier to achieve if the level of diversification is relatively low.

- *Evaluation.* The centre allocates funds to the individual divisions, and must monitor the subsequent use of funds. Traditional accounting rates of return may be too crude to measure the true contribution of individual divisions to the corporation as a whole. For example, division A may be instructed to send resources to division B, but if this were likely to compromise division A's financial performance, A's cooperation might not be forthcoming. A more sophisticated method of evaluation may be required, recognizing each division's total contribution to the corporation's performance.

■ *Selection*. This reflects the ability of the corporation to select managers who are sympathetic to its strategies, ideals and culture. Effective selection is easiest when the level of diversification is relatively low, and the centre is informed about of the specific needs of individual divisions.

■ *Rotation*. The rotation of resources, especially management, helps spread best practice and develops networks. Rotation encompassing all aspects of the corporation's activities is more difficult in large diversified conglomerates.

■ *Motivation*. In large conglomerates, financial criteria tend to determine incentives, since the centre may be unable to access other information. In less diversified corporations, it may be easier to develop incentive structures based not only on financial criteria, but also on strategic criteria reflecting the performance of the entire organization.

■ *Coordination*. Coordination of joint activities among divisions tends to be easier in less diversified corporations. In highly diversified conglomerates, central coordination may be impeded if it is seen as damaging to the interests of the individual division, and consequently resisted by its management.

■ *Support*. Functions such as human resources, research and development, and legal services can be organized centrally, but the level of diversification is likely to influence the extent of central provision. There is less scope for central provision in a corporation with a diversified range of activities.

Summarizing these arguments, Van Oijen and Douma anticipate that as the level of diversification increases, the centre becomes less involved in planning business strategies and in the day-to-day management of the divisions; relies more on financial criteria when evaluating performance; becomes less involved in the selection of staff; reduces the level of staff rotation; tends to rely increasingly on financial incentives; and offers fewer centralized services.

The conglomerate as a vehicle for the exploitation of specific assets

Penrose (1995) argues that firms' opportunities for growth derive from their possession of resources and assets that can be exploited in other markets. If these resources could be sold to other firms through the market, the rationale for diversification would disappear. Specific assets include new technologies, trade secrets, brand loyalty, managerial experience and expertise (Gorecki, 1975; Markides and Williamson, 1994; Sutton, 1980; Teece, 1982). In the management science literature, assets of this kind are termed core competences by Prahalad and Hamel (1990) and core capabilities by Stalk *et al.* (1992). In order to capitalize on its specific assets, the firm can either sell the assets in the market, or diversify into the relevant industry and exploit the asset itself. The decision whether to sell or diversify depends on the presence of market imperfections which increase the transaction costs incurred by selling the assets in the market.

■ A market may not exist because the property rights in the asset cannot be protected. Basic knowledge which is non-patentable is an example of a specific asset of this kind.

■ It may be too difficult to transfer a specific asset independently of its owner. A team of managers or a group of skilled workers may be uniquely loyal to an owner and unwilling to transfer to another organization.

■ The transaction costs of transferring the asset may be too high. For example, if the technology is complex, it may not be possible to find a buyer with the skills and facilities needed to exploit the asset. It may be necessary to transfer not only the blueprints and recipes for a new product or process, but also skills that are learnt through experience. This would require the training of staff in the buying firm, whose technical background may be unsuitable.

■ Market transactions may be subject to externalities. For example, if B purchases A's brand or trademark, but B is unable to maintain A's standards of service, A's reputation and profitability may suffer. Negotiations between a seller and a buyer may reveal production methods and strategies sufficient for the buyer to contemplate entry into the seller's industry, even if the sale and purchase are not completed. To guard against externalities or spillovers of these kinds, strict and complex contractual relations, perhaps involving high monitoring and policing costs, would be required.

In view of these market imperfections and the associated transaction costs, firms might find it more beneficial to diversify than to trade their specific assets in the market. For example, Gillette's acquisition of the battery manufacturer Duracell in 1996 can be interpreted in terms of the exploitation of specific assets. At first glance there appears to be no obvious potential for economies of scope: capital equipment and technology are very different for the two products. Douma and Schreuder (1998) suggest Gillette wished to exploit its marketing and sales operations in emerging markets such as Brazil, China and India by selling batteries as well as razors.

Montgomery and Wernerfelt (1988) see diversification as a means for extracting rents in related activities. Rents are the returns or rewards to owners of unique factors. Potential diversifiers have excess capacity in their factor inputs, which can be exploited beyond their current use. As a firm diversifies it transfers this excess capacity to the adjacent market which yields the highest rents. Should any spare capacity remain, the firm diversifies into markets further afield, until the marginal rents disappear. Davis and Devinney (1997) suggest three ways in which the desire to make better use of specific assets might propel firms towards diversification. First, supply conditions relate to the potential for economies of scale and scope, created by the possibility of spreading the costs of production, marketing and distribution over a greater number of activities. Second, synergies are created by various customer switching costs. For example, if a firm has built up brand loyalty, and consumers perceive the brand as representing high-quality, then this perception can be exploited in other markets. Third, and perhaps most importantly, is the exploitation of managerial skills, such as technical expertise, the ability to marshal skilled labour and knowledge of the workings of supply industries.

Managerial motives for diversification

As we have seen in Section 3.4, one of the most important characteristics of the large corporation is the separation of ownership from control. According to Marris's (1966) managerial theory of the firm, diversification is the principal method by which growth in demand is achieved in the long run. Similarly, Mueller (1969) suggests conglomerate merger is a strategy that may be pursued by managers who are more concerned with the maximization of growth than with the maximization of shareholder value. If the regulatory authorities make it difficult for firms to expand horizontally or vertically, conglomerate merger may represent the best available alternative strategy.

There may be several reasons why the managers (the agents) might wish to pursue growth at a faster rate than would be chosen by the owners or shareholders (the principals). First, the managers' power, status and remuneration might be related to the growth of the organization. Second, diversification into new activities might complement the talents and skills of the managers, increasing their value to the organization. Third, unlike shareholders, who are able to reduce risk by diversifying their portfolios, the managers' job security depends on the fortunes of the firm. Diversification might provide a means of reducing the risk of failure facing the firm and its managers. Income from employment represents a large proportion of the managers' remuneration, and this income is correlated with the firm's performance. The risks to the managers' income are closely related to the risks facing the firm. Since their employment risk cannot easily be reduced by diversifying their personal portfolios, managers diversify their employment risk by supporting strategies of diversification or conglomerate merger. Amihud and Lev (1981) find manager-controlled firms are more likely to pursue conglomerate merger than owner-controlled firms.

Any firm that wishes to grow within its existing markets is eventually likely to find these markets incapable of expanding sufficiently quickly. Investment opportunities in new markets may offer better prospects than those in existing markets. These opportunities may reflect not just changes in prices, tastes and other market conditions, but also the development of skills and knowledge within the firm (Penrose, 1995). Furthermore, the firm might find expansion within its existing markets triggers increasing rivalry from its competitors. Case study 16.1 presents historical examples which illustrate these kinds of constraint.

In a survey of US firms, Rose and Shepard (1997) find managers' salaries were 13 per cent higher in diversified firms than those in similar specialized firms. However, some caution is required in interpreting this finding. It could be because diversified firms are more complex to manage, and require managers with greater ability. Incumbent managers who pursue diversification strategies are not necessarily rewarded with higher salaries; instead, newly appointed managers of diversified firms might be paid more than managers of specialized firms because the job is more demanding.

16.4　Corporate coherence

Teece *et al.* (1994) develop an interesting approach to the question as to why some firms diversify and some do not. Most firms are coherent in the sense that they do not diversify at random; to do so would reflect an incoherent strategy. Furthermore **corporate coherence** is usually stable over time. Companies such as Shell Oil, ICI and Boeing have all focused on a narrow range of activities for close to a century. For example, Shell has never attempted to diversify into jewellery, Boeing into buses or ICI into supermarkets. Coherence suggests the products of most conglomerates tend to be related, and the challenge is to develop a theory which explains why these firms usually tend to diversify coherently.

Few firms are truly specialized in the sense that they produce only one product. Owing to natural variation in market demand, at the very least firms are likely to offer products in more than one size, colour, flavour, or other relevant characteristic. However, diversification refers to product extension, which is more variegated than these examples. Firms add new products over time with technical or market similarities to existing product lines. In order to develop a measure of coherence, Teece *et al.* first construct a measure of relatedness. This is computed on the basis that frequently observed combinations of activities on the part of firms in the same industry should be related. If firms in a given industry almost always involve themselves in specific combinations of activities, then these activities are related. A measure of relatedness is computed on the basis of a sample of over 18,000 US manufacturing firms, active in 958 different four-digit SIC industries involved in close to 67,000 activities in total. For example, the highest relatedness was between SIC 5181 (beer wholesalers) and SIC 5182 (spirit wholesalers). The measure of coherence is the weighted-average relatedness of one activity to all other activities in the firm. As diversification increases, firms tend to add activities that relate to their existing activities, and the degree of relatedness does not tend to change as firms diversify further. Therefore coherence appears to be a major characteristic of diversified business operations.

In an attempt to develop a theory of corporate coherence, Teece *et al.* redefine the firm in terms of enterprise learning, path dependency and selection. Below, each of these is considered briefly.

Enterprise learning

Learning is an important part of any economic and business activity. Through learning, processes are improved and new opportunities identified. Learning takes place not only through the traditional trainer–trainee interaction, but also through group interaction. Successful learning results in the development of two types of organizational routine: static and dynamic. Static routines are activities which are copied or replicated, with refinements, modifications and the development of new routines taking place gradually over time. Dynamic routines are activities through which the organization develops new processes and practices. Research and development activities are an obvious example. These routines may be difficult to replicate and apply in other situations. Therefore dynamic routines can be thought of as a specific asset which differentiates the firm from its competitors.

Path dependency

The value of enterprise learning depends largely on what the firm has achieved in the past. Past investments and routines tend to shape the future, because learning tends to be local in the sense that the firm is most likely to develop opportunities based on its existing knowledge and skills (Lockett and Thompson, 2001). In respect of new products, the two most important aspects of the learning process are the technology and the market in which the new product is to be launched. To enter a completely new market with a radically different product may overextend a firm's learning capabilities; consequently, the strategy may fail. Teece *et al.* identify three aspects of path dependency:

- *Complementary assets* help construct paths for future growth. In many cases, assets have alternative uses which can be exploited vertically and horizontally. For example, Singer sewing machines diversified into the furniture business partly because of its ability to build wooden cabinets to house its machines.

- *Technological opportunities* determine how far and how fast a firm moves down any particular path. The firm's research and development effort identifies the technological opportunities available for existing products, as well as possible alternatives.

- *Convergence of paths* occurs when there are major shifts in basic knowledge. As the core technological characteristics of different industries change, paths may converge or diverge. For example, the development of digital electronics has led to convergence between computers and telecommunications. Products once aimed at different markets and based on different technologies now share the same core technology.

Selection

Selection refers to the natural tendency for efficient firms to survive and prosper, and for inefficient firms to decline and fail. The rate at which this selection takes place depends on the level of competition, public policy, technology and the firm's accumulated debt. The more debt the firm accumulates, the greater the threat of discipline from the capital market. Teece *et al.* argue the more rigorous the selection process, the greater the reliance the firm places on its core competences or specific assets.

Based on these characteristics, Teece *et al.* identify three types of firm:

- *The specialist firm* is characterized by rapid learning with high technological opportunity and narrow path dependency. This type of firm tends to be younger, because the extent of technological opportunity tends to diminish over time.

■ *The coherent diversifier* is characterized by quick learning, a broad path dependency based on generic technologies and rigorous selection. These firms tend to be older than specialist firms, and to have successfully weathered periods of recession.

■ *The conglomerate* is characterized by slow learning, low path dependency and weak selection. Should selection become stronger, the survival of some of the less dynamic conglomerates is likely to be threatened.

In general, Teece *et al.* do not view conglomerates in a positive light. Two responses are offered to the question as to why some conglomerates seem to have prospered. First, as discussed in Section 16.3, conglomerates may serve as internal capital markets, and may generate savings in the costs of collecting information and monitoring performance (Williamson, 1975). Second, some conglomerates may have evolved almost accidentally, through some form of organizational mutation. By chance, some conglomerates may develop characteristics which allow them to survive for a period of time, but eventually selection eliminates all but a few.

16.5 Corporate focus and deconglomeration

In the management science literature, the term corporate focus refers to the extent to which a firm specializes in its core activity. In a study of 33 large US firms over the period 1950–86, Porter (1987) notes most had divested more acquisitions than they had retained; in other words, most had become increasingly focused. Similar conclusions are drawn by Scharfstein (1998), who analyses a US sample of 165 conglomerates that were diversified into at least one other unrelated activity in 1979. By 1994, 55 of these firms had become focused on their core activity; 57 firms that had not become more focused had been acquired by other firms; and only 53 firms still existed as conglomerates in 1994.

Why did many large conglomerates tend to divest activities during the 1980s and 1990s? The fundamental reason is that in many cases, firms that had become increasingly diversified also became less profitable (Rhoades, 1974). Conversely, average profitability often tended to increase among firms that became more focused. There is some evidence of a tendency for the stock market prices of parent firms that divested some activities to have risen (Daley *et al.*, 1997). Furthermore, this tendency was more pronounced for firms that sold unrelated activities than for firms that sold related activities. In a study of 1,449 US firms in the 1980s, Lang and Stulz (1994) find Tobin's q (the ratio of the market value of a firm to its replacement cost of assets; see Box 9.1) was greater for specialized firms than for diversified firms.

If the share prices of diversified firms are consistently lower than those of specialized firms (relative to the underlying value of assets), it appears shareholders tend to penalize diversified firms. This might suggest that unrelated diversification is a strategy intended to benefit managers and not shareholders. Analysing the profitability of the parent firms that divested themselves of their acquisitions, as well as the units that were divested, Daley *et al.* (1997) find profitability increased for both types of organization. This appears to justify the observed tendency for capital markets to be optimistic about firms that have become more focused.

The issue of focus is approached from a different angle in Siggelkow's (2003) study of US mutual fund providers. Some providers offer a broad range of funds, including specialized equity, bond and index funds; while others focus on a narrower range of funds. Using data for the period 1985–96, Siggelkow finds the mutual funds of focused providers outperformed those of diversified providers. Similar findings are reported by Comment and Jarrell (1995), Haynes *et al.* (2002), Kaplan and Weisbach (1992) and Ravenscraft and Scherer (1987). Martin and Sayrak (2003) survey the literature on diversification and shareholder value.

Berger and Ofek (1995) test for the existence of a diversification discount, measured by comparing the performance of individual divisions of a conglomerate with that of specialized firms in the same industry. The diversification discount is the difference between the sum of the hypothetical stand-alone market values of each constituent division of the conglomerate, and the actual market value. The stand-alone values exceeded the market values by about 15 per cent on average.

Agreement as to the existence and magnitude of the diversification discount is not universal. Hyland (2003) tests the hypothesis that a diversification discount may already exist before a firm decides to diversify. A firm that diversifies may have a relatively low value of Tobin's q for reasons other than diversification, such as inferior management. Accordingly, Hyland examines the diversification discount over the three years before and the three years after the diversification decision. On average, Tobin's q tends to fall in the first year after diversification; but the value for the subsequent two years is not lower than that for the preceding three years. In an international study, Lins and Servaes (1999) find evidence of a diversification discount for Japan and the UK, but not for Germany. It is suggested the different results might reflect different levels of concentration of ownership.

Nevertheless, the consensus seems to be that a diversification discount does exist, and if the discount is as large as some studies suggest, it is perhaps unsurprising that shareholders have encouraged managers to implement strategies of divestment or **deconglomeration**. Haynes *et al.* (2002) suggest the following reasons for improved performance following divestment from diversified activities. First, the diversified firm may be overstretched in so far as its organizational structure is unable to cope with the complex demands of its divisions. Second, if diversification was originally undertaken in order to realize managerial objectives such as growth or sales revenue maximization, then divestment may enable the firm to regain previous levels of profitability performance. Third, for an underperforming firm, a divestment announcement may signal that management are addressing the problem and that changes are imminent. The stock market may view such an announcement in a positive light. Finally, if the divesting firm is acquired by a new owner, the potential for cost savings may generate gains which flow to the vendors via a higher purchase price. An improvement in performance is therefore linked with divestment.

Porter (1990) draws a similar conclusion, and suggests another reason for poor performance: the neglect of innovation in the various divisions of the conglomerate. Innovation stems from focus and commitment to sustained investment in a specific activity. In contrast:

Unrelated diversification, particularly through acquisition, makes no contribution to innovation. Unrelated diversification almost inevitably detracts from focus, commitment and sustained investment in the core industries, no matter how well-intentioned management is at the outset. Acquired companies, where there is no link to existing businesses, often face short-term financial pressures to justify their purchase price. It is also difficult for corporate managers of a diversified firm to be forward-looking in industries they do not know.

(Porter, 1990, p. 605)

I will continue to hold the view that management too often underestimates the problems in carrying through mergers, especially of companies in unrelated fields. It has indeed been one of the more welcome developments of recent years that companies have been increasingly concentrating on their core activities, divesting themselves of some of the enterprises they have acquired in earlier diversifications. It is the very pressures of competition I referred to earlier that have forced so many companies to re-examine their structure.

(John Bridgeman, Director-General of Fair Trading, speech to the European Policy Forum, 30 January 1996)

In the light of most of this evidence, it is natural to wonder why companies ever diversified into unrelated activities, and why some still do. One possibility is that the diversification discount may not have been as high in the past (Matsusaka, 1993; Servaes, 1996). Changes in the external environment might be partly responsible. For example, the attitudes of policy makers towards highly concentrated industries and horizontal mergers generally became more relaxed during the 1980s than they had been during the 1960s and 1970s. Consequently, firms wishing to grow could do so more easily within their existing markets. Furthermore, the increasing scope and efficiency of capital markets may have reduced the need for the conglomerate to act effectively as an internal capital market. In the US and UK in particular, the refocusing of many conglomerates during the 1980s and 1990s was made possible by leveraged buyouts, in which unsecured junk bonds and loans were used to buy up large diversified conglomerates. Typically, the less profitable parts of the target firm would be sold off, leaving only the more profitable core activities. The receipts from the sale of unrelated activities would be used to service and repay the unsecured loans. An example of this type of buyout was Hoylake's attempt to buy British and American Tobacco, which in 1989 was the ninth largest company in Europe. In another case, Hanson's purchase of a 2.8 per cent share in ICI was interpreted by the markets as a prelude to a full takeover bid. Investors inferred that to finance the takeover, Hanson would be forced to sell off some ICI divisions, and refocus the remaining activities. ICI fought back by splitting into two independent companies: one (ICI) concentrating on chemicals, and the other (Zeneca) on pharmaceuticals and agriculture. As a result of this strategy, the profitability and share prices of both companies increased.

The myth of the mega-bank: after the failures of diversification, wary lenders scale back their global ambitions

At the dawn of this decade there seemed no limits to the ambitions of the global banking industry. In the US the Gramm-Leach-Bliley Act dismantled Depression-era barriers between banks and other businesses, clearing the way for the creation of more 'financial services supermarkets' that would tempt customers with a one-stop outlet for everything from managed funds to travel insurance. In Europe, the advent of the eurozone seemed set to herald sweeping cross-border consolidation. That has not happened. While bankers worldwide have been pursuing deals, their ambitions have grown humble. They are building scale in businesses they like and abandoning those that prove disappointing; but they are avoiding attempts at diversification.

To some extent, the banks' caution reflects the collapse of the stock market bubble in 2000 and the resulting pressure to cut costs and reduce capacity. But banks have also tested the idea of the financial supermarket in the real world and found it wanting. 'Visionary restructuring is finding it hard to gain support', PwC [PricewaterhouseCoopers] concluded in a recent report on the financial sector. 'A warmer reception is given to those [deals] that concentrate on filling in specific gaps in [an institution's] portfolio and getting rid of awkward fits.' The pace of mergers and acquisitions picked up significantly last year in the financial services industry and accounted for about a third of global M&A volume. But it mainly involved companies sticking to what they know best. Insurers are combining with insurers: Manulife with John Hancock; Travelers Property Casualty with the St Paul Companies. Citigroup, a market leader in credit cards and sub-prime lending, bought a card portfolio from Sears and a consumer finance unit from Washington Mutual. Even Bank of America's US$47bn (£26bn, €37bn) proposed purchase of FleetBoston Financial – the biggest deal in the world last year – had a prosaic quality. By buying Fleet, BofA sought refuge in the US branch banking businesses that produce most of its profits. It turned away from the temptations that tantalised commercial banks in the 1990s – Wall Street, fund management, insurance, or bold overseas expansion.

BofA's thoughts of a pioneering transatlantic deal to buy Barclays in the UK appear to have been shelved and Ken Lewis, chairman and chief executive, told investors last month that he had little appetite for a brokerage or an investment bank acquisition. Other bankers are likely to do even less. Chuck Prince, Citigroup's new chief executive, told investors they should expect 'fill-in' acquisitions from him. Goldman Sachs analysts concluded last month that 'small bank deals [were] likely to remain the trend'. Rodgin Cohen, the influential US banking lawyer, told a conference organised by Prudential Financial that he tended to doubt 'we will ever see' financial institutions such as AIG, American Express, Goldman Sachs, Morgan Stanley, Merrill Lynch or Prudential buy commercial banks. 'Most of the bank deals you are going to see are going to be about cost saves', said Mark Sirower, head of North American M&A at the Boston Consulting Group. 'A lot of deals are going to be boring in a sense, because they will be about scale and capabilities in business the banks are already in.'

The global banking sector ought to be primed for a furious round of mergers: banks are suffering from low revenue growth, yet remain highly profitable and are therefore awash with excess capital. But many banks have decided against deploying their capital to make acquisitions, preferring to return it to shareholders through dividends or share buy-backs.

So why is diversification out of favour? For a start, the evidence that banks gain from being big is not conclusive. Some bankers speak of the need to be giant – with market capitalizations of more than US$100bn – if they are to be large enough to provide the multi-billion-dollar credit lines demanded by some of the world's biggest corporations. Yet new research by analysts at Morgan Stanley has found that 'there's no statistical relationship between size of assets and returns that we can see. The data might suggest size brings its own inefficiencies or, just as likely, that "returns to scale" run out at relatively low levels of market share.' Underlying banks' new-found risk aversion is an acknowledgement that the diversification strategies fashionable during the 1990s seem to have produced minimal benefits for investors. Attempts at cross-selling – marketing as many products as possible to a customer – have proved disappointing in many cases. According to Morgan Stanley: 'Investor doubts on bank managements' core competences have risen in recent years . . . the value to shareholders of banks increasing the diversity of the business model – fanning out in both geographic and activity terms – has given way to wholly legitimate concerns on both the risks and value added of diversity as an end in itself.'

In Europe, diversification has produced many casualties, particularly where banks' ventures into insurance are concerned. Indeed, the market risk acquired by banks has recently proved a bigger problem than the credit risk that is their stock in trade. Since Lloyds TSB of the UK bought Scottish Widows, the life assurer, in 2000, losses on its investment funds have been just as heavy as the group's hits on bad loans in both 2001 and 2002. Lloyds TSB, now under new leadership, has since tried to sell Scottish Widows but found no takers at the price it wanted. Equally, Switzerland's Credit Suisse came to rue the day in 1997 when it took over the Winterthur insurance company. When combined with the disastrous consequences for earnings of having bought Donaldson Lufkin & Jenrette, the investment bank, at the top of the market, Credit Suisse found that its acquisitions had created a serious capital risk. Officially, the bank remains wedded to its investment bank, despite dissent on the board. But it has been much quicker to sell off large parts of its insurance operation, sometimes for excellent prices.

Nor has the argument for diversification been bolstered by the results when insurers have bought banks. Allianz has seen its reputation as one of Germany's finest companies shattered by its takeover of Dresdner Bank. Declining revenues and bad loans at the bank forced the insurer into a humiliatingly discounted equity raising this year. Ironically, the move away from diversification probably began with Citigroup, the company most closely associated with the financial supermarket idea. One big reason for the 1998 merger between Travelers and Citicorp that created Citigroup was to make cross-selling easier. This has happened in businesses ranging from branch banking to corporate finance. But Citigroup has run into curious results in other areas. When it offered vehicle and home insurance to banking customers, it attracted the wrong kind of people: bad drivers, for example. As a result, Citigroup last year spun off Travelers Property Casualty, its vehicle and home insurance underwriter, in what was then the fifth biggest US initial public offering. 'It just didn't play well together', Sandy Weill, Citigroup's chairman, said at the time.

Source: The myth of the mega-bank: after the failures of diversification, wary lenders scale back their global ambitions, *Financial Times*, 6 January 2004. © Financial Times Limited. Reprinted with permission. (Abridged.)

16.6 Empirical evidence

In this section we examine some of the empirical evidence concerning the reasons for diversification, and its direction. We begin by examining the measurement of the extent of diversification.

In a technical sense, the measures of the extent of diversification are quite similar to the measures of concentration that were reviewed in Section 6.4. Concentration measures reflect the number and relative sizes of the firms operating in an industry. Diversification measures reflect the number of industries in which one firm is involved, and the relative scale of its involvement in each case (Gollop and Monahan, 1991; Lacktorin and Rajan, 2000). Some of the most widely used diversification measures are as follows:

■ *A count of activities*. One possibility is to simply count the number of three- or four-digit Standard Industrial Classification (SIC) activities in which the firm is involved. This is perhaps too simple for most purposes: one would naturally wish to discount or disregard activities in which the firm's involvement is very small.

■ *Ratio of non-primary activities to all activities*. A simple measure of the extent of diversification is the ratio $DR = B/(A + B)$, where A represents the firm's primary activity and B represents all other non-primary activities. A and B might be measured in terms of sales or employees. A specialized firm has $DR = 0$; and the greater the extent of diversification, the closer is DR to its maximum value of one. However, DR does not reflect the relative importance of each of the non-primary activities.

■ *Herfindahl index of specialization, H(S)*. This index is based on a weighted sum of the share of each activity in the total of all of the firm's activities (Berry, 1971, 1974). It is defined in the same way as the Herfindahl–Hirschman (HH) index of concentration (see Section 6.4). For a firm involved in N activities, let x_i denote the share of sales or employment in activity i in the firm's total sales or employment. The H(S) index is calculated as follows:

$$H(S) = \sum_{i=1}^{N} x_i^2$$

The index is influenced by both the number of activities and their relative importance. The more specialized the firm, the greater is H(S). As in the case of the HH index of concentration, a numbers equivalent of the H(S) index is defined as $1/H(S)$. The numbers equivalent is an inverse measure of diversification. For a firm with N activities (and using a sales-based measure), the minimum possible value of the numbers equivalent is $1/H(S) = 1$, when virtually all of the firm's sales are derived from one activity, with a negligible proportion split between the other $N - 1$ activities. The maximum possible value is $1/H(S) = N$, when the firm's sales are split equally between the N activities.

Using 1963 UK manufacturing data, Gorecki (1975) examines the direction and determinants of diversification. Measurement of the **direction of diversification**

Table 16.1 Calculation of Gorecki's T-value

Order X	Total number of firms	Firms diversified into any industry within order X	Firms diversified into any industry within any manufacturing order, including X
Industry A	30	13 (in B, C or D)	16
Industry B	20	9 (in A, C or D)	17
Industry C	80	53 (in A, B or D)	61
Industry D	20	11 (in A, B or C)	18
		Total = 86	Total = 112

distinguishes between diversification within and outside a firm's two-digit industry group. To measure direction, Gorecki calculates the extent of participation of diversified firms in other industries within a broadly defined industry, known as an order. An order roughly corresponds to a two-digit industry group. Gorecki's data set comprises 14 orders and 51 industries. The measure of direction is the T-value, the summation of the total number of enterprises that own establishments in each of the other industries within the same order, divided by the summation of the total number of enterprises that own establishments in any other manufacturing industry.

The calculation of the T-value is illustrated in Table 16.1, where it is assumed the (broadly defined) order X is composed of four (narrowly defined) industries A, B, C and D. Of the 30 industry A firms, 13 are diversified into at least one of industries B, C or D within order X. Three further industry A firms are not diversified into any of B, C or D, but are diversified into at least one industry from another manufacturing order. Therefore in total, 16 of the 30 industry A firms are diversified. The T-value for order X is the ratio of the summation across industries A to D of the number of firms diversified within order X to the summation of the number of firms diversified within any manufacturing order, or $86/112 = 0.76$. The minimum possible T-value is zero (all diversification is outside the order), and the maximum possible T-value is one (all diversification is within the order).

The actual T-value can be compared with the T-value expected if diversification occurs randomly across the other 50 industries. If a firm in industry A were to diversify randomly (in order to reduce risk), the probability that it would diversify into one of industries B, C and D would be $3/50 = 0.06$. In the majority of cases examined by Gorecki, the actual T-value was greater than the expected T-value. In only a handful of cases, including building materials, footwear and furniture, was the actual value less than the expected value. Gorecki's overall conclusion, that the direction of diversification was not random, is unequivocal.

In a regression model that seeks to identify the determinants of the decision to diversify, Gorecki's dependent variable is the ratio of employment in non-primary activities to total employment. Two types of independent variable are used to explain diversification. The first covers activities determined by the firm, such as advertising and research and development, which produce specific assets (brands, trademarks, innovation) that can be exploited through diversification. Advertizing is measured using an advertising-to-sales ratio, and research and development is measured using the number of research employees. Dummy variables control for differences between consumer and non-consumer goods industries. The second category of variables covers environmental factors, such as industry growth and concentration. Firms in low-growth industries are more likely to diversify in order to exploit their specific assets; therefore a negative relationship between growth and the extent of diversification is expected (although this relationship might be offset if firms in declining industries are unable to finance diversification). Firms in highly concentrated industries face higher costs of further expansion within the same industries. Firms in more highly concentrated industries are therefore expected to be more likely to diversify.

The estimation results do not support all of the hypotheses advanced above. The results are consistent with the hypothesis that diversification and research and development expenditure are positively related. However, the coefficient on the advertising-to-sales ratio is negative, and not positive as expected. Gorecki suggests firms in consumer goods industries characterized by heavy advertising might vertically integrate forwards in order to protect their brands, and this type of strategy might be at the cost of diversification. The coefficients on industry growth and concentration are both statistically insignificant.

Using a sample of 200 of the largest UK manufacturing firms in 1974, Utton (1977) examines the level of specialization and the extent and characteristics of diversification. The 200 firms are classified into 14 orders, and their activities into 121 three-digit industries. The degree of involvement at these stages is calculated by the level of employment. The extent of specialization is measured as the ratio of the percentage employment in each firm's primary three-digit activity. Comparing industry averages based on this measure, the lowest level of specialization is 38 per cent for textiles and the highest is 75 per cent for shipbuilding. These results seem at variance with the received wisdom at the time, that large firms are almost by definition eager diversifiers. '[T]he picture that emerges is of enterprises that, on the whole, are still rather more highly specialized than some recent comment would suggest' (Utton, 1977, p. 100).

Utton's measure of the extent of diversification is:

$$W = 2 \sum_{i=1}^{N} ip_i - 1$$

where N is the number of activities in which the firm is involved, p_i is the proportion of the firm's employment in activity i, and activities are ranked in order of the firm's employment data (so $i = 1$ for the activity in which the firm has the most employees, $i = 2$ for the activity in which the firm has the second-highest number of employees, and so on). W is a numbers equivalent diversification measure. The minimum value of W is one (virtually all of the firm's employment is in one activity, with a negligible proportion of total employment split between the other $N - 1$ activities), and the maximum value is N (the firm's total employment is split equally between the N activities). The higher the value of W within the range 1 to N, the greater the extent of diversification. A weighted average is calculated for each order. For the 14 orders the range runs from 9 (coal, petroleum, chemicals and allied products) to 1.7 (instrument engineering), with a weighted average of 4.4.

[T]he data . . . on the whole run counter to the popular view of a small number of very large conglomerates with tentacles stretching into every corner of industry and able to strangle existing competitors should the need arise. Where the largest enterprises are diversified to the equivalent extent of operating equally in only about four fairly narrowly defined industries, inclusive of vertical integration, we may question whether they are likely to have much scope for practices such as cross-subsidization, predatory reciprocal purchases and avoidance of competition which some authorities have envisaged.

(Utton, 1977, p. 106)

Utton also finds a relationship between firm size and the extent of diversification. In the sample of 200 firms, the largest firm has some 12 times as many employees as the smallest firm. The index of diversification (W) averages 3.85 for the 50 largest firms, and 2.63 for the 50 smallest firms. There is a positive relationship between firm size and the average value of W, but the differences in average W by size group are smaller than the differences between orders.

Table 16.2 summarizes Utton's findings concerning the direction of diversification. Activity in three-digit industries within the same order as a firm's primary activity is termed narrow-spectrum diversification, and activity in three-digit industries outside the order of the firm's primary activity is broad-spectrum diversification. In food, drink and tobacco, for example, 73 per cent of secondary activities were located in the same order. In metal goods, the corresponding figure was only 15 per cent. Excluding shipbuilding and instrument engineering as special cases,

Table 16.2 Direction of diversification in UK top 200 manufacturing enterprises, 1974

Enterprises (SIC order)	No. of enterprises	Narrow-spectrum diversification	Broad-spectrum diversification
Food, drink and tobacco	31	0.729	0.271
Coal, petroleum, chemicals, etc.	18	0.378	0.622
Metal manufacture	10	0.210	0.790
Mechanical engineering	31	0.318	0.682
Instrument engineering	3	0.000	1.000
Electrical engineering	22	0.556	0.445
Shipbuilding and marine engineering	6	0.000	1.000
Vehicles	17	0.065	0.935
Metal goods	6	0.149	0.851
Textiles	13	0.605	0.395
Clothing and footwear	6	0.452	0.548
Bricks, pottery, glass, cement, timber	14	0.141	0.859
Paper, printing and publishing	13	0.731	0.269
Other manufacturing	10	0.254	0.746
Total	200	0.446	0.554

Source: Adapted from Utton, M.A. (1977) Large firm diversification in the British manufacturing industry, *Economic Journal*, 87, 109. Used with permission.

seven of the remaining 12 orders had a broad-spectrum diversification percentage of more than 60 per cent. For the whole sample, 45 per cent of all secondary activities were narrow spectrum and 55 per cent were broad-spectrum. Although at first sight this result appears to be at odds with Gorecki's (1975) earlier findings, it is important to note the two samples are very different. Furthermore, Utton finds no correlation between W and broad-spectrum diversification. Prolific diversifiers are as likely to diversify narrowly as broadly. Much secondary activity is in orders that are closely related technologically. For example, if the mechanical engineering, electrical engineering, vehicles and metal goods orders were combined, 73 per cent of secondary activity in these orders would be classed as narrow; and narrow spectrum diversification for the whole sample of 200 firms would increase from 45 per cent to 58 per cent.

Writing from a strategic management perspective, Luffman and Reed (1984) examine diversification by UK firms during the 1970s, using a four-category methodology suggested by Rumelt (1974):

■ In a single business, more than 95 per cent of sales are accounted for by one product.

■ In a dominant firm, between 70 per cent and 95 per cent of sales are accounted for by one product.

■ In a related firm, no one product accounts for more than 70 per cent of sales, all products are related.

■ In an unrelated firm, no one product accounts for more than 70 per cent of sales, the products are unrelated.

Luffman and Reed (1984) find there was a trend towards increased diversification during the 1970s, although the trend was not as strong as in the decades immediately after the Second World War. There was significant movement into unrelated (conglomerate) activities.

Rondi *et al.* (1996) measure the extent of diversification among major firms producing within the EU, and attempt to identify the major determinants of diversification. Their sample is based on the five leading EU firms in each manufacturing industry. Although both EU and non-EU firms are considered, any production activity located outside the EU is ignored. The diversification measures used are those described at the start of Section 16.6: first, a simple count of different industry involvement, N; second, the ratio of secondary production to total production, DR; and third, the Berry (1971, 1974) index, $D = 1 - H(S)$. All three measures are calculated at the two-digit and three-digit levels, to allow a distinction to be drawn between product extension (related) and pure (unrelated) diversification. Production outside the two-digit level implies pure diversification.

Table 16.3 summarizes the results. The average firm is involved in almost five three-digit industries, and almost three two-digit industries. Around 28 per cent of output is produced outside the primary two-digit industry, and 17 per cent is produced outside the primary two-digit industry. By country, the highest levels of diversification at the three-digit level were for the UK and the Netherlands, and the lowest levels were for Italy and Germany.

Table 16.3 Measures of diversification, large EU manufacturing enterprises

	Two-digit industry definition	Three-digit industry definition
Average number of industries, N	2.9	4.9
% Production outside primary industry, DR	17.1	28.3
Berry index, $D = 1 - H(S)$	0.23	0.37

Source: Adapted from Rondi, L., Sembenelli, A. and Ragazzi, E. (1996) Determinants of diversification patterns, in Davies, S. and Lyons, B. *Industrial Organisation in the European Union*. Oxford: Oxford University Press, 171.

In examining the determinants of diversification, Rondi *et al.* (1996) focus on three theories of diversification. The first, attributed to Marris (1964) and Penrose (1959), suggests managers seek to maximize the growth of the firm. The exploitation of specific assets such as marketing skills and technical expertise in other industries provides a convenient vehicle for the pursuit of a growth objective. The second theory, attributed to Bain (1959), focuses on the conditions that make entry possible or attractive. These include industry-level characteristics such as average profitability, growth and concentration, as well as barriers to entry. The third theory, attributed to Rumelt (1984) and Williamson (1975), focuses on relatedness between industries that makes diversification attractive. Relatedness refers to similarities between technologies, markets and organizational structures.

Rondi *et al.*'s empirical model is:

$$P(F,P,S) = f\{W(F), X(P), Y(S), Z(P,S)\}$$

The dependent variable P(F,P,S) is the probability that firm F with primary activity P diversifies into secondary activity S. The independent variables are W(F), a vector of characteristics of firm F; X(P), a vector of characteristics of primary activity P; Y(S), a vector of characteristics of secondary activity S; and Z(P,S), a vector reflecting the degree of relatedness between P and S.

The vector W(F) includes a firm size measure, to reflect the ease with which a firm can acquire resources; a measure of the size of the firm's domestic market, to reflect the opportunities for growth; and dummy variables to capture relevant characteristics of each country's capital markets. X(P) includes indicators of advertising intensity, research and development, human resources and capital intensity, to reflect the firm's specific assets. Y(S) includes measures of the attractiveness of secondary industries and the height of entry barriers, captured using industry growth, profitability, advertising intensity, research and development, human resources and capital intensity indicators. Z(P,S) includes measures of the relatedness of each secondary and primary industry, also based on advertising, research and development, human resources and capital intensity indicators.

The estimation results suggest firm size matters: larger firms are more likely to diversifiy than smaller firms. Firms originating from countries where there is a separation of ownership from control (proxied by capital market characteristics) are more likely to diversify. However, the size of the domestic market has no effect on the probability of diversification. Diversification is more likely if levels of advertising, research and development and specific human capital skills are high in both the primary and secondary activities. Specific assets play an important role in determining the rate and direction of diversification, as does the degree of relatedness: diversification often involves entry into secondary industries with characteristics similar to the primary industry. The coefficients on capital intensity are negative, supporting the notion that entry barriers influence the direction of diversification.

In general, the empirical evidence on the direction and determinants of diversification in the UK and Europe suggests firms tend to be relatively cautious in their diversification strategies, preferring in most cases to remain close to their technological and market bases. Perhaps the single most important motive for diversification is the opportunity to exploit specific assets within related industries.

16.7   Summary

Chapter 16 has examined the topic of diversification. There are three basic types of diversification. Diversification by product extension implies a firm supplies a new product that is closely related to its existing products. Diversification by market extension implies a firm supplies its existing product in a new geographic market. Finally, pure diversification involves a movement into a completely unrelated field of activity. There are two ways in which a diversification strategy can be implemented: first, through internally generated expansion; and second, through conglomerate merger. While diversification through internal expansion leads to an increase in the total productive capacity in the industry concerned, diversification through conglomerate merger involves only a transfer of ownership and control over existing productive capacity.

A number of theories have been developed to explain why a firm might decide to pursue a diversification strategy.

■ *Enhancement of market power*. The diversified firm may be in a strong position to compete against a specialized rival by drawing on cash flows or profits earned elsewhere within the organization, effectively cross-subsidizing the costs of engaging the rival in either price or non-price forms of competition. Reciprocity and tying may be attractive strategies for a diversified firm that is seeking to generate sales across several distinct product lines.

■ *Cost savings*. Diversification can result in cost savings in three ways. First, economies of scope are realized when the costs of indivisibilities are spread over the production of several goods or services, or when the diversified producer is able to realize other types of average cost saving. Second, diversification reduces the firm's exposure to adverse fluctuations in demand in any one of its product markets. The ability to manage risk through diversification may reduce the firm's cost of raising finance. Third, by offsetting profits earned from one activity against losses in another, a diversified firm may be able to reduce its tax exposure.

- *Reduction of transaction costs.* If investors are unable to access reliable information in order to judge the performance of managers, the efficient allocation of investment funds may be impeded. Within a diversified firm or conglomerate, central managers at head office undertake the task of allocating funds between the divisions of the conglomerate. Effectively, the conglomerate acts as a miniature capital market, but enjoys better access to information and is able to monitor performance more effectively. Most firms possess specific assets that are of value if exploited in other markets. If the transaction costs incurred in trading specific assets through the market are high, it may be better for the firm to exploit the assets itself by implementing a diversification strategy.

- *Managerial motives for diversification.* According to several of the early managerial theories of the firm, diversification is the principal method by which growth in demand is achieved in the long run. Managers might target growth rather than profit because their compensation and prestige are related to the size or growth of the organization. Diversification might increase the managers' value to the organization, and it might enhance their job security by reducing risk.

According to the corporate coherence approach, most conglomerates pursue a coherent diversification strategy in the sense that they do not diversify at random; instead, the products of most conglomerates tend to be related. Learning is a crucial factor. Successful learning results in the development of static and dynamic organizational routines: static routines are activities that are easily copied or replicated; while dynamic routines leading to the development of new processes and practices are a type of specific asset. The value of enterprise learning depends largely on what the firm has achieved previously; in other words, there is path dependency. Finally, a process of natural selection enables successful firms to survive and prosper, while unsuccessful firms tend to decline and fail. In general, the empirical evidence on the direction and determinants of diversification suggests most firms are cautious in their diversification strategies, usually preferring to remain close to their current technological and market bases.

During the 1980s and 1990s there was a shift of emphasis away from diversification, and in some cases towards the divestment of unrelated activities in pursuit of increased focus. There is some empirical evidence of a diversification discount: a tendency for conglomerates to underperform relative to specialized firms in terms of profitability and stock market valuation. This may explain why shareholders encouraged managers to implement a strategy of divestment or deconglomeration.

There are several reasons why a diversified firm might underperform, or why a policy of divestment might be expected to bring about an improvement in performance. First, some conglomerates may simply be too large, and their organizational structures overstretched. Second, if diversification was originally undertaken in pursuit of non-profit objectives, divestment might enable the firm to recover previous levels of profitability. Third, a divestment announcement may signal to the stock market that the problems of an underperforming conglomerate are being addressed. Finally, in the more market-oriented environment of the late twentieth and early twenty-first centuries, the economic rationale for the existence of large, highly diversified conglomerates is perhaps less persuasive than it may have been during the decades up to the 1970s, when the trend towards corporate diversification was apparently at its strongest.

Discussion questions

1. Explain the distinction between diversification through product extension, diversification through market extension, and pure diversification.

2. For what reasons might a firm's choice of diversification strategy depend on the stage achieved in the industry life cycle?

3. In what ways might a strategy of diversification enhance the market power exercised by a conglomerate in some of its product markets?

4. The argument that diversification benefits a firm through the realization of economies of scale by spreading the costs of indivisible inputs over a larger output is of limited appeal, according to some economists. Explain why.

5. With reference to Case study 16.1, quote examples of successful and unsuccessful diversification strategies.

6. Williamson argued that a common motive for conglomerate merger is the opportunity to take over inefficiently managed and undervalued firms. Owing to information impactedness, capital markets and shareholders may be unable to discipline weak management effectively. Why might a cadre of corporate managers be better positioned than shareholders to exercise effective control over an unsuccessful firm?

7. For what reasons might a non-profit-maximizing firm be expected to diversify at a faster rate than a profit-maximizing firm?

8. In what ways might a strategy of continued diversification eventually weaken the control exercised by central management over the divisions of a large conglomerate?

9. Suggest examples of firms that correspond to Teece *et al.*'s categorization of the specialist firm, the coherent diversifier and the conglomerate.

10. Describe the methods that can be used to measure the extent of diversification in a particular industry.

11. Why have strategies of deconglomeration and the quest for greater corporate coherence become more fashionable than the strategy of continued diversification for many large conglomerates since the 1980s? Discuss with reference to Case study 16.2.

Further reading

Berger, P.G. and Ofek, E. (1995) Diversification's effect on firm value, *Journal of Financial Economics*, 37, 39–65.

Blackstone, E.A. (1972) Monopsony power, reciprocal buying, and government contracts: the General Dynamic case, *Antitrust Bulletin*, 17, 445–66.

Comment, R. and Jarrell, G. (1995) Corporate focus and stock returns, *Journal of Financial Economics*, 37, 67–87.

Gorecki, P. (1975) An inter-industry analysis of diversification in the UK manufacturing sector, *Journal of Industrial Economics*, 24, 131–46.

Luffman, G.A. and Reed, R. (1984) *The Strategy and Performance of British Industry, 1970–80*. London: Macmillan.

Montgomery, C. (1994) Corporate diversification, *Journal of Economic Perspectives*, 8, 163–78.

Penrose, E. (1995) *The Theory of the Growth of the Firm*, 3rd edn. Oxford: Oxford University Press.

Rondi, L., Sembenelli, A. and Ragazzi, E. (1996) Determinants of diversification patterns, in Davies, S. and Lyons, B. (eds) *Industrial Organization in the European Union*. Oxford: Oxford University Press, ch. 10.

Teece, D., Rumelt, R., Dosi, G. and Winter, S. (1994) Understanding corporate coherence, theory and evidence, *Journal of Economic Behaviour and Organization*, 23, 1–30.

Utton, M.A. (1977) Large firm diversification in the British manufacturing industry, *Economic Journal*, 87, 96–113.

Utton, M.A. (1979) *Diversification and Competition*. Cambridge: Cambridge University Press.

Analysis of Public Policy

Competition policy

Learning objectives

This chapter covers the following topics:

- theory of competition policy
- the case for and against monopoly
- three branches of competition policy: monopoly, merger and restrictive practices policy
- competition policy in the UK, EU and US
- assessment of UK competition policy

Key terms

Article 81	Monopoly policy
Article 82	Restrictive practices policy
Chapter I prohibition	Rule of reason
Chapter II prohibition	Vertical agreement
Horizontal agreement	Workable competition
Merger policy	

17.1 Introduction

Chapter 17 examines competition policy. As we have seen in previous chapters, there are strong associations between competition and the theoretical notions of productive and allocative efficiency. Firms operating in competitive markets may be compelled to achieve full efficiency in production, or face the prospect of being driven out of business by more efficient competitors. The long-run market equilibrium in perfect competition is also consistent with allocative efficiency, since the industry operates at the point where price *equals* marginal cost. Accordingly, the economic case for competition policy rests largely on the theoretical arguments for and against perfect competition and monopoly. These arguments are examined in Section 17.2.

The idea that competition is always preferable to monopoly has not gone unchallenged. If the monopolist is able to operate on a lower average or marginal cost function than the firms comprising a perfectly competitive industry, social welfare could be higher under monopoly than under perfect competition. The theories of natural monopoly and price discrimination can also be used to make a case for monopoly based on social welfare criteria; while the Schumpeterian hypothesis suggests market power and monopoly status may be interpreted as a reward for successful past innovation.

Section 17.3 discusses some of the more practical aspects of competition policy. Competition policy deals with three principal areas: monopoly, restrictive practices and merger. The implementation of **monopoly**, **restrictive practices** and **merger policy** requires a practical method for measuring market power. Seller concentration and market share measures are obvious candidates. Issues of product and geographic market definition have major implications for the measurement of market power using concentration or market share measures. The notion of **workable competition**, which may provide a more realistic target than the theoretical ideal of perfect competition, is examined.

Section 17.4 traces the historical evolution of competition policy in the UK since the 1940s, with particular emphasis on current arrangements. At the time of writing, competition policy in the UK is the responsibility of the Office of Fair Trading and the Competition Commission. The respective roles of these two agencies are described. One of the objectives of the most recent competition policy legislation, especially the Competition Act 1998 and the Enterprise Act 2002, was to harmonize the UK's arrangements with those effective at EU level. Section 17.5 describe the EU's current competition policy arrangements. A major objective is the promotion of competition within the European Single Market. The cornerstones of EU competition policy are **Articles 81** and **82** of the Treaty of Amsterdam, which was concluded in 1999, and which replaced earlier competition policy provisions under the Treaty of Rome.

The main current emphasis in UK competition policy is examination of the consequences of anticompetitive behaviour, rather than the form taken by any particular agreement or restrictive practice. The most recent legislation, together with the provisions operative at EU level, has strengthened the UK's competition policy regime, in comparison with earlier decades. This chapter concludes in Section 17.6 with a brief assessment of the effectiveness and strengths and weaknesses of the UK's current competition policy arrangements.

17.2 Competition policy: theoretical framework

According to the structure–conduct–performance (SCP) paradigm, perfect competition is the market structure with the most favourable efficiency and welfare properties. In much of the theoretical and policy debate, there is an implicit assumption that competition is good and monopoly bad. In this section, we examine the economic case for and against monopoly in some detail. Several of the arguments have already been rehearsed in previous chapters of this book. As we have seen on several occasions, not all economists agree that monopoly is necessarily a worse state of affairs than competition.

Abnormal profit, allocative and productive inefficiency

A comparison between models of perfect competition and monopoly in the neoclassical theory of the firm has been drawn in Section 2.5. Figures 2.13 and 2.14 make the case for perfect competition and against monopoly, on the grounds of allocative and productive efficiency. In Figure 2.13 it is assumed the monopolist and the perfectly competitive industry both face the same horizontal LRAC (long-run average cost) and LRMC (long-run marginal cost) function. Some of the consumer surplus achieved under perfect competition is converted into producer surplus (abnormal profit) under monopoly; and the rest becomes deadweight loss. Therefore monopoly is allocatively inefficient. In Figure 2.14 it is assumed that a complacent monopolist, shielded from competitive pressure emanating either from rival firms or from actual or potential entrants, operates on a higher LRAC and LRMC function than it would if it were fully efficient in production. This leads to a further increase in the deadweight loss. The main findings of this analysis can be summarized as follows.

■ Under monopoly, market price is higher and output is lower than under perfect competition. If LRAC is U-shaped or L-shaped, the monopolist typically fails to produce at the MES (minimum efficient scale), and therefore fails to produce at the lowest attainable long-run average cost (LRAC). In contrast, the perfectly competitive firm produces at the MES in long-run equilibrium. The monopolist earns an abnormal profit in the long run, while the perfectly competitive firm earns only a normal profit.

■ Under monopoly, there is allocative inefficiency because price exceeds marginal cost. This implies the value society would place on an additional unit of output (measured by the price the most marginal consumer is prepared to pay) exceeds the cost of producing that unit. Therefore industry output is too low, and welfare could be increased by producing more output. In contrast, under perfect competition there is allocative efficiency, because price *equals* marginal cost.

■ Under monopoly, there may also be productive inefficiency, if a lack of competitive pressure enables the monopolist to become complacent or lazy. A complacent monopolist may fail to make the most efficient use of its factor inputs (technical inefficiency), or it may fail to employ the most cost-effective combination of inputs (economic inefficiency). Under perfect competition, intense competitive pressure compels all firms to be efficient in production, since any firm that fails to minimize its LRAC will to realize a loss and be forced out of business.

■ The sum of consumer surplus and producer surplus is lower under monopoly than it is under perfect competition. Therefore under monopoly there is a deadweight loss, due to industry output being lower than it is under perfect competition. The existence of a deadweight loss is a corollary of the monopolist's preference to produce an output level at which price exceeds marginal cost (allocative inefficiency). The size of the deadweight loss is increased if the monopolist is also inefficient in production.

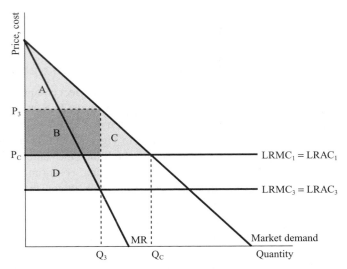

Figure 17.1 Consumer and producer surplus: perfect competition versus a monopolist with a cost advantage

However, a further possibility that is not considered in Figures 2.13 and 2.14 is that the monopolist could operate on a *lower* LRAC and LRMC function than the firms comprising the perfectly competitive industry. For example, by exploiting economies of scale in research and development, the monopolist might be able to gain access to a production technology that is not available to a group of perfectly competitive firms. This argument is developed by Williamson (1968a,b), and has often been used to support the case of large firms seeking to merge horizontally, despite the fact that the merged entity would acquire enhanced market power. This efficiency defence for mergers forms part of the US Department of Justice Merger Guidelines.

Figure 17.1 considers prices, costs and output under conditions of monopoly and perfect competition, in the case where the monopolist's costs are below those of the firms under perfect competition. The perfect competitors' cost functions are $LRMC_1 = LRAC_1$, and the monopolist's cost functions are $LRMC_3 = LRAC_3$. As in Figure 2.13, the perfectly competitive industry operates at (P_C, Q_C). Consumer surplus is A + B + C, and producer surplus (abnormal profit) is zero. The monopolist operates at (P_3, Q_3). Consumer surplus is A, and producer surplus is B + D. Comparing the sum of consumer surplus and producer surplus in the two cases, welfare is higher under monopoly than it is under perfect competition if D > C. Whether this condition is satisfied depends on the size of the difference between $LRMC_1 = LRAC_1$ and $LRMC_3 = LRAC_3$: the larger the difference, the more likely it is that welfare is higher under monopoly than it is under perfect competition.

Overall, the theoretical evidence as to whether monopoly leads to a reduction in efficiency and social welfare is inconclusive. Consequently, the case for and against the continuation of any particular monopoly must be assessed on an individual basis.

The regulatory problems posed by dominant positions in the private sector can be brought into focus by considering the distinction between technical efficiency and allocative efficiency. In many markets the need of technical efficiency may threaten allocative efficiency by allowing firms to attain dominance due to economies of large size to bolster their position by restrictive or exclusionary practices. Success in this respect may then also create x-inefficiency and thus reduce welfare still further.

(Utton, 1986, p. 135)

Harberger (1954) estimates the welfare loss from monopolization accounted for 0.1 per cent of US gross national product over the period 1921–28. Kamerschen (1966) reports a much larger estimate of almost 6 per cent of national income for the period 1956–61. Cowling and Mueller (1978) adopt several measures of welfare loss for the US (1963–66) and the UK (1968–69). They find that in the former case, welfare losses arising from monopoly range from 4 per cent to 13.1 per cent of national income, while in the latter they range from 3.9 per cent to 7.2 per cent. Jenny and Weber (1983) find welfare losses for France ranging from 0.14 per cent to 8.9 per cent for the period 1967–74. Hay and Morris (1991) argue many of these studies were carried out at national level, and so provide little information concerning the welfare effects of monopoly at industry level. Littlechild (1981) argues monopoly profits are a temporary phenomenon, and short-run welfare losses should not be overemphasized.

Natural monopoly

As we have seen in Section 2.5, a **natural monopoly** is a market in which long-run average cost (LRAC) is decreasing as output increases over the entire range of outputs that could conceivably be produced, given the location of the market demand function. This case is illustrated in Figure 2.15. There is insufficient market demand for any firm to exploit all possible opportunities for savings in average costs through economies of scale; in other words, there is insufficient market demand for any firm to attain the MES (minimum efficient scale) of production. In a natural monopoly, monopoly is always more cost-effective than competition. LRAC is lower if one firm services the entire market than if two (or more) firms share the market between them. In natural monopolies, fixed costs tend to constitute a large proportion of total costs. The utilities (water, gas, electricity) and telecommunications are the most obvious examples of industries that tend to conform, to some extent, to the textbook case of natural monopoly. Competition would tend to lead to wasteful duplication of infrastructure and delivery systems. The regulation of utilities is examined in Chapter 18.

Price discrimination

As we have seen in Section 10.3, a monopolist can practise price discrimination in several ways. Under **first-degree** (perfect) **price discrimination**, the price per unit of output depends on the identity of the purchaser and on the number of units purchased. Under **second-degree price discrimination**, the price per unit of output depends on the number of units purchased, but not on the identity of the purchaser. All consumers who buy a particular number of units pay the same price per unit. Under **third-degree price discrimination**, the price per unit of output depends on the identity of the purchaser, but not on the number of units purchased. Any consumer can buy as few or as many units as he or she wishes at the same unit price. In each case, the market for the product must be divisible into sub-markets, within which there are different demand conditions (or different price elasticities of demand). These sub-markets must be physically separate either through space or time, so that secondary trade or resale between consumers in different sub-markets is not possible. For example, according to the European Commission (1995b), European car manufacturers have practised a form of price discrimination that has resulted in large price disparites between different countries.

Perhaps surprisingly, however, price discrimination should not always be judged pejoratively. The monopolist who adopts a policy of first-degree price discrimination earns an even higher abnormal profit than the monopolist who charges a uniform price; but on allocative efficiency criteria, the outcome in the former case is preferable. Total output is higher under first-degree price discrimination than under monopoly with uniform pricing, and in the former case the last unit of output produced is sold at a price equivalent to its marginal cost. In the less extreme but more realistic cases of second- and third-degree price discrimination, it is not possible to generalize about the social welfare implications, which can be either positive or negative.

Entry barriers and vertical restraints

As we have seen in Section 8.4, an incumbent monopolist might pursue various strategies in an attempt to raise entry barriers and deter potential entrants. These might include limit pricing, predatory pricing, and product differentiation or brand proliferation. For example, Myers (1994) argues predatory pricing in the deregulated UK bus industry led to a decline in the number of bus operators. Another example involves a case brought by the European Commission against Deutsche Post in 2001, in which the company was alleged to have used its monopoly profit from mail delivery to subsidize its prices in the business parcel service market, where it was exposed to competition from United Parcel Services (UPS). The commission found the company had failed to cover its costs in parcel delivery for five years, suggesting a form of predatory pricing.

As we have seen in Section 15.7, vertical restraints are conditions and restrictions on trade that are imposed by firms that are linked vertically. Principal forms of vertical restraint include retail price maintenance, foreclosure, territorial exclusivity and quantity-dependent pricing (tying or bundling). Case study 17.1 discusses the recent Microsoft case in the US, which involves several forms of anticompetitive behaviour, including vertical restraints. Case study 17.2 discusses the nature of competition in the airlines industry following the growth of low-cost or budget airlines.

Case study 17.1

The Microsoft monopoly in the US

In 1998, the US Department of Justice launched an investigation that accused the Microsoft Corporation of operating a monopoly in the computer industry. Specifically, Microsoft was accused of:

■ Operating a monopoly in operating systems in the personal computer industry.

■ Using its market power to distort competition in other markets by preventing firms from offering applications that could run on the Microsoft Windows operating system.

■ Using its market power to prevent rival firms from developing alternative operating systems.

■ Engaging in vertical restraints to trade by bundling software products (such as its internet Explorer application) with operating systems licenced to third-party users.

Microsoft's market power was due to its position as a vertically integrated firm that supplied not only the Windows operating system, but also thousands of applications which ran on this system. Any firm wishing to compete with Microsoft by producing a rival operating system would have to produce a huge number of applications compatible with the alternative operating system. These were described by the Department of Justice as 'applications barriers to entry'. On the supply side, competitors faced barriers to entry due to the cost of capital, while on the demand side competitors faced difficulties in persuading consumers to switch from the numerous established Microsoft products to alternatives.

Microsoft argued that due to the fast pace of technological change in the computing industry, its dominance had arisen naturally, as the outcome of fair competition. Microsoft pointed to the success of other companies in developing rival software systems. It defended itself against charges of bundling by arguing that adding internet Explorer to Windows represented a technological advance, resulting in the availability of an improved product for end-users. However, the Department of Justice contended that such a strategy had enabled Microsoft to displace the former market leader for internet browers, Netscape Navigator, by anticompetitive means.

In 2000, Microsoft was found guilty of operating a monopoly in the operating systems market, of using this position to restrain competition, and of the effective monpolization of the internet browser market (by bundling internet Explorer with Windows). However, the remedies and penalties were not determined immediately. Possible remedies were structural and conduct-based. Structural remedies would influence the market structure of the computing industry. Conduct-based remedies would impose limits on Microsoft's business activities. Specific remedies suggested at the time included the following:

■ Breaking the company into two parts: first, an operating systems company to supply the Windows system; and second, a software applications company. However, this would still leave the operating systems company with a monopoly position in its own market.

■ Breaking Microsoft into several smaller vertically integrated companies that would provide competing operating systems and software applications. However, whether these companies would actually compete is questionable. There would be obvious incentives for collusion. Furthermore, opportunities to exploit technical and learning economies of scale and scope might be lost; or if there was genuine competition, this might result in wasteful duplication of effort.

■ Force Microsoft to publish or provide details of the Windows code to software producers wishing to develop applications to run on Windows.

■ Force Microsoft to license Windows to any company wishing to buy it, and allow licensees to alter or improve the software as they see fit. This option might lead to a fall in standards and a fragmentation of operating systems.

■ Impose limits on the ways in which Microsoft conducts its business, for example by preventing the extension of its monopoly position into other areas of the computing business. However, this option could prove costly to monitor and enforce.

Microsoft argued that breaking the company into smaller companies would reduce efficiency and stifle future innovation in the computing industry. Talks between a mediator (Judge Richard Posner) and Microsoft regarding a suitable remedy broke down in April 2000. Subsequently, Judge Jackson ruled that Microsoft should split its Windows operating systems division from its software applications division. Microsoft appealed against this decision, and in 2001 the Court of Appeal declared the initial judgement was too severe. While Microsoft was guilty of some anticompetitive practices, such as bundling, these should be assessed on a *rule of reason* basis, weighing the benefits to consumers (an efficient, integrated browsing system), against the costs imposed by the lack of effective competition. In November 2002, the Court of Appeal reversed the verdict concerning monopolisation of the internet browser market, on the grounds that the relevant market had not been properly defined in the initial judgement. However, Microsoft would be required to remove many of the restrictions preventing competitors from offering applications that would run on Windows. Microsoft would also be required to provide more flexible conditions to third party users wishing to offer alternative configurations of Windows. Microsoft was also asked to disclose certain technical information to allow rival applications to run on the Window platform.

Source: Various issues of *The Economist* throughout 1999–2002 provide details of the Microsoft case, as does the US Department of Justice website www.usdoj.com (last accessed July 2004). Useful overviews of the economics of the Microsoft case can be found in Evans, D. (2000) An analysis of the government's economic case in US v Microsoft, *Antitrust Bulletin*, 46: 2, 163–251; Fisher, F. and Rubinfield, D. (2001) US v Microsoft, *Antitrust Bulletin*, 46, 1–69; Gilbert, R. and Katz, M. (2001) An economist's guide to US v Microsoft, *Journal of Economic Perspectives*, 15, 25–44.

Technological progress

As we have seen in Section 14.2, according to the **Schumpeterian hypothesis**, market power and monopoly status should be interpreted as the reward for successful innovation. For a time the successful innovating firm becomes a monopoly supplier of a new product; or its mastery of a new process enables it to produce at a lower cost than its rivals, perhaps capturing some or all of their market share by setting a price they are unable to match. However, the market power conferred by successful innovation is always temporary, because in time the new technology will itself be superseded by further technological progress. Successful innovation brings benefits to society, in the form of new products or more efficient production processes. In the past, the competition authorities have often tended to take a benign or favorable view of firms that are perceived to invest heavily in research and development.

Case study 17.2

Competition in the airlines industry

Introduction

Prior to the 1980s, competition in the European airlines industry was limited. Most major airlines were state-owned, and regulatory barriers to entry severely limited the ability of individual airlines to operate outside their home territory. A more integrated EU-level regulatory approach has involved extensive deregulation, including the privatization of many formerly state-owned airlines. Since the liberalization of Europe's domestic airline market was completed in 1997, the intensity of competition has increased significantly, mainly due to the emergence of budget airlines. The pioneers, Ryanair and easyJet, mimicked a business model originally developed by low-cost airlines in the US, involving aggressive price-cutting, ticketless booking via the internet, use of cheap airports, fast airport turnaround times, and 'no frills' service standards. However, historical advantages that are still enjoyed by some incumbent airlines, together with some of the fundamental structural characteristics of the airlines industry, means competition is in some respects still limited.

Economics of the airlines industry

Airlines can be described as a network industry. A certain number of airports are connected through a very much larger number of routes. Airlines incur high fixed costs (the expense of acquiring a fleet of aircraft) and low marginal costs (the cost of adding one more passenger to a flight with some spare capacity is minimal). Economies of scale are available to airlines that use larger aircraft (reducing the average cost per passenger), and airlines that operate over longer geographic distances (reducing the costs associated with take-off, landing and airport turnaround time). Economies of scope can be achieved by combining air passenger and cargo handling and transportation services on the same route. Economies of density can also be achieved when an airline increases it presence in a geographic area. This can be achieved by operating a hub-and-spoke network, whereby the airline channels the majority of its passengers through a central point, known as the hub airport, from which it operates connecting services, or spokes, to passengers' final destination airports. 'The lower number of routes in the hub-and-spoke network means that by transforming its network from a point-to-point network into a hub-and-spoke network, an airline is able to reduce its costs without lowering the number of served destinations' (NCA, 2002, p. 46).

There are significant barriers to entry into the airlines industry. Over many routes, the minimum efficient scale of operation exceeds half of total consumer demand. Any entrant is likely to operate at a cost disadvantage relative to an incumbent airline. Economies of scope may also act as a barrier to entry, as a new firm needs to offer a large number of routes to compete with incumbent airlines. The prevalence of the hub-and-spoke system effectively assures an incumbent airline considerable monopoly power (through control over landing slots) at or around its hub. On the demand side, customers tend to prefer an airline that offers a large number of routes, particularly when connecting flights are required.

Firm-level strategic behaviour

Airlines use a variety of price and non-price competitive strategies. Pricing practices include versioning and corporate discount schemes. Versioning involves airlines charging different prices for tickets based on differences in quality or flexibility. Under such a strategy customers wishing to buy flexible tickets pay higher prices than those buying less flexible tickets. With corporate discount schemes, airlines recognize the buying power of large customers, by charging lower prices than those available to small individual customers. Such discounts are often subject to lock-in periods, which effectively prevent large customers from switching to other airlines.

Non-price competitive strategies include airmiles or frequent flyer programmes and travel agent agreements. Airmiles programmes reward customers with points each time they travel with a given airline. Once customers reach some points threshold, they are eligible to exchange their points for additional services (such as free or discounted flights, or accommodation). Airmiles programmes are designed to encourage customers to fly with a single airline, by imposing switching costs on those who go elsewhere. Naturally, airlines with extensive routes are likely to have the most successful airmiles programmes. Under travel agent agreements, a travel agent sells tickets on behalf on an airline. Payment for this service is determined based on the quantity sold, encouraging agents to concentrate their selling activities on one airline. In a number of European countries, airlines have become vertically integrated into the travel agency business, and can offer their own agencies favourable terms for promoting their tickets. 'The more the agreements favour the concentration of ticket sales on a single airline company, and the more dependent the travel agencies are on a such a company, the more effectively the agreements prevent entry into the market' (NCA, 2002, p. 89).

Policy concerns

Demand and supply side conditions in the airlines industry, together with the types of price and non-price competitive strategies commonly employed pursued by incumbent airlines, often lead to the concentration of market power on any particular route in the hands of a small number of airlines. The availability of landing slots to budget airlines varies considerably throughout Europe; for example, the obstacles to the expansion of budget airlines are much greater in France and Germany than in the UK. There is considerable scope for incumbent airlines to adjust capacity and cut prices when faced with the prospect of increased competition. In the UK and Ireland, incumbents such as British Airways, BMI (British Midland) and Aer Lingus offer fares that are competitive with Ryanair and easyJet on some services. In order to increase competition, the NCA report recommends an active competition policy to monitor changes in capacity, pricing and use of airmiles programmes, together with a review of the system used to allocate landing slots. '[W]ithout a more vigorous competition policy at the national and Community levels, the welfare losses stemming from an insufficient competitive pressure on airlines are due to increase rather than diminish over time' (NCA, 2002, p. 118).

Source: This case study is based on Nordic Competition Authorities (2002) *Competitive Airlines: Towards a More Vigorous Competition Policy in Relation to the Air Travel Market*. Report Number 1/2002. Stockholm: Nordic Competition Authorities. For further analysis of the European and global airlines industry, see Johnson, P.S. (2003) Air transport, in Johnson, P. (ed.) *Industries in Europe*. Cheltenham: Edward Elgar, *The Economist*, 8 July 2004.

17.3 Competition policy: practical implementation

In general, competition policy aims to promote competition and to control abuses of market power by firms. More specifically, competition policy may seek to increase efficiency, promote innovation, or improve consumer choice.

> Competition policy has its central economic goal as the preservation and promotion of the competitive process, a process which encourages efficiency in the production and allocation of goods and services over time, through its effects on innovation and adjustment to technological change, a dynamic process of sustained economic growth.
>
> *(OECD, 1984, para. 232)*

> The role of competition policy is to ensure that competition is indeed effective. To this end, competition policy stops, penalizes and deters anti-competitive actions by suppliers. It extends also to the unnecessary restrictions on competition stemming from government laws and regulation. And a full effective competition policy also embraces measures to make markets work more competitively by enhancing the power of consumer choice.
>
> *(Vickers, 2002, p. 3)*

Competition policy deals with three principal areas: monopoly, restrictive practices and merger. First, **monopoly policy** addresses existing monopolies. If a firm has sufficient market power, its dominant position may enable it to pursue policies detrimental to competition or the wider public interest. The competition authorities must weigh this danger against the possible benefits (such as cost savings through economies of scale) of large-scale operation. Second, **merger policy** deals with situations where two or more firms propose a merger that may create a dominant position in the market for the newly merged entity. Merger policy considers whether the increased concentration of market power arising from a merger is in the public interest. For example, the possible benefits of rationalization must be weighed against the possible cost in terms of potential abuse of market power. Merger policy should not be so restrictive as to provide inefficient management with complete protection from the threat of being taken over; the threat of merger or takeover can in some cases act as a spur to managerial efficiency (Marris, 1964).

Third, **restrictive practices policy** examines cases where a firm or a group of firms is involved in restrictive practices of one type or another that may prove damaging to competition or the wider public interest. Such practices might include price fixing agreements, predatory pricing and vertical restraints (Pickering, 1982). As we have seen in Chapter 5, the agreement to collude may be formal (explicit) or informal (implicit or tacit). **Horizontal agreements** involve firms in the same industry, and are primarily aimed at reducing competition. Examples include common pricing policies, production quotas, market allocation, or sharing of information on prices, output and quality. **Vertical agreements** involve firms operating at successive stages of production or distribution, such as exclusive dealing contracts and resale price maintenance.

> If companies seek to eliminate or at least to reduce competition between themselves, they will normally try to do so by some form of agreement or concerted practice; these are classified as horizontal since they are made by undertakings operating at a similar level, for example as manufacturers or retailers. By contrast vertical agreements are those where relationships of the parties are complementary, for example when a supplier makes a distribution agreement with a dealer or a patent owner enters into a licence agreement with a licensee.
>
> *(Goyder, 2003, pp. 11–12)*

The implementation of monopoly, restrictive practices and merger policy requires a practical method for measuring market power. Seller concentration and market share measures are the most obvious candidates (see Section 6.4). According to Shepherd (1997), abuses of market power are most likely to take place in industries with four-firm concentration ratios (CR_4) exceeding 0.6, and the attentions of the competition authorities should be focused on such cases. Of course, the market share of an individual firm is also highly relevant as an indicator of market power. As a rule-of-thumb, a firm with a market share exceeding 30 per cent has at many times been assumed by the UK competition authorities to be dominant. However, as we have seen in Section 8.5, according to the contestable markets approach of Baumol *et al.* (1982), provided entry barriers are not insurmountable and markets are contestable, the threat of entry and competition constrains the pricing policy of a firm that might appear to have market power according to a standard seller concentration measure, perhaps even to the extent that only a normal profit can be earned. In assessing the degree of market power, it is therefore relevant to ask questions concerning the ease of entry.

In order to assess whether an abuse of market power is taking place, it is first necessary to define the extent of the relevant market. Naturally, this decision has major implications for the values of the market power indicators mentioned above, seller concentration and market share. If a narrow market definition is employed, market power may be overstated. Conversely, if a wide market definition is employed, market power may be understated, and genuine abuses might not even be investigated. As we have seen in Section 6.2, the definition of any market contains both a product dimension and a geographic dimension. The product market definition should include all products that are close substitutes for one another, both in consumption and in production. In practice, however, it is not usually straightforward to decide which products to include within this definition. Fosters lager might be included in the same market as Tennants lager; but do other beers (bitter and real ale) belong in the same product market? Should other beverages, such as soft drinks, tea, coffee, wines and spirits, be included? Geographic market definitions present similar problems. Is the relevant geographic market defined at a local, regional, national or international level? The market definition should reflect the true competitive situation. If it fails to do so, competition policy decisions will be biased. In practice, the competition authorities in the UK and elsewhere tend to rely on a range of market definitions.

It is also relevant to note that market definitions are not static, but are subject to change over time due to changes in technology or consumer tastes. Therefore in some cases, it might be appropriate to incorporate a dynamic element into market definitions. For example, in 2002, Tetra (a carton packaging firm with a world market share of around 80 per cent) sought to merge with Sidel (a plastics packaging firm with a world market share of around 60 per cent). While the European Commission concluded the relevant markets were separate, it was likely they would tend to converge over time. Therefore the proposed merger would reduce competition in the long run.

Most economists would recognize that perfect competition is a theoretical ideal, which is highly unlikely to prevail in practice (Clark, 1940; Reid, 1987; Sosnick, 1958). Therefore a more realistic objective for competition policy might be to foster **workable competition**. This approach searches for aspects of structure and conduct that can be adjusted in order to bring about a favourable performance outcome. In other words, competition policy should start from a definition of good performance, and aim to bring into being the forms of industry structure and conduct that are most likely to produce good performance.

The workable competition approach has several drawbacks. First, the weights that should be attached to each dimension of performance are not specified. Second, any definition of favourable performance is subjective to some extent. There is scope for disagreement as to the appropriate criteria for the implementation of competition policy based on the concept of workable competition. Stigler (1968) criticizes the workable competition approach for its serious ambiguity. According to the Austrian school, 'departures from the optimality conditions of perfectly competitive equilibrium are not a threat to any relevant notion of economic efficiency. Equilibrium is not an attainable ideal, nor are perfect or "near perfect" competition attainable' (Kirzner, 1997b, p. 59).

17.4 Competition policy in the UK

Goyder (2003) summarizes the essential elements of competition policy as follows:

> There has to be a substantive law setting out . . . the basic rules to be applied . . . the adoption of procedures for ascertaining the relevant facts of each case, from which fair and properly reasoned conclusions can be drawn about the application of the substantive law to the case . . . the maintenance and development of institutions capable of enforcing the substantive rules in a way which is both fair and effective.
>
> *(Goyder, 2003, pp. 14–15)*

At the time of writing, competition policy in the UK is the responsibility of the Office of Fair Trading (OFT) and the Competition Commission. The OFT investigates complaints of anticompetitive practices, and if these complaints are upheld, refers the findings to the Competition Commission. In this section, we review the historical evolution of the UK competition policy framework since the 1940s.

Monopolies and Restrictive Practices Act 1948

The Monopolies and Restrictive Practices Act 1948 was the first major piece of UK legislation concerned with the regulation of monopolies and restrictive practices. The act defined a monopoly as a firm or a cartel controlling one-third or more of total industry supply. The Act founded the Monopolies and Restrictive Practices Commission. The Board of Trade (now the Department of Trade and Industry) could refer cases to the Monopolies and Restrictive Practices Commission for investigation.

The act accepted that if a monopoly was acting in the public interest, it should be allowed to continue to operate. A monopoly was deemed to be in the public interest if the firm(s) in question were:

■ Efficient.
■ Making full use of scarce resources (operating with no excess capacity).
■ Meeting the wishes of the public in terms of price, quantity and quality.
■ Developing new technologies.
■ Expanding the market.

Because each case of monopoly had different defining characteristics, the act recommended that outcomes should be determined on a case-by-case basis.

> [T]he new system was administrative, directed more toward researching and publicizing problems of monopoly than enforcing rules against them. The very general 'public interest' approach was to avoid legalism and encourage negotiation.

(OECD, 2002, p. 8)

Critics complain that this pragmatic approach has led to inconsistency in the decision making of the UK competition authorities (Clarke *et al.*, 1999). The public interest could be satisfied if a monopoly position was associated with lower prices, higher-quality goods or more efficient production techniques than would be the case under competition. On balance, the reports of the Monopolies and Restrictive Practices Commission tend to suggest monopoly power did not by itself signify anticompetitive behaviour; rather this depended on how monopoly power was being exercised. However, the reports also find restrictive practices were quite widespread, and many did not operate in the public interest. Indeed, a 1955 report on *Collective Discrimination* argues restrictive practices should be outlawed (Monopolies and Restrictive Practices Commission, 1955).

Restrictive Trade Practices Act 1956

The Restrictive Trade Practices Act 1956 attempted to ban most restrictive practices. The act required trade association agreements with respect to price, conditions surrounding the sales of goods and production techniques employed to be registered, in a Register of Restrictive Trading Agreements. A Registrar was appointed, one of whose functions was to bring these registered agreements before the newly established Restrictive Trade Practices Court. The court would decide whether the agreement was in the public interest. If not, the court could declare an agreement void, and issue orders that the parties should cease any practices covered by the agreement. The court's presumption was that registered agreements were against the public interest, and the onus of proof was placed on the parties to the agreement. Firms could decide to terminate an agreement voluntarily, or attempt to mount a public interest defence in the court.

A number of specific defences or gateways were defined, through which exemption could be claimed and granted. An agreement could be deemed admissible if it helped:

■ Protect the public against injury.
■ Provide specific benefit to the public.
■ Prevent other restrictive practices.
■ Secure fair terms from suppliers or purchasers.
■ Protect jobs.
■ Promote exports.
■ Support another agreement acceptable to the court.

Even if an agreement was deemed to be valid through one or more of these gateways, this did not necessarily mean the court would allow an exemption. The agreement still had to be shown to serve the public interest *on balance*. For example, it was argued that terminating the Yarn Spinners agreement of 1959 would result in unemployment. This point was conceded, but the court still ordered that the agreement should cease, since it took the view that on balance the costs associated with reduced competition outweighed the costs associated with higher unemployment (Stevens and Yamey, 1965).

In practice the criteria adopted by the court were strict, and the 1956 act is regarded as one of the more draconian pieces of legislation in UK competition policy history. Many agreements were terminated voluntarily, once the parties realized that expensive litigation was likely to prove unsuccessful. Over the period 1956–65, of around 4,500 agreements that were registered, no more than 50 came before the court, and only 12 were successfully defended (Lipczynski, 1994).

Resale Prices Act 1964

The Resale Prices Act 1964 imposed restrictions on the practice of resale price maintenance (RPM): the practice whereby a producer requires retailers or other distributors not to cut their selling price below a prescribed minimum level (see Section 15.7). The act extended the powers of the Restrictive Practices Court to cover cases where RPM was thought to operate against the public interest. Consequently, firms wishing to operate RPM had to obtain permission from the court. Again, the presumption was that such arrangements operated against the public interest, unless the parties could prove otherwise. A new set of gateways enabled an RPM agreement to be endorsed if its termination would:

- Reduce the quality and choice of goods produced.
- Lead to a decline in retail outlets.
- Lead to injury to the public.
- Lead to increased prices.
- Reduce the quality or level of service provision.

The act led to the scrapping of RPM in most cases. Important exceptions were medicines and books. In the latter case, the Net Book Agreement between publishers and booksellers enabled the publisher to set a resale price for each book, which booksellers had to follow. The agreement was designed to allow publishers a reasonable return on books with a limited print run, and protect small retailers from price competition from the larger chains. The Net Book Agreement was eventually abolished in 1995. The medicines agreement is discussed in Case study 17.3.

Monopolies and Mergers Act 1965

The Restrictive Practices Act 1956 placed restrictions on the scope for successful collusion between UK firms. However, it seems highly likely that the court's successes in breaking up anticompetitive practices contributed significantly to the UK's 1960s merger boom, as firms looked for alternative methods (other than collusion) to increase their market power. Accordingly, the Monopolies and Mergers Act 1965 sought to strengthen the regulation of monopoly, the common consequence of consolidation involving formerly independent producers. The Monopolies Commission

Case study 17.3

The end of RPM in medicines

Medicine prices set to tumble after court ruling

The last bastion of restrictive practices on the high street fell yesterday when a court abolished price fixing on over-the-counter medicines.

Britain's leading supermarkets immediately moved to slash prices on a range of branded pain killers, vitamins and cold and flu remedies – some by as much as 50 per cent. One supermarket group estimated the change would save consumers £300m a year.

The decision by the Restrictive Practices Court sparked warnings that many independent pharmacists could be put out of business, restricting access to medicines, especially in rural areas and among the elderly and infirm.

Yesterday's decision overturned 30 years of restrictive practices under the resale price maintenance rules. Books, the other area that had been protected, lost its status two years ago. Consumers will now save hundreds of millions of pounds in a market worth about £1.6bn a year. Tesco, the UK's biggest supermarket group, and its rivals J Sainsbury and Asda said they would cut prices by between 40 and 50 per cent.

For example, a packet of 16 Nurofen tablets from today will cost £1.14, instead of £2.29. Six sachets of Calpol, the popular children's medicine, will fall from £2.75 to £1.37.

The ruling came after the Community Pharmacy Action Group, an umbrella body campaigning for the retention of RPM, withdrew from the High Court case after the judge said there was insufficient proof to back its claims.

The CPAG had argued RPM protected the viability of the UK's network of community pharmacies. Yesterday it said it still felt it had a strong case, but with a clear indication a victory was unlikely it did not make sense to continue.

John D'Arcy, chief executive of the National Pharmaceutical Association, the community pharmacy trade body, said supermarkets would indulge in headline-grabbing price-cuts across a small range of drugs.

'Supermarkets will be able to use this to cherry pick where they want to offer price cuts', he said. 'That will push independents out of business and as they offer a wider range of drugs than supermarkets the medicine range will contract.'

Mr D'Arcy said viable independent stores in economically successful areas would always thrive. Under more pressure would be smaller stores in secondary and tertiary retail sites – particularly those in rural and socially deprived areas.

'Pharmacies often go into a lot of areas where other retailers fear to tread', he said.

The Office of Fair Trading, which brought the court case, said it was delighted with the result. The OFT said: 'We felt that like every other product, there ought to be competition. We thought it was bad news for consumers that they couldn't shop around.'

The OFT said it would now remain on the look-out for any underhand practices across the retail sector. 'This is the end for legal price fixing, but we would love to hear about anyone who is illegally trying to fix prices.'

Source: The end of RPM in medicines: medicine prices set to tumble after court ruling, *Financial Times*, 16 May 2001. © The Financial Times.

now became the Monopolies and Mergers Commission, and was granted new powers to regulate prices and break up monopolies. The Board of Trade could refer a proposed merger to the commission if it would create a monopoly, defined as a situation where a single firm controlled one-third of a market, or had annual turnover exceeding £5m. This threshold was later increased to £30m in 1984. The commission's findings were presented to the Secretary of State of the Board of Trade, who made the final decision as to whether the merger would be permitted.

The apparent inconsistency between the Monopolies and Mergers Act 1965 on the one hand, and a separate strand of government policy that sought to promote consolidation in order to improve efficiency and promote innovation on the other hand, has been widely noted. The need for the modernization of UK industry was a central part of the platform of the Labour government that was elected in 1964 and re-elected in 1966. Accordingly, the Industrial Reorganization Act 1966 established the Industrial Reorganization Corporation (IRC), which sought opportunities for rationalization and consolidation that would help improve efficiency and productivity. The IRC was active in promoting mergers: support ranged from providing general advice to suggesting merger opportunities and assisting with implementation. Any IRC-sponsored merger was automatically exempt from reference to the Monopolies and Mergers Commission. In 1971, following extensive criticism for its focus on industries that were already highly concentrated, and for its tendency to further increase market power, the IRC was disbanded by the Conservative government that had been elected in 1970.

Restrictive Trade Practices Act 1968

Following the Restrictive Trade Practices Act 1956, agreements to share information on prices, quality and costs of production became widespread. As long as these agreements were limited to information sharing only, they were permitted under the provisions of the act. As we have seen in Chapter 5, however, the dividing line between the mere exchange of information on the one hand, and stronger forms of collusion on the other, is a relatively fine one. The Restrictive Trade Practices Act 1968 made the registration of information-sharing agreements compulsory and subject to the supervision of the Restrictive Practices Court. The 1968 act also strengthened the existing regime of fines for failure to register agreements that fell within the court's remit.

Fair Trading Act 1973

The Fair Trading Act 1973 established the Office of Fair Trading (OFT). A Director-General of Fair Trading was appointed to oversee competition policy relating to monopoly, merger and restrictive practices. According to new definitions contained in Section 84 of the Act, a merger was in the public interest if:

■ It promoted or maintained competition.
■ It was in the overall interest of consumers and other market participants.
■ It led to a reduction of costs through economies of scale.
■ It promoted innovation and technical progress.

A reference to the Monopolies and Mergers Commission could be made if either a scale monopoly or a complex monopoly existed. A scale monopoly existed if one firm had a market share of 25 per cent; formerly, the threshold had been set at 33 per cent. A complex monopoly involved two or more firms with a combined market share of 25 per cent that were cooperating in some manner that would affect competition. A merger could be referred if the worldwide assets being taken over exceeded £70m.

The OFT advised the Secretary of State for Trade and Industry as to whether a merger should be referred to the commission. If investigated, the commission's role was to assess whether the proposed merger operated against the public interest. The final decision as to whether the merger should proceed still rested with the Secretary of State. In 1980, the coverage of the act was extended to service industries such as banks, travel agents and estate agents, nationalized industries and local monopolies.

Restrictive Trade Practices Act 1976

The Restrictive Trade Practices Act 1976 consolidated previous legislation relating to restrictive practices. The act required registration of all verbal and written agreements to the Director-General of Fair Trading. The details of these agreements were entered in a public register. The Director-General referred agreements that appeared to affect competition to the Restrictive Practices Court. At the end of 1999, over 15,000 agreements were disclosed on the public register, but only about 1 per cent of these agreements had been referred to the court.

Competition Act 1980

The Competition Act 1980 replaced much of the previous legislation that dealt with anticompetitive practices. The Act extended the provisions of the Fair Trading Act 1973, defining clearly what constituted restrictive and anticompetitive practices. The definition included price-fixing, price discrimination, predatory pricing, vertical squeezes, exclusive dealing and tie-in sales. It specified the process for investigation of complaints received by the OFT from the Secretary of State of the DTI or a member of the public. The act allowed firms an opportunity to comply voluntarily with OFT recommendations before any case was referred to the Monopolies and Mergers Commission. The act also made it easier for nationalized industries to be investigated.

Companies Act 1989

The Companies Act 1989 codified several procedures for the investigation and administration of mergers. The Act required firms to notify the OFT of any proposed merger before it took place. The Director-General then decided whether a reference to the Monopolies and Mergers Commission was required. If no reference was made within 21 days of the notification, the merger was allowed to proceed. If an investigation ensued, the acquiring firm could not acquire shareholdings in the target firm during the investigation.

Competition Act 1998

The Competition Act 1998 rationalized and consolidated competition policy in the UK, and brought it into line with EU competition policy. The Act significantly increased the powers of investigation and intervention of the Director-General. The act dissolved the Restrictive Practices Court, and set up a new Competition Commission to take over from the Monopolies and Mergers Commission and a Competition Appeals Tribunal (CAT) to hear appeals arising from any decisions made under the Act.

The Competition Act consists of two main components, known as chapter prohibitions. The **Chapter I prohibition** deals with anticompetitive (restrictive) practices, and the **Chapter II prohibition** deals with abuses of dominant (or monopoly) positions. Both chapters are concerned with promoting competition in the UK, but Section 60 requires that the enforcement of the act and any investigations to be consistent with EU competition policy.

The Chapter I prohibition applies to (formal or informal) agreements between firms which prevent, distort or otherwise affect trade within the UK. Agreements which fall under the remit of the act include:

■ Agreements to fix buying or selling prices.
■ Agreements to share markets.
■ Agreements to limit production.
■ Agreements relating to collusive tendering.
■ Agreements involving the sharing of information.

Exemptions can be granted if the agreement improves the production or distribution of goods and services, or promotes technological progress, leading to substantial benefits for consumers.

The Chapter I prohibition is closely related to **Article 81** of the EU's Treaty of Amsterdam (see pp. 644–6). In cases of investigative overlap under the terms of Chapter I and the equivalent Article 81, the Competition Directorate-General IV takes charge of the investigation. An exemption granted under Article 81 automatically implies a parallel exemption from the Chapter I prohibition. However, an exemption from the Chapter I prohibition does not automatically lead to an exemption from Article 81.

The Chapter II prohibition is based on **Article 82** of the Treaty of Amsterdam, and deals with the possible abuse of market power by monopolies. The investigation of a dominant position comprises a two-stage test, to assess whether the firm is dominant in the relevant market; and if so, whether the firm is abusing its position. Practices that constitute abuse include charging an excessive price, price discrimination, various forms of predatory competition, vertical restraints and refusals to supply. For example, in 2001 Napp Pharmaceuticals was fined £3.2m for over-charging NHS hospitals and pharmacies for the supply of morphine. Napp was convicted of charging between 33 per cent and 67 per cent more than other firms that were selling simlar products in other markets. Section 36 of the act specifies the penalties for violation of either of the chapter prohibitions. The maximum penalty is 10 per cent of annual turnover for each year that the violation takes place, up to a maximum of three years.

The 1998 Competition Act significantly strengthened the UK competition policy regime. The emphasis has shifted towards the examination of the consequences of anticompetitive behaviour, rather than the form taken by any particular agreement or restrictive practice (Bloom, 1999; Maitland-Walker, 1999). Case study 17.4 provides a recent application in banking for small business.

Case study 17.4

Banking for small business

In 2002, the UK's Competition Commission published a report on an investigation into the supply of banking services to small and medium-sized businesses in the UK. The report found that competition in this market was impeded due to the large market shares of the big clearing banks. In each geographic market examined (Scotland, England, Northern Ireland and Wales), the four largest banks accounted for up to 90 per cent of certain financial services offered to small firms. This market power meant there was a high degree of similarity across services offered and prices charged. New providers faced significant barriers to entry. General sources of entry barrier in banking include a high MES (minimum efficient scale) relative to total market size. Econometric estimates suggest entrants operating below the MES may face average costs around 5 per cent higher than those of incumbents operating at the MES. Minimum capital and licensing requirements may make it difficult for entrants to compete with incumbents.

Specific problems

With specific reference to the market for banking services to small and medium-sized businesses, three types of entry barrier were identified. First, a bank that had built up a reputation over time was more likely to enjoy the benefits of customer loyalty. There was some evidence that incumbent banks offered preferential services to new customers or to those who threatened to switch to another bank. Second, substantial switching costs incurred by customers when changing banks acted as an entry barrier and restricted competition. Third, incumbent banks operated many branches across large geographic areas, making it difficult for entrants to compete on an equal basis.

Solutions

The entry barriers outlined above contributed to high prices being charged and excessive profits being earned by incumbent banks in England and Wales. The Competition Commission proposed a number of behavioural remedies, including the abolition of certain bank charges, the introduction of interest on current accounts, and improved information flows to customers. Collectively, these remedies would make it easier for customers to switch banks, leading to increased competition in this part of the banking sector.

Source: Competition Commission (2002) *The Supply of Banking Services*. London: HMSO.

Enterprise Act 2002

The Enterprise Act 2002 strengthened further the regulatory framework for UK competition policy. The act established the OFT as a legal entity, and provided guidelines with respect to the OFT's day-to-day running, investigative powers and operating and reporting procedures. The act sought to improve the use of quantitative and qualitative analysis in reaching expert and independent decisions. For example, merger control regulations should be based on economic analysis of the likely effects on competition, rather than vague public interest concerns. The process of investigation and enforcement has been made more transparent, in line with EU practice. The act also strengthened the punishment regime for managers convicted of anticompetitive practice. Harsh penalties (up to five years' imprisonment) can be imposed on managers found guilty of price fixing and related offences.

17.5　Competition policy in the EU

A major objective of EU competition policy is the promotion of competition within the European Single Market (Motta, 2003). Historically, the EU competition policy regime has been stricter than that of the UK. The cornerstones of EU competition policy are Articles 81 and 82 of the Treaty of Amsterdam, which was concluded in 1999. These articles incorporate Articles 85 and 86 of the earlier Treaty of Rome. Goyder (2003) reviews the historical development of EU competition policy. In accordance with the principle of subsidiarity, the scope of Articles 81 and 82 is confined to firms based in EU member states that trade in other EU states. These articles do not apply to the activities of domestic firms trading within the domestic market. Cases are investigated and the articles are enforced by the Competition Directorate-General IV, which has the power to fine companies up to 10 per cent of their annual worldwide turnover (Whish, 2003). The Directorate-General IV Leniency program offers reductions in fines of between 10 per cent and 100 per cent for cooperation or provision of information relating to violations of Article 81 (Pena-Castellot, 2001).

Article 81 of the Treaty of Amsterdam deals with restrictive practices. Article 81 prohibits agreements between firms from EU member states that prevent or restrict competition. The prohibition covers both horizontal and vertical agreements. For example, agreements to fix prices, production quotas or to share markets are all deemed illegal. However, exemptions are available if it can be shown the benefits outweigh the costs to consumers. For example, an agreement might be exempt if it led to higher production, resulting in economies of scale, improvements in efficiency in distribution, or technological progress, with consumers ultimately benefiting from lower prices or improvements in quality. Block exemptions are also available, typically with respect to vertical agreements between firms at different stages of the supply chain, in cases where the parties involved do not exercise significant market power. For example, it is accepted that agreements between a manufacturer and a distributor do not necessarily reduce competition. At the end of 2000, a new block exemption covering distribution agreements (EC2790/1999) was introduced, following a European Commission study of vertical restraints. This permits agreements between firms at different stages of the supply chain, as long as the seller (buyer) does not account for at least a 30 per cent market share of the relevant seller (buyer) market. Agreements covering market partitioning, price fixing and resale price maintenance are still deemed illegal.

Article 82 of the Treaty of Amsterdam regulates possible abuses of monopoly power, such as monopoly pricing, predatory pricing and price discrimination. An individual firm occupies a dominant position if it can prevent competition, behave independently of competitors, and exercise control over production and prices. In practice, an investigation is triggered if a single firm has a 40 per cent share of the relevant market. Price fixing, the restriction of production or technical development to the detriment of consumers, a refusal to trade with certain customers, and the imposition of unfair terms or restrictions are recognized forms of abuse of a dominant position. A landmark case in 1978 involved the prices charged for bananas by the United Brands company to distributors in EU countries. Higher prices charged to distributors in Denmark and Germany than to those in Ireland, Belgium, Netherlands and Luxembourg were found to be unjustifiable on criteria such as cost or risk. In contrast to Article 81, Article 82 does not allow for any exemptions.

Mergers are regulated by Regulation 139/2004, which came into force in May 2004, and replaces the previous merger regulation (Regulation 4064/89, *European Council Merger Regulation (ECMR), The Control of Concentrations*), which was passed in 1989, and subsequently amended by Council Regulation 13/10/97. Regulation 139/2004 covers mergers, acquisitions and joint mergers. A horizontal merger qualifies for investigation if it has a fundamental effect on competition within the EU. Regulation 139/2004 is intended to streamline and improve the transparency of merger investigations. It contains new guidelines for the assessment of mergers based on economic indicators, and new guidelines for firms concerning their rights in the event of a merger being disallowed. The Merger Task Force, which previously had responsibility for investigating proposed mergers, was disbanded. Lyons (2003) suggests these changes were motivated by increased recognition of the usefulness of economic analysis in informing competition policy, and a need to streamline procedures following the accession of ten new member states to the EU in May 2004. Lyons cites three successful appeals (Airtours/First Choice; Schneider/Le Grand; and Tetra/Sidel) against decisions taken under the pre-2004 arrangements. In each case the Merger Task Force was criticized for using inappropriate economic theory, failing to take account of changing industry conditions, and misinterpreting documentary evidence.

Notification of any merger should be made to Competition Directorate-General IV not more than one week after a bid is placed or a deal announced. Failure to notify may result in a fine. The Directorate reviews any proposed merger in two phases. Phase I, the initial investigation, is completed within one month, and may or may not trigger a more detailed Phase II investigation. Phase II, which is normally completed within four months, examines the implications of the proposed merger for competition (based on the dominance test) and the single market. During the investigation, interested parties are given the opportunity to attend a series of state-of-play meetings with investigators. This provides Directorate-General IV with the opportunity to collect additional information and entitles the interested parties to assess the progress of the investigation. The investigation invites views and written submissions from customers, suppliers and competitors. The Directorate-General IV takes the final decision as to whether an investigation takes place, and whether a merger is permitted to proceed.

Most merger investigations weigh the implications for competition and the single market against any possible benefits, which might include scale economies or technological advance. It is unusual for a merger to be allowed to proceed if it creates or strengthens a dominant position. However, any investigation will take account of the extent to which buyer power acts as a countervailing force against the competitive dominance brought about by the proposed merger. If a merger is disallowed, the parties involved can appeal to the Court of First Instance, and ultimately to the European Court of Justice. Case studies 17.5 to 17.7 describe several cases of EU competition policy in action.

Case study 17.5

ABB fined heavily over role in cartel

European Commission: ten companies penalised for fixing prices of insulated steel heating pipes

The European Commission yesterday slapped an €70m (£50m) fine on ABB, the Swedish–Swiss engineering multinational, for its critical role in a price-fixing cartel, which from 1994 controlled the entire European market for insulated steel heating pipes. Nine other companies were fined a total of €22.21m.

The Commission, the European Union's executive branch, also accused the cartel of trying to force out of business the Swedish company Powerpipe, the only competitor not part of the 'ring'. 'It is difficult to imagine a worse cartel', said Karel Van Miert, the EU competition commissioner. 'The main producers tried to bankrupt the only competitor who was willing to take them on. They deliberately flouted EU public procurement rules . . . and they continued the violation nine months after Commission investigators caught them red handed.'

ABB said yesterday it had not yet decided whether to appeal against the fine, among the largest imposed on an individual company.

The other companies involved in the case were Logstor, Tarco, and Starpipe of Denmark; Isoplus, Pan-Isovit, Brugg Rorsysteme and Ke-Kelit of Austria and Germany; KWH Tech of Finland, and Sigma Tecnologie di Rivestimento of Italy. Logstor got the second biggest fine of €8.9m.

According to the Commission the cartel began in Denmark in 1990, but soon spread to cover the entire European market worth around €400m. In Germany and Denmark, the two biggest markets, the cartel operated a sophisticated system of bid rigging under which one company was nominated to win the contract and other cartel members deliberately put in higher offers. Brussels investigators were tipped off by Powerpipe in 1995 after the cartel members, furious that Powerpipe had won a big project in Germany, refused to deliver supplies to the Swedish company.

Yesterday was the third time in less than two months that the Commission, which acts as Europe's antitrust enforcer, has imposed fines on companies involved in market-rigging. Earlier this month it punished two British sugar companies and last month it imposed its biggest ever antitrust fines on 15 of the largest shipping lines. The Commission said the fines would have been higher if the companies had not owned up to their violations.

Source: Emma Tucker, ABB fined heavily over role in cartel, *Financial Times*, 22 October 1998, p. 3.
© Financial Times.

Case study 17.6

Not so sweet
Abuse of dominant position by Irish Sugar

In 1997, the European Commission concluded an investigation under Article 86 into abuse of a dominant position in the Irish sugar market by Irish Sugar Plc over the period 1985–95. Irish Sugar is the main sugar supplier in Ireland, with a market share exceeding 90 per cent. It is the only company with an extensive distribution network. Distribution is carried out by Sugar Distributors Ltd, a wholly owned subsidiary of Irish Sugar since 1990. Most retail and industrial customers in Ireland obtained granulated sugar supplies from Irish Sugar. Sugar imports came from Northern Ireland, France, Germany and Belgium. In the industrial market for granulated sugar, there was competition from French sugar imports, supplied by ASI International Foods Ltd. In the retail market, there was competition from Round Tower Foods and ASI. However, ASI withdrew from the retail market in 1994. Overall, the prices of sugar in Ireland are among the highest in the EU.

Irish Sugar, in conjunction with Sugar Distributors Limited, was accused of the following abuses of its monopoly position:

- *Transport restrictions*. Irish Sugar was accused of impeding competition from imported French sugar by threatening to withdraw Irish Sugar's business from the British and Irish Shipping Line company, if it continued to import French sugar on behalf of ASI.

- *Selective pricing and potential customers*. The Commission uncovered evidence that Irish Sugar offered reduced prices to ASI's customers. There was also evidence to suggest customers close to the Ireland–Northern Ireland border were offered Irish Sugar at a 5.5 per cent discount, in an attempt to restrict cross-border imports.

- *Selective pricing and target rebates*. Irish Sugar offered customers discounts on sugar if they increased their purchases of Irish Sugar products. This had the effect of tying customers to Irish Sugar, to the detriment of other competitors.

- *Selective pricing and export rebates*. Irish Sugar offered discounts to customers who were exporting sugar from Ireland. The same terms were not available to firms buying sugar for resale within Ireland. Accordingly, a policy of cross-subsidization was suspected.

- *Product swapping*. When ASI introduced *Eurolax* sugar (with ingredients imported from France), Irish Sugar arranged to exchange its own products for *Eurolax* with wholesalers and retailers. This had the effect of eliminating competition in the retail market.

Irish Sugar argued it had only engaged in these practices to meet the challenges of increased competition. Therefore it argued that it not infringed Article 86. However, Irish Sugar was found guilty of abuses of its dominant position, discouraging sugar imports, and distorting competition with Irish Sugar's rivals. The firm was fined an amount equivalent to €8,800,000.

Source: European Commission (1997e) Irish sugar, *Official Journal of the European Communities*, L258, 22 September.

Microsoft got what it deserved in Europe **FT**

The remedies demanded by the European Commission in the Microsoft case are far-reaching and go well beyond the fairly tepid relief obtained by the US government when it chose to settle its own case against the company.

What explains this difference in regulatory outcomes? Is it, as Microsoft's defenders suggest, that European competition authorities (unlike their US counterparts) fail to appreciate the difference between an 'injury to competition' (conduct that harms consumers) and 'injury to competitors' (conduct that may make life difficult for rivals but operates to the benefit of consumers)? Or is it that the US settlement was inadequate?

The Commission's case alleges that Microsoft is improperly using its near-monopoly position in personal computer operating systems to achieve market power in two adjacent markets: the market for operating systems on workgroup servers and the market for media companies.

Workgroup servers are the computers in an organization's network that have responsibility for everyday network tasks such as allowing users to sign on, enabling users to share files, routing jobs to printers, and so on. Workgroup servers typically cost less than US$25,000 and frequently cost less than US$10,000.

How is Microsoft trying to obtain control over the market for workgroup server operating systems? Workgroup servers, by their nature, need to work, or 'interoperate', with PCs. Since Windows is the operating system on more than 90 per cent of PCs, this means that a workgroup server cannot be commercially viable unless it can work with Windows. This is where the problem arises. Microsoft is good about disclosing information that will enable software developers to write programs that run on Windows but is highly reluctant to disclose information that would enable a workgroup server running Linux or another operating system to interoperate fully with other computers that have Windows as their operating system.

Microsoft's response to complaints about 'interoperability' is on two levels. First, the company denies that interoperability is a problem; this response, however, is inconsistent with Microsoft's own marketing material (which emphasizes that Microsoft products work 'better together') and the experience of Microsoft's competitors.

Its second response is more fundamental. Microsoft has invested significant amounts in developing Windows and part of the company's business strategy is to increase the use of Windows on corporate servers. Why should Microsoft be forced to make disclosures that would frustrate this strategy by making it easier for competitors to compete with Windows on servers? Microsoft argues that, if these become the rules of the game, its incentive to make future investments in innovation will be sharply reduced.

Microsoft's argument is incomplete as a matter of economics and ignores important policy issues. Microsoft's near-monopoly in PC operating systems provides it with the opportunity, if unchecked, to migrate its initial monopoly to any adjacent market in which interoperability is important. And, once a monopoly is established in the adjacent market, this creates the opportunity to achieve a monopoly in neighbouring markets. This process of using a monopoly over one part of an integrated, interconnected network to extend monopoly into complementary parts of the network has been carefully studied in modern economics. There is now no doubt that in the right conditions – present in the Microsoft case – a monopolist can capture whole markets far beyond the value of its initial invention and, potentially, regardless of the intrinsic merits of its product. The public policy question is whether such a scenario promotes or retards innovation. Intervention would reduce Microsoft's profits and might reduce its incentive to invest. But against this one must consider – which Microsoft does not – the effect of intervention on other companies with bright ideas and good products that might otherwise limit their investment because of interoperability problems.

The Commission is not being draconian by ordering Microsoft to provide interoperability information to its rivals in the server market. We see and benefit from just such requirements every day in telecommunications markets. In Europe, North America and elsewhere any telecoms operator must interconnect smoothly with rival telecoms companies. Encouraging interoperability clearly benefits consumers and we also see continuing innovation in the industry.

Against this background, it is difficult to imagine BT or France Telecom arguing that they should be allowed to offer inferior interconnection to rivals because an obligation to provide interconnection information would violate their intellectual property rights and damp industry-wide incentives to innovate. Yet this is the proposition that Microsoft argues is somehow self-evident in the case of computers. The basis for this claim is a mystery to us.

Source: William Bishop and Robert Stillman, Microsoft got what it deserved in Europe, *Financial Times*, 29 March 2004, p. 21. © The Financial Times.

Box 17.1

Competition policy in the United States

Competition law was first introduced in the US in the late nineteenth century, in response to the growth in corporate trusts. The trust was an arrangement whereby shareholders of different companies signed over the ownership of their shares to a single group of trustees. Consequently, there was a tendency for independent competitor firms to be consolidated into large entities, which rapidly came to dominate their respective industries. Anticompetitive practices of these large consolidated firms included price fixing and price discrimination.

In response, a series of antitrust laws was passed, with the intention of lessening the impact on competition of the growth of corporate trusts. Enforcement of these laws is carried out by the Antitrust Division within the US Department of Justice and by the Federal Trade Commission (FTC), set up by the Federal Trade Commission Act 1914. The FTC's remit was strengthened by the Wheeler–Lea Act 1938, which extended its investigative powers to cover not only antitrust issues, but also consumer protection. The Antitrust Division's traditional role was that of prosecutor, rather than policy maker. The FTC, on the other hand, is an independent body, charged with providing economic analysis of various competition issues and conducting formal investigations and prosecutions. It is also possible for private parties to bring prosecutions for violations of antitrust law. Under private prosecutions, plaintiffs are entitled to three times the value of the economic damages caused by the defendant (Shepherd, 1997).

Landmark acts that have shaped the evolution of US competition policy include the following.

Sherman Act 1890

The Sherman Act comprised two main sections. Section 1 made it illegal for firms to pursue strategies aimed at reducing competition. Such activities included price fixing and the allocation of production quotas. Section 2 made it illegal for any firm to monopolize an industry. The Act empowered the courts to impose fines of up to US$5,000 for each violation. By 1992 the maximum fine had increased to US$10 million. However, from the content of the act it was unclear what constituted an illegal monopoly position; and this has been left for the courts to interpret.

The most famous early prosecution under the terms of the Sherman Act was against the Standard Oil Company in 1911, for monopolization of the crude and refined oil and petroleum goods industries. Standard Oil had a market share exceeding 80 per cent in the market for refined oil, and was accused of practising price discrimination and attempting to eliminate rivals. The company had also used its market power to obtain preferential transport rates from railway operators. The court found Standard Oil had abused its monopoly position, and ordered the break-up of the firm into 34 separate companies. The oil firms Exxon (Esso), Mobil and SoCal (Standard Oil of California) were all part of the original Standard Oil Company.

The finding in the Standard Oil case was an example of courts referring to the **rule of reason** doctrine, whereby the firm's conduct, and the consequences for competition and welfare, are more important than structural features such as the firm's size or market share. The courts reversed the rule of reason doctrine in 1945 in favour of a more straightforward assessment of monopoly. In another landmark case, Alcoa (Aluminum Company of America) was found guilty of operating a monopoly in the virgin ingot production market, where its market share exceeded 90 per cent. This decision reversed an earlier judgement in Alcoa's favour. The earlier decision was based on a broad market definition (including other types of aluminium product), while the later one used a narrower definition. Although there was no evidence that the firm was abusing its market power, it was deemed to have acted illegally simply by being a monopoly.

The American Tobacco case of 1946 provides an early example of a prosecution for collusive behaviour under the Sherman Act. The US tobacco industry was dominated by three firms: American Tobacco, Reynolds and Ligget and Myers. Over a period of 20 years, these firms had charged almost identical prices for their retail products, and had contrived to bid identical prices for supplies of tobacco at auctions. Although there was no evidence of a collusive agreement to fix prices, observed behaviour suggested tacit collusion was occurring. The courts imposed a fine of US$255,000, but did not impose any remedies to change the structure or conduct of firms in the tobacco industry.

In 1974, AT&T (American Telephone and Telegraph Company), at the time the world's largest company, was accused of monopolizing the markets for telephone equipment and local and long-distance calls. In the telephone equipment market, AT&T had restricted competition by purchasing equipment only from its own manufacturing divisions. The company was also accused of restricting the access of independent telephone equipment and services suppliers to its telephone networks. In 1982, AT&T agreed to divest itself of its 22 local telephone companies, accounting for around two-thirds of AT&T's total assets. The competitive environment in the US telecommunications industry was transformed. However, AT&T was permitted to retain its manufacturing divisions and its long-distance services. It was also allowed to diversify into cable television and computing (Shepherd, 1997). At the time, AT&T was one of the largest antitrust cases ever filed; but even this has been overshadowed recently by the Microsoft case, described in Case study 17.1.

Clayton Act 1914

The Clayton Act supplemented the Sherman Act, outlining specific instances of abuses of monopoly power, and restricting the legality of practices such as exclusive supply agreements, tied arrangements and price discrimination. The latter would only be allowed in cases where there were differences in the quantities purchased; differences in product quality; and differences in transport or distribution costs sufficient to justify different prices being charged. These provisions were strengthened in the Robinson–Paton Act 1936. The Clayton Act also limited cross-share ownership between firms, and mergers which created monopolies through share acquisition between firms operating in the same industry. These provisions were extended in 1950 in the Celler–Kefauver Act, which prevented any merger between firms at different stages of the same production process (vertical mergers), or in unrelated activities (conglomerate mergers), that would impede competition.

In 1957 DuPont–General Motors (GM) case was prosecuted under the terms of the Clayton Act. DuPont, at the time a dominant supplier of fabrics, paints and other chemicals, acquired a 23 per cent shareholding in GM. It was claimed this move reduced competition in the supply of paint and fabrics to car manufacturers, and placed other suppliers at a competitive disadvantage. DuPont was deemed guilty of violating the Clayton Act, and was required to divest itself of its GM shareholding.

Antitrust Improvements Act 1976

The Antitrust Improvements Act was passed with the specific aim of improving the regulation of mergers. Firms with assets exceeding US$100m that wished to merge with firms with assets exceeding US$10m were required to notify the appropriate regulatory authority 30 days before the merger was due to take place. This act made it much easier for regulators to investigate and act against proposed mergers. This act was supplemented by further merger guidelines and amendments introduced in 1982, 1992 and 1997. The 1982 guidelines made it easier for mergers to be investigated with reference to standard concentration measures (for example, the HH index). The 1992 and 1997 amendments reduced the emphasis on concentration, but allowed for consideration of the implications for costs and product prices, taking account of some of the theoretical arguments in favour of large-scale mergers.

The US was the first country to develop a comprehensive body of competition law. However, penalties for abuses of market power and restrictive practices have varied considerably over time. Remedies have included breaking up large firms into smaller constituent parts (Standard Oil), limiting expansion (Alcoa), and large fines (American Tobacco). Antitrust policy has been relatively stringent in the 1900s, 1920s, 1930s to 1950s, 1970s and 1990s (Kovacic and Shapiro, 2000). Restrictive practices policy (in particular price fixing) has always been stringent. However, instances of tacit collusion are difficult to prove. Changes over time in the interpretation of various laws have made it difficult to achieve consistency in decision making. More than 100 years after the passing of the Sherman Act, Demsetz (1992) comments that more still needs to be done to ensure effective competition in all sectors of the US economy.

17.6 Assessment of UK competition policy

In an assessment of the effectiveness of UK competition policy, Shaw and Simpson (1986) find firms that were investigated by the Monopolies and Mergers Commission over the period 1959–73 tended to lose market share over a 10-year period following the investigation. To assess whether this was as a direct consequence of competition policy, the sample of 28 investigations is matched by a sample of 19 similarly structured cases that were not investigated. The results were similar for both the Monopolies and Mergers Commission sample and the matched sample. Increased competition from foreign and domestic firms appears to have had a greater effect on the performance of dominant firms than any remedies imposed by the Monopolies and Mergers Commission.

Davies *et al.* (1999) examine the determinants of Monopolies and Mergers Commission decisions against monopolies. The commission ruled against roughly two-thirds of the 73 cases examined in the study, most of which were investigated under the provisions of the Fair Trading Act 1973. Of these cases, 36 referred to pricing issues (monopoly pricing, predatory pricing, collusion), and 37 referred to vertical restraints (vertical integration, resale price maintenance, tie-in sales, exclusivity in distribution and purchasing). Among the cases where the commission ruled against the firms, recommendations included the termination of a restrictive practice (34 cases), price controls (9 cases) and divestment of assets (9 cases).

Davies *et al.* develop a statistical model to identify the factors most likely to influence the probability of the commission ruling against a firm or group of firms.

Explanatory variables include indicators of market structure, such as concentration, rates of entry and market shares; indicators of conduct covering areas such as vertical integration, exclusive purchasing, exclusive distribution, monopoly, predatory pricing, price discrimination and collusion; and variables to allow for changes in the commission's decisions over time, and to identify whether or not the investigation was a repeat referral. The estimated model suggests the greater the market share of the biggest firm in the industry, the more likely it was that the commission would be to rule against the monopoly practice. The commission was more likely to rule against in cases involving exclusive dealing, but less likely to do so in cases involving vertical restraints. The commission was more likely to rule against in the 1970s and 1980s than in the 1990s.

It is often easier to prevent an increase in seller concentration by preventing a merger before it takes place than by breaking up an incumbent firm that already occupies a dominant position. Weir (1992, 1993) analyses commission decisions on referred mergers using a sample of 73 published reports covering the period 1974–90. The sample is split into two groups: cases where the commission thought the merger would reduce competition; and cases where the commission thought the merger would have no effect on competition.

Regression analysis is used to identify the factors that influence the judgement as to whether a merger was in the public interest. Factors investigated include the effects of the merger on prices, market shares, profits, product quality, efficiency, research and development expenditure, and the UK balance of payments. The analysis distinguishes between horizontal, vertical and conglomerate mergers. Unsurprisingly, mergers were more likely to be permitted in cases where the commission thought competition would increase. Expectations of lower prices, cost savings, increased expenditure on research and development, or a benefit to the balance of payments increased the likelihood of a positive verdict.

For most of the post-war period, the policy approach of the UK authorities towards the regulation of monopoly and merger has been relatively cautious, and has been implemented on a case-by-case basis. The question posed by regulators is not whether a firm has monopoly power, but whether or not this power is used in a way that is detrimental to the wider public interest. In contrast, the approach taken towards the regulation of restrictive practices has usually been more stringent in principle, although it has encountered difficulties in its execution.

It seems highly likely that tacit forms of collusion are widespread, and difficult for the authorities to uncover (O'Brien *et al.*, 1979; Rees, 1993a,b). For most of the post-war period, the risk of detection has been small, and penalties in the event of detection light (Utton, 2000). For example, prior to the Competition Act 1998, there were no fines at all for first offenders: 'it is as though the police having captured a bank robber red-handed, inform him that he has broken the law and should not do it again, but then let him go with the fruits of his crime' (Williams, 1993, cited in Utton, 2000, p. 276).

A number of studies have attempted to assess the performance of the UK's competition policy regime. In 2001, the DTI commissioned Price Waterhouse to carry out an assessment of UK competition policy, in comparison with other EU and OECD countries including the US, Germany, Australia, France, Italy, Ireland, Netherlands, Spain, Sweden and Switzerland (Department of Trade and Industry,

2001). Experts (including senior officials from competition authorities, multi-national companies, competition lawyers, academic economists and representatives of consumer bodies) were asked to assess a number of factors relating to the effectiveness of competition policy, including:

- Clarity of policy objectives.
- Competence of economic and legal analysis.
- Political independence.
- Quality of leadership within competition authorities.
- Transparency of procedures.
- Communication with the general public.

The experts were also invited to suggest improvements to the UK's arrangements. Each country was assigned a score relative to an EU benchmark. The UK was deemed to have a competition policy regime less effective than the US and Germany, but more effective than the average for the other OECD countries included in the study. The UK was praised for its economic analysis, transparency of procedures and speed of decision making in investigations of monopolies. However, relative to the EU, UK merger policy was criticized as being less politically independent, providing a lower quality of legal analysis, and slower in taking decisions. The report suggested abandoning the vague notion of public interest in favour of a competition-based test for the assessment of proposed mergers. A follow-up report (Department of Trade and Industry, 2004) finds UK merger policy has improved relative to the EU since 2001. This may be partly as a consequence of difficulties experienced by the EU, in the form of successful appeals by the firms involved in several high-profile merger cases (Lyons, 2003). While UK monopoly policy was rated as strong, policy towards cartels still lacks some clarity; although the introduction of the Competition Appeals Tribunal has improved transparency.

Overall, the most recent legislation (specifically, the Competition Act 1998 and the Enterprise Act 2002), together with the stricter provisions that are effective at EU level, has strengthened the UK's competition policy regime significantly. Emphasis is placed on serving the needs of consumers and enhancing the productivity and competitiveness of UK industry. At the start of the twenty-first century, the UK's competition policy regime is more robust than any that has operated previously.

17.7 Summary

The economic basis for competition policy rests in large measure on the theoretical case for and against monopoly. According to the neoclassical theory of the firm, under monopoly, market price is higher and output is lower than under perfect competition. The monopolist typically fails to produce at the minimum efficient scale, and therefore fails to produce at the lowest attainable average cost. The monopolist earns an abnormal profit in the long run, while the perfectly competitive firm earns only a normal profit. Under monopoly, there is allocative inefficiency because price exceeds marginal cost. Industry output is too low, and welfare could be increased by producing more output. Under monopoly, there may also be productive inefficiency, if a lack of competitive pressure implies a monopolist becomes complacent or lazy, failing to achieve full technical or economic efficiency. Monopoly produces a dead-weight loss, and the sum of consumer surplus and producer surplus is lower than it is under perfect competition.

On the other hand, if the monopolist is able to operate on a lower average or marginal cost function than the firms comprising a perfectly competitive industry, social welfare could be higher under monopoly than under perfect competition. Overall, the theoretical evidence as to whether monopolies lead to a reduction in efficiency and social welfare is inconclusive.

A natural monopoly is a market in which average cost decreases as output increases over the entire range of realistic output levels. In natural monopoly, monopoly is always more cost-effective than competition. In this case, it is not at all obvious that competition is a more desirable state of affairs than monopoly. On theoretical grounds, a policy of price discrimination practised by a monopolist should not always be judged pejoratively. Although in this way the monopolist earns an even higher abnormal profit than is possible by charging a uniform price, total output is higher and the last unit of output produced is sold at a price equivalent to its marginal cost. Therefore a policy of first-degree price discrimination may be consistent with social welfare maximization. With other forms of price discrimination, it is not possible to generalize about the social welfare implications.

An incumbent monopolist might pursue various strategies in an attempt to raise entry barriers and deter potential entrants. Monopolists might also seek to impose vertical restraints on other firms that are vertically linked (suppliers of the monopolist's inputs or purchasers of its outputs). Such practices might be expected to attract the attention of the competition authorities. According to the Schumpeterian hypothesis, market power and monopoly status should be interpreted as the reward for successful past innovation. Successful innovation brings benefits to society, in the form of new products or more efficient production processes. In the past, the competition authorities have often taken a benign or favourable view of firms that are perceived to invest heavily research and development.

Competition policy deals with three principal areas: monopoly, restrictive practices and merger. The implementation of monopoly, restrictive practices and merger policy requires a practical method for measuring market power. Seller concentration and market share measures are obvious candidates. However, provided entry barriers are not insurmountable and markets are contestable, the threat of entry and competition may constrain a monopolist's pricing policy. It is therefore relevant to ask questions concerning the likelihood of entry. Issues of product and geographic market definition have major implications for the measurement of market power using concentration or market share measures. Most economists recognize that perfect competition is a theoretical ideal, which is unlikely to be attainable in practice. A more realistic objective for competition policy might be to foster workable competition, which seeks to create aspects of structure and conduct that are most likely to deliver good performance.

In this chapter, we have traced the historical evolution of competition policy in the UK from the 1940s through to the present. At the time of writing, competition policy in the UK is the responsibility of the OFT (Office of Fair Trading) and the Competition Commission. The OFT investigates complaints of anticompetitive practices, and if these complaints are upheld, refers the findings to the Competition Commission. The Competition Act 1998 and the Enterprise Act 2002 consolidated current arrangements for the conduct of competition policy, and harmonized the UK's arrangements with those operative at EU level. The Chapter I prohibition deals with restrictive practices, and corresponds to Article 81 of the EU's Treaty of Amsterdam. The Chapter II prohibition deals with abuses of dominant (or monopoly) positions, and corresponds to Article 82 of the Treaty of Amsterdam. In UK competition policy, the current emphasis is on the examination of the consequences of anticompetitive behaviour, rather than the form taken by any particular agreement or restrictive practice. The most recent legislation, together with the provisions operative at EU level, has strengthened the UK's competition policy regime considerably, in comparison with previous decades.

Discussion questions

1. Compare the long-run equilibrium values of output, price and average cost under perfect competition and monopoly, assuming cost structures are identical in both cases. What conclusions can be drawn concerning productive and allocative efficiency?

2. With reference to Q1, is the assumption of identical cost structures reasonable? If a monopolist operates on a lower long-run average cost function than a perfectly competitive industry, what are the implications for the comparison between the productive and allocative efficiency properties of perfect competition and monopoly?

3. What factors should be taken into account by the competition authorities in determining whether a particular market is under monopoly control?

4. With reference to Case study 17.1, outline the key components of the US Department of Justice Case against Microsoft.

5. What is meant by workable competition, and what are its implications for the interpretation of competition policy?

6. 'The emphasis of UK competition policy has shifted away from the examination of the form taken by any restrictive practice, and towards examination of the consequences of anticompetitive behaviour.' By making reference to the content of specific pieces of legislation during the post-Second World War period, assess the validity of this claim.

7. Outline the relationship between the chapter prohibitions contained in the UK Competition Act 1998, and Articles 81 and 82 of the EU Treaty of Amsterdam.

8. With reference to Case study 17.2, identify structural characteristics of the airlines industry that may give rise to impediments to competition.

9. From a public policy perspective, present a supplier's possible defence of the practice of RPM (resale price maintenance). Illustrate your answer with reference to the debate surrounding the effects of the abolition of RPM in medicines in the UK, summarized in Case study 17.3.

10. With reference to Case study 17.4, examine the sources of impediments to competition in the market for banking services for small businesses. What remedies are available to the competition authorities?

11. With reference to Section 5.6 and Case study 17.5, what factors do you think were conducive to the formation of a price fixing cartel in the European insulated pipes industry?

12. With reference to Section 15.7 and Case study 17.6, identify the forms of vertical restraint that constituted the main substance of the European Commission's case against Irish Sugar.

13. With reference to Case study 17.7, do you agree Microsoft 'got what it deserved in Europe'?

14. To what extent has competition policy legislation in the UK during the post-Second World War period provided an effective deterrent to anticompetitive behaviour?

Further reading

Audretsch, D., Baumol, W.J. and Burke, A. (2001) Competition policy in a dynamic economy, *International Journal of Industrial Organization*, 19, 613–34.

Burke, J. (1991) *Compeitition in Theory and Practice*. London: Routledge.

Goyder, D.G. (2003) *EC Competition Law: Text and Cases*. London: Oxford University Press.

Kwoka, J.E. and White, L.J. (2003) *The Anti-Trust Revolution*, 4th edn. London: Oxford University Press.

Motta, M. (2003) Competition Policy: Theory and Practice. Cambridge: Cambridge University Press.

Neven, D., Nuttall, R. and Seabright, P. (1993) *Merger in Daylight: The Economics and Politics of European Merger Control*. London: Centre for Economic Policy Research.

Neven, D., Papandropoulos, P. and Seabright, P. (1998) *Trawling for Minnows: European Competition Policy and Agreements Between Firms*. London: Centre for Economic Policy Research.

Office of Fair Trading (1999a) *Quantitative Techniques in Competition Analysis*. London: Office of Fair Trading.

Pickering, J.F. (1982) The economics of anti-competitive practices, *European Competition Law Review*, 3, 253–74.

Pickering, J.F. (1999) Competition policy and vertical relationships: the approach of the UK Monopolies and Mergers Commission, *European Competition Law Review*, 20, 225–39.

Shepherd, W.G. (1997) *The Economics of Industrial Organization*. Englewood Cliffs, NJ: Prentice-Hall.

Whish, R. (2003) *Competition Law*, 4th edn. London: Butterworth.

Learning objectives

This chapter covers the following topics:

- the rationale for government regulation
- resource allocation under conditions of natural monopoly
- public ownership and privatization
- price cap and rate of return regulation
- franchise agreement
- compulsory competitive tendering and best value

Key terms

Best value
Compulsory competitive tendering
Conduct regulation
Franchising
Natural monopoly

Price cap regulation
Privatization
Rate of return regulation
Regulatory capture
Structural regulation

18.1 Introduction

Chapter 18 examines government or public sector involvement in the provision of goods and services. Government provision is often motivated by a desire to correct various types of market failure. More specifically, we examine the relative merits of organizing production in the private and public sectors, particularly in cases where average costs tend to fall over the entire range of industry output; in other words, when the industry operates under cost conditions that give rise to a **natural monopoly**. Advantages sometimes attributed to organizing production within the public sector include the elimination of wasteful competition, and the exploitation of the full potential for economies of scale and scope. Disadvantages include a lack of competitive discipline or incentive to minimize costs and maximize productivity. With these and other factors in mind, during the 1980s and 1990s the pendulum swung away from state ownership and towards **privatization** in many countries. If privatization involves the break-up of monopolies into smaller units, an element of competition may be introduced automatically. In cases where this is not feasible, regulation may be required in order to ensure outcomes mimicking those that may have occurred under (hypothetical) competitive conditions.

The chapter begins in Section 18.2 with a review of the policy issues raised by natural monopolies, including an overview of the range of options open to policy makers seeking to reduce or eliminate the scope for a natural monopolist to abuse its market power. These options are examined in more detail in the next four sections. Section 18.3 discusses the policy of nationalization, which involves taking an industry into state ownership. Section 18.4 considers the reverse policy of privatization, whereby state-owned enterprises are transferred to private ownership and control. These two sections discuss the economic case for and against nationalization and privatization, and review the empirical evidence concerning the performance of state-owned enterprises, and of those that have been transferred to private ownership during their pre- and post-privatization stages.

In cases of natural monopolies in particular, privatization often does not involve the creation of a competitive market structure. In such cases, regulation of the newly privatized industry provides an alternative method for avoiding various forms of market failure, and achieving outcomes that might have resulted had the introduction of competition been a feasible option. Section 18.5 examines regulation, and draws comparisons between the types of regulatory regime most widely used in the US and in Europe. These are known as **rate of return regulation** and **price cap regulation**, respectively. Finally, Section 18.6 discusses the policy of franchising, involving the allocation of exclusive rights to supply certain goods and services. Consideration is also given to the widespread local government practice of competitive tendering, under which in-house public sector providers compete against private contractors to retain or acquire the rights to provide public services.

18.2 The problem of natural monopoly

One of the main arguments in favour of the regulation of industry is based on the notion that some industries are natural monopolies. As we have seen in Section 2.5, a **natural monopoly** exists when production at the minimum possible long-run average cost can take place only if one firm controls the industry's total production; or in other words, when the minimum efficient scale (MES) is roughly equivalent to (or longer than) the total market size.

In the case of a natural monopoly with a large fixed cost, entry may well be uneconomic. Suppose, for example, a water company supplies an entire geographic region through a network of pipes. It might well be uneconomic for an entrant to set up its own infrastructure and start supplying a segment of the same market, because the entrant would have difficulty in claiming a sufficient share of the market to cover its fixed cost. According to Ogus (1996), in the UK 'a degree of scepticism of the merits of competition developed, particularly in relation to water and gas, as the duplication of facilities funded by major capital outlays and often surplus capacity, was perceived to be wasteful' (Ogus, 1996, p. 265).

Regulation may therefore be viewed as a substitute for competition in cases where competition, by reducing the nautral monopolist's market share, would prevent the full exploitation of economies of scale (Waterson, 1987). Regulation is required to ensure the monopolist does not abuse its market power. For example, a diversified firm that has a natural monopoly in one line of business might cross-subsidize loss-making activities in other lines of business using monopoly profits from the business in which the firm is a natural monopolist. In the UK, several of the utility furms have diversified into other lines of business, offering new services at below-cost prices and attracting accusations of unfair competition from incumbent firms in the service industries concerned. Case study 18.1 provides an overview of the changing role of regulation in the UK since the 1980s.

Case study 18.1

Government and regulation

The past 20 years have seen a marked shift in regulators' role – towards helping businesses and markets to function

It was not long ago that government–business relations were associated with taxation, investment incentives, public enterprises and regional development. The government was viewed as a substitute for markets where markets failed to operate. The classic examples were utilities, whose natural monopoly characteristics demanded supply by public enterprises. Though this view of government prevails in certain areas, there has been a marked shift in the past 20 years. Now business–government relations conjure up views of regulation, competition policy and public-private partnerships.

These developments have been driven by a changing perception of the function of government. In the postwar period, industrial policy aimed to correct 'market failures'; more recently there has been a growing appreciation of government failures. Thus the focus of government involvement in business has moved from substituting for markets to assisting them to function.

Alongside this change in attitudes, governments have acquired new analytic techniques for designing and evaluating policy tools, which permit the implementation of more sophisticated public policies at the microeconomic level.

Privatisation has been a big spur to change. During the 1980s and 1990s, some 2,500 deals worth approximately US$1,100bn were reported in 120 countries. Huge segments of corporate activity around the world were transferred from public to private sector control. But the retreat of public sector ownership has coincided with the expansion of a new form of public sector activity – regulation.

Utilities

Regulation has been primarily associated with the utilities. In the absence of competition, the charges that utilities levy on customers had to be regulated. Regulation was originally conceived as a temporary expedient that would wither as competition emerged. In some sectors, such as electricity and telecommunications, this has occurred, but for the most part regulation has actually intensified. There are several reasons for this.

First, it is difficult to introduce competition into certain areas, for example, water services and the core part of utilities, such as electricity and gas transmission systems. Second, the tools available to regulators have become increasingly sophisticated, for example, in benchmarking performance and comparing costs. The belief that regulators can replicate the incentive mechanisms of competitive markets remains widespread.

There is little doubt that privatisation has brought considerable gains in efficiency, particularly in reducing the costs of running utilities. However, providing the right incentives for utilities to invest has been a tougher nut for regulators to crack. It is formidably difficult to determine the rates of return that utilities need to earn and it is even more complex to ensure that they are able to earn these returns over the long life of their investments.

The US has attempted to solve this by fixing the rate of return that utilities earn (the so-called 'rate of return regulation') while the UK and much of the rest of the world has opted for 'price regulation'. Price regulation has encouraged the pursuit of operating efficiencies but potentially at the expense of investment.

Competition policy

The deficiencies of regulation have prompted policymakers to promote competition instead where possible. For example, in energy, competitive markets in supply have been developed separately from the core activities of transmission.

The emergence of potentially competitive markets in utilities has been one factor encouraging a greater emphasis on competition policy. Another has been the recognition that a tough public policy stance is required to avoid anti-competitive practices. As governments' role as provider of goods and services has diminished so their function as protector of the consumer has increased.

As in regulation, the tools of competition policy have become increasingly sophisticated. The principles of competition policy have been one of the greatest successes of economics in the past 20 years. While anti-trust regulation has been a focus of public policy in the US for the past 100 years, it has only recently risen to prominence in Europe, led by the European Commission. The focus of US policy is on consumer protection, promotion of competition and arbitration through the courts. In Europe, however, many argue that policy has had a wider remit of the protection of small and medium-sized enterprises, employment and market integration. Critics suggest this is a source of confusion in European decisions.

In summary, the past 20 years have witnessed a pronounced shift in the role of government in business away from substituting for markets towards promoting them. This is happening at various speeds in different countries. It has been the focus of policy in the US for a long time. It is being rapidly adopted in the UK and there is a growing appreciation of its relevance in Brussels.

These developments reflect not only a realization of the limits of government but also the emergence of new tools of analysis. While it has not been widely appreciated, advances in microeconomic analysis over the past 20 years have given rise to more sophisticated policies towards corporate sectors. The US leads the world in the quality of its economic analysis, so it is not surprising that it has been the source of most policy innovations. But these innovations offer policymakers around the world the opportunity of modernizing the government of business.

Source: The past 20 years have seen a marked shift in regulators' role – towards helping businesses and markets to function, *Financial Times*, 28 August 2002, p. 9. © The Financial Times. (Abridged.)

If a natural monopolist is abusing its market power, there are several possible solutions. The first is public ownership, which normally involves granting statutory rights to a single firm. In doing so, the firm can be required to price its products in a reasonably competitive manner. A second solution is to open up the relevant market to competition. In many countries, the privatization of previously nationalized industries, involving the transfer of state-owned assets to the private sector, has been accompanied by efforts to create more competitive post-privatization market conditions. A final solution is to allow temporary monopoly rights through the granting of a franchise. In this case, competition takes place prior to the award of the franchise during the bidding process, with stipulations concerning matters such as price and quality of service written into the successful bidder's contract. The merits of these three approaches have been summarized as follows:

> First, the firm can be publicly owned . . . , the expectation being that the mechanics of political direction and accountability will be sufficient to meet public interest goals. Secondly, the firm may remain in, or be transferred to, private ownership but be subjected to external constraints in the form of price and quality regulation . . . Thirdly, firms desiring to obtain a monopoly right may be forced to compete for it . . . As part of their competitive bid, they are required to stipulate proposed conditions of supply, relating especially to prices and quality; and those conditions then become terms of the licence or franchise under which they exercise the monopoly right.
>
> *(Ogus, 1996, p. 5)*

In Sections 18.3 to 18.6, each of these solutions to the problem of natural monopoly is examined in turn.

In most cases, nationalization involves the creation of a statutory monopoly owned and controlled by the government. Usually, competition is prohibited: new firms cannot enter and compete with the established monopolist. Domberger and Piggot (1986) argue there is a strong case for public ownership of natural monopolies. By assuming ownership, the government can instruct the firm to pursue certain objectives or adopt certain policies. The aim is to correct market failures associated with market power, externalities and asymmetric information, and to satisfy the necessary conditions for allocative efficiency. In practice, however, allocative efficiency may be difficult to achieve, if a marginal cost pricing policy causes the natural monopolist to realize a loss (see Section 2.5, Figure 2.15). Therefore second-best policies are sometimes used: the firm might adopt average cost pricing; or the government might provide a subsidy to cover the losses entailed by marginal cost pricing (Lipsey and Lancaster, 1956).

Nationalization involving the creation of a statutory monopoly may result in the elimination of wasteful competition, or it may allow the full exploitation of economies of scale. In some cases, nationalization may be justified in terms of social objectives, such as the provision of services that would otherwise be deemed uneconomic by the private sector: for example, postal or telephone services to rural areas.

However, the public provision of goods and services does raise a number of difficult issues. Nationalized firms are generally shielded from the rigours of competition. Therefore there is little or no threat of bankruptcy, as losses are effectively recovered by means of government subsidy. Nationalized firms are also protected from the threat of being taken over. Consequently there may be little or no incentive for the managers of nationalized firms to achieve full productive efficiency, especially if the managers' remuneration is not directly linked to the organization's performance. In many cases, conflict between political and economic objectives has made nationalized firms difficult to manage. Nationalized firms may be instructed to follow non-commercial objectives, in order to further the pursuit of policy objectives concerning employment, procurement and trade.

Foster (1992) suggests higher priority was attached to political objectives than to objectives relating to economic efficiency in the management of nationalized industries in the UK. Rees (1984) suggests the efforts of UK nationalized industries to pursue commercial objectives were stifled by excessive trade union power in the labour market. Bos (1991, 2003) suggests underperformance was due to various imperfections in the structure of ownership and control: for example, lack of clarity concerning objectives, financial constraints on borrowing and investment, inadequate incentives for efficient performance, and excessive interference by politicians. However, empirical evidence concerning the performance of the UK's nationalized industries is rather more varied than the views of some critics might suggest. Below, a selection of empirical studies is reviewed briefly.

Pryke (1981, 1982) examines trends in productivity in nine nationalized industries over the period 1968–78. In industries subject to rapid technological change, including airlines and telecoms, labour or total factor productivity increased. The rate of increase was slower in utilities such as gas and electricity. However, productivity in several nationalized industries, including steel, coal, postal services, bus and rail services declined.

> What public ownership does is to eliminate the threat of takeover and ultimately of bankruptcy and the need, which all private undertakings have from time to time, to raise money from the market. Public ownership provides a comfortable life and destroys commercial ethic.

> *(Pryke, 1982, p. 81)*

Molyneux and Thompson (1987) carry out a similar analysis for the same nine nationalized industries for the period 1978–85, and find productivity increased in all nine cases. The improvement is attributed to greater workforce flexibility, tighter controls over subsidy (which stimulated cost savings), increased investment, technological progress, rationalization and learning economies of scale. Millward (1990) compares the productivity of nationalized firms with privately owned firms in the gas, electricity, water and transport industries. Over the period 1950–86, in many cases productivity measures for publicly owned firms increased faster than those for privately owned firms. Finally, Lynk (1993) examines productivity differences between private and publicly owned water companies, prior to privatization in 1989. The publicly owned companies were found to be more productive. Overall, the empirical evidence provides a rather mixed view of the productivity and performance of the UK's nationalized industries.

18.4 Privatization

There is some confusion surrounding the use of the term **privatization**. This term has been widely used to refer to (at least) three distinct policies: denationalization, deregulation and franchising.

- *Denationalization.* This involves the transfer and sale of assets from the public to the private sector. The transfer of assets may or may not be accompanied by a process of deregulation (or market liberalization). Where capital markets are developed, the transfer of assets can be implemented by means of a sale of shares to financial institutions and the general public.

- *Deregulation and market liberalization.* Policies of deregulation and market liberalization aim to increase competition (Winston, 1993, 1998). This may involve altering the market structure, perhaps by reducing or eliminating barriers to entry. Some re-regulation might be required, in order to control the behaviour of incumbent firms towards new entrants. Advantages of deregulation are that inefficient firms, previously protected from competition, may eventually be superseded by more efficient competitors (Saal, 2003). However, Winston (1998) notes this is by no means an instantaneous process.

> It is not surprising that deregulated (or partially deregulated) industries are slow to achieve maximum efficiency. When regulatory restrictions on pricing, operations and entry (especially from new firms), has been

enforced for decades, managers and employees of regulated firms settle
into patterns of inefficient production and missed opportunities for
technological advance and entry into new markets . . . [I]t takes firms a
long time to tear down decades-old barriers to efficiency and to adopt
more efficient production and marketing practices.

(Winston, 1998, pp. 89–90)

The negative effects of deregulation are experienced if the process results in
the transfer of surplus from consumers to producers (see Case study 18.2 and
The Economist, 2002 for an extended discussion). For example, Crandell (2003)
discusses the recent deregulation of the electricity industry in California.

In 2000–2001, California's failed approach to deregulation allowed
generators to exploit the short term scarcity of power created by natural
forces, such as shortfall in precipitation and a rise in fossil fuel prices,
because California forbade utilities to enter into long term contracts.
The result was an increase in the state's electricity bill of approximately
$12 billion per year.

(Crandell, 2003, p. 78)

■ *Franchising.* This involves the contracting out to private contractors (often by
means of some form of auction) of services that were previously provided from
within the public sector. Franchising is often used in cases where direct competition is deemed impossible or undesirable. In the UK, examples include local
bus services and commercial passenger train services. The aim is to increase
competition indirectly, by encouraging firms to bid competitively for contracts
and licences to provide the relevant goods or services.

Case study 18.2

Reforms that have failed to work a power of good

Liberalization of the market has brought the UK industry to crisis point

Deregulation has caused persistent problems for energy markets. They go far beyond erratic
trading stemming from Enron misaccounting or California's peculiar market structure. And
they are not confined to nuclear power, or to the UK.

But the situation has apparently reached crisis point with British Energy in the UK, where
since electricity privatization in 1990 liberalization has probably been pushed furthest.

Wholesale power prices have fallen by 40 per cent since 1998 when reforms to the old
electricity spot market – known as the Pool – were first mooted. These reforms culminated
with the introduction last year of the new electricity trading arrangements (Neta).

Neta has accelerated the decline in prices, but without so far reducing the 25 per cent over-capacity in the industry that was sustained by the Pool, a system dominated and, to some extent, rigged by the big generators.

This over-capacity, or reserve margin, has made life difficult for British generators, particularly the nuclear ones with higher fixed costs than gas or coal-fired plants.

Indeed, because of the legacy of the Pool, the UK reserve margin today is, ironically, just as high as the 24 per cent level aimed for by the old Central Electricity Generating Board, which was widely considered to be a rather gold-plated monopoly with sizeable redundant back-up capacity.

Elsewhere, deregulation's downward pressure on prices has generally been less severe. A recent study by the International Energy Agency, which surveyed deregulation effects in its 26 member countries, reported generating reserves had declined in most markets since liberalization.

So, in contrast to the UK, nuclear companies even in liberalized markets like the US are able to make money out of their existing reactors. The big question mark is over new reactors. It is no accident that those built in recent years have been mainly in regulated markets like China. Last February's energy review by Downing Street's performance and innovation unit raised the question bluntly by saying: 'Nowhere in the world have new nuclear stations yet been financed with a liberalized electricity market.' It is not clear whether the government's forthcoming energy White Paper will provide an answer.

While the attraction of deregulation is lower prices, it can pose a problem for security of supply and for cleaner, but more expensive, forms of energy, like nuclear and renewable power. European gas liberalization, for instance, has unsettled the prospects for the import of gas through new long-distance pipelines from Russia and Algeria. These pipelines, like nuclear reactors, require large upfront investments, and there has been a concern that funding them would be undermined by a move away from long-term gas contracts. Companies wanting to pipe gas from Alaska through Canada to the rest of the US confront the same funding problem in the face of volatile gas prices.

Governments that have signed the Kyoto protocol on climate change have also begun to realize the need to rig the market in favour of renewable energy if they are to reduce carbon emissions. In the UK this has taken the form of a 'renewable obligation' requiring utilities to draw 10 per cent of their power from sources such as wind power by 2010.

In these circumstances, independent energy regulators are finding it increasingly hard to reconcile these environmental and security of supply considerations with their primary task of assuring full and fair competition in liberalized markets.

In the UK, Callum McCarthy, the OFGEM regulator, has made clear his main task is to provide cheaper energy to consumers, and that government should find other means of helping renewable energy producers.

A not dissimilar clash over the security of supply issue has occurred in Germany where the cartel office banned the takeover by Eon of Ruhrgas on grounds of preserving competition, only to find its ban overruled by the German government. The latter is keen to create a large German energy company capable of negotiating long-term gas supplies with countries like Russia.

Source: David Buchan, Reforms that have failed to work a power of good, *Financial Times*, 7 September 2004, p. 4. © Financial Times.

Table 18.1 Selected UK privatizations by industry and year of first sale

Enterprise	Industry	Year privatized
British Aerospace	Aerospace	1981
Cable & Wireless	Telecommunications	1981
Britoil	Oil	1982
National Freight Corporation	Transport	1982
Associated British Ports	Ports	1983
British Telecom	Telecommunications	1984
British Leyland (Austin–Rover)	Cars	1984
Jaguar	Cars	1984
British Gas	Gas	1986
National Bus Company	Buses	1986
British Airports Authority	Airports	1987
British Airways	Airlines	1987
British Steel	Steel	1988
Water authorities (10 companies)	Water	1989
Electricity distribution (12 companies)	Electricity	1990
Electricity generation	Electricity	1991
British Rail (Railtrack)	Railways	1995
British Energy	Nuclear energy	1996

In the UK, denationalization, deregulation and franchising were all implemented with enthusiasm by the Conservative goverments led by Margaret Thatcher (1979–90) and John Major (1990–97). In this chapter, we use the term **privatization** to describe the first of these three policies: denationalization, or the transfer of state owned assets to the private sector. The policy of privatization is examined in Section 18.4.

Table 18.1 lists a selection of the UK's largest privatizations. In total, the UK's privatization programme transferred assets exceeding £100bn from public to private ownership (Helm and Jenkinson, 1997). The policy of privatization was motivated partly by a desire to widen share ownership among the general public. Between 1979 and 1988, the proportion of adults in the UK holding shares increased from 7 per cent to 21 per cent (Fraser, 1988). The sale of state-owned assets also provided windfall gains to the Treasury, which helped finance tax cuts. In cases where the sale of state-owned assets involved the break-up of nationalized industries into smaller constituent parts, an element of competition was introduced. In several industries where direct competition is not feasible, such as rail services, a relatively tough regulatory regime has been introduced (Parker, 2003a). In contrast, deregulation has been implemented in a number of industries where competition prevails (such as telecommunications services).

The perceived success of the UK privatization programme persuaded many other industrialized countries to follow suit (Megginson and Netter, 2001). Table 18.2 shows the receipts of the privatization programmes of other selected OECD countries. Telecommunications and financial intermediation account for approximately half of all privatization proceeds. Privatization proceeds in OECD countries reached a peak

Table 18.2 Privatization proceeds for OECD countries (US$ million)

Country	1990	1991	1992	1993	1994	1995	1996	1997	1998	1999	2000	2001
Belgium	–	–	–	956	548	2,745	12,222	1,842	2,288	10	–	–
Canada	1,504	808	1,249	755	490	3,998	1,768	–	11	–	–	–
France	–	–	–	12,160	5,479	4,136	3,096	10,105	13,596	9,478	17,438	429
Germany	11	351	–	73	678	191	1,421	3,125	11,357	2,754	1,750	3,343
Greece	–	–	–	35	73	44	558	1,395	3,960	4,880	1,384	1,305
Ireland	–	515	70	274	–	157	293	–	–	4,846	1,458	773
Italy	–	–	759	3,039	9,077	10,131	11,230	23,945	15,138	25,594	9,729	2,653
Japan	–	–	–	–	13,875	–	2,039	–	6,641	15,115	–	–
Netherlands	716	179	–	780	3,766	3,993	1,239	842	335	1,481	310	831
New Zealand	3,895	17	967	630	29	264	1,839	–	441	1,331	–	–
Spain	172	–	830	3,222	1,458	2,941	2,680	12,532	11,618	1,128	1,079	741
Sweden	–	–	378	252	2,313	852	785	2,390	172	2,071	8,082	–
UK	4,219	5,346	7,923	8,114	4,632	5,648	24,246	4,500	–	–	–	–
US	–	–	–	–	–	–	–	3,650	3,100	–	–	–
Total (30 OECD countries)	16,112	20,925	25,586	40,461	55,885	54,599	53,022	96,282	100,633	96,735	67,119	20,583

Source: Adapted from OECD (2001) Privatization: recent trends, *Financial Market Trends*, 79, June.

of US$100.6bn in 1998. Subsequently, proceeds appear to have fallen sharply, with an estimate of $20.6bn reported for 2001. OECD (2001) notes signs of a policy reversal away from privatization in some countries. For example, in 2001 the New Zealand government bailed out the troubled (and previously privatized) Air New Zealand by acquiring an 80 per cent stake. In 2002, the UK government placed Railtrack, the country's rail network operator, into receivership, prior to effective renationalization. Plans to privatize the UK's postal services, one of the few remaining state-owned industries, have been repeatedly postponed.

The following points contribute to the economic case for privatization.

■ *Increased competition.* Privatization may encourage firms that were previously in state ownership to search for methods of reducing costs and eliminating x-inefficiencies for several reasons. If privatization is accompanied by a change in market structure, perhaps through the break-up of a previously state-owned monopoly into a number of competing units, the resulting competitive pressure may dictate that the newly privatized firms engage vigorously in the search for cost savings (Moore, 1983, Price Waterhouse, 1989). Increased competition may help deliver lower prices, improved product or service quality and greater choice for consumers.

■ *Increased capital market discipline.* Following privatization, the creation of a tier of profit-motivated shareholders may force management to attach higher priority to objectives related to profitability. Therefore pressure from shareholders may also motivate the search for methods of reducing costs, through the elimination of bureaucracy, waste and inefficiency (Wolfram, 1998). In privatized firms, the shareholder is the principal and the manager is the agent. Reward and incentive structures can be created to encourage managers to perform well.

> Efficiency gains from privatization arise essentially out of the interaction of product and capital market pressures. Competition in product markets means that the persistent underperformance will ultimately lead to bankruptcy. Competitive capital markets mean that if management is not successful in averting a downward performance trend, it will be displaced through takeover well before the company has reached the point of no return.
>
> *(Domberger and Piggott, 1986, p. 150)*

In nationalized industries, the government is the principal and the manager is the agent. This principal–agent relationship is mediated through a complex bureaucracy. Direct communication between principal and agent is difficult, and information flows tend to be distorted. Direct incentives for the manager to maximize performance, and penalties in the event of underperformance, tend to be weak. The capital market discipline that threatens underachieving managers with the possibility of takeover is absent in the case of state-owned enterprises. In contrast, by the end of 1997, 10 of the UK's 12 privatized regional electricity distribution firms had been acquired by domestic or foreign rivals (Helm and Jenkinson, 1997).

- *Reduction in government borrowing.* During the 1980s and 1990s, the UK's privatization programme had the intended side-effect of reducing the national debt. The total borrowing requirement of the nationalized industries shifted from a deficit of £1.1bn in 1984 to a surplus of £1.35bn in 1987 (Foster, 1992). This contributed to a reduction in the overall public sector borrowing requirement (PSBR), making the conduct of monetary and fiscal policy easier than would otherwise have been the case. For example, the availability of privatization proceeds increased the scope for the large cuts in income tax rates that were implemented in successive budgets between 1986 and 1988.

- *Elimination of government controls.* Nationalized enterprises are subject to various controls over their operations or financing, which may be eliminated as a result of privatization. For example, borrowing by nationalized enterprises in the UK contributed to the PSBR, and accordingly was subject to public sector borrowing rules. Privatized enterprises have the same freedom to raise finance via the capital markets as any other companies.

There are a number of counter-arguments against privatization. If privatization simply leads to the transfer of a monopoly from public to private ownership, with the privatized firm free to exploit its market power in pursuit of shareholder profit, this is likely to work against the interests of consumers. On the other hand, if privatization involves the break-up of a state-owned monopoly into smaller components, costs might increase if the smaller units are unable to realize the full benefits of economies of scale or scope. The use of privatization proceeds to finance current government spending or tax cuts can also be criticized. The proceeds from the sale of a state-owned assets are effectively the capitalized value of the future profit flows those assets are expected to yield. There is an element of short-termism in the policy of using such windfall gains to finance current expenditure, which is likely to lead to a gap appearing in the public finances in future years when no further saleable assets remain.

There is now an extensive literature that evaluates the impact of privatization. Yarrow (1986, 1989) examines changes in performance and productivity in seven privatized firms. Productivity and profitability increased in only three of the seven cases (Associated British Ports, Cable & Wireless and the National Freight Corporation). Similarly, Parker (1991) examines the performance of several privatized firms over the period 1987–90. Profitability increased for British Gas, British Telecom and Rolls-Royce, but declined for Associated British Ports, Jaguar and Enterprise Oil. Bishop and Thompson (1992) examine changes in productivity and profitability over the period 1970–90 for nine privatizations: British Airports Authority, British Airways, British Telecom, British Coal, electricity supply, British Gas, Post Office, British Rail and British Steel. While productivity and profitability improved, there is no direct evidence that the privatizations were solely or primarily responsible. Similarly, Price and Weyman-Jones (1993) compare productivity measures for British Gas in the late 1970s (several years before privatization in 1984) and early 1990s. The data were split into 12 geographic areas covered by British Gas's distribution network. Productivity was found to have increased following privatization.

Parker (1994) examines the effects of privatization on the performance of BT (formerly British Telecom) over the period 1984–94. Performance indicators include price changes, service quality indicators, employment, research and development and productivity measures. Prices fell by 11 per cent on average, but there was considerable variation in price changes across BT's full range of products and services. The reliability of network equipment and quality of installation improved. Employment increased during the late 1980s, but decreased subsequently as the firm searched for cost savings. Profitability increased but investment in research and development declined post-privatization. This latter trend may be due to short-term pressure to maximize profit. Labour productivity improved, but the productivity of other factors of production declined.

> [N]oteworthy gains have been achieved by BT in terms of service, overall prices, profitability and labour productivity since privatization. However, it is important to treat these results with some caution. In reviewing BT's restructuring and performance over the past ten years, it is not possible to say with certainty that the same changes would not have occurred had BT remained state owned.
>
> *(Parker, 1994, p. 108)*

Parker and Martin (1995) measure the trend in labour and total factor productivity for 11 privatized firms. Labour productivity is measured by changes in output in response to changes in labour inputs. Similarly, total factor productivity is measured by changes in output in response to changes in various inputs, including capital, raw materials, energy and labour. There was typically a substantial improvement in performance during the lead-up to privatization. However, performance did not always continue to improve after privatization, especially for privatizations that preceded the recession of the early 1990s, and in cases where there was intense competition or underinvestment in the privatized firm's capital assets.

Parker and Wu (1998) use data covering the period 1979–94 to assess the performance of British Steel before and after privatization in 1988. Labour and total factor productivity indicators, and profitability, are used as performance measures. Performance appears to have improved immediately before privatization, but the rate of improvement slowed considerably after privatization. Comparisons between British Steel and the steel industries of Australia, Canada, France, Germany, Japan and the US suggest that before privatization, British Steel was more efficient than several of its international competitors, but this position had been reversed by the early 1990s.

> [T]he results suggest that British Steel achieved considerable efficiency gains in the years immediately before privatization. One interpretation is that the prospect of privatization spurred management to improve performance. An alternative interpretation is that major efficiency gains can occur under state ownership, given a government and management determined to bring about change.
>
> *(Parker and Wu, 1998, p. 45)*

Borcherding *et al.* (1982) survey the results of 52 studies that compare the performance of publicly and privately owned firms in the US, Germany, France, Canada and Australia in a wide range of industries. Forty-three of the 52 studies suggested that private enterprises outperformed their public counterparts. In comparisons involving 18 countries, Megginson *et al.* (1994) find that privatization led to cost savings, increased investment and higher profitability. Dewenter and Malatesta (2001) compare the performance of a number of large state-owned and privately owned firms in 1975, 1985 and 1995. The privately owned firms were generally more profitable and more efficient than the state-owned firms.

Overall, the empirical evidence seems to suggest the productivity and profitability of some, but not all, privatized firms improved as a result of privatization. In some cases, productivity gains achieved in the run-up to privatization exceeded any further improvements post-privatization. In most cases, it is difficult to determine whether some or all of the improvements would have taken place anyway, without the transfer of ownership from the public to the private sector.

> In practice, the effects of privatization have been complex. There have been significant reductions in costs. Staffing levels have fallen, in some cases dramatically, and with these reductions in operating costs, prices have typically fallen too. Some of these reductions have been due to incentives created by regulation, some by new management practices, some by the reduction in union power, and some by the application of the new information technologies, which were particularly relevant to networks. It is impossible to estimate with much precision how great the changes would have been in the state sector if privatization had not taken place.
>
> *(Helm, 2001, p. 299)*

18.5 Regulation

Regulation may be required when one or more forms of market failure lead to allocative inefficiency. Possible causes of market failure include the following:

- *Market power.* Under perfect competition firms set prices equal to marginal cost and there is allocative efficiency: no one can be made better off without making someone else worse off. At the opposite end of the competitive spectrum, the monopolist restricts output and charges a price higher than marginal cost and there is allocative inefficiency. Therefore there is a case for regulation to prevent or curb the exercise of market power.

- *Asymmetric information.* Asymmetric information arises when buyers and sellers have access to different information. For example, regulation of sellers through licensing or certification might be required in order to provide buyers with assurances concerning the quality of the product or service.

- *Externalities.* An externality exists when a transaction confers benefits or costs on parties other than the buyer or seller, who are not compensated under the terms of the transaction. There is likely to be overproduction of goods that produce negative externalities (such as pollution), and underproduction of goods that produce positive externalities (such as education, training or research and development). In both cases there is allocative inefficiency, and a case for regulation to alter behaviour in a way that results in an efficient allocation of resources.

■ *Public goods.* The non-exclusivity characteristic of services such as policing, fire protection and street lighting makes it difficult to charge directly for their provision: if the service is provided at all, it is provided to everyone regardless of willingness-to-pay. Consequently private contractors are unlikely to provide such services, unless there is some form of regulatory intervention.

The potential for market failure due to the exercise of market power has raised particular concerns in the case of privatizations (in the sense of denationalization) of state-owned monopolies. While privatization may create incentives for cost savings, this will not guarantee allocative efficiency unless there is also competition. In cases where the introduction of genuine competition may be infeasible (perhaps because cost conditions approximate to those of natural monopoly), a stringent regulatory regime may be required to deliver outcomes that mimic those that would hypothetically be achieved under competitors.

> The first phase of privatization is associated with regulating the incumbent monopoly; a second stage involves policing the developing competition and establishment and monitoring infrastructure access rules to ensure that the dominant firm does not crush new entrant to the industry; and a third stage is concerned within maintaining the effective competition that eventually develops.
>
> *(Parker, 2003b, p. 548)*

In the US, the utilities have traditionally been in private ownership, and there is a long regulatory tradition. In the UK, where the utilities were in state ownership prior to privatizations during the 1980s and 1990s, the regulation of utilities is a more recent phenomenon. Accordingly, the state has moved from being primarily concerned with production towards a greater emphasis on regulation (Helm, 1994). Kay and Vickers (1990) characterize regulation with reference to principal–agent theory. The regulator can be regarded as a principal, and the regulated firms are the agents that are expected to follow the principal's instructions in pursuit of the principal's objectives. However, the regulated firms also have their own objectives, which differ from those of the regulator. The firms are likely to have more information than the regulator, making it difficult for the latter to construct a suitable framework to ensure its objectives are met.

Furthermore, over time the regulator's objectives are influenced by the actions of regulated firms. Ultimately this process may lead to the regulator representing the interests of the industry rather than those of consumers. Regulated firms tend to be better organized than consumers. Often, regulators are themselves industry insiders, who may have worked in the industry previously or who may hope to do so again in the future (Asch and Seneca, 1985). Consequently, regulated firms are able to influence the regulator, leading to **regulatory capture**. For these reasons, Stigler (1971) and Peltzman (1976, 1989) argue regulation tends to distort, more than it promotes competition. Becker (1983) suggests regulators will tend to respond to lobbying by the regulated firms, as long as the gains arising from the resulting changes in regulation are not outweighed by the possible loss of votes from consumers or others who lose out as a result. Regulatory capture may be less likely if the regulatory framework and objectives are clear, consistent and transparent. For legitimacy, regulation should be proportional to the extent of any perceived distortion in competition, and accountable to the various interest groups, especially consumers (Parker, 2003b).

There are two basic types of regulation: structural and conduct regulation. **Structural regulation** focuses on market structure. Measures include the functional separation of firms into complementary activities (for example, electricity generators and distributors), restrictions on entry, and rules regarding the operation of foreign firms. Structural regulation may tend to make entry difficult, and may tend to protect incumbent firms from competitive pressure. In contrast, **conduct regulation** seeks to influence the behaviour of firms, through measures such as price controls, regulated fees and commissions, controls on the levels of advertising or research and development expenditure, or restrictions on the rate at which distribution networks can be expanded. '[Structural regulation] aims to create a situation in which the incentives or opportunities for undesirable behaviour are removed, while [conduct regulation] addresses not the underlying incentives, but the behaviour that they would otherwise induce' (Kay and Vickers, 1990, p. 233).

For regulation to be effective, the regulator requires information on changes in costs and market conditions. In a stable market, this requirement is relatively straightforward. In a dynamic market, where conditions tend to change rapidly, it may be difficult to maintain an accurate picture. The main regulatory regimes adopted in the US and UK are **rate of return regulation** and **price cap regulation**, respectively.

Rate of return (or cost plus) regulation

In the US, rate of return regulation is the main regulatory regime. The regulator fixes a required rate of return on capital, denoted R*, as follows:

$$R^* = \frac{\text{Total revenue} - \text{total cost}}{\text{Capital employed}}$$

Under rate of return regulation, the regulator allows the firm to set a price that covers costs and allows a mark-up for profit. Price reviews can be carried out frequently. However, there may be little incentive for the firm to minimize its costs, given that the rate of return on assets is effectively guaranteed, and in the event of an increase in costs the firm can simply apply to be allowed to increase price. The frequency of contact between the regulator and the regulated firms makes it likely that a relationship will develop over time. This increases the likelihood of regulatory capture, which may create opportunities for the firm's managers to maximize their own utility, for example by spending on pet projects. US regulators have sought to address this problem by creating a time-lag between any request for a price change, and its implementation. In this case, a firm that fails to control its costs is penalized by earning a reduced return during the waiting period. Similarly if costs were to fall, the firm would earn a return exceeding the required rate during the waiting period. Therefore a regulatory lag provides an incentive for firms to exercise effective cost control.

Another drawback with rate of return regulation is that if the required rate of return is set at an inappropriate level, this can encourage either over- or underinvestment in assets (Averch and Johnson, 1962). A required rate of return that is set too high encourages overinvestment, since the more capital the firm employs, the more profit is required in order to achieve the required rate of return. Klevonich (1966) suggests this tendency can be avoided by reducing the required rate of return in cases where the firm's capital base has recently been increased dramatically. However, this may simply introduce other distortions into the way in which firms use their factors of production (Sherman, 1985). If the required rate of return is set too low, firms may seek economies (perhaps by reducing the quality of their inputs or outputs) in order to earn an adequate return.

Finally, rate of return regulation is often problematic because regulators find it difficult to value the firm's capital employed. For example, should capital be valued on a historical cost basis, or should it be calculated as the replacement cost of assets? Technical decisions on matters affecting the calculation of the firm's declared rate of return for regulatory purposes may have major implications for the firm's true profitability.

Price cap regulation

In the UK and most other European countries, price cap regulation is the most widely practised regulatory regime. Price cap regulation imposes a specific limit on the prices firms are permitted charge. In the UK, price changes are commonly determined by a formula of the form RPI *minus* an X-factor, where RPI denotes the change in the retail price index, and the X-factor allows for productivity gains and other factors affecting costs. Therefore if inflation is expected to be 5 per cent, but productivity gains of 3 per cent are expected over the same period, a price rise of 2 per cent would be permitted. In the UK and many other European countries, price caps are generally reviewed every four or five years. In addition to price cap regulation, there may be a need for regulation of the quality of products or services, especially if the search for cost savings creates a temptation to compromise on product or service quality. In the UK, the Competition and Service Utilities Act 1992 represents an attempt to extend the scope of regulation to cover quality as well as price.

Price cap regulation seeks to ensure cost savings are passed on to consumers in the form of lower prices. In the short run there is an incentive for the firm to minimize costs, if profitability is boosted by savings that were unanticipated by the regulator at the time of the last price review. In the long run, however, the regulator may simply increase the X-factor in order to incorporate the cost saving, in which case the firm fails to benefit. In this case, there may be disincentives for long-run investment in cost saving technologies. 'RPI *minus* X regulation encouraged a management style based upon cost minimization rather than investment' (Helm, 2001, p. 300). Critics argue that in some countries, price cap regulation has resulted in a tendency for long-term underinvestment in the infrastructure of network industries such as rail, water and energy.

Factors influencing the regulator's decision when setting the X-factor include the firm's cost structure and capital structure, its investment plans, expected productivity gains and expected changes in market demand, and the implications of the chosen X-factor for competition. It may be necessary to set the initial value of X at the time of privatization, when the firm is still state-owned and before competition has been introduced. In cases where there is likely to be public opposition to the privatization decision, there may be a temptation to allow consumer interests to weigh heavily in determining the initial value of X; however, successful privatization requires the expected profitability of the newly privatized firm to be sufficient to attract private shareholder investment. Similarly, in reviewing the X-factor after privatization, the regulator must strike a balance between consumer and shareholder interests. If a state-owned monopoly has been broken up into smaller components, the impact of competition on prices may provide useful information for the regulator in determining the appropriate price cap during the post-privatization phase (Shleifer, 1985).

Littlechild's (1983) study of the UK telecommunications industry was influential in determining the UK's approach to regulation. Littlechild analyses five possible types of regulation: no interference; rate of return regulation (as in the US); profit ceilings; an output-related profit levy (firms producing low output are unlikely to be operating at the minimum efficient scale, and are subject to a high levy in order to encourage expansion); and price cap regulation. Each regulatory regime is evaluated regarding its ability to protect consumers from abuses of market power; to promote cost savings and increase productivity; to promote competition; and ease of implementation. Littlechild concludes in favour of price cap regulation with an RPI *minus* X pricing formula, because it provides greater incentives for firms to search for cost savings than the other regulatory regimes, and because it is both simple to operate and transparent.

In the UK, separate acts of Parliament have created agencies responsible for the regulation of newly privatized and formerly state-owned industries. In general, these agencies are responsible for:

- Collecting and publishing information on competitive conditions.

- Advising the Office of Fair Trading or Competition Commission of possible abuses of market power or anticompetitive practices.

- Enforcing competition law.

- Setting price and quality levels and investigating complaints.

- Specifying conditions under which individual firms are licensed to trade.

Helm and Jenkinson (1997) characterize the UK regulatory approach as one of contracts and discretion. Effectively, firms are contracted to operate within price and quality guidelines imposed by the regulator, who retains the discretion to intervene in order to promote competitive outcomes. Under free competition, entry and exit would normally ensure profit rates gravitate towards competitive levels in the long run. In privatized industries, this process does not always happen spontaneously, and it is the regulator's responsibility to ensure compliance, not necessarily with the process, but with the consequences of competition. '[I]n principle, the regulator can intervene to lower prices or increase costs to keep the actual rate of return at or around the normal level – to mop up excess returns' (Helm, 1994, p. 25).

In many European countries, regulators have attempted to foster competition; and in the long run this should lessen the need for regulation. However, as yet there is no integrated EU-wide policy for the regulation of privatized industries; consequently different countries have implemented different policies.

> For as long as the creation of European regulatory bodies to oversee European networks is resisted, the incoherence of current policies is likely to remain, and therefore the focus will continue to be on the national interest of member countries. The result is the loss of the additional economic benefits, which potentially arise at the European level.
>
> *(Helm, 2001, p. 310)*

> [A] renewed commitment to establish an internal market for goods and services (if not capital and technology) of network industries is essential for such a strategy. Today's inconsistencies, omissions, and distortions hinder the fully fledged development of competition and, in causing uncertainty, inhibit especially the infrastructural investment required.
>
> *(Pelkmans, 2001, p. 455)*

Beesley and Littlechild (1997) point out a number of key differences between US-style rate of return regulation and European-style price cap regulation.

- Under price cap regulations, if X is set for a defined period, the firm faces an element of risk over this period. Under rate of return regulation, the firm can apply for a price review at any time if its rate of return falls below the required rate.

- With rate of return regulation, calculations are based on historic costs, revenues and capital valuations. Cost savings are likely to lead to price reductions being imposed quickly. In contrast, price cap regulation incorporates assumptions concerning the firm's future trading conditions. Cost savings in excess of those built into the X-factor can be appropriated by the firm between reviews.

- With price cap regulation, the regulator can exercise greater discretion, by selecting assumptions concerning any of the variables thought to affect the X-factor.

- In Europe, the X-factor is often set by the regulator without much consultation. In contrast, the more legalistic US approach demands explicit justification for the regulator's decisions.

- With price cap regulation as widely practised in Europe, the firm exercises discretion over the prices charged for individual products, provided the average price of the firm's portfolio of products complies with the price cap (Armstrong *et al.*, 1994, p. 168). With rate of return regulation as practised in the US, the prices of individual products require regulatory approval.

Box 18.1

Regulation of privatized industries in the UK

Box 18.1 examines the evolution of regulation in four privatized industries in the UK: telecommunications, energy, water and rail.

Telecommunications

Telecommunications was the first major privatization in the UK during the 1980s. The incumbent, British Telecom or BT, was privatized in 1984 as a single entity. Initially, the post-privatization market structure was a duopoly in telephone networks, consisting of BT and Mercury Communications, an entrant which was given permission to use parts of the BT network. However, Mercury failed to achieve sufficient scale to compete effectively with BT. An alternative competitive regime was introduced in the early 1990s, which focused on competition in call services, rather than networks. By 1998, there were more than 200 call service operators. Regulation has been most active in the areas of national and international calls, and fixed line rentals (Butler, 1998). Television broadcasters have been encouraged to develop network services, using their own communications networks. The post-privatization regulatory regime was established in the 1984 Telecommunications Act, which assigned responsibility for regulation to the newly-created Office of Telecommunications (OFTEL). The X-factor for the purposes of price cap regulation of the form 'RPI *minus* X' was initially set at 3 per cent for the period 1984–89: in other words, the maximum price increase was 3 per cent below inflation. X was subsequently increased to 4.5 per cent (1989–91), 6.25 per cent (1991–93) and 7.5 per cent (1993–98), before being reduced to 4.5 per cent (1998–2002). Since privatization, competition in the telecommunications industry has become much more intense, with a rapid pace of technological change creating numerous opportunities for innovation and the provision of new products and services.

Energy

The Office of Gas and Electricity Markets (OFGEM) is responsible for regulation of energy markets in the UK, under the terms of the Gas Act (1986), Electricity Act (1998) and Utilities Act (2000), and in conjunction with Energywatch, an independent organization set up in 2000, OFGEM aims to promote competition and protect consumers.

British Gas was privatized under the terms of the Gas Act of 1986 as an integrated firm, with operations in exploration and in the production and supply of gas. The Office of Gas Supply (OFGAS), a forerunner of OFGEM, was the original regulator. Price cap regulation was implemented through an 'RPI *minus* X *plus* Y' formula, in which an additional variable Y-factor allowed for changes in cost conditions which could be passed on to consumers. The X-factor was set at 2 per cent (1987–92), 5 per cent (1992–97), 4 per cent (1997–2002) and 2 per cent (2003–07). The Y-factor was dropped from the formula for 2003–07.

An element of competition was introduced in 1992, when other suppliers were permitted to use British Gas's distribution network to supply large customers (consuming more than

2,500 therms per year). Between 1991 and 1996, British Gas's share of this market fell dramatically, from 91 per cent to 29 per cent. The Gas Act of 1995 extended competition to the rest of the market. Other firms were allowed to use pipeline systems, for the shipping and supply of gas. Charges for the use of British Gas's pipelines were capped at RPI *minus* 5 per cent (1995–97) and RPI *minus* 6.5 per cent (1997–2001). By 1998, around 70 new suppliers had obtained a combined market share of more than 70 per cent. Following a 1996 Monopolies and Mergers investigation, in 1997 British Gas voluntarily split its operations into a gas supply company (British Gas, comprising Transco and several other units) and an exploration and production company (Centrica). In 2000 Transco was sold, and became the major constituent of a new supply company, the Lattice Group. OFGEM assumed responsibility for regulation in 1998. Between 1986 and 2002, prices had fallen by 37 per cent in real terms, and price cap regulation was eventually abandoned in 2002.

The electricity industry in England and Wales was privatized in the 1989 Electricity Act. This unbundled the Central Electricity Generating Board (which had previously operated generation and transmission, with 12 area boards responsible for distribution) into separate units responsible for generation, transmission and regional distribution. In Scotland, the two electricity providers were privatized as fully integrated firms. The Office of Electricity Regulation (OFFER) was the original regulator, before being superseded by OFGEM in 1998. Post-privatization, the National Grid Company assumed responsibility for transmission, while generation was under the control of a duopoly, comprising National Power and Powergen.

The wholesale market for electricity used the electricity pool after privatization. Electricity suppliers purchased electricity at wholesale prices from the pool, while the generators sold electricity to it. The National Grid Company set prices so as to balance the demand and supply of electricity. Within each day, demand was estimated for half-hour periods. Generators were then asked to submit bids, stating how much electricity each of their power stations would produce, and at what price. The bids were arranged in ascending order, until demand was satisfied. If demand exceeded supply, the generators were required to increase production. Concern over alleged abuses of market power by the generators (making low-cost generating plants unavailable; claiming emergency maintenance programmes) led to enforced sales of power stations to new entrants or distributors. In 2001, the New Electricity Trading Arrangements (NETA) came into force. Electricity is traded forward in bilateral contracts between buyers and sellers. Prices are agreed today for quantities of electricity to be purchased in future. NETA has led to a further reduction in prices. In transmission, price cap regulation of the form 'RPI *minus* X' has been used. The X-factor was set at 0 per cent (1990–92), 3 per cent (1992–96), 20 per cent (1996–97) and 4 per cent (1997–2000). In April 2002, most price controls in the retail market were removed.

Water

Privatization of the water industry involved the creation of ten regional companies, responsible for water supplies and sewage. The Water Industry Act of 1991 set up the Office of Water Services (OFWAT) to oversee regulation. Regulation of prices was based on comparisons of the performance of the regional water companies (known as yardstick competition). The Competition and Service Utilities Act of 1992 allowed rival firms to supply domestic customers from outside their original regions, and competition was extended to large corporate customers. In the period 1989–94, price cap regulation was based on an 'RPI *plus* Y *plus* K' formula, where the Y-factor allowed for cost increases and the K-factor allowed for expenditure on the maintainance, renewal or expansion of the distribution network. From 1995 an 'RPI *minus* X' formula was adopted. The Water Industry Act of 1999 introduced new consumer protection measures, and a one-off 10 per cent price cut was imposed by OFWAT in 2000. Although investment has increased following water privatization, in some cases users have also been required to pay increased prices.

Rail

The Railways Act of 1993, the Transport Act of 2000 and *Transport 2010* (Department of Environment, Transport and the Regions, 2000) established the framework for the past and future regulation of the UK's rail industry. Privatization was a highly complex operation, involving the division of the state-owned British Rail into a number of separate components. A single firm, Railtrack, owned and operated the rail network, with responsibilities for the track, stations and the coordination of timetables. Responsibility for the supply of rolling stock was split between three firms. Train services are provided by a number of operators, which compete with one another to secure franchises to operate specific routes on an exclusive basis. The nature of the bidding process depends on the expected profitability of the route: lump-sum payments are required for profitable routes, while subsidies are available for loss-making routes. Subject to various commitments on service quality, the firm offering the highest lump-sum payment or requiring the lowest subsidy secures the franchise. Fares are set by the individual train service operators.

Railtrack was regulated by the Office of the Rail Regulator (ORR). Railtrack charged individual operators for use of its network. These charges were subject to an 'RPI *minus* X' formula. The X-factor was set at 8 per cent (1995–96) and 2 per cent (1996–2001). However, with Railtrack on the verge of financial collapse, in October 2002 its assets and responsibilities were transferred to a new not-for-profit body, Network Rail. This decision amounted to effective renationalization of the network operation. Meanwhile, regulation of the privately owned (but in several cases heavily subsidized) train operating franchises is the responsibility of the Strategic Rail Authority (SRA). SRA monitors the performance of franchise operators, and has the power to levy fines for failure to meet the terms of their contracts. In November 2002, as part of the UK government's *Transport 2010* initiative, the SRA announced a package of measures aimed at improving quality of service.

Rail privatization makes a strong claim to be considered the UK's least successful privatization of the 1980s and 1990s. A lack clarity in the formulation of policy, the division of decision-making authority between bodies with overlapping responsibilities, unrealistic targets for the network provider and the train operators, a lack of investment, and a series of highly publicized accidents, have all contributed to the post-privatization difficulties of the UK's railway industry (Glaister, 2003).

18.6 Franchising and competitive tendering

As we have seen in Section 15.5, franchising involves the allocation of exclusive rights to supply certain types of goods and services. This right or licence protects the franchisee from competition for the duration of the contract. Governments sometimes award franchises in cases where there are grounds for doing so based on efficiency or welfare considerations. For example, restrictions on entry might be needed to allow incumbents the opportunity to realize the full benefits of economies of scale. An example is the practice of franchising the rights for sole provision of passenger train services on specific routes or sections of the rail network to individual firms (see Box 18.1).

Franchises can be characterized as *ownership* or *operating*. Ownership franchises grant the holder control over an asset in perpetuity. Operating franchises grant the holder temporary control, for a limited period of time. Both types of franchise shield the holder from competition while the franchise is effective, but in the case of an operating franchise this benefit is of limited duration. It has been argued operating franchises discourage long-term investment, because the franchise holder is aware of the risk that the franchise will not be renewed when it expires. For example, it has been suggested this factor has discouraged long-term investment by passenger train service operators on the UK rail network. Winston (1993, 1998) argues that by eliminating entry barriers, franchising tends to make markets contestable. To win a contract, the future monopoly provider has to charge a competitive price for its services. A successful bid overcomes what was previously a government-imposed entry barrier.

Once the franchise has been awarded, the franchisor retains an element of control, either by threatening that the franchise might not be renewed when it expires; or, in extreme cases, by retaining the right to revoke the franchise in the event of the franchisee's non-compliance with the terms and conditions. Although the franchisee is shielded from competition once the franchise has been awarded, competition during the bidding process may be intense (Demsetz, 1968). If the franchise is expected to be profit-making, bidders are invited to pay to secure the franchise. Conversely, if the franchise is expected to be loss-making, bidders are invited to state the payment or subsidy they would require to supply the product or service. As we have seen in Chapter 11, the design of the auction under which the franchise is to be awarded may have significant implications for the size of the proceeds the franchisor can expect to realize from the auction.

There are several ways in which bids for a franchise contract might be invited (McAfee and McMillan, 1987; Milgrom, 1989).

■ *Bidding by the lowest cost per unit.* In this case, the winning bidder is the one that offers to perform the service at the lowest average cost. Competition in the bidding process may cause the price to reach a level at which the franchisee can earn only a normal profit. Certain problems can arise under this bidding method. First, if cost savings are achieved after the award of the franchise, perhaps due to technological advance, consumers do not necessarily see any benefit in the form of lower prices. Second, if the franchise covers several products or services, it may be difficult to determine which bid is the lowest overall. Third, in order to secure the franchise, a firm may submit a bid below its average cost. After the award of the franchise, the franchisee may claim that costs have risen, and attempt to renegotiate the agreement.

■ *Bidding by the lowest lump-sum subsidy*. In this case, the winning bidder is the one that offers to perform the service for the lowest lump-sum subsidy. Some privatized industries were loss-making before privatization, and were expected to remain so afterwards. Private contractors would therefore require a subsidy in order to provide the service.

■ *Bidding by lump-sum payment*. In this case, bidders offer a lump-sum payment to secure the franchise. This method of franchise allocation is often used in cases of natural monopoly, where it is likely an abnormal profit will be earned, but breaking the industry up into constituent parts is not feasible. Effectively, this system allows the franchisor the opportunity to appropriate some of the abnormal profit the successful bidder expects to earn once it becomes the monopoly supplier. If potential franchisees can be induced to submit bids equivalent to or near to the full value of the abnormal profit they expect to earn, all or most of the abnormal profit may revert to the franchisor. In the short term, the lump-sum payment provides funds for the government, but if the franchisee secures the right to exploit its market power over the duration of the franchise, this may work against the interests of consumers. Regulation may be required to avoid this outcome; although bidders who know they will be subject to stringent regulation are unlikely to bid less aggressively to secure the franchise.

Issues that arise when inviting bids for the award of franchises include the following:

■ *Setting the length of the contract*. This may be important in determining the degree of competition at the bidding stage. On the one hand, if the duration of the contract is too short, bidders may be deterred; but on the other hand, short-term contracts offer the franchisor greater control over the franchisee's activities. Long-term contracts may attract more bidders, but they may also allow the winning bidder the opportunity to abuse its market power, or to underperform for a long period.

■ *Collusion among bidders*. Bidders may decide to collude to ensure the contract goes to a particular firm, or to maximize the financial benefit to the winning bidder by limiting competition among bidders. The gains from collusion might be split between the colluding firms. Collusion is more likely when the duration of a contract is short, and when sealed bids are required, leaving the winning bidder at greater risk of experiencing the winner's curse (Schmalensee, 1979); see Section 11.3.

■ *The level of fixed investment*. If the franchisee needs to incur significant sunk cost investment expenditure in order to operate the franchise, bidding is likely to be discouraged, especially if this investment is non-recoverable in the event of non-renewal of the franchise. To avoid this difficulty, the franchisor might need to make arrangements for the transfer of ownership of industry-specific assets at the end of the contract. However, this might prove difficult in cases where the assets are also firm-specific.

■ *Asymmetric information between bidders*. If the bidding is for the renewal of an existing franchise, an incumbent franchisee's specialized knowledge may place it at an unfair advantage relative to other bidders, making it difficult for the latter to displace the incumbent.

■ *Measuring quality of product or service*. In cases where the franchisor is concerned about quality as well as cost, it may be possible to invite bids based on price–quality combinations. In this case, an 'RPI *minus* X' price cap might be amended to 'RPI *minus* X *plus* ΔQ', where ΔQ represents quality improvements. Effectively, the franchisee is permitted to charge for introducing improvements in quality. In practice, however, measurement of quality can be problematic (Baldwin and Cave, 1998; Rovizzi and Thompson, 1995).

Compulsory competitive tendering (CCT) is a practice similar to franchising. In this case, existing local government (in-house) providers and private contractors are invited to tender for contracts to provide services for local government (Lavery, 1997). For provision to remain in-house, the local government department has to demonstrate it can provide the service more cheaply than any alternative private contractor (UK Cabinet Office, 1996). CCT was introduced under the terms of the 1988 Local Government Act; although previously, many local authorities had practised some form of competitive tendering (Domberger, 1999; Wilson, 1994). The 1988 Act covered service provision in areas such as catering (schools, hospitals, residential care centres), cleaning (of local authority buildings, hospitals, schools) and refuse collection.

It has been suggested CCT represents 'a convenient halfway house between public production and private ownership by retaining public sector control over the activity whilst simultaneously introducing commercial discipline through a formal contracting process' (Domberger and Rimmer, 1994, p. 441). The debate surrounding CCT focuses on the following issues:

■ In-house teams or private contractors may perceive increased incentives to strive for cost savings and productivity improvements, due to the threat of losing the contract on the next occasion it is renewed.

■ By helping to trim local government expenditure on the services concerned, CCT may provide opportunities for increased spending elsewhere, tax cuts, or a reduction in the public sector borrowing requirement (Domberger and Jenson, 1997).

■ CCT encourages flexible working practices such as part-time work, job sharing and casualization. However, this may be interpreted as a euphemism for a deterioration in the working conditions of local government employees (Ascher, 1987).

■ Substantial transaction costs are involved in specifying the terms of the contract, the method of bidding, and monitoring the contract after it has been awarded. Contracting out should only be considered if the expected cost saving exceeds these transaction costs (Domberger and Hall, 1995). Monitoring costs may tend to be higher for contracts awarded to private contractors. The latter are more profit-motivated than their in-house counterparts, and may seek to minimize costs at the expense of quality (Prager, 1994).

In an early study of the effectiveness of competitive tendering in reducing costs, Domberger *et al.* (1986) examine the efficiency of refuse collection services that were subject to competitive tendering in 1984 and 1985. Regression analysis is used to identify the relationship betwen 16 variables describing the volume, type and quality of refuse services, and the costs of providing the service. Services that were contracted out following competitive tendering were delivered 20 per cent more cheaply on average than those for which there was no competitive tendering. Even in cases where in-house teams had submitted successful tenders, costs fell by 17 per cent on average. Ganley and Grahl (1988) argue these results are biased, because the sample was unrepresentative. However, Szymanski and Wilkins (1993) obtain results similar to those of Domberger *et al.* for the period 1984–88; see also Szymanski (1996).

Domberger and Rimmer (1994) survey international evidence on the effectiveness of CCT by national and local government departments. In most cases, CCT was associated with significant cost savings. However, assessing the magnitude of cost savings due to CCT can be controversial.

> It is difficult to place a monetary value on the results of competitive tendering. How, for example, does one assess how much any budgetary change should be attributed to competitive tendering rather than restraints upon public sector expenditure and wages, or the use of new management techniques?
>
> *(Jackson, 1997, p. 230)*

The effect of CCT on the quality of service provision is also difficult to assess (Domberger *et al.*, 1995; Hall and Rimmer, 1994; McMaster, 1995; Walsh, 1992; Walsh and Davis, 1993). Hartley and Huby (1986) examine competitive tendering by local government departments, the National Health Service and private firms. In many cases there was a tendency for private contractors to submit low bids on the first occasion tendering took place, in an effort to eliminate in-house competition; and then submit higher bids on subsequent occasions. Quality was often compromised in order to produce cost savings. 'Cost savings, if any, are short lived and offset by reductions in the quality of services supplied' (Hartley and Huby, 1986, p. 289). The UK Cabinet Unit Office (1996) assesses the impact of the 1991 White Paper *Competing for Quality* on competition during the period 1992–95 in areas where CCT was used. The estimated average cost saving was 18 per cent. However, there was also evidence of a decline in quality. Perceptions of a decline in standards were stronger among workers than among users of services, but in both cases significant numbers of survey respondents noticed a drop in quality. On the other hand, Stevens (1984) and Albin (1992) find competitive tendering had little impact on quality in the US and Australia, respectively.

Following the election of the Labour government in the UK in 1997, CCT was replaced by a new system known as *Best Value* (DETR, 1998). Best Value places greater emphasis than CCT on quality as well as cost criteria in determining the provision of local government services. Local government departments are required to demonstrate continuous improvement measured by specific performance indicators.

Departments formulate annual organizational plans and conduct service reviews, in which a wide range of interested parties are encouraged to participate. Departments are no longer required to invite tenders from private contractors, but are expected to demonstrate that provision is efficient, and that quality benchmarks are being achieved. In the event of underachievement, the system allows for competitive tendering of existing in-house provision (Boyne *et al.*, 1999).

18.7	**Summary**

Chapter 18 has examined regulation, in particular the regulation of natural monopolies. If a natural monopolist is abusing its market power, there are several possible solutions. The first is public ownership, which normally involves granting statutory rights to a single firm. In doing so, the firm can be required to price its products in a reasonably competitive manner. A second solution is to open up the relevant market to competition. In many countries, particularly in the UK, the privatization of previously nationalized industries, involving the transfer of state-owned assets to the private sector, has often been accompanied by efforts to create more competitive post-privatization market conditions. Regulation may be viewed as a substitute for competition in cases where competition is impractical. A final solution is to allow temporary monopoly rights through the granting of a franchise. In this case, competition takes place prior to the award of the franchise during the bidding process, with stipulations concerning matters such as price and quality of service written into the successful bidder's contract.

In most cases, nationalization involves the creation of a statutory monopoly owned and controlled by the government. By assuming ownership of a natural monopoly, the government can instruct the firm to pursue certain objectives or adopt certain policies. The aim is to correct market failure and satisfy the necessary conditions for allocative efficiency. Nationalization may eliminate wasteful competition, or it may allow the full exploitation of economies of scale. Nationalization may be motivated by social objectives, such as the provision of services that would be deemed uneconomic by the private sector. However, without a profit motive, and in the absence of competitive discipline, incentives to operate efficiently may be lacking. Confusion or conflict between economic and non-economic objectives has often made nationalized firms difficult to manage. Overall, the empirical evidence presents a rather mixed picture of the performance of the UK's nationalized industries before most of them were privatized during the 1980s and 1990s.

The economic case for privatization, in the sense of the sale or denationalization of state-owned enterprises, rests on the following arguments.

■ Privatization accompanied by the introduction of competition may help deliver lower prices, improved product or service quality and greater consumer choice, as firms subject to competitive pressure search for cost savings and productivity gains.

■ The creation of a tier of profit-motivated shareholders, and increased capital market discipline, may force management to attach higher priority to objectives related to profitability.

- In the short term, privatization proceeds make a positive contribution to the public finances, creating new options for increasing public expenditure, cutting taxes or reducing borrowing.

- Privatized firms have the same freedom to raise finance from capital markets as any other private sector firms. In contrast, state-owned firms may be subject to public sector borrowing constraints.

On the other hand, if privatization simply leads to the transfer of a state-owned monopoly into private ownership, this may work against the interests of consumers. Following a privatization involving the break-up of a state-owned monopoly into smaller components, costs might increase if the smaller units fail to realize the full benefits of economies of scale or scope. The use of proceeds from the sale of capital assets to finance current expenditure or tax cuts suggests unsound management of the public finances. In general, the benefits and costs of privatizations are difficult to evaluate. In some cases, staffing levels, costs and prices have fallen, sometimes dramatically. However, in several cases, privatization has been accompanied by rapid and far-reaching technological progress. It is usually difficult or impossible to estimate with any certainty what might have happened had the enterprises concerned remained in state ownership.

Regulation is an option when one or more types of market failure result in allocative inefficiency. Sources of market failure include the abuse of market power, asymmetric information between buyers and sellers, various types of externality and the non-exclusivity characteristic of public goods. The potential for market failure due to the exercise of market power has raised particular concerns in the case of privatized natural monopolies. In several cases a stringent regulatory regime has been introduced, in an attempt to deliver outcomes that mimic those that would (hypothetically) be achieved under competitive conditions. Structural regulation includes the functional separation of firms into complementary activities, restrictions on entry, and rules regarding the operation of foreign firms. Conduct regulation seeks to influence the regulated firms' behaviour, through measures such as controls on price, or product or service quality, or other conduct variables.

The main regulatory regime used in the US is rate of return regulation. The regulator specifies a required rate of return on capital, and allows regulated firms to set their prices accordingly, subject to frequent price reviews. In the UK and most other European countries price cap regulation is widely used. Price changes are dictated by an 'RPI *minus* X' formula, where X can be adjusted to allow for productivity savings or improvements in quality. Reviews of the price cap usually take place at intervals several years apart. Price cap regulation may provide stronger incentives for firms to search for cost savings than other regulatory regimes, because the firm keeps the saving (at least until the next review). Effective regulation requires clear policy objectives, accurate information and accountability. In the long term, any regulatory regime is subject to the possibility of regulatory capture: a tendency for the regulated firms to exercise undue influence over the regulator's decisions.

Franchising involves the allocation of exclusive rights to supply a particular good and service. Bidders may be invited to pay to secure a profit-making franchise; or to state the minimum subsidy they would require to run a loss-making franchise.

Although the franchisee is shielded from competition once the franchise has been awarded, competition to secure the franchise may be intense. After the award the franchisor retains an element of control, by threatening non-renewal when the present franchise expires, or by terminating the franchise in the event of non-compliance with the terms and conditions. Competitive tendering is a practice similar to franchising, in which in-house local government providers and private contractors are invited to tender for contracts to provide services for local government. There is evidence that compulsory competitive tendering has produced substantial cost savings in some cases, although there are concerns about the implications for quality and standards of service, as well as the pay and employment conditions of local government employees and those hired by private contractors.

Discussion questions

1. If a natural monopolist is suspected of abusing its market power, what remedies short of full-scale nationalization might be available?

2. The author of Case study 18.1 wrote: 'the focus of government involvement in business has moved from substituting for markets to assisting them to function'. With reference to examples drawn from this case study and elsewhere in Chapters 17 and 18, describe the evolution of regulation and competition policy in the UK since the 1980s.

3. Assess the arguments for and against the public ownership of key industries.

4. On what economic grounds can the policy of privatization be justified?

5. With reference to Case study 18.2, assess the impact of the deregulation of the UK's electricity industry.

6. It is often argued that regulation is justified in cases where some form of market failure would otherwise create an inefficient allocation of resources. Identify possible sources of market failure that might give rise to a need for regulation.

7. What is meant by regulatory capture?

8. Distinguish between structural and conduct regulation. With reference to regulation in the UK or elsewhere, provide specific examples of each of these forms of regulation.

9. Explain the difference between rate of return (cost plus) regulation and price cap regulation, and assess the advantages and disadvantages of each.

10. Compare and contrast the UK's approach to the regulation of the following privatized industries: telecommunications, energy, water and rail.

11. What are the main issues an intending franchisor should consider when framing the bidding rules and drafting the terms and conditions under which the franchise will be awarded.

12. Assess the effectiveness of compulsory competitive tendering and best value initiatives in improving efficiency and quality in public services.

Further reading

Ball, A., Broadbent, J. and Moore, C. (2002) Best value and the control of local government: challenges and contradictions, *Public Money and Management*, 22, 9–16.

Beesley, M.E. (ed.) (1997) *Privatization, Regulation and De-Regulation*, 2nd edn. London: Routledge.

Domberger, S. and Hall, C. (1995) *The Contracting Casebook: Competitive Tendering in Action*. Canberra: Australian Government Publishing Service.

Green, R. (1999) Checks and balances in utility regulation: the UK experience, *Public Policy for the Private Sector*, May. World Bank.

Helm, D. and Jenkinson, T. (1997) The assessment: introducing competition into regulated industries, *Oxford Review of Economic Policy*, 13, 1–14.

Kay, J., Mayer, C. and Thompson, D. (eds) (1986) *Privatization and Regulation: The UK Experience*. Oxford: Clarendon Press.

Megginson, W.L. and Netter, J.M. (2001) From state to market: a survey of empirical studies on privatization, *Journal of Economic Literature*, 39, 321–89.

Newberry, D. (2000) *Privatization, Restructuring and Regulation of Network Utilities*. Cambridge, MA: MIT Press.

Parker, D. (2000) *Privatization and Corporate Performance*. Cheltenham: Edward Elgar.

Vickers, J. and Yarrow, G. (1988) *Privatization: An Economic Analysis*. Cambridge, MA: MIT Press.

Wilson, J. (1994) Competitive tendering and UK public services, *Economic Review*, April, 12, 31–5.

Winston, C. (1993) Economic deregulation: days of reckoning for microeconomists, *Journal of Economic Literature*, 31, 1263–89.

Winston, C. (1998) US Industry adjustment to economic deregulation, *Journal of Economic Perspectives*, 12, 89–110.

Analytical Tools

Mathematical methods

Appendix 1 contains mathematical derivations of selected results from chapters of this book. To follow these derivations, a knowledge of elementary calculus is required. The section numbers and headings containing each result are identified at the start of each derivation.

2.3 Demand, revenue, elasticity and profit maximization

This section demonstrates the relationship between marginal revenue and price elasticity of demand.

Symbols
P = price
Q = output
TR = total revenue
MR = marginal revenue
PED = price elasticity of demand

The formal definition of price elasticity of demand is:

$$PED = \frac{dQ}{dP} \times \frac{P}{Q}$$

where $\frac{dQ}{dP}$ is the derivative of the market demand function with respect to price.

The definition of total revenue is:

$$TR = PQ$$

Using calculus, the definition of marginal revenue is the derivative of TR with respect to Q.

According to the Product Rule, if $y = uv$, $\dfrac{dy}{dx} = u\dfrac{dv}{dx} + v\dfrac{du}{dx}$

Let $y = TR$, $x = Q$, $u = P$ and $v = Q$.

$$MR = \frac{dTR}{dQ} = P\frac{dQ}{dQ} + Q\frac{dP}{dQ}$$

$$MR = P + Q\frac{dP}{dQ}, \text{ because } \frac{dQ}{dQ} = 1$$

Multiplying top and bottom of the second term on the right-hand-side by P:

$$MR = P + P\left(\frac{dP}{dQ} \times \frac{Q}{P}\right)$$

$$MR = P + P\frac{1}{\left(\frac{dQ}{dP} \times \frac{P}{Q}\right)} = P\left(1 + \frac{1}{PED}\right) = P\left(1 - \frac{1}{|PED|}\right)$$

2.4 Theory of perfect competition and monopoly

This section derives the long-run profit-maximizing equilibrium in monopoly for the case where the market demand function is linear, and the long-run average cost (LRAC) and long-run marginal cost (LRMC) functions are horizontal (constant returns to scale production technology).

Symbols
P = price
Q = output
c = marginal cost
TR = total revenue
π = profit

Market demand function (in inverse form) is:

$$P = a - bQ$$

By definition, total revenue is:

$$TR = PQ = (a - bQ)Q = aQ - bQ^2$$

Total cost is:

$$TC = cQ$$

By definition, profit is total revenue *minus* total cost:

$$\pi = TR - TC = aQ - bQ^2 - cQ$$

$$\pi = (a - c)Q - bQ^2$$

To find the value of Q at which π is maximized, differentiate π with respect to Q, set the derivative to zero, and solve the resulting equation for Q.

$$\frac{\partial \pi}{\partial Q} = (a - c) - 2bQ$$

$$(a - c) - 2bQ = 0$$

Therefore the profit-maximizing output level is:

$$Q = \frac{a - c}{2b}$$

The profit-maximizing price and profit are as follows:

$$P = a - bQ = a - b\left(\frac{a - c}{2b}\right) = \frac{a + c}{2}$$

$$\pi = PQ - cQ = (P - c)Q = \left(\frac{a + c}{2} - c\right)\left(\frac{a - c}{2b}\right) = \left(\frac{a - c}{2}\right)\left(\frac{a - c}{2b}\right) = \frac{(a - c)^2}{4b}$$

4.3   Models of output determination in duopoly

This section provides an algebraic derivation of the Cournot–Nash, joint profit maximization and Stackelberg equilibria for a two-firm (duopoly) model and an N-firm (oligopoly) model. It is assumed the firms produce identical products, the market demand function is linear, and the long-run average cost (LRAC) and long-run marginal cost (LRMC) functions are horizontal (constant returns to scale production technology).

Symbols
P = price
q_i = output of firm i
$Q = \sum_i q_i$ = total output of all firms
c = marginal cost
TR_i = total revenue of firm i
π_i = profit of firm i

Two-firm model (firms A and B)

Market demand function (in inverse form) is:

$$P = a - bQ$$

Substituting for Q in the market demand function, we can write:

$$P = a - b(q_A + q_B)$$

Therefore:

$$\text{TR}_A = Pq_A = [a - b(q_A + q_B)]q_A = aq_A - bq_A^2 - bq_A q_B$$
$$\text{TR}_B = Pq_B = [a - b(q_A + q_B)]q_B = aq_B - bq_A q_B - bq_B^2$$
$$\pi_A = \text{TR}_A - cq_A = aq_A - bq_A^2 - bq_A q_B - cq_A = (a - c)q_A - bq_A^2 - bq_A q_B$$
$$\pi_B = \text{TR}_B - cq_B = aq_B - bq_A q_B - bq_B^2 - cq_B = (a - c)q_B - bq_A q_B - bq_B^2$$

Reaction functions

To derive the expression for firm A's reaction function: take the partial derivative of π_A with respect to q_A (holding q_B constant, in accordance with the zero conjectural variation assumption), set this partial derivative to zero, and solve the resulting expression for q_A.

$$\frac{\partial \pi_A}{\partial q_A} = (a - c) - 2bq_A - bq_B$$

$$(a - c) - 2bq_A - bq_B = 0$$

Therefore firm A's reaction function is:

$$q_A = \frac{a - c}{2b} - \frac{q_B}{2}$$

Firm B's reaction function is derived in the same way:

$$q_B = \frac{a - c}{2b} - \frac{q_A}{2}$$

Cournot–Nash equilibrium

The Cournot–Nash equilibrium occurs at the intersection of the two firms' reaction functions. To locate the Cournot–Nash equilibrium, substitute the expression for q_B from firm B's reaction function into firm A's reaction function, and solve the resulting expression for q_A. Let q_A^* and q_B^* denote the Cournot–Nash equilibrium values of q_A and q_B.

$$q_A = \frac{a - c}{2b} - \frac{1}{2}\left[\frac{a - c}{2b} - \frac{q_A}{2}\right] \implies q_A = \frac{a - c}{4b} + \frac{q_A}{4} \implies \frac{3q_A}{4} = \frac{a - c}{4b}$$

$$q_A^* = \frac{a - c}{3b}$$

Substituting q_A^* into firm B's reaction function:

$$q_A = \frac{a - c}{2b} - \frac{a - c}{6b}$$

$$q_B^* = \frac{a - c}{3b}$$

The equilibrium total output and price are:

$$Q_n = q_A^* + q_B^* = \frac{2(a - c)}{3b}$$

$$P_n = a - bQ_n = a - \frac{2(a - c)}{3} = \frac{a - 2c}{3}$$

If $a = b = 1$ and $c = 0$, $q_A^* = q_B^* = \frac{1}{3}$, $Q_n = \frac{2}{3}$ and $P_n = \frac{1}{3}$, as in Section 4.3.

Joint profit maximization

Let $q_A^M = q_B^M = \frac{Q}{2}$, where Q is total output, shared equally between firms A and B under joint profit maximization.

Let $\pi = \pi_A + \pi_B$ denote joint profits:

$$\pi = PQ - cQ = (a - bQ)Q - cQ = (a - c)Q - bQ^2$$

To find the value of Q that maximizes joint profits, differentiate π with respect to Q, set the derivative to zero, and solve for Q.

$$\frac{\partial \pi}{\partial Q} = (a - c) - 2bQ$$

$$(a - c) - 2bQ = 0$$

The equilibrium total output and price are:

$$Q_M = \frac{a - c}{2b}$$

$$P_M = a - bQ_M = a - \frac{a - c}{2} = \frac{a + c}{2}$$

Let q_A^M and q_B^M denote the corresponding values of q_A and q_B.

$$q_A^M = q_B^M = \frac{a - c}{4b}$$

If $a = b = 1$ and $c = 0$, $q_A^M = q_B^M = \frac{1}{4}$, $Q_M = \frac{1}{2}$ and $P_M = \frac{1}{2}$, as in Section 4.3.

Stackelberg equilibrium

Let firm A be the Stackelberg leader, and firm B be the follower. Firm A chooses q_A to maximize π_A, subject to the constraint that (q_A, q_B) must lie on firm B's reaction function. From the above, the relevant functions are firm A's profit function and firm B's reaction function:

$$\pi_A = (a - c)q_A - bq_A^2 - bq_A q_B$$

$$q_B = \frac{a - c}{2b} - \frac{q_A}{2}$$

Substitute firm B's reaction function for q_B in firm A's profit function:

$$\pi_A = (a - c)q_A - bq_A^2 - bq_A \left(\frac{a - c}{2b} - \frac{q_A}{2} \right)$$

$$\pi_A = \left(\frac{a - c}{2} \right) q_A - \frac{bq_A^2}{2}$$

To find the value of q_A that maximizes π_A subject to the constraint that firm B must operate on firm B's reaction function, differentiate π_A with respect to q_A, set the derivative to zero, and solve for q_A.

$$\frac{d\pi_A}{dq_A} = \frac{a - c}{2} - bq_A$$

$$\frac{a - c}{2} - bq_A = 0$$

Let q_A^L and q_B^F denote the equilibrium output levels of firms A and B as Stackelberg leader and follower respectively.

$$q_A^L = \frac{a - c}{2b}$$

To find q_B^F, substitute q_A^L for q_A in firm B's reaction function:

$$q_B = \frac{a - c}{2b} - \frac{a - c}{4b}$$

$$q_B^F = \frac{a - c}{4b}$$

The equilibrium total output and price are:

$$Q_S = q_A^L + q_B^F = \frac{3(a - c)}{4b}$$

$$P_S = a - bQ_S = \frac{a + 3c}{4}$$

If $a = b = 1$ and $c = 0$, $q_A^L = \frac{1}{2}$, $q_B^F = \frac{1}{4}$, $Q_S = \frac{3}{4}$ and $P_S = \frac{1}{4}$, as in Section 4.3.

N-firm model (firms 1 . . . N)

As before, substituting for Q in the market demand function, we can write:

$$P = a - b\sum_{j=1}^{N} q_j$$

Therefore for firm i:

$$TR_i = Pq_i = \left(a - b\sum_{j=1}^{N} q_j\right)q_i = aq_i - bq_i^2 - bq_i\sum_{j\neq i} q_j$$

$$\pi_i = TR_i - cq_i = aq_i - bq_i^2 - bq_i\sum_{j\neq i} q_j - cq_i = (a-c)q_i - bq_i^2 - bq_i\sum_{j\neq i} q_j$$

Reaction functions

To derive the expression for firm i's reaction function:

$$\frac{\partial \pi_i}{\partial q_i} = (a-c) - 2bq_i - b\sum_{j\neq i} q_j$$

$$\frac{\partial \pi_i}{\partial q_i} = 0 \quad \Rightarrow \quad (a-c) - 2bq_i - b\sum_{j\neq i} q_j = 0$$

Therefore firm i's reaction function is:

$$q_i = \frac{a-c}{2b} - \frac{\displaystyle\sum_{j\neq i} q_j}{2}$$

Cournot–Nash equilibrium

The Cournot–Nash equilibrium occurs at the intersection of the reaction functions of all N firms. Let q_i^* denote the Cournot–Nash equilibrium value of q_i. Since all firms are identical, q_i^* is the same for all N firms. Therefore it is possible to solve for q_i^* by substituting for q_i and q_j in the expression for firm i's reaction function:

$$q_i^* = \frac{a-c}{2b} - \frac{(N-1)q_i^*}{2}$$

$$\frac{(N+1)q_i^*}{2} = \frac{a-c}{2b}$$

$$q_i^* = \frac{a-c}{(N+1)b}$$

The equilibrium total output and price are:

$$Q_n = Nq_i^* = \frac{N(a - c)}{(N + 1)b}$$

$$P_n = a - bQ_n = a - \frac{N(a - c)}{N + 1} = \frac{a - Nc}{N + 1}$$

Note that the perfectly competitive output level at which price *equals* marginal cost, denoted Q_C, is given by the following expression:

$$P = a - bQ \quad \Rightarrow \quad Q_C = \frac{a - c}{b}$$

Accordingly, we can write:

$$Q_n = \left(\frac{N}{N + 1}\right)Q_C$$

Joint profit maximization

Let $q_i^M = \dfrac{Q}{N}$, where Q is total output, shared equally between all N firms under joint profit maximization.

As before, the equilibrium total output and price are:

$$Q_M = \frac{a - c}{2b}, \quad P_M = a - bQ_M = \frac{a + c}{2}$$

Therefore for each firm:

$$q_i^M = \frac{a - c}{2Nb}$$

Stackelberg equilibrium

Let firm i be the Stackelberg leader, and let the other firms be followers. Firm i chooses q_i to maximize π_i, subject to the constraint that all other firms must be located on their own reaction functions. Firm i's profit function and firm j's reaction function are as follows:

$$\pi_i = (a - c)q_i - bq_i^2 - bq_i \sum_{j \neq i} q_j$$

$$q_j = \frac{a - c}{2b} - \frac{q_i}{2} - \frac{\sum_{k \neq i,j} q_k}{2}$$

Since all of the followers are identical, firm j's reaction function can be written as follows:

$$q_j = \frac{a-c}{2b} - \frac{q_i}{2} - \frac{(N-2)q_j}{2}$$

$$\frac{Nq_j}{2} = \frac{a-c}{2b} - \frac{q_i}{2}$$

$$q_j = \frac{a-c}{Nb} - \frac{q_i}{N}$$

Substitute into firm i's profit function:

$$\pi_i = (a-c)q_i - bq_i^2 - bq_i(N-1)q_j$$

$$\pi_i = (a-c)q_i - bq_i^2 - \frac{(N-1)(a-c)q_i}{N} + \frac{(N-1)bq_i^2}{N}$$

As before, differentiate π_i with respect to q_i, set the derivative to zero, and solve for q_i.

$$\frac{d\pi_i}{dq_i} = (a-c) - 2bq_i - \frac{(N-1)(a-c)}{N} + \frac{(N-1)2bq_i}{N}$$

$$(a-c) - 2bq_i - \frac{(N-1)(a-c)}{N} + \frac{(N-1)2bq_i}{N} = 0$$

$$\frac{a-c}{N} = \frac{2bq_i}{N}$$

Let q_i^L and q_j^F denote the equilibrium output levels of the leader and each of the followers, respectively:

$$q_i^L = \frac{a-c}{2b}$$

$$q_j^F = \frac{a-c}{Nb} - \frac{a-c}{2Nb} = \frac{a-c}{2Nb}$$

The equilibrium total output and price are:

$$Q_S = q_i^L + (N-1)q_j^F = \frac{(2N-1)(a-c)}{2Nb}$$

$$P_S = a - bQ_S = \frac{a + (2N-1)c}{2N}$$

| 10.3 | **Price discrimination** |

This section derives the profit-maximizing equilibrium under third-degree price discrimination for the case of two sub-markets, and demonstrates that the total profit under third-degree price discrimination exceeds the total profit under uniform monopoly pricing.

Symbols
Q_1, Q_2 = quantities sold in sub-markets 1 and 2, respectively
P_1, P_2 = prices in sub-markets 1 and 2
Q = total quantity under uniform monopoly pricing
P = uniform monopoly price
c = marginal cost
TR_1, TR_2 = total revenues in sub-markets 1 and 2
π_1, π_2 = profits in sub-markets 1 and 2
π = profit under uniform monopoly pricing

The sub-market demand functions (in inverse form) are as follows:

$$P_1 = a_1 - b_1 Q_1 \qquad\qquad P_2 = a_2 - b_2 Q_2$$

Therefore the total revenue and profit functions for each sub-market are:

$$TR_1 = a_1 Q_1 - b_1 Q_1^2 \qquad\qquad TR_2 = a_2 Q_2 - b_2 Q_2^2$$

$$\pi_1 = (a_1 - c)Q_1 - b_1 Q_1^2 \qquad\qquad \pi_2 = (a_2 - c)Q_2 - b_2 Q_2^2$$

For profit maximization:

$$\frac{d\pi_1}{dQ_1} = (a_1 - c) - 2b_1 Q_1 \qquad\qquad \frac{d\pi_2}{dQ_2} = (a_2 - c) - 2b_2 Q_2$$

$$a_1 - c - 2b_1 Q_1 = 0 \qquad\qquad a_2 - c - 2b_2 Q_2 = 0$$

$$Q_1 = \frac{a_1 - c}{2b_1} \qquad\qquad Q_2 = \frac{a_2 - c}{2b_2}$$

The prices and profits in each sub-market are as follows:

$$P_1 = a_1 - b_1\left(\frac{a_1 - c}{2b_1}\right) = \frac{a_1 + c}{2} \qquad P_2 = a_2 - b_2\left(\frac{a_2 - c}{2b_2}\right) = \frac{a_2 + c}{2}$$

$$\pi_1 = P_1 Q_1 - cQ_1$$

$$\pi_1 = \left(\frac{a_1 + c}{2}\right)\left(\frac{a_1 - c}{2b_1}\right) - c\left(\frac{a_1 - c}{2b_1}\right) = \frac{(a_1 - c)^2}{4b_1}$$

Similarly, $\pi_2 = \dfrac{(a_2 - c)^2}{4b_2}$

To show that the total profit under third-degree price discrimination exceeds the total profit under uniform monopoly pricing, we begin by rearranging the sub-market demand functions:

$$Q_1 = \frac{a_1}{b_1} - \frac{P_1}{b_1} \qquad\qquad Q_2 = \frac{a_2}{b_2} - \frac{P_2}{b_2}$$

Let P denote the uniform monopoly price, and Q denote the total quantity.

$$Q = Q_1 + Q_2 = \frac{a_1}{b_1} + \frac{a_2}{b_2} - \left(\frac{1}{b_1} + \frac{1}{b_2}\right)P = \frac{a_1 b_2 + a_2 b_1}{b_1 b_2} - \left(\frac{b_1 + b_2}{b_1 b_2}\right)P$$

Therefore the inverse demand function is:

$$P = \frac{a_1 b_2 + a_2 b_1}{b_1 + b_2} - \left(\frac{b_1 b_2}{b_1 + b_2}\right)Q = \alpha - \beta Q$$

where $\alpha = \dfrac{a_1 b_2 + a_2 b_1}{b_1 + b_2}$, $\beta = \dfrac{b_1 b_2}{b_1 + b_2}$

The total revenue and profit functions are:

$$TR = \alpha Q - \beta Q^2$$
$$\pi = (\alpha - c)Q - \beta Q^2$$

For profit maximization:

$$\frac{d\pi}{dQ} = (\alpha - c) - 2\beta Q$$

$$\alpha - c - 2\beta Q = 0$$

$$Q = \frac{\alpha - c}{2\beta} \quad \Rightarrow \quad P = \frac{\alpha + c}{2}; \quad \pi = \frac{(\alpha - c)^2}{4\beta}$$

The condition for profit under third-degree price discrimination to exceed profit under uniform monopoly pricing is:

$$\frac{(a_1 - c)^2}{4b_1} + \frac{(a_2 - c)^2}{4b_2} - \frac{(\alpha - c)^2}{4\beta} > 0$$

$$\frac{a_1^2 - 2a_1 c + c^2}{4b_1} + \frac{a_2^2 - 2a_2 c + c^2}{4b_2} - \frac{\alpha^2 - 2\alpha c + c^2}{4\beta} > 0$$

It is trivial to show the following:

$$-\frac{2a_1 c}{4b_1} - \frac{2a_2 c}{4b_2} + \frac{2\alpha c}{4\beta} = 0; \qquad\qquad \frac{c^2}{4b_1} + \frac{c^2}{4b_2} - \frac{c^2}{4\beta} = 0$$

Therefore it is sufficient to show:

$$\frac{a_1^2}{4b_1} + \frac{a_2^2}{4b_2} - \frac{\alpha^2}{4\beta} > 0$$

$$\frac{a_1^2}{4b_1} + \frac{a_2^2}{4b_2} = \left(\frac{1}{4b_1b_2}\right)(b_2a_1^2 + b_1a_2^2)$$

$$\frac{\alpha^2}{4\beta} = \frac{(a_1b_2 + a_2b_1)^2}{4b_1b_2(b_1 + b_2)} = \left(\frac{1}{4b_1b_2}\right)\left[\left(\frac{b_2}{b_1 + b_2}\right)b_2a_1^2 + \left(\frac{b_1}{b_1 + b_2}\right)b_1a_2^2 + \frac{2a_1a_2b_1b_2}{b_1 + b_2}\right]$$

Therefore:

$$\frac{a_1^2}{4b_1} + \frac{a_2^2}{4b_2} - \frac{\alpha^2}{4\beta} = \left(\frac{1}{4b_1b_2}\right)\left[\left(\frac{b_1}{b_1 + b_2}\right)b_2a_1^2 + \left(\frac{b_2}{b_1 + b_2}\right)b_1a_2^2 - \frac{2a_1a_2b_1b_2}{b_1 + b_2}\right]$$

$$= \frac{a_1^2 + a_2^2 - 2a_1a_2}{4(b_1 + b_2)} = \frac{(a_1 - a_2)^2}{4(b_1 + b_2)} > 0$$

11.3 The pure common value model and the winner's curse

This section discusses the derivation of the expected value of the highest signal obtained by any bidder in the pure common value model.

Symbols

N = number of bidders

$S_{(1)}$ = highest signal obtained by any bidder

$E[S_{(1)}]$ = expected value of $S_{(1)}$

$\underline{v}$, $\bar{v}$ = minimum and maximum values (respectively) any bidder's signal can take

Section 11.3 makes use of the following result: if the bidders' signals are distributed uniformly over the interval $\underline{v}$ to $\bar{v}$:

$$E[S_{(1)}] = \underline{v} + [N/(N + 1)]\bar{v}$$

Below and with reference to independent private values model, we prove the result $E[V_{(1)}] = N/(N + 1)$ for the cases $N = 2$ and $N = 3$, where $E[V_{(1)}]$ is the expected value of the highest private valuation, and bidders' private valuations are distributed uniformly over the interval 0 to 1. This proof is equivalent to the proof required in the present case (simplified, but unaffected in any important way, by setting $\underline{v} = 0$ and $\bar{v} = 1$). This proof is presented on pp. 706–7, and to avoid repetition the proof is not shown here.

Optimal bidding strategies and revenue equivalence in the independent private values model

Optimal bidding strategies

This section derives a bidder's optimal bidding strategy in a first price sealed bid auction in the independent private values model.

Symbols

V_i = independent private valuation of bidder i

B_i = submitted bid of bidder i

b_i = ratio of bidder i's submitted bid to bidder i's private valuation

R_i = bidder i's economic rent

N = number of bidders

Two bidders

Bidder 1's economic rent is:

$$R_1 = (V_1 - B_1) \times \text{Probability that bidder 1's bid is the winning bid}$$

$$R_1 = V_1(1 - b_1) \times P(B_1 > B_2)$$

$$R_1 = V_1(1 - b_1) \times P(b_1 V_1 > b_2 V_2) = V_1(1 - b_1) \times P\left(V_2 < \frac{b_1 V_1}{b_2}\right)$$

$$R_1 = V_1(1 - b_1) \frac{b_1 V_1}{b_2} = \frac{V_1^2}{b_2}(b_1 - b_1^2)$$

To find the value of b_1 that maximizes R_1, take the partial derivative of R_1 with respect to b_1, set this derivative to zero, and solve for b_1.

$$\frac{\partial R_1}{\partial b_1} = \frac{V_1^2}{b_2}(1 - 2b_1)$$

$$\frac{V_1^2}{b_2}(1 - 2b_1) = 0$$

$$b_1 = \frac{1}{2}\left(= \frac{N-1}{N} \text{ with } N = 2\right)$$

Similarly, it can be shown that the value of b_2 that maximizes R_2 is $b_2 = \frac{1}{2}$

N bidders

Bidder 1's economic rent is

$$R_1 = V_1(1 - b_1) \times P(B_1 > B_2) \times \ldots \times P(B_1 > B_N)$$

$$R_1 = V_1(1 - b_1) \times P(b_1 V_1 > b_2 V_2) \times \ldots \times P(b_1 V_1 > b_N V_N)$$

$$R_1 = V_1(1 - b_1) \times P\left(V_2 < \frac{b_1 V_1}{b_2}\right) \times \ldots \times P\left(V_N < \frac{b_1 V_1}{b_N}\right)$$

$$R_1 = V_1(1 - b_1)\frac{(b_1 V_1)^{N-1}}{b_2 \ldots b_N} = \frac{V_1^N}{b_2 \ldots b_N}(b_1^{N-1} - b_1^N)$$

$$\frac{\partial R_1}{\partial b_1} = \frac{V_1^N}{b_2 \ldots b_N}[(N-1)b_1^{N-2} - Nb_1^{N-1}]$$

$$\frac{V_1^N}{b_2 \ldots b_N}[(N-1)b_1^{N-2} - Nb_1^{N-1}] = 0$$

$$b_1 = \frac{N-1}{N}$$

Similarly (or by symmetry), $b_2 = \ldots = b_N = \dfrac{N-1}{N}$

The revenue equivalence theorem

This section demonstrates the revenue equivalence theorem in the independent private values model for the cases where the number of bidders is two or three, and the private valuations are distributed uniformly over the interval zero to one.

Symbols
V_i = independent private valuation of bidder i
$V_{(1)}$ = highest private valuation of any bidder
$V_{(2)}$ = second-highest private valuation of any bidder
$E(V_{(1)})$, $E(V_{(2)})$ = expected values of $V_{(1)}$ and $V_{(2)}$
N = number of bidders
x_i = possible values of V_i over which integrals are evaluated.

To demonstrate the results summarized in Table 11.2, it is necessary to demonstrate (i) $E(V_{(1)}) = \dfrac{N}{N+1}$; (ii) $E(V_{(2)}) = \dfrac{N-1}{N+1}$. Below, these results are derived for the cases $N = 2$ and $N = 3$.

Two bidders

$$E(V_{(1)}) = \int_{x_1=0}^{1} \int_{x_2=0}^{x_1} x_1 dx_2 dx_1 + \int_{x_1=0}^{1} \int_{x_2=x_1}^{1} x_2 dx_2 dx_1$$

$$E(V_{(1)}) = \int_{x_1=0}^{1} [x_1 x_2]_0^{x_1} + \int_{x_1=0}^{1} [x_2^2/2]_{x_1}^{1} = \int_{x_1=0}^{1} (x_1^2 + 1/2 - x_1^2/2)dx_1$$

$$E(V_{(1)}) = \int_{x_1=0}^{1} (x_1^2/2 + 1/2)dx_1 = [x_1^3/6 + x_1/2]_0^1 = 1/6 + 1/2 = 2/3$$

$$E(V_{(2)}) = \int\limits_{x_1=0}^{1} \int\limits_{x_2=0}^{x_1} x_2 dx_2 dx_1 + \int\limits_{x_1=0}^{1} \int\limits_{x_2=x_1}^{1} x_1 dx_2 dx_1$$

$$E(V_{(2)}) = \int\limits_{x_1=0}^{1} [x_2^2/2]_0^{x_1} + \int\limits_{x_1=0}^{1} [x_1 x_2]_{x_1}^{1} = \int\limits_{x_1=0}^{1} (x_1^2/2 + x_1 - x_1^2) dx_1$$

$$E(V_{(2)}) = \int\limits_{x_1=0}^{1} (x_1 - x_1^2/2) dx_1 = [x_1^2/2 - x_1^3/6]_0^1 = 1/2 - 1/6 = 1/3$$

Three bidders

$$E(V_{(1)}) = \int\limits_{x_1=0}^{1} \int\limits_{x_2=0}^{x_1} \int\limits_{x_3=0}^{x_2} x_1 dx_3 dx_2 dx_1 + \int\limits_{x_1=0}^{1} \int\limits_{x_2=0}^{x_1} \int\limits_{x_3=x_2}^{x_1} x_1 dx_3 dx_2 dx_1$$

$$+ \int\limits_{x_1=0}^{1} \int\limits_{x_2=0}^{x_1} \int\limits_{x_3=x_1}^{1} x_3 dx_3 dx_2 dx_1 + \int\limits_{x_1=0}^{1} \int\limits_{x_2=x_1}^{1} \int\limits_{x_3=0}^{x_1} x_2 dx_3 dx_2 dx_1$$

$$+ \int\limits_{x_1=0}^{1} \int\limits_{x_2=x_1}^{1} \int\limits_{x_3=x_1}^{x_2} x_2 dx_3 dx_2 dx_1 + \int\limits_{x_1=0}^{1} \int\limits_{x_2=x_1}^{1} \int\limits_{x_3=x_2}^{1} x_3 dx_3 dx_2 dx_1$$

Evaluating the innermost integrals only:

$$[x_1 x_3]_0^{x_2} + [x_1 x_3]_{x_2}^{x_1} + [x_3^2/2]_{x_1}^{1} = x_1^2/2 + 1/2$$

$$[x_2 x_3]_0^{x_1} + [x_2 x_3]_{x_1}^{x_2} + [x_3^2/2]_{x_2}^{1} = x_2^2/2 + 1/2$$

$$E(V_{(1)}) = \int\limits_{x_1=0}^{1} \int\limits_{x_2=0}^{x_1} (x_1^2/2 + 1/2) dx_2 dx_1 + \int\limits_{x_1=0}^{1} \int\limits_{x_2=x_1}^{1} (x_2^2/2 + 1/2) dx_2 dx_1$$

Evaluating the innermost integrals only:

$$[x_1^2 x_2/2 + x_2/2]_0^{x_1} + [x_2^3/6 + x_2/2]_{x_1}^{1} = 2/3 + x_1^3/3$$

$$E(V_{(1)}) = \int\limits_{x_1=0}^{1} (2/3 + x_1^3/3) dx_1 = [2x_1/3 + x_1^4/12]_0^1 = 2/3 + 1/12 = 3/4$$

$$E(V_{(2)}) = \int_{x_1=0}^{1}\int_{x_2=0}^{x_1}\int_{x_3=0}^{x_2} x_2\,dx_3\,dx_2\,dx_1 + \int_{x_1=0}^{1}\int_{x_2=0}^{x_1}\int_{x_3=x_2}^{x_1} x_3\,dx_3\,dx_2\,dx_1$$

$$+ \int_{x_1=0}^{1}\int_{x_2=0}^{x_1}\int_{x_3=x_1}^{1} x_1\,dx_3\,dx_2\,dx_1 + \int_{x_1=0}^{1}\int_{x_2=x_1}^{1}\int_{x_3=0}^{x_1} x_1\,dx_3\,dx_2\,dx_1$$

$$+ \int_{x_1=0}^{1}\int_{x_2=x_1}^{1}\int_{x_3=x_1}^{x_2} x_3\,dx_3\,dx_2\,dx_1 + \int_{x_1=0}^{1}\int_{x_2=x_1}^{1}\int_{x_3=x_2}^{1} x_2\,dx_3\,dx_2\,dx_1$$

Evaluating the innermost integrals only:

$$[x_2x_3]_0^{x_2} + [x_3^2/2]_{x_2}^{x_1} + [x_1x_3]_{x_1}^{1} = x_1 - x_1^2/2 + x_2^2/2$$

$$[x_1x_3]_0^{x_1} + [x_3^2/2]_{x_1}^{x_2} + [x_2x_3]_{x_2}^{1} = x_2 + x_1^2/2 - x_2^2/2$$

$$E(V_{(2)}) = \int_{x_1=0}^{1}\int_{x_2=0}^{x_1} (x_1 - x_1^2/2 + x_2^2/2)\,dx_2\,dx_1 + \int_{x_1=0}^{1}\int_{x_2=x_1}^{1} (x_2 + x_1^2/2 - x_2^2/2)\,dx_2\,dx_1$$

Evaluating the innermost integrals only:

$$[x_1x_2 - x_1^2x_2/2 + x_2^3/6]_0^{x_1} + [x_2^2/2 + x_1^2x_2/2 - x_2^3/6]_{x_1}^{1} = 1/3 + x_1^2 - 2x_1^3/3$$

$$E(V_{(2)}) = \int_{x_1=0}^{1} (1/3 + x_1^2 - 2x_1^3/3)\,dx_1 = [x_1/3 + x_1^3/3 - 2x_1^4/12]_0^1 = 1/3 + 1/3 - 2/12$$
$$= 1/2$$

11.5　Extensions and additional topics in auction theory

This section derives the formula for the optimal reserve price in the independent private values model, for the case of an English auction with two bidders, where the bidders' private valuations are distributed uniformly over the interval zero to one.

Symbols
r = seller's reserve price
V_0 = seller's private valuation
R_0 = seller's economic rent
$E(R_0)$ = expected value of R_0
V_1, V_2 = private values of bidders 1 and 2
x_1, x_2 = possible values of V_1 and V_2 over which integrals are evaluated.

The optimal reserve price is the value of r that maximizes $E(R_0)$.

If $r > V_1 > V_2$ or $r > V_2 > V_1$, both bidders drop out before the reserve price is attained. No sale takes place, so the seller retains the item worth V_0.

If $V_1 > r > V_2$ or $V_2 > r > V_1$, one bidder drops out before the reserve price is attained, but one bidder remains. A sale takes place at the reserve price, r.

If $V_1 > V_2 > r$ or $V_2 > V_1 > r$, both bidders remain when the reserve price is attained. Bidding continues until the bidder with the lower private valuation drops out. A sale takes place, with the remaining bidder paying a price equivalent to the lower of the two private valuations.

$$E(R_0) = \int_{x_1=0}^{r} \int_{x_2=0}^{x_1} V_0 dx_2 dx_1 + \int_{x_1=0}^{r} \int_{x_2=x_1}^{r} V_0 dx_2 dx_1 + \int_{x_1=0}^{r} \int_{x_2=r}^{1} r dx_2 dx_1$$

$$+ \int_{x_1=r}^{1} \int_{x_2=r}^{x_1} x_2 dx_2 dx_1 + \int_{x_1=r}^{1} \int_{x_2=0}^{r} r dx_2 dx_1 + \int_{x_1=r}^{1} \int_{x_2=x_1}^{1} x_1 dx_2 dx_1$$

Evaluating the innermost integrals only:

$$[V_0 x_2]_0^{x_1} + [V_0 x_2]_{x_1}^{r} + [r x_2]_r^1 = V_0 r + r - r^2$$

$$[x_2^2/2]_r^{x_1} + [r x_2]_0^r + [x_1 x_2]_{x_1}^1 = x_1^2/2 + r^2/2 + x_1 - x_1^2$$

$$E(R_0) = \int_{x_1=0}^{r} (V_0 r + r - r^2) dx_1 + \int_{x_1=r}^{1} (x_1^2/2 + r^2/2 + x_1 - x_1^2) dx_1$$

$$E(R_0) = [V_0 r x_1 + r x_1 - r^2 x_1]_0^r + [x_1^3/6 + r^2 x_1/2 + x_1^2/2 - x_1^3/3]_r^1$$

$$E(R_0) = (1 + V_0) r^2 - 4r^3/3 + 1/3$$

To find the value of r that maximizes $E(R_0)$, differentiate $E(R_0)$ with respect to r, set the derivative to zero, and solve for r.

$$\frac{dE(R_0)}{dr} = 2(1 + V_0) r - 12r^2/3$$

$$2(1 + V_0) r - 4r^2 = 0$$

$$r = \frac{1 + V_0}{2}$$

12.5 Hotelling's location model

This section derives the equilibrium prices in the collusive and non-collusive versions of the Hotelling model with fixed locations and endogenous prices.

Symbols

P_A, P_B = prices charged by firms A and B

P = common price charged by both firms (where applicable)

TR = total revenue

d = consumers' addresses, measured on a scale of d = 0 to d = 1

k = parameter reflecting magnitude of transport cost (per unit of distance), or degree of substitution between the products of firms A and B

$\tilde{P}$ = price at which the consumer located at address d = 0.5 is indifferent between buying from either firm

Collusive model: joint profit maximization

$\tilde{P} = 1 - k/4$ denotes the price at which the consumer located at address d = 0.5 is indifferent between buying from either firm or withdrawing from the market. Let $P = P_A = P_B$ represent the common price charged by firms A and B under a policy of joint profit maximization. We examine the implications for joint total revenue (and therefore joint profit) of variations in P around $\tilde{P}$.

For $0 \leq P < \tilde{P}$, firms A and B each supply one half of the market. Total quantity demanded = 1, and total revenue = P.

For $\tilde{P} \leq P < 1$, firm A supplies consumers at addresses d such that $P + kd^2 \leq 1$.

The consumer at address $d = \sqrt{\dfrac{1 - P}{k}}$ is indifferent between buying from firm A or withdrawing from the market.

Therefore firm A's quantity demanded $= \sqrt{\dfrac{1 - P}{k}}$. By symmetry, firm B's quantity demanded is given by the same expression.

Total quantity demanded $= 2\sqrt{\dfrac{1 - P}{k}}$, and total revenue $= TR = 2P\sqrt{\dfrac{1 - P}{k}}$

To find the value of P that maximizes TR, differentiate TR with respect to P, set the derivative to zero, and solve for P.

$$TR = \frac{2}{\sqrt{k}}P(1 - P)^{1/2}$$

To differentiate TR with respect to P, use both the Product Rule and the Chain Rule. It can be shown:

$$\frac{dTR}{dP} = \frac{2}{\sqrt{k}}\left(-\frac{P}{2(1 - P)^{1/2}} + (1 - P)^{1/2}\right)$$

$$\frac{2}{\sqrt{k}}\left(-\frac{P}{2(1 - P)^{1/2}} + (1 - P)^{1/2}\right) = 0$$

$$(1 - P)^{1/2} = \frac{P}{2(1 - P)^{1/2}} \Rightarrow 1 - P = \frac{P}{2} \Rightarrow 1 = \frac{3P}{2}$$

$$P = 2/3$$

When $\tilde{P} \geq \dfrac{2}{3}$ or $k \leq \dfrac{4}{3} = 1.33$, total revenue is maximized by setting $P = \tilde{P} = 1 - k/4$

When $\tilde{P} < \dfrac{2}{3}$ or $k \geq \dfrac{4}{3} = 1.33$, total revenue is maximized by setting $P = \dfrac{2}{3}$

Non-collusive model: Bertrand (or Nash) equilibrium

For the mathematical derivation of the Bertrand (or Nash) equilibrium, we assume both firms' prices are sufficiently low that no consumer is priced out of the market.

The address at which a consumer is indifferent between purchasing from firm A or from firm B is d such that:

$$P_A + kd^2 = P_B + k(1 - d)^2$$

To solve for d:

$$P_A + kd^2 = P_B + k(1 - 2d + d^2)$$

$$P_A - P_B - k = -2kd$$

$$d = \frac{P_B - P_A + k}{2k}$$

This expression represents firm A's quantity demanded. Therefore firm A's total revenue is:

$$TR_A = \frac{P_A P_B - P_A^2 + kP_A}{2k}$$

Similarly, firm B's total revenue is:

$$TR_B = \frac{P_A P_B - P_B^2 + kP_B}{2k}$$

To determine the Bertrand (or Nash) equilibrium, at which each firm sets its price to maximize its own profit treating the other firm's price as fixed: take the partial derivatives of TR_A and TR_B with respect to P_A and P_B respectively, set the partial derivatives to zero, and solve the resulting simultaneous equations for P_A and P_B.

$$\frac{\partial TR_A}{\partial P_A} = \frac{P_B - 2P_A + k}{2k} \qquad\qquad \frac{\partial TR_B}{\partial P_B} = \frac{P_A - 2P_B + k}{2k}$$

From the expression for $\dfrac{\partial TR_A}{\partial P_A}$:

$$\frac{P_B - 2P_A + k}{2k} = 0 \Rightarrow 2P_A = P_B + k$$

$$P_A = \frac{P_B + k}{2}$$

Substituting P_A into the expression for $\dfrac{\partial TR_B}{\partial P_B}$ and multiplying through by 2k:

$$\frac{P_A - 2P_B + k}{2k} = 0 \Rightarrow \frac{P_B + k}{2} - 2P_B + k = 0$$

$$P_B + k - 4P_B + 2k = 0$$

$$P_B = k$$

$$P_A = k$$

Therefore the Bertrand (or Nash) equilibrium is $P_A = P_B = k$. As noted above, this result is based on the assumption that no consumer is priced out of the market altogether at the Bertrand (or Nash) equilibrium. For the consumer located at $d = 0.5$, this assumption is valid under the following condition:

$$k + kd^2 \leq 1 \Rightarrow k + \frac{k}{4} \leq 1 \Rightarrow \frac{5k}{4} \leq 1 \Rightarrow k \leq \frac{4}{5} = 0.8$$

For $k > 0.8$, both firms operate as local monopolists, and their quantities demanded are not dependent on the other firm's price. Each firm maximizes profit within its own market. The solution is the same as in the collusive model. Therefore the full set of solutions (see also Figure 12.12) is as follows:

For $k \leq 0.8$, $P_A = P_B = k$

For $0.8 < k \leq 1.33$, $P_A = P_B = 1 - k/4$

For $k > 1.33$, $P_A = P_B = 2/3$

14.4 Diffusion

With reference to the Mansfield model, this section demonstrates the equivalence between the following expressions:

$$\text{Pace of diffusion:} \quad n_{i,t+1} - n_{i,t} = k_i \left(\frac{n_{i,t}}{N_i}\right)\left(1 - \frac{n_{i,t}}{N_i}\right)$$

$$\text{Solution for } \frac{n_{i,t}}{N_i}: \quad \frac{n_{i,t}}{N_i} = \frac{1}{1 + e^{-(\alpha_i + \beta_i t)}}$$

Symbols

N_i = total number of firms that will eventually adopt innovation i,

$n_{i,t}$ = number of firms that have adopted by time t.

k_i, α_i, β_i = constants

To simplify the notation, we drop the subscripts on all variables and coefficients, and define the time-dependent variable y as follows:

$$y = \frac{n_{i,t}}{N_i} = \frac{1}{1 + e^{-(\alpha+\beta t)}}$$

We can think of $n_{i,t+1} - n_{i,t}$ as the rate of change of y with respect to time, $\frac{dy}{dt}$.

Therefore the original expression for the pace of diffusion can be rewritten as follows:

$$\frac{dy}{dt} = ky(1 - y)$$

The equivalence between the two previous expressions is shown by demonstrating that when $y = \frac{1}{1 + e^{-(\alpha+\beta t)}}$, $\frac{dy}{dt} = ky(1 - y)$.

To differentiate $y = \frac{1}{1 + e^{-(\alpha+\beta t)}}$ with respect to t, use the Chain Rule.

In general, if $y = f[g(t)]$, $\frac{dy}{dt} = f'[g(t)]g'(t)$, where $f[\ ]$ and $g(\ )$ are functions, and $f'[\ ]$ and $g'(\ )$ are the derivatives of $f[\ ]$ and $g(\ )$.

In this case, $g(t) = (1 + e^{-(\alpha+\beta t)})$ and $f[g(t)] = (1 + e^{-(\alpha+\beta t)})^{-1}$

$$f'[g(t)] = -(1 + e^{-(\alpha+\beta t)})^{-2}$$
$$g'(t) = -\beta e^{-(\alpha+\beta t)}$$

Applying the Chain Rule:

$$\frac{dy}{dt} = \frac{\beta e^{-(\alpha+\beta t)}}{(1 + e^{-(\alpha+\beta t)})^2}$$

This expression is equivalent to $ky(1 - y)$ if $k = \beta$:

$$\frac{dy}{dt} = ky(1 - y) = k\left(\frac{1}{1 + e^{-(\alpha+\beta t)}}\right)\left(1 - \frac{1}{1 + e^{-(\alpha+\beta t)}}\right) = k\left(\frac{1}{1 + e^{-(\alpha+\beta t)}}\right)\left(\frac{e^{-(\alpha+\beta t)}}{1 + e^{-(\alpha+\beta t)}}\right)$$

$$\frac{dy}{dt} = ky(1 - y) = \frac{ke^{-(\alpha+\beta t)}}{(1 + e^{-(\alpha+\beta t)})^2}$$

Econometric methods

Introduction

Several chapters in this book refer to empirical studies, which examine whether economic hypotheses based on theoretical reasoning are supported empirically using data from the real world. In many cases, this evidence is obtained by applying regression analysis to industrial organization data. Appendix 2 provides a brief survey of the essentials of regression analysis at an introductory and non-technical level. Any reader requiring a comprehensive treatment of this topic is advised to consult one (or more) of the following textbooks:

Stock, J.H. and Watson, M.W. (2003) *Introduction to Econometrics*, International edn. Harlow: Pearson Education.
Studenmund, A.H. (2000) *Using Econometrics: A Practical Guide*, International edn. Harlow: Pearson Education.
Vogelvang, B. (2004) *Econometrics: Theory and Applications with E-Views*. Harlow: Financial Times Prentice Hall.

Types of industrial organization data set

Data sets used for empirical research in industrial organization may have been compiled by government agencies or commercial organizations. There are two basic types of data set: time series and cross-sectional.

■ A time-series data set contains observations on a specific 'unit' over a number of time periods, which might be days, months or years. The 'unit' might be a single firm, or a particular industry.

■ A cross-sectional data set contains observations on a number of 'units' at one particular point in time. The 'units' might be a group of firms classified as members of one industry, or a number of industries that comprise a larger grouping, such as an entire manufacturing or service sector.

Some data sets include both a time series and a cross-sectional dimension. For example, we might have several time-series observations on each member of a group of firms or industries. This type of data set is known as pooled cross-sectional time-series data, or alternatively as panel data.

The two-variable linear regression model

Most empirical studies seek to explain observed facts about the real world. One of the most important questions that can be investigated using appropriate data is whether there is empirical evidence of a relationship between some specific economic variables. For example, if we have cross-sectional data on the levels of advertising expenditure and the sales revenues of a number of firms in the same year, we can investigate whether the data reveals any evidence of a relationship between advertising and sales revenue.

More generally, a two-variable linear regression model takes the following form:

$$y_i = \beta_1 + \beta_2 x_i + u_i$$

The definitions of variables and symbols are as follows:

y_i is the dependent variable;
x_i is the independent or explanatory variable;
u_i is the error term;
β_1, β_2 are the regression coefficients.

The dependent variable y_i is the variable whose behaviour the model seeks to explain. The independent variable x_i is a variable thought to influence or determine y_i. The coefficient β_2 identifies the impact on y_i of a small change in the value of x_i. For example, if x_i increases by one unit, the numerical adjustment to the value of y_i is given by the coefficient β_2. The coefficient β_1 can be interpreted as the expected value of the dependent variable y_i when the independent variable x_i *equals* zero. Finally the error term u_i allows for any variation in the dependent variable that is not accounted for by corresponding variation in the independent variable. In most regression models, the error term is assumed to be purely random. For purposes of statistical inference (see pp. 718–19) it is often useful to assume the error term is drawn from some specific probability distribution, such as the normal distribution.

So far, everything we have said refers to what is known as the 'population' or 'true' regression model. β_1 and β_2 are unknown parameters which describe the true relationship between x_i and y_i. In order to know β_1 and β_2, we would need complete information about every member of the population of firms or industries. In practice we do not have this much information. However, we can take a random sample of observations of y_i and x_i, and use it to obtain estimates of β_1 and β_2. If we take a random sample and using only these observations, fit a line as best we can through them, we obtain the sample regression line. Because no sample is ever perfectly representative of the population from which it is drawn, the sample regression line will never coincide precisely with the (true but unknown) population regression line: we will always slightly over- or underestimate β_1 and β_2.

The sample regression model is specified as follows:

$$y_i = \hat{\beta}_1 + \hat{\beta}_2 x_i + e_i$$

In the sample (estimated) model, $\hat{\beta}_1$ and $\hat{\beta}_2$ are the sample estimators of β_1 and β_2. e_i is the sample estimator of u_i, known as the estimated error term or residual. $\hat{y}_i = \hat{\beta}_1 + \hat{\beta}_2 x_i$ are known as the estimated values or fitted values of the dependent variable, y_i.

Consider the following table, which records the levels of advertising expenditure and sales revenue for a sample of nine firms, observed in 2005:

Firm	y_i = Sales revenue of firm i, 2005, £m	x_i = Advertising expenditure of firm i, 2005, £m
A	14	8
B	4	1
C	12	8
D	14	6
E	6	2
F	16	9
G	12	7
H	10	5
I	10	4

These data can be plotted on a graph, with y_i = sales revenue shown on the vertical axis, and x_i = advertising expenditure shown on the horizontal axis. The resulting graph is shown as Figure A.1.

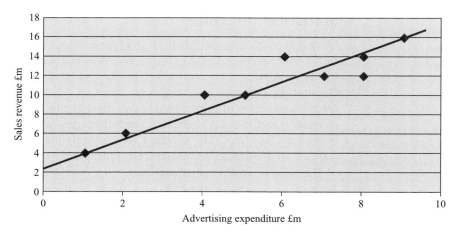

Figure A.1 Sample regression line for advertising-sales model

The simplest way of thinking about regression analysis is in terms of using a ruler to draw a 'line-of-best-fit' through the centre of the set of plotted points. The estimation technique known as Ordinary Least Squares (OLS) is the mathematical method that is used to locate the line-of-best-fit precisely. Numerical estimates of the regression coefficients β_1 and β_2 can be obtained from any computer package that includes OLS estimation. The estimation results are shown below, together with a few additional pieces of information which will be explained below.

	Coefficient	Standard error	t-statistic
Intercept $\hat{\beta}_1$	3.607	1.102	3.27
Advertising $\hat{\beta}_2$	1.311	0.179	7.21

N = number of observations = 9
Total variation, $\Sigma(y_i - \bar{y})^2 = 120.9$
Explained variation, $\Sigma(\hat{y}_i - \bar{y})^2 = 106.9$
Unexplained variation, $\Sigma e_i^2 = 14.0$
R-square = 0.884 (=106.9/120.9)

Therefore the fitted regression model is:

$$\hat{y}_i = 3.607 + 1.311 x_i$$

In many empirical studies, it is standard practice to write down an estimated regression model using a slightly different notational convention, in which the dependent and independent variables are identified by names (which are often abbreviated). Therefore we might use SALES to denote sales revenue and ADVERT to denote advertising expenditure. Using this alternative notation, the same fitted regression model would be written:

$$SALES = 3.607 + 1.311 \ ADVERT$$

Statistical inference

Once a regression model has been estimated, the signs and numerical magnitudes of the estimated coefficients convey information about the direction and strength of the relationship between the independent variable and the dependent variable. Because the estimated coefficients are based on a limited sample of data, there is always a suspicion of imprecision or unreliability attached to them. For this reason, estimation methods for regression coefficients provide a standard error for each estimated coefficient. The standard error reflects the reliability of the estimated coefficient: the smaller the standard error, the greater the reliability.

The ratio of an estimated coefficient to its standard error, usually known as a t-statistic or z-statistic (depending on precisely which type of regression model is being fitted), provides a convenient method for assessing whether the estimation has succeeded in identifying a relationship between variables that is reliable in a statistical sense. This is one of the main tasks of statistical inference. The t-statistic (or z-statistic) for the estimated coefficient $\hat{\beta}_2$ is calculated as $t = \hat{\beta}_2/se(\hat{\beta}_2)$, where $se(\hat{\beta}_2)$ is the standard error of $\hat{\beta}_2$. If the absolute value of the t-statistic exceeds a certain critical value, we say that $\hat{\beta}_2$ is statistically significant or significantly different from zero. This means we have sufficient statistical evidence to reject the hypothesis that the true value of the coefficient β_2 is zero.

Whenever a hypothesis test is carried out, it is usual to quote an accompanying significance level, such as 1, 5 or 10 per cent. This expresses the probability that the test may cause us to draw a wrong inference, by rejecting a hyothesis that is actually true. With a significance level of 5 per cent, if β_2 really were zero, the test would run a 5 per cent risk of incorrectly concluding that β_2 is non-zero. The smaller the significance level, the greater the degree of confidence we can have in any decision to reject the hypothesis that the true value of the coefficient is zero.

In the advertising–sales example, suppose we wish to test the hypothesis that advertising has no effect on sales revenue. This is equivalent to testing the hypothesis that the true value of the unknown coefficient β_2 *equals* zero. We will use a significance level of 5 per cent.

■ The t-statistic is $\hat{\beta}_2/\text{se}(\hat{\beta}_2) = 1.311/0.179 = 7.21$.

■ The critical value for the test is taken from statistical tables for the t-distribution with $n - k = 7$ degrees of freedom, where $n = 9$ is the number of observations used to estimate the model, and $k = 2$ is the number of estimated regression coefficients. For a test at the 5 per cent significance level, this critical value is 2.365.

■ If the t-statistic is numerically smaller than the critical value, we accept the hypothesis we are testing. If the t-statistic is numerically greater than the critical value, we reject the hypothesis.

■ In this case, the t-statistic of 7.21 exceeds the critical value of 2.365. Therefore we reject the hypothesis that the true value of the coefficient β_2 *equals* zero. We infer β_2 is non-zero, and advertising does therefore have a significant effect on sales revenue.

Multiple regression

The two-variable linear regression model that is described above can easily be extended to allow for cases where there is more than one independent variable. We might wish to expand the model that seeks to explain the variation in sales, by adding more independent variables. For example, we might believe that for any particular firm, sales will depend not only on the firm's own advertising expenditure, but also on a number of other factors such as price, product quality, or rivals' pricing and advertising decisions.

For a multiple regression, the population or 'true' model is defined as follows:

$$y_i = \beta_1 + \beta_2 x_{2i} + \beta_3 x_{3i} + \ldots + \beta_k x_{ki} + u_i$$

The definitions of variables and symbols are as follows:

y_i is the dependent variable;
$x_{2i}, x_{3i}, \ldots, x_{ki}$ are the independent or explanatory variables;
u_i is the error term;
$\beta_1, \beta_2, \beta_3, \ldots, \beta_k$ are the regression coefficients.

As before, the dependent variable y_i is the variable whose behaviour the model seeks either to explain or to predict. The independent variables $x_{2i}, x_{3i} \ldots x_{ki}$ are other variables thought to influence or determine y_i. The coefficients $\beta_2, \beta_3 \ldots \beta_k$ identify the impact on y_i of small changes in the values of each of $x_{2i}, x_{3i} \ldots x_{ki}$, respectively.

The sample/estimated model is written as follows:

$$y_i = \hat{\beta}_1 + \hat{\beta}_2 x_{2i} + \hat{\beta}_3 x_{3i} + \ldots + \hat{\beta}_k x_{ki} + e_i$$

This type of regression cannot be presented graphically, but computer software can be used to obtain estimated regression coefficients denoted $\hat{\beta}_1, \hat{\beta}_2 \ldots \hat{\beta}_k$, as well as their standard errors and t-statistics.

So far, we have assumed the dependent variable, y_i, is influenced by a number of independent variables, $x_{2i} \ldots x_{ki}$, which are quantitative (measurable) in nature. However, in some cases we might also want to incorporate certain non-quantitative or qualitative information as well.

With reference to our earlier example of a model for the sales revenues of firms in 2005, it might be the case that some of the firms have introduced a new model in 2005, while others are continuing to sell an old model. For each firm, the information as to whether or not a new model has been introduced can be captured by defining a 0–1 dummy variable d_i:

$d_i = 1$ if firm i introduced a new model in 2005
$d_i = 0$ if firm i did not introduce a new model in 2005

In our earlier example, suppose firms A, D, F and I introduced new models in 2005, while firms B, C, E, G and H continued to sell old models. The extended data set is as follows:

Firm	y_i = Sales revenue of firm i, 2005, £m	x_i = Advertising expenditure of firm i, 2005, £m	d_i = Dummy variable identifying firms that introduced a new model in 2005
A	14	8	1
B	4	1	0
C	12	8	0
D	14	6	1
E	6	2	0
F	16	9	1
G	12	7	0
H	10	5	0
I	10	4	1

Running a multiple regression, in which the dependent variable is y_i and the independent variables are x_i and d_i, the estimation results (presented in the same format as before) are as follows:

	Coefficient	Standard error	t-statistic
Intercept, $\hat{\beta}_1$	3.567	0.680	5.25
Advertising, $\hat{\beta}_2$	1.138	0.121	9.40
New model, $\hat{\beta}_3$	2.254	0.640	3.52

N = number of observations = 9
Total variation, $\Sigma(y_i - \bar{y})^2 = 120.9$
Explained variation, $\Sigma(\hat{y}_i - \bar{y})^2 = 116.3$
Unexplained variation, $\Sigma e_i^2 = 4.6$
R-square = 0.962 (= 116.3/120.9)

Therefore the fitted regression model is:

$$\hat{y}_i = 3.567 + 1.138x_i + 2.254d_i$$

Using the alternative notation, and letting NEW denote the new product dummy variable, the same fitted regression model would be written:

$$\text{SALES} = 3.567 + 1.138\ \text{ADVERT} + 2.254\ \text{NEW}$$

Suppose we now wish to test the hypothesis that the introduction of a new model has no effect on sales revenue. This is equivalent to testing the hypothesis that the true value of the unknown coefficient β_3 *equals* zero. As before, we will use a significance level of 5 per cent.

■ The t-statistic is $\hat{\beta}_3/\text{se}(\hat{\beta}_3) = 2.254/0.640 = 3.52$.

■ The critical value for the test is taken from statistical tables for the t-distribution with $n - k = 6$ degrees of freedom (there are $n = 9$ observations and $k = 3$ estimated regression coefficients). For a test at the 5 per cent level, this critical value is 2.447.

■ The t-statistic of 3.52 exceeds the critical value of 2.447. Therefore we reject the hypothesis that the true value of the coefficient β_3 is zero. We infer the introduction of a new model does have a significant effect on sales revenue.

Coefficient of determination, R^2

When we fit a regression model using a sample of data, we are attempting to explain as much as possible of the variation in y_i (the dependent variable). The variation in y_i is explained by corresponding variation in x_i (the independent variable). However, not all of the variation in y_i can be explained by variation in x_i. This is why we have an error term, u_i, which allows for all other (random) influences on y_i.

Consider Figures A.2a and A.2b. In both cases, the same regression line has been fitted. Both lines have the same intercept and the same slope. However, it is clear that the regression line in Figure A.2a fits the data more accurately than the one in Figure A.2b, because in the latter case the data are more widely dispersed around the fitted regression line. It is natural to ask what proportion of the total variation in y_i is explained by x_i, and what proportion is left unexplained.

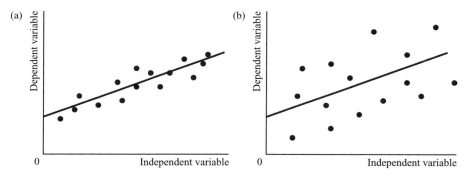

Figure A.2 Regression models with different degrees of explanatory power

In the case of a multiple regression, the estimated model may be written:

$$y_i = \hat{y}_i + e_i \qquad \text{where } \hat{y}_i = \hat{\beta}_1 + \hat{\beta}_2 x_{2i} + \hat{\beta}_3 x_{3i} + \ldots + \hat{\beta}_k x_{ki}$$

Subtracting the sample mean of the dependent variable, denoted $\bar{y}$, from both sides we can write:

$$(y_i - \bar{y}) = (\hat{y}_i - \bar{y}) + e_i$$

For the i'th observation, we can interpret the components of this expression as follows:

$y_i - \bar{y}$ = total variation in the i'th observation of the dependent variable (difference between the actual value and the sample mean).

$\hat{y}_i - \bar{y}$ = explained variation in the i'th observation (difference between the fitted value and the sample mean).

e_i = unexplained variation (error, or difference between the actual and fitted values).

It can be shown that a similar relationship exists between the sums (over all observations in the sample) of squares of these terms. By squaring, we make all the terms positive and therefore comparable with each other. By summing we obtain measures of variation over the entire sample.

$$\Sigma(y_i - \bar{y})^2 \quad = \quad \Sigma(\hat{y}_i - \bar{y})^2 \quad + \quad \Sigma e_i^2$$

Total variation in y_i = Explained variation + Unexplained variation

This relationship allows us to define R^2 ('R-square') or goodness-of-fit, also known as the coefficient of determination, as follows:

$$R^2 = \frac{\text{Explained variation}}{\text{Total variation}}$$

$$R^2 = \frac{\Sigma(\hat{y}_i - \bar{y})^2}{\Sigma(y_i - \bar{y})^2}$$

R^2 must lie between 0 and 1. As we have seen, its interpretation is quite simple: R^2 is the proportion of the variation in y_i that is explained by the model.

For the first of our two fitted regression models, SALES = 3.607 + 1.311 ADVERT:

$$\Sigma(\hat{y}_i - \bar{y})^2 = 106.9 \text{ and } \Sigma(y_i - \bar{y})^2 = 120.9 \Rightarrow R^2 = 0.882$$

For the second of our two models, SALES = 3.567 + 1.138 ADVERT + 2.254 NEW:

$$\Sigma(\hat{y}_i - \bar{y})^2 = 116.3 \text{ and } \Sigma(y_i - \bar{y})^2 = 120.9 \Rightarrow R^2 = 0.962$$

Therefore advertising expenditure by itself is capable of explaining 88.2 per cent of the variation in sales revenue. When the information about which firms are selling new models is added to the data set, the proportion of the variation in sales revenue that is explained by the model increases to 96.2 per cent.

Difficulties and pitfalls in the interpretation of regression results

In practice, there are a number statistical issues that can create difficulties or cloud the interpretation of an estimated regression model. This survey concludes with a brief discussion of a few of the issues that arise most frequently.

■ *The direction of causation.* Although regression analysis may be able to confirm the existence of significant relationships between economic variables, it may be unable to determine the direction of causation. For example, one might find evidence of a positive relationship between research and development and the level of seller concentration. However, it might still be difficult to decide whether high concentration leads to high research and development expenditure, or whether a high level of research and development expenditure tends to create a highly concentrated industry structure.

■ *Multicollinearity.* Multicollinearity describes the case where some or all of the independent variables included in a multiple regression model are highly correlated with one another. Collectively, the independent variables are successful in explaining the variation in the dependent variable, but the estimation is unable to pinpoint the individual relationships between each independent variable and the dependent variable. For example, suppose the quantity demanded of a firm's product depends on its own price, and on a rival's price (as well as other variables). If the two firms always tend to change their prices in the same direction at the same time, it becomes difficult for the regression model to isolate the separate effects of each of the two prices on the quantity demanded.

■ *Autocorrelation.* Autocorrelation or serial correlation arises when the assumption of a random error term is violated. This problem commonly arises in regression models estimated using time-series data. The randomness assumption requires that all random disturbances affect the dependent variable for one time period only, and then disappear completely. However this requirement may not be satisfied in practice. For example, the demand for a particular product may be affected by many factors that change slowly through time, such as lifestyles, tastes, customs, habits. If these factors are not captured explicitly among the model's independent variables, their effects will be incorporated into the error term. Because these factors change slowly over time, the values of the error term in successive periods will be correlated, violating the randomness assumption. If uncorrected, autocorrelation may result in t-statistics and R-square giving an exaggerated impression of the precision of a fitted regression model.

■ *Heteroskedasticity.* If the amount of variation in the random error term (measured by its variance) changes as the values of the independent variables change, there is a problem of heteroskedasticity. Heteroskedasticity is a common problem in regression models estimated using cross-sectional data. For example, over a large cross section of firms, one might expect to find greater variation in growth rates at the lower end of the firm size distribution than at the upper end. Starting from a very low base, a successful small firm might record a year-on-year growth rate of several hundred per cent, whereas an unsuccessful small firm might just as easily shed most of its sales or assets in any one year. It is unlikely that pro-portionately, a very large firm would experience such a large (positive or negative) year-on-year growth rate. Therefore a cross-sectional regression model using growth as a dependent variable might be subject to a heteroskedasticity problem, if the variation in the dependent variable feeds through into similar variation in the error term. If uncorrected, heteroskedasticity can lead to incorrect inferences being drawn from hypothesis tests.

■ *Misspecification.* Misspecification errors arise when independent variables that actually have no effect the dependent variable are included in a multiple regression model, or when variables that do have an effect are omitted. Another possible source of misspecification error is the selection of an incorrect functional form for the estimated equation. For example, if the true relationship between seller concentration and advertising expenditure is quadratic, but a linear specification is estimated instead, misleading inferences about the existence or nature of this relationship may be obtained. In practice, finding the correct specification for a regression model is often a difficult task. There are hundreds of economic variables, many of which are interrelated to a greater or lesser extent. Researchers may need to estimate and compare many different versions of a model before a final specification is accepted.

Glossary

Abnormal profit. The return in excess of the minimum required to prevent the owner from closing the firm down, equivalent to revenue *minus* accounting costs *minus* **normal profit**.

Absolute cost advantage entry barrier. An incumbent incurs a lower long-run average cost than a potential entrant at any output level.

Accounting profitability approach. An indirect method of testing for economies of scale, based on the correlation between firm size and accounting profitability.

Accounting rate of profit. A profit measure based on company accounts data. Normally calculated as the ratio of profit to assets (return on capital), equity (return on equity), or sales revenue (return on sales).

Adverse selection. Arises when a principal is unable to verify an agent's claims concerning the agent's own ability or productivity.

Advertising elasticity of demand. A measure of the sensitivity of quantity demanded to changes in advertising expenditure. Measured as the ratio of the proportionate change in quantity demanded to the proportionate change in advertising expenditure.

Advertising intensity. See **advertising-to-sales ratio**.

Advertising response function. Measures the responsiveness of sales revenue to the volume of advertising expenditure.

Advertising-to-sales ratio. The ratio of advertising expenditure to sales revenue.

Affiliated valuations model. In auction theory, the case where information about one bidder's valuation of the item would influence other bidders' valuations. Represents an intermediate case between the **independent private values model** and the **pure common value model**.

Agency theory. The study of relationships between principals and agents. For example, a manufacturing firm, acting as principal, contracts a supplying firm, the agent, to produce its inputs.

Aggregate concentration. The share of the largest firms in total sales, assets or employment (or other appropriate size measure) for the economy as a whole.

Allocative efficiency. Describes an allocation of resources such that no possible reallocation could make one agent (producer or consumer) better off without making at least one other agent worse off.

Article 81. Part of the Treaty of Amsterdam dealing with the regulation of restrictive practices on the part of firms located within the boundaries of the European Union. Article 81 deals with restrictive agreements, collusion and vertical restraints.

Article 82. Part of the Treaty of Amsterdam dealing with abuses of monopoly power. A monopoly is said to exist if a single firm has a 40 per cent market share. Article 82 deals with monopoly pricing, predatory pricing and price discrimination.

Ascending bid auction. See **English Auction**.

Asset specificity. An asset that is specific to a contractual relationship, and which has little or no value outside that relationship.

Austrian school. A school of thought originally identified with the University of Vienna. Views competition as a dynamic process, driven by the acquisition of new information. Tends to be hostile to government intervention.

Average cost. The ratio of total cost to output.

Average fixed cost. The ratio of total fixed cost to output.

Average product of labour. The ratio of total output to the number of workers employed.

Average revenue. The ratio of total revenue to quantity demanded, equivalent to price.

Average variable cost. The ratio of total variable cost to output.

Backward vertical integration. Expansion upstream into an activity at an earlier stage of a production process (further away from the final market). For example, a manufacturer starts producing its own inputs. Also known as **upstream vertical integration**.

Barometric price leadership. One firm announces a price change, which is followed by other firms in the same industry. The leader is not necessarily a dominant firm, and does not necessarily have market power.

Barrier to entry. Any factor which makes the average cost of a would-be entrant higher than that of an incumbent, or which impedes entry in any other way.

Barrier to exit. Any cost incurred by an incumbent wishing to exit from an industry.

Bertrand model. A duopoly model in which each firm sets its own price treating its rival's price as fixed at its current level (zero **conjectural variation**). Each firm sells as much output as it can at its chosen price.

Best value. Has recently replaced **compulsory competitive tendering** as a method for determining the provision of local government services in the UK. Local government departments are expected to demonstrate that provision is efficient.

Bounded rationality. Recognizes that decision making takes place within an environment of incomplete information and uncertainty.

Bundling. The practice of selling several goods together as a single package.

Business unit effects. The component of profitability that derives from a particular division or line of business within a firm.

Buyer concentration. A measure of the number and size distribution of buyers, reflecting the degree of market power on the demand side.

Cartel. A group of firms that acts collectively, often in order to increase their joint profitability by exploiting their (collective) market power.

Chapter I Prohibition. Part of the UK's 1998 Competition Act dealing with restrictive practices. Closely related to Article 81 of the EU's Treaty of Amsterdam.

Chapter II Prohibition. Part of the UK's 1998 Competition Act dealing with abuses of monopoly power. Closely related to Article 82 of the EU's Treaty of Amsterdam.

Chicago school. A school of thought originally identified with the University of Chicago. Tends to view high profitability as a reward for superior efficiency, rather than symptomatic of abuses of market power. Argues government intervention in the form of active competition policy tends to lead to less rather than more competition.

Cluster. A group of interdependent firms that are linked through close vertical or horizontal relationships, located within a well defined geographic area.

Collusion. Firms agree, either tacitly or explicitly, to limit competition through the coordination of price, output or other decisions.

Collusion hypothesis. The view that a positive association between concentration and profitability constitutes evidence of the abuse of market power in an effort to enhance profitability.

Committed incumbent. A firm that signals intent to resist entry by increasing its own sunk cost expenditure.

Complements. Goods with a negative cross-price elasticity of demand: an increase in the price of one good leads to an decrease in the demand for the other good.

Compulsory competitive tendering. In-house providers and private contractors tender for contracts to provide services to local government.

Concentration measures. Measures of the number and size distribution of the firms in an industry. Size is usually measured using data on sales, assets, employees or output.

Concentration ratio. The share of an industry's n largest firms in a measure of total industry size, for some specific value of n.

Conduct regulation. Regulation designed to influence firms' behaviour directly, through measures such as price controls, regulated fees and commissions, controls on advertising, or restrictions on the expansion of distribution networks.

Conglomerate. A firm that produces a number of unrelated products or operates in a number of unrelated markets.

Conglomerate merger. A merger between firms that produce unrelated products or operate in unrelated markets.

Conjectural variation. The assumption one firm makes about its rivals' reactions to its own decisions, often with respect to decisions on price or output.

Constant returns to scale. If the use of all inputs increases by k per cent, output also increases by k per cent. Long-run average cost is constant with respect to changes in output.

Constant-sum game. In game theory, a game in which the sum of the payoffs to all players is always the same, whatever actions are chosen.

Consumer surplus. The difference between the maximum price a consumer would be willing to pay and the market price.

Contestable market. A market with free entry and exit conditions. An outside firm can enter temporarily, and cover its costs when it subsequently exits. Consequently, the behaviour of incumbents is constrained not only by actual competition, but also by potential competition.

Contractual incompleteness. Firms are unable to conclude contracts that specify outcomes under every possible contingency, due to incomplete information.

Convenience good. A good that is relatively cheap and purchased frequently.

Cooperative game. In game theory, a game in which the players cooperate when deciding their actions.

Core competences. Firm-specific skills deriving from specialized knowledge, and the manner in which this knowledge is employed by the firm.

Corporate coherence. Achieved by diversification into closely related activities in which **core competences** can be exploited.

Corporate effects. The component of profitability that derives from membership of a larger corporate group.

Cost plus pricing. The firm calculates or estimates its average variable cost, and sets its price by adding a percentage mark-up to average variable cost. The mark-up includes a contribution towards firm's fixed cost, and a profit margin.

Cournot–Nash equilibrium. A duopoly or oligopoly equilibrium in which all firms make their output decisions based on a zero **conjectural variation** assumption: each firm optimizes assuming its rivals' actions are given or fixed.

Creative destruction. Term coined by Schumpeter to describe the economic impact of technological change. The creative aspect results in new and improved goods and services being brought to market, and cost-saving technologies being used in production. The destructive aspect refers to the displacement of obsolete goods, services and technologies.

Credence good. A good whose quality cannot easily be assessed before or after consumption, because a judgment about quality requires specialized knowledge.

Cross-price elasticity of demand. A measure of the sensitivity of the quantity demanded of Good A to changes in the price of Good B. Measured as the ratio of the proportionate change in quantity demanded of Good A to the proportionate change in price of Good B.

Cross-subsidization. The practice of using revenue or profit earned from one activity to support or subsidize another activity.

Deadweight loss. The loss of social welfare (the sum of **consumer surplus** and **producer surplus)** attributable to the fact that an industry is monopolized, or to some other source of market failure or misallocation of resources.

Decreasing returns to scale. If the use of all inputs increases by k per cent, output increases by less than k per cent. Long-run average cost is increasing with respect to an increase in output. See also **diseconomies of scale**.

Deconglomeration. Cessation of production of some products by a conglomerate, on order to focus more on its core products.

Degrees of collusion. Measures of the strength and effectiveness of collusion.

Descending bid auction. See **Dutch auction**.

Diffusion. The imitation and adoption of new technologies (products or processes) by firms other than the original innovating firm.

Direction of diversification. Describes whether a firm diversifies within the same (broadly defined) industry, or into an unrelated industry.

Diseconomies of scale. Long-run average cost is increasing with respect to an increase in output. See also **decreasing returns to scale**.

Distinctive capabilities. A firm's unique or specialized competences.

Dominant price leadership. The dominant firm acts as leader by setting the market price. Firms on the competitive fringe adopt **price taking behaviour** with respect to the price set by the dominant firm.

Dominant strategy. In game theory, a strategy which always produces the best outcome for one player, no matter what strategies are selected by other players.

Dorfman–Steiner condition. The profit-maximizing advertising-to-sales ratio *equals* the ratio of **advertising elasticity of demand** to **price elasticity of demand**.

Double marginalization. Two stages of the same production process are both under the control of monopoly producers, and each producer adds its own monopoly mark-up to the price. The price of the finished product is higher than it would be if the two producers were vertically integrated.

Downstream vertical integration. See **forward vertical integration**.

Dumping. The practice of charging a lower price in poorer countries than in richer countries for the same product.

Duopoly. A market that is supplied by two firms. A special case of oligopoly.

Dutch auction. An auction in which the price is lowered successively until a level is reached which a bidder is prepared to pay. Also known as a **descending bid auction**.

Economic efficiency. A firm is economically efficient if it has selected the combination of factor inputs that enable it to produce its current output level at the lowest possible cost, given prevailing factor prices.

Economies of scale. Long-run average cost is decreasing with respect to an increase in output. See also **increasing returns to scale**.

Economies of scale entry barrier. An incumbent incurs a lower long-run average cost than an entrant by virtue of producing at a larger scale, and benefiting from economies of scale.

Economies of scope. Long-run average cost when two or more goods are produced together is lower than long-run average cost when the goods are produced separately.

Edgeworth model. A duopoly model of price competition with a production capacity constraint. The model predicts there is no stable equilibrium.

Efficiency hypothesis. The view that a positive association between concentration and profitability derives from a tendency for the most efficient firms to dominate their own industries.

Elasticity. A measure of the responsiveness of one economic variable to a small change in another variable. See **price elasticity of demand, price elasticity of supply, cross price elasticity of demand, advertising elasticity of demand**.

Engineering cost approach. Method for estimating a production function or cost function based on hypothetical rather than actual data. Expert (engineering) estimates are used to quantify relationships between inputs and outputs.

English auction. An auction in which the price is raised successively until a level is reached which only one bidder is willing to pay. Also known as an **ascending bid auction**.

Entropy coefficient. Concentration measure based on a weighted sum of market shares: the weights are the natural logarithms of the reciprocals of market shares.

Experience good. A good whose qualities can only be ascertained when it is consumed, and not by inspection prior to purchase and consumption.

Experimental economics. A branch of economics which uses laboratory experiments to test economic theories.

Explicit collusion. Collusion that is organized through a formal, explicit contract or other agreement between the colluding parties.

First-degree price discrimination. Price depends on the number of units purchased and on the identity of the buyer. Also known as **perfect price discrimination**.

First-mover advantage. An advantage that rewards a firm for being the first to enter a market, or the first to take some other strategic action.

First price sealed bid auction. An auction in which each bidder independently submits a single bid, without seeing the bids submitted by other bidders. The highest bidder secures the item, and pays a price equivalent to his or her winning bid.

Five forces model. A model used by Porter (1980) to describe competition. The five forces are: the extent and intensity of direct competition; the threat of entrants; the threat of substitute products and services; the power of buyers; and the power of suppliers.

Fixed cost. Cost that does not vary with the quantity of output produced.

Foreclosure. The practice of refusing to supply downstream firms or to purchase from upstream firms.

Forms of collusion. Organizational structures, as well as custom and practice, that characterize collusive agreements.

Forward vertical integration. Expansion downstream into an activity at a later stage of a production process (closer to the final market). For example, a manufacturer starts selling its own products direct to consumers. Also known as **downstream vertical integration**.

Franchise agreement. The allocation of exclusive rights to supply a particular good or service. The franchisee is protected from competition for the duration of the franchise.

Game theory. A theory of decision making under conditions of uncertainty and interdependence. Components of a game include players, strategies, actions, payoffs, outcomes and an equilibrium.

Geographic concentration. Measures whether a large share of an industry's total output is produced in a small number of countries or regions, or whether the industry is widely dispersed geographically.

Geographic market definition. Involves determining whether an increase in the price of a product in one geographic area significantly affects either demand or supply, and therefore price, in another area. If so, both areas are in the same geographic market.

Geographic entry barrier. Any entry barrier affecting foreign firms attempting to enter a domestic market. Examples include tariffs, quotas, frontier controls, national standards, regulations and exchange controls.

Gibrat's Law. Describes the implications for industry concentration if the growth rate of each firm is random, or more specifically, unrelated to the current size of the firm. If firm sizes are subject to random growth, the firm size distribution becomes increasingly skewed and concentration increases over time. Also known as the **Law of Proportionate Effect**.

Gini coefficient. A measure of inequality based on the **Lorenz curve**, which can be applied to data on firm sizes or market shares.

Governance. Describes the manner in which an organization manages its contractual relationships between shareholders, managers, employees and other relevant parties.

Hannah and Kay index. Generalization of the **Herfindhal–Hirschman index**, based on the sum of market shares raised to some exponent, for all member firms of an industry.

Herfindhal–Hirschman index. Concentration measure based on the sum of the squared market shares of all member firms of an industry.

Hit-and-run entry. A situation in which an entrant has sufficient time to sell its product profitably and withdraw before the incumbent has time to react.

Horizontal agreement. An agreement between firms in the same industry, which may result in reduced competition. Subjects of such agreements may include common pricing policies, production quotas or information sharing.

Horizontal product differentiation. Products or brands are of the same or similar overall quality, but offer different combinations of characteristics, and may be valued differently by different consumers.

Horizontal merger. A merger between two firms that produce the same or similar products.

Imperfect competition. Market structures that fall between the polar cases of perfect competition and monopoly. Includes **monopolistic competition** and **oligopoly**.

Incomplete contracts. A contract for which the parties cannot identify in advance every possible contingency which might affect their contractual relationship. Most contracts are incomplete contracts.

Increasing returns to scale. If the use of all inputs increases by k per cent, output increases by more than k per cent. Long-run average cost is decreasing with respect to an increase in output. See also **economies of scale**.

Independent action. Competing firms take decisions without consulting one another, or colluding in any other way.

Independent private values model. In an auction, each bidder independently forms an opinion of the value of the item to himself or herself. These private valuations differ between bidders, and there is no single, intrinsic valuation that all bidders can agree on.

Industrial district. A geographic area containing a number of firms producing similar products, including firms operating at different stages of a production process.

Industry. A group of firms producing a similar product, using similar technology, and perhaps obtaining factors of production from the same factor markets.

Industry concentration. Measure of importance of the largest firms in an industry. See also **seller concentration**.

Industry effects. The component of profitability that derives from involvement in a particular industry.

Industry life cycle. Describes the long-run evolution of an industry and its constituent firms through the introduction, growth, maturity and decline phases of the life cycle.

Informative advertising. Advertizing that provides consumers with factual information about the existence, attributes or price of a product, service or brand.

Innovation. Bringing a new idea or invention to the stage of commercial application, through the applied research, development and commercial production stages.

Interdependence. A situation in which the outcome for each firm depends not only on its own actions, but also on the actions of its rivals. A defining characteristic of the market structure of **oligopoly**.

Internal capital market. An organization's procedures for allocating investment funds internally, between departments or divisions that are competing for access to such funds.

Internal rate of return. In investment appraisal, the discount rate at which the net present value of all cash flows associated with the project under consideration *equals* zero.

Intertemporal price discrimination. Price depends on the point in time when a good is sold, but production costs do not depend on the point in time when the good is produced and sold.

Invention. The creation of an idea and its initial implementation, through basic research.

Isocost line. All combinations of two factor inputs which produce an identical total cost.

Isoprofit curve. All combinations of quantities produced or prices charged by two firms which produce an identical profit for one of the firms.

Isoquant. All combinations of two factor inputs which produce an identical level of output.

Joint profit maximization. Two or more firms set their combined output level and price as if they were a single monopolist. The firms share the resulting monopoly profit among themselves.

Joint venture. Two or more independent firms cooperate over a specific project.

Kinked demand curve. An **oligopoly** model that explains price rigidity, arguing that a firm in a situation of **interdependence** may be reluctant either to raise or lower its price, because in both cases it expects its rivals to react in a way that reduces its own profit.

Law of diminishing returns. As the use of a variable factor input increases progressively while the use of other factor inputs is fixed, beyond some point successive increases in output become smaller.

Law of Proportionate Effect. See **Gibrat's Law**.

Legal entry barrier. Any entry barrier created by government, for example through franchised state-sponsored monopolies, patents, and registration, certification or licensing requirements.

Lerner index. Price *minus* marginal cost expressed as a proportion of price. The extent to which price exceeds marginal cost can be interpreted as a measure of market power.

Limit pricing. A pricing strategy by an incumbent firm intended to prevent entry. The incumbent sacrifices some profit by setting a price sufficiently low to make it impossible for an entrant to operate profitably.

Location model. A model of product differentiation in which consumers' tastes or preferences are expressed in terms of the characteristics embodied in goods or services. Also known as a **spatial model**.

Long run. A time period of sufficient duration that the quantities of all factor inputs used in production can be varied.

Lorenz curve. When plotted using firm size or market share data, shows the cumulative sizes or market shares of all firms up to firm n, for n = 1 . . . N (where N is the total number of firms), when the firms are numbered in descending size or market share order.

Marginal cost. The additional cost of producing one extra unit of output.

Marginal product of labour. The additional output obtained by employing one extra unit of labour.

Marginal revenue. The additional revenue obtained by selling one extra unit of output.

Mark-up test. A test suggested by Bresnahan (1982, 1989) and Lau (1982), which involves estimating a structural model incorporating demand and cost equations, and drawing inferences about the nature of competition by observing each firm's **conjectural variation** under an assumption of profit maximization.

Market concentration. See **seller concentration** and **industry concentration**.

Market demand function. The relationship between market price and the number of units of a product or service consumers wish to buy at that price.

Market equilibrium. At the equilibrium or market-clearing price, quantity demanded *equals* quantity supplied.

Market power. A firm's ability to charge a price higher than marginal cost, because the market structure is one of imperfect competition or monopoly.

Merger policy. A branch of competition policy dealing with mergers. Examines whether a merger should be permitted, or prevented on the grounds that it may lead to abuses of market power.

Minimum efficient scale. The output level beyond which the firm can achieve no further saving in long-run average cost by means of further expansion of production.

Minimum profit constraint. In managerial theories of the firm, a minimum profit level demanded by shareholders, which limits managers' discretion to pursue objectives such as sales revenue, growth or managerial utility.

Mixed strategy. In game theory, a player adopts a mixed strategy by choosing his actions randomly, using fixed probabilities.

Monopolistic competition. A market structure with a large number of firms producing similar but not identical products, and with free entry. Falls between the polar cases of perfect competition and monopoly.

Monopoly. A market structure with a single firm, producing a unique product and protected from competition by insurmountable entry barriers.

Monopoly policy. A branch of competition policy dealing with abuses of market power when a single firm or group or firms has a large market share.

Moral hazard. Arises when an agent has the opportunity to act in his own private interests but against the principal's interests, in contravention of the terms of the contract between the two parties. It is difficult for the principal to detect and punish opportunistic behaviour on the part of the agent.

Multiple-period game. In game theory, a game that is repeated a number of times. Also known as a **repeated game**.

Nash equilibrium. In game theory, all players maximize their own actual or expected payoffs, subject to a zero **conjectural variation** constraint: each player takes the other players' current strategies as given. No player can improve his actual or expected payoff given the strategies currently chosen by the other players. See also **Cournot–Nash equilibrium**.

Natural monopoly. An industry in which long-run average cost is decreasing in output over all output levels the market is capable of absorbing. The definition depends on both the cost structure and the position of the **market demand function**.

Natural product differentiation. The distinguishing characteristics of products or services derive from their inherent or natural attributes.

Near-neighbour brands. Brands with similar characteristics.

Network. A group of firms that is linked through regular contact or other types of informal relationship.

New empirical industrial organization. An approach which attempts to draw inferences about market structure and competitive conditions from direct observation of conduct at firm level.

New industrial organization. Theories of industrial organization which focus primarily on strategy and conduct at firm level, rather than on market or industry structure.

Non-constant sum game. In game theory, the sum of the gains and losses of all players depends on the actions chosen by the players.

Non-linear pricing. See **quantity-dependent pricing**.

Normal profit. The minimum return a firm's owner must earn to prevent the owner from closing the firm down, equivalent to the **opportunity cost** of running the firm.

Numbers equivalent. An inverse measure of concentration, which compares the structure of an observed N-firm industry to a hypothetical industry comprising N equal-sized firms.

Oligopoly. A market structure with a small number of firms, whose products may be identical or differentiated, and where there are barriers to entry. The firms recognize their **interdependence**.

Opportunity cost. The cost of allocating scarce resources to some economic activity, measured as the return that could be earned by allocating the same resources to the next best available alternative activity.

Organizational slack. In the behavioural theory of the firm, resources held by the organization which permit **side payments** in excess of the minimum required to prevent individuals or groups withdrawing from the organization.

Passive incumbent. A firm that does not signal intent to resist entry.

Patent. The award of a patent to the inventor of a new product, process, substance or design confers a property right over the knowledge that is embodied in the invention.

Payoff. In game theory, a player's return, which is dependent on the strategies and actions chosen by all players.

Peak load pricing. Demand varies over time for a good which cannot be stored, but production capacity does not vary over time. The peak-period price charged by the producer exceeds the off-peak period price.

Pecuniary economies of scale. Economies of scale arising when large firms find it easier or cheaper than small firms to obtain or purchase inputs or raise finance.

Perfect competition. A market structure with a large number of firms producing identical products, and with free entry.

Perfect price discrimination. See **first-degree price discrimination**.

Persistence of profit. The extent to which profits or losses above or below average levels tend to be sustained, either in the short run or in the long run.

Persuasive advertising. Advertizing that aims to change consumers' perceptions of a product, service or brand with a view to stimulating sales. May include claims that are not objectively verifiable.

Porter's Diamond Model. A model of the determinants and dynamics of competitive advantage, based on analysis of competitive rivalry, factor and demand conditions, and the existence of related and supporting industries.

Predatory competition. A dominant firm engages in certain aggressive forms of price or non-price competition, aiming to force a weaker competitor to withdraw from the market.

Predatory pricing. A dominant firm adopts price-cutting as an instrument of **predatory competition**.

Price cap regulation. Regulation in the form of a specific limit on the price a firm is permitted to charge.

Price–cost margin. The ratio of profit to sales revenue, or price *minus* average cost to price.

Price elasticity of demand. A measure of the sensitivity of quantity demanded to changes in price. Measured as the ratio of the proportionate change in quantity demanded to the proportionate change in price.

Price elasticity of supply. A measure of the sensitivity of quantity supplied to changes in price. Measured as the ratio of the proportionate change in quantity supplied to the proportionate change in price.

Price leadership. See **barometric price leadership** and **dominant price leadership**.

Price rigidity. A tendency for oligopolists to avoid frequent changes of price, perhaps preferring instead non-price forms of competition.

Price taking behaviour. Each firm's market share is sufficiently small that the firm believes its output decision has no bearing on the market price. Therefore the firm treats the market price as being beyond its control.

Prisoner's dilemma. In game theory, refers to a case in which players select their dominant strategies and achieve an equilibrium in which they are worse off than they would be if they could all agree to select an alternative (non-dominant) strategy.

Privatization. The sale and transfer of assets from the public sector to the private sector.

Process innovation. The commercial application of a new piece of cost-saving technology.

Producer surplus. The difference between the market price and the minimum price a producer would be willing to accept.

Product differentiation. The practice of making close substitutes appear different, so that customers no longer regard them as similar or identical.

Product differentiation entry barrier. Arises when a potential entrant incurs advertising or other marketing costs in order to achieve a viable market share, because consumers are loyal to the established brands of incumbents. Both **natural** and **strategic product differentiation** may give rise to entry barriers.

Product innovation. Production of a new product on a commercial basis.

Product market definition. Includes all products that are close substitutes for one another, both in consumption and in production.

Production function. A technological relationship between the quantities of inputs and the level of output.

Productive efficiency. A firm is efficient in production if it has achieved both **technical efficiency** and **economic efficiency**.

Pure common value model. In auction theory, there is a single, intrinsic value of the item being sold, that is the same for all bidders.

Pure strategy. In game theory, a strategy whereby one player always chooses a certain action, regardless of the actions chosen by other players.

Quantity-dependent pricing. The price per unit depends on the number of units purchased. Also known as **non-linear pricing**.

Quantity forcing. A seller with market power forces buyers to purchase more units of a good than they would wish if they had the choice.

Quasi rent. Rent arising from the creation of an asset that is specific to some particular relationship, but with little or no value outside that relationship.

Rate of return regulation. Regulation in the form of a limit on the rate of return on capital a firm is permitted to earn. Price must be set so that the target rate of return is achieved.

Reaction function. Shows the profit-maximizing response of one firm to a price or output decision taken by a rival firm, treating the rival's decision as fixed.

Real economies of scale. Economies of scale arising from technological relationships between inputs and output embodied in a firm's long-run production function.

Reciprocity. An agreement whereby firm A purchases inputs from firm B, on condition that firm B also purchases inputs from firm A.

Regional concentration. See **geographic concentration**.

Regulatory capture. A tendency for lobbying by a regulated firm to succeed in influencing the regulator in the regulated firm's favour.

Repeated game. See **multiple-period game**.

Representative consumer model. A model of product differentiation in which consumers' tastes or preferences are expressed in terms of goods or services (rather than characteristics), and firms compete to attract buyers by differentiating the goods or services they offer.

Resale price maintenance. A practice whereby an upstream firm sets a minimum (or possibly a maximum) price to be charged in a downstream (usually retail) market.

Reserve price. In auction theory, a minimum bid that must be registered for the sale of the item to proceed.

Residual rights. Rights to whatever resources are left after a firm's contractual obligations have been satisfied and all **specific rights** to the firm's resources have been assigned.

Restrictive practices policy. A branch of competition policy dealing with single firms or groups or firms that engage in practices that may be detrimental to consumer welfare, such as price fixing, output quotas, predatory pricing and vertical restraints.

Returns to scale. See **increasing returns to scale** and **decreasing returns to scale**.

Revenue equivalence theorem. In auction theory, in the case where bidders form independent private valuations of the item that is for sale, all four basic auction types (English, Dutch, first price sealed bid and second price sealed bid) yield the same expected proceeds to the seller.

Revenue test. A test proposed by Rosse and Panzar (1977), which examines whether firm conduct is in accordance with the models of perfect competition, imperfect competition or monopoly, based on observation of the impact of variations in factor prices on profit-maximizing firm-level revenues.

Rule of reason. The principle that competition policy should be concerned with the practical consequences for competition and welfare of specific abuses of market power or other restrictive practices, rather than with the structural characteristics of markets which might, in theory, create opportunities for anticompetitive practice.

Sample selection bias. Bias arising in statistical analysis if the data has been chosen non-randomly. For example, if five years' data is required for each firm, and only those firms that traded continuously for five years are included, a non-random sample of survivors is obtained, excluding all firms that entered and exited during the five-year period. This specific form of sample selection bias is known as **survivorship bias**.

Satisficing. In the behavioural theory of the firm, a firm aims for a satisfactory profit but does not necessarily maximize profit.

Schumpeterian hypothesis. Describes the view that a fast pace of innovation is more likely to be associated with monopoly than with competition.

Search good. A good whose qualities can be ascertained by inspection prior to purchase and consumption.

Second-degree price discrimination. The price per unit of output depends on the number of units purchased, but not on the identity of the buyer. All buyers who purchase a given number of units pay the same price per unit.

Second price sealed bid auction. An auction in which each bidder independently and privately submits a single bid. The highest bidder secures the item, but pays a price equal to the second-highest submitted bid. Also known as a **Vickrey auction**.

Seller concentration. A measure of the number and size distribution of sellers, reflecting the degree of market power on the supply side. May refer either to **aggregate concentration** (for the economy as a whole) or to **industry concentration** (for one particular industry).

Semi-collusion. Firms collude over certain areas of activity (for example, pricing or production), but compete in other areas in which it may be more difficult to specify, conclude or enforce an agreement (for example, research and development).

Sequential game. In game theory, players choose their actions sequentially (in turn). A player who moves later knows which actions were chosen by players who moved earlier.

Shopping good. A good that is expensive and is purchased infrequently.

Short run. A time period during which only one factor input used in production can be varied, while other factor inputs are fixed.

Side payment. In the behavioural theory of the firm, a payment in excess of the minimum required to prevent an individual or group from withdrawing from the organization.

Simultaneous game. In game theory, all players choose their actions simultaneously. When choosing, no player knows the actions chosen by other players.

Spatial model. See **location model**.

Specialization. Refers to the extent to which a country's production is composed mainly of a small number of products or services, or is more widely dispersed.

Specific rights. Rights that are specified explicitly in the terms of a contract.

Stackelberg equilibrium. A solution to a **duopoly** or an **oligopoly** model, in which one firm anticipates its rivals' tendencies to act in accordance with a zero **conjectural variation** assumption, and exploits this awareness to increase its own profit.

State-sponsored collusion. Collusion that is encouraged or dictated by government. The justification might be to promote rationalization, or to assure a steady supply.

Statistical cost approach. An industry production function or cost function is estimated using data on the inputs, input prices and outputs of the industry's member firms. The results can be interpreted to obtain an estimate of the minimum efficient scale of production.

Strategic group. A group of firms from the same industry whose conduct is similar, and which tend to view other firms from the same group as their main competitors.

Strategic product differentiation. The distinguishing characteristics of products are consciously created by suppliers, for example through advertising or other types of marketing campaign.

Strategy. In game theory, a set of rules defining which action a player should choose under each possible set of circumstances that might exist at any stage in the game.

Structural regulation. Regulation that seeks to influence market structure. Measures include the functional separation of firms into complementary activities, restrictions on entry, and restrictions on the operation of foreign firms.

Structure–conduct–performance paradigm. A methodological approach for research in industrial organization, in which the structural characteristics of industries are assumed to influence or dictate the conduct and performance of the industry's member firms. More sophisticated models allow for feedback effects, whereby conduct and performance variables help shape the industry's future structure.

Substitutes. Goods with a positive cross price elasticity of demand: an increase in the price of one good leads to an increase in demand for the other good.

Sunk cost. Expenditure on items such as advertising and research and development that is non-recoverable in the event that the firm exits from the industry.

Survivor approach. The most efficient scale of production is inferred from data on the growth and survival of firms in different size bands over time.

Survivorship bias. See **sample selection bias**.

Switching cost. Cost associated with switching from one supplier to another.

Tacit collusion. Collusion that is not organized through a formal, explicit contract or other specific agreement between the colluding parties.

Tangency solution. Long-run equilibrium under **monopolistic competition**, at which each firm's average revenue function is tangential to its average cost function. Accordingly, each firm earns only a normal profit.

Technical efficiency. A firm is technically efficient if it is producing the maximum quantity of output that is technologically feasible, given the quantities of the factor inputs it employs. A technically efficient firm operates on (and not within) its own production function. Also known as **x-efficiency**.

Third-degree price discrimination. Price depends on the identity of the buyer, but not on the number of units purchased. Any buyer is offered as many or as few units as he or she wishes at a constant price.

Tie-in sale. See **tying**.

Tit-for-tat. In game theory, a strategy whereby one player punishes another for non-cooperation in a previous period.

Tobin's q. The ratio of a firm's stock market value to the replacement cost of its capital.

Total cost. Variable cost *plus* fixed cost.

Total revenue. Price *times* quantity sold.

Trade association. An organization that represents the interests of the member firms of an industry. It usually differs from a cartel in that it has no monopolistic intent.

Transaction costs. Costs incurred when using the market to allocate resources, arising from the acquisition of information or the negotiation, monitoring and enforcement of contracts.

Transfer pricing. The pricing of intermediate products traded internally between the divisions of a single firm.

Two-part tariff. A price structure requiring the payment of a fixed fee (mandatory if any purchases are to be made) and an additional uniform price for each unit purchased.

Tying. A firm with market power in the market for Good X requires buyers also to purchase Good Y in order to obtain Good X. Also known as a **tie-in sale**.

Type 1 industry. An industry in which growth in the size of the market leads to fragmentation of industry structure and deconcentration (Sutton, 1991). The level of sunk cost investment expenditure is determined exogenously, by product characteristics and technological conditions.

Type 2 industry. An industry in which growth in the size of the market leads to growth in the size of the largest firms, and no tendency for fragmentation of industry structure or deconcentration (Sutton, 1991). The level of sunk cost investment expenditure is determined endogenously, by incumbent firms' decisions on advertizing and research and development.

Upstream vertical integration. See **backward vertical integration**.

Value chain. A technique devised to disaggregate a firm into its strategically relevant activities, in order to appraise each activity's contribution to the firm's performance.

Variable cost. The component of total cost that varies with output.

Variance decomposition analysis. A statistical technique involving the decomposition of the variation in a firm's profitability into components deriving from the industries in which the firm operates, and from each division or business unit within the firm.

Vertical agreement. Agreements between firms operating at successive stages of a production process, such as exclusive dealing contracts and resale price maintenance.

Vertical product differentiation. One product, service or brand differs from another in terms of overall quality. If the prices were the same, all consumers would choose the superior product.

Vertical integration. Ownership or control over two or more stages of a production process.

Vertical restraint. Conditions or restrictions on trade between firms that are linked vertically.

Vickrey auction. See **second price sealed bid auction**. Due to Vickrey (1961).

Winner's curse. A tendency for the winning bid to exceed the intrinsic value of the item being auctioned, common in sealed bid auctions.

Workable competition. An approach to competition policy which seeks to adjust aspects of structure and conduct in order to bring about a favourable performance outcome.

X-efficiency. See **technical efficiency**.

Zero-sum game. A constant sum game in which the sum of the gains and losses of all players is always zero.

References

Aaronovitch, S. and Sawyer, M.C. (1975) Mergers, growth and concentration, *Oxford Economic Papers*, 27, 136–55.

Abernethy, A. and Franke, G.R. (1996) The information content of advertising: a meta-analysis, *Journal of Advertising*, 25, 1–17.

Acemoglu, D., Aghion, P., Griffiths, R. and Zilibotti, F. (2003) Vertical integration and technology, theory and evidence, *Working paper*, www.iies.su.se/~zilibott/aagz20031117.pdf (accessed 7 May 2004).

Acs, Z.J. and Audretsch, D.B. (1990) *Innovation and Small Firms*. Cambridge: Cambridge University Press.

Adams, W.J. and Yellen, J. (1976) Commodity bundling and the burden of monopoly, *Quarterly Journal of Economics*, 90, 475–98.

Adelman, M.A. (1949) Integration and antitrust policy, *Harvard Law Review*, 63, 27–77.

Adelman, M.A. (1955) Concept and statistical measurement of vertical integration, in Stigler, G.J. (ed.), *Business Concentration and Price Policy*. Princeton, NJ: Princeton University Press.

Adelman, M.A. (1959) *A & P: A Study in Price–Cost Behaviour and Public Policy*. Cambridge, MA: Harvard University Press.

Adner, R. and Helfat, C.E. (2003) Corporate effects and dynamic managerial capabilities, *Strategic Management Journal*, 24, 1011–25.

Advertising Association (2003) *Advertising Statistics Yearbook 2003*. Oxford: NTC Publications.

Aharonson, B.S., Baum, J.A.C. and Feldman, M.P. (2004) Industrial clustering and the returns to inventive activity: Canadian biotechnology firms, 1991–2000, DRUID Working Paper No. 03-16, www.druid.dk/wp/pdf_files/04-03.pdf (accessed 15 May 2004).

Aiginger, K. (1999) Do industrial structures converge? A survey of empirical literature on specialization and concentration of industries, WIFO, mimeograph. Vienna: WIFO.

Aiginger, K. and Davies, S.W. (2000) Industrial specialization and geographic concentration: two sides of the same coin? Not for the European Union. Department of Economics Working Paper 23/2000, University of Linz.

Aitchison, J. and Brown, J.A.C. (1966) *The Lognormal Distribution*. Cambridge: Cambridge University Press.

Akerlof, G.A. (1970) The market for lemons: quality uncertainty and the market mechanisms, *Quarterly Journal of Economics*, 39, 489–500.

Albæk, S., Møllgaard, P. and Overgaard, P.B. (1997) Government-assisted oligopoly coordination? A concrete case, *Journal of Industrial Economics*, 45, 429–43.

Albin, S. (1992) Bureau shaping and contracting out: the case of Australian Local Government, *Public Policy Program Discussion Paper*, No. 29. Canberra: Australian National University.

Albion, M.S. and Farris, P. (1981) *The Advertising Controversy*. Boston, MA: Auburn House.

Alchian, A.A. (1963) Reliability and progress curves in airframe production, *Econometrica*, 31, 679–93.

Alchian, A.A. (1965) The basis of some recent advances in the theory of management of the firm, *Journal of Industrial Economics*, 14, 30–41.

Alchian, A. and Demsetz, H. (1972) Production, information costs, and economic organisation, *American Economic Review*, 62, 777–95.

Alexander, D.L., Flynn, J. and Linkins, L. (1995) Innovation, and global market share in the pharmaceutical industry, *Review of Industrial Organisation*, 10, 197–207.

Altunbas, Y. and Molyneux, P. (1993) Scale and scope economies in European banking, *Research Papers in Banking and Finance*, RP 93/18. Bangor: University College of North Wales.

Amato, L. and Wilder, R.P. (1990) Firm and industry effects in industrial economics, *Southern Economic Journal*, 57, 93–105.

Amel, D. and Froeb, L. (1991) Do firms differ much? *Journal of Industrial Economics*, 39, 323–9.

Amihud, Y. and Lev, B. (1981) Risk reduction as a managerial motive for conglomerate mergers, *Bell Journal of Economics*, 12, 605–17.

Amiti, M. (1997) Specialisation patterns in Europe, *Centre for Economic Policy Research, Discussion Paper*, No. 363.

Amiti, M. (1998) New trade theories and industrial location in the EU: A survey of the evidence, *Oxford Review of Economic Policy*, 14, 45–53.

Andrews, P.W.S. (1951) Industrial analysis in economics, in Wilson, T. and Andrews, P.W.S. (eds) *Oxford Studies in the Price Mechanism*. Oxford: Clarendon Press.

Angelini, P. and Cetorelli, N. (2000) Bank competition and regulatory reform: the case of the Italian banking industry, Federal Reserve Bank of Chicago, Working Paper, 99–32.

Archibald, G.C. and Rosenbluth, G. (1975) The new theory of consumer demand and monopolistic competition, *Quarterly Journal of Economics*, 89, 569–90.

Archibald, R.B., Haulman, C.A. and Moody, C.E. (1983) Quality, price, advertising and published quality ratings, *Journal of Consumer Research*, 9, 347–56.

Armentano, D.T. (1975) Price fixing in theory and practice, in Brozen, Y. (ed.), *The Competitive Economy*. Morristown, NJ: General Learning Press.

Armstrong, M. (1999) Price discrimination by a many-product firm, *Review of Economic Studies*, 66, 151–68.

Armstrong, M., Cowan, S. and Vickers, J. (1994) *Regulatory Reform: Economic Analysis and British Experience*. Oxford: Oxford University Press.

Aron, D.J. (1993) Diversification as a strategic preemptive weapon, *Journal of Economics and Management*, 2, 41–70.

Arrow, K.J. (1962) Economic welfare and the allocation of resources for invention, in *The Rate and Direction of Inventive Activity*, National Bureau of Economic Research Conference Report, Princeton, NJ: Princeton University Press, 609–25.

Arrow, K.J. (1975) Vertical integration and communication, *Rand Journal of Economics*, 6, 173–83.

Arterburn, A. and Woodbury, J. (1981) Advertising, price competition and market structure, *Southern Economic Journal*, 47, 763–75.

Asch, P. (1969) Collusive oligopoly: an antitrust quandary, *Antitrust Law and Economic Review*, 2, 53–68.

Asch, P. and Seneca, J. (1975) Characteristics of collusive firms, *Journal of Industrial Economics*, 23, 223–37.

Asch, P. and Seneca, J. (1976) Is collusion profitable? *Review of Economics and Statistics*, 58, 1–10.

Asch, P. and Seneca, R. (1985) *Government and the Market Place*. New York: Dryden.

Ascher, K. (1987) *The Politics of Privatisation: Contracting Out Public Services*. London: Macmillan.

Audretsch, D.B., Baumol, W.J. and Burke, A. (2001) Competition policy in a dynamic economy, *International Journal of Industrial Organization*, 19, 613–34.

Audretsch, D.B., Klomp, L. and Thurik, A.R. (2003) Gibrat's Law: are the services different, *Erasmus Research Institute of Management (ERIM) Report Series Research in Management*, January 2003.

Aust, P. (1997) An institutional analysis of vertical co-ordination versus vertical integration: the case of the US broiler industry, Department of Agricultural Economics, Michigan State University Staff Paper 97–124.

Averch, H. and Johnson, L.L. (1962) Behaviour of the firm under regulatory constraint, *American Economic Review*, 52, 1052–69.

Axelrod, R. (1984) *The Evolution of Cooperation*. New York: Basic Books.

Ayres, I. (1987) How cartels punish: a structural theory of self-enforcing collusion, *Columbia Law Review*, 87, 295.

Baake, P., Kamecke, U. and Norman, H. (2004) Vertical foreclosure versus downstream competition with capital precommitment, *International Journal of Industrial Organisation*, 22, 185–92.

Bagwell, K. (2005) The economics of advertising, in Armstrong, M. and Parter, R. (eds) *Handbook of Industrial Organization*, vol. 3. Amsterdam: Elsevier.

Bagwell, K. and Staiger, R.W. (1997) Collusion over the business cycle, *Rand Journal of Economics*, 28, 82–106.

Bailey, D. and Boyle, S.E. (1971) The optimal measure of concentration, *Journal of the American Statistical Association*, 66, 702–6.

Bain, J.S. (1948) Output quotas in imperfect cartels, *Quarterly Journal of Economics*, 62, 617–22.

Bain, J.S. (1951) Relation of profit rate to industry concentration: American manufacturing, 1936–1940, *Quarterly Journal of Economics*, 65, 293–324.

Bain, J.S. (1956) *Barriers to New Competition*. Cambridge, MA: Harvard University Press.

Bain, J.S. (1959) *Industrial Organisation*. New York: John Wiley.

Bain, J.S. (1960) Price leaders, barometers, and kinks, *Journal of Business of the University of Chicago*, 33, 193–203.

Bajari, P. and Hortacsu, A. (2004) Economic insights from internet auctions, *Journal of Economic Literature*, 42, 457–86.

Baldwin, J.R. and Gorecki, P.K. (1987) Plant creation versus plant acquisition: the entry process in Canadian manufacturing, *International Journal of Industrial Organisation*, 5, 27–41.

Baldwin, R. and Cave, M. (1998) *Understanding Regulation*. Oxford: Oxford University Press.

Ball, A., Broadbent, J. and Moore, C. (2002) Best value and the control of local government: challenges and contradictions, *Public Money and Management*, 22, 9–16.

Banerjee, S. and Lin, P. (2003) Downstream R&D, raising rivals' costs, and input price contracts, *International Journal of Industrial Organisation*, 21, 79–96.

Baptista, R. (2000) Do innovations diffuse faster within geographical clusters? *International Journal of Industrial Organization*, 18, 515–35.

Barback, R.H. (1964) *The Pricing of Manufactures*. London: Macmillan.

Barney, J.B. (1991) Firm resources and sustained competitive advantage, *Journal of Management*, 17, 99–120.

Barney, J.B. and Hoskisson, R.E. (1990) Strategic groups: untested assertions and research proposals, *Managerial and Decision Making Economics*, 11, 187–98.

Bartelsman, E., Scarpetta, S. and Schivardi, F. (2003) Comparative analysis of firm demographics and survival: micro level evidence for OECD countries, *Economics Department Working Paper*, No. 348. OECD: Paris.

Bartlett, F.C. (1932) *Remembering*. New York: Cambridge University Press.

Battisti, G. and Stoneman, P. (2003) Inter- and intra-firm effects on the diffusion of new process technology, *Research Policy*, 32, 1641–55.

Battisti, G. and Stoneman, P. (2005) The intra-firm diffusion of new process techniques, *International Journal of Industrial Organization*, 23, forthcoming.

Baumol, W. (1959) *Business Behaviour, Value and Growth*. New York: Harcourt Brace Jovanovich.

Baumol, W.J. (1962) On the theory of the expansion of the firm, *American Economic Review*, 52, 1078–87.

Baumol, W.J. (1982) Contestable markets: an uprising in the theory of industry structure, *American Economic Review*, 72, 1–15.

Baumol, W.J. (2001) When is inter-firm coordination beneficial? The case of innovation, *International Journal of Industrial Organization*, 19, 727–37.

Baumol, W.J., Panzer, J. and Willig, R.D. (1982) *Contestable Markets and the Theory of Industry Structure*. New York: Harcourt Brace Jovanovich.

Bazerman, M.H., and Samuelson, W.F. (1983) I won the auction, but I don't want the prize, *Journal of Conflict Resolution*, 27, 618–34.

Bearne, A. (1996) The economics of advertising: a re-appraisal, *Economic Issues*, 1, 23–38.

Beath, J. and Katsoulacos, Y. (1991) *The Economic Theory of Product Differentiation*. Cambridge: Cambridge University Press.

Beath, J., Katsoulacos, Y. and Ulph, D. (1994) Innovation, in Cable, J. (ed.) *Current Issues in Industrial Economics*, ch. 8. London: Macmillan.

Beaudry, C. and Breschi, S. (2003) Are firms in clusters really more innovative? *Economics of Innovation and New Technology*, 12, 325–42.

Becattini, G., Bellandi, M., Dei Ottati, G. and Sforzi, F. (2003) *From Industrial Districts to Local Development*. Cheltenham: Edward Elgar.

Becker, G. (1983) A theory of competition among pressure groups for political influence, *Quarterly Journal of Economics*, 98, 371–400.

Becker, G. and Murphy, K.M. (1993) A simple theory of advertising as a good or bad, *Quarterly Journal of Economics*, 108, 941–64.

Beder, S. (1998) Is planned obsolescence socially responsible? *Engineers Australia*, November, 52.

Beesley, M.E. (ed.) (1997) *Privatization, Regulation and De-regulation*, 2nd edn. London: Routledge.

Beesley, M.E. and Littlechild, S.C. (1997) The regulation of privatised monopolies in the United Kingdom, in Beesley, M.E. (ed.) *Privatisation, Regulation and Deregulation*, 2nd edn. London: Routledge.

Beise, M. (2004) Lead markets: country-specific drivers of the global diffusion of innovations, *Research Policy*, 33, 997–1018.

Bell, G.G. (2005) Clusters, networks and firm innovativeness, *Strategic Management Journal*, 26, 287–95.

Benham, L. (1972) The effect of advertising on the price of eyeglasses, *Journal of Law and Economics*, 15, 337–52.

Benton, W. (1943) *Cartels and Peace*. University of Chicago Round Table, No. 277. Chicago: University of Chicago Press.

Benz, G. and Wolkomir, S. (1964) A decision-making framework within an oligopolistic group structure, *American Journal of Economics and Sociology*, 24, 291–9.

Berger, A.N. (1995) The profit–structure relationship in banking: tests of market power and efficient structure hypotheses, *Journal of Money, Credit and Banking*, 27, 404–31.

Berger, A.N. and Hannan, T.H. (1998) The efficiency cost of market power in the banking industry: a test of the quiet life and related hypotheses, *Review of Economics and Statistics*, 80, 454–65.

Berger, A.N. and Humphrey, D. (1997) Efficiency of financial institutions: international survey and directions for future research, *European Journal of Operational Research*, 98, 175–212.

Berger, P.G. and Ofek, E. (1995) Diversification's effect on firm value, *Journal of Financial Economics*, 37, 39–65.

Bergstrom, T.C. and Miller, J.H. (2000) *Experiments with Economic Principles*, 2nd edn. New York: McGraw Hill.

Berle, A.A. and Means, G.C. (1932) *The Modern Corporation and Private Property*. London: Macmillan.

Berlin, M. (1999) Jack of all trades? Product diversification in nonfinancial firms, *Federal Reserve Bank of Philadelphia Business Review*, May, 15–29.

Bernheim, B. and Whinston, M. (1998) Exclusive dealing, *Journal of Political Economy*, 106, 64–103.

Berry, C.H. (1971) Corporate growth and diversification, *Journal of Law and Economics*, 14, 371–83.

Berry, C.H. (1973) Corporate growth and diversification, in Yamey, B.S. *Economics of Industrial Structure*, Middlesex: Penguin.

Berry, C.H. (1974) Corporate diversification and market structure, *Rand Journal of Economics* (formerly the *Bell Journal of Economics and Management Science*), 5, 196–204.

Bertrand, J. (1883) Théorie mathématique de la richesse sociale, *Journal des Savants*, 67, 499–508.

Bikhchandani, S. and Huang, C. (1993) The economics of treasury security markets, *Journal of Economic Perspectives*, 7, 117–34.

Bikker, J.A. and Groeneveld, J.M. (2000) Competition and concentration in the EU banking industry, *Kredit und Kapital*, 33, 62–98.

Binmore, K. and Klemperer, P. (2002) The biggest auction ever: the sale of the British 3G Telecom licences, *Economic Journal*, 112, C74–C96.

Bishop, M. and Thompson, D. (1992) Regulatory reform and productivity growth in the UK's public utilities, *Applied Economics*, 24, 1181–90.

Bishop, S. and Walker, C. (2002) *The Economics of EC Competition Law*, 2nd edn. London: Sweet & Maxwell.

Blackstone, E.A. (1972) Monopsony power, reciprocal buying, and government contracts: the General Dynamic case, *Antitrust Bulletin*, 17, 445–66.

Blair, B.F. and Lewis, T.R. (1994) Optimal retail contracts with asymmetric information and moral hazard, *Rand Journal of Economics*, 25, 284–96.

Blair, J.M. (1972) *Economic Concentration*, New York: Harcourt Brace Jovanovich.

Blaug, M. (1963) A survey of the theory of process-innovations, *Economica*, 30, 13–22.

Blaug, M. (2001) Is competition such a good thing? Static efficiency versus dynamic efficiency, *Review of Industrial Organization*, 19, 37–48.

Blecherman, B. and Camerer, C.F. (1998) Is there a winner's curse in the market for baseball players? New York: Brooklyn Polytechnic University, mimeograph.

Blinder, A. (1992) Why are prices sticky? *American Economic Review*, 81, 89–96.

Bloch, H. (1974) Advertising and profitability: a reappraisal, *Journal of Political Economy*, 82, 267–86.

Blonigen, B.A. and Tomlin, K. (2001) Size and growth of Japanese plants in the United States, *International Journal of Industrial Organization*, 19, 931–52.

Bloom, M. (1999) A UK perspective on the Europeanisation of national competition law. Paper presented at the Centre for the Law of the European Union, University College of London, 17 September 1999.

Boerner, C.S. and Macher, J.T. (2001) Transaction cost economics: an assessment of empirical research in the social sciences. Unpublished working paper, retrieved from Macher's website at www.msb.georgetown.edu/faculty/jtm4/Papers/JLEO.pdf, Georgetown University (accessed 11 February 2004).

Bolton, P. and Bonanno, G. (1988) Vertical restraints in a model of vertical differentiation, *Quarterly Journal of Economics*, 103, 555–70.

Bolton, P. and Scharfstein, D.S. (1998) Corporate finance, the theory of the firm and organisations, *Journal of Economic Perspectives*, 12, 95–114.

Bolton, P. and Whinston, M. (1993) Incomplete contracts, vertical integration, and supply assurances, *Review of Economic Studies*, 60, 121–48.

Bonanno, G. and Vickers, J. (1988) Vertical separation, *Journal of Industrial Economics*, 36, 257–65.

Borcherding, T.E., Burnaby, T., Pommerehne, W.W. and Schneider, F. (1982) Comparing the efficiency of private and public production: evidence from five countries, *Zeitschrift für Nationalökonomie* (Supplement 2), 127–56.

Borden, N. (1942) *The Economic Effects of Advertising*. Chicago, IL: Irwin.

Bork, R. (1978) *The Antitrust Paradox: A Policy at War with Itself*. New York: Basic Books.

Bornstein, S. and Netz, J. (2000) Why do all flights leave at 8am? Competition and departure differentiation in the airline markets, *International Journal of Industrial Organisation*, 17, 611–40.

Bos, D. (1991) *Privatisation: A Theoretical Treatment*. Oxford: Clarendon Press.

Bos, D. (2003) Regulation: theory and concepts, in Parker, D. and Saal, D. (eds) *International Handbook on Privatization*. Cheltenham: Edward Elgar.

Bosch, J.C. (1989) Alternative measures of rates of return: some empirical evidence, *Managerial and Decision Making Economics*, 10, 229–339.

Bougheas, S., Holger Görg, H. and Strobl, E. (2003) Is R & D financially constrained? Theory and evidence from Irish manufacturing, *Review of Industrial Organization*, 22, 159–74.

Bourlakis, C.A. (1997) Testing the competitive environment and the persistence of profits hypotheses, *Review of Industrial Organization*, 12, 203–18.

Bowman, E.H. and Helfat, C.E. (2001) Does corporate strategy matter? *Strategic Management Journal*, 22, 1–23.

Boyne, G., Gould-Williams, J., Law, J. and Walker, R. (1999) Competitive tendering and best value in local government, *Public Money and Management*, 19, 23–9.

Bradley, M., Desai, A. and Kim, E.H. (1988) Synergistic gains from corporate acquisitions and their division between the stockholders of target and acquiring firms, *Journal of Financial Economics*, 21, 3–40.

Braithwaite, D. (1928) The economic effects of the advertisement, *Economic Journal*, 38, 16–37.

Brems, H. (1951) Cartels and competition, *Weltwirtschaftliches Archiv*, 66, 51–67.

Bresnahan, T.F. (1982) The oligopoly solution identified, *Economics Letters*, 10, 87–92.

Bresnahan, T.F. (1989) Empirical studies of industries with market power, in Schmalensee, R. and Willig, R.D. (eds) *Handbook of Industrial Organisation*, 2. Amsterdam: Elsevier Science Publishers, 1011–58.

Bresnahan, T. (1992) Sutton's sunk costs and market structure: price competition, advertising and the evolution of concentration. Review article, *Rand Journal of Economics*, 23, 137–52.

Bresnahan, T.F. and Schmalensee, R.C. (1987) The empirical renaissance in industrial economics: an overview, *Journal of Industrial Economics*, 35, 371–8.

Briggs, H. (1996) Optimal cartel trigger strategies and the number of firms, *Review of Industrial Organisation*, 11, 551–61.

Brod, A. and Shivakumar, R. (1999) Advantageous semi-collusion, *Journal of Industrial Economics*, 47, 221–30.

Brofenbrenner, M. (1940) Applications of the discontinuous oligopoly demand, *Journal of Political Economy*, 48, 420–7.

Brozen, Y. (1971) Bain's concentration and rates of return revisited, *Journal of Law and Economics*, 13, 279–92.

Brozen, Y. (1975) *The Competitive Economy*. Morristown, NJ: General Learning Press.

Brulhart, M. (1998) Economic geography, industry location and trade: the evidence, *World Economy*, 21, 775–801.

Brush, T.H. and Bromiley, P. (1997) What does a small corporate effect mean? A variance components simulation of corporate and business effects, *Strategic Management Journal*, 18, 10, 825–35.

Bryson, B. (1994) *Made in America*. London: Minerva.

Bunch, D.S. and Smiley, R. (1992) Who deters entry? Evidence on the use of strategic entry deterrence, *Review of Economics and Statistics*, 74, 509–21.

Burke, T. (1991) *Competition in Theory and Practice*. London: Routledge.

Butler, J. (1998) Regulating telecommunications: lessons from the UK, in Vass, P. (ed.) *Network Industries in Europe*. London: CIPFA.

Button, K. and Stough, R. (2000) *Air Transport Networks*. Cheltenham: Edward Elgar.

Butz, D.A. and Kleit, A.N. (2001) Are vertical restraints pro- or anticompetitive? Lessons from 'Interstate Circuit', *Journal of Law and Economics*, 44, 131–59.

Buxton, A.J., Davies, S.W. and Lyons, S.R. (1984) Concentration and advertising in consumer and producer markets, *Journal of Industrial Economics*, 32, 451–64.

Cable, J. (1972) Market structure, advertising policy and intermarket differences in advertising intensity, in Cowling, K. (ed.) *Market Structure and Corporate Behaviour: Theory and Empirical Analysis of the Firm*. London: Gray Mills.

Cable, J. and Schwalbach, J. (1991) International comparisons of entry and exit, in Geroski, P.A. and Schwalbach, J. (eds) *Entry and Market Contestability: An International Comparison*. Oxford: Blackwell.

Cable, J., Henley, A. and Holland, K. (2002) Pot of gold or winner's curse? An event study of the auctions of 3G telephone licences in the UK, *Fiscal Studies*, 23, 447–62.

Cady, J. (1976) An estimate of the price effects of restrictions on drug price advertising, *Economic Inquiry*, 14, 493–510.

Call, G.D. and Keeler, T.E. (1985) Airline deregulation, fares and market behaviour: some empirical evidence, in Daugherty, A.H. (ed.) *Analytical Studies in Transport Economics*. Cambridge: Cambridge University Press.

Caloghirou, Y., Protogerou, A., Spanos, Y. and Papagiannakis, L. (2004) Industry-versus firm-specific effects on performance: contrasting SMEs and large-sized firms, *European Management Journal*, 22, 231–43.

Campbell, J.R. and Hopenhayn, H.A. (2005) Market size matters, *Journal of Industrial Economics*, 53, 1–25.

Canepa, A. and Stoneman, P. (2004) Comparative International Diffusion: Patterns, Determinants and Policies, *Economics of Innovation and New Technology*, 13, 279–98.

Capen, E.C., Clapp, R.V. and Campbell, W.M. (1971) Competitive bidding in high risk situations, *Journal of Petroleum Technology*, 23, 641–53.

Carlton, D. (1979) Vertical integration in competitive markets under uncertainty, *Journal of Industrial Economics*, 27, 189–209.

Carlton, D.W. and Waldman, M. (2002) The strategic use of tying to preserve and create market power in evolving industries, *Rand Journal of Economics*, 33, 194–220.

Carroll, G. and Hannan, M.T. (1999) *The Demography of Corporations*. Princeton, NJ: Princeton University Press.

Cassing, J. and Douglas, R.W. (1980) Implications of the auction mechanism in baseball's free agent draft, *Southern Economic Journal*, 47, 1110–21.

Casson, M. (1982) *The Entrepreneur: An Economic Theory*. Oxford: Oxford University Press.

Caves, R.E. (1986) *American Industry: Structure, Conduct and Performance*, 6th edn. Englewood Cliffs, NJ: Prentice-Hall.

Caves, R.E. (1992) Productivity dynamics in manufacturing plants: comments and discussion, *Brookings Papers on Economic Activity*, 187–267.

Caves, R.E. (1998) Industrial organization and new findings on the turnover and mobility of firms, *Journal of Economic Literature*, 36, 1947–82.

Caves, R.E. and Greene, D.P. (1996) Brands, quality levels and advertising outlays, *International Journal of Industrial Organization*, 14, 29–52.

Caves, R.E. and Porter, M.E. (1977) From entry barriers to mobility barriers: conjectural decisions and contrived deterrence to new competition, *Quarterly Journal of Economics*, 91, 241–62.

Caves, R.E. and Porter, M.E. (1980) The dynamics of changing seller concentration, *Journal of Industrial Economics*, 29, 1–15.

Caves, R.E. and Williamson, P.J. (1985) What is product differentiation really? *Journal of Industrial Economics*, 113–32.

Chamberlin, E. (1933) *The Theory of Monopolistic Competition*. Cambridge, MA: Harvard University Press.

Chamberlin, E. (1957) On the Origin of Oligopoly, *Journal of Economics*, 67, 211–18.

Chandler, A.D., Jr (1977) *The Visible Hand: The Managerial Revolution in American Business*. Cambridge, MA: Harvard University Press.

Chandler, A.D. (1990) *Scale and Scope: The Dynamics of Industrial Capitalism*. Cambridge, MA: Harvard University Press.

Chang, H.J. and Singh, A. (2000) Corporate and industry effects on business unit competitive position, *Strategic Management Journal*, 21, 739–52.

Chawla, M. (2002) Estimating the extent of patient ignorance of the health care market, *World Bank Economists' Forum*, 2, 3–24.

Chen, Y. (1997) Multidimensional signalling and diversification, *Rand Journal of Economics*, 28, 168–87.

Chen, Y. and Riordan, M. (2003) Vertical integration, exclusive dealing, and ex post cartelization, www.csio.econ.nwu.edu/Conferences/IO-2003/vertical-rev3.pdf (accessed 22 June 2004).

Chen, Z. and Ross, T.W. (1999) Refusals to deal and orders to supply in competitive markets, *International Journal of Industrial Organisation*, 17, 399–418.

Chesher, A. (1979) Testing the law of proportionate effect, *Journal of Industrial Economics*, 27, 403–11.

Cheung, S.N. (1983) The contractual nature of the firm, *Journal of Law and Economics*, 26, 386–405.

Chipty, T. (2001) Vertical integration, market foreclosure, and consumer welfare in the cable television industry, *American Economic Review*, 91, 428–53.

Choi, J.P. (1998) Information concealment in the theory of vertical integration, *Journal of Economic Behaviour and Organisation*, 35, 117–31.

Choi, J.P. and Stefanadis, C. (2001) Tying investment, and dynamic leverage theory, *Rand Journal of Economics*, 32, 52–71.

Christie, W.G. and Schultz, P.H. (1995) Policy watch: Did Nasdaq market makers implicitly collude? *Journal of Economic Perspectives*, 9, 199–208.

Church, J. and Gandal, N. (2000) Systems competition, vertical merger and foreclosure, *Journal of Economics and Management Strategy*, 9, 25–51.

Church, J. and Ware, R. (2000) *Industrial Organization: A Strategic Approach*. New York: McGraw Hill.

Clanton, D.A. (1977) Trade associations and the FTC, *Antitrust Bulletin*, 22, 307.

Clark, J.B. (1899) *The Distribution of Wealth*. London: Macmillan.

Clark, J.B. (1904) *The Problem of Monopoly*. New York, Columbia University Press.

Clark, J.M. (1940) Towards a concept of workable competition, *American Economic Review*, 30, 241–56.

Clarke, D.G. (1976) Econometric measurement of the duration of advertising effect on sales, *Journal of Marketing Research*, 13, 345–57.

Clarke, R. (1979) On the lognormality of firm and plant size distribution: some UK evidence, *Applied Economics*, 11, 415–33.

Clarke, R. (1985) *Industrial Economics*. Oxford: Blackwell.

Clarke, R. (1993) Trends in concentration in UK manufacturing, 1980–9, in Casson, M. and Creedy, J. (eds) *Industrial Concentration and Economic Inequality*. Aldershot: Edward Elgar.

Clarke, R., Davies, S. and Driffield, N.L. (1999) *Monopoly Policy in the UK: Assessing the Evidence*. Cheltenham: Edward Elgar.

Clarke, R., Davies, S. and Waterson, M. (1984) The profitability–concentration relation: market power or efficiency? *Journal of Industrial Economics*, 32, 435–50.

Claver, E., Molina, J. and Tari, J. (2002) Firm and industry effects on firm profitability: a Spanish empirical analysis, *European Management Journal*, 20, 321–8.

Clerides, S.K. (2002) Book value: intertemporal pricing and quality discrimination in the US market for books, *International Journal of Industrial Organisation*, 20, 1385–408.

Clowes, J. and Clements, N. (2003) An examination of discriminatory ticket pricing practice in the English football Premier League, *Managing Leisure*, 8, 105–20.

Coase, R.H. (1937) The nature of the firm, *Economica*, 4, 386–405.

Coase, R.H. (1972) Durability and monopoly, *Journal of Law and Economics*, 15, 143–9.

Coase, R.H. (1991) The nature of the firm: meaning, in Williamson, O.E. and Winter, S.G. (eds) *The Nature of the Firm, Origins, Evolution and Development*. Oxford: Oxford University Press.

Coate, M.B. (1989) The dynamics of price–cost margins in concentrated industries, *Applied Economics*, 21, 261–72.

Cockburn, I. and Henderson, R. (1994) Racing to invest? The dynamics of competition in the ethical drugs market, *Journal of Economics and Management Strategy*, 3, 481–519.

Cockerill, T. and Johnson, P. (2003) Industry in the EU: trends and policy issues, in Johnson, P. (ed.) *Industries in Europe*. Cheltenham: Edward Elgar.

Cohen, A. (2002) *The Perfect Store: Inside eBay*. London: Piatkus Publishers.

Cohen, K.J. and Cyert, R.M. (1965) *Theory of the Firm*. Englewood Cliffs, NJ: Prentice-Hall.

Cohen, W.M. (1995) Empirical studies of innovative activity, in Stoneman, P. (ed.) *Handbook of the Economics of Innovation and Technical Change*, ch. 8. Oxford: Blackwell.

Cohen, W.M. and Levin, R.C. (1989) Empirical studies of innovation and market structure, in Schmalensee, R. and Willig, R. (eds) (1989) *Handbook of Industrial Organisation*, vol. 2. Amsterdam: North Holland, 1059–107.

Cohen, W.M., Nelson, R.R. and Walsh, J. (2002) Links and impacts: the influence of public research on industrial R&D, *Management Science*, 48, 1–23.

Colangelo, G. (1995) Vertical vs horizontal integration: pre-emptive merging, *Journal of Industrial Economics*, 43, 323–37.

Colangelo, G. (1997) Vertical vs horizontal integration: pre-emptive merging: a correction, *Journal of Industrial Economics*, 45, 115.

Collins, N.R. and Preston, L.E. (1966) Concentration and price–cost margins in food manufacturing industries, *Journal of Industrial Economics*, 15, 271–86.

Comanor, W.S. (1967a) Market structure, product differentiation and industrial research, *Quarterly Journal of Economics*, 18, 639–57.

Comanor, W.S. (1967b) Vertical mergers, market power and the antitrust laws, *American Economic Review, Papers and Proceedings*, 57, 254–65.

Comanor, W.S. (1985) Vertical price-fixing, vertical market restrictions, and the new antitrust policy, *Harvard Law Review*, 98, 983–1002.

Comanor, W.S. and Frech, H.E., III (1985) The competitive effects of vertical agreements, *American Economic Review*, 75, 539–46.

Comanor, W.S. and Leibenstein, H. (1969) Allocative efficiency, X-efficiency and the measurement of welfare losses, *Economica*, 36, 304–9.

Comanor, W.S. and Scherer, F.M. (1969) Patent statistics as a measure of technical change, *Journal of Political Economy*, 77, 392–8.

Comanor, W.S. and Wilson, T. (1967) Advertising, market structure and performance, *Review of Economics and Statistics*, 49, 423–40.

Comanor, W.S. and Wilson, T. (1974) *Advertising and Market Power*. Cambridge, MA: Harvard University Press.

Comanor, W.S. and Wilson, T. (1979) Advertising and competition: a survey, *Journal of Economic Literature*, 17, 453–76.

Combs, J., Michael, S.C. and Castrogiovanni, G.J. (2004) Franchising: a review and avenues to greater theoretical diversity, *Journal of Management*, 30, 907–31.

Comment, R. and Jarrell, G. (1995) Corporate focus and stock returns, *Journal of Financial Economics*, 37, 67–87.

Competition Commission (2001) *A Report on the Acquisition by Interbrew SA of the Brewing Interests of Bass Plc*. London: HMSO.

Competition Commission (2002) *The Supply of Banking Services*. London: HMSO.

Compte, O., Jenny, F. and Rey, P. (2002) Capacity constraints, mergers and collusion, *European Economic Review*, 46, 1–29.

Conner, K.R. and Prahalad, C.K. (1996) A resource-based theory of the firm: knowledge versus opportunism, *Organization Science*, 7, 477–501.

Contini, B. and Revelli, R. (1989) The relationship between firm growth and labour demand, *Small Business Economics*, 1, 309–14.

Coriat, B. and Dosi, G. (1998) Learning how to govern and learning how to solve problems: on the co-evolution of competences, conflicts and organisational routines, in Chandler, A.D., Hagström, P. and Sölvell, Ö. (eds) *The Dynamic Firm: The Role of Technology, Strategy, Organisation and Regions*. Oxford: Oxford University Press, 103–33.

Corts, K.S. (1999) Conduct parameters and the measurement of market power, *Journal of Econometrics*, 88, 227–50.

Cosh, A., Hughes, A. and Singh, A. (1980) The causes and effects of takeovers in the United Kingdom: an empirical investigation for the late 1960s at the microeconomic level, in Mueller, D.C. (ed.) *The Determinants and Effects of Mergers: an International Comparison.* Cambridge, MA: Oelgeschlager, Gun & Hanin.

Cournot, A. (1838) Recherches sur les principes mathématiques de la théorie des richesses, published in Cournot, A. (ed.) *Researches into the Mathematical Principles of the Theory of Wealth.* London: Macmillan, 1897.

Coursey, D., Isaac, M.R. and Smith, V.L. (1984) Market contestability in the presence of sunk costs, *Rand Journal of Economics*, 15, 69–84.

Cowan, S. (1997) Competition in the water industry, *Oxford Review of Economic Policy*, 13, 83–92.

Cowan, T. and Suuter, D. (1999) The costs of cooperation, *Review of Austrian Economics*, 12, 161–73.

Cowling, K. and Mueller, D.C. (1978) The social costs of monopoly power, *Economic Journal*, 88, 727–48.

Cowling, K. and Sugden, P. (1998) The essence of the modern corporation: markets, strategic decision-making and the theory of the firm, *The Manchester School*, 66, 1, 59–86.

Cox, J.C. and Hayne, S. (1998) Group versus individual decision making in strategic market games, mimeograph. Tucson, AZ: Arizona University.

Cox, S.R. (1982) Some evidence on the early price effects of attorney advertising in the USA, *Journal of Advertising*, 1, 321–31.

Cox, S.R., De Serpa, A. and Smith, S. (1982) Attorney advertising and the pricing of legal services, *Journal of Industrial Economics*, 30, 305–18.

Crandell, R.W. (2003) An end to economic regulation? in Robinson, C. (ed.) *Competition and Regulation in Utility Markets.* Cheltenham: Edward Elgar.

Croteau, J.T. (1963) *The Economics of the Credit Union.* Detroit, MI: Wayne State University Press.

Cubbin, J.S. and Geroski, P.A. (1990) The persistence of profits in the United Kingdom, in Mueller D.C. (ed.) *The Dynamics of Company Profits: An International Comparison.* Cambridge: Cambridge University Press.

Curry, B. and George, K. (1983) Industrial concentration: a survey, *Journal of Industrial Economics*, 31, 203–55.

Cuthbert, N. and Black, W. (1959) Restrictive practices in the food trades, *Journal of Industrial Economics*, 8, 33–57.

Cyert, R. (1955) Oligopoly behaviour and the business cycle, *Journal of Political Economy*, 63, 41–51.

Cyert, R. and March, J.G. (1964) *A Behavioural Theory of the Firm.* Englewood Cliffs, NJ: Prentice-Hall.

Daley, L., Mahotra, V. and Sivakumar, R. (1997) Corporate focus and value creation: evidence from spinoffs, *Journal of Financial Economics*, 45, 257–81.

Darby, M. and Karni, E. (1973) Free competition and optimal amount of fraud, *Journal of Law and Economics*, 16, 67–88.

Das, B.J., Chappell, W. and Shughart, W. (1993) Advertising, competition and market share instability, *Applied Economics*, 25, 1409–12.

D'Aspremont, C. and Jacquemin, A. (1988) Joint R&D ventures, cooperative and non-cooperative R&D in duopoly with spillovers, *American Economic Review*, 78, 1133–7.

D'Aspremont, C., Jacquemin, A., Gabszowiez, J. and Weymark, J. (1983), On the stability of collusive price-leadership, *Canadian Journal of Economics*, 16, 17–25.

D'Aveni, R. and Ravenscraft, D. (1994) Economies of integration versus bureaucracy costs: does vertical integration improve performance? *Academy of Management Journal*, 37, 1167–206.

Davidson, K. (1983) The competitive significance of segmented markets, *California Law Review*, 71, 445–63.

Davies, S.W. (1979) Choosing between concentration indices: the iso-concentration curve, *Economica*, 46, 67–75.

Davies, S.W. (1989) Concentration, in Davies, S. and Lyons, B. (eds) *The Economics of Industrial Organisation.* London: Longman.

Davies, S.W. and Geroski, P.A. (1997) Changes in concentration, turbulence and the dynamics of market shares, *Review of Economics and Statistics*, 79, 383–91.

Davies, S.W. and Lyons, B.R. (1982) Seller concentration: the technological explanation and demand uncertainty, *Economic Journal*, 92, 903–19.

Davies, S.W. and Lyons, B.R. (1996) *Industrial Organisation in the European Union.* Oxford: Clarendon Press.

Davies, S.W. and Morris, C. (1995) A new index of vertical integration: some estimates for UK manufacturing, *International Journal of Industrial Organisation*, 13, 151–77.

Davies, S.W., Driffield, N.L. and Clarke, R. (1999) Monopoly in the UK: what determines whether the MMC finds against the investigated firms, *Journal of Industrial Economics*, 47, 263–83.

Davies, S., Rondi, L. and Sembenelli, A. (2001) European integration and the changing structure of EU manufacturing, 1987–1993, *Industrial and Corporate Change*, 10, 37–75.

Davis, J. and Devinney, T. (1997) *The Essence of Corporate Strategy: Theory for Modern Decision Making.* Sydney, St Leonards, NSW: Allen & Unwin.

Davis, L.E. (1974), Self-regulation in baseball 1909–71, in Noll, R.G. (ed.) *Government and the Sports Business*. Washington, DC: Brookings Institute.

Dawkins, R. (1998) *Unweaving the Rainbow, Science, Delusion and the Appetite for Wonder*. London: Penguin.

De Bandt, O. and Davis, E.P. (1999) Competition, contestability and market structure in European banking sectors on the eve of EMU, *Journal of Banking and Finance*, 24, 1045–66.

Degryse, H. (1996) On the interaction between vertical and horizontal product differentiation: an application to banking, *Journal of Industrial Economics*, 44, 169–86.

De Jong, H.W. (ed.) (1993) *The Structure of European Industry*. Dordrecht: Kluwer Academic.

Demmert, H.H. (1973) *The Economics of Professional Team Sports*. Lexington, KY: DC Heath.

Demsetz, H. (1968) Why regulate utilities? *Journal of Law and Economics*, 11, 55–65.

Demsetz, H. (1969) Information and efficiency: another viewpoint, *Journal of Law and Economics*, 12, 1–22.

Demsetz, H. (1973) Industry structure, market rivalry and public policy, *Journal of Law and Economics*, 16, 1–9.

Demsetz, H. (1974) Two systems of belief about monopoly, in Goldschmid, H.J., Mann, H.M. and Weston, J.F. (eds) *Industrial Concentration: The New Learning*. Boston, MA: Little, Brown.

Demsetz, H. (1982) Barriers to entry, *American Economic Review*, 72, 47–57.

Demsetz, H. (1992) How many cheers for antitrust's 100 years? *Economic Inquiry*, 30, 202–17.

Deneckre, R., Marvel, H.P. and Peck, J. (1996) Demand uncertainty, inventories and resale price maintenance, *Quarterly Journal of Economics*, 111, 885–913.

Denicolò, V. (1996) Patent races and optimal patent breadth and length, *Journal of Industrial Economics*, 44, 249–65.

Dennis, P.T. (1992) Practical approaches: an insider's look at the new horizontal merger guidelines, *Antitrust Bulletin*, 6:6, 6–11.

Department of the Enviroment, Transport and the Regions (2000) *Transport 2010 – The Ten-Year Plan*. London: Department of the Enviroment, Transport and the Regions.

Department of the Environment, Transport and the Regions (1998) *Modern Local Government: in Touch with the People* (Best value White Paper). London: DETR.

Department of Trade and Industry (2001) *Peer Review of Competition Policy*. London: Department of Trade and Industry.

Department of Trade and Industry (2003) *Innovation Report: Competing in the Global Economy: The Innovation Challenge*. London: HMSO.

Department of Trade and Industry (2004) *Peer Review of Competition Policy*. London: Department of Trade and Industry.

Deutsch, L. (1984) An examination of industry exit patterns, *Review of Industrial Organisation*, 1, 60–8.

Dewenter, K. and Malatesta, P.H. (2001) State owned and privately owned enterprises: an empirical analysis of profitability, leverage and labor intensity, *American Economic Review*, 91, 320–34.

Diamond, A.M. (2003) Edwin Mansfield's contributions to the economics of technology, *Research Policy*, 32, 1607–17.

Dick, A.R. (1996) When are cartels stable contracts? *Journal of Law and Economics*, 39, 241–83.

Disney, R., Haskel, J. and Heden, Y. (2003) Entry, exit and establishment survival in UK manufacturing, *Journal of Industrial Economics*, 51, 91–112.

Dixit, A.K. (1982) Recent developments in oligopoly theory, *American Economic Review, Papers and Proceedings*, 72, 12–17.

Dixit, A.K. (1996) *The Making of Economic Policy: A Transaction–Cost Politics Perspective*. Boston, MA: MIT Press.

Dixit, A.K. and Norman, G. (1978) Advertising and welfare, *Bell Journal of Economics*, 9, 1–17.

Dixit, A.K. and Stiglitz, J.E. (1977) Monopolisitic competition and optimum product diversity, *American Economic Review*, 67, 297–308.

Dobson, P. (1997) The EC green paper on vertical restraints: an economic comment, *Competition and Regulation Bulletin, London Economics*, No. 7.

Dobson, P. and Waterson, M. (1996) *Vertical Restraints and Competition Policy*, Office of Fair Trading Research Paper No. 12. London: OFT.

Dobson, P. and Waterson, M. (1997) Countervailing power and consumer prices, *Southern Economic Journal*, 64, 617–25.

Dobson, P. and Waterson, M. (1999) Retailer power: how regulators should respond to greater concentration in retailing, *Economic Policy*, 28, 135–64.

Dobson, S. and Goddard, J.A. (2001) Revenue convergence in the English Soccer League, *Journal of Sports Economics*, 2, 257–76.

Dodgson, M. and Rothwell, R. (eds) (1994) *The Handbook of Industrial Innovation*. Cheltenham: Edward Elgar.

Dolan, R.J. (1977) How an association is investigated and what the government is looking for – a Federal Trade Commission perspective, *Antitrust Bulletin*, 22, 273–86.

Dolbear, F.T., Lave, L.B., Bowman, G., Lieberman, A., Prescott, E., Reuter, F. and Sherman, R. (1968) Collusion in oligopoly: an experiment on the effect of numbers and information, *Quarterly Journal of Economics*, 82, 240–59.

Domberger, S. (1986) Economic regulation through franchise contracts, in Kay, J., Mayer, C. and Thompson, D. (eds) *Privatisation and Regulation: The UK Experience.* Oxford: Clarendon Press.

Domberger, S. (1999) *The Contracting Organization: A Strategic Guide to Outsourcing.* Oxford: Oxford University Press.

Domberger, S. and Fiebig, D.G. (1993) The distribution of price changes in oligopoly, *Journal of Industrial Economics*, 41, 295–313.

Domberger, S. and Hall, C. (1995) *The Contracting Casebook: Competitive Tendering in Action.* Canberra: Australian Government Publishing Service.

Domberger, S. and Jenson, P. (1997) Contracting out by the public sector: theory, evidence, prospects, *Oxford Review of Economic Policy*, 13, 67–78.

Domberger, S. and Piggott, S. (1986) Privatisation policies and public enterprise: a survey, *Economic Record*, 62, 145–62.

Domberger, S. and Rimmer, S. (1994) Competitive tendering and contracting in the public sector: a survey, *International Journal of the Economics of Business*, 1, 439–53.

Domberger, S., Meadowcroft, S. and Thompson, D. (1986) Competitive tendering and efficiency: the case of refuse collection, *Fiscal Studies*, 7, 69–87.

Domberger, S., Meadowcroft, S. and Thompson, D. (1987) The impact of competitive tendering on the costs of hospital domestic services, *Fiscal Studies*, 8, 39–54.

Domberger, S., Hall, C. and Li, E. (1995) The determinants of price and quality in competitively tendered contracts, *Economic Journal*, 105, 1545–70.

Donsimoni, M.P., Economides, N.S. and Polemarchakis, H.M. (1986) Stable cartels, *International Economic Review*, 27, 317–27.

Dorfman, R. and Steiner, P.O. (1954) Optimal advertising and optimal quality, *American Economic Review*, 44, 826–36.

Dosi, G., Malerba, F., Marsila, O. and Orsenigo, L. (1997) Industrial structures and dynamics: evidence interpretations and puzzles, *Industrial and Corporate Change*, 6, 3–24.

Douma, S. and Schreuder, H. (1998) *Economic Approaches to Organisations*, 2nd edn. Hemel Hempstead: Prentice Hall.

Droucopoulos, V. and Lianos, T. (1993) The persistence of profits in the Greek manufacturing industry, 1963–1988, *International Review of Applied Economics*, 7, 163–76.

Dunne, P. and Hughes, A. (1994) Age, size, growth and survival: UK companies in the 1980s, *Journal of Industrial Economics*, 42, 115–40.

Dunne, T., Roberts, M.J. and Samuelson, L. (1988) Patterns of firm entry and exit in US manufacturing industries, *Rand Journal of Economics*, 19, 495–515.

Dyer, D., Kagel, J.H. and Levin, D. (1989) A comparison of naive and experienced bidders in common value offer auctions: a laboratory analysis, *Economic Journal*, 99, 108–15.

Eccles, R. (1985) *The Transfer Pricing Problem.* Lexington, MA: D.C. Heath.

Eckard, E.W. (1987) Advertising, competition and market share instability, *Journal of Business*, 60, 539–52.

Eckard, E.W. (1995) A note on the profit-concentration relation, *Applied Economics*, 27, 219–23.

The Economist (1991) The purest treasure, 7 September 1991.

The Economist (1998) The economics of antitrust, 18 May 1998.

The Economist (1999) The brand's the thing, 16 December 1999.

The Economist (2001) Brands: who's wearing the trousers, 4 September 2001.

The Economist (2002) Coming home to roost: privatization in Europe, 29 June 2002.

The Economist (2002) Economics focus: bidding adieu, 29 June 2002.

The Economist (2004a) Just as mobile phones have changed dramatically in recent years, the industry that makes them is being transformed too, 29 April 2004.

The Economist (2004b) The future of advertising, 26 June 2004.

The Economist (2004c) Turbulent skies, 8 July 2004.

The Economist (2005) Target practice: Advertising used to be straightforward. 2 April 2005.

The Economist Technology Quarterly (2004a) A brief history of Wi-Fi, 12 June 2004.

The Economist Technology Quarterly (2004b) Shape of phones to come, 12 June 2004.

Edgeworth, F. (1897) La teoria pura del monopolio, *Giornale degli Economisti*, 15, 13–31. Reprinted as The pure theory of monopoly, in *Papers Relating To Political Economy*, London: Macmillan, 1925.

Edwards, J., Kay, J.A. and Mayer, C.P. (1987) *The Economic Analysis of Accounting Profitability.* Oxford: Clarendon Press.

Efroymson, C.W. (1955) The kinked demand curve reconsidered, *Quarterly Journal of Economics*, 69, 119–36.

Eichner, A.S. (1987) Prices and pricing, *Journal of Economic Issues*, December, 21, 1555–84.

Elango, B. and Sambharya, R.B. (2004) The influence of industry structure on the entry mode choice of overseas entrants in manufacturing industry, *Journal of International Management*, 10, 107–24.

Ellison, G. (1994) Theories of cartel stability and the Joint Executive Committee, *Rand Journal of Economics*, 25, 37–57.

Elzinga, K.G. and Hogarty, T.F. (1973) The problem of geographic delineation in anti-merger suits, *Antitrust Bulletin*, 18, 45–81.

Elzinga, K.G. and Hogarty, T.F. (1978) The problem of geographic delineation revisited: the case of coal, *Antitrust Bulletin*, 23, 1–18.

Emerson, M., Aujean, M., Catinat, M., Goybet, P. and Jacquemin, A. (1988) *The Economics of 1992: The EC Commission's Assessment of the Economic Effects of Completing the Single Market*. Oxford: Oxford University Press.

Emons, W. (1996) Good times, bad times, and vertical upstream integration, *International Journal of Industrial Organisation*, 14, 465–84.

Enright, M.J. (1998) Regional clusters and firm strategy, in Chandler, A., Hagstrom, P., and Sovell, O. (eds) *The Dynamic Firm: the Role of Technology Strategy, Organizations and Regions*. New York: Oxford University Press.

Enright, M.J. (2000) The globalization of competition and the localization of competitive advantage, in Hood, N. and Young, S. (eds) *Globalization of Multinational Enterprise Activity and Economic Development*. London: Macmillan.

Erickson, W.B. (1969), Economics of price fixing, *Antitrust Law and Economic Review*, 2, 83–122

European Commission (1985) *Completing the Internal Market* (White Paper), COM(85)310, 14 June 1985.

European Commission (1994) Evolution of mergers in the community, *European Economy*, 4, 13–40.

European Commission (1995a) *Green Paper on Innovation*, COM(95)688.

European Commission (1995b) *Car Price Differentials in the European Union on 1 May 1995*, IP/95/768. Brussels: European Commission.

European Commission (1997a) Competition issues, *The Single Market Review*, Subseries 5:3.

European Commission (1997b) Economies of scale, *The Single Market Review*, Subseries 5, vol. 4. London: Kogan Page.

European Commission (1997c) *Panorama of EU Industry: The Key to European Industry*, vols 1 and 2. Luxemburg: Office for Official Publications of the European Communities.

European Commission (1997d) *Green Paper on Vertical Restraints in EU Competition Policy*, COM(96)721.

European Commission (1997e) Irish sugar, *Official Journal of the European Communities*, L258, 22 September.

European Commission (1998) *Communication from the Commission on the Application of the Community Competition Rules to Vertical Restraints*, COM(98)544.

European Commission (1999a) *Draft Guidelines on Vertical Restraints* europa.eu.int/comm/dg04/antitrust/others/vertical_restraints/reform/consultation/draft_guidelines_en.pdf (last accessed October 1999).

European Commission (2000) *Panorama of EU Business.* Luxembourg: Office for Official Publications of the European Communities.

European Commission (2002a) Business demography in Europe, *Observatory of European SEMs*, 5, 1–58. Luxembourg: Office for Official Publications of the European Community.

European Commission (2002b) Regional clusters in Europe, *Observatory of European SMEs*, No. 3. Luxembourg: Enterprise Publications.

European Commission (2003a) *EU Business: Facts and Figures.* Luxembourg: Office for Official Publications of the European Communities.

European Commission (2003b) *Directorate General for Enterprise*, Euroabstracts Vol. 41, August 2003. Luxembourg: Office for Official Publications of the European Communities.

European Commission (2003c) European Innovation Scoreboard 2003, *Cordis Focus*, 20, 1–40.

European Commission (2004) *Financial Services Action Plan: Progress and Prospects. Final Report. May 2004.* Luxembourg: Office for Official Publications of the European Communities.

Evans, D.S. (1987a) Tests of alternative theories of firm growth, *Journal of Political Economy*, 95, 657–74.

Evans, D.S. (1987b) The relationship between firm growth, size and age: estimates for 100 manufacturing industries, *Journal of Industrial Economics*, 35, 567–81.

Evans, D.S. (2000) An analysis of the government's economic case in US v Microsoft, *Antitrust Bulletin*, 46, 2, 163–251.

Evely, R. and Little, I.M.D. (1960) *Concentration in British Industry*. Cambridge: Cambridge University Press.

Fare, R., Grosskopf, S., Seldon, B.J. and Tremblay, V.J. (2004) Advertising efficiency and the choice of media mix: a case of beer, *International Journal of Indusrial Organization*, 22, 503–22.

Farrell, J. and Shapiro, C. (2000) Scale Economies and Synergies in Horizontal Merger Analysis (October 1, 2000). *Competition Policy Center*. Working Paper CPC00-015. repositories.cdlib.org/iber/cpc/CPC00-015.

Fellner, W.J. (1949) *Competition Among the Few*. New York: Alfred Knopf.

Fellner, W.J. (1965) *Competition Among the Few*. London: Frank Cass.

Ferguson, C. and Mckillop, D. (1997) *The Strategic Development of Credit Unions.* Chichester: John Wiley.

Fischer, T. and Kamerschen, D.R. (2003) Measuring competition in the US airline industry using the Rosse-Panzar test and cross sectional regression analysis, *Journal of Applied Economics*, 6, 73–93.

Fisher, F.M. and McGowan, J.J. (1983) On the misuse of accounting rates of return to infer monopoly profits, *American Economic Review*, 73, 82–97.

Fisher, F.M. and Rubinfeld, D. (2001) US v Microsoft, *Antitrust Bulletin*, Spring, 46, 1, 1–69.

Fisher, I. (1898) Cournot and mathematical economics, *Quarterly Journal of Economics*, 12, 119–38.

Fluent, C. and Garella, P.G. (2002) Advertising and prices as signals of quality in a regime of price rivalry, *International Journal of Industrial Organization*, 20, 965–94.

Fog, B. (1956) How are cartel prices determined? *Journal of Industrial Economics*, 5, 16–23.

Fog, B. (1960) *Industrial pricing policies*. Amsterdam: North Holland.

Foss, N.J. (2003) The strategic management and transaction cost nexus: past debates, central questions, and future research possibilities, *Strategic Organization*, 1, 139–69.

Foss, N.J. and Eriksen, B. (1995) Competitive advantage and industry capabilities, in Montgomery, C.A. (ed.) *Resource-based and Evolutionary Theories of the Firm: Towards a Synthesis*. Dordrecht and Boston, MA: Kluwer Academic, 43–69.

Foster, C.D. (1992) *Privatisation, Public Ownership and the Regulation of Natural Monopoly*. Cambridge: Cambridge University Press.

Fraas, A.G. and Greer, D.F. (1977) Market structure and price collusion: an empirical analysis, *Journal of Industrial Economics*, 26, 21–44.

Fraser, R. (ed.) (1988) *Privatisation: The UK Experience and International Trends*. Cambridge: Cambridge University Press.

Freeman, C. and Soete, L. (1997) *The Economics of Industrial Innovation*, 3rd edn, London: Pinter.

Friedman, M. (1953) *Essays in Positive Economics*. Chicago, IL: Chicago University Press.

Friedman, M. (1962) *Capitalism and Freedom*. Chicago, IL: Chicago University Press.

Fritsch, M. and Meschede, M. (2001) Product innovation, process innovation, and size, *Review of Industrial Organization*, 19, 335–50.

Fung, M.K. and Cheng, A.C.S. (2004) Diffusion of off balance sheet financial innovations: information complementarity and market competition, *Pacific Basin Finance Journal*, 12, 525–40.

Furman, J.L. (2000) Does industry matter differently in different places? A comparison of industry, corporate parent, and business segment effects in four OECD countries. Boston, MA, MIT Sloan School of Management Working Paper.

Gabszewicz, J.J., Laussel, D. and Sonnac, N. (2005) Does advertising lower the price of newspapers to consumers? A theoretical appraisal, *Economics Letters*, 87, 127–34.

Galbraith, J.K. (1952) *American Capitalism: The Concept of Countervailing Power*, Boston, MA: Houghton-Mifflin.

Galbraith, J.K. (1956) *American Capitalism*. Boston, MA: Houghton Mifflin.

Galbraith, J.K. (1958) *The Affluent Society*. Boston, MA: Houghton Mifflin.

Galbraith, J.K. (1967) *The New Industrial Estate*. Boston, MA: Houghton Mifflin.

Gallini, N.T. (2002) The economics of patents: lessons from recent US patent reform, *Journal of Economic Perspectives*, 16, 131–54.

Gal-Or, E. (1991) Optimal franchising in oligopolistic markets with uncertain demand, *International Journal of Industrial Organisation*, 9, 343–64.

Gal-Or, E. (1999) Vertical integration or separation of the sales function as implied by competitive forces, *International Journal of Industrial Organisation*, 17, 641–62.

Ganley, J. and Grahl, J. (1988) Competitive tendering and efficiency in refuse collection: a critical comment, *Fiscal Studies*, 9, 81–5.

Genovese, D. and Mullin, W.P. (1998) Testing static oligopoly models: conduct and cost in the sugar industry, 1890–1914, *Rand Journal of Economics*, 29, 355–77.

Geroski, P.A. (1990) Modelling persistent profitability, in Mueller, D.C. (ed.) *The Dynamics of Company Profits: An International Comparison*. Cambridge: Cambridge University Press.

Geroski, P.A. (1991a) *Market Dynamics and Entry*. Oxford: Blackwell.

Geroski, P.A. (1991b) Domestic and foreign entry in the United Kingdom, in Geroski, P.A. and Schwalbach, J. (eds) *Entry and Market Contestability: An International Comparison*. Oxford: Blackwell.

Geroski, P. (1994) *Market Structure, Corporate Performance and Innovative Acitivity*. Oxford: Clarendon Press.

Geroski, P.A. (1995) What do we know about entry? *International Journal of Industrial Organization*, 13, 421–40.

Geroski, P.A. (1999) *The Growth of Firms in Theory and Practice*, Centre of Economic Policy Research Discussion Paper Series, No. 2092. London: Centre of Economic Policy Research.

Geroski, P.A. (2003) *The Evolution of New Markets*. Oxford: Oxford University Press.

Geroski, P.A. and Gugler, K. (2001) *Corporate Growth Convergence in Europe*. CEPR Discussion Paper No. 2838. London: Centre for Economic Policy Research.

Geroski, P.A. and Jacquemin, A. (1988) The persistence of profits: a European comparison, *Economic Journal*, 98, 375–89.

Geroski, P.A. and Mazzucato, M. (2001) Learning and the sources of corporate growth, mimeograph. London: London Business School.

Geroski, P.A., Machin, S. and Van Reenen, J. (1993) The profitability of innovating firms, *Rand Journal of Economics*, 24, 198–211.

Geroski, P.A., Lazarova, S., Urga, G. and Walters, C.F. (2003) Are differences in firm size transitory or permanent? *Journal of Applied Econometrics*, 18, 47–59.

Gertner, R. and Stillman, R. (2001) Vertical integration and internet strategies in the apparel industry, *Journal of Industrial Economics*, 49, 415–40.

Ghemawat, P. (2002) Competition and business strategy in historical perspective, *Business Strategy Review*, 76, 37–74.

Ghemawat, P. (2003) Semiglobalization and international business strategy, *Journal of International Business Studies*, 34, 138–52.

Gibrat, R. (1931) *Les Inégalités économiques*. Paris: Sirey.

Gil, R. (2004) Decision rights and vertical integration in the movie industry, Working paper home.uchicago.edu/~rgil/jmpmarch.pdf (accessed 7 May 2004).

Gilbert, R. (1984) Bank market structure and competition – a survey, *Journal of Money Credit and Banking*, 16, 617–45.

Gilbert, R. and Katz, M. (2001) An economist's guide to US v Microsoft, *Journal of Economic Perspectives*, 15, 25–44.

Gilligan, T.W. (1986) The competitive effects of resale price maintenance, *Rand Journal of Economics*, 17, 544–56.

Gini, C. (1912) *Variabilità e Mutabilità*. Bologna: Tipografia di Paolo Cuppini.

Glaister, S. (2003) UK Trasport policy, 1997–2001, in Robinson, C. (ed.) *Competition and Regulation in Utility Markets*. Cheltenham: Edward Elgar.

Glazer, A. (1985) The advantages of being first, *American Economic Review*, 75, 473–80.

Glen, J., Lee, K. and Singh, A. (2001) Persistence of profitability and competition in emerging markets: a time series analysis, *Economic Letters*, 72, 247–53.

Glen, J., Lee, K. and Singh, A. (2003). Corporate profitability and the dynamics of competition in emerging markets: a time series analysis, *Economic Journal*, 113, F465–84.

Glover, F.J. (1977) Government contracting, competition and growth in the heavy woollen industry, in Tucker, K.A. (ed.) (1977) *Business History Selected Readings*. London: Frank Cass.

Goddard, J.A. and Wilson, J.O.S. (1996) Persistence of profits for UK manufacturing and service sector firms, *Service Industries Journal*, 16, 105–17.

Goddard, J.A. and Wilson, J.O.S. (1999) Persistence of profit: a new empirical interpretation, *International Journal of Industrial Organisation*, 17, 663–87.

Goddard, J.A., Blandon, P. and Wilson, J.O.S. (2002a) Panel tests of Gibrat's Law for Japanese manufacturing, *International Journal of Industrial Organization*, 20, 415–33.

Goddard, J.A., McKillop, D.G. and Wilson, J.O.S. (2002b) The growth of US credit unions, *Journal of Banking and Finance*, 22, 2327–56.

Gollop, F.M. and Monahan, J.L. (1991) A generalised index of diversification: trends in US manufacturing, *Review of Economics and Statistics*, 73, 318–30.

Gorecki, P. (1975) An inter-industry analysis of diversification in the UK manufacturing sector, *Journal of Industrial Economics*, 24, 131–46.

Gort, M. (1962) *Diversification and Integration in American Industry*. Princeton, NJ: Princeton University Press.

Goyder, D.G. (2003) *EC Competition Law: Text and Cases*. London: Oxford University Press.

Grabowski, H. and Mueller, D. (1970) Industrial organization: the role and contribution of econometrics, *American Economic Review*, 60, 100–4.

Graham, C. (2003) Methods of privatization, in Parker, D. and Saal, D. (eds) *International Handbook on Privatization*. Cheltenham: Edward Elgar.

Graham, D.R., Kaplan, D.P. and Sibley, R.S. (1983) Efficiency and competition in the airline industry, *Bell Journal of Economics*, 14, 118–38.

Grant, R.M. (1991) The resource-based theory of competitive advantage: implications for strategy formulation, *California Management Review*, 33, 114–35.

Grant, R.M. (1996) Toward a knowledge-based theory of the firm, *Strategic Management Journal*, 17, 109–22.

Green, E.J. and Porter, R.H. (1984) Non-cooperative collusion under imperfect price information, *Econometrica*, 52, 87–100.

Green, R. (1999) Checks and balances in utility regulation: the UK experience, *Public Policy for the Private Sector*, May. Washington, DC: World Bank.

Greuner, M.R., Kamerschen, D.R. and Klein, P.G. (2000) The competitive effects of advertising in the US Automobile industry, 1970–1994, *International Journal of the Economics of Business*, 7, 245–61.

Griliches, Z. (1958) Research costs and social returns: hybrid corn and related innovations, *Journal of Political Economy*, 66, 419–31.

Grimes, W.S. (2002) GTE Sylvania and the future of vertical restraint law, *Antitrust Magazine*, Fall 2002, 27–31.

Grossman, S. and Hart, O. (1986) The costs and benefits of ownership: a theory of vertical and lateral integration, *Journal of Political Economy*, 94, 691–719.

Gugler, K., Mueller, D.C., Yurtoglu, B.B. and Zulehner, C. (2003) The effects of mergers: an international comparison, *International Journal of Industrial Organisation*, 21, 625–53.

Gupta, B. (1995) Collusion in the Indian tea industry in the Great Depression: an analysis of panel data. *Explorations in Economic History*, 34, 155–73.

Haan, M.A. (2003) Vaporware as a means of entry deterrence, *Journal of Industrial Economics*, 51, 345–58.

Haffer, S. and DiSalvo, J. (1994) Conduct in a banking duopoly, *Journal of Banking and Finance*, 18, 1063–82.

Hagedoorn, J. (2002) Inter-firm R&D partnerships – an overview of major trends and patterns since 1960, *Research Policy*, 31, 477–92.

Hague, D. (1971) *Pricing in Business*. London: George Allen & Unwin.

Hall, B.H. (1987) The relationship between firm size and firm growth in the US manufacturing sector, *Journal of Industrial Economics*, 35, 583–606.

Hall, B.H. and Ziedonis, R.H. (2001) The patent paradox revisited: an empirical study of patenting in the US semiconductor industry, 1979–1995, *Rand Journal of Economics*, 32, 101–28.

Hall, C. and Rimmer, S.J. (1994) Performance monitoring and public sector contracting, *Australian Journal of Public Administration*, 53, 453–61.

Hall, R.L. and Hitch, C.J. (1939) Price theory and business behaviour, *Oxford Economic Papers*, 2, 12–45.

Hall, S., Walsh, M. and Yates, T. (1996) How do UK companies set prices? *Bank of England Quarterly Bulletin*, May, 36, 180–92.

Hallett, M. (2000) Regional specialisation and concentration in the EU, *European Commission Working Paper*, No. 141.

Haltwanger, J. and Harrington, J. (1991) The impact of cyclical demand movement on collusive behavior, *The Rand Journal of Economics*, 22, 89–106.

Hamberg, D. (1966) *Essays in the Economics of Research and Development*. New York: Random House.

Hamel, G. and Prahalad, C.K. (1994) *Competing for the Future*. Cambridge, MA: Harvard Business Press.

Hannah, L. (1983) *The Rise of the Corporate Economy*. London: Methuen.

Hannah, L. and Kay, J.A. (1977) *Concentration in Modern Industry*. London: Macmillan.

Hannah, L. and Kay, J.A. (1981) The contribution of mergers to concentration growth: a reply to Professor Hart, *Journal of Industrial Economics*, 29, 305–13.

Hannan, T.H. and McDowell, J.M. (1984) The determinants of technology adoption: the case of the banking firm, *Rand Journal of Economics*, 15, 328–35.

Hansen, R.G. and Lott, J.R. (1991) Winner's curse and public information in common value auctions: comment, *American Economic Review*, 75, 156–9.

Hanson, W. (1992) The dynamics of cost-plus pricing, *Managerial and Decision Economics*, 12, 149–61.

Harberger, A.C. (1954) Monopoly and resource allocation, *American Economic Review, Papers and Proceedings*, 44, 77–87.

Harbord, D. and Hoehn, T. (1994) Barriers to entry and exit in European competition policy, *International Review of Law and Economics*, 14, 411–35.

Hardt, M. (1995) Market foreclosure without vertical integration, *Economic Letters*, 47, 423–9.

Harrigan, K.R. (1983) A framework for looking at vertical integration, *Journal of Business Strategy*, 3, 30–7.

Harrington, J.E. (1989) Collusion among asymmetric firms: the case of different discount factors, *International Journal of Industrial Organization*, 7, 289–307.

Harrington, J.E. (1991) The determination of price and output quotas in a heterogeneous cartel, *International Economic Review*, 32, 767–92.

Harris, M. and Raviv, A. (1996) The capital budgeting process: incentives and information, *Journal of Finance*, 51, 1139–74.

Harrison, B., Kelley, M. and Gant, J. (1996) Innovative firm behaviour and local milieu: exploring the intersection of agglomeration, firm effects, industrial organization and technical change, *Economic Geography*, 72, 233–58.

Harrod, R. (1952) *Economic Essays*. London: Macmillan.

Hart, O. (1995) *Firms, Contracts and Financial Structure*. Oxford: Oxford University Press.

Hart, O. and Moore, J. (1990) Property rights and the nature of the firm, *Journal of Political Economy*, 98, 1119–58.

Hart, P.E. (1962) The size and growth of firms, *Economica*, 29, 29–39.

Hart, P.E. (1981) The effects of mergers on industrial concentration, *Journal of Industrial Economics*, 29, 315–20.

Hart, P.E. and Clarke, R. (1980) *Concentration in British Industry: 1935–1975*. Cambridge: Cambridge University Press.

Hart, P.E. and Oulton, N. (1996) The size and growth of firms, *Economic Journal*, 106, 1242–52.

Hart, P.E. and Oulton, N. (1999) Gibrat, Galton and job generation, *International Journal of the Economics of Business*, 6, 149–64.

Hart, P.E. and Prais, S.J. (1956) The analysis of business concentration: a statistical approach, *Journal of the Royal Statistical Society*, Series A, 119, 150–91.

Hart, P.E., Utton, M.A. and Walshe, G. (1973) *Mergers and Concentration in British Industry*. Cambridge: Cambridge University Press.

Hart, R.A., Hutton, J. and Sharot, T. (1975) A statistical analysis of Association Football attendances, *Applied Statistics*, 24, 17–27.

Hartley, K. (2003) Defence industries, in Johnson, P. (ed.) *Industries in Europe*. Cheltenham: Edward Elgar.

Hartley, K. and Huby, M. (1986) Contracting out policy: theory and evidence, in Kay, J., Mayer, C. and Thompson, D. (eds) *Privatisation and Regulation: The UK Experience*. Oxford: Clarendon Press.

Haskel, J. and Scaramozzino, P. (1997) Do other firms matter in oligopolies? *Journal of Industrial Economics*, 45, 27–45.

Hawawini, G., Subramanian, V. and Verdin, P. (2003) Is performance driven by industry or firm-specific factors? A new look at the evidence, *Strategic Management Journal*, 24, 1–16.

Hawawini, G., Subramanian, V. and Verdin, P. (2004) The home country in the age of globalization: how much does it matter for firm performance? *Journal of World Business*, 24, 1–16.

Hay, D. and Morris, D. (1991) *Industrial Economics and Organization*, 2nd edn. Oxford: Oxford University Press.

Hay, G.A. and Kelley, D. (1974) An empirical survey of price fixing conspiracies, *Journal of Law and Economics*, 17, 13–38.

Haynes, M., Thompson, S. and Wright, M. (2002) The impact of divestment on firm performance: empirical evidence from a panel of UK companies, *Journal of Industrial Economics*, 50, 173–96.

Healy, P.M., Palepu, K. and Ruback, R.S. (1992) Does corporate performance improve after mergers? *Journal of Financial Economics*, 31, 135–75.

Heide, J.B., Dutta, S. and Bergen, M. (1998) Exclusive dealing and business efficiency: evidence from industry practice, *Journal of Law and Economics*, 41, 387–407.

Helfat, C.E. and Teece, D.J. (1987) Vertical integration and risk reduction, *Journal of Law, Economics and Organisation*, 3, 47–68.

Helm, D. (1994) British utility regulation: theory, practice and reform, *Oxford Review of Economic Policy*, 10, 17–39.

Helm, D. (2001) The assessment: European networks – competition, interconnection, and regulation, *Oxford Review of Economic Policy*, 17, 17–39.

Helm, D. and Jenkinson, T. (1997) The assessment: introducing competition into regulated industries, *Oxford Review of Economic Policy*, 13, 1–14.

Hendricks, K., Porter, R.H. and Boudreau, B. (1987) Information, returns, and bidding behavior in OCS auctions: 1954–1969, *Journal of Industrial Economics*, 35, 517–42.

Hennessy, D.A. (1997) Information asymmetry as a reason for vertical integration, in Caswell, J.A. and Cotterill, R.W. (eds) *Strategy and Policy in the Food System: Emerging Issues*, Proceedings of NE-165 Conference, Washington, DC.

Herfindahl, O.C. (1950) Concentration in the US steel industry. Unpublished PhD thesis, Berkeley, CA: University of California.

Herling, J. (1962) *The Great Price Conspiracy, the Story of the Antitrust Violations in the Electrical Industry*. Washington, DC: Robert Luce.

Herman, E. and Lowenstein, L. (1988) The efficiency effects of hostile takeovers, in Coffee, J. Jr., Lowenstein, L. and Ackerman, B.A. (eds) *Knights, Raiders and Targets: the Impact of The Hostile Takeover*. New York: Oxford University Press.

Herold, A.L. (1977) How can an association avoid antitrust problems – a private practitioner's perspective, *Antitrust Bulletin*, 22, 299–306.

Hersch, P.L. (1994) The effects of resale price maintenance on shareholder wealth: the consequences of *Schwegmann, Journal of Industrial Economics*, 42, 205–16.

Hertzendorf, M.N. (1993) I'm not a high quality firm, but I play one on TV, *Rand Journal of Economics*, 24, 236–47.

Hexner, E. (1946) *International Cartels*. Chapel Hill, NC: University of North Carolina Press.

Hirschleifer, J. (1956) On the economics of transfer pricing, *Journal of Business*, 29, 172–84.

Hirschleifer, J. (1971) The private and social value of information and the reward of inventive activity, *American Economic Review*, 61, 561–74.

Hirschman, A.O. (1945) *National Power and the Structure of Foreign Trade*. Berkeley, CA: University of California Bureau of Business and Economic Research.

Hondroyiannis, G., Lolos, S. and Papapetrou, E. (1999) Assessing competitive conditions in the Greek bank system, *Journal of International Financial Markets, Institutions and Money*, 9, 377–91.

Horstmann, I. and MacDonald, G. (2003) Is advertising a signal of product quality? Evidence from the compact disc player market, 1983–1992, *International Journal of Industrial Organization*, 21, 317–45.

Hoschman, J. and Luski, I. (1988) Advertising and economic welfare: comment, *American Economic Review*, 78, 290–6.

Hotelling, H. (1929) Stability in competition, *Economic Journal*, 39, 41–57.

Howard, T. (1998) Survey of European advertising expenditure, 1980–1996, *International Journal of Advertising*, 17:1, 115–24.

Howe, W.S. (1978) *Industrial Economics*. London: Macmillan.

Huck, S., Normann, H. and Oechssler, J. (2001) Two are few and four are many: number effects in experimental oligopolies, *Bonn Econ Discussion Papers* bgse12_2001, University of Bonn, Germany. ideas.repec.org/p/bon/bonedp/bgse12_2001.html (accessed 19 April 2004).

Hunter, A. (1954) The Monopolies Commission and price fixing, *Economic Journal*, 66, 587–602.

Hurdle, G.J., Johnson, R.L., Joskow, A.S., Werden, G.J. and Williams, M.A. (1989) Concentration, potential entry, and performance in the airline industry, *Journal of Industrial Economics*, 38, 119–39.

Hyland, D.C. (2003) The effect of diversification on firm value: A pre- and post-diversification analysis, *Studies in Economics and Finance*, 21, 22–39.

Hymer, S. and Pashigan, P. (1962) Firm size and rate of growth, *Journal of Political Economy*, 52, 556–69.

Jackson, P.M. (1997) Planning, control and the contract state, in Corry, D. (ed.) *Public Expenditure: Effective Management and Control*. London: Dryden.

Jacobson, D. and Andréosso-O'Callaghan, B. (1996) *Industrial Economics and Organisation: A European Perspective*. Maidenhead: McGraw-Hill.

Jacobsson, S. (2002) *Universities and Industrial Transformation: An Interpretative and Selective Literature Study with Special Emphasis on Sweden*. Brighton, United Kingdom: SPRU – Science and Technology Policy Research.

Jacquemin, A. and Slade, M.E. (1989) Cartels, collusion and horizontal merger, in Schmalensee, R. and Willig, R.D. (eds) *Handbook of Industrial Organization*. Cambridge, MA: MIT Press.

Jaffe, A.B. (1986) Technological opportunity and spillovers of R&D, *American Economic Review*, 76, 984–1001.

Jagtiani, J., Saunders, A. and Udell, G. (1995) The effect of bank capital requirements on bank off balance sheet financial innovations, *Journal of Banking and Finance*, 19, 647–58.

James, L.M. (1946) Restrictive agreements and practices in the lumber industry 1880–1939, *Southern Economic Journal*, 13, 115–25.

Jarrell, G.A., Brickley, J.A. and Netter, J.M. (1988) The market for corporate control: the empirical evidence since 1980, *Journal of Economic Perspectives*, 2, 49–68.

Jenny, F. and Weber, A.P. (1983) Aggregate welfare loss due to monopoly power in the French economy: some tentative estimates, *Journal of Industrial Economics*, 32, 113–30.

Jenny, F. and Weber, A.P. (1990) The persistence of profits in France, in Mueller, D.C. (ed.) *The Dynamics of Company Profits: An International Comparison*. Cambridge: Cambridge University Press.

Jensen, M. and Meckling, W. (1976) Theory of the firm: managerial behaviour, agency costs, and capital structure, *Journal of Financial Economics*, 3, 305–60.

Jensen, M.C. (2000) *Foundations of Organizational Strategy*. Cambridge, MA: Harvard University Press.

Jevons, W.S. (1871) *The Theory of Political Economy*, 5th edn. New York: Kelley & Macmillan (1957).

Jewkes, J., Sawers, D. and Stillerman, R. (1969) *The Sources of Invention*, 2nd edn, London: Macmillan.

John, G. and Weitz, B.A. (1988) Forward integration into distribution: an empirical test of transaction cost analysis, *Journal of Law, Economics and Organisation*, 4, 337–56.

Johnson, P.S. (2003) Air transport, in Johnson, P. (ed.) *Industries in Europe*. Cheltenham: Edward Elgar.

Joskow, P.L. (2003) Vertical integration, in *Handbook of New Institutional Economics*, Forthcoming, Kluwer. econ-www.mit.edu/faculty/download_rpdf.php?id=833 (accessed 27 April 2004).

Joskow, P.L. (1985) Vertical integration and long-term contracts: the case of coal-burning electric generating plants, *Journal of Law, Economics and Organisation*, 1, 33–80.

Joskow, P.L. (1987) Contract duration and relationship-specific investments: empirical evidence from coal markets, *American Economic Review*, 77, 168–85.

Julien, B. and Rey, P. (2000) Resale price maintenance and collusion, CEPR Discussion Paper No. 2553. London: Centre for Economic Policy Research.

Kagel, J.H. and Levin, D. (1986) The winner's curse and public information in common value auctions, *American Economic Review*, 76, 894–920.

Kagel, J.H., Levin, D., Battalio, R. and Meyer, D.J. (1989) First price common value auctions: bidder behavior and winner's curse, *Economic Inquiry*, 27, 241–58.

Kagel, J.H. and Richard, J.F. (2001) Super-experienced bidders in first price auctions: rules of thumb, Nash equilibrium bidding and the winner's curse, *Review of Economics and Statistics*, 83, 408–19.

Kaldor, N. (1950) The economic aspects of advertising, *Review of Economic Studies*, 18, 1–27.

Kalnins, A. (2001) Hamburger prices and spatial econometrics: implications for firm strategy and public policy, *Working Paper*, San Diego, CA: University of Southern California.

Kalnins, A. and Lafontaine, F. (2004) Multi-unit ownership in franchising: evidence from the Texan fast food industry, *Rand Journal of Economics*, forthcoming. Originally NBER Working Paper Series (1996) 5859, papers.nber.org/papers/W5859 (accessed 10 May 2004).

Kamerschen, D.R. (1966) An estimation of the 'welfare losses' from monopoly in the American economy, *Western Economic Journal*, 4, 221–36.

Kamien, M. and Schwartz, N. (1970) Market structure, elasticity of demand and incentive to invent, *Journal of Law and Economics*, 13, 241–52.

Kamien, M. and Shwartz, N. (1982) *Market Structure and Innovation*. Cambridge: Cambridge University Press.

Kantzenbach, E., Kottman, E. and Krüger, R. (1995) New industrial economics and experiences from European merger control – new lessons about collective dominance? *European Commission*, Luxembourg: Office for Official Publications of the European Communities.

Kaplan, S. and Weisbach, M. (1992) The success of acquisitions: evidence from divestitures, *Journal of Finance*, 47, 107–38.

Kaplan, S., Schenkel, A., von Krogh, G., and Weber, C. (2001) Knowledge-based Theories of the Firm in Strategic Management: A Review and Extension. *Submitted to Academy of Management Review*, www.mit.edu/people/skaplan/kbv-0301.pdf (accessed 11 March 2004).

Karshenas, M. and Stoneman, P. (1995) Technological diffusion, in Stoneman, P. (ed.) *Handbook of the Economics of Innovation and Technical Change*, ch. 7, Oxford: Blackwell.

Kashyap, A. (1995) Sticky prices: new evidence from retail catalogues, *Quarterly Journal of Economics*, 110, 245–74.

Kato, A. (2005) Market structure and the allocation of R&D expenditures, *Economics Letters*, 87, 127–34.

Katz, M.L. (1989) Vertical contractual relations, in Schmalensee, R. and Willig, R.D. (eds) *Handbook of Industrial Organisation*, vol. 1. Amsterdam: North Holland, ch. 11.

Kaul, A. and Wittink, D.R. (1995) Empirical generalisations about the impact of advertising on price sensitivity and price, *Marketing Science*, 14, 151–60.

Kay, J.A. (1976) Accountants, too could be happy in a golden age: the accountants' rate of profit and the internal rate of return, *Oxford Economic Papers*, 28, 447–60.

Kay, J.A. (1990a) Identifying the strategic market, *Business Strategy Review*, 1/2, 2–24.

Kay, J.A. (1990b) Vertical restraints in European competition policy, *European Economic Review*, 34, 551–61.

Kay, J.A. (1993) *Foundations of Corporate Success*. Oxford: Oxford University Press.

Kay, J.A. (1999) Mastering Strategy, *Financial Times*, 27 September 1999 www.johnkay.com/strategy/135 (accessed 2 March 2004).

Kay, J.A. (2003) A brief history of business strategy, in Kay, J. (ed.) *Economics of Business Strategy*. Cheltenham: Edward Elgar.

Kay, J.A. (2004) *The Truth about Markets: Why some Nations are Rich, but Most Remain Poor*. London: Penguin.

Kay, J.A. and Mayer, C.P. (1986) On the application of accounting rates of return, *Economic Journal*, 96, 199–207.

Kay, J.A. and Vickers, J. (1990) Regulatory reform: an appraisal, in Majone, G. (ed.) *Deregulation or Reregulation? Regulatory Reform in Europe and the United States*. London: Pinter.

Kay, J.A., Mayer, C. and Thompson, D. (eds) (1986) *Privatization and Regulation: The UK Experience*. Oxford: Clarendon Press.

Keating, B. (1991) An update on industries ranked by average rates of return, *Applied Economics*, 23, 897–902.

Kessides, I.N. (1990) Internal versus external conditions and firm profitability: an exploratory model, *Economic Journal*, 100, 773–92.

Khanna, T. and Rivkin, J.W. (2001) Estimating the performance of business groups in emerging market, *Strategic Management Journal*, 22, 45–74.

Khemani, R.S. and Shapiro, D.M. (1990) The persistence of profitability in Canada, in Mueller, D.C. (ed.) *The Dynamics of Company Profits: An International Comparison*. Cambridge: Cambridge University Press.

Kihlstrom, R.E. and Riordan, M.A. (1984) Advertising as a signal, *Journal of Political Economy*, 92, 427–50.

King, S. (1983) Advertising and market entry, in Bullmore, J.J.D. and Waterson, M.J. (eds) *The Advertising Association Handbook*. London: Holt, Rinehart & Winston.

Kirzner, I. (1973) *Competition and Entrepreneurship*. Chicago, IL: Chicago University Press.

Kirzner, I. (1997a) Entrepreneurial discovery and the competitive market process: an Austrian approach, *Journal of Economic Literature*, 35, 60–85.

Kirzner, I. (1997b) *How Markets Work: Disequilibrium, Entrepreneurship and Discovery. IEA Hobart Paper No. 133*. London: Institute of Economic Affairs.

Klein, B. (1995) The Economics of Franchise Contracts, *Journal of Corporate Finance*, 2, 9–37.

Klein, B. (2000) Fisher – General Motors and the nature of the firm, *Journal of Law and Economics*, 37, 105–41.

Klein, B. and Murphy, K. (1988) Vertical restraints as contract enforcement mechanisms, *Journal of Law and Economics*, 31, 265–97.

Klein, B., Crawford, R. and Alcian, A. (1978) Vertical integration, appropriable rents, and the competitive contracting process, *Journal of Law and Economics*, 21, 297–326.

Klein, N. (2000) *No Logo*. London: Flamingo Press.

Kleit, A.N. and Palsson, H.P. (1999) Horizontal concentration and anticompetitive behavior in the central Canadian cement industry; testing arbitrage cost hypothesis, *International Journal of Industrial Organisation*, 17, 1189–202.

Klemperer, P. (1987) Markets with consumer switching costs, *Quarterly Journal of Economics*, 102, 375–94.

Klemperer, P. (1995), Competition when consumers have switching costs, *Review of Economic Studies*, 62, 515–39.

Klemperer, P. (1999) Auction theory: a guide to the literature, *Journal of Economic Surveys*, 13, 227–86.

Klemperer, P. (2002a) What really matters in auction design, *Journal of Economic Perspectives*, 16, 169–89.

Klemperer, P. (2002b) How not to run auctions: the European 3G telecom auctions, *European Economic Review*, 46, 829–45.

Klemperer, P. (2002c) The wrong culprit for telecom trouble, *Financial Times*, 26 November 2002.

Klemperer, P. (2003) Using and abusing economic theory, *Journal of the European Economic Association*, 1, 272–300.

Klemperer, P. (2004) *Auctions: Theory and Practice*. Princeton, NJ: Princeton University Press.

Klepper, S. (1996) Entry, exit, growth, and innovation over the product life cycle, *American Economic Review*, 86, 562–83.

Klepper, S. (1997) Industry life cycles, *Industrial and Corporate Change*, 6, 145–81.

Klepper, S. and Simons, K. (2005) Industry shakeouts and technological change, *International Journal of Industrial Organization*, 23, forthcoming.

Klevorick, A.K. (1966) The graduate fair return: a regulatory proposal, *American Economic Review*, 56, 477–84.

Klevorick, A.K., Levin, R.C., Nelson, R. and Winter, S. (1995) On the sources and significance of interindustry differences in technological opportunities, *Research Policy*, 24, 185–205.

Klimenko, M.M. (2004) Competition, matching, and geographical clustering at early stages of the industry life cycle, *Journal of Economics and Business*, 56, 177–95.

Knight, F. (1921) *Uncertainty and Profit*, Boston, MA: Houghton Mifflin.

Kogut, B. and Zander, U. (1992). Knowledge of the firm, combinative capabilities and the replication of technology, *Organization Science*, 3, 383–97.

Koller, R.H. (1975) On the definiton of predatory pricing, *Antitrust Bulletin*, 20, 329–37.

Koppl, R. (2000) Fritz Machlup and behavioralism, *Journal of Industrial and Corporate Change*, 9, 4.

Kor, Y.Y. and Mahoney, J.T. (2005) How dynamics, management and governance of resource deployments influence firm-level performance, *Strategic Management Journal*, 26, 489–96.

Kortum, S. and Lerner, J. (2000) Assessing the contribution of venture capital to innovation, *Rand Journal of Economics*, 31, 674–92.

Koutsoyannis, A. (1982) *Non-price Decisions, The Firm in a Modern Context*. London: Macmillan.

Kovacic, W.E. and Shapiro, C. (2000) Anti-trust policy: a century of economic and legal thinking, *Journal of Economic Perpsectives*, 14, 43–60.

Kranton, R.E. and Minehart, D.F. (2000) Networks versus vertical integration. *Rand Journal of Economics*, 31, 570–601.

Krattenmaker, T.G. and Salop, S.C. (1986) Anticompetitive exclusion: raising rivals' cost to achieve power over price, *Yale Law Journal*, 96, 209–93.

Kreps, D., Milgrom, P., Roberts, J. and Wilson, R. (1982) Rational cooperation in the finitely repeated prisoners' dilemma, *Journal of Economic Theory*, 27, 245–52.

Krickx, G.A. (1995) Vertical integration in the computer main frame industry: a transaction cost interpretation, *Journal of Economic Behaviour and Organisation*, 26, 75–91.

Krugman, H.E. (1965) The impact of television advertising, *Public Opinion Quarterly*, 29, 349–56.

Krugman, P. (1991) *Geography and Trade*. Cambridge, MA: MIT Press.

Krugman, P. (2000) Where in the world is the new economic geography? in Clark, G.L., Feldman, M.P. and Gertler, M.S. (eds) *Oxford Handbook of Economic Geography*. Oxford: Oxford University Press.

Kuehn, D.A. (1975) *Takeovers and the Theory of the Firm*. London: Macmillan.

Kuhlman, J.M. (1969) Nature and significance of price fixing rings, *Antitrust Law and Economic Review*, 2, 69–82.

Kumar, M.S. (1985) Growth, acquisition activity and firm size: evidence from the United Kingdom, *Journal of Industrial Economics*, 33, 327–38.

Kwoka, J.E. (1981) Does the choice of concentration measure really matter? *Journal of Industrial Economics*, 29, 445–53.

Kwoka, J.E. (2002) Vertical economies in electric power: evidence on integration and its alternatives, *International Journal of Industrial Organisation*, 20, 653–71.

Kwoka, J.E. and White, L.J. (2003) *The Anti-Trust Revolution*, 4th edn. London: Oxford University Press.

Lacktorin, M. and Rajan, M. (2000) A longitudinal study of corporate diversification and restructuring activities using multiple measures, Academy of Business and Administrative Sciences Conference, July 2000, Prague, Czech Republic,

Lambin, J.J. (1976) *Advertising, Competition and Market Conduct in Oligopoly over Time*. Amsterdam: North Holland.

Lancaster, K. (1966) A new approach to consumer theory, *Journal of Political Economy*, 74, 132–57.

Lang, L.H. and Stulz, R.M. (1994) Tobin's q, corporate diversification, and firm performance, *Journal of Political Economy*, 102, 1248–80.

Langinier, C. (2004) Are patents strategic barriers to entry? *Journal of Economics and Business*, 56, 5, 349–61.

Langlois, R.N. and Foss, N.J. (1997) Capabilities and governance: the rebirth of production in the theory of economic organization, *DRUID Working Paper*, 97–2.

Langlois, R.N. and Robertson, P.L. (1989) Explaining vertical integration: lessons from the American automobile industry, *Journal of Economic History*, 49, 361–75.

Larner, R.J. (1966) Ownership and control in the 200 largest non-financial corporations, 1929 and 1963, *American Economic Review*, 56, 777–87.

Lau, L. (1982) On identifying the degree of competitiveness from industry, price and output data, *Economics Letters*, 10, 93–9.

Laurenson, K. and Salter, A. (2003) Searching low and high: What types of firms use universities as a source of innovation? DRUID working paper No. 03-16.

www.druid.dk/wp/pdf_files/03-16.pdf (accessed 15 May 2004).

Lavery, K. (1997) *Smart Contracting for Local Government Services: Processes and Experience*. Westport, CT: Praeger.

Lawler, K. and Lee, K-P. (2003) Brewing, in Johnson, P. (ed.) *Industries in Europe*. Cheltenham: Edward Elgar.

Layson, S. (1994) Third degree price discrimination under economies of scale, *Southern Economic Journal*, 61, 323–7.

Leahy, A.S. (1997) Advertising and concentration: a survey of the empirical evidence, *Quarterly Journal of Business and Economics*, 36, 35–50.

Lee, C.Y. (2002) Advertising, its determinants, and market structure, *Review of Industrial Organization*, 21, 89–101.

Leech, D. and Leahy, J. (1991) Ownership structure, control type classifications and the performance of large British companies, *Economic Journal*, 101, 1418–37.

Leibenstein, H. (1950) Bandwagon, snob, and Veblen effects in the theory of consumers' demand, *Quarterly Journal of Economics*, 64, 183–207.

Leibenstein, H. (1966) Allocative efficiency versus X-efficiency, *American Economic Review*, 56, 392–415.

Leone, R.P. (1995) Generalising what is known about temporal aggregation and advertising carryover, *Marketing Science*, 14, G141–50.

Lerner, A.P. (1934) The concept of monopoly and the measurement of monopoly power, *Review of Economic Studies*, 1, 157–75.

Lerner, J. and Tirole, J. (2002) Some simple economics of open source, *Journal of Industrial Economics*, 52, 197–234.

Levenstein, M.C. (1996) Do price wars facilitate collusion? A study of the bromine cartel before World War I, *Explorations in Economic History*, 33, 107–37.

Levenstein, M.C. (1997) Price wars and the stability of collusion: a study of the pre-World War I bromine industry, *Journal of Industrial Economics*, 45, 117–37.

Levenstein, M.C. and Suslow, V.Y. (2004) What determines cartel success?, in Grossman, P. (ed.) *How Cartels Endure and How They Fail: Studies of Industrial Collusion*. Cheltenham: Edward Elgar.

Levin, R.C., Klevorick, A.K., Nelson, R.R. and Winter, S.G. (1987) Appropriating the returns from industrial R&D, *Brookings Papers on Economic Activity*, 3, 783–820.

Levine, P. and Aaronovitch, S. (1981) The financial characteristics of firms and theories of merger activity, *Journal of Industrial Economics*, 30, 149–72.

Levy, D. (1987) The speed of the invisible hand, *International Journal of Industrial Organisation*, 5, 79–92.

Levy, D., Bergen, M., Dutta, S. and Venable, R. (1997) The magnitude of menu costs: direct evidence from large supermarket chains, *Quarterly Journal of Economics*, 112, 791–825.

Lewis, P. and Thomas, H. (1990) The linkage between strategy, strategic groups, and performance in the UK retail grocery industry, *Strategic Management Journal*, 11, 385–97.

Liebeskind, J.P. (1996) Knowledge, strategy, and the theory of the firm, *Strategic Management Journal*, 17, 93–107.

Liefmann, R. (1932) *Cartels, Concerns and Trusts*. London: Methuen.

Lind, B. and Plott, C.R. (1991) The winner's curse: experiments with buyers and with sellers, *American Economic Review*, 81, 335–46.

Link, A.N. and Scott, J.T. (2003) US Science Parks: the diffusion of an innovation and its effects on the academic missions of universities, *International Journal of Industrial Organization*, 21, 1323–56.

Lins, K. and Servaes, H. (1999) International evidence on the value of corporate diversification, *Journal of Finance*, 54, 2215–39.

Lintner, V.G., Pokorny, M.J., Woods, M.M. and Blinkhorn, M.R. (1987) Trade unions and technological change in the UK mechanical engineering industry, *British Journal of Industrial Relations*, 25, 19–29.

Lipczynski, J. (1994) Selected aspects of cartel stability. Unpublished PhD thesis, London School of Economics.

Lipsey, R. and Lancaster, K. (1956) The general theory of second best, *Review of Economic Studies*, 24, 11–32.

Littlechild, S. (1981) Misleading calculations of the social costs of monopoly power, *Economic Journal*, 91, 348–63.

Littlechild, S. (1982) *The Relationship between Advertising and Price*. London: Advertising Association.

Littlechild, S. (1983) *Regulation of British Telecommunications' Profitability*. London: HMSO.

Littlechild, S. (2003) Electricity: developments worldwide, in Robinson, C. (ed.) *Competition and Regulation in Utility Markets*. Cheltenham: Edward Elgar.

Lockett, A. and Thompson, S. (2001) The resource-based view and economics, *Journal of Management*, 27, 723–54.

Lorentzen, J., Møllgaard, P. and Rojec, M. (2003) Host-country absorption of technology: evidence from automotive supply networks in eastern Europe, *Industry and Innovation*, 10, 415–32.

Lorenz, M.O. (1905) Methods of measuring the concentration of wealth, *American Statistical Association Journal*, 9, 209–19.

Love, J.H. and Stephen, F.H. (1996) Advertising, price and quality in self regulating professions: a survey, *International Journal of the Economics of Business*, 3, 227–47.

Low, R.E. (1970) *Modern Economic Organisation*, Homewood, IL: Irwin.

Lucking-Reiley, D. (1999) Using field experiments to test equivalence between auction formats: magic on the internet, *American Economic Review*, 81, 1063–80.

Lucking-Reiley, D., Bryan, D., Prasad, N. and Reeves, D. (2000) Pennies from eBay: the determinants of price in online auctions, Vanderbilt University Economics Department Working Paper.

Luffman, G.A. and Reed, R. (1984) *The Strategy and Performance of British Industry, 1970–80*. London: Macmillan.

Luik, J. and Waterson, M.J. (1996) *Advertising and Markets: A Collection of Seminal Papers*. Oxford: NTC Publications.

Lundvall, B. and Johnson, B. (1994) The learning economy, *Journal of Industry Studies*, 1, 23–42.

Lynk, E. (1993) Privatisation, joint production and the comparative efficiencies of private and public ownership: the UK water case, *Fiscal Studies*, 14, 98–116.

Lyons, B.R. (1996) Empirical relevance of efficient contract theory: inter-firm contracts, *Oxford Review of Economic Policy*, 12, 27–52.

Lyons, B.R. (2003) Reform of European merger policy, *Centre for Competition and Regulation*, Working Paper, 03-05. Norwich: University of East Anglia.

Lyons, B.R., Matraves, C. and Moffatt, P. (1997) Industrial concentration and market integration in the European Union, *Wissenschaftszentrum Berlin für Sozialforschung*, Discussion Paper FSIV 97–21.

MacGregor, D.H. (1906) *Industrial Combination*. London: Bell & Sons.

Machlup, F. (1946) Marginal analysis and empirical research, *American Economic Review*, 36, 519–54.

Machlup, F. (1952a) *The Economics of Sellers' Competition*. Baltimore, MD: Johns Hopkins University Press.

Machlup, F. (1952b) *The Political Economy of Monopoly*. Baltimore, MD: Johns Hopkins University Press.

Machlup, F. (1967) Theories of the firm: marginalist, behavioural, managerial, *American Economic Review*, 57, 1–33.

Machlup, F. and Taber, M. (1960) Bilateral monopoly, successive monopoly and vertical integration, *Economica*, 27, 101–19.

Macho-Stadler, I. and Perez-Castrillo, J.D. (1998) Centralised and decentralised contracts in a moral hazard environment, *Journal of Industrial Economics*, 46, 489–510.

Mackintosh, D.R. and Frey, S. (1978) The prices of prescription eyeglasses under advertising restraints, *Journal of Consumer Affairs*, 12, 323–32.

Maclaurin, W.R. (1950) The process of technological innovation: the launching of a new scientific industry, *American Economic Review*, 40, 90–112.

Madu, C., Chu-Hua, K. and Madu, A. (1991) Setting priorities for the IT industry in Taiwan – a Delphi study, *Long Range Planning*, 24, 105–18.

Maitland-Walker, J. (1999) The new UK competition law regime, *European Competition Law Review*, 20, 51–4.

Mansfield, E. (1961) Technical change and the rate of imitation, *Econometrica*, 29, 741–66.

Mansfield, E. (1962) Entry, Gibrat's Law, innovation, and the growth of firms, *American Economic Review*, 52, 1023–51.

Mansfield, E. (1968) *Industrial Research and Technological Innovation*. New York: Norton.

Mansfield, E. (1969) Industrial research and development: characteristics, costs and diffusion results, *American Economic Review, Papers and Proceedings*, 59, 65–79.

Mansfield, E. (1975) *Microeconomics, Theory and Applications*, 2nd edn. New York: Norton.

Marayuma, N. and Odagiri, H. (2002) Does the persistence of profits persist? A study of company profits in Japan, 1964–1997, *International Journal of Industrial Organization*, 20, 1513–33.

Markham, J.W. (1951) The nature and significance of price leadership, *American Economic Review*, 41, 891–905.

Markides, C. and Williamson, P.J. (1994) Related diversification, core competencies and corporate performance, *Strategic Management Journal*, 15, 149–65.

Markusen, A. (1996) Sticky places in slippery space, a typology of industrial districts, *Economic Geography*, 72, 293–313.

Marquez, J. (1994) Life expectancy of international cartels: an empirical analysis, *Review of Industrial Organization*, 9, 331–41.

Marris, R. (1964) *The Economic Theory of Managerial Capitalism*. London: Macmillan.

Marshall, A. (1890) *Principles of Economics*, 8th edn. London: Macmillan (1920).

Marshall, A. (1892) *Elements of Economics of Industry*, 3rd edn. London: Macmillan (1964).

Marshall, R. and Meurer, M.J. (2001) Economics of bidder collusion, in Chatterjee, K. and Samuelson, W.F. (eds) *Game Theory and Business Applications*, Norwell, MA: Kluwer.

Martin, J.D. and Sayrak, A. (2003) Corporate diversification and shareholder value: a survey of recent literature, *Journal of Corporate Finance*, 9, 37–57.

Martin, R. and Sunley, P. (1997) Paul Krugman's geographical economics and its implications for regional theory, *Regional Studies*, 77, 259–92.

Martin, S. (1984) The misuse of accounting rates of return: comment, *American Economic Review*, 74, 501–6.

Martin, S. (1988) *Industrial Economics*. New York: Macmillan.

Martin, S. (2002) *Advanced Industrial Economics*, 2nd edn. Cambridge, MA: Blackwell.

Martínez-Ros, E. and Labeaga, J.M. (2002) Relationship between firm size and innovation activity: a double decision approach, *Economics of Innovation and New Technology*, 11, 35–50.

Marvel, H. and McCafferty, K. (1984) Resale price maintenance and quality certification, *Rand Journal of Economics*, 15, 346–59.

Marx, L.M. and Shaffer, G. (2004) Opportunism and menus of two-part tariffs, *International Journal of Industrial Organization*, 22, 1399–414.

Mason, E.S. (1939) Price and production policies of large scale enterprise, *American Economic Review*, 29, 61–74.

Mason, E.S. (1949) The current state of the monopoly problem in the United States, *Harvard Law Review*, 62, 1265–85.

Massini, S. (2004) The diffusion of mobile telephony in Italy and the UK: an empirical investigation, *Economics of Innovation and New Technology*, 13, 251–77.

Masten, S. (1984) The organization of production: evidence from the aerospace industry, *Journal of Law and Economics*, 27, 403–17.

Mathewson, F. and Winter, R.A. (1998) The law and economics of resale price maintenance, *Review of Industrial Organisation*, 13, 57–84.

Matsui, A. (1989) Consumer-benefited cartels under strategic capacity investment competition, *International Journal of Industrial Organisation*, 7, 451–70.

Matsusaka, J.G. (1993) Takeover motives during the conglomerate merger wave, *Rand Journal of Economics*, 24, 357–79.

Mauri, A. and Michaels, M.P. (1998) Firm and industry effects within strategic management: an empirical examination, *Strategic Management Journal*, 19, 211–19.

Maurizi, A., Moore, R.L. and Shepard, L. (1981) The impact of price advertising: the California eyewear market after one year, *Journal of Consumer Affairs*, 15, 290–300.

McAfee, R. and McMillan, J. (1987) Auctions and bidding, *Journal of Economic Literature*, 25, 699–738.

McCloughan, P. (1995) Simulation of industrial concentration, *Journal of Industrial Economics*, 43, 405–33.

McGahan, A.M. (1999a) The performance of US corporations: 1981–1994, *Journal of Industrial Economics*, 47, 373–98.

McGahan, A.M. (1999b) Competition, strategy and business performance, *California Management Review*, 41, 74–101.

McGahan, A.M. (2000) How industries evolve, *Business Strategy Review*, 11, 1–16.

McGahan, A.M. and Porter, M.E. (1997) How much does industry matter really? *Strategic Management Journal*, 18, 15–30.

McGahan, A.M. and Porter, M.E. (1999) The persistence of shocks to profitability, *Review of Economics and Statistics*, 81, 143–53.

McGahan, A.M. and Porter, M.E. (2002) What do we know about the variance in accounting profitability? *Management Science*, 48, 834–51.

McGahan, A.M. and Porter, M.E. (2003) The emergence and sustainability of abnormal profits, *Strategic Organization*, 1, 79–108.

McGee, J. and Thomas, H. (1986) Strategic groups: theory, research and taxonomy, *Strategic Management Journal*, 7, 141–60.

McGee, J.S. (1958) Predatory price cutting: the Standard Oil (NJ) case, *Journal of Law and Economics*, 1, 137–69.

McMaster, R. (1995) Competitive tendering in the UK health and local authorities. What happens to the quality of service? *Scottish Journal of Political Economy*, 42, 407–27.

Mead, W.J., Moseidjord, A. and Sorensen, P. (1983) The rate of return earned by energy leases under cash bonus bidding in OCS Oil and Gas leases, *Energy Journal*, 4, 37–52.

Meeks, G. (1977) *Disappointing Marriage: A Study of the Gains from Merger*. Cambridge: Cambridge University Press.

Megginson, W.L. and Netter, J.M. (2001) From state to market: a survey of empirical studies on privatization, *Journal of Economic Literature*, 39, 321–89.

Megginson, W.L. and Netter, J.M. (2003) History and methods of privatization, in Parker, D. and Saal, D. (eds) *International Handbook on Privatization*. Cheltenham: Edward Elgar.

Megginson, W.L., Nash, R. and von Randenborgh, M. (1994) The financial and operating performance of newly privatized firms: an international empirical analysis, *Journal of Finance*, 49, 403–52.

Melitz, J. (1965) Friedman and Machlup on testing economic assumptions, *Journal of Political Economy*, 73, 37–60.

Midgley, D.F., Morrison, P.D. and Roberts, J.H. (1992) The effect of network structure in industrial diffusion processes, *Research Policy*, 21, 533–52.

Milgrom, P. (1989) Auctions and bidding: a primer, *Journal of Economic Perspectives*, 3, 3–22.

Milgrom, P. (2004) *Putting Auction Theory To Work*. Cambridge: Cambridge University Press.

Milgrom, P. and Roberts, J. (1982) Predation, reputation and entry deterrence, *Journal of Economic Theory*, 27, 280–312.

Milgrom, P. and Roberts, J. (1986) Price and advertising signals of product quality, *Journal of Political Economy*, 94, 796–821.

Milgrom, P. and Roberts, J. (1988) Economic theories of the firm: past, present, and future, *Canadian Journal of Economics*, 21, 444–58.

Milgrom, P. and Weber, R.J. (1982) A theory of auctions and competitive bidding, *Econometrica*, 50, 1485–527.

Miller, D. and Shamsie, J. (1996) The resource-based view of the firm in two environments: the Hollywood Film Studios from 1936 to 1965, *Academy of Management Journal*, 39, 519–43.

Miller, R.A. (1969) Market structure and industrial performance: relation of profit rates to concentration, advertising intensity and diversity, *Journal of Industrial Economics*, 17, 95–100.

Millward, R. (1990) Productivity in the UK services sector: Historical trends 1956–1985 and comparisons with the USA, *Oxford Bulletin of Economics and Statistics*, 52, 423–35.

Milne, R.G. and McGee, M. (1992) Competitive tendering in the NHS: a new look at some old estimates, *Fiscal Studies*, 13, 96–111.

Milyo, J. and Waldfogel, J. (1999) The effect of price advertising on prices: evidence in the wake of the 44 liquormart, *American Economic Review*, 89, 1081–96.

Minehart, D. and Neeman, Z. (1999) Termination and coordination in partnerships, *Journal of Economics and Management Strategy*, 8, 191–221.

Minkes, A. and Foxall, G. (1982) The bounds of entrepreneurship: inter-organisational relationships in the process of industrial innovation, *Managerial and Decision Economics*, 3, 31–43.

Mixon, F.G. (1994) The role of advertising in the market process: a survey, *International Journal of Advertising*, 13, 15–23.

Molyneux, P. and Shamroukh, N. (1996) Diffusion of financial innovations: the case of junk bonds and note issuance facilities, *Journal of Money, Credit and Banking*, 28, 502–22.

Molyneux, P., Lloyd-Williams, M. and Thornton, J. (1994) Competitive conditions in European banking, *Journal of Banking and Finance*, 18, 445–59.

Molyneux, P., Altunbas, Y., Gardener, E.P.M. and Moore, B. (2001) Efficiency in European banking, *European Economic Review*, 45, 1931–55.

Molyneux, R. and Thompson, D. (1987) Nationalised industry performance, *Fiscal Studies*, 8, 48–82.

Monopolies Commission (1968) *Supply of Man-made Cellulose Fibres*, HC 130. London: HMSO.

Monopolies Commission (1973) *British Match Corporation Ltd and Wilkinson Sword Ltd: A Report on the Proposed Merger*, Cmnd. 5442. London: HMSO.

Monopolies and Mergers Commission (1966) *Household Detergents: A Report on the Supply of Household Detergents.* London: HMSO.

Monopolies and Mergers Commission (1981) *Bicycles: A Report on T.I. Raleigh Industries.* London: HMSO.

Monopolies and Mergers Commission (1993) *A Report on the Supply of National Newspapers in England and Wales, December 1993*, Cm 2422.

Monopolies and Mergers Commission (1997) *London Clubs International and Capital Corporation PLC: A Report on the Merger Situation.* London: HMSO.

Monopolies and Restrictive Practices Commission (1955) *Collective Discrimination.* London: HMSO.

Monteverde, K. and Teece, D. (1982) Supplier switching costs and vertical integration in the automobile industry, *Bell Journal of Economics*, 13, 206–13.

Montgomery, C.A. (1994) Corporate diversification, *Journal of Economic Perspectives*, 8, 163–78.

Montgomery, C.A. and Wernerfelt, B. (1988) Diversification, Ricardian rents, and Tobin's q, *Rand Journal of Economics*, 19, 623–32.

Moore, J. (1983) Why privatise? in Kay, J., Mayer, C. and Thompson, D. (eds) *Privatisation and Regulation: The UK Experience.* Oxford: Clarendon Press.

Moore, T.G. (1986) US airline deregulation: its effect on passengers, capital and labour, *Journal of Law and Economics*, 29, 1–28.

Morosini, P. (2004) Industrial clusters, knowledge integration and performance, *World Development*, 32, 305–26.

Morrison, S.A. and Winston, C. (1987) Empirical implications of the contestability hypothesis, *Journal of Law of Economics*, 30, 53–66.

Moss, S. (1984) The history of the theory of the firm from Marshall to Robinson and Chamberlin: the source of positivism in economics, *Economica*, 51, 307–18.

Motta, M. (2003) *Competition Policy: Theory and Practice.* Cambridge: Cambridge University Press.

Mueller, D.C. (1969) A theory of conglomerate mergers, *Quarterly Journal of Economics*, 84, 643–59.

Mueller, D.C. (1977) The persistence of profits above the norm, *Economica*, 44, 369–80.

Mueller, D.C. (1986) *Profits in the Long Run.* Cambridge: Cambridge University Press.

Mueller, D.C. (1990) The persistence of profits in the United States, in Mueller, D.C. (ed.) *The Dynamics of Company Profits: An International Comparison.* Cambridge: Cambridge University Press.

Mueller, W.F. and Hamm, L.G. (1974) Trends in industrial concentration, *Review of Economics and Statistics*, 56, 511–20.

Mueller, W.F. and Rodgers, R.T. (1980) The role of advertising in changing concentration of manufacturing industries, *Review of Economics and Statistics*, 62, 89–96.

Mund, V.A. and Wolf, R.H. (1971) *Industrial Organisation and Public Policy*, New York: Appleton-Century-Crofts.

Myers, G. (1994) *Predatory Behaviour in UK Competition Policy*, Office of Fair Trading, Research Paper 5. London: Office of Fair Trading.

Nathan, A. and Neave, E.H. (1989) Competition and contestability in Canada's financial system: empirical results, *Canadian Journal of Economics*, 22, 576–94.

National Economic Development Council (NEDC) (1983) *Innovation in the UK.* London: National Economic Development Office.

National Economic Research Associates (NERA) (1992) *Market Definition in UK Competition Policy*, Office of Fair Trading Research Paper, No. 1. London: Office of Fair Trading.

National Economic Research Associates (NERA) (2003a) Switching costs. *Office of Fair Trading Economic Discussion Papers*, No. 5. London: OFT.

National Economic Research Associates (NERA) (2003b) Switching costs Annexe A – literature review, economic discussion paper 5, prepared for the OFT and DTI. www.oft.gov.uk/nr/rdonlyres/989eb3c9-38f6-446c-9563-471604d50d8f/0/oft655aannexea.pdf (accessed 10 April 2004).

Nawaz, M. (1997) The power of the puppy – does advertising deter entry? *London Economics – Competition and Regulation Bulletin*, 6, April, 1–7.

Nayle, T. (1984) Economic foundations of pricing, *Journal of Business*, 57, 23–39.

Nebesky, W.E., Starr McMullen, B.S. and Lee, M. (1995) Testing for market power in the US motor carrier industry, *Review of Industrial Organization*, 10, 559–76.

Needham, D. (1976) Entry barriers and non-price aspects of firms' behaviour, *Journal of Industrial Economics*, 25, 29–43.

Needham, D. (1978) *The Economics of Industrial Structure Conduct and Performance.* Edinburgh: Holt, Rinehart & Winston.

Nelson, M.N. (1922) *Open Price Associations.* Urbana, IL: University of Illinois.

Nelson, P. (1974a) The economic value of advertising, in Brozen, Y. (ed.) *Advertising and Society.* New York: New York University Press.

Nelson, P. (1974b) Advertising as information, *Journal of Political Economy*, 82, 729–54.

Nelson, P. (1975) The economic consequences of advertising, *Journal of Business*, 48, 213–41.

Nelson, P. (1978) Advertising as information once more, in Tuerck, D.C. (ed.) *Issues in Advertising: The Economics of Persuasion*. New York: New York University Press.

Nelson, R. (1994) The role of firm difference in an evolutionary theory of technical advance, in Magnusson, L., (ed.) *Evolutionary and Neo-Schumpeterian Approaches to Economics*. Dordrecht: Kluwer.

Nelson, R. and Winter, S.G. (1982) *An Evolutionary Theory of Economic Change*. Cambridge, MA: Harvard University Press.

Nemoto, J. and Goto, M. (2002) Technological externalities and economics of vertical integration in the electric utility industry, *International Journal of Industrial Organisation*, 22, 67–81.

Neuberger, D. (1998) Industrial organization of banking: a review, *International Journal of the Economics of Business*, 5, 97–118.

Neumann, J. von and Morgenstern, O. (1944) *The Theory of Games and Economic Behaviour*, Princeton, NJ: Princeton University Press.

Neven, D.J. (1989) Strategic entry deterrence: recent developments in the economics of industry, *Journal of Economic Surveys*, 3, 213–33.

Neven, D.J., Nuttall, R. and Seabright (1993) *Merger in Daylight: The Economics and Politics of European Merger Control*. London: Centre for Economic Policy Research.

Neven, D.J., Papandropoulos, P. and Seabright, P. (1998) *Trawling for Minnows: European Competition Policy and Agreements Between Firms*. London: Centre for Economic Policy Research.

Nevins, A. (1953) *Study in Power: John D. Rockefeller*. New York: Scribner's.

Newberry, D. (2000) *Privatisation, Restructuring and Regulation of Network Utilities*. Cambridge, MA: MIT Press.

Newman, H.H. (1978) Strategic groups and the structure–performance relationship, *Review of Economics and Statistics*, 60, 417–27.

Nichols, L. (1985) Advertising and economic welfare, *American Economic Review*, 75, 213–18.

Nickell, S.J. (1996) Competition and corporate performance, *Journal of Political Economy*, 104, 724–46.

Nightingale, J. (1978) On the definition of industry and market, *Journal of Industrial Economics*, 27, 1–12.

Nightingale, P. (2003) Pharamceuticals, in Johnson, P. (ed.) *Industries in Europe*. Cheltenham: Edward Elgar.

Noll, R.G. (1974) Attendance and price setting, in Noll, R.G. (ed.) *Government and the Sports Business*. Washington, DC: Brooking Institution.

Nordic Competition Authorities (2002) *Competitive Airlines: Towards a More Vigorous Competition Policy in Relation to the Air Travel Market*. Stockholm: Nordic Competition Authorities.

Notta, O. and Oustapassidis, K. (2001) Profitability and media advertising in Greek food manufacturing industries, *Review of Industrial Organization*, 18, 115–26.

Nyman, S. and Silbertson, A. (1978) The ownership and control of industry, *Oxford Economic Papers*, 30, 74–101.

Obi, C.P. (2003) Bank holding company expansion into nonbank functions: is the rise in systematic risk rewarded? *Managerial Finance*, 29, 9–22.

O'Brien, D.P. and Swann, D. (1969) *Information Agreements, Competition and Efficiency*. London: Macmillan.

O'Brien, D.P., Howe, W., Wright, D. and O'Brien, R. (1979) *Competition Policy, Profitability and Growth*. London: Macmillan.

Odagiri, H. and Yamawaki, H. (1990) The persistence of profits in Japan, in Mueller D.C. (ed.) *The Dynamics of Company Profits: An International Comparison*. Cambridge: Cambridge University Press.

O'Donoghue, T., Scotchmer, S. and Thisse, J. (1998) Patent breadth, patent life, and the pace of technological progress, *Journal of Economics and Management Strategy*, 7, 1–32.

OECD (1965) Glossary of Terms Relating to Restrictive Business Practices, B-2. Paris: OECD.

OECD (1984) *Competition and Trade Policies*. Paris: OECD.

OECD (1989) *Predation*, www.oecd//dat/clp/Publications/PREDA.PDF, Paris.

OECD (1993a) *Competition Policy and a Changing Broadcasting Industry*. Paris: OECD.

OECD (1993b), *Competition Policy and Vertical Restraints: Franchising Agreements*. Paris: OECD.

OECD (1999) *Oligopoly*, Committee on Competition Law and Policy DAFFE/CLP(99)25. Paris: OECD.

OECD (2001) Privatisation: recent trends, *Financial Market Trends*, 79, June. Paris: OECD.

OECD (2002) *The Role of Competition Policy in Regulatory Reform: UK*. Paris: OECD.

OECD (2003) *Bank Profitability Statistics*. Paris: OECD.

Office of Fair Trading (1994) *Predatory Behaviour in UK Competition Policy*, Research Paper No. 5. London: Office of Fair Trading.

Office of Fair Trading (1995) *An Outline of United Kingdom Competition Policy*. London: Office of Fair Trading.

Office of Fair Trading (1997) *Competition in Retailing*, Research Paper No. 13. London: Office of Fair Trading.

Office of Fair Trading (1999a) *Quantitative Techniques in Competition Analysis*. London: Office of Fair Trading.

Office of Fair Trading (1999b) *The Major Provisions*, OFT 400. *The Chapter I Prohibition*, OFT 401. *The Chapter II Prohibition*, OFT 402. *Market Definition*, OFT 403. *Powers of Investigation*, OFT 404. *Concurrent Application to Regulated Industries*, OFT 405. *Transitional Arrangements*, OFT 406. *Enforcement*, OFT 407. *Trade Associations, Professions and Self-regulating Bodies*, OFT 408. *Director General of Fair Trading's Procedural Rules*, OFT 411. *Assessment of Individual Agreements and Conduct*, OFT 414. *Assessment of Market Power*, OFT 415. *Mergers and Ancillary Constraints*, OFT 416. *The Application of the Competition Act to the Telecommunications Sector*, OFT 417. *Intellectual Property Rights*, OFT 418. *Vertical Agreements and Restraints*, OFT 419. *Land Agreements*, OFT 420. *General Economic Interest*, OFT 421. London: Office of Fair Trading.

Office of Fair Trading (2002) *BSkyB: The Outcome of the OFT's Competition Act Investigation, December 2002, OFT62*. London: Office of Fair Trading.

Office of Fair Trading (2003) *The Control of Entry Regulations and Retail Pharmacy services in the UK*. London: Office of Fair Trading.

Ogus, A.I. (1996) *Regulation: Legal Form and Economic Theory*. Oxford: Oxford University Press.

Oi, W.Y. (1971) A Disneyland dilemma: two-part tariffs for a Mickey Mouse monopoly, *Quarterly Journal of Economics*, 85, 77–96.

Oi, W.Y. and Hunter Jr, A.P. (1965) *Economics of Private Truck Transportation*. New York: William C. Brown, reprinted in Yamey, B.S. (ed.) (1973) *Economics of Industrial Structure*. Harmondsworth: Penguin.

Ordover, J., Saloner, G. and Salop, S. (1990) Equilibrium vertical foreclosure, *American Economic Review*, 80, 127–42.

Ornstein, S.I. (1985) Resale price maintenance and cartels, *Antitrust Bulletin*, 30, 401–32.

Orr, D. (1974) The determinants of entry: a study of the Canadian manufacturing industries, *Review of Economics and Statistics*, 56, 58–65.

Osborne, D.K. (1976) Cartel problems, *American Economic Review*, 66, 835–44.

Oster, S.M. (1999) *Modern Competitive Analysis*, 3rd edn. New York: Oxford University Press.

Oster, S.M. and Quigley, J.M. (1977) Regulatory barriers to the diffusion of innovation: some evidence from building codes. *Bell Journal of Economics*, 8, 361–77.

Ozanich, G.W., Hsu, C-W. and Park, H.W. (2004) 3G Wireless auctions as an economic barrier to entry: the western European experience, *Telmatics and Informatics*, 21, 225–35.

Ozga, S.A. (1960) Imperfect markets through lack of knowledge, *Quarterly Journal of Economics*, 74, 29–52.

Palda, K.S. (1964) *The Management of Cumulative Advertising Effects*. Englewood Cliffs, NJ: Prentice-Hall.

Palmer, J. (1972) Some economic conditions conducive to collusion, *Journal of Economic Issues*, 6, 29–38.

Panzar, J.C. and Rosse, J.N. (1982) Structure, conduct and comparative statistics, *Bell Laboratories Economics Discussion Paper*. Stanford, CA: Bell Laboratories.

Panzar, J.C. and Rosse, J.N. (1987) Testing for monopoly equilibrium, *Journal of Industrial Economics*, 35, 443–56.

Papandreou, A.G. (1949) Market structure and monopoly power, *American Economic Review*, 39, 883–97.

Parker, D. (1991) Privatisation ten years on, *Economics*, 27, 155–63.

Parker, D. (1994) A decade of privatisation: the effect of ownership change and competition on British Telecom, *British Review of Economic Issues*, 16, 87–115.

Parker, D. (2000) *Privatization and Corporate Performance*. Cheltenham: Edward Elgar.

Parker, D. (2003a) Privatization in the European Union, in Parker, D. and Saal, D. (eds) *International Handbook on Privatization*. Cheltenham: Edward Elgar.

Parker, D. (2003b) Privatization and the regulation of public utilities: problems and challenges for developing economies, in Parker, D. and Saal, D. (eds) *International Handbook on Privatization*. Cheltenham: Edward Elgar.

Parker, D. and Martin, S. (1995) The impact of UK privatisation on labour and total factor productivity, *Scottish Journal of Political Economy*, 42, 201–20.

Parker, D. and Wu, H.L. (1998) Privatisation and performance: a study of the British steel industry under public and private ownership, *Economic Issues*, 3, 31–50.

Parsons, P. (2003) Horizontal integration in the cable television industry: history and context, *Journal of Media Economics*, 16, 23–40.

Patel, P. and Pavitt, K. (1987) The elements of British technological competitiveness, *National Institute Economic Review*, 122:4, 72–83.

Patel, P. and Pavitt, K. (1995) Patterns of technological activity: their measurement and interpretation, in Stoneman, P. (ed.) *Handbook of the Economics of Innovation and Technical Change*. Oxford: Blackwell, ch. 2.

Patinkin, D. (1947) Multiple-plant firms, cartels, and imperfect competition, *Quarterly Journal of Economics*, 61, 173–205.

Paton, D. (1998) Who advertises prices? A firm level study based on survey data, *International Journal of the Economics of Business*, 5, 57–75.

Paton, D. and Conant, N. (2001) The determinants of internet advertising: evidence from UK firms, *Nottingham University Business School Working Paper*.

Paton, D. and Vaughan Williams, L. (1999) Advertising and firm performance: some evidence from UK firms, *Economic Issues*, 4, 89–105.

Pavitt, K.L.R. (2001) Public policies to support basic research: What can the rest of the world learn from US theory and practice? (And what they should not learn), *Industrial and Corporate Change*, 10, 761–79.

Pelkmans, J. (2001) Making EU network markets competitive, *Oxford Review of Economic Policy*, 17, 432–56.

Peltzman, S. (1976) Toward a more general theory of regulation, *Journal of Law and Economics*, 2, 211–40.

Peltzman, S. (1989) The economic theory of regulation after a decade of deregulation, *Brooking Papers on Economic Activity: Microeconomics*, 5, 1–41.

Pena-Castellot, M.A. (2001) An overview of the application of the leniency notice, *EC Competition Policy Newsletter*, February, 11–15.

Penrose, E. (1959) *The Theory of the Growth of the Firm*, London: Basil Blackwell.

Penrose, E. (1995) *The Theory of the Growth of the Firm*, 3rd edn. Oxford: Oxford University Press.

Perren, R. (1979) Oligopoly and competition: price fixing and market sharing among timber firms in northern Scotland 1890–1939, *Business History*, 213–25.

Perry, M.K. (1980) Forward integration by Alcoa: 1888–1930, *Journal of Industrial Economics*, 29, 37–53.

Pescetto, G. (2003) Financial services, in Johnson, P. (ed.), *Industries in Europe*. Cheltenham: Edward Elgar.

Pesendorfer, M. (2003) Horizontal mergers in the paper industry, *Rand Journal of Economics*, 34, 495–515.

Peston, M.H. (1959) On the sales maximisation hypothesis, *Economica*, 26, 128–36.

Phelan, S.E. and Lewis, P. (2000) Arriving at a strategic theory of the firm, *International Journal of Management Reviews*, 2, 305–23.

Phillips, A. (1962) *Market Structure, Organisation and Performance*, Cambridge, MA: Harvard University Press.

Phillips, A. (1966) Patents, potential competition and technical progress, *American Economic Review*, 56, 301–10.

Phillips, A. (1972) An econometric study of price-fixing, market structure and performance in British industry in the early 1950s, in Cowling, K. (ed.) *Market Structures and Corporate Behaviour Theory and Empirical Analysis of the Firm*. London: Gray Mills, 177–92.

Phillips, A. (1976) A critique of empirical studies of relations between market structure and profitability, *Journal of Industrial Economics*, 24, 241–9.

Phimister, I.R. (1996) The Chrome Trust: the creation of an international cartel, 1908–38, *Business History*, 38, 77–89.

Phlips, L. (1983) *The Economics of Price Discrimination*. Cambridge: Cambridge University Press.

Phlips, L. (ed.) (1998) *Applied Industrial Economics*. Cambridge: Cambridge University Press, sections II and III.

Phlips, L. and Thisse, J.-F. (1982) Spatial competition and the theory of differentiated markets, *Journal of Industrial Economics*, 31, 1–9.

Pickering, J.F. (1974) *Industrial Structure and Market Conduct*. London: Martin Robertson.

Pickering, J.F. (1982) The economics of anticompetitive practices, *European Competition Law Review*, 3, 253–74.

Pickering, J.F. (1999) Competition policy and vertical relationships: the approach of the UK Monopolies and Mergers Commission, *European Competition Law Review*, 20, 225–39.

Pigou, A.C. (1920) *Economics of Welfare*. London: Macmillan.

Pindyck, R.S. (1977) Cartel pricing and the structure of the world bauxite market, *Rand Journal of Economics*, 8, 343–60.

Pindyck, R.S. and Rubinfeld, D.L. (1992) *Microeconomics*, 2nd edn. New York: Macmillan.

Piotrowski, R. (1932) *Cartels and Trusts*. London: Allen & Unwin.

Plott, C.R. (1989) An updated review of industrial organization: applications to experimental methods, in Schmalensee, R.C. and Willig, R. (eds) *Handbook of Industrial Organization*, vol. 2. Amsterdam: North Holland.

Podolny, J.M. and Scott Morton, F.M. (1999) Social status, entry and predation: the case of British shipping cartels 1879–1929, *Journal of Industrial Economics*, 47, 41–67.

Porter, M.E. (1976) Interbrand choice, media mix and market performance, *American Economic Review*, 66, 398–406.

Porter, M.E. (1979a) How competitive forces shape strategy, *Havard Business Review*, July–August, 1–10.

Porter, M.E. (1979b) The structure within industries and companies performance, *Review of Economics and Statistics*, 61, 214–27.

Porter, M.E. (1980) *Competitive Strategy: Techniques for Analysing Industries and Competitors*. New York: The Free Press.

Porter, M.E. (1985) *Competitive Advantage: Creating and Sustaining Superior Performance*. New York: The Free Press.

Porter, M.E. (1987) From competitive advantage to corporate strategy, *Harvard Business Review*, May–June, 43–59.

Porter, M.E. (1996) What is strategy? *Harvard Business Review*, 74, 61–78.

Porter, M.E. (1998a) Locations, clusters and company strategy, in Clark, G.L., Feldman, M.P. and Gertler, M.S., *Oxford Handbook of Economic Geography*. Oxford: Oxford University Press.

Porter, M.E. (1998b) Clusters and the new economics of competition, *Harvard Business Review*, 76, 77–90.

Porter, M.E. (2001) Regions and the new economics of competition, in Scott, A.J., *Global-City Regions*. Oxford: Oxford University Press.

Porter, M.E. and Sovall, O. (1998) The role of geography in the process of innovation and the sustainable competitive advantage of firms, in Chandler, A., Hagstrom, P. and Sovell, O. (eds) *The Dynamic Firm: The Role of Technology Strategy, Organizations and Regions*. New York: Oxford University Press.

Porter, R. (1983) A study of cartel stability: the Joint Executive Committee 1880–1886, *Bell Journal of Economics*, 14, 301–25.

Posner, R.A. (1970) A statistical study of antitrust enforcement, *Journal of Law and Economics*, 13, 365–419.

Posner, R.A. (1976) *Antitrust Law – An Economic Perspective*. Chicago, IL: University of Chicago Press.

Posner, R.A. (1979) The Chicago school of anti-trust analysis, *University of Pennsylvania Law Review*, 127, 925–48.

Posner, R.A. (1981) The next step in the antitrust treatment of restricted distribution – per se legality, *University of Chicago Law Review*, 48, 6–26.

Powell, T.C. (1996) How much does industry matter? An alternative test, *Strategic Management Journal*, 17, 323–34.

Prager, J. (1994) Contracting out government services: lessons from the private sector, *Public Administration Review*, 54, 176–84.

Prahalad, C.K. and Hamel, G. (1990) The core competence of the corporation, *Harvard Business Review*, 68, 79–91.

Prais, S. (1976) *The Evolution of Giant Firms in Britain*, National Institute of Economic and Social Research, Economic and Social Studies, 30. Cambridge: Cambridge University Press.

Pratten, C.F. (1971) *Economies of Scale in Manufacturing Industry*. Cambridge: Cambridge University Press.

Pratten, C.F. (1988) A survey of the economies of scale, in *Research on the Costs of Non-Europe*, Vol. 2. Luxembourg: Office for Official Publications of the European Communities.

Price, C. and Weyman-Jones, T.G. (1993) *Malmquist Indices of Productivity Change in the UK Gas Industry Before and After Privatisation*, Department of Economics, Research Paper 93/12, Loughborough University.

Price Waterhouse (1989) *Privatization: Learning the Lessons from the UK Experience*. London: Price Waterhouse.

Prokop, J. (1999) Process of dominant-cartel formation, *International Journal of Industrial Organisation*, 17, 241–57.

Pryke, R. (1981) *The Privatised Industries: Policies and Performance since 1968*. Oxford: Martin Robertson.

Pryke, R. (1982) The comparative performance of public and private enterprise, *Fiscal Studies*, 3, 68–81.

Pryor, F.L. (2001a) New trends in US industrial concentration, *Review of Industrial Organization*, 18, 301–26.

Pryor, F.L. (2001b) Dimensions of the worldwide merger boom, *Journal of Economic Issues*, 35, 825–40.

Pryor, F.L. (2002) News from the monopoly front: changes in industrial concentration, 1992–1997, *Review of Industrial Organization*, 20, 183–5.

Qualls, D. (1974) Stability and persistence of economic profit margins in highly concentrated industries, *Southern Economic Journal*, 40, 604–12.

Quandt, R.E. (1966) On the size distribution of firms, *American Economic Review*, 56, 416–32.

Radice, H.K. (1971) Control type, profitability and growth in large firms: an empirical study, *Economic Journal*, 81, 547–62.

Ravenscraft, D.J. (1983) Structure–profit relationships at the line of business and industry level, *Review of Economics and Statistics*, 65, 22–31.

Ravenscraft, D.J. and Scherer, F. (1987) *Mergers, Sell Offs and Economic Efficiency*, Washington, DC: The Brookings Institution.

Reder, M.W. (1982) Chicago economics: permanence and change, *Journal of Economic Literature*, 20, 1–38.

Rees, R. (1984) *Public Enterprise Economics*. London: Weidenfeld & Nicolson.

Rees, R. (1993a) Collusive equilibrium in the great salt duopoly, *Economic Journal*, 103, 833–48.

Rees, R. (1993b) Tacit collusion, *Oxford Review of Economic Policy*, 9, 27–40.

Reid, G.C. (1987) *Theories of Industrial Organization*. Oxford: Blackwell.

Reid, G.C. (1992) *Small Firm Growth and its Determinants*, Department of Economics Discussion Paper No. 9213. University of St Andrews.

Resnick, A. and Stern, B.L. (1977) An analysis of information content in television advertising, *Journal of Marketing*, 41, 50–3.

Rey, P. (2002) Collective Dominance in the Telecommunications Industry, University of Toulouse, mimeo. europa.eu.int/comm/competition/antitrust/others/telecom/collective_dominance.pdf (accessed 19 April 2004).

Rey, P. and Stiglitz, J.E. (1988) Vertical restraints and producers' competition, *European Economic Review*, 32, 561–8.

Rey, P. and Tirole, J. (1986) The logic of vertical restraints, *American Economic Review*, 76, 921–39.

Rhoades, S.A. (1974) A further evaluation of the effect of diversification on industry profit performance, *Review of Economics and Statistics*, 56, 557–9.

Richardson, G.B. (1966) The pricing of heavy electrical equipment: competition or agreement? *Bulletin of the Oxford University Institute of Economics and Statistics*, 28, 73–92.

Rizzo, J. and Zeckhauser, R. (1992) Advertising and the price, quantity and quality of primary care physician services, *Journal of Human Resources*, 27, 381–421.

Robbins, L. (1932) *An Essay on the Nature and Significance of Economic Science*. New York: New York University Press.

Roberts, B. and Thompson, S. (2003) Entry and exit in a transition economy: the case of Poland, *Review of Industrial Organization*, 22, 225–43.

Roberts, P. and Eisenhardt, K. (2003) Austrian insights on strategic organization: from market insights to implications for firms, *Strategic Organization*, 1, 345–52.

Robertson, D.H. (1930) *Control of Industry*, Cambridge Economic Handbooks, 4. London: Nisbet.

Robertson, P.L. and Langlois, R.L. (1995) Innovation, networks, and vertical integration, *Research Policy*, 24, 543–62.

Robinson, J. (1933) *The Economics of Imperfect Competition*. London: Macmillan Press.

Robinson, J. (1969) *The Economics of Imperfect Competition*, 2nd edn. London: Macmillan.

Robinson, W.T. and Chiang, J. (1996) Are Sutton's predictions robust? Empirical insights into advertising, R&D and concentration, *Journal of Industrial Economics*, 44, 389–408.

Robinson, W.T., Kalyanaram, G. and Urban, G.L. (1994) First-mover advantages from pioneering new markets: a survey of empirical evidence, *Review of Industrial Organisation*, 9, 1–23.

Roll, R. (1986) The hubris hypothesis of corporate takeovers, *Journal of Business*, 59, 197–216.

Roller, L., Stennek, J. and Verboven, F. (2001) Efficiency gains from mergers, Centre for Economic Policy Research, Report for EC Contract II/98/003. London: Centre for Economic Policy Research.

Romeo, A.A. (1975) Interindustry and interfirm differences in the rate of diffusion of an invention, *Review of Economics and Statistics*, 57, 311–19.

Rondi, L., Sembenelli, A. and Ragazzi, E. (1996) Determinants of diversification patterns, in Davies, S. and Lyons, B. *Industrial Organisation in the European Union*. Oxford: Oxford University Press, ch. 10.

Roquebert, J.A., Phillips, R.L. and Westfall, P.A. (1996) Markets versus management: what drives profitability? *Strategic Management Journal*, 17, 653–64.

Rose, N.L. and Shepard, A. (1997) Firm diversification and CEO compensation: managerial ability or executive entrenchment? *Rand Journal of Economics*, 28, 489–514.

Rosenberg, J.P. (1976) Research and market share: a reappraisal of the Schumpeter hypothesis, *Journal of Industrial Economics*, 25, 133–42.

Ross, T.W. (1992) Cartel stability and product differentiation, *International Journal of Industrial Organisation*, 10, 1–13.

Rosse, J. and Panzar, J. (1977) *Chamberlin versus Robinson: An Empirical Test of Monopoly Rents, Studies in Industry Economics*, Research Paper No. 77. Stanford, CA: Stanford University Press.

Rotemberg, J.J. and Saloner, G. (1986) A supergame-theoretic model of price wars during booms, *American Economic Review*, 76, 390–407.

Roth, A.E. (1991) Game theory as a part of empirical economics, *Economic Journal*, 101, 107–14.

Rothschild, K.W. (1942) The degree of monopoly, *Economica*, 9, 24–40.

Rothschild, K.W. (1947) Price theory and oligopoly, *Economic Journal*, 57, 299–302.

Rothschild, R. (1999) Cartel stability when costs are heterogeneous, *International Journal of Industrial Organisation*, 17, 717–34.

Rothwell, G. (1980) Market coordination by the uranium oxide industry, *Antitrust Bulletin*, 25, 233–68.

Rotwein, E. (1962) On the Methodology of Positive Economics, *Quarterly Journal of Economics*, 73, 554–75.

Rovizzi, L. and Thompson, D. (1995) The regulation of product quality in public utilities, in Bishop, M., Kay, J. and Mayer, C. (eds) *The Regulatory Challenge*. Oxford: Oxford University Press.

Rubinfeld, D.L. and Singer, H.J. (2001) Vertical foreclosure in broadband access? *Journal of Industrial Economics*, 49, 299–318.

Rudholm, N. (2001) Entry and the number of firms in the Swedish pharmacuticals market, *Review of Industrial Organization*, 19, 351–64.

Ruefli, T.W. and Wiggins, R.R. (2003) Industry, firm and business unit effects on performance: a non-parametric approach, *Strategic Management Journal*, 24, 861–79.

Rumelt, R.P. (1974) *Strategy, Structure and Economic Performance*. Boston, MA: Harvard Business School (Division of Research).

Rumelt, R.P. (1984) Towards a strategic theory of the firm, in Lamb, R.B. (ed.) *Competitive Strategic Management*. Englewood Cliffs, NJ: Prentice-Hall, 556–70.

Rumelt, R.P. (1991) How much does industry matter? *Strategic Management Journal*, 12, 167–86.

Rydén, B. and Edberg, J. (1980) Large Mergers in Sweden, 1962–1976, in Mueller, D.C. (ed.) *The Determinants and Effects of Mergers: an International Comparison*. Cambridge, MA: Oelgeschlager, Gun & Hanin.

Saal, D. (2003) Restructuring, regulation and the liberalization of privatised utilities in the UK, in Parker, D. and Saal, D. (eds) *International Handbook on Privatization*. Cheltenham: Edward Elgar.

Salop, S. (1979) Monopolistic competition with outside goods, *Bell Journal of Economics*, 10, 141–56.

Salter, A. and Martin, B.R. (2001) The economic benefits of publicly funded basic research: a critical review, *Research Policy*, 30, 509–32.

Salvanes, K.G., Steen, F. and Sorgard, L. (2005) Hotelling in the air? Flight departures in Norway. *Regional Science and Urban Economics*, 35, 193–213.

Samuals, J.M. (1965) Size and growth of firms, *Review of Economic Studies*, 32, 105–12.

Samuals, J.M. and Chesher, A.D. (1972) Growth, survival, and size of companies, 1960–69, in Cowling, K. (ed.) *Market Structure and Corporate Behaviour*. London: Gray–Mills.

Sandy, R., Sloane, P.J. and Rosentraub, M.S. (2004) *The Economics of Sport: An International Perspective*. Basingstoke: Palgrave Macmillan.

Sargent, F.P. (1933) *The Logic of Industrial Organization*. London: Kegan Paul.

Sargent, F.P. (1961) *Ownership, Control and Success of Large Companies*. London: Sweet and Maxwell.

Sawyer, M.C. (1985) *The Economics of Industries and Firms*, 2nd edn. London: Croom-Helm.

Schankerman, M. (1998) How valuable is patent protection? Estimates by technology field, *Rand Journal of Economics*, 29, 77–107.

Scharfstein, D.S. (1998) *The Dark Side of Internal Capital Markets*, 2, NBER Working Paper No. 6352.

Schary, M.A. (1991) The probability of exit, *Rand Journal of Economics*, 22, 339–53.

Scherer, F.M. (1965) Firm size, market structure, opportunity, and the output of patented inventions, *American Economic Review*, 55, 1097–125.

Scherer, F.M. (1967a) Research and development resource allocation under rivalry, *Quarterly Journal of Economics*, 81, 359–94.

Scherer, F.M. (1967b) Market structure and the employment of scientists and engineers, *American Economic Review*, 57, 524–31.

Scherer, F.M. (1980) *Industrial Market Structure and Economic Performance*, 2nd edn. Chicago, IL: Rand McNally.

Scherer, F.M. (1992) Schumpeter and plausible capitalism, *Journal of Economic Literature*, 30, 1416–33.

Scherer, F.M. and Ross, D. (1990) *Industrial Market Structures and Economic Performance*, 3rd edn. Boston, MA: Houghton Mifflin.

Scherer, F.M., Beckenstein, A., Kaufer, E. and Murphy, R.D. (1975) *The Economics of Multi-plant Operation: An International Comparisons Study*. Cambridge: Cambridge University Press.

Schick, F. (1997) *Making Choices, A Recasting of Decision Theory*. Cambridge: Cambridge University Press.

Schmalensee, R.C. (1972) *The Economics of Advertising*. Amsterdam: North-Holland.

Schmalensee, R.C. (1973) A note on the theory of vertical integration, *Journal of Political Economy*, 81, 442–9.

Schmalensee, R.C. (1978) Entry deterrence in the ready-to-eat cereal industry, *Bell Journal of Economics*, 9, 305–27.

Schmalensee, R.C. (1979) *The Control of Natural Monopolies*. Lexington, MA: DC Heath.

Schmalensee, R.C. (1981) Output and welfare implications of monopolistic third-degree discrimination, *American Economic Review*, 71, 242–47.

Schmalensee, R.C. (1982) Antitrust and the new industrial economics, *American Economic Review*, Papers and Proceedings, 72, 24–8.

Schmalensee, R.C. (1985) Do markets differ much? *American Economic Review*, 74, 341–51.

Schmalensee, R.C. (1987) Competitive advantage and collusive optima, *International Journal of Industrial Organization*, 5, 351–67.

Schmalensee, R.C. (1988) Industrial economics: an overview, *Economic Journal*, 98, 643–81.

Schmalensee, R.C. (1989) Inter-industry studies of structure and performance, in Schmalensee, R.C. and Willig, R.D. (eds) *Handbook of Industrial Organization*, vol. 2. Amsterdam: North-Holland, ch. 16.

Schmalensee, R.C. (1990) Empirical studies of rivalrous behaviour, in Bonanno, G. and Brandolini, D. (eds), *Industrial Structure in the New Industrial Economics.* Oxford: Clarendon Press.

Schmalensee, R.C. (1992) Sunk costs and market structure: a review article, *Journal of Industrial Economics*, 40, 125–34.

Schmitt, N. and Weder, R. (1998) Sunk costs and cartel formation: theory and application to the dyestuff industry, *Journal of Economic Behaviour and Organisation*, 36, 197–220.

Schmookler, J. (1952) The changing efficiency of the American economy, 1869–1938, *Review of Economics and Statistics*, 34, 214–31.

Schohl, F. (1990) Persistence of profits in the long-run: a critical extension of some recent findings, *International Journal of Industrial Organisation*, 8, 385–403.

Schonfield, A. (1965) *Modern Capitalism.* Oxford: Oxford University Press.

Schroeter, J., Smith, S. and Cox, S.R. (1987) Advertising and competition in routine legal service markets: an empirical investigation, *Journal of Industrial Economics*, 36, 49–60.

Schumpeter, J. (1928) The instability of capitalism, *Economic Journal*, 30, 361–86.

Schumpeter, J. (1942) *Capitalism, Socialism, and Democracy.* New York: HarperCollins.

Schwalbach, J. (1991) Entry, exit, concentration and market contestability, in Geroski, P.A. and Schwalbach, J. (eds) *Entry and Market Contestability: An International Comparison.* Oxford: Blackwell.

Schwalbach, J., Grasshoff, U. and Mahmood, T. (1989) The dynamics of corporate profits, *European Economic Review*, 33, 1625–39.

Schwartz, B. (2004) *The Paradox of Choice: Why More is Less.* New York: Harper Collins.

Schwartz, M. (1986) The nature and scope of contestability theory, *Oxford Economic Papers* (Special Supplement), 38, 37–57.

Schwartz, M. and Reynolds, R. (1983) Contestable markets: an uprising in industry structure: comment, *American Economic Review*, 73, 488–90.

Schwartzman, D. (1963) Uncertainty and the size of the firm, *Economica*, 30, 287–96.

Schwed, F. (1955) *Where are the Customers' Yachts?* New York: John Wiley.

Schwert, W.G. (1981) Using financial data to measure the effects of regulation, *Journal of Law and Economics*, 24, 121–58.

Schwert, W.G. (1996) Markup pricing in mergers and acquisitions, *Journal of Financial Economics*, 29, 153–92.

Scitovsky, T. (1950) Ignorance as a source of monopoly power, *American Economic Review*, 40, 48–53.

Scitovsky, T. (1971) *Welfare and Competition* (revised edition). London: Allen & Unwin.

Scotchmer, S. (1991) Standing on the shoulders of giants: cumulative research and the patent law, *Journal of Economic Perspectives*, 5, 29–41.

Scott, J.T. and Pascoe, G. (1986) Beyond firm and industry effects on profitability in imperfect markets, *Review of Economics and Statistics*, 68, 284–92.

Scott Morton, F.M. (2000) Barriers to entry, brand advertising, and generic entry in the US pharmaceutical industry, *International Journal of Industrial Organization*, 18, 1085–104.

Sedgewick, J. (2002) Product differentiation at the movies: Hollywood, 1946 to 1965, *Journal of Economic History*, 62, 676–705.

Servaes, H. (1996) The value of diversification during the conglomerate merger wave, *Journal of Finance*, 51, 1201–25.

Shaffer, S. (1982) A non-structural test for competition in financial markets, in *Bank Structure and Competition*, Conference Proceedings. Chicago, IL: Federal Reserve Bank.

Shaffer, S. (1989) Competition in the US banking industry, *Economics Letters*, 29, 321–23.

Shaffer, S. (1993) A test of competition in Canadian banking, *Journal of Money, Credit and Banking*, 25, 49–61.

Shaffer, S. (1996) Viability of traditional banking activities: evidence from shifts in conduct and excess capacity, *International Journal of Economics of Business*, 3, 125–43.

Shaffer, S. (2001) Banking conduct before the European single banking license: a cross country comparison, *North Amercian Journal of Economics and Finance*, 12, 79–104.

Shaffer, S. and DiSalvo, J. (1994) Conduct in a banking duopoly, *Journal of Banking and Finance*, 18, 1063–82.

Shalit, S.S. and Sankar, U. (1977) Measurement of firm size, *Review of Economics and Statistics*, 59, 290–8.

Shaw, R.W. and Simpson, P. (1986) The persistence of monopoly: an investigation of the effectiveness of the United Kingdom Monopolies Commission, *Journal of Industrial Economics*, 34, 355–69.

Shelanski, H.A. and Klein, P.G. (1995) Empirical research in transaction cost economics: a review and assessment, *Journal of Law, Economics and Organisation*, 11, 335–61.

Shepherd, W.G. (1972) Structure and behaviour in British industries with US comparisons, *Journal of Industrial Economics*, 20, 35–54.

Shepherd, W.G. (1986) Tobin's q and the structure–performance relationship: comment, *American Economic Review*, 76, 1205–10.

Shepherd, W.G. (1997) *The Economics of Industrial Organisation*. Englewood Cliffs, NJ: Prentice-Hall.

Sherif, M. and Sherif, C.W. (1956) *An Outline of Social Psychology*. New York: Harper.

Sherman, R. (1977) Theory comes to industrial organisation, in Jacquemin, A. and de Jong, H.W. (eds) *Welfare Aspects of Industrial Markets*. Amsterdam: Martinus Nijhoff.

Sherman, R. (1985) The Averch and Johnson analysis of public utility regulation twenty years later, *Review of Industrial Organization*, 1, 178–91.

Shipley, D. (1981) Primary objectives in British manufacturing industry, *Journal of Industrial Economics*, 29, 4, 429–43.

Shipley, D. and Bourden, E. (1990) Distributor pricing in very competitive markets, *Industrial and Marketing Management*, 19, 215–24.

Shleifer, A. (1985) A theory of yardstick competition, *Rand Journal of Economics*, 16, 319–27.

Sibley, D. and Weisman, D.L. (1998) Raising rivals' costs: the entry of an upstream monopolist into downstream markets, *Information Economics and Policy*, 10, 451–69.

Siegfried, J.A. and Evans, L. (1994) Empirical studies of entry and exit: a survey of the evidence, *Review of Industrial Organisation*, 9, 121–55.

Siggelkow, N. (2003) Why focus? A study of intra-industry focus effects, *Journal of Industrial Economics*, 51, 121–50.

Silberman, I.H. (1967) On lognormality as a summary measure of concentration, *American Economic Review*, 57, 807–31.

Simon, H.A. (1959) Theories of decision-making in economics and behavioural science, *American Economic Review*, 49, 253–83.

Simon, H.A. and Bonini, C.P. (1958) The size distribution of business firms, *American Economic Review*, 48, 607–17.

Singer, E.M. (1968) *Antitrust Economics*, Englewood Cliffs, NJ: Prentice-Hall.

Singh, A. (1971) *Takeovers*. Cambridge: Cambridge University Press.

Singh, A. and Whittington, G. (1975) The size and growth of firms, *Review of Economic Studies*, 42, 15–26.

Singh, S., Utton, M.A. and Waterson, M. (1998) Strategic behaviour of incumbent firms in the UK, *International Journal of Industrial Organization*, 16, 229–51.

Slade, M. (2004). Competing models of firm profitability, *International Journal of Industrial Organization*, 22, 289–308.

Sleuwaegen, L. and Dehandschutter, W. (1991) Entry and exit in Belgian manufacturing, in Geroski, P.A. and Schwalbach, J. (eds) *Entry and Market Contestability: An International Comparison*. Oxford: Blackwell.

Smiley, R. (1988) Empirical evidence on strategic entry deterrence, *International Journal of Industrial Organisation*, 6, 167–80.

Smirlock, M., Gilligan, T.W. and Marshall, W. (1984) Tobin's q and the structure-performance relationship, *American Economic Review*, 74, 1051–60.

Smith, A. (1776) *An Inquiry into the Nature and Causes of the Wealth of Nations*. New York: Modern Library (1937).

Smith, V. (1989) Theory, experiment and economics, *Journal of Economic Perspectives*, Winter, 2, 151–69.

Smyth, D., Boyes, W. and Pesau, D.E. (1975) Measurement of firm size: theory and evidence for US and the UK, *Review of Economics and Statistics*, 57, 111–13.

Snyder, C.M. (1996) A Dynamic Theory of Countervailing Power, *Rand Journal of Economics*, 27, 747–69.

Solberg, E.J. (1992) *Microeconomics for Business Decisions*. Lexington, MA: DC Heath.

Sonkondi, L. (1969) *Business and Prices*. London: Routledge.

Sosnick, S.H. (1958) A critique of concepts of workable competition, *Quarterly Journal of Economics*, 72, 380–423.

Spanos, Y., Zaralis, G. and Lioukas, S. (2004) Strategy and industry effects on profitability: evidence from Greece, *Strategic Management Journal*, 25, 139–65.

Spence, M. (1981) The learning curve and competition, *Bell Journal of Economics*, 12, 49–70.

Spencer, J.W. (2001) How relevant is university-based scientific research to private high-technology firms? A United States–Japan comparison, *Academy of Management Journal*, 44, 432–40.

Spengler, J.J. (1950) Vertical integration and antitrust policy, *Journal of Political Economy* 68, 347–52.

Spiller, P.T. (1985) On vertical mergers, *Journal of Law, Economics and Organisation*, 1, 285–312.

Spulber, D.F. (1992) Economic analysis and management strategy, a survey, *Journal of Economics and Management Strategy*, 1, 535–74.

Spulber, D.F. (1994) Economic analysis and management strategy, a survey continued, *Journal of Economics and Management Strategy*, 3, 355–406.

Spulber, D.F. (2003) Entry barriers and entry strategies, *Journal of Strategic Management Education*, 1, 55–80.

Sraffa, P. (1926) The laws of returns under competitive conditions, *Economic Journal*, 36, 535–50.

Stackelberg, H. von (1934) *Marktform und Gleichgewicht*, Vienna: Julius Springer. Trans. A. Peacock, *Theory of the Market Economy*. New York: Oxford University Press (1952).

Stalk, G., Evans, P. and Shulman, L.E. (1992) Competing on capabilities, resources and the concept of strategy, *Harvard Business Review*, March–April, 57–69.

Stanley, M.H.R., Buldyrev, S.V., Havlin, S., Mantegna, R.N., Salinger, M.A. and Stanley, H.E. (1995) Zipf plots and the size distribution of firms, *Economics Letters*, 49, 453–7.

Steen, F. and Sørgard, L. (1999) Semicollusion in the Norwegian cement market, *European Economic Review*, 43, 1775–96.

Steiner, M. (2002) Clusters and networks – institutional setting and strategic perspectives, in McCann, P. (ed.) *Industrial Location Economics*. Cheltenham: Edward Elgar.

Stephen, F. (1994) Advertising, consumer search costs and prices in a professional service market, *Applied Economics*, 26, 1177–88.

Stern, L.W. (1971) Antitrust implications of a sociological interpretation of competition, conflict, and cooperation in the marketplace, *Antitrust Bulletin*, 16, 509–30.

Stevens, B. (1984) Comparing public and private sector productive efficiency: an analysis of eight activities, *National Productivity Review*, Autumn, 395–406.

Stevens, R.B. and Yamey, B.S. (1965) *The Restrictive Practices Court: A Study of Judicial Process and Economic Policy*. London: Weidenfeld and Nicholson.

Stigler, G.J. (1947) The kinky oligopoly demand curve and rigid prices, *Journal of Political Economy*, 55, 432–47.

Stigler, G.J. (1951) The division of labor is limited by the extent of the market, *Journal of Political Economy*, 59, 185–93.

Stigler, G.J. (1952) *The Theory of Price*. New York: Macmillan.

Stigler, G.J. (1955) *Business Concentration and Price Policy*. Princeton, NJ: Princeton University Press.

Stigler, G.J. (1957) 'Perfect competition, historically contemplated', *Journal of Political Economy*, 65, 1–17.

Stigler, G.J. (1958) The economies of scale, *Journal of Law and Economics*, 1, 54–71.

Stigler, G.J. (1961) The economics of information, *Journal of Political Economy*, 69, 213–25. Reprinted in Stigler, G.J. (1968) *The Organization of Industry*, 171–90.

Stigler, G.J. (1963) United States v. Loew's Inc.: a note on block booking, *Supreme Court Review*, 152–7.

Stigler, G.J. (1964) A theory of oligopoly, *Journal of Political Economy*, 72, 44–61.

Stigler, G.J. (1966) *The Theory of Price*, New York: Macmillan.

Stigler, G.J. (1968) *The Organisation of Industry*. Holmwood, IL: Irwin.

Stigler, G.J. (1971) The theory of economic regulation, *Bell Journal of Economics*, 2, 3–21.

Stigler, G.J. (1978) The literature of economics: the case of the kinked oligopoly demand curve, *Economic Inquiry*, 16, 185–204.

Stiglitz, J. (1991) Imperfect information in the product market, *Handbook of Industrial Organization*, vol. 1, ch. 13.

Stock, J.H. and Watson, M.W. (2003) *Introduction to Econometrics*, International edn. Harlow: Pearson Education.

Stocking, W. and Mueller, W. (1957) Business reciprocity and the size of firms, *Journal of Business*, 30, 73–95.

Stokey, N.L. (1979) Intertemporal price discrimination, *Quarterly Journal of Economics*, 94, 355–71.

Stole, L. (2005) Price discrimination in competitive environments, in Armstrong, M. and Porter, R. (eds) *Handbook of Industrial Organization*, vol. 3. Amsterdam: Elsevier Publishing, forthcoming.

Stoneman, P. (1989) Technological diffusion, and vertical product differentiation. *Economic Letters*, 31, 277–80.

Stoneman, P. (1995) *Handbook of the Economics of Innovation and Technical Change*. Oxford: Blackwell.

Storey, Sir R. (1979) Technology and the trade unions, in Henry, H. (ed.) *Behind the Headlines*. London: Associated Business Press, ch. 4.

Strassmann, D.L. (1990) Potential competition in the deregulated airlines, *Review of Economics and Statistics*, 72, 696–702.

Stuckey, J. (1983) *Vertical Integration and Joint Ventures in the Aluminium Industry*. Cambridge: Cambridge University Press.

Studenmund, A.H. (2000) *Using Econometrics: A Practical Guide*, International edn. Harlow: Pearson Education.

Suetens, S. (2005) Cooperative and non-cooperative R&D in experimental oligopoly markets, *International Journal of Industrial Organization*, 23, forthcoming.

Sultan, R.G.M. (1974) *Pricing in the Electrical Oligopoly*, vol. 1. Cambridge, MA: Harvard University Press.

Sundqvist, S., Frank, L. and Puumalainen, K. (2005) The effects of country characteristics, cultural similarity and adoption timing on the diffusion of wirless communication, *Journal of Business Research*, 58, 107–10.

Sutton, C.J. (1980) *Economics and Corporate Strategy*. Cambridge: Cambridge University Press.

Sutton, J. (1991) *Sunk Costs and Market Structure*. London: MIT Press.

Sutton, J. (1997) Gibrat's legacy, *Journal of Economic Literature*, 35, 40–59.

Sweezy, P. (1939) Demand under conditions of oligopoly, *Journal of Political Economy*, 47, 568–73.

Sylos-Labini, P. (1962) *Oligopoly and Technical Progress*. Boston, MA: Harvard University Press.

Symeonides, G. (1999) Cartel stability in advertising-intensive and R&D-intensive industries, *Economics Letters*, 62, 121–9.

Symeonides, G. (2003) In which industries is collusion more likely? Evidence from the UK, *Journal of Industrial Economics*, 51, 45–74.

Szymanski, S. (1996) The impact of compulsory competitive tendering on refuse collection services, *Fiscal Studies*, 17, 1–19.

Szymanski, S. and Wilkins, S. (1993) Cheap rubbish? Competitive tendering and contracting out in refuse collection – 1981–88, *Fiscal Studies*, 14, 109–30.

Takalo, T. (2001) On the optimal patent policy, *Finnish Economic Papers*, 14, 33–40.

Taylor, C. and Silberston, Z.A. (1973) *The Economic Impact of the Patent System*. Cambridge: Cambridge University Press.

Tedlow, R.S. (1993) The fourth phase of marketing: marketing history and the business world today, in Tetlow, R.S. and Jones, G. (eds) *The Rise and Fall of Mass Marketing*. London: Routledge.

Teece, D.J. (1982) Toward an economic theory of the multiproduct firm, *Journal of Economic Behaviour and Organisation*, 3, 39–63.

Teece, D.J. (1984) Economic Analysis and Strategic Management, *California Management Review*, 26, 87–110.

Teece, D.J., Rumelt, R., Dosi, G. and Winter, S. (1994) Understanding corporate coherence, theory and evidence, *Journal of Economic Behaviour and Organisation*, 23, 1–30.

Tellis, G.J. and Fornell, C. (1988) The relationship between advertising and product quality over the product life cycle: a contingency theory, *Journal of Marketing Research*, 25, 64–71.

Telser, L. (1960) Why should manufactureers want fair trade? *Journal of Law and Economics*, 3, 86–105.

Telser, L. (1964) Advertising and competition, *Journal of Political Economy*, 72, 537–62.

Telser, L. (1966a) Cut throat competition and the long purse, *Journal of Law and Economics*, 9, 259–77.

Telser, L. (1966b) Supply and demand for advertising messages, *American Economic Review*, 56, 457–66.

Thaler, R. (1991) *The Winner's Curse: Paradoxes and Anomalies of Economic Life*. Princeton, NJ: Princeton University Press.

Thomas, L.A., Shane, S. and Weigett, K. (1998) An empirical examination of advertising as a measure of product quality, *Journal of Economic Behaviour and Organization*, 37, 415–30.

Tirole, J. (1988) *Theory of Industrial Organization*. Cambridge: Cambridge University Press.

Tremblay, V.J. (1985) Strategic groups and the demand for beer, *Journal of Industrial Economics*, 34, 183–98.

Tufano, P. (2003) Financial innovation, in Constantinides, G., Harris, M., and Stulz, R. (eds) *Handbook of the Economics of Finance*. Amsterdam: North-Holland.

UK Cabinet Office (1996) *Competing For Quality Policy Review: An Efficiency Unit Scrutiny*. London: HMSO.

UK Science Parks Association (UKSPA) (1999) www.ukspa.org.uk/htmfiles/aboutus.htm

Uri, N.D. (1987) A re-examination of the advertising and industrial concentration relationship, *Applied Economics*, 19, 427–35.

Utton, M.A. (1970) *Industrial Concentration*. Harmondsworth: Penguin.

Utton, M.A. (1971) The effect of mergers on concentration: UK manufacturing industry 1954–1965, *Journal of Industrial Economics*, 20, 42–58.

Utton, M.A. (1972) Mergers and the growth of large firms, *Bulletin of Oxford University Institute of Economics and Statistics*, 34, 189–97.

Utton, M.A. (1977) Large firm diversification in the British manufacturing industry, *Economic Journal*, 87, 96–113.

Utton, M.A. (1979) *Diversification and Competition*. Cambridge: Cambridge University Press.

Utton, M.A. (1982) Domestic concentration and international trade, *Oxford Economic Papers*, 34, 479–97.

Utton, M.A. (1986) *Profits and the Stability of Monopoly*. Cambridge: Cambridge University Press.

Utton, M.A. (2000) Fifty years of UK competition policy, *Review of Industrial Organization*, 16, 267–85.

Van Oijen, A. and Douma, S. (2000) Diversification strategy and the roles of the centre, *Long-Range Planning*, 33, 560–78.

Vanlommel, E., de Brabander, B. and Liebaers, D. (1977) Industrial concentration in Belgium: empirical comparison of alternative seller concentration measures, *Journal of Industrial Economics*, 26, 1–20.

Veblen, T. (1923) *Absentee Ownership and Business Enterprise in Recent Times*. New York: B.W. Huebsch.

Vernon, J.M. and Graham, D.A. (1971) Profitability of monopolisation in vertical integration, *Journal of Political Economy*, 79, 924–5.

Vernon, J.M. and Nourse, R.E. (1973) Profit rates and market structure of advertising intensive firms, *Journal of Industrial Economics*, 22, 1–20.

Vickers, J. (2002) Competition is for consumers, *Fair Trading Magazine*, May, 32, 6–8.

Vickers, J. and Yarrow, G. (1988) *Privatization: An Economic Analysis*. Cambridge, MA: MIT Press.

Vickrey, W. (1961) Counterspeculation, auctions and competitive sealed tenders, *Journal of Finance*, 16, 8–37.

Villalonga, B. (2004) Intangible resources, Tobin's q and sustainability of performance differences, *Journal of Economic Behavior and Organization*, 54, 205–30.

Vogelvang, B. (2004) *Econometrics: Theory and Application with E-Views*. Harlow: Financial Times Prentice Hall.

Vos, E. and Kelleher, B. (2001) Mergers and takeovers: a memetic approach, *Journal of Memetics – Evolutionary Models of Information*, 5, jom-emit.cfpm.org/2001/vol5/vos_e&kelleher_b.html (accessed 2 May 2004).

Wagner, J. (1992) Firm size, firm growth and the persistence of chance, *Small Business Economics*, 4, 125–31.

Walker, M. (1997) RIP for RRP, *London Economics – Economics in Action*, No. 2.

Walsh, K. (1992) Quality and public services, *Public Administration*, 69, 503–14.

Walsh, K. and Davis, H. (1993) *Competition and Service: The Impact of the Local Government Act, 1988*. London: Department of the Environment.

Wang, H. (2004) Resale price maintenance in an oligopoly with uncertain demand, *International Journal of Industrial Organisation*, 22, 389–411.

Waring, G.F. (1996) Industry differences in the persistence of firm-specific returns, *American Economic Review*, 78, 246–50.

Waterson, M. (1987) Recent developments in the theory of natural monopoly, *Journal of Economic Surveys*, 1, 59–80.

Waterson, M. (1988) On vertical restraints and the law: a note, *Rand Journal of Economics*, 29, 293–7.

Waterson, M. (1993) Are industrial economists still interested in concentration?, in Casson, M. and Creedy, J. (eds) *Industrial Concentration and Economic Inequality*. Aldershot: Edward Elgar.

Waterson, M. (1994) Models of product differentation, in Cable, J. (ed.) *Current Issues in Industrial Economics*. London: Macmillan.

Weir, C. (1992) The Monopolies and Mergers Commission merger reports and the public interest: a probit analysis, *Applied Economics*, 24, 27–34.

Weir, C. (1993) Merger policy and competition: an analysis of the Monopolies and Mergers Commission's decisions, *Applied Economics*, 25, 57–66.

Weiss, L.W. (1963) Factors in changing concentration, *Review of Economics and Statistics*, 45, 70–7.

Weiss, L.W. (1965) An evaluation of mergers in six industries, *Review of Economics and Statistics*, 47, 172–81.

Weiss, L.W. (1974) The concentration–profits relationship and antitrust, in Goldschmid, H., Mann, H.M. and Weston, J.F. (eds) *Industrial Concentration: The New Learning*. Boston, MA: Little, Brown, 183–233.

Weiss, L.W. (1989) *Concentration and Price*. Boston, MA: MIT Press.

Werden, G.J. and Froeb, L.M. (1993) Correlation, causality and all that jazz: the inherent shortcomings of price tests for antitrust markets, *Review of Industrial Organization*, 8, 329–53.

Wernerfelt, B. (1984) A resource-based view of the firm, *Strategic Management Journal*, 5, 171–80.

Wernerfelt, B. and Montgomery, C.A. (1988) Tobin's q and the importance of focus in firm performance, *American Economic Review*, 78, 246–50.

Weston, J.F. (1970) Conglomerate firms, *St John's Law Review*, 44, 66–80, reprinted in Yamey, B.S. (ed.) (1973) *Economics of Industrial Structure*. Middlesex: Penguin, 305–21.

Whinston, M. (1990) Tying, foreclosure and exclusion, *American Economic Review*, 80, 837–59.

Whish, R. (2003) *Competition Law*, 4th edn. London: Butterworth.

White, L.J. (1981) What has been happening to aggregate concentration in the United States, *Journal of Industrial Economics*, 29, 223–30.

Wilcox, C. (1960) *Public Policy Toward Business*, Homewood, IL: Irwin.

Wildsmith, J.R. (1973) *Managerial Theories of the Firm*. London: Martin Robertson.

Williams, M. (1993) The effectiveness of competition policy in the United Kingdom, *Oxford Review of Economic Policy*, 9, 94–112.

Williamson, J. (1966) Profit growth and sales maximisation, *Economica*, 33, 1–16.

Williamson, O.E. (1963) Managerial discretion and business behaviour, *American Economic Review*, 53, 1032–57.

Williamson, O.E. (1967) Hierarchical control and optimum firm size, *Journal of Political Economy*, 75, 123–38.

Williamson, O.E. (1968a) Economies as an anti-trust defence: the welfare trade-offs, *American Economic Review*, 58, 18–36.

Williamson, O.E. (1968b) Economies as an anti-trust defence: correction and reply, *American Economic Review*, 58, 1372–6.

Williamson, O.E. (1971) The vertical integration of production; market failure considerations, *American Economic Review*, 61, 112–27.

Williamson, O.E. (1975) *Markets and Hierarchies*. New York: The Free Press.

Williamson, O.E. (1983) Credible commitments: using hostages to support exchange, *American Economic Review*, 73, 519–40.

Williamson, O.E. (1985) *The Economic Institutions of Capitalism*. New York: The Free Press.

Williamson, O.E. (1989) Transaction cost economics, in Schmalensee, R. and Willig, R.D. (eds) *Handbook of Industrial Organisation*, vol. 1. Amsterdam: North-Holland, ch. 3.

Williamson, O.E. (2002a) The theory of the firm as governance structure: from choice to contract, *Journal of Economic Perspectives*, 16, 171–95.

Williamson, O.E. (2002b) The lens of contract: private ordering, *American Economic Review*, 92, 438–43.

Willis, M.S. and Rogers, R.T. (1998) Market share dispersion among leading firms as a determinant of advertising intensity, *Review of Industrial Organization*, 13, 495–508.

Wilson, J. (1994) Competitive tendering and UK public services, *Economic Review*, April, 12, 31–5.

Wilson, J.O.S. and Morris, J.E. (2000) The size and growth of UK manufacturing and service firms, *Service Industries Journal*, 20, 25–38.

Wilson, J.O.S. and Williams, J.M. (2000) The size and growth of banks: evidence from four European countries, *Applied Economics*, 32, 1101–9.

Winston, C. (1993) Economic deregulation: days of reckoning for microeconomists, *Journal of Economic Literature*, 31, 1263–89.

Winston, C. (1998) US Industry adjustment to economic deregulation, *Journal of Economic Perspectives*, 12, 89–110.

Winter, S.G. (2003) Understanding dynamic capabilities, *Strategic Management Journal*, 24, 991–5.

Wolfram, C. (1998) Increases in executive pay following privatization, *Journal of Economics and Management Strategy*, 7, 327–61.

www.druid.dk/wp/pdf_files/97-2.pdf (accessed 11 March 2004).

Yamey, B.S. (1970) Notes on secret price cutting in oligopoly, in Kooy, M. (ed.) *Studies in Economics and Economic History in Honour of Prof. H.M. Robertson.* London: Macmillan, 280–300.

Yamey, B.S. (1972a) Do monopoly and near monopoly matter? A survey of the empirical studies, in Peston, M. and Correy, B. (eds) *Essays in Honour of Lord Robbins.* London: Weidenfeld & Nicolson, 294–308.

Yamey, B.S. (1972b) Predatory price cutting: notes and comments, *Journal of Law and Economics*, 15, 137–47.

Yamey, B.S. (1973) Some problems of oligopoly, *paper presented to International Conference on International Economy and Competition Policy*, Tokyo, Japan.

Yamey, B.S. (1974) Monopolistic price competition and economic welfare, *Journal of Law and Economics*, 17, 377–80.

Yang, C. and Tsou, T. (2002) Do stronger patents induce more patents? Evidence from Taiwan's 1994 patent reform, *Paper presented to the Second International Conference of the Japanese Economic Policy Association*, Nagoya, Japan.

Yarrow, G. (1986) Privatisation in theory and practice, *Economic Policy*, 2, 319–78.

Yarrow, G. (1989) Privatisation and economic performance in Britain, *Carnegie Rochester Conference Series on Public Policy*, 31, 303–44.

Yoon, S. (2004) A note on the market structure and performance in Korean manufacturing industries, *Journal of Policy Modelling*, 26, 733–46.

Young, G., Smith, K.G. and Grimm, C.M. (1996) Austrian and industrial organization perspectives on firm-level activity and performance, *Organization Science*, 7, 243–54.

Youssef, M.I. (1986) Global oil price war is expected to affect the industry for years, *Wall Street Journal* (18 February 1986).

Index